1 MONTH OF
FREE
READING

at

www.ForgottenBooks.com

By purchasing this book you are eligible for one month membership to ForgottenBooks.com, giving you unlimited access to our entire collection of over 1,000,000 titles via our web site and mobile apps.

To claim your free month visit: www.forgottenbooks.com/free921064

ISBN 978-0-266-99864-8
PIBN 10921064

A MANUAL OF THE WRITINGS IN
MIDDLE ENGLISH

1050-1400

A Manual of the Writings in Middle English

1050-1400

By

JOHN EDWIN WELLS, M.L., M.A., Ph.D.

Professor of English Literature in Beloit College

Published under the Auspices of the
Connecticut Academy of Arts and Sciences

NEW HAVEN: YALE UNIVERSITY PRESS
LONDON: HUMPHREY MILFORD
OXFORD UNIVERSITY PRESS
MDCCCCXVI

PR
2535
W H

TO

PROFESSOR ALBERT STANBURROUGH COOK

PREFACE

This manual makes the first attempt to treat all the extant writings in print, from single lines to the most extensive pieces, composed in English between 1050 and 1400. At times, as with the Romances, the Legends, and the Drama, a desire for greater completeness has led to the inclusion of pieces later than 1400.

The work is not a history, but a handbook. It seeks to record the generally accepted views of scholars on pertinent matters, and does not pretend to offer new theories or investigations. It is unique in that, besides attempting to deal with all the extant writings of the period in print, it groups each piece with the others of its kind; indicates its probable date, or the limitations as to its date, its MS. or MSS., the probable date of its MS. or MSS., its form and extent, commonly the dialect in which it was first composed, and its source or sources when known; presents comments on each longer production, with an abstract of its contents; and supplies a bibliography for each composition.

The book includes the data available up to September, 1915. A few recent German dissertations and University prints may be omitted because of delays in the forwarding of foreign mails.

The manual is devoted primarily to the English pieces of the period; yet general directions to the associated writings in other languages will be found in the Text and the Bibliographical Notes.

The exclusion of any treatment of Ballads (see Index, *s.v.* *Ballads*) as a class is justified by the fact that apparently the extant form of but one genuine popular ballad, *Judas*, dates from before 1400, and by the existence of comprehensive studies and bibliographies of this type of literature.

For the first time, as is stated above, an attempt is here made to arrange and classify all the pieces noted. The cross-

references in the Text, and many of the entries in the Index,
may contribute to a more perfect future classification. As a
rule, at the head of the consideration of a group in the Text,
are indicated the more obvious features common among the
individual representatives of the group. Within the groups
the discussion usually follows a chronological order; but this
order is sometimes modified for the sake of clearness or the
exhibition of similarity.

The abstracts and indications of contents are offered in
the hope of interesting the general reader in the literature of
the period, and of affording the special student means for a
readier apprehension and comparison of the individual pro-
ductions.

For the first time, too, an effort is here made to present
bibliographical notes (see pages 749 ff.) on each of the extant
writings. The limitations of these notes are indicated on pages
751 and 866. The bibliographical note for a given item is
indicated in the Text by the number inserted in brackets after
the title or the mention of the item. The chapter-number at
the head of the right-hand page, and the note-number in
brackets in the body of the page, direct attention to the bibliographical note on the piece. The notes for groups are usually
not numbered; they are found at the head of the notes on the
chapter or the group concerned. This method of numbering
will enable students, on occasion, to refer to individual items by
mere statement of chapter or type or group and number.

The Index is designed to facilitate the identification of each
writing, and refers (see the explanations on pages 751 and
885) to each mention of it and to the special discussion of it
in the Text, and to the bibliographical note or notes on it.

All the pieces dealt with have been read especially for this
book. With the exception of fewer than a dozen rare prints,
all the editions and studies mentioned in the Bibliographical
Notes have been examined. Excepting those starred, all the
periodicals listed in the Table of Abbreviations on pages 753 ff.
have been gone over from their beginnings; and even of the
periodicals starred, most of the issues have been examined for

pertinent matter. It is hoped that few printed pieces or versions of texts have escaped notice. In the MSS., however, there are, no doubt, texts still unnoted in print.

In a word, the manual affords a handy general view of the materials in the field, which, it is hoped, will make possible more immediate appreciation of those materials, and will open the way to a fuller recognition of the problems regarding them. It offers at a glance much that has hitherto been accessible only to the careful special student of particular writings, or to the maker of private bibliographies. The most cursory examination will show that much remains to be worked out regarding even some of the most prominent pieces in Middle English, and that often the most frequently repeated notions are questionable. Though I have ventured silently to correct many obvious errors, I may be permitted to disclaim responsibility for misstatements by editors and special investigators.

Despite intermittent study of the Middle English period during almost twenty years, and several years of application to the present undertaking, I must suppose that many omissions and mistakes will be discovered in this work. For these, and for slips in the transcription of data, I ask kindly forbearance. Those who have the closest acquaintance with the conditions will be foremost in recognizing the difficulties that I must have encountered in accumulating and arranging the widely scattered materials. It is gratifying to be able to feel that future students will be spared these particular trials.

It is my purpose to extend the usefulness of the book by printing from time to time in the periodicals supplementary notices of later studies in this field. In anticipation of this, and of a possible reprinting of the manual, I shall be heartily obliged for any communications regarding errors or omissions, and for information concerning new publications.

I desire to express my appreciation of the courtesies shown me in the loan of books by the Library of Harvard University, and for the liberties and gracious service accorded me for months at a time in the Libraries of Yale University and of the Universities of Chicago and Wisconsin.

PREFACE

To Messrs. D. C. Heath & Company I am obliged for permission to incorporate in the notice of the *Owl and the Nightingale* passages from the introduction to my edition of that poem.

To Professor Albert S. Cook of Yale University I am most deeply indebted for the suggestion of a manual of Middle English literature, his encouragement and kind insistence toward its accomplishment, his interest in the publication of the work as actually completed, his reading of the proofs, and his many helpful suggestions during the printing. He must, however, be held in no way responsible for the matter or form of anything that appears in the book.

I am profoundly grateful for the honor done me by the Connecticut Academy of Arts and Sciences in generously making possible the immediate publication of the manual, under the auspices of the Academy, and at its expense.

JOHN EDWIN WELLS.

Beloit, Wisconsin,
    December, 1915.

CONTENTS

CHAPTER I

CHAPTER II

CHAPTER XI

CHAPTER XII

CHAPTER XIII

CONTENTS

CHAPTER XIV

CHAPTER XV

CHAPTER XVI

A MANUAL OF THE WRITINGS IN
MIDDLE ENGLISH

1050-1400

CHAPTER I

ROMANCES

Though the romances regarded as a class are commonly judged to be the most literary of the products in English of the Middle English period, they are generally declared inferior as compared with the romances in French.

Practically all the extant versions are based on French originals. Usually the English author follows only one source, but in some instances apparently several earlier works have been drawn on. Difficulty in ascertaining just the amount of originality evinced in the pieces is caused by the fact that undoubtedly often the actual originals used are not the versions now extant. Commonly the English pieces, as they have come to us, were composed with the originals before the writers' eyes; but in some cases, and perhaps more frequently than is supposed, they were made from memory, perhaps from recitation—conditions that may account for many of the variations from extant earlier treatments. Most of the surviving pieces seem to have been composed, not by persons of the courtly class, but by more humble members of society; and some were made by minstrels or gleemen. Indeed, it may be said rightly that, certain notable exceptions being admitted, much of the best of the English romances is due to simpler and humbler origins and aims. Yet it must be recognized that, when, after 1350, the English romance came largely into the hands of the common folk and the minstrels, it degenerated and became debased.

The authors of the English romances seem to have aimed at preserving the incidents of their originals, but they treated them from an English point of view. They invented little; they abridged and condensed freely. The English pieces are less unified than are their French sources, and are inferior in

structure to them. As a class they are sounder in morals than
are the French. The best are generally more homely, less
sophisticated; their conditions and their conceptions are more
primitive and natural. They exhibit love for sports, and often
a response to the larger or severer aspects of nature. They
are more sincere, more direct, than the French. As a rule,
in matter and in manner they lean to the more 'popular,' and
from the elegant and courtly; except in the later years of
decay, they show little liking for the elaboration and refinements of the French. In their representative nature, they
prefer incident, deeds, vigorous action, the blood and bone of
life, the realistic, the melodramatic, the marvelous, often the
rude and the grotesque. Though not infrequently his sense
of the dramatic leads an author to turn the flowing narrative
of his original into direct discourse, the long speeches and
extended dialogues of the French are usually greatly condensed
or even eliminated. The English romances employ few refinements of diction; they use scarcely any metaphors, and introduce but rarely short phrase similes. Generally they have
little sympathy with the French sensibility and sentimentality.
The representative pieces disregard the polite casuistry, the
introspection, the analysis of feeling and situation, of the
French; and they exhibit little fondness for the elaborated
description, the minor details, and the lists, with which French
writers sought to adorn their narratives. True it is, that
most of the qualities and materials of the French romances
are found more or less in isolation, now here and now there,
in the English pieces, and that they appear more frequently
and more to the given romance as the period advances; but
those elements that are the product of the more sophisticated
and courtly French muse, are to be met with little in the representative English tales, and are actually cultivated considerably
only in the later and more decadent of the English pieces.

The metre of the English romances is commonly the short
couplet. Several early romances are in the twelve-line tail-
rime stanza, and from about 1350 both the shorter and the
longer tail-rime were popular. The pieces of this later period
are generally inferior, and, as Chaucer's *Sir Thopas* indicates,

were probably realized to be so by the cultivated. From about 1350, too, the alliterative verse, sometimes rimed and commonly bound up into stanzas, was employed. This revival and these modifications of the old measure, were used in some of the best of the English poems. The English prose romances are all after 1400.

Though the general purpose of this book is to deal with only works before 1400, for the sake of completeness in this chapter are discussed all the romances in English (except the tales of Chaucer and Gower) composed before the practice of printing in England. The following tables afford a notion of the family relationships, the chronology, and the dialect of the various pieces.

GROUPS OF ROMANCES ACCORDING TO THEME AND ORIGIN

This table includes only romances discussed in this chapter, and gives a general view of the arrangement of the discussion.

1. ENGLISH AND GERMANIC LEGENDS

King Horn, Horn Childe and Maiden Rimnild, Havelok, Guy of Warwick, William of Palerne, Beues of Hamtoun, Athelston, The Tale of Gamelyn.

2. ARTHURIAN LEGENDS

I. The Whole Life of Arthur—Layamon's *Brut, Arthur, Morte Arthure;* II. Merlin and the Youth of Arthur—*Arthour and Merlin,* the prose *Merlin,* the verse *Merlin;* III. Lancelot and the Last Years of Arthur—*Le Morte Arthur, Lancelot of the Laik;* IV. Gawain—*Sir Gawayne and the Grene Knight, The Grene Knight, The Turke and Gowin, Syre Gawene and the Carle of Carelyle, The Awntyrs of Arthure, Golagrus and Gawain, The Avowynge of Arthur, Ywain and Gawain, The Weddynge of Sir Gawen and Dame Ragnell, The Jeaste of Syr Gawayne, Libeaus Desconus;* V. Perceval—*Sir Percyvelle of Galles;* VI. The Holy Grail— *Joseph of Arimathie,* Lovelich's *History of the Holy Grail;* VII. Tristram—*Sir Tristrem.*

3. CHARLEMAGNE LEGENDS

I. Firumbras—*The Sowdone of Babylone, Sir Firumbras, Charles the Grete;* II. Otuel—*Roland and Vernagu, The Sege of Melayne, Otuel, Duke Rowlande and Sir Ottuell,* the Fillingham

Otuel; III. Detached Romances—*The Song of Roland, The Taill of Rauf Coilȝear, The Foure Sonnes of Aymon, Huon of Burdeux.*

4. LEGENDS OF GODFREY OF BOUILLON

Chevalere Assigne, Helyas, Godefroy of Boloyne.

5. LEGENDS OF ALEXANDER THE GREAT

The Lyfe of Alisaunder or *King Alisaunder;* the Alliterative Fragments, *Alisaunder, Alexander and Dindimus, The Wars of Alexander;* the *Alexander-Cassamus Fragment;* the prose *Alexander;* the Scottish *Alexander Buik;* Hay's *Buik of King Alexander;* the fragments of a printed Alexander piece.

6. LEGENDS OF TROY

The Gest Historiale of the Destruction of Troy, The Seege of Troye, the Laud *Troy-Book,* Chaucer's *Troilus and Criseyde,* Lydgate's *Troy-Book,* the Barbour *Troy-Book,* the Rawlinson prose *Siege of Troy, The Recuyell of the Historyes of Troye.*

7. LEGENDS OF THEBES

Lydgate's *Siege of Thebes,* the Rawlinson prose *Siege of Thebes.*

8. EUSTACE-CONSTANCE-FLORENCE-GRISELDA LEGENDS

Sir Isumbras, Sir Eglamour of Artois, Sir Torrent of Portyngale, Octovian, Sir Triamour, The King of Tars, Le Bone Florence of Rome (and Chaucer's *Man of Law's Tale* and *Clerk's Tale,* and Gower's *Confessio Amantis,* Book II 3).

9. BRETON LAIS

Lai le Freine; Sir Orfeo; Emare; Sir Launfal, Sir Landeval, Sir Lambewell, Sir Lamwell; Sir Degare; Sir Gowther; The Earl of Toulous; Chaucer's *Franklin's Tale.*

10. MISCELLANEOUS ROMANCES

I. Romances of Greek or Byzantine Origin—*Apollonius of Tyre, Floris and Blauncheflur;* II. Composites of Courtly Romance— *Sir Degrevant, Generydes, Parthenope of Blois, Ipomadon, The Lyfe of Ipomydon, Ipomedon, The Squyr of Lowe Degre;* III. Romances on Historical Themes—*Richard Coer de Lyon, Titus and Vespasian* or *The Siege of Jerusalem* (couplet and alliterative versions), Barbour's *Bruce;* IV. Romances from Family Tradition— *Partenay, Melusine, The Knight of Curtesy;* V. Legendary Romances of Didactic Intent—*Amis and Amiloun, Sir Amadace, Sir Cleges, Roberd of Cisyle.*

GROUPS OF ROMANCES ACCORDING TO PROBABLE CHRONOLOGY AND DIALECT OF ORIGINAL COMPOSITION

1100-1250

South-East or Midland: *King Horn* (extant version c. 1225 or earlier).
South: *Beues of Hamtoun* (beginning 13th century).

1250-1350

North: *Ywain and Gawain* (1300-1350); *Octovian* (later version, c. 1350).
North Midland: *Roland and Vernagu* (before 1325); *Guy of Warwick* (after 1300); *Horn Childe* (1300-1325).
North-West Midland or North: *Sir Tristrem* (end of 13th century).
North-East Midland: *Havelok* (before 1275); *Amis and Amiloun* (c. 1300).
Midland: *King of Tars* (before 1325).
East Midland: *Guy of Warwick*, story of *Reinbrun* (before 1325); *Floris and Blauncheflur* (c. 1250); *Tale of Gamelyn* (c. 1340 or 1350).
West Midland: *Alisaunder*, Fragment A, and *Alexander and Dindimus*, Fragment B (both extant in West Midland of c. 1340).
South-West Midland: *Sir Degare* (before 1325).
South-East Midland: *Otuel* (beginning 14th century); *Guy of Warwick* (after 1300).
South-East: *Sir Launfal* (1325-1350); *Libeaus Desconus* (1325-1350); *Octovian* (earlier version, c. 1350).
Kent: *Arthour and Merlin* (1250-1300, not after 1325); *Richard Coer de Lyon* (reign of Edward I); *King Alisaunder* (1275-1300, not after 1325).
Southern: *Lai le Freine* (perhaps South-East Midland; beginning 14th century); *Sir Orfeo* (perhaps South Midland; beginning 14th century).

1350-1400

North or Scotland: *Gest Historiale of the Destruction of Troy* (1350-1400).
North: *Sege of Melayne* (1350-1400); *Sir Eglamour* (1350-1400); *Morte Arthure* (1350-1400); *Sir Percyvelle* (1350-1400); *Sir Degrevant* (1350-1400); *Duke Rowlande and Sir Ottuell* (c. 1400).
North, near Carlisle: *Awntyrs of Arthure* (c. 1350, 1350-1400); *Avowynge of Arthur* (c. 1350, 1350-1400).
North or North-West: *Chevalere Assigne* (end of 14th century); *Sir Amadace* (1350-1400).

North or North Midland: *Le Bone Florence* (c. 1400).
North-West Midland: *Sir Gawayne and the Grene Knight* (c. 1370); *Le Morte Arthur* (end of 14th century); Laud *Troy-Book* (c. 1400).
North Midland: *Ipomadon* (earlier version, c. 1350 or earlier); *Athelston* (c. 1350).
North-East Midland or North Midland: *Sir Gowther* (c. 1400 or early 15th century).
North-East Midland: *Emare* (1375-1400); *Sir Isumbras* (1350-1400).
West Midland: *William of Palerne* (c. 1350).
West or South-West Midland: *Joseph of Arimathie* (c. 1350).
South-West Midland: *Song of Roland* (1350-1400).
South-East Midland: Tales of Chaucer and Gower; *Titus and Vespasian* (couplet version, c. 1375-1400).
East Midland: *Sowdone of Babylone* (c. 1400 or soon after).
South Midland: *Roberd of Cisyle* (before 1380).
South: *Arthur* (1350-1400); *Seege of Troye* (1380-1400); *Sir Firumbras* (1375-1400).

After 1400

Scotland: Troy poem by Barbour (15th century); *Alexander Buik* (? c. 1438); *Golagrus and Gawain* (1450-1500); *Taill of Rauf Coilƺear* (1475-1500); *Sir Lancelot of the Laik* (1475-1500); Hay's *Buik of Alexander* (before 1494).
North: Thornton Prose *Alexander* (before 1430).
North or North Midland: *Syre Gawene and the Carle of Carelyle* (14th or 15th century); *Turke and Gowin* (15th century); *Foure Sonnes of Aymon* (printed c. 1481); *Huon of Burdeux* (printed ? 1534).
North Midland: *Sir Triamour* (1400-1450); *Sir Cleges* (beginning 15th century); *Partenay* (1400-1450).
East Midland: *Lyfe of Ipomydon* (beginning 15th century); *Squyr of Lowe Degre* (c. 1450); Lydgate's *Troy-Book* (c. 1410) and *Siege of Thebes* (1420-1422).
North-East Midland or North: *Torrent of Portyngale* (1400-1450); *Earl of Toulous* (beginning 15th century).
Midland: *Generydes* (c. 1430).
South Midland: *Grene Knight* (15th century); *Weddynge of Sir Gawen* (15th century); *Jeaste of Syr Gawene* (15th century).
South or South Midland: Lovelich's *History of the Holy Grail* (c. 1450) and *Merlin* (c. 1450); *Partonope of Blois* (two versions, 1400-1450).
South: Rawlinson fragments of prose *Siege of Troy* and *Siege of Thebes* (1420-1450); *Tale of Beryn* (1400-1450). ✔

Among other pieces after 1400 that may be mentioned, are: *King Ponthus and the Fair Sidone* (after 1450); Malory's *Morte Darthur* (1469-1470, printed 1485); the Scottish *Roswall and*

Lillian and *Sir Eger, Sir Grime, and Sir Gray-Steel* (first mentioned 1497); Caxton's editions of *The Recuyell of the Histories of Troye* (c. 1474), *Godefroy of Boloyne* (1481), *Charles the Grete* (1485), *Paris and Vienne* (1488), *Blanchardyn and Eglantine* (c. 1489), *Eneydos* (1490), and *The Three King's Sons* (MS. c.1500); *Melusine* (near 1500); de Worde's editions of *Apollyn of Tyre* (1510) and *Joseph of Arimathy;* Pynson's editions of *De Sancto Joseph Ab Arimathia* (1516) and *Joseph of Arimathia* (1520); Lord Berners' *Arthur of Little Britain; Clariodus* (MS. c. 1550); *Valentine and Orson;* Copland's editions of *The Knight of Curtesy* (1568) and *Helyas.*

1. ENGLISH AND GERMANIC LEGENDS

A number of allusions in early writings support the conjecture that many Germanic heroes became, as did Wade, Waltheof, and Hereward, the subjects of legends which circulated orally among the English, and that some of these were themes of written treatment. The few stories that have survived are, then, to be valued not only for their own worth, but also as the representatives of a considerable body of heroic tales. The common qualities of the extant pieces will be sufficiently evident from the discussions of the individual poems.

HORN seems to have been a favorite in story. He is the hero of the English *King Horn*, the French twelfth-century *Horn et Rymenhild*, the English fourteenth-century *Horn Childe and Maiden Rimnild*, the fifteenth-century French prose *Pontus et Sidoine* that was translated into English and into German prose, the Norse *Pontus-rímur*, and a number of Scottish, and several Norse, ballads.

Apparently the story is primarily of Danish origin, reaching back to the Danish invasions of England and dominance in Dublin. It is composed of two groups of incidents, those in England and those in Ireland. The former group centres in the love of Horn and Rimenhild, is novelistic, and is born of French and Norman elements. The second group of incidents is warlike; it centres in the 'exile-and-return' motive, and dominion in Ireland. The nature of the material and the form of the proper names, show the second group to be the earlier. Strong argument has been offered by Deutschbein for association of the story with Horm the Dane, who, having been expelled by Norwegians, landed in Ireland in 851, was aided by Cearbhall, King of Ossory, and in succeeding enterprises fought with Cearbhall against their common enemies the Norwegians, the Saracens of the tale.

The English *King Horn* and *Horn Childe*, and the French *Horn et Rymenhild*, have a common general plot. The English poems agree little in details, but each has a number of details in common with the French piece. The precise relationship of the three versions has not been determined. Evidently *King Horn* is the earliest. Possibly all are developed from a group of variant ballad versions.

KING HORN [1], the earliest of the extant English romances, is preserved in MS. Cbg. Univ. Libr. Gg 4, 27, 2 (c. 1250-1260) 1530 lines, MS. Laud Misc. 108 part II (c. 1300-1320) 1569 lines, MS. Harley 2253 (c. 1310) 1546 lines. MS. Gg is the best. The relationship of the MSS. is uncertain. Brandl and Wissmann regard them as independent of each other. Zupitza and Hall assign a common source to Laud and Harley. Hall believes that Laud and Harley are each one remove from this source, which, in turn, is directly from the common source of all these MSS. He holds that this common source is one remove from Gg, and that Gg is independent of the other extant MSS. The surviving version appears to be Midland or South Midland of about 1225.

Horn is the son of Murray and Godhild, King and Queen of Suddene. When the boy is fifteen years old, a band of Saracens land, and slay the King. The mother takes refuge under a rock. Because of his beauty, the pagans spare the boy's life; but fear of his strength causes them to send him away in a vessel alone with his boy friends, Athulf and Fikenhild. The youths row to the fair land of Almair, King of Westernesse. The King cares for them, and educates them. Horn becomes greatly beloved. Rymenhild, the King's daughter, sends the steward Athelbrus to bring Horn to her chamber where she lies sick for love of him. Athelbrus substitutes Athulf for the hero. The lady makes love to the supposed Horn. On learning of the cheat, she becomes furiously angry. Athelbrus finally brings Horn to her. She clips and kisses him, and declares she will be his wife. The youth urges his inferior birth; he would be knighted. By intercession of Athelbrus, he is dubbed. Rymenhild insists that he relieve her of her pain, but he protests that he must prove his prowess. The lady gives him and Athulf magic rings whose stones when looked upon protect from all blows. Horn slays a band of pagans that have come to ravage the country. The next day, the King goes a-hunting. Horn finds Rymenhild weeping because she has dreamed that, as she was fishing, a great fish that she desired to catch broke her net. The lovers plight troth, Horn explaining that the fish is one who will do them harm. Fikenhild betrays the lovers to the King, and accuses Horn of plotting to kill the King. Horn is banished. He takes ship, and arrives in Ireland. Under the name 'Cutberd,' he enters the service of the King of that country. At Christmas, aided by thought of his lady, he slays in single combat the giant champion of the Saracens that are besetting the King. Subse-quently, all the pagans are slain, but the King's sons fall. The King offers Cutberd his realm and his daughter. The hero post-pones acceptance for seven years. Meanwhile, Rymenhild is sought in marriage by a King whom she dares not refuse. Her messenger finds Horn, who sends back word that he will come to her at prime on Sunday. But the body of the messenger is washed up to Rymen-hild's door, and the lady is distracted. Horn arrives. He leaves his folk under a woodside. Disguised as a palmer, he forces his way into the castle, and, by dropping the magic ring into a cup, makes himself known to Rymenhild. He sends the princess to his folk, and summons Athulf. The knights slay the would-be hus-band and his fellows. To the King, Horn reveals his birth. With him he leaves the lady, while he goes to Suddene to win back his realm. With Athulf, he lands in Suddene. He finds Godhild is still living, summons the people, and slays the Saracens. Then he proceeds to build chapels and churches. Meanwhile, Fikenhild bribes the nobles, fortifies a castle, and demands Rymenhild as wife. Warned in a dream, Horn sets off to the aid of the princess. On his arrival he learns that Rymenhild is wedded to Fikenhild. Disguised as a harper, with his two companions he makes his way into the castle, and slays the traitor at his board. He rewards Athelbrus and Athulf, and with Queen Rymenhild lives happily in Suddene.

The origin and the structure of the verse of *King Horn* have been much discussed. Suggestions of possible original strophic form have been detected. The poem is in couplets that are a result of influence of the French short couplet on the Old Eng-lish long alliterative metre. The verses have now three, now four, stresses; a few exhibit survivals of the old two-stressed half-line. There appear some traces of alliteration within the line and between successive lines. A number of alliterative expressions in the poem are found in Layamon, and are perhaps from a considerable body of stock phrases current at the time.

The opening lines show that the poem was composed to be sung or, more probably, recited in public, evidently not so much to cultivated as to popular audiences. In form and in matter it is primitive, simple, homely, and unsophisticated—quite free from the courtly elements in the French, and in some of the later English, romances. It exhibits no embellishment for its own sake. Description, casuistry, and discussion of motive or situation, are absent. The love-element is unelaborated and without any of the courtly notions of the French. It is the maid, not the man, who pines for the loved one. The conditions of life in the poem are on a small scale; the domestic environment is limited; the royalty is restricted, its retinues are small. There is nothing of feudal relations.

The poem is vigorous, virile, straightforward. It has indeed much of the ballad quality. The poet suppresses himself. He is concise, sometimes even to a fault. He prefers to take for granted and to allude, rather than to narrate. He presents the essential fact of each incident, and speeds from one incident to the next, often omitting the ordinary connective material, and often neglecting to present adequate motives for important incidents or deeds. But these very tendencies add to the spirit, the dignity, the freshness, and the native power, that make the poem one of the most notable pieces of Middle English literature.

HORN CHILDE AND MAIDEN RIMNILD [2] is preserved in MS. Auchinleck f. 317 v (1330-1340). It consists of 1136 verses in twelve-line tail-rime stanzas normally aabaabccbddb. Some ten stanzas show variation from the normal rime scheme, and several others are defective. Assonance and alliteration often appear. The work is probably of 1300-1325, and perhaps originally of the North Midland.

Hatheolf, King of all the North of England, has but one child, Horn, whom he rears with eight other boys as his companions. Arlaund is their instructor in all manly sports. In assisting the King to overcome a band of pagan invaders at Clifland, the fathers of the eight boys are slain. To each youth the King gives his father's property; and he swears all to fidelity to Horn. Nine months later, Hatheolf is slain after a dreadful combat with some Irish invaders. Arlaund flees with the boys to Houlac, a King in the South of England, who receives them well and cares for them. Horn is famed for fairness and manly attainments. The King's daughter, Rimnild, falls in love with him. She summons him to her chamber. Arlaund substitutes Hatherof, one of the other youths. But Hatherof reveals the trick. Horn is given fair gifts in the chamber—a horse, a horn, and a sword. He promises he will fight for the lady's sake. Within a fortnight, he is knighted. Soon after, he wins the prize at a joust. The King offers Horn any maiden in his court. The eight companions depart on adventures. Two of Horn's companions, Wiard and Wikel, declare to the King that Horn and Rimnild are carrying on improper relations. The King beats the innocent maiden, and decrees Horn's death. The lovers part, promising seven years of fidelity. Horn bears away Rimnild's magic ring. He goes to Wales, where he overcomes a valiant knight, and, later, conquers the king of the country. In Ireland, he rescues the realm of King Finlac from pagan invaders. Finlac rewards him with land; and his daughter bestows her love on the hero. Seven years pass. Warned by his ring, Horn returns to England. He finds Rimnild about to be married. Clothed as a beggar, he has a colloquy with the King, is admitted to the feast in the hall, and reveals himself to Rimnild through the ring. Hatherof supplies him with equipment and knights. In a tournament Horn overthrows the would-be bridegroom. He slays Wiard, and puts out Wikel's eyes. He is wedded to Rimnild.

Chaucer rightly included *Horn Childe* in his parody in *Sir Thopas*. The poem is of the decadence of the story. In details of matter and in expression, it is conventional. Its verse is sing-song and monotonous, with all the triteness and triviality of the tail-rime stanza in a romancer's hands. Perhaps from anxiety for novelty, perhaps largely from the nature of the version used by the author, possibly from a remodeling after stories other than that of Horn, the details of the poem vary greatly from those in *King Horn*. Most of the variations are, to say the least, not improvement. It should be noted that the hero of *Horn Childe* is not a Dane, but a Northumbrian; that

his father wars against the Irish; and that, on leaving Rimnild, Horn goes first to Wales, and later aids the King of Wales
in Ireland.

All the simplicity, force, directness, conciseness, and dignity
of the earlier piece, are lost in *Horn Childe*. The author
has little appreciation of quality, little discrimination; of
vigor of expression and intrinsic worth of matter, he knows
nothing. He ekes out lines or meets the needs of rime with
stock phrases, and with circumlocution and redundancy. For
essential worth and pith, he substitutes everywhere elaboration of unimportant detail. He has the late romancer's weakness for the specific. Losing sight of perspective at the very
beginning, he devotes a fifth of his poem to the contests of
Horn's father. He carefully localizes definitely the incidents
of the story at 'Clifland bi Teseside,' at 'Blakerowemore,' at
'Pikering'; he enumerates the associates of Horn; he elaborates
the charm of Rimnild's ring; he introduces gifts and food and
description of each into the account of Rimnild's reception of
Hathcrof; he details the appearance of Rimnild's bower, and
the dishes she prepares for Horn's reception; he names the
hero's sword 'Blauain.' In contrast to the abundance of
matter, the native power, and the unconscious spontaneity of
King Horn, the poem exhibits poverty, inefficiency, and anxious
effort.

Hind Horn [3] is the name under which the banquet scene of
Horn Childe is dealt with in the Scottish ballads.

King Ponthus and the Fair Sidone [4], in MS. Digby 185
and MS. Douce 384 (a fragment), is a fifteenth-century prose
translation of the French *Ponthus et Sidoine* composed before
1445 by Ponthus de la Tour Landri, who, in glorification of
his family, turned the French romance of Horn into a sort of
text-book for training to perfect knighthood. Ponthus was a
son by second marriage of the wife of Geoffrey de la Tour
Landri, who, for the instruction of his daughters, wrote the
French original of the English prose *Book of the Knight of
La Tour Landri*, that was translated in the reign of Henry VI.

THE LAY OF HAVELOK [5] is preserved in MS. Laud Misc. 108 part II ff. 206-19 (c. 1300-1320), and in four fragments in MS. Cbg. Univ. Libr. 4407 (19) (14th century), corresponding to Laud ll. 341-64, 537-44 (with ten added lines), 545-46 (with one added line), 547-49, but from a text earlier than that of Laud. There are two French versions, one in ll. 37-818 of Gaimar's *L'Estorie des Engleis* (1141-1151), the other the *Lai d'Havelok* (12th century). A third version is indicated by interpolation made in mention of the story in the Lambeth MS. of Robert of Brunne's *Chronicle* (see page 199). The Laud version is probably fourth in descent from the common French original of all the extant versions, and is independent of the extant French versions. It consists of 3001 four-stress lines, normally in couplets, with occasional occurrence of a group of 4 or 6, and once of 19, verses on one rime. Alliteration is rare, and the couplets are clearly affected by the French short couplet. The verse was apparently intended for recitation, not for singing.

The original of the *Lay* is possibly from the days of the invasions and dominance of the Danes in England, perhaps from the early tenth century. Possibly the early development of the story arose from concern of the Danes to justify their rule in the island. Close association of at least some elements of the story with Lincolnshire, is indicated by occurrence in the English poem of a number of local place-names, by use of local traditions, and by presence of the name of the city Grimsby, whose ancient seal contains labeled effigies of 'Habloc,' 'Gryem,' and 'Goldeburgh.'

The fact that Havelok is dealt with in Gaimar's *Estoire*, and is mentioned in several chronicles (*e.g.*, those of Robert of Brunne, Pierre de Langtoft, and de Boun), suggests that, perhaps even earlier than the time of these chronicles, Havelok was regarded as a historical personage. 'Habloc,' on the Grimsby seal, has been shown to be a variant of 'Olaf,' from 'Anlaf.' In the *Metrical Chronicle of England* (see page 198), line 797, Olaf Tryggvason is called 'Haveloc'; and in the ballad of *Guy and Colbrande*, Olaf Cuaran is styled 'Auelocke.' Perhaps the hero and the tale of Havelok are rightly to be asso-

ciated with the personality and history of this Olaf or Anlaf
Cuaran (Olaf with the leather buskin). Gaimar applies to
Havelok the epithet 'Cuherun,' and the French *Lai* applies
that of 'Cuaran.' It is perhaps more likely that the original
of Havelok was Reginwald, uncle of Anlaf, who in the course
of the development of the saga was displaced by Anlaf. Exiled
from his home in Northumbria by Athelstan; become son-in-
law of Constantine III of Scotland; head of the league against
Athelstan beaten at Brunanburh; after Athelstan's death,
King of Northumbria; driven into exile, to return and again
to be driven out; subsequently, many years a king at Dublin;
Anlaf died a monk at Iona in 981.

In his *Handlyng Synne*, published in 1303, Robert of Brunne
echoes *Havelok*, lines 679-80, 819-20. In his *Le Bruit Dengle-
terre* (1310), Rauf de Boun cites the English version. The
part of MS. Laud containing *King Horn* and *Havelok*, is of
about 1310, and not later than 1320. Perhaps the conjectured
fourth MS. back of Laud is of about 1275-1280. The language of MS. Laud is mixed, having suffered much from confusion of dialects and scribal peculiarities. The original dialect
is doubtful, but is probably North-East Midland.

Dying, King Æthelwold of England gives his only child Goldborough to Godrich, Earl of Cornwall, to foster and to marry to
the best, fairest, and strongest man in the realm. On his death-
bed, Birkabeyn, King of Denmark, leaves his son Havelok and his
two daughters to the guardianship of Earl Godard. Godard murders the maidens, and hands over Havelok to a fisherman, Grim,
to be drowned. At night, by the bright flame that issues from his
mouth, and by the King's mark on his shoulder, Grim recognizes
Havelok as future King of Denmark. With his family and the boy,
he sails to England, lands at the mouth of the Humber, and founds
Grimsby. Havelok grows very strong, works earnestly at menial
tasks with his foster-father, becomes servant to the cook of Earl
Godrich, and wins renoun for his diligence and for his ability in
sports. To degrade Goldborough, yet to fulfil his oath to Æthelwold, Godric, against the will of the pair, weds the princess to
Havelok. The couple go to Grimsby. There in bed, grieving at
her disgrace, Goldborough sees the light from Havelok's mouth
and the King's mark, and is assured by an angel's voice that Havelok is of royal birth and that he and she shall rule England and
Denmark. She is reconciled. Havelok relates a dream that within
a year he shall be a great king. With Grim and his sons, the lovers

go to Denmark. Havelok gains the favor of the mighty earl, Ubbe. He valiantly defends himself and his wife from assailants. Ubbe recognizes his kingly stock by the flame and the mark, dubs him knight, and aids him to an army. Godard is beaten and hanged. Havelok becomes King. Later, he overcomes Godrich. England submits to Havelok's rule. Godrich is burned at the stake. The daughters of Grim are married off nobly.

The frank, familiar, offhand opening is characteristic of all the story. The poem is without polish; it is blunt, bluff, hearty, direct. It was probably told by a wandering gleeman in kitchen or at village gathering-place, not in bower or in hall. It is a story of a king's son and a king's daughter, told for the common people from the point of view of the populace, of the day-worker of the period. The poet touches little on kingship and knightly prowess or courtly behavior. Havelok is a youth after the heart of the common folk. He is stalwart and lusty, a hero of the kitchen and the fisher's boat, a champion at good old English sports. His life, like that of his foster-parents and foster-brethren, is the life of the simple fisher. The environment of the incidents is homely. It is at Bernard Brown's house that Earl Ubbe shelters Havelok, and Griffin Galle is the chief of those who attack him there. The opening passage concerning the reforms made by King Æthelwold, would come home to the people, who in the thirteenth century were complaining more and more of the wretchedness of the poor, the prevalence of robbers, and the uncertainty of the law. The poet utters many proverbs. He calls his villain 'Judas.' His vocabulary is unpolished, his few figures are born of humble conditions. Yet withal his hero is a king's son. The poem has not the simple dignity of *King Horn*. But it is vigorous, direct, full of power and of genuine feeling; it is sound and true. As were its thirteenth-century hearers, the reader of to-day is caught and held by the quick succession of its incidents, the realness of its situations, the swing and go of its action, and the hearty sincerity and the primitive soundness of its concerns and its attitudes.

GUY OF WARWICK [6] became one of the most popular of the mediæval romances. In addition to the numerous MSS.

in French, there exist in English a version in (A) the Auchinleck MS. (c. 1330-1340), (C) MS. Caius College Cbg. 107
(beginning 15th century) containing also all the continuations
of incident after Guy's marriage, and (S) MS. Sloane 1044 (a
fragment, 14th century); a second version, the continuation of
Guy's story after marriage, and also the story of Reinbrun, in
(a) the Auchinleck MS.; a third version, fragments, in (P)
Br. Mus. MS. Addit. 14408 (14th century; fragment); and a
fourth version in (c) MS. Cbg. Univ. Libr. Ff II 38 (15th
century) and in several parts of MS. Caius College Cbg. 107.
All of these English versions are translations, often very
close, from the French. The French versions may go back
to the twelfth century; the earliest extant English version was
made first probably at about 1300. Version (a) is in the
twelve-line tail-rime stanza aabaabccbddb or aabccbddbeeb;
the rest of the versions are in short couplets. (A) has about
7100 lines, with a little over 200 more lines missing; (a) has
299 strophes, the story of Reinbrun having 127 more strophes;
(c) has 11976 lines; (S) has 216 lines; (C) has 11095 lines.
(A) is perhaps of South Warwickshire; (a) is from a little
north of (A); (c) and (P) are perhaps of the North Midland; and the story of Reinbrun is probably from the East
Midland. The following is a synopsis of the oldest versions,
those in MS. Auchinleck.

Guy, son of Siward, steward of Rohand, Earl of Warwick, is
cupbearer to the Earl. He falls in love with the daughter of
Rohand, Felice, who scorns the steward's son. Finally impressed
with his love, the lady agrees that if he were knighted she would
grant him favor. Roland knights Guy. Felice declares Guy must
prove his prowess. The Knight goes oversea, and wins great glory
in various lands. On his return, Felice refuses to marry him, for
marriage might prevent him from adding to his glory; when he
is peerless she will wed him. Guy goes back to the Continent.
After proving his supremacy in various enterprises, among which
are his relations with the Emperor of Germany, his saving of Constantinople, and his association with Sir Tirri, he returns again,
to be received with honor by King Æthelstan, and to kill a dragon
that has been infesting Northumberland.

Here the couplets end, and the strophic version (a) begins.
Felice is wedded to Guy. There is much joy for fifteen days.
Then Guy is suddenly struck with remorse for his undevout life.

Abandoning his wife and unborn child, he becomes a pilgrim. Journeying in the East, he fights a Saracen giant, Amorant. In Germany, he again aids Sir Tirri. An old man, he returns to England, where near Winchester he champions England against the African giant Colbrand, representative of the Danes under Anlaf. He kills the giant, in disguise visits his wife, becomes a hermit, and later dies in his wife's arms.

Reinbrun, Gy sone of Warwike, which follows in the (a) version, illustrates the romance tendency to satisfy popular demand for more matter concerning a hero, by giving accounts of his relations or descendants.

At the age of seven years, Reinbrun, son of Guy, is stolen and presented to Argus, King of Africa. Heraud, to whom Guy on his first departure has bidden Felice to give their son, goes in quest of the child, but is wrecked, and finally imprisoned, in Africa. He champions the cause of Amiral Parsan against Argus, who, through the valor of a youthful knight, has almost conquered Parsan. After a mighty duel with the youth, Heraud beseeches him to declare his name. He learns that the hero is Reinbrun. The knights are reconciled. Reinbrun frees his friend Amis from an enchanted castle. In Burgundy, he fights a duel with a powerful knight, whom luckily he discovers to be Haslak, son of Heraud, in quest of his father. The three knights go to England, where Æthelstan welcomes them with honor. Reinbrun is received at Warwick with great rejoicing.

No doubt much of the detail of this long-drawn-out story of Guy is a product of imagination or of combination of common romance material. Possibly Guy is to be connected with a certain Wigod of Wallingford, a cupbearer of Edward the Confessor, and a favorite of William the Conqueror. Perhaps Guy's father was Siward, son of Thurkill, the last Saxon lord of Warwick and the founder of the house of Arden. Felice may be connected with Filicia or Letitia, granddaughter of Thurkill. That the great event of Guy's life, the combat with Colbrand, is based on some historical episode, seems probable; but the episode has not been identified.

The romance proper falls into two parts—the incidents preceding Guy's marriage to Felice, and those following it. The popularity of the story may be partly accounted for by its double appeal, first to those who loved narratives of warlike

achievement and courtly behavior, and secondly to those of religious inclination. It would appear that an earlier version
fell into the hands of an ecclesiastic, who for his own ends
added the ascetic second part. A strong patriotic appeal is
manifest in the notable episode of the duel with Colbrand in
defense of England.

The romance is a long-winded narrative of insignificant incidents, many of which might be omitted without detriment to
the plot. The first episode of Sir Tirri, for example, is purely
gratuitous, yet occupies over twenty-five hundred lines. Triteness of matter, overlapping of phrases, and sheer wordiness,
add to the tediousness of the piece. As his expression at the
outset shows, the author was evidently a reader of books, who
wrote up various details and effects that he had encountered.
Fondness for elaboration is manifest in numerous passages—
e.g., the description of the personages, the exposition of the
education of the heroine, the details of the various encounters
in jousts and in combats, the description of the ornaments of
Guy's shield, and the items of Colbrand's equipment. There
are a number of recognition-scenes. In contrast with the holding to bare facts of incident in *King Horn, Guy* carries over
the French concern for analysis of feeling. For direct narrative, it substitutes conversation. Protest, lamentation, and
meditation in soliloquy, are employed for presentation of inner
experience. Except in the accounts of the duel with Colbrand and the contest with Amorant, there is little vigor or
spirit in the romance. Perhaps it is merely the change of
metre that causes one to get the impression of a better manner
in the opening of the strophic portion of the tale.

From the sixteenth and seventeenth centuries are extant
among others the following pieces: *Guy and Phillis* [7]; *Guy
and Colebrande* [8]; *Guy and Amarant* [9]; some seventy-four
eight-line stanzas of a version by Lydgate [10], dealing with
Guy's fight with the giant and his experience at the hermitage;
John Lane's version [11] (1621) of the story, in some 17500
lines; Samuel Rowlands' *Famous History of Guy, Earl of Warwick*, printed in twelve cantos in 1630, and partly represented
in *Guy and Amarant*.

The Speculum Guy (see page 275) is the product of a handling of the story for religious ends, carrying farther the aim manifested in the addition to the romance of the account of Guy's life as pilgrim and as hermit.

WILLIAM OF PALERNE [12], the earliest, or after *Joseph of Arimathie* the next to earliest, romance of the fourteenth-century alliterative revival (see page 240), is preserved in MS. King's College Cbg. 13 (1350, or soon after). It consists of 5540 alliterative long lines, in which generally the alliteration is not so regularly sustained as in the later alliterative romances. It is composed probably in the West Midland. Near the beginning and at the end of the poem we learn that the author was a certain 'William,' who translated the piece from the French at command of Sir Humphrey de Bohun, Earl of Hereford. As Bohun died in 1361, and in 1349 returned from a trip to France, the date of the translation may be fixed at about 1350.

Just what is the ultimate source of the story, is uncertain. The werwolf motive was known among Romans, Scandinavians, and Celts. The title of the romance and the names of the cities referred to, seem to point to Italy and to support the ascription of the French poem to a Latin source, composed perhaps in Italy or in Sicily. The love-matter between the hero and the heroine is derived from later Greek romance (see page 139), and its treatment gives to the story much of the atmosphere of the Greek tales. The French romance, *Guillaume de Palerne* (1150-1200), is by its author said to be translated from Latin into Romance by command of Yolande, daughter of Baldwin IV, Count of Hainault. The English romance shows in details extraordinary independence of the extant French poetical version; but, since it is much closer to the sixteenth-century French prose version by Durand, possibly some or many of its variations may be derived from a lost French source.

The English MS. is defective at the beginning. From the French one learns that William is son of a King of Apulia, Sicily, Palermo, and other lands. His uncle plots to poison the child. A werwolf, who in his childhood has been enchanted by his step-mother, the Queen of Spain, saves the boy by carrying him off and fostering him. One day (and here the English begins), William is found and carried home by a cowherd. Childless, the peasant and his wife adopt the boy, whom they come to love dearly. Attracted by his appearance, the Emperor of Rome takes the youth under his patronage. His daughter, Melior, and the boy fall in love. Through Alisaundrine, the girl companion of Melior, who acts as go-between, the lovers are brought together and long enjoy each other in secret. William exhibits great prowess in battle in Saxony and in Lombardy. Marriage is arranged between Melior and the Emperor of Greece. The lovers flee, sewed in bearskins. In the forest, the werwolf supplies them with food, and misleads their pursuers; finally, he guides them into Sicily, clothed as hart and hind. There they find William's half-brother and his father, the King of Spain. William overcomes the Spaniards, and acts for the Queen in the stead of her lost son. Ultimately, he captures the King of Spain and his son. Learning from the King of the enchantment of the werwolf, William compels the Queen to undo her magic. The restored Alphonse reveals the identity and the past history of William. William and Melior are wedded. Alphonse marries William's sister. Alisaundrine is advantageously matched. William becomes Emperor of Rome, and rewards his foster-parents.

Underlying the machinery of the plot as a whole is the widely known werwolf theme. Love is the chief motive of the romance; war is introduced only so far as it is needed to exhibit the prowess of the hero and to untie the plot. The tale is a good love-story made up by combination of familiar elements. The earlier part is characterized by introspection and elaborate analysis of feeling through soliloquy, meditation, and dialogue. The passages dealing with the relations between the cowherd and his wife and William and the peasant boys, between the lovers, and between William and his mother, exhibit able sympathetic handling of affecting situations. The devotion of the werwolf is well presented. From his apology at the end of the poem one may infer that the author recognized somewhat that the vigorous, rougher, alliterative verse was not so appropriate for his sophisticated matter as was the fluent couplet of the French romances. Yet the verse is surprisingly well composed, and at times notably smooth. In the piece there is evinced no realization that the relations between the lovers are reprehensible. Warnings in dreams and through magic, recognition-scenes of several types, and, especially at the conclusion, the giving of advice as to conduct by most of the personages, play a prominent part in the poem. Now and again, as in the behavior of the Emperor after his daughter's flight, there is struck a surprisingly realistic, one may say modern, note. The poem is interesting and attractive, and gets on well to an effective climax in the midst of a scene of recognition between William and his mother; but the catastrophe, consisting of nine hundred lines, is made up of quite unimportant and non-essential details. Unnecessary narrative by personages of series of events already related, mars the story.

SIR BEUES OF HAMTOUN [13] celebrates a hero who was little less popular than Guy of Warwick. Of his story, there are extant at least nine MSS. in French verse, and two in French prose. There are six versions in Italian, and versions in Dutch, Cymric, Irish, Yiddish, Russian, Norse, and Roumanian. The Anglo-Norman *Boeve de Haumtone* is of the early thirteenth century. The original of the story is no doubt much earlier than the extant French version and the original English version. The tale seems to be a composite from various sources, Anglo-Norman, Celtic, Oriental, and Germanic. The nature of some of its elements, joined with its general resemblance to the story of *King Horn*, makes acceptable an ascription of it to Germanic origin. Association of an early form of it with the Hamlet story, has been urged.

Sir Beues of Hamtoun, the English romance, is as it stands probably of about 1300. It was first translated perhaps near Southampton and perhaps as early as the beginning of the thirteenth century. It is preserved in MSS. Auchinleck (1330-1340), Caius College Cbg. 175 (15th century), Duke of Sutherland (now Egerton 2862; end of 14th century), Royal Libr. Naples XIII, B, 29 (15th century), Cbg. Univ. Libr. Ff II 38 (15th century), and Chetham Libr. 8009, Manchester (15th century). The Auchinleck MS., the oldest of the MSS., has 4620 verses. The first 474 verses are in tail-rime strophes aabaab or aabccb, the tails of two, the other verses of four, stresses each. As Kölbing notes, Chaucer seems to have bor-

rowed the basis for his Sir *Thopas* metre from *Sir Beues*
rather than from *Guy*. After line 474, the poem is in short
couplets.

Having induced the Emperor of Germany to murder her husband, Guy, Earl of Southampton, and having married the mur-
derer, the mother of Bevis eventually sells her protesting son as a
slave. The youth is given to the King of Armenia, who offers him
his daughter, Josian, as wife. The Christian hero refuses the offer.
He saves the realm from a devastating boar, and preserves Josian
from a violent suitor, Brademond. Pressing her love by promise
of becoming a Christian, Josian wins Bevis' favor. Misinformed
of the lovers' relations, the King sends Bevis to Brademond with
a sealed letter. Brademond imprisons the knight in a dungeon for
seven years. There he must with a stick protect himself from
dragons. Josian is compelled to marry Yvor, King of Mombrant;
but by magic she preserves her virginity. Bevis finally escapes.
He kills a giant. He visits Jerusalem, where the Patriarch bids
him wed only a virgin, and where he learns that Josian is married.
Disguised as a palmer, he visits Mombrant. With Josian, he flees
to Cologne. Thence he goes to aid his foster-father, Saber, against
the German Emperor. Meanwhile, Josian is forced to marry Earl
Miles. On the wedding-night she hangs her husband. Bevis rescues her from punishment at the stake, and conveys her to England.
There, with Saber, he defeats and executes the Emperor. The
Empress comes to a violent end. Bevis and Josian are married.
But King Edgar forces Bevis to leave England. Josian bears two
boys on the journey, and is carried off by partisans of Yvor. Bevis
leaves the boys with foster-fathers. His prowess at a tournament
wins him the heart of a princess. The lady proposes that Bevis
be her lord in virginity; if they hear that Josian is not dead, the
princess will marry Terri, a son of Saber. Saber rescues Josian.
She travels with him, and is finally united with Bevis and the boys.
Bevis slays Yvor, and takes his realm. With Saber, Bevis wins
back for the latter's son his property taken by King Edgar. Bevis
and his sons overcome the Londoners, and one of the sons is promised the King's daughter. Bevis and Josian go back to the East,
and die together.

Probably because Chaucer mentioned Sir Bevis in his *Sir
Thopas*, general commentators have given the romance much
less approval than it merits. The story is much superior to
that of Guy. Though many of the incidents could be omitted,
and though the tale could be ended with the death of the evil
mother, the plot is well worked out to the punishment of the
villains and the glory and happiness of the heroes. The suc-

cessive incidents are at times introduced somewhat abruptly; but the action is rapid, and interest does not flag. There is little tendency to over-elaboration; the dialogue is to the point; as a rule the writer deals with his matter and has done. He frequently refers to his 'romance' original; but, unless he used a version that varies much from any of those extant in French, he did not merely translate. He appears to introduce details freely at every turn, adding vividness and picturesque_ ness. Three extended passages making up some eight hundred and fifty lines, or over a sixth of the whole, are apparently his own. These narrate the fight with the Dragon of Cologne; the contest with the Londoners; and the Christmas Day battle with the Saracens and the boar hunt. With them is to be joined the vivid picture of the abused, fierce-eyed, lonely, wounded boy in the attic, fearful of punishment and warning off all who approach. The matter and the expression are homely and plain. Almost every detail counts in vivifying the scene or the feeling.

The story is full of intimate human nature, of warm life, of genuine sympathy, that manifest themselves in direct, spontaneous, even blunt utterance that is surprisingly realistic. Again and again, as it were, life blurts out. That the writer had no little humor is shown by his account of the giant page, Asclopard, and his 'baptism.' The matter of the tale, as well as these qualities, was sure to make it popular. It is a story of an evil mother, of a base stepfather, of an illtreated child passionate under abuse; of a boy and man devoted to Christian customs and a champion of the Faith; of a man robbed of his glory and his liberty and his lover, and cruelly tormented for seven years; of a man who cannot be bribed to abandon a friend; of a savior of nations from cruel beasts; of jousts and battles; of magic and of giants and dragons; and of the warm love of a devoted woman.

ATHELSTON [14], in MS. Caius College Cbg. 175 (15th century), was composed in the North Midland dialect at about 1350. It consists of 811 verses, mostly in twelve-line tail- rime stanzas usually aabccbddbeeb. Though no original of

the poem is extant, the history of the other English romances
would lead to inference that the author's frequent references
to oral and to 'romance' written versions, are not mere reflection of the common mediæval device for gaining credence and
weight for narrative.

Four messengers, meeting by chance in a forest, swear to be
brothers. One of them, Athelstan, becomes King of England. He
makes one brother Archbishop of Canterbury, another Earl of
Dover, and the third Earl of Stane and husband of his sister.
Dover becomes jealous of Athelstan's fondness for Stane and his
children, and, under oath of secrecy, falsely accuses Stane and his
wife of plotting against the King. Enraged, Athelstan entices
Stane and his family to London, and imprisons them. The Queen
intercedes for them. Her furious husband kicks her, and so kills
her unborn child. The Queen sends for the Archbishop, who comes
and intervenes. Angered, the King orders the Archbishop to give
up his office. The priest excommunicates the King, and bans the
realm. The people prepare to rise; the King quickly sends submission. The Archbishop assumes control of affairs, and by ordeal
exculpates the Count of Stane and his family. The Countess gives
birth to a son, the future Saint Edmund. The King names the boy
his heir. The false accuser of Stane is exposed in confession. He
fails at the ordeal, and is executed.

The romance has been strangely neglected. It is an excellent piece of narrative, well told and interesting from first to
last. The opening incident of the messengers and their oath of
brotherhood, is striking; the account of the ride of the messenger from the palace to Canterbury, is spirited. Very effective, too, are the Archbishop's ride to London and his quarrel
with the King. Though the tail-rime cloys somewhat, the
verse is smooth and vigorous as well, moving admirably to
the sense. The situations lay hold of one; the emotion is
intense and genuine, despite the fact that, as in all the Germanic
romances in English, there is a tendency to high coloring of
incident and character. Much of the ballad quality is evident.
Perhaps it was in ballads that the author met the oral version
or versions to which he refers.

The fundamental element in the plot, the scheme against
Stane, reminds one of William of Malmesbury's narrative of the
reign of Æthelstan, under the dates 924-932. It has been suggested that the relations between the King and the Archbishop

reflect the quarrel between Henry II and Becket in 1163-1170, and that the characters and behavior of the King and the Archbishop in the story are closely similar to the characters of Henry and Becket, and to what would probably have been their behavior in identical circumstances. Whatever be the case here, the poem was made under ecclesiastical influence. The first two-thirds of it are the tale of a hot-headed, brutal king whose violence brings its own punishment through the killing of his unborn heir, and through public humiliation before the power of the Church. The last third deals with the detection of the truth, and the assignment of reward and punishment; but it is really illustrative of the supremacy of the Archbishop, and of the justice of Heaven through trial by ordeal. Historically inaccurate, the introduction of the birth of St. Edmund and of his acceptance as heir by the bereft Athelstan, points to the same ecclesiastical influence.

THE TALE OF GAMELYN [15], probably originally of the East Midland and of about 1350, is preserved in a number of the MSS. of the *Canterbury Tales*. It consists of some 900 verses in couplets. The verse is divided by a metrical pause. Normally, the first half of the verse has four stresses, and the second three, without regard to number of unstressed syllables, and often with stress immediately following stress.

Sir John de Boundys leaves his property in equal parts to his three sons. The eldest son undertakes the education of the youngest, Gamelyn. He lets the youth's property run down, takes the income, and feeds and clothes Gamelyn wretchedly. But the boy grows up mighty in strength and much beloved. One day, harshly chidden, he accuses the brother of abuse of the wardship. With a pestle he beats off men who are called in to punish him. The brother promises to deliver the property as he received it. To the general delight, Gamelyn wins the prize at wrestling. Shut out of their home by the brother's orders, the youth forces entrance. He breaks the porter's neck, and throws the body into a well. The brother being in hiding, for a week the hero entertains the neighborhood at a great feast on the brother's goods. He makes reparation by giving the brother the profits of the estate that he has wrongfully enjoyed for fifteen years. To save the brother from failure to keep an oath, Gamelyn submits to being bound to a post in the hall. There for two days he is starved as a madman. On promise of a part of Gamelyn's property, Adam, the spencer (officer in charge of provisions), agrees to free and feed him. At a feast given by the brother, Gamelyn vainly prays the abbots and the priors to pity him. Then he casts off his bonds, 'assoils' the clergy and the rest with a drubbing, and breaks the brother's back and binds him by the post. He and Adam repulse the sheriff's posse that seek to take him. A new troop arriving, they flee to the woods. There Gamelyn becomes lieutenant and, later, 'king,' of a band of outlaws. The brother (now identified with the sheriff) has the hero outlawed. Hearing of this, Gamelyn appears at the moothall, and is cast into jail. His second brother, Sir Ote, pledges himself as bail. Gamelyn returns to the wood. Priests he mulcts of their property, but he spares all others. The eldest brother bribes the jury to condemn Gamelyn. Ote is seized as Gamelyn's substitute. The hero appears, sets him free, throws the Justice over the bar, and sits on the bench. Justice, sheriff, and jurors are all hanged. Ote and Gamelyn make their peace with the King. Ote is appointed Justice; Gamelyn is made Chief Justice of all the Free Forest; the outlaws receive good offices. The piece *states* finally that later Gamelyn wedded a wife fair and good.

Beyond its intrinsic merit, the piece has interest through its association with Chaucer and Shakespeare. Most of the material for *As You Like It* came from Lodge's *Rosalynde*, the first part of which is based on *Gamelyn*. The MS. copies of *Gamelyn* are all in MSS. of the *Canterbury Tales* (see page 676), and all seem to go back to one original copy. The tale always appears in the gap left by the uncompleted *Cook's Tale;* in some of the MSS. it is styled *The Cook's Tale of Gamelyn*. Probably it was found among the MSS. of Chaucer, who had it by him intending to rewrite it as a Canterbury tale. Possibly the scribe wrote it after the *Cook's Tale* because of the gap at that place. Its wildwood setting would make the *Tale* more appropriate for Chaucer's Yeoman. The outlaw-matter connects, of course, with the Robin Hood theme. There is a ballad of *Robyn and Gandeleyn*. In *Robin Hood and the Stranger* a young Gamwell takes the name of 'Will Scadlock,' and so becomes the famous Scarlet. The fact that the chief of the outlaws is not named in the *Tale*, points to an early date, before the latter half of the reign of Edward III. Robin Hood is first named in the *Vision of Piers Plowman*, B-text (1377). The absence in the *Tale* of designation of a definite locality for the outlaw activity, points to the same conclusion. Possibly the *Tale* is less indebted to ballads than are ballads to the *Tale*. The verse, like the ballad measure, is irregular in number of unstressed syllables, and the pairs of verses are practically the 'ballad stanza' written in long lines. The various divisions of the poem open with the conventional minstrel appeal for attention and designation of a new stage. Connection with *Havelok* is suggested in Gamelyn's prowess as a wrestler, and in his beating of his opponents with the pestle and with a staff. Finally, the *Tale* has a number of verbal resemblances to the poem *On the Times of Edward II* (see page 231), of which line 475 is very similar to lines 277 and 764 of *Gamelyn*. But too much must not be made of these last parallels.

The poem has genuine merit. It is primitive and unsophisticated in all its details; in its attitude as well as in its matter and its manner, it is to be associated with the ruder Germanic romances—with *Havelok* and *Horn,* and with the ballads. The tale is the favorite story of the abused child and the villainous and unnatural relative; of the simple and confiding youth and the treacherous and scheming elder brother. The matter is boisterous and rough. Right wins because of superior might; and it wins by blows and maiming and murder, and by execution under guise of law. The glory in physical prowess, the praise of hospitality and generosity, are large elements of the theme. There is no love-motive, there are no refinements. The piece is a well-told tale of hearty, out-of-doors, almost animal, life, brutally crude in its ethical and social ideals and conduct. But its genuineness, its heartiness and freshness, make it of great appeal now, as they did in its own day.

2. ARTHURIAN LEGENDS

It is now generally admitted that the figure of Arthur is in some degree historical, and that a chieftain 'Arthur' probably lived in the fifth century. Perhaps he fought in defense of Britain against the Saxons; perhaps the chroniclers' and the romancers' accounts of his activity in that struggle are but

fruit of later invention. Whether the tradition that transmitted his fame to later ages originated on the Continent or in
insular Britain, is still, and perhaps ever will be, a matter of
debate; probably at a very early period the hero became a
favorite of Celts on both sides of the Channel. Whatever be
the truth on these points, dealt with by tradition, associated
with myths and fairy tales, made a theme of popular narrative, and treated by chroniclers, historians, and romancers,
Arthur gradually became a king, a conqueror of nations, one
of the greatest heroes of the world, the foremost of the three
Christian representatives among the Nine Worthies, and greatest of the nine. About him gathered a vast body of literature
in all civilized tongues. Gradually, there came to be associated
with his story and that of his court, cycles of romance that
developed in connection with a number of originally independent heroes—Gawain, Perceval, Eric, Lancelot, Tristram—and
also with the Holy Grail. Most of these cycles, as wholes and
as individual tales, were but loosely connected with the story
of Arthur himself. But, in later treatments, the history of
Lancelot, through the *liaison* of the knight with Guinevere, became intimately bound up with the main story of the last days
of Arthur's rule.

Much of our present popular conception of Arthur as the
perfect king, the matchless knight, the model of honor and
purity and ideal purpose, is beyond the conception of the
romancers. It is only in the accounts of his early years up to
and immediately following his coronation and marriage (if
indeed so far), in those of his last efforts to preserve his realm,
and in those of his death, that Arthur is a central figure. It
is only in the versions of the Merlin story bound up with the
enfances of Arthur, and in the romances dealing with the
King's death, that he is not a subordinate personage. True,
in the romances he is conventionally a perfect king, ever conventionally spoken of as such, with a magnificent court and
vast dominions. But, outside of the versions of the Merlin
matter and of the last days of the King, his court is but a place
for the young knight to visit in search of a quest, and for the
real hero to start from at the beginning of his adventure, and

to return to at the end. Moreover, in most of the versions, and especially in the later prose romances, he is actually as loose in morals as are many of his knights. From Geoffrey of Monmouth on through a number of the tales, he is father of a son, Modred, begotten in incest, whose treason against the realm and whose mortal blow to his father in the last great battle in the West, are but the working out of Nemesis. In the Welsh tales, Arthur, as are his knights, is homely, crude, and grotesque. In some versions, as in the German *Diu Krône*, he dwells in sloth and luxury. In many of the later versions, he is beaten in jousting. In some, he is a lover of practical jokes. Often, as in Malory, he is represented as the complaisant spouse who, from weakness and a desire to keep Lancelot by his side, condones his wife's adultery. In some, this last culpable behavior takes place in a court that is thoroughly cognizant of the whole affair, as it is of the loose conduct of Guinevere with knights other than Lancelot. Even in the tales of the last days of Arthur, all of them of later growth, the King is sacrificed to preserve the greatness and supremacy of Lancelot, and, in a less degree, of Gawain—just as in the prose romances Gawain is sacrificed to the glory of Lancelot and Galahad. He is a puppet in the hands of Gawain, who, to avenge the killing of his brothers by Lancelot, drives Arthur, lamenting the loss of his best knight and lamenting naught else, to war with the Queen's lover and to pursuit of vengeance— despite his protests, despite his reception of the Queen from the hands of her lover, and despite his willingness to take the lover back to favor and to let the *liaison* go on. We shall see that all these features of the developed story of Arthur are preserved, some in one, some in another, of the extant English romances.

The facts just indicated concerning the development of the stories of Arthur, and the nature of the material of the extant pieces in English, lead to discussion of the Arthurian romances under the following heads: I. The Whole Life of Arthur; II. Merlin and the Youth of Arthur; III. Lancelot and the Last Years of Arthur; IV. Gawain; V. Perceval; VI. The Holy Grail; VII. Tristram.

I. The Whole Life of Arthur

The story of the whole life of Arthur is related in Middle English in Layamon's *Brut;* the *Arthur* in the Latin chronicle of the British Kings; the alliterative *Morte Arthure;* the chronicles of Robert of Gloucester, Robert Mannyng, and Thomas Bek of Castelford; Malory's *Morte Darthur;* and the ballad *The Legend of King Arthur.* The treatments in the chronicles are not of sufficient importance to be discussed separately from the general remarks on those works (see pages 195, 199). Malory's *Morte Darthur* is so late and so well known, that it will not be treated at length in this book.

Before proceeding to the *Brut, Arthur,* and the *Morte Arthure,* some general statements concerning the forerunners of these works must be made.

Into his Latin prose *Historia Britonum* (c. 800, or somewhat later) Nennius [16] introduced a brief passage that is probably a close reproduction of a passage in a lost Latin chronicle of the date 697. Here he speaks of Arthur as a 'dux bellorum' of the Britons, who, fighting under a banner bearing the image of the Virgin, overthrew in twelve great battles the pagan invaders of his country. This is the first mention of Arthur in extant literature.

Between 1135 and 1147 Geoffrey of Monmouth [17] composed his Latin prose *Historia Regum Britanniæ.* Into this supposed history Geoffrey introduced the story of Arthur, expanding the matter in Nennius by using traditions and tales current in his day, but apparently chiefly by drawing on a very fertile imagination. In forty-one sections of his book (Bk. 8 Ch. 19-Bk. 11 Ch. 2), a total of 49 printed pages in the modern English translation, he recounts the life of the hero from his conception to his departure for Avallon.

He tells of Uther's love for Igerna, wife of the Duke of Cornwall; the begetting of Arthur through the magic aid of Merlin; the death of the Duke; the marriage of Uther and Igerna; the wars of Uther, and his death; Arthur's coronation; his wars to protect the realm from the pagans, and to subdue the rebels who would not believe the story of his birth and acknowledge his rule; his subjugation of the Scots and Picts; his marriage of Guanhumara; his conquest of Ireland, Iceland, Gothland, the Orkneys, Norway, Dacia, Aquitania, and Gaul; and his final triumphant public coronation in the City of Legions. Then are recounted at great length Arthur's preparations for the war with Rome, which claimed tribute of the Britons; the commission of the regency to his nephew Modred; his dream of the dragon and the bear; his slaying of the giant of Michael's Mount; and his contests with the Romans, leading up to their defeat under Lucius Tiberius. Then follows an account of Modred's usurpation of the throne; the marriage of the base Guanhumara to the traitor; the wars against the rebels; the great battle in Cornwall, wherein Modred was slain and the King mortally wounded; and Arthur's departure to Avallon to be healed.

Geoffrey's narrative became directly or indirectly the chief ultimate source for the later accounts of Arthur. From Geoffrey was derived the version in the Latin hexameter poem *Gesta Regum Britanniæ*; the enthusiastic treatment in the English chronicle associated with Robert of Gloucester; the account in Bek's *Chronicle*; and the matter in Langtoft's French *Chronicle* composed in the reigns of Edward I and Edward II. At about 1150 Geoffrey Gaimar wrote his French metrical *Estorie des Bretons*, now lost but known to be a translation of Geoffrey of Monmouth. In 1155, in his French verse *Roman de Brut* or *Geste des Bretons*, Wace [18] freely worked over Monmouth's story. Wace's book was composed rather for lovers of romantic narrative, than for readers of chronicles. He followed the order, and presented the matter, of the *Historia*; but he dealt with the material in the Norman spirit. His contributions are chiefly effort at regard for fact, eloquence of treatment, play of imagination, elaboration of detail, development of the elements of courtly love and the chivalric virtues, and introduction of current fables of Arthur—especially his insertion of the first mention of the Table Round and the first specific literary record of the hope of the Britons that Arthur should come again.

In its turn, Wace's work became a source for later treatments. Only two of these need be dealt with here. Robert Mannyng's account in his *Chronicle* finished in 1338, is a version of Wace. His book is discussed at its proper place (see page 199). The great fruit of Wace's poem is the splendid story of Layamon, completed at about 1205.

LAYAMON'S BRUT [19] as a whole is to be discussed with
the other English chronicles (see page 191). But in Arthur
the first great Middle English poet found his chief hero; to
the story of the King he devotes over ten thousand lines, or a
little less than a third, of his noble work. After his account
of the rule and death of Aurelius, Layamon enters upon the
reign of Uther Pendragon.

Through the aid of Merlin's magic, Uther begets Arthur on
Ygaerne, wife of Gorlois of Cornwall. Gorlois is slain, and Uther
and Ygaerne marry. At his birth the elves take Arthur and
enchant him, bestowing on him riches, long life, and princely virtues so that he is the most generous of men. Uther wars in defense
of his kingship, and dies by poison.

Arthur is summoned from Brittany, and, at the age of fifteen
years, is made King. He wars against the rebels and the Scots
and Picts and Saxons; and, with French allies, despite aid sent
from the Continent, he crushes them. While he is subduing
Orkney and Galloway, Man and Norway, the pagans treacherously
land and commit depredations in the South. In his splendid
helm 'Goswhit,' with his shield adorned in red gold with the
image of the Virgin, fighting with his good sword 'Caliburn' made
by an elvish smith, Arthur defeats the heathen at Bath, and slays
Childric, their chieftain. | Then he conquers Scotland, whose miser-
able people he spares. Returning to York, he re-establishes the
churches and the priesthood, restores their land to those bereft, commands his knights to give doom, and distributes parts of the realm
to Urien and Angel and Loth, the husband of Arthur's sister, whose
sons are Walwain and Modred. In Cornwall, he weds Wenhaver
(Gwenayfer), a relative of Cador of Cornwall. He brings under
his rule Ireland, Iceland, the Orkneys, and Gutland. A crafty
workman makes for him a wonderful table that can be carried from
place to place, yet at which all his knights high and low may be
seated equally. This board was made in four weeks, and is the
same that Britons boast of and say many lies about with respect
to Arthur. | The King becomes the most esteemed in all the world,
the theme of knights and poets. He makes Loth King of Norway,
and receives the subjection of Denmark. He conquers Flanders
and Boulogne's land, and wins France by single combat with Frollo
on an island. After dwelling in France for nine years, he returns
to England to maintain at Caerleon on Usk a court more splendid
than that of Rome. | At a great feast, twelve ambassadors from
Rome summon Arthur to tribute and subjection to the Emperor
Luces. Arthur declares war. Wenhaver is left with the realm
in care of Modred. On the way to Rome, Arthur slays the giant
of Mount St. Michael who has caused the death of his intended
victim, the daughter of Howel. Arthur proceeds toward Rome.

As ambassador of Arthur, Walwain utters a noble defiance of the Emperor, and manfully repulses his pursuers. Arthur gradually subdues the country. The Emperor is slain. | The King is about to enter Rome, when he has a dream which is later verified, that Modred has seized Wenhaver and the realm as his own. With the faithful Walwain, Arthur returns, intending to slay Modred and to burn his Queen who has gone over to her 'dearest of men.' Walwain wins a landing for the King, but is slain in the fight. Arthur laments his loss. Modred is repulsed, and is besieged at Winchester. He steals away to Cornwall. Having taken and burned the city, Arthur goes in pursuit of Modred. Wenhaver takes the veil at Caerleon, and becomes lost to men's knowledge. The hostile armies engage upon the Tambre. Modred and all his knights are slain. Two knights and the King, who is wounded in eleven places, are all that survive on the royal side. | To Constantine, son of Cador, Arthur gives his realm. He declares that he must go to Avalun, where Argante, the Queen of Elves, shall cure his wounds with healing draughts; afterwards, he shall come to his kingdom, and dwell with joy among the Britons. He is borne off in a short boat containing two queens 'wondrously formed'—and Britons believe that he is yet alive and dwells in Avalun with the fairest of all elves, and they ever expect him to return.

From whatever sources Layamon got material for his story of Arthur, his account expands greatly the version of Wace that is commonly familiar to us. Notable among his additions is the slight but vitally important bit concerning the activity of the elves at Arthur's birth. What in Wace is but a hint of the Table Round, Layamon develops to an incident of much prominence. Moreover, in his hands Arthur becomes an Englishman. Again, whatever were his sources, true to his great interest in the valorous and the patriotic, Layamon deals with the heroic and warlike aspects of the King. So, as in the first part of the *Brut* he dwells especially on the conquest of Rome by the early Britons, here the special theme is Arthur the conquering warrior, the war with Rome being developed at great length as the climax of the hero's career.

Moreover, Layamon was much less concerned with the activity of Merlin than were others who dealt with the rule of Arthur as a whole or with only the earlier years of the hero. The mystery of Merlin's birth and the early incidents of his career, are related dramatically, and at several momentous points Merlin appears actively engaged. But the sage is properly repressed; he is not the dominating figure, the centre of interest; he is always subordinate to Arthur, and has little part in the story áfter the death of Uther. Of course, none of the extreme refinements of the courtly codes of war and of love is in the *Brut*. The matter is on the more primitive Germanic basis. Arthur is not much the king of chivalry, but is rather the Germanic chieftain with his *comitatus*. Yet, though sometimes the hero 'gabs' after the fashion of the less courtly chieftain, he is never the boisterous and crude hero of the Welsh, is always generous and kind, and is of a courtesy that manifests itself even in refusal to attack the brutal giant of St. Michael 'without giving fair warning. In contrast with some other treatments, he is ever noble and valiant, consistently elevated in word and act; he exhibits none of the carnal looseness of some of the later versions, and none of the weakness of nature or baseness of conduct manifested in his last days by the Arthur of the later accounts. The fairy elements of the birth and the passing of the hero, lend a mystic touch little Germanic.

It must not be passed over that Layamon's Arthur marries and cherishes Wenhaver from love. The poem has nothing of the vicious character of the Queen in the later romances, until the exigencies of the story require that in Arthur's absence she surprise us with a sudden transfer of her affections to Modred. Lancelot does not have part in the tale. Modred is nephew of Arthur. In the last battle he dies of wounds not inflicted by Arthur, and the King is not wounded by Modred. In Arthur's loss of the realm and in his passing, Layamon saw nothing of the motive of punishment for former evil conduct. Again, Beduer is one of Arthur's chief knights, but he is slain at Rome. In the *Brut* Kay is not a braggart; he is a valiant knight, a 'noble man,' who dies fighting in the last battle against the Emperor. Walwain is the glorious hero of the earlier treatments of Gawain—'full well was given that Walwain was born to be man, for he was full noble of spirit, in every quality was he good, he was liberal and knight with the best.' Layamon's treatment of him is consistent throughout to his death on the strand fighting out a way for the last landing of Arthur, whose grief-stricken lament for him is a heart-felt tribute to a really flawless hero.

ARTHUR [20]. As if feeling the impropriety of dealing with the matter in any tongue other than English, the author of an incomplete Latin chronicle of the British Kings in the Marquis of Bath's MS. (1430-1440), after speaking of Uther Pendragon and the sword Brounsteele (Excalibur), gives an account of Arthur's life in 642 four-stress irregular English verses in couplets. The piece is in the Southern dialect and of 1350-1400. It appears to be a brief·abstract of Geoffrey of Monmouth's story or of a similar version; but at the end the writer expresses a purpose of continuing the account of the Kings, and refers his readers to 'the Frensche boke' for information.

The poem tells rapidly of Arthur's begetting; his birth; his coronation; his establishment of the Table Round; his invasion of France and killing of Frollo in single combat; his conquests; the Easter feast at Caerleon and the summons to pay tribute to Rome; the expedition to Rome; the killing of the Spanish giant by Arthur; the conquest of the Romans in battle; the burial of Lucius and Bedivere in Rome; the treason of Modred; the retreat of the Queen into a nunnery; the death of Modred in Cornwall; and the convey-ance of Arthur to Avalon or Glastonbury, where he is buried. The author takes care to tell that Arthur was attended by an ordinary leech, and that he died and is buried at Glastonbury.

The piece is of little value beyond its presenting at a com-paratively late date a form of the story in which there is noth-ing of Lancelot or of Arthur's incest, and in which the King is still the hero of single combat. The author had little imagi-nation, no sense of proportion, no poetical power. He admits that he found his lines difficult to compose. His main purpose was to inform. He exhibits a schoolmaster's tendency to explain, as when he pauses to comment on the name 'Pen-dragon,' to tell just why Arthur's Table was round, and to elaborate on the difference between Great and Little Britain and on the attitude of the Welsh toward the English. One smiles at his precise lists of persons and forces, and at the statement that Lucius' host numbered 400,124 men.

MORTE ARTHURE [21] covers much more elaborately
the same general ground as *Arthur*. This highly poetical piece
is in the Thornton MS. (1430-1440), and consists of 4346
alliterative long lines composed in the North of England or the
South of Scotland probably between 1350 and 1400. Much
effort has been expended to show that the poem is the *Gret
Geste of Arthure* that, with the *Awntyre of Gawane* and the
Pystyl of Swete Swsane, is ascribed by Wyntoun in his *Crony-
kil of Scotland* to Huchown of the Awle Ryale. The case
seems to be against this assignment to Huchown (see page
400).   .

The poet speaks of 'cronycles' and 'romawns' as sources
of his matter (ll. 3200, 3218, 3440, 3445). Geoffrey of Monmouth's *Historia* is probably the basis of the story. Elements
are adopted from Layamon's *Brut,* now in preference to Geoffrey's account, now by addition to it. It would seem that
some French romance connected with the Arthurian story
may have afforded the boasts of Arthur and his knights at
lines 320, 2044, 3164, and that some other not associated with
Arthur was drawn on for material for the conquest of Lor-
raine (ll. 2385-3205). Apparently the poet was very independent in his handling of his originals. At every turn he
seems to have adapted and developed his material, sometimes
perhaps combining matter from several sources, often adding
from his own imagination. His own are, apparently, some
of the most notable bits in the piece—such as the vivid scene
of the Roman envoys terrorstricken before Arthur's anger,
Modred's desire not to be left as regent of England, Guinevere's grief at her separation from Arthur, the vivid description of the dragon of Arthur's dream, Arthur's fight with the
second giant, and much of the dream of Fortune and her wheel.
After the point where Arthur learns of Modred's treachery,
the poet often departs especially far from any extant chronicle. He records Arthur's burial at Glastonbury, and says
nothing concerning the mythical account of his passing.

The author of the *Morte Arthure* was one of the most notable
of the romance writers in English. That he had appreciation
for nature, and power to describe it, is evinced by the passages

on the grove at St. Michael's Mount, and on the meadow in the early morning near Metz. His humor is shown in Arthur's jeers at the second giant, and in Bedever's comment when he finds that the 'Saint' whom Arthur ostensibly has gone to visit is really the St. Michael giant. His capacity for pathos is manifested in Gawayne's laments for his warriors who are in sore straits, and in Modred's and Arthur's grief at the death of Gawayne; and for deeper feeling of the significance of the story than is often shown, in Arthur's cry on hearing of Modred's treachery, 'I am with treason betrayed, for all my true deeds! and all my travail is lost. I am none the better for it!', as well as in his grief over the slaughter of his knights and in his dying words, after the last battle in Cornwall.

The poet has the chronicler's rather than the romancer's eye and attitude. He affects always with impression of accuracy and truth, suggesting fact, rather than fiction; for he never writes mechanically, he sees vividly and sees definitely and in detail, and he evidently draws on a considerable experience. His accounts of preparations for siege, of embarkations, of marshaling of forces, and of fights on sea and on land, are like those of an eye-witness. At every turn he presents much detail, but always detail that is significant, consistent, constructive, and picturesque. He yields nowhere to the vague, loose, conventional phrasing and elaboration of matter, common in the romances. The poem is a series of vivid scenes, of astonishingly veracious dramatic situations, from the opening where the terrified ambassadors from Rome cower before the awful countenance and flaming eyes of Arthur, to the last sad moments of the dying hero at Glastonbury. Of passages other than those already mentioned, especially to be noted are the accounts of the embarkation of Arthur's forces and the sailing of the fleet from Britain, Arthur's dream of the dragon and the bear, Arthur's approach to the cave of the giant in Mount St. Michael, the scene on the Mount between Arthur and the old woman, the pathetic death of the giant's victim, the monstrous behavior and appearance of the giant, the fight, the gorgeous camp of the Romans, Gawayne before Lucius and the succeeding combat, Cador's exploits, the arrangement of

the forces, the duel with the Viscount of Valence, the effect of
the storm of arrows, the horrors of the battle-field, Arthur's
message to Rome with the coffins of the heathen dead, the gath-
ering of the host and the accumulation of provisions at the siege
of Metz, the great seafight with Modred's forces, Gawayne's
last battle on the English strand, Arthur's dream of Fortune,
and Modred's remorse.

The alliterative verse is admirably adapted to the martial
material and the picturesque and dramatic nature of the theme.
The poet writes it as a master, having no less control of it
than of his matter. The opening prayer and the summons of
the Roman envoys, are remarkable pieces of sustained expression in the metre.

In this poem Lancelot is but mentioned four times as active
among other knights. He is not the great champion and not
the lover of the Queen. It is of interest, too, that Modred is
still the nephew of Arthur, and of special interest that the
expression leaves the way open to the notion that the Queen
was a not unwilling victim of Modred. Further, Gawayne is,
after Arthur, the great hero, the most noble and valiant of
knights, one worthy to be King in Arthur's place. As a matter
of fact, he is the central figure in the third quarter of the poem
and in part of the last.

In addition to its own intrinsic worth and to its preservation
of elements of the Arthur story not encountered elsewhere, the
poem is important because Malory followed it very closely in
the fifth book of his compilation, owing to it most that is of
worth in many passages of that part of his work.

The Legend of King Arthur [22], a ballad summary in one
hundred verses of the story of Arthur, is in the Percy Folio
MS. (c. 1650).

II.   Merlin and the Youth of Arthur

The accounts of the earlier events of the life of Arthur deal
also with the story of Merlin [23]. The incidents of these
accounts fall into two groups: those that extend up to, and

include, the coronation of Arthur; and those that deal also with the attempts of Arthur after his coronation to pacify, defend, and extend his realm. Again, these accounts are of two kinds: (A) those of the *historical* or *chronicle* type, and (B) those of the *literary* or *romance* type.

(A) Among the Welsh, Merlin or Myrddin was famous as a bard, prophet, and magician—perhaps also as a deceived lover. In his *Historia Britonum* Nennius prepared for later conceptions of the sage by telling a story of the British King Vortigern and a gifted boy Ambrosius.

Beset by Hengist and his Saxons, Vortigern is advised by his magicians to build a citadel and a city for his defense. As fast as the foundations of the citadel are laid, they are swallowed up in the earth. The magicians declare that the blood of a boy born without a father must be sprinkled on the site. The King's mes. sengers find Ambrosius, whose mother asserts that his was no mortal sire. Brought before the King, Ambrosius confounds the magicians by explaining that beneath the site of the citadel is a pool in which dwell two dragons, one red and one white. The earth is dug up, and the dragons are discovered. They fight, and the white dragon is put to flight. Then the boy interprets the omen as prophetic of the expulsion of the Saxons by the British, and warns Vortigern to build his citadel elsewhere. The King gives Ambrosius the city and all the western provinces of Britain.

Matter in Ordericus Vitalis' *Historia Ecclesiastica* shows that before December 1135, Geoffrey of Monmouth wrote a *Book of Merlin*. The *Book* is lost, and the nature of its contents is but to be inferred from Ordericus' quotations and from the account of the prophecies of Merlin to which is devoted the seventh book of Geoffrey's *Historia Regum Britanniæ* (see page 30). It is in the latter work that Merlin appears first as definitely associated with the story of Arthur. Geoffrey's account in the *Historia* is partly an elaboration of Nennius' story of Ambrosius, and combines Ambrosius and Myrddin.

It recites Nennius' tale of the citadel, the finding of the boy Merlin 'who was also called Ambrosius,' the discovery of the dragons, and the discomfiture of the magicians—who here are execit'd (Bk. 6 Chs. 17-19). Then it tells of the combat of the dragons, and bases on it a long, detailed prophecy of the future of Britain, that is but suggested by Nennius (Bk. 7). Then follows the matter not at all in Nennius. Merlin prophesies the manner of death of Vortigern and his successors, Aurelius and Uther (Bk. 8 Ch. 1). He advises Aurelius to remove the Giant's Dance from Ireland, and aids Uther to convey it to Britain and to set it up there (Bk. 8 Chs. 10-12). He assists Uther to beget Arthur on Igerna, and to accomplish the death of Igerna's husband Gorlois (Bk. 8 Ch. 19).

Geoffrey's account of the life of Arthur has been outlined already (see page 30).

Another Latin work, *Vita Merlini,* ascribed questionably to Geoffrey and of date about 1148, presents a treatment of Merlin that differs greatly from the *Historia* and that led to a conception of two Merlins, Geoffrey's Ambrosius Merlin and Merlin Silvester or Caledonicus. For the student of the English pieces, the *Vita* and the resultant dual identity of Merlin are not important.

Also of the historical or chronicle work dependent on Geoffrey, are lines 2052-3005 of the Latin poem *Gesta Regum Britanniæ* (see page 31), an account of Merlin and of the early years of Arthur close to the *Historia*. Lines 2271-3480 of Robert of Gloucester deal with the Merlin matter, and are a translation of Geoffrey. The Norse *Breta Sögur* is a condensed translation of Geoffrey's account, and lines 6585-9265 of Wace's *Roman de Brut* (1155; see page 31), are a free version of Geoffrey. The first part of Pierre de Langtoft's French *Chronicle* slightly condenses the *Historia* material, adding some minor details. In lines 12884-19961 of his *Brut*, Layamon doubled the extent of the Merlin material in Wace, but really added little to the incidents in the latter (see page 32). Lines 6989-9768 of Robert Mannyng's *Chronicle* follow Wace's Merlin story pretty closely.

(B) The line of *literary* or *romance* treatments of Merlin goes back to Robert de Borron's poem *Merlin*, of the end of the twelfth century. Only a fragment of 504 lines of the piece is extant, but the French works based on it afford good indications of its nature. Robert's *Joseph d'Arimathie* had dealt with the early part of the Grail story. In the *Merlin* Robert apparently carried the narrative through the coronation of Arthur—in other words, his work represented the first group of the Merlin-Arthur material (see page 38). In his *Perceval*, which is wholly lost, Robert had told of the attainment of the Grail by Perceval, and (following Geoffrey) the last battle of Arthur and the ruin of his achievements.

At the end of the twelfth or the beginning of the thirteenth century, Robert's *Merlin* was turned into French prose. At least two continuations of his work, one the 'Ordinary' or 'Vulgate' *Merlin*, the other the *Livre du Roi Artus* or *Livre d'Arthur* or *La Suite de Merlin*, were made in French in the thirteenth and fourteenth centuries. These continuations were composed for the purpose of filling in the matter between the coronation of Arthur and the appearance of Lancelot at Arthur's court. Upon the story as made over in prose from de Borron and the continuations of de Borron, were based the Provençal, the Italian, and the Dutch prose versions. On them, too, were based the English representatives of the legend—the verse *Arthour and Merlin*, Lovelich's verse *Merlin*, the English prose *Merlin*, and the correspondent section of Malory's *Morte Darthur*.

ARTHOUR AND MERLIN [24] survives in an earlier and in a later version, both in four-stress couplets. The former (A) is in MS. Auchinleck (1330-1340). It was composed in the neighborhood of Kent not later than 1325 and probably between 1250 and 1300. It consists of 9938 lines, and extends from the death of Constans to the defeat of Rion immediately after the betrothal of Arthur and Guenever. The second (Y) version is in (L) MS. Lincoln's Inn Libr. 150 (end of 14th or beginning of 15th century), (P) the Percy Folio MS., (H) MS. Harley 6223 (c. 1560), and (D) MS. Douce 236 (beginning 15th century). L consists of 2490 verses, P of 2378 verses; both extend from the death of Constans the elder to the death of Uther Pendragon (*i.e.*, to about line 2700 of the A version). H is a fragment of but 62 verses. D consists of 1278 verses dealing with the death of Constans the elder, and extending to the landing of Arthur and Aurelius to reclaim their heritage from Fortiger. L, P, and H are from a common

antecedent, but are independent of each other; H is closer to
L than to P. L, P, H, and D go back to a common original.

The following remarks are based mainly on the earlier (A)
version. The part of the poem ending with the coronation of
Arthur (l. 3133), appears to represent a transition between
the chronicle and the romance versions of the incidents; it is
apparently from the lost first form of de Borron's poem (see
page 40), or from a version used by de Borron. Citation of
'the Brout' at lines 538 and 2730, suggests that the translator
or his original had access to a verse treatment. The part of
Arthour and Merlin following the coronation, is based on the
Livre d'Arthur or *Suite de Merlin*. The poem seems to be little
more than an abbreviated translation.

Constaunce, King of England, has three sons, Constant or Constantine, Aurelis Brosias, and Uter Pendragon. At his death,
Constaunce names as his successor his eldest son, Constant, who
has been a monk. His steward, Fortiger, swears to aid the children. Dissatisfied with Constant, the people call him King
Moyne. Moyne makes a poor defense against the Danes and
Saxons under Angys. After learning that Fortiger would accept
the throne were the King dead, the barons murder Constant. Fortiger drives out the Danes. Aurelis and Uter are spirited out of
his reach. Fortiger executes the murderers, and civil war ensues.
Aided by Angys, Fortiger defeats the rebels. He gives land to the
Danes, and weds Angys' daughter. After some years, fearful of
Aurelis and Uter, Fortiger attempts to build a great castle at
Salisbury. Each night the work of the day is overthrown. Ten
wise clerks declare that the blood of a child not of man's begetting,
must be smeared on the work. Fortiger sends to seek the child.
The devils in Hell plan to beget a babe that shall do as much
harm as Christ did good. The Devil destroys the family of a
girl, begets on her a boy, and makes her a woman of the town. The
pious girl is brought to judgment; but her confessor, the hermit
Blasi, has the decision postponed until her child shall be two and
a half years old. Blasi christens the boy 'Merlin.' The hideous
infant at once speaks in defense of his mother. He is good, not
evil. He exhibits wonderful knowledge of secrets, and phenomenal
sagacity. The mother he makes a nun; Blasi he engages to write
down what he reveals, and what he shall perform as master of
four kings to come. At the age of five years, he is large and
bold. He is brought before Fortiger, on the way manifesting pre-
ternatural knowledge. He explains that a white dragon and a red
one fight every night beneath the foundations of the castle. The
dragons are dug up; they fight, and the white dragon destroys the

red, and flees. Merlin confounds the sages by interpreting the omen. The white dragon is the rightful heir who shall drive out Fortiger. When effort is made to seize him, Merlin disappears. Aurelis and Uter defeat Fortiger, burn him and his family in his castle, and, by aid of Merlin, slay Angys. Uter becomes King. 'Denmark Saracens' land, and slay Aurelis; but they are destroyed by Uter. With Merlin's counsel, Uter rules for many years and conquers much of France; by his discretion, he founds the Round Table at which may sit only the noblest, wisest, most courteous, and most valiant, and establishes a code of conduct to which the knights are bound. Merlin aids Uter to beget Arthur on Ygerne, wife of Duke Hoel of Cornwall. Hoel is slain by Uter's forces, and Uter weds Ygerne. At his birth, Arthur is given by Merlin to a foster-father, Antour, who brings him up as his own child with his son, Kay. Uter dies. Arthur proves his right to the throne by pulling out of a stone that appears before the church door a sword, Estalibore. Merlin reveals his true parentage. Arthur is crowned.
ꞏ Many kings refuse to accept Arthur's rule. By advice and magic aid from Merlin, Arthur overwhelms his foes. He begets a child on Earl Siwein's daughter. For five years the land is distressed with civil war and invasion by Danes. Galathin, son of King Nanters and Blasine, learns from his mother the truth of Arthur's birth. He and Wawain (Gawain), son of King Lot, seek to reconcile their fathers with Arthur. With Wawain's brothers, Agreuein, Gueheres, and Gaheriet, they set off to Arthur at London, overcoming on the way three pagan armies. Arthur, with Merlin's aid, performs great deeds of valor against King Rion, the enemy of King Leodegan of Carohaise, and wins the love of Leodegan's daughter, Gvenour. There follows a tedious series of contests in which pagans and rebels are destroyed through the valor of Galathin, Wawain, Ywain, and the brothers of Wawain, and the magic of Merlin. Through the embassy of Merlin, Arthur is betrothed to Gvenour. Again, with Merlin and the dragon standard in the van, Arthur defeats Rion. The victors rejoice at Carohaise.

The poem is usually not rated high, and is regarded as showing little independence. Though it has not the boldness and dash of the verse of *Ywain and Gawain*, the couplet here is admirably smooth. The piece has a coherence and even flow rare among English romances. Pleasing is the passage recounting Gvenour's arming of Arthur for the last battle in the poem. Pleasing, too, are the lyrical verses on the Seasons and Love, that occur at the openings of the sections of the story, somewhat as similar passages occur in *Kyng Alisaunder* (see page 102), and at the beginning of the second part of *Richard Coer de Lyon* (see page 152). Hints for some of these pas-

sages in *Arthour and Merlin* were derived from the French original, but some of them are probably the poet's own. Partly
because the incidents themselves are attractive, partly because
they are presented fluently, realistically, and dramatically, the
first part of the poem is interesting. The speeches and behavior of the child, Merlin, are very effective. The second
part, that after the coronation, deals with accounts of battles,
which, though vigorous, are too numerous, too prolonged, and
too like each other and the general run of romance passages
at arms. It is to be noted that Arthur begets an illegitimate
son; that Gawain is next most prominent in the story after
Arthur, and is indeed the hero of several thousand lines in the
second part; that Modred is the son of Lot and Belisent; that
Merlin's relations with Nimiane (Nimue or Vivien) are touched
on only in a reference to the lady as 'Nimiane, who with her
cunning craft beguiled the good clerk Merlin' (l. 4446); and
that the Holy Grail is but referred to, thrice merely by mention of its name (ll. 2222, 2750, 4294), and once by mention of
Celidoine's and Naciens' experience (ll. 8899-8918). Resemblances in material and in the lyrical introductory passages,
led Kölbing to hold that *Kyng Alisaunder, Richard Coer de
Lyon,* and the present poem are by one author. Some critics
seem disposed to admit identity of authorship to *Kyng Alisaunder* and *Arthour and Merlin.*

THE PROSE MERLIN [25]. Though Laurence Minot
opens one of his songs with matter concerning Merlin, and
though the seventh tale of the *Seven Sages* deals with the theme
Herowdes and Merlin that has verbal agreements with *Arthour
and Merlin,* the other actual romances in English on Merlin
are the English prose *Merlin* of about 1450-1460 and Lovelich's verse *Merlin* of about 1450. The lateness of these pieces
necessitates restriction of our remarks on them.

The prose *Merlin* is in a fifteenth-century MS. in the Cambridge University Library. As Mead has indicated, this
romance and *Arthour and Merlin* parallel each other more or
less exactly to the end of the latter work, so that a general
synopsis of the one might serve for the other. But the prose

continues the story, telling of the incidents leading up to the marriage of Arthur; the marriage; the reconciliation of Arthur and Lot; the taking of vows by the Table Round; the war with the Saxons; the wars on the Continent; Arthur's fight with the giant; the war with Rome; Arthur's fight with the great cat of Losane; the enchantment of Merlin by Nimiane; and, finally, the birth of Lancelot, son of King Ban of Benoyk. The piece has been shown to be a very close translation of the French original, which is not exactly the same as the original of *Arthour and Merlin*.

LOVELICH'S MERLIN [26], about 28000 lines in couplets, is preserved in MS. Corpus Christi College Cbg. 80 (later 15th century). Only the first 15556 lines of it have been printed. It was composed at about 1450 by the London skinner Henry Lovelich, author of the *Holy Grail* (see page 77). The work is distressingly tedious. Comparison of the first 6200 lines with the correspondent part of the prose *Merlin*, has shown that the two pieces agree in incidents and vary but little in details. They are independent of each other, but are apparently derived from one original, or from originals with almost identical readings.

III.   Lancelot and the Last Years of Arthur

The story of Lancelot is a late development as compared with the stories of the other chief heroes associated with Arthur. Lancelot is not in Wace's *Brut*, or in the Welsh Arthurian tales. Apparently he is mentioned first in the *Erec* of Chrétien de Troyes, where, as in the work of Hartmann von Aue, he is but a name in a list of heroes, holding rank after Gawain and Erec. In Chrétien's later *Cliges* he is named as next in rank after Gawain and Perceval. But in Chrétien's still later *La Chevalier de la Charrette* he is Gawain's superior, and his relations with Guinevere as lover are the central theme. Oddly, in Chrétien's next poem, *Le Chevalier au Lion*, Lancelot appears only in connection with the *Charrette* matter; and in the succeeding poem, *Perceval*, he is quite ignored. The *Charrette* and the *Lion* were composed between 1164 and 1173. It would appear that a number of *lais* and a lost French poem, a version of which is in Ulrich von Zatzikhoven's *Lanzelet* of the first of the thirteenth century, caused Lancelot to be listed high among the heroes, and to be a reasonable candidate for special office when need occurred. It would seem, further, that the relations of Lancelot and the Queen in the *Chevalier de la Charrette*, written at command of Marie de Champagne, who supplied an outline of the story, were introduced to satisfy, and perhaps to promote, the ideas of courtly love prevalent in the circles of Eleanor and Marie. Chrétien's dropping of the Lancelot matter after the *Charrette*, suggests that he was not much interested in it. The evidence seems to show that, originally, the Queen's lover was Gawain; that, later, as in the chronicles, when Gawain's character had been elevated, this rôle was shifted to Modred, Gawain's brother; that, later still, the Queen's character was elevated, and Modred was represented as an unwelcome suitor; and that, finally, a feeling of rivalry between Tristram and Lancelot as prime heroes, aided by the demands of the conditions of courtly love, led to the introduction and development of Lancelot as lover, Modred still remaining in the story. Of course, the assignment of this rôle to Lancelot, led to intimate association of his story with the story of the last years of Arthur.

In the thirteenth century was composed an interminable Dutch version of the story, extant only as a fragment of some fifty thousand lines. But the great influential work was the vast thirteenth-century French prose *Lancelot*, of which versions were made in all the cultivated European tongues. In its vulgate form, this romance, often styled *Le Livre d'Artus*, is commonly, though probably wrongly, ascribed to Walter Map. It is made up of four parts: (1-2) Lancelot, dealing with the life and deeds of Lancelot, and the deeds of Gawain, Agravayne, and other knights of the Round Table; (3) the Quest of the Grail; (4) the Death of Arthur.

Lancelot seems never to have attained in English the place attained by Gawain. Most of the English Arthurian pieces have little to do with him; the *Awntyrs of Arthur, Sir Gawayne and the Grene Knight*, and the *Avowynge*, do not mention him. In *Golagrus and Gawain*, the *Carle of Carelyle*, the *Marriage of Gawain*, and *Libeaus Desconus*, he is mentioned, but has no important part. His story is dealt with in but three English romances of before 1500—*Le Morte Arthur, Lancelot of the Laik*, and Malory's *Morte Darthur*. To these pieces may be joined the ballads *Sir Lancelot du Lake* and *King Arthur's Death*, in the Percy Folio MS.

LANCELOT OF THE LAIK [27], in Lowland Scotch with many Southern forms due at least partly to influence of Chaucer, was composed 1475-1500. It is in MS. Cbg. Univ. Libr. Kk I 5 (15th century) in 3486 pentameter couplets. Brandl has suggested that the theme and the form of the language and verse, are due to influence of the court of James IV of Scotland, who attempted to keep up the chivalric tradition by holding tournaments in imitation of those of Arthur.

The poem paraphrases very loosely a portion of the first part of the French prose *Lancelot*, now omitting much, now expanding suggestions into lengthy passages. The poet displaces the French prologue with one of his own, in which, after an April nature passage imitative of Chaucer, he relates how, overwhelmed with love, he fell asleep, and in a vision was charged by the God of Love in form of a bird to write a treatise for his lady's pleasure. Accordingly, though aware of his incapacity, he finally decides to translate the story of Lancelot of the Lake. As he cannot adequately translate the French, he gives a list of the principal facts of the knight's career that he will *not* recount, and states that he will tell of the wars of Arthur and Galiot, of how Lancelot won glory in the contest and finally pacified the foes, and of how Venus rewarded him. The author prays for the support of a great poet, of which he is quite unworthy. The poet's name he will not tell—just as three of his personáges could tell of various matters of no moment, but will not. It is notable that, though the outline at the beginning calls for response by the Queen to Lancelot's passion, the poem presents her as indifferent to his love and even unwilling to ask him to aid Arthur. Further, as far as the poem extends, Gawain is as prominent as Lancelot.

The first book tells of Arthur's dreams of impending ill; a clerk's evasions, and final equivocal interpretations of the dreams; Galiot's summons to Arthur to pay tribute, and Arthur's refusal; Lancelot's imprisonment by the Lady of Melyhalt; Gawain's valor against Galiot's forces; and the Lady's permitting of Lancelot to fight for Arthur disguised in red, his deeds in sight of the Queen, and Galiot's granting of a truce for a twelvemonth.—Most of the second book is a development of a suggestion in the French—a painfully tedious set of discourses on the proper conduct of a king, directed at Arthur by a clerk. It is not impossible that the passage was aimed at contemporary Scottish monarchs and political conditions. Finally, Lancelot obtains permission to fight as a black knight on renewal of the war.—The third book deals with a battle. Gawain does great deeds, but his wounds force him to withdraw. Reluctantly requested by the Queen to do his best, the black knight performs before her eyes prodigies of valor. The fragment ends with him just about to eclipse all his previous achievements.

The author's protestations of incapacity are nearer the truth than they were intended to be. Except in the nature-matter and the dream at the opening of the prologue, and the nature-matter (cp. *Kyng Alisaunder, Arthour and Merlin,* and *Richard Coer de Lyon*) at the opening of each of the three books, all openly imitative of Chaucer, there is scarce a bit to relieve the dullness of the work. The writer was run away with by trivial details. He was wonderfully impressed by the cheap mystery of 'I could tell you, but I will not.' Without feeling, enthusiasm, originality, or taste, he took himself and his commonplaces with a garrulous seriousness probably painful to his lady and to all his friends. He is just about beginning when he ends.

Sir Lancelot du Lake [28] is the title of a defective ballad of 124 verses in the Percy Folio MS., dealing with Lancelot's duel with Sir Tarquin.

LE MORTE ARTHUR [29], in MS. Harley 2252 (late 15th century), is the Middle English poetical rendering of the love of the Maid of Astolat, and of the culmination and the end of the loves of Guinevere and Lancelot and of the rule of

Arthur—an admirable treatment, apparently for the first time in English, of themes that have caught and held the spirit of poet and of reader through more than five hundred years since. The poem was composed at the end of the fourteenth century, probably in the North-West Midland, the two scribes of the extant MS. being one of the North and one of the South of England. It consists of 3834 four-stress lines (usually numbered 3969 to allow for about 136 lines supposed to be lost after line 1181) in stanzas normally riming abab004bab, with extensive use of alliteration. There seems to be little ground for the suggestion that *The Lyfe of Ipomydon* in the same MS. is by the author of the poem. *Le Morte Arthur* deals with matter very similar to much in Malory's Books XX and XXI. Both versions seem to have had as source a lost version of the French *Mort Artu*, the last part of the French *Vulgate Lancelot* (see page 46). Close resemblances in phrasing at points where there is no original in the French, indicate that probably Malory was acquainted with the English poem.

Four years after the quest of the Grail, at the Queen's suggestion, Arthur proclaims a tournament at Winchester. Launcelot remains behind to be with the Queen. Agravaine watches. Fearful of discovery, Genure sends her lover to the jousts. Though disguised, Launcelot is recognized on the road by Arthur and Evwayne. He is well received by the Lord of Ascolot, conceals his name, is lent the armor of a sick son of the lord, and is given the other son as a companion. The lord's fair daughter falls in love with the knight. In her chamber, where he visits her with her brother to comfort her, she declares her passion. The hero cannot be unfaithful to the Queen, but promises to wear the maid's sleeve, though he has never before worn lady's favor. At the jousts, Launcelot takes the weaker side, and performs great feats of arms; but his kinsman, Sir Ector, overthrows and severely wounds him. With his companion, Launcelot takes refuge in the near-by castle of the sister of the Lord of Ascolot. Arthur eventually learns of the hero's wounds, and goes to Kamelot, strangely expecting to find Launcelot with the Queen. The Knight is borne to Ascolot, where he is found by several knights. Genure rejoices that her lover will soon return. Launcelot leaves his armor as a keepsake with the lord's daughter. Gawayne visits Ascolot, is told by the maid that she is Launcelot's love, and is shown the armor as proof. To Arthur in full court he declares what he has learned. Genure remains in her chamber sore sick from loss of her lover. Launcelot returns, and is joyfully received. Reproached by the Queen, he indignantly leaves the court. The Queen is heartbroken. Gawayne and others set out in search of the hero. Genure is accused of poisoning a Scottish knight. Arthur and she seek in vain for a champion. The maid of Ascolot is borne in a barge to Arthur's palace. A note in her purse tells that she has died for love of Launcelot. She is· buried as a duke's daughter. Gawayne confesses that he has lied unintentionally in stating that Launcelot loved the maid.. Launcelot slays the Queen's accuser, and the lovers are reconciled. Though his brothers, Gawayne, Gaheriet, and Gueheres, will have no part in the act, Agravaine in open hall betrays the lovers to the King. By arrangement with Arthur, Agravaine and twelve knights surprise the guilty pair together. Launcelot slays all but Modred, and escapes. The Queen is condemned to be burned, but her lover rescues her and bears her away. Unluckily, in doing so he slays the brothers of Gawayne. Seeking vengeance, Arthur and Gawayne besiege the lovers in Joyous Garde. At the Pope's intercession, Launcelot restores Genure to Arthur. He returns to his possessions in Brittany. Thither the King and Gawayne follow him. Launcelot proposes peace; he will abide in the Holy Land. Arthur would accept this, but Gawayne will not have it so. They besiege the hero. Twice Gawayne and Launcelot fight. Profiting by the waning of Gawayne's strength after noon, Launcelot wounds him severely. Modred seizes Arthur's realm, and attempts to wed Genure. The Queen shuts herself up in the Tower of London. At the landing of Arthur at Dover, Gawayne is slain. Arthur wins several battles. Modred retreats to Cornwall. There, by previous arrangement, occurs the last great battle. All on both sides are slain but Arthur, Sir Bedwer, Sir Lucan, and Modred. Modred and the King engage; each mortally wounds the other. After vainly attempting to save Excalibur, Bedwer obeys Arthur and hurls the sword into the sea, where a hand receives it. In a boat full of beautiful ladies Arthur is borne away to Avalon. At a chapel, Bedwer finds Arthur's body in a tomb. He takes orders, and remains to help watch over the grave. Genure takes the veil at Ambresbury. Launcelot comes with an army to aid Arthur. Hearing of the deaths of Arthur and Modred, he seeks the Queen. At Ambresbury, Genure declares her vows irrevocable, and counsels her lover to marry, and live at peace in France. Launcelot comes upon the tomb of Arthur. He becomes a priest, and dwells for seven years with the other guardians of the grave. When he dies, visions reveal that he is received in heaven. He is conveyed to Joyous Garde. The Queen is buried with Arthur. On the spot grows up the Abbey of Glastonbury.

Both its form and its matter make the poem one of the most notable of Middle English romances. As has been indicated, its themes are in modern times among the widest known and most dearly cherished of the group of Arthurian stories. The

work is remarkably unified: it begins well, it ends well; it keeps
to its subject, practically all its episodes contributing directly
to the effect of the main theme, which cumulates as the poem
advances. It is remarkably concise: the ballad-manner, that is
so frequently suggested in the work, is reflected in the speed
with which the poet proceeds, in his omission of non-essential
connective details. Stock phrases are used freely, but they
are so aptly employed as to be little objectionable—indeed,
often scarcely obtrusive. The expression is direct, and free
from diffuseness. The poem is simple, unpretending, sincere.
The writer lent himself to the human appeal of his material,
and told his story with an earnestness and a sincerity of feeling
that make it true and real and warm, winning a response as
immediate and as profound to-day as it must have won in the
fourteenth century. It is to be noted that in this poem
Gawayne, though dominant over Arthur and the real champion
of the King's rights after the revelation of the Queen's guilt,
loses status. He is represented as attempting to beguile the
Maid of Ascolot, as lying about Launcelot to the Queen, and
as compelled to acknowledge his guilt. Launcelot becomes the
hero.

King Arthur's Death [30], a fragment (180 verses) of a
ballad account of the last battle and the end of Arthur, is in
the Percy Folio MS.

IV. Gawain

It seems now generally agreed that, though its development
is due to North French poets, the story of Gawain is of Celtic
and mythic origin. The special characteristics of the hero are
the waxing of his strength until noon, and the waning of it
after noon; his possession of a steed with a special name,
'Gringalet'; and his ownership of a sword (in the early
romances 'Excalibur') that gives out a great light when
unsheathed.

Gawain was the first of the heroes to be associated with
Arthur. He is a nephew of the King on his mother's side, and
is closely connected with Arthur at all times. While in many

tales and versions of tales the other great knights are not mentioned, he is spoken of in all, and occupies a prominent place in
many. Often in a romance he is much more prominent than
the ostensible hero. He appears in the pseudo-historical
accounts. In 1125 William of Malmesbury described his tomb
at Ross in Pembrokeshire, and declared him nephew of Arthur,
and 'not unworthy' of the King. In Italian deeds of the twelfth
century still extant, his name with Arthur's appears frequently,
evincing an extended circulation and popularity of his fame on
the Continent at that date. There is no doubt that very early
there clustered about him a body of story of considerable extent
and importance. In Wace and in Geoffrey of Monmouth (see
pages 30, 31) he is Arthur's emissary to Rome, and by his
deportment contributes greatly to the outbreak of war with
Rome; and he is the great champion of Arthur on the return
from the Continent to check Modred, his death on the sands
being a notable piece in the *Historia*. These two episodes,
always greatly emphasized, appear in most of the accounts that
deal with the war against Rome and with the death of Arthur.
Moreover, though rather oddly he is not the hero of any of
Chrétien's romances, he is almost always first in his lists of
knights. There is good reason for supposing that he preceded
Perceval as hero of the Grail quest.

In all the early versions, in Chrétien's poems and in the early
prose romances, he is the perfect knight, the pink of courtesy,
the invincible paladin against whom but few have the happy
fortune to fight a drawn battle. In all the English Arthurian
romances except *Le Morte Arthur* and Malory's *Morte
Darthur*, he is a model of purity, of courtesy, and of valor.
Indeed, he is the actual hero of the Middle English Arthur
romances. In the greatest of these pieces, *Sir Gawayne and
the Grene Knight*, he has the chief rôle. He is the only knight
of Arthur concerning whom a cycle of poems was composed in
English; but two other knights have even single poems (*Sir
Percyvelle of Galles* and *Lancelot of the Laik*) chiefly devoted
to them. As we have seen, he is actually the prominent figure
of the latter poem, as he is of others not of the Gawain cycle;
in these pieces he is given rôles that lend him supreme weight,

and in them great reaches of matter are devoted to the exhibition of his prowess.

But in the French continuation of the *Merlin*, in the *Tristan*, in the *Lancelot*, and as the ecclesiastical ideal of the Grail develops, Gawain becomes strangely degraded. As time goes by, though he preserves his courtesy, he becomes but a shell; he is a libertine, deceitful and cruel; he loses even his physical superiority. It would seem that Gawain, the figure of the perfect gentleman, the model of chastity, and the champion peerless in arms, interfered with the supremacy of the later hero, Lancelot, and was a rebuke to the latter's adulterous intrigue, as he was to that of Tristram. Moreover, he stood in the way of the development of Galahad, the representative of the later ecclesiastical Grail doctrine. No doubt, too, misinterpretation of some of the survivals of myth associated with him, lent aid or pretext. Unhappily, the modern notion fostered by Tennyson has grown out of the later conception. *Le Morte Arthur* and Malory's work are the only Middle English romances that exhibit such degradation. In both these works the treatment wavers between the two conceptions of the hero. In the poem (see page 51) Gawain is guilty of duplicity in his relations with Launcelot and the Maid of Ascolot, and lies and acknowledges his lie; but there, as in Malory, he is at the end the director of Arthur's policy, the power that determines war and peace for the weak king, the hero of the landing at Dover, and the subject of a great lamentation by Arthur that declares him to be one of the noblest and highest figures of the world and among the first in Heaven.

The romances of the Gawain cycle in English are *Sir Gawayne and the Grene Knight, The Grene Knight, The Turke and Gowin, Syre Gawene and the Carle of Carelyle, The Awntyrs of Arthur, Golagrus and Gawain, The Avowynge of Arthur, Ywain and Gawain, The Weddynge of Sir Gawen and Dame Ragnell, The Jeaste of Syr Gawayne*, and *Libeaus Desconus*.

Reference has just been made to the unique cycle of English poems on Gawain. Miss Weston has argued that the French parallels to a number of these poems, *The Jeaste of Syr*

Gawene, The Carle, Sir Gawayne and the Grene Knight, The Weddynge of Sir Gawene, Golagrus and Gawain, and the early part of *Libeaus Desconus,* are found in Wauchier de Denain's continuation of the French *Perceval.* She urges that *Jeaste* is a misreading of *Geste;* that the matter of the English poems just named, and perhaps of others, the matter of the Wauchier *Perceval,* and that of the Prologue (*Eluciderius*) of the Mons MS. of *Perceval,* are all survivors of one very early collected form of Arthurian tradition, most primitively preserved in the English poems; and that this group had the common title *The Jeaste of Sir Gawayne,* dealt with Gawain and his kindred, was of insular origin, was of widespread circulation, and was popularly ascribed to Bleheris or 'famosus ille fabulator Bledhericus.'

SIR GAWAYNE AND THE GRENE KNIGHT [31], generally declared to be the best of the English romances, is preserved in MS. Cott. Nero A X (now X+4; hand of 14th or early 15th century), and is possibly by the author of the *Pearl, Purity,* and *Patience* (see pages 578, 583, 584). It was composed at about 1370 in the West Midland. It consists of 2530 verses in strophes of varying length, the strophe being made up of alliterative long lines concluding with five short riming lines ababa, the first of one stress, the rest of three stresses each. The poem is divided into four 'fyttes,' not arbitrarily, but in close accord with division of the matter. It is composed of two main themes, a beheading and a test of chastity. The former or chief motive is found in the Irish *Bricriu's Feast,* connected with Cuchulinn; in the German *Diu Krône* and the French *La Mule sans Frein* and *Gauvain et Humbart,* attached to Gawain; in the French prose *Perceval,* attached to Lancelot; in Gautier de Doulens' continuation of Chrétien's *Conte del Graal,* associated with Carados, nephew of Arthur. The chastity-test has many parallels. It is probable that *Sir Gawayne* is derived, with much individual variation, from a French source that made the beheading theme the chief element, and not merely an incident as in the other versions. It seems generally admitted that the special charm of

treatment in manner and details of matter in *Sir Gawayne* is
due to the English poet.

On New Year's Day Arthur sits with his knights at feast in
Camelot, eager for an adventure. Scarcely is the first course
announced, than in bursts a gigantic knight clad all in green, riding
a green steed, and bearing a huge axe and a holly bough. He scornfully and impudently challenges any knight to a game: the knight
shall strike him a blow with the axe, on condition that a year hence
the Green Knight shall give a return blow. All are amazed.
Taunted further, Arthur starts up. But Gawayne obtains the
office of champion. He swears to observe the Knight's condition,
and strikes off his head. The stranger gathers up his head, mounts
his horse, calls on Gawayne to keep his appointment at the Green
Chapel a year hence, and rides away. The year fleets by. Near
the date fixed, Gawayne leaves the grieving court, and goes in
quest of the Green Chapel. He is beset with perils of weather
and wild beasts and giants. On Christmas Eve, bitter cold and
almost exhausted, in a vast dreary forest, he prays. In response
to the prayers he sees before him a splendid castle. Learning that
the Green Chapel is but two miles farther on, he agrees to abide
with the Lord of the castle until the New Year. On each of the
three successive days, the Lord proposes that Gawayne remain in
bed while he goes hunting; at night each shall give the other what
he has gained. On each of the three mornings, the Lady of the
castle tempts the Knight in his chamber to unchastity. By his
courteous and artful speech, Gawayne, though more and more
tempted, withstands her approaches. On the first day he receives a
kiss; on the second, two kisses; on the third, three. These he gives
to the Lord as he has agreed. He receives on the first day the
spoils of a deer-hunt; on the second, those of a boar-hunt; on the
third, those of a fox-hunt. On the third day, the Lady offers him a
ring as a token of love. This he refuses, but he accepts a magic
girdle that protects from all wounds. He keeps this gift secret
from the Lord. On New Year's Day Gawayne proceeds to the
dreadful chapel, a fearful cave in a green mound, whence issue
sounds of a grindstone making sharp the axe. Gawayne prepares
to receive the blow; but he flinches at the first feint of the Green
Knight, and is reproached for cowardice. After another feint, the
Green Knight strikes, but in such manner as to do little injury.
Gawayne proceeds to defend himself. The Knight explains that
he is the Lord of the castle; the challenge, the wooing by the Lady,
the feigned blows, were only tests of the hero's fidelity, chastity,
and courage. Gawayne, however, has feared for his life, and has
not kept faith in regard to the girdle. Remorseful, Gawayne offers
the girdle to the Knight. Urged, he agrees to keep it; he will
wear it as a reminder against pride. He learns the name of the
Knight, and is told that Morgan le Fay instigated all the tests

with an ultimate purpose of proving the Round Table and frightening the knights and Guinevere. Gawayne goes to Camelot, where he tells his story and wears the girdle as mark of his shame. All the knights and ladies agree to wear a like girdle of green for the sake of the hero. Thereafter, whoever received it was greatly honored.

It was indeed fortunate that, before the older conception of Gawayne had passed, this poet came to delineate the knight. In the poem the hero is mighty in arms, courageous of heart, true to his word, faithful to duty, pure of body and of mind, courteous in even the most trying conditions, fine of spirit and of ideal, devout in act, and strong in trust in the five wounds of Christ and in the power derived from the five joys of the Virgin, all of which he bears in symbol in his equipment. True it is, that at base the poem has didactic purpose that obtrudes itself especially in the elaborately explained allegory of Gawayne's armor, and, at the end of the story, in the comments of the Green Knight and the wearing of the girdle. It is true, too, that, having finished, one feels that the adventures of the beheading and the chastity-test both fall rather flat—after all, they were but tests in which there was not great peril. But this is little in face of the great merit of the poem.

The piece is admirably constructed. Though it tends to over-elaborate description, it proceeds with little digression and with much variety. The third fitt is a very skilful handling of parallel elements—Gawayne's quest for the Grene Chapel, the working out of the agreement between Gawayne and the Lord of the castle, the hunting by the Lord, and the temptation by the Lady. The poet's skill is shown at the same places in his presenting three hunting episodes and three tests of chastity with a variety that few writers in a much later period could approach. He had a keen eye, a vivid imagination, and a love for external phenomena, that gave him a power for description unequaled in Middle English literature. He was a lover of details; but he handled the details with a constructive power and a picturesqueness that create vivid impressions or realistic scenes. His observation of dress, of color, of position, of relative location, of deportment, enabled him at the opening of the piece to make of a conventional situation an intense, rich, dramatic scene with a splendid background. His observation of details of architecture is shown in his description of the castle; of sports, in the remarkable hunting scenes, in the account of the brittling of the deer and the unlacing of the boar; and of armor, in the account of the arming of Gawayne, and in that of the equipment of the Green Knight. He caught, and makes us feel, the very spirit of nature in varied moods, spring, summer, autumn—but especially nature in her wilder aspects, the biting winter, the icy rain, the dreary forest, the rugged rocks, the snow-covered country, and the cold hills lost in mist. All this he makes us not so much see as feel; he inducts us into the atmosphere of the very scene. No little effect is lent the poem by the Christmas and New Year setting, which enhances the joyous life indoors, and makes more bitter the hardships of the lonely seeker for the Green Chapel. And one must not disregard the fineness of nature that, in such contradistinction to the common run of mediæval writers, particularly those of imagination and talent, is manifested in the handling without coarseness of the three delicate situations with the Lady of the castle that had to be made to grow in effect as they progressed. Judged even by strict modern standards, the romance must be rated very high. Unfortunately, the dialect and the unusual vocabulary (due largely to the requirements of alliteration) make the language somewhat difficult to follow. Happily and unhappily, a number of modernizations have been made in recent years.

Of much interest are the efforts that have been made to show that *Sir Gawayne* is a 'Garter poem,' composed by a courtly poet to compliment Edward III and his sons. The conclusion of the piece and many of its details, lend support to such interpretation. The association of the contemporary alliterative *Wynnere and Wastoure* with the Garter (see page 244), and the direct statement at the end of *The Grene Knight* that that poem accounts for the wearing of the 'lace' by the Knights of the Bath (see page 58), afford confirmation of the Garter interpretation.

THE GRENE KNIGHT [32], a fifteenth-century South Midland poem, is evidently a modernization and abridgment of *Sir Gawayne and the Grene Knight,* perhaps through an intermediate version. It is in the Percy Folio MS. (c. 1650), and consists of 528 verses in tail-rime stanzas aabccb. The poem modifies much the details of Sir Gawayne.

The writer explains in advance that the Green Knight is Sir Bredbeddle of the West Country, whose wife, as he knows, loves Sir Gawain, though she has never seen him, and whose witch mother-in-law transforms him, and induces him to go to court to test Gawain. A porter parleys with the Green Knight, and announces his entrance to Arthur and his court. The Knight is very courteous and complimentary to the company, and his challenge loses force by being delayed. The dignity of the older version is partly destroyed by the fact that the crabbed Kay boastfully threatens to cut off the stranger's head, and has to be suppressed. The blow is postponed until after the meal, of which the Green Knight partakes. The recovery of the head is explained as by enchantment. Moreover, in advance the writer lets the reader into the secret of the chastity-test, for, as Gawain comes to the castle, he tells that it is the abode of the Green Knight. The Lady tempts Gawain but once, giving him three kisses and the magic lace or girdle. The Green Knight hunts boars, deer, and foxes, all on one day. The knights exchange the kisses and the venison. Gawain sets off for the chapel by one way, the Knight by another. The Knight strikes at Gawain once, whereupon Gawain draws sword to prevent farther assault. The Knight explains who he is, and shows that Gawain has lost his three chief virtues, truth, gentleness, and courtesy; but he will forgive him if he takes him to Arthur's court. At court they are joyfully received.—All this is why Knights of the Bath wear the lace until they have won their spurs, or until a lady takes off the lace. King Arthur decreed this custom by request of Sir Gawain.

The poem has interest; but, of course, it loses all the mystery and suspense and surprise of the older piece. The changes noted destroy the splendid effect of the opening scene of *Sir Gawayne.* There is no fearful journey of Gawain. The tempting is trivial. The descriptive features are gone. All that makes *Sir Gawayne and the Grene Knight* an enthralling piece of high poetical imagination, has disappeared.

Of much importance is the open declaration of association of the story with the Order of the Bath. The connection with the Order of the Garter, suggested from *Sir Gawayne and the*

Grene Knight (see page 57), and evident in Wynnere and Wastoure (see page 244), must be recalled.

THE TURKE AND GOWIN [33], in the Percy Folio MS. (c. 1650), is a fifteenth-century Northern or North Midland piece. It consists of 335 verses in tail-rime aabccb, with much alliteration. Parts of the MS. of the tale are missing. The opening of the poem overlaps from the Grene Knight.

As Arthur is at table, a huge Turk enters and challenges to an exchange of buffets. Kay derides him, and offers to beat him to the ground. Gawain reproves Kay for lack of courtesy. The Turk challenges the better of them.—Here is a break in the MS. Apparently Gawain strikes the Turk.—With the Turk, Gawain travels to the North for over two days. Distressed with hunger and taunted by the Turk, Gawain accompanies the giant into a hill, where they find terrible, stormy weather.—Here is another break in the MS.—They enter a splendid castle. Gawain is fed by the Turk. Strangely, the Turk now asks to receive a second buffet, and to be permitted to go his way.—Here is a break in the MS.—The pair sail over a sea, and enter the castle of the King of Man and his company of giants. Gawain is taunted about Arthur and his knights and the clergy. He plays at tennis with a troop of giants, the Turk acting as his boy. Trials of strength are engaged in: Gawain lifts a huge fireplace, and the Turk seizes it and swings it about his head. The King and one of the giants attempt to boil Gawain; but the Turk, in an invisible coat, throws the chief giant into the caldron, and the King into the fire. Then the Turk brings a basin, and begs Gawain to strike off his head. After persuasion, Gawain does as he is asked. In place of the Turk, rises a knight, Sir Gromer, who devoutly sings a Te Deum. Many captives are released. Gromer causes Arthur to make Gawain King of Man; but, at the hero's request, Gromer is crowned.

This grotesquely marvelous piece has been connected with traditions current in the Isle of Man, the scene of part of the story, which was long held to be inhabited by giants and to contain underground dwellings of wonderful magnificence.

SYRE GAWENE AND THE CARLE OF CARELYLE [34] is in the Porkington Library MS. 10 (Phillipps 8336; c. 1460). It was composed probably in the North Midland or the North in the fourteenth or the fifteenth century. It consists of 660 verses in tail-rime aabccbddbeeb.

With a great troop of knights, Arthur goes hunting. Kay, Gawain, and Baldwin seek shelter for the night at the castle of the Churl of Carlisle. From the fireplace, a boar, a bull, a lion, and a bear rise to slay the visitors; but the monstrous Churl restrains his pets. Gawain kneels to his host, who bids him get up—this is no place for courtesy. The knights drink from a huge nine-gallon cup. Kay and Baldwin go out to see to their horses. They find a foal beside the steeds. They push it away, and are beaten by the Churl. Gawain leaves the hall. Finding the foal out in a storm, he brings it into the stable, and covers it with his green mantle. The Churl thanks him. At table, Kay admires much the beautiful wife of their host, who tells him that he thinks more than he dares utter. At the Churl's bidding, Gawain hurls a spear full at his face. The Churl lowers his head, and the spear breaks against a wall. Gawain falls in love with the lady. The Churl taunts him with his passion. After supper, the Churl's daughter plays the harp, and sings of love and Arthur's arms. The Churl puts Gawain in bed with his wife, bidding him kiss her. Then he gives him his daughter as companion for the night. The next morning, the Churl tells that twenty years back he swore that whoever took lodging with him should do as his host wished, or die; and he exhibits the bones of his many victims who have failed in the test. He will do better hereafter, and will have masses said for those whom he has slain. The three knights, with the daughter, go to Arthur's court. By invitation, Arthur dines next day with the Churl. The decorations and the dinner are magnificent. Arthur makes the Churl a knight of the Round Table and lord of all the country about Carlisle. Gawain weds the daughter. That masses may be said for the souls of his victims, the Churl builds at Carlisle a rich abbey, which becomes a bishop's seat.

The piece seems to be parallel in general features with the first part of the French *fabliau Le Chevalier à l'Epée*. It represents a primitive form of the story, and was probably composed by a minstrel for an uncultivated audience.

The Carle off Càrlile [35], a ballad in the Percy Folio MS. (c. 1650) based on this poem, is probably of the sixteenth century. In it is an incident supposed to be of very primitive origin, and to have been suppressed by the author of the earlier poem. After dinner on the day following the arrival of the knights, the Churl takes Gawain to a chamber hung with swords. There, by direction of his host, Gawain beheads the Churl. As in *The Turke and Gowin*, a handsome knight rises in place of the hideous Churl; he has been enchanted until a knight of the Table Round shall smite off his head.

THE AWNTYRS OFF ARTHURE AT THE TERNE WATHELYNE [36], largely to the glory of Gawain, was composed probably in the North of England near Carlisle, at the middle, or in the latter half, of the fourteenth century. It is in MS. Ireland at Hale, Lancashire (15th century); MS. Thornton (1430-1440); MS. Douce 324 (15th century); and MS. Lambeth 491 ff. 275-86 (1400-1450). It consists of 702 verses in stanzas abababbcdddc, made up of nine long alliterative lines each with two stresses to the half-line, and four short lines of two or three stresses each. As in the *Pearl*, stanzas are connected by repetition in a second stanza of a word or of words in that just preceding (see Index, *Repetition*). In the *Awntyrs* one finds in the first and ninth lines of each stanza a word or several words repeated from the line next preceding or sometimes from some other earlier line. The alliteration and the repetition are very regular in the first part of the poem, but are irregular in the second part. The question whether the poem is the *Awntyre of Gawane* ascribed by Wyntoun to Huchown of the Awle Ryale, has been much discussed (see page 400).

From Carlisle Arthur goes a-hunting. Accompanied by Gawain, Guinevere rides out and rests under a laurel. A terrific storm bursts upon them. A flame breaks forth, and a horrible female figure, blackened as from fire, and covered with toads and snakes, appears groaning and yelling. The dogs and the birds are terrified. Gawain demands the creature's purpose. The spirit would see her daughter Guinevere. She urges the Queen to take warning by her evil state, which is due to incontinence, and urges the transitoriness of power, place, and beauty, and the inevitable punishment of sin. If thirty trentals are said for her soul, the mother may ultimately reach Heaven. Guinevere promises that the masses shall be said. Questioned, the spirit declares that Pride is the worst sin, and that the duty of Man is to be meek and merciful and to do almsdeeds. She states that the King is too courteous; and prophesies that a knight by treason shall be made King. Gawain shall be slain, and Arthur and the Table Round shall be destroyed on the coast of Cornwall. The storm clears off; Arthur and his train, with Guinevere and Gawain, go to supper in Rudolf's hall. While they are at table, a beautiful lady enters with a gorgeously armed knight. The latter is Sir Galleroune of Galway, who comes to fight for his lands taken in war by Arthur and given to Gawain. To the regret of the Queen, Gawain undertakes the

duel.   The contest is long doubtful.   The lady laments when the
Knight is hurt; the Queen grieves when Gawain is wounded.
Gawain is overpowering his opponent, when, at the lady's request,
the Queen induces Arthur to stop the fight.   Galleroune yields his
rights to Gawain.   Arthur makes Gawain duke and lord of Wales,
and, at request of Gawain, gives Galleroune his former territory.
At Carlisle, Galleroune weds his lady, and is received into the
Table Round.   The last stanza states that the Queen ordered a
million masses said for her mother.

No source for the poem as a whole, is known.   Perhaps
because the versions were committed to memory by minstrels,
and because they circulated long before being written down,
the MSS. vary much in details of expression.   The piece exhibits
pretty close acquaintance with the geography of the neighborhood of Carlisle, Inglewood Forest, and Tarn Wadling, but a
somewhat confused notion of the South of England.

The poem falls into two parts connected only in time and
place and personages.   Up to the last stanza the second part
ignores the first.   In the first part there is an obvious religious purpose, with perhaps the end of exhorting (as in *Lancelot of the Laik*) some prince to proper kingly conduct.   The
theme of this part is the not uncommon mediæval Latin one of
a woman in torment to be freed only after a definite number
of masses are said for her.   The somewhat popular *Trental of
St. Gregory* (see page 172), preserved in several English versions, makes the Pope's guilty mother warn her son and beg
masses of him.   The general situation of the second part of
the *Awntyrs* is common in romances.   The story is very simple,
and is told artlessly.   Gawain is still the favored attendant of
the Queen, still the courteous and the mighty.   Guinevere is
now the vain and licentious Queen of later romance, who must
be warned of her evil ways.   With all his desire to preach the
vanity of things material, the author had an eye for color and
glitter and show.   He had much imagination, and was given to
elaboration of external appearance.   The details and the
excellent setting of the ghost scene, the appearance of Guinevere going hunting, the aspects of the halls in the second part,
and the description of the splendid Galleroune and his lady,
are presented well.

GOLAGRUS AND GAWAIN [37], a Scottish poem assigned to 1450-1500, is extant in a text printed in Edinburgh in 1508 and preserved in the Advocates' Library. On very doubtful grounds, it has been ascribed by some to Clerk of Tranent, who died not later than 1507, and by others to Huchown (see page 400). It consists of 1362 verses in stanzas abababababcdddc. The first nine lines of the stanza are the regular long alliterative metre with medial cæsura, lines 10-12 have three stresses, and line 13 has two stresses. The poem is made up of two quite independent tales (ll. 1-234, 235-1362). Both are based on the French *Perceval*, but exhibit much independence.

In the first part the churlish Kay is contrasted with the courteous Gawain. On the way to the Holy Land, Arthur and his host lack food and shelter. At his own request, Kay is sent to a city to supply their needs. His boorishness wins him a sound beating in a castle hall. Having urged a more seemly embassy, Gawain is sent on the mission. By courtesy he obtains food and thirty thousand troops.—In the second part, Arthur continues the march. He comes to a castle whose masters have never acknowledged an overlord. The King leaves the castle, promising that on his return he will have homage of its lord, Golagrus. On the way back, he sends Gawain, Lancelot, and Ywain, to demand submission. Golagrus replies that he would do for the great King anything except submit. A siege, with many duels, follows. Golagrus is finally overcome by Gawain; but, despite the latter's beseeching, he will not preserve his life by admitting defeat. In the end, he suggests that Gawain go with him to his castle as if beaten, and he shall be rewarded. To save him, Gawain, to the grief of Arthur's host, pretends defeat. In the castle, Golagrus and all his people yield to Gawain; they accompany him to acknowledge fealty to Arthur. After a feast of nine days, the King liberates Golagrus from allegiance, and departs.

The poem is for the glorification of Gawain, for the exposition of fine courtesy and gentle nobleness, and for the inspiring of knightly prowess. It is interesting, full of life, and picturesque. As are other writers of the alliterative stanza, the poet is fond of description. The painfully intricate artificial verseform is well handled. In some respects it is well fitted for expression of the stress and strife of the second part of the piece. No doubt the best of the poem is in the combats,

though here and there in these all the writer's skill could not
save him from tediousness. The use of Sir Spinogras, a knight
of Arthur, who, as a sort of expositor, from time to time
explains the history, nature, motives, and probable behavior
of Golagrus, is an interesting means of avoiding third personal
omniscient declarations by the author, and other less economi-
cal methods of presentation. Unhappily, however, these
speeches of Spinogras become rather tiresome.

THE AVOWYNGE OF KING ARTHUR, SIR GAWAN, SIR KAYE, AND SIR BAWDEWYN OF BRETAN [38],

of the latter half of the fourteenth century, is preserved in the
Ireland MS. at Hale in the same hand (15th century) as the
Awntyrs. It consists of 72 sixteen-line tail-rime stanzas
arranged aaabcccbddddbeeeb. Alliteration is used much.

While at Carlisle, Arthur hears of a great boar. The King and
his three knights hunt him to his lair in Inglewood Forest. Arthur
vows to kill the boar alone before morning. By command of the
King, Gawain vows to watch all night at Tarn Wadling; Kay,
to ride the forest till day, and to slay any who would restrain
him; Baldwin, never to be jealous of his wife or any fair woman,
never to refuse his food to any man, and not to fear any threat of
death. After a hard fight, Arthur slays the boar, cuts him up,
and devoutly thanks the Virgin. Kay attempts to rescue a maiden
from Sir Menealfe of the Mountain, whom he meets in the forest;
but he is easily made captive—Menealfe will free him if Gawain
will run a course with him. At the Tarn, Gawain runs the course
and frees Kay; and then he runs another, and frees the maiden.
Menealfe and the maiden he sends to the Queen, who gives them
to the King. Arthur admits Menealfe to the Table Round. At
Kay's urging, the King sends Kay and five other knights to
test Baldwin's valor. Baldwin overthrows all of them. An elaborate test of the Knight's hospitality is arranged by the King, and
is satisfied equally well. So, too, is proved Baldwin's faith in his
wife. At Arthur's urging, Baldwin tells of three incidents of his
experience in a besieged castle, that begot the convictions at base
of his triple vow.

The poem belongs to the literature of boasting, most widely
known through *Le Pèlerinage de Charlemagne*. No source for
the work as a whole has been traced. Baldwin's story of the
soldiers and the women belongs to the class represented in
Johannes de Garlandia's *Poetria* and the twenty-sixth *fabliau*

of Montaiglon's *Recueil Général*. The poem presents an extraordinary combination of stories of various types from varying sources, skilfully accomplished without unduly distracting attention from the framing plot, or destroying the unity of the piece as a whole. The matter is all dealt with in a popular spirit quite free of sophistication, and more in the tone of the ballad or of the Welsh Arthurian tales than in that of the romances. The characters are individualized and definite. Arthur is not the King, but a hunter, a good fellow with his knights, quite ready with practical jokes on his associates. Kay, as in other tales of this group, is much like Malory's Kay, a boaster, a discourteous and untimely jeerer and taunter, incapable in arms. Gawain, in the episode with Menealfe contrasted with Kay, is the servant of the Queen as in the *Le Morte Arthur, Lancelot of the Laik*, and the *Awntyrs*, a champion of dauntless skill, a gracious, courteous gentleman, ever considerate of the feelings of others. Baldwin is a well-rounded, large nature, serene from a broad and full experience. He appears in the Welsh and in Malory, but is not dealt with in the extant French tales.

YWAIN AND GAWAIN [39], in MS. Galba E IX (early 15th century), consisting of 2016 short couplets with some use of alliteration, was composed in the Northern dialect probably in 1300-1350. It falls into two parts, the second beginning at line 1449.

To his fellows of the guard at the door of Arthur's bedchamber, Colgrevance relates some of his adventures. The Queen joins the group. Taunted by Kay and urged by the Queen, the abashed knight tells of meeting in a wood a monstrous creature, at whose direction he went to the forest of Broceliande, and there poured out a basin upon a rock. At once, a terrible storm burst upon him. When it subsided, a strange knight appeared, jousted with him, overthrew him, and bore him away on his horse. This story arouses the interest of Arthur, who swears to seek the adventure. Ywain secretly precedes him. He overcomes the knight of the rock, and pursues him to his castle. But Ywain is caught between the two portcullises. A damsel, Lunet, whom he has treated well at Arthur's court, preserves him by means of a magic ring. Ywain sees the lady of the castle mourning for her dead husband, and falls

in love with her. With much art, Lunet wins her finally to forgive
the Knight, and to marry him. Made guardian of the rock by the
marriage, Ywain responds when Arthur pours the water. He overthrows Kay, the scoffer and easily defeated jouster; reveals his
identity; and for several weeks entertains Arthur, Gawain, and the
others at the castle. Urged by Gawain, Ywain leaves his wife,
Alundyne, to go in search of glory; if he is gone over a year, the
lady shall cease to love him. He forgets her. Lunet appears at
Arthur's court, declares his recreancy, and takes back the magic
ring. Ywain goes mad with grief. Naked and fed by a hermit, he
roams the wood. A lady anoints and cures him. He defends her
castle, and ultimately weds her. From a fire-breathing dragon he
rescues a lion, which becomes his attendant. So devoted is the
creature, that it plans suicide when it supposes its master dead.
Ywain rescues the family of the sister of Gawain from a giant, and
preserves Lunet from burning for treason. The elder of two sisters
obtains Gawain's assistance to gain for her all her father's property. The younger sister makes similar application to Gawain.
Finding him engaged, through her damsel she obtains Ywain's
championship. With the Knight, the damsel is shut up in the Castle
of Heavy Sorrow. Aided by the lion, Ywain overcomes two giants
who have long held the castle, liberates many maiden captives,
and wins the lord's daughter and all the country. But he will
not wed, and goes with the damsel to fulfil his promise. Neither
knowing the other, Ywain and Gawain fight till night falls; as they
are about to break off, they learn each other's names, and are
reconciled. The King divides the property between the sisters.
Overcome with love of his lady, Alundyne, Ywain goes to the fountain, and raises the storm. Alundyne has no knight to answer the
summons. Craftily Lunet persuades her to swear to make peace
between 'the Knight of the lion' and his wife, and so reconciles
her and Ywain. With the pair, Lunet lives thereafter in peace and
power.

The poem is one of the most interesting, and in many other
respects one of the best, of the romances in English. Its
theme in the first part is the quick consolation of the widow; in
the second part, fidelity in love. Arthur appears only to afford
a framework for the story. As the synopsis shows, Ywain
is the hero, Gawain being introduced only to magnify his worth.
Oddly, the writers of English appear to have neglected Chrétien
de Troyes. *Ywain and Gawain* is the only extant Middle English romance that was surely translated and paraphrased from
him. It is a somewhat close but free version of Chrétien's best
composition, the culmination of the French court-epic, *Yvain,
ou Le Chevalier au Lion.* The English poet cuts down the orig-

inal by nearly three thousand lines. As a consequence, the narrative proceeds with speed and vividness. Though the psychological analysis for which the French romance is famous, is in the English less extended and fine, it is represented well in dialogue, soliloquy, and meditation, especially in the earlier part of the poem. Direct discourse is employed frequently and naturally, with excellent dramatic effect. All the elements of form and manner are well controlled. Despite the number of incidents, interest is admirably sustained through the excellence of the narrative and through skilful holding back of one episode while another is related. The method of beginning the story with the narrative of Colgrevance to the watch at the door of the King's bedchamber, is striking and dramatic, as is the discussion among the personages there. The interviews between the clever Lunet and Alundyne, are remarkable for their dramatic truth. The character-drawing is good. All in all, the poem is singularly smooth and finished. The admirable verse puts the writer in the class of Gower and Chaucer. It is fluent, and shows masterful control of the run-on line with shift of pause to the cæsura of the second, or even of the third, line. Chaucer's characteristic stopping of the sense at the end of the first line of the couplet and carrying of the second line over into the next couplet, occurs frequently, as at one place does his use of this device to connect paragraphs. Very often, in periodic manner, the sense is carried on with run-on lines and with shift of pause through four or five or six consecutive lines. The arrangement of the elements of the sentence, shows notable boldness and originality, and is often very similar to practice in the modern short couplet. But, notable as is his finish, the poet is not the courtly Frenchman. A natural fondness for direct, even rude, expression, often exhibits itself in his conversations. Pithy utterance of homely wisdom reminds of the popular saws that appear incidentally in the *Owl and the Nightingale* and in other English pieces (see page 374).

THE WEDDYNGE OF SIR GAWEN AND DAME RAGNELL [40], a fifteenth-century South Midland poem, is in MS. Rawlinson C 86 (16th century). Allowing for a missing leaf, it consists of about 925 lines (actually extant, 853 lines) in tail-rime aabccb.

Hunting in Inglewood Forest, Arthur leaves his retinue and pursues a great hart. As he stands by the slain deer, there appears a stalwart knight, who threatens to kill him for giving his lands to Gawain. Arthur pleads the shame of slaying an unarmed knight, and promises amends. Having required him to appear that day twelvemonth, alone and in the same garb, and to show, on pain of death for failure, what it is that women love best, the Knight permits the King to go. Though he has promised to keep the matter secret, when pressed by Gawain Arthur reveals the situation to the knight. Independently the twain travel far and wide, questioning the folk and keeping record of the replies. When they return, a month before the fatal day, they find that, though each has a great book full of answers, their quest has been in vain. Encouraged by Gawain, Arthur goes to the forest. There he meets the hideous Dame Ragnell. She will aid him if he gives her Gawain for husband. The King protests, but agrees to try to persuade Gawain to her will. Gawain declares that, to save the King who has honored him so much, he would wed the lady were she foul as Beelzebub. Ragnell tells the King that women most love sovereignty. After trying other answers, the King offers Ragnell's to the mysterious Knight. The Knight curses his sister (Ragnell) for revealing the secret, and permits Arthur to depart. At the lady's request, Gawain weds her in the open church. She gorges at the feast. But in the bridal-chamber she becomes young and lovely. Her stepdame has enchanted her: will Gawain have her fair by day and foul by night, or *vice versa?* The hero bids her choose. Given the sovereignty, she wills to be always fair. The court is delighted with the outcome. The King becomes reconciled with Ragnell's brother. The lady bears a son, Gyngolyn. Love causes Gawain to forget knightly glory. The author proposes to make a quick end of the lady, and states that she died five years later. He adds that Gawain was married often, but the five years with Ragnell were his greatest wedded bliss.

The piece contains much excellent dialogue and good description of behavior. It is not humorous, is vivid, and progresses well.

Before this piece was composed, the story had been told by Gower in the *Tale of Florent* in the *Confessio Amantis*, and by Chaucer in the *Wife of Bath's Tale* (see page 719). The three versions seem to be independent of each other, all perhaps being derived from some very old tale, perhaps a Breton *lai*.

Analogues are found in Oriental, African, Gaelic, and Scandinavian tales. The earliest extant form is in an Irish version in a twelfth-century MS., where sovereignty is personified as a lady who has transformed herself in order to test the man she loves.

The Marriage of Sir Gawain [41] is an English ballad based probably on *The Weddynge*. Another ballad, *King Henry*, has parallels with the latter, and may well have antedated it.

THE JEASTE OF SYR GAWAYNE [42], of the South Midland and probably of the fifteenth century, is in MS. Douce 261 (1564), apparently from an early print. It consists of 541 verses of tail-rime aabccb; the first lines are missing.

Gawain is enjoying the love of a lady whom he has found in a pavilion. Her father appears, and requires the Knight to fight with him. Gawain offers amends, but is forced to fight. He overcomes the father, who warns him to be on his guard. One after the other, two brothers of the lady are beaten. A third brother, Sir Brandles, a splendidly attired knight of great prowess, fights with the hero until night falls. With honors equal, they part, agreeing to continue the duel when next they meet. The brother administers a severe beating to the lady, and helps his wounded father and brothers to their home. The lady flees, and wanders in the woods. To the gratification of the court, Gawain never meets Brandles again.

The piece deals with the first part of a story that appears in the first continuation of Chrétien's *Perceval*. In the French, a second part follows Gawain's departure from the lady and Brandelis. According to this, the knights meet and continue the duel at Brandelis' castle, which Arthur and his train have visited unaware; the lady appears with her child, Giglain, and pleads for peace; Brandelis kicks the boy, but is overcome by Gawain; he is persuaded to yield, is made a member of the Table Round, and forgives the penitent Gawain.

LIBEAUS DESCONUS [43], the story of 'The Fair Unknown' or Guinglain (English Gingelein), son of Gawain, originated from the desire for more stories concerning famous personages of romance, that called forth accounts of the early

life of many heroes, and narratives of the history of their associates or kindred or offspring. A number of versions of the
original *Libeaus* were produced. There survive the French
Le Bel Inconnu by Renaud de Beaujeu, of the end of the
twelfth century; the Italian *Carduino*, of about 1375; the
Middle High German *Wigalois*, of about 1210; and the English
romance.

The English poem was composed in the neighborhood of Kent
at about 1325-1350, and is commonly ascribed to Thomas
Chestre, author of *Sir Launfal* (see page 131) and possibly of
Octovian (see page 120). It is in MSS. Lincoln's Inn Libr.
150 (end of 14th or beginning of 15th century), Cotton Caligula A II (15th century), Royal Libr. Naples XIII, B, 29
(1457), Ashmole 61 (15th century), Lambeth 306 (end of 15th
century), and the Percy Folio MS. (1650). These in Kaluza's
critical text afford a whole of 2232 verses, generally of three
stresses, in stanzas usually aabaabccbddb. In verses 1-42 and
1705-32, which are perhaps interpolated, the tails are of
three, and the other verses of four, stresses each.

Gingelein, the bastard son of Gawain, is brought up in seclusion
by his mother. One day, while hunting, he dons the armor of a
knight whom he finds dead, and goes to Arthur at Glastonbury
demanding knighthood. As he does not know his name, he is
knighted as 'Libeaus Desconus.' Gawain trains him. Doubtfully
Arthur grants his request for the 'first fight' that shall develop at
court. A maiden, Elene, and a dwarf appear at mealtime, and
request a rescuer for the imprisoned lady of Sinadoune. Reluctantly and jeering, they accept Libeaus. Mocking him, the maid
rides to encounter William Salebraunche. Libeaus overcomes the
knight, and sends him to Arthur. The maid apologizes, and is
reconciled. Then he overthrows and sends to Arthur several
nephews of William who overtake him to avenge their uncle. Next
he rescues a maid from two giants, one red, one black, whose heads
he sends to Arthur. He declines an offer of the maid in marriage.
He matches Elene for beauty against the lady of Sir Giffroun le
Fludus, and, losing the judgment, challenges and defeats the
knight. The prize, a gerfalcon, is sent to Arthur. He overcomes
Sir Otes de Lile and twelve companions, and sends Otes to Arthur.
The King elects Libeaus to the Round Table.—As the author
remarks, 'Nou . . . telle we other tales.' He wanders from his
theme; he states that Libeaus had many adventures in Wales and
in Ireland. On a June day, the hero slays a giant who besieges a

fair lady of the Isle d'Or. Through the sorcery of the lady, for a year he forgets in her arms all his honor and his quest. At last Elene makes him realize his disgrace; and he sets off once more. At Sinadoune, Libeaus overcomes the steward, Sir Lambard. The lady is imprisoned by two brothers, magicians, Maboun and Irain, who seek to force her to wed Maboun. Libeaus enters the magic hall; the music ceases, the lights are quenched, the building shudders and rocks. He slays Maboun; wounded, Irain disappears. A serpent with a woman's face enfolds him. As she kisses him, she becomes a lovely lady. She was enchanted until she should kiss Gawain or one of his kin. The Knight and the lady are wedded. We are not told whether Libeaus' parentage was revealed.

The author refers (l. 246) to a French original, probably a poem older than *Le Bel Inconnu*. Much of the detail of the story reaches far back into folk-lore. The English poem is not of high quality. Its only unity lies in the general framework of the quest to free the lady of Sinadoune. The various combats, and the adventure with the lady of the Isle d'Or (analogous to the well-known Bower of Bliss episode familiar in Tasso, Aristo, and Spenser), have no essential connection with each other or with the general theme. The incidents might with as much reason have been multiplied interminably from the many adventures in Ireland and Wales that the author, forgetting his theme, says Libeaus had. But the extraordinary number of the MSS. extant, and the frequency of references in later works up into the sixteenth century, prove that the story was very popular. This popularity probably arose from the variety of the incidents, the prowess of the hero, the mystery of his parentage, the magic elements, the giants, and the combats against odds. The poet is fond of describing, but his products consist of stock generalities of matter and of phrase that make no picture. The jingling verse adds to the general tediousness. Its popularity and its verse-form led Chaucer to include the piece in his list in *Sir Thopas*.

V. Perceval

Though very important, the story of Perceval was made the theme of but few romances. In English, it was dealt with only in *Sir Percyvelle of Galles* and in Malory. It was originally a folk-tale that was diffused widely among various peoples. Apparently, the general lines of the early story corresponded fairly closely with *Sir Percyvelle*. In the early versions, the court to which the boy came was merely that of a 'king.' But comparatively early, in the twelfth century, the tale was connected with Arthur. In time, the Perceval and the Grail lines came together, and Perceval displaced Gawain as hero of the Grail quest.

The *Perceval* or *Conte del Graal*, left unfinished by Chrétien de Troyes, is the earliest extant Perceval poem, though a number of pieces must have preceded it. This *Perceval* was continued by Wauchier de Denain, Gerbert de Montreuil, and Manessier. In German, the tale is represented by Wolfram von Eschenbach's *Parzival*. Moreover, there are two French prose romances, one the *Perlesvaus*, the other the Didot and Modena *Perceval*. The latter, in both the Didot MS. and the Modena MS., is a part of a great whole, being preceded by de Borron's *Joseph d'Arimathie* (see page 74) and *Merlin* (see page 40), and followed by a *Mort Artus* (see page 75). In both of these French Perceval pieces, the original element of the tale, the *enfances*, is omitted. Further, there must be mentioned a Welsh tale *Peredur, son of Evrawc*, where matter from Chrétien, or parallel to Chrétien, is mingled with Welsh tradition. In *Peredur*, however, as in the English *Sir Percyvelle*, the Grail theme has no part.

SIR PERCYVELLE OF GALLES [44], in the Thornton MS. (1430-1440), was composed in 1350-1400 in the North of England. The MS. contains a number of Midland forms. It consists of 2286 verses in sixteen-line tail-rime stanzas usually aaabcccbdddbeeeb. Usually, stanzas are connected by repetition, in the first line, of a word or a phrase in the last line of the next preceding stanza (see *Repetition*, Index). There is irregular alliteration.

Percyvelle, father of the hero and brother-in-law of Arthur, soon after his son's birth is slain in combat by a red knight. The mother rears the child in the woods, ignorant of men and of all knightly customs. The boy becomes expert with the dart. One

day, he learns of God from his mother, and sets out to seek Him.
He meets Ywain, Gawain, and Kay, one of whom he assumes must
be the Deity. Kay jeers; Gawain courteously declares they are all
of Arthur's court. The boy would be knighted. On his way to
his mother, he catches and mounts a wild mare. The next day,
he sets out for Arthur's court. He rests at a hall, takes a ring
from the finger of a sleeping lady, and leaves one that his mother
has given him as a recognition token. He demands knighthood of
Arthur. The red knight enters the hall, drinks a cup of wine,
and, to the distress of the King, makes off with the goblet. Percyvelle declares he will get back the cup if he is knighted. Arthur,
suspecting his parentage, is about to dub him, when he bursts off
after the thief. He kills the red knight with his dart, and, on foot,
catches his horse. Unable to get off the knight's armor, he undertakes to burn him out. Gawain appears, and helps him don the
harness. The boy sends the cup back to Arthur, and goes on
adventures. The witch mother of the red knight he kills and burns
in the fire in which he has put the body of her son. He takes
shelter with an old knight and his twelve sons, who are oppressed
by the red knight. Learning from a messenger on his way to
Arthur that the Lady Lufamour is besieged by a sultan who seeks
her hand and her lands, with three of the sons the hero sets off
to raise the siege. Informed by the messenger of the situation,
Arthur and three knights set off to aid the youth. Percyvelle
fights his way into the city, where he is welcomed by the lady. The
next day he cuts down a host of besiegers, and rides against Arthur,
Ywain, Gawain, and Kay. He runs a drawn course with Gawain
before they recognize each other. Percyvelle is knighted, defeats
the sultan, and weds the lady. After a year, he seeks his mother.
He finds bound to a tree the lady with whom he left his ring. The
ring he took away from her is a magic one; the exchange has led
her lover to deem the lady faithless. Percyvelle overthrows the
lover; an explanation follows. The hero slays the present holder
of his mother's ring, a giant brother of the sultan. The ring glides
out of the giant's treasure-box toward the Knight. Learning that,
believing her son dead, his mother wanders the woods naked, Percyvelle dons goat-skins, and seeks her. He comes upon her, is recognized, and takes her home to his lady. At the end of the last stanza,
the author states that Percyvelle later won many countries in the
Holy Land, and was slain there.

The poem has no reference to the Grail quest. Unlike most
of the Perceval pieces, it is especially brief and simple. It
exhibits a number of very primitive elements associated with
popular lore. The writer may have been a minstrel who knew
something of Chrétien's *Conte del Graal*, with which the poem
corresponds up to the end of the red knight theme, but who,

with poor judgment and with no knowledge of the significance of the Grail material, rejected the greater elements of the story in favor of a version not now extant. So, the piece seems to represent a form of the legend that, with those represented by the Welsh and by Chrétien's work in the *Conte del Graal*, is the earliest that has survived. Possibly, as a recent investigator has suggested, the poem is a minstrel's versification of a folk-tale current in his home in Northwestern England. The romance has no high literary value. The verse is jerky. The expression is frequently redundant. The best parts are the homely elements, especially the naïve, indeed grotesque, simplicity of the boy evinced in conversation with his mother, in his interview with the three knights, in the entrance to Arthur's court when he rides up his horse so that its head is thrust into the King's face, and in his attempts to burn the red knight out of his armor.

VI. The Holy Grail

The earliest extant form of the Grail romances is found in *Perceval* or *Le Conte du Graal* or *Le Conte del Graal*, begun before 1188 by Chrétien de Troyes, probably at the request of Count Philip of Flanders. Chrétien left the story unfinished in 10601 verses. Perhaps soon after Chrétien's death, Gautier or Gauchier de Doulens carried on the work to 34934 verses. Probably between 1214 and 1227, Manessier or Mennessier finished it, completing a total of 45379 verses. Another writer, Gerbert, composed in 15000 verses a continuation of Gautier, and so a parallel of Manessier, that is usually found interpolated between Gautier's and Manessier's portions of the *Conte*. Probably in the last years of the twelfth century, not before 1170 or after 1212, Robert de Borron wrote in verse his *Joseph d'Arimathie* and *Merlin* and *Perceval*. The verse *Perceval* is lost. The *Joseph* and the *Merlin* are preserved in a fragmentary metrical version, the former in 3514, the latter in 504, verses; and in prose in the Cangé MS. and the Didot MS. Another *Perlesvaus*, probably originally in prose of the early thirteenth century, is preserved. In prose, and perhaps later than any of the pieces just mentioned, was composed the *Queste del Saint Graal*. In the MSS. it is found commonly alone with the *Lancelot* and the *Mort Artus*, and has been ascribed, though with little probability, to Walter Map, archdeacon of Oxford. Dating in its present form from about 1240, is the prose *Grand Saint Graal*, in the MSS. found sometimes preceding the *Merlin* and the *Queste*, and sometimes preceding the *Queste* and the *Mort Artus*. In the MSS. this romance is ascribed to Robert de Borron. It treats of what is styled the Early History of the Grail, and is an amplification and a modification of its basis, de Borron's *Joseph d'Arimathie*. With other versions of the Grail legend we are not concerned here.

The story of the Grail, as it is dealt with in these various pieces, falls on basis of contents into two groups: the first and earlier developed treats of the Quest of the Grail; the second is dependent on the former group, and treats of the Early History of the Grail.

The legend of the Grail is the theme of but two pieces in English before Malory, *Joseph of Arithmathie* and Lovelich's *History of the Holy Grail*. Both of these poems are versions of parts of the *Grand Saint Graal*; both deal with the second or Early History group of material; and the more extensive (that of Lovelich) does not go beyond the deaths of the immediate successors of Joseph of Arimathea in Britain. Consequently, for the consideration of the actual pieces in English, our attention need not be given to the various shifts of significance of the Grail itself, and the changes in personality of the hero of the quest, but is to be fixed upon the limited field of the Early History material. The nature of this material is sufficiently indicated in the abstracts of the two pieces in English that follow.

JOSEPH OF ARIMATHIE [45] is preserved in the Vernon MS. (1370-1380) as a fragment of 709 alliterative long lines, about one hundred preceding lines being lost. It was composed originally in the West or South-West Midland at about 1350, the present form being affected by a Southern scribe. It follows the main lines of the correspondent part of

the French *Grand Saint Graal*, effectively omitting many
details and greatly condensing the treatment of the original, but
adding some slight elements not in that version.

(After burying Christ, Joseph of Arimathea was imprisoned by
the Jews for forty-two years. In his confinement he was comforted by Christ, who brought to him the dish containing His blood
shed on the Cross. Joseph was finally released by Vespasian.)
The fragment opens with Joseph's statement that his long imprisonment seems as but three nights. He and Vespasian and fifty
others, are baptized. The Jews are punished. By direction of
a voice, Joseph, his wife, his son Josaphe, and the fifty others, go to
Sarras, bearing the dish containing Christ's blood in a box that
they make for it. To Evalak, King of Sarras, Joseph tells the
story of Christ's life, and preaches the Trinity. The King doubts
the doctrine, but at night has two visions of Christ on the Cross,
and later a vision of Christ with the Lance, the Nails, and the
Grail. Josaphe is consecrated bishop by Christ. A clerk whom
Evalak appoints to dispute with Joseph, is stricken dumb and blind.
The heathen idols are defeated. Tholomer, King of Babylon,
invades Evalak's dominions. Joseph reveals Evalak's past history,
and gives him a shield marked with a red cross, before which he
shall pray to Christ if he is in distress. At first Evalak is successful, but later he is taken prisoner. Praying as Joseph directed,
he is rescued by an angel, who, in the form of a white knight, slays
Tholomer, and aids Evalak to victory. Joseph finds Evalak's queen
to be a Christian, converted by a miraculous healing of her mother.
Evalak and his brother-in-law, Seraphe, are baptized as Mordreins
and Naciens. Five thousand of their subjects are baptized with
them. Joseph and Naciens go on a missionary journey, leaving
the Grail in the care of two specially appointed guardians. The
poem ends with a brief mention of Joseph's later imprisonment
in North Wales, and his release by Mordreins.

The writer evidently aimed to treat only an episode that he
felt to be of great importance, and that he was qualified to deal
with. Though now and then unnecessarily harsh, the verse is
well handled, and is especially appropriate to the matter. The
piece is one of the earliest of the extant Middle English alliterative poems. The expression is concise and impressive. All the
matter, except the battle pieces, is full of mystic fervor.
There is nowhere anything trivial. There is no effort, and no
attempt at ornamentation. A reverential, simple dignity, a
solemn elevation, suffuses all with a quasi-Scriptural spirit.
The battle pieces evince extraordinary power; they are delin-

eated with laconic vigor, with realistic detail, in phrasing often strikingly suggestive and picturesque. The poet wrote them with his imagination active, and with his ears ringing with Biblical accounts of warfare rather than with the narrative of the romances.

THE HISTORY OF THE HOLY GRAIL [46], by the skinner Henry Lovelich, author of the English verse *Merlin* (see page 45), dates from about 1450, and is preserved in MS. Corpus Christi College Cbg. 80 (later 15th century) in 11892 short couplets in the Southern or South Midland dialect. The opening of the piece is lost, the MS. beginning with the correspondent to the last lines of Chapter XI of its original, the French *Grand Saint Graal*.

An outline of the poem section by section is given in the Early English Text Society edition. An outline of the original, which will answer for Lovelich's version also, is in Nutt's *Studies*. The *History* begins a little before the preparations of Evalak to resist Tholomer, paralleling thence *Joseph of Arimathie* to the end of that poem; and then it continues the story of Joseph, Naciens, Mordreins, and their children, up to the death of the immediate successors of Joseph.

The piece has little or no artistic or literary value. Its theme exhibits one of the least interesting phases of the growth of the legend, due largely to the infusion of Christian legendary elements that are best represented in the *Grand Saint Graal;* that, at the time of the composing of the work, had such popular appeal; and that contributed greatly to the continued growth of the Grail story as a whole.

Later English treatments [47] of the Grail material are the version of Malory's *Morte Darthur;* the prose *Lyfe of Joseph of Armathy* printed by de Worde; the prose *De Sancto Joseph Ab arimathia* printed by Pynson in 1516; and the legend *Here begynneth the lyfe of Joseph of Arimathia* with *A praysing to Joseph*, all in 456 verses, printed by Pynson in 1520.

VII. Tristram

The story of Tristram and of the passionate love between the hero and Iseult, antedated long the now better-known tale of the love of Lancelot and Guinevere, which by some scholars is supposed to have been invented partly to supplant it in popular approval. Though the whole problem of sources is very complicated and is unlikely ever to be solved finally, the prevalent present view is that the legend is of insular or British origin. Perhaps some of its elements go back to the Viking period, and originated in tradition of actual events of the ninth or the tenth century. Some of its motives are certainly of Celtic birth.

Probably, the incidents of the story were dealt with in literature first in the form of short *lais,* just as one incident of it is treated in Marie de France's *Chèvrefeuille.* Whatever be the fact here, in the twelfth century the legend was composed into longer poems. In England and Germany and Italy have been discovered various fragments of Anglo-Norman verse making up a total of about three thousand lines, that give a fair notion of the nature and quality of a great poem of some twenty thousand lines that was composed by an Anglo-Norman writer, Thomas. Apparently the poem was of great merit, and either directly or indirectly gave birth to a number of redactions. Very early in the thirteenth century, Gottfried von Strasburg composed from it, in 19573 verses in irregular short couplets, one of the greatest mediæval German poems. His work was carried only as far as Tristram's marriage to Ysonde of the White Hands; but it was later completed from the French, both by Ulrich von Türheim and by Heinrich von Freiburg. Heinrich added a number of incidents connected with the court of Arthur. Early in the thirteenth century (1226), the version of Thomas was translated into Norse prose for King Hakon by a certain Brother Robert. Later the story underwent great modification in another Norse prose version. Thomas' Anglo-Norman poem was the ultimate source of the English *Sir Tristrem.*

A different version of the legend is represented by a fragment of a Norman-French poem by Béroul, and by a German poem of 1175-1200 by Eilhart von Oberge. Moreover, there are extant two MSS. of a short poem, *La Folie Tristan*, prob_ ably of the twelfth century, wherein Tristram, disguised as a fool, gives a résumé of the story by relating to Mark the inci_ dents of his relations with Ysonde. Lost poems on phases of the legend were composed by Chrétien de Troyes and a certain La Chièvre. The Gerbert continuation of the French *Perceval* (see page 74) contains matter stated therein to be based on two short poems styled *Luite Tristran*. Finally, the legend was written in the great French prose *Tristan*, a vast work corresponding to the prose *Lancelot*. There it is mingled with incidents of the Arthurian story, its chief element being rivalry between Tristram and Lancelot. From this romance Malory probably obtained much material.

SIR TRISTREM [48] is the only Middle English romance version of the Tristram and Iseult story outside of Malory. This piece, so closely associated with Sir Walter Scott, because of his edition of it and his filling out of its defective ending, is in MS. Auchinleck (1330-1340) in 3344 verses in stanzas of eleven lines abababab cbc, the tenth verse having one stress, and each of the others three stresses. It was composed in the North Midland or the North, probably in the last years of the thirteenth century. Writing at about 1330, Robert of Brunne in his *Chronicle* mentions the poem, referring to its author in such fashion as to leave open the question whether he is Thomas of Erceldoun or Thomas of Kendale. At lines 397, 412, 2787, the romance cites 'Thomas' as authority, and in its first stages the writer says that at Erceldoun he spoke with 'Thomas,' and heard him tell the story of Tristrem. A 'Thomas' is referred to as author in the early French and German versions. The general present opinion is that it was the reputation of Thomas of Erceldoun (see page 223) that led the writer of the English piece and Mannyng to connect him with the narrative. The writer of the extant text does say distinctly that he heard Thomas of Erceldoun tell the story.

Rouland of Erminia begets a boy on Blaunchefleur, sister of King Mark of England. Morgan, one of his lords, treacherously slays Rouland, and seizes the kingdom. Blaunchefleur bears a boy, who is named Tristrem. She dies, leaving the child, with a ring received from Mark, in the care of Rouhand. Rouhand rears the boy as his own, training him to expertness in hunting and music and law. At fifteen, Tristrem beats at chess a sea captain who has put into Norway. The seamen bear off the boy, and deposit him and his winnings on a strange coast, really England. On the way to Mark's court, he shows hunters how to brittle deer. At the court, he exhibits his skill as musician, and is entertained well. Rouhand finds the boy with Mark, and reveals his parentage. Mark knights Tristrem. The hero slays Morgan, and wins Germany and Erminia, which he gives to Rouhand and his sons as his underlords. Every few years Mark must send to Ireland as tribute a hundred youths. Tristrem and the Irish King Moraunt sail to an island, and fight to settle the question of tribute. Tristrem slays Moraunt, but leaves in his head a piece of his sword. He is himself hurt with a wound that will not heal. After three years' sailing, he is borne to Deluelin in Ireland. Ysonde, sister of Moraunt, cures him. Tristrem returns to England, and tells Mark of the lady. Mark sends him to request her in marriage. Tristrem wins the lady's hand by killing a dragon at Dublin. Ysonde recognizes Moraunt's slayer by his broken sword. She and her mother arrange to kill the knight; but, learning his mission, they put aside the plan. By mistake, on the way to England, Tristrem and Ysonde drink a magic draught prepared by the mother for Ysonde and Mark. Thereafter they love without restraint. Mark weds Ysonde, who substitutes her maid for herself on the wedding night, and afterwards attempts to have her murdered. Tristrem rescues Ysonde from a minstrel who has won her from the King. A knight, Meriadok, informs the King of the *liaison*. By craft, the King is present at the interview between the lovers. They detect him, and by their conversation deceive him as to their relations. At last they are caught. At Westminster, through Tristrem's artful phrasing of her oath, Ysonde proves her innocence by ordeal. Tristrem wins the daughter of the King of Wales by slaying a giant. He is received with great joy at Mark's court. But soon Mark discovers the relations of the lovers, and banishes them. For about a year, Ysonde and Tristrem live happily in a forest. One day, Mark comes upon them asleep with a naked sword between them. Believing them true, Mark welcomes them back to court. But soon Tristrem has to flee again. He bears as token a ring of Ysonde. Mark forgives his wife. Tristrem weds Ysonde with the White Hand, daughter of the Duke of Brittany; but sight of his ring causes him to withhold himself from his wife. He defeats a giant whose lands border on his own. By aid of the giant, a hall is made, with images of the chief actors of Tristrem's story. Ganhardin, his brother-in-law, reproaches the hero for neglecting his wife. Sight of the images satisfies him, and leads him to fall in love with Ysonde of Ireland's maid, Brengwain. Tristrem and Ganhardin set off for England to get Brengwain for the latter. Seeking her love, a knight, Canados, reveals to Ysonde of Ireland Tristrem's marriage. She is much distressed. But Tristrem and Ganhardin meet her and Brengwain in the forest, and are with them for two nights. They are detected. The knights flee. Brengwain persuades Mark that all is well. Ysonde and Tristrem meet again. At a tournament, Tristrem and Ganhardin overthrow Meriadok and Canados and many other knights; then they go to Brittany. There, fighting in behalf of a knight of his own name, Tristrem bears away an arrow in his old wound.—Here ends the poem.

His choice of an intricate and immelodious stanza-form, with his efforts at alliteration, led the poet into frequent obscurity of expression, and confined him chiefly to the satisfying of metre. Unskilful use of elliptical and transposed expression and of abrupt transitions, contributes to render the piece unpleasing. With little judgment, beset with anxiety to condense, the poet cut down details, and hurried from incident to incident, paying little attention to clearness, neglecting proportion, and slurring or even omitting vital elements. It has been well suggested that the piece was intended for recitation to a general audience, and that, in the characteristics that have just been indicated, it shows how ballads may have developed from metrical romances. Though the metre is elaborate, the general tone of the poem is 'popular.' The story is in many places very close to the French work of Thomas, but seems to have been copied from memory. Proverbs occur, stock phrases are very common, and expletives are used liberally to eke out the metre and rime. The detailed description of the brittling of the deer by Tristrem, reminds of the similar account in *Sir Gawayne and the Grene Knight* (see page 57), and of the importance of the art in *Ipomydon* (see page 146). The piece exhibits no moral sense; the author is thoroughly in sympathy with the lovers, and feels no need to justify or to explain away their unrestrained passion and their other obliquities. Their behavior is its own justification; chivalric courtesy, faith, honor, religion, all bend before their desire. The treachery to uncle and patron and husband, the plotting against the life of

Brengwain, the cheat in the oath at ordeal, falsehood, adultery—all these prosper, without recognition by the personages or the author of anything reprehensible in them. Christianity and chivalric honor made practically no impress on the principles of the tale.

3. CHARLEMAGNE LEGENDS

Of all the actually historical personages in the Middle Ages, Charlemagne was the most widely famed in romance. Probably, during his lifetime his deeds and those of his associates were sung in *cantilènes*, short popular songs uttered by the people in their ordinary daily intercourse. These pieces evidently were lyric, and dealt with isolated adventures or episodes, much as the later English ballads treated contemporary events. After the death of Charles, imagination worked upon his story, and the *cantilènes* carried on a growing body of traditional matter. In the eleventh century the professional *jongleurs* took up the theme, traveling about reciting their pieces to the accompaniment of the viol. In their hands and in those of the professional *trouvères*, who put their matter into writing, the stories were expanded and modified according to the will of the poet or the supposed demands of the audience.

The romances of Charlemagne fall into several groups. First is the *Royal* or *National* material, preceding the development of feudalism, devoted to wars against enemies of the nation, and represented by *Les Saisnes, Aspremont, Les Enfances Ogier le Danois, Fierebras, Le Pèlerinage de Charlemagne, Roland,* and the other poems dealing with the wars with Spain, etc. Next is the *Feudal* material, falling into two groups, the former of which is the struggle of the rebellious barons against the royal power, the latter the wars of the barons with each other. Of the former are *Renaud de Montaudon* or *Les Quatre Fils Aimon, Huon de Bordeaux,* etc. Connected with this Feudal matter is the *Biographical* matter devoted to the deeds of individual heroes who experience various changes of fortune that finally end happily. Next is the *Adventitious* matter, stories gathered from various sources and slenderly attached to the main theme. Finally, there is the *Genealogical* matter, stories of the early deeds (the *enfances*, see pages 17, 69) of more noted heroes, or accounts of their parents or their children.

All the English Charlemagne romances derive their principal elements directly from the French, though sometimes they introduce new details. Since, at the date of their composition, the comprehension of French among Englishmen had diminished greatly, and since the older and better versions had been lost or forgotten or made over, the translators, with exception of the author of the English *Roland*, used as bases poorer French pieces of the fourteenth and fifteenth centuries.

As we are concerned with them, the Charlemagne romances extant in English, fall into three groups: I. those connected with *Firumbras* (French *Fierebras*), consisting of *The Sowdone of Babylone*, *Sir Firumbras*, and Caxton's *Charles the Grete* (1485); II. those connected with *Otuel* (French *Otinel*), consisting of *Roland and Vernagu*, *The Sege of Melayne*, *Otuel*, *Duke Rowlande and Sir Ottuell*, and the Fillingham *Otuel*; III. four *detached* romances, two in verse, *The Song of Roland* and *The Taill of Rauf Coilʒear*, and two late prose pieces, *The Four Sons of Aymon* and *Huon of Burdeux*. These will be discussed in the order just indicated.

I. Firumbras

The Firumbras matter seems to go back to a lost French poem designated sometimes as *Balan*, a version of which is seen in Philippe Mousket's riming chronicle of c. 1243. The abrupt ending and several allusions in the extant French verse *Fierebras*, make probable the existence of such a poem, of a portion of the second part of which the verse *Fierebras* is a modified and expanded version. The French *Destruction of Rome* may have represented wholly or partly the first part, or may have been composed as an introduction to *Fierebras*. In English *The Sowdone of Babylone* and *Sir Firumbras*, with Caxton's *Charles the Grete*, represent the *Fierebras* group.

THE SOWDONE OF BABYLONE [49] has its first part correspondent with the French *Destruction of Rome,* and the rest (ll. 940 ff.) with the French *Fierebras.* It is evidently a loose, condensed paraphrase of a French version, probably of the *Balan.* It is in a MS. formerly owned by Sir Thomas Phillips, from whom it passed to the Rev. J. E. A. Fenwick. An early nineteenth-century copy of this MS. by G. Ellis is referred to as Douce 175. The poem dates from the East Midland of about 1400 or shortly thereafter. It consists of 3274 four-stress verses abab with lapses into stanzas of eight lines. Now and then there are verses, sometimes in considerable passages, containing but three stresses. When these verses occur as *b* lines they make the stanza approach the regular 'ballad stanza.' Indeed, in many parts the relation to the ballad form is very interesting.

Laban, Sultan of Babylon, with his son, Firumbras, and daughter, Floripas, besieges Rome. Lukafer of Baldas, after capturing a thousand Christian maids (whom the Sultan destroys), asks the hand of Floripas on promise of capturing the city. The war rages; the city weakens. The Pope sends messengers to Charlemagne, and sallies out against the enemy. Firumbras disarms him, and, after lecturing him concerning his unpriestly behavior, sends him home. The city is betrayed by the treacherous porter, Isres. Firumbras removes the holy relics; the city is burned; the Saracens return to Spain. His forces having arrived too late to succor Rome, Charles sails for Spain. There, in battle he inflicts great losses on the Saracens under Firumbras. He gives thanks to God, and counsels the young knights to imitate the twelve peers.

At this point there is an obvious shift, for lines 939-62 are a prayer to Mars for aid of the Saracens, with no designation of who it is who makes the prayer. The passage varies in rime arrangement from the rest of the poem, and appears as if lifted from some source other than the general original. It is paralleled in Chaucer's *Knight's Tale* and in the opening of his *Anelida and Arcite.* Moreover, there follows in the *Sowdone* at lines 963-78 a quite incongruous and irrelevant passage on the joys of Spring and its effect in inspiring love, insisting that only the lover can be a good warrior. This last, and lines 41 ff. of the *Sowdone,* seem to be paralleled in the opening of the *Canterbury Tales,* of which they may be imitations. Further, lines 979 ff. sound like a quite fresh beginning.

The Sultan assembles his forces, and sends Firumbras against the Christians. Firumbras offers single combat to any of Charles' peers. Roland bids Charles depend for a champion on his old knights whom he has so praised. Oliver finally overcomes Firumbras. But the pagans capture Oliver. Later they take Roland, who has gone to his aid. Firumbras is baptized as Floreyn. Clearly, here is another shift of the piece. The author apparently conceived of Firumbras as done with, for he briefly speaks of his later history, and states that God manifested many miracles for his sake, so holy a man did he become. After some fifteen hundred lines, the hero suddenly reappears to rescue Charles.

The passages from about line 1500 to the end are the most interesting of the story. The hero is really Floripas, the daughter of the Sultan. She murders her duenna and a jailer, and obtains the care of Roland and Oliver. The purpose of Charles' war with the Sultan is reverted to in an embassy sent to the latter to urge return of the relics to Rome. The ambassadors are imprisoned, and are cared for by Floripas. Long in love with Guy of Burgundy, the lady demands his hand in payment for her protection. Guy weds her. By Floripas' suggestion and aid, the prisoners slay many of the Saracens at a feast. The Sultan escapes, and besieges the Christians. The latter hold out through the cunning of Floripas, who by means of her magic girdle supplies them with food. The girdle is stolen. The Sultan's treasure is cast down to crush the besiegers. The Christians make a sortie. A message is got to Charles, who has been advised by the traitor, Ganelyn, to return to France. Charles goes to the aid of his knights. He is caught helpless between the gates of the city. Ganelyn urges the army to retreat and to make him King. Firumbras comes back into the story, and rescues Charles. The besieged are liberated. The Sultan is captured, and, refusing baptism, is executed. Floripas is baptized, and formally wedded to Guy. Guy and Firumbras are given all Spain. Ganelyn is drawn and hanged. The holy relics are located in Paris, St. Denis, and Boulogne.

As has been intimated, the interesting part of the poem is not the battle and duel matter, but the passages following the capture of Oliver and Roland. In these the craft of woman inspired by love becomes the controlling force. The naïve acceptance of the treason of Floripas to her father and her faith, and her murder of her governess and the jailer, all for the sake of the Christians, is representative of the attitude of mediæval romances toward Saracen maidens. No impropriety was perceived in such demonstrations of conversion to Christianity. Here, as elsewhere in these romances, Charles is a minor figure, and appears to no advantage. He is forced to receive aid in combat, and to endure impudence from Roland.

Of much interest are Firumbras' chiding of the Pope for fighting; the scene of the drowning of the governess; the prison scenes, especially those of the burning of Naymes' beard and of the roasting of Lukafer; the episode of the giant, Algolofer; and the quite gratuitous incident of the giantess, Barrok, and her two sons, that appears also in *Sir Firumbras*. With the passages reminding of Chaucer, is to be connected that (not in *Sir Firumbras*) of Floripas in her garden, picking flowers beneath the window of the two prisoners.

SIR FIRUMBRAS [50], from the South of England and probably 1375-1400, is in MS. Ashmole 33 (end of 14th century). Some lines are missing from the beginning and the end. As printed, it consists of 5852 verses. Lines 1-3410 are septenary couplets with internal rime, that might be written as 'ballad measure.' This measure often develops in the *Sowdone of Babylone*, but the number of unstressed syllables is much less irregular here than in the *Sowdone*. Lines 3411 to the end are in tail-rime stanzas aabaab. Much alliteration occurs.

The themes, and most of the episodes, of *Sir Firumbras* are the same as those of the second part (*i.e.*, ll. 979 ff.) of the *Sowdone*. But *Sir Firumbras* is assumed to be a rather close translation of a version of the French verse *Fierebras*, and the *Sowdone* a translation of a MS. of the French *Balan*. The synopsis of the *Sowdone* will give a notion of *Sir Firumbras* sufficient for this book. But it must be noted that the latter poem, to little advantage, has devoted to the matter about five times the lines devoted to it in the former. Many episodes and collateral incidents are not in the *Sowdone*. The names of the persons differ in the two pieces—the Saracen King in *Sir Firumbras* is not 'Laban,' but 'Balan.' In *Sir Firumbras*, Floripas' influence over her father is much diminished, and the details of her behavior vary much from those in the *Sowdone;* there are descriptive passages of which scarcely anything appears in the *Sowdone;* the prayer to Mars, the passages on Spring, and 'the incident of Floripas in the garden, are not in *Sir Firumbras*.

The story of Firumbras was the most popular of the Charlemagne tales; it was translated into most of the European tongues, and was carried on from the twelfth century almost to the present day. In his *Bruce,* Barbour has his hero relate the story to encourage his soldiers as they pass over Loch Lomond. The tale is probably a composite of a legend of the taking of Rome, and a legend of the relics of the Passion, the whole based on Mousket and a later story made up from vari. ous, sources, especially the *chansons de geste.* It came into being perhaps from a desire of a jongleur to account for the worship of relics of St. Denis at the fair of l'Endit.

CHARLES THE GRETE [51], an elaborate prose translation of Jean de Bagnyon's extended prose version of *Fierebras,* was made by Caxton and was printed by him in 1485. The work deals with the whole life of Charlemagne, sketches the lives of the early French kings, and treats the incidents met with in *Sir Firumbras,* the *Sowdone, Roland and Vernagu,* and the *Song of Roland.*

II. Otuel

The second group of English Charlemagne romances are probably versions of tales represented in an assumed great cyclic poem *Charlemagne and Roland,* dealing with Charlemagne's wars against the Saracens, and divided by Gaston Paris into four elements: (1) The journey of Charlemagne into the Holy Land, according to the Latin legend; (2) the beginning of the war with Spain, including the episode of Ferragus (Vernagu); (3) *Otuel,* but in a version other than that represented in the Auchinleck MS., and badly written; (4) the end of the narrative of Turpin. In English, the first two of these elements are represented in *Roland and Vernagu.* The first half of the third element is represented in the *Sege of Melayne, Otuel,* and *Roland and Otuel.* Representation of the second half of the third element survives only in Ellis' analysis of a version in a MS. formerly owned by a W. Fillingham. The fourth element is represented only through the Fillingham version and the *Song of Roland.*

ROLAND AND VERNAGU [52], in MS. Auchinleck (1330-1340), seems to have been drawn from a lost French version based on an eleventh-century Latin verse chronicle, *Descriptio, qualiter Carolus Magnus Clavum et Coronum Domini,* . . . The poem is of the North Midland, and was copied by a Southern scribe. It consists of 880 three-stress verses in tail-rime aabccbddbeeb. A part of a stanza is missing at the beginning.

The piece begins with the miseries of the Emperor of Constantinople. The Emperor beseeches Charles for aid against the Saracens. Charles marches to the city, is given rich relics, and comes back. Not a word is told of what he did in regard to the Saracens. Then follow lists of the victories won by Charles in Spain. To no advantage to the plot, and with little point beyond a surrounding of the hero with the approval of Heaven, are introduced accounts of a series of miracles by which Charles' pious progress is accompanied. Finally, after one half the poem is ended, after Charles (for no obvious ultimate purpose) has been described as the gigantic hero piously wont to sit crowned with thorns, and with a drawn sword on his table, on the feast days of the Christian year—suddenly the pagan giant, Vernagu, appears. He is of twice the stature of Charles, and is accustomed to bear off his opponents under his arm. Roland encounters and daunts him. They fight to the end of the day, and continue on the next day. Roland graciously adjourns the combat to permit the giant to sleep, and under his head he puts a stone to relieve his snoring. Charmed with this act, the giant inquires of the faith that has prompted it, and has explained to him the mysteries of the Trinity, the Incarnation, the Resurrection, and the Ascension. The giant declares that, having mastered these points, he is ready to go on with the fight, and see which religion is better. He is slain by Roland.

The piece has no poetical merit. The jingling of the metre and rime is accentuated by the pauses at the end of the lines. That the work is but part of a larger story, is suggested by the statement in the last three lines that word of all this soon came to the stern Saracen, Otuel. The piece is an effort of a pious writer who had little idea of unity or coherence, who sought to achieve doctrine through romance, and to whose mind the grotesquely diverting episode of Vernagu probably was heroic.

THE SEGE OF MELAYNE [53], representative of a part of the third element of the Otuel group, is in MS. Additional 31042. (15th century), and was written probably in the Northern dialect in 1350-1400. Incomplete, it consists of 1602 verses in tail-rime aabccbddbeeb. The text refers a number of times to 'the Cronekill.' No original is extant. The piece was probably translated from a lost French poem that was an introduction to the French *Otinel*, and that so occupied to *Otinel* the position that the *Destruction of Rome* occupies to *Fierebras*.

The Saracen Arabas has overrun Lombardy, and conquered Rome and Milan. Dreams lead Alantyne, ruler of Milan, to apply to Charles for aid; dreams cause Charles to grant the aid. The traitor Ganelon suggests that Roland be sent to recover Milan. The French are beaten, and Roland and many of his noble associates are captured. Brought before the exultant Saracen, Roland prays for a miracle. A cross that the impudent King tries to burn, sends sparks into the Saracen's eyes; the peers slay the King, and burn many Saracens. Meanwhile, Archbishop Turpin abuses the Virgin for letting all but four of the French be slain. Ganelon advises Charles to submit to the new Sultan. Turpin will have none of this, and cries a crusade. Charles takes Ganelon's advice to let Turpin conduct the war. Turpin curses Charles, excommunicates him, shuts him in Rome, and advances to destroy and burn the city. Charles submits, and is absolved. The French approach Milan. Turpin accomplishes a miracle at the mass, and his clergy win a battle with the Saracens. Turpin is wounded, but will neither attend to his wounds nor eat before Milan is captured. He singly charges a relief force of French supposed to be Saracens; then he leads the force to defeat the pagans. Turpin has fasted three days, and is most seriously injured. The French prepare to assault the city.—Here the piece ends abruptly.

Up to the escape of the French to Paris, the hero of the story is Roland. Thereafter he appears but once, and then in a very minor rôle; Archbishop Turpin now occupies the place of prominence. Charles is but the King necessary for the story. He is sacrificed for the plot, and to give opportunity to the virtues of Turpin and others of his knights. He is ever subject to advice. He fights but once, and then, though encouraged vigorously by Turpin, overcomes his opponent only with the greatest difficulty. He scarcely ever rises to dignity or force of action or of speech. He lets Roland go alone to Milan; he would remain at Paris, and have Turpin and his clergy avenge the French. At Milan, he seeks a messenger to go for aid for his forces, and is refused by his knights, who are too valiant to ask for help. Ganelon is the double-dyed villain without motive, always on the alert to misadvise—the stock villain whose viciousness is taken to be self-explanatory. The Church predominates. In the first part visions are most influential. Miracles are prominent, and make rather unnecessary the prowess of Roland and his associates. The Archbishop gradually becomes the controlling force in the action, and the central figure on the stage. His dominance in the poem and his relations with Charles, make an interesting parallel with the dominance of the Archbishop and his relation with the King in *Athelston* (see page 24). He is a well-drawn, masterly spirit. He fears naught. He openly abuses the Virgin for permitting the French to be defeated. He avenges France by his crusade. To his face he taunts and curses Charles for cowardice and recreancy; and he personally defends himself against the furious King, whom he shuts up in his own city, and compels to submission and to participation in the war. He directs the campaign, prevents plundering, sustains the spirits of the forces, and wins battles. He it is who supports and endures. In the passages just alluded to, in spite of stock features, the piece has much spirit and genuine power. Good specimen passages are Turpin's scenes with Charlemagne (ll. 667 ff.) and with the squire (ll. 973 ff.).

OTUEL [54], said to be the earliest Charlemagne romance in English, is in MS. Auchinleck (1330-1340). It was composed in the South Midland, probably at the opening of the fourteenth century. It is in 869 short couplets grouped in short unequal paragraphs. It seems to be a rather free reproduction of a version similar to the French *Otinel* in the Middlehill MS.

The story of *Otinel*, an episode between two of Charlemagne's expeditions into Spain, seems to have originated in France at about 1200. Its source is doubtful, and its plot is not a part of the early Charlemagne legend. Possibly it was created and recited to satisfy the demand for more Charlemagne stories. The name 'Otinel' has been suggestively identified with 'Hospinellus' of the *Pseudo-Philomela*. Versions are extant in Norse and in Danish, as well as in the English *Otuel·* and *Roland and Otuel*.

Rightly in his first lines the author summons those who would hear of 'battles bold'; the story is made up wholly of duels, combats, and battles. The first third deals with the conversion of Otuel, nephew of Vernagu, who would avenge the death of his uncle. He is sent as messenger to summon Charles to surrender to Garcy, the pagan King of Lombardy. Otuel dares all the court of Charles, fights a drawn duel with Roland on an island, becomes converted by miracle, and agrees to marry Charles' daughter after the war with Lombardy is over. The last thousand lines tell of a combat of Roland, Oliver, and Ogier with four Saracens, and of their rescue from the heathen army by Otuel; the slaying of Clarel by Otuel in a duel which (like that between Roland and Vernagu) is presented as a test of the relative worth of the Saracen faith and Christianity; and the capture of Garcy, and presentation of him to Charles.—Here the MS. breaks off.

The whole piece is dull, despite the writer's effort to vary the general nature and the details of his contests. For the benefit of Otuel, Roland is lowered in ability. Charles is full of womanish fear for Roland. Rather interesting is the entrance of the love-element for the first time in these English Charlemagne romances. Clarel makes Ogier captive, and sends him to his leman, Aufange, daughter of King Garcy, to be healed. This episode consists of but seventeen lines, and is undeveloped.

DUKE ROWLANDE AND SIR OTTUELL OF SPAYNE

[55], in MS. Additional 31042 (15th century), was composed probably in the North of England at about 1400. It consists of 1596 verses in tail-rime aabaabccbccb. Its general theme is that of *Otuel*, but in details it varies much from that poem. It appears to be a fairly close translation of a French version somewhat different from the original of *Otuel*. In this poem his lady, Belisant, arms Otuel for his duel with Roland, is elaborately described, and, in response to Otuel's query, declares

she is much pleased with him; Otuel and Belisant are actually
wedded; and Otuel makes a vow to fight hereafter for the lady's
sake. Moreover, the episode of Clariel's lady, who is given now
a speaking part, is expanded to forty-eight lines; and, as he
goes to the duel with Clariel, Otuel is kissed thrice by Belisant.

THE FILLINGHAM OTUEL [56] has been lost. It was
in six-line stanzas in a MS. formerly owned by W. Fillingham,
and was paraphrased by Ellis in his *Specimens of Early English Metrical Romances*. Ellis' paraphrase led Gaston Paris
to infer the former existence of the cyclic poem already mentioned (see page 87). The Ellis version completes the story
left unfinished in *Otuel*, and carries on the general epic theme,
paralleling Turpin's *Chronicle*, from the death of Ferragus
(Vernagu) to the end of Roland at Roncesvalles, the defeat of
the Saracens by Charlemagne, and the punishment of Ganelon.

III.　Detached Romances

THE SONG OF ROLAND [57] is a translation of a version of the French epic, composed in the South-West Midland
toward the end of the fourteenth, or perhaps in the fifteenth,
century. It exists as a fragment of 1049 lines in MS. Lansdowne 388 (1450 or later). Perhaps from desire to reflect the
epic movement of his original, the poet varied the verse-length
of his couplets. The rimes are poor; alliteration occurs, but
is not structural. Possibly the irregularities are due to general incapacity. The beginning and the end are missing, lines
are omitted, minor passages are confused and unintelligible.

In Spain, Ganelon appears before Charles with a troop of Saracen maidens. He informs him that the King of Saragossa has
agreed that, if Charles goes home within three days, he will be
baptized with his best knights; the ladies are gifts. Charles
agrees, and sets off for Germany. After a journey of ten miles,
he pitches his camp. The knights all drink, and have their way
with the damsels. Charles dreams of besieging Saragossa, and of
Ganelon treacherously trying to murder him; of a boar that bit
off his right hand; and of a leopard that tore off the boar's right
ear. At the Gates of Spain, he decides to establish a van- and

a rear-guard. Ganelon urges him to leave Roland with the rear-guard. The King perceives the traitor's anxiety for Roland's death. Roland offers to take the rear; all the other knights refuse. Charles leaves half the twelve peers with Roland, and starts for France with Ganelon in the van. With forty thousand troops, the Sultan attacks Roland. Ten thousand men sent to reconnoitre are slain by the infidels; only the leader, Sir Gauter, escapes to warn Roland. The French lament, but the hero encourages them. Charles is alarmed at the failure of the rear-guard to come up. The knights accuse Ganelon, who urges that Roland has probably gone hunting. The main army advances to Cardoile. About the rear some hundred thousand Saracens assemble. Oliver urges Roland to blow his horn for aid. Roland will not blow; are they afraid? The French beseech him; but, on his still refusing to blow, they all swear to support him. Morning dawns. Turpin conducts mass. Roland prays for success, and cheers his men. Oliver and the rest declare Roland should blow for help. Roland slays the Saracen champion, Amaris; various duels follow. A terrific battle rages until sunset, when not a Saracen survives. The French thank God. But now the main body of the infidels approaches. The day is overcast, and a fearful slaughter ensues in the darkness. The field is strewn with dead and dying. The Saracens are hard pressed. The Sultan rallies his men in vain. Again he attacks; but he is beaten into a valley. A new host of infidels approaches. The Christians are few, and are sore wounded. Roland bids them rest while he sends to Charles for help—unless help comes, all is lost! Angry in heart, Oliver cries, 'Broder, let be all siche sawes!' and the piece ends.

Intrinsically the poem has little value. As compared with the French *Song*, all its elements are badly thinned out, emasculated. Charles becomes commonplace; Roland exhibits little prowess; Ganelon is no longer a man of genuine worth who yields to desire for vengeance—but an unqualified villain. The plot against Roland is suspected from the first by Charles and his knights, and the evil nature of Ganelon and his animus against the hero are well known; yet the story goes on. The terse speeches of the heroes in the French are weakly expanded. The martial elements are diminished. The fire and spirit of the original are gone. The matter is not let speak for itself; comment and explanation are introduced. Employment of certain learned and religious material supports the idea that the translator was a well-intentioned but incapable church-man, who, however, (unless he followed a lost version) showed enterprise unusual for the date in adopting from the *Pseudo-Turpin* the episode of the Saracen women at the opening of the fragment, and some details apparently from other variants.

THE TAILL OF RAUF COIL3EAR [58], a Scottish poem of 1475-1500, is preserved in a unique copy of a text printed by Robert Lekpreuik in 1572. It is in 975 verses in the Gawain-school stanza, predominantly ababababcdddc, the first nine lines each of four stresses and alliterative, the next three each of three stresses, the last line of one stress. No French original is known. The piece is generally accepted as of insular origin; nothing but the place-names and the general suggestion from them, is foreign; the storm and the mountains afford Scottish atmosphere. The piece is but externally connected with the Charlemagne legends. Slight consideration of language, phrasing, and structure, shows the untenableness of the theory that the author of the poem wrote *Golagrus and Gawain*, the *Awntyrs of Arthur*, and the *Pistill of Susan*.

Separated from his retinue during a storm in the mountains, Charlemagne at night meets Rauf the Collier, leading a horse. Though suspicious of the stranger, Rauf takes him to his home seven miles away. Rauf proceeds, in well-intentioned but rough manner, to teach courtesy to his guest. When he leaves the next day, the King is rebuked for impoliteness in offering to pay for his entertainment. After persuasion, Rauf consents to bring his goods to court, and to ask for Wymond. On the next day, Christmas, Charles sends Roland to bring to him whoever first appears on the moor-road. Roland meets Rauf, who refuses to accompany him, but agrees to fight him on the morrow. Ultimately, Rauf arrives at the palace. Inquiring for 'Wymond,' he enters the hall where the King and the Queen are at dinner. Rauf recognizes the King, and is abashed. The King recounts his experiences at the hut. The knights laugh, and advise hanging the peasant. But the King knights him, and gives him an estate. The next morning, Rauf goes out to meet Roland. He encounters, instead, a Saracen, Magog, on a camel. Roland parts the duelists. He converts the Saracen, who weds a Lady Jane Anjou. Rauf is made Marshal of France, and sends for his wife to share his fortune.

The subject of the poem, the meeting of a king and a peasant, is common in English, Continental, and Eastern tales. In English there illustrate it at least ten ballads [59], *King*

Henry II and the Miller of *Mansfield*, *King Henry and the Soldier*, *James I and the Tinker*, *William III and the Forester*, *King Edward and the Shepherd*, *Edward IV and the Tanner of Tamworth*, *Henry VII and the Cobbler*, *John the Reeve*, *King Edward and the Hermit*, and *Henry II and the Cistercian Abbot*.

The writer of *Rauf* has his story under control, saying just enough for his purpose. The tale is well constructed, is told with dramatic effect, and proceeds with ease. Rauf is admir. ably characterized. No longer is the lord or the king the source of courtesy; in the peasant hero speak out the Scotch democracy and a new standard—a standard that appears in the ballads. The work is thoroughly humorous; but one has difficulty in accepting the view that it was intended as a parody of the romances, and that the contest between Rauf and the Saracen is a burlesque of the stock hero-giant duel of the knightly tales. As Amours has suggested, the piece may have won its way because of its realistic presentation of Scotch manners and life.

The Right Plesaunt and Goodly Historie of the Foure Sonnes of Aymon [60] was printed at about 1489 by Caxton. It deals with the wars of Charlemagne against his rebel vassals, and is a prose translation of the French *Les Quatre Fils Aymon*, often styled *Renaud de Montauban*, the earliest extant text of which is of the end of the twelfth century.

The Boke of Duke Huon of Burdeux [61] was translated from the French by Sir John Bourchier, Lord. Berners, and printed by de Worde at about 1534.

4. LEGENDS OF GODFREY OF BOUILLON

Godfrey of Bouillon was one of the three Christian heroes of the Nine Worthies so celebrated in the Middle Ages. He was represented as the son of a descendant of a swan-maiden— another Lohengrin. To his fame was dedicated a cycle of poems, the *Cycle of the Knight of the Swan* or *Le Chevalier au Cygne* or the *Cycle of Antioch*. This series of poems, devel-

oped probably in the twelfth century, falls into five divisions:
(1) *Chanson d'Antioche*, dealing with the expedition of Peter
the Hermit and the conquest of Antioch; (2) *Chanson de Jérusalem*, dealing with the conquest of Jerusalem; (3) *Les Chétifs,
The Captives*, based perhaps on narratives of the luckless expedition by William of Poitiers to the Holy Land; (4) *Hélias*,
the story of the Knight of the Swan; and (5) *Les Enfances de
Godefroy de Bouillon*. So, the series reaches from the beginning of the Crusades and the ancestry of Godfrey, to the Conquest of Jerusalem.

CHEVALERE ASSIGNE [62], the only representative of
the cycle in English before the fifteenth century, is a condensed
version of the material, if not of the verses themselves, of the
first part of the story of the Swan Knight represented in the
first 1083 lines of a French poem of six thousand lines of the
twelfth or the thirteenth century, that is one of two distinct
versions of the *Chevalier au Cygne*, and that is an amalgamation of the *Jérusalem*, the *Hélias*, and the *Enfances*. Though
the story was known at Feversham near Canterbury early in the
thirteenth century, the extant English piece is of the end of
the fourteenth century. It consists of 370 alliterative long
lines in MS. Cotton Caligula A II (15th century), an East
Midland copy of an apparently Northern or North-Western
original.

For declaring adulterous any woman who bears more than one
child at a birth, Beatrice, wife of King Oryens, gives birth at one
time to six sons and a daughter. Each child has a silver chain
about its neck. Matabryne, the evil mother of the King, sends
her man, Marcus, to drown the children, and substitutes seven newborn whelps for the babies. She accuses the Queen to the King,
and ultimately has her imprisoned with threat of burning. For
eleven years the King resists Matabryne's efforts to bring the
Queen to the stake. Moved by the beauty and the helplessness of
the babes, Marcus leaves them wrapped in a mantle. A hermit
cares for them. Malkedras, a forester, discovers the children, and
reports the fact to Matabryne. Matabryne puts out Marcus' eyes.
She orders Malkedras to kill the children, and to bring to her the
seven chains. Malkedras finds one of the boys absent with the
hermit. He cuts the chains from the throats of the six children.

At once the children become swans, and fly away. The chains he bears to Matabryne, who orders them made into a cup. In the fire the silver increases so far that a half of one chain proves enough to make the cup. The goldsmith declares that a half-chain is all that remains over. He receives it as pay for his work. Finally Matabryne persuades Oryens to burn the Queen. An angel warns the hermit that the surviving boy shall fight for and save his mother, and reveals to him all the story of the children. Informed by the hermit, the boy, quite ignorant of all culture and knightly practices, makes his way to the procession that escorts the Queen to the stake. He stops the King, learns from him what the preparation means, and warns him against Matabryne. After an altercation with Matabryne, he demands a champion to fight with for his mother. Malkedras is chosen to oppose him. The boy is christened Enyas, is knighted, and is armed. He is instructed as to use of his horse and armor, and the methods of jousting. During the desperate duel that follows, the bells of the abbey ring without human aid. Malkedras mocks the cross on Enyas' shield: he is struck by an adder that darts from the shield, and is blinded by a flash from the cross. Enyas decapitates him. Then he burns Matabryne in the bale-fire. He tells the King the story of the children. The goldsmith produces the five chains and the half-chain. When the chains are put on the necks of the five swans, one swan becomes a girl, the others become boys. The sixth swan, having no chain, remains thereafter a swan, and is called *Chevalere Assigne.*

The poem is replete with incident. All is, of course, very highly colored and melodramatic; the plot depends on unqualified villainy, supernatural intervention, and the operation of mysterious underforces. There is little of the atmosphere of romance, and much of the folk-tale. Strong and effective appeal is made to wonder, indignation, pity, and desire for punishment of villainy. The behavior and speech of the forest-reared boy in his efforts to acquaint himself with the common details of sophisticated life, are thoroughly well presented and make a strong humorous appeal—stronger and more humorous, indeed, than is attained in a similar case in *William of Palerne.* The pathetic picture at the end of the poem—that of the sixth swan biting himself with his bill so that his breast bled, because of grief that he too could not be transformed—and the statement, contrary to the French, that 'the one was always a swan for the loss of his chain,' give a conclusion that remains firmly imprinted on the reader's memory.

At a considerably later period, a version of the whole story of the Swan Knight conducted on his adventures by his swan-brother, his marriage to the Duchess of Boulogne, and his begetting of Ydein, who was to become mother of Godfrey of Bouillon, was made in English, and was printed by Copland early in the sixteenth century under the title *Helyas, the Knight of the Swan* [63].

To be mentioned here is *Godefroy of Boloyne* or *The Last Siege of Jerusalem* [64], Caxton's translation, printed in 1481, of the historical work, *The Siege and Conquest of Jerusalem* made by William, Archbishop of Tyre (1175-1184), dealing with the First Crusade and the sequent French activity in the Holy Land.

5.   LEGENDS OF ALEXANDER THE GREAT

The extensive popularity in Latin and in French of the romantic accounts of Alexander the Great, gave rise to several poems on the same theme in English.

About the life of Alexander in the East gathered a body of fiction born of popular imagination caught up and supplemented by the invention of the learned.   All of the Western versions of the life of the hero go back to a Greek account, the *Pseudo-Callisthenes*, in which apparently culminates the popular creation, and from which are derived the mediæval versions. From the *Pseudo-Callisthenes* issued at about 340 a Latin work of Julius Valerius, of which a Latin epitome was made in the ninth century.   In the early ninth century were composed a Latin *Letter* of Alexander to Aristotle, and five other *Letters* between the hero and the sage.   In the tenth century was composed by Archpresbyter Leo, who got material when in Constantinople on embassy from John and Marinus, Dukes of Campania, a fabulous Latin *Historia Alexandri Magni, Regis Macedoniæ, de Prœliis*, known as *Historia de Prœliis*, that had a great vogue.   To these works is to be added a little Latin *abc* poem of a date perhaps somewhat earlier than the *Historia*, and a Latin *Alexandri Magni Iter ad Paradisum* of the first

of the twelfth century. These pieces were used in various compilations of historical material, which spread the accounts, but
which need not detain us here.

In French the matter early received attention. A fragment
of a version by Alberic de Besançon is in a MS. of the twelfth
century. A little later appeared a version in decasyllabic
verse, which serves as a connecting link between Alberic's poem
and the great *Roman d'Alixandre*. The *Roman* consists of
some 20000 twelve-syllable lines composed in the twelfth century by Lambert le Tort, Alexandre de Bernai (surnamed 'de
Paris'), and others. From the verse of the *Roman* comes our
use of the term *alexandrine*. Thereafter followed, from the end
of the twelfth century, *La Vengeance d'Alexandre*, by Jean le
Venelais and Gui de Cambrai, which gave birth to a group of
poems. Eustache or Thomas of Kent wrote *Le Roman de
Toute Chevalerie* at about the middle of the thirteenth century.
In 1310-1315 Jacques de Longueyon added a popular episode,
the *Vœux du Paon*. French prose versions were made, the
first in the second half of the thirteenth century, and two
others in the fifteenth century.

Into Old English prose were made a version of the *Epistola
Alexandri* and one of the *Wonders of the East* (*De Rebus in
Orienti Mirabilis*). The Middle English pieces on Alexander
are: three fragments in long alliterative verse—A known as
Alisaunder, B known as *Alexander and Dindimus*, C known as
The Wars of Alexander; a fragment in stanzas at Cambridge;
a *Lyfe of Alisaunder* in short couplets; an *Alexander Buik*,
printed by Arbuthnot, and sometimes ascribed to John Bar-
bour; a prose *Alexander* in the Thornton MS.; Gilbert Hay's
Buik of King Alexander; and four fragments of a sixteenth-
century print apparently connected with the matter of the
Lyfe of Alisaunder.

All in all, the versions of the Alexander story in English of
before 1400, are admirable pieces of work. They are interesting, full of effective episodes, vigorous, swift, picturesque. The
versification is good. The purpose of instruction is prominent
in the poems, but is fulfilled with interest to the reader and
without objectionable didacticism. The considerable travel

material is varied, and must have been very attractive at the date of composition. No attempt is made to produce or to maintain the ancient atmosphere. Yet in all the pieces a bookish note is obvious, as is the impression of dependence on books. Moreover, in none of the English tales of before 1400, including the *Wars*, is Alexander an actually mediæval knight representative of the spirit of chivalry. He is a great conqueror, a mighty hero, a rather isolated superhuman figure— a type, indeed, not an individualized man. His personality is vague and remote. Its dignity and majesty never suffer the degradation to which Arthur and Charlemagne are subjected in romances. The love-element is found only in the relations of the magician with Olympias, and in Candace's seduction of Alexander. The latter is represented as a shameful outwitting of the hero, who yields only perforce and with disgust at his defeat. Instead of celebrating the relations leading to the marriage to Roxana, as would the romances of other groups, the *Lyfe* ignores the episode, and the *Wars* merely states that the marriage took place. The military spirit prevails. But the battle pieces, good as some of them are, have not the supreme importance that similar matter occupies in the Charlemagne tales. They are usually struck off with vigor, and are not tediously elaborated. The best parts of the *Lyfe* and of the *Wars* are the accounts of Olympias and of Alexander's youth, and the experiences of Alexander in the Far East. The best of Fragment A has naught of battles, and Fragment B has no battle.

THE LYFE OF ALISAUNDER or KING ALISAUNDER [65], probably the earliest of the English romances of the group, is in MSS. Laud I 74 (now Misc. 622; c. 1400; ll. 4772-5989), Lincoln's Inn L 150 (end of 14th or beginning 15th century; ll. 1-4772, 5989 to end), and Auchinleck (1330-1340; a fragment). It consists of 8033 verses in short couplets of before 1330, and perhaps originally Kentish of the latter part of the thirteenth century. It is based on Eustache's *Roman de Toute Chevalerie*, and contains a number of French phrases.

At lines 2199-202, the writer states that he fills in from Latin material that is lacking in the French.

The poem deals with the mysterious begetting of the hero; his youth; the discomfiture and death of Philip; Alexander's succession to the throne of his father; and the conquest of Carthage and other cities. The rest of the first part (to l. 4748) recounts the wars with, and conquests of, Darius. The second part tells of Alexander's travels and conquests in India and far Eastern countries; the geography of those realms, their wondrous creatures, and the perils of Alexander in face of them; the outwitting of Alexander by Candace; and the death of the hero by poison.

The poem is unusually good for the period. The poet shows great control of the couplet, which moves fluently and with grace. The language is free from redundancy. The writer has plenty of matter, and does not linger long on single details. The tale drags only in the latter half of the first part, where the contest with Darius is too long drawn out and too little varied. The descriptions of battles are usually general in character, and are hurried along with picturesqueness and suggestiveness. They follow the ancient epic, rather than the romance, style. Often very vivid, they tend to consist of lists of contests told in very few lines. Conferences between leaders, with speeches by various heroes, occur. The conventional duel is represented only in Alexander's fight with Porus, which occurs toward the end of the piece, and is hurried over. The author inclined somewhat to sentiment; at a number of places he is concerned for the families and the lovers of those slain in battle, and once exhibits great sympathy for the sufferings of the poor during a siege (ll. 1229-38). Love enters only in the episode with Candace, whose enticing of Alexander to sloth is made into something of a lesson. Toward the beginning there are several brief passages of analysis of feeling and of expression of feeling in soliloquy, as well as several bits of detailed description. Interesting is the lengthy series of lessons in geography and travel in the East, dealing with astonishing details of animal life, and reminding somewhat of Mandeville. Miracle appears in the saving of the hero's life by an angel (ll. 5088-89), and in the pacifying of the barons by a gentle bird (ll. 7996 ff.). Magic is prominent early in the tale.

Especially to be noted is the division of the poem into short sections each headed by a lyrical passage, often charmingly graceful, of from two to ten verses, that is not connected with the story, but is introduced purely to please the audience. Similar use of such matter is seen in the introduction to the second part of the *Sowdone of Babylone* (see page 84), the second part of *Richard Coer de Lyon* (see page 152), and a number of lines in *Arthour and Merlin* (see page 43). These admirable bits sometimes suggest a nature piece at a specific time of day or year; sometimes add to this a love element, as in *Alysoun* (see page 493); sometimes to one or both of these add a bit of homely wisdom. The pithy proverbial expression here and at a number of other places, is sometimes thoroughly humorous, and suggests immediate extraction from the popular store whence came the *Proverbs of Alfred*, the *Proverbs of Hendyng*, and the scraps in the *Owl and the Nightingale* (see pages 374 ff.). Didactic inclination is manifested also in remarks for the instruction of the reader—as in the Prologue to Part I where Alexander is said to have been conqueror because he obeyed his master's teaching, and in the last couplet of the poem where the author laments that the hero did not die 'in Cristenyng.' But such passages are controlled, and add to the attractiveness of the narrative.

THE ALLITERATIVE ALEXANDER FRAGMENTS [66] are three in number: Fragment A, sometimes styled *Alisaunder*, 1249 long lines in MS. Bodley Greaves 60 (16th century); Fragment B, known as *Alexander and Dindimus*, 1139 long lines in MS. Bodley 264 (15th century, c. 1450); Fragment C, known as *The Wars of Alexander*, 5677 long lines in the fifteenth-century MSS. Ashmole 44 and Dublin Trinity College D, 4, 12. The Dublin MS. of C corresponds to Ashmole lines 678-3426, and fills in a gap in Ashmole of 122 verses after verse 722, but itself has a gap of lines 3296-356.

Trautmann has shown that A and B are from one poem of great length. A and B are by one translator, who did not translate C. A, B, and C are connected in content, all being founded on some common Latin version of Leo's *Historia de*

Prœliis. A parallels verses 23-722 of C; B parallels verses 4020-67 and 4188-715 of C. C, of date 1400-1450 or about 1450, and perhaps originally pure Northumbrian, is a close translation of the Latin, with material from other sources, and with an original prologue of 22 verses. A and B, of the West Midland and of about 1340, supplement the Latin with poetical interpolations and with material from other sources, the translator telling the story in his own way, and seeking to add interest to the narrative.

Fragment A, *Alisaunder*, consists of two elements. The first is matter from the Latin chroniclers, Orosius, Rudolphus, and others. It tells of Philip's early conquests, and his marriage with Olympias (ll. 1-451); Thermopylæ, and Philip's cruelty to the Thebans (ll. 900-55); and the beginning of the siege of Byzantium (ll. 1202-49). None of this is in Fragment C or *Kyng Alisaunder*. In these passages the account proceeds as a chronicle; the elaborate description of Olympias is of interest, and at its end appeals to one's humor (ll. 178 ff.); and the account of the siege of Methone is vigorous and picturesque (ll. 255 ff.).

The second element is composed of the lines not devoted to the first, and deals with the legend of Alexander as based on the *Historia de Prœliis.*

It relates that, in Philip's absence, Nectanabus, King of Egypt, fled from the Persians to Macedonia, by magic tricked Olympias and begot on her Alexander, and later as a dragon aided Philip against his enemies; Philip returned; Nectanabus by magic proved the greatness of the child to be born; Alexander grew up (the account of the hero's birth and youth is omitted); to prove false Nectanabus' prophecy of his own death by his son's hand, he drowned his father; and he tamed Bucephalus.

So the fragment, exclusive of the passages about Philip, really completes the first stage of the legend, the 'infancy' of Alexander. This matter corresponds closely with lines 23-722 of Fragment C. The romance part of the fragment is more interesting than the chronicle part, the best passages being those of the relations of Nectanabus and Olympias, and of the drowning of Nectanabus. The expression in both A and B moves smoothly and directly, the rules of the older alliterative line being closely observed.

Fragment B, *Alexander and Dindimus,* is as follows:

Having slain Porus in single combat, Alexander comes to the country of the Oxydracæ, who, in reply to his offer of peace on submission, bid him give them everlasting life. Alexander sees trees that disappear at sundown, and that are guarded by birds that spit deadly fire. At the Ganges, passable only in July and August, he corresponds with Dindimus, the king of the people on the other side of the river. The rest of the piece consists of the five letters between the kings, really an episode added by ecclesiastics for moral purpose. Alexander erects a pillar to mark his farthest progress, and turns homeward.

The letters are really a presentation of all the author can say on the old theme of the contrast and relative worth of the Active Life and the Contemplative Life. With this is inter-mingled an opposition of the life of Christians and the life of idolaters, asceticism and use of the goods of the world. The piece, then, in a general sense belongs to the contention litera-ture. Without doubt, the original intention was to instruct. The matter is presented effectively and interestingly. The whole is cleverly manipulated so as to exhibit the excellent quali-ties of each of the opposing elements, without seeking to per-suade to conclusion in favor of either. Particularly in the first two letters, the text is eloquent. At times satire on manners enters. A pleasing passage is that (ll. 473 ff.) on the Brah-min's love of the heavens, the woods, the waters, the flowers, the song of birds. But one must not forget that the most of the matter is taken from the Latin, and that only in his expression and in his elaboration of the details, can the author claim merit.

Fragment C, *The Wars of Alexander,* is much less original and effective than Fragment B in its treatment of the general matter common to the two pieces. It parallels the romance portions of Fragment A (see page 103). It then proceeds much upon the general lines of matter indicated (see page 101) for the *Lyfe of Alisaunder,* but with much variation in details, filling in the gap between the death of Nectanabus and the correspondence with Dindimus that represents Fragment B. After the correspondence, it continues the story upon the general lines of the *Lyfe*, but with much variation, up to the death of Bucephalus and the conquest of Babylon shortly after the Candace episode. A description of the throne at Babylon inscribed with Alexander's conquests, closes the fragment. The verse is good; interest is well sustained; many scenes are admirably delineated. In whole, it compares favorably with the earlier fragments.

THE CAMBRIDGE ALEXANDER-CASSAMUS FRAGMENT [67] is in MS. Cbg. Univ. Ff I 6 f. 142 (15th century). It consists of 566 verses ababbcbc, and is said to be based directly on the French *Vœux du Paon* (see page 99). The extent of the complete work, it seems impossible to determine. In view of its lateness, further discussion of the fragment is unnecessary here.

THE PROSE ALEXANDER [68], in MS. Thornton (1430-1440), covers in print about 108 pages averaging 36 lines each. It is a Northern translation from the Latin. The opening is missing.

It tells of the putting to death of Anectanabus, the subduing of Bucephalus, the conquest of the Arridons, Philip's separation from Olympias, the reconciliation by Alexander, the accession of Alexander, the conquest of Rome and all Western Europe and Africa, the founding of Alexandria, the defeat of the Jews and the destruction of Tyre, the conquest of Judæa, the war with Darius, the conquest of Darius and ascension of the throne of Cyrus, the wedding to Roxana, the war with Porus of India, the defeat of Porus, the land of the Amazons and its subjection, the strange adventures with strange beasts in the East, the slaying of Porus, the Gymnosophists, a farther adventure in India, the correspondence with Dindimus across the Ganges, the habits and beliefs of the Brahmins, adventures with strange animals and trees and dragons, etc., the slaying of the Basilisk, the Phœnix, the episode with Candace, the punishment of Gog and Magog or the ten tribes of Israel, the death of Bucephalus, the taking of Babylon, Aristotle's letter to Alexander, Alexander's throne, the poisoning of the hero, and the death and funeral of Alexander.

THE SCOTTISH ALEXANDER BUIK [69] is preserved only in Lord Panmure's copy of the text printed in 1580 by

Alexander Arbuthnot. It is in three parts: first, *The Foray of Gadderis*, based on Eustache's *Fuerre de Gadres* (Gaza), a version of which is in the *Wars*, lines 1193 ff.; second and third, *The Avows of Alexander* and *The Battle of Effesoun*, based on Jacques de Longueyon's *Vœux du Paon* (see page 99)—the *Avows* dealing with the vows made over a peacock shot by Porus, and the *Battle* telling of the accomplishment of the vows against Alexander's host. The epilogue assigns the work to 1438. Passages of the poem are said to be almost identical with passages in Barbour's *Bruce*. The efforts to ascribe the piece to Barbour are not acceptable.

GILBERT HAY'S BUIK OF KING ALEXANDER [70] is preserved in a MS. in Taymouth Castle written in 1493 after Hay's death. It consists of some twenty thousand lines in couplets covering the whole of Alexander's life. Only some selections have been printed.

FOUR FRAGMENTS OF AN OLD PRINT [71] of about (?) 1550 are on six leaves in the British Museum. They make up a total of 417 four-stress verses in couplets, and appear to be connected with the matter of the *Lyfe of Alisaunder*.

6. LEGENDS OF TROY

To the Middle Ages Homer was known but little, and only through Thebanus' *Epitome*. He was often despised as utterly untrustworthy. The great sources of the mediæval versions of the legends of Troy, though probably none was used directly by most of the writers, were Virgil, Dares Phrygius, and Dictys Cretensis.

In the fourth century was issued, with a letter by a Lucius Septimius, *Dictys Cretensis Ephemeris Belli Trojani*, purporting to be from a Greek version. Recent discovery of a part of a Greek original, supports this derivation. The piece is in Latin prose, extends from the rape of Helen to the return of the Greeks, and professes to be the journal of a follower of

Idomeneus. *Dictys Cretensis de Bello Trojani Libri VI*, a Latin prose epitome of this work, was made in the fourth century.

Between 400 and 600 an unknown writer composed *Daretis Phrygii de Excidio Trojæ Historia* in Latin prose purporting to be from a Greek original. Dares is said to have been present on the Trojan side during the siege. His work begins with the voyage of the Argonauts.

The fiction of descent from Trojan heroes was a favorite with Western peoples; the founder of Britain was Brutus, son or great-grandson of Æneas. Nennius and Geoffrey of Monmouth emphasize the tradition; Wace and Layamon and the historians carry it on; it extends into the time of Elizabeth.

At about 1184 Benoît de Sainte-More, a North-French poet, finished his *Roman de Troie*, a poem of thirty thousand Anglo-Norman verses beginning with the voyage of the Argonauts and concluding with the wanderings of Ulysses. Benoît used Dares and Dictys, but all the poetry in his work is his own. The poem is ·the great masterpiece of the mediæval classical romances; but, until comparatively recent times, it has received little of the recognition that is its due.

·At about 1187 Joseph of Exeter wrote in Latin six books of verse of considerable excellence, influenced much by Benoît. In 1287 Guido delle Colonne, a Sicilian, finished in Latin prose his *Historia Destructionis Troiæ*, really a very close but abridged translation of Benoît. Though it is dull and in bad style, and though it has none of the poetry of its original, this work became the popular authority; and, since Guido did not acknowledge his indebtedness to Benoît, it stole from the latter his just meed.

It is impossible and, indeed, undesirable, to consider here the many versions of the legends in different mediæval languages. The four chiefly influential writers are Dictys, Dares, Benoît, and Guido. The Middle English versions are *The Gest Historiale of the Destruction of Troy*, *The Seege of Troye*, the Laud *Troy-Book*, Chaucer's *Troilus and Criseyde*, Lydgate's *Troy-Book*, the fragments of the Scottish Troy-Book ascribed to a 'Barbour,' the prose piece in MS. Rawlinson Misc. D 82, and *The Recuyell of the Historyes of Troye* printed by Caxton at about 1474.

THE GEST HISTORIALE OF THE DESTRUCTION OF TROY [72] consists of 14044 long alliterative lines in a MS. (c. 1450) in the Hunterian Museum of the University of Glasgow. It is probably of 1350-1400, and probably originally Northern or Scottish, though the extant MS. is in the West Midland dialect.

After speaking contemptuously of Homer because he is untrustworthy and feigns much falsehood (as that the gods fought in the field like folk, and other 'trifles'), the writer declares that Guido is the author of the following story, which was got from Dares and Dictys, historians. The poem deals with the quest and the winning of the Golden Fleece; the destruction of the first Troy by Jason and Hercules; the founding of the second Troy, and Priam's efforts to obtain from the Greeks redress for the wrongs done the city; Priam's councils and preparations for war on the Greeks, and Cassandra's warnings; Paris' expedition to Greece, the rape of Helen, the rejoicing in Troy, the imprisonment of Cassandra; the plan of the Greeks for revenge, the drowning of Castor and Pollux, the natures of various royal personages; description of the Greek fleet; the Greeks' testing of the Delphic oracle; the voyage to Troy; the Greeks' demand for reparation; Achilles' expedition after food and the royal allies of Troy; the details of the siege and the fighting; the betrayal and destruction of the city; the departure of Æneas; the return of the Greeks; and the adventures of Ulysses, and his death by the hand of his son, Telegonus.

The poem preserves the various incidents of Guido's account; but it is very independent, amplifying, omitting, and condensing, with much good judgment. The matter is treated with a power that makes from the dull prose an excellent poem that ranks well among the English alliterative romances. Notable are the descriptive passages, especially those of the storm, which suggest close familiarity with the sea. Again and again one is struck with the vividness, liveliness, and dramatic clearness of scenes and incidents in the piece.

THE SEEGE OF TROYE [73] is in MS. Harley 525 (beginning 15th century) in 1922 verses in short couplets, originally Southern; MS. Lincoln's Inn 150 (end of 14th or

beginning 15th century) in 994 short couplets by a Southern
scribe from a Northern version; and a MS. (now Egerton
2862; end of 14th century) of the Duke of Sutherland, not yet
printed, in 914 short couplets by a Southern scribe from a
Northern original. The poem is independent of the other
English Troy pieces. It has probably as direct source a recension of Benoît's *Roman de Troie*, perhaps longer than that
extant. Perhaps it is little more than an epitome of this
lost recension. The Harley and Lincoln's Inn texts appear to
be independent of each other, but to be derived from an ultimate English original probably of 1350-1400. The Lincoln's
Inn version is less artistic than the Harleian, and exhibits less
subordination of detail to a larger purpose, and more effort
toward reproducing its original.

The piece deals successively with the quest of the Golden Fleece,
and the first destruction of Troy; the rebuilding of the city; the
embassy of Ector to Greece to require the restoration of Isyon;
the ravishing of Elyn by Alisaunder; the preparations for war, and
the first three years of the strife; the arrival of Achilles; the death
of Ector; the love of Achilles for Pollexene; the deeds and the death
of Troyel; the plot of Ekeuba and the death of Achilles; the death
of Alisaunder and Aiax; the betrayal of the city by Entemore and
Eneus; and the return of the Greeks.

In rude and irregular verses the details of the extensive
story are hurried over without dallying, but with much effect.
The piece has no high literary quality; yet the rapid succession
and the variety of its incidents, and the energy of the narrative, whose impression of realness is assisted greatly by the
liberal employment of direct discourse, could have had great
appeal to a reader or a hearer of the fourteenth century.

THE LAUD TROY-BOOK [74] obtains its name from its
preservation in MS. Laud 595 (beginning 15th century). It
is in 9332 short couplets with frequent use of alliteration, and
was composed probably at about 1400 in the North-West
Midland. The extant MS. is a copy.

The author goes back mainly to Guido delle Colonne, but was
probably acquainted with the poem of Benoît. The poem begins
with the story of Jason and the Fleece, and covers the general

ground of the *Gest Historiale;* but it omits the after-history of Ulysses, and hurries over in a few lines the return of the Greeks. The poet has no great genius. He is notable for the vigor and the flow of his narrative, and particularly for the interest and power of his description, and for the concreteness, definiteness, and realness of his treatment. He is fond of imagery, and employs it effectively in many instances, drawing from a great variety of sources.

LYDGATE'S TROY-BOOK [75], a version in 30117 verses in heroic couplets of Guido's *Historia,* amplified, as the author states, from a French piece, was probably begun in 1412 and finished in 1420. It was presented to Henry V, at whose suggestion it was composed. It covers the ground of Guido and the *Gest Historiale,* beginning with the expedition of the Argonauts, and concluding with the death of Ulysses by the hand of Telegonus. The piece is perhaps the most poetic of the Middle English Troy poems. It is notable for its vivid presentation of psychological motives, and for its descriptions of nature and of artificial features—feasts, buildings, and the like.

THE SCOTTISH TROY FRAGMENTS [76] are in the MSS. declared to be by a 'Barbour,' who has been shown to be not the author of the *Bruce* (see page 202). The fragments were inserted into texts of Lydgate's *Troy-Book* to fill up gaps in the MSS. (both 15th century) that the scribes were copying. The poem is probably of the fifteenth century. The first fragment is in 596 verses, eleven verses being missing at the beginning, in MS. Cbg. Univ. Libr. Kk V 30 ff. 1-9. The second fragment opens on f. 304 v of the same MS., with the words, 'Here endis the monke ande begynis Barbour'; it ends with line 1562 of the 'Barbour' version. In MS. Douce 148 ff. 290-300 are correspondents of Kk lines 1-918, after which follows the text of Lydgate, up to f. 306; then follow verses corresponding to Kk lines 1181-562; thence the piece is continued to the end of the story or what would be line 3118 of this 'Barbour' poem.

THE RAWLINSON MISC. D 82 PROSE TROY PIECE
[77] is a probably fifteenth-century epitomized Southern version of Guido's *Historia*. Brie has recently judged that it is a rehandling of the materials in Lydgate's *Troy-Book*, and that the prose *Sege of Thebes*, which precedes it in the MS., is a making over of Lydgate's *Siege of Thebes*. It makes up some twenty-six pages of modern print, and deals with the story from the quest for the Fleece to the fall of Troy. The MS. is of c. 1450.

THE RECUYELL OF THE HISTORYES OF TROYE
[78], in prose, the first printed book in English, was issued at about 1474 by Caxton, who translated it in 1471 from Raoul de Fevre's French prose *Le Recueil de Troyennes Ystoires*. The work had a great vogue, being printed more than a dozen times before 1750.

7. LEGENDS OF THEBES

The story of Thebes was familiar to the Middle Ages through Statius' *Thebaid*, the French verse *Roman de Thèbes* of c. 1150, several French prose romances, and Boccaccio's *Teseide*. In Middle English a single phase of it was dealt with nobly by Chaucer in his *Knight's Tale* (discussed on page 692) ; and the whole story was treated by Lydgate in his *Siege of Thebes* and by the author of the Rawlinson prose *Siege*.

LYDGATE'S SIEGE OF THEBES [79] is preserved in twenty-one MSS. and two old editions, which have been enumerated by its editor. John Lydgate composed the piece between the latter part of 1420 and the death of Henry V on August 31, 1422. It is in heroic couplets, and as printed consists of 4716 lines. According to Koeppel, Ten Brink, and Erdmann, the source of about two-thirds of the poem is a lost French prose romance (the nearest extant version being the *Sensuyt le Roman de Edipus*) based on the French *Roman*. The Bible, Seneca, Martianus Capella, Boccaccio, and Chaucer are drawn on. More than a fourth of the piece is said to be from Lydgate's own imagination.

The poem was written as a supplementary Canterbury tale. The imitation of Chaucer is laborious. In the prologue the author imagines himself among the pilgrims at the inn in Canterbury the night before the party sets out for London. The *Siege* is told at the Host's command as the first tale on the departure the next morning. The story proper extends from the building of Thebes through the history of Œdipus (Part 1); the labors of Œdipus' sons (Part 2); the siege of the city, the election of Creon, the slaying of the Greeks, and the expedition of Theseus to satisfy the prayers of the Greek widows (Part 3).

THE RAWLINSON MISC. D 82 PROSE SIEGE OF THEBES [80] follows the prose story of Troy (see page 111) in MS. Rawlinson D 82 (c. 1450). It is an epitome of the story from the founding of the city to the death of Adrastus, and consists of about 7500 words. Its editor has felt that it is a making-over of Lydgate's *Siege*.

8. EUSTACE-CONSTANCE-FLORENCE-GRISELDA LEGENDS

A group of romances composed in the North of England in twelve-line tail-rime, have in form, subject-matter, and purpose, a number of close connections. They embody variants (some of all, some of several) of the St. Eustace or Placidas, the Constance, the Florence, and the Griselda themes. In purpose they all emphasize the virtue of patience, of meek endurance. The Eustace story is of Placidas, an officer of Trajan, who was converted by the appearance of Christ between the antlers of a hart that he was hunting. With his wife and two sons he is baptized. He receives the name 'Eustache.' His property is destroyed, and the family are driven to a wandering life. The wife is carried off by shipmen. The children are borne away; one by a lion and one by a leopard. For long the saint works as a journeyman, until messengers take him to Trajan.

While leading an expedition against the Dacians, he finds his wife in a cottage. Near by he discovers his sons, who, after being brought up as shepherds, have become soldiers. The family return to Rome, and are burned because they will not sacrifice to heathen gods.

The typical Constance story is of an innocent maiden who is banished by or flees from an unnatural father, and reaches a strange land where she marries the ruler. In her husband's absence she is falsely accused of bearing monstrous offspring, and is banished with her child or children. Ultimately, she is reunited to her husband, and in some cases to her father also (see page 130).

The former of these themes occurs alone in the English *Sir Isumbras*, the latter alone in *Sir Triamour*. Combinations of the two are in *Sir Eglamour, Sir Torrent of Portyngale*, and *Octovian*. Resemblances in matter and form and manner have suggested that *Sir Isumbras* and *Octovian* are by one author. It is urged that a form of the story of Octovian was a bridge between the Eustace tale and *Sir Eglamour* and *Sir Torrent*. It has been claimed by some that *Sir Torrent* is a making-over of *Sir Eglamour*, and by others that the two are from a common source. In *Octovian* little part is played by Octovian; in *Sir Triamour*, the general plot of which is very similar to that of *Octovian*, the hero is the son, Triamour. Very close resemblances in content and expression, and even in wording at places, are found between *Sir Eglamour, Sir Torrent, Octovian*, and the lay *Emare*. Though this is true, and though *Emare* is one of the best representatives in English of the Constance theme, it is preferable to discuss *Emare* with the other pieces based on Breton *lais* (see page 124). The Constance theme is most familiar in Chaucer's *Man of Law's Tale* (see page 701).

The ideas of the self-sacrifice of a Christian maid, of her patience, and of her monstrous offspring, connect *The King of Tars* with others of these pieces, and with the Florence theme that is represented especially in the English *Le Bone Florence of Rome*. The Griselda theme, familiar through Chaucer's *Clerk's Tale* (see page 726), the story of the patient wife subjected to tests of devotion by her husband or lover, reflects

certain of the elements of the other themes just mentioned. It
is seen in *Lai le Freine* (see page 126) and the *Nut-brown
Maid*. *Chevalere Assigne* (see page 96), the *Earl of Toulous*
(see page 137), and the *Lady of Faguell* (see page 157), contain elements that connect them with the pieces in this present
group.

SIR ISUMBRAS [81] is in MSS. Caius College Cbg. 175
(15th century), Thornton (1430-1440), Cotton Caligula A II
(15th century), Ashmole 61 (15th century), Advocates' Libr.
Edbg. 19, 3, 1 (15th century), and Royal Libr. Naples XIII,
B, 29 (1457); and fragments are in a Gray's Inn MS. and in
MS. University Coll. Oxf. 142 (ll. 1-17). Fragments or copies
of early prints are extant. The romance was composed in 1350-
1400, probably on the Northern border of the East Midland.
In Schleich's edition it consists of 804 verses in twelve-line tail-
rime aabccbddbeeb.

Isumbras is strong and handsome, a patron of gleemen, a most
generous king of courtesy. Prosperous and happy with his wife
and three sons, he neglects God. In a wood, a bird sent by God
gives him choice of suffering in youth or in old age; suffer he must.
Isumbras chooses carefree age. His horse falls dead, his hawks
fly away, his property is burned. Only his wife and children are
left him. The Knight cheerfully recognizes all as punishment for
sin. The family wander begging. A lion bears off the eldest son,
a leopard the second. The Knight is patient. Though starving,
at the Greeks' Sea the family refuse succor by the Saracen Sultan.
The Sultan beats Isumbras, and sets him with a bag of money and
his son on the shore. The wife is sent off as the Sultan's queen.
An eagle bears away the money, and a unicorn the son. For seven
years the Knight is a porter of iron and stone, and for seven
more a blower in a smithy. Then, on a horse used for bearing coals,
Isumbras fights for three days and nights in a battle between Christians and heathen. He slays all the Saracens, and is rewarded by
the King. For seven years he dwells in hunger and pain at Acris
(Acre?). Near Bethlehem, an angel announces to him that his sins
are forgiven. He wanders long, and finally is sheltered by a queen.
He proves his prowess at heaving the stone; and, on a broken steed,
he wins a tournament. In a nest he finds the gold stolen by the
eagle. The Queen recognizes it, and a reunion follows. Isumbras
seeks to compel all his subjects to become Christians. They rebel,
and the Knight and his lady, fighting alone, slay many of them.
Led by an angel, three knights appear, respectively riding a lion,

a unicorn, and a leopard. They slay the pagans, and declare them_
selves to be Isumbras' sons. Happy ever after, they win five lands
to Christianity, and after death all go to Heaven.

The poem has many similarities in plot to *King Robert of
Sicily, Sir Eglamour, Sir Torrent,* and *Octovian.* The loss of
the gold and its recovery remind of one of the *Arabian Nights'*
tales. The number of the MSS. extant, the many allusions to
the poem, from the *Cursor Mundi* to Drayton's *Dowsabell* and
The Cobbler of Canterbury in 1608, and the printing of it in
the sixteenth century, indicate the popularity of the piece.
The trials of Job are at once suggested to the reader. The
story is over-didactic, and at no time credible. Its popularity
must have been due to the preposterousness of incidents, the
marvels of patience, and the obtrusive didacticism, that repel
us to-day. The piece has no real excellence. Suggestion has
been made that the author composed *Octovian,* and also that
the piece is a bad imitation of *Octovian.*

SIR EGLAMOUR OF ARTOIS [82] is in MSS. Thornton
(1430-1440), Cotton Caligula A II (15th century), Cbg. Univ.
Libr. Ff II 38 (15th century), and a leaf in a MS of the Duke
of -Sutherland (now Egerton 2862; end of 14th century).
The piece was composed 1350-1400, probably in the Northern
dialect, and consists of 1335 verses in twelve-line tail-rime
aabccbddbeeb.

Eglamour and the daughter of the Earl of Artois discover their
love for each other. They appeal to the Earl. He agrees to give
Eglamour the princess and his realm, if he will perform three feats.
With the aid of two hounds and a magic sword given him by his
lady, Eglamour performs the first feat of bringing to the Earl one
of a herd of deer watched by a giant keeper. Then, in Sedonia he
performs the second feat: after four days of fighting, he slays a
boar; and he aids the King of Sedonia by slaying a giant who besets
him. He refuses the King's daughter, and returns to Artois. The
now angry and fearful Earl grants him twelve weeks of rest. The
Knight performs the third feat by slaying the Dragon of Rome.
Meanwhile, the Lady Cristabelle bears a son, Degrebelle. The Earl
sets her adrift with her son. A griffon bears off the boy. The
King of Israel finds him, and, being childless, brings him up as his
heir. Cristabelle is borne to Egypt, where she is cared for as
daughter of the King. Eglamour returns to Artois, learns of the

exile of his wife and child, and sets off in search of them. When the boy is fifteen years old, the King of Israel takes him to Egypt, and marries him to Cristabelle. Immediately his mother recognizes him by means of the mantle in which he was found. In a tournament he defends her from would-be husbands; but he is beaten by Eglamour. Eglamour is recognized, and is married to Cristabelle. The Earl falls out of his tower, and breaks his neck. The lovers inherit his realm.

As was *Sir Isumbras, Sir Eglamour* was very popular. The poem is a composite of details found in various sources, and has many resemblances to other pieces. The trials of the wife are paralleled in the Constance saga, generally familiar in Chaucer's *Man of Law's Tale.* The carrying off of the boy is paralleled in *Sir Isumbras, Sir Torrent,* and *Octovian.* The marriage of son and mother is possibly from *Sir Degare,* and reminds of the *Œdipus* of Sophocles. Possibly an *Octovian* in French or English was a chief source. The duel between son and father is a common theme, familiar in the tale of *Sohrab and Rustum.* The relation of confidant that his squire bears to Eglamour, is similar to that between the hero and the squire in *Sir Degrevant,* and accords with the common confidant device in many of the later romances and in novels. There is close relationship between *Sir Eglamour, Sir Torrent,* and *Emare.* Lines and couplets agree, with but slight variants in such places. As has been stated, *Sir Eglamour* has been said to be an original of *Sir Torrent,* or at least to be from the same original as *Sir Torrent.* It is closer to *Emare* than is *Torrent.* Both *Sir Eglamour* and *Emare* may go back to a common original source. In spite of the jingling verse and the general unreality of the story, the piece has much interest. The account of the exile of the mother and the child is related not without pathos. Proverbial expression occurs at several places. Especially early in the story, direct discourse is used freely in place of narrative. The discussion between Eglamour and his squire as to whether the hero shall declare his love, is of particular interest. Exquisitely ludicrous is the lament of the giant of Sedoyne as he addresses the slain boar, 'my litell spotted hogelyn.'

SIR TORRENT OF PORTYNGALE [83] is in MS. Chetham 8009, Manchester, f. 76 (15th century), and in several fragments of an early printed text in the Douce collection. It was composed in 1400-1450, probably in the North-East Midland or the North. It consists of 2668 verses in the twelve-line tail-rime of *Sir Eglamour, Sir Isumbras, Sir Torrent,* and *Sir Amadace.* There are so many blunders and omissions in the text as to suggest that the MS. was written from recitation.

The splendid youth Torrent performs great deeds in honor of Desonell, daughter of the King of Portugal. The King promises the lady to Torrent, provided he kill a giant by the Greek Sea. The feat is performed, and the hero is given rich gifts. The King treacherously suggests in an anonymous letter that Torrent get a falcon for Desonell. In search of the bird, the hero slays a dragon and its master, a giant. On his return, Desonell gives him her heart. The King plots to marry the lady to the Prince of Aragon, and induces Torrent to go to fight the giant of Calabria. Torrent slays the giant, and refuses a king's daughter and two duchies. He is knighted by the King of Provyns. He defeats the Prince of Aragon in single combat, produces the giant's head, and claims his reward. The King of Aragon declaring that Desonell is wedded to the Prince, Torrent on an island kills with cobblestones the giant champion of the Prince. Desonell is now divorced. The King of Portugal suggests that Torrent wait six months before marriage. After three months the hero goes to Norway to slay a giant, leaving to Portugal his lands for Desonell, and two rings for the lady in case a child is born. He kills two dragons and a giant, and refuses the Princess of Norway. One of his false squires bears false news to Portugal. Desonell faints, and is discovered to be with child. She bears two boys. The King, to the general grief, has her set adrift with her two sons. When they come to land, a griffon bears off one son, a leopard the other. The King of Jerusalem finds and fosters one child. The other boy is borne to St. Anthony, who induces his father, the King of Greece, to adopt the child. Desonell arrives at the court of the King of Nazareth, where she is cared for. On learning of the fate of his family, Torrent drowns the King of Portugal. He sets off to the Holy Land. After long sieges, he takes two cities, killing or starving the inhabitants. At Antioch, he fights every Friday against the Saracens. The King of Jerusalem sends his foster-son against Torrent. The hero is captured, and is imprisoned in Jerusalem. His son overhears his prayers, and has him freed. At a great tournament, Torrent defeats his son and 'wins the gre.' Desonell recognizes her lover by his arms. At a joust at Nazareth, Torrent and the two sons prove to be the best knights, and Desonell is declared to be the fairest lady. Desonell tells her story at a feast, and all are united. The lovers are married in Portugal. Ultimately, Torrent is chosen Emperor of Rome.

Similarity of incidents and identity of phrases indicate that the poem is a direct elaboration of *Sir Eglamour*. Possibly, however, both poems are from a common source. The writer of *Torrent* multiplies by two or three the incidents or the details of incident, and elaborates minor elements, of *Sir Eglamour*. The piece is of poor quality. It is replete with stock phrases. The writer's forte is trivialities. The prayers at every important turn, the indications of divine interposition, Desonell's concern about her children's baptism, the matter about masses and the sacraments, and the praises of founding of abbeys and churches, indicate a working over and a padding out of an original for ecclesiastical ends.

OCTOVIAN [84] is preserved in two wholly independent versions. The former of these, of the South-East of England and of about 1350, is in MS. Cotton Caligula A II (15th century). It consists of 1962 verses aaabab, of which the *b* verses have two, and the *a* verses have four, stresses each. The second, of the North and of about 1350, is in MSS. Cbg. Univ. Libr. Ff II 38 (15th century; 1731 lines), and Thornton (Lincoln Cathedral Libr. A 5; 1430-1440; 1628 lines), in twelve-line tail-rime aabccbdddbeeb.

Octovian, Emperor of Rome, weds Florence, daughter of the King of France. The lady bears twin sons. His mother leads Octovian to believe his children to be bastards. Florence and her babes are driven away into a wild forest. An ape bears off the child Florentyn. A knight rescues him. Outlaws seize the boy, and sell him to a palmer, Clement, who is a butcher of Paris. Clement informs his wife that Florentyn is his bastard son, and rears the boy with his family. The other son is borne off by a tiger, which with its prey is caught up by a griffon. A lioness kills the griffon, and rears the child with her whelps. Florence makes her way to a city by the sea, and sails for the Holy Land. Seeking water, the mariners come upon the lioness, and rescue the child. The lioness accompanies Florence to Jerusalem, and dwells with her there. Florence works embroidery, and becomes chief lady to the Queen. When he is fifteen years old, Florentyn is sent to drive cattle to market. He trades the animals for a sparhawk. The butcher beats

him. Sent to change money, the youth gives the gold for a colt.
Clement's wife will no longer believe the boy is a bastard. Suspecting his parentage, Clement devotes Florentyn to sport. The
youth becomes an adept at wrestling and casting the stone, and
grows to be the idol of the Parisians and their King. The Sultan
besets the King. His giant champion slays the twelve peers. In
a dream, the Virgin bids Florentyn support the Christian cause.
The youth is knighted. At his own request taunted by Clement
with the epithet 'butcher's son,' he kills the giant. He bears off
the sleeve of the Sultan's daughter. Paris honors as first the
butcher's craft. In love with Florentyn, the Sultan's daughter so
plans that the hero carries her off to Paris. She will be christened
only after Clement has preached to her in the Saracen language.
The lovers are married. Clement plays a joke on the guests. The
Sultan gathers new forces. At the daughter's direction, Clement
goes to the Sultan, and poses as warden of Arthur's horses. Invited
to mount the Saracen's precious unicorn, he swims it over the
Seine, and gives it to the King of Paris. In battle, the King,
Florentyn, Octovian, and a hundred thousand nobles, are made captive. The other son of Octovian becomes a valiant knight. He is
always accompanied by the lioness. He fights the Saracens, and
frees the prisoners. The brothers slay thousands of pagans. At
Paris, Clement is knighted. Florence recognizes Octovian, and tells
her story. Florentyn is recognized; Clement tells his story. The
old mother of Octovian is burned.

Such is the Southern version. It is based on the French
romance of the same name, often following it word for word,
but often happily condensing it much. The modifications in
the first part are largely for realism. The variations are
greatest in the second part, and suggest writing down from
memory. The references at lines 935 and 1359 to a Latin
source, are probably the common device for attaining authority.
The piece exhibits considerable narrative power. The passages dealing with Clement are related with much appreciation.
The realistic humorous treatment of the butcher makes the incidents in which he is concerned the most striking in the poem.
The attitude of the author is 'popular.' The love-matter of
the original is practically eliminated; the psychological analysis, the utterances of lamentation and introspection, are
omitted. The personages are given middle-class or lower-
class activity: at Jerusalem, Florence teaches sewing; her son
is sent to school to learn grammar and to 'Ayscryue the
Donet'; the other son is a poacher, and, like Havelok, is a cham-

pion at wrestling and at putting the stone. The author would
appear to be a minstrel who could tell a story with spirit and
homely realism. It has been urged that he was Thomas Chestre,
author of *Sir Launfal.*

The Northern version is much closer to the French. It
agrees in general with the Southern version, but differs much
from it in details. It preserves from the French a recognition-
scene between Florent and the Emperor, just after the giant
is slain; an embassy of Florent to the court of the Sultan,
whence, having at request of the Sultan's daughter, Marsabelle,
revealed that he is the giant's conqueror, the hero has to fight
his way free; extended love-matter between Florent and Marsabelle; a ludicrous episode where Clement puts on the boy
his dirty armour, and, attempting with his wife's aid to remove
the sword from the scabbard, comes down hard on the ground;
a humorous .episode, where, meaning to be very generous,
Clement lavishly casts down thirty florins at a banquet, and is
heartily laughed at by the knights. The writer departs from
the French and the Southern version in making Octovian and his
wife childless for seven years; in making them endow an abbey,
and in consequence have the twin sons; in having the father
of the Empress condemn her; and in telling continuously, first
the story of the Empress and her one son, and thereafter the
story of the other son. Much is made of the love story. The
daughter of the Sultan is given much space, and has a confidante, as have heroines of more sophisticated romances. Moreover, though he here obtains high honor, and is a burgess of
Paris, Clement is made the butt of burlesque incidents, and is
not taken with the seriousness, or given the prominence, that
he receives in the Southern version. It has been claimed that
the author was a churchman. It is rather difficult to approve
of the repeated statement that this poem is greatly superior to
the Southern piece.

SIR TRIAMOUR [85], preserved in MS. Cbg. Univ. Libr.
Ff II 38 (15th century) and in the Percy Folio MS. (c. 1650),
is closely associated in general plot with *Octovian.* It consists of 1719 verses in twelve-line tail-rime normally aabccbddb-

eeb, and was composed in the North Midland in 1400-1450. A fragment of 75 lines, probably from one of the several early printed texts, is in a Rawlinson MS.

Hoping for an heir, Ardus, King of Aragon, vows to go to the Holy Land. Having unawares begotten a boy, he sets off, leaving his Queen, Margaret, in care of a steward, Marrok. Marrok vainly makes advances to the Queen, and covers them by pretense that they aré a test of her virtue. After doing great deeds, Ardus returns. Marrok declares he has caught the Queen with a knight, has slain the lover, and has been offered the lady's favors. The King drives Margaret into a forest with an old horse, an old knight, Sir Roger, and thirty pounds of money. Marrok, with a troop, attempts to seize the Queen, but Roger and his dog, True-love, hold them off while Margaret flees. Roger is murdered. The dog stays by the body, and tries to bury it. In a forest in Hungary, Margaret bears a boy. Sir Barnard Messengere succors her. The boy is christened 'Triamour.' The mother and the child are beloved throughout the neighborhood. After dwelling twelve years on his master's grave, True-love goes to the King's palace, and kills Marrok at table. He is followed to the grave of his master, who is given proper burial. The body of Marrok is hanged. The King sends in search of Margaret. A joust is cried for the hand of the seven-year-old daughter of the King of Hungary. Triamour performs great deeds on the side of his father, the King of Aragon; the next day, fighting on the other side, he overcomes his father; the third day, he wins the joust and is chosen governor for the lady. But there is opposition; Triamour is wounded, and the son of the Emperor of Germany is slain. Triamour disappears. The lady is given two years in which to find him. The Emperor besieges Ardus. The case is submitted to decision by duel. Ardus vainly sends for Triamour. Finally, the hero appears, is knighted, and slays Moradas, the Emperor's champion. He sets off to visit his lady, wins many jousts, slays the brothers of Moradas that hold the road to prevent him from coming to the aid of his lady, and reaches the palace. From his mother Triamour learns that Ardus is his father. He invites the King to the wedding. Ardus and Margaret are united, and rule in Aragon. Triamour ·has two children, one of whom succeeds Ardus in Aragon.

No French original of the poem is extant. The story is really a composite of incidents to be met with in earlier romances. Even minor details are borrowed. But the tale is well put together, and exhibits good narrative power. It moves fluently, without abruptness or crude breaks. The verse is smooth. Dialogue is used freely, and, as are many passages of the narrative, is full of color and very realistic. The story is told sympathetically, with much controlled sentiment. The passages on the faithful hound (paralleled in the twelfth-century French *Macaire*), are very effective, as is all the first part of the tale up to Triamour's departure for Hungary.

THE KING OF TARS [86] (Tarsus) is in MSS. Auchinleck (1330-1340; 1228 verses), Vernon (1370-1380; 1122 verses), and Br. Mus. Additional 22283 (1380-1400; 1122 verses), in twelve-line tail-rime aabaabccbddb. The original dialect is difficult to determine; it is probably Midland of not after 1325.

The Saracen Sultan of Dammas sues for the hand of the daughter of the King of Tarsus. Because of his faith, he is scornfully rejected. He invades the country, massacres many Christians, and besieges Tarsus. Overwhelmed with grief, to prevent further suffering for her sake, the Princess obtains her parents' consent to give herself to the Sultan. She is splendidly received. She has a horrible dream of black hounds; but the largest hound assumes the appearance of a knight in white, and assures her of Heaven's protection. The Sultan insisting, outwardly she becomes a Saracen. They are married. A child is born without limbs or face, and quite inert. Chidden by the Sultan, the lady bids him see if his gods can make a perfect child of the lump of flesh. The gods fail; the Sultan destroys their images; if God will perfect the babe, he will forsake Mahoun. At the lady's direction, a priest from among the prisoners christens the child. At once it becomes fully formed. The Sultan is delighted; but the lady declares he has no part in mother or child unless he becomes a Christian. She instructs him in the faith. He is christened, and his black and loathly countenance becomes fair and clear. He summons the King of Tarsus to aid him to compel all his land to Christianity. The Christian prisoners all are freed. The heathen are converted or slain. Five kings make a good fight, but are defeated. The survivors are baptized or executed.

The story of the poem is paralleled in the very brief account of the King of Tarsus in Thomas of Walsingham's *Historia Anglicana* and in Matthew of Westminster's *Flores Historiarum* under the date 1299. It is not improbable that the poem is based on a French original. Its didactic purpose is obvious. It affords a good example of the close relationship between the Romance and the Saint's Life. As a whole the piece is dull.

The latter half is quite too long drawn out; the last two hundred and seventy-five lines, after the christening of the Sultan, are extremely uninteresting. The miracles and conversions are incredible and trite. But the earlier passages dealing with the relations between the heroine and her parents, are not lacking in dramatic truth; and the pathetic sacrifice of the maiden is told with some sympathetic power.

LE BONE FLORENCE OF ROME [87], in MS. Cbg. Univ. Libr. Ff II 38 (15th century), consists of 2187 verses of twelve-line tail-rime aabccbddbeeb, composed probably on the Northern border of the Midland at about 1400.

Garcy, the aged and debilitated Emperor of Constantinople, sends to Otes, Emperor of Rome, for his daughter, Florence, to console him. The lady is refused. Rome is besieged. Miles and Emere, sons of the King of Hungary, fight valiantly for Rome. The lady falls in love with Emere. Distressed by thought of the sufferings that will be caused by continuation of the war, she proposes to yield herself to Garcy. Otes refuses, and offers her hand to the knight who bears him best. Otes is slain; Emere is captured. Miles, who has falsely accused Emere of favoring Garcy, is invited to wed Florence. He hesitates, and is rejected by the indignant lady. Relations with the King of Hungary lead Garcy to free Emere. The Knight is wedded to Florence, and becomes Emperor of Rome. But the lady will be fully his wife only after he has slain or captured Garcy. Emere defeats Garcy, and pursues him over the sea. Miles, left behind, usurps Emere's power, leads Florence to suppose her husband is dead, and gives her a false message from Emere urging her to marry Miles. Wishing to become a nun, Florence is shut up in the palace. Egravayne confesses to the Pope, who arms the clergy, rescues the Empress, and confines Miles. They discover that Emere is not dead. Emere defeats and captures Garcy, and is crowned Emperor of Constantinople. Florence for love of Emere, frees Miles, and conceals his guilt. Miles rides to meet Emere, and accuses Florence of adultery with Egravayne. Returning, he entices Florence to a forest, and forces her to promise to keep her identity secret. Her prayers to Heaven preserve her from Miles' embraces. Sir Tyrry rescues her and cares for her. Foiled in attempts on her honor, a knight of Tyrry cuts the throat of the latter's daughter, and puts the knife in the hand of the sleeping Florence. Florence is condemned; but Tyrry sends her away into a forest. There she obtains as page a man who is about to be hanged. The page and a burgess sell her to a mariner, who pays them lead instead of gold. The lady's prayers preserve her honor. The ship sinks, all the crew except the mariner are drowned, Florence floats to a rock. She reaches a nunnery, and heals one of the nuns. Her fame spreads. To her for healing come Emere, Miles, the burgess, the mariner, and the page. Florence compels her four foes to confession as preliminary to cure. She heals all the five men. Emere and Florence, and Tyrry and his wife, are gloriously received at Rome. A son, Otes, is born to Florence and Emere. Pope Symonde wrote this story in the Chronicles of Rome. Let all who would be false bethink themselves; evil cunning is always punished.

Resemblance to the opening of the *King of Tars,* and similarities to the Constance story, will be noticed. The piece seems to be an abbreviated translation of a lost text of the French *Florence de Rome.* Survival of much good descriptive matter is seen in the early parts. Elaboration of details extends the story greatly; this produces, however, not distraction and tediousness, but greater reality and interest. A number of personages, both major and minor, stand out very distinctly. The extraordinary miracles of protection and of healing, and the delineation of the Seven Sins on the walls of the Emperor's palace, suggest the cleric who speaks out plainly in the final lines of the piece. The character, behavior, experience, and achievements of the heroine, remind again of the slightness of the division between Saint's Life and Romance. The author is more interested in the heroine than in the hero. Miles is at first a rather incompetent villain, but he improves as the story progresses. Well touched in is the episode of the pardoned candidate for the gallows, and the burgess, from the point where the former 'twinkled with his eye as who seyth holde the stylle.' All in all, despite its didactic intent, the story is vivid and interesting.

9. Breton Lais

Some seven or eight English pieces have been grouped together because of their evident dependence on Breton *lais*— short poems of romantic content intended to be sung, represented best in the *lais* of Marie de France. Actual French originals for but two of these English tales, *Lai le Freine* and *Sir Launfal,* are extant. But in each of six of them, the *Earl of Toulous* (ll. 1219-21), *Emare* (ll. 1030-32), Chaucer's

Franklin's Tale (ll. 709-15), *Sir Gowther* (ll. 28-29, 751-53), *Lai le Freine* (ll. 1-26), and *Sir Orfeo* (ll. 1-22), deliberate mention is made of a lay of Britain in connection with the story. In *Sir Launfal* (ll. 4-5) Britain is not mentioned, but a lay is.

Each of these poems fits well the description of *lais* that is prefixed to *Sir Orfeo* in the Harley and Ashmole MSS., omitted in the Auchinleck MS., and written almost word for word at the opening of *Lai le Freine* in the Auchinleck MS.

> We redyn ofte and fynde ywryte,
> As clerkes don us to wyte,
> þe layes þat ben of harpying
> Ben yfounde of frely (ferly) þing.
> Sum ben of wele and sum of wo,
> And sum of joy and merþe also,
> Sum of trechery and sum of gyle,
> And sum of happes þat fallen by whyle,
> Sum of bourdys and sum of rybaudry,
> And sum þer ben of þe feyre.
> Of alle þing þat men may se,
> Most o lowe (love) forsoþe þey be.
> In Brytain þis layes arne ywryte,
> Furst yfounde and forþe ygete,
> Of aventures þat fillen by dayes
> Whereof Brytouns made her layes.
> When þey myght owher heryn
> Of aventures þat þer weryn,
> þey toke her harpys wiþ game,
> Maden layes and ȝaf it name.
> Of aventures, þat han befalle,
> Y can sum telle, but nought all.

Most of the classes of theme here indicated are found in the seven English pieces. Suggestion, here adopted, has been made that *Sir Degare*, though it does not mention a Breton original, be added to the group. Probably by influence of their originals, all of the eight poems are short, simple, direct, unified, coherent, and free from the diffuseness characteristic of most of the English romances. The short couplet, the general verse-form of the French *lais*, is preserved only in *Sir Orfeo*, *Lai le Freine*, *Sir Launfal*, and *Sir Degare*. *Emare*, *Sir Gowther*, and the *Earl of Toulous*, are in the favorite Northern tail-rime aabccbddbeeb. The *Franklin's Tale* is, of course, in heroic couplets. It is dealt with in the discussion of Chaucer (see page 734).

LAI LE FREINE [88], in MS. Auchinleck (1330-1340), consists of 340 verses (including a gap of thirteen verses) in short couplets. It is probably of the beginning of the fourteenth century. The original dialect, though uncertain, appears to be Southern or South-East Midland.

In the West Country dwell two rich knights, close neighbors. The wife of one bears boy twins. Envious, the wife of the other declares that a woman who bears twins must have been unfaithful. Soon she herself bears girl twins. Fearful of the consequences of her own declarations, she plots with a midwife to do away with one of the children. A maid bears off the babe wrapped in a rich robe from Constantinople, and having fastened on its arm a gold ring as a token of rank. The maid carries the infant through the winter night. As the cocks are crowing and the dogs are barking, she comes to a nunnery. She prays for aid. Looking up, she sees a hollow ash-tree. Into the hollow she puts the babe, and makes off. Having rung the bells and lighted the fires and laid out the books, the porter undoes the church door. He catches sight of the robe in the trunk. He finds the child, gives it to his daughter, and reports to the abbess. The ring is discovered; the foundling is baptized 'Frain,' 'because she was found in the ash-tree. When twelve years old, the maiden asks, and is told, of her history, and is given the robe and the ring. A young rich Knight hears of her, sees her, artfully gets access to her, wins her love, and persuades her to run away to his home and be his mistress. For long she dwells with him as if she were his wife, demeaning herself perfectly and winning universal love. But his knights urge her lover to forsake her, and to marry. He arranges to wed Le Freine's twin-sister. The bride is brought to the groom's house. With her come her parents and the bishop to perform the marriage.

Unhappily, the fragment ends here. From the original, Marie de France's *Lai de Fresne*, the conclusion may be filled out.

Le Freine is all gentleness and self-forgetfulness. She is so kind and serviceable, that she wins the mother's heart. Thinking the bridal-bed too plainly decked, she lays over it her beautiful robe. The mother enters with the bride, recognizes the robe, learns of the ring, and confesses to the father. The marriage of the Knight is undone. Le Freine is wedded to her lover. Soon after, the sister marries another knight.

The poem is written simply and tenderly, with much circumstantial detail that makes the matter real and close. The writer gives himself to the story; in the midst of it he even forgets that his scene is laid in Brittany, and says that the maid is the fairest 'in England.' The shrewishness of the mother, her accusation of the other knight's lady (similar to that in *Chevalere Assigne*), and her subsequent predicament, are presented effectively. The journey of the maid with the infant through the clear moonlit winter-long night, her resting under the forest-side until the cocks crow and the dogs begin to bark, the gradual appearance of the outlines of the walls and the house and the church with its steeple fair and high, her hurried prayer, her folding the child in the hollow ash, and her hastening away as day dawns and the birds begin to sing and the acre-men go to the plough, are most vividly and sympathetically related. So, too, is the circumstantial account of the porter in the early morning performing his various duties in the close; ringing the bells; then, within the church, lighting the tapers, and laying out the books; finally opening the door, catching sight of the fair cloth, and fearing robbers have been about; and his taking to his daughter of the poor babe that cannot be suckled because it is so cold. The manner in which the lover beguiles the maid from the nunnery, arouses warm feeling. It is unfortunate that we have not the writer's treatment of the last part of the story. The piece, with *Sir Orfeo*, contains the best that is in this group of tales. It exhibits a fineness of conception and a delicateness of taste and touch, that raise it far out of the mass of Middle English literature.

The story belongs to the widespread mediæval cycle of tales of the patient woman, and reminds particularly of the Griselda group that is most familiar to us in Chaucer's *Clerk's Tale* (see pages 113, 726). The matter of the Ash, and that of Boccaccio and Petrarch on which Chaucer's story rests, probably go back to a common source. The tale of Patient Grisell became the theme of a number of English poetical and dramatic treatments reaching down to modern times (see page 726). The prologue of *Le Freine*, found also in *Sir Orfeo*, has already been spoken of (see page 125).

SIR ORFEO [89], composed in the South Midland or the
South, probably at the beginning of the fourteenth century, is
in MSS. Auchinleck (1330-1340), Ashmole 61 (15th century),
and Harley 3810 (early 15th century). In Zielke's critical
edition it consists of 301 short couplets. It is contended that
the prologue, found also in *Lai le Freine,* properly belongs with
the French original of *Sir Orfeo* (see page 125).

On a beautiful flowery May morning, Heurodis, Queen of Orfeo,
King of the city Traciens, makes merry with her maidens in her
garden. She falls asleep under a tree, and slumbers till afternoon.
She awakes in great agony. Borne to her bed in the palace, to
Orfeo's loving inquiries she replies that they must part. As she
lay asleep knights summoned her to speak with their King. She
refused. With a great troop of knights and damisels all in white
and on snowwhite steeds, the strange King came, and bore her to
his palace. Then he brought her home again with the warning that
the next day she be under the tree, whence she shall go with him
to stay forevermore. The distressed Orfeo takes counsel in vain.
The next morning, he surrounds the lady under the tree with his ten
hundred knights; but she is spirited away. The King, heartbroken, gives over his realm to his steward; and, dressed as a pilgrim, with only his harp, he goes to dwell in the woods. For ten
years he lives an outcast, hairy and emaciated, almost starved on
roots and bark and berries, only now and again inspiriting himself
by playing on his harp. When he plays, so sweet is his music that
birds and beasts draw near him for joy. Often in the heat he
sees and hears the King of Fairies and his rout hunting; but
he knows not whither they go. Often he sees ten hundred knights
all armed draw their swords under displayed banners—and lo!
they vanish. Sometimes he sees knights and ladies dancing. On
a day, he beholds a band of ladies hunting with falcons, every
falcon slaying its prey. He laughs with delight, and draws near—
and he sees Heurodis, and she sees him, and the ladies ride away
with her. With his harp he hurries after them, and in at a rock,
and on for three miles into a most beautiful level country all sunny
and green, with a great castle all crystal and gold and precious
stones. The ladies enter the gates, and the porter admits the
minstrel too. There he sees all the people as they were taken
by fairies, without heads, wounded, strangled, drowned, burned—
and his lady asleep under a tree. He hastens to the hall before
the King and the Queen, and begs that he be permitted to play. The
King is amazed that he is there; but Orfeo pleads, Whoever refused
to hear a minstrel? And he charms the King with his lovely
melody, and is offered whatever reward he will ask. Heurodis
he would bear home. The King will not have her in such loathly
company. But Orfeo persists, it is a foul thing for a king to

break his promise; and he wins the lady, and takes her by the hand and leads her to Traciens. The steward still holds his lands. Orfeo goes to the castle, and is welcomed; all minstrels are welcomed for the sake of the lost King, the sweet player. He harps before the lords. Questioned, he tells that he found his harp in a wood beside a man torn to pieces by lions. The steward faints with grief; Orfeo is dead! The minstrel now tells that he is Orfeo, and relates all the tale of his wanderings and his recovery of Heurodis. The lovers are crowned again, and they live long and happily. For his faithfulness, the steward is made King after Orfeo. And the harpers in Bretaine heard of it, and they made of it a pleasant lay, and the lay is called 'Orfeo.'

The little story is one of the most attractive pieces in Middle English, charmingly graceful and fanciful. It is the tale of Orpheus and Eurydice handed down through popular tradition and folk-lore. The classical becomes the Celtic. The ancient is completely made over into the mediæval; if one did not know the old story, one could scarce suppose the tale other ✓ than a fairy tale. It is a tale of harping—as are many lays, the prologue tells us; and it is a tale of true love—as are most lays, says the same authority. And true love and minstrelsy win their reward of happiness. With fatal forgetfulness like that of the classic 'Orpheus,' mediæval literature was sufficiently familiar—but permanent separation and woe were not for such a lady and such a king.

EMARE [90], in MS. Cotton Caligula A II (15th century), is of the Northern East Midland toward the end of the fourteenth century. It consists of 1035 verses of twelve-line tail-rime, two-thirds of which are aabccbdddbeeb or variants, and one-third aabaabccbddb or variants. The mixture of stanza-forms is unusual.

Emare is daughter of the Emperor Artyus, a most handsome, courteous, brave, and just man, the best in the world. Artyus obtains the Pope's permission to marry Emare. He has made into a robe for her a gorgeously embroidered and jeweled cloth wrought in the East by a lady of high rank, and given him by the King of Sicily. Emare will not sin by marrying her father. In her beautiful garment, she is cast adrift. As soon as the vessel is out of sight, Artyus repents. Emare is found on the shore of Galys by the steward of the King of that place. Recovered, she teaches

embroidery, and is much beloved. Falling in love with her at a
feast, the King weds her despite the protests of his old mother,
who insists that her beauty proves her of unearthly origin. The
King goes off to fight the Saracens. A child, Segramour, is born.
The messenger bearing word to the King stops at the castle of the
old mother Queen, who for his letter substitutes one declaring the
child is a monster. The King is heartbroken, but sends orders that
the mother be cared for diligently. The old Queen substitutes
directions that the lady be set adrift with her robe and her son.
Amid general grief, the order is fulfilled. The lady reaches Rome.
There, under the name of Egarye, she is succored by a merchant.
For several years she instructs her son, and works embroidery. Her
husband returns from the wars, learns of the plot against Emare,
and exiles his mother. For seven years he sorrows. Finally, he
goes to Rome for penance. The merchant, protector of Emare,
entertains him. By Emare's direction, her son serves the King at
table, then conducts him to his mother. The reunion is joyful.
Artyus comes to Rome for penance. The boy serves him, too, and
leads him to Emare.

One observes at once the close similarity of the general story
to that of Constance as related by Chaucer and Gower from
Nicholas Trivet's *Chronique Anglo-Normande* (see pages 113,
701). It is the best Middle English representative of the Constance saga, of which versions are extant in Latin, French,
German, Italian, Spanish, and Catalan, and which still persists in folk-lore in widely separated localities. The characteristic features of the typical Constance story, have been indicated on page 113. Similarities between *Emare* and the stories
of *Sir Eglamour*, *Sir Torrent*, *Octovian*, and *Sir Triamour*,
will be observed at once (see pages 113 ff.). It would seem that
Sir Eglamour, the probable chief original of *Sir Torrent*, goes
back to the source of *Emare*. Remarkable coincidences of
whole lines and couplets, as well as of details of story, occur
in these three pieces.

The poem is full of sentiment and sensibility. Even the
unnatural Artyus is a most perfect fine gentleman; he is in
bitter tears of remorse as soon as his daughter has drifted away.
Stress is put on the training of the lady, the fineness of her
demeanor, and the superior nature of her child. Emare's
ability in silk work is made much of, as are her courtesy and
her personal charm. This charm and her beauty, enhanced by

the wonder of the gorgeous robe, cause repeated declaration
that she is of 'únearthly' nature. These declarations open
the way to the theory that the original lady was a fairy. Her
robe is described in 109 lines or over a tenth of the whole, introduced perhaps by the minstrel in accord with his general interests. With all its sensibility, the poem does not run over into
sentimentality. The grief of the father for his wife and child,
is presented effectively; and the pathetic tenderness of the
mother caring for her child on the drifting vessel, is well on
the way to the scene in Chaucer. ·

SIR LAUNFAL or LAUNFALUS MILES [91], is the
first of two Middle English versions of the story of Launfal.
The second version is represented in three pieces, *Sir Landeval*,
Sir Lambewell, and *Sir Lamwell*. Both versions are from a
common source, an English translation of Marie de France's
Lai de Lanval.

The poem *Sir Launfal* is by Thomas Chestre. It is an amalgamation of the *Lai de Lanval* with the anonymous *Lai de
Graelent*, and contains two interpolated episodes—the tournament at Caerleon (ll. 433-92), and the combat with Valentine
(ll. 505-812). It is in MS. Cotton Caligula A II (15th century), and consists of 1044 verses in twelve-line tail-rime
aabccbddbeeb. It was composed in the South-East. Various
dates, from the first half to the last quarter of the fourteenth
century, are assigned to it.   ·

Sir Launfal, a knight of Arthur's Table Round and a steward of
the King, is famed for his largesse. Arthur marries Qwennere.
Launfal dislikes the Queen because she is reputed as having an
endless list of lovers under her lord. Moreover, at the wedding
she gives gifts to all the knights except Launfal. So the Knight
makes an excuse to leave the court. Arthur insists that he take
with him two of the King's kinsmen. The three, with their retinue,
come to Caerleon, where the Mayor, an old servant of Launfal,
receives them with fair words. But when Launfal asks harborage,
he makes an excuse to refuse. Launfal remarks to his knights on
the situation; the Mayor, shamed, offers them a fair chamber.
There for a year Launfal dwells, distributing such bounty that he
is left in poverty. The two knights go to court, under promise
to keep secret his indigence. To Arthur they explain away their

raggedness, and represent Launfal as in good circumstances. The Queen is much annoyed. Launfal is in complete poverty, so that he cannot show himself abroad. The Mayor gives a feast; the Knight is invited only at the last moment, and only by the pitying daughter. Launfal refuses to go; but he begs a horse, that he may ride out. With no retinue and mocked, he rides to a forest. Two maidens, most beautifully clad and wearing gorgeous crowns, appear to him, and conduct him to a pavilion, where Tryamour, 'the King's daughter of Olyroun,' the King of Fairy, declares her love for him. Launfal is passionately enamored of the lady. She promises him wealth, a steed, a page, and arms that keep the wearer from all injury. The next morning they part, the lady promising to come to him invisible to all others, whenever he calls her, but warning him that, if he speak of her to anyone, her love shall cease. He returns to Caerleon. A troop of youths and the page, Gifre, bring him great wealth and the horse and the armor. The Mayor at once becomes cordial. Launfal wins a great tournament. News of his fame reaches Lombardy, whence Sir Valentine challenges him to a duel. In Lombardy, with the aid of Gifre, Launfal slays Valentine. He is received with much joy at Arthur's Court. The Queen declares that she has loved him for seven years, and asks his love in return. The Knight will not be a traitor to the King. To the Queen's taunts that he loves no one, he replies that he loves a lady whose maids are fairer than the Queen. Furious, the Queen accuses him before Arthur of tempting her to infidelity. Because of his speech to the Queen, all Launfal's wealth and his steed and his page disappear. He is brought to trial; but, because of the well-known lasciviousness of the Queen, and his great liberality, it is judged that if, within a year and a fortnight, he exhibit the lady of whose beauty he has boasted, he shall be pardoned. The time expires without his being able to produce the lady. The lords are rebelling against executing the Knight, when there appear a troop of lovely ladies, who bid the King prepare à bed for their royal mistress. Then come another troop splendidly clad, who bid Arthur deck the halls for the Lady Tryamour. Then comes the lady, alone, in gorgeous garb, transcendently beautiful. She declares the Knight to be true, and states that the Queen has been the aggressor. Then she blows on the Queen's eyes such a breath that thereafter she is blind. With Launfal she rides away to the Isle of Olyroun, where she dwells still with her lover. Once a year men hear Launfal's steed neigh, and see the Knight. Who desires jousts needs to go no farther. 'Thomas Chestre made this tale of a noble Knight Sir Launfal.'

It was probably to satisfy the demand for exhibition of military prowess that were interpolated the jousts and the duel with *Sir Landeval* enhances the unity and the effect of the story there. Of great interest are the open declarations of the Queen's lasciviousness, the attitude of the knights toward her, and her punishment. As in several others of the pieces of this group of lays, a thread of abstract purpose runs through the poem. In Launfal are stressed bounty and largesse; and in the relations of the Queen and Launfal to Arthur, and of Launfal to Tryamour, is emphasized fidelity to troth pledged. A note of irony is struck in the variations in the behavior of the mayor to his former master as Launfal's fortunes fall and rise. In the paragraphs on Tryamour and her maidens there is much charming description, which, since it appears as admirably in *Sir Landeval*, is probably from the original. The claims that *Octovian* and *Libeaus Desconus* also are by Chestre, seem not well supported.

SIR LANDEVAL [92], one of the representatives of the second version, is in 535 verses in short couplets in MS. Rawlinson C 86 (16th century). It is of the South and the fifteenth century. Excluding the departure from Arthur's court, the sojourn at Caerleon, the jousts, the duel, and all incidentally connected with them, it is in matter close to *Sir Launfal*.

Largesse brings to indigence Landeval, a generous knight of Arthur's court. He rides to a wood, lamenting that in his poverty none will consort with him. Then comes the episode of the fairy lady, much as it is in *Sir Launfal*. In the city he gives rich gifts. Then follow, much as in *Sir Launfal*, the Queen's offer of her love, the disappearance of the fairy wealth, the accusation of the Knight, and the rest of the matter to the fairy lady's appearance and declaration of the Queen's guilt. There is no word of punishment of the Queen. The fairy rides off. Landeval rides after her, beseeching forgiveness. At first obdurate, she finally pardons him. They ride to Amylyone, that every Briton knows about. This is all the author can tell.

Sir Lambewell [93], 316 couplets in the Percy Folio MS. (c. 1650), is from the same original as *Sir Landeval*, and in matter very close to the latter. It makes the fairy lady's forgiveness less prompt than does *Sir Landeval*.

Sir Lamwell [94], a damaged fragment of eight printed leaves, probably of the sixteenth century, close in matter to *Sir Lambewell* and *Sir Landeval*, is MS. Malone 941 in the

Bodleian. A printed leaf of 61 lines, probably a reprint of
Sir Lamwell, is in MS. Douce II 95. Another fragment of 90
lines is in MS. Cbg. Univ. Libr. Kk V 30 (15th century). All
these pieces are in short couplets.

SIR DEGARE [95], in short couplets, is preserved in MSS.
Auchinleck (1330-1340; the most perfect; 993 verses), Cbg.
Univ. Libr. Ff II 38 (15th century; imperfect; some 602
verses), Selden C 39 (c. 1564; imperfect; some 352 verses),
the Percy Folio MS. (c. 1650; 900 verses), Duke of Sutherland (now Egerton 2862; end of 14th century; two fragments),
and in prints by de Worde, Copland, and John King in 1560.
The poem is not later than 1325, and is probably of the South-
West Midland.

The daughter of a king of England is lost in a forest with her
maid. She wanders from her woman. A knight ravishes her, and
leaves with her a pointless sword for the boy who shall be born.
When her time for delivery comes, she fears her father will be
accused of incest with her, for she has known no other man. With
one of her maidens she arranges that the birth be kept secret.
The maid bears off the child with thirty pounds of money, a pair
of gloves, and a letter asking the finder to bring up the boy, and
directing that the child shall marry only the lady whose hands the
gloves will fit. A hermit finds and christens the babe, and gives
it into his sister's care. The hermit educates the boy in clerkly
lore from his tenth to his twentieth year. Then he gives him the
money, the gloves, and the letter. Armed only with a sapling,
Degare sets off to find his father. He rescues an earl by slaying
a dragon. The Earl knights him, and offers him his daughter and
half his lands. But the gloves will not fit the lady or any other
woman in the castle. The King offers his lands and his daughter
to whoever will joust with him. None will accept, for the King
has already slain many opponents. Degare, after a stiff fight,
overthrows the King. Forgetting the gloves, he marries the Princess. But the Princess can put on the gloves: she tells him she is
his mother. She relates the story of his begetting, and gives him
the pointless sword. Degare sets off in search of his father. He
enters a castle empty of inhabitants, and sits by the great fire in
the hall. Maiden huntresses appear with venison, and will not
speak to him. A dwarf all in green sits at the table, but will not
respond to his advances. A beautiful lady and many maidens clad
in red and in green, take supper with him, but will not notice him.
He follows them to the lady's bower. There, as he looks at the
lady, and listens to her harping, he falls asleep. The next morning

he learns that the lady is unprotected, and is beset by a giant. She and all hers shall be his, if Degare will help her. The Knight slays the giant, but defers the wedding for a year. In a wood, he contends with a knight. The knight notices that the hero's sword is pointless. He produces the missing point, and declares he is the youth's father. They go to England. The parents are wedded, and Dagare marries the lady of the castle.

The piece is a composite of motives and incidents to be found scattered in romance and folk-lore. The materials are wrought into a coherent whole without digression or unnecessary expansion. The union of the parents is somewhat hasty, and, in view of the early part of the story, insufficiently motived; but, as a rule, the various incidents are well prepared for. All in all, the poem deserves the popularity that its repeated reprinting in the sixteenth century indicates it to have enjoyed. The mysterious begetting of the boy has much similarity with that of *Sir Gowther*, and is a feature common to a number of mediæval works. No doubt, it goes back to fairy material, to folk-lore, whence certainly came suggestions for the elements and appurtenances of the admirably presented episode of the night in the castle.

SIR GOWTHER [96], is in the fifteenth-century MSS. Advocates' Libr. Edbg. 19, 3, 1, and Royal 17 B XLIII. It was composed in the North-East Midland or the North at about 1400 or shortly thereafter, and consists of 757 verses in twelve-line tail-rime aabccbddbeeb. The number of unstressed syllables is very irregular.

After over ten years of wedded life, a duke in Estryke is childless. The Duke regretfully declares he must marry again in order to have an heir. The lady prays for a child begotten in any manner whatever. A fiend in a form very like her lord possesses her in her garden, and then, assuming his proper shape, announces that the youth born of the union shall be wild and a powerful wielder of weapons. Cleverly the lady brings it about that her lord seems father of the child. When the boy is born he is christened 'Gowther.' He kills nine wet-nurses, and injures his mother, and grows with great rapidity. He is wicked in every fashion, and so strong that he cannot be punished. The Duke makes him a knight, but dies of grief because of his evil nature. The mother flees with the boy to an out-of-the-way castle. Gowther harasses

all the neighborhood; he kills men and horses on the high roads,
strikes down priests, prevents religious services, enters a nunnery
and defiles the nuns and burns all together, and ravishes wives and
maids. One day, an old earl faces him, and accuses him of being
a fiend's son. Gowther is shocked. He wrings from his mother
the truth of his birth. Remorseful, he goes to Rome, and accepts
the Pope's penance that, until he receives from God assurance of
forgiveness, he shall eat only food from a hound's mouth, and
shall speak no word. Gowther travels to Almeyn. There, to the
wonder of the court, he eats under the high table food that he
wrests from the hounds. The knights style him 'the Fool.' The
Emperor has a single child, a daughter, who is dumb. A sultan
demands her in marriage. The lady is refused, and war ensues.
In response to Gowther's prayers, on three successive days he is
given arms, black, red, and white; and, to the relief of the Emper-
or's forces and the joy of the lady, who loves him, each day he
defeats the enemy. Only the lady knows that the strange champion
is the fool. But at the end of the third day Gowther is severely
wounded. The lady faints at the sight, and falls from her tower.
All suppose her dead. The Pope and the cardinals are assembled
for the funeral, when she arises and speaks, declaring to Gowther
that God forgives him. Gowther and the lady are wedded; Gowther
returns to Estryke, gives the old Earl all his property there, and
marries him to his mother. He founds an abbey and convent in
further reparation for the evil he has done. He becomes Emperor
of Germany, and at his death a corsaint. At his tomb miraculous
cures are wrought.

As the prologue suggests, the birth of Gowther is to be connected with that of Merlin. The Breton lay to which the
author alludes is probably the *Lay of Tydorel*. The poem
belongs to a large group of pieces in various languages generally designated as the *Legend of Robert the Devil*, already
extensively developed in the thirteenth century. It apparently
has no historical foundation, but is a making over of two folk-
lore strains; first, the 'Kinder-Wunsch' theme, according to
which a child long desired is begotten by supernatural means,
ultimately discovers the fact of his parentage, and, by his own
power or by the aid of the Virgin, frees himself from the forces
of evil; and, second, the 'male Cinderella' theme, according to
which the youth lives long at a ruler's court as a beggar or a
scullion, and finally, still disguised, saves the realm in war, and
is wedded to the princess. It has been urged that the priests
of the Middle Ages, found and made of the story an embodi-

ment of the problem of sin and forgiveness; and presented in the first part an extreme case of evil-doing, and in the second the adequate expiation for it. If this be so, it must be admitted that all through *Sir Gowther* the hero has the advantage of the situation. The ecclesiastical handling is obvious throughout the piece. But the ill deeds of Gowther are told with a certain satisfaction in his thorough viciousness, that is equaled only by the gusto with which is related his eating with the dogs to the delight and scorn of the court, and by the gratification with which are narrated the blessings that the saint bestows after death on pilgrims to his tomb. Attempts at doctrine and popularization go hand in hand. Again one is led to think of the influence of ecclesiastical handling in transferring in the direction of the Saint's Life myth and legend of whatever type. The three battles in black, red, and white armor, connect the tale with the Three Days' Tournament theme represented in *Ipomadon* (see page 146).

It is to be noted that at about 1510 Wynkyn de Worde printed a later English prose version of the legend, 'The Lyfe of the most Myscheuoust Robert the Deuyll whiche was afterwarde called the Seruaunt of God.' A metrical version of this prose was made in the sixteenth century. A prose romance by Thomas Lodge was printed in 1591.

THE EARL OF TOULOUS [97] is in MSS. Cbg. Univ. Libr. Ff II 38 (15th century), Ashmole 45 (15th century) and 61 (16th century), and Thornton (1430-1440). It dates from the first of the fifteenth century and the Northern East Midland, and in the most complete MS., Ashmole 45, consists of 1224 verses in twelve-line tail-rime aabccbddbeeb. It exhibits much alliteration.

The Emperor of Almayne wrongfully seizes property of Barnard, Earl of Toulous, and, despite his wife's protests and warnings, attempts to defend the wrong. The Earl defeats him with heavy loss. From Sir Tralabas, one of his captives and a favorite of the Emperor, Barnard hears of the great beauty of the Empress. He offers Tralabas his ransom and gifts, if he will enable him to see the lady. Tralabas takes him to the city, and there betrays him to the Empress. She bids Tralabas keep faith and bring the

Earl to the chapel next day. She carefully shows herself, so that Barnard who is clad as a hermit may view her fully, and has given him money and a ring. Full of love and hope, the Earl rejoices in the ring. Tralabas and two others attack him on the way home. Barnard slays all three, and reaches his castle in safety. Two knights successively fail to seduce the Empress. They induce a youth to hide in her chamber. Then they burst in, and kill the young knight. When he learns of his wife's supposed unfaithfulness, which confirms a dream that he has had, the Emperor attempts suicide. A council finds the lady guilty, but grants her trial by champion. With a merchant, who assures him of the Empress' innocence, Barnard goes to Almayne. They stay with an abbot, the lady's confessor, who declares the lady pure, though she has made innocent gift of a ring to the Earl of Toulous. On the day of ordeal, dressed as a monk, Barnard receives the Empress' confession of innocence and of the gift of the ring. He defeats the evil knights, who are burned at the stake. The abbot obtains safe conduct for the Earl, and reveals his identity. Reconciliation follows. Barnard serves as steward to the Emperor. On his lord's death, he succeeds to the throne, and weds the lady.

The poem states that 'this gest' is 'Chronycled' in Rome and is a 'lay of Bretayn.' It seems to be a combination of a lay and a modified account of a Barnard, Count of Toulouse, who at about 830 was accused of relations with the Empress Judith, wife of Louis le Débonnair.

The piece has, apparently, a central purpose: that of enforcing, through the behavior of the heroine, the duty of keeping faith in wedlock and in word given; and, in the fates of Tralabas and the two false accusers, and the discomfiture of the Emperor in his wrongful war, the sinfulness and the punishment of unjust and evil conduct. These points are stressed in the speech of the lady, who, though she is beautiful and virtuous, is somewhat too didactic. The piece has not high literary worth. Its great interest is in its exemplification of the intermingling of folk-lore, legend, and actual history, that existed in both romantic and pseudo-historical accounts of the Middle Ages.

10. Miscellaneous Romances

To avoid undesirable classification as major groups, a number of romances shall be dealt with as 'Miscellaneous Romances.' These may be grouped, however, as follows: I. *Romances of*

Greek or Byzantine Origin; II. *Composites of Courtly Romance;* III. *Romances on Historical Themes;* IV. *Romances from Family Tradition;* V. *Legendary Romances of Didactic Intent.*

I.   Romances of Greek or Byzantine Origin

At an early date Late-Greek and Byzantine literature had come to the knowledge of the French and the English.   Through the Crusades—now, as whole tales ; again, as single incidents or episodes—it was transmitted into the Western vernaculars by oral tradition or by Latin versions.   So, in the history of Western romances it played a considerable part, influencing not only plot, but also style, form, and attitude.   Before the Norman Conquest a Latin version of the tale of *Apollonius of Tyre* was translated into Old English prose, a portion of which survives.   *Partonope of Blois,* in both the French and the English versions (see page 144), shows possible influence of the Byzantine *Cupid and Psyche.*   In *William of Palerne* have been seen Late-Greek elements (see page 19).   But the special Middle English representative of Byzantine influence in our period, is *Floris and Blauncheflur.*

APOLLONIUS OF TYRE [98], reprobated by Chaucer in the head-link to his *Man of Law's Tale,* was chosen by Gower for the concluding story of his *Confessio Amantis* in illustration of unlawful love.   His version was based on Godfrey of Viterbo's *Pantheon,* which was here derived from the eleventh-century Latin prose *Apollonii Tyrii Historia.*   The story is extant in several MSS. of an English version of the *Gesta Romanorum* of the reign of Henry VI.   In 1510 de Worde printed the English *Chronicle of Apolyn of Tyre,* translated from a French prose romance.   Shakespeare drew on Gower's story for his *Pericles of Tyre.*

FLORIS AND BLAUNCHEFLUR [99], in verses of three or four stresses in short couplets, was composed at about 1250 in the East Midland, farther north than *King Horn.*   It is preserved in the Duke of Sutherland's MS. (now Egerton 2862; end of 14th century) in 1083 lines, MS. Cotton Vitellius D III in 451 lines (180 imperfect; 1250-1300), MS. Auchinleck (1330-1340) in 861 lines, MS. Cbg. Univ. Libr. Gg 4, 27, 2 (1250-1275 or 1250-1300; 824 lines, beginning with l. 373 of Egerton and l. 1001 of the French). The beginning of the poem is missing in each MS. Hausknecht's critical text comprises 1296 verses.

The children, Floris, son of the King of Spain, and Blauncheflur, a captive maiden, love each other so dearly that they are inseparable. Fearing possible marriage in the future, his parents send Floris away for a time; then, learning of his grief, they sell the maiden to merchants of Babylon for a great sum of money and a golden cup. Blauncheflur is sold to the Sultan of Babylon, into whose harem she is put as his prospective Queen. The parents of Floris erect a tomb marked with Blauncheflur's name. On his return, Floris is so grief-stricken that he attempts suicide. Fearful for their only surviving child, the parents reveal the truth, and equip the youth to go in quest of Blauncheflur. At Babylon, the lover learns that the maiden is held in an inaccessible tower. By advice of a bridge-warden, through losing money and giving gifts to the porter, he is conveyed into the tower in a basket of flowers. There he is ultimately united to Blauncheflur. The lovers are found sleeping together. They are ordered to be burned. But the unwillingness of either to survive the other through aid of a magic ring that preserves from death, and their rivalry as to which shall die first, along with their beauty and their pathetic story, win their pardon. The Sultan knights Floris. The lovers are married. The Sultan takes as his Queen, Clarice, the friend of Blauncheflur. The King of Spain dies; and the lovers, to the regret of the Sultan, go to rule their home country.

In two general versions, probably first developed in the East—one in its original form, and the other in an adaptation for the more common folk—the story spread over all Western Europe, from the extreme South to the far North. In France, the original version took two forms—the 'aristocratic version,' developed for a select audience, and the 'popular version,' composed for the lower orders. The former emphasizes the effeminate, the amorous, the sentimental, the decorative; the latter neglects sentiment, cares little for description, and presents Floris as a hero of physical prowess winning his lady by force of arms.

The English piece is one of the most charming of the extant English romances. It lacks the characteristics of the 'popular' French version. Close parallels with the texts preserved show that the writer followed very closely, and frequently translated word for word, the main elements of some lost French original of the 'aristocratic' type, antecedent to any text now extant. But this poem has probably but two-fifths the length of the French pieces. With English feeling, for an English audience, the author qualified the sentiment of his original; he condensed the descriptive matter—such as the accounts of the cup, the garden by the harem, the flowers, and the equipment of Floris; and he omitted nonessential decorative pieces, such as the French account of the hero's knife. The tale is not of passion, but of tender, gentle, devoted love. There are no combats, there is no villain. Love and beauty win their way over all obstacles. The parents yield; the not unrighteously enraged Sultan gives way in face of the devotion and beauty of the children, and, contrary to his previous notions, makes a permanent marriage. The piece rests on the charming presentation of the essential need of the children for each other: love is all in all; there is nothing without the loved one.

II.   Composites of Courtly Romance

A few English romances, all of late origin, are in great part artificial composites of elements derived from sophisticated courtly romances. These pieces are *Sir Degrevant, Generydes, Parthenope of Blois, Ipomadon,* and the *Squyr of Lowe Degre.*

SIR DEGREVANT [100], in MSS. Thornton (1430-1440) and Cbg. Univ. Libr. Ff I 6 (15th century), composed in the North in 1350-1400, consists of 1904 verses in sixteen-line tail-rime aaabcccbdddbeeeb.

Degrevant of the Table Round has vast estates, and is famed for prowess, music, hunting, almsdeeds, and aid of the unfortunate. While he is in the Holy Land, a neighbor earl kills his game, injures his tenants, and spoils his estates. Degrevant returns, repairs the damages, and sends to ask reparation. The Earl

threatens farther injury. Degrevant assembles forces. With a
host, the Earl slays many deer on the Knight's estate. The hero
and his band come upon the thieves with the deer stretched on the
ground. The Earl's men are slain, and their leader barely escapes.
Degrevant and twelve other knights take position at the Earl's
gates, and vainly challenge him and his men to joust. The Countess
appears on the walls with her daughter, Melydore, and protests
to Degrevant. The hero falls in love with the maiden. With his
squire, he enters the castle through a postern, and has an interview with Melydore. The lady threatens the hero with death, but
permits her maid to entertain him for the night. At a joust, the
hero overthrows the Duke of Gerle who pretends to Melydore's
hand. Later, he enters the hall of the castle and challenges for
the lady. Again he vanquishes the Duke, who goes home. Through
the maid, he is received by Melydore in her gorgeous 'chamber of
love,' and feasted magnificently. The lady confesses she loved
him at first sight. For long Degrevant visits her nightly. At last
he is detected and ambushed; but he kills or puts to flight all his
opponents. The Countess persuades the Earl to grant the hero
his daughter. The lovers live together for thirty years, and have
seven children. After Melydore's death, Degrevant goes to the
Holy Land. There he is slain.

The first part of the poem reminds of the *Hunting of the
Cheviot*. The verse is poor, exigencies of rime lead to obscurity and to use of forced meanings. There is much conversation. The whole is highly sophisticated and artificial. The
writer has an eye for color and show, and runs to the decadent
elaboration of details, especially of physical appearance and
ornament. His hero kisses the lady ardently thirty times;
then, chairs are brought with sweet cushions, and the lovers sit
down to converse. There is lengthy minute description of
details of the dress of Melydore on her first appearance, of the
rich paintings and embroidery and jewel-work of her chamber
and of its furnishings, of the table-fittings, and of the dainties
on which the lovers feast. 'Courtly' modes prevail. The lovers
are enamored at first sight. The lady pretends hatred of the
knight, and yields only after he has done great deeds for her
sake. The knight is all devotion, most subject, most punctiliously polite and considerate. He carefully conceals from the
loved one his feats of prowess. Great stress is laid on the
influence of 'love paramour' on knightly valor.

GENERYDES [101] is preserved in two English versions, both probably of about 1430, though perhaps of later date. One is in 5043 short couplets in the Helmingham MS. (1400-1450), the other consists of 6995 verses in rime-royal in MS. Trinity College Cbg. Gale O, 5, 2 (15th century, perhaps c. 1440). A few fragments of a sixteenth-century print are extant. In all essentials of matter the two texts agree, though they differ in some minor details, especially the names. The story is generally admitted to be from a French original, though no such piece has been discovered. The Helmingham version, of which a synopsis follows, states that it was translated from Latin into French.

The wife of Aufreus of Ynde is unfaithful to him. On a magic stag-hunt, he begets on the Princess of Surre a child, Generydes. The boy is educated by his mother. He goes to Aufreus' court, and is beaten by the paramour of the Queen. Too young to have vengeance, he retires to the court of the Sultan of Perse. There is kindly received, and he and the Princess Clarionas fall in love at first sight. By envy of a knight, Malachias, Generydes is caught at the lady's window. He is sentenced to be hanged. Bellyns, King of Kings, summons the Sultan to pay tribute, and demands his daughter as concubine. Generydes is accepted as champion. After two great battles, Bellyns is beaten in a duel with the hero, and dies on his way home. Aufreus' wife betrays herself and the castle to her paramour. Aufreus flees to Tharse, of which he ultimately becomes King. Here he marries the mother of Generydes. Bellyn's son, Gwynan, has Clarionas abducted and conveyed to Egypt. He is about to marry her, when Generydes appears in the guise of a leper, and rescues her. Leaving the lady with her father, the hero goes to aid Aufreus to regain Ynde. A battle is fought, and a truce is declared. Generydes defeats Gwynan, who has invaded Perse. Aufreus' first wife persuades each of the lovers, Clarionas and Generydes, that the other has married. Her scheme is foiled by Clarionas' confidante. Generydes defeats the usurper of Ynde, who dies with his paramour. Generydes succeeds his parents in Ynde, and weds his lady. On the Sultan's death, he assumes his throne.

The rime-royal version is by much the more condensed. In verse it is inferior to the other version. But its incidents are presented effectively. Its language shows apparent Chaucerian influence.

In *Generydes* two lines of story are carried on and finally

united, one of the father, the other of the son. The story seems
to be a composite of various elements borrowed from earlier
romances, some of the principal features being derived, probably, from the East, especially Persia. So it affords great
variety. There are Saracen villains, adulterers, Christian
traitors, the coming of an unknown youth to court, love at first
sight, secret meetings, a betrayal, imprisonment of the hero,
an abduction, a rescue in disguise, a misunderstanding between
the lovers, several tremendous battles, a duel, and many other
attractive features. The stories are well told. The battle
matter is made much of in the English pieces, and apparently
was a cherished feature of the original. Especially prominent
in the couplet version is the begetting of the hero, when the
King pursues the hart, and ultimately comes to the fair place
with ivory work, where dwell the wonderful lady with the
jeweled gates and jeweled chamber, and the strange old man
who is one of the Seven Sages. The episode is comparatively
flat in the rime-royal.

PARTHENOPE OF BLOIS [102] is preserved in two fifteenth-century English versions. The first, in couplets composed in the Southern dialect, is in MS. Br. Mus. Additional
35288 (late 15th century, in three hands), 12195 verses; MS.
University College Oxford C 188 (c. 1450), in 7257 verses
(actually 7096 verses) with a number of gaps, and with the
beginning and the end missing; MS. Bodley Engl. Poetry C 3 ff.
6-7 (formerly the property of New College, Oxford; 15th
century), a fragment of 162 lines (now 158 lines), a piece
from the binding of a book, that helps to fill up the missing
end of the University College text; MS. Rawlinson Poetry 14
(1450-1500), in about 6280 verses, imperfect but supplying
many deficiencies in the University College MS.; and a fragment of about 200 verses in Lord Robart's MS. (15th century).
The second version, in quatrains abab of four-stress verses, is
represented in a fragment of 308 lines in the MS. (c. 1450)
of Lord Delamere at Vale Royal. The first version is very
long, and its details are multitudinous. It is from a French
treatment of the story that is represented in the extant

Partonopeus de Blois. Only a brief general synopsis of this version may be given here.

Parthenope, hunting, is borne on an enchanted boat to a city. There he enters a magnificent palace. The lady Melior informs him that she has visited France, and has judged of him. He shall be her lover. She must be unseen by him and by all men for two and a half years; then she will wed him. Meanwhile, she will visit him every night, and he shall have possessions and luxuries of all sorts. If he seeks to see her, he shall be dead and she disgraced. For a year he abides in the magic palace; then he is borne, splendidly equipped, to Blois. His father is dead. The hero is a second Hector against the Saracens who have invaded France. As he is fighting a duel with the Saracen King, he is borne off a captive. The pagan King becomes hostage for Parthenope, who is ultimately released. Parthenope tells his mother about Melior. By a magic potion, the mother makes the hero love the niece of the King of France. After betrothal the Knight recovers in terrible remorse. Ultimately, he is conveyed to Melior's castle. He confesses, and is held blameless. He returns to Blois to help the King and his mother against their enemies. The Bishop of Paris vainly preaches to him on his relations with Melior, and is instructed by the hero in Christian courtesy and bounty. By his mother's persuasion, Parthenope goes to Melior, and turns the light of a lamp on her. Melior reveals that their love-affair has been carried on by magic in the midst of her court. The morning makes her disgrace public. Urak, sister to Melior, enables the Knight to escape. Parthenope, in the depths of remorse, goes to the forest of Ardennes, in the hope of being devoured by beasts. Urak finds him, and bears him to Solence, an island of delights. There he recovers. Urak and another maiden fall in love with him. Urak and Melior arrange that Parthenope fight in a three days' joust for the hand of Melior. Parthenope is blown to sea in a boat, and is driven to an island where he is imprisoned by a tyrant, Armaunt. Armaunt goes to the jousts; his lady permits Parthenope also to go, on agreement that he return afterward. Parthenope fights valiantly, and is adjudged one of the six best contestants. Ultimately, after a variety of experiences, the story comes to a happy end.

The second piece is a fragment, evidently of a very condensed version. It extends to the end of Melior's statement of the conditions on which she will be the hero's lover. To this are added, without a break, thirty-two lines that deal with an utterly different part of the story. This version varies considerably from the longer piece.

Possibly, the earlier relations of Parthenope and Melior were affected by those of the Late-Greek story of Cupid and Psyche; but, probably, the matter is a development of a story of relations between a mortal and a fairy, such as are suggested in *Chevalere Assigne*. One wishes that the author had kept to, and made still more of, this earlier material. The writer of the fuller English romance follows his original rather closely; but he has cut down the descriptive matter somewhat, and several times he indicates that the original goes quite too much into detail. Yet the piece is tremendously long and tedious and slow. It is full of minor elements that are of no avail. Practically every episode is related mainly by direct discourse in long inconsequential speeches and conversations and meditations and discussions, that try the soul of the reader. Scarcely any incident or situation is let go by without remarks on it by the personages. Even in the best part of the piece, that of the early relations of the lovers, the lady delivers to the knight counsel that, however admirable it be, certainly indicates over-fondness for didactic effect. The dull love-casuistry enters more after the middle of the poem. Of interest are a number of passages where the author discourses in the first person on some general view of the subject at issue. At each of a number of such places, the poet states that he gives only the gist of the original there; but actually he preserves much of it. At several points he openly disagrees with the original, particularly where he takes up the defense of the truth and the purity of women against the original's repetition of the common mediæval view of woman. Much description is retained. Very remarkable is the passage on the experience of the hero on the strand at the edge of the woods by night (ll. 4181-95).

IPOMADON [103] is extant in three Middle English versions: (A) *Ipomadon*, of the North of Lancashire at about 1350 or earlier, in 8890 verses of twelve-line tail-rime aabccbddbeeb, in MS. Chetham 8009, Manchester (15th century); (B) *The Lyfe of Ipomydon*, of the East Midland at the beginning of the fifteenth century, in 2343 four-stress verses in couplets, in MS. Harley 2252 (late 15th century); and (C) *Ipomedon*, in prose, composed in a dialect not yet determined,

in the Marquis of Bath's MS. 25 (MS. end of 14th or beginning of 15th century), where the dialect is very much mixed.

Ipomadon, after preliminary exposition, proceeds as follows:

The daughter of the Duke of Calabria will wed only the most
capable knight in the world. Ipomadon, son of the King of Apulia,
is educated under the master Tholomeus. Enamored, the youth
conceals his birth, and acts as cupbearer to the lady. He devotes
himself to hunting and not to arms. The lady loves him; but,
to prevent the inevitable revelation of passion, chides her relative,
Jason, the friend of Ipomadon. So she inspires the hero with a
desire for glory and arms. He goes to Apulia, is knighted, and
wins fame in many lands. Her nobles insist that his lady marry.
She delays long, but finally declares a three days' tournament
for her hand. Hearing of this, and desiring to be unknown.
Ipomadon goes to Sicily, obtains from his uncle, Meleager, permission to act as Platonic servant of his Queen, and devotes himself to that service and to hunting. On each of the three days of
the tournament, he departs early, fights all day, returns in the
evening with the spoils of a hunt that Tholomeus has conducted,
and is mocked as a coward and fool. The Queen, who really loves
him, is much distressed; but she finally sees the truth. On each
of the three days, in white, in red, in black, Ipomadon wins the
jousts. Each day at the end of the contests, he gets word to his
lady of his identity. Other refinements of confusion for the lady,
are invented. After the tournament, Ipomadon departs from his
uncle's court with Tholomeus and his maiden cousin. The Queen
accuses him of abducting the maiden. He overthrows the seneschal
who pursues him. His father being dead, the hero becomes King
of Apulia. He renders subject the brother of the King of France,
and promises to marry his daughter. But he slips away, and
learns that his princess is besieged by a hideous Indian, Lyolyne,
who shall have her as wife if a champion does not appear within
a month. Unwilling, as usual, to be known, the hero plays the
fool at Maleager's court, but obtains grant of the first adventure
that shall befall. The princess' confidante, Imayne, requests a
champion, and is given the foolish Knight. She is disgusted; but,
after the hero has saved her from emissaries of Lyolyne, she falls
in love with him. She vainly pleads her passion. Near the castle,
the Knight sends her forward to represent him as a foolish
incompetent. The princess is hopeless. She arranges to flee with
a fleet, if Lyolyne slays the fool. Ipomadon dresses in Lyolyne's
favorite color, black. He drives the Indian to his vessel, where he
dies. The hero makes it appear, through his black armor, that he
is Lyolyne. The princess takes refuge on her fleet. Capaneus,
heir of Meleager, who has been active all through the story, appears
as champion against the supposed Lyolyne. A terrible duel ensues.

Ipomadon's head is exposed. Capaneus recognizes him, and declares he is his brother. The lovers are united, and the various persons are rewarded.

Nothing but a careful reading of the romance itself can give a proper notion of its contents or of its nature. The personages are numerous; the incidents and the details of the incidents are innumerable and minutely complicated. The motives are various. Hue de Rotelande, the author of the French original, *Ipomedon*, which the text attempts to follow more faithfully than is usual in Middle English romances, apparently looked up effective elements and made an elaborate composite of those that appeared most striking. The localities are unusual, Calabria, Sicily, Apulia; the names are largely borrowed from classical sources. Notable among the themes are those of the three days' tournament in armor of varying colors, the fair unknown, and the court fool. The piece is interesting. It is full of action. Much of each episode is made up of direct discourse. Though this sometimes makes the matter tedious, the dialogue is commonly, like most of the constituents of the piece, mature, formed, sophisticated. It is direct and natural, and commonly consists of rapid interchange of speeches each of a line or part of line without narrative connection. Here are found more extensively than anywhere else in Middle English romance, analysis of feeling, elaborate introspection, and lengthy soliloquy or lamentation expressive of subtle conflicting emotions at crises. Subtleties of sentiment and *finesse* of behavior, are at the basis and on the surface of most of the poem. Though it is so close to its original, and because it is so close to its original, which is a representative 'secondary romance' of the French, the poem is one of the most notable romances of Middle English. Unfortunately, the writer chose the tail-rime instead of the couplet that is employed in the second English poetical version.

The Lyfe of Ipomydon is a greatly condensed version of the ten thousand lines of the French, apparently produced from memory. The general story follows closely the episodes in *Ipomadon* in the order they have in that piece. As is usual with English translators of romances, the writer practically eliminates the sentiment and the introspection, and cuts down the conversation to slight proportion. The piece is vigorous and rapid. Though greatly inferior to *Ipomadon*, it is, as compared with that poem, much more interesting and admirable than several critics have judged it to be. The once suggested ascription of the *Lyfe* to the author of *Le Morte Arthur*, seems not acceptable.

The prose *Ipomedon* is in matter closer to *Ipomadon* than to the *Lyfe*. As was *Ipomadon*, it was probably written from a manuscript. It consists of about 1700 lines in print, cut down much on the general principles of the writer of the *Lyfe*; but it introduces some slight additions for expansion of details and for closer motivation.

THE SQUYR OF LOWE DEGRE [104], composed in short couplets at about 1450 and probably in the East Midland, is preserved in Copland's edition of about 1555-1560 in 1132 verses, and in two fragments (180 verses, corresponding to Copland's lines 1-60, 301-420) of an edition by de Worde of about 1520, in the possession of Mrs. Christie-Miller of Burnham, Buckinghamshire. In the Percy Folio MS. ff. 444-46, there is a short version of 170 lines in short couplets, styled *The Squier*. In general, the incidents of the Copland and Percy versions are substantially the same, though the Copland is almost seven times as long as the Percy. It is conjectured that both versions go back to a lost metrical version based on the lost original piece.

A squire of low degree in the service of the King of Hungary, loves his master's daughter. The lady overhears his lamenting beneath her window, and comforts him, accepts his love, and directs him as to his deportment in the seven years of trial that she imposes on him. A steward in love with the lady overhears the conversation, and reports it to the King. The latter declares his confidence in the Squire, but gives his men permission to capture him if he attempts to enter the lady's chamber. The Squire obtains permission to go abroad to gain glory. But he returns by night to say farewell to the lady. Perceiving the watchers in ambush, he cries to the lady to open the door. When the princess recognizes him, she holds a long colloquy with him without letting him in. Attacked, the youth slays the steward and several men. The body of the steward is disfigured and clad in the Squire's clothes. The lady finds the body, and, supposing that it is her lover's, embalms it and keeps it at her bed's head throughout seven years. The Squire is imprisoned; but the King visits him, and, under pledge of secrecy, gives him permission to go abroad for seven years, with promise of the lady and the realm when he returns. The time expires; the Squire returns. The steward's body is dust, and the lady is about to become a nun. Satisfied with her constancy, the King tells her the truth; and the lovers are married.

The motives of the lovers of unlike rank, and of the woman faithful during many years, were common. Study has shown that the poem is composed largely of elements employed in many other romances. Close similarities to the story of the *Emperor Polemus* in the *Gesta Romanorum* and to the *Knight of Curtesy* have been shown; still greater resemblances to *Guy of Warwick* indicate that perhaps the *Squyr* was modeled somewhat on the B version of *Guy*. The plot has little or no novelty. The behavior of the personages is singularly accommodating. Incident is cut down to the lowest minimum. There is the least possible action. The author develops little the emotional possibilities of the crises in the story. Little is made of the characters of the persons. The piece gives the impression of existing for the insupportably lengthy discourse in which the persons indulge at every turn, and for the numerous descriptive catalogues of foods and drinks, musical instruments, armor, birds, plants, and the like, that are introduced on the slightest occasion. Yet the elaborateness of some of these passages affords valuable glimpses of conditions of life and manners in the middle of the fifteenth century.

III. Romances on Historical Themes

Several English pieces are romance treatments of historical themes. These are *Richard Coer de Lyon, Titus and Vespasian* or *The Siege of Jerusalem,* and Barbour's *Bruce.* Because of its effort at historical accuracy, the *Bruce* is discussed with the Chronicles (see page 202).

RICHARD COER DE LYON [105] is in MSS. Auchinleck (1330-1340; fragments), Duke of Sutherland (now Egerton

2862; end of 14th century; 44 leaves), Br. Mus. Additional
31042 (15th century; 6380 verses), Harley 4690 (15th century; fragment of 1608 verses), Douce 228 (a fragment; late
15th century), College of Arms LVIII (H D N 58; 1400-
1450), and Caius College Cbg. 175 (1350-1400; the most complete and best; 3568 short couplets). The piece is probably
of the reign of Edward I, and Kentish.

Seeking the most beautiful lady in the world for King Henry
of England, messengers meet a vessel bearing the daughter of the
King of Antioch mysteriously bound to satisfy their very quest. The
Queen cannot endure the presence of the Host at Mass. She bears
Richard, John, and a daughter. One day, Henry permits her to
be prevented from leaving the church at the Elevation of the Host.
She flies up the through the roof, dropping John (whose leg is
injured), and bearing off her daughter. Richard succeeds Henry.
To test his knights, he jousts with them at a tournament, disguised successively in black, red, and white armor. With the
best two, Sir Thomas Multon and Sir Fulk Doyly, in pilgrim's
guise he visits and studies the Holy Land. He is imprisoned by
the Emperor of Germany, has intercourse with the Emperor's
daughter and kills his son, tears out the heart of a lion sent to
devour him, and finally is ransomed with half the wealth of England. With an army, he sets off on the Crusade preached by
Urban. He is unfavorably received on the Continent. He resumes
relations with the German princess, who reconciles him with her
father on agreement of return of the ransom. At Messina, the
King of France tries traitorously to arouse hostility to him.
Finally, the two kings are reconciled. After many losses, Richard
reaches Cyprus. The German Emperor abuses his messengers,
and cuts off the nose of his own steward because he protests against
his lack of courtesy. The steward betrays the daughter and the
treasure and many knights, into Richard's hands. Richard defeats
and imprisons the Emperor. After adventures at Acre, he learns
of the terrible losses of the Christians there. He is ill, and longs
for pork. A Saracen's head is boiled, and he is fed on it. Strength-
ened, he kills a host of Saracens. When he learns of the true
nature of his 'pork,' he laughs heartily and remarks that the Christians need not starve as long as a Saracen is left. Acre yields.
A great battle ensues. Saladin sends messengers to Richard, who,
to intimidate them, has served for dinner the heads of their friends
executed for the purpose, each head being labeled with its former
owner's name. The King dines heartily on the head set before him.
Saladin offers to bribe Richard to renounce his faith. The Christian
hero will have none of it. When the pagans refuse to give up the
Cross, he slays all his prisoners except twenty reserved to tell the
news. So ends Part I.

Part II opens with a lyrical May passage reminding of those in *Arthour and Merlin* (see page 43) and *Kyng Alisaunder* (see page 102). The allied armies proceed with the war. The French King, Philip, spares several cities for money. Richard and Multon take their cities, and for treason slay all the inhabitants. Doyly takes Ebedy. Richard abuses Philip for sparing the cities, and himself goes and executes all their inhabitants. He gains great victories at Caiphas and the city of Palestine and Arsour. Nineveh is surrendered after a combat of three against three, and all its people are baptized. The English and the French besiege Babylon. By heavenly direction, Richard is enabled to slay hosts of pagans with a magic steed given him by Saladin. The city is taken, and the forces proceed to Jerusalem. Philip quarrels with Richard, falls ill, and, by medical advice, goes home. After a dispute, the Duke of Austria and his forces depart. Richard takes many cities. Word coming of John's rebellion, Richard decides to return to England; but first he conquers many more cities. Henry of Champagne flees at sight of a great pagan host. After capturing Jaffa and winning another battle, Richard obtains a three years' truce with Saladin, and sails for England. The author states in four lines that Richard reigned in England for ten years; he was shot in Castel-Gaylard.

The piece is probably, as it itself asserts a number of times, a translation from the French. The original is lost; strong opposition has been offered to the judgment that it was a compilation from the *Itinerarium Peregrinorum et Gesta Regis Ricardi* as chief source, with use of Roger of Hovenden, Ricardus Divisienis, Walter of Hemingburgh, John of Brompton, and others. The story is a well-unified combination of historical and romantic materials; the chronicle matter can be seen here and there in the definite statement of minute detail of equipment and of siege operations, and in the consistent regard for geography in the progress from incident to incident. To increase interest, and to avoid breaking the sequence of narrative, the author put the captivity of his hero before the Crusade. The Crusade affords the chief incidents; there is no account of the youth of Richard; the pilgrimage to the East is cut short; the history of the hero after the Crusade is disposed of in four lines. Yet the real theme is the marvelous personality of Richard. The author, like his King, is much more interested in fighting than in Christianity. The poem is an account of brute violence, and of the triumph of physical force. The writer tells with special gusto of Richard's eating of the Saracens' heads, and of the cutting off of the steward's nose right down to the gristle. Richard is superhuman, almost demoniac. The pagans cannot stand against him; they are merely for slaughter. To account for his nature, his mother is represented as supernatural, just as to other heroes like Lancelot was given similar parentage to account for their high prowess. To be noted are the use of magic in the case of the Devil transformed into a horse (l. 5490), and in the appearance twice of angels as directors (ll. 5308, 6886), and once of St. George fighting for the hero's forces. In view of the probable French original, of importance is the English view exhibited in the careful presentation of the French King and the King of Champagne as cowards and takers of bribes, and in the author's deliberate lengthy utterance (ll. 3821-37) damning the French as a nation of braggarts and cowards and covetous rascals. The piece is spirited, and proceeds with speed and directness. The central interest, the character and personality of the hero, is well preserved; Richard stands out admirably distinct. On the basis of similarity of manner, this poem, *Arthour and Merlin,* and *Kyng Alisaunder* have been ascribed to one author. While many scholars favor assignment of the last two pieces to one writer, the ascription of *Richard* also to him seems very questionable.

TITUS AND VESPASIAN or THE DESTRUCTION OF JERUSALEM [106], of which at least ten French MSS. are preserved, is extant in two Middle English versions, one in short couplets and one in alliterative verses.

The Bataile of Jerusalem or *The Vengeaunce of Goddes Deth* or *The Sege of Jerusalem,* are the titles given the couplet version in the MSS. It is in MSS. Br. Mus. Additional 10036 f. 2 (15th century), 1420 lines, imperfect at the beginning; Laud 622 (c. 1400); Douce 78 (1450-1475); Digby 230 (15th century); Magdalene College Cbg. Pepys 37 (new number 2014; see below), 3114 verses, the preceding 812 verses missing; Harley 4733 (15th century); Douce 126 (1400-1450), a fragment. A critical text would make up a total of 5770 verses. The Pepys text has been printed under the confusing title *Vindicta Salvatoris*. The couplet version is claimed to be quite independent of the alliterative version, and has been said to be of the vicinity of London at about 1375-1400. The Pepys MS. has been assigned to about 1300, but Mr. M. R. James has dated it at the beginning of the fifteenth century. The sources of the poem are said to be the French *La Venjance Nostre Seigneur*, the *Gospel of Nicodemus* or the *Gesta* or *Acti Pilati* (see page 326), and the *Legenda Aurea* of Jacobus a Voragine.

The piece opens with a review of the chief incidents of the life of Christ, including the first wrath of the Jews, the Passion, the Resurrection, and the wonders that accompany these last scenes. Then are related the chiding of the Jews by Joseph of Arimathea and Nicodemus, and Joseph's imprisonment and marvelous liberation. Then follows a general declaration of the nature and power of Christ, His murder by the Jews, and the punishment of Pilgrimage, Servitude, and Dispersion, that the Jews shall suffer. Seven years after the Ascension of Christ, Jacob is sent to give the Jews their first warning. He becomes a famous bishop. Day and night he prays for the people. The Jews forbid him to preach, and finally murder him. King Vespasian is terribly afflicted with leprosy. At the time of the Crucifixion, Tiberius was Emperor at Rome. The Jews complained of Pilate, but failed because Pilate sent rich gifts to Titus. On a mission to Nero to pay the tribute, Nathan is asked for advice to cure Vespasian. He relates to Titus, the son of Vespasian, the story of Christ, belief in whom will bring healing. Nathan presents to Nero the tribute and a letter of defense from Pilate blaming the Jews for Christ's death. The story of the birth and the life of Pilate, follows. Velosian tells Vespasian of Nathan's words to Titus. He is sent to Jerusalem to inquire of the cure. From Jacob, a secret Christian, he learns fully of the Passion and the Resurrection. Through Jacob, Veronica is introduced as the savior of Vespasian. Her story and that of her napkin and its powers, are told. Velosian pledges vengeance against the Jews. He takes Veronica to Gascony. Clement, the Pope, is rejoiced. To Vespasian it is explained that if he believe on Christ he shall be whole; and Clement tells of Heaven and Earth and Hell, the Fall, and the Birth and Life and Death and Resurrection of Christ. Vespasian believes, and is healed with the napkin. Titus and Vespasian propose to destroy Jerusalem, and with Nero's permission gather a hundred thousand men and proceed to the Holy Land. They take Jaffa. The Christians flee from Jerusalem. The city is besieged just thirty-four years after the Crucifixion. Pilate defies the Romans. After five

years of siege, Vespasian goes to Rome to be crowned. He returns.
Jacob prophesies the fall of the city, and is imprisoned by Pilate.
His daughter Mary prays for him, and he is freed by an angel.
At his suggestion, a ditch is dug about the city so that no Jews
may escape. After defeat in a sortie, the Jews suffer terrible
famine. ˙ Pilate and the other leaders have magic stones that dispel
hunger. The Jews kill each other, and finally urge Pilate to
capitulate. Jacob calls to the walls Josephus, who is a secret Christian, and informs him that only Christians shall be spared. Josephus
advises Pilate to call an assembly of the people, and learn their
views. They decide to surrender. Josephus escapes to the
besiegers. Pilate attempts vainly to gain time. He is deprived
of the seamless coat of Christ, is imprisoned at Vienna, and finally
commits suicide. Buried in a cask, his body causes much trouble
until a rock swallows it up. Now follows the story of Judas from
birth to death, and an account of the choice of the twelfth Apostle.
Titus and Vespasian destroy Jerusalem. They return to Rome,
where Vespasian and many of his followers are baptized. Clement
is given the Papal power and insignia. Vespasian and his successor, Titus, rule long and do much good.

With the stories of Judas, Pilate, Veronica, the Creation and
Fall to the Resurrection, Joseph of Arimathea, and the Fall of
Jerusalem, should be compared the *Temporale* matter of the
Southern Legendary, especially that of the St. John's College
Cbg. complete *Temporale*, which extends to the end of the fall
of Jerusalem (see page 299).

*Distructio Jerusalem per Vespasianum et Titum, The Sege of
Jerusalem, La Sege de Jerusalem*, and *Distruccio Jerusalem*,
are the titles given the alliterative version respectively in MSS.
Vespasian, Caligula, and Additional. The piece is in MSS
Cotton Caligula A II f. 111 (15th century), 1213 lines, imperfect in the middle; Cotton Vespasian E XVI f. 70 (15th century), the last 147 lines of Passus VI and all of Passus VII, a
total of 362 lines; Laud 656 f. 1 (15th century), 1332 lines;
Br. Mus. Additional 31042 f. 50 (c. 1450), originally about
1300 lines, of which 1224 remain; Cbg. Univ. Libr. Mm V 14 f.
185, 1266 lines; Ashburnham CXXX (end of 14th century);
and Lambeth 491 f. 206 (1400-1450). The piece is probably
more or less from a French version with perhaps direct or
indirect dependence on the Latin paraphrase of Josephus
(*Hegesippus de Excidio Hierusalem*), and on the Latin *Vin-*

dicta Salvatoris. The claim that the Old English legend of St. Veronica is a source of the poem, seems not acceptable.

The piece begins with a brief account of the Passion of Christ. Forty years after the Passion, rage produced by hearing the story from the Greek Nathan, causes Titus, a vassal lord of Nero, to be healed of leprosy. His sick father at Rome is cured by the napkin of Veronica. Titus and Vespasian are baptized; they swear vengeance against the Jews. Nero sends an army under their command to force tribute of the Jews. Jerusalem is besieged. In an open battle, the Romans, who are represented as Christians, capture Caiaphas and other priests, torture them to death, and burn their bodies. The city is hard pressed. Vespasian is elected Emperor, and reluctantly goes to Rome, leaving Titus to represent him. The sufferings of the Jews are terrible. Finally, the city falls, the earth is ploughed up and sowed with salt, and the Jews are sold as slaves, thirty for a penny. Condemned to captivity, Pilate commits suicide. Josephus goes to Rome, and writes of the history and the fall of Jerusalem.

IV. Romances from Family Tradition

MELUSINE and PARTENAY are late English versions of French romances dealing with the family of Lusignan.

Melusine [107] is from a French piece of the same name. In 1387 the Duc de Berri, brother of Charles V of France, commanded his secretary, Jean d'Arras, to compose for the pleasure of the Duchess de Bar the romance of the Fairy Mélusine, the lamia, records of whom were preserved in documents in the castle of Lusignan. Jean's work was probably in Latin; but it was soon turned into French, perhaps by Jean himself. Among the first products of the press, was a French version printed at Geneva in 1478. The English prose *Melusine* (in print, 371 pages) corresponding very closely to this printed text, and probably made from it, is preserved in MS. Royal 18 B II of about 1500.

The Romauns of Parthenay or *Lusignen* [108], in 6615 verses of rime-royal in MS. Trinity College Cbg. R, 3, 17 (late 15th century), is a North Midland English version from before 1500 of a later French handling of the story of *Melusine.* This French treatment was composed by La Coudrette at the request of William, Duke of Partenay, and continued after 1401 at the request of William's successor, John.

The story of *Melusine* takes its title and large interest from the heroine Melusine, one of the daughters of Helmas, Duke of Albany. Helmas broke his vow to his fairy wife, Presine, never to visit her at time of childbirth. His three daughters, Melusine, Melior, and Palestine, all gifted with fairy powers, punish him by shutting him up in a mountain until he dies. The mother causes Melusine every Saturday to become partly a serpent; Melior is exiled to the Sparrow-Hawk Castle in Armenia; Palestine is compelled to guard Helmas' treasure on a mountain in Aragon. The story falls into five parts: 1. (located first in *Melusine,* and near the end in *Partenay*) deals with Helmas and the incidents first mentioned; 2. treats the married life and unhappy end of Melusine; 3. tells of the ten sons of Raymond and Melusine; 4. deals with Melior and Sparrow-Hawk Castle; 5. treats of Palestine and the treasure.

The story has had wide popularity. Tieck composed an excellent modern version of it that still has a sale as a cheap 'volksbuch' in Germany.

THE KNIGHT OF CURTESY AND THE FAIR LADY OF FAGUELL [109], extant in a print by Copland in 1568, but dating perhaps from 1450-1500, may be mentioned here because it is perhaps ultimately based on the story of the love of the Chastellain of Couci and La Dame de Faïel, Gabrielle de Vergi, of the twelfth century. The piece is in 504 four-stress verses abab.

V. Legendary Romances of Didactic Intent

Four romances, *Amis and Amiloun, Sir Amadace, Roberd of Cisyle,* and to a less degree *Sir Cleges,* were written evidently largely for teaching. All depend on supernatural intervention in behalf of a pious hero. *Sir Amadace* and *Sir Cleges* are rather tales than romances; *Roberd of Cisyle* illustrates the close similarity that frequently existed between the Romance and the Saint's Legend.

AMIS AND AMILOUN [110] is preserved in MSS. Auchinleck (1330-1340), Douce 326 (15th century), Harley 2386

(16th century), and a MS. of the Duke of Sutherland (now Egerton 2862; end of 14th century). It is from the end of the thirteenth century, and the northern border of the East Midland. It consists of 2508 verses in twelve-line tail-rime aabaabccbddb.

Amis and Amiloun are the only sons of neighboring barons, and are born on the same day. They are adopted by the Duke of Lombardy, and become notable for beauty, courtesy, and strength. They are to be distinguished from each other only through their clothing. They pledge faithfulness to each other in absolutely all details of life. The Duke knights them, and gives them high office. After much service, Amiloun is forced by the death of his parents to go home to manage his estate. The friends renew their troth, each bearing one of two gold cups that Amiloun has had made as tokens. Amiloun marries. At Court, Amis is watched by an evil steward hostile to the friends. The daughter of the Duke falls in love with Amis. Ultimately, by pleadings and threats, she forces Amis to do her will. The steward sees the lovers together, and reports to the Duke. Amis insists that he is not guilty, and a day is fixed for trial by combat. Conscience-stricken, Amis fears to fight for the wrong. He goes to the land of Amiloun, meets the knight on the way, and obtains his consent to fight in his place. Amis fills the office of Amiloun at home. Amiloun, though warned by a voice from Heaven of punishment by leprosy and poverty, fights and wins the duel. The Duke's daughter is married to Amis, and bears two children. After a time, the Duke dies, and Amis rules in his stead. Amiloun is afflicted with leprosy, is cast out by his wife, and suffers dreadful hardships from poverty and starvation. But he is tenderly cared for by a youth, Owaines or Amoraunt. Ultimately, Amoraunt bears him in a cart to the gates of Amis. There the behavior of Amoraunt causes Amis to send out wine in his token-cup. This Amiloun receives in his own token-cup. The fact is reported to Amis, who, believing that his friend has been slain by the leper, rushes out and beats the sick man. Learning that he is Amiloun, Amis and his wife cherish him in the lady's chamber. Both of the friends are warned from Heaven that, if the leper were bathed in the life-blood of Amis' two children, he would be healed. Agonized but faithful, Amis cuts his children's throats, and recovers Amiloun. He tells his wife, who, though heartbroken, approves of his devotion. When they visit the bodies, they find the children alive and well. The lady of Amiloun marries. The friends with their forces break up the bridal, and shut the lady in a great lodge, where she is fed on bread and water till her death. Amiloun gives his lands to Amoraunt, and lives happily united with Amis.

The story of Amicus and Amelius was one of the most popular tales of the Middle Ages. Latin versions are extant; versions were made in French prose and verse, in Celtic, German, and Norse. In the twelfth century the story was connected with the Charlemagne saga, the friends entering Charles' service, and the steward being a relative of Ganelon. The English version was made probably from a redaction of an Anglo-Norman version. In the English poem war and valor play but a slight and incidental part. The piece is devoted to presentation of the devotion of the friends, their faith to each other and sacrifice for each other. The metre is smooth, but the stanza is spoiled by a tendency to full pause at the end of each tail. The expression contains many stock phrases. The story is told with directness, simplicity, and affecting sympathy. The important incidents are exhibited in forceful climactic scenes, where the narrative yields to natural and impressive dialogue. The love and self-forgetfulness of the friends, and the generosity of the devoted Amoraunt, are so treated as to come home to us to-day. As is frequently the case in mediæval literature, the sympathy of the writer and his stress on the excellence of his heroes, lead to loss of moral distinctions. The steward, though fighting for a rightful cause, is slain by the false representative of the wrong. The evildoers, Amis and his lady, are left unpunished to profit by their false conduct, though an attempt at justice is made in the heaping of afflictions on the agent, Amiloun, and in the need to kill the children. The piece is, of course, rather melodramatic.

SIR AMADACE [111], probably of the North-West of England and 1350-1400, is in MS. Ireland (15th century) at Hale, Lancashire, with the *Awntyrs of Arthur* and the *Avowynge of Arthur*, and also in MS. Auchinleck (1330-1340). Some stanzas are missing in both the MSS. In MS. Ireland the piece consists of 72 twelve-line tail-rime stanzas aabccbddbeeb.

Sir Amadace has spent almost all his property in knightly entertainment of his peers, and in lavish gifts to his inferiors and the poor. Ashamed to remain on his estates in poverty, he mortgages all, gives rich gifts to his acquaintances and servants, and leaves the country with but forty pounds and a small retinue. He comes upon a chapel in which a lady sits grieving by the body of her lord. The body is refused burial, because, having lived a life of largesse as has Sir Amadace, the knight has died owing thirty pounds. Sir Amadace dines with the creditor, and seeks to soften his heart. Failing, he pays him the thirty pounds, and gives his remaining ten pounds to bury the knight. Unable longer to support them, he dismisses his few retainers, giving them their horses. Proceeding on his way dejected, he is met by a knight all in white. The knight commends his conduct, encourages him, and directs him to several wrecked vessels whence he may obtain equipment for suit to a king's daughter who dwells near by. Amadace shall give him a half of all he gains. The hero is favorably received at the King's court, proves himself a gallant jouster, gives the King half the wealth he wins with his lance, and is wedded to the Princess. He lives happily with his wife and child. Ultimately, the white knight appears. He claims as his share not only half the property gained, but half the wife and half the child. Heartbroken, but encouraged by his wife, Amadace finally yields. He is about to cut in two first his wife as the dearer, when the white knight stops him, tells him that he is the grateful spirit of the knight whose body Amadace has given burial, and commends his generosity and his own and his lady's honor in fulfilling pledges.

The piece is rather a tale than a romance. Its notion of the dead held for debt is found among the Egyptians. Certainly the story has Eastern connections, and is associated with the legend of 'the grateful dead' extensively treated in the Middle Ages. The poem is obviously didactic, its purpose being to commend and inculcate true knightly conduct, liberality, philanthropy, and fidelity to pledges; the point of several elements of the story is deliberately indicated. The verse is loose and irregular; the manner has many popular features. The writer is genuinely sympathetic and concerned. To be noted are the analysis of situation and the introspection manifested in the utterances of Amadace and the widow in the chapel. It has been supposed that the poem represents the often referred to lost French *Idoyne and Amadas;* but the references (as in *Emare, Confessio Amantis,* Bk. 6, and *Sir Degrevant,* l. 1478) suggest that that poem dealt especially with fidelity in love.

SIR CLEGES [112], in 531 verses in MS. Advocates' Library Edbg. Jac. V, 7, 27 (now 19, 3, 1; 15th century), and in 570 verses (6 lost) in MS. Ashmole 61 (15th century), apparently originated in the North Midland at the beginning of the fifteenth century. It is in tail-rime, normally aabccb-ddbeeb. The Advocates' text has lost some stanzas at the end. The two MSS. agree in 180 lines; in nearly half the lines they differ in several words or are quite unlike.

Sir Cleges, a knight of Uther Pendragon, resembles Sir Amadas and Sir Launfal, in that he has distributed largesse and charity most liberally. In the end, he is reduced to poverty, and is abandoned. Christmas comes around, the season that he was wont to celebrate with great good cheer. Through prayer and through consolation of his wife, he patiently bears the meagre fare and the loneliness. On Christmas Day he prays in his garden. He is amazed to behold cherries growing on a tree above him. He plucks some of the fruit. By advice of his wife, with his son bearing the basket, he walks to Court, hoping for gifts in return for his present to the King. The porter, the usher, and the steward, each in turn, before admitting him to Uther, demands a third of what he shall receive from the King. The King offers him anything that he asks. He asks twelve blows to be bestowed on anyone he names. The King reluctantly grants the request. Cleges gives each of the three evil servants his due share. Then, at the request of Uther, Cleges tells why he has asked such a boon. The courtiers are delighted. Uther asks the stranger's name, and learns that the poor man is Cleges, whom he has supposed to be dead. The King gives Cleges the Castle of Cardiff and property suitable to support a knight, and makes him his steward.

The matter of the poem and the form in which it is preserved in the MSS., suggest that it is a minstrel's tale, probably for Christmas and for encouragement of liberality at that season. In the Edinburgh MS. it is headed with a drawing of a minstrel singing of the knight to Uther. The resemblances to *Sir Amadace* and *Sir Launfal* have been indicated. The piece is an interesting combination of the Pious Tale, the Humorous Tale or *Fabliau*, and the Romance, with an Arthurian background. Obviously, the piece has two main elements, which bring out a moral from two sides—the reward of liberality and the punishment of covetousness. Many analogues to the gift and punishment theme in Oriental as well as European tongues, have been pointed out. The miracle of the cherries is not uncommon in mediæval literature. An original containing the two elements has not been found. The union in *Sir Cleges* is so well made that it seems difficult to declare which of the two themes was intended as the principal one. It is perhaps the nature of its matter that causes the story of the greedy servants to be told with more spirit, and to stand out the more vividly in the reader's memory. The characterization is not distinctive; yet the nature of the wife and her encouragement of Cleges, and the grief of the hero because he cannot celebrate fittingly the festival of the Savior, are presented most sympathetically. Very suggestive are the details of customs and of domestic life reflected in the piece.

ROBERD OF CISYLE [113], is in MSS. Vernon (1370-1380), Trinity College Oxf. 57 (late 14th or beginning of 15th century), Br. Mus. Additional 22283 (1380-1400), Harley 1701 (? c. 1360) and 525 (15th century), Cbg. Univ. Libr. Ff II 38 (15th century) and Ii IV 9 (15th century), and Caius Coll. Cbg. 174 (15th century). It is in short couplets, and in Horstmann's edition consists of 444 lines. It was composed probably in the South Midland, at latest before 1380.

Robert of Sicily, brother of Emperor Valmounde and Pope Urban, is a king and knight of supreme ability and repute. But he is possessed with pride, regarding no one as his peer; and he gives himself to contemplation of his high estate rather than to regard for Christ. He attends evensong, hears the Magnificat, and declares that God has not power to put down the high and to exalt the humble; who could bring Robert low? He falls asleep, to awake in the empty church. An angel in his likeness has passed out, and Robert is accused by the sexton of an attempt to rob the church. Furious, the King rushes out to his palace. At the gate, he strikes the porter, and is beaten and cast into filth. Before the Angel, he claims his throne, and is told that he is a fool; he shall be the court fool, shall live the fool's life, with a fool's apparel and with an ape, the fool's counsellor. Despite his protests, his hair is mutilated, and he is clad as a fool, and is forced to sleep with the hounds. The Angel rules the land so that it is full of prosperity and love. He is invited to visit Valmounde and Urban at Rome. He goes with a great retinue, among whom is the fool. Robert bursts out and claims his own of his brother, and is laughed at. He repents his pride, and submits to his punishment. The Sicilians return home. The Angel summons Robert, and questions him;

'What art thou?' 'Sire, a fool; and worse than a fool, if such may be.' The Angel dismisses the attendants. Then he announces that he is an angel sent to chasten Robert for his pride; in the sight of God, the King is but a fool. He vanishes; Robert is King once more, and goes out to his court.

The story is very attractive. Its simple, earnest feeling, its high dramatic quality, and its distinct atmosphere, account for much of Longfellow's success with his modernization of it. It proceeds directly and swiftly, growing in effect. The point of the piece is carefully held to, and kept forward throughout; and all the elements of importance are stressed fittingly with good proportion. The verse is fluent and spirited; the vocabulary and the arrangement of words, are unforced; the sense is frequently carried on from line to line, and the pauses are shifted, with remarkable control and success. The poem is a good example of truly artistic, large, sane handling of a moral story. One has to make little allowance for the fact that it is not a modern piece.

CHAPTER II

TALES

The Middle Ages, like every other time among all peoples, were fond of stories. Certainly, through the period were composed and circulated hosts of tales of 'popular' and secular origin and cultivation, whose broad humor made them little acceptable to the more serious clergy, commonly prevented their being committed to writing, and made unlikely their preservation when they were written down. Again, speakers and writers with a didactic purpose early seized on the short narrative for illustration and enforcement of their matters. The results are the *exempla*, the apologues, the fables, the pious tales, the stories of the saints, that are found scattered through the greater number of the graver works of the period. As time went by, these narratives gained more weight, were more developed, were recognized more fully for their own sake as well as for their furthering of external ends. Their value for instruction was acknowledged through extraction of them from their matrices, and utterance of them in individual form as independent units or as members of more or less extensive collections of kindred pieces compiled as cyclopædias or source-books. It was such treatment that begot, for example, the collections of fables; the bestiaries and the lapidaries; the collections of *exempla*, of moralized tales, of miracles of the Virgin; and the legendaries. Finally, both pieces of the humorous and pieces of the serious type were united by narrative connection into large wholes, as in the *Seven Sages*, the *Decameron*, the *Confessio Amantis*, and the *Canterbury Tales*.

Representatives of all these classes of narrative, in the various stages, are extant in Middle English. This present chapter, however, must be confined almost exclusively to discussion of tales that are preserved as independent units, as members of independent groups of such units, or as parts of larger narrative wholes. For tales or germs of tales but incidentally employed in graver works, and for legends of the saints, one must turn in this book to the discussions of Homilies and Legends (see page 271), Works of Religious Information and Instruction (see page 338), Precept Pieces (see page 374), and Contention Poetry (see page 411).

The English pieces will be dealt with in the following groups: 1. Pious Tales; 2. Humorous Tales; 3. Fables, Bestiaries, and Animal Tales; 4. Unified Collections of Tales.

1. .PIOUS TALES

Current in the Middle Ages in all Christian countries were short tales of religious import, the *contes dévots* or *pious tales.* These short pieces, usually in verse, were composed by members of the clergy, who seized on the popular liking for a story to inculcate and confirm faith, devoutness, and right conduct toward God, the Virgin, and Man. To the reader of the present day, most of these pieces are trivial, exaggerated, incredible, grotesque, and crude; yet one who reads with but slight care, realizes that undoubtedly their writers were most sincere, and that their auditors were impressed and edified. A few of these tales are extant in English of our period.

I. Miracles of the Virgin

Miracles of the Virgin were popular throughout Europe. In the eleventh and twelfth centuries were made extensive Latin collections that soon were translated into French in the form either of collections or of isolated tales. A certain Guiot wrote in French in the twelfth century a number of pieces, of which but a few fragments, if any, survive. Gautier de Coinci, who died in 1236, made a French collection of 30000 verses. Jean le Marchant finished in 1262 a great French collection of miracles of Our Lady of Chartres. Everard de Gateley, of the region of Lyons, at about 1250 wrote sixty miracles. In the twelfth century, a monk, Adgar, translated into Anglo-Norman a Latin collection; and another Anglo-Norman group was composed in the thirteenth century. No doubt many miracles were written in England and in English; but only a few of our period are preserved. Barbour is said to have written a collection of sixty-six pieces, all of which are lost.

THE VERNON MIRACLES [1] are the best known and the most representative group of Mary miracles in English. The index to the Vernon MS. f. 123 ff. (1370-1380) gives the titles of 42 miracles of Our Lady that were incorporated, or were intended for incorporation, into the collection. Unfortunately, but nine of these are in the MS., and the ninth is incomplete. All but the fourth and the fifth of the extant pieces are in short couplets. The shortest piece has 74 verses, the longest has 186 verses. The group comprises a total of 1064 lines. The fourth piece was originally in eight-line stanzas, but now is generally in quatrains abab of four-stress verses. The fifth piece is in long seven-stress lines, with cæsura after the fourth foot. The representative nature of the collection justifies the following synopsis of the pieces:

1. *The Deliverance of the City of Crotey.* Rollo conquered many Northern lands; he subdued Normandy, became its first Duke, and besieged Crotey. Bishop Watelin bade the citizens pray, and, after praying himself, bore in procession the kirtle of Our Lady into the host of the besiegers. The enemy were blinded by the sight, and the townsmen captured them all. 2. *The Child Slain by the Jews.* A poor child in Paris gained his living by singing 'Alma redemptoris Mater.' The Jews were incensed because he sang the song on his way to and fro through their quarter. One of them enticed the child into his house, cut his throat, and cast him into a privy. But the child still sang on, so that the mother, seeking him, heard his voice, and asked for him. The Jew denied that he was there. Summoned by the mother, the Mayor and the people came, heard the voice, burst into the house, and found the boy. The Jew was condemned. The Bishop found in the child's throat a lily with golden letters reading 'Alma redemptoris Mater.' When the lily was removed, the child lay dead. Buried in the minster, at the requiem mass the body sang 'Salve sancta Parens.' 3. *The Harlot's Prayer.* A harlot at Rome tempted a hermit. He prayed for her. She abused him, and declared that she had no need for prayers. He asked that she pray for him. She prayed in a chapel of Our Lady. The Christ Child was angry that such an one prayed for His friend; but He forgave the harlot at Mary's

intercession. The Virgin urged the harlot to repent and be shriven, for in forty days she should die and pass to everlasting bliss. 4. *A Jew Boy in an Oven.* A Jew's child who was wont to play with Christian children, went with the Christians to mass at Easter-tide. He knelt and prayed to the images of the Virgin and the Child. His father saw him come from the church, and cast him into an oven. The mother raised the citizens, who found the boy in the oven unharmed. The boy declared that, through the Virgin and her infant, the coals were as sweet flowers and spices beneath him. The mother and all the Jews were converted, and the father was condemned to the oven. 5. *How a Man Got a New Leg.* The leg of a man in Vivary burned like fire. He prayed for relief at Our Lady's minster. Acting on advice, he had the leg cut off. Still he prayed to the Virgin; but, though others were aided, he was not. He dreamed that a lady pulled a new leg from his knee. When he awoke, he found his leg whole. 6. *The Virgin a Surety for a Merchant.* Theodorus, a merchant of Constantinople, obtained money from a Jew by pledging the Virgin as surety. At Alexandria, he thought of the payment the night before it was due. He cast a chest containing the money into the sea, praying the Virgin that it might come safely to the Jew. The Jew received it, knew whence it came, and hid it away. On Theodorus' return, the Jew denied the payment. At the church where the Virgin was pledged, the image of Our Lady revealed the cheat, to the chagrin of all the other Jews. 7. *The Fornicating Priest.* The Virgin wished to cleanse the conscience of a priest who had lain by a nun, and who was one of her faithful servants. The priest confessed to a friendly brother, asked his prayers, and died. For a year, the friend prayed every day for the priest. On the anniversary, Mary announced to the friend that she had obtained forgiveness for the priest, who now knelt behind him. The friend gave the dead man the Sacrament, and the Virgin led him out of the church. 8. *The Monk with the Quinsy.* A monk, who was a true servant of the Virgin, learned and uttered all the matins, hours, and special prayers that he could find. He was so afflicted with the quinsy that he was supposed to be dead. The Virgin cured him by sprinkling milk from her breast into his mouth, and by stroking his swelling. Then she disappeared. The monk chid the bystanders for not worshipping her and for driving her away by their noise. Then he wept for joy, and was ever after her servant. 9. *The Incontinent Monk.* A lecherous sacristan was wont ever to greet the image of the Virgin as he passed. One night, on an evil expedition, he was drowned. Devils wrested him from angels because of his ill deeds. The Virgin defended him; he had ever greeted her kindly. She besought God, who returned the sacristan's soul to his body that he might have opportunity to repent and reform. His brethren awoke; they wondered why the sacristan was so long away. Here the piece breaks off.

Several of the pieces delay too much in unnecessary preliminary details or in exhortation that the story proper is intended to illustrate. But at least half of them begin directly, and hold to the point straight to the end. Each piece concludes with exhortation to the service of Mary, who will ever care for her servants. The genuine devoutness and earnestness of the writer make him naïvely obtuse to the grotesqueness and incongruity between incident and attitude, in the tales. The pieces are full of that simple devotion to the lovely and potent protector, and of confidence in her loving grace, that are among the most grateful features of mediæval literature.

OTHER MIRACLES OF THE VIRGIN [2] are in the *Northern Homily Cycle* MSS. (see pages 291, 292) Harley 4196 f. 166 (four miracles) and Cotton Tiberius E VII (one miracle, Theophilus; see page 314). Others are in the *Southern Legendary* MSS. (see page 294 ff.). Trinity College Cbg. R, 3, 25 Items 97 (one miracle) and 103 (two miracles) separated from Item 40; Harley 2277 Item 46 (eight miracles); Additional 10301 (the eight Harley miracles); Cotton Cleopatra D IX (the first seven Harley miracles); Cotton Julius D IX (Harley miracles 2, 3, 4, 5, 1); and Harley 2250 (The Taper Left by an Angel). As illustrative *Narrationes* for his *Festial* (see page 301), John Mirk introduced a number of tales that hinge on miraculous intervention by the Virgin. These are in the homilies numbered as follows in the E. E. T. S. edition: 4, 14 (two), 16, 17, 24 (three), 53 (three), 54, 57 (two), 74. In MS. Lambeth 432 f. 85 (15th century) are fifteen prose sketches [3] of miracles of the Virgin.

HOW THE PSALTER OF OUR LADY WAS MADE [4], 252 three-stress verses aabccb, is in MSS. Digby 86 (1272-1283) and Auchinleck (1330-1340).

A monk, son of a rich man, every day prayed a hundred *Aves.* One Saturday, Mary appeared, declared him redeemed for his good deeds, and directed him to pray a hundred and fifty *Aves* daily. This was her *Psalter.* The first fifty *Aves* were for joy at the annunciation that she should bear God-in-Man; the second fifty, that she should bear Christ; the third, that she should go to

Him for bliss. The monk learned that she had no petticoat because
the cloth he gave her with his prayers was too little. He fulfilled
the directions; and, in a week, Mary came fully clothed. She
declared he should be an abbot, and should preach her *Psalter*
everywhere; all who said it should be saved; in seven years the
monk should die. The monk preached the message everywhere.
'All you, say the *Psalter* every day.'

THE CLERK WHO WOULD SEE THE VIRGIN [5] is
a fragment of 200 four-stress verses abababababcdcd, the beginning missing, in MS. Auchinleck (1330-1340). Horstmann
thought this piece may be from a twelfth-century Midland collection on which the Vernon collection may have been based.
The tale is used as *exemplum* in the prose homily for the
Assumption of Mary in Mirk's *Festial* (see page 301).

A clerk who would see the body of Mary, is told by an angel
that he may have his will, on penalty of death or of loss of sight.
The clerk agrees to lose sight, but plans to look with only one eye.
Mary shows herself, and the clerk's eye is blinded. The next day,
remorseful, he confesses and begs for total blindness. At night,
Mary, in a band of angels, appears and forgives him. She warns
of the ills of total blindness; but the clerk is content—he has seen
her, and asks only to be admitted to Heaven. She grants his
prayer. The next morning his sight is restored.

THE EFFICACY OF AVE MARIAS [6] is the theme of
62 verses, the end of a piece apparently originally aabccb, the
tails of two, the other verses of three, stresses each. The lines
are on a fly-leaf of MS. Laud Latin 95 in a hand of about 1380.

Evidently Mary has bidden a monk to say *Aves* thrice a day.
She leaves him with counsel of silence, and promise of Christ's
favor. The monk prays. Mary returns with her robe all white,
and thanks him for the prayers that have cleansed it. She promises he shall be an abbot; he shall say the *Aves* thrice a day; whoever so says them shall not die unshriven. The abbot is said by
this news and preaching to have brought many folk to God. All
you, with good cheer say your *Aves* thrice a day, and may God soon
bring us all to Heaven.

DE MIRACULO BEATE MARIE [7], in MS. Thornton
f. 147 (1430-1440), consists of 140 verses of tail-rime aabccbddbeeb, with a small gap after line 57, and a larger one after
line 97.

A vicious knight ravished wives and maidens, and would have naught to do with religion. In the land was a clerk who plucked the Devil out of men's hearts as one plucks apples from a tree. In Latin and in English he preached at the knight, who, finally aroused, rushed at him to scorn God and Mary. The MS. is defective here. Apparently the priest struggled with the fiend through the night, and the Virgin intervened. The knight was saved, repaired the injuries he had done, and ultimately went to Heaven.

THE GOOD KNIGHT AND THE JEALOUS WIFE [8] is in MS. Ashmole 61 (15th century) along with the *Tale of an Incestuous Daughter* (see page 176). It is probably much earlier than the MS., and consists of 396 lines of tail-rime aabccb, the end being missing.

After seven years, a knight and his wife have two children. When the wife is again with child, the Devil, envious of their bliss, prompts her to ask if the knight loves anything better than her. He declares he loves another woman more—it is the Virgin. Every night he leaves his wife asleep, and goes to the chapel to pray to Mary. The devils have a witch inform the wife that nightly her husband visits another woman. The lady finds the knight does leave her side; she kills her children, and stabs herself to the heart. The knight finds the bodies, and prays to the Virgin. The fiends, in horrible guise, rejoice about the corpses. Mary attempts to drive them off, but they claim their own. Mary declares the bodies shall be alive at the Angelus. Angels catch up a devil, whose ribs crack. The devils flee. They burn the house of the witch, and leave her almost dead. The neighbors make off. So the fragment ends.

II. Other Tales

THE GAST OF GY [9], in 2064 four-stress verses in couplets, is in MSS. Cotton Tiberius E VII (c. 1400) and Rawlinson F 175 (c. 1350). A prose version is in MS. Vernon (1370-1380) and in a short fragment in MS. Caius College Cbg. 175 (1350-1400). The verse is of the North of England at about 1325-1350. It is said to be a version of the prose (also originally Northern), which was made from a Latin *De Spiritu Guidonis* in the form preserved in MS. Cotton Vespasian A VI. The Latin tract is also in the older MS. Cotton Vespasian E I and in MS. Harley 2379.

God shows us many examples on earth to establish our faith. Guy, a great burgèss of Alexty, died on the twelfth calends of December, 1323. Harassed by his ghost, his wife summons the priests. With two hundred soldiers all shriven and bearing the Sacrament, the clergy go to the house. After religious exercises are held, the ghost argues with the prior, a master of geometry, and a master of philosophy, who seek to confuse and to entrap him. He demonstrates at length that he is a good ghost; that, though a soul die shriven, it may be called evil until it completes its purgation; that neither he nor anybody else could reveal who have been saved or damned, unless he had been in all the three realms of the Hereafter; that the revelations by prophets have no bearing on the capabilities of ghosts; that being in the house and in Purgatory, is not being in two places at once. Then he replies, and defends his replies, to questions as to why he is punished; what is the greatest distress and what the best aid to a man on point of death; who, about to die, may actually see Christ and Mary and the saints; whether spirits know what is done on earth for them; how many souls a priest may pray for effectively at one time; and many other topics. The wife is in terrible distress. The ghost says this is because they both have not done proper penance for sin; he has come that the wife may complete the penance. He explains, in response to questions, how a ghost may speak without a tongue; where a spirit dwells until Doomsday; how quickly a soul gets from the body to Hell or Heaven or Purgatory; what deeds best help to Heaven; what men are most in Purgatory; what kinds of pains are suffered in Purgatory; how a spirit may suffer from fire; that he is sure men ought to believe in the Incarnation; what are the most common sins; etc. He agrees that if his wife pray for him and live chastely, he will disturb her no more. He declares he cannot reveal when Antichrist will come; and he meets the argument that, since he can hear, he has ears. The company disperses, the prior directing publication of what has occurred. Later, the ghost reveals to the priests at his house that their prayers have freed him from common Purgatory. He will reveal no marvels, and refuses to tell how many Popes shall rule in Rome.—All these marvels were told to Pope John, who sent investigators. As no farther response could be got, the authorities concluded that Guy had reached Heaven.

The tale has no literary merit. Some of it is to be compared with *A Revelation of Purgatory* in the Thornton MS. The argument that is carried on at a number of places, makes possible its classification with contention poems. The writer wished to present and to offer solutions to, various problems connected with the nature of the hereafter, conduct on earth, the value of the offices of the Church, and duty to the Church and its offices. The device of questioning the ghost enabled him to put the questions, and to have them met with the authority of experience in the other world. By having a prior and masters of mathematics and philosophy seek in vain to discredit and to refute the ghost, he gave special weight to the ghost's declarations. Though the arguments offered in the piece had no novelty among the ecclesiastics of the day, they are of curious interest to the uninitiated reader.

TRENTALLE SANCTI GREGORII [10] is preserved in two versions in short couplets. The first is in MSS. Vernon f. 230 and f. 303 (1370-1380), 200 verses in two copies with but slight verbal variants; Cotton Caligula A II f. 86 (15th century), 240 verses; Garrett in Princeton University Library f. 38 v (15th century), 258 verses; and Lambeth 306 f. 110 (15th century), 240 verses. The second version is in two redactions: the first is in MS. Advocates' Library Edinburgh Jac. V, 7, 27 (now 19, 3, 1) f. 213 (15th century), 190 verses; the second is in MSS. Cbg. Univ. Libr. Kk I 6 f. 242 (15th century), 202 verses, and Harley 3810 f. 75 v (hand of end of 15th century), 350 verses. The two versions are independent treatments, probably of a common original. The first version is of 1300-1350. It employs much alliteration and many 'popular' formulas. The second version is difficult to date; its two redactions are independent of each other; alliteration is rare. The Harley MS. is the longest and most complete of the texts of this version. It is more closely related to Kk than to Edinburgh, and is probably from a source common with Kk, which perhaps is written from oral transmission.

According to the first version, Pope Gregory's mother was regarded as of pure life, and as sure of residence in Heaven. But secretly she had borne a child out of wedlock, and had murdered it. Not confessing, she was sent to torment. She appeared at night to Gregory in monstrous form, confessed her case and its cause, and declared she could be freed only if three masses were said for her on each of the ten chief feasts of the year. Gregory said the masses, and at the end of the year the mother appeared to him in such lovely form that he took her for the Virgin. An angel bore her to Heaven. The piece ends with exhortation and instruction as to masses.—The second version has not the concluding exhortation and instruction. MSS. Kk and Harley introduce several supernatural attempts to draw Gregory away from the final masses on the Nativity of Mary.

Perhaps the original of the first version is a Latin or a French text correspondent to the French in MS. Cbg. Univ. Libr. Ff VI 15. Resemblances to the second version are in Odo de Ceritona, in Hervieux's *Les Fabulistes Latins*, and in a French version of Odo. The story should be compared with Northern Homily 30, lines 112-84, in MS. Harley 4196 (see page 291), the Venetian legend of the *Knight in the Chapel*, the Venetian story of the *Steadfast Penitent*, and the *Awntyrs of Arthure* (see page 62).

NARRATIO DE VIRTUTE MISSARUM [11] consists of 59 short couplets, originally Southern of 1350-1400, in MS. Harley 3954 f. 77 v (c. 1420).

A poor man, tempted, was persuaded by his wife to go to the priest. The latter bade him come to mass each day, leaving his work and receiving a penny in compensation for his loss of labor. One day, when taking swine to market, he passed the church and asked the clerk for the mass. The clerk took his tabard in pay, and then declined to conduct the service, giving the man all the merit of three services he himself had heard. As the man came homeward, he learned of the suicide of the clerk who had sold the merits of the mass. He went on home, and was good ever after.

NARRATIO SANCTI AUGUSTINI [12], 84 originally Southern verses in tail-rime aabccb, is in MS. Harley 3954 f. 75 r (c. 1420). The piece is in illustration of the notion that fiends record all evil speeches.

St. Gregory was conducting mass. While St. Austin was reading the Gospel, he saw from a window a devil striving with tremendous speed to write down the gossip of three women. In his agitation, the fiend struck his head against a pillar. Greatly amused, Austin laughed out loudly. Later, he told Gregory of the matter. They found the pillar all bloody. Thereafter, the miracle was used as a warning to folk to be quiet at mass.

The account of the devil's efforts as stenographer is very amusing. Similar matter is in *Tutivillus the Devyl of Hell* (see page 234). In favor of women, are the pieces noted on page 233.

THE SMITH AND HIS DAME [13], preserved in a print
of Copland, is held by Horstmann, since it is in the same dialect
and stanza as the *Disputisoun bytwene a Christeneman and a
Jew* (see page 417), to be by the author of the latter piece, and
to date from about 1360. The story consists of 580 verses,
part being missing, in tail-rime aaabcccbdddbeeeb. The metre
is rude. The tails are normally three-stressed; the other verses
have three or four stresses.

A smith was very proud of his art. The Lord came and asked
him if he could make a rod that would guide a blind man. The
smith called Him a madman for proposing such a thing. The
Lord said He could do it, and could make an old man young.
The smith bade Him make his beldame young. The Lord put her
in the fire, and forged her out a lovely maid. The smith wished to
learn the art. The Lord declared he should not; He came to show
him he was not so able as he boasted. When the Lord was gone,
the smith thrust his wife into the fire, and hammered her until
she was dead. Then he pursued the Lord, and begged mercy for
his presumption in seeking to imitate Him. The Lord pitied him,
and restored his wife to life and beauty.

Much of this mixture of rude jest and pious tale is broadly
comic and certainly of low appeal. The author saw no impropriety in the colloquy between the smith and the Lord, or in
the smith's impudence to Him.

THE EREMYTE AND THE OUTELAWE [14], com-
posed in the Midland at 1350-1375, is in MS. Br. Mus. Additional 22577, a copy (c. 1806) from the lost Fillingham MS.
that contained an *Otuel* (see page 92). The piece consists of
387 verses in tail-rime aabccbdddbeeeb.

There were two brothers, one a hermit (who lived as a genuine
hermit, not 'as other hermits do now-a-days'), one an outlaw who
had dwelt long in evil-doing. On a Good Friday, the outlaw went to
church, was affected to remorse by the vicar's sermon, and asked
absolution. The vicar assigned the penance of going barefoot for
seven years, fasting on bread and water, saying a *Pater* and *Ave*
daily, and making a pilgrimage. The outlaw would have none of
these. Learning that all his life long to drink water had been the
thing he most disliked, the vicar assigned as penance that he should
not drink water that day. The devil possessed the outlaw with a
terrible thirst, and caused him to meet successively three women

bearing water. The outlaw resisted, and opened a vein in his arm to quench his thirst. He died of the flow of blood. Angels bore his soul singing to Heaven. In a vision the hermit recognized his brother; he protested his own life of privation, and his brother's vicious career—he would turn outlaw. An angel declared the outlaw had suffered more in the one day than the hermit in all his years, and bade him bury the body, and persevere in right living. The hermit obeyed, and finally attained Heaven.

The piece is based on a union of two stories widely known as *exempla.* Each of these, the legend of the penitent outlaw and the tale of the easy penance, is represented in Jacques de Vitry's *Exempla* and Étienne de Bourbon's *Recueil.* The whole is very like the remarkable French legend *Du Chevalier au Barizel.* The story aims to offer hope to the most abandoned, and to emphasize the doctrine of the parables of the Lost Sheep and the Workers in the Vineyard. Unhappily, the excessive consideration shown the sinner, would rather lead the reader to the hermit's conclusion, 'Why not be an outlaw?'

THE CHILD OF BRISTOWE [15], probably originally Northern of 1350-1400, is in MS. Harley 2382 f. 118 v (15th century), and consists of 558 verses of tail-rime aabccbdddbeeb.

A squire who dwelt near Bristol gathered a vast estate by evil deeds. His son was well educated, and grew up good. He refused the law, and was apprenticed to a Bristol merchant. When the squire was on his death-bed, unable to obtain another as executor, he insisted that the son manage the property. The boy agreed so to act, if the father would appear to him within a fortnight. He sold the property, and disposed of it in philanthropy and in purchase of thirty trentals for his father's soul. At the time fixed, the father appeared, all on fire and led by a chain in the Devil's hand. He agreed to appear a fortnight later. The youth sold his own property, and devoted it to remedy of the father's evil deeds. The spirit appeared, free of the chain, and no longer on fire. The son sold himself to his master, and paid up his father's tithes and offerings. He gave his clothing to the last poor creditor. As he prayed, he saw an angel in a great light leading a little child, the father's soul newborn to bliss. Learning of the youth's devotion, the merchant made him his partner and heir and attorney, and gave him his daughter.

Spare the poor, avoid the law, get wealth honestly, pay tithes and offerings in due season, spend your all on masses for the departed, and all shall be blessed to you; fail in these, and your reward shall be torment—such is the doctrine of the tale. One credits the piece for its purpose, not for literary merit.

THE TALE OF AN INCESTUOUS DAUGHTER [16], emphasizing the efficaciousness of repentance in winning for the most abandoned the mercy of Christ, stresses the possibility of vicious practice and easy remedy illustrated in the *Eremyte and the Outelawe*. It is in the fifteenth-century MSS. Cbg. Univ. Libr. Ff V 48 f. 44 (288 verses), Ashmole 61 f. 66 (from verse 118 on, with 18 added verses), and Rawlinson 118 (264 verses), in tail-rime aabccb. It is urged that MSS. A and R must represent one group of texts, and MS. C another, and that the tale is from a thirteenth-century piece made up of two 'exempla contritionis,' one by Jacobus de Vitriaco, and the other by Thomas Cantipratanus.

A beautiful young woman has a child by her father. To hide their guilt, she breaks the babe's neck. The wife discovers the guilty pair together, and is murdered by the daughter. The father repents, and is bidden go on a pilgrimage. The daughter murders him. Taking his wealth, she goes to a city, where she lives riotously. One day she enters a church. The sermon so moves her, that in the midst of the preaching she publicly confesses her sins. The bishop bids her wait till the sermon is over. She falls down dead. An angel announces to the bishop that her soul is now in Heaven before Christ, that she shall be given Christian burial, and that any man who asks mercy of Christ shall have it. Let no man fall into despair because he has done great sin.

Versions of the story are in both English and Latin MSS. of the *Gesta Romanorum*, and a text of it is extant in Norse. The story is very close to that of the curious and important dramatic fragment *Dux Moraud* (see page 545).

TWO STORIES FROM HELL (*The Lament of the Soul of William Basterdfeld, Knight* [17], and *Against Breaking of Wedlock* [18]), directed against adultery, are in one of the MSS. of the *Incestuous Daughter*, and apparently are of the fifteenth century. The former is in MSS. Rawlinson C 813 (c. 1525, 96 lines), Ashmole 61 f. 136 (15th century, 99 lines), Thornton (1430-1440, 81 verses in a later hand), and Lambeth 560 f. 98 (? 16th century, 17 verses). It is in stanzas generally ababcbc, and of 1400-1450. The second piece is in the fifteenth-century MSS. Cbg. Univ. Libr. Ff II 38 f. 48 r, Ff V 48 f. 14, Ee IV 35, Ashmole 61 f. 136 (194 verses), Lambeth 306 f. 107, Harley 5396 f. 276, and Rawlinson 118 (224 verses). It consists of irregular four-stress verses abab.

A LEGEND OF THE CRUCIFIX [19] consists of 58 short couplets in MS. Ashmole 61 f. 26 v (15th century). A version of the story is told in *Handlyng Synne*.

A young knight besieged the castle of the slayer of his father. On a Good Friday, contrary to his custom, the guilty knight went to church. The young man beset him on the way thither, but was placated by his prayers. The twain pledged friendship, and went to church together and knelt before the Cross. When they kissed it, the Cross bent down and kissed the young knight. The consequence was that all the country lived in charity. So all men should forgive, and dwell in peace.

2. HUMOROUS TALES

That tales corresponding in matter to the extant French *fabliaux* were current in England from an early period, would on its face seem probable. The probability is confirmed by the caution issued against such pieces by the University of Oxford in 1292, and by reference to them at the opening of the *Cursor Mundi*, in *Octovian* (sts. 2, 3), in *Weping haueth myn wonges wet* (st. 4; see page 496), repeatedly in *Piers Plowman*, in the *Canterbury Tales*, and in other writings. The attitude of condemnation or of apology in each of such references, with the natural attitude of the serious clergy and copyists, accounts for the fact that scarcely any representatives of humorous tales in English before 1400 are extant. The list consists of *Dame Siriʒ* and the associated *Interludium de Clerico et Puella*, *A Peniworþ of Witte*, the humorous metrical romance *Sir Cleges* (see page 160), and the animal tale of the *Fox and the Wolf* (see page 183). To these are to be added Chaucer's tales by the Miller, the Reeve, the Merchant, the Shipman, and the Summoner (see Index).

DAME SIRI3 [20] is in MS. Digby 86 f. 165 (1272-1283)
in 450 verses, copied by a scribe of the South-West from an
East Midland MS., the original being probably Southern.
About 300 lines are tail-rime aabccb, the tails of three or two
stresses each. The rest of the piece is in couplets, usually of
four-stressed verses. The uses of the several forms of verse
appear to be arbitrary.

In the absence of her husband, a merchant, 'at the fair of
Botolfston (Boston) in Lincolnshire,' a clerk, Wilekin, makes
advances to Margeri. The lady will have none of him. In great
grief, Wilekin meets a friend, who sends him to a procuress, Dame
Siri3. Approached, the Dame protests pious unwillingness and
inability; but, on being pressed, she agrees to help the lover. She
feeds her dog pepper and mustard to make its eyes water. Weeping
and lamenting, she goes with it to Margeri. Urged to tell the cause
of her grief, she declares that her daughter was approached by a
clerk. She repulsed his advances. In revenge, the clerk has by
magic turned her into a bitch, the very one that now stands here,
its eyes running tears. She declares that such is likely to be the
fate of women who refuse clerks their will. Margeri tells the Dame
of Wilekin, and begs Siri3 to go find him, and bring him to her; he
shall have his way. The Dame brings the clerk, who is enthusiastic-
ally received by the wife.

Here are to be seen many of the characteristics of *fabliaux:*
the piece is a story of middle-class life; the personages are
favorites of the genre—a merchant, his wife, a clerk; the plot
depends on illicit sex relations, and rests chiefly on a trick; the
effect aimed at is one of broad humor; the speech is open and
free, the matter undisguised. Realism and definiteness are
chief qualities of the tale. With exception of the husband, who
does not participate in the action, each personage has a name.
The merchant goes to a fair at Botolfston in Lincolnshire.
The characterization is striking, especially that of Siri3, manifested in her behavior and utterance. Though he disregarded
proportion, the writer plunged at once into his story, and told
it chiefly by means of conversation. The transitions between
scenes are very brief; of connectives between speeches there is
one of three words in one place, and one of nine words at
another; elsewhere the speeches are interchanged without connection. All of this, with the realism of the whole, and the

naturalness and crudeness of the language, makes the piece almost more of a drama than a narrative. So far is this true, and so great are the similarities in incident and in wording between the tale and the very early English *Interludium de Clerico et Puella*, that the theory has been urged that *Dame Siriȝ* is, like the *Interludium*, really a later form of an earlier dramatic piece, and that it was written down from oral presentation. The story came indirectly from a Latin *exemplum* derived from a collection such as the *Gesta Romanorum* or the *Disciplina Clericalis*. The theme is of Indian origin, and is common in Latin and in Western vernaculars.

A PENIWORÞ OF WITTE [21] is preserved in two versions. The former, not later than 1325, consists of 200 short couplets in MS. Auchinleck (1330-1340). The latter, *How a Merchande dyd hys Wyfe Betray*, of much later date, is in MSS. Cbg. Univ. Libr. Ff II 38 (15th century), 136 couplets, and Harley 5396 (15th century), a fragment of 175 verses in couplets.

A merchant neglects his wife, and leaves her unadorned, while he devotes himself to a leman whom he decks out gorgeously. About to go abroad, he inquires what gifts the courtesan would have. To his wife he suggests that he will get for her what she will pay for. She gives him a penny, with the request that he buy with it a pennyworth of wit and knit it fast in his heart. From a wise man he buys for the penny the advice to appear before the women singly, ill-clad and pretending he has done murder. He follows the advice. His leman will not see him. The wife cherishes him most lovingly, and undertakes to obtain his pardon on her knees. She is rejoiced to learn the truth. The leman attempts to make up to the merchant again; but he strips her of his gifts, and casts her off. He is delighted with his pennyworth, and dwells happily with his wife thereafter.

The second version as a whole is much the more condensed. Possibly it is an abbreviated version of the earlier piece. Here the ill behavior of the leman is greatly intensified; and, at the end, the merchant is caused to confess to his wife his ill conduct. The great irregularity of the metre of this later piece, and the several conventional appeals to hearers to give attention, point to composition by a minstrel for oral recitation.

The idea of the story is old, that of the test of the true and the false friend. The English versions are possibly independent of the French; but they are probably derived from a lost French original—not, however, from the extant *fabliau,* Jean de Galois' *De la Bourse Pleine de Sens.* The English pieces are not very spirited; scarcely any attempt is made to suggest individuality of character. The persons fulfil their rôles; the stories convey the point of the test.

CHAUCER'S TALES by the Reeve, the Miller, the Merchant, the Shipman, and the Summoner, are treated in Chapter XVI.

Later pieces [22] that may be but mentioned here, are Adam Cobsam's *The Wright's Chaste Wife, The Lady Prioress and her Suitors,* once assigned to Lydgate, *The Pardoner and the Tapster, The Freiris of Berwyk, Sir Corneus, The King and the Barker, The Tale of the Basin, The Wife in a Morelles Skin, The Vnluckie Fermentie, The Friar and the Boy, How the Plowman Learned his Pater Noster* (see page 353), *The Hunting of the Hare, The Felon Sowe, The Miller of Abingdon, Dan Hewe Monk, The Tournament of Totenham, How a Sergeant Would Learn to be a Friar.*

3. Fables, Bestiaries, Animal Tales

I. Fables

Mall and Joseph Jacobs have shown that England was the home of the mediæval fable. Here was made the lost twelfth-century collection of Alfred of England, used, through a lost English version, by Marie de France, who herself wrote in England. Here, also, in the same century, Walter of England wrote the collection *Anonymus Neveleti.* Here, too, probably were composed some of the French collections known as *Ysopets.* Jacobs' genealogical table shows that scarce a single mediæval collection was unaffected by the works of Walter, Alfred, or Marie. The popularity of fables in England is indicated by the preservation there of a number of the earliest MSS. of the various versions. The Bayeux Tapestry has a dozen fables wrought on its border. Composers of sermons and collectors of *exempla* employed them freely. Odo of Cheriton's thirteenth-century *Narrationes*, and John of Sheppey's fourteenth-century work, consist largely of fables. Neckam's *De Naturis Rerum*, the poems ascribed to Walter Mapes, and John of Salisbury's *Polycraticus*, contain fables. The *exempla* of Holkot, Bromyard, and Nicole Bozon, use fables freely.

SURVIVING ENGLISH FABLES [23]. But what of all this has come down to us, is in Latin or in French. There survive in English to the death of Chaucer scarcely a dozen fables. These are used singly and incidentally in the midst of larger writings; yet, occurring as they do, they support the idea of a large interest in such pieces in England.

The crab who would swim backwards, is told of in Lambeth Homily 5 of the twelfth century (see page 280). In the *Owl and the Nightingale* (c. 1220) are the fables of the fox with many tricks, and of the nest defiled by the young cuckoo (see page 418). In the *Song on the Times of Edward II* (see page 213) is the fable of the lion, the wolf, and the ass. In the *Aȝenbite of Inwyt* (c. 1340) is the fable of the hound and the donkey (E. E. T. S. 23. 155; see page 345). In *Barlaam and Josaphat* (Vernon MS. ll. 421 ff.), of the South-West Midland, 1300-1350, is the fable of the nightingale who escaped under promise of giving wise counsel. Bozon's French fable of the wolf and the sheep ends with English words, and his version of the belling of the cat must not be forgotten. The fable of the belling of the cat is admirably allegorized in the B-text of *Piers Plowman*, and is referred to in *On the Times* (1. 99; see page 238). In Barbour's *Bruce* (Bk. 9) is the fable of the fox and the fisher. Gower's *Confessio Amantis* (2. 291 ff.; 5. 4937 ff.) uses fable matter, as do Chaucer's *Reeve's Tale* (ll. 133-34), *Tale of Melibeus* (1. 2370 ff.), *Troilus and Criseyde* (1. 257; 2. 1387), *Knight's Tale* (ll. 319-22), and *Truth* (1. 12).

The earliest extant collection of fables in English, is the seven of Lydgate, probably of the early fifteenth century. In the last quarter of the same century, Henryson wrote thirteen fables in English. But the most notable early collection is that printed by Caxton in 1484.

II. Bestiaries

At a very early period the Church began to employ exposition of the natures and qualities of animals, for presenting and enforcing moral and religious doctrine. Probably all due originally to a *Physiologus* composed among the Christians in Alexandria, were written in the Middle Ages many collections of accounts of the sort. Extant versions and allusions in Latin and in French, show that such works were as popular in England as elsewhere. The Old English poem on the *Panther and the Whale* still survives. Of the twelfth century, is Philippe de Thaon's Anglo-Norman *Physiologus;* of the thirteenth century, are Guillaume le Clerc's *Bestiare Divin* and Richard de Fournival's more worldly *Bestiare d'Amour.*

THE BESTIARY [24], in MS. Arundel 292 f. 4 (late 13th century), is the only surviving collection of the sort in Middle English. It is from the East Midland (some authorities say the South-East, others the North-East, Midland) of 1200-1250. Its 802 lines exhibit an interesting stage of transition from the older alliterative verse to the new rimed forms. The collection is a translation of the Latin *Physiologus* of Theobaldus, a text of which is preserved in MS. Harley 3093. The Latin consists of accounts of the lion, the serpent, the eagle, the ant, the fox, the hart, the spider, the whale, the mermaid, the centaur, the elephant, the turtle-dove, and the panther. The English shifts somewhat the order of the original, omits the passage on the centaur, and appends one on the culver or dove. The nature and the habits (largely fictitious) of each creature are stated. Then follows an application or interpretation. The passage on the elephant will illustrate the work.   ʹ

Elephants are in India. They are burly, and go in herds. Only when they have eaten mandrake, have they sexual desire. They go two years with their young, and bear one at a birth, standing in water. They take heed not to fall, for they cannot get up of themselves. The elephant rests by leaning against a strong tree. Accordingly, ·the hunter saws the tree half through; then he watches. The beast leans against the tree, and both go to the ground. The creature calls loudly for help. His fellows seek vainly to raise him. They cry out like the blast of a horn or the music of a bell. A young elephant approaches. With his snout, he helps up the old one. Thus the hunter is cheated.—So Adam fell through a tree. Moses and the prophets vainly sought to raise him. They all cried to Heaven. Christ came down as a man, and by death went under Adam and raised him and all mankind that were fallen into 'dim hell.'

SCATTERED BESTIARY MATERIAL is in several extant English pieces from before 1400. Such are the passages on the serpent with the jewel in its head, and the serpent that drinks and bursts, in Trinity Homily 31 (see page 281); the reference to the serpent, in the *Vices and Virtues* (E. E. T. S. 89. 101; see page 413); and the Vernon and Dulwich *La Estorie del Euangelie* (see page 324), on books about beasts, birds, stones, herbs, etc., written by clerks of old for the instruction and solace of men. The lion and the dragon are themes of two scraps among the religious fragments in MS. Harley 7322 f. 163 of the end of the fourteenth century.

Such matter had vast influence on the symbolism in mediæval art of all forms; had great effect on natural science up to a late date; and prepared for acceptance of fabulous accounts like that of Mandeville (see page 433), and for the Euphuism of Elizabeth's time.

III. Animal Tales

The animal epic, so highly developed and extensively cultivated on the Continent, seems to have received in England but little treatment in any of the current languages.

THE FOX AND THE WOLF [25] is, with Chaucer's *Nun's Priest's Tale*, the only survival in Middle English, up to the latter part of the fifteenth century, of the animal story told for its own sake. This lively poem consists of 295 four-stress verses in couplets in MS. Digby 86 (1272-1283), the MS. of *Dame Siriʒ*, and is of the South of about 1250 or 1250-1275.

A very hungry and thirsty Fox, who would rather meet one hen than half a hundred women, makes his way into the enclosure of some friars. After an attempt to inveigle from his perch a cock who sits aloft with two hens, the Fox, seeking water, leaps into one of the well-buckets, and sinks to the bottom of the well. There he laments his unhappy state, until his gossip, Seagrim, the Wolf, appears. To the latter, who wonderingly inquires why he is so situated, Reynard pictures his state as the bliss of Paradise. Envious, Seagrim begs to join him. The Fox declares he is too sinful, he must be shriven. The Wolf replies that there is none to shrive him; will the Fox do it? Reynard consents; Seagrim confesses, is absolved, and is bidden get into the upper bucket. Being the heavier, he descends while the Fox rises. The next morning, the friar who draws the water finds the Devil in the bucket! All the community with dogs and staves sorely tear and drub the creature.

The general theme of the Fox deceiving the Wolf was widespread throughout the Middle Ages, and is popular even to-day on the Continent of Europe. The English poem is based probably on some version of the French *Roman de Renard;* but, apparently, no extant version of the *Roman* has the tale just as it is in the *Fox.* The theme is the subject of an episode in *Reynard the Fox*, and of a fable of Odo of Cheriton. The piece is a worthy predecessor of the *Nun's Priest's Tale.* It is well constructed and is told with spirit. The setting is admirably suggested and full of 'color.' Material, situation, action, characterization, phrasing, and comment by the author, all contribute to exquisite humorous and realistic effects. The personages are thoroughly humanized and well individualized. Especially notable are the colloquy between the Fox and the Wolf, the confession of the latter, and the scene of the finding and the beating of the Devil (!) at the well. Whatever the author got from sources, the greater number of his effects are due to his own personality, his own way of looking at things, and his own aptness of expression.

THE FALSE FOX [26] may be dealt with here, though it was evidently intended to be sung. It is in MS. Cbg. Univ. Libr. Ee I 12 (15th century), associated with a version of the

Psalms (see page 401) said in the MS. to be of 1342. The poem consists of 18 five-stress couplets each with a couplet refrain, the first line of which has six, the second seven, stresses. In crude song, it tells with much humor of the visits of the fox to croft, sty, yard, hall, and coop, stealing 'our geese'; of the good wife stoning him, and the good man beating him; of the fox's escape; of his merry feast; and of his purposed visit next week to carry off hen and chick.

CHAUCER'S NUN'S PRIEST'S TALE is dealt with on page 712.

4. UNIFIED COLLECTIONS OF TALES

In the Middle Ages it was not at all uncommon to make collections of material of a single general type, usually for some larger purpose. So were grouped into single MSS. popular saws (see page 374), recipes (see page 428), homilies (see page 277), fable (see page 180), *exempla* (see page 164), anecdotes (as in Neckam's *De Naturis Rerum*), moralized tales (see page 164), fabulous accounts of animals (see page 182), miracles (see page 165), saint's legends (see page 303), and various other classes of writing. These collections were, however, generally of an encyclopædic character; they were series of individual pieces juxtaposed because of common traits of matter or of form, or because of availability for a common use.

Representative of the last mentioned types of grouping, is the English version of the *Gesta Romanorum* in MS. Harley 7333 (c. 1450). Sometimes stories were extracted from larger wholes, as were pieces from the *Handlyng Synne* (see page 344). Again, tales of kindred nature were preceded with an introduction—either narrative, as in Chaucer's *Legend of Good Women* (see page 665); or expository of purpose, as in Chaucer's *Monk's Tale* (see page 709). But narrative pieces were sometimes united more closely. Sometimes pieces were wrought over and fitted together as component parts of a single great continuous narrative, as in the English *Cursor Mundi* (see page 339). Sometimes, as in the *Handlyng Synne* (see page 342), really a treatise on the Seven Sins, they were introduced as illustrative of phases of a large general theme. One of the chief bonds of connection between the tales of Gower's *Confessio Amantis*, is of this class; and it has been urged recently that the *Canterbury Tales* evince a basis of union of a similar sort (see page 687). But the widely popular *Proces of the Seven Sages of Rome*, the *Confessio*, and the *Canterbury Tales*, represent use of still a different type of union. In these works, as in Boccaccio's *Decameron*, the single tales are told incidentally by personages in a large narrative whole which is introduced by a prologue, is completed by a conclusion, and sustained in the intermediate parts by narrative connections between the individual tales—in other words, in each of such works the single stories are narratives within a narrative.

With one exception, each of the English works of these types up to 1400, is in this book discussed under the appropriate one of the general headings adopted for consideration of the literature of the period. The exception is the *Seven Sages*.

THE SEVEN SAGES OF ROME [27]. In India originated the collection of stories known in the East as the *Book of Sindibad*, and in the West as the *Seven Sages of Rome*. Versions of the 'Eastern group' (of which are extant ten, ranging up to the latter part of the fourteenth century) were composed in Hebrew, Syriac, Greek, Spanish, Persian, and Arabic. It is assumed that the 'Western group' is descended from a lost twelfth-century original. The oldest form in which the Western type exists, is seen in the *Dolopathos*, which survives in two versions, one in the Latin prose (c. 1207-1212) of Johannes de Alta Silva, the other in the thirteen thousand lines of French verse (c. 1220-1226) made by Herbert from the Latin of Johannes. But few copies of the *Dolopathos* survive. The later form of the Western type, *Les Sept Sages de Rome* of before 1150, preserves more closely the form and the contents of the common original, and influenced the later treatments. There are extant over a hundred French or Italian MSS. of the *Sept Sages*, in at least five sub-groups. Versions in manuscript, or in print, or in both, are found in nearly every European language. The norm of these contains fifteen tales, seven by the Queen, one by each of the seven Sages, and one by the Prince. The scene is generally Rome, the Emperor being Diocletian.

The *Seven Sages* did not become so popular in England as on the Continent. The English versions fall into two groups— the Middle English, and the Early Modern English. There are eight Middle English versions in nine MSS., MSS. Cotton and Rawlinson being copies of one text. Seven of these versions are from one thirteenth-century original now lost. MS. Aslone is from a separate French version. The eight English versions fall into three, perhaps four, groups. Group 1, originally Kentish of 1300-1325, is in short couplets; it is represented by MS. Auchinleck (1330-1340), 2646 lines, beginning and ending lost, Kentish; MS. Egerton 1995. (1450-1500), 3588 lines, complete, probably Kentish; MS. Arundel 140 (15th century), 2565 lines, fragmentary and defective, Kentish; MS. Cbg. Univ. Libr. Ff II 38 (c. 1450), 2555 lines, incomplete and defective, dialect mixed but Southern; MS. Balliol College Oxford 354 (early 16th century), 3708 lines, complete, Southern. Group 2 is originally South-East Midland; it is represented by MS. Cbg. Univ. Libr. Dd I 17 (end of 14th century), in short couplets, 3453 verses, complete, South Midland with many Northern forms. Group 3 is originally Northern of 1300-1350 in short couplets; it is represented by MS. Cotton Galba E IX (1400-1430), 4328 verses, complete; and MS. Rawlinson Poetry 175 (c. 1350), 3974 verses, incomplete. Representing a Scottish version, and perhaps a fourth group, is MS. Aslone (beginning 16th century) in the Library of Malahide Castle, Ireland, about 2800 verses, incomplete, Scottish probably from a French prose original.

A synopsis of the Cotton text will give a sufficient notion of the versions in general.

Diocletian, Emperor of Rome, sends his only son to be educated by seven wise men. The boy acquires vast learning. The Emperor weds a lady. Jealous that the child shall be her husband's heir, the Queen persuades the Emperor to send for the boy. She arranges by magic that, if he speak within seven days after his arrival, he shall die and his masters shall suffer. By his craft, one of the masters discovers the plot. The youth promises that he will be silent during the seven days. He goes to court. The Queen attempts to lead him to speak by making love to him. This failing, she accuses him to the Emperor of attempting her honor. The boy is ordered to punishment. The courtiers persuade the Emperor to be lenient. Then follow a series of seven tales told by the Queen, one on each of seven nights; and another of seven tales told by the seven sages, one on each of the succeeding mornings. The Queen's tales are to convince the Emperor of the danger of his son's supplanting him; the sages' tales are all to show that one should not trust women. Every night, the Emperor sides with the Queen; and at the succeeding dawn he orders the boy to execution. Every morning, he sides with the sages, and orders the youth to be delivered. The Queen tells of the small tree that brought about the destruction of the larger one; of the boar that was beguiled and slain by the herdsman; of the son who, caught stealing treasure, concealed his guilt by decapitating his father; of the steward who for gold gave his wife as concubine to a king, and was banished; of the emperor who through cupidity lost the tower made by Virgil at Rome; of the child Merlin's curing of Herod's blindness by revealing the tricks of his seven wise men; of seven wise men who by craft saved Rome from her pagan besiegers, and so supplanted the rightful emperor. The wise men tell of the faithful hound unjustly slain by his master because of women's counsel; of Ypocras who from jealousy slew his apt pupil; of the husband who shut out his unfaithful wife at night, but suffered from his own craft; of the young wife who through her mother learned that she had better be true to her unloving old husband; of the trick played by a wife and her lover on a friar, and how the husband found out the truth too late; of the wife who maimed the body of her husband and hung it on the gallows, but failed to win the knight she loved; of the knight who won the wife of an earl who shut her in an inaccessible tower.—The seven days being passed, the youth Florentine speaks out and tells a tale of a king who, jealous of the prophesied superiority of his son, attempted to drown him, but finally acknowledged the child's greater achievements. The false Queen confesses, and is burned at the stake.

Reading the series of stories, one does not wonder at the popularity of the *Seven Sages*. The tales are varied; each is interesting and, though without poetical merit, is well told. The weakness is in the general frame, in the pliancy of the Emperor, who, accommodatingly for the plot, shifts between favor and hostility to his son in accord with the purpose of each narrator.

f the later English versions may be mentioned that printed
de Worde before 1520; the edition by Copland between
8 and 1561; John Rolland's Scottish version in heroic
plets of about 1560, reprinted five times before 1625; the
matic piece by Dekker, Chettle, Haughton, and Day; and
many chap-books based on de Worde.

CHAPTER III

CHRONICLES

During the greater part of the Middle English period English writers of histories or of chronicles naturally composed their matter in Latin or, in the earlier years, in French. Despite the patriotic example set by the writers of the *Old English Chronicle* before the Conquest and even up to the middle of the twelfth century, the historical writers in English before the death of Chaucer are few. Yet there survive from the period eight or nine chronicles in the vernacular, some of them of great importance. These are the continuations of the *Old English Chronicle*, Layamon's *Brut*, Robert of Gloucester's *Chronicle*, the *Short Metrical Chronicle*, Thomas Bek of Castelford's *Chronicle*, Robert Mannyng of Brunne's *Story of England*, Barbour's *Bruce*, Trevisa's translation of Higden's *Polychronicon*, and the *Brut* or *Prose Chronicle*.

THE OLD ENGLISH CHRONICLE [1], which is extant in seven MSS., was carried on after the Conquest at Winchester (MS. Corpus Christi College Cbg., the Parker MS.), at Worcester (MS. Cotton Tiberius B IV), and at Peterborough (MS. Laud 636). The Winchester additions (Parker MS.) are eleven short statements of local occurrences between 1005 and 1070. The Worcester continuation consists of a series of careful entries up to 1079, and probably contained entries up to 1107, apparently taken over from the Peterborough text. The extant Worcester items are in the standard Wessex English, and were composed probably by, or under the direction of, Wulfstan, who was Bishop of Worcester in 1062-1095. After the burning of the monastery at Peterborough in 1116, and the rebuilding of the minster in 1121, a full edition of the chronicle based on the Worcester, the Winchester, and the Abingdon versions, was undertaken at Peterborough, and was continued, probably by one hand, to 1131. From 1132 a second hand carried it to 1154. The former writer is somewhat romantic in his tendencies, and is especially interested in the events connected with the Church; his account of his own monastery and its misfortunes is particularly impressive. The second writer concludes the whole with an affecting picture of the anarchy in the land, the cruelty of the nobles, and the misery of the people, under Stephen.

A PROSE FRAGMENT [2] of an Old English chronicle of the twelfth century, covering one page of MS. Cotton Domitian A IX f. 9, and dealing with the years 1113-1114, needs but to be mentioned here.

LAYAMON'S BRUT [3] is not only the most prominent of the English chronicles, but, from a literary and linguistic ✓ point of view, one of the most important works of the Middle English period. The *Brut* is in two MSS., the second of which is not dependent on the first. The earlier, A, originally a separate MS., but now the first part of MS. Cotton Caligula A IX, is of the first quarter of the thirteenth century. It contains 32241 short lines in the South-Western dialect. The second MS., B, is Cotton Otho C XIII, some fifty years later than A, and South-Western, the Midland traits often spoken of having been shown to be not such. This MS. was badly damaged in the fire of 1731; of the original, estimated at 26960 short lines, but 23590 complete lines and about a thousand imperfect lines, remain. B is a recension different from A; it is not based on A, and it does not present the original as Layamon wrote it; it is a modified text corrected apparently by reference to a version of Wace.

The original text was written probably in the mixed dialect of North Worcestershire. The evidence for the date, some of it very questionable, points to completion in 1205. In his charming first lines the author tells that he was Layamon, a priest, son of Leovenath, and dwelt at Ernleȝe at a noble church on the bank of the Severn near Radestone. There he read

books (A *bock*, B *bokes;* taken by some to mean that he was a
'reading clerk'), and it came into his mind to write of the noble
deeds of the English—their names, their origin, who first possessed the land, from the time of the Flood. So he journeyed
over the country, and he procured the noble books that he took
as patterns—the English book that St. Bede made, and another
in Latin by St. Albin and St. Austin; and he laid in the midst
a third made by a French clerk, Wace, who knew well how to
write, and who gave his work to Eleanor 'who was the high King
Henry's Queen.' Layamon lovingly read the books, and took
pen and wrote on bookskin, compressing the three works into
one.

Ernley, near Redstone, has been identified as Lower Arley or
Arley Regis, three and a half miles from Bewdley in Worcestershire. The books that Layamon procured were the Old English translation of Bede's *Historia Ecclesiastica*, the original
Latin of the same work, and Wace's *Le Roman de Brut*, the
Anglo-Norman version of Geoffrey of Monmouth's *Historia
Britonum* (see page 31), completed in 1155 and dealing with
the supposed history of Britain from the fall of Troy to the
death of Cadwallader in 689. The title 'Brut' was not uncommonly applied to chronicles of Britain; it originated probably
from the fact that to Brutus, grandson of Ascanius, was
ascribed the founding of the British race in Britain.

The latest investigation points to the conclusion that Layamon did draw chiefly from Wace—not, however, from the well-
known version of *Le Roman*, but from some later recension in
which were combined substantial elements from the rimed
chronicle of Gaimar (see page 31), with influence from other
sources, such as the Lancelot and Tristram poems. At least, it
would appear that this redaction of Wace was supplemented
with Breton material derived from Norman composition. The
suggestion that Layamon used works other than those he mentions, is supported by a passage not in Wace, where (1.24276)
he remarks 'some books say certainly'; by another (1. 4249) to
the effect that manifold examples of the glory of Dunwale is 'in
books'; and by another (1. 28869) after the name 'Carric,' 'in
many books men so write his name.' Of course, effort to gain

authority by reference to pretended works, was common in the period. All of this bears on the question of how much of the matter in Layamon not in Wace, was due to the English poet himself. Layamon's A-text has 32241 short lines; Wace has 15300 lines. A list of the more important passages not in Wace, is given in the introduction of Madden's edition. Until recently it has been assumed that most of what is not in Wace was added by Layamon largely from contemporary traditions of the West of England and the border of Wales. But if an at present inaccessible version of Wace be accepted as direct source of the *Brut*, one cannot be at all sure of what Layamon did do with his bases, especially if one admit the theory that much of his supposed Welsh traditional matter is really from a Norman source that is Gaimar or that is similar to Gaimar. To influence of Gaimar have been ascribed certain tendencies of Layamon—for instance, something of his use of direct discourse, his diffuseness, his invocations of the gods, his assurances of the truth of what he relates. It is little necessary to suppose that Layamon used Geoffrey of Monmouth directly; the evidence for such use is slight, especially since we have not for study the actual version of Wace used by Layamon. Bede, either in Latin or in English, Layamon seems not to have used. Perhaps right are the contentions that the poet cited Bede merely after the common practice of claiming the authority of a celebrated writer on the subject dealt with, and that the mention of three works in three different languages is merely conventional. Possibly Layamon's original, the made-over version of Wace, had some such list of authorities, and Layamon merely took them over. It is to be noted that text B ascribes the three works respectively to Bede, Albin, and Austin.

Whatever be the truth as to the sources and the nature and the extent of Layamon's borrowings, the work as it stands is extremely valuable and attractive. It is a tremendously long story of the Britons, from the ancestors of Brutus, the founder of Britain, to the final driving out of the Britons to Wales under Cadwallader, ending with 689. The beginning and the ending of the work are, then, not arbitrary, but are in accord with a unified plan. The poem falls into three chief parts:

lines 1-18532, dealing with the early history from the fall of Troy to the begetting of Arthur; lines 18533-28651, dealing with the story of Arthur (see page 32); lines 28652-32241, dealing with the history from the passing of Arthur to the final expulsion of the Britons by Æthelstan.

That the Arthurian material should occupy a third of the whole *Brut*, is in accord with Layamon's ideals and his method, as they are exhibited throughout the poem. Probably he believed in the truth of what he dealt with—but he was always interested especially in the heroic and the romantic aspects of a theme. At the opening of his work he declares that he would tell of the 'noble deeds of the English.' It is these of which he ever tells, the noble deeds. He loves valor, vigor, energy, power, bold speech, a heroic fight. He is a good hater, a strong lover. He is enthusiastic, responsive, wrapt up in each incident with which he deals. He hates evil and all vicious conduct with a hearty hatred, and he leaps warmly to admiration and reverence for the good and the brave. He is a devoted partisan of the Faith; his heroes are champions of Christianity, his villains are crafty but valiant heathen. He is a patriot filled with all the Englishman's love of his island home, and pride in her defense and her conquests. It is true that this religious and patriotic spirit produces some curious anachronisms and confusions; but that is to be expected of every vigorous and earnest mediæval soul—'so doth every man that can another love,' he says of the Britons' perhaps exaggerated boasting of Arthur, and in saying it he speaks for all time.

Vigor, vividness, realness, intenseness, dramatic effectiveness—these characterize Layamon's work everywhere. He is no dull proser in narrative; something is always happening in his accounts, they are full of life and incident. It has been shown that the poet had no little ability in the use of effective figures; his work is studded with sage bits out of a large fund of homely wisdom; page after page glows with the color of intense participation in life; the large part of his accounts is made up of direct discourse, of rousing exhortation, of ringing defiance. The piece manifests a ready eye for the picturesque and for descriptive possibility—as in the account of the splendor of Caerleon upon Usk and of the festivities there (ll. 24258 ff.), in Arthur's comparison of Childric's flight to that of the fox hunted to earth (ll. 20840 ff.), and in the account of the episode of the St. Michael giant (ll. 25636 ff.). The last two of these three passages, and part of the first, are not in Wace. Of decoration there is little, of adornment for its own sake there is nothing, in Layamon. He speaks out of his heart, with a simple and direct utterance learned from the common folk and from the older English poets. Without doubt, he followed French originals in much that he wrote, but he wrote out of himself; the unsophisticated patriotic and devout nature of the man is everywhere in absolute dominion. This is what made possible the remarkable phenomenon of the earlier version of 32241 short lines with but 87 words of Romance origin, and the later version with but 63 more. It is this, too, that gave him the power to compose the vigorous ringing lines that make him, despite the changed notions of verse by which he was influenced, a worthy successor of the Old English heroic poets.

The lines of the *Brut* are an extremely interesting and valuable monument of the spirit of Old English alliterative verse incarnated in a curiously Protean form. The verse is divided into two staves, as is the Old English line. It is controlled predominantly by the presence of but two stressed important syllables in the stave, though at times three or four such stressed syllables occur in the stave. Alliteration usually marks stresses, though not infrequently the alliterative sequence is confined to but the one stave, or to but one syllable in each of the two staves. Now and again syllable-counting seems to be prominent. Rime of end of stave with end of stave is common. Sometimes, when two or three or four of these phenomena occur together, the result approaches the short couplet. The versification is a precious record of a stage of the transition from the old ideals to the new.

The Arthurian matter in Layamon has been discussed already (see page 32).

ROBERT OF GLOUCESTER'S RIMED CHRONICLE

[4] exists in two recensions. The earlier is in MSS. Cotton

Caligula A XI (earlier 14th century), Harley 201 (c. 1400), Br. Mus. Additional 19677 (1390-1400), and several later MSS.; the later recension is in MSS. Trinity College Cbg. R, 4, 26 (late 14th century), Digby 205 (14th or early 15th century), Cbg. Univ. Libr. Ee IV 31 (c. 1430-1440), Lord Mostyn's Library Flintshire 259 (c. 1440), Magdalene College Cbg. Pepys 2014 (beginning 15th century), and several other later MSS. The chronicle as printed by Wright consists of 12046 verses, to which are to be added the extensions of the later redaction, and the continuation of the possible third author, C. The verses are of six stresses with cæsura at the middle, and rime in couplets. The two recensions agree substantially up to line 9137; the later, however, gives but one fifth of the space devoted by the earlier to the events from the beginning of Stephen's reign to the end of the rule of Henry III, and has no parallels to some eight hundred lines of the earlier recension.

Strohmeyer concludes that the chronicle has three authors: A, probably a monk of Gloucester, who, toward the end of the thirteenth century, wrote a verse history of England from the destruction of Troy to the death of Henry I (1135) in 9137 lines; B, probably of the same abbey, and named 'Robert' (l. 11748), who wrote up the first part and carried on the history to the end of Henry III, lines 9138-12046; C, probably also a Gloucester monk of the beginning of the fourteenth century, who wrote up the chronicle to the death of Henry I, and added an independent extension of 572 lines to follow line 9137. It has been suggested that possibly A and B wrote independently of each other.

The sources for the work are Geoffrey of Monmouth, Henry of Huntingdon, William of Malmesbury, Matthew of Westminster, Ailred of Rievaux, the Annals of Winchester, Tewksbury, and Waverley, the Southern Legend Collection, and possibly Roger of Hovenden. The author or the authors undoubtedly drew largely from tradition. The end of the chronicle shows independent first-hand testimony concerning almost contemporary events, and is apparently reliable.

The Robert who wrote at least the second form of the chronicle, lived through the civil war of Henry III. When he names himself (l. 11748), he describes vividly the battle of Evesham (1265), thirty miles from which he was sore afraid in the gloomy, dreadful weather, dark with heavy clouds from which fell a few drops of rain. The author (for a moment for brevity we may assume a single author) was not a poet, indeed seems to have made no pretense at poetry. He wrote in verse because most vernacular work was so composed; he wrote in English because he would popularize the story of the land he loved so well. He was not learned, but he was more of the scholar than was Layamon. The list of the sources shows that he looked widely for materials. His judgment in choice of source and of matter is not always very good, but he was careful and anxious for the truth, and sought to be impartial. Arthur was the hero; to him he devotes a large part of the chronicle. The mysterious, however, as associated with him, he had little patience with. The mystery of the proof of Arthur's birth he does not touch; he protests against the common belief that Arthur is to come again—he is dead, only recently his bones were uncovered by the altar in Glastonbury! Among the best of the poet's work are his not infrequent comments on the events that he has dealt with, and his effective description. He is an ardent admirer and lover of England and Englishmen. The note struck in the first lines accompanies all the story: 'England is the best land,' the fairest, the richest; the nobility and purity and beauty of Englishmen are so manifest that everywhere in other lands men point out the native of the island. Simplicity, guilelessness, warmth and generosity of feeling, goodness, enthusiastic love of purity and truth, exultant pride in the physical nature and the institutions and the men of England, ardent patriotism—these are the great characteristics of the work. Genuine, artless, sincere, direct, warm, these adjectives characterize best the poem, to which one is drawn more by sympathetic feeling than by admiration. Notable passages are the account of the town and gown riot in Oxford in 1263, and the descriptions of the battle of Evesham and the death of Simon de Montfort.

The Southern collection of Saint's Lives sometimes ascribed

to Robert, are not his, though, since they were composed in
Gloucestershire in the thirteenth century, it is quite possible
that he had some connection with some of the pieces. It has
been urged that he wrote the *Becket* in this collection (see page
301).

THE SHORT METRICAL CHRONICLE OF ENGLAND
[5], in short couplets, is in five recensions in five MSS. The
recensions fall into three groups according to the ground they
cover. The first group, which is without episodes, is in MS.
Cbg. Univ. Libr. Ff V 48 (15th century), probably written
down at about 1307, extending to the death of Edward I; and
in MS. Royal 12 C XII (c. 1340), South-West Midland, probably written down in the reign of Edward II, extending to the
death of Piers Gaveston. The second group, extending to
Edward I without episodic details, is in MS. Br. Mus. Additional 19677 (14th century), probably written down first at
about 1307; and in MS. Auchinleck (1330-1340), first written
down in 1327-1328 and probably near London. The representative of the third group is in MS. Cbg. Univ. Libr. Dd XIV
2 (15th century), extends into the reign of Henry VI, and
was probably written down in 1424-1428. A version of a
chronicle in MS. College of Arms LVII, finished in 1448, seems
connected with this chronicle.

The Royal MS., which contains 1037 four-stress verses in
couplets, is the only one that has been printed. Consequently,
most of the questions connected with the versions are unsettled.
The Royal version has as its principal source Robert of
Gloucester's *Chronicle* as represented in the later redaction,
and as source for a part of it William of Malmesbury's *Gesta
Regum*. It shows also acquaintance with Wace, the B-text of
Layamon, and Geoffrey of Monmouth. The Auchinleck text is
a later working over of the original chronicle, and shows apparent influence of the French *lai Des Grauntz Jiauntz*, a Latin
treatise *De Dedicatione Eccl. Westmon.*, the St. Edmund
story, and *Richard Coer de Lyon.*

The Royal text bears everywhere the marks of priestly interest. But the writer was a sympathizer with reforms; he is

opposed to Peter's Pence, favors Stephen Langton and Simon de Montfort, and evidently approves of the execution of Gaveston. The piece was composed to give a rapid *résumé* of the history of England, from the giants before the coming of Brutus, to the death of Gaveston. The verse is very regular for the short couplet in English at the first of the fourteenth century. The story proceeds rapidly and with enthusiasm. The piece is interesting; it is nowhere a mere tedious abstract. Certainly, it would admirably accomplish its end to interest, and so to inform, the unlearned.

THOMAS BEK OF CASTELFORD'S CHRONICLE OF ENGLAND [6] is in the Göttingen Library Codex MS. Hist. 664 (end of 14th or beginning of 15th century). The piece has not yet been printed. It consists of about twenty thousand short couplets. It has been assigned to the Southern border of the North of England; Castelford is near Pontefract in Southern Yorkshire. After a prologue of 225 lines dealing with the story of Albion and her sisters as the first settlers in England, the piece is made up of eleven books extending from the account of Brutus to the accession of Edward III. As ignorance of the events of 1327 is suggested, the work may have been completed at about that year. On other grounds it is asserted that the piece is perhaps rather to be assigned a more general dating—*i.e.*, before 1350. The first 27464 verses appear to follow, often verbally, Geoffrey of Monmouth's *Historia*. The bases for the later verses are not definitely ascertained. The prologue is probably from a French source. The author shows much familiarity with the local conditions and the history of the neighborhood of York.

ROBERT MANNYNG OF BRUNNE'S RIMED STORY OF ENGLAND [7], in the East Midland dialect, was finished, as the author declares at the end of the piece, between three and four o'clock on the afternoon of Friday, May 25, 1338. The work consists of two parts, from Noah and the Deluge to Cadwallader and 689, and from Cadwallader to the death of Edward I. The first consists of 8365 short couplets; the second is made up of about 9000 alexandrines in couplets. Though at the beginning of the first part the author speaks against *rime couée* and artificial versing, in the second part he uses frequently, to the detriment of his work, both internal rime and tail-rime. The alexandrines sometimes fall into pentameters, and so make pentameter couplets.

The chronicle is in Inner Temple Library Petyt MSS. No. 511 No. 7 (before 1400), MS. Lambeth 131 (c. 1350), MS. Cotton Julius A V (end of 13th or 14th century), and a MS. in Lincoln Cathedral Library. A fragment of 176 verses (ll. 13018-193) is in MS. Rawlinson Misc. 1370 (end of 14th century). The first part is a close translation of Wace's *Brut*, and exhibits some acquaintance with Dares Phrygius, Bede, Gildas, Henry of Huntingdon, and William of Malmesbury. It has been shown that the second part is a faithful but not slavish rendering of the Anglo-Norman *Chronicle* of Pierre de Langtoft, of Bridlington in Yorkshire, who wrote at the end of the thirteenth and the beginning of the fourteenth century; that Robert expands and interpolates considerably, and frequently introduces connective material; that this added material is largely from other writers, such as Bede, Ailred of Rievaux, Henry of Huntingdon, and Nicolas Trivet, with some from *Havelok*, *Richard Coer de Lyon*, the *Life of St. Edmund*, and popular songs, and some again certainly from oral tradition and the experience of the writer himself.

In 1303 Robert had composed his *Handlyng Synne*. Now, thirty-five years later, he undertook this other long work. At the opening of the chronicle he declares that he turns the originals into English, not for the learned, but for the uncultivated— to give solace and pleasure and knowledge of their country's history, to companies of those who know no Latin or French. So he undertakes to tell all the story, beginning with Noah. 'Piers of Langtoft tells of the English; all the story to Cadwallader Wace put into French from Latin. The Latin original Piers overleaps many times, so I follow Wace; and where Wace ends, and Piers begins the English history, I take up and follow Piers. It is all written in as plain English as I know how to use, and for the love of simple men who cannot make out stranger English. It is not for praise, but for the good of the unlearned. I will write in plain terms, for too many authors, like the tellers of *Sir Tristrem*, spoil their story by trying to show off. My reward shall be my reader's prayers. Of Brunne I am, and Robert Mannyng is my name. I wrote the story in the third Edward's day in the house of Sixille, where I was for a time; and Dan Robert of Malton caused me to write it.'

It would appear, then, that Robert of Bourne in Lincolnshire was apparently connected at about 1338 with the Gilbertine establishment at Sixhill in Lincolnshire, which was under the same management as the Priory at Sempringham with which he seems to have been connected when he wrote *Handlyng Synne* (see page 342). His evident high respect for the clergy has led to suggestion that he was not in full orders. The rules of the Gilbertine order were extremely strict, but were perhaps relaxed in Robert's time.

Mannyng disclaims all attempts at originality; in independence he is inferior to Robert of Gloucester. But he is a much more attractive figure than is Gloucester. Simple, cheerful, earnest, sympathetic, alluringly garrulous about himself and his aims and his methods, expending many of the last days of his life in toil to bring to the unlearned and the idle matter that will instruct them in right notions of their country and of its past rulers, and that will entertain and comfort them when they gather in fellowship, Robert makes a charming person. Though its worth as literature or as history is slight, his work is a valuable monument of the language. Beyond his personality, of appeal to us are his interest in and his remarks about romances and ballads. He is impatient (Part II, ll. 93 ff.) with singers and seggers of Erceldoun and Kendale, and reciters of *Sir Tristrem*, all of whom spoil their original by attempting to exhibit their imagined skill in expression. He stops once to remark in surprise on the omission by Bede and Gildas of mention of Arthur, who, except the saints, was the most important personage they could have had occasion to deal with; and to regret that the French know the hero better than do the English. He is amazed and distressed that none of the historians has written of how Havelok won England, or of Athel-

wold or Goldeburgh. Why, says he, the 'lewid' tell of this in
English, and at Lincoln Castle is the very stone that Havelok
cast, and the chapel still stands wherein Havelok wedded Golde-
-burgh, and men still <u>read</u> the story in rime! The romance of
Richard Coer de Lyon (see page 150) he knew well and used
to advantage; and in his work he drew from, and partly quoted,
a number of popular songs (see page 210).

THE BRUCE [8] may be said to be practically the beginning of Scottish literature. Wyntoun attests that the author
–is John Barbour. Barbour was born at about 1320. More
details of his life are known than of that of any other writer
in English of the period, except Chaucer. On August 13,
1357, as Archdeacon of Aberdeen he was granted safe-conduct
by Edward III to go to Oxford with three other scholars to
study for a year. A month later, the Archbishop of Aberdeen
appointed him one of a commission to meet at Edinburgh to
arrange for the ransom of David II. In November, 1364, he
received a safe-conduct to pass through England with four
knights to study at Oxford or elsewhere. In October, 1365,
and in November, 1368, he was granted safe-conducts to travel
with companions through England to France. In 1372, at
Perth, he was appointed Clerk of Audit of the King's Household. In 1373 he was one of the auditors of the Exchequer. In
1376 or 1377 he was granted ten pounds by the King. In
1382-1384 he was an auditor of the Exchequer. In 1378,
possibly in recognition of the *Bruce*, Robert II granted him a
pension of twenty pounds, which was paid regularly, and which
after his death was continued until at least 1479 to his assignees
the Dean and Chapter of Aberdeen. In 1380 he assigned to the
Dean and Chapter a pension of one pound. In 1386 he received
from the King two gifts of money, and in 1388 a pension of ten
pounds. Various other details of minor importance are known
of him. Good evidence shows that he died on March 13, 1395;-
Wyntoun ascribes to Barbour the *Bruce;* a lost poetical
Brut with a theme apparently similar to that of Layamon;
and another lost poem, *The Stewartis Orygenalle* or *The
Stewarts' Genealogy.* Probably the works were composed in

the order *Bruce, Brut, Orygenalle.* In the *Bruce,* Book XIII, lines 699 ff., Barbour dates the poem 1375. The 'Barbour' who wrote the *Troy-Book* (see page 110) seems not to be the author of the *Bruce.* The suggestion that Barbour composed the Scottish Legendary, is unproved (see page 304). Similar-ity of phraseology has led several critics questionably to assign the *Buik of Alexander* to Barbour (see page 106), Brown's idea of a late redaction of the *Bruce,* has won little if any acceptance.

The *Bruce* is in MS. St. John's College Cbg. G 23 (1487; defective at beginning), and in a MS. in the Advocates' Library Edinburgh (1489). It consists of twenty 'Books' comprising a total of 13549 four-stress verses in couplets. After a pro-logue dealing with the events between 1290 and 1304, the poem proper begins with the offering of the crown to Bruce, and extends to July 20, 1332. The opening of the poem states the two purposes of the work, the giving of pleasure and the con-veyance of truth. The writer undertakes his story, and pro-ceeds to tell it, in the romance rather than in the chronicle manner. The first line after the preliminary to the prologue, is from a ballad; the poem proper opens (ll. 445-46) with the declaration, 'The romaunys now begynnys her.' Perhaps it is this, and the somewhat unfortunate identifying in Book I of Robert the Bruce with his grandfather, along with a number of minor errors, that has led to the common opinion that Barbour is not at all a reliable historical authority. But careful inves-tigation has caused Bain to declare that, besides the *Chronicon de Lanercost* and the *Gesta Annalia* of Fordun, Sir Thomas Gray's *Scala Chronica* and the *Bruce* are of the highest value as authorities for the period; that Barbour slips often in regard to details, and mistakes names; that, because of his distance from the dates of the incidents recorded, he sometimes confuses the order of events and gives wrong dates; but that the defects' detract little from the historical value of the work. Appar-ently Barbour had access to much oral tradition and to written accounts, that have perished. He states a number of times that various versions of incidents were in circulation. For the most part, he seems to have tried hard and honestly to present the facts as they were.

The Barbour who made so many expeditions for study is suggested in the many signs of wide reading in the poem. The author had acquaintance with the story of Troy (I 395, 521), the story of Thebes (II 528, VI 183), the Maccabees (I 465), the story of Julius Cæsar (I 537, III 277), the story of Arthur (I 549), the prophecies of Thomas of Erceldoune (II 86), the story of Hannibal (III 208), the story of Fiere- bras, which Bruce read to his men as he was rowed to refuge on an island on Loch Lomond (III 436), the war between the French and the Flemings (IV 240), Dionysius Cato, Virgil, and Lucan (I 343, II 520, III 561, 705, V 87, III 281). He had no sympathy with astrology or necromancy, and little regard for the supernatural. The common leaning to a sneak- -ing belief in prophecies, however, he sometimes evinces. Now and again appear traces of humor. He remarks that Edward was liberal with other men's lands (XI 148). When relating O'Dymsy's letting out of a loch in Ireland in an attempt to drown the Scottish forces, he notes that O'Dymsy entertained the Scots well, for if they had not enough to eat they had plenty to drink (XIV 366). Amusing is Earl Warren's remark to a band of foragers who returned with a single cow, 'This is the dearest beef I ever saw, for certainly it cost a thousand pounds or more' (XVIII 282).

Barbour knows how to tell a story well. Skeat has culled from the poem many examples of admirable narrative. The *Bruce* is a simple, direct, picturesque, spirited, dignified pres- entation of a series of striking episodes out of the story of the period that is covered, composed by an earnest man of noble and patriotic impulse and purpose, who, for the inspira- tion of a declining nationality, sought to tell alluringly the story of the heroism, the lofty spirit, the chivalry, of a genera- tion not long passed away.

TREVISA'S TRANSLATION OF HIGDEN'S POLY- CHRONICON [9] is of less importance than are the other chronicles.

In the earlier half of the fourteenth century Ranulph or Ralph Higden, a Benedictine monk of St. Werburg's at Chester, wrote in Latin prose his *Polychronicon*, a universal history carried down to his own days. The work was the most complete of the kind up to that date, and was popular into the sixteenth century. More than a hundred MSS. of it are extant.— Several continuations were composed. Two translations were made in English prose, one in the fifteenth century, the other by John de Trevisa. Trevisa states that his work was composed by direction of Sir Thomas of Berkeley, and was completed April 18, 1387, 'Deo Gracias.' This version is in MSS. St. John's College Cbg. H 1, Br. Mus. Additional 24194, Harley 1900, and Cotton Tiberius D VII.

Trevisa was born at Carados in Cornwall. He was a fellow of Exeter College (1362-1369), and later a fellow of Queen's College, Oxford. In 1379, with the Provost and a number of others, he was expelled by the Archbishop of York for unworthiness. Before he completed the *Polychronicon*, Trevisa had become vicar of the parish of Berkeley. He also held the position of canon of the collegiate church of Westbury-on-Severn in Gloucestershire. He died at Berkeley in 1412, and is said to lie in the chancel of the church there.

Trevisa seems to have made no effort at originality, and to have confined himself to translation. He admits that he found Higden's Latin difficult, and does actually make some careless blunders in translation. He held very literally to his original, adding only now and then brief explanations of the text. But he wrote a very short continuation that would fill about four printed pages, carrying Higden's work down to 1360, the last date mentioned being 1357; and he composed as an introduction *A Dialogue on Translation between a Lord and a Clerk.* This dialogue, as well as *The Epystle of Sir Johan Treuisa . . . upon the Translation of Polychronycon into our Englysshe Tongue*, is interesting and somewhat amusing. The latter piece contains the sentence: 'Yf ony man make of these bookes of Cronykes a better Englissh translacion and moore prouffytable, God do hym mede.'

Trevisa's work is one of the earliest pieces of English prose, and is of value chiefly to the student of language. It must be borne in mind that Caxton in his edition displaced words with others, and systematically modified Trevisa's spelling. The second translation, already mentioned as made in the fifteenth century, and Caxton's edition with ·his continuation, present, interesting stages in the development of the language.

In addition to the work already mentioned, Trevisa translated Bartholomew de Glanville's *De Proprietatibus Rerum,* finished February 6, 1398; *Dialogus inter Militem et Clericum,* ascribed incorrectly to William of Occam; Vegetius' *De Re Militaris* and Nicodemus' *De Passione Christi,* done at Berkeley's request in 1408; Ægidius Romanus' *De Regimine Principum,* preserved with the Vegetius; a sermon of Fitzralf, Archbishop of Armagh, preached at Oxford against the mendicant friars; and a spurious tract of Methodius, *On the Beginning and End of the World.* Caxton, Bale, and others ascribe to Trevisa a translation of the Bible, and Bale assigns to him several other translations.

THE BRUT OF ENGLAND or THE CHRONICLES OF ENGLAND [10], in the various forms of its French, Latin, and English versions, is preserved in some 167 MSS. Two English translations are extant, with numerous continuations. The first part of the chronicles, the common *Brut,* a prose translation of the *Brut d'Engleterre,* extends from the time of Albina and Brutus to the Battle of Halidon Hill in 1333. The best MSS. of this part are Rawlinson B 171 (c. 1400), Douce 323 (c. 1450), and Trinity College Dublin 490 (beginning 15th century). From 1333 to the death of Edward III in 1377, the chronicles are carried on in one version, the MSS., agreeing. Thereafter the accounts are continued in two independent versions. The work has no literary merit; but claims have been advanced for the historical worth of some of its details. That it was highly valued for centuries, is clear not only from the number of the extant MSS., and from the printing of it thir —teen times between 1400 and 1528, but from the fact that it was drawn on by most of the chronicle writers of the sixteenth

euth centuries. Of interest are the poetical
ge 217) of the Battle of Halidon Hill, included
4690 f. 82 v (32 short couplets) and Arundel
short couplets).

CHAPTER IV

WORKS DEALING WITH CONTEMPORARY
CONDITIONS

From the thirteenth century on, there are extant a number of writings that, because of their many variations from each other in form and extent, are difficult to classify, but that may well be grouped together on the basis of their predominating concern with contemporary political, social, ecclesiastical, or moral conditions, or with several or all of these classes of theme. The fact that a number of these pieces deal primarily or wholly with political conditions, justifies discussion of the writings in two separate groups, 1. *Political Pieces* and 2. *Satires and Complaints*. Again, the fact that many of the political pieces are prophetic, supports a sub-classification of the members of the first group as I. *Non-Prophetic Writings* and II. *Prophetic Writings;* and the fact that some of the group of satires and complaints are in long alliterative lines with notable family similarities of form and matter, supports a sub-classification of the second group into I. *Works Not in Alliterative Long Lines* and II. *Works in Alliterative Long Lines*. This general and subordinate grouping cannot be satisfactory in all respects, yet may be accepted as sufficiently adequate for such general consideration as should be given in a work like the present one.

1.   POLITICAL PIECES

Among the most interesting pieces of English verse of the period before 1400, are the political songs and ballads. Most of these are rude, many are coarse, and few are to be dignified with the name of literature. But they are right out of the life of the time—they are full of the hot passion and the bitter scorn of the participant or of the concerned onlooker; or they are the intense utterance of the more cultivated and accomplished clerk or minstrel striving to express the feeling of the day, or so to present the events of the time as to influence others to his own attitude.

I.   Non-Prophetic Writings

FRAGMENTS IN CHRONICLES.   Many political and satirical pieces were composed in the twelfth, thirteenth, and fourteenth centuries.   Fragments of a few of these, in forms modified by transmission, are preserved in several of the chronicles.

In the *Old English Chronicle* (see page 190) are passages that are conjectured to represent songs.   Of these the following are from after 1050: the *Death of Edward the Prince* or the *Son of Ironside*, 1057; the *Dirge of King Edward the Confessor*, 1065; the *Wooing of Margaret*, 1067; the *Baleful Bridal*, 1076; and the *High-Handed Conqueror*, 1086.

In Matthew of Paris [1], along with some tags in English in an entry for 1075, an account of a dream of Bartholomew, Bishop of Exeter, in 1173, and a gloss of *Terræmotus*, there is a scrap in the Battle of the Standard, 1138, and one on songs of Flemish soldiers under the Duke of Leicester, 1173.

Wyntoun preserves in his *Chronicle* [2] an eight-line stanza on the times following the death of Alexander III of Scotland. Though the extant lines are of about 1420, they probably represent a piece from soon after Alexander's death, and are so the earliest extant Scottish poetry.

Fabyan quoted in his *New Chronicle* [3] five lines of a 'mokkysshe ryme' made by the Scots against King Edward after they had driven the English forces back from Berwick; six lines of tail-rime made by the English 'in reproche of ye Scottes' whom they had beaten in the attempt to relieve Dunbar; a six-line tail-rime stanza with a refrain like that sung by the mariners in *Richard Coer de Lyon* ('with heue a lowe— with rumbylowe'; see page 150), made by the 'Scottis enflamyd with pryde in dèrysyon of Englysshe men' after Bannockburn; and four lines 'specially remembryd' from 'dyuerse truffys, roundys, and songys' made in derision by the Scots when Robert the Bruce married to the King of England his sister Jane—'Jane make peace,' they styled her.

William of Malmesbury drew from such songs, as did Robert of Gloucester and Pierre de Langtoft and his translator, Robert Mannyng of Brunne. The two latter chroniclers [4] quote from such pieces, Langtoft sometimes in French, sometimes partly in English and partly in French, and sometimes in English only. Apparently, often such compositions were paraphrased, as is the case with the first stanzas of the fourth fragment noted hereafter. All of these songs in Langtoft and Robert were probably originally in some form of English, since the English in Langtoft always occurs at the end of his quotation, as if the chronicler had tired of translating. It is difficult to say whether Robert translated back into English at all, or gave the original in every case. All of the fragments are in six-line tail-rime.

The first of these pieces, quoted in French by Langtoft, is a single stanza against John Balliol. The second, two English stanzas in Langtoft, and three stanzas with one intermediate additional stanza in Robert, is in mockery of the Scots after the battle of Berwick. The third piece, in three stanzas, of which the first two are in French in Langtoft, attacks the English after a truce at Dunbar. The fourth piece is against the Scots after the fight at Dunbar; each version consists of two English stanzas, with an introductory English stanza in Robert, that is apparently not a part of the original song. The fifth piece is a single English stanza on the same theme and against the Scots. The sixth piece urges Edward to vengeance, since John Balliol is in his power. In Langtoft this consists of eight French and two English stanzas, but in Robert it has only seven stanzas—a difference due perhaps to Robert's recollection of a variant version, and to his substitution from it for parts of what he found in Langtoft. The seventh piece is against the Scots, in Langtoft five French and two English stanzas, in Robert seven English stanzas not wholly agreeing with Langtoft and suggesting use of a variant version. The eighth piece depicts the successes of Edward, and declares the fulfilment of Merlin's prophecies. Here Langtoft's six French stanzas are paraphrased by Robert, who opposes the notion that Merlin's prophecy of the union of the three realms has been fulfilled. The ninth piece, two stanzas in English against the Scots, appears only in Langtoft. The tenth piece is in exultation over the execution of Wallace; Langtoft has one French and one English stanza; Robert inserts an interesting third stanza. All of these pieces are rough and primitive, but they let us hear directly the very voices of the rude fighting men and of the no less rude populace, in jeers and cries of exultation.

THE SONG AGAINST THE KING OF ALMAIGNE [5] was composed in the South shortly after the Battle of Lewes, and probably not later than the winter of 1264-1265. It is in MS. Harley 2253 f. 58 v (c. 1310) in eight stanzas aaaabcb, the fifth verse having three, the other verses four, stresses each, the unstressed syllables varying in number. The stanza proper concludes with the fifth verse, which usually ends with 'Wyndesore' mocking the efforts of Henry and Richard to make a stronghold of Windsor Castle by filling it with foreign troops. The last two verses of each stanza are a refrain: 'Richard, though thou be ever a tricker, trick shalt thou never more.' The piece voices the exultation of the partisan of the barons and Simon de Montfort over the defeat and capture of Henry III, his son, and Richard, Earl of Cornwall, who had been King of Germany since 1258. It mocks the King's and Richard's importation of foreign forces, jeers at Richard's really valiant defense of himself in the mill at the conclusion of the Battle of Lewes, voices de Montfort's threats against the Earl of Warren and Sir Hugh de Bigot, and promises that Prince Edward shall ride spurless on his hack to Dover and to banishment. The piece has a catching swing and a rude force of expression that must have won its hearers to enthusiastic utterance of its refrain.

THE SONG ON THE FLEMISH INSURRECTION [6] is in MS. Harley 2253 f. 73 v (c. 1310), and in the Southern dialect. It consists of seventeen eight-line tail-rime stanzas normally aaabaaab, the *a* verses of four, the *b* verses of three, stresses each, with irregular number of unstressed syllables. It voices the national hostility to France in exultation over the slaughter, by the Flemish burghers under Peter Coning, of the army of the Comte d'Artois at the Battle of Courtrai in July, 1302. The verses must have originated soon after that date; but the final stanza, which speaks of the Prince of Wales as the avenger who shall punish France, is probably an addition of about 1305. The author of the song was probably a minstrel. With rude mockery and almost brutal jests, he jeers at the proud French as 'bought and sold' by Peter Coning and his weavers and fullers; at Sir Jacques de St. Paul and his sixteen hundred knights, whose 'basins of brass' the burghers 'began to clinke' and 'broke all to pieces as a stone breaks glass,' until the French 'lay in the streets stuck like swine'; at the proud boasts of King Philip and his officers; and at the slaughter of the sixty thousand French, whose heads were 'dabbed' and 'dodded off' without ransom, all heaped huggermugger, knights and lords and men, into pits—this by a few fullers!

THE SONG ON THE EXECUTION OF SIR SIMON FRASER [7] is in MS. Harley 2253 f. 59 v (c. 1310) in 233 verses in stanzas normally aabbcddc. The first four lines of the stanza have a cæsura and five stresses each; the *d* verses have three stresses; the fifth verse has one stress; and the eighth verse has five stresses. An extra *d* verse is added to the last stanza. The piece is in the Southern dialect. It was composed after September 7, 1306, when Fraser was executed. It ante-dates November 7, 1306, the day of execution of the Earl of Athole, who at verse 218 is mentioned as not yet taken. Author-ship by a minstrel is evinced in the opening 'Lystneth, Lord-ynges,' by several occurrences of the gleeman's favorite address to his hearers, and by the rather incoherent arrangement of the material. The song expresses the English feeling toward the Scotch, all of whom are traitors to the realm. It presents vividly

the trial of Fraser and his fellows, their execution, the hanging
and the beheading, the burning of the bowels, and the drawing
and the quartering; and it points its hearers to the parts of the
bodies hanging on London Bridge close guarded, a warning to
all other traitors.   The treacherous Scots planned to bring
the English barons to death, and Charles of France would
willingly have given them aid:

> 'Tprot, Scot, for thy strife!
> Hang up thy hatchet and thy knife
> While to him lasts the life
> With the long shanks!'

AN ELEGY ON THE DEATH OF EDWARD I [8],
preserved in MS. Harley 2253 f. 73 r (c. 1310), was composed soon after the King's death on July 7, 1307.   Three
fragments of the piece, with four new lines, are in MS. Cbg.
Univ. Libr. 4407 (19) (end of 14th century).   The poem consists of 91 four-stress verses normally ababbcbc, and is in the
Southern dialect with some West Midland forms.   Unlike the
other political pieces considered here, it is a (loose) translation.   The original appears to be a French poem in MS. Cbg.
Univ. Libr. Gg I 1.   The piece is much more finished than are
most of the other English political poems.   It stresses less
Edward's martial and political achievement than his religious
attitude and purpose.   The greater number of the verses are
occupied with the lament of the Pope of Poitiers, with dramatic
narrative presentation of Edward's dying bequest and directions for a crusade, and with the thwarting of his purpose,
which the singer ascribes with characteristic Englishness to the
machinations of the King of France.   The song rings throughout with sincere emotion in face of the passing of the great
personality that had been so potent—'Though my tongue were
made of steel, and my heart wrought out of brass, never might
I tell the goodness that was with King Edward; King, as thou
art called conqueror, in every battle hadst thou glory!'

A SONG ON THE TIMES OF EDWARD II [9], in MS.
Harley 913 f. 44 v (1308-1318, before 1325), is one of the

group of poems (see pages 228, 522) associated with the name of Michael Kildare. The piece consists of 198 four-stress verses, the first two stanzas ababcbcb, the last stanza ababcc, the rest ababcdcd. Evidently the poem was composed in the early years of tHe fourteenth century.

The point of the piece is complaint against the prevalent lawlessness, and the oppression of the poor by the powerful and ruthless rich. The world is full of sorrow and strife; hate and wrath are dominant; true love is rare; and the highest are most charged with sin. Covetousness controls the law; pride and contention rule. Holychurch and Law should exert themselves against the oppressors of the poor, who should not be buried in church, but should be cast out like dogs. The King's ministers favor who bribes them; the upright man loses his possessions, and is borne to death. Now the writer connects the piece with the animal-fable: these folk are like the animals in the parable. The Lion, King of beasts, summoned the Wolf and the Fox before him, under charge of evil-doing. Men joined with the culprits the simple innocent Ass. The Fox and the Wolf sent fowls as a present to the Lion; the Ass sent nothing. The guilty were pardoned; the innocent was condemned. God and the Trinity preserve us; one can live only through covetousness and contention, and pride is master. As a man comes, so shall he go—alone and with nothing. Yet the beggar scorns his crust, and curses the giver. Trust no one, not even sister or brother. Honor God and Holychurch; give to the poor—so, do God's will, and win Heaven.

The piece is direct, and is crisp in expression. The lines predominantly have initial truncation; the recurrence of accented and unaccented syllables is notably regular. The sermonizing side by side with the satire, is obvious. Reflection of the proverb and precept literature (see page 374), and connection (st. 20) in expression with the popular *Erthe upon Erthe* (see page 387), should be noted.

ON THE KING'S BREAKING OF MAGNA CHARTA

[10], in MS. Auchinleck (1330-1340), was written probably toward the end of 1311, when Edward II was joined in the North by the recently banished Peter de Gaveston, and broke his confirmation of the Charter made in October. The piece consists of 98 verses. It opens with 20 lines, some French, some English: at a great parliament at Westminster the King made a charter of.wax, that was held too near the fire, and is now

melted away—and all goes the Devil's road. Then, in four English stanzas aabccbdddeee (the *a* and *c* verses of four, the *b* verses of three, the *d* verses of two, and the *e* verses of five, stresses each), follow the bitter, somewhat balanced declarations of four wise men, that in their pithy utterance and parallelisms remind of the saws in *Hendyng* (see page 377). Then come five English stanzas of tail-rime aabccb in fours and threes, pleading for goodness and love and Christian brotherhood.

PERS OF BIRMINGHAM [11], one of the Kildare poems, is in MS. Harley 913 f. 50 (1308-1318, before 1325). In 132 three-stress verses aabccb, rude and without any artistic merit, the balladist laments the death on April 20, 1308, of Peter of Birmingham, the really ruthless champion of the English settlers in Ireland, and extols his suppression of thieves and his relentless pursuit of the Irish. Nearly half the piece is given to exultant narrative of Peter's outwitting and destroying of a body of Irish who plotted to undo the English. 'He that this song let [? did] make' had gone on pilgrimages two hundred days and more, and got good pardon. Brandl assigns the piece to the South-West Midland.

LAURENCE MINOT [12], who gives his name twice (5 l. 1; 7 l. 20), wrote eleven poems on the wars of Edward III, preserved in MS. Galba E IX f. 49 r ff. (early 15th century). The poems were written between 1333 and 1352, each apparently soon after the event that it commemorates. Later the author revised them, and united them by placing at their heads metrical titles that link the neighboring pieces together. The opening of the last poem, the reference to Henry of Derby as Duke of Lancaster in the fifth, the inserted link at the end of the third, and several lines in the sixth, indicate that the revision and the union of the pieces were made during, or soon after, 1352.

Beyond the name, nothing is known of Minot. The poems as extant are in the Northern dialect with some Midland forms. Their themes are: 1 and 2, the Battle of Halidon Hill; 3, the expedition to Brabant; 4, the first invasion of France; 5, the sea-fight at Sluys; 6, the siege of Tournay; 7, the Battle of Crécy; 8, the siege and capture of Calais; 9, the Battle of Neville's Cross; 10, the defeat of the Spanish fleet in 1350; 11, the taking of Guisnes. The wholé, excluding the couplet links, makes up a total of 923 lines. Poems 2, 5, 9, 10, 11 are in alliterative long lines aaaabb with prevailing trochaic or dactylic rhythm. The last couplet of each stanza of 2 has refrain effect, with rime-words *wile, gile*. Poem 3 and ll. 1-20 of 7, are in short couplets. Poems 7, ll. 21-172, and 8, are in four-stress verses ababbcbc. Poem 4 is in tail-rime aabccb. Poem 1 is in regular four-stress verses abababab. Poem 6, ll. 1-48, are three-stress verses abababab; ll. 49-81 are three stanzas like the rest, but each with three lines added, the first of one stress, the last two of three stresses each. In 1, 6, 7, ll. 21-172, Minot connects stanzas by repeating in the first line of a second stanza a word or phrase used in the last line of the preceding stanza. This device, probably of popular origin, and frequent in mediæval romance lyrics, is employed in the *Pearl*, the *Awntyrs of Arthur*, and *Sayne John* (see page 311; Index, *Repetition*). The poet exhibits everywhere great fondness for alliteration and for well known alliterative phrases. Though none of the elements of his verse is original, he makes interesting combinations. The poems in long lines are metrically the best, but most of the verse is hard and unmusical—qualities to forgive when one regards the theme and the purpose of the pieces. The poems add little to knowledge of the incidents with which they deal. They exhibit animation, and often vigor and spirit. Minot has little turn for figurative speech; his style is simple, but realistic, with much of the bald unfeelingness of the other political lyrics that we have dealt with. For the French and the Scots he has the scorn and mockery of the other writers. The religious coloring seen in some of these writers is markedly observable in his work. In contrast to the ballad objectivity, his personal feeling, his own intense anxiety for the welfare of his King and his country, speaks out all through the lines. Notable are the absence of the outcry against the abuses in the realm, so common in the other political poets, and the dominance in his poems of passionate enthusiasm for the nation as a whole, and of exultation in her successes. Earnest, enthusias_tic, patriotic, mingling in himself the minstrel and the more cultivated singer, epic but dominantly lyric, of rather limited interests and of no extensive capacities, Minot is much more worthy of consideration, especially when his aims and the class of his work are regarded, than recent critics have been willing to admit.

It is to be noted that Hall claims for Minot, on the basis of resemblances in style and language with Poem 1, the *Hymn to Jesus Christ and the Virgin*, 'Fadur and Sone and Holigost' (see page 522).

THE BATTLE OF HALIDON HILL [13] (1333) is the theme of 32 short couplets in MS. Harley 4690 f. 82 v (15th century), and of 12 short couplets in MS. Arundel 58 f. 336 v (see page 207). In Harley the piece is styled a 'romance.' It presents incoherently and redundantly an account of the pursuit and slaughter and plundering of the Scots by Edward and his forces. The lines have no merit.

ON THE DEATH OF EDWARD III [14] (1377), in MSS. Vernon (1370-1380) and Br. Mus. Additional 22283 (1380-1400), consists of fourteen stanzas ababbcbc of four-stress verses, with the refrain 'Seldom seen and soon forgotten.' The piece is permeated with the gloom that marks all the verse dealing with the social and political events of the date.

All wears and wastes away. Formerly we had a noble English ship, strong against storms, a defense of the land, feared through all Christendom. A rudder governed the ship. While rudder and ship held together, they feared naught, and sailed all seas in all weathers; but now they are flitted asunder, and all is ill. The ship had a sure mast and a strong, large sail, and to it belonged a barge that set all France at naught, and was a shield to us all. The rudder was the noble King Edward the Third; the helm was borne up by the Prince of Wales, never discomfited in fight; the barge was Duke Henry (of Lancaster), who ever chastised his enemies; the mast was the Commons; the wind that bore the vessel on, was good prayers. But all these are gone. A promising impe (Richard II) of the stock of these lords, is beginning to grow. I hope he will prove to be a conqueror. Meanwhile, let both high and low aid and maintain him. The French are bragging, and are scorning us.

Take heed of your doughty King who died in his age, and of his son Edward; two lords of such worth I know not—and they are being forgotten!

LETTERS AND SPEECHES OF REBELS IN 1381 [15]. In Thomas Walsingham's *Historia Anglicana* under date 1381, is *Littera Johannis Balle, Missa Communibus Essexiœ*—some seventy-five words of prose and nine lines of doggerel rime from 'John Carter,' bidding to beware of guile and to stand together. In Knighton's *Chronicon* under 1381, are three short English prose addresses of from eighty to a hundred words each, declared to have been delivered in London by the insurgent leaders, Jack Milner, Jack Carter, and Jack Trueman; and along with these are a letter of some sixty words, and another of some ninety words, purporting to be from John Ball.

THE REBELLION OF JACK STRAW [16], in alternating English and Latin verses, was composed probably by a clerk, and apparently soon after the putting down of the outbreak in 1381. The piece is in MSS. Corpus Christi College Cbg. 369 (later 14th century) and Digby 196 (15th century), the latter supplementing the former, and bringing the total of verses up to seventy. The first six and the ninth of the nine stanzas are abababab, the English or *a* lines of three stresses sometimes with feminine ending, the Latin or *b* lines each of three stresses with feminine ending. Stanzas 7 and 8 (and 6 of Digby) are ababab. A Latin couplet concludes the piece. In a few rapid verses (the Latin lines being usually a sort of chorus or comment), the writer outlines the rebellion, from the beginnings in Kent to the overthrow of Straw in Smithfield by the King. The author has no sympathy with the uprising and the violent behavior of the churls. He feels ardently with the King; he regards him as not at all responsible for the distresses of the land, but as, like the rest of the realm, in the grasp of the evil—may God ever defend and guide him!

ON KING RICHARD'S MINISTERS [17], in a MS. formerly owned by W. Hamper, Esq., of Deritend House, Birmingham, was composed, as its contents show, in 1399. It consists of fifteen tail-rime stanzas aabccb.

By punning on 'a busch that is forgrowe,' 'the long gras that is so grene,' and 'the grete bagge that is so mykille,' the writer utters his feeling against the King's three most objectionable ministers, Bushey, Greene, and Bagot. Designating the persons by the features of their arms, he declares that Bushey caused the death of the swan (the Duke of Gloucester, murdered in 1397); that Greene slew the horse (the Earl of Arundel); that a bearward (the Earl of Warwick) found a rag, and made a bag through which he is undone (*i.e.*, he aided to raise up Bagot, who became instrumental in his banishment). The swan's mate is grief-stricken, her eldest bird (Humphrey Plantagenet) is taken from her; the steed's colt (Thomas of Arundel) has escaped, and has joined the heron (the Duke of Lancaster); and the bearward's son (Richard Beauchamp) has been married off, but is watching to join the heron. The heron and the colt are up in the North in company with the geese and the peacocks (the Percies and the Nevilles). The heron will alight on the bush, and will fall upon the green. The bag is full of rotten corn; the geese and peacocks and many other birds will be fed. The bush is bare and waxes sere, it puts forth no new leaves—there's no remedy but to hew it down. The long grass, though green, must be beaten out if it is to become nourishing. The great bag is so torn that it will hold naught; when it is hung up to dry, it may be improved enough to buy a beggar. May God grant us to see that sight, and give peace to our lean beasts that were like to be ruined.

By his allegory, whose point was quite obvious to all who heard, the writer found means to please the taste of the times, to gratify his own ingenuity, and superficially to veil his intense expression of the bitter hatred and the ardent hope for vengeance against the agents of oppression, that he felt with the people.

THE SIEGE OF CALAIS [18], 'Her biginyth the seige off Calays in the yer off our Lord j M l iiii c,' is in a fifteenth-century hand on the fly-leaf of MS. Cotton Galba E IX. It consists of 172 verses chiefly in tail-rime aabccb. The conclusion of the piece shows that when it was composed Calais was still England's. After a July nature introduction, the poem tells in very irregular metre how the Duke of Burgundy assembled his forces, besieged Calais, and was beaten off with heavy losses. The narrative is vigorous, with close details that show that the writer's heart and eye were on the work, and that give an excellent picture in action of the various features of a fourteenth- or fifteenth-century siege. The accounts of the Irishman who did such scathe to the French, and of the hound belonging to the water-bailey that rushed out and attacked the besiegers, horse and man, are more specific examples of the picturesque narrative that carries one right into the midst of the scene.

Here may be mentioned a group of political pieces [19] of the opening years of the fifteenth century in MS. Digby 102, another group of the same period printed by Wright, and the alliterative *Crowned King* of about 1415.

II.   Prophetic Writings

In England during our period, as in the rest of Western Europe, political prophecies were popular. Several Latin pieces, the *Vision of Edward the Confessor* and the *Omen of the Dragons,* date from before the twelfth century. But the great influential early prophecies are those in Geoffrey of Monmouth's Latin *Book of Merlin* (partly preserved in fragments in Ordericus Vitalis, and in the seventh book of Geoffrey's *Historia;* see page 39), and his Latin narrative *Vita Merlini,* both of the first half of the twelfth century and both from earlier materials. From a little later, is another treatment of the matter in the Latin verse *Prophecy of Ambrosius Merlin concerning the Seven Kings.* This has the form of question and answer, and purports to have been made by John of Cornwall from the Welsh. Giraldus Cambrensis preserved traces of another group, and planned treatment of the prophecies, in the third book of his *Expugnatio Hibernica* (see page 40). The so-called *Prophecy of the Eagle,* under the name of Merlin Silvester or Caledonicus, is in several thirteenth-century MSS. Following these, came various pieces in French or Latin or both, with some in English, extending up to a date several centuries beyond 1400, and cherished widely for guidance as to the political future of the nation or of its parties. All of these pieces are confused and, from their very nature and their method, obscure. Probably from Geoffrey's practice, use of birds and animals to designate personages or parties dealt with, was especially preferred in England over the other types of symbolism in compositions of this class. To lend weight to them, the prophecies were commonly fathered on eminent personages, as Bede, Gildas, Merlin, Thomas à Becket, John of Bridlington, and Thomas of Erceldoune.

We are here concerned with the pieces in English composed wholly, or probably partly, before 1400—the *Here Prophecy*, Adam Davy's *Five Dreams*, the *Prophecy of the Six Kings*, *Thomas of Erceldoune*, the Northumbrian *Ballad on the Scottish Wars*, and the so-called *Scottish Prophecies* connected with à Becket.

'HATEST THOU URSE, HAVE THOU GOD'S CURSE' [20], are the first two verses (all that are quoted in English) of a metrical prophetic curse ascribed by William of Malmesbury to Aldred, last Saxon Archbishop of York. Urso had encroached on ecclesiastical land.

THE HERE PROPHECY [21], five riming lines preserved in two versions by Benedict of Peterborough, is very obscure in sense. It is concerned with conditions of about the time of the accession of Richard I, and was composed probably near the beginning of 1191—at least soon after Ralph Fitz-Stephen, in 1189, raised the image of a hart on a dwelling given him by Henry II.

ADAM DAVY'S FIVE DREAMS ABOUT EDWARD II [22], consisting of 83 short couplets, is in MS. Laud 622 f. 26 v (c. 1400). The piece speaks of Edward (1307-1327) as still living, and prophesies that he shall become Emperor. It has been urged that line 76 shows that the verses were written during the interregnum (1314-1316) after the death of Clement V. The author thrice names himself 'Adam Davy,' and twice declares he is 'the Marshal of Stratford-atte-Bowe' and well known far and wide. The verses are not very interesting, and have no poetical value.

Adam dreamed first that, armed in steel and crowned with gold, Edward stood before the shrine of St. Edward; that two knights laid on him with swords—yet, though he did not resist, he was not wounded; that the knights departed, and from each of Edward's ears issued four streams of light.   Then he dreamed that Edward rode on an ass as a pilgrim to Rome; he wore a gray cap, his feet and legs were bare, and his shanks were blood-red.   Next he dreamed of the Pope at Rome in his mitre preceding Edward, who walked crowned in token that he should be Emperor.   Then he dreamed that, in a chapel of Mary, the Christ unnailed His hands, and obtained from the Virgin permission to accompany the pious Edward on a crusade.   Finally, he dreamed that Edward, clad all in red, stood before the high altar at Canterbury.   After the fourth dream, a voice warned Adam to make known his vision.   After the fifth dream, an angel directed him on pain of punishment to communicate to the King what he had seen.   Adam declares, 'Therefore, my lorde sir Edward the Kyng, I shewe you this ilke metyng, as the Aungel it shewed me in a visioun.'

THE PROPHECY OF THE SIX KINGS TO FOLLOW KING JOHN [23], headed in the MS. Cotton Galba E IX f. 49 r (early 15th century), 'Here begins prophecies of Merlin,' is a translation, in 139 short couplets, of a French version of a piece that is extant in Latin and in several French texts. The date is doubtful: the MS. is of the early fifteenth century; but the matter on the end of the reign of Edward II suggests that perhaps the original piece was written before the death of that monarch in 1327.   The framework is derived from the influential *Book of Merlin* (see page 220) of Geoffrey of Monmouth, alluded to in the heading in the MS.   The matter indicates that, as it stands, the piece is an attack on Henry IV by the Percy-Glendower-Mortimer faction.   The prophecies begin with the Lamb of Winchester (Henry III), who is to be succeeded by his heir, the Dragon (Edward I), who is to be followed by a Goat (Edward II), after whom shall come a Lion (Edward III), who shall be followed by an Ass (Richard II), to whom shall succeed a Mole (Henry IV).   A closely related English prose version of the *Six Kings* is in the fifteenth-century *Brut* (see page 206).

A BALLAD ON THE SCOTTISH WARS [24], as Ritson styled it, beginning 'As y yod on ay mounday' and composed in

Northumberland, is in MS. Cotton Julius A V f. 180 (end of
13th century, and 14th century) in 252 four-stress verses abab.
The general setting of the poem has some similarity to that of
Thomas of Erceldoune. The speaker tells of meeting a
strangely dressed little man, who, despite him, leads him into
a garden where are lords and ladies at pleasure. His inquiry
of what shall be the outcome of 'this war' between the Northern
folk and 'ours,' brings him prophetic declarations as to the
Mole, the Tup, the Bear, the Lion, and the Leopard. It is
difficult to make out much of the sense of the piece.

THOMAS OF ERCELDOUNE [25]. Thomas Rymour of
Erceldoune, the reputed composer or singer of an earlier version of the English *Sir Tristrem* (see page 79), was made the
hero of a romantic narrative, and was famed from the thirteenth century to the seventeenth as author of various prophecies concerning England and Scotland. That an actual
Thomas dwelt at Erceldoune in Berwickshire on the Leader, is
attested by contemporary legal documents, and by tradition
known to Barbour, Fordun, Mannyng, Henry the Minstrel, and
Andrew of Wyntoun. His fame as a poet is shown perhaps by
the name 'Rymour,' possibly by Mannyng's reference to
'Thomas' as author of *Sir Tristrem,* certainly by the *Tristrem*
writer's declaration that he had heard him recite the story of
Tristrem, and by the same writer's reference to him as authority. Before his death, which must have occurred earlier than
1294, Thomas had great celebrity for prophecy, his supposed
prediction of the death of Alexander III in 1286 being perhaps the most notable exhibition of his gift. MS. Harley 2253
(not later than 1310) contains a cryptic prose prophecy said
to have been made by Thomas to the Countess of Dunbar. MS.
Arundel 57 (c. 1340) contains a prophecy of ten lines by
Thomas to Alexander concerning the 'birth of the King
Edward that now is': 'To-ny3t is boren a barn. . . .' With
Thomas were associated utterances of contemporary origin,
and about him clustered vague and mysterious predictions of
greatly later date—as similar matter clustered about the name
of Merlin, and proverbial utterance about that of Alfred. To

these predictions the English and the Scotch for three centuries
looked for light. In *King Lear* Shakespeare, or an interpolater,
parodies these obscure and confused declarations.

TOMAS OF ERSSELDOUNE [25] is the chief representa-
tive of these prophecies. It is in three 'fitts,' and was probably
originally Northern English.· It is preserved in MSS. Thornton (1430-1440), 636 verses; Cbg. Univ. Libr. Ff V 48 (15th
century), 492 verses; Cotton Vitellius E X (late 15th century),
very defective, 564 verses; Lansdowne 762 (1500-1550), 491
verses; and Sloane 2578 (c. 1550), 321 verses, only fitts 2
and 3. Scattered fragments are found in various MSS. The
verses are four-stress abab; the prologue (in MS. Thornton)
has 24 verses ababbcbcbdeddedefgfgfgfg.

Though the MSS. agree in general as to their matter, they
supplement each other in a number of cases. The total number of unrepeated lines culled from the various texts, is 700.
The Thornton MS., the best and the oldest, has 636 lines.

A prologue (only in Thornton) begs attention to the difficulty of
telling of fighting, and promises to recount battles of the past and
prophecies of battles in the future. The first fitt opens after the
fashion of *Piers Plowman* and the *Parlement of the Thre Ages.*—
One glad May morning, I wandered out by Huntley banks [on the
Eildon Hills near Melrose] listening to the birds. As I lay under
a tree, I saw riding on a dapple-gray steed, a lovely lady most
richly clad, with hounds and arrows and a hunting horn. Thomas
[the text shifts to the third person] took her for Mary, and hastened
to her and knelt in prayer for mercy. The lady declared she was
not the Virgin. Thereupon, Thomas, enamored, asked her love.
Sin, she declared, would destroy her beauty. Thomas persisted;
the lady became a hideous hag. She bore him with her down to
middle earth, where she showed him a vision of the roads to Heaven,
Paradise, Purgatory, and Hell, and of the fair country over which
she was queen. Then she took him to the palace. Thomas lived
there most joyously for three years that seemed but three days.
Then, that he might not be taken by a fiend who was coming for his
annual tribute, the lady brought him up again to earth. As she
was taking farewell, Thomas begged a token of her. She predicted
to him various events of 1332-1345, and the principal events between
1298 and 1388.—Thereafter follows a confused passage with allusion to Black Agnes of Dunbar.—Thomas and the lady parted with
great grief, the lady promising to meet him at some time hereafter.
She disappeared on the way to Helmsdale.

The first 72 lines of the piece, as numbered in Murray's parallel-text edition, are in the first person; lines 73-272 are in the third person; in three MSS. line 274 is in the first person; the prophecies in lines 317-672 are in the third person without clear indication of the speaker, just like independent pieces written into the text; lines 672-700 are third-personal narrative. This, supported by the nature of the prophecies, assists the idea of cumulative authorship. Line 83 implies former existence of an earlier version in which was designated the place where Thomas and the lady met. The latest identifiable reference is to the Battle of Otterbourne (1388), at line 469—or possibly to Henry IV's invasion of Scotland in 1400, at line 505. As the first group of prophecies covers 1332-1345 in chronological order, it was composed after 1345, and probably before the next group. As the second group disregards the first and covers 1298-1388 in chronological order, it was composed probably after 1388, and after the first group. The possible allusion to 1400 would put the piece in its present form after that date. The Thornton MS. is 1430-1440. Recent argument fixes the date of the poem between 1388 and 1400. Lines 521 ff. consist of a mixture of stock traditional prophecies. Apparently the piece as it appears in the various MSS. is the result of a choice from earlier materials by various persons, with additions made at will without regard to unity. This is borne out by the appearance of the prologue only in MS. Thornton, inclusion of some passages in only one or two of the MSS., and omission of the first fitt in MS. Sloane. The earlier matter would appear to be represented by lines 1-356 and 521 to the end. Professor Child urged that the first fitt, dealing with Thomas and the lady, was originally an independent poem. This fitt seems too long and too detailed to have been written merely as an introduction to the prophecies, and may well have existed long before they were composed.

To us the important part of the piece is the first fitt, the wonder-story of fairy visitation and transfer into the underworld, a remarkable poem of fancy and mystery that throws about us to-day an atmosphere of mystic glamour. But to the fifteenth century and later periods the prophecies were more than this was. The writer of MS. Sloane copied only fitts 2 and 3. The prophecies fathered on Thomas were held in high esteem through all the fifteenth and sixteenth centuries, and even in the uprisings of 1715 and 1745. Thomas' name was associated with those of Merlin and Bede and Gildas, and in many cases his authority supplanted that of the other sages. Collections were made. Notable is the *Whole Prophesie of Scotland,* printed in Edinburgh in 1603, containing the *Prophecie of Thomas Rymour.* Interesting, too, are the *Prophecies of Rymour, Reid, and Marlyng* that are associated with Sir David Lyndesay and the young James V. Ballads seem to have been composed on the romantic story of Thomas; two of them of somewhat questionable authenticity were published by Jamieson and Sir Walter Scott.

PROPHECIES ASCRIBED TO À BECKET [26] are extant. Most of these are in Latin, and are associated with the reign of Richard II. But an English alliterative piece (with the two dealt with in the next paragraph, making up the so-called *Scottish Prophecies*) of about 100 lines is in MS. Hatton 56 f. 45 r (dialect of London, c. 1450); and in a much longer (last 256 lines extant) Northern or perhaps Scottish version in MS. Cbg. Univ. Libr. Kk I 5 (1450-1500), in its present state probably of the fifteenth century. The two versions agree generally in matter; both are defective, one aiding to fill out the other; both together give less than the whole. The piece was written apparently soon after the Battle of Poitiers (1356), which is the latest event alluded to. It has been suggested that the piece was composed to arouse confidence in Edward III, and to encourage the English in the expedition of 1360. Close relationship of features to the *Prophecy of the Six Kings* has been noted.

TWO NORTHERN ALLITERATIVE PROPHECIES [27] are with the Becket in MS. Kk, and with it make up the so-called *Scottish Prophecies*. The one is a mixture of prophecies beginning with matter on the Cock of the North. A version of this in 73 lines is in MS. Harley 1717 f. 249 v, in a fifteenth-century hand. The other piece is a mixture of Northern alliterative lines and couplets opening with prophecy of what will happen 'when Rome is removed into England.'

2. Satire and Complaint

Of what may be called satire in the limited sense of the term, there is little in English before the sixteenth century. Yet extant from before 1400 are a number of English writings that deal with contemporary distresses, abuses, or ill conduct, with an ultimate object of correction. These pieces are but the vernacular products of a great activity that found its voice in a host of similar compositions in French or in Latin, where are treated similar themes with like purposes and often in much the same general forms. This use of the three tongues for the common material, is illustrated in the several occurrences, that will be noted, of use of two or three of the languages in a single piece.

The English writings will be discussed in chronological order, those in the long alliterative verse, with their special family peculiarities, being' dealt with in a group after the others.

I. Works Not in Alliterative Long Lines

HWON HOLY CHIRECHE IS VNDER UOTE [28], in 18 pentameter couplets with cæsural pauses, composed in the South-West of England in 1225-1250, is in MS. Jesus College Oxford 29 f. 254 v (c. 1275). It is directed against the prevalent simony, and is one of the many outbursts against abuses by the clergy, that we are wont to regard as uttered not before a much later date.

Whilom Christ called St. Peter a stone, and upon him set the Church. Now those who should be her protectors are her foes; she has no friends, and her honor is almost gone. For Simon, Simony rules. After Peter, came Clement and Gregory, who suffered much, but preserved the Church aright; for some time after them, she stood firm. Now with silver and gold men seek to fell her to the earth. None will suffer for her as did Stephen and

Thomas, or honor her as did Edmund. High and low, clerks and laymen, hold her in hatred. The Pope takes gifts. May God send her salvation, that we in this life may see it!

The piece has no poetic merit. Its worth consists in its theme, in the earnestness of its author, and in the widespread feeling of which it is a voice.

THE LAND OF COCKAYGNE [29], often styled a *fabliau*, consists of 95 short couplets of 1250-1300 in MS. Harley 913 f. 3. The MS. was written probably between 1308 and 1318, at latest before 1325. With several French bits, it contains Latin and English (see pages 214, 215, 232, 274, 324, 328, 352, 354, 382, 387, 392, 394, 503, 516, 522) pieces composed probably in or about the Abbey of Kildare in Ireland, by emigrants from Southern or South-Western England. So it is sometimes called 'the Kildare MS.'

'Bi weste Spaygne' is the Land of Cockaygne, compared with which Paradise is naught. There is every joy, free from strife and all ill. The rivers are oil and milk and wine and honey. There are a fine abbey of white monks and gray, and a cloister and a church, whose walls and roofs are flesh and pastry and pudding. In the cloister a tree bears all kinds of pleasant spices. There are wells of balm and wine. Birds sing sweetly. Geese fly roasted to the abbey, crying, 'Geese all hot! all hot!', and the larks fly down to one's mouth all ready to be eaten. The glass windows turn to crystal when more light is needed for the Mass. The monks here and in the neighboring abbey have fine doings with the nuns that dwell with them. Who would come to that land must perform the penance of wading for seven years in swine's ordure.

The theme of the Land of Fair-Ease was known widely. The extant French treatment varies greatly from the English, which possibly is from a lost French source. Of the 95 English couplets, 70 are devoted to the abbeys and the life of the clergy. As the ecclesiastical matter and other details (*e.g.*, the seven-year test) are not a part of the general Cockaygne theme, they may be the English poet's additions. Several striking features suggest satire against specific conditions, possibly some at the Abbey of Kildare. But the satire would as well be accepted as of more general application. Certainly, the writer, possibly a Goliardic clerk of specially lively imagination, was actually sympathetic, rather than hostile, toward the proceedings of the monks and the nuns.

THE SONG OF THE HUSBANDMAN [30], in Southern English of before 1310 and perhaps of about 1297, is in MS. Harley 2253 f. 64 r (c. 1310). It consists of 72 four-stress verses with irregular number of unstressed syllables, and with prevalent alliteration on the stresses. The lines are in stanzas alternately abababab and abab. Usually the final verse of a stanza is bound to the first verse of the next by repetition of a word or of words (see Index, *Repetition*), as in the *Pearl*, the *Awntyrs of Arthur*, etc. The wars of Edward I caused the imposition of crushing taxes that in some cases among the lower orders made existence almost impossible. In passionate bitterness, as from the bottom of his soul, the author of the *Song* raises a powerful plaint of despairing misery.

> Men on the earth make lamentation; the good years and the corn are both gone—now must we work without hope. I can no longer live by my gleanings, yet ever the fourth penny must to the King. It is hard to lose from so little; yet hayward and woodward and bailiff oppress us—there remains to us neither riches nor repose. The poor are robbed and picked full clean; barons and bondmen and clerks and knights and clergy are borne down; many who once wore robes, now wear rags. More than ten times I paid you tax, yet I must give feasts for the beadles when they come to collect. What I used to save, I must spend in anticipation of the coming of these catchpoles. The master-beadle arrives rough as a boar, he declares he will make my house bare; I must bribe him with a mark or more. They hunt us as a hound doth a hare on the hill. I sold my seed to get silver for the King, so my land lies fallow. Since they took away my fair cattle from the fold, I well nigh weep when I think on my weal. Thus breed they bold beggars. Our rye is rotted ere we reap, because of the evil weather. Consternation and woe awake.—It were as well to perish at once, as so to labor.

AGAINST THE PRIDE OF THE LADIES or LUXURY OF WOMEN [31], in the Southern dialect of not later than 1310, is an intense outburst against the vanity of women of the middle and the lower classes in their efforts to deck themselves in the elaborate garb made the mode in the latter half of the thirteenth century. The piece is in MS. Harley 2253 f. 61 v (c. 1310), in five stanzas aaaabbb. The *a* verses have each six

stresses with cæsura after the third stress, the syllables ending
the first halves of the lines riming with each other.   The fifth
line has one stress; the seventh, three stresses; the sixth, from
two to four stresses.   Driven by intense moral feeling, and filled
with disgust, the author attacks the offenders with bitter,
passionate invective, expressive of the attitude of the clergy
of the day toward the excesses of fashion, and anticipates what
one would expect of an especially narrow Puritan of the middle
seventeenth century.   One feels that the humor of a gleeman
would have accomplished more, in the situation, than would this
abusive onslaught.

ON THE RETINUES OF THE GREAT [32], ten stanzas
abcbdbeb, is in MS. Harley 2253 f. 124 v (c. 1310).   It is in
the Southern dialect, and was written before 1310—perhaps
before the death of Edward I (1307).   There are two stresses
to the verse, and alliteration is so common as to suggest that
the stanza is really composed of four alliterative lines with one
end-rime.

In galloping rhythm the minstrel vents his wrath against the
swarm of horse-boys and pages and hangers-on that accompany
those who 'ride on horses.'   Bitterly he inveighs against the ribald,
impudent knaves, who rise early, scraping their scabs, and cramming
their crops before cockcrow; who ape the fashions, going about
with buttons as if they were brides, wearing low-laced shoes, and
content with only the pick of fine food.   Christ walked; He would
have no snarling, jawing gadelings attend Him.   'Hearken this
way, horsemen . . . ; ye shall hang, and lodge in Hell.'

A SATIRE ON THE CONSISTORY COURTS [33], in
MS. Harley 2253 f. 70 v̇ (c. 1310), consists of five elaborately
wrought stanzas, each aabccbddbeebffgggf.   Alliteration is
extensive, the *a, c, d, e* and first two *f* verses representing the
old long alliterative line of two staves, the others a single stave
of the long line.   The poem is of the reign of Edward I, and is
a Southern making-over of an original in mingled Northumbrian and East Midland speech.   It is a coarse and abusive
attack on the minor ecclesiastical courts by one purporting to
be a culprit summoned for trial, apparently for illicit behavior
with women.   Very realistically are presented the 'old churl in

a black robe' presiding like a lord, 'laying his leg along,' with his forty clerks that 'pink with their pens on their parchment'— all ready to take bribes; the half-dozen summoners who reach forth their rolls—the banes of the peasantry; the court-crier in yellow, who jigs with his rod and calls in Mag or Mall, who enters covered with mould like a moor-hen, ashamed in face of the assembly of men, but screeching out that the culprit must marry her; the black thralls, who order the marriage; the priest proud as a peacock, who, after the man has been driven like a dog through the market, weds the pair.

The consistory courts perhaps were evil, and worked woe to the poor man; but one judges that this culprit got his deserts. Not the moral question in the case, but the general oppression and injustice wrought by the ecclesiastics, is the real point of the piece.

A SONG ON THE TIMES [34], in MS. Royal 12 C XII f. 7 r (c. 1340), consists of eighteen quatrains abab of three- or four-stress intermixed Latin, French, and English verses. It is a complaint of the corruption of the age (apparently the first years of Edward II), generally phrased after the precept or monitory fashion (see pages 374 ff.).

ON THE EVIL TIMES OF EDWARD II [35] exists in two versions, one in MS. Auchinleck (1330-1340), the other in a folio volume of homilies by Radulphus Acton (fl. 1320) in St. Peter's College Cbg. The versions vary from each other considerably in phrasing, metre, matter, and arrangement. The Auchinleck text consists of 476 verses in 79 stanzas aabbcc, of which the fifth verse has one foot with feminine ending, and the other verses have seven, or sometimes six, feet. At the end of the piece are the first two verses of an eightieth stanza. The Cambridge version has 468 verses; is in the same form of stanza as the other, but has the longer lines six-stressed; stops with a stanza whose beginning corresponds with lines 391-92 of Auchinleck; inserts earlier some of the later Auchinleck matter; and adds matter not in the Auchinleck text. Stanzas 71-72 of the Cambridge version complete the defective eightieth stanza of Auchinleck; and possibly some of the additional matter in Cambridge represents the lost ending of Auchinleck.

The piece is of very great importance, because of its presentation of the conditions of the first quarter of the fourteenth century; because of its reflection of the attitude of many persons of the time toward those conditions; and because of its anticipation, by perhaps fifty years, of much of the motive and the spirit that animated Langland. It is a powerful invective by an ardent, patriotic, devout nature indignant at the disgrace of the Church, the higher classes, and his fellow men.

Why the land is full of violence, why hunger and dearth have laid low the poor, why beasts perish, why corn is so dear—this the satirist will tell, and will tell truly, if you will but hear. All the clergy, all the lay classes, are vicious. Covetousness and simony and pride and lewdness, possess all churchmen. Pope, archbishops, bishops, archdeacons, abbots; priors, Minorites, Jacobins, Carmelites, Augustinians, deans and officers of chapters—all the clergy in turn, he shows at length to be selfish oppressors and false livers. Earls and barons and knights and squires, are untrue to their professions and base in conduct. Justices, sheriffs, mayors, bailiffs, beadles, all the civil officials, are rogues and self-seekers. Merchants are cheats; the members of the crafts are thieves. For this God has cursed the land with vexation and sorrow, has inflicted dearth and pestilence and strife and slaughter. Pride and falseness are the cause of it all. Each man knows the cause, but each blames others; did each but ransack himself, all were well done.

THE SONG OF NEGO [36], one of the pieces connected with the name of Michael Kildare (see pages 228, 522), in MS. Harley 913 f. 58 v (1308-1318, before 1325), consists of twelve short couplets. The verses, which have no poetical worth, are directed against the trickery of dialecticians. 'Nego' is taken as the most representative and objectionable of the terms (among others, 'Dubito,' 'Concedo,' 'Obligo,' 'Verum Falsum') employed by the clerical hair-splitters, as, knowing nothing, they conceal their ignorance, and, pretending search for truth, distort the truth. Truth draweth to the bliss of Heaven; 'Nego' surely doth not so.

A SATIRE ON THE PEOPLE OF KILDARE [37], one of the Kildare poems (see page 228), in MS. Harley 913 f. 7

(1308-1318, before 1325), consists of twenty stanzas aabcdd, composed in the early years of the fourteenth century. The last two lines of each stanza are a sort of refrain in which the poet comments on his piece; as, 'This verse is very well wrought, it is from very far brought,' 'Surely he was a clerk who made this crafty work,' 'Fitting it were that he were king who composed this noble thing.' The metre is doggerel, the first line of the stanza prevailingly five-stressed, the next three varying between five and seven stresses, the last two of two stresses. The author devotes the first verse of each of the first nineteen stanzas to address (as, 'Hail, seint Michael with the longe sper!') to Michael, Christopher, Mary, Dominic, Francis, the friars, the monks, the nuns of St. Mary's, the priests, the merchants, the tailors, the souters, the skinners, the potters, the bakers, the brewsters, etc., individually. The rest of the stanza he devotes to comments on the individual or the group addressed. His remarks to the saints are, to say the least, extremely familiar and free. The criticism of the clergy is bold. The characterization of the lay crafts exposes vicious practices of each, or personal qualities little creditable. The last stanza bids its hearers not sit quiet too long; they have heard of the lives of those who dwell in the land, now let them drink deep and make merry. The piece may indeed be directed not at the people of Kildare, whom the generally accepted title indicates, but at inhabitants of some other locality—if a specific locality be really intended. With their loose galloping swing, and their impudent irresponsible humor, the verses must have carried their hearers along in a rollicking mood. They were composed by a devil-may-care scamp, who, whether gleeman or clerk, must have been hail-fellow-well-met in popular circles.

THE PRAISE OF WOMEN [38] is to be connected with the question of the worth of women, dealt with so commonly in the various languages of the Middle Ages, the theme of the *Thrush and the Nightingale* (see page 421) and the *Nut-brown Maid*, the Vernon lyric No. 16 'In worschupe of that mayden swete' (see page 512), and various other English pieces. The poem is in MS. Auchinleck (1330-1340). It consists of 324 verses ababababcdc. The ninth verse of the stanza contains one iambic foot, usually with feminine ending; the eleventh has three iambics, usually with feminine ending; the other verses have each four feet. The last two lines of each stanza are reserved for specially emphatic statement of conclusion, reason, hope, or the like.

The piece is a translation of a French lyric printed by Holthausen, whose metre and rime-system it preserves. Both versions are ABC poems. The first three and a half stanzas of the English are lost. After the introduction of two stanzas, the French opens with a stanza whose first word begins with the letter *A.* In similar manner the initials of the succeeding stanzas in the two pieces proceed down the alphabet through Z, the English failing to observe *Y.* In the French follow five more stanzas; in the English follow eight stanzas, three not in the French, and the others not in the order of the French. The translation is free, often a very loose paraphrase. In contradiction of most of the mediæval literature on the subject, the poets urge the great worth of Woman, her fairness, her sweetness, her constancy, the consolation she affords to Man and the service she does to him, her office as mother of the race, her bearing of kings and emperors and especially of Christ, and, above all, the fact that Mary was a woman. The last is urged repeatedly and chiefly, in the pieces. The matter is uttered as it chanced to occur to the writers, and repetition is frequent. One feels sometimes that the English poet is over-doing, and suspects that the whole is ironical. The English stanzas move with much grace, especially for translation. Suggestion has been made that the passage (l. 235, not in the French) 'out of that lond in-to Linne' connects the translator with the Linne of the Towneley Mysteries or that of the *Heir of Lynne*, or with Lynne Regis in Norfolk. Brandl assigns the English to the South-East Midland.

TUTIVILLUS, THE DEVYL OF HELL [39] is in MS. Douce 104 (1427), following the *Vision of Piers Plowman.* It consists of 18 lines in groups of two four-stress English verses and one three-stress Latin verse with feminine ending, the groups being connected by rime of the Latin lines. The piece is against the gossiping of women ('Thei beth al of the develis nowte') at church, and on the notion of the devils' taking down their talk—elements met with in *Narratio Sancti Augustini* (see page 173). 'Better is it to be at home, than at service to gossip yourself into the Devil's clutches. Be still, that you may win the bliss of Heaven.' 'Unde Beda.—Qui osculatur meretricem pulsat campanam inferni,' the scribe or the poet adds.

The clever infernal satirist of the Towneley *Judgment* (see page 560) bears the name 'Tutivillus.'

MADDAMYS ALLE AS 3E BEE [40] is a scrap of four rude couplets warning ladies as to conduct, written on the margin of a fourteenth-century psalter.

Later pieces on women are *Of Women's Horns*, a *Song on Women* in MS. Lambeth 306, and *Praise of Women* in MS. Harley 4294. Reference should be made also to *Advice to the Fair Sex* and *Weping haueþ myn wonges wet* in MS. Harley 2253 (see page 496).

A SATIRE AGAINST THE BLACKSMITHS [41] is written as prose on a fourteenth-century leaf of MS. Arundel 292 (late 13th century). The 22 long alliterative lines voice the author's wrath at the noise made by the smiths. The alliteration is used to mimic the crash of the hammers. The onomatopoetical representation of the rattle and clatter of the smaller hammers, the clang of the sledges, the roaring of the bellows, the shouts of the men, is admirable. The scene, with its hurry and noise, and its gaunt leathery-skinned actors, is strikingly real, and gives an excellent picture of the activity of smiths before an expedition in the days when armor was worn generally. For all time is the indignation of the disturbed poet, from the beginning 'Swarte smekyd smethes smateryd wyth smoke Dryue me to deth wyth den of here dyntes,' to the end 'Cryst hem gyue sorwe! May no man for brenwateres a nyght han hys rest!'

This piece is discussed here because its general character and its motive relate it more closely with the members of the present group than with the other poems in alliterative long lines (see page 240).

AGAINST THE MINORITE FRIARS [42], in MS. Cotton Cleopatra B II (1382), consists of seven stanzas aabbcc, of which the first four lines have seven stresses, and the last two have six, each. The last two lines of the stanza are a refrain that connects the poem with the 'With an O and an I' series grouped together by Heuser (see pages 359, 381, 408, 498, 506, 527, 528). Heuser contends that the form of the speech points to Ireland, as does the phrase in stanza 3 'Armachan distroy ham,' Richard Fitz Ralph, Archbishop of Armagh, usually styled 'Armachanus' (died 1360), being a great opponent of the Irish mendicant friars. The writer is intensely hostile to the friars, who were formerly so low, and now are so high. The offenses that he enumerates show that his immediate feeling grew largely from use of theatrical representations (see page 539 ff.) of the Passion and of the Bible story for impressing the common folk.

The friars hang one of their number on a green cross with bright leaves and blossoms—men judge them to be mad! They fasten on him wings as if he were to fly—may Armachan destroy them! Another fellow comes down out of the sky in a gray gown, as if he were a hog-herd hieing to town—why should they not be burned? there wants but a fire! I saw another representing Christ bleeding at His side, and with great wounds in the hands—and the Pope is a party to it! Another gray friar representing Elijah was in a cart made of fire—just as he ought to be! Well ought they all to be burned! May God grant me grace to see it! They preach wholly of poverty, but like it not themselves; the town is ransacked for victuals for them; their dwellings are spacious and wondrously wrought—murder and whoredom have paid for them—slay thy father and betray thy mother, and they will assoil thee for sixpence!

AGAINST THE FRIARS [43], in MS. Cotton Cleopatra B II (1382), is full of intense feeling arising from personal experience. The piece is in fifteen stanzas aaabcccbdede. The *a* and *c* lines are of four stresses, the *b* lines are of three stresses, the last four lines are two split seven-stress verses. The poem is of 1350-1375.

The friars surpass all other religious in devotion, for they apply themselves to chivalry, riot, and ribaldry, to great standing, and to long prayers. Who keeps their rule, shall have Heaven's bliss. Their appearance shows their great penances and simple sustenance; in my forty years I never saw men fatter about the ears; they are so meagre that each is a horse-load. Their founder was a man of simple ordinance; they have to wander, alas! from town to town in pairs selling purses, pins, knives, gloves, and the like, to wenches and wives. The husband fares ill if he's from home, for the friar does his will wherever he comes; with fine dress finishings and spices he catches women's fancy. They are masters of tricks beyond all pedlars. Let each man who has a wife or a daughter, watch them, for they can win them away. Were I a householder, no friar should come near. They declare they destroy sin; but they foster it, for if a man has slain his kin, they will shrive him for a pair of shoes. What men in many lands say of them seems true, that Caym (Cain) founded them—Carmelites come of K, Augustinians of A, Jacobins of I, Minorites of M. There isn't room in Hell, it's so full of friars. They labor to bring down the clergy and abuse them. But soon they shall be made low as were the Templars. They cheat in chantries. No possessioners can equal their array. They were to live by begging, and to pray for those who gave them alms; but they have supplanted the secular priests. They preach wisely, but do not practise. I was long a friar, and I know. When I saw they did not as they taught, I cast off the garb and went my way, commending prior and convent to the Devil. I am no apostate, for I lacked a month and nine or ten odd days of my twelve months. Lord God, who with bitter pain redeemed men, let never a man desire to become a friar.

ON THE EARTHQUAKE OF 1382 [44], in 88 four-stress verses ababbcbc, is in MSS. Vernon f. 411 r (usually dated just before 1380) and Br. Mus. Additional 22283 f. 132 v (1380-1400). To pestilence, bloodshed, famine, and oppression, Nature added in 1382 the terrors of earthquake. It is probably this earthquake that the poet seizes upon as his theme, and that he plays upon in the refrain of each stanza as a 'warning to be ware.'

God is a courteous lord, who knows to show His might meekly; He would lead men all in accord to live rightly. Many warnings has He given. First was the outbreak of the commons, when no lord however great was not afraid. Had they had grace the lords might have crushed the insurrection at once, but God showed them the slightness of their power. Then He sent the earthquake, when all forgot worldly goods, and, alike terrified, burst out of their abodes as chambers and chimneys were hurled asunder, and churches and castles, steeples and pinnacles, toppled to the ground. Yet men went back to their evil living. The pestilence and these other two great curses were enough to warn all to beware, but they had no lasting effect. Apparently, nothing can avail; men are so lost that for gain they would destroy father and mother and all their kindred. 'Beware! beware! and make amends!' 'our bag hangs on a cliper pin.'

Like almost all the other contemporary pieces of the class, these verses are little poetical. But they ring with intense sincerity, and are permeated with the awful darkness and foreboding that encompassed many a serious thinker on the social and religious conditions of the day.

ON THE TIMES [45], a satire on manners and costume, and on the state of the nation at large, is in MSS. Harley 536 and 941, and Trinity College Dublin E, 5, 10. It was written probably in 1388, the retreat of 'Jack' and 'Jack Noble' mentioned in it probably referring to the flight to the Continent of the King's favorite, Robert de Vere, Duke of Dublin, and Michael de la Pole, Earl of Suffolk. The piece consists of 236 irregular three-stress verses (MS. Trinity having an added Latin couplet) alternately English and Latin, in quatrains abab, the Latin lines with feminine ending.

England and the English have lost all their former glory. Lechery and pride reign. The land is full of violence; those who feared us, now press upon us. The fear of God is departed; the speaker of truth is shent; whisperers and flatterers have their way. The rich make merry; worn out, the people grieve. Spiritual forces decay; God's holy days are not observed. The laws are perverted; the evil go unpunished. The King knows not the truth; men fear to 'bell the cat.' Jack and Jack Noble are gone; but plenty of the evil remain. Penniless gallants roam the cities. The people assume ridiculous fashions—they pad out their shoulders to make them seem broad; they have wide and high collars, as if making their necks ready for the axe; they wear spurs and long pointed shoes; their hose has a straight band, as if their thighs were fastened to their bodies. They dare not try to bend, for fear of hurting their hose; for this and their long toes, they pray standing. The women are as bad as the men, or worse than they. Drinking and cursing prevail everywhere. Simony is loose; the Church is vicious, not a clear light. May God rule and grant that as the King grows in years he shall learn the grief of England. 'Oh King, if thou art King, rule thyself, or thou shalt be a king without a realm!'

A DISTICH ON THE YEAR 1391 [46], in MS. St. John's College Oxford 209;

> 'The axe was sharp, the stock was hard,
> In the fourteenth year of King Richard,'

should be connected with the allusion to the youth of the King in *On the Times*.

NARRACIO DE DOMINO DENARII and SIR PENNY [47] are on the influence of money, the theme of a number of pieces, some in Latin, some in French, some in English, from the time of Walter Mapes to the sixteenth century. Early are the Latin *De Cruce Denarii* and *De Nummo;* of the thirteenth century is the Latin *Versus· de Nummo* and the French *De Dan Denier*. In MS. Cotton Galba E IX (early 15th century) is the English *Narracio de Domino Denarii*, probably of the late fourteenth century, consisting of 123 verses in tail-rime aabaab. In MS. Caius College Cbg. Moore 147 (15th century) is the English *Sir Penny* in 93 verses of tail-rime aabaab. The first six and seven stanzas of these two last pieces agree closely, but thereafter the poems diverge. The general content of one is practically the content of the other, all being matter common in the period.

Sir Penny rules wherever he goes. Clergy and laymen, rulers and people, bend before him. He changes men's spirit; he influences the court; he wins women; he buys Heaven and Hell, and looses and binds. The *Narracio* declares that he makes bold the meek, and meek the bold; he binds doomsmen; he makes peace from strife, friends of foes; he buys judgment and false-swearing, and so loss of life and soul; he may lend and give, may slay and grant life. He is a good fellow, welcomed and served as a guest, however often he comes. He serves every need, and gives his owner his way when others are set aside. He goes in rich weeds, and makes merry. He ever gets the gree.—Yet covetousness is not well; delight not in treasure, but spend as thou canst in perfect charity to God and to man. God grant us wisely to spend our goods, that we have the bliss hereafter.

A fifteenth-century English address to Penny in 21 verses, quite unlike the preceding pieces, is in MS. Sloane 2593; and there is also a sixteenth-century Scottish poem of seven strophes ababbcbc.

II.   Works in Alliterative Long Lines

1066

After the Norman Conquest, the Old English alliterative measure gave way before the French and the Latin verse forms. In the twelfth and thirteenth centuries, the rimed couplet and the stanza appear to have held almost complete sway in English verse. The *Brut* of Layamon and the *Proverbs of Alfred* exhibit the long line going to pieces in favor of rime. But, though the actual texts are wanting, there is adequate evidence that, certainly among the people, and perhaps in more dignified hands, the practice of the old alliterative verse persisted, and the tradition of the long line was preserved. Fondness for alliteration in religious prose, is evinced throughout the period. That shortly before, and shortly after, 1300 alliteration in verse was highly esteemed in the West Midland, is manifested by the steady and often excessive use of it in the rimed stanzas of most of the Harley 2253 lyrics (see page 488). From this time to beyond the limits of our period, it is a practically constant element in the rimed stanzaic English poems, both religious and secular—extending to the far North, and reaching into the dialects of London and the South. Moreover, at about 1350 emerged in the West Midland a remarkable group of poems, among the best of the whole period, composed in alliterative long lines that preserve the essentials of the old measure, or in stanzaic forms made up largely of such lines. As did the favor for alliteration in stanzas consisting wholly of rimed verses, predilection for these uses of the long line in all classes of poetry spread over all the English districts. The importance during the next hundred years of the several forms of alliteration that have been indicated, may be apprehended from mention of *Joseph of Arimathie, William of Palerne, Morte Arthure, Titus and Vespasian, Chevalere Assigne,* the *Alexander Fragments,* the *Gest Historiale of the Destruction of Troy,* the *Parlement of the Thre Ages, Wynnere and Wastoure,* the *Pistill of Susan, Patience, Purity,* the various Piers Plowman poems, *Erkenwalde, St. John the Evangelist,* the *Pearl, Sir Gawayne and the Grene Knight,* the *Awntyrs of Arthure, Golagrus and Gawain,* the *Tale of Gamelyn,* the *Satire on the Black-*

smiths, *Death and Life, Scottish Feild,* the *Houlate,* and the *Scottish Prophecies.* A full list of the alliterative pieces of the several types, may be made up from the references in the Index under *Alliteration.*

Of the poems on contemporary conditions before 1400, the following are in alliterative long lines: the Worcester Cathedral Fragment, the *Satire on the Blacksmiths,* the *Parlement of the Thre Ages, Wynnere and Wastoure,* the *Vision concerning Piers the Plowman, Pierce the Ploughmans Crede,* and *Richard the Redeless.* It has seemed most appropriate to discuss the *Satire* at an earlier place (page 235). All the other pieces, except the very early Worcester Fragment, are closely related to each other in general subject-matter, and through dependence in origin and form.

WORCESTER CATHEDRAL FRAGMENT [48]. In a twelfth-century MS. in Worcester Cathedral, is a fragment of a piece whose contents can hardly be determined. It begins 'Sanctus Beda was i-boren her on Breotene mid us.' Ten alliterative long lines tell how Bede and 'Ælfric abbot, whom we call Alquin,' turned books into English for the education of the people. Line 10 introduces a list of bishops. Eight final verses declare these taught the people in English, their light shone; but now their lore is lost, and the folk are forlorn—others teach our folk, and many of the teachers perish and the folk forthwith.

THE PARLEMENT OF THE THRE AGES and WYNNERE AND WASTOURE are perhaps the earliest extant representatives of the West Midland alliterative revival of the fourteenth century. They are ascribed to one author because of similarity of form, and because they are preserved together in MS. British Museum Additional 31042 (15th century). The date of the poems is fixed at about 1350 by two allusions in *Wynnere,* one to the twenty-fifth year of Edward III (l. 206), the other to William de Shareshull as chief Baron of the Exchequer (l. 317). This dating would seem to indicate indebtedness of *Piers Plowman* to the two poems, or at least

✓to one of them. The three pieces have the vision form; there is
remarkable similarity between the openings of the *Parlement*
and *Piers Plowman;* and there are striking parallels in lines of
the *Parlement* and *Wynnere* on the one hand, and *Piers Plowman* on the other.

The *Parlement of the Thre Ages* [49] consists of 665 alliterative long lines. A copy of verses 226-665 is in MS. British
Museum Additional 33991. The poem appears to be a development of a plan to treat the theme of the Nine Worthies widely
popular in mediæval literature from a period antedating
Longueyon's *Vœux du Paon* (see pages 99, 105, 106). The
Worthies are listed in the prologue of the *Cursor Mundi;* the
first six are mentioned in *Golagrus and Gawain* (ll. 1253 ff.).
They are dealt with in Arthur's Dream in the *Morte Arthure*
(ll. 3220 ff.; see page 36), in Arbuthnot's and Hay's *Buiks*
(see pages 99, 106), the Scottish version of the *Vœux,* and *Ane
Ballet of the Nine Nobles.* They were the subject of a fifteenth-
century mumming-play whose popularity is attested in *Love's
Labour's Lost.* Caxton refers to them in his preface to
Malory's *Morte Darthur.*

At dawn of a beautiful day in May, on the bank of a stream, the
poet lay in wait for deer, enjoying the loveliness of the flowers,
the song of the birds, and the movements of foxes and hares and
other wild creatures. A most stately deer appeared, accompanied
by a buck that watched to protect it from hunters. The poet slew
the deer, brittled it, and concealed the parts that the forester might
not be aware. Then, as he watched his spoils, he fell asleep and
had a vision of three men. One was a young knight on horseback,
most elaborately decked with jewels and embroidery; the second, of
middle age and clad in ill-shaped russet and gray, sat meditating
on his possessions; the third, clothed in black, with a white beard,
bald, blind, and crippled, lay on his side mumbling his beads and
crying to God for mercy. The youth exclaimed long of the joys of
the hunt, of ladies' love, of reading of romances, of revel in hall.
The man in russet chid his folly. Old Age in black warned both:
the pleasures of Youth and the thrift of Middle Age fail; all must
come to his own condition, and all must die. This he enforced with
short accounts of each of the Nine Worthies, and with a list (the
longest in Middle English) of the most famous heroes of Romance.
'Vanity of vanities!' he cries: 'Death takes all! Go shrive you,
Youth and Middle Age!' A bugle-call awakened the poet. The
sun was setting. He made his way toward town.

The poem ranks high because of its elaborate and effective descriptions of Nature, of hawking and hunting, and of the outer appearance of the personages, and because of its interesting summaries of the stories of the heroes. But these passages are out of proportion, and are over-stressed as compared with the treatment of the real theme of the poem. Like the reader, the poet is more interested in them than in the doctrine that the verses were meant to bring home. The descriptions of deer-stalking and of hawking, the detailed account of the brittling of the deer, and the author's susceptibility to the charm of material things, connect the piece with *Sir Gawayne and the Grene Knight*.

A Tretys and God Schorte Refreyte by-twixe Wynnere and Wastoure [50] consists of 503 alliterative long lines.

In a short prologue the author complains of the decay of the times and of the prevalent neglect of the true poet for the mere prattler of the words of others. Then he tells at length that he wandered in the West. He lay down by a burn's side under a hawthorn. The birds sang so loud and the stream made such a rushing noise, that he fell asleep only as night was coming on. He dreamed that he was in a fair green land shut in by a hill a mile long. On each of two sides was an army ready for battle. All prayed for a truce until the Prince should come to pacify them. On a cliff was a cabin, its roof railed with red, and its sides decked with English besants (gold coins) each tied round with garters made of gold and inscribed 'Honi soit qui mal y pense.' There was also a man garbed like a satyr, with a golden leopard on his helmet which was adorned with the arms of England and of France. A King appeared bearing the blue belt of the Garter. He summoned a Knight (the Black Prince) to bid the armies withhold from fighting. The Knight harangued the hosts at length, with many allusions to social and political and ecclesiastical conditions. A representative of each party followed him to the King: one was Wynnere (gainer, hoarder), the other was Wastoure (spendthrift). Before the King they argued the merits of their respective natures and activities. The King ordered Wynnere to the Pope at Rome; Wastoure he sent to London until the King should return from his wars in France.—Here the work breaks off unfinished.

The poem is an interesting composite of dream-vision, allegory, debate, occasional poem, and satire or complaint. In view of the incompleteness of the MS., the confusion of the matter, and the obscurity of many of what evidently were meant to be significant allusions, the primary object of the piece is difficult to perceive.   The connection with the Order of the Garter, is of great interest, because of the contention that *Sir Gawayne and the Grene Knight* is a Garter poem (see page 57), and because of the connection with the Order of the Bath declared in the *Grene Knight* (see page 58).   The descriptive passages are composed carefully and effectively.   The prologue twice mentions the 'West' from the point of view of a man of that district; but, like the poet or poets of *Piers Plowman*, the author knew London and its conditions.   The poem is full of satire much after the manner of *Piers Plowman*—on questions of labor, prices, wages, food, dress, on the friars and the power of the Pope, on the moneyed classes, etc.

THE VISION CONCERNING PIERS PLOWMAN [51] was in its own and the succeeding century one of the most valued pieces of literature in the English language.   Forty-seven MSS. of it are extant.   It is preserved in three general forms known respectively as the A-text, the B-text, the C-text. All of the forms are in alliterative long lines.

The statements made on the following pages as to the relationships of the MSS., especially of the A-text MSS., are on the authority of Skeat, corrected and augmented by that of Chambers and Grattan (see pages 256, 258).   On page 263 are noted Knott's recently printed general conclusions regarding the A-text MSS., and his adverse criticism of the work of Chambers and Grattan.

The A-text consists of 2567 verses divided as a Prologue and 12 Passus.   These are in two groups: (1) A Prologue and 8 Passus, composed of a Prologue and 4 Passus of the Vision concerning the Field of Folk, Holy Church, and Lady Meed, and 4 Passus of the Vision concerning Piers the Plowman—in all 1833 lines; and (2) 4 Passus of the Vision concerning Dowel, Dobet, Dobest—in all 734 lines.

Nine MSS. (RUEIDAsVHL) contain the A-text only; four (TH₂DigW) follow the A-text with Passus of the C-text; one (H₃) has a B-text to the end of Passus V, followed by Passus VI-XI from the A-text.   In many of the A-text MSS., the parts of the text that are for convenience styled by scholars since Skeat A Passus IX ff., are numbered as a Prologue and Passus I, II ff. But three of the MSS. have any of Passus XII: (R) Rawlinson Poetry 137 contains all of it with the additions of John But; (U) University College Oxf. 45 breaks off at line 19 with two leaves lost at the end; (I) Ingilby breaks off at line 88. MS. (E) Trinity College Dublin D, 4, 12, closely related to R and U, breaks off at Passus VII line 45. MSS. (T) Trinity College Cbg. R, 3, 14, (H₂) Harley 6041, (Dig) Digby 145, and (W) Duke of Westminster, end the A-text with the last of Passus XI, and add the later portion of the C-text—T, H₂, Dig, C-text Passus XII 297 to end of C; W, C-text Passus XIII 1 to end of C. MS (D) Douce 323 has only the A-text to the end of Passus XI, a final couplet stating that there ends 'þis litel book.' D and the A-text parts of TH₂DigW are from a common source. The carelessly copied MS. (As) Ashmole 1468, which is unlike any other MS. and has interpolations from a B- or a C-text, stops at the end of Passus XI. MS. (H₃) Harley 3954 also stops at the end of Passus XI; it has a B-text to the end of Passus V, and a contaminated A-text thereafter. MSS. (V) Vernon and (H) Harley 875 end imperfectly, V at Passus XI 180, H in Passus VIII. MS. (L) Lincoln's Inn 150 contains Passus I-VIII, the last imperfect. It appears that RUTH₂DigDIAs are from one original archetype which had a Latin colophon (see page 262) after Passus VIII connecting the *Visio de Petro Plowman* and the vision of Dowel. The connecting colophons of TH₂DDigRIAs (*i.e.*, all that have this-part of A-text, except VUW) style Passus IX, etc., 'Vita de dowel, dobet, dobest'; and those of TUH₂DDigRI (*i.e.*, all that have this part, except VWAs) add after 'dobest' 'secundum wyt and resoun' (see page 262).

Only R contains Passus XII 89-117. This passage has been made the subject of much discussion. In it is the declaration of John But (l. 106) that 'he made þis ende.' That But did append lines to Passus XII, is generally admitted. How much of the Passus is his, is debated: Skeat originally allowed him lines 106-17, and later lines 99-117, Manly assigns to him lines 55-117, Chambers gives him lines 89-117 or else all the

Passus. Chambers has shown that But added his lines to a transcript; they were not in the parent MS. of RUTH₂Dig-DIAs. Lines 101-05 state that 'Wille' 'wrouȝthe þat here is wryten and oþer werkes boþe Of peres þe plowman and mechel puple al-so And whan þis werk was wrouȝt ere wille myȝte a-spie deþ delt him a dent and drof him to þe erþe And is closed vnder clom crist haue his soule.' According to this, 'Will' (the actual writer or the hypothetical author assumed in the poem) was dead when (*i.e.*, while Richard II was still living, l. 113) But wrote his lines—or, as Skeat assumed, he deliberately killed himself off in order to make an end of the poem. Bradley thought that 'þat here is wryten' means 'this book,' and that 'oþer werkes boþe' are the Vision of Piers Plowman and the Vision of the Field of Folk ('mechel puple'); and he suggested that the twelve Passus 'must have been published in three instalments, comprising respectively Passus I-V, VI-VIII, IX-XII.' Chambers has argued with more apparent probability that 'þat here is wryten' is the A-text, and 'oþer werkes boþe' are the B-text additions.—In January, 1913, Bradley announced that a 'king's messenger' named 'John But' is frequently mentioned in the Patent Rolls of Richard II, the first notice being of 1378, the latest being a record of his death in 1387. He suggested that this man might be the Rawlinson But. In July, 1913, Miss Rickert argued for the identity of the two men.

The date of the A-text is accepted as 1362-1363 or soon after 1362. Tyrwhitt correctly identified the 'south-westerne wynt on a Seterday at even' (A V 14 ff.) as the terrible storm of January 15, 1362. The passage on the wars with France (A III 200 ff.) clearly points to the treaty of Brétigny in 1360. Reference is made (A IV 40) to abuses such as were especially denounced in the Parliament of 1362. Allusions to evils of papal 'provisions' (A III 142, II 148) point to the same date, an Act being passed in 1364-1365 to confirm that of 1350-1351 which had become ineffective.

The B-text consists of the vision of Piers Plowman, etc., and that of Dowel, Dobet, Dobest. The former has a Prologue and 7 Passus; the latter has 3 Prologues and 10 Passus—*i.e.*, a

Prologue and 6 Passus of Dowel, a Prologue and 3 Passus of Dobet, a Prologue and 1 Passus of Dobest. In some MSS. the whole is styled *Liber de Petro Plowman*, without mention of Dowel, Dobet, Dobest in the titles, and is divided as a Prologue and 20 Passus. The MSS. containing the B-text alone are, according to Skeat's classification: (a) Laud Misc. 581, Rawlinson Poetry 38 (four leaves in Lansdowne 398), Ashburnham 129 (now Br. Mus. Addit. 35287); (b) Trinity College Cbg. B, 15, 17, Crowley's printed text of 1550, Caius College Cbg. 201 (a poor transcript of Rogers' edition of 1561), Ashburnham 130; (c) Oriel College Oxf. 79, Cbg. Univ. Libr. Ll IV 14 and Gg IV 31, H. Yates Thompson; (d) Corpus Christi College Oxf. 201, Phillipps 8252; (e) Cbg. Univ. Libr. Dd I 17. MSS. containing mixed B-text and C-text readings, are, according to Skeat: Bodley 814, British Museum Additional 10574, Cotton Caligula A XI. Chambers and Grattan have found that MS. Harley 3954 (H_3) is a B-text to the end of Passus V, and thence a contaminated A-text.

For the B-text an A-text was taken as a basis, and thoroughly made over. Passus XII of A was practically ignored; A Passus V and VI were combined to make B Passus V. A number of A passages were suppressed, but more matter was added; for the total of 2567 lines up to the end of A Passus XI, there are 3206 lines in B. Further, B expands and develops the *Vita de Dowel*, etc., by adding B Passus XI-XX and so bringing the total of B-text verses up to 7242.

The date of the B-text is generally accepted as 1376-1377. The fable of the Belling of the Cat (Prol. 146 ff.; not in A) is taken as an allegory of the political crises of 1376-1377, particularly June 8, 1376, to June 21, 1377. New allusions are made to the famine of 1370 (B XIII 269); to the papal wars remonstrated against by the Good Parliament in 1376 (B XIII 173); and to the plague, probably that of 1375 (B XIII 244).

The C-text is a revision of the B-text, not a making-over with additions of numbers of passus as is the B-text. It makes many minor omissions; rearranges many passages; and inserts many passages, some of considerable importance (*e.g.*, that in

VI 1 ff. on the dreamer's life). It has no new passus, but re-
divides several of the B-text. It is arranged as 23 Passus, all
prologues as such being ignored: 10 Passus of Piers Plowman,
etc.; and 7 Passus of Dowel, 4 Passus of Dobet, 2 Passus of
Dobest. The whole comprises 7357 lines. Some of the more
remarkable additions are listed in Skeat's Oxford edition, and
all are indicated in Skeat's notes there.

The MSS. containing C-text alone are, according to Skeat's
classification: (a) Phillipps 8231, Laud 656, Harley 2376;
(b) Earl of Ilchester, Douce 104, Digby 102 (and British
Museum Additional 35157, not known to Skeat when he made
his editions); (c) Bodley 851; (d) Digby 171 (ends with
XVI 65), Cotton Vespasian B XVI, Cbg. Univ. Libr. Ff V 35;
(e) Corpus Christi College Cbg. 293, Trinity College Dublin
D, 4, 1, Cbg. Univ. Libr. Dd III 13, Royal 18 B XVII; ? (f)
Phillipps 9056. Skeat states that the mixed A and C, and
B and C, MSS. belong to the (b) group of the C-text MSS.

The date of the C-text is 'about 1393,' or between '1393 and
1398 as the extreme limits,' according to Skeat, and 1398-
1399 according to Jusserand. Skeat bases his dating on C
IV 203-10, whose complaints against the king he feels to reflect
the general dislike of Richard II, especially that arising from
the quarrel with the Londoners in 1392; on the passage (C V
191) against the King's application to the Lombards for
money, which he feels fits in with 1392; and on the passages
on gross misgovernment (C IV) and on the difference between
Bribery and Wages (C IV 287 ff.). Jusserand feels that the
complaint against Richard fits better 'the more important
events of 1397-1398,' when the King became practically absolute monarch through the Parliament held at Shrewsbury,
January 28, 1398. Manly has remarked that 'Jusserand's view
seems the more probable,' but has quoted a complaint of Parliament against the King from as early as 1386.

There are, then, the three general versions of *Piers Plowman*.
There are, too, the seven MSS. containing combinations of A-
and C-texts, and B- and C-texts. MS. Harley 3954 has a combination of B- and A-texts. Further, some MSS., such as Ashmole and Rawlinson 38, Harley 6041, and Harley 3954, have

what appear to be contaminated texts. By selecting certain MSS., Skeat observed ten varieties of form. No doubt other varieties will be discovered. At least in the cases of some MSS., Chambers (who, with Grattan and Knott, is most familiar with the MSS.) does not approve of Skeat's and Jusserand's theories of a continued succession of minor modifications by the author. How far the numerous variations are due to scribal modification, how far to editing by others than the author, and how far to a series of changes made by one author or by several authors, can be determined only when all the MSS. have been gone over thoroughly.

Until recently, knowledge of the contents and relationships of the MSS. has rested chiefly, and in many cases wholly—indeed, for many MSS. it still rests—on the statements of Skeat. There are a number of MSS. that Skeat had not studied or collated thoroughly; one he does not mention. Some years ago Messrs. Chambers and Grattan, and independently Mr. Knott, undertook a study of the MSS. The investigations of the former gentlemen have already resulted in most important conclusions (see pages 256, 258, 261). The results of Knott's studies have not been printed in full. Some of his conclusions, and some of his statements regarding the MSS., differ greatly from those of Chambers and Grattan (see pages 258, 263). The solutions of most of the questions that have recently been raised concerning the poem, must wait upon the completion and thorough assimilation of such studies of the MSS.

Piers Plowman belongs to vision literature. It purports to be a series of visions or dreams (in the fullest text, eleven) by a lonely wanderer, the first vision being on the Malvern Hills. It has a slight narrative introduction, and between the visions has generally, but not always, slight narrative connections indicating the dreamer's waking and again falling asleep. The poem is made up of two general parts: (1) the *Vision concerning Piers the Plowman* (A Prol. and Passus I-VIII, now styled A_1; B Prol. and Passus I-VII; C Passus I-X), and (2) *Vita de Dowel, Dobet, Dobest* (A Passus IX-XII, really only

Dowel, Passus IX-XI or IX-XII styled A₂; B Passus VIII-XX; C Passus XI-XXIII). The *Vision of Piers the Plowman* contains *two* dreams: the *Fair Field Full of Folk, Holy Church,* and *Lady Meed* (A Prol. and Passus I-IV; B Prol. and Passus I-IV; C Passus I-V), and the *Seven Deadly Sins and Piers the Plowman* (A Passus V-VIII; B Passus V-VII; C Passus VI-X). *Vita de Dowel,* etc., contains *nine* dreams. *Dowel* has *four* dreams and part of a fifth: *Wit, Study, Clergy, and Scripture* (A Passus IX-XII; B Passus VIII-X; C Passus XI-XII 162); *Fortune, Nature, Recklessness, and Reason* (B Passus XI; C Passus XII 163-XIV); *Imaginative* (B Passus XII; C Passus XV); *Conscience, Patience, and Activa Vita* (B Passus XIII-XIV; C Passus XVI-XVII 157); *Free-will and the Tree of Charity,* part a prologue of *Dobet* (B Passus XV to 253; C Passus XVII 158 to end). *Dobet* contains the rest of the dream of *Free-will and Charity* (B Passus XV 253-XVI; C XVIII-XIX), the dream of *Faith, Hope, and Charity* (B Passus XVII; C Passus XX), and the dream of the *Triumph of Piers the Plowman* (B Passus XVIII; C Passus XXI). *Dobest* contains the dream of *Grace* (B Passus XIX; C Passus XXII), and that of *Antichrist's Attack on Unity* (B Passus XX; C Passus XXIII).

The length of the work, the multiplicity of its incidents, and the many variations between the three general versions, make practically impossible any adequate synopsis of the poem that would be within reasonable limits for such a manual as this. Good synopses have been given by Skeat in his three-text edition (chiefly the C-text, with indications of important variants), by Morley (*English Writers* IV, over sixty pages; C-text), and by Manly (*Cambridge History* II; A-text and B-text).

Until the last decade, *Piers Plowman* has regularly been regarded as the work of one writer, who at about 1362-1363 composed the A-text, in 1376-1377 revised and supplemented this to the B-text, and in 1392-1393 or 1398-1399 revised the B-text to the C-text. Such disagreements in interests, points of view, opinions, style, and method, as were noted between the various texts or parts of the texts, were regarded as the natural fruits of changes in the man and the poet with the advance of years. A number of uses of the name 'Wille,' most of them applied apparently to the author, in the several texts (A VIII 43, IX 118, XII 51, 89, 99, 103; B V 62, VIII 124, XV 148; C II 5, VII 2, XI 71); the colophon between A VIII and IX in many A MSS., and at corresponding location in MSS. of other texts; the colophon at the end of the Digby-Douce-Ilchester (and Addit. 35157) C-text; the note in Dublin D, 4, 1, concerning 'Stacy de Rokayle pater Willelmi de Langlond qui Stacius fuit generosus et morabatur in Schipton vnder Whicwode tenens domini le Spenser in comitatu Oxoniensi qui predictus Willelmus fecit librum qui vocatur Perys ploughman'; and the Ashburnham note to the effect that 'Robert or william langland made pers ploughman'—these led to acceptance of the author's name as 'William.' The B XV 148 'I haue lyued in londe, quod I, my name is long Wille'; the notes in Dublin D, 4, 1, and Ashburnham 130; and the notes - of John Bale in his *Scriptorum Illustrium* and Ashburnham 130, led to acceptance of the name 'Langland.' Pearson's argument for the name 'Langley,' based on the fact that there were many Langleys connected with Wychwood, but no Langlands, was generally dismissed as a hypothesis unsupported by tradition. Little weight was given to the colophon in the C-text group of MSS. IDDig (and Addit. 35157) and probably in their archetype: 'Explicit visio Willelmi W. de Petro Plowman. . . .' 'W.' was explained as 'Whicwode' or 'Wigorniensis' (of Worcester). The 'Robert' of Ashburnham 130, of Bale's note in that MS., and of Bale's notes in *Scriptorum Illustrium* and its *Index*, was put aside as perhaps a misreading of 'i-robed' (A IX 1, first line of *Dowel*, written as 'y-Robt' in one MS.) as 'I Robert.' The attribution of the poem to John de Malverne, based on Stow's assertion, has usually been regarded by scholars as resting on an error.

It was accepted that the poet was born at Cleobury Mortimer in Shropshire (Bale's notes); and (by Skeat and others) that his father was Stacy de Rokayle, who later held a farm under the Despensers in Shipton-under-Wychwood in Oxford-

shire. Upon passages scattered through the poem were based
a number of conclusions concerning the life and the condition of the poet. From C VI 63 Skeat inferred that his father
was a franklin, and that the poet himself was born in lawful
wedlock. From B XI 46 and XII 3 ('Coueityse-of eyghes
. . . folwed me fourty wynter and a fyfte more'; and Imagy-
natyf's declaration, 'I haue folwed the in feithe this fyue and
fourty wyntre'—the former not in C, the latter in C reading
'more than fourty wynter') it was concluded that he was born
at about 1332. On C II 73 ('Ich vnder-feng the formest and
fre man the made') Jusserand very questionably based inference
that he was a child of a bondman, and that he obtained freedom through ecclesiastical connection. From C VI 36-37
('Whanne ich ȝong was,' quath ich, 'meny ȝer hennes, My
fader and my frendes founden me to scole, Tyl ich wiste wyter-
liche what holy writ menede') it was concluded that he was early
sent to school, perhaps to the Benedictine convent at Malvern,
to become a clerk; and from B X 300, C VI 153 ('For if heuene
be on this erthe and ese to any soule, It is in cloistre or in scole
be many skilles, I fynde,' etc.), that there he found a most con-
genial life. It was accepted that in 1362-1363 he wrote the
A-text, or at least the first eight Passus of it, partly in May
while wandering over the Malvern Hills (A Prol. 5). The Malvern Hills are mentioned in A and B Prol. 5, C I 6 and 163,
A Prol. 88, B Prol. 214, C VI 110, A VIII 130, B VII 141,
C X 295. It was accepted that later he came to London,
where he lived in a 'cot' idly in Cornhill, clothed as a Lollard but
unpleasing to Lollards, with his wife Kytte (C VIII 304, VI
1 ff.) and a daughter Calote (B XVIII 426, C XXI 473) for
many years (C XVII 286). The text mentions Cornhill (C
VI 1), Cock Lane (A V 162, B V 319, C VII 166), Cheapside
(A V 165, B V 322), the Flanders women who haunted London (A V 163, B V 321, C VII 367), Tyburn (B XII 190, C
VII 368, XV 130), Shoreditch (B XIII 340), Garlickhithe
(B V 324), Stratford (B XIII 267), Southwark (B XIII
340, C VII 83), Westminster (A II 131, B II 160, C III 174;
A and B III 12, C IV 13). It was held that the passages con-
cerning the wanderings of the dreamer were really reflections

of a wandering life of the author (*e.g.*, Prol. 1 ff.; A IX 1, B
VIII 1, 62, C XI 1, 61; B XIII 2, C XVI 2; etc.). In 1376-
1377 he at least began the B-text. It was asserted that he
obtained much learning and was eager to know all science (B
XV 48, C XVII 210), that he was acquainted with French (see
page 262) and Latin, but that what he had he owed more to wit
than to application (A XII 6). In 1392-1393 or 1398-1399 he
wrote the C-text. He was judged to have been tall of stature
(A IX 61, B XV 148, C VI 24). He was said to have been
proud, and to have been regarded as a fool (B XV 3-10). He
wore long robes in London (C VI 41), was tonsured (C VI 54,
56) but had taken only minor orders, and stalked about the city
a marked figure. The dreamer refers often to his poverty (cp.
B XX 3). From C VI 44 ff. it was concluded that he held a
position as singer in a chantry in London. It was recognized
that this idleness and begging and singing for men's souls, was
all in direct contradiction of doctrines preached persistently
in the poem (cp. C I 84, VI 44, 51, IX 124-28, 139, 158; C I
53, VI 24; C VI 142; B XII 51). Excuse for the poet was
found on the basis that he was a poet who had to keep body
and soul together; that many of his declarations were utterances of Old Age exaggerating the faults of Youth; and that
he was an example of the but too common conjunction of weakness of will with strength and vigor of insight and judgment.

With modification of details, this was and is now the orthodox view of the general facts of authorship of the poem, and
of the life of the poet.

In 1901 Jack argued that the time statements in *Piers Plowman* are not to be taken literally, that 'we have no basis for
certainty nor even for probability, as to the date of the poet's
birth, nor age at any time of writing any of the texts nor
length of wandering'; that the dreams are but a literary device;
that the wandering of the dreamer is but a conventional motive;
that the poet's statements of his idleness, his vagabondage, his
begging, and his singing in a chantry, are all absolutely contrary to his persistent teaching, and that all these statements,
except those on his vagabondage, are in C VI 1-50—a passage
possibly interpolated or written in a whimsical or semi-humor-

ous mood; that the place-names are casual, and that the
accounts of low life in London presuppose no extensive direct
acquaintance with such life; that the wife and daughter, Kitte
and Calote, are merely conventional; and that the poet could
not have been a well known figure in London without some
mention of him being preserved. Jack qualified his sweeping
conclusions by admitting that the poet was perhaps a priest,
possibly in the country; that he led a meditative life, sym-
pathized with the struggles of the common people, and kept in
obscurity because of fear, or at least dislike, of publicity. The
critic felt that some of the poet's own direct experiences might
be drawn on for the poem; yet that the work is autobiographical
as regards the poet's inner life, not as regards his outer life.

In January, 1906, Professor Manly printed a short article
that inaugurated a new era in the study of the poem. He
announced that he had, and would at an early date publish in
a book, proofs that the B- and C-texts are by two different
authors, each other than the authors of the A-text; that the
A-text to Passus IX (*i.e.*, A$_1$) is by one author; that the A-
text from Passus IX to not beyond the middle of Passus XII
(*i.e.*, A$_2$) is the work of another; and that John But (see page
245) wrote not only the Rawlinson Passus XII 101-12
allowed him by Skeat, but at least half of Passus XII. He
stated that he would try to show that the autobiographical
details were, even by the writer of C, intended to be taken as
attributes of the *dreamer*, who was as much a fictional character as the other persons in the dreams. The conclusions were
to be supported by differences in language, in versification, in
use and kind of figurative language, and above all by striking
differences in the mental qualities and powers of the authors;
and the probabilities derived from these classes of evidence
were to be made certainties through evidence of misunderstanding of the earlier texts by each of the later writers.—
Meanwhile, as a specimen, Manly offered for consideration A-
text V 236-41. This passage he believed to be out of place,
and really to belong to Robert the Robber, not to Sloth; and
he urged that its displacement (common to all the A MSS.)
argues a lost leaf in the archetype of the A MSS. The handling

of the passage in B seemed to him to be unsatisfactory, and so to point to authorship other than that of A. The questions so raised concerning this passage have been debated by Bradley, Hall, Jusserand, Brown, Knott, Manly, and R. W. Chambers, with the issue still doubtful, and with disagreements among the holders of each of the two general sides.

In 1908, in the *Cambridge History of English Literature,* Volume II, Professor Manly repeated his theories as to authorship, now indicating that the differences demonstrating the fivefold authorship were in diction, metre, sentence structure, methods of organizing material, number and kind of rhetorical devices, power of visualizing objects and scenes presented, topics of interest to the author, and views on social, theological, and various miscellaneous questions. The nature of the *History* precluded entering into polemics or detailed proofs. So, after statement of his theories, Manly confined himself to a paraphrase of A and B, to general statement of some of the differences he believed to exist between the different sections as he divided them, and to the offering of certain selected instances in evidence of some of the supposed differences.

In January, 1909, M. Jusserand published a lengthy article in which he commended Manly's discovery in regard to the so-called misplaced passage; but he did not agree with the assumed implication of independence of the author of B. He differed categorically with Manly as to his other contentions, opposing each of his theories and specimens of proof.—In July, 1909, Manly replied to this criticism in an equally long article, confining himself almost wholly to the meeting of Jusserand's arguments, and offering little new evidence for the original contention.—In January, 1910, Jusserand replied to this article, meeting *seriatim* his opponent's replies. Further, he called attention to the inherent uncertainty of evidence of the classes that Manly had announced that he would ultimately offer, and indicated the great difficulty of obtaining from MSS. so obviously modified and so remote from the original text as are those of *Piers Plowman,* reliable evidence of such kinds as Manly promised.—Since then Manly has printed nothing on the subject, probably being still engaged, as in his third article he stated he was, in marshaling his materials.

Meanwhile, to an article printed October, 1908, T. D. Hall prefaced a note stating that the article had been written before the publication of the *Cambridge History*, Volume II; approving Manly's ideas of an independent author of the C-text, and his inferences from the Robert the Robber passage of an independent author of the B-text; expressing feeling that Manly 'perhaps scarcely does justice to the high merits of B'; and questioning the theory of separate authorship of A_1 and A_2.— In his article proper Hall declared 'that not only is the C-text a debasement of the author's own work, but that the nature of many of the changes precludes the supposition of their being from the hand which penned either the original (A) or the enlarged (B) *Vision*.' This he supported by discussion of examples of three classes of 'the more serious changes'—*i.e.*, (1) *Omissions* (C I 6-8; B III 188-99; C 63 ff.; C IX in the discourse of *Wit*, and X in that of *Dame Study;* C XV in the discourse of *Ymaginatyf;* B XIII-XIV, the episode of *Haukyn*);—(2) *Additions*, futile or inconsistent (C I 94-124, II 112 ff., IV 317 ff., VI 1-108);—(3) *Structural Changes* (needless and vexatious alterations of arrangement, as in the case of the Prologue to Passus I; freedom in shifting the location of blocks of text, as in C VI; modification, with inconsistency, of B XI; redistribution of parts of the Haukyn episode, and abridgement and emasculating of the rest of it). Further, he *stated* that he found confirmation in 'certain obvious dialectical peculiarities of C,' and in the fact that the C writer 'would seem to have been a man of somewhat different temperament and convictions from his predecessor or predecessors.'

A new stage of the discussion was inaugurated in April, 1909, by R. W. Chambers and J. H. G. Grattan in a most important article communicating some of the results of their collation and study of all the fourteen MSS. of the A-text (see page 263 for Knott's adverse criticism). They pointed out that the received A-text (that of Skeat) is not a reconstruction of the original text of the author, but is a result of printing MS. Vernon as closely as possible, yet with some two hundred necessary corrections, or one in every dozen lines ('excluding cases where a whole line or passage is inserted from other MSS.'), taken from other MSS. (primarily Harley 875 (H), and from others where V and H both have an impossible reading); that with his reprint of Vernon, Skeat printed complete collations of but three other MSS. (Harley 875, H; Trinity College Cbg., T; and University College Oxford, U); that of some MSS. no collations have ever been printed; that the writers of the MSS. are not exact copyists, but editors, although working without an editor's sense of responsibility; that V and H are 'derived from an original' which 'we cannot reconstruct with any degree of certainty,' and that this original is at least one remove from the poet's autograph MS.; that MSS. T and U are from another tradition, they being at least two removes from the author's MS.; that the TU tradition, though it has been practically neglected, is nearer in readings to the original A-text than is the VH tradition; that T, Harley 6041 (H_2), Digby 145 (Dig), and Westminster (W), continue after Passus XI with C-text material; H_2 has corrections by a later hand familiar with the earlier passus of a B or C version; Dig is from an A MS. (with or without C continuations) and a C MS.; MSS. Rawlinson Poetry 137 (R), Trinity Dublin D, 4, 12 (E), and T, are from one common source, E less directly; that Skeat's and Jusserand's theories of transitional texts produced by a series of minor changes by the author between A and B, are certainly not supported by the bulk of the phenomena that at first sight seem to support them; that URE as sub-class joins without much difference with sub-class TH_2W-Dig to form a second group of MSS.; that MS. Douce 323 (D) belongs to the TU group, but to neither the T nor the U subgroup distinctly from the other; that MS. Lincoln's Inn (L) is a garbled copy of a good MS. independent of both the VH and the TU groups; that MS. Ingilby (I) is another corrupt copy (less so than L) independent of the VH and TU groups; that MS. Ashmole 1468 (As) is imperfect, corrupt, and contaminated by B and C influence; that MS. Harley 3954 (H_3) up to Passus V is a B MS., thereafter a contaminated A MS.; that MS. Ilchester is mainly a C-text, but has an A passage

apparently from the TU group; that approach to the original
readings of the A-text must be through the TU group as basis,
and to a less degree through the VH group, assisted in still
doubtful cases by the independent MSS. with care against
readings due to correction from a B- or a C-text; that 'a text
so formed will be found to approximate much more closely to
the received B-text than the received A-text does'; that only
when we know what is the 'diction, metre, and sentence structure
of the original A-text, can we argue with certainty whether
these are, or are not, materially different from those of the B
additions, or decide whether B's treatment of the A-text is
really inconsistent with unity of authorship.'

In January, 1910, R. W. Chambers argued against Manly's
shifted-leaf theory to the conclusion that there 'would seem to
be no ground for disturbing the order of the MSS. in so far
as Robert the Robber is concerned'; that it is a question
whether A's Sloth in the Robert the Robber passage is anything worse than incoherent, or whether A was incapable of
incoherency; that Manly's argument (accepted by Furnivall
and Jusserand) that the lines about Piers' wife and children
(VII 89-90) were not properly placed by B, does not hold good;
that the critics who approve the misplaced-leaf theory, do not
agree as to where the misplaced passage belongs; that the rearrangements proposed are not more satisfactory than the present location; that, therefore, these supposed defects in the A-
text, more or less accepted by B, cannot be used as a basis for
argument that the two texts are by different authors. He
rejected Manly's several examples of B's misunderstandings of
A. He showed the impossibility of testing at present differences
of dialect between the three texts, since out of 47 MSS. there
are [evidently taking no notice of collations] in print but four
(Vernon, of A-text; Laud and Trinity, of B-text; Phillipps, of
C-text), and these were selected for print on bases quite other
than quality or form of dialect. He indicated that in the only
case where we have the readings of all the MSS. (*i.e.*, a passage of eleven lines printed by Skeat), the dialectical argument
for difference between the authors of the several texts 'breaks
down utterly.' He pointed out the complexity and inconsist-

ency of the dialectical features of the A MSS., and the tremendous difficulty—almost impossibility—of fixing the dialect of the MSS. behind the extant copies, and thence piercing to that of the archetype, which in turn may be far removed from the author's autograph; he indicated that much the same difficulty would be encountered in determining the hypothetical dialect of the original B-text; and he noted the practical impossibility, if all this were accomplished, of proving inconsistency between the hypothetical dialects of the theoretically reconstructed original texts that were composed fifteen years apart and, according to the commonly accepted view, by a man who, some years before he composed the B-text, had moved from a Western bordering on Southern dialectical district and had resided in London. He pointed out that 'any statistics of metre or alliteration are without value, until we have before us full collations of all the MSS.'; and that the same holds true of contentions that B took over variant readings of A—though 'the more the MSS. are examined, the more probable' it appears 'that these variants from the received text of A, adopted by B, are, in fact, the true readings.' To the assertion of difference in methods, interests, and mental powers and qualities, between the writers of A and B, he opposed 'many other' critics' convictions 'of the exact contrary.' He further presented the evidence for 'Will' as the name of the author of all three texts; and he urged that acceptance of multiple authorship calls for much more evidence than had been presented up to that time.

In April, 1910, because of Chambers' article, Bradley modified somewhat his views in regard to the Robert the Robber passage, and, though he felt the evidence conclusive for dislocation of text at that place, admitted that Chambers had weakened the effect of dislocation as argument against singleness of authorship of the texts. He still rejected Manly's idea of a lost counterfoil after A V 235. He held to a neutral attitude in the authorship dispute. He noted that unity of authorship does not imply that elaboration of the early poem was the author's main preoccupation during the thirty years.

And he suggested the publication of the A-text in three instalments (see page 261).

In July, 1909, Miss Deakin published the results of her study of alliteration in the three texts in Skeat's edition: 'the alliteration gives no support to Professor Manly's theory'; it 'gives no conclusive evidence one way or the other'; 'the gradual increases and decreases' of similarities between the texts are 'especially striking and suggestive of the gradual development of a single artist.'—Miss Dobson's study (published July, 1910, dated May, 1909), under ten heads, of the vocabulary of the A-text Prologue-Passus IV, Passus V-VIII 131, Passus VIII 132-XII 58, based also on the printed editions, led her to declare that 'all the tests taken together cannot be said to prove conclusively that the whole of the A-text of "Piers the Plowman"—leaving out of consideration the work of "John Butt"—is the work of one author, but the larger part of the evidence tends in that direction, and there are certainly no differences of vocabulary which need a theory of dual authorship to explain them.'

In April, 1910, Macaulay printed a note favoring the Ashburnham-Bale (apparently on authority of Nicholas Brigham)-Crowley designation of the author's name as 'Robert.'

In July, 1910, Mensendieck approved of Chambers' argument as to the Robert the Robber passage, and felt that 'the old tradition of a single author seems to be not yet seriously disturbed.' Following up his studies of 1900, he sought to show that the 'Visions of Dowell, etc., contain experiences and confessions of the author in autobiographical chronology, where the different periods appear disguised as allegorical figures and following each other from passus to passus in the same order as they had followed each other in the actual life of the author.' *Thought* reveals the *poet's* thoughts, *Wit* gives us *his* knowledge, *Dame Study* acquaints with *his* studies, *Clergy* with *his* experiences when in clerical orders, etc. This effort the critic carried through A Passus IX-XII. He found confirmation of identity of authorship of A and B in the fact that he perceived concord between certain of the B writer's revelations of personal experience and those of the A writer.

In July, 1911, Chambers opposed Bradley's suggestion of publication of the A-text in three instalments. He argued that the 'other werkes boþe' mentioned by But were the parts of the B version, and that 'þis werk' was the complete A-text (see page 246). He argued further that But's contribution must be all of Passus XII of A, or only from line 89 onwards.

Following up remarks of Warton, Skeat, Jusserand, Manly, and others as to indebtedness to the French and to French allegory, in a study finished in April, 1909, and published in book-form in 1912, Miss Owen made a careful comparison of *Piers Plowman* and *Li Romans de Carité, Le Songe d'Enfer, La Voie de Paradis* of (?) Raoul de Houdenc, *Le Roman de la Rose, Le Tournoiement de l'Antecrist, La Voie de Paradis* of Ruteheuf, *Le Pèlerinage de Vie Humaine, Salut d'Enfer,* and *De Dame Guile.* She concluded as follows: There was a common stock of allegorical material that could be drawn on for *Piers Plowman;* part of the material was supplied to French and English poets independently by commentaries on Scripture, and by other educational and theological works; no external proof is forthcoming that the French allegories, except the *Roman,* were known in England at the date of writing of *Piers;* no similarities to the allegories studied are so striking as to justify conclusion that the English writer certainly borrowed from the French, though there are some likenesses close enough to suggest reading or remembrance of some of the French allegories. Miss Owen found evidence for unity of authorship in the facts that such reminiscences of certain French allegories are in all parts of *Piers;* that the same methods of personification, the same kind of allegorical action, and, in many cases, the same allegorical devices, are used in all parts of *Piers;* that in respect to allegory the same strongly marked personality is exhibited in all the texts; that the same curious personification (as in *Thought* and *Ymagynatyf*) of an aspect of the writer's own personality, is in all the texts; that the manner in which the common allegorical material is treated, is similar in all the texts, and quite different from the manners of the French writers. She found the author of *Piers* one to whom the unseen is more than the seen, to whom moral and spiritual truths are matters of experience rather than of dogma, to whom his personages are realities, and not mere abstractions of intellect; and in all this saw qualities that distinguish the author from all the French allegorists studied by her.

There is difference of opinion as to whether the author or the authors of *Piers Plowman* could speak or read French. Miss Owen's comparison with the French allegories proves nothing either way. It has been urged that French was the language of the law courts until 1362, and that the author of the A-text seems to have obtained his contempt for lawyers from personal acquaintance with them. The B-text (XV 369; not in C-text) condemns the 'newe clerkes' of whom 'nouȝt on amonge an hundreth' can 'rede a lettre in any langage but in Latyn or English.' French expressions are in all parts of the poem—*e.g.*, A Prol. 103 (B Prol. 224; C I 225), VII 299 (B VI 313; C IX 335), VIII 148 (B VII 162; C X 311); B X 439, XI 376-77 (Rawlinson only; C XIV 205-07), B XIV 122 (C XVI 303), XV 113 (C XVII 269), XVIII 229 (C XXI 241); C XVIII 163-64, XX 166. These are rather catchphrases and scraps of songs of the day.

The articles of Chambers and Grattan having shown the probable futility of much of the effort that might be based on readings of the texts themselves before collations of all the MSS. were accessible, and, in any case, the possible uncertainty as to the readings of the original MSS., the way was open to another field of investigation. In two carefully written articles (1913, 1914) Moore has gone over the question of antecedent probability of single authorship, the scholarly tradition, the external evidence of the texts and the MSS., and the evidence extant concerning the name of the author. This investigation led him to find: (1) No presumption in favor of single authorship founded on antecedent probability or scholarly tradition; (2) no evidence tending to prove or to disprove that A_1 and A_2 are by one author; (3) possible evidence that the author of A_2 wrote the B-text, the argument being based on the facts that the Latin link between A_1 and A_2 in the 10 MSS. has the opening of Passus IX of A and probably of the archetype of the 10 MSS., styling A_2 *Vita de Dowel, Dobet, et Dobest, secundum Wyt et Resoun,* whereas Reason does not appear in A, and appears first in B XI; (4) no evidence as to the authorship of the C-text; (5) no evidence in favor of a single authorship of all the texts; (6) the evidence regarding the author's name to point, not to a single author or to one named '*Will,*' but rather to the hypothesis that at least two persons—one being Robert Langland, a Shropshire man; and the other being a son of Stacy de Rokayle—were concerned in the composition of *Piers Plowman.* Further, Moore has preferred to accept *all* of Passus XII of the A-text as by John But.

As has been indicated (see page 244), the statements made on the preceding pages as to relationships of MSS., especially of the A-text MSS., are on the authority of Skeat, corrected and augmented by that of Chambers and Grattan. In an article printed January, 1915, Knott has presented some of the results of his study of the A-text MSS. preparatory to a critical edition of the A-text. He differs much from the conclusions of Chambers and Grattan, asserting, 'First, the method employed by these students has been at fault; secondly, they have stated their opinions before they have had the necessary material in hand to formulate sound opinions; and, thirdly, they have not collected the evidence afforded by MS. readings which were perfectly accessible.'

Knott concludes that the A-text MSS. fall into two principal groups: x, V and H; and y (four sub-groups), (1) L, (2) I, (3) W and Dig, (4) TH_2DURT_2 (Trinity Dublin D, 4, 12, styled E by the other scholars) AH_3—y (4) falling into two sub-groups, which are TH_2D complete, and T_2AH_3 almost complete, UR falling with T_2AH_3 at the beginning of the poem, and with TH_2D through the remainder. Knott believes that 'y furnishes a much better tradition than x'; and he adopts MS. Trinity Cbg. R, 3, 14 (T) as 'basis' for his proposed critical text.

Apparently the interesting question of the authorship of *Piers Plowman* will be settled, if it is settled, only after extended discussion of very complicated evidence, the bases for which are not now generally accessible. Whatever be the final decision, the work itself will remain practically as it is. The discussion of authorship, however, will have centred on the poem the attention, and (in place of the actually but cursory consideration that it has been given until only recently) will have won to it something of the close study, that it richly merits.

Piers Plowman is, after the *Canterbury Tales*, the greatest piece of Middle English literature; it is one of the greatest of the mediæval vision poems, and, as a vision poem, in many respects second only to the *Divine Comedy;* it is one of the foremost of the writings in English in which allegory is used.

The work is everywhere glowing, often flaming, with immediate noble feeling. It is a poem, born of enthusiasm and imagination working on personal experience. Its visions are really visions, not mere figments of the intellect. Its achievements are not through conscious selection or skilful management toward a clearly preconceived design, but through sheer native aspiration and power. Indeed, it knows little of formal art. Swept along by the impulse of the moment, it forgets that it has a reader, it interrupts its story, it neglects transitions, it breaks up its pictures, it confuses its aims. Yet in its very faults lies much of its tremendous force. Its utterances appear to spring spontaneously from an uncontrollable passion, an exhaustless reservoir that pours itself out prodigally.

Its verse is the irregular alliterative long line that must have been cherished in popular tradition since the Conquest, and that in the West from about 1350 had come again into splendid use in literature. No more fitting form could be imagined for the work. Its language, too, is simple and direct—commonly blunt, harsh, rough. Its vocabulary is the vocabulary of the day. French and Germanic derivatives appear side by side—and, when it will avail, Latin is used. There is no labor for the phrase, the word is born of the thought. For elegance, the poem has not patience or desire.

The work deals with the great issues of life, the under-realities that endure. But it is rarely abstract; it sees all concretely. It employs allegory, not as a fashionable or graceful medium, but because it is the naturally appropriate medium, and because the writer sees things alive. This allegory is not subtle or devious; it is proclaimed plainly, its sense cannot be escaped. Comparison with notable earlier and contemporary French writings, has shown that, of all so studied, only *Piers Plowman* uses allegory to record the writer's own mental and spiritual experiences. Its personifications are realities, are individual; few of them are not of flesh and blood. Yet even this creative capacity is inadequate to the poet; persistently it fails to satisfy him. Then, regardless of narrower consistency, often with true mediæval grotesqueness, enter actual human figures out of the roads, the ale-houses, the marts, the churches, the law-courts. Everywhere in the poem realism rules, the general is exhibited in the individual, the abstract is vivified in the concrete—all is objectivized, is seen in action. The poem is a great series of portraits, of scenes from life. Rightly it is acclaimed as the only adequate direct representation of the evils and the sufferings and the aspirations of the common life of the times.

This same freedom and sincerity and vitality is evinced, too, by the independence of learning shown in the poem. Each of the parts of the work manifests authorship by a cleric, but by one who never could have been a scholar or even a careful or wide student of books. No definite sources beyond those of some of the Latin phrases have been discovered. There is no evidence of any knowledge of French other than catch-phrases and songs of the day. Ovid, Aristotle, and (several times) Plato, are mentioned, as are a number of the Fathers; but the ascriptions at these places are so vague as to make questionable any definite knowledge, at the time of composition at least, of more than the names. Scriptural quotations and allusions are very numerous, but they are often inaccurate; most of them seem from memory, and from memory that is treacherous. Whatever is said comes out of the writer. Everywhere the poem penetrates to the heart of things; there is its concern, there it dwells. It not only cares little, but appears to know little, of the letter. And again and again, in all of its parts, from a native insight and an intuitive faculty of utterance, it blurts out the very essence of truth in a line or a phrase that is unforgettable.

Almost every critic of the poem has styled the poet a reformer, but a reformer not in the usual sense of the term. The work reflects at all points the general current realization of the monstrous abuses in Church and in State and in common social and industrial conditions. But it gathers these up and expresses them on a scale and with a power unapproached by any other contemporary English writing. King and knight and bourgeois and peasant, pope and all the grades of priesthood, friar and summoner and pardoner and hermit, it exposes with sardonic bitterness and often with consuming wrath. It spares, no class, no condition of life. In all it finds baseness that damns itself and that makes miserable its neighbors and dependents. It is little the respective natures of the themes, it is chiefly the intensity of the writer's conviction against evil, that causes the ill-doers to stand out most vividly, while often the good are comparatively tame and remote. Yet, with all its fiery passion, the poem is full of a large charity and a melancholy mildness of nature. Never are the exposures and the invectives in the poem for the gratification of a carping or a furious spirit, or for satisfaction of an æsthetic end. There is little humor in the work, and there is little direct effort to minister pleasure. The origin and the object of the poem are burning zeal for righteousness, and labor for its fulfilment in all the earth.

The poem does aim at reform, but not at revolution. Its appeal is to the inherent nobility and goodness of the human spirit, to its yearning that Truth and Purity shall prevail. It sees in detail, individual evils and individual ill-doers. But, however wrapt in the particular it may be for the moment, it ever returns to the larger issues that are its real concern. It preaches no overturning of the State, no demolition of any portion of the structure of the Church. It speaks out emphatically against John Ball and the movement that he represented. It is not Wycliffite, as Bale deemed. A lunatic it styles its poet; but he is a madman only to those who have not his ideal. The poem is singularly conservative. To it the State, the Church, organized Society, are the media through which human-

ity acts; they are not the life. It ever distinguishes tacitly
between the system and the operation of the system and its
agents. The existence and the prosperity of creeds and constitutions, it knows to be dependent on the ideals and the practice of the folk. The evils and the miseries that every part of
the poem harps on with bitterness born of agony of heart for a
world gone wrong, it sees as the fruits of human souls self-
perverted, self-debased. Its remedy is through neither physical
violence nor asceticism, the favorite modes of the period. It
offers no definite code of life, no formulated programme for
perfect conduct. It foresees no millenium. To it life is a
pilgrimage through uncharted regions, every step beset with
perils without and insidious weakness within, the haven but
vaguely apprehended, and the earthly journey bound to fail
unfulfilled. Yet God is; Truth and Love and Duty and honest
Work are ever transcendent—and the Soul true to itself is
unconquerable. Its guides are found, not in philosophies or in
the priesthood or in creeds, but in Man's own self—Reason and,
greater, Conscience. And its model is Piers the Plowman—now
the simple, righteous peasant giving his days in patient
devotion to the pursuance of Duty through hard toil for sustenance of his fellow man; now Christ, the Divine exemplar of
sacrifice, of service, of triumphant victory, the human nature
in its supreme manifestation—both offering to every man of
every class the essentials of right living that he should practise
in the manner his own proper sphere demands; and, finally, it
is the perfect universal body of Christians, the beloved of God,
the recipients of the Holy Spirit's lavish benefactions.

Apparently, from the date of the B-text up into the sixteenth
century, *Piers Plowman* was very popular and either begat or
influenced greatly many writings. The letters of the rebels of
1381 use the names of Piers Plowman and Dowel and Dobet for
the designation and concealment of their intents (see page
218). At about 1394 appeared *Pierce the Ploughman Crede;*
at about 1399, *Richard the Redeless;* perhaps before 1400, the
Lollard poem that was expanded in the sixteenth century to
the *Complaint of the Plowman* or the *Plowman's Tale* [52], in

stanzas, printed in 1532 or 1535 with Chaucer's works.   In 1401 or 1402 was composed *Jacke Upland* [52], a Wycliffite attack on the friars, possibly originally in alliterative verse. This was followed by the alliterative *Reply of Friar Daw Thopias* [52], to which was made the *Rejoinder of Jacke Upland* [52], similar in form to *Jacke Upland*.   Of the many other pieces listed by Skeat, are to be mentioned the alliterative *Crowned King* [52] (1415); *Death and Liffe* [52] in the Percy Folio MS.; and *Scottish Feilde* [52], chiefly an account of the Battle of Flodden, written soon after the event, and perhaps rewritten later.

Of these pieces, we are concerned with only *Pierce the Ploughmans Crede* and *Richard the Redeless.*

PIERCE THE PLOUGHMANS CREDE [53] consists of 850 alliterative long lines preserved in MSS. Royal 18 B XVII (reign of Henry VIII) and Trinity College Cbg. R, 3, 15 (after 1600), and in Wolfe's edition of 1553.   All these copies go back to a common original MS.   Trinity is the best copy.   The two MSS. have five lines (822-23, 828-30) omitted by Wolfe, apparently because of their doctrine of transubstantiation.   Wolfe inserts five spurious verses (817-21).   Mention (l. 657) of the persecution of Walter Brute, fixes the date after the latter part of 1393; and the allusion to flattering kings (ll. 364-65) may indicate composition before the death of Richard II.   Skeat accepts the date 1394.   The author was a Wycliffite (see l. 528, etc.).   The general plan of the poem would seem derived from *Piers Plowman*—particularly from the prologue to *Vita de Dowel,* where the dreamer sets out on his quest, and falls in first with two Minorites whom he questions as to the whereabouts of Dowel.   Skeat identified the author with the writer of the *Complaint of the Plowman.*   But Bradley has shown that, though some elements of it may be of the fourteenth century, the *Complaint* as it stands is practically wholly of the sixteenth.

The poet knew his *Pater Noster* and *Ave,* but was ignorant of the Creed.   In great distress he set out in search of one who would teach him.   Successively from representatives of the Minorites, the Dominicans, the Augustinians, and the Carmelites, he obtained

extended abuse of each other's order, and direct evidence of the
mercenary and carnal ends of all—but no knowledge of the Creed.
As he proceeded hopeless, he caught sight of Piers at the plow, all
in tatters, urging his emaciated nags through the muddy field. With
a goad walked his wife miserably clad, her bare feet leaving blood-
tracks on the ice. The youngest child was sheltered in a bowl, and
the two others lay beside it in bits of garment, all moaning sorrow-
fully. Yet Piers comforted the traveler, and offered him sustenance from his poor scraps. He exposed at length the viciousness
of the friars, showing in detail their lack of all that Christ commended and enjoined. Finally, he taught the poet his Creed.

Direct discourse prevails. Particularly to be commended are
the descriptive passages, especially the detailed account of the
buildings and luxury of the Dominicans (ll. 155-215), the portrait of the fat friar with a double-chin big as a goose-egg (ll.
220-30), and the picture of Piers and his family (ll. 421 ff.).

RICHARD THE REDELESS [54] is the title given by
Skeat to the poem styled by Wright *Poem on the Deposition of
Richard II*, and known in the sixteenth century to Nicholas
Brigham, and perhaps at the time of its composition, as *Mum,
Sothsegger* (Silence, Truth-teller). The piece consists of 857
alliterative long lines comprising a Prologue and 4 Passus,
the ending being missing, in the *Piers Plowman* MS. Cbg. Univ.
Libr. Ll IV 14 (c. 1450). Lines 23-29 of the Prologue indicate composition after Richard was taken prisoner (September
18, 1399) and before receipt of news of his deposition (September 30). There is allusion to the execution of Scrope at
Bristol (July 29), and to the release of the Earl of Warwick
(just before August 25). The abrupt breaking off of Passus
IV may indicate interruption by receipt of news of Richard's
deposition. But the MS. is a copy, and the Prologue seems to
imply that the poem was completed. Its excellence and its
location in the MS., have led Skeat and others to ascribe the
poem to the author of *Piers Plowman*. The work should be
connected with the political poems, especially with *Of King
Richard's Ministers* (see page 218).

The poet dedicates the poem to the King, and assumes the rôle
of devoted and anxious counselor of Richard. Yet the work is
certainly strongly partial to Henry. It is not a vision, but purports

to have originated from strange news of Henry's invasion that the poet heard at Christ Church as he was passing through Bristol. Passus I discourses to the King on the ill-doings of his favorites. Passus II inveighs against the King's servants (styled the White Harts, from their badges) as plagues of the people; it reproves the King for failing to favor the good Greyhound (Westmoreland), who would have preserved to him a multitude of retainers. Meanwhile, the Eagle (Bolingbroke) was cherishing his own nestlings. In puns similar to those in *Of King Richard's Ministers* (see page 218), the poem tells of the punishment of Bushy, Green, Scrope, and Bagot. Passus III holds forth on the unnatural attacks of the White Harts on the Colt (Fitz-alan), the Horse (Earl of Arundel), the Swan (Gloucester), and the Bear (Earl of Warwick), and how so they came to grief. It then deals at length with the luxurious and wasteful lives and practices of Richard's courtiers and favorites. Passus IV continues the reprehension of Richard's enormous expenditures, and violently abuses the Parliament of 1397 for its cowardly subservience. Here the piece breaks off.

CHAPTER V

HOMILIES AND LEGENDS

Some sermons or homilies extant from the Middle English period are unaffected by legends. There are preserved legends composed with little or no idea of delivery in church services. Yet in history, in matter, or in form of preservation, the extant homilies and legends commonly intermingle. It would seem that clearness in exposition of the facts concerning the extant pieces, would best be attained through a grouping of the homilies and the legends under one large head. Moreover, further classification must be made to recognize properly the fact that homilies and legends were composed or preserved either as independent units or as members of groups.

Consequently, in this chapter the pieces are dealt with as follows: 1. Sermons or Homilies, I. Independent or Isolated Sermons or Homilies, II. Groups or Cycles of Sermons or Homilies; 2. Collections or Cycles of Homilies and Legends Intermixed; 3. Legends, I. Collections or Groups of Legends, II. Legends Treated in at least One Separate Piece.

It must be understood that, of course, in many cases these groups and their members overlap. The classification is primarily for clearness in dealing with the phenomena as they are *manifested in the extant* pieces. It will not be misleading, especially if the statements just made be borne in mind.

1. Sermons or Homilies

The Middle English sermons and homilies were written down either independently or in cycles or groups. Further, they were composed for one or both of two purposes—for use on special occasions by the author, for use as stock material affording discourse to less capable or unequipped ecclesiastics.

I.   Independent or Isolated Sermons or Homilies

Sometimes it is difficult to determine whether a given English piece of the period was intended by its author to be of the homily or sermon class, or to be merely monitory. The use of verse for many of the writings adds to the difficulty. Critics tend to speak of individual items as 'homilies' or 'sermons,' without recognition of the distinction, and to accept as homilies or sermons pieces certainly not originally intended as such. The following writings seem to justify treatment as homilies. Of pieces that have been at times erroneously designated as homilies, some are, because of their content and manner, discussed in this book as monitory pieces (see page 385); others, on the same bases, are treated as writings for religious information or instruction (see page 338); and some others, because of their form or impulse, are considered as religious lyrics (see page 498).

HALI MEIDENHAD [1], of the middle South or the South-West and the beginning of the thirteenth century, is one of four pieces (see *Juliana*, page 312; *Margaret*, page 314; *Katherine*, page 312) of alliterative prose, all in exaltation of virginity. The theory that the four pieces are by one author is not tenable. Little more acceptable is the idea that *Juliana* and *Margaret* are by one hand. *Hali Meidenhad* is in MS. Cotton Titus D XVIII f. 112 v (1200-1250). In print it covers twenty-three pages. It dwells intemperately on the thraldom, the vexations, and the miseries of marriage; the baseness of carnal desires, and the avoidance of any incentives to such; the woes of childbirth; the troubles that children bring; and the troubles of the wedded who have no children. It urges the mystic marriage with Christ with its offspring of virtues, and a resolution to remain a maiden as if the opposite were Hell. With the matter of the piece should be connected that in *A Luue Ron* (see page 529) and in *Of Clene Maydenhod* (see page 530).

SAWLES WARDE [2], a very pleasing prose homily making in print some ten pages, is from the South-West of

1200-1250 and perhaps 1200-1225. It is in MSS. Cotton
Titus D XVIII (1200-1250), Royal 17 A XXVII (c. 1230)
and Bodley 34 (c. 1230). The Bodley text stops a little short
of the Royal, to which are appended also nine four-stress verses
asking of the reader 'a pater noster for John who wrote this
book.' The piece is a rendering, with considerable variations,
additions, and elaborations, of Hugo de St. Victor's *De Anima
et Ejus ad Sui et ad Dei Cognitionem et ad Veram Pietatem
Institutione Libri Quatuor*, Book 4, Chapters 13-15. To the
Kentish *Aȝenbite of Inwyt* (see page 346) is appended another
version of the material in St. Victor. This latter piece is
Kentish, and is a close verbal translation apparently directly
from the Latin—not, as some have urged, a revision of the
English version.

Sawles Warde is an allegory on its text, Matthew 24. 43: 'But
know this, that if the goodman of the house had known in what
watch the thief would come, he would have watched and would not
have suffered his house to be broken up.' The house is Man's self
within; the husband is Wit, Will is the untoward wife, the Five
Senses are the servants, Man's Soul is the treasure of the house.
The Vices ever beset the house. Wit guards it with God's four
daughters—Prudence is the doorkeeper, Spiritual Strength is the
guard close by the door, Moderation is Mistress of the household,
and Righteousness or Equity, as judge, punishes and rewards the
Senses. To keep all alert, Prudence sends in Fear, who declares
he is messenger of Death; he is from Hell, and describes its terrors.
Prudence announces that if the house be well kept, Death has no
terrors, but warns against trust in the world and the wiles of the
flesh. Strength fears only worldly prosperity; Moderation fears
poverty and hardship, and praises the Golden Mean. Righteousness
advises that all be humble and meek, and fearful of her power. Wit
thinks of God; Will is silent;—the household turn to Wit. Then
Prudence sends in Love of Life or Mirth, come straight from
Heaven. He tells of Heaven's bliss; of God's glory; of the Trinity;
of Christ and the Virgin making intercession; of the hosts of the
angels, patriarchs, prophets, apostles, martyrs, confessors, and holy
virgins, whose prayers win salvation for souls, and who dwell in
love of God and of each other. Prudence and Strength bid cast out
Fear. Fear protests that his message is as true as Mirth's. Moderation supports him—he shall depart when Mirth speaks, but be
present when Mirth is silent. Will and the household become subject to Wit—all through listening to the two messengers and the
four Sisters. So should each man listen, and defend his soul from
the Thief of Hell.

The personification is excellent. The great amount of direct discourse gives the piece a dramatic quality approaching that of the much later Moralities. In that it is a religious allegory, it is to be connected with the *Castel of Love*, the *Abbey of the Holy Ghost*, and other pieces of that kind (see pages 366, 368). The elements in the account of Hell differ greatly from the stock features of the *Vision of St. Paul* (see page 332). The figure of the wife, Will, who is added to the 'familias' of the Latin, reminds of Anselm of Canterbury's *Liber de Similitudinibus*, Cap. 2 *Similitudo inter Mulierem et Voluntatem*. In their modifications and additions over the original, the matter and the expression of the piece show much imagination and artistic sense. All in all, the homily is well conceived, consistently executed, and forceful. It is written with strong feeling, and it holds the reader as can few allegories of the same or of later date.

A LUTEL SOTH SERMUN [3], one hundred irregular short verses abcb with much alliteration, of the South Midland not later than 1230, is in MSS. Cotton Caligula A IX f. 248 v (before 1250) and Jesus College Oxford 29 f. 258 r (c. 1275).

Let all good men sit and listen to a good sermon. We all know that Adam fell by the forbidden apple, and remained in Hell until Christ relieved him. All backbiters and man-slayers and thieves and lechers shall go to Hell. Let cheating bakers and butchers leave their evil dealings. All priests' wives shall be damned. The proud youths who love Malkin, and the maids in love with Jankin, come to church and market but to prate of illicit love, with thoughts set only on self. They go to the alehouse, and then off together in the evening. Though her parents beat her, Jilot will not give up her Robin. For God's love, leave your sins, and let us pray the Virgin to intercede for us.

The piece is not poetry. Its earnestness and its satire connect it with the other attacks on the times (see page 227).

A SARMUN [4], probably of the end of the thirteenth century, consists of 240 four-stress verses abab in MS. Harley 913 f. 16 (1308-1318, before 1325). It urges the vanity of pride, the uselessness and the punishment of covetousness, the

inevitable coming of death, and the pains of Hell and the correspondent joys of Heaven. Brandl assigns the piece to the
South.

SPECULUM GY DE WAREWYKE [5] is in MSS.
Auchinleck f. 39 r (1330-1340), Royal 17 B XVII f. 19 r
(c. 1370-1400), Harley 1731 f. 134 r (1440-1460), Harley
525 f. 44, Arundel 140 f. 147, Cbg. Univ. Libr. Dd XI 89 f.
162 (last three of 15th century), and two others not now
located. Its principal source is Alcuin's *De Virtutibus et
Vitiis Liber*, with dependence on Augustine's discourses, and
with indirect dependence on various other literary or traditional
bases. It supplements, or represents a lost section of, the perhaps least attractive treatment of the story of Guy of Warwick
indicated in Lydgate's *Guy* and Copland's printed text (see
page 18). As printed it consists of from 511 to 517 short
couplets. The original was probably of the South-West Midland, and of about 1300 or perhaps an earlier date.

An introduction announces the purpose of teaching soul's health;
to win Heaven, love God and your fellow-man, and avoid the world's
net. An earl, Guy of Warwick, feeling disgust at the world, begged
of the devout Alcuin a sermon to free him from its enticements.
Alcuin taught him to distinguish the Vices and the Virtues. He
told of the Virtues in order, of the baseness of the Seven Sins, of
Wisdom attained through pain, of Faith, of true Love, of Hope, of
reading of the Scriptures, of Peace, of Mercy, of Forgiveness, of
Patience, of Humility, of Confession, of Penance, of the Fear of
God, of Almsgiving—concluding with the illustrative tale of the
widow of Zarephath (I Kings 17. 9). Guy forsook the world, and
betook him to Christ.

The piece should be connected with the various treatises of
religious information and instruction (see pages 338 ff.).

A LUYTEL SARMOUN OF GOOD EDIFICACIOUN [6]
is in 80 four-stress verses abcbdbeb (st. 1 abcbdded) in MS.
Vernon (1370-1380).

The author states that he heard Friar Henry preach a sermon:
'Shrive you of your sins; prepare for Doomsday; in Hell are heat,
cold, thirst, darkness; with the worm, Woman, Man is caught as

the fisher catches the fish with his bait; we should listen to the preachers, and be shriven; I would be with Christ in Heaven; may God have mercy on men.'

SERMO IN FESTO CORPORIS CHRISTI [7], in short couplets, is in MSS. Vernon.f. 195 v (1370-1380; 632 verses, Southern), Cbg. Univ. Libr. Dd I 1 f. 32 v (15th century; 674 verses, with added introduction of 38 verses, Southern), and Harley 4196 (15th century; 664 verses, Northern). The last 62 verses of Dd and Vernon are abab, chiefly fours and threes. The piece is probably of Northern origin (see page 289). Brandl assigns it to 1300-1350.

The feast of Corpus Christi is new; yet it is really old, for David said Man ate angels' food, and God gave manna to the Israelites. Here is a warning to usurers who buy up corn to raise the price; they shall pay at Doomsday. God slew hundreds of thousands of the Israelites who gathered more manna than they needed. In God's body we have richer food than angels. A Jew at mass saw the priest hold above his head a child, whence flew a bleeding child to each Christian in the church. Each ate his child. The Jew's Christian companion explained that God had made him see a bleeding child in order to hide the Sacrament. The Jew was converted. Break a mirror, and one face in it becomes three; so God's body prevails against each of the Seven Sins.—Now follows an account of the institution of the Supper, and explanation and comment. Once the Supper was taken each Sunday, now it comes but once a year. An impure English priest fell ill. A child put in his hand one from a number of burning Sacramental wafers. The wafer burned a hole through the hand, but did not maim it. The priest sinned no more, and went to Heaven.—There follows a detailed history of the service of the Supper, with repetition of the *Pater Noster,* a list of the Apostles, and a list of the martyrs for the Bread. Worthily taken, the Body will keep you till the great feast on Resurrection Day, when the food shall be sight of the Trinity.—Then follows indication of the indulgence given through partaking of the Sacrament.

To the text in MS. Vernon f. 196 v is added *Seven Miracles of Corpus Christi* [8] (only six miracles in the text), which is a Southern version of the *Handlyng Synne,* lines 9891-10811 (see page 344).

A SERMON AGAINST MIRACLE-PLAYS [9], really a tract, in MS. Br. Mus. Additional 24202, is discussed on page 483.

HOMILETIC PIECES BY ROLLE AND WYCLIFFE
AND THEIR FOLLOWERS are discussed with the other
works of those writers (see pages 444, 465).

THE FEAST OF ALL SAINTS [10] is theme of a homily
in 300 short couplets in MS. Ashmole 61 f. 73 (15th century).

II. Groups or Cycles of Sermons or Homilies

At a very early period it was permitted to substitute a reading in the vernacular of a homily of 'one of the Fathers for the
sermon after the Gospel of the Mass. The practice extended:
collections of homilies more or less original were made, some,
like Bede's hundred and fifty *Homiliæ de Tempore,* covering the
whole *Church Year.* For use of this sort were composed in
Old English the *Blickling Homilies* and Ælfric's *Homiliæ
Catholicæ* (c. 990). In Middle English, groups are extant in
MSS. Bodley 343, Lambeth 487, Trinity College Cbg. B, 14,
52, and the *Ormulum,* the Kentish Sermons, the pieces in MS.
Cotton Vespasian A 22, and possibly the original Northern
Homily Cycle. In view of its history, the last group
is dealt with under Collections or Cycles of Homilies and
Legends Intermixed (see page 285). Wycliffe's homilies are
discussed with his other works (see page 468).

THE BODLEY HOMILIES [11], in MS. Bodley 343 f. 4
v, consist of fourteen prose pieces in a twelfth-century hand,
and comprise in print a total of about twelve pages. The pieces
are as follows:

1. The Gospel account of Christ's interview with Nicodemus,
with comments on the passage and on baptism; 2. Christ's last
discourse, especially His assurance concerning prayer, with *exempla*—Gregory moving a mountain, the lake dried up by prayer,
Julian the Apostate foiled by prayer of Publius; 3. the healing of
the ruler's son of Capernaum, with exposition and running comments; 4. the parable of the Talents, with exposition 'from Augustine' and explanation out of Augustine of the significance of Bible
use of numbers; 5-6. the three Christian Virtues and the six Duties
of Lent, with illustrations from the Bible and citations of Fathers;
7. the healing of the man born blind, with exposition of spiritual

meaning from Augustine; 8. a discourse developed from John 12. 24, on physical death and spiritual fruition; 9. for Christmas Day, on the birth of Christ, the nature and office of Christ, the nature and virtues of the soul; 10. the tempting of Christ by the Devil, with comment in preparation for Lent; 11. the Transfiguration, with comment, exposition, and final exhortation; 12. on the vanity of worldly things; 13. on covetousness and desire only for the truly good; 14. on the three dead raised by Christ, illustrating the three ways of death of the soul, and Christ's power to bring life.

Usually the sermons present the Gospel story at much length, then announce that, the story having been told in plain English, there shall follow the 'exposition' or 'exposition from the commentary.' The latter expression points to what several pieces acknowledge, dependence in the Fathers—*i.e.*, Augustine, Jerome, Isodore. Some of the pieces are somewhat lengthy. But all are direct, with little rambling; in several is expressed concern against length and diffuseness. There is little elaboration of allegory or symbolism. Characteristic is effort toward careful, thorough, easy explanation of the words and the ideas of the Gospel basis, and toward simple comment. Direct exhortation appears only in 11, 12, and 14, and then only in a minor degree. *Exempla* occur only in 2; a brief *bysen* is in 12. There is no application to contemporary conditions or specific needs. The tone of 1-4 is cold, rather impersonal, and patronizing in address; the attitude of the other pieces is warmer, more personal, with kindly tone and repeated address of 'dearest men' and 'brethren.' There is no vehemence or exaggeration; all is sensible and controlled.

THE LAMBETH HOMILIES [12] consist of seventeen pieces, one in verse on the *Pater Noster* (see page 280), followed by a text of the *Poema Morale* (see page 385) and *On Ureisun of Oure Louerðe* (a defective version of *On Wel Suiðe God Ureisun of God Almihti*, see page 528). The pieces are in MS. Lambeth 487 f. 1 r, in a hand of before 1200, and make up seventy-nine pages in print. The themes are as follows:

1. The Gospel narrative of Palm Sunday; 2. the law of the Hebrews and the law of mercy, Christ's law and its obligations; 3. true confession, restitution, and repentance; 4. the privileges and virtues of Sunday, with Paul's and Michael's descent into Hell

and winning of rest for the damned on the Sabbath (see page 333);
5. Jeremiah in the pit of serpents; 6. the *Pater Noster,* with exposition, comment, and exhortation (see page 280); 7. the Creed, with
introduction and exposition (see page 353); 8. the Nativity, with
the parable of the Good Samaritan; 9. Pentecost, with explanation
especially of the Holy Ghost and the Trinity; 10. the eight Cardinal
Sins and the eight Cardinal Virtues, and the twelve abuses of this
age; 11. Fifth Sunday in Lent; 12. praise due Christ for our
redemption; 13. pure life of clergy and laity and its reward, the
parable of the Sower, almsgiving; 14. Sunday and the Bible events
that occurred on it; 15. deserting all and following Christ, with
explanation of the three crosses of the faithful; 16. being strong
against the Serpent, and donning the spiritual armor; 17. the Psalmist's account of the holy men weeping for their own and their
fellows' sins.

In all the pieces the themes and the application are broad
and general. There are no attempts to correct merely local
or contemporary evils. The topics and the treatment are
always abstract; only in the first five pieces are concrete
instances introduced. The pieces consist of from 1200 to 3000
words each. Only in several does the writer relate at length the
Gospel story of the text. Beyond the fable of the Crab, such
illustrations as occur are but mentioned in a few words. Symbolism is a mainstay of the collection; yet rarely is a Bible
theme related and then interpreted in detail as in the Kentish
Homilies (see page 283). Morris claimed that the extant
pieces are 'only a portion of a much larger and probably complete collection of Homilies compiled' 'from older documents of
the eleventh century'—especially since 10 and 11 are 'trans-
literations,' with minor substitutions, of Ælfric's sermons with
the same titles (*In Die Pentecosten* and *De Octo Uiciis & de
Duodecim Abusiis Huius Seculo*), and since 11 contains a
passage from Ælfric's homily for Palm Sunday. As Old English originals for the other homilies have not been traced, and
as some of the twelfth-century Trinity Homilies were influenced
by Latin pieces written by French or Norman authors, probably the Lambeth Homilies are from various sources, and contain original additions.

Perhaps the first five of these pieces are by one author. All
the five use frequently the same modes of address, 'good men'

and 'dear men,' a use that does not occur in the other homilies. All are on the theme of Confession and Thrift. All exhibit a kindly intimacy and a feeling of concern for the auditors, which are absent in the other items. Not infrequently in these five pieces, and not at all in the others, occur brief, homely applications and illustrations—as, the castle well garrisoned, but lost because of one small hole in the wall (2) ; the apple rosy without and rotten within, and what the man long in prison would give for freedom (3) ; the fable of the young crab whose mother chid it for swimming backwards, yet herself swam backwards in illustrating the proper manner of progressing (5) ; and the comparison of slanderers to spotted adders, of misusers of wealth to black toads, and of women in their yellow robes to yellow toads and to devil's mouse-traps baited with yellow cheese.

The *Pater Noster* (see page 353) is the earliest known poem in English composed consistently in the short couplet. It consists of recital and exposition of the Prayer, in 305 verses, feminine and masculine rimes occurring, with some instances of four or five successive verses on one rime.

THE TRINITY COLLEGE HOMILIES [13], thirty-four prose items making in print a total of 109 pages, are in MS. Trinity College Cbg. B, 14, 52 f. 1 (early 13th century). A text of the *Poema Morale* follows them. The homilies are probably of the South-East Midland and of the twelfth century. Items 4, 25, 26, 30, 32, correspond to Lambeth Homilies 7, 17, 13, 16, 15. But none of the Trinity pieces is from Ælfric. Probably a twelfth-century collection of Latin sermons by a French or a Norman clergyman, rather than a Latin collection by an Anglo-Saxon, was their source. Perhaps some of the collection is original. The matter of the five pieces in the Lambeth collection has been indicated (see page 279). The number and the rambling nature of the other twenty-nine, make it impossible here to give a synopsis of each of them.

The matter of the pieces is as follows: 1. The Advent; 2. the need for immediate repentance; 3. the call of Paul to eschew the deeds of night, and to put on the weapons of right; 4-5. recital and exposition of the Creed and the *Pater Noster;* 6. exposition of the Shepherds at the Nativity; 7. the Epiphany; 8. the purification of Mary; 9. Lent compared with the ceasing of the Jews from song in Babylon, and the body likened to a city inhabited by vices; 10. the need to hasten to shrift; 11. the need to turn to God; 12. the need of repentance and confession, and the ten hindrances from true shrift; 13. the need for patience to bear penance and to overcome sin; 14. Christ's reply to those who demanded a sign; 15. the procession of Palm Sunday; 16. the significance of the feast of Easter Day; 17. the Resurrection; 18. James' letter against blaming God for sins; 19. for Ascension Day, Habakkuk's declaration of the risen sun, with explanation; 20. the wonders of Pentecost; 21. Christ's mercy and men's hostility to God; 22. the birth and life of John the Baptist; 23. Christ's estimate of John; 24. Christ's forgiveness of Mary; 25. as in Lambeth 17, but applied to St. James; 26. as in Lambeth 13, but applied to St. Laurence; 27. the Assumption of Mary; 28. the dead, Death, Doomsday; 29. the calling of Andrew and Peter; 30. as in Lambeth 16; 31. Peter's directions to be prudent, wary, and cautious; 32. as in Lambeth 15; 33. the Devil likened to a hunter laying snares; 34. Isaiah's prophecy of the rod of the root of Jesse.

These homilies exhibit little of method or of general plan. Especially as compared with the other twelfth-century series, the pieces are rambling and incoherent, the author being guided only by the momentary suggestions of memory or imagination as he wrote. The failure to master a single theme, to hold to it, and to bring it home forcefully, often makes the special point of a homily difficult to perceive. The homilies exhibit a yielding to weak subtleties in subdivision, and to trivial and thin-drawn symbolic interpretation, from which the Bodley, the Lambeth, and the Vespasian homilies are practically free. The connections are often far-fetched, and frequently produce an effect hardly that intended. The Gospel narrative so freely used in the other series, is employed but little. There are no *exempla.* Some few quaint illustrations like that of the washerwoman (10) occur; there are some developed figures like that of Mary the sea-star (24, 27; see the *Ave Stella Maris,* page 532); and there occur some odd expositions, as where the Devil is likened to the hunter who sets his snares of Play, Drink, Market, Church, for men the wild beasts (33). Very interesting is the bestiary illustration (31) of the adder with the jewel in her head, who, pursued for her treasure, finds a stone

and lays to it one ear and holds her tail to the other, and so
shuts out the alluring song of her foes; and of the serpent that,
thirsty, comes to a well and drinks until she bursts, then vomits
her venom, and creeps into a pierced stone, so leaving her old
skin behind her.   Curious, too, is the frequent use of folk-
etymology—as when Easter or *Estrene* Day is derived from
Aristes (resurrection) Day; and when God is styled *father*
because He *feide* (joined) us here, or because He *fet* (feeds)
all things; and when *housel* is associated with *hu* (how) and
seely (happy, blessed).   With exception of one allusion to evil-
doing by the clergy (23), there is no reference to abuses of
the day.   In unity, in logical form, in directness, in dignity, in
impressiveness, the collection is inferior to the other twelfth-
century groups.

THE ORMULUM [14] (so named because Orm made it,
says the author) is preserved in what is probably the composer's
own MS., Bodley Junius 1.   The work is of the North-East
Midland and about 1200.   It consists of 19992 complete verses
(including the dedication) with fragments of 67 more thereafter.   The lines are based on the Latin *septinarius*, are
unrimed, and are absolutely and monotonously regular—the
odd verses of four unstressed and four stressed syllables, the
even of three iambic feet with feminine ending.

In the 342 lines of his dedication the author (whose name
suggests Scandinavian kinship) addresses Walter, his brother
in the flesh and in the Faith, and his fellow canon-regular of
the order of St. Augustine.   He explains that he intends to
present in English the Gospels in the Mass-Book for all the
year, and after each to give its interpretation and applications;
and he protests that he has held closely to the original, insert-
ing words only where the metre required such.   After the dedication follows a table of contents in Latin listing 242 homilies,
of which apparently only the first 32 were finished.   Then comes
a preface of 108 English verses.   Thereafter follow the 32
extant homilies.   Each of these consists of a translation of the
Gospel for the day, followed by explanation and application of
it.

Orm did not seek literary excellence. He wrote, as he says, that simple men might understand the doctrines of the Church. He is diffuse, redundant, intolerably monotonous. Yet that he was painstaking and methodical in an extraordinary degree, is evinced everywhere in his matter and in his form. Particular evidence of this is seen in his care in inventing and punctiliously practicing a system of spelling, which he earnestly bids every copyist scrupulously to observe. This spelling consists in the doubling of a consonant following a short vowel in the same word; the substituting of *t* for *þ* after a word ending in *d*, *dd*, *t*, or *tt*—except in the case of initial *þ* after the cæsura, and when *u* follows initial *þ;* and the use of single, double, and triple strokes of the pen like acute accents, above letters. The language of the *Ormulum*, and the information concerning pronunciation of the time afforded by the spelling, are of great value to the scholar; but beyond these, the work is of little worth. Orm's sources appear to be Bede, Gregory I, and Isodore; and, indirectly, Augustine (through Bede) and Ælfric. Romance notions and the French language have practically no influence in the work.

FIVE KENTISH SERMONS [15] in prose, making in print a total of ten pages, date from before 1250. They are in MS. Laud 471 f. 128 v (end of 13th century) with their French originals by Maurice de Sully.

Sermon 1, for the Epiphany, tells of the appearance of the star to the three kings, of their dealing with Herod, of their gifts to Christ. The star manifested the birth of Christ; to-day should be made special offerings; the gold signified Christ's kingship, the incense His priesthood, the myrrh His mortality—now they signify good belief, prayer, good works that mortify the flesh. Offer God daily not only worldly gifts, but these spiritual ones; and may Christ give us to believe, to pray, to work, that finally we have Heaven's bliss.—Sermon 2 tells the story of the marriage at Cana. The water is the bad Christian—he is cold in love of God, and cools all that he touches; wine, hot in itself, warms the drinker, and betokens those fired with love of God; Christ once touched water to wine, but often He has spiritually made good men of evil. Let each test if he is water or wine.—Sermon 3 tells of the healing of the leper after the Sermon on the Mount. Leprosy indicates deadly sins, scab indicates minor sins; the leper loses fellowship of men, the sinner loses

fellowship of God. Pray God for spiritual health; come to shrift.—
Sermon 4 tells of the stilling of the tempest. That miracle should
confirm our faith in Christ, and lead us to call on Him; He will aid
us. Tempted by the Devil, let us cry to Him as did the shipmen,
that we be saved at Doomsday.—Sermon 5 relates the parable of
the employment of the workers in the vineyard. The good man is
God; the vineyard is His service; the times of day are the ages of
the world; the penny is the bliss of Heaven; if we die not in deadly
sin, we shall have that bliss, whatever be our age. See that ye be
true servants of God, lest ye be cast out of the vineyard.

The pieces are all on one general plan: *a* Gospel story, *b*
(allegorical) exposition, *c* exhortation. They are all brief,
direct, earnest, simple, without ornament or factitious appeal
of any sort. The language is of special value because it preserves forms that at the date were archaic in other dialects,
and has a vocabulary exhibiting an admixture of notably modern phrases derived from the French.

THE COTTON VESPASIAN HOMILIES [16] consist of
three prose pieces and a scrap of a fourth: *De Initio Creature,
An Bispel, Induite Uos Armatura Dei,* and *Erant Appropin-
quantes.* They are in MS. Cotton Vespasian A 22 f. 54, and
are probably from the South-West at 1200-1250.
De Initio Creature is a slightly abridged transliteration of
Ælfric's *Sermo de Initio Creaturæ, ad Populum, quando
Volueris,* with an added preface.

In direct, forceful sentences the piece declares God to be the
beginner of all, the King of Kings, the Trinity in one. It tells
of the creation of the ten orders of Angels, of which the tenth fell
and were cast as devils into Hell; the creation of Adam and Eve
to fill out the tenth order; the Fall, the Expulsion, the Condemnation
to Hell; the world become evil, the Flood, Babel, the origin of
idolatry; the rise of the Hebrews, the giving of the Laws, the passing of the Red Sea; the Incarnation, the Passion, the Resurrection,
and the Ascension.

An Bispel, as its name indicates, is a parable.

A rich king would tell his friends from his foes. He sent messengers to five districts to summon both. The friends were kindly
received at the castle, and fed; the foes were beaten and imprisoned.
The King came and inquired why his foes were hostile; then he
declared they should have naught to eat, and he cast them out into

darkness. He feasted his friends on bread and wine and seven dishes. The King is God; the five realms are the five laws—the natural, the Mosaic, the Prophetic, the Christian, and the law of the Holy Spirit. The gate of the castle is the day of death; angels receive the good, devils the evil. At Doomsday the evil shall be damned; God shall then go to feast with the good, who shall have Christ who is the bread and the true wine.

The deficiency in treatment of the wine and the messengers at the end, suggests that the piece is abbreviated, or was concluded very hurriedly. The parable proper is closely paralleled in, and is perhaps a retelling of, Anselm's *De Similitudine inter Deum et Quemlibet Regem Suos Judicantem.* The antiquity of the *Bispel* suggests that both go back to a common source.

Induite Uos Armatura Dei makes one page of print.

It tells of the armor of the Christian warrior; and it enumerates his foes, the World, the Flesh, and the Devil, who contend against him like three robbers. If they prevail, they take, not gold and silver, but life. If we overcome, we shall be praised and rewarded as good soldiers. Our leaders are the Holy Ghost and Christ. Eight weapons (not interpreted) must we have, and our shield shall be Faith.

Erant Appropinquantes is a scrap of a few lines telling of Christ's reception of the lepers and the sinful, the anger of the Scribes and the Pharisees thereat, and Christ's reply in the parable of the Lost Sheep.

WYCLIFFE'S HOMILIES [17] are discussed with his other writings (see page 468).

2. COLLECTIONS OR CYCLES OF HOMILIES AND LEGENDS INTERMIXED

At an early period the Mass came to include the *Lectio*, a reading of an Epistle, a Prophecy, or a Gospel. Gradually, particularly through the Benedictines, the *Lectio* was included in services of the Church other than the Mass, and came to consist of three kinds of passage—from the Scriptures other than the Gospels for the Mass, from commentaries or homilies by

the Fathers, and from the *Acta Sanctorum.* Ultimately, provision was made for a *regular series* of Scripture selections, one
for each of the days of the Church Calendar, for general use.
For the second sort of readings were drawn up *collections of
commentaries and homilies* like that of Paulus Diaconus with
its later version incorrectly ascribed to Alcuin. The writings
of Bede were in England extensively drawn on for these purposes. The *Acta Sanctorum* made their way from a brief
passage in the Liturgy before the Epistle with a brief exposition of the legend, first to a reading at the close of *Prime* of a
chapter of the acts of the saint for the following day, and then
to introduction into the *Nocturnes,* where they developed *from
concise notices to elaborated accounts.*

Gradually, the actual facts of the life and the significance of
the saint were neglected, and were lost in apocryphal invention
and modification. The great period of development was in the
twelfth and thirteenth centuries. From decade to decade, saint
after saint was added to the canon, and feast after feast to the
calendar. In addition to the festivals of more or less general
observance, various churches had their special local celebrities
and local celebrations. The life of the saint became the great
issue in the service for his day, as the saints' days came to make
up the great bulk of the Church Year. Gradually, too, the
legends pushed aside the Scriptures and the homilies in the *Lectiones*—though often only a part of the legend was read. To
meet these conditions, to satisfy enthusiasm for an individual
story or the needs for a particular common or local occasion,
isolated or *special legend pieces* were composed.

Another condition assisted the vogue of the Legend. From
an early time, on the saints' feast-days the Latin sermons were
devoted largely to the saints concerned. Naturally, corresponding pieces in the vernacular for delivery to the congregation, were composed or translated. Ælfric's *Homeliæ Catholicæ* contain homilies for certain saints' days. The *Blickling
Homilies* have discourses on the Annunciation, the Assumption
of Mary, the Birth of John Baptist, Peter and Paul, Michael,
Martin, and Andrew. The Trinity College Homilies (see page
280) have pieces on John Baptist (2), Mary Magdalene,

James, Laurence, Andrew, and the Assumption of Mary. The
tendency from this was to *compose or collect special groups of
discourses on saints covering all, or large sections, of the festivals of the year*. This Ælfric exemplified when, as far back
as about **996**, he appended to his *Homeliæ Catholicæ*, or collection of homilies, his *Passiones Martyrum*, a collection of pieces
on the saints.

Still another condition enhanced the vogue of the Legend.
Up to the thirteenth century the homilies of whatever sort,
preserved their original nature of sermons, and as such dominated even the saints' days. But in the thirteenth and the fourteenth centuries another stage was entered on—the *saints'
legends commonly displaced the homilies proper for the festivals
of the saints* (so making up a *Proprium Sanctorum* or *Legendary*) and *crowded the homilies proper over to the Sundays and
the festivals of Christ* (so making up a *Temporale*). The
intrusion went even farther, for in the expository portion of
the Sunday homily often a legend or several legends came to be
used as *exemplum* or illustrative narrative. Indeed, as time
passed, except in the homilies of Wycliffe and his immediate
followers, who were opposed to appeal by narrative from other
than the Bible itself (see page 469), the vogue of the Legend
by the end of the fourteenth century caused *the homily to be
composed largely of stories or tales* from other than Scriptural
sources.

The procedure that has just been sketched is illustrated by
the various phenomena of form and of content in the stages
and sub-stages of growth seen in the English Northern Homily
Cycle, in the Southern Legend Collection, in the *Festial* of
John Mirk, in the Collections or Cycles of legends, and in the
separate legends, of which discussion follows.

THE NORTHERN HOMILY CYCLE [18]. The tend-
ency toward production of cyclopædic works in the thirteenth
century, led in the South to collaboration in the compilation of
the Gloucester collection of legends; the same tendency in the
North, after causing the completing of the *Cursor Mundi* (see

page 339), led to the production of a homily cycle to which was added later a legendary.

It has been estimated that the MSS. of the Northern Cycle were ten times as numerous as those still preserved. The extant MSS. exhibit notable variations and inconsistencies due to rewriting or copying by ecclesiastics in accord with individual needs, and without regard for any close preservation of originals. The pieces of the cycle are all in short couplets. The cycle is extant in three general forms.

1. In its *earliest form* the cycle, or *Evangelia Dominicalia*, is a prologue and a series of discourses for the Sundays of the Church Year, extending from Advent to Advent, with addition of Christmas, the Epiphany, Easter-Monday, Whit-Monday, the Ascension, the Purification, and the Annunciation. The complete series, then, comprises a Prologue and 59 items. The homilies are made up usually of a paraphrase of the Gospel for the day, followed by a largely allegorical exposition of the Gospel based on the Fathers (especially Gregory and Bede), usually succeeded by a *narratio* or tale (legendary or 'popular') as *exemplum* for some teaching drawn from the Gospel. Gerould has shown that 'excluding the Bible and counting each saint's biography by itself, twenty-two different works are represented' as sources in the 55 *narrationes*. It would seem that the author wrote the tale sometimes from memory, perhaps sometimes from oral tradition; and that he was not learned, and had not much literary skill. The *homilies* are not merely discussions of the Gospel text, as are the older homilies; they are closer to the type of Orm's pieces with addition of the *narrationes*.

Gerould has declared recently that the pieces were not intended for reading in church services, and were not so read. The actual composition of the original cycle of homilies, seems to have been by one hand, though material may have been gathered by collaborators. The work was done at the beginning of the fourteenth century, and probably in the neighborhood of Durham. It has been held that the Gospels of the Durham Missal are those on which the original cycle is based. The French *dominicalia* in short couplets in MS. Cbg. Univ. Libr.

Gg I 1, has a number of resemblances to these English homilies, and so suggests that some of the material came from a similar French *dominicalia*. Gerould has recently given opinion that the source of a considerable portion of the original cycle is Robert of Gretham's *Miroir* or *Les Evangiles des Domées*.

The oldest MS., and probably the closest to the original, is in the Royal College of Physicians in Edinburgh (Northern; early 14th century), unfortunately containing only the Prologue and the first 13 items.—MS. Ashmole 42 (Northern; early 15th century) has a lacuna from *Dom. XX* to *Dom. XXII post Trin.* It adds the Purification (properly Item 13 of the cycle), the feast of St. John Baptist (in two parts, for the Vigil and for the Day of St. John), and the feast of Peter and Paul. Ashmole is said to offer the text next best after that of the Edinburgh MS.—MS. Cbg. Univ. Libr. Gg V 31 (Northern; early 15th century) has the homilies with omission of the Annunciation to *Dom. II post Pasche* inclusive, and of *Dom. XIV-XVII post Trin.* inclusive. The Purification is Item 13; there is an insertion in the Christmas homily; and there are the Ashmole additions for St. John Baptist and Peter and Paul. The writer of this version is said to have treated the text very freely, omitting and substituting words and short passages at will.—MS. Lambeth 260 (Northern; near 1450) is close to Ashmole, and perhaps was copied from it, though with many defects.—MS. Br. Mus. Additional 38010 (c. 1450) has an imperfect text of the cycle that is said to agree closely with Lambeth.—MS. Cbg. Univ. Libr. Dd I 1 (Southern; c. 1450) has before Item 1 of the cycle proper a late homily for Corpus Christi Day (included in MS. Harley 4196 in Northern form, and in MS. Vernon with an additional part; see page 276) with its prologue; has a number of pages missing; rearranges some of the items; drops *narrationes* 22, 52, 55; inserts, instead of appending, the day of John Baptist and that of Peter and Paul, and inserts also an *Assumptio Mariæ* with the text of the old Southern *Assumptio* (see page 298). The MS. represents a Southern version from a peculiar Northern version of the original, follows a good archetype and offers often the preferable reading. The version is a special base for the Ver-

non version of the second form of the cycle.—MS. Phillipps
8122 (Northern; not before 1375-1400) begins with Item 7 *In
Epiphania,* and extends to include the last item, 59, omitting
Items 9 and 24 (*Dom. II post Epiph.* and *In Die Pasche,*
neither originally in the MS.), and having a lacuna of Items 32
(*Dom. inf. Oct. Asc.*) to 35 (*In Die S. Trin.*) inclusive, with
only the *narratio for Dom. XX post Trin.*—MS. Phillipps
8254 (Northern; 1400-1450) has the Prologue and Items 1-55
inclusive, omitting Items 25 (*Feria II*) to 31 (*In Ascensione*)
inclusive, omitting also Item 9 (*Dom. II post Epiph.,* not originally in the MS.), and having only the *narratio* of Item 55.—
MS. Harley 2391 f. 156 v (Northern; 1450-1500) has only
narrationes, and these only of Items 2 (at end), 4 (at end), 5,
6, 8, 10, 11, 12, 13 (*Abbess* only), 14-16, 18-24 (order partly
shifted), 26-28, 30-35, 37-39, 46, 48-54, and 56-58. The tales
omitted from Item 7 on, were not originally in the MS.—To be
added are several fragments: MS. Br. Mus. Additional 30358
(late 15th century), not noted by Gerould or Horstmann, a
fragment of the Prologue and the first three Sundays in Advent; MS. Bodley Engl. poet. C 4, containing the story of St.
Oswald from *Dom. XI post Trin.* in part, following closely Ashmole; and a Robartes fragment not described.

The modifications and additions noted in the later MSS.,
indicate that the cycle was growing. But more was to come.

2.   The *second great form* of the cycle is represented in MS.
Vernon ff. 165-227 (1370-1380) and its sister MS., Br. Mus.
Additional 22283 (1380-1400). The latter MS. preserves but
35 pieces, has great gaps caused by loss of leaves, is as
it exists literally the same text as Vernon, and has no peculiar
value. The dialect of Vernon is Southern of 1370-1380. Just
as the text of the Southern Legend Collection in this MS. (see
page 297) is made up of a compilation from various versions
with new additions, so here various versions of the Northern
Cycle are drawn from, as is also foreign material, to make up a
combination version with additional new items. This version
contains the Northern *Dominicalia* transcribed into the Southern dialect, partly from the Dd version, partly from older
Northern MSS.; and contains also a group of later homilies

originally composed in the South.   Often Vernon has better readings than Dd.

MS. Vernon contains only homilies proper; legends are deliberately excluded—perhaps because of the extensive Southern collection in the earlier part of the MS. (see page 297). This version falls into two great divisions, a *Temporale* and a *Proprium Sanctorum* (see page 287).   The *Temporale* represents a composite version of the Northern homilies on the bases already noted, with omissions, substitutions, and rearrangements.   A number of additional homilies are inserted—notably vigils before Christmas, Epiphany, the Ascension, and Pentecost; and week-day homilies, especially for the week before Easter and that before Whitsunday.   There are in the *Temporale* 78 homilies as compared with the 59 of the earlier form of the cycle.   The *Proprium Sanctorum* is new.   It names 35 titles; 29 pieces are actually written down in the MS.   The pieces are homilies, not legends—the Gospels appropriate for the feasts, with exposition of each.   Only the more important saints' days are included.

3.   The *third great form* of the cycle is represented in MSS. Harley 4196 ff. 1-205 (early 15th century) and Cotton Tiberius E VII ff. 101 v ff. (c. 1400).

This third redaction, like the second, is in two parts—now a *Temporale* and a *Legendary*.   In the *Temporale* the two MSS. agree verbally, but Tiberius arranges the items differently from Harley, and on a historical basis rather than on that of the calendar; and it omits the legends inserted in the Christmas week in Harley.   The Harley *Temporale* contains 121 items, partly from the original cycle, partly new matter.   Most of the items of the *Dominicalia* are from the original cycle, but the texts are more or less recast; some are displaced by others; and the Prologue, the introductory piece, and some other items, are dropped.   As can be seen from the total of 121 items, the additions in Harley are numerous.   These are mostly from sources other than the redactions represented by the extant MSS.   Two facts are of extreme importance.   The first is, that Harley *introduces a group of legends* (see page 287) as readings for the Christmas week.   The second is, that only some twenty-odd *narrationes* are kept. It seems that for the *Temporale* the Gospels were the chief issue; the narrative itself of Gospel story had *pushed the homiletic element into the background* (see page 287). It has been urged that the homogeneous character of the collection indicates that the making-over of the older pieces and the additions, are by one writer of the North of England.

The *Legendary* of this recension in Harley consists of 31 items. Tiberius omits Items 1-8, 11, 13-14, 25-26, and 31; but it has three added pieces between 30 and 31. There is difference of opinion as to which of the two MSS. presents the older version. The items are confined to the principal common Church festivals; yet its interest and its instructive character have caused the legend of Barlaam and Josaphat to be appended to Harley, though theirs was not actually a feast day. The introduction to Harley states that the legends are 'drawn out of Latin.' Expressions in the text lead to impression that the original must have been an extensive work. Apparently, it is not the *Legenda Aurea*, at least not the commonly known version of it. The editor of the *Cecilia* has shown that the source of that legend had a text fuller than that of the *Legenda*.

THE SOUTHERN LEGEND COLLECTION [19].

A few years before, or at the same time with, the *Legenda Aurea* (see page 306)—*i.e.*, in the latter half, and probably the last quarter, of the thirteenth century—was undertaken the Southern Legend Collection. Apparently, the *Legenda* and the English pieces had no influence on each other; the agreements (*e.g.*, in the accounts of *Christopher* and *Margaret*) that occur between them, are probably due to use of common originals. The various parts of single MSS. of the Southern collection manifest peculiarities of manner and of preference as to matter, that indicate participation of collaborators in the composition. Again, the earlier MSS. fall into several quite distinct groups, exhibiting the collection in a course of development through several stages. Moreover, the single MSS. of the same general class contain special modifications and additions of their own. All of this suggests that the collection is the result of the work of a number of writers, perhaps of a number of groups of writers in somewhat separated places; and that its first completed form came into being only after years of labor, and as a consequence of a gradually developing plan.

The characteristics of the language indicate that the earlier stages of the work were done in the Southern dialect, and that the enterprise probably originated among the monks at Gloucester, or at least became defined and developed at Gloucester. Possibly Robert of Gloucester, the chronicler (see page 197), had a part in the undertaking. The fact that items of the collection bear the marks of composition much antedating the earliest extant MS. of the collection (*e.g.*, the old *Assumption;* the old *Magdalen,* as in Laud Item 66, Lambeth Item 4, Trinity Cbg. Item 66; and the old *Margaret*—see pages 330, 294, 298, 313, 314), suggests that perhaps the first steps toward the collection were taken farther back than is usually assumed. At least, it must be admitted that some very old pieces were taken over into the collection.

The measure is, with few exceptions, the long couplet, generally of septenary verses with pause after the fourth stress. Not uncommonly the line becomes alexandrine or eight-stressed; sometimes there is added rime of the stressed syllables next preceding the cæsuras of the couplet. In Laud 108 the *Magdalen* is a survival of an old version originally in four-line stanzas with middle-rime; the same with more middle-rimes is represented in Lambeth and Trinity Cbg. The *Childhood of Jesus* in Laud 108 is in couplets of chiefly four-stress lines. The Laud 108-Vernon *Alexius* and the Trinity Oxf. and Laud L 70 (*i.e.,* 463) *Alexius,* are in tail-rime aabccb. The Vernon *Gregory* is in eight-stress lines whose fourth stresses rime from couplet to couplet or in groups of four lines, and whose eighth stresses rime in similar fashion. But *Alexius* and *Gregory* are apparently intruders into the collection.

The collection was widely copied and modified. The MSS. extend from the late thirteenth into the sixteenth century. They fall into *eight groups,* the first six of which illustrate stages in the development of the collection. A full list of the items of all the MSS. is in E. E. T. S. Pub. 87 pp. xiii ff.

The groups of MSS. are as follows:

1. The oldest MS., the one exhibiting the earliest stages of the collection, is Laud 108 (part 1; c. 1280-1290)—a copy, and perhaps a somewhat made-over copy, of an earlier text. It is certainly independent of the other earlier MSS. It contains a number of pieces that apparently represent a recension earlier than that used for the making-up of the Harley and Corpus completed series. This Laud MS. begins with the eighth item of a series of pieces originally 67 in number. The first seven lost pieces appear to have comprised a part of a *Temporale*, for Item 8 is on the later incidents of the Life and the Passion of Christ. Then follows an inserted *Infancy of Christ* in different metre; after which come 58 pieces, followed by an appendix of two (*Blase* and *Cecile*) and one (*Alexius*) more, written by later hands. The whole in Laud comprises sixty pieces plus the added three. When this recension was composed, the idea for the collection had not developed to the stage of completeness for the whole Church Year, or of arrangement according to the calendar. The MS. pays no attention to the chronology of the holy days. It appears to be a copy of the pieces that were at hand in complete form. It is barely possible that the hit-or-miss arrangement indicates the order in which the pieces were composed. A full list of the Laud items and synopses of Items 10 to the end, are in E. E. T. S. Pub. 87 pp. xiii and xxv.

2. The second group falls into four divisions: a, b, c, d.

a. MSS. Harley 2277 (c. 1300) and Corpus Christi College Cbg. 145 (c. 1320) represent the completed cycle for the whole Church Year. Harley arranges the pieces in the order of the calendar, and presents the standard that was followed with modifications in the later MSS. It is, however, a copy—and it is defective, already representing a considerable corruption of the completed version or full *annus festivalis*. Originally, this redaction contained 91 items; but Items 1-24 and 59, and several beginnings and endings, are lost or omitted.—MS. Corpus is very close to Harley 2277, but is not derived from that MS.

It has the same series of legends, and supplies the first twenty-four pieces and some other parts, that are missing in Harley; but it has some of the defects of that earlier MS., has defects of its own, and omits the *Passion* (Harley Item 29) and 10 items from *Quintin* at October 31 to *Lucy* at December 13. The full recension represented by these MSS. consisted of 91 items (or 92, if *Judas and Pilate* be separated) and a Prologue, beginning with the *Circumcision* at January 1 and working through the calendar to *Judas and Pilate* after *Thomas of Canterbury* at December 29. Corpus has appended in a later hand *Guthlac* (apparently from memory; see Bodley 779 and Julius D IX) for April 11. A full list of the items of Harley 2277 and Corpus is in E. E. T. S. 87 pp. xiv ff.

Here may be mentioned the fact that the accounts of the Passion and the Resurrection *inserted* in the *Cursor Mundi* Cotton MS. at lines 16749 and 17288 in addition to the regular accounts of the *Cursor* MSS., are from the Southern Collection (see page 341).

b.   MS. Ashmole 43 (c. 1300) has close to it MS. Cotton Julius D IX (15th century). The Harley-Corpus list and order are followed in these MSS., with the following variants: omission in Ashmole of the Prologue, Items 1-3 and part of 4, *Longius*, the *Passion*, *Theophilus* with miracles of Mary, *Martha*, the third part of *Michael*, *Judas and Pilate*; omission in Julius of *Longius*, *Albon*, *Swithin*, *Kenelm* and *Oswald*; addition in both MSS. of the *Seven Sleepers*, *Ipolitus*, *Justine*, *Leger* (also in Laud), *Francis* (also in Laud), *Fei* (also in Laud), *Fredeswide*, *Eustace* (shorter text in Ashmole), *Brice*, *Cecilia*, *Edward the King*; insertion in Ashmole alone of the *Advent*; addition at end in Julius alone of *Egwine*, *Silvester*, *Albriჳt* (also in place of Ashmole's *Albon*), *Ignatius*, *Guthlac* (the original form, said to be from the *Vita Sancti Guthlaci*; appended to Corpus—see above—much modified, perhaps from memory, and to Bodley 779—see page 299—much condensed after line 85), *Miracula Ste. Marie*, and insertion of *Jakes* and *Birin*; in both MSS. change of order of *Exaltacio Crucis* and the second part of *Michael*; change of order in

Ashmole of *Oswald* and *Albon;* and, among the added pieces in
Julius, insertion of the third part of *Michael,* and *Theophilus*
with the Mary miracles. Several of the additions in Ashmole are
appended items of Julius. A full list of the items is in E. E.
T. S. 87 pp. xiv ff.

c.   MS. Stowe 669 (c. 1340 ?) has but 35 items, beginning
with *Michael,* which corresponds to Item 66 in Harley 2277. It
follows the last-named four MSS. in general, differing from
Harley and Corpus in the following: it omits *Leonard, Anas-
tasius, Judas and Pilate;* it adopts all the insertions of Ashmole
after *Michael,* except the *Advent, Edward* and *Oswald,* but supplies a longer text for *Eustace* and a different text for *Frides-
wide;* it inserts the *Conception of Mary,* the *Conception of
Christ,* the *Nativity of Christ, Fremund* (also in Vernon),
Petronelle (as in Egerton), *Moses de 10 Preceptis* (part of Old
Testament); and it adopts the Julius insertion of *Egwine* (cp.
Egerton).

d.   Later MSS. with the items and order of Harley 2277,
are the following: MS. Br. Mus. Additional 10301 (late 14th
century), omits the *Passion* and all after the opening of the
third part of *Michael* (Item 68); MS. Trinity College Oxford
57 (late 14th or beginning 15th century), omits Items 1 to
middle of 23 *Edward,* 87-90, and the first days of the *Passion,*
locates *Judas and Pilate* after the *Passion,* and inserts *Birin*
(in different metre; see Laud L 70) and *Alexius;* MS. Laud
L 70 (*i.e.,* Laud 463) is complete, locates *Judas and Pilate*
after the *Passion,* inserts *Alexius* (text of Trinity Oxf.) and
Celestyn (different metre, aaabb, three fours, one two, one six,
said to be from the North), *Birin,* and *In Principio in English;*
MS. Tanner 17 (beginning 15th century), contains Items 1-44
(to *Austin* l. 66), inserts *Letania* after the Resurrection in
the *Passion,* and locates *Judas and Pilate* after the *Passion.*

3.   The third group is represented in MS. Egerton 1993
(14th century). It omits words, contracts phrases and sentences, and turns the septenary verses common in the collection into alexandrines. It consists of 85 items, others at the end
being lost. It begins with a portion of a *Temporale* (the Old

Testament story from the Creation to Habakkuk, with Zecba-
rias and Elizabeth, an abridged *Life of Christ*, and a *Passion*
different from Harley), the *Advent* (ll. 1-278 parallel to Ashmole), and Christmas Gospels. Then, after the *Prologue*, the
cycle begins, not with January 1, but with November 30
(*Andrew*) correspondent to Harley Item 83. Thence it goes on
down through *Becket*, and then begins the year with *Yeres
Day, Twelfth Day*, and *Hillary*. Besides the additions before
the Prologue, it adds in calendar order *Albriȝt* (cp. Julius Item
97), *Purnele, Eadborw, Botolf, Aedri, Mildride*, and *Egwine*
(cp. Julius Item 95, Stowe Item 31). It preserves the Ashmole additions *Seven Sleepers, Justine, Ypolit, Leger*, and
Francis; and adds *Dominic* (paralleled in Laud 108). Interestingly, *Brandan* is omitted as it is in Vernon.

4. MSS. Stowe and Corpus are seen to contain a list of
items to be made up only by going to versions 2a, 2b, and 3, or
1, 2a, 2b, and 3, while Egerton's list must be made up by
turning to 1, 2a, 2b, 2c. There is a group of later MSS. that
are made up of farther combinations. These are MSS. Vernon,
Lambeth 223, and Trinity College Cbg. R, 3, 25.

a. MS. Vernon (1370-1380) has 101 items extant, with 11
lost items noted in the index. The general order is the order
of Harley. The extant portion ends with *Thomas of Canterbury*. The cycle begins with a version of Old Testament story
parallel with that in Egerton, followed by an account of the
prophecies, the conception and nativity and life of Mary, and
the birth and life and death of Christ. Then come the Prologue, New Year's Day, the *Epiphany*, with the rest in calendar
order. In the items all the older texts are represented: for
example, *Fabyan* and *Sebastian, Brigide*, and *Alexius* represent Laud 108; the *Passion* represents Harley; *Purnell, Ed-
burgh, Ælbrith, Etheldrede, Botulf, Mildred*, and *Egwyn*, represent Egerton; the *Seven Sleepers, Justyne, Brys*, and *Cecile*
represent Ashmole; and *Fremund* represents Stowe. Vernon
contains, too, a new item, *Æthelwold*, and new texts of *Kenelm·*
and *Gregory*.

b. MS. Lambeth 223 (c. 1400) is in two great divisions, a

Temporale and a *Sanctorale.* The items of the *Temporale* are *Movable Feasts, Septuagesima, Lent, Easter, Holy Thursday, Litany;* Old Testament story from Adam to Abacuc (cp. Egerton and Vernon); *Fifteen Tokens from the Life of Christ;* the *Conception of Mary* (cp. Vernon); *Joachim and Anna, Life of Mary, Conception of Christ, Nativity, Purification, Childhood of Christ* (cp. Egerton and Vernon); and *Assumption of Mary* (new; based on the short-line version, see page 331). The *Passion* is omitted.—The *Sanctorale* proceeds from the Prologue and Year's Day through the calendar in the usual order, with 76 items. The MS. contains texts otherwise peculiar to Laud 108 and Vernon. Of the Harley list but a few pieces are omitted. The additions of Ashmole (mostly in Laud and Egerton) are largely preserved. *Maudelayn* has the peculiar text in Laud. A number of the Laud texts are kept. The *Conversio Pauli* is paralleled only in Laud. *Elyne* joined with the legend of the Cross, is new. The *Assumptio Mariæ* goes back to the Old Southern *Assumptio* used in the Northern Cycle (see pages 289, 331). In general, the Lambeth version is a free treatment of the texts, with abbreviations, omissions of couplets, shifts of arrangement, and substitution of phrasing. The contents of the MS. are listed in E. E. T. S. 87 pp. xx-xxi.

c. MS. Trinity College Cbg. R, 3, 25 (beginning 15th century) has 116 items. It opens with a review of the Old Testament from Adam to Daniel. Then, under title of *Salutatio Mariæ,* comes the story of the Advent (cp. Ashmole and Egerton). Then, after the *Prologue* and *Year's Day,* follow the items in the usual order up to Item 42, after which the arrangement is greatly changed. This version has the legends of Harley with additions of Ashmole except *Justine.* The peculiar Laud-Lambeth *Magdalen* is preserved, but the influence of the Laud recension does not appear in the MS. Many of the Egerton additions are omitted. The texts are mostly those common to several versions. Except for the Old Testament material and the *Conception,* the *Temporale* items are split up, and the parts are located, according to the dates of the calendar.

There is a general tendency to shift location. The contents of the MS. are listed in E. E. T. S. 87 pp. xxi-xxii.

5. In MS. Bodley 779 (15th century) is the latest version, made up from the various earlier versions, with many new additions, especially lives of the popes. It has 135 items. The arrangement seems quite arbitrary. Various larger groups, as the *Passion* and the *Advent*, are split up and separated. There are several new texts (*e.g.*, those of *Fraunceys* and *Fey*). The contents of the MS. are listed in E. E. T. S. 87 pp. xxii-xxiii.

6. It will be perceived that the *Temporale* gradually developed. But none of the MSS. yet mentioned contains it complete. The complete form is in only MS. St. John's College Cbg. B 6 (Northern; c. 1400). The MS. has none of the other items. The *Temporale* is as follows: a review of Old Testament history from the Creation to the rescue of Daniel by Habakkuk; the *Life of Jesus* to the finding in the Temple; the *Later Life of Jesus* from the preaching by John and the baptism of Christ to the raising of Lazarus; the *Passion*, the *Resurrection*, the *Ascension*; *Longius*; *Pilate*; the *Harrowing of Hell* (abstract from *Evangelium Nicodemi*), the experiences of *Joseph of Arimathea* and the *Destruction of Jerusalem* (see page 155); finally, *Movable Feasts, Septuagesima, Lent, Easter, Holy Thursday,* and *Litany*. So there is a full Bible history from the Creation to the destruction of Jerusalem, reminding of the *Cursor Mundi* (see page 339). For the *Advent* was used apocryphal matter, especially the *Evangelium de Nativitate Mariæ*. The *Life of Jesus* is from the Gospels arranged chronologically and worked into a whole; the Gospels are not literally translated, but are given only in outline with copious comments (see page 405). The version of the *Harrowing of Hell* is said to be unique (see page 327).

7. Besides the above texts, there are fragments in MSS. Kings College Cbg. 15 (c. 1350), twelve items; Br. Mus. Additional 10626 (c. 1380, perhaps by the scribe of 10301), one complete item and several defective pieces; Harley 2250

(Northern; 15th century), part of a *Temporale*, and six other items.

8. Further, *single legends* from the Southern group are in the following MSS.: Auchinleck (1330-1340) *Joachim and Anna* and the other *Advent* stories, ending with Joseph comforted by the angel; Cotton Caligula A II (ff. 135, 137; 1400-1450), *Jerome* and *Eustas* (imperfect at end); Harley 4012 (c. 1500), *Joachim and Anna* (different text) and *Patrick;* Bedford (now Br. Mus. Additional 36983; 15th century), the third part of *Michael;* Royal 17 C XVII (1400-1450), *Mary Egypt* and *Magdalen;* Cotton Cleopatra D IX (14th century), last 8 lines of *John the Evangelist, Thomas à Becket, Theophle,* and *Cecile.*

Since only a part of the MSS. of the Southern Collection has been printed, our knowledge of the relations of the versions and of their originals is very restricted. A synopsis of the items of the various redactions is impracticable here. In his four volumes of texts of Legends, Horstmann has described the MSS. and itemized their contents, and has given a synopsis of all the items of MS. Laud 108 after Item 9, in his edition of that MS.

The range of material in the collection is, of course, very great, even in the earlier and shorter recensions. The developed design is comprehensive, like that of the *Cursor Mundi.* Taking all the versions together, we have a synopsis of all the important Old and New Testament material and of apocryphal matter, from the Creation to the Fall of Jerusalem, accounts of the lives of all the chief saints and of some of the popes, and cycles for the Advent and the Passion and Easter. A great deal of instruction other than what is purely religious is wrought into the work. In the third part of *Michael* is presented an extensive body of matter concerning the constituents of the physical world, a cosmology, and a theory of demons (see *Fragment on Popular Science*, page 438). In *Brandan* is given a view of contemporary notions concerning the sea and the unknown parts of the world.

The love of wonders is evident everywhere; miracles of marvelous nature are frequent. But sometimes the writer of a piece intimates that he has his own doubts concerning the truth of what he relates. Though now and then a finer element appears, the mediæval crude pleasure in more lurid incidents and more physical sufferings and torments, is amply represented. Effort to work in collaboration seems to have crushed out, for the most part, personal idiosyncrasies and individuality. The metre is generally irregular, the language plain, the work without polish, the narrative monotonous. There is practically no spirit, no elevation, except what comes occasionally as a reflection of the inherent quality of the material. The account of Becket (by some critics ascribed to Robert of Gloucester, see page 198), whose festival on December 29 is a sort of concluding mark for a number of the versions, is perhaps the best of the collection.

THE FESTIAL OF JOHN MIRK [20], author of the *Instructions for Parish Priests* (see page 361), is a complete fusing of Homily Cycle and Legendary. The head-note of the Cotton MS. states that Mirk was a canon-regular of the monastery of Lulshull (Lilleshul), which is in Shropshire. Repeatedly head-notes and end-notes in the MSS. remind that the work must be styled *Festial*. It is in prose from the West of England. It dates from about 1400, certainly from before 1415, for St. Winifred's Day, made a Church festival in 1415, is declared 'not ordeynyd by holy churche to be halowed.' The prologue says the sources are the '*Legenda Aurea* with more addyng-to.' Most of the sermons are made up of selections from the *Legenda*, freely chosen and freely worked over, with additions of many *narrationes* (especially from the *Gesta Romanorum*) and comments. Frequently Mirk mentions his sources, among which are Bede, Augustine, Neckam, Josephus, Melitus, Higden's *Polychronicon*, Gregory's *Dialogues*, the *Acts of the Apostles*, 'Gestes' of the Romans, 'Gestes' of France, *Vitæ Patrum*, and John Belet. Of the sermons not from the *Legenda*, those on *Winifred* and *Alkmund*, Patron of Lilleshul, are from local sources. Much of the narrative is apparently from local oral tradition.

The *Festial* is in MSS. Cotton Claudius A II (15th century), 71 items and a Prologue; Bodley Gough Eccl. Top. 4 (15th century), 69 items following the list and the order of Claudius, but omitting Items 34 and 68-70, adding *Prima Quadrigesime* after 19, and splitting Item 45 (*Peter and Paul*, and *Nero*); Caius College Cbg. 168 (15th century), corresponding in contents with Claudius, but omitting Items 34, 26, 70, 71; Harley 2403 (15th century), close in contents to Claudius, omitting Item 55 *Alkmund*, revising Items 70 (with a longer text, an added *narratio*, and an added Mary miracle) and 71; Lansdowne 392 (15th century), a series close to Claudius, with several large gaps, and with its conclusion in the midst of Item 66 (*Katherine*); Douce 108 (1450-1500), with changes of order and but 44 items; Douce 60 (15th century), with but 45 items; Harley 2247 (1450-1500), a much expanded version presenting the text printed by Caxton, but having several new sermons for each festival; and Harley 2381 (1450-1500), with the matter arranged as a *Temporale* and a *Sanctorale*, a total of 62 items stopping at *Katherine*. The text represented by this last MS., allowing for dialectical variations, is close to Caxton's first edition; with change of dialect it was used in that edition. By Caxton and his successors, from 1483 to 1532, nearly a score of editions were printed. Again, some of the tales were copied out separately: MS. Harley 1288 f. 88 (c. 1450) has five whole tales and part of a sixth; MS. Harley 2250 f. 84 (15th century) has some tales.

The *Festial* provides a full *annus festivalis*. As has been intimated, the work combines and fuses the Homily Cycle and the Legendary. The sermons are all intended to provide material for delivery by ill-equipped priests, of whom, says the *Præfatio*, 'mony excuson ham by defaute of bokus and sympulnys of lettrure.' The language and the method are plain; the whole undertaking aims consistently at comprehension by the simple audience, and appeal to it. There is no predominant formula for the pieces. Sometimes the matter is largely explanation of the meaning and the name of the day celebrated. The sermons for the saints' days are given over to narrative of the incidents

of the lives of the saints honored. Narrative of a Bible story
·and exhortation to proper conduct in conformity with Divine
ordinance, make up the other chief types. Symbolism is infrequent. Definiteness of point and directness of procedure and of
statement, characterize the collection. But especially notable
is the extensive use of narrative, not merely in the main line ⌣
of the discourse, but in the hundred or more illustrative *narrationes*. Clearly, unlike Wycliffe and his followers (see page
469), Mirk approved heartily of employment of tales in preaching: indeed, he directly defends the practice. But he shows
control and judgment in use of them. The *narrationes*, sometimes as many as five in a sermon, are always closely connected
with the theme; they are introduced with the declared purpose
of enforcing the issue through conviction or stimulation; and,
the story ended, the hearers are usually brought back to the
point illustrated. The tales vary much in kind; some are
over-marvelous, some have local flavor. It is not at all wonderful that these simple pieces of prose full of narrative, caught the
popular taste, and that, when the other native collections and
cycles were on the wane, these were copied into many MSS.,
and (unlike any of the other groups), as soon as the press was
available, were printed in edition after edition.

Attention must be called to the forty-eight lines of tail-rime
to Mary on her blessed union with Christ, that, in the sermon
on the Assumption of Mary, Mirk quotes for repetition by the
people (see page 538).

3. Legends

As has been intimated (see page 286) isolated legends were
composed to meet individual predilections or special exigencies.
Some of these pieces and some items extracted from regular
series, were selected and were copied or worked over in groups or
collections irrespective of location in church calendars. For
clearness and brevity we deal first with the groups or collections
of such pieces, and thereafter with each legend that is treated
or copied at least once as a separate piece.

I. Collections or Groups of Legends

THE SMALLER VERNON COLLECTION [21] is a group of nine pieces in the Southern dialect, that follows the Southern Collection in MS. Vernon f. 89 (1370-1380), and that was inserted perhaps as an appendix to that collection. It is in short couplets, probably of between 1350 and 1375. The first eight pieces, *Paula* (some 250 lines missing from the beginning), *Ambrosius, De Quadam Virgine in Antiochia, Theodora, Bernard, Augustin, Savinian & Savina, Barlam et Josaphat*, are almost word for word from the *Legenda Aurea*. The ninth piece, *Eufrosyne* (674 lines), is word for word from the *Vitæ Patrum*, and apparently did not originally belong to the group. The pieces have special linguistic interest in that they carry over a number of Latin words, and attempt to preserve some of the Latin constructions. Treatment of the Fathers does not occur in the other Middle English collections; yet here the accounts of Ambrose, Bernard, and Augustine are by all odds the longest of the first eight pieces, and occupy 3142 of the total of 6443 verses.

THE SCOTTISH COLLECTION OF LEGENDS [22] is preserved in a somewhat defective text in MS. Cbg. Univ. Libr. Gg II 6 in a fifteenth-century hand with two other principal hands filling in omissions and additions. The former ascription of the group to John Barbour (see page 203) was on very questionable bases, and now seems wholly given up. The work was written at the end of the fourteenth century—according to some critics, in the dialect of Aberdeen, and according to others, in Lowland Scotch. The language of the MS. is mixed, and is styled in Item 18, line 1471, 'ynglis townge.'

The group consists of 50 items with a prologue, making a total of 33533 four-stress verses in couplets. These fall into eight groups: 1, the Prologue and twelve legends of the Apostles; 2, legends of the Evangelists, Mark, Luke, and Barnabas; 3, legends of Mary Magdalene and Martha, who are, after the Virgin, the two principal women in the Gospels; 4, the legend of Mary of Egypt; 5, nine legends—Christopher,

Blaise, Clement, Laurence, the Seven Sleepers, Alexius, the three Julians and the Emperor Julian, Nicholas, and Machor; 6, eight legends, chiefly of women—Margaret, Theodora, Eugenia, Justina, Pelagia, Thais, Eustace, and George; 7, five legends—John the Baptist, Vincent, Adrian, Cosmas and Damian, and Ninian; 8, ten legends of virgins—Agnes, Agatha, Cecilia, Lucy, Christina, Anastasia, Euphemia, Juliana, Thecla, and Katherine. Only two Scottish saints are treated. No English saints are dealt with; but, oddly, St. George (in 1349 adopted as patron-saint of England, and in 1350 made patron of the Garter) was included. The members of the first three groups are arranged, as the author indicates, according to the relative importance of the persons celebrated. The order of the rest of the items seems to be largely by chance.

The legends of Julian, George, Mathias, and James the Less, are very close to the *Legenda Aurea*, which is the chief source of the series. The *Speculum Historiale* of Vincent of Beauvais, the *Vitæ Patrum*, the Latin *Acts of Thecla*, the *Martyrology* of Ado, the *Passio S. Andreæ*, Ailred de Rievaux's *Vita Niniani*, and the lost Latin *Vita S. Macharii*, are some of the other sources. Often the originals identified have been followed very closely, indeed translated almost literally—often, however, omissions and insertions are made, comments are added, and other sources are drawn on. Parts of *Ninian* (ll. 37-84, 781-814) are similar to parts of *Machor* (ll. 333-74, 1581-1614), one of the pieces appearing to be made over from the other.

The prologue and the first items give a number of details concerning their author. He is a minister of Holy Kirk, but old age and feebleness prevent him from his duties. So, to avoid idleness and to afford good examples to others, he writes the lives of divers saints. He tells that he has already written a work based on translations, dealing with the Conception and Life of Mary; the Conception, Life, Death, and Resurrection of Christ; the Harrowing of Hell; the story of Longius; the Later Life, the Compassion, the Assumption, the Coronation of Mary; and sixty-six Miracles of the Virgin—now he will tell of the Twelve Apostles.—Interestingly, this lost work, which reminds of the *Cursor Mundi,* begins and ends with the Virgin, as do the *Cursor* and the Vernon poem on the Birth (see page 323). Perhaps the aged (see also Item 4, l. 390; 7, l. 12; 10, l. 585) priest wrote all the extant legends; but his authorship of more than the first dozen or fourteen has been questioned.

It would appear that the collection was written for reading, not for use in church-services; there is no sign of address to a congregation, no calendar order, no mention of saints' days. The poet's confidences give the work a warm personal touch. The writer is really interested in his themes, and (whatever the prologue says conventionally) interested for their own sake. The work is by all odds superior as literature to the other collections. The couplet is fluent, sometimes dashing almost headlong, yet keeping the measure with notable skill. The use of run-on lines, shift of pauses, and the split couplet, and the clever but natural arrangement of phrases, merit admiration and study. The expression is very simple, indeed even colloquial; what the matter offers, the writer puts down with ready frankness of vocabulary and phrasing. Yet the expression is surprisingly precise and sharp in its form and its suggestion. The stories are told with swiftness and spirit. Digressions and comments are few and brief. Selection and mastery are evident everywhere. Each piece (however many authors wrote the items) begins with the story, holds to the story, ends with the story.

LEGENDS BY LYDGATE [23]. To John Lydgate are ascribed a *Life of Our Lady,* and accounts of Edmund, Albon and Amphabel, Austin at Compton, Edmund and Fremund, George, Giles, Margaret, Petronilla, and others.

VERSIONS OF THE LEGENDA AUREA. At about 1260-1270 Jacobus a Voragine, to meet a demand for a cycle of pieces that could be used in church-services for all the festivals of the year, wrote in Latin the great collection of legends known as *Legenda Aurea* [24]. The *Legenda* at once became very popular, being drawn upon as a source-book by writers in Latin and by others in the vernaculars. In English the Scottish Legendary, Mirk's *Festial,* the smaller Vernon collection, and Osbern Bokenam's *Lives of Saints,* were largely based on it or were translated from it, while writers of innumerable single pieces of various types drew from it.

An English Prose Translation [25] of the *Legenda* made in 1438, consists of 177 items. It is preserved in MSS. Egerton 876, Harley 4775 and 630, and Douce 372. It has close resemblances to the French translation made by Jehan de Vignay at about 1380.

Caxton's Prose Golden Legend [26] was printed in 1484 and (?) 1487. For this Caxton worked over the translation of 1438, making many additions, some perhaps from older separate English poetical pieces.

OSBERN BOKENAM'S LIVES OF SAINTS [27], composed 1443-1446 in stanzas ababbcbc with a prologue in short couplets, and written in 'language of Suthfolk speche' (*St. Agnes* l. 17), is in MS. Arundel 327. The source is the *Legenda Aurea* followed 'fro sentence to sentence.' The thirteen lives are all of women: Margarete, Anne, Crystyne, the Eleven Thousand Virgins, Feyth, Agneys, Dorothye, Marye Magdeleyn, Kateryne, Cecilye, Agas, Lucye, Elyzabeth.

THE DOUCE GROUP [28], in MS. Douce 114 ff. 1-148 (15th century), perhaps in the Nottinghamshire dialect, consists of prose lives of Elizabeth of Spalbeck, Cristyne . . . of St. Trudous in Hasbon, and Marye of Oegines (Oignies), and a 'Letter' on Kateryn of Senis. These are followed by *A Tretys of the Seuene Poyntes of Trewe Loue and Euerlastynge Wisdame* from the Latin *Orologium Sapienciæ.*

NOVA LEGENDA ANGLIÆ [29] is a fifteenth-century collection of legends translated by John of Tynemouth, John Capgrave, and others, and printed with additions by de Worde in 1516.

THE STOWE LIVES OF WOMEN SAINTS [30] in MS. Stowe 949 (c. 1610) have been edited.

II.   Legends Treated in at Least One Separate Piece

In the following pages are brief notices of legends of which at least one treatment is found *outside* of the various groups or collections already discussed. Effort is made to note as well under each such item the collections in which the theme is treated.

A. *Legends of Saints*

The various legends of saints of which a treatment exists in Middle English outside of the collections, are here arranged in alphabetical order.

ALEXIUS [31] was a favorite subject. The versions have been grouped as follows: (1) aabccb, in Southern Legendary MSS. Laud 108 and Vernon, in a Naples MS., and MSS Royal 13 B XXIX (1457) and Durham Cathedral Libr. 5, 2, 14 (c. 1450-1475); (2) aabccb, of end of fourteenth century, a different text from (1), in Southern Legendary MSS. Laud 463 and Trinity College Oxf. 57 (see page 296); (3) aabccbddbeeb, in MS. Laud 622 (1375-1400); (4) short couplets, in MS. Cotton Titus A XXVI (1400-1450); (5) short couplets, in Northern Homily Cycle MSS. Ashmole 42, Cbg. Univ. Libr. Gg V 31, and Lambeth 260 (see page 289); and (6) short couplets, in the Scottish Collection. All of these versions are essentially different from each other. Furnivall mentioned also an aabccb text in the Cosin's Library MS. V ii 14 f. 92. There is a prose version in Caxton's *Golden Legend.*

ANNA [32] is treated outside of the collections in a rime-royal version in MS. Chetham 8009 ff. 19-30 (15th century).

ANTONIUS [33] is dealt with in prose of the West Midland, in MS. Royal 17 C XVII f. 124 v (15th century), in the 1438 English *Golden Legend,* and in Caxton's *Golden Legend.*

CATHARINE, see KATHERINE below.

CECILIA [34] is treated in the Southern Legendary, the Northern Homily Cycle, the Scottish Collection, Bokenam's *Lives*, the 1438 English *Golden Legend*, and Caxton's *Golden Legend*. She is the heroine of Chaucer's *Second Nun's Tale* (see page 739).

CHRISTINA [35] is subject of a legend in the Southern Legendary, the Northern Harley-Tiberius Legendary, the Scottish Collection, Bokenam's *Lives*, the 1438 English *Golden Legend*, and Caxton's *Golden Legend*. Moreover, along with a *Dorothea*, Lydgate's *Life of Mary*, and Capgrave's *Catherine*, there is in MS. Arundel 168 f. 2 (15th century) an account in 528 four-stress verses ababbaba by William Paris (see I. 515). Identification of 'Brawchaump' (ll. 500-01) as the Earl of Warwick, fixes the date during the imprisonment of the Earl on the Isle of Man, October, 1397-August, 1399.

CHRISTOPHER [36] is dealt with not only in the Southern Legendary, the Scottish Collection, the 1438 English *Golden Legend*, and Caxton's *Golden Legend*, but also in 1013 lines in short couplets in MS. Thornton f. 122 v (1430-1440). This last text might perhaps be regarded as an extension for the Northern Cycle, in the MSS. of which the saint does not appear.

CUTHBERT [37] is treated in the Southern Legendary, in Caxton's *Golden Legend*, and in a version (c. 1450) in a MS. in the library of Castle Howard.

DOROTHEA [38] is told of in Bokenam's *Lives* and Caxton's *Golden Legend*. There is a prose account in MS. Lambeth 432 f. 90 (15th century), and one in MS. Chetham 8009 Manchester f. 1 (15th century). A free translation of the *Legenda Aurea* is in 334 four-stress verses ababbcbc (the end lost) in MS. Harley 5372 (15th century), and in a very defective text, much being lost, in MS. Arundel 168 (15th century).

EDITHA and ETHELDREDA [39] are themes of pieces (1131 irregular long lines, end missing) apparently by two authors, in the Wiltshire dialect, in MS. Cotton Faustina B III

(c. 1420). A short legend of *Etheldreda* is in the Southern
Legendary MSS. Vernon Item 49, Egerton 1993 Item 58, and
Bodley 779 Item 124.

ERASMUS [40] is dealt with in 87 short couplets at the end
of the Northern Homily Cycle in MS. Cbg. Univ. Libr. Dd I 1
f. 295 (Southern; 15th century). The piece is addressed to a
congregation, and contains prayers to Erasmus and to God.
It would seem to be perhaps a homily for a saint's day, with
use of the story to enforce doctrine. A defective text is in
MS. Bedford f. 280 (now Br. Mus. Additional 36983; 15th
century) in 50 verses followed by a list of fifty-two 'passiones'
suffered by the saint. This copy is closer to Dd than is the
more perfect text (172 lines) in MS. Harley 2382 (15th
century).

ERKENWALD [41], fourth Bishop of the East Saxons
(†695 ?), is hero of a miracle in 352 long alliterative lines in
MS. Harley 2250 f. 72 v (15th century). The poem belongs
to the group of North-West alliterative pieces of 1350 or 1350-
1400 (see pages 240 ff.). It is dignified and elevated, one of
the best of the legends in English. It tells of the finding of the
grave of a judge of 'New Troy' in the year 1033 B. C. and in
the reign of King Belin; of the recovery of speech by the body
at the command of Erkenwald; and of the saving of the judge's
soul through the pitying tears of the saint. It has been suggested that the Hatton alliterative *Becket* (see page 226) is
by the same author. Caxton's *Golden Legend* has a section on
Erkenwald.

EUSTACE [42] is treated in the Southern Collection, the
Northern Homily Cycle, the Scottish Collection, and the 1438
and the Caxton *Golden Legends*. In MSS. Digby 86 f. 122 v
(1272-1283) and Ashmole 61 f. 1 (15th century) is a Southern
version in tail-rime aabccb. In 1561 a legend by John Partridge was printed. The tales based on the Eustace or Placidas
story are discussed with the romances (see pages 112 ff.).

GEORGE [43] is theme of pieces in the Southern Collection, the Scottish Collection, and the versions of the *Golden Legend*. He is the subject of a piece attributed to Lydgate (see page 306). A version is also in Ælfric's Old English *Lives of the Saints*.

GREGORY [44] is dealt with (1) in lines of seven or six stresses aaaa (sometimes aabb) with medial rime aaaa (sometimes aabb) of the stresses immediately preceding the cæsura, inserted as Item 64 in the Southern Legendary MS. Vernon f. 44 (1370-1380; 750 lines), but probably going back to before 1250 and to a French source—and also in MS. Rawlinson Poetry 227 (1450-1500) with a *Theophilus;* (2) in strophes of four-stress verses ababcdcd, in the Southern Legendary MS. Cotton Cleopatra D IX (14th century; 1314 lines); (3) in MS. Auchinleck (1330-1340), in 1056 four-stress lines abababab; (4) in lines of seven or six stresses in couplets, in the Southern Legendary MSS. Laud 108, Harley 2277 (and its cognates), Corpus, Ashmole 43, Julius D IX, Lambeth 223, Egerton 1993, Trinity Cbg., and Bodley 779; (5) in prose in the 1438 and Caxton *Golden Legends*.

JEROME [45] is told about in the Southern Legendary, and in the 1438 and Caxton *Golden Legends*. In MS. Lambeth 432 (15th century) is a prose legend of *Hieronymus*.

ST. JOHN THE EVANGELIST [46] is dealt with in the Southern Legendary, the Northern Homily Cycle, the 1438 and Caxton *Golden Legends*, the Scottish Collection, and Mirk's *Festial*. In MS. Thornton f. 231 v (1430-1440) is a version that, though preserved in the Northern dialect, belongs to the cycle of alliterative poems of the North-West at 1350 or 1350-1400 (see page 240). It consists of 266 verses in stanzas of fourteen lines, the first eight being long alliterative lines abababab, the last six being alliterative half-lines aabaab.

JUDAS AND PILATE [47] (*maledictorum Jude & Pilati*, is the Harley heading) oddly are dealt with in the Southern

Legendary MSS. Harley 2277 and Corpus (at the end);
Trinity Oxford 57, King's College Cbg. 15, Laud 463 (L 70),
and Tanner 17 (after the *Passion*); and Trinity Cbg. R, 3, 25
at the end. The stories of the birth and life and death of Pilate
and of Judas, are inserted in the couplet version of *Titus and
Vespasian*—*i.e.*, *The Bataile of Jerusalem* or *The Vengeaunce
of Goddes Deth* (see page 154).

JUDAS [48] is theme of a fragment of 33 verses of seven or
six stresses in couplets. Child printed these as the ballad
quatrain, and classed the piece as a thirteenth-century, and
hence very early, example· of a ballad. The piece is in MS.
Trinity College· Cbg. B, 14, 39 (13th century). Of much
interest is the addition to the story of a sister of Judas, and of
a motive for the selling of Christ to the Jews—namely, desire
of Judas to reimburse himself for thirty pieces of silver of
which he had been robbed.

JULIANA [49] is dealt with in the Scottish Collection, and
in the 1438 and Caxton *Golden Legends*. But her story is
known best from the alliterative prose piece of the 'Katherine
Group' to which belong also the alliterative prose *Katherine,
Marherete,* and *Hali Meidenhad* (see pages 314, 272). Each
of the two texts of this prose *Juliana*—one in MS. Royal 17 A
XXVII f. 56 (c. 1230), and one in MS. Bodley. 34 f. 36 v (c.
1230)—covers about eighteen printed pages. The texts vary
much from each other in language, the Bodley text producing
the more modern impression. The story is probably from
some Latin piece, with no dependence on the Old English
Juliana.

KATHERINE [50] is heroine of a number of treatments.
(1) The alliterative prose *Katherine* in MSS. Royal 17 A
XXVII, Bodley NE, A, 3, 11, and Cotton Titus D XVIII,
gives name to the 'Katherine Group' just indicated under
Juliana (see also pages 314, 272). Printed as verse, the
text makes 2505 half-lines. The MSS. are of 1200-1250; the
first two are probably copies of one archetype, which with the

third is a copy of a lost text. This version, perhaps because it has long been generally accessible, is the best known of the English Katherine pieces. The other texts are: (2) abcbdbeb, in MSS. Auchinleck f. 21 (1330-1340; 660 lincs) and Caius College Cbg. 175 f. 107 (15th century; 796 lines, sometimes ababcbcb); (3) short couplets, in MS. Cbg. Univ. Libr. Ff II 38 (c. 1420; 446 lines), perhaps originally in six-line stanzas; (4) lines of seven or six stresses in couplets, in Southern Legendary MSS. Laud 108, Harley 2277 and Corpus and the cognate MSS., Ashmole 43 and Julius D IX, Vernon, Lambeth 223, Trinity Cbg., and Bodley 779; (5) short couplets, in the Scottish Collection; and (6) a text in MS. Harley 5259 (early 15th century). There are also prose treatments in MS. Chetham 8009 Manchester f. 31 (15th century), Mirk's *Festial*, the 1438 and Caxton *Golden Legends*, Bokenam's *Lives*, and Capgrave's collection. In MS. Bodley Rolls 22 (1400-1450) is a hymn to Katherine by Richard Spalding.

MARY MAGDALENE [51] was treated very widely and from an early period. (1) In the Southern Legendary MSS. Laud 108, Lambeth 223, and Trinity Cbg., is incorporated an early version in verses of seven or six stresses aaaa, having medial rime aaaa of the stress preceding the cæsura with the similar stress in each of the other three verses. (2) The regular Southern Legendary version in verses of seven or six stresses in couplets, is in MSS. Harley 2277 and Corpus and the cognate MSS., Ashmole 43 and Julius D IX, Egerton 1993, Vernon, Bodley 779, and Royal 17 C XVII. (3) A *narratio* of Mary for *Dom. I in Adventu*, is in short couplets in the Northern Homily Cycle MSS. Cbg. Univ. Libr. Gg V 31 and Dd I 1, Royal College of Physicians, Phillipps 8254, Vernon, and Additional 22283. (4) Another text in short couplets is in MS. Auchinleck f. 62 (1330-1340; 680 lines, end lost). (5) A short couplet version is in the Scottish Collection. Prose treatments are in Mirk's *Festial*, in the 1438 and Caxton *Golden Legends*, in a Cosin's MS. V ii 14, and in MS. Durham Cathedral Library 5, 2, 14 (East Midland of c. 1450-1475; incomplete; from an English version of Jean de Vignay's

Legenda, or from a French version of the *Legenda Aurea.*)   A
Lamentatyon of Mary Magdalena was printed first in Thynne's
edition .of Chaucer.   An unprinted treatment is said to be in
MS. Harley 6211.

MARGARET [52] also was a favorite.   (1) A treatment in
alliterative prose, *Seinte Marherete the Meiden ant Martyr,* is
one of the members of the 'Katherine Group' composed in
exaltation of virginity (see pages 272, 312).   This is in MSS.
Royal 17 A XXVII f. 37 (c. 1230) and Bodley 34 (c. 1230),
and covers in print 22 pages.   (2) An early treatment preserved in verses of seven and six stresses in stanzas aaaa with
medial rimes aaaa (c. 1270), is in MS. Trinity College Cbg.
B, 14, 39 (13th century), MS. Auchinleck (1330-1340), and
Southern Legendary MS. Bodley 779 (Item 84; 15th century).
(3) The regular Southern Legendary version in verses of seven
or six stresses in couplets, is in MSS. Harley 2277 and Corpus
and cognate MSS., Ashmole 43 and Julius D IX, Egerton
1993, Lambeth 223, and Trinity College Cbg.   (4) A short
couplet version of before 1450 is in MSS. Ashmole 61 f. 145
and Brome Hall.   Further, there are the short couplet version
in the Scottish Collection; the ababbcc text attributed to Lydgate, in MS. Durham Cathedral Library 5, 2, 14 (1450-1475);
and the prose pieces in Mirk's *Festial,* the 1438 and Caxton
Golden Legends, Bokenam's *Lives,* and the Cosin's Library MS.
V ii 14.   The sources of the four numbered versions are probably: (1) The *Sanctuarium* of Mombritius, (2) a slight Latin
variant from Mombritius, (3) the *Legenda Aurea* and several
other Latin texts, (4) the English version numbered (2).

MARINA [53] is dealt with in 114 short couplets in the
Vernon (1370-1380) text of the Northern Homily Cycle, and
the 1438 and Caxton *Golden Legends.*   She is the theme of
116 short couplets in MS. Harley 2253 f. 64 v (c. 1310).

THEOPHILUS [54] is treated in the Southern Legendary
(long couplets) MSS. Laud 108, Harley 2277 and Corpus
(and the Harley cognates), Trinity Cbg., and Cleopatra D IX;

in a later version in the Northern Homily Cycle (short couplets) MSS. Vernon, Harley 4196, Tiberius E VII; and in the
still later version in MS. Rawlinson Poetry 227 f. 11 (642
verses of tail-rime aabccb), the MS. of 1450-1500 but the
poem perhaps much earlier, since in the MS. is a *Gregory*
agreeing closely with the Vernon *Gregory*. In MS. Harley
1703 is a version by William Forrest, completed in 1572.
Attention must be called to the fact that in the MSS. with
Theophilus are commonly joined miracles of the Virgin (see
the items noted on page 168).

THOMAS À BECKET [55] is the hero of accounts in the
Southern Legendary, the Vernon Northern *Proprium Sanctorum*, the Northern Harley-Tiberius *Temporale*, and the
1438 and Caxton *Golden Legends.* He is treated also as a
prophet in some alliterative long lines composed probably about
1360, and preserved in MS. Hatton 56 and MS. Cbg. Univ.
Libr. Kk I 5 (see page 226). It has been suggested that this
piece is by the author of the Harley alliterative *Erkenwald*
(see page 310). An epic account of à Becket written by
Laurentius Wade in 1497, is in MS. Corpus Christi College
Cbg. 298.

WERBERGE [56] is theme of a *Life* translated into English in 1513 by Henry Bradshaw, and printed by Pynson in
1521.

WOLFADE AND RUFFYN [57] are treated in 382 verses
of seven or six stresses in couplets in the dialect of Stafford-
shire, preserved in the defective MS. Cotton Nero C XII (c.
1450).

B.   *Other Legends*

. The legends other than Saints' Legends are discussed under
the following heads: a. The Cross; b. The Saga of Adam and
Eve; c. Old Testament Story, and Christ and Mary; d. Visions,
and Visits to the Under-World.

a. The Cross

Around the Rood or the Cross clustered a body of stories that were dealt with widely in various tongues in the Middle Ages. As we were concerned with them the versions fall into two groups, the *Rood-Tree* and the *Legend* groups. The Rood-Tree Group is represented by the *History of the Rood-Tree* in MS. Bodley 343 (c. 1150-1175), part of the *Cursor Mundi* accounts, two Latin prose versions in MSS. Cbg. Univ. Libr. Mm V 29 (12th century) and Harley 3185 (early 14th century), a French prose text of Andrius in MS. Bibl. Nat. Paris 95, a French poem in MS. Bibl. Nat. Paris fr. 763, a Dutch poem *Dboec van den Houte* (14th or 15th century), and a Low German poem. The Legend Group is represented by the Latin *Legend* preserved in a number of MSS. from the thirteenth century on, from which are derived directly, with retention of some of its representative elements, the English Southern Legend Collection poems, the Trinity Oxford *Canticum de Creatione*, and the Northern Homily Cycle pieces. Translations of the *Legend* are in the various other vernaculars. As the Rood-Tree and Legend groups have a number of features in common, it has been urged that probably they are from an ultimate common original. The features of the two groups, as we are concerned with them, may be seen sufficiently in the following accounts of the English pieces.

THE HISTORY OF THE ROOD-TREE [58], a prose piece making in print 17 pages, is in MS. Bodley 343 (c. 1150-1175).

After the passage of the Red Sea, Moses, on successive mornings, on waking found three rods grown up around him. He dug up the rods, and took them with him. They sweetened bitter springs. Moses and David met; David asked for the rods, and obtained them. He wrought many miracles with them. In a garden between Gethsemane and Olivet, he planted the rods. They could not be removed, and grew up into one tree. Solomon attempted vainly to build the tree into the Temple. Thereafter it was kept in that holy place, working miracles. A part of the tree was used for the Cross. Three hundred and thirty years later, Helena found the Rood, and in the Temple came upon the rest of the tree. These she bore to Constantinople.—Now the piece tells that Judas (not before mentioned) 'who had shown St. Helena the Rood,' was baptized as 'Ciriacus' and made Archbishop. The next day, Helena gave him parts of the Rood to bear to Jerusalem, Alexandria, and Rome, she keeping the fourth part at Constantinople. Three days later, Ciriacus 'gave' Helena the five Nails of the Cross. These she had made into a bridle for Constantine, who performed miracles with it. Ultimately, by Divine command Constantine hung up the Nails with the Cross in Constantinople.

The last part of the piece, that covering the finding of the Cross and the events thereafter, contains contradictions of statement, and is hurried over in a few lines. Quite disproportionate treatment is given many incidents of the earlier parts.

THE SOUTHERN LEGENDARY ROOD POEMS [59] make up an account based on the Latin *Legend* with some use of lines 157-84 of the *Legenda Aurea*. The version is in four sections, *The Early History of the Rood, How the Rood was Found, The Exposition of the Cross, The Life of St. Quiriac* (Ciriacus). All the parts are together in MSS. (see pages 294 ff.) Laud 108 Item 3 (Item 10 of original copy; arranged somewhat differently from the rest of the MSS.), Ashmole 43 and Cotton Julius D IX Item 36, Egerton 1993 Item 48, Vernon Item 40. The parts are dealt with in MSS. Harley 2277 and Corpus and cognate MSS. (Additional 10301, Trinity Oxford, Laud 463, Tanner 17, Phillipps 8253; see pages 294 ff.) in Items 39, 40, 64; in MS. Lambeth 223 in Items 29, 30, 48; in MS. Trinity Cbg. R, 3, 25 in Items 51, 52; in Bodley 779 in Items 52, 128. MS. Harley 2250 (15th century; Northern) has a *St. Quiriac* and a *St. Elayne*.

This account tells of the Fall of Adam and Eve, and the promise of ultimate mercy; Seth's journey to Paradise, and return with three kernels of an apple from the Tree of Mercy; the planting of the seeds, and the growth of three trees; the transplanting of the trees by Moses at Mt. Tabor, and again by David at Jerusalem; the union of the three into one tree; Solomon's vain attempt to build the tree into the Temple; the making of the Rood from the tree; the hiding of the Rood by the Jews; Constantine's inquiries, and Helena's finding of the Rood through Judas; Judas' finding of the nails; Judas' baptism as Quiriac; the miracles of the Cross; and Helen's building of a church for the Cross. Then is told how the

pagan conqueror Cosdre took a part of the Cross, and set himself
up as God, but was overcome and slain by the Roman Emperor
Eraclius; and how the latter restored the Rood to the Temple at
Jerusalem.   Then follows an account of Quiriac's martyrdom at the
hands of the Emperor Julian.

THE CURSOR MUNDI ROOD VERSION [60] (see page
339) is inserted in sections at the fitting places—lines 1237-
1432 (Seth's mission to Paradise); lines 6301-68, 6659-66,
6937-46 (the account of Moses); lines 7973-8978 (the
account of David and Solomon); lines 15961 ff. (Judas and his
mother); lines 16543 ff. (the Crucifixion); lines 16861 ff. (the
hiding of the three crosses); and lines 21347 ff. (the finding of
the Cross).   All the matter preceding the account of Moses, is
from the Legend Group, as are parts of lines 8923 ff. and 8206-
30.   The general story, however, follows the Rood-Tree
Group.   Judas appears only at the end of the account of the
finding of the Cross.   There he is connected with the pound
of flesh story that anticipates the *Merchant of Venice.*

CANTICUM DE CREATIONE [61], in 1200 verses of
tail-rime aabccb in MS. Trinity College Oxford 57 f. 156 (late
14th or beginning 15th century), follows the Latin *Legend,*
with some use of the *Vita Adæ et Evæ.*   The author states at
lines 1185 ff. that it was first made in Hebrew, then it was
turned into Latin, and he now turns it into English in the
year A. D. 1375.   It is from the East Midland toward the
South.   It falls into two parts, *How Adam and Eve Lost
Paradise* and *Of the Rood Tree.*   It is greatly drawn out, with
much elaboration and expansion of details, and with much use
of direct discourse.   The earlier version of the *Canticum* is
discussed on page 319.

THE NORTHERN HOMILY CROSS STORY [62] fol-
lows the general matter of the Legend Group, with use of the
Vita Adæ et Evæ.   It is in three parts, *The Story of the Holy
Rood, The Finding of the Cross,* and *The Exposition of the
Holy Rood,* in MSS. Harley 4196 Items 10 and 22, and Cotton
Tiberius E VII Items 2 and 11 (see page 291).

Further are to be mentioned the treatments of the Cross material in Mirk's *Festial* (*De Invencione* and *De Exaltacione*), and in the 1438 and Caxton *Golden Legends* [63] (the same parts).

To be connected with the story of the Cross are the Passion pieces (see Index) and several of the Contention pieces (see pages 414 ff.).

b.   The Saga of Adam and Eve

The saga of Adam and Eve, that was drawn upon for the part of the *Canticum de Creatione* (see page 318) preceding the account of the Rood Tree, and that afforded material for the Cross series of the Southern Legend Collection (see page 317) and of the Northern Homily MSS. Harley 4196 and Tiberius E VII (see page 318), was treated in several Middle English pieces.

AN EARLIER VERSION OF THE CANTICUM DE CREATIONE [64] (see page 318) consists of two fragments, 780 short couplets, in MS. Auchinleck (1330-1340). It is of 1300-1325 and the East Midland toward the North, and is said to be from the Latin Vulgate and a Latin legend-book, or from a source combining these two. The fragments tell of the Creation, the Fall, the subsequent life of Adam and Eve, the writing of Adam's life, and the revelation to Solomon of the tables bearing the record. They conclude with brief statement of the facts of the Redemption and of the Harrowing of Hell.

Þᴇ LYFF OF ADAM AND EUE [65], some 4000 words of prose in MS. Vernon f. 393 (1370-1380), tells of the Creation, the Fall, the subsequent woes of Adam and Eve, Seth's journey to Paradise and obtaining of the seeds of the apple (as in the Southern Legendary; very brief—see page 317), the death of Adam, Seth's writing of Adam's life on tables of stone that were found after the Flood, and the revealing of the tables to Solomon.

THE LIFE OF ADAM AND EVE [66], in prose from an originally independent work, is appended to the 1438 prose translation of the *Legenda Aurea* in MSS. Harley 4775, Egerton 876, and Douce 872 (see page 307), and was printed in Caxton's *Golden Legend* (see page 307). It contains much the same matter as the Vernon version. Seth's journey to Paradise and his obtaining of the *promise* of mercy (not the seeds of the apple), are told at length. In MS. Bodley 596 (c. 1430) is a prose *Life of Adam* that varies little from this version.

Later pieces on Adam and Eve, or on elements associated with the story, are in MSS. Ashmole 802 and 244 (c. 1610), Cbg. Univ. Libr. Dd XII 41 and Ff VI 33, Douce 15, and Harley 1704.

Matter on Adam and Eve is found, of course, in the appropriate items of the various *Temporales* in the collections, and in such of the Bible translations as cover the beginnings of the Old Testament (see pages 397 ff.). See the Harley 913 *Fall and Passion* (see page 324).

c. Old Testament Story, and Christ and Mary

Of course the Old Testament and the Gospel stories are found in the Bible translations of the period (see pages 397 ff.). The Passion of Christ and the Compassion of Mary are themes of contention pieces (see pages 414 ff.), of lyrical poems (see pages 515 ff.), and of meditations (see Index).

Legendary narratives of *both* Old Testament story connected with the Fall and the Redemption, *and* the various elements of the stories of Christ and Mary, comprise a great part of the *Cursor Mundi* (see page 339). Both classes of matter are dealt with in the *Temporales* of the collections, in appropriate items of the Caxton *Golden Legend,* and in the pieces noted in the discussion of the legends of the Cross and of Adam and Eve (see pages 316, 319). The Gospel and legendary materials concerning the life of Christ and the story of Mary, are themes of appropriate items of the various homily collections (see pages 277 ff.) and of the 1438 English *Golden Legend*. Examination of the Advent, the Christmas, and the Easter pieces, of those on the Circumcision and the Epiphany, and of those on the Conception, the Nativity, the Annunciation, and the Assumption of Mary, and on John the Baptist, in these various legend and homily collections, will afford the matter on Christ and Mary. The tables of contents in the editions of the homilies, the lists of contents of the legend MSS. in Horstmann's editions of *Altenglische Legenden* 1875, 1878, 1881, of the Scottish Collection, and of the Laud 108 legends, and the lists in Gerould's *North-English Homily Collection*, will introduce to the items that must be considered. The *Miracles of Mary* have already been discussed (see pages 165 ff.).

The following statement of the Old Testament material, and the matter on Christ and on Mary in the MSS. of the Southern Legend Collection, will give a sufficient notion of the general nature of the material that is in the various collections. Thereafter will be discussed the *separate* pieces—the Harley 913 *Fall and Passion, La Estorie del Euangelie*, the Harley 3954 *Childhood of Christ*, the Ashmole 61 *Resurrection and Apparitions*, the Pepys prose *Life of Christ*, the *Holy Blood of Hayles*, the *Gospel of Nicodemus*, the *Harrowing of Hell*, the *Fifteen Signs*, Lydgate's *Life of Mary*, the *Festival of the Conception of Mary*, and the *Assumption*.

THE SOUTHERN LEGENDARY MATERIAL [67] on Old Testament story and Christ and Mary, is best gathered up in the only complete Southern *Temporale*, that in MS. St. John's College Cbg. B 6 (see page 299). The contents of this *Temporale*, as given by Horstmann, are: (1) narrative of Old Testament story from Adam to Habakkuk; (2a) the Advent and Christmas series—Joachim and Anna, the Conception of Mary, her Offering, her early life in the Temple, her Marriage, the Annunciation; Zacharias and Elisabeth, the Birth of John Baptist, Mary's Trial before the Bishop; the Birth of Christ, Tebel and Salome, signs in heaven and earth; the Epiphany; the Purification, Simeon and Anna; the Circumcision; the

Slaughter of the Innocents; the Flight to Egypt, with miracles; the Return from Egypt; and Jesus in the Temple; (2b) the later Life of Christ according to the Gospels and Sunday Lessons (part in MS. Laud 108 Item 8; omitted in other MSS.); (2c) the Passion, the Resurrection, the Ten Apparitions, the Sending of the Holy Ghost; followed by Longius (in Harley 2277), Pilate (as in Harley 2277), the Descent into Hell (from the *Evangelium Nicodemi*), and the Destruction of Jerusalem; (3) the Movable Feasts, Septuagesima, Lent, Easter, Holy Thursday, and Litany.

The following treatments of portions of the material are in other MSS. of the Southern Legend Collection. In MS. Laud 108 Item 8 is a fragment of 141 lines correspondent to (2b) of MS. St. John's; Item 9 is on the Infancy of Christ, a narrative in 1854 verses of marvels and miracles performed by the Child, and extending from the manger through the Disputing in the Temple.—In MS. Harley 2277 and Corpus Christi College Cbg. 145 are Item 1 on the Circumcision; Item 2 on the Epiphany; Item 29 on the Passion (not in Corpus), the Resurrection, the Ascension, and Pentecost; and Item 61 on the Assumption. Having the items of Harley, are MSS. Additional 10301, omitting the Passion; Laud 463 (L 70); Tanner 17, omitting the Assumption; and Trinity College Oxford 57, omitting the Circumcision and the Epiphany. MS. Phillipps 8253 is said to contain the Harley material.—MS. Cotton Julius D IX has correspondents to Harley Items 1, 2, 29 (only ll. 803-62) and 61.—MS. Ashmole 43 agrees with the Julius correspondents to Items 29 and 61, and has an Item 86 on the Advent and the Life of Mary correspondent to Egerton 1993 Item 2 lines 1-276 (earlier text).—MS. Egerton 1993 has Item 1a, the Old Testament story to Habakkuk, with Zacharias and Elisabeth; Item 1b on the Life of Christ abridged, from the promise of the Birth of John to and including the Death of Christ; Item 2, the Advent and Christmas Gospels—*i.e.*, on the Birth of Mary, her Life, her Marriage, the Birth and the Childhood of Christ with miracles of the Child, to the Division of the Kingdom of Herod; Item 38, Easter; Item

77, the Assumption.—MS. Stowe **669** has Items **25-27** on the Conception of Mary, the Nativity of Christ, and the Conception of Mary (account of the institution of the festival)—parts of Egerton Item 1b and Vernon Item 1.—MS. Vernon Item 1 has Old Testament story that is in Egerton Item 1a, the Prophecies of Christ, the establishment of the festival of the Conception of Mary, her Birth, her Life, the Birth and Life of Christ through the Death on the Cross; Item 4 on the Epiphany; Items **27, 30, 31, 33**, on the Annunciation, Easter, the Ascension, the Passion (the last like Harley); Item **71** on the Assumption.—MS. Lambeth **223**, after the Movable Feasts, has Item b1 of the *Temporale* correspondent to Vernon Item 1 and Egerton Item 1a; Item b2 is on the Fifteen Tokens; Item b3 is on the establishment of the feast of the Conception of Mary, as in Vernon Item 1; Item b4 treats Joachim and Anna, the Life of Mary, the Conception, the Nativity, the Purification, and the Childhood of Christ, correspondent to Egerton Item 1b and Vernon; Item b5 is the Assumption.—MS. Trinity College Cbg. R, 3, 25 has Item 1 on the Old Testament story and the Birth of Christ; Items **28-30** on the Movable Feasts; Item **53** on the Assumption; Items **86-89**, parts of the Christmas matter of Egerton Item 2; Items **90** and **91**, the Passion and the Resurrection; Item **92**, the Fifteen Signs correspondent to Lambeth Item b2; Item **112** on the Conception of Mary; and Item **114**, the *Pater Noster* from the Life of Christ.—MS. Bodley has Item 6 on the Birth of Christ, correspondent to Egerton Item 2 lines 495-649; Item 8 on the Passion; Item **57** on the Assumption; Item **65** on the Ascension; Item **111** on the Conception of Mary, a part of Vernon Item 1; Item **114** on the Birth of Our Lord, lines 1-110 from Egerton Item 1b, lines 111-250 from part of Egerton Item 2 lines 495-649.—MS. King's College Cbg. 15 treats the Movable Feasts, the Passion, and the Resurrection.—MS. Additional 10626 has a fragment of the Birth of Christ.—MS. Harley 2250 has a *Temporale*.— MS. Auchinleck treats Joachim and Anna and the Advent stories, stopping at Joseph comforted by the Angel.—MS. Harley 4012 has a different text of Joachim and Anna.

THE FALL AND THE PASSION [68] is the theme of
one of the Kildare poems (see page 228), 216 four-stress
verses abab in MS. Harley 913 f. 29 v (1308-1318, before
1325). The poem tells rapidly of the Rebellion and the Fall
of the Angels, the Creation and the Fall of Adam and Eve,
the Incarnation and the Life of Christ, the Harrowing of Hell,
the Resurrection, and the Ascension.

LA ESTORIE DEL EUANGELIE [69], in four-stress
verses aaaa, probably of the South-East Midland and 1250-
1300, is preserved in MSS. Dulwich College XXII (c. 1300;
East Midland, probably from a Northern MS.; first 519 lines),
Vernon (1370-1380; Southern, with West Midland traces;
392 lines of beginning), and Bodley Additional C 38 (1410-
1420; South Midland; 1703 lines, complete). Passages from
the poem are in the Rawlinson C 655 (Southern, c. 1350) text
of the *Northern Passion* (see page 287). The three texts are
independent of each other. Bodley and Vernon represent an
abridged text; completed, Dulwich would probably consist
of 3000 lines.

The piece opens with address to Christ, declaring devotion to
Him and intention to write His story in English. Wise men of
old wrote rules of conduct, but knew not Christ. Clerks wrote
books of instruction about beasts, birds, stones, herbs, especially
the wonders and the transformations of beasts (see *Bestiaries,*
page 182); but Christ surpasses all creatures. Before His coming,
the good were imprisoned, the evil tormented, in Hell.—Then
follows the life of Christ from the Annunciation to the Ascension,
with the Judgment.

The chief source is probably rather a compilation of Biblical
material, than the Vulgate directly. Apocryphal and homiletical material, probably from Comestor (apparently cited in
Dulwich l. 461), is added. The reference to bestiary and
lapidary writing, and the bestiary passages introduced in
Dulwich (ll. 69-170), should be noted.

THE CHILDHOOD OF CHRIST [70] from the manger
to the taking up of the Ministry, is the theme of a North Midland poem of 694 four-stress verses commonly abababababcdcd

with frequent variation in the last four verses of the stanza, in MS. Harley 3954 f. 74 (15th century). Agreeing much with this, and dealing with the Life from the manger through the Baptism, are 842 four-stress verses, in similar stanzas with similar irregularities, in MS. Harley 2399 f. 47 (15th century). A third version from the North, with like stanzaic basis, in 925 four-stress verses with irregular number of unstressed syllables, is in MS. Br. Mus. Additional 31042 f. 163 v (15th century). The three pieces are apparently from one ultimate common original; but the third is independent of the other two, which appear to have a common original.

THE RESURRECTION AND THE APPARITIONS [71] are dealt with in 605 four-stress verses aabccb, with gaps, in MS. Ashmole 61 f. 138 (15th century). The matter is worked over in romance form on the mediæval chivalric basis. The guards at the tomb are knights, as is Sir Pilate.

A PROSE LIFE OF CHRIST, made up by arranging chronologically matter of the Gospel Lessons, is in MS. Pepys 2498 (see page 405).

THE HOLY BLOOD OF HAYLES [72] is in two parts in 400 four-stress verses abab in the dialect of (?) Cornwall in MS. Royal 17 C XVII f. 147 (1400-1450).

The first part, declared to be from the Latin of Pope Urban IV, tells of Joseph of Arimathea's catching the blood as it issued from Christ's side, and of his imprisonment with the vessel in a stone house outside Jerusalem for forty-two years. When they besieged Jerusalem, Titus and Vespasian found Joseph. When they took the blood from Joseph, he fell dead as a stone. They bore the blood to Rome with the Vernicle. There it was preserved until Charles the Great took half of it to Germany. The second part of the poem tells how Edward, son of Richard, Earl of Cornwall and King of Germany (see page 211), learned of the portion of the blood in Germany, and by permission of his father brought it to England and ultimately to Hailes, where he nobly enshrined it. At the shrine many miracles are performed.

With the piece should be connected the romances *Joseph of Arimathie* and *Titus and Vespasian*, and the *Song Against the King of Almaigne* (see pages 75, 153, 211).

THE GOSPEL OF NICODEMUS [73], in its complete form composed of two parts, *Acti Pilati* and *Descensus Christi ad Inferno*, had a tremendous influence on mediæval faith, on mediæval art of all kinds, and on mediæval drama. Though no version is located back of 400 A. D., it was a potent document in the controversies between the Greek and the Roman Churches as to the purpose of Christ's mission to Hell. The popularity of its matter is attested by pictorial representation in miniatures, mosaics, manuscript illuminations, ivory carvings, enamel, stained glass, and painting. Practically every one of the extant Easter cycles of miracle-plays contained a version of the Harrowing of Hell. Caught from such versions, Satan and his satellites became stock figures of the stage, and prepared the way for some of the comic personages of later drama. Hell-mouth became a regular part of the stage equipment.

In addition to the several Old English translations of the Gospel, of which the chief is that in MS. Cotton Vespasian D XIV of the early twelfth century, there are *a strophic version* and *several prose versions* in Middle English.

The *strophic version*, of four-stress verses abababcdcd, is in at least four MSS. of the fifteenth century: Cotton Galba E IX and Harley 4196 (each 1764 verses), Br. Mus. Additional 32578 (1812 verses), and Sion College arc L, 40, 2^a+^2 (1752 verses). Galba and Harley are Northern, and form a group closer to the original than do the other MSS., which show a Northern tendency. The original was written probably as early as 1300-1325; certain parts of the York Plays that have been put back as far as 1340-1350, follow it rather than the Latin *Evangelium*. The version seems to have arisen independently of the French versions, and to go back to the Latin. It relates the incidents of the Passion from the accusation by the Jews to the death of Christ, the activity of Joseph of Arimathea, the Resurrection, the Ascension, the history and the contents of the account of the Harrowing of Hell written by Carin and Lentin, the reception of the document by Pilate and Caiaphas and Annas, and the revelation of the Resurrection to the Roman Emperor by the soldier messengers.

The *prose versions* of the Gospel are in six groups, in MSS. as follows: (1) Egerton 2658 f. 15 v (c. 1450), Stonyhurst College B XLIII f. 83 (c. 1460), Bodley 207 f. 120 v (c. 1470); (2) Salisbury Cathedral Library 39 f. 129 v (15th century), Br. Mus. Additional 16165 f. 94 v (15th century, before Salisbury); (3) Magdalene College Cbg. Pepys 2498 f. 459 (late 14th or early 15th century); (4) Harley 149 f. 255 (1450-1500); (5) Worcester Cathedral Library 172 f. 4 (late 15th century); and (6) Cbg. Univ. Libr. Mm I 29 f. 8 (late 15th or early 16th century). Groups 2 and 4 have the whole *Gospel*, as originally had Group 5. The rest hold to fairly literal translation of parts especially connected with Joseph of Arimathea. A statement in John Shirley's MS. (Additional 16165), and characteristic appearance of Trevisa's name in both MSS., have caused the second version to be ascribed to John Trevisa (see page 204).

Versions of the *Gospel* were printed in black letter by Julian Notary in 1507, de Worde in 1509, John Skot in 1529, *et al.*

THE HARROWING OF HELL [74], composed not later than 1250, is in four-stress verses in couplets in MSS. Digby 86 f. 119 (256 lines; these sheets are late 13th century), Harley 2253 f. 55 v (249 lines; these leaves c. 1300), Auchinleck f. 35 (201 lines, parts lost; 1330-1340).

After a short narrative introduction, the piece proceeds as a drama, by speeches assigned by name to the personages, Christ, Satan, the Door-Keeper, and the persons in Hell—Adam, Eve, Abraham, David, John, and Moses. Christ tells of His sufferings on earth, is threatened by Satan, reproves Satan for the Fall, and claims Adam as His own. Satan threatens to seduce as many men as Christ takes away patriarchs. Christ retorts that He will bind Satan so that he will be impotent until Doomsday. He breaks in the door, and binds the Devil. Adam and Eve confess their guilt, and are freed. Abraham is promised release. John declares he has died in advance to announce the freeing of the souls in Hell. Christ states to John and Moses that all His servants shall dwell with Him, but unbelievers shall remain evermore with Satan. A prayer closes the piece.

The assumption frequently offered that the poem was written as a play for actual dramatic performance, calls for supposition that the beginning and the end are later additions. This supposition has to justify it little beyond the assumption it seeks to prove.

THE FIFTEEN SIGNS BEFORE JUDGMENT [75], one occurring on each of fifteen days ending with Doomsday, were very extensively treated in six groups (Augustinian-Acrostic, Bede, Comestor, Aquinas, Old French, Miscellaneous) in Latin and the vernaculars of the Middle Ages. The theme was dealt with in English as part of larger works, as in the *Cursor Mundi*, lines 22427-710, of which a separate copy is in MS. Royal College of Physicians Edinburgh f. 1; the homily for the Second Sunday in Advent in the Northern Homily Collection MSS. (more extended in the Harley 4196 version); the Southern Legend Collection MS. Lambeth 223 Item b2, and the same in MS. Trinity College Cbg. R, 3, 25 Item 92; the *Pricke of Conscience*, lines 4738-817 (see page 447); the first homily of Mirk's *Festial* (see page 301); *Ezechiel* in the Chester Plays; the Halliwell (Bodleian Library Additional B 107) version of the *Castel of Love*, lines 1523 ff. (see page 367); Sir David Lyndesay's *Monarchie*, etc.

But the Signs were treated in a number of separate pieces, the Signs varying somewhat and being not always arranged in the same order. (1) In MS. Harley 913 f. 20 (1308-1318, before 1325) are 180 four-stress verses abab.

After eight stanzas of preliminary warning, the signs are enumerated: the stars shall fall and become black; the dead shall rise; the sun shall be green and wan and black; the sun shall become red; all creatures shall quake and pray to Heaven; hills and mountains and castles and towers and trees shall fall; the trees shall grow roots on high and tops in earth, and shall bleed, and men high and low shall die; the waters shall all draw together in a wall, and cry to God; the skies shall cry out for mercy; the saints, the angels, the fiends, shall all be afraid; four winds shall rise, and the rainbow shall fall, and the fiends shall be chased into Hell; and the four elements shall cry in one voice, 'Mercy, Jesus!'—Here the piece ends abruptly with the twelfth sign.

(2) In MS. Digby 86 f. 120 v (1272-1283) are 208 four-stress verses in couplets, an incomplete Southern version. (3)

In MS. Laud 622 f. 70 v (c. 1400), in 22 seven-stress verses in couplets with cæsura after the fourth stress, is a list of the Signs; and in 32 similar lines there is a statement of the incidents of the Judgment. (4) In MS. Trinity College Cbg. B, 11, 24 (c. 1450) is a complete version in 134 short couplets. (5) In MS. Harley 2255 f. 117 (time of Edward IV) are 10 stanzas ababbcbc, pentameter, incomplete with thirteen Signs. (6) In MS. Cbg. Univ. Libr. Ff II 38 f. 42 v (15th century) are 199 short couplets which, after four lines of prayer and twenty-five lines of preface to the reader, present diffusely the fifteen Signs and the Judgment, with final prayer for escape from damnation. (7) In MS. Cotton Caligula A II f. 89 r (15th century) is a complete version in 178 short couplets closely related to the Digby version. Lines 1-74 are prayer dealing with the Creation and Fall, and the Redemption, and offering entreaty for God's grace. Then follow the Signs. At the end Christ gives judgment, Mary's intermediation saving the good souls.—Of these pieces, 1, 2, 4, 6, 7, and the *Cursor Mundi*, belong to the Old French Group derived from a twelfth-century French poem; the *Pricke of Conscience* belongs to Bede's Group; poems 3, 5, the Northern homily, the Chester *Ezechiel*, and Mirk's *Festial* (by way of the *Legenda Aurea*, which is a branch of the Comestor Group), belong to the Comestor Group. In MS. Cotton Vespasian D XIV f. 102 r (here ? 12th century) is a prose statement of the Signs. In the Brome Hall MS. (15th century) is another version.—In the *Debate of the Body and the Soul* (see page 411) in MSS. Harley 2253 and Digby 86, *seven* Signs are indicated.

LYDGATE'S LIFE OF MARY [76] in four books (15th century) is to be noticed (see pages 306, 309).

THE ORIGIN OF THE FESTIVAL OF THE CONCEPTION OF MARY [77] may be mentioned here because texts of it have been printed as if they were separate pieces.

The legend tells how Helias, Abbot of Ramsay, returning from an embassy to placate the King of Denmark on behalf of William the Bastard, was almost lost in a storm at sea; how an angel offered him safety if he would vow with all his monks to celebrate annually the conception of the Virgin, and urge others to do so; how he learned that the feast should be on December 18, the Nativity of Mary, the service being the same as that for the Nativity, the word 'Conception' displacing 'Nativity'; and how he kept the vow at Ramsay.

The legend is told in the Southern Legend MSS. Vernon Item 1, Lambeth 223 Item b3, Trinity College Cbg. R, 3, 25 Item 112, Bodley 779 Item 111, Stowe 669 Item 27; in the *Cursor Mundi*, lines 24733-972 (see page 339); and in the homily on the Conception in Mirk's *Festial* (see page 301). The ultimate original is the *Miraculum de Conceptione Beatæ Mariæ* inserted by Gerberon in the Benedictine edition of the works of Anselm. Wace wrote the French *L'Établissement de la Fête de la Conception Notre Dame* (c. 1125-1150).

THE ASSUMPTION OF OUR LADY [78] goes back to the fourth century, perhaps even farther. Early Greek, Syriac, Arabic, Sahidic, and Ethiopic versions are extant. In Latin are the *Transitus Mariæ* in two forms, the *De Assumptione Beatæ Mariæ* of the *Legenda Aurea,* and *De Modo Assumptionis Beatæ Mariæ.*

The earliest extant Middle English version of the *Assumption* (see the Blickling Homilies, *Assumptio Sanctæ Mariæ Virginis*) is in four-stress couplets in MSS. Cbg. Univ. Libr. Gg IV, 27, 2 (1250-1300; 240 verses of beginning), Chetham 8009 Manchester f. 4 (15th century), Cbg. Univ. Libr. Dd I 1 (c. 1350; Southern, in Northern Homily MS.; unprinted, 544 lines), Cbg. Univ. Libr. Ff II 38 (15th century; Southern; unprinted, 770 lines), Harley 2382 (15th century; 710 verses), Br. Mus. Additional 10036 (15th century; 904 verses). This version is Southern, not later than 1250. MS. Additional, line 893, states that Archbishop St. Edmund (Rich) has granted forty days' pardon to all who will hear and learn 'this vie.' Probably by false inference from this, the *Cursor Mundi* (ll. 20057 ff.) repeats the offer, and says that Edmund himself wrote the piece in Southern English. The latest investigation indicates that this version is from a single source, probably a mixed redaction of the apocryphal *Pseudo-Johannes, Pseudo-*

Joseph, and *Pseudo-Melito;* or it is a composite from some five
or six varying sources—for in no one of the possible available
sources are there more than a few of the features as found in
this version.

Another English version is in 736 verses of tail-rime aabccb
in MS. Auchinleck (1330-1340). The variations of matter
from the older version are slight; there are many verbal agreements with it. The text appears to go back to the earlier
version.—A third version, based perhaps on the *Legenda Aurea*
or an original common with the *Legenda,* is in the Southern
Legend MSS. Harley 2277 and Corpus Item 61, in 123 couplets of verses of seven or six stresses. Another late copy is in
MS. Bodley 779 Item 57. Other copies are in the Southern
Legend MSS. Ashmole 43, Egerton, Vernon, Trinity Cbg., Br.
Mus. Additional 10301, Laud 463 (L 70), and Trinity Oxford
57.—A fourth version, 271 short couplets probably dependent
on the first (not the first on this one), is in the Northern
Homily MSS. Harley 4196 and Cotton Tiberius E VII.—
A fifth version is in lines 20065 ff. of the *Cursor Mundi,* following the first version almost line for line but with some addi-
tions. The text says it was made in Southern English by St.
Edmund, and the author puts it into the Northern dialect.—
Another version is in the Southern Legend MS. Lambeth 223
(beginning 15th century) *Temporale* Item b5. It apparently
goes back to the first version.

d.   Visions, and Visits to the Under-World

Widespread in the period was interest in dreams and visions.
The extensive use of such interest for allegorical exposition or
as a framework for narrative (see Index, *Dream-Visions*), can-
not be discussed here: mention of the *Divine Comedy,* the
Roman de la Rose, the *Pearl, Piers Plowman,* the *House of
Fame,* the *Legend of Good Women,* the *Parlement of the Thre
Ages, Wynnere and Wastoure,* and the political, prophetic, and
satirical pieces, is sufficient to indicate its great importance.

Of especial interest were accounts of visits to Hell or 'the
other world' or 'the under-world.' Apparently, but few of these

were carried over into English. A Latin *Vision of the Monk of
Evesham* (revealed by St. Nicholas from Good Friday night to
Easter Eve, 1196, and written by Adam, sub-prior of Evesham,
later made abbot and deposed in 1228, and chaplain of St.
Hugh of Lincoln) apparently did not get into English before
the version of William Machlenia of about 1482. The Latin
account of the *Vision of Thurcill* (revealed in 1206 to a farmer
of Stisted, Essex), questionably ascribed by Ward to Ralph of
Coggeshale, apparently was not turned into English. The
pieces that found their way into English before 1400, are the
Vision of St. Paul, St. Patrick's Purgatory, and the *Vision of
Tundale* (probably before 1400). 'Vision' in the first two of
these pieces is not used in the usual sense of the word; the hero
of each of the two actually visits the lower world in the flesh.
Attention must be directed to the visits to strange scenes employed in the English *Thomas of Erceldoune* (see page 224),
the *Ballad on the Scottish Wars* (see page 222), the *Turke and
Gowin* (see page 59), the legend of *Brandan* (see Legend Collections), etc. The *Harrowing of Hell* (see page 327) is, of
course, of fundamental importance in connection with these
pieces.

THE VISION OF ST. PAUL or THE ELEVEN PAINS
OF HELL [79] was a favorite theme of the Middle Ages in
various languages. It satisfied the general fondness for visits
to the under-world, and for information as to the sufferings
of the damned. 'Vision' in the versions of this theme, is not
used in the sense of 'dream'; Paul actually visits Hell. The
original was Greek, in at least two versions of the fourth century, of which but one is extant. There exist at least twenty-
two Latin MSS., that fall into six redactions.

Of English versions there are the following, grouped according to the redactions: (1) MS. Laud 108 (part I, c. 1290),
46 tail-rime stanzas aabccb, Southern; (2) MS. Jesus College
Oxford 29 (c. 1275), 290 verses in short couplets, South-
Western, and MS. Digby 86 (1272-1283), 308 lines in short
couplets, Southern; (3) MS. Vernon (1370-1380), 346 lines
in short couplets of about 1360-1370, Southern, and MS. Br.

Mus. Additional 22283 (1380-1400), a verbal copy of Vernon lines 1-124; (4) MS. Douce 302 (15th century), 28 stanzas ababbcbcdeeed; (5) MS. Lambeth 487, Lambeth Homily 4 (see page 278), before 1200, prose, three pages in print; (6) MS. Br. Mus. Additional 10036 (15th century), perhaps of the fourteenth century, prose, dialect not determined, over two pages in print.

The Vernon-Additional 22283 and Douce texts agree closely, and probably come independently from the same original. The Jesus text varies greatly from them, and agrees much with the Digby text; its opening suggests that it is from a French source. The Laud text is comparatively short, and is concise, abrupt, often somewhat obscure. It and the Lambeth and Additional 10036 versions all come probably from the Latin redaction numbered IV by Brandes. All the features of the various English versions, are in MSS. Vernon and Jesus College.

The Vernon text tells that Paul visited Hell in the company of Michael, and viewed its torments. On burning trees hung souls (Jesus, of those who did not attend church). In a heated caldron, wherein are plagues of snow, ice, clotted blood, poisonous reptiles, lightning, and stench, suffered those who would not repent (Jesus, who were lascivious, or makers of evil laws, or false judges). On a burning wheel were punished others (Jesus, who made evil laws). In a horrible lake full of venomous reptiles (Jesus, environed by fiends who thrust back those who would escape), suffered backbiters, wedlock-breakers, whores and whore-mongers, rejoicers in others' ill, brawlers in church, and the like, each submerged according to his guilt. In a deep pit, gnawing their tongues, were usurers. In another place, boiling in pitch, bitten by serpents, and tormented by devils, were unchaste women who had slain their offspring. Those who broke fasts were subjected to starvation. Devils tormented an old man who was unchaste, covetous, and proud. In a deep stinking pit sealed with seven seals, suffered those who did not believe in Christ's birth from Mary, or in Baptism, or the Eucharist. Paul saw tormented a soul who despised God's commands, and lived in foolishness; and then a soul of a righteous man welcomed by angels, brought before God, and borne to Paradise. The damned called to Paul and Michael, who prayed to the angels. In response Christ granted that the lost souls should have rest each week from Saturday at noon until the second hour on Monday. He who hallows Sunday shall have part in the angels' eternal rest.—The Jesus text preserves, with more specific additions and

with explicit designation of the eleven pains and of the sins of those
who suffer, the general punishments of the Vernon version. But
the Jesus account is rather gratuitously narrated to Satan by a soul
that has been permitted to return to earth; Paul is merely mentioned at the opening of the piece. The Jesus MS. omits all of
the account of the prayers of Paul and Michael and of the winning
of rest for the damned, the fact of the weekly respite being merely
referred to at the beginning.

ST. PATRICK'S PURGATORY [80] was written down
first probably in the Latin prose of Henry, a monk of Saltrey
in Huntingdonshire. The work was taken up quickly. Many
Latin MSS. from the twelfth to the fifteenth century, falling
generally into two groups, are extant. The story was told in
varying forms by Roger of Wendover, John of St. Albans,
Matthew of Paris, Ranulph Higden, and John of Brompton.
It was dealt with somewhat by Jacobus a Voragine, Petrus de
Natalibus, Vincent of Beauvais, Cæsarius of Heisterbách,
Jacques de Vitry, and Giraldus Cambrensis. There exist at
least thirteen French MSS., of which that of Marie de France is
the most notable.

Three Middle English versions are preserved. The first, in
seven-stress verses in couplets, is in the Southern Legendary
MSS. Laud 108 (c. 1280-1290; 673 verses), Egerton 1993
(14th century; 712 verses), Cotton Julius D IX (15th cen-
tury; 624 verses), and Ashmole 43 (624 verses); see also MSS.
Harley 2277 and Corpus Christi College Cbg. 145 and the
cognate MSS. (pages 292 ff.). A second version, *Owayn
Miles*, in 198 tail-rime stanzas aabccb of the thirteenth or
early fourteenth century, is in MS. Auchinleck (1330-1340).
A third version consists of 341 short couplets in MS. Cotton
Caligula A II, and of 342 similar couplets in MS. Brome of
Brome Hall, Suffolk; both MSS. are of the fifteenth century.

St. Patrick drove the poisonous snakes from Ireland, and did
other wonders. Then he drew a circle on the ground. In it was
formed a great pit, which is his 'Purgatory.' Hereabout he set
up a great religious establishment. The sinful while alive might
purge themselves by descending into the pit. But few who made
the attempt returned. Sir Owayn, guilty of all the deadly sins,
despite the remonstrances of the clergy, went into the pit. He
came upon a splendid hall. There a group of fair men warned him

that he should soon be tempted and tormented by devils, and that his salvation lay in prayer. Yawning and grinning, the devils beset and tortured him, and dragged him bound from world's end to world's end. Then he was taken through the various places of torment—first into a waste where men and women were spiked out prone, with nails of fire driven through their bodies; next, where, spiked to the earth, souls were devoured by serpents, and tortured with awls and scourges; then, where the souls were full of burning nails, and played upon by a bitter wind; then, where souls were hung up by arms and feet and neck, etc., and burned in fire and brimstone; then, where souls were fixed on a wheel that whirled about burning and stinking of brimstone; and to several other places of torture. To all the torments the knight was subjected; but he escaped each by prayer. Then he was borne into a pit that the devils declared to be Hell. His prayers caused him to be expelled by a blast of wind. Then he was forced to cross a narrow, sloping, high bridge under which was really Hell. Now the devils left him, and he entered the Earthly Paradise with its sweet odors and flowers and gem-paved roads, where a great procession welcomed him to a great hall. After a time he was directed to return to earth. At the opening of the pit the ecclesiastics welcomed him with much joy. He became a holy man.

Apparently the legend was suggested by the cave 'Purgatory' near Lough Derg, Donegal, with which were connected some of the many traditions of descent into the under-world. The piece resembles the *Vision of St. Paul* in that the hero actually visits the evil land, and the *Vision of Tundale* in that he is subjected (here, however, in the flesh) to the torments there. Good reasons have been offered for supposing that the original author modified a version of the *Vision of St. Paul* with elements from visions of Drihthelm and Tundale. The cave 'Purgatory' had a great vogue up to the end of the fifteenth century, being visited by pilgrims from England and the Continent. Even to-day it is sought by some of the pious. But the methods of the priests in charge gave it ill favor, and after 1500 it fell into decline. The story was treated considerably in Spain, England, and France, up into the eighteenth century, the most notable literary result being Calderon's *El Purgatorio de San Patricio.*

THE VISION OF TUNDALE [81] is one of the best known, and certainly one of the most elaborate, of the mediæval 'visions.' There are many MSS. in Latin, French, German, and Norse. In 1882 Wagner listed fifty-four Latin MSS. dating between the twelfth and the fifteenth centuries. The prologue to the piece says it was composed in 1149. An English version in short couplets is in four fifteenth-century MSS.: Edinburgh Advocate's Library 19, 3, 1 (East Midland), Cotton Caligula A II (North Midland), Royal 17 B XLIII (North of West Midland), and Ashmole 1491 (East Midland) two fragments—lines 2307-26 + 115-386, and 700-1165. The composite text of Wagner consists of 2354 lines. The English original was probably of the North and the end of the fourteenth or beginning of the fifteenth century.

Tundale, a rich man of Ireland, was guilty of the seven deadly sins, and disregarded God and Holy Church—no man lived worse. One day, he went to collect money due him for three horses. The debtor could not pay; but he gave security by oath, mollified Tundale by fair words, and invited him to dinner. At the meal Tundale was stricken, and he lay as dead for four days. Horrid demons gathered about his spirit and reviled him—where was now his pride and wealth! A bright star appeared, Tundale's guardian-angel, who became to him guide and expositor.—They pass a gloomy valley stinking and strewn with hot coals over which murderers are melted on iron plates—to trickle through, re-form, and again be melted. Successively, they pass a mountain, one side covered with fire and smoke, the other with ice and snow, between which thieves are tossed back and forth; a stinking abyss spanned by a narrow bridge, where the proud and boastful are tormented; a huge beast, Acharon, who swallows the covetous, and torment by adders and fire and ice and stench, suffered also by the guilty Tundale; a lake full of terrible creatures, where Tundale has to lead a cow he has stolen over a bridge a band's-breadth wide and set with spikes; an oven where fiends mutilate the gluttonous; in the midst of a frozen lake, a great beast into whose fiery mouth are cast the gluttonous; a smithy where souls are heated and hammered out, to recover and be torn to pieces; a pit whence issues a pillar of fire bearing up and burning to ashes souls that fall back to re-form and be re-burned; the horrid and vast Satan crushing souls in his hands like grapes, and suffering terrible torments; hunger and thirst punishing the negatively good; the Earthly Paradise, a jeweled golden house where infidelity in wedlock suffers fire to the waist three hours every day; the abode of the chaste and liberal beyond a silver wall; beyond a golden wall, the jeweled golden thrones of the saints and martyrs, sweet melody and pleasant odors; a fair tree (Holy Church) full of fruits, flowers, and spices, beneath which live souls in golden cells and wearing crowns; beyond a wall of jewels, the nine orders of angels, the Trinity, and God.—Tundale recovered; he repented, was shriven, and spent his days in penance and alms-deeds; and ultimately he went to God.

The writer adopted practically all the elements of the other visions, usually elaborating the details. Interestingly, he differentiates Hell, Purgatory, a sort of Earthly Paradise, Paradise, and Heaven. Greater precision and definiteness in presentation of the features are exhibited here than in most of the other visions. The various refinements of physical torment are presented with a vivid intensity that must have been a most horrible delight and terror to the mediæval reader or hearer. The survival of so many MSS. indicates the popularity of the legend.

CHAPTER VI

WORKS OF RELIGIOUS INFORMATION AND INSTRUCTION, AND AIDS TO CHURCH SERVICES

Necessity for making accessible and for disseminating the principal elements of Christian knowledge, for assisting to comprehension and practice of Christian conduct, and for directing to understanding of the services of the Church and to due regard for them, led to production in Middle English of a number of writings ranging from volumes of elaborated composition to mere translation of the *Pater Noster* or mere statement of the names of the Seven Sins.

Some of these pieces deal especially with the more formal elements of religious life and knowledge; others are based on and deal with the spiritual or the devotional. It is with the former of these types that the present chapter is concerned; the pieces of the latter class are discussed with the works of Rolle and his followers (see pages 444 ff.), with whom and with whose writings in the MSS. the surviving pieces are regularly associated and copied.

The pieces of the former class—as well as that general compèndium of knowledge and information, the *Cursor Mundi*— are devoted largely to statement and exposition of the Seven Sins, the Sacraments, the Articles of the Creed, the Petitions of the *Pater Noster*, the Works of Mercy, the *Ave Maria*, the Ten Commandments, the Gifts of the Holy Ghost, the Virtues of the Gospel, and the like—individually or in groups. In some instances these elements are incorporated in presentation of a mode of perfect living. In addition to such pieces there are aids toward the comprehension, the justification, and the proper conducting, of Church offices—as of the Mass, the

Hours, the chief festivals, and the like. With these pieces are to be joined the several writings that instruct as to the manner of life of those dedicated to religion—of monks and nuns. Finally are to be added, on the basis of content and of purpose, a group of religious allegories.

The works indicated will be discussed as follows: 1. Comprehensive Works of Religious Information and Instruction; 2. The Seven Sins, the *Pater Noster*, the Creed, etc.; 3. Service Pieces and Offices of the Church; 4. Instruction for the Life of Monks and Nuns; 5. Allegorical Works of Instruction.

1. COMPREHENSIVE WORKS OF RELIGIOUS INFORMATION AND INSTRUCTION

THE CURSOR MUNDI or CURSOR O' THE WORLD [1] is an encyclopædic work containing, gathered together and woven into a whole, the great part of the religious material of the period. It is in MSS. Cotton Vespasian A III (end of 14th and beginning of 15th century; the most complete version; ll. 1-29547), Göttingen University Library Theol. 107 (14th century; next most complete version; ll. 1-25766), Trinity College Cbg. R, 3, 8 (15th century; ll. 1-23898), Fairfax 14 (15th century; ll. 1-27899; with many gaps, but with some added matter), Bedford Library (15th century; now Br. Mus. Additional 36983; ll. 1-22004), Laud 416 (15th century; ll. 1-23898); Arundel 57 (c. 1350; ll. 153-23898). Fragments are in MSS. Cbg. Univ. Libr. Gg IV, 27, 2 f. 13 v (1250-1300; 240 lines, *Assumption of Our Lady*, cp. *Cursor* ll. 20065-848; see page 330), Royal College of Physicians Edinburgh (14th century; cp. ll. 18989-23644), Br. Mus. Additional 10036 f. 62 (beginning 15th century; 904 lines, *Assumption of Our Lady*, cp. *Cursor* ll. 20065-848 of main text, at beginning and end a total of 200 new lines; see page 330).

The poem is almost wholly in short couplets. But at places (*e.g.*, ll. 17189 ff.) it has four-stress verses in series on one rime. Moreover, ll. 14937-17113, on the Passion and the Death of Christ, are long seven-stress verses in couplets, or sometimes in longer series on one rime, each verse having a cæsura after the fourth stress.

Very little final investigation of the problems connected with this work has been made. Some of the most elementary and surface facts are unsettled. Even the dates of the MSS. seem to have been incorrectly or questionably assigned by the editors.

The work was composed in the North, probably in 1300-1325. It consists (1) of a prologue and seven parts divided according to the Seven Ages of the World; and (2) four appendices—with seven further additions, of which some are in some MSS., some in others.

The prologue declares that men yearn to hear rimes and to read romances of knights of antiquity, or of early Britain, or of France; or tales of pious heroes like Isumbras (see page 114) or Amadas (see page 159);—stories of any princes or prelates or kings. Each will hear what pleases him best—the wise, wisdom; the fool, folly. The lover 'paramour' is now the popular ideal; but the Virgin is the best lover, 'tis of her men should sing. The author would write an enduring work in her honor, that men may know her and her kin. Then follows an outline of the whole, the prologue concluding with statement that the work should be called *Cursor o' werld* because 'almost it over-runs all.'

The First Age deals with the Trinity and the Creation; the fall of the angels, the nature and the qualities of Man's soul, the name 'Adam' and Paradise, the plot of the Temptation and the Fall, the world after the Fall, the curse of Cain, Seth's gaining of the seeds of the Rood-tree (see page 318), the genealogy of Adam, and the corruption of the world. The Second Age proceeds from Noah and the Flood to the confusion of tongues. The Third Age covers the reigns of David and Solomon and their successors. The Fifth Age deals with the family of Mary, Isaiah's prophecy of Christ, the points of the scheme of salvation, the parables of the King and his daughters and the Castle of Love and Grace (the theme of the *Chasteau d'Amour,* the *Castel of Love,* etc.; see page 366), the conception and childhood and marriage of Mary, the Annunciation, the birth and childhood of Christ with their miraculous incidents (see Index) up to the Baptism. The Sixth Age treats thoroughly the chief themes of the life of Christ from the Baptism to the Ascension, with the chief incidents of the Book of Acts, of the Assumption of Mary (see page 330), of the works and death of each of the Apostles, the works and virtues of each of the Evangelists, the finding of the Cross (see page 318), and the virtues and symbols of the Cross (see page 359). The Seventh Age deals with the Day of Doom and Antichrist (see Index), the fifteen Signs before Doomsday (see page 328), the incidents of Doomsday (see Index), the joys of Heaven (see Index), and the world after Doomsday. The work proper closes with a gentle exhortation to the folk to repentance and to right living, and a humble declaration that God has given the writer one talent that he has sought to use for men as best he may; and concludes fitly, according to its original purpose, with a prayer to the Virgin. MSS. Trinity and Laud stopped just before the final prayer (1. 23898).

Then follow a passage on the Sorrows of Mary, an apostrophe to St. John, and the story of Elsey and the origin of the festival of the Conception of Mary (see page 329). Additions to these, some in some, some in others, of the MSS., are an exposition of the Apostles' Creed (see page 471), the Lord's Prayer and its exposition (see Index), a prayer to the Trinity (see page 522), a prayer for the Hours of the Cross (see Index), a song of the Five Joys of Mary (see page 536), a Book of Penance (see Chaucer's *Parson's Tale,* page 745) that deals with the three requisites of Penitence—Contrition, Confession, and Satisfaction—and with Absolution and Cursing. In the Fairfax MS. is finally a version of Cato's *Morals* (see page 379).

Space fails to describe this encyclopædic poem, which deals at length with all the principal incidents of Old and New Testament story, and includes treatments of almost all the religious topics of any considerable interest to the folk of the age. The general resemblance to the miracle-play cycles, on ✓ some of which the *Cursor* had influence, is apparent.

As the nature of his undertaking required, the writer derived material from various sources, perhaps most largely from the Vulgate and from Peter Comestor's Bible story-book, *Historia Scholastica.* He used Wace's *L'Établissement de la Fête de la Conception Notre Dame* (for ll. 10123-11232, with use perhaps of one or more of the *Evangelium de Nativitate Mariæ, Pseudo-Matthæi Evangelium, Protevangelium Jacobi Minoris*), Grostête's *Chasteau d'Amour* (for ll. 9517 ff.), the *Pseudo-Matthæi Evangelium* (for ll. 11595 ff.), the *Evangelium Nicodemi* (for ll. 17289 ff., etc.), the Southern *Assumption* (for ll. 19993 ff., see page 330), Isodore's *De Vita et Morte Sanctorum* (for ll. 20849 ff.), the *Legenda Aurea,* and other works. The passages on the Resurrection and on the sufferings of Christ, inserted in MS. Cotton at lines 16749 ff. and 17288 ff., are probably from the Passion in the Southern

Legend Collection. In MS. Bedford (Br. Mus. Additional 36983) is said to be interpolated the *Meditations of the Supper of Our Lord,* sometimes ascribed to Robert Mannyng (see page 358).

In handling and in completing his tremendous enterprise, the author manifests for the period an unusual sense of form and order and consistency with purpose. From a wide reading he brought together into a whole very diverse materials, selecting what would have popular appeal, without doubt supplementing from other writings his chief sources in various sections, holding to facts and controlling his imagination far beyond the capacity of his contemporaries, keeping ever to the point, observing throughout excellent proportion, and writing in plain and straight-forward language fluent and fairly regular verse. The material and the clever adaptation of it and of its live treatment to the general taste, account for the wide popularity of the *Cursor*—but, beyond these, a great cause for its appeal must have been the sympathetic humanity of the writer that is everywhere manifest.

HANDLYNG SYNNE [2], preserved in MSS. Harley 1701 (c. 1360) and Bodley 415 (c. 1400) in 12630 four-stress lines in couplets, was written by Robert Mannyng of Brunne (Bourne) in Lincolnshire, author of a version of Langtoft's *Chronicle* (see page 199). In the opening of his poem (ll. 57 ff.) Robert addresses all good men of Brunne, especially the fellowship of the priory of Sempringham. He tells that for fifteen years he was connected with the priory, dwelling at Brymwake in Kestevene for ten years in the time of *Dan John* of Camelton, and for five years in the time of Dan John of Clynton. There, in 1303, under Dan Philip he began the *Handlyng Synne.* As he indicates (ll. 80 ff.), his book is a version of the *Manuel des Péchiez* or *Péchés* of William of Wadington. He states that he would have men ever handling or considering the sins, so that they might be on guard against them. He tells that he wrote for the common people, for the many who would gladly listen to tales and rimes at games and feasts and at the ale-house, and who, hearing what he treats, would be restored from sin or other folly. So he took Wadington's *Manuel*, whose general treatment of the sins with its numerous illustrative stories made it especially suitable for his purpose, and made, not a translation, but an adaptation of it. Robert would appeal to the 'lewed'; so he omitted much that appeared not practical or likely to be interesting to such folk. He dropped out William's opening on the Articles of Faith, the sermon at the end of the passage on the Sacraments, much of the matter on Shrift, and the articles of the conclusion following Shrift. With the same end, though he omitted six of William's tales, he added fourteen (two from Bede), besides a number of shorter bits, and made many skilful modifications of the original to give it liveliness and appeal. In all, Robert sought to avoid pedantry, dullness, remoteness, and repellant over-didacticism and abstraction, and to attain practicalness, freshness, simplicity, directness, and concreteness.

The work as it stands is really a collection of stories (see page 185)—an epitome of the various sins, each illustrated most liberally with attractive tales and anecdotes. After the prologue follows an exposition of the Ten Commandments severally, each illustrated with from one tale to three; the Seven Deadly Sins severally, each with from one illustrative tale to eight; the Seven Sacraments severally, with similarly extensive illustrative narrative; and the Twelve Requisites of Shrift, and the Twelve Graces of Shrift, both with illustration. It will be seen that while the *Handlyng Synne* is similar to Chaucer's *Parson's Tale* and the *Aȝenbite of Inwyt* in the fact that it is an extensive work dealing largely with the Sins, it is unlike these writings, and is an antecedent of Gower's *Confessio Amantis*, in its extensive use of stories as illustrative of the Sins.

In all of the matter of the work is evinced a close contact with life itself, with the manners and social and moral conditions of rich and poor of the day, and a considerable knowledge of human nature. The work is direct and practically specific in its applications and its injunctions. Repeatedly it parallels and anticipates the attitude of the fourteenth-cen-

tury political pieces (see page 208) and of Langland and his
fellows, toward the hardships and abuse of the poor, and the
oppressiveness and viciousness 'of the rich (cf. ll. 2195 ff.,
5980 ff.) ; yet it sees and reprobates the wrong-doing of servants and of the poor, as well as that of the wealthy.   It
attacks folly in fashions of·dress and of wearing the hair, of
both men and women (cf. ll. 3202 ff.).   It speaks out against
the ills attending out-of-door performance of miracle-plays
(ll. 4643 ff.), the vicious associations of tournaments (ll.
4550 ff.), impious minstrels (ll. 4696 ff.), slothful parsons (ll.
4821 ff.), merchants who give false measure (ll. 5951 ff.),
worldly and adulterous priests, vicious children (ll. 4856 ff.),
and idle youths (ll. 5048 ff.).   A thousand and one are the sins
and the follies that it 'handles'; each it treats with kindly touch,
yet with convincing moderate good-sense.   The stories are
remarkably varied.   Their pertinence is apparent, and the
application is always made and made well.   It is significant of
the nature of Mannyng's method and attitude that he declares (independently of the French) that some of the incidents he introduces he has himself seen and known, and it is
significant that of the tales that he adds a number are to a
greater or less degree local, and so of immediate impressiveness to his prospective audience.   Of these last are the stories
of Bishop Grostête of Lincoln and how he loved music, of the
Cambridgeshire miser-parson who died trying to devour his
gold, of the punishment of the two Kesteven executors, of a
Norfolk bondman's reproof of a knight for letting his beasts
defile the churchyard, and of the Suffolk man who was freed
from Purgatory by two masses his wife had sung for him.

Septem Miracula de Corpore Christi [2] (see page 276),
in MS. Vernon f. 196 v (1370-1380), is a Southern version
of the *Handlyng Synne* beginning with the Third Sacrament
of the Altar, and ending where the Fourth Sacrament begins
(ll. 9891-10811).

R. Englyssh's Manual of Sin, in MS. Arundel 20 f. 43
(late 15th century), is a treatise on the Ten Commandments,
Sacrilege, the Seven Sins, etc., with illustrative tales based
on Mannyng.

THE PRICKE OF CONSCIENCE [3] might, on certain
grounds of similarity with the pieces now discussed, be considered here.   But, for convenience of reference and because
of its more spiritual aim, it is discussed with the writings
ascribed to Rolle and his followers (see page 444).

AƷENBITE OF INWYT [4] ('Remorse of Conscience'),
making about 270.pages in print, a literal prose translation
of Friar Lorens' *Le Somme des Vices et des Vertues* or *Li
Libres Roiaux de Vices et de Vertues* or *Le Livre des Com-
mandmens* or *Le Somme le Roi* or *Le Miroir du Monde,* is in
MS. Arundel 57 f. 1.   The MS. opens, 'Þis boc is dan Michelis
of Northgate y-write an englis of his oƷene hand.   þet hatte:
Ayenbyte of inwyt.   And is of the boc-house of saynt Austines
of Canterberi.'   Michael does not indicate that he translated
the work; he leaves us to infer that it is his own.   He concludes
to the effect that the piece was completed on the eve of the
Apostles Simon and Judas, by a brother of the cloister of St.
Anselm of Canterbury, in the year 1340.   The piece is a
most important monument of the Kentish dialect, but has little
or no literary value.   Michael was very careless, or he was a
poor French scholar; for he fell into innumerable errors, and
his expression is often almost, if not quite, incomprehensible.
The author tells us that the book is written in the local
dialect of Kent that it may reach fathers and mothers and
other kindred of the neighborhood, and may keep them from
sins—the ultimate motive of the *Pricke of Conscience* and the
Handlyng Synne.   But the *AƷenbite* is very bare and very dull.
After a short preface and an elaborate table of contents, the
author gives expositions of the Commandments and of the
Twelve Articles of the Creed; a narrative interpretation of
John's vision of the beast with seven heads and ten horns—the
heads are the Seven Sins, the horns are the sins against the
Commandments; and an enumeration of the Sins with elaborate
sub-division—each kind being styled a 'bough,' for it is like a
bough sprung from an evil root (see *Desert of Religion,* page
371).   Next is instruction how to die, then how to distinguish
between good and evil, with sub-division and specification.

Exposition severally of the Seven Petitions of the *Pater Noster*
follows. Finally come lengthy analysis and exposition one by
one of the Seven Gifts of the Holy Ghost.

To the *Aӡenbite* is appended a Kentish version of the matter
of *Sawles Warde*, that is quite independent of that work (see
page 273). Interestingly, the prayer at the end of the
appended piece, and that at the beginning of the MS., are in
tail-rime.

The *Aӡenbite* seems to have had little popularity, especially
as compared with the *Pricke of Conscience* (see page 447), for
only the author's own MS. is preserved. Yet to the English of
the period there were worth and interest in the material—for
in MS. Br. Mus. Additional 17013 there is a Midland prose
treatment of about 1400, styled *Þe boc of vices and vertues;*
and there is another prose treatment in MS. Bodley 283, of
about 1440, *The mirroure of the worlde that some calleth vice
and vertu.* Chaucer's *Parson's Tale* (see page 745) is an
adaptation of a *summa* of Vices and Virtues. Of the French
Somme Caxton made a prose version, *The Book Royal* or *The
Book for a Kyng.*

THE MIRROR OF ST. EDMUND [5], prose comprising
in print 33 pages, is in MS. Thornton f. 197 r (1430-1440).
It is a Northern copy of a translation (possibly Southern),
made at about 1350, of the Latin *Speculum S. Edmundi,* which
had been composed or finished at Pontigny by Edmund Rich,
Archbishop of Canterbury.

The author exhorts 'us folke of religioune' to a life of perfection, which means living *honorably, meekly, lovingly. Honorably*
implies doing God's will, being holy. Holiness consists in knowing
and loving, attained through prayer to Christ and through contemplation of the works of God, of His goodness to His creatures, and
of Holy Writ. The last teaches what are the Deadly Sins, the
Christian Virtues, the Commandments, the Articles of the Creed,
the Cardinal Virtues, the Gifts of the Holy Ghost, the Works of
Mercy, the Virtues of the Gospel, and the Prayers of the *Pater
Noster.* The items of each of these groups are enumerated and
explained. The subjects of Contemplation of God are considered,
with their hours and distribution; Christ's life on earth and resurrection and ascension; God as God; God's manifestation of Himself

within by revelation and reason, without by Holy Writ and His creation; one God in three Persons; the ultimate contemplation through the spirit which magnifies God. The second element, *Love,* must be lived by loving men in God for goodness or righteousness or truth; by doing all good that is asked, by taking all that men give, by suffering all men say.—Then is urged living *meekly* by knowledge of self and by example of Christ.

The piece keeps coherently to the points; but it so develops the first great topic, living honorably, as to hurry over the last two in a single page. In this last matter the reader is addressed as 'dere syster and frende,' whereas previously the from of address is only 'dere frende.' The intense asceticism of the original no doubt contributed largely to the popularity of the *Speculum* in the period.

Another Southern prose version of the *Speculum* is in MS. Vernon f. 355 (1370-1380). This agrees in some places with the Thornton version, but is a closer rendering of the Latin.

In MS. Cbg. Univ. Libr. Ff VI 40 f. 207 is said to be a translation of part of the *Speculum* in a very corrupt text.

How a Man Schal Lyue Parfytly [6], an English version of the first part of the *Speculum* made perhaps from a prose translation like those of the Vernon and Thornton MSS., is in 579 short couplets in MS. Vernon f. 227 (1370-1380). The analysis of the prose already given affords a sufficient idea of the matter here. The text is often corrupt and obscure. It breaks off at the warning to the rich after the enumeration of the Works of Mercy.

The Pricke of Love [7] (as its heading reads) or *The Spur of Love* (as ll. 21, 1081 name it), in 541 short couplets in MS. Vernon f. 283 v, is a very free version of the *Speculum* with much omission, addition, and condensation. After a short address to the reader, the author begins with Chapter 3 of the *Speculum,* and works through the general topics of the original. Mention at lines 163-68 of Duke Henry who built the new work at Leicester, may aid to the date and place of composition.

THE MIRROR OF LIFE [8], a Northern translation of John de Waldeby's *Speculum Vitæ*, consists of 8000 short couplets, of which the first 185 have been printed from MS. Cbg. Univ. Libr. Ll I 8 f. 1 (end of 14th century). Other copies are in MSS. Stowe 951, Br. Mus. Addit. 22283 and 22558 and 33995, Sloane 1785, Harley 435, Trin. Coll. Cbg. 593 and 603, Univ. Libr. Cbg. Ff IV 9 and Gg I 7 and Gg I 14 and Ii 36 and Ll I 8, Cott. Tib. E VII, Rawlinson A 356 and C 884 and C 890, Vernon, and eight or nine other MSS. that are now difficult to trace. Some MSS. assign it to Rolle, and others, with more probability of truth, to William of Nassyngton (see page 463). The author would hold up a glass in which everyone might see his life. The treatise offers exposition of the Seven Prayers of the *Pater Noster*, the Gifts of the Holy Ghost, the Deadly Sins, the Seven Virtues, the Seven Blessings of Heaven, etc.

DAN JON GAYTRYGE'S SERMON [9] on Shrift and what should be considered in Shrift, a prose piece probably of 1350-1400 (some 14 pages in print), is in MS. Thornton f. 189 r (1430-1440; Northern) and in a somewhat later little variant copy in MS. Trinity College Cbg. B, 10, 12 (15th century). The arrangement of words in both the MSS. has suggested that at least parts of the piece were originally in alliterative verse. Portions of the *Sermon* are in MS. Br. Mus. Additional 24202 (see page 483).

As a great Doctor shows in his book, God made His creatures through His mercy and goodness—some of them to have eternal bliss. To share this, man must have knowledge. Adam had it, but fell; since his fall, all must be instructed by hearing and learning. The Bishop has ordered all who have care of souls to instruct their people in English in the six groups of necessary knowledge: the fourteen points of the Creed, the Commandments, the Sacraments, the Works of Mercy, the Seven Virtues, and the Deadly Sins—and shall require that they know them at Lent. The piece then enumerates and explains briefly each of the constituents of each of these six groups. These must be known, it concludes, if we would have Heaven's bliss.

Of þe Seuen Vertewes, a part of the 'Sermon,' is in MS. Cbg. Univ. Libr. Dd XII 39 f. 1 (latter part of 14th century) and

MS. Br. Mus. Additional 24202 f. 36 v (imperfect at end; 14th century, see page 484).

Another part of the 'Sermon' is in MS. Rawlinson C 285 (15th century).

WILLIAM OF SHOREHAM'S POEMS [10] are in the second part of MS. Br. Mus. Additional 17376 f. 150, a careless copy of the pieces. The MS. differs in hand, vellum, and ornamentation from the earlier MS. of the West Midland Psalter (see page 402), with which it is bound. It is by some said to be of 1375-1400, by others of before 1350. The poems consist of seven pieces or groups, the seventh breaking off incomplete. In the colophons to 1, 4, 5, William of Shoreham is mentioned as the author. William was of Kent, probably of Shoreham, near Otford, close to Sevenoaks. He is said to have been a vicar of Chart near Leeds in Kent. The incumbency must have been after, probably soon after, 1320.

Four of the pieces are didactic. The first poem (2240 lines abcbded, *a, c, e* of four feet, *b* of three feet, *d* with feminine ending, line 5 of one foot, line 7 of three feet) has an introduction of 189 lines, after which it deals elaborately with the Seven Sacraments, one after another. The third poem (344 verses abcbdbeb, the lines alternately of four and three stresses) is devoted to presentation and exposition of the Commandments, and to exhortation to obey them. The fourth piece (424 four-stress verses abab) discusses Sin in general, the need for instruction against sin, and 'original' and 'actual' sin; and concludes with exposition of the Deadly Sins. The seventh poem (894 verses aabccb, the third and sixth lines of two feet with feminine ending, the rest of four feet) presents what the Christian must believe and what must be his creed, and explains the Trinity, the Creation, the origin and purpose of Evil, the Fall, and the Redemption.

Of the other three pieces, the second, 178 verses alternately of four and three stresses abab, is devotional. It is translation of the *Horæ Canonicæ Salvatoris* 'Patris sapientia, veritas divina.' Each 'hour' is followed by an apostrophe to the Virgin based on her sorrows at Christ's sufferings (see page 518).

The fifth poem (354 verses of tail-rime aabccb) is in glorification of the Virgin and in exultation over her *Five Joys* (see
page 537). The sixth piece (84 verses aaabab, the *b* lines of
three, the others of four, feet) is apostrophe to Mary as Queen
of Paradise and Heaven and Earth, Dove of Noah, Bush of
Sinai, true Sarah, David's Sling, Aaron's Rod, Temple of
Solomon, Judith the Fair, etc. The colophon states that this
piece is a translation from Robert Grostête. As it is the only
purely lyric poem of the group, Shoreham's authorship of it
has been questioned.

William was evidently a devout man and a scholar, learned
in the theology of the day and earnestly concerned for the
weal of the folk. At times he enters into discussion of theological points quite beyond the needs of the common people of his
cure, and thereby suggests that he wrote for the more cultivated also. Yet in these passages he employs a clear and
simple expression easily comprehensible to folk of the lower
order. Though his pieces compare favorably with others of
the period on the same themes, William was not much of a
poet. The defects of his rime and metre are probably due
partly to his copyist.

2. The Seven Sins, the Pater Noster, the Creed, Etc.

THE SEVEN SINS, THE PATER NOSTER [11], etc.,
in *groups*, are treated in a number of MSS. as follows, the
comprehensive works just discussed being excluded: (1)
Arundel 292 f. 3 (late 13th century), Creed, *Pater Noster, In
Manus Tuas*, 19 short couplets, *Ave Maria* in four verses
aaaa, and two other short bits of verse; (2) Cotton Cleopatra
B VI f. 201 v (c. 1250), *Ave* in four-stress verses, Creed in
prose, several prayers, *Pater Noster* in five couplets of irregular verses; (3) Cbg. Univ. Libr. Hh VI 11 (13th century),
Ave in three short couplets, a *Pater Noster* in 8 seven-stress
verses aaabbcaa; (4) Harley 3724 f. 44 (13th century), prose
Creed and *Pater Noster* in 6 short couplets; (5) Caius College
Cbg. 44 (13th century), Creed, *Pater Noster, Ave, In Manus*

Tuas, prose, a total of 18 lines in print; (6) Auchinleck f. 70 r
(1330-1340), introduction, the Sins, Commandments, *Pater
Noster, Ave,* the Passion (at greater length), 154 short couplets; (7) Arundel 57 f. 94 r (c. 1340), Kentish prose, in print
18 lines, *Ave,* Creed, *Pater Noster;* (8) Halliwell 219 (14th
century), prose *Pater Noster, Ave,* Creed (originally followed
by Commandments), Deeds of Mercy, Gifts of the Holy Ghost,
Blessings of Christ; (9) Laud 463 f. 157 (beginning 15th
century), account of Sins in 230 short couplets, and paraphrase of Commandments in 145 short couplets; (10) Cbg.
Univ. Libr. Gg IV 32 (time of Henry IV), metrical *Pater
Noster* and Creed; (11) Makculloch (after 1477), metrical
Pater Noster and Creed; (12) Cathedral Library Sarum 126
f. 5, perhaps by Thomas Cyrcetur (†1452), a prose Creed with
two couplets on Sins, and five couplets epitomizing the Commandments; (13) Arundel 20 f. 43 (late 15th century),
ababbcc expositions of Commandments and Sins with comments and *exempla;* (14) Laud 416 (15th century), ababbcc
paraphrase of Commandments and Sins with *narrationes;* (15)
Harley 1706 (15th century), verse Commandments, Sins,
Works of Mercy, Cardinal Virtues, Beatitudes; (16) Harley
2346 f. 1 (toward 1450), *Compendium of Christian Doctrine*
on Seven Sacraments, Works of Mercy, etc.; (17) Rawlinson
B 408 f. 3 (c. 1450), in the *Register of Godstow Nunnery,*
an *ABC of Devotion* composed of *Pater Noster* (paraphrase),
Creed, *Ave,* Confession of Sins, Prayers, *In Manus Tuas,* etc.,
and a Calendar, in all 617 verses ababbcc; (18) Garrett in
Princeton University Library (15th century), preceding a
Trentalle Sancti Gregorii (see page 172) and versions of three
Vernon-Simeon refrain poems (see pages 511, 513, 514), a
prose *Treatise of the Ten Commandments* containing matter
on the Commandments, Sins, Five Wits, Works of Mercy, etc.;
(19) University Coll. Oxf. 97 (end of 14th or beginning 15th
century), exposition of the *Pater Noster,* Twelve Articles of
Faith, and the Commandments. To be added are the items on
page 471. See also the treatments in groups in the larger
works discussed in divisions 1, 3, and 4 of this chapter.

THE SEVEN SINS *alone* [12] are treated in the following MSS.: (1) Harley 957 f. 27 (13th century), 12 four-
stress lines abab forbidding commission of the first three sins;
(2) Cotton Vespasian A III (Northern; end of 13th or beginning of 14th century), 229 short couplets, elaborately developed presentation and exposition of the Seven Sins; (3) Harley 913 f. 48 ff. (1308-1318, before 1325), after 60 verses in
tail-rime aabccb of introductory exposition, 60 short couplets
of exposition of Pride, Covetise, Onde, breaking off in the midst
of the last; (4) Cotton Tiberius E VII (c. 1400), just preceding the Northern Homily cycle at f. 101 r, a Northern
piece on the Seven Sins; (5) Laud 463 (*i.e.*, L 70; early 15th
century), after an introduction, 232 short couplets naming
each of the sins and explaining them at length; (6) Jesus
College Cbg. Q, T, 3 (15th century) and Balliol College Oxf.
354 (16th century), 15 and 14 couplets respectively, the
author exhibiting the sins by declaring that who would abide
in Hell should do as he tells, and then presenting himself as
viciously confessing guilt of each sin in turn. (7) An allegorical piece in 11 stanzas of four-stress verses abababbbcbc
with a refrain 'And gyf me lycens to lyve in ease,' is in MS.
Cbg. Univ. Libr. Ff I 6 f. 56 v (15th century): walking one
May morning the poet heard a man who prayed to Jesus for
aid that he might never creep to the cabin where Lucifer was
locked; declared none could cure his wounds but a 'knight'
who knew his sickness; and enumerated the Seven Sins, their
efforts against him, and the remedy for each.—Again may be
mentioned Shoreham's poem No. 4 on the Seven Sins (see page
349). In the *Vision of Piers Plowman* are two passages on the
Sins that have played a considerable part in the recent discussion of the authorship of the versions of the *Vision* (see pages
254 ff.). A treatment is in the *Disputison bitwene a God Man
and the Deuel* (see page 423). There are also treatments in
the *Handlyng Synne* (see page 342), the *Aȝenbite* (see page
345), Chaucer's *Parson's Tale* (see page 745), the *Cursor
Mundi* ll. 27524-28065 (see page 339), the *Lay-Folks' Catechism* (see page 355), *et al.*

THE PATER NOSTER is dealt with *separately* [13] in the following MSS.: (1) Lambeth 487 (before 1200), 305 verses in short couplets, recital and exposition in a Lambeth homily (see page 278); (2) Cotton Vitellius A XII f. 181 v (early 12th century), the Prayer in prose; (3) Corpus Christi College Cbg. 54, D, 5, 14 f. 66 (before 1300), a *Hymn to God* 'Hit bilimpeð forte speke, to reden & to singe,' 36 seven-stress verses aaaa with aaaa rime at the cæsuras—after the introductory verse on God's power, a very loose paraphrase of the Prayer addressed to God; (4) Auchinleck f. 72 r (1330-1340), 68 short couplets with fragments of about 40 additional verses, an introduction followed by statement and exposition of each of the clauses of the Prayer; (5) Cathedral Library Sarum 82 f. 271 v (late 13th-century hand), a rimed *Pater Noster* (? 10 four-stress lines in couplets) copied as prose with peculiar spelling due perhaps to an Anglo-Norman scribe; (6) Corpus Christi College Cbg. 296 f. 172 (late 14th or early 15th century), a prose exposition of the Prayer clause by clause, concluding with praise of the Prayer—sometimes ascribed to Wycliffe; (7) Trinity College Cbg. R, 3, 25 f. 270 (early 15th century), an exposition of the Prayer, from the Life of Christ, Item 114 of the Southern Legendary (see pages 298 ff.); (8) Thornton f. 209 v (Northern; 1430-1440), a prose exposition in 1200 words; (9) Harley 4172 f. 50 v, an exposition similar to Thornton. (10) A Northern metrical exposition is in Cott. Galba E IX f. 73 (early 15th century). Of much interest is the fifteenth-century narrative *How the Plowman Learned his Pater Noster*. Ascribed to Lydgate are an exposition in MSS. Laud 683, Harley 2255, and Jesus College Cbg. 56; and a translation in MS. Trinity College Cbg. R, 3, 21 f. 274. See also pages 471, 479.

THE CREED is treated *separately* [14] in early thirteenth-century prose (16 lines in print) in a Latin MS. in the Library of Blickling Hall containing Gregory's *Dialogues*. *Þe Lesse Crede*, prose (some 10 lines in print), is in MS. Cotton Nero A XIV f. 131 r (13th century). Lambeth Homily 7 is exposition of the Creed (see page 279). MS. Lambeth 853 f. 39 (c. 1430) has a strophic Creed.

THE COMMANDMENTS *alone* [15] are dealt with in the following MSS.: (1) Harley 913 f. 31 v (1308-1318, before 1325), an introduction of 24 verses against great oaths, then each commandment in brief with comment and explanation, in 20 four-stress Southern verses abab of 1250-1300; (2) Cbg. Univ. Libr. Ff VI 15 f. 21 (before 1300), 10 four-stress lines in couplets summarizing the Commandments; (3) Trinity College Cbg. B, 1, 45 f. 42 r at the end of a homily, in a hand shortly after 1300, 5 short couplets summarizing the Commandments; (4) Vernon f. 408 v (1370-1380), Br. Mus. Additional 22283 (1370-1380), and Lambeth 853 f. 49 (c. 1430), *Kepe Wel Christes Comaundement* 'I warne vche leod þat liueþ in londe,' one of the 'Vernon-Simeon refrain group' (see page 510), 104 four-stress verses ababbcbc, an introductory and a final stanza, one stanza to each of the first nine, and two to the tenth, of the Commandments; (5) Lambeth 853 f. 47 (c. 1430), 48 four-stress verses abab, introductory and final stanza, one stanza to each Commandment; (6-7) Royal 17 A XXVI f. 4 and Harley 218, a treatise on the Commandments; (8) Harley 5396 (15th century), a version of the Commandments; (9) Harley 665 f. 90 (end of 15th century), a paraphrase in 46 four-stress verses, one couplet, the rest abab; (10) Jesus College Cbg. Q, T, 3 (15th century) and (11) Ashmole 61 f. 16 (15th century), 44 four-stress verses abab, with prefixed couplet in Cbg.; (12) St. John's College Cbg. 94 f. 119 (first half 15th century), a prose treatise making 34 pages in print; (13) Thornton (1430-1440), a prose treatise of 800 words.

THE AVE MARIA *alone* is discussed on pages 530 ff.

3. Service Pieces and Offices of the Church

There are extant a number of writings composed as aids toward the comprehension, the justification, and the proper conducting of Church offices, Church festivals, and the like.

THE LAY-FOLKS' MASS-BOOK [16], is in MS. Advocates' Library Jac. V, 7, 27 (*i.e.*, 19, 3, 1; 15th century; 130 verses), Royal 17 B XVII (Midland; 1370-1400; 629 lines), Corpus Christi College Oxf. 155 (Northern; 15th century; 374 lines), Cbg. Univ. Libr. Gg V 31 (15th century; 364 lines), Gonville and Caius College Cbg. 84 (West Midland; c. 1450; 614 lines), and a MS. of H. Yates Thompson (West Midland; c. 1450; 364 lines). The original English version was probably of about 1300, and probably Northern. The work explains the value of the Mass and the stages of the service, and gives directions for the behavior of the layman. The MSS. declare it to be a translation (probably from the French) and the author to be a Dan Jeremy (later changed in two MSS. to St. Jerome). With exception of the general Confession (in tail-rime aabccb), the Creed (abab, the *a* verses of four, the *b* verses of two, stresses each), and the Prayer at the Levation (aabaabbaa, three-stress verses; identical with a piece in Rolle's *Form of Living;* see page 449), it is in short couplets. The Gonville and Royal versions appear to reproduce the matter of the original; the other copies are revisions for special purposes.

THE LAY-FOLKS' CATECHISM [17]. To improve his clergy and to instruct his lay-folk, John de Thoresby, Archbishop of York, caused to be composed a Latin catechism based on Archbishop Peckham's corresponding Lambeth Canons of 1281. This he issued from his manor at Cawood, November 25, 1357, with an expanded English version, *Lay-Folks' Catechism* (preserved in Thoresby's *Register* at York), of 576 rude unrimed lines by John de Garryk or Gaytrik, *alias* Taystek, a monk of the Abbey of St. Mary's, York. The piece indicates Thoresby's concern for the salvation of all; gives a brief exposition of the Creed, the Commandments, the Sacraments, the Works of Mercy, the Seven Virtues, and the Seven Sins; and promises forty days of indulgence to all who learn the articles.

Wycliffites, perhaps Wycliffe himself, possibly with Thoresby's approval, took up and expanded this Catechism to an equivalent of 1429 lines. This version (in MS. Lambeth 408 and York Minster XVI, L, 12) varies much from Gaytrik's, adding the Creeds, treatment of the physical and the spiritual Senses, and great expansion in prose of the Commandments. In the midst of the Virtues is a Lollard passage.

THE PRIMER or LAY-FOLKS' PRAYER-BOOK [18], in MS. Cbg. Univ. Libr. Dd XI 82 (c. 1420-1430), presents rhythmically the fundamental contents of the *Primarium* without the additions that crept into some versions. It contains (1) the Hours of the Virgin (Matins, Lauds, Prime, Tierce, Sext, None, Evensong, Compline, Concluding Directions), (2) the Seven Penitential Psalms (see page 403), (3) the Fifteen Gradual Psalms, (4) the Litany, (5) the Office for the Dead, and (6) Commendations. It is probably of 1350-1400.

HOW TO HEAR MASS· or A TREATISE OF THE MANNER AND MEDE OF THE MASS [19], in 688 verses aabccbddbeeb, tail-rime, in MS. Vernon f. 302 v (1370-1380), offers homely and earnest counsel, with several interesting anecdotes or *exempla* urging the necessity for hearing the Mass; explains the proceedings of the service; and gives directions for the behavior of laymen. It appears to be a general paraphrase of the *Lay-Folks' Mass-Book*.

MERITA MISSÆ [20], a later piece ascribed to John Lydgate, in MS. Cotton Titus A XXVI f. 154 (15th century), gives counsel with illustrative anecdotes, for behavior in connection with the Mass.

SOME YORK BIDDING PRAYERS [21], of date after 1400, have been printed—as have the York *Horæ* in MS. York Minster XVI K 6 (15th century), and the order for Nuns for Trinity Sunday according to the Use of York in MS. York Minster XVI A 9 (c. 1425).

PRÆPARATIO EUCHARISTIÆ [22], a prose presentation of matters for consideration before and after receiving the Sacrament, is in MS. Ashmole 1286 f. 223 (c. 1400).

OF THE SACRAMENT OF THE ALTAR [23], 'I wole be mendid ʒif y say mis,' sixteen stanzas abababab in MS. Digby 102 f. 123 v (early 15th century), explains the Eucharist.

TWO PRAYERS AT THE LEVATION [24] are in MS. Vernon (1370-1380). The former is 'Welcome, lord, in fourme of bred' in 36 verses of tail-rime aabccb; the latter is 'I þe honoure wiþ al my miht' in 18 four-stress verses ababab- abcbcbcbdbcb.

Narratio de Virtute Missarum and *Narratio Sancti Augustini* are concerned with the Mass, but are rather tales (see page 173).

THE ATHANASIAN CREED (*Symbolum Athanasianum*) [25], the correspondents to sections 17 and 18 being omitted, is translated closely in 51 couplets of loose four-stress verses 'Who so wil be sauf in blis,' in MS. Bodley 425 f. 69 v (Northern; 14th century).

THE PASSION OF CHRIST [26] is the subject of homilies in the Northern Cycle (see page 321). It is dealt with in appropriate items in some of the Southern Legend MSS. (see page 321), whence were derived the accounts of the Passion and the Resurrection in the Cotton MS. of the *Cursor Mundi* (see pages 339, 342). In MS. Jesus College Oxf. 29 is the *Passion of Our Lord* (see page 409). The Passion was dealt with also in several dialogue pieces (see pages 414 ff.), and afforded basis for many religious poems in lyrical forms (see pages 498 ff., 515 ff.).

The six items next following are especially to be mentioned at the present place, because of their form and purpose.

AN ABC POEM ON THE PASSION OF CHRIST [27], in 226 verses çhiefly tail-rime aabccb, is in MS. Harley 3954 f. 87 (c. 1420; Southern, original perhaps North Midland). It tells of use in school of an *ABC* nailed on a slab of wood, and rubricated with five paraffes to remind of Christ's five wounds. Then, after the selling by Judas, stanzas beginning successively with the successive letters of the alphabet tell of the incidents of the Passion. Thereafter follows a statement of the Resurrection and the Doom, with an appropriate prayer to be offered for realization of the Passion and for gratitude for it.

THE MEDITATIONS OF THE SUPPER OF OUR LORD JESUS, AND ALSO OF HIS PASSION, AND ALSO OF THE PAINS OF HIS SWEET MOTHER [28], has frequently been ascribed to Robert of Brunne (see page 342) because it is East Midland of 1300-1325 and follows the *Handlyng Synne* in each of the complete MSS. (Harley 1701, Bodley 415) of that work. The grounds seem inadequate to demonstrate Robert's authorship. The poem is worked into the Bedford MS. (now Br. Mus. Additional 36983; 15th century) of the *Cursor Mundi,* and is also in MS. Trinity College Cbg. B, 14, 19 (15th century). A prose version is in MS. Bodley 789. As printed by Cowper from Harley 1701 (c. 1360), it consists of 1142 irregular four-stress verses in couplets. It deals with the Supper and the events following thereafter up to and including the entombment; tells of the return and the grief of the disciples and Mary; and finally has a passage on the Harrowing of Hell. The writer sees in detail the events and acts, and feels intensely the sufferings, of which he tells. His exhortations at every vital point are vigorous and impressive. These, with the careful grouping of the matter according to episodes marked to be used at the various hours of the Passion period, and the dividing of many of the chief topics into numbered points, indicate that the members of this group of 'meditations' were intended for delivery at sequent stages of the two days that it covers. Of course, much of the character of the piece was determined by the *Meditationes Vitæ Christi* ascribed to Bonaventura, of Captions 75-85 of which it is a translation; but the writer treated his original freely, with modifications and additions that improve the Latin much. It has been urged that he used with freedom Bernard's sermon on the Passion.

The Privity of the Passion and *Meditations on the Passion*, in English from Bonaventura and ascribed to Rolle (see pages 456, 451), may be mentioned here.

The Myrrour of the Blessed Lyf of Iesu Crist [29] was made in English from Bonaventura by Nicholas Love early in the fifteenth century, and printed by Caxton in 1488 and de Worde in 1525.

PATRIS SAPIENCIA, SIVE HORÆ DE CRUCE [30] is in 118 English verses in MS. Vernon (1370-1380), each hour having its Latin original followed by the English in a stanza aaaabb (line 5 one stress to three, the rest seven stresses) followed by the 'verse' (a couplet) and the 'prayer' aaaabb (line 5 three, lines 1 and 2 eight, 3 and 4 seven, stresses) and the 'verse' (a couplet of irregular four-stress verses).—In MS. Caius College Cbg. 175 (15th century) is a version in eight stanzas aaaabb (line 5 of four, the rest of seven, stresses). Each of the first seven stanzas is preceded by the appropriate Latin catch-phrase. The 'verse' and the 'prayer' are always omitted. The piece is a making-over of the Vernon version or of a common original. It preserves most of the rime-sounds, and many of the rime-syllables, of Vernon. The first half of the fifth line of the stanza, 'Wiþ an O and an I,' connects the piece with the other 'O and I' poems (see page 236).—Another English piece in MS. Bodley Misc. Lit. 104 f. 50 (time of Edward II or III) consists of 34 lines of six or seven stresses in couplets, each hour being preceded by a part of the Latin version.—Shoreham's version of the *Horæ* has been discussed already (see page 349).

THE SYMBOLS OF THE PASSION [31] is in MSS. Royal 17 A XXVII f. 72 v (116 short couplets), Br. Mus. Additional 22029 and 11748 (both 15th century; respectively 76 and 84 short couplets). It characterizes severally the various objects associated with the Passion (vernicle, nails, pelican, thirty pieces of silver, lantern, swords and staves, etc.), and connects a prayer with each. At the head of each section of the two first MSS., is a drawing of the object concerned. Royal has finally a brief *résumé* of the sufferings of Christ, with prayer for salvation in the name of the symbols.

A FORM OF CONFESSION [32] in prose (five pages in print), probably originally Northern, is in the Southern MS. Vernon f. 366 (1370-1380). First is a detailed confession item by item of guilt of each of the Seven Sins, of breaking of each Commandment, of failure to fulfil any of the Deeds of Mercy, of evil use of each of the Senses. This is followed by a catechism with questions and answers, on the Commandments, the Deadly Sins, the Senses, the Works of Mercy, and the Cardinal Virtues. It has been suggested that Richard Rolle, author of a Latin *De Modo Confitendi*, wrote this piece. But works of the sort are not rare (note those in MSS. Laud 210 and Harley 1706).

ON THE VISITING OF THE SICK [33] (*Visitatio Infirmorum*), some 2400 words of prose made up of extracts from St. Augustine's work on the subject, and from Anselm, is in MSS. University College Oxf. 97 (end of 14th or beginning 15th century), Laud 210 (c. 1370), Bodley 938, Harley 2398, and Caius College Cbg. 209 (15th century). A shorter text is in MS. St. John's College Oxf. 117.

THE BOOK OF THE CRAFT OF DYING [34], some 8000 words of prose, is in MSS. Rawlinson C 894, Harley 1706, Douce 322, Royal 17 C XVIII, and others, of the fifteenth century. It is a later translation of the Latin *De Arte Moriendi*, and gives instruction under six heads for the 'teaching and comforting of those on the point of death':—commendation of Death and of knowing how to die well, temptations of men dying, interrogation of the dying, obsecrations of the dying, instruction of the dying, and prayers for the dying.

SEVEN QUESTIONS TO BE ASKED OF A DYING MAN [35] is a prose piece (in print two pages) in MS. Lansdowne 762 f. 21 v (1500-1550).

EXITACION OF CUMFORT TO THEM THAT BE IN PARELL OF DETHE [36], in prose, is in MS. Lambeth 432 f. 68 (15th century).

THE FESTIVALS OF THE CHURCH [37] is a fragment of 334 verses ababababbccccb, with some stanzas of four or five or eight verses interspersed, in MS. Royal 18 A X f. 130 (1350-1400 or after 1400).

'The Lord, that is a householder,' clothes his folk, and feasts them on His flesh and with blood from His breast that was broached as a tun.   He ordained for the year eight feasts: Christmas, New Year, Epiphany, Easter, Holy Thursday, Whitsunday, Trinity, and Corpus Christi.   At much length and with much detail reminding of the crude realism of the miracle-plays, follows explanation of Christmas, the Circumcision, Epiphany, and Easter, breaking off in the midst of the last.

INSTRUCTIONS FOR PARISH PRIESTS [38] by John Mirk, author of the *Festial* (see page 301), is in MS. Claudius A II f. 127 (perhaps before 1450) in 1934 verses in short couplets.   It is also in the fifteenth-century MSS. Douce 60 and 103.   The piece is from after 1400.

THE POINTS AND ARTICLES OF CURSING [39] gives directions for pronouncing the ban of the Church.   It is probably from after 1400, and is in MS. Claudius A II f. 123 (perhaps before 1450) following Mirk's *Festial*.

4.   INSTRUCTION FOR THE LIFE OF MONKS AND NUNS

THE ANCREN RIWLE [40], the most significant piece of earlier Middle English prose, is preserved in English in the following MSS.—(B) Corpus Christi College Cbg. 402 (1230-1250); (T) Cotton Titus D XVIII (1230-1250); (N) Cotton Nero A XIV (1230-1250); (C) Cotton Cleopatra C VI (13th century, a little later than the preceding); (G) Caius College Cbg. 234 (13th century); (V) Vernon f. 371 (c. 1370-1380); (P) Magdalene College Cbg. Pepys 2498 (14th century); and a leaf of about 1330-1340 in possession of Lord Robartes, said in dialect to resemble (N). A French version is in MS. Cotton Vitellius F VII f. 1. This MS. suffered in the great fire, but is said now to be legible except for a line or two at the top of each page. There is also a Latin version represented in MS. Magdalen College Oxf. 67 and the remains of MS. Cotton Vitellius E VII, only 34 leaves of the latter being restored. Notes that were made on a copy of Smith's Catalogue (1696) before the fire, indicate that the Latin text of the *Riwle* covered ff. 61-133 of the perfect MS. In the Latin, Part 1 of the *Riwle* is almost wholly omitted; many passages are left out, notably those containing personal reference to the sisters; there is a persistent effort to eliminate the personal character of the address to the sisters; and there is a curious attempt to adapt the work to men.

Until recently scarcely any problem connected with the *Riwle* has been thoroughly investigated; scarcely any can be said to have been convincingly settled. For the study of the work itself there have been generally available only Morton's edition of Nero with his notes of a number of readings from Cleopatra and Titus; Napier's print of the Robartes fragment; Pahlsson's text of Pepys; and a collation of Morton's Nero with the MS. Scholars appear to have been but imperfectly acquainted with even the condition of some of the MSS. and with the existence of Vernon.

For long Morton's arguments caused assumption that the piece was originally in English. Investigations based on study of a copy of the Latin Magdalen text, led Bramlette to conclude that the Latin was the original, and that Nero was derived from it. Macaulay's recent studies are the first that are based on thorough collation of the MSS. They lead their maker to the conclusions that the English text is 'actually a translation from the French'; that the French treatise 'is identical with that which we have in English under the name of *Ancren Riwle* or *Ancrene Wisse*'; that Bramlette has invalidated little of Morton's arguments; that the Latin is not the original of the English or of the French; and that the Latin appears rather to be a translation from the English. The following remarks on the MSS. are based on Macaulay's articles.

Of the English texts BCG represent a Southern dialect bordering on Midland, seen in the lives of St. Katherine and St. Juliana (see page 312), the purest and most correct form being in the earliest MS., B. T is based on a similar kind of text; it was written by a North Midland scribe from a Southern version. N is characterized by purely South-Western features of language. V is South-Western. P is Midland with South-Western features.—In many cases N disagrees with readings common in the other MSS.; it has similarities to C and T; it agrees with C and T, and with G, in omission of a number of passages found in B and of some in V and P. Of nineteen added passages in B, eleven occur in B alone, seven occur also in V, one is in a later hand in C, and four are in P. Apparently, CTNG are more primitive as regards interpolations than is B, though B is more generally correct in text. So, there are the two groups of MSS., BVP and CTNG; and the original English text is earlier than MS. B. The first four interpolations are in the French text.

Of the original author of the *Ancren Riwle* we know nothing. √ At the head of the Magdalen Latin version, the work is said to have been written by Simon of Ghent, Bishop of Salisbury, 'sororibus suis Anachoritis apud Tarente.' This heading was probably in the archetype of the Magdalen MS. It indicates merely that Simon may have been the maker of the Latin version; he lived too late to compose the English version. This heading is the only evidence connecting the *Riwle* with Tarente, which is in Dorsetshire. Yet from this heading it has been customary to connect with the *Riwle* Richard Poor, born at Tarente, benefactor of a nunnery in that place, and buried there in 1237.

An introduction addressed to three 'dear sisters' directs attention to the 'inward rule' that relates to right conduct of the heart, and the 'outward rule' that regulates the outward life; presents the qualifications for profession; recommends that the ladies declare themselves of the order of St. James; and gives an outline of the work that follows. The *Riwle* falls into eight parts. The first part, 'Of Divine Service,' and the eighth, 'Of Domestic Matters,'

deal with the 'outward rule'; the 'inward rule' is treated in the other
six parts, 'On Keeping the Heart,' 'Moral Lessons and Examples,'
'Of Temptations,' 'Of Confession,' 'Of Penance,' 'Of Love.' In
the course of the work are given directions for services, devotions,
and meditations, and liturgical directions; counsel as to worship of
the Virgin and glorification of the 'Joys' of Mary (see page 536);
intimate and detailed counsel as to food, intercourse with the outer
world, alms, traffic, keeping of animals and pets, dress, industry,
correspondence, deportment, etc., within the nunnery; caution and
advice as to the Senses; urgence of patience, sincerity, confession,
mortification of the flesh, watchfulness and diligence, modesty, soli-
tary meditation, retirement from the world; discussion, with advice,
of the Deadly Sins (see page 352); elaborate consideration of Confession (see pages 351, 360)—its efficacy, its nature, the immediate
need for it, and the cautions to be regarded concerning it; the
attainment of Heaven's bliss through affliction on earth; exposition
of purity of heart as essential to Love, of what Christ has given
and what He will give for our love, of the requiting of Christ's
love, and of Spiritual Love as the supreme rule.

So, much of the *Riwle* deals with religious themes common in
the period. These were taken from various previous works,
such as Cæsarius' *Exhortatio ad Virginem Deo Dedicatam* and
Ailred de Rievaux's *Epistola ad Sororem Inclusam* (referred
to several times, and the source of a number of directions).
A large familiarity with the Fathers is shown in the frequent
apposite quotations, in Latin as well as in English, introduced from them. A fondness for allegory and symbolism is
evident. Parables are admirably employed. Notable is the
story of Christ, the mighty King, wooing the Soul, a lady beset
in her castle. Fine distinctions are utilized; from names are
extracted profound truths; puns afford doctrine. Bestiary
materials are drawn on. The features are remarkably varied.
The work is ever concrete with images and illustrations, sometimes beautiful, sometimes tender, sometimes naïvely humorous—always appropriate and illuminating. Popular homely
elements abound. Legends and history, sacred and profane,
illustrate the points. Details from contemporary daily life
are not infrequent. Though the theme is restricted, the occasion limited, and the material largely borrowed, the matter and
the manner are at every turn perfectly adapted to the purpose
of the writer. The work is never pedantic, never stiff, never

dull.· It is broad, free, liberal, spontaneous, sincere, fresh, familiar, kindly, tender, devout, simple, dignified. But its singular charm resides less in the qualities of its matter and its style, than in the personality that they characterize and that breathes upon the reader at every turn—a fine, elevated, pious, catholic, lovable spirit, full of knowledge of the heart, of a mystical and even a romantic nature, wise and good, and rich in that love that to him was the centre of all.

The *Ancren Riwle* must, of course, be remembered as a very prominent representative of tendencies in the South that at the time were advancing and elevating Woman—the cult of the Virgin, the enthusiastic glorification of the virgin saints, and the passionate urgence of the wooing by the Heavenly Lover (see pages 273, 312, 314, 520 ff., 529 ff.).

THE RULE OF ST. BENEDICT [41], written in Latin at about 516, went into a number of English versions. The West Saxon or Common version is in MSS. Corpus Christi College Cbg. 178 (c. 1000); Corpus Christi College Oxf. 197 (c. 1000); Cotton Tiberius A III f. 103 (beginning 11th century), only Chapter IV; Durham Cathedral Library B, 4, 24 (c. 1050); Cotton Titus A IV (end of 11th century); and Cotton Faustina A X (c. 1100). All of these are in Latin and English—except Faustina, which is only in English. They are for monks; but feminine pronouns suggest derivation from a text made for nuns. A version of most of Chapters 50-64 for monks, in Latin and West Saxon, is on some loose leaves (beginning 11th century) belonging to the Chapter of Wells. The *Interlinear* version is in Latin and Kentish-West Saxon for monks in MS. Cotton Tiberius A III f. 105 (beginning 11th century). The *Winteney* version for nuns is in Latin and Hampshire English in MS. Cotton Claudius D III (beginning 13th century). The *Northern Prose* version, at the beginning for monks, later for nuns, is in English with some Latin catch-words in MS. Lansdowne 378 (beginning 15th century). The *Northern Metrical* version for nuns, 1292 short couplets, in English with Latin catch-words, of a more Southerly character than the *Northern Prose*, is in MS. Cotton

Vespasian A XXV (earlier 15th century). Caxton printed an abstract of the *Rule* for men and women.

The pieces undertake elaborately to designate the offices and the whole behavior of life of monks or nuns or both. The topics include specification as to the orders of monks and nuns, their relative ranks and duties; the elements of a good life, obedience, silence, humility, poverty, regularity, industry, etc.; the performance of divine offices; dormitories, food and meals, clothing, visitors, working out of doors or traveling; punishments and penances; admission and ordination; etc.

A RITUAL FOR ORDINATION OF NUNS [42] is in English prose in MS. Lansdowne 378 (beginning 15th century). Another in English and Latin prose is in MS. Cotton Vespasian A XXV (earlier 15th century). Both are with the versions of the *Rule of St. Benedict.*

INFORMACIO ALREDI ABBATIS MONASTERIJ DE RIEUALLE [43] is an almost verbal English translation ('per Thomam N.,' says the MS.) of Ailred de Rievaux's *De Vita Eremitica ad Sororem Liber* prefixed to MS. Vernon ff. a-k (c. 1370-1380). In close print the piece covers some forty pages. The original dialect has not been determined.

EPISTOLA AD SIMPLICES SACERDOTES [44], in MS. Royal 17 B XVII f. 96 v (West Midland; 1370-1400), consists of some 200 words of advice on establishing a religious body, the number of the members, and the occupations of the priests.

5. ALLEGORICAL WORKS OF INSTRUCTION

In several English works of instruction allegory or symbolism is employed. Now and again one or the other of these media appears in homiletic pieces. Already have been discussed *Sawles Warde* and a *Bispel* (see pages 272, 346, 285).

THE CASTEL OF LOVE (*Chasteau d'Amour* or *Carmen de Creatione Mundi*) [45] of Bishop Grostête was translated from French into at least three Middle English versions. The

earliest of these, probably of 1350-1400 and South-East Midland, is in MSS. Vernon f. 292 (1370-1380) and Br. Mus.
Additional 22283 (1380-1400) in 762 short couplets preceded
by a quatrain abab announcing the poem as translated from
'Grostey3t.'

After a rather lengthy preface, the author tells of the Creation,
the fall of the angels, the Creation of Man, Man's fall and subjection to Satan. So, a free man had to be had to take Adam's
lost place. Here follows the tale of the King who had a Son, his
equal, and four daughters named Mercy, Truth, Right, and Peace.
His thrall, Adam, did amiss, and was imprisoned and punished.
Mercy pleaded that he had fallen through a woman. Truth urged
that he deserved his punishment. Justice said the same—indeed,
that he merited death. The thrall was stripped, and enslaved in sin.
Mercy and Peace fled, and all the world were drowned but Noah
and his family. Then Peace declared the end of Truth and Justice ever should be Peace; no judgment should be unless all four
sisters approved of it; the thrall should be ransomed. The King's
Son pitied the prisoner; He said He would take his clothes, and
make Peace and Right kiss, and save the folk. So God had to
become a man. The patriarchs and the prophets heard of it. The
Child from Heaven alighted in a fair castle of Love (Mary) on
a high rock (her pure heart) defended by four forts (the Cardinal
Virtues) and three baileys (her maidenhood, her chastity, her wedding) with seven barbicans (the Seven Virtues) and painted green
(Faith) below, blue (Hope) in the middle, red (Love) above, all
white within. Inside was a well (Springs of Grace), and an ivory
throne with seven steps, with a rainbow over it and a chair on it.
Here Christ made His seat, but He left her immaculate.—The
writer now cries to God for help against the Three Foes and the
Seven Sins. Christ became a man, and bade men have faith in His
aid. Wealthy folk disregard Him, though a good man may have
riches.—Then follows a dramatic presentation of the tempting of
Christ. Then are dealt with the Passion, the Grief of Mary, the
nature of the Trinity, the Harrowing of Hell, the Redemption, the
Resurrection, and the Ascension.

The translation is often very loose, with mistakes of sense
and with omissions. It may well have been composed originally
in the Southern dialect.—A version printed by Halliwell
'chiefly' from an unnamed MS. (Bodleian Library Additional
B 107; 14th century) varies much from the earlier Vernon MS.,
and substitutes for its lines 1512-24 a set of 310 lines, part of
which is in the French. Of these substituted lines verses 1523 ff.
are on the Fifteen Signs before Judgment (see page 328),

the greater part not in the French; verses 1693 ff. are on the Pains of Hell; and verses 1745 ff. are on Jesus as Prince of Peace.

Another version, probably from Yorkshire, in MS. Egerton 927 (15th century), is ascribed in its preface to a monk of Sallay or Sawley in Craven, where was a Cistercian monastery. The language points to 1350-1400. The text comprises 1250 verses varying between four and seven stresses in length. This version is a loose paraphrase, with condensation of the original, and with additions (usually unfortunate) from other sources. It is inferior to Vernon and the French.

After an introduction, the piece tells of the Creation; the Fall; the Commandments; the story of the King, His Son, and His daughters, much condensed; the Temptation; the Passion; the Sorrows of Mary; Christ as almighty; the Sacrament of the Altar; Christ the Father; the Creed; the Sacraments; the Gifts of the Holy Ghost; the Coming of Antichrist and the Day of Doom; the Pains of Hell; and the Joys of Heaven.

Another translation of the first part of the *Chasteau* is represented in MS. Ashmole 61 f. 78 (15th century) in 220 short couplets. The piece concludes with the kiss of Justice and Peace at the end of the story of the King and His children.

A translation of the story of the King and His four daughters is in the *Cursor Mundi*, lines 9517 ff. (see page 340).

THE ABBEY OF THE HOLY GHOST [46], a prose piece making in print some eleven close pages, is in MSS. Laud 210 f. 180 (c. 1370), Vernon (1370-1380), and Thornton (c. 1430-1440). It is in at least six other MSS. that are mostly derived from the Laud-Vernon version, though several show influence of a Northern MS. MS. Thornton is Northern; the other MSS. are Southern. MS. Lambeth 432 (15th century) alone ascribes the piece to Rolle. A Latin *Abbacia de St. Spiritu* is extant in several MSS.

The author will write a book of the religion of the heart, of the Abbey of the Holy Ghost, that all may at least be spiritually religious members. Conscience is the site of the Abbey. God sends two maidens, Righteousness and Purity, to clear the ground; and two others, Meekness and Poverty, to prepare the cellars. The

Abbey is by the River of Tears. The walls are reared by Obedience and Mercy. The cements are Love of God and steadfast Faith. The pillars are raised by Patience and Strength. A cloister must enclose from evil. Shrift shall make the chapter-house; Preaching, the chapel; Contemplation, the dormitory; Ruefulness, the infirmary; Devotion, the cellar; and Meditation, the storehouse. The Holy Ghost shall be warden and visitor; Charity, the abbess; Wisdom, the prioress; etc. The author now conceives of the Abbey as completed and in operation. A tyrant sent into it four daughters, Envy, Pride, Gambling, and Evil-thinking, who harmed the convent much. On advice of Discretion, the Council prayed to the Visitor, the Holy Ghost. He drove out the evil damsels, and made the Abbey better than ever before. If evil come into your hearts, pray and let the Holy Ghost drive it out.

In MS. Thornton the *Abbey* stands alone; but in MS. Vernon and the other later MSS. there is joined to the *Abbey* the *Charter of the Abbey of the Holy Ghost* [47] (not complete). This is written separately in MS. Laud 432 f. 136 (15th century). The *Charter* in print covers twelve close pages of prose.

An abbey must have deeds and charters for maintaining its property. So, the author makes a book telling of the founding of the Abbey, its destruction and the expelling of the convent, its restoration and the reassembling of its people, and God's installation of His four daughters in place of the fiend's daughters driven out by the Holy Ghost. After a short statement, somewhat in form of a charter, of God's gift to men of a holy abbey, Conscience, the piece tells at length of the Fall, the patriarchs and prophets, God's ordaining of a way of salvation, His four daughters pleading for Man's soul, Christ's coming and founding of the Abbey of the Holy Ghost (an account of His life, death, and harrowing of Hell), and how God put His daughters into the Abbey, which should be kept fair and clean.

The allegory in the *Abbey* is well sustained. That in the *Charter* is poorly worked out, and is broken into by the details of the history of the Fall and the Redemption that the writer is anxious to present.

THE CHARTERS OF CHRIST [48] are written in general imitation of the mediæval legal charters or grants, and purport to represent a grant to Man by Christ of the bliss of Heaven, on condition that Man give love to God and to his neighbor. The Charters exist in five general forms: (1) some 20 lines of Latin prose, *Carta Nomini Nostri Iesu Christi*, in MS. Br. Mus. Additional 21253 f. 186 (15th century), and probably part of a homily; (2) 36 or 38 Latin verses in MSS. St. John's College Cbg. E 24 f. 22 (14th century) *Carta Libera d. n. Ihesu Christi*, and D 8 f. 174 (15th century) *Carta Redempcionis Humane*; (3) 21 English short couplets, *Carta Dei*, on the back of MS. Bodley Kent Charter 233 (1395; *Carta* probably later); (4) 16 English short couplets, for convenience to be styled the *Short Charter*, under various titles in thirteen MSS., of which the earliest seems to be Br. Mus. Additional 37049 (1400-1450), though the piece apparently originated in the fourteenth century; and (5) what has been styled the *Long Charter* (*Testamentum Christi* in MSS. Vernon, Harley 2382, Ashmole 61). There are three versions of the *Long Charter*: (a) normally 117 English short couplets, in seven MSS., of which all but Rawlinson Poetry 175 (c. 1350) and Vernon (1370-1380) are of the fifteenth century; (b) 209 short couplets (comprising almost all of (a) with some 200 added lines) in the best form, in six fifteenth-century MSS.; (c) 309 short couplets in MS. Royal 17 C XVII (1400-1450) with but 57 lines of (b), and with 257 lines not in (a) or (b). In the *Long Charter* the deed is the crucified body of Christ, the parchment is Christ's skin inscribed by the scourges, the letters are His wounds, the wax is His blood, etc. The relationships of the five forms of Charters have not been definitely determined. Address by Christ directly to Man connects some of the texts with the Christ on the Cross pieces (see page 515). The dialogue between the Virgin and Mary Magdalene in MS. Royal, seems taken over from the *Lamentation of Mary to St. Bernard*, second version (see page 415). The idea of a charter is used in the *Charter of Favel to Falsehood* in *Piers Plowman* (see page 249), and in the *Charter of the Abbey of the Holy Ghost* (see page 369).

THE TESTAMENT OF LOVE [49], three books of prose making up in print 145 pages, goes back to Thynne's edition of Chaucer in 1532. The sections of the piece arranged in

their correct order make by their initial letters an acrostic:
'Margaret of Virtw, have merci on thin Usk.' Hence it is
supposed that the piece was written probably about 1387 by
Thomas Usk, the confidential clerk who betrayed his master,
John of Northampton, in 1384, and who was executed March
4, 1388. The autobiographical details in the *Testament* agree
closely with what is known of Usk. The piece is obscure and
loose-jointed, lacking unity both of matter and of form.

In the piece the word 'testament' is used in the Scriptural
sense of 'a witnessing'; 'love' is Divine Love or the Christian
spirit that impels the wish for the Grace of God, which is Margaret. But the last paragraph says that 'Margaret, a woman,
betokeneth grace, lerning, or wisdom of God, or els holy
church.'

The writer is in prison hoping for a change of fortune, and praying for aid to Margaret, the Grace of God. Heavenly Love comes
to succor him. He tells how he once wandered in a wood at the end
of Autumn, and was attacked by some animals that suddenly
became wild. To escape, he embarked on the vessel of Travail.
Driven on an island, he caught sight of Love, and found Margaret,
a pearl of price. To Love he appeals for comfort. Love reproves
him, then consoles him, then advises the contemning of those who
have spoken against him. He laments that he has served seven
years, and would have comfort for the eighth. Love bids him persevere. He tells how, on compulsion, he revealed a certain secret.
He was justified, because his gage of battle was not taken up.
Love states that earthly fame is to be despised, and declares the
greatness and goodness of God and His providence.—In Book II
the writer discusses his purpose. Love sings a Latin song with
complaints against the clergy. Then comes a discourse on women,
owing much to Chaucer's *House of Fame*. This is followed by a
long discussion of the way to the bliss of Heaven, largely from
Chaucer's *Boethius*. Then in three stanzas the excellence of Margaret (here the Church Visible) is declared.—In Book III 'Margaret in virtue is likened to Philosophy with her three kinds.' The
book is dedicated to Joy, and (with debts to Chaucer's *Boethius*)
deals with Predestination and Free-will. Love shows that continuance in good-will produces Grace, and then shows how Grace
is attained. Then, after recurrence to Predestination, the piece ends
with apologies for its defects.

THE DESERT OF RELIGION [50], originally probably
Northern, perhaps of Scotland, consists of 940 four-stress

verses in couplets in MSS. Br. Mus. Additional 37049 f. 46, Cotton Faustina B VI pars II f. 1, and Stowe 39 f. 11, all of 1400-1450. In the MSS. the piece is ascribed with pictorial illustrations to Rolle of Hampole.

The *Desert* is an allegory developed from the *Psalter:* 'Fleand I fled fra mare and les and dwelled in herd wylderness.' The opening and the closing lines explain it. The wilderness or desert is 'Hard Penaunce,' a forest of temptation. The poem is to show how virtues grow—what to cherish, what to shun. In this spiritual forest are trees with branches and boughs (see *A3enbite of Inwyt,* page 345), some reaching upward to heaven, some downward to hell, some to preserve, some to destroy. The rest of the piece describes in detail the trees and their various branches: the tree of Virtues rooted in Meekness; Vices rooted in Pride; Meekness; Pride; Abuses of Religion; Seven Points of Christ's Godhood, and Seven Points of His Manhood; the Seven Sacraments and Seven Virtues; the Deeds of Mercy; the Ten Commandments; the Five Senses; Shrift; Six Things Good to Avoid; Chastity; Evil Tongue; Prowess; Perfection; the Twelve Virtues; the Fourteen Pains of Hell; and the Seven Blisses of Heaven.

A TREATISE OF GHOSTLY BATTLE [51], some 9000 words of prose, is in MSS. Douce 322, Harley 1706, Rawlinson C 894, Royal 17 C XVIII, and Corpus Christi College Oxf. 220 (all apparently of the 15th century). It is seemingly based on a chapter in the *Pore Caitif* (see page 482), on *Of Three Arrows* (see page 453), or on some other similar writings. It is an elaboration of a passage in Job, 'Milicia est vita hominis super terram,' and of Paul's 'clothe yow in trewe armoure of Gode.' Section by section the piece allegorically exposes the details of the spiritual knight's equipment—the horse, bridle, reins, saddle, shield, sword, spear, spurs, etc.; tells why men should fight; and describes Doomsday and its 'three arrows,' the pains of Purgatory (cp. *Pricke of Conscience* l. 2892, see page 447), and the joys of Heaven.

In MS. Arundel 286 is said to be a *Milicia Christi* with quotations from Rolle.

THE QUATREFOIL OF LOVE [52] is in MSS. Br. Mus. Additional 31042 (15th century) and Bodley Additional A 106 (later than 31042). It is from the North of England, and is in metrical form similar to the earlier *Pistill of Susan* (see page 399). It consists of 40 strophes abababab-cdddc, the strophe comprising eight long alliterative lines, the ninth line of one stress, the tenth and eleventh and twelfth lines each of three or four stresses with alliteration, the thirteenth line of three stresses with alliteration.

On a May morning the poet overhears a lady complaining to a turtle-dove that she has sought in vain for 'a true-love,' and asking counsel. The dove replies that, when found growing, a true-love will be surrounded with four leaves, God the Creator, Christ, the Holy Ghost, and Mary. Then in this leaf symbolism it tells of the Creation, the Fall, the Annunciation, the Conception, the Birth and Life and Passion of Christ, inevitable Death, and Doomsday; and finally urges the lady to repentance. The lady blesses the dove. The poet counsels to appeal to Mary for intercession.

CHAPTER VII

PROVERBS AND PRECEPTS, AND MONITORY PIECES

There are preserved a number of Middle English pieces that consist of pithy utterances of comment on or declaration concerning life, sometimes with more, sometimes with less, didactic or monitory intent. Some of these are extensive, others are but mere scraps written on the margins or other vacant spaces in MSS. Though the nature of some of these pieces might justify classification in each group, they are here differentiated as 1. Proverbs and Precepts, or as 2. Monitory Pieces.

1. PROVERBS AND PRECEPTS

SCATTERED PROVERBS [1] of a line or a couplet are to be met with in the most unpromising parts of Middle English literature. Skeat has listed a number imbedded in the twelfth-century English Homilies, Layamon's *Brut*, the *Ancren Riwle*, the *Owl and the Nightingale*, the *Cursor Mundi*, *Havelok*, *Kyng Alisaunder*, the *Handlyng Synne*, *Piers Plowman*, Barbour's *Bruce*, Gower's *Confessio Amantis*, and Wycliffe's works. Several writers have recorded Gower's and Chaucer's considerable use of saws.

COLLECTIONS OF PROVERBS were made—some mere lists, others bound into units by various devices. Commonly they were ascribed to some person of experience, and frequently they were connected with revered names—Alfred, Bede, Bernard, Cato, Aristotle, and the like.

THE TRINITY COLLECTION [2], dating from 1200-1250, is in MS. Trinity College Cbg. O, 2, 45 (13th century, after 1248). It consists of twenty proverbs in French and Latin parallel, with parallel English versions of eighteen of them.

PROUERBES OF DIUERSE PROFETES AND OF POETS AND OF OÞUR SEYNTES [3] is the title given in the index of the MS. to a collection of wise sayings in MS. Vernon f. 306 (1370-1380). The collection opens with a prologue in French stating that the maker translates it from Latin into French. It consists of a series of quotations in Latin, generally of one line, each item paraphrased in from four to eight lines of French followed by an English equivalent of an equal number of lines in couplets of four-stress verses. There are 452 English lines. Over each item is written the name of the personage to whom it is attributed—David, Solomon, Isaiah, Jeremiah, Jacob, Tobias, Raphael, Seneca, Serafyn, Saul, Samuel, Job, Augustine, Ipocras, Ecclesiastes, Reuben, Samson, Sirach, James, Jerome, Christ, and others. Of these, Seneca and Solomon are the favorites; the Christian Fathers cut scarce any figure. Many of the sayings are really from the book of *Ecclesiasticus*. In MS. Harley 4733 is an English version (Latin and French omitted) of 1450-1475 in 201 short couplets.

THE DOUCE COLLECTION [4], in MS. Douce 53 ff. 13-32 (15th century), consists of English proverbs with translations in Latin hexameters arranged in roughly alphabetical order, with some Latin proverbs.

THE PROVERBS OF ALFRED [5] is the principal Middle English proverb collection. It is in the Southern dialect, and is preserved in MS. Jesus College Oxford 29 (c. 1275; 456 lines) and MS. Trinity College Cbg. B, 14, 39 (beginning of 13th century; 709 lines). Fragments of a version are preserved from a text in MS. Cotton Galba A XIX now destroyed. The original of these MSS. is probably of about 1150. The lines have each two stresses without regard to the number of

unstressed syllables; alliteration is frequent; rime is not uncommon—so, the verse is a valuable example of transition
stages between the old English alliterative verse and the newer
regular rimed verse. The lines are in paragraphs (23 in MS.
Jesus, 37 in MS. Trinity; the parallel paragraphs are not in
like order in the two MSS.) of irregular length determined in
each case by completion of the topic under consideration.

The piece opens with an introductory paragraph stating
that at Seaford sat many thanes, bishops, book-learned men,
and proud earls and knights; there were Earl Alurich, very wise
in the law, and Alfred, King of England, guardian and darling
of the English, the wisest man in the land—and Alfred began
to teach this company how to live. Each of the following paragraphs, except the last three in Trinity, begins, 'Thus says
Alfred . . . ' There is no narrative conclusion.—The piece
falls into three divisions: I, lines 1-210—prologue (ll. 1-24),
exordium (ll. 25-60), and ten proverbs (ll. 61-210); II,
lines 211-572—exordium (ll. 211-25), and sixteen (only
ten of which are in MS. Jesus) sayings (ll. 226-572); III,
lines 573-709 (only in MS. Trinity)—exordium (ll. 573-
605), and four pieces of advice (ll. 606-709), the last of
which falls into three groups. Each section of the third division (ll. 573-681) opens, 'Thus said Alfred . . . ,' followed by
'Sone mine so leue' or similar address. Thus this division is
connected with the unifying medium of advice of a wise man or
a father to a youth, and so fails to keep up the plan of the
prologue. Possibly this last part (only in Trinity), is an addition from a source other than the original of the other parts,
and lines 682-709 (only in Trinity) may represent further
addition. Though Alfred did make a collection of useful quotations, it is unlikely that he had any direct connection with
these *Proverbs.* Undoubtedly, it was his widespread reputation for wisdom that led to the common practice of attributing
to him scraps of popular lore (as in the *Owl and the Nightingale,* see page 421), just as it has been the custom in all ages
to father wise sayings or jests or anecdotes on celebrated
personages.

The *Proverbs* urge men to love and fear the Lord; kings shall seek learning; nobles, clerks, and knights shall administer law justly; knights shall protect the land, giving peace to the Church and to the people. They urge men individually to add wisdom to wit; to work hard, and to lay up for old age; to remember that life is short, and that death comes unexpected; not to be proud of wealth; to keep one's self; to choose a wife for character, not for looks; not to confide secrets to a wife, to rule her and keep her busy, and not to yield to her counsel; not to be too trusting; to avoid lying and vice; to remember that worldly wealth perishes; not to speak unnecessarily; to teach the child to obey, and not to spare the rod; to avoid drunkenness; to keep thought secret; to hold fast to friends; to be generous, and liberal in old age; to be grateful to God, and kind to all; and to avoid a drunken man, a deceitful man, a false friend, and a man who is short or tall or red.

It will be seen that the piece is a mingling of religious admonition, popular wisdom as to conduct, and some traditional superstition.

THE PROVERBS OF HENDYNG [6] are in MSS. Digby 86 f. 140 v (1272-1283), 47 stanzas; Harley 2253 f. 125 r (c. 1310), 39 stanzas; Cbg. Univ. Libr. Gg I 1 f. 475 (1300-1330), 46 stanzas. In MS. Bodley 920 is a record that there was once in the library of the Priory of St. Martin at Dover a MS. containing a version of the *Proverbs*. The first line of this as quoted differs from that of each of the extant versions. In MS. Cbg. Univ. Libr. 4407 (19) (end of 14th century) is the opening of a version that is more like that in MS. Harley than any of the others. The original of the *Proverbs* is of about 1250, and probably from the Midland. The MSS. vary much in their contents; taken together they make up a composite piece of 51 stanzas. The stanza consists of a statement of fact or experience in six verses usually aabccb (the *b* verses of three, the others of four, stresses), and a proverb in one line followed by 'Quoþ Hendyng.'

The tone of these *Proverbs* is, as compared with that of the other Middle English collections, especially worldly and bitter. The form of the collection may well have been taken from the Old French *Proverbes del Vilain* or the *Proverbes au Conte de Bretaigne*. The piece contains some proverbs similar to saws in the *Proverbs of Alfred*, and others parallel to several in the *Owl and the Nightingale*. Ascription of these to Hendyng indicates the decline of the popularity of Alfred as father of proverbs. MS. Harley declares Hendyng to be Marcolf's son. So, the collection is connected with the widely celebrated contention between Solomon and Marcolf, a version of which is extant in the Old English *Solomon and Saturn* (see page 425). The derivation of the name 'Hendyng' is not yet determined.

THE WISE MAN'S PROVERBS [7], 106 loose four-stress verses in couplets, is in MS. Bodley 9 (14th century). It begins, 'The wysman seyde to hys sones, Thenk on þise proverbis þat after comes.' Then follows a series of wise saws or proverbs, each in a couplet or a single verse. The bitterness and the cynicism of *Hendyng* are absent from the lines.

THE DISTICHS OF CATO [8], composed originally in Latin in about the fourth or the fifth century, relate 'How the wyse man tauhte his sone that was of tendere age.' The Latin was very popular in the Middle Ages, and was used as a schoolbook. An Anglo-Norman version ascribed to a monk Everard, was made apparently originally in 1150-1200. The *Distichs* are in two divisions, *Great Cato* and *Little Cato*. They are merely an extensive collection of pithy counsel concerning conduct.

In addition to the Old English version in MS. Cotton Julius A II *et al.*, there are several Middle English versions, all of about the same contents. The earliest of these, translated directly from Latin in the Northern dialect of the fourteenth century, is in MSS. Rawlinson G 59 (1450-1475; 607 verses) and Sidney Sussex College Cbg. Δ, IV, 1 (1450-1475; 654 verses), both close to each other and from one original text. This version is in short couplets usually grouped as quatrains, each group corresponding to a distich of the Latin; in several instances tail-rime is used. The text begins with a Latin prologue, and ends with a Latin epilogue which corresponds to the lines 633-36 of the second version.—The second version is in the sister MSS. Vernon (1370-1380) and Br. Mus. Additional

22283 (1380-1400). Here an English introduction largely correspondent to the French, precedes the Latin prologue. Then section follows section, first in Latin, next in Anglo-Norman, last in English. There are 644 English verses abab alternately of four and three stresses, each quatrain corresponding to a distich of the Latin. This version has an eight-line conclusion of its own.

Furnivall mentions a 'Cato in verse' in MS. Cosin's Libr. V ii 14.

The conclusion of a version (without the Latin or the French) in which, apparently, the two *Cato's* were regarded as one, is at the end of the Fairfax *Cursor Mundi* (see page 341). This piece consists of 378 verses aabccb (the *b* verses of three, the rest of four, stresses) of the late fourteenth or the early fifteenth century, and from the French.

The continued popularity of the *Distichs* is indicated by the existence of several still later English versions—the pieces in rime-royal in the fifteenth-century MSS. Chetham 8009 and Arundel 168, and another by Benedict Burgh printed by Caxton.

HOW THE WYSE (GODE) MAN TAUGHT HYS SONE [9], probably originally of the fourteenth century, is preserved in five fifteenth-century MSS., and one (Balliol) sixteenth-century MS. These MSS. represent three groups or versions, all of which are in four-stress verses ababbcbc: the first, in MSS. Cbg. Univ. Libr. Ff II 38 and Harley 5396, had 24 stanzas, 4 now being lost; the second, in MSS. Lambeth 853 and Balliol College Oxford 354, has 19 stanzas; the third has in MS. Harley 2399, 17 stanzas, and in MS. Ashmole 61, 13 stanzas. An abstract of the first version follows:

The piece is written to aid young men. A wise father counseled a son fifteen years of age, fair, gentle, good and noble: Begin the day with worship of God; desire moderation; do not talk too much; do not seek office; avoid new-fangledness and frequent changes; avoid drinking and dicing and following common women; be more humble as you have more; do not laugh too much; pay your debts; avoid late eating and drinking; avoid serving on an 'enqueste'; marry for love, and regard naught but the wife's goodness and honesty and wisdom; cherish your wife for her good deeds; chide not servants too hastily on the wife's accusation; avoid jealousy; though she is in rank a servant, the wife is somewhat your fellow; do not beat or curse her, rule her gently; pay your tithes, and give alms; the day of death approaches, when all shall be leveled—think on it.—The greater number of directions are urged on the basis of policy—if you do not practice this advice you shall suffer.

The device of the wise man's or father's counsel to the youth is employed in the Old English *Fæder Larcwidas*, the *Disciplina Clericalis*, the *Distichs of Cato* (see page 378), the *Wise Man's Proverbs* (see page 378), the third part of the *Proverbs of Alfred* (see page 376), and the fifteenth-century *Ratis Raving* in MS. Cbg. Univ. Libr. Kk I 55.

HOW THE GOOD WIFE TAUGHT HER DAUGHTER [10] is in eight MSS., and in three or four versions. The first group consists of MSS. Norfolk, printed in 1597, 231 lines; Lambeth 853 (c. 1430), 219 lines; Trinity College Cbg. R, 3, 19 (late 15th or early 16th century), 316 lines; and Ashburnham CXXX (Loscombe MS.; end of 14th century), 175 lines. These are in stanzas aabbccd, the verses of the first two couplets in sixes or sevens, the *c* verses of three or four stresses and proverbial in nature, the last line a refrain 'My leue child' or 'Mi dere child.'

The mother advises the child as follows: Go to church, and spare not for rain; pay tithes and do alms-deeds; at church pray, and prattle not; mock none, and be courteous; when asked to wed, consult friends, do not despise the offer or be too close with the lover; love your husband most, and answer him meekly; be glad and true and free from all ill; have good manners, control yourself, laugh quietly; walk demurely; talk little, and do not swear; in town do not run about, or drink up your money; do not go to public games; do not talk with strange men, or accept gifts; be not too easy or too strict in house-keeping. Then follows advice as to household affairs, hospitality, economy, and management of children.

The version in MS. Ashmole 61 f. 7 (15th century) is in 104 couplets of verses usually four-stressed. The matter is similar to what is in the first group.

In MS. Cbg. Univ. Libr. Kk I 5 (15th century) is a version

in 316 four-stress verses in couplets, the *Thews of Gudwomen*. This, though in different language, is in general sense close to the *Documenta Matris ad Filiam* in 153 couplets in MS. St. John's College Cbg. G 23, copied in 1487. This version begins: 'The good wife shows as best she can what are the manners of a good woman, what causes her to be held dear and makes poor women the peers of princes.' Then in the third person follow directions as to proper conduct of a woman, much resembling the synopsis already given. The versions dispense with dramatic effect, and, as they proceed, abandon the idea of utterance by a 'good wife.'

The Good Wyfe Wold a Pylgremage, in MS. Porkington 10 (Phillipps 8336; c. 1460), consists of 168 verses in stanzas abcbdbeb of verses alternately of four and three stresses with an abcb refrain of fours and threes beginning 'With an O and an I' (see page 236) and concluding with an appropriate proverb in the last two lines.

The directions are by the wife as she is departing on her journey. She cautions her daughter not to run about like St. Anthony's pig; not to show off before men; not to laugh lightly, or be free of looks; not to sit with men, or talk too much, or change friends too often, or swear, or give pledges hastily, or cherish slander; not to gad about, or drink much, or spend beyond her means.

To be mentioned here is the Scottish version in 102 short couplets of Bernard's *De Cura Rei Famuliaris* dedicated to a knight, Raymond. The piece is in MS. Cbg. Univ. Libr. Kk I 5 f. 2 r (15th century).

THE ABC OF ARISTOTLE [11], in alliterative long lines probably of 1400-1450 or perhaps of 1350-1400, is in nine East Midland MSS. of 1450-1500. It may have originated in the North or the North-West. MSS. Harley 541 f. 213, Harley 1304 f. 103, and Lambeth 853 f. 30, have introductions respectively of 12, 10, and 13 verses, varying considerably from each other in expression. These urge him who would be wise and have honor, to cherish the *ABC* of Aristotle.

There are two versions of the *ABC* itself. In the first are

22 verses each opening with 'Too,' the first 21 having the second word begin with the letters of the alphabet successively. The reader is urged not to be too amorous, too bold, too angry, too eager, too courteous, etc. The last line urges a moderate mean as best for all. In MS. Harley 1304 f. 103, after the introduction of ten lines and before the first *ABC* version (here 21 lines, *W* omitted), is inserted the second version of the *ABC* consisting of 21 lines with an added conclusion of 7 lines. The first 20 lines of the second version begin directly with the letters of the alphabet successively. As contrasted with the first version, which urges pagan or worldly virtue, the second version urges especially Christian notions, with less stress on Temperance, and more on reliance on and devotion to God and Christian conduct. The concluding lines state that books and rolls tell that God is maker of all, and teacher of moderation in all His works; manhood' and moderation are the golden means. The last eleven lines of this Harley 1304 version are in a seventeenth-century hand, but appear to be from an old original.

The title was taken to give it the weight of the all-admired Aristotle. The ABC device was adopted to bind into a unit the scattered precepts, and to afford with the alliteration a sort of substitute for end-rime. The superscription of Harley 1706 f. 94 designates a 'Mayster Benett' as author—certainly not Benett or Benedict Burgh. A 'Benedictus Anglus, doctor theologus,' 1333-1346, Bishop Suffragan of Norwich and Winchester, is connected by Bale with an 'Alphabetum Aristotelis'; but apparently this is not the present English version or its Latin original.

MISCELLANEOUS SCRAPS OF PITHY UTTERANCE [12] are found in odd spaces in MSS.

In MS. Cotton Cleopatra C VI f. 22 (13th century; c. 1250) is 'Liþir lok and tuingling,' five four-stress verses aaaaa repeated in MS. Trinity College Cbg. B, 1, 45 f. 24 r (early 14th century). Following this in Cleopatra are seven verses of two or three stresses aaabbcc, 'King conseilles,' which has been shown to be a selection from the favorite *Duodecim Abusiones*. In MS. Harley 913 f. 6 v (1308-1318, before 1325)

is 'Bissop lorles,' a variant of 'King conseilles,' seven lines of
two or three stresses aaaaabb; in MS. Rawlinson Poetry 32
(15th century) is 'A yong man a rewler recheles,' six lines of
four or five stresses on one rime. With 'Liþir lok,' in Cleopatra,
are four rude verses aabb of six or seven stresses, warning
ladies with double meaning that, no matter how splendid be
their clothing by day, they shall to bed naked as they were
born. *Ten Abuses*, 'Hwan þu sixst on leode,' in 14 verses of
two or three stresses in MSS. Cotton Caligula A IX f. 248 v
(before 1250) and Jesus College Oxford 29 f. 257 v (c. 1275),
reminds of part of 'Liþir lok.' The metrical form of some
of these pieces reminds of 'Wytte is trechery; Love is lechery,'
an epigram on the times, 6 verses in MS. Ashmole 750 f. 100
(15th century), and 8 verses in MS. Worcester Cath. Libr.
F 154 f. 110b (15th century).

Will and Wit [13], 'Hwenne so wil wit ofer-stieð,' eight four-
stress verses abababab in MS. Cotton Caligula A IX f. 246 v
(before 1250), declares pithily the supremacy Will should
have over Wit.

In MS. Royal 17 B XVII (West Midland, 1370-1400)
among a set of Latin sentences, are two short couplets 'Heuen
is wonnen with woo & shame' [14]: Woe and shame win
Heaven; joy and merriment win Hell—should one in this world
better have weal or woe? In the same group is a set of mixed
English and Latin verses on the evils of the times: The law is
dead; Fraud reigns; Love is little; Right goes afoot; Guile is in
every band; Truth is locked up, and none may unlock it unless
he sings 'si dedero.'

In MS. Arundel 507 f. 76 v (14th century) are three couplets of septenary verses, 'Thynk oft with sare hart' [15], urging contemplation of one's sins, the woe of Hell, the joys of
Heaven, the Passion, Doomsday, the falseness of the world, etc.

In MS. Cbg. Univ. Libr. Gg IV 32 (time of Henry IV) are
four scraps [16]. 'Sori is the fore,' in four couplets of two-
stress verses, declares it's a sorry journey from bed to floor,
a sorrier from floor to pit, and for sin from pit to torment—

alas, then all joy is gone! This is the same matter as in the longer 'If man him biðocte' [17], ten verses of two stresses aabbccdddd in MS. Arundel 292 f. 3 (late 13th century). Another of the Cambridge scraps, 'Be the lef other be the loth,' three short couplets, declares the world's wealth will depart and life-days fleet away—these conditions hold every man 'in hand.' Another, 'Suo sit fairhed in womman sot,' two couplets, one of four-stress verses, the other of three-stress lines, declares a man shall rightly lead his life between hope and fear.

In MS. Arundel 220 f. 301 v (early 14th century) is a saw [18]: 'Levere is the wrenne, Abouten the schowe renne, Than the fithel draut Other the floute craf.'

In MS. Harley 2316 f. 25 (later 14th century) are [19] 'ʒis is ʒi sete, domes man,' 'He is wys ʒat kan be war or him be wo,' 'Hope is hard ʒer hap is fro,' 'Men hem bimenin of litel trewthe,' 'Now goot falshed in everi flok' (cp. scrap in MS. Royal 17 B XVII, page 383), 'Mercy is hendest whose sinne is mest.'

Several scraps [20] are in MSS. Bodley 622 (early 14th century) flyleaf and Cotton Cleopatra D VIII f. 1 (end of 14th century). 'That in thi mischef forsakit the noʒth,' four loose four-stress verses on one rime, and a fifth verse of two stresses, defines a friend. 'Wan y was pore, then was y fre,' three rude short couplets, indicates the ill effect of riches on character, and the quickness of their disappearance. 'A scheld of red, a crosse of grene,' three similar couplets, declares that he need not fear among his enemies, who will take into his heart a shield of red emblazoned with a green cross and the symbols of the Passion.

On the back of the last leaf of MS. Harley 3724 (13th century), in a later hand, is 'Silly sicht i seich, unsembly forte se, As wil as hit was fetherto, fundind forte fle' [21].

In a number of fifteenth-century MSS. are written various similar scraps [22], some of which are printed in *Reliquiæ Antiquæ*.

A group of moral songs of about the time of Henry VI, is in MS. Sloane 2593 f. 54 (c. 1450) [23]; and another is in MS. Cbg. Univ. Libr. Kk I 5 f. 4 (15th century) [24]. In Kk is also a prose piece, *The Wisdom of Solomon* [24] (see pages 397 ff.), a digest of passages of *Ecclesiastes*. The metrical *King Solomon's Book of Wisdom* [24] (see page 399) is in the Bible-story MS., Laud 622 f. 69 (c. 1400).

2. MONITORY PIECES

Writers of the period were fond of dwelling on the transitoriness of wealth and the mutations of Fortune, the vanity of human life and endeavor, the decay of physical powers and the repulsive aspects of old age, the inevitable coming of death, the loathsome details of the rotting in the grave of the body as the food of worms, and the terrors of Doomsday. This fondness begat in our period many monitory pieces, mostly of slight extent, but all certainly favorably regarded by copyists, and many of them apparently popular.

These topics—now singly, now several at a time—were made the themes of a number of the religious lyrics (see pages 498 ff.).

POEMA MORALE or A MORAL ODE [25] is the most considerable of these pieces, and one of the most important of the early Middle English poems. It is in couplets of septenary verses with one unstressed syllable or two such syllables between stresses, and a cæsura after the fourth stress. It is preserved in MSS. Égerton 613 f. 7 (13th century), 398 lines; Egerton 613 f. 64 (somewhat earlier than the text on f. 7), 370 lines; Jesus College Oxford 29 f. 242 (c. 1275), 390 lines; Lambeth 487 f. 59 (late 12th or early 13th century), first 270 lines; Trinity College Cbg. B, 14, 52 f. 2 (early 13th century), 400 lines; Cbg. McClean 123 f. 123 (soon after 1300), 337 lines; and Digby A 4 f. 97 (beginning 13th century), 764 short lines in quatrains corresponding to 382 long lines of the other MSS. MSS. J, E, e, and L are from one ultimate version; MSS. T and D form one other group. McClean is apparently from a text that is brother to the common original of the two groups just mentioned. D is Kentish, T is nigh-Kentish, M is Kentish with a strong intermixture of more westerly forms; all the MSS. are Southern; E and e are perhaps of Hereford. The poem would appear to be from perhaps as early as about 1150.

With much feeling the poet looks back over his past life with what he regards as its waste and failure; and sadly he contemplates the slightness of attainment and the imperfection of his present old age. Thence he proceeds in single lines or in couplets to exhibit the specific forms of ill-conduct to which men are prone, and to give counsel as to right behavior toward men and toward God. He admonishes to use opportunity, while one has it, to lay up a sure treasure in Heaven, whither our efforts all should tend, and where is a safe storehouse and a secure harbor. God is ready to recognize every effort; He judges by Man's intention, not by his accomplishment; and He gives a hundredfold for all good that is done. He made all and holds all in His hands. He knows all. How shall we appear at Doomsday if we have not labored at all, and if we have been evil? The poet pictures the last Judgment, and he tells of the torments of Hell. He advises as to how to avoid damnation. Let Man pursue the spirit of God's teaching, let him love God and love his fellows. Let him avoid the broad and easy road, and follow the straight and narrow path. And he declares the happiness of Heaven, which is of the Spirit and has naught of mere physical or earthly delights.

The popularity of the poem is evinced through its preservation in the seven MSS. and the several recensions, and through its obvious influence on other writings. It is simple, direct, dignified, and elevated. While its matter has little novelty, it is so dealt with as to convict the reader, and to arouse him to a realization of the tremendous issues of life. Though the piece has not the imagination or the majesty of much of the Old English religious verse, it has its sincerity and a great deal of its convincing power. Sane judgment born of profound experience, and large wisdom that is the fruit of earnest contemplation, are its essence. While it deals with the errors and sins of men, and while it presents the physical torments of Hell, it treats these with a notable temperance. Its underlying conceptions, like its Heaven, are spiritual. In all these features, as in its subjective and personal quality, it is a striking contrast to most of the other religious and monitory verse of the Middle English period.

ERTHE UPON ERTHE [26], a very popular set of verses beginning 'Whan erþ haþ erþ iwonne wiþ wow,' or similar expression, is preserved in at least 24 MSS. ranging from the early fourteenth to the seventeenth century. On tombstones and in mural inscriptions portions of it have been employed almost up to the present time. The purport of all the texts is that all earthly conditions are born of the earth and must return to earth: 'Memento homo quod cinis es et in cinerem reverteris.' The matter is dealt with in three versions. The first, that with which we are concerned especially, is in MS. Harley 2253 (c. 1310) in four irregular five-stress verses on one rime; and in MS. Harley 913 (1308-1318, before 1325) in 84 verses aaaabb, each odd stanza English, and each even stanza the Latin equivalent of the preceding English one. The first four lines of the stanza in Harley 913 are loose four-stress verses; the final couplet is on the septenarius basis; and at the cæsuras the Latin lines always, and the English usually, rime with each other aaaabb. The four verses of Harley 2253 may be the opening of a transcript made from memory, or they may be an older version. Both poems are South Midland.—The texts of the two later versions are in metre quite different from the earliest version, and range in length between 20 and 82 verses. The second version is in 18 MSS. ranging from 1400 to 1623. The texts are usually in irregular four-stress verses aaaa. They vary greatly in length, the normal extent being seven stanzas. The third version, in MS. Cbg. Univ. Libr. Ii IV 9 f. 67 r (15th century), has 82 lines, combining parts of both the other versions.

SIGNS OF DEATH [27] in the form of decay of physical powers, are enumerated in 12 South Midland verses of irregular length in MS. Jesus College Oxford 29 f. 262 v (c. 1275). A list of similar kind is in nine couplets of irregular length in MS. Harley 7322 f. 121 r (14th century; see page 396). Similar matter is in MS. Harley 7322 f. 7 v, 'Whanne þe ffet

coldet3,' 7 short couplets; in the same MS. f. 169 v, 'Wonne
þin eren dinet,' 4 quatrains abab of usually three-stress verses;
and in MS. Arundel 507 f. 76 v (14th century), 'When þe hee
beginnis to turne,' three couplets of irregular three-stress
verses.   In Harley 7322 f. 79 r are four couplets, 'Kinge I sitte
and loke aboute,' on the mutations of earthly experience—now
king, now poor man; now king, now dead.

THREE MESSENGERS OF DEATH [28], a version of a
theme widely treated in the several tongues, in four-stress
verses abab, is in the sister MSS. Vernon f. 297 (1370-1380;
224 verses) and Br. Mus. Additional 22283 f. 88 v (1380-
1400; 216 verses).   It has been suggested that the piece is
an imitation of the *Saws of St. Bernard* (see page 389).   The
author quotes two Latin quatrains, and cites Job, Paul, and
Augustine.   The verses were written probably at about 1350,
and in the Midland.

Man's life is but brief; young and old, rich and poor, fall before
Death.   His messengers are Disasters, Sickness, and Old Age.
Disasters chance to all as a thief in the night; woe to him to whom
unshriven they come.   Sickness comes openly, and is God's courteous warning; when ill, we love God—but we soon forget; we
should pray for sickness.   Old Age is like a man kept out of his
Lord's gate by a porter; though one live to be four-score, one's life
is woeful, all must die; all should fear who pass a churchyard, where
in 'poor-hall' lie the bodies full of maggots.   Earthly life is as
nothing to eternity.   In Hell a man shall weep more than all the
water in the earth—alms, masses, and prayers shall not avail him.
Heaven is for those who serve God.

THE ENEMIES OF MAN [29], 'Þe siker soþe who so
says,' is in MS. Auchinleck f. 303 v (1330-1340).   It consists
of seven Northern stanzas aaabcccbddddbeeeb with alliteration
of the important syllables, and often with alliteration uniting
pairs of lines.   In short, pithy, crabbed utterance whose sense
is sometimes obscure, the piece warns of the three foes of Man,
the World, the Flesh, and the Devil—but more of the fourth,
who is Death.   'Now have I found thy foes; find thou thy
friends.'

THE SAYINGS OF ST. BERNARD [30], in tail-rime aabccb, is in MSS. Harley 2253 f. 106 r (c. 1310), 156 lines; Vernon f. 304 v (1370-1380), 216 lines; Laud 108 f. 198 r (part I of MS., c. 1290), 186 lines; Digby 86 f. 125 v (1272-1283), 186 lines; and Auchinleck f. 280 r (1330-1340), a fragment of 42 lines correspondent to Laud lines 121-32, 157-86. The piece is of 1250-1300. The original form is assigned by some scholars to the West Midland, and by others to the South-East Midland. The first four MSS. agree in general in matter, though Vernon varies from the others in introduced matter in lines 79-138, and in arrangement from line 150 to the end. MSS. Harley, Laud, and Digby are close to each other, the first two being especially close. At lines 133-56 Laud has material not in the rest. A section (II), 'Wher beþ hue þat byforen vs were,' occurs at Harley lines 121-44, Laud 121-74, and Vernon 181-210. This is written at the end of Digby (ll. 127-80) with a separate title 'Ubi sount qui ante nos fuerount,' and is in the Auchinleck fragment. Perhaps this section was originally a separate piece; perhaps, however, it was transposed or written separately merely because of the nature of its contents.

I. Bernard says in his book that Man must die, and his body must be eaten by worms; human life is transitory; flesh and soul are ever at strife; the soul shall rule; fleshly life is vile; Man's three foes are the World, the Flesh, and the Devil; you wrong your soul by favoring your body; the World tempts with pleasures, of which Death strips you bare; beware of the Devil's tricks; tempted, take Christ for your shield, the Cross for your staff, and fight for the bliss of Heaven.—II. Where are those who were before us, who made merry with hawks and hounds and rich garb and splendid ladies and eating and drinking and song? They had their Paradise here, and now burn in Hell forever. But, Mary, protect us from the fiend, and help us to flee sin and see thy Son world without end!

The 'ubi sunt' formula, on which is based the second section of this piece, has well been said to be 'as universal as the themes of mutability and mischance'; it has been utilized both in humorous and in grave literature from the Far East to America, and from before the period of Classical Greece to the present generation. It was a special favorite of mediæval writers.

In Old English it occurs in the *Wanderer* (ll. 92-93) and the *Metres of Boethius* (10. 33) ; and in Middle English it appears not only in the *Sayings of St. Bernard*, but also in *Death* (see page 392), *A Luue Ron* (see page 529), *Of Clene Maydenhod* (see page 530), the *Debate between the Body and the Soul* (*e.g.*, Vernon ll. 23 ff., Harley 2253 ll. 14 ff., Laud ll. 11 ff.; see page 411), Lydgate's *Like a Midsummer Rose*, Ryman's fifteenth-century poem No. 85, and other pieces.

THE SAWS OF ST. BEDE [31] is in MS. Digby 86 f. 127 v (1272-1283) in 373 lines usually of three stresses and usually aabaab, and in MS. Jesus College Oxford 29 f. 248 (c. 1275) in 59 similar stanzas printed by Morris under the title *Sinners Beware*.

After a passage beseeching aid of the Holy Ghost to save us from the Devil, the piece urges confidence in Christ and a pure life, and assurance of the bliss of Heaven and the pains of Hell. It enumerates and warns against the Deadly Sins; admonishes those proud of wealth, and warns that poverty will not save; declares that to Hell shall go sinful ecclesiastics, knights who have slain Christians, evil lawyers, cheating merchants, false bondmen, proud adulteresses and wearers of fine gowns, and lecherous monks and nuns. We think to sin, and to repent on our death-beds; but repentance is not easy. Each gets his deserts at death, when the body rots and is ground to ashes by worms. Naked we came, naked we shall go. Let us forsake sin, and turn to shrift! Let us not be ashamed of shrift; the proud confess falsely, and suffer in Hell.— Then are recounted the proceedings of the Last Judgment. If we live rightly, we shall on Doomsday be companions of angels. Let us pray that we be with them.

Here, then, is an interesting combination of common themes—the joys of Heaven; the pains of Hell; the Deadly Sins; pride of the rich; sins of the clergy and of fine ladies; the value of shrift; the terrors and joys of Doomsday; and the complaint of the Soul to the Body.

DOOMSDAY [32], 'Hwenne ich þenche of domes-dai,' is the theme of eleven South Midland stanzas abcbdbeb, the *b* verses of three stresses, the others of four, in MSS. Cotton Caligula A IX f. 246 (before 1250) and Jesus College Oxford 29 f. 255 (c. 1275).

The writer expresses his fear as he thinks of Doomsday, of the all-consuming fire and the last trump. Then the piece shifts to declaration that the rich shall lament, weapons nor alms-deeds shall avail them; they shall see the Virgin, and Christ with the good on His right and the evil on His left.—He shall welcome the good, and damn the evil. Let us all pray the Virgin to beseech Christ to bring us to Heaven.

ON SERVING CHRIST [33], 'Hwi ne serue we crist,' in 78 verses of six or seven stresses riming in *laisses* of from 6 to 16 lines, is in MS. Jesus College Oxford 29 f. 258 v (c. 1275; South Midland).

Why do we not serve Christ? Doom impends, which shall level all. Pray to Christ and Mary; contemplate the Passion; forsake war; consider the saints and the martyrs. Inevitable is the dwelling with the worms, where gay garments and hounds shall be naught.

A SONG ON DEATH [34], so-called, 'Esto memor mortis, jam porta fit omnibus ortis,' is in MS. Cbg. Univ. Libr. Ee VI 29 (c. 1400). Its 86 verses open with two couplets of three-stress Latin verses. Then comes a stanza of alternating English and Latin lines abababab, the *a* verses of four stresses, the *b* verses of three stresses with feminine ending. Thence it proceeds abababab, normally alternating English verses of three or four stresses with Latin verses of two stresses. The piece reminds of the stealthy approach of Death, the inevitable decay of the body, the pains of Hell, and the need of present penitence and shrift.

In MS. Royal College of Physicians Edinburgh f. 2 v, after the *Fifteen Signs before Judgment* (see page 328), is a Northern piece of some 650 short couplets on the Judgment, that is really an extract from the *Cursor Mundi* (see page 339). In MS. Rawlinson C 285 f. 39 (15th century), after Hilton's *Scala Perfectionis* (see page 460) and in MS. Cbg. Univ. Libr. Dd V 55 f. 92 v (15th century), is a piece on Doomsday, 'þai þat withoutene lawe dos syne,' extracted from the *Pricke of Conscience* (see page 449).

OLD AGE [35], a favorite theme of the period, is dealt with in 72 verses, 'Elde makiþ me geld, and growen al grai,' in

MS. Harley 913 f. 54 v (1308-1318, before 1325). As they stand, the verses compose a mixture of alliterative long lines, of continuous interlaced riming lines, and of tail-rime. Bitterly and with a hard, brutal realism, the writer presents in the first person the loathsomeness of appearance and the repulsiveness of deportment of the body shattered and rotten with years.

DEATH [36], 'Ihereþ of one þinge,' consists of 264 three-stress lines abcbdbeb of the South-West, in MSS. Cotton Caligula A IX f. 247 (before 1250) and Jesus College Oxford 29 f. 255 v (c. 1275). It combines features of the pieces on Doomsday, Old Age, the Body and the Soul, and the Pains of Hell. The shortness of the lines and the use four times of each rime-sound, make the verses monotonous. The detailed picture of the horrible Devil must have been very effective. On the use of the 'ubi sunt' formula see page 389.

The rich are reminded that they cannot escape Death; with naught Man enters the world, and with naught he departs; our joy shall be gone at Doomsday; the pains of Hell are terrible; the body is sewn up and buried; and friends forget the man, and strive for his property. Then the soul shall curse the body, shall taunt it with the loss of all its worldly joys and power, and shall tell of its decay in the grave and of its own torment in Hell. Let us, then, repent and do alms-deeds, and pray for salvation.

THREE SORROWFUL TIDINGS [37], in MS. Jesus College Oxford 29 f. 262 (c. 1275), consists of three short couplets: 'Vyche day me cumeþ tydinges þreo'—I must go hence, I know not when, I know not whither. A variant of this is in MS. Arundel 292 f. 3 (late 13th century), 'Wanne I ðenke ðinges ðre,' three short couplets following a Creed, etc. (see page 350). Another variant in three short couplets, 'Hit beoþ þreo tymes on þo day,' is in MS. Harley 7322 f. 8 (in a piece of end of 14th century). Similar matter is incorporated into Poem 24 of the Vernon-Simeon refrain group (see page 513).

CAMBRIDGE 4407 (19) FRAGMENTS [38]. In the collection of fragments known as MS. Cbg. Univ. Libr. 4407

(19) (end of 14th century), are some scraps of a poem ababab containing didactic declaration of loss of good times, and of decline into evil days.

GHENT 317 FRAGMENTS [39].   On the back leaf of MS. Ghent Univ. Libr. 317, with other scraps (14th century) in Latin, French, and English (see pages 395, 534), is 'Ye flour of hour gerlond es doun falle,' consisting of three couplets, the first of five-stress verses, the second of three-stress verses, the third of four-stress verses.   This pessimistic bit was written apparently as a motto to be placed above the heads of those imagined to be suffering in Hell for adultery.

HARLEY 2316 PIECES [40].   To be connected with the verses on Old Age and Death are some short pessimistic pieces in MS. Harley 2316 f. 25 (1350-1400): 'Kyndeli is now mi coming,' 'Ded is strong and maystret alle thing,' 'Sey, sinful man, what is ȝyn thowht,' 'Man, loke ȝow troste ȝe nowght to fele,' 'Riche mannis riflowr,' and 'Blisse it were in londe to haven wrchipe and miht.'

MAXIMIAN [41], originally in a Midland dialect, is preserved in two Southern versions in MSS. Digby 86 f. 134 v (1272-1283) and Harley 2253 f. 82 r (c. 1310).   The piece is in three-stress verses probably originally, as now, in twelve-line stanzas.   Lines 3, 6, 9, 12 are on one rime; and the other lines are in couplets, all of which in some stanzas were on one rime.   By chance each MS. has 273 verses.   Digby appears to preserve the original fairly closely; but one stanza has less than twelve verses.   The sense and the coherence of Digby are good.   Harley may have been written from memory; its stanzas are of various lengths; the sense and the connection in it are often poor; and the coherent order of Digby is frequently departed from.—The chief ideas of the piece are from the first of the six Latin elegies of Cornelius Maximianus Gallus of the sixth century, lines 1-4 and 223-28 of which Chaucer imitated in lines 727-33 of his *Pardoner's Tale.*

The poem makes Maximian its hero. He was a good clerk, the handsomest of men except Absalom. But old age came upon him, and he composed a plaint. Thence (st. 5 to end) follows the lament: Youth, physical powers, capacity for enjoyment, are gone; he who was so vigorous, so proud, so handsome, so capable, so beloved, is decayed and broken down, and is shunned by wife and friends. He has lived too long, and would rather be dead than so to retain life.

A TREATISE OF PARCE MICHI DOMINE [42], 'By a forest syde, walkyng as I went,' follows *Pety Iob* in the fifteenth-century MSS. Douce 322 f. 15 and Harley 1706. It consists of 19 stanzas of 8, 12, or 16 lines, made up of quatrains of alternate rime, each stanza ending 'Parce michi, domine.'

In a forest the poet hears a bird pray the Lord to spare it, for it has lost its feathers. Questioned by the poet, it tells that Old Age has bereft it of its four principal feathers—Youth, which led it to sinful pleasures; Beauty, which induced it to lechery; Strength, which begat selfish greed and desire for mastery; Wealth, which turned it to worldly goods and from God. The poet thanks the bird for the lesson; 'parce' is the word to win mercy from God.

AL ES BOT A FANTUM ÞAT WE WITH FFARE [43], in MS. Cotton Galba E IX (15th century), consists of 94 verses of six or seven stresses (verses 23-27 being repeated as 30-34) in stanzas of from 4 to 8 lines on one rime. The first five stanzas, and stanzas 9 and 14, begin with the title-line; and the piece ends with a variant of it. The theme is the worthlessness of earthly matters. All worldly goods are snares, and shall vanish; he is a fool who yields to them; let us pray for salvation to the Justice who knows all.—A scrap of four lines aaaa beginning, 'Al it is a fantam that we mid fare,' is in MS. Cbg. Univ. Libr. Ee I 5 (15th century).

TWO LULLABIES [44] may be dealt with here (see pages 499, 504) because of their matter. The first, 'Lollai, lollai, litil child, whi wepistou so sore,' is in MS. Harley 913 f. 32 r (1308-1318, before 1325). It consists of 36 verses of six or seven stresses aaaabb, the fifth line of the stanza being a variant of the opening line of the piece.

Unlike other creatures, the child is born to sorrow because of Adam's sin; it shall remember whence it came, what it is, what it shall be; let it not trust the world that makes rich poor, woe weal, and *vice versa;* it is a pilgrim in a false land, its days are told, death surely shall befall it.

The fourth stanza agrees closely with a scrap, 'Þe leuedi fortune is boþe frend and fo,' four lines in MS. Cbg. Univ. Libr. Oo VII 32 (time of Edward II). Of this a four-line variant, 'The levedy dame fortune, . . . ,' is among the Ghent 317 fragments (see page 393), in a fourteenth-century hand.

The other lullaby, whose every strophe begins 'Lollay, lollay, þu lytel child, Wy wepys þou so sore,' is in MS. Harley 7358 (14th century). It consists of 36 verses abaaab, the *a* verses of four, the *b* verses of three, stresses.

The child is likened to Christ who suffered for Man; then it is represented as grieving because it took an apple from a tree forbidden by its father, and so lost its heritage; then Mankind is declared to be the cause of its weeping; finally, the babe is represented as the Christ-child that shall suffer to save the lost.

'WEOLE Þu ART AWARIED ÞING' [45] is a scrap of four seven-stress verses aaaa in MS. Jesus College Oxford 29 f. 252 v (c. 1275) declaring the unfairness of Fortune.

LONG LIFE [46], 'Mon mai longe liues wene,' is in 50 four-stress verses in ten-line stanzas of irregular rime, in MSS. Cotton Caligula A IX f. 246 (before 1250) and Jesus College Oxford 29 f. 252 v (c. 1275), and in 49 verses (l. 26 lost) in MS. Laud 471 f. 65 r (hand of end of 13th century). C and J are closer to each other than either is to L. The last line of the stanza has in C and J four stresses, in L two stresses. Nine verses corresponding to the ten of the first stanza are inserted in the *Aȝenbite of Inwyt*. Close to the end of the Kentish Sermons (see page 283) is 'Man mai longe liues wene and ofte him leghep se wrench.'

The piece declares: Man may expect a long life, but Death comes suddenly; all must die; world and weal deceive us, and are our foes; take Solomon's counsel, prepare for the end, and do not let trivial transitory pleasure interfere.

HARLEY 7322 SCRAPS [47]. Imbedded in several of a collection of Latin prose pieces probably for the use of preachers, in MS. Harley 7322 (various hands of the 14th century), are a number of short English bits, some prose, some verse, all on themes similar to those dealt with in this section. Some of them have been mentioned (see pages 387, 388, 392, 518) with the pieces to which they are most similar.

AUGUSTINUS DE CONTEMPTU MUNDI [48] is the title of 250 words of prose followed by forty irregular verses alternately of six and seven stresses in couplets in MS. Harley 1706 f. 142 v and f. 92 (15th century). The theme is the vanity and transitoriness of worldly conditions.

CONSILIA ISODORI [49] consists of some 3500 words of prose in the fifteenth-century MSS. Harley 1706 f. 140 and f. 90, Rawlinson C 894, and Royal 17 C XVIII f. 104. It is a close translation of a Latin text represented in MS. Cbg. Univ. Libr. Mm VI 17. It is made up of a number of paragraphs of advice on Evil Thoughts, Fasting, Chastity, Continual Prayer, Drink, Manhood, Peace, Conscience, and other similar topics. The piece has been assigned to Rolle, to Hilton, and to followers of each.

Other pieces of monitory effect are discussed with the lyrics (see pages 486 ff.).

CHAPTER VIII

TRANSLATIONS AND PARAPHRASES OF THE BIBLE, AND COMMENTARIES

The translations and paraphrases of the Bible and commentaries on the Scriptures, will be discussed according as the material is of the Old Testament or of the New Testament. The Wycliffite version of the Bible will be considered at the end.

1. THE OLD TESTAMENT

GENESIS AND EXODUS [1] is the name given to 4162 (*Genesis*, 2536; *Exodus*, 1626) four-stress verses in couplets with frequent alliteration and irregularity in number of unaccented syllables, preserved in MS. Corpus Christi College Cbg. 444 f. 1 (c. 1300). The poem is in the South-East Midland dialect of about 1250, and is apparently by one author. It is a paraphrase of the accounts of the principal incidents in the Biblical *Genesis* and *Exodus*, portions of *Numbers* and *Deuteronomy* being inserted to complete the story of Moses and of the wanderings of the Israelites. It follows, rather than the Bible itself, Peter Comestor's popular epitome and commentary, *Historia Scholastica*. In his prologue the author declares that one ought to love the course of rimes that well instructs the unlearned how to love God and to serve Him, though the hearer be quite ignorant of books; this 'song' (apparently the piece was intended for oral delivery) was drawn out of Latin into English, and told in the common tongue and in 'wordes smale,' a kind of composition all should be glad to hear. Then, after invocation of the Father, the work proceeds with its story. The piece has little or no poetical value; it exhibits a great falling-off from the Old English verse paraphrases. The style is simple and somewhat bald. The expression is heavy and sometimes clumsy, though now and again it rises to earnest elevation.

THE STORY OF JOSEPH [2], in MS. Bodley 652 f. 1 (beginning 15th century), is told in 270 couplets of verses sometimes of seven, sometimes of six, stresses, with medial cæsura and with some alliteration. The piece is probably from before 1300, and of a dialect bordering on the South-East. The poem is of the earlier, more epic type; it was composed probably for recitation at lodging-places by a traveling min- strel-clerk (see last couplet). The verses tell of Joseph's dream, the selling into captivity, the stewardship and tempta- tion, the imprisonment, the elevation, the visit of the brethren, and the reconciliation. The story is a complete unit, is vigor- ous, and is full of action and direct speech; the incidents impress as told for their own sake, with no obvious theological or direct didactic intent.

A STROPHIC VERSION OF OLD TESTAMENT PIECES [3], in MS. Bodley Selden Supra 52 (beginning 15th century), paraphrases the Scriptural books *Genesis* to *Second Kings* inclusive, *Third* and *Fourth Kings, Job, Tobias, Esther, Judith,* and *De Matre cum VII Filiis* and *De Anthiaco* (from *Maccabees*). The strophes are abababababcdcd, the first eight lines of four, the last four of three, stresses each. As it stands, this strophe appears to be unique in Middle English. Another copy excluding *Genesis* and *Leviticus,* is in the Mar- quis of Bath's MS. 25 f. 119 (end of 14th or beginning 15th century). The work is probably of 1350-1400, and was origi- nally Northerly. The verse is well handled, with very elaborate alliteration between pairs of lines. The general quality of the. pieces is excellent. Only the *De Matre,* the *De Anthiaco,* and the first 48 lines of *Genesis* have been printed.

A VERSE VERSION OF OLD TESTAMENT PAS- SAGES [4] is in MS. Laud Misc. 622 (c. 1400). The verses are of seven stresses with cæsura. There have been printed part of the account of the life of Solomon in 64 verses; the abstracts of the Book of Wisdom in 110 verses; the accounts of Rehoboam and Jeroboam in 36 verses, of Elijah in 64 verses, of Elisha in 22 verses, of Daniel in 32 verses; and a passage on Antichrist and the Signs of Doom in 32 verses.

PETY IOB or PARCE MIHI DOMINE [5] is in the fifteenth-century MSS. Douçe 322 f. 10, Harley 1706 f. 10, Merton College 68 f. 97, and Cbg. Univ. Libr. Ff II 38 f. 19 (see page 394). It consists of 684 irregular four-stress verses abababbcbc, the stanza being headed with its Latin theme and ended with 'Parce michi domine.' The whole is divided into nine parts or 'lessons,' each a series of expanded paraphrases of a portion of the laments of Job. The MS. headings connect with the piece the name of 'Richard Hampole.' The verses were probably based on Rolle's *Parvum Iob sive Lectiones Mortuorum* (see page 446) by a later East Midland writer— Richard Maidenstone (see page 404), according to Horstmann.

The repetend 'Parce michi domine' is used in 'By a forest syde, walkyng as I went' [6] that follows *Pety Iob* in MSS. Douce and Harley (see page 394).

THE LESSONS OF THE DIRIGE [7] is in MS. Digby 102 f. 124 v (early 15th century) in 52 stanzas abababab. The piece is another paraphrase of Job's lamentations, divided into ten 'lessons.'

SUSANNAH or SEEMLY SUSAN or THE PISTILL OF SUSAN [8], a version of the story of Susannah and Daniel, is in MSS. Vernon f. 317 (1370-1380), Br. Mus. Additional 22283 (1380-1400), Phillipps 8252 f. 184 r at Cheltenham (15th century), Cotton Caligula A II f. 1 (c. 1430), and Ingilby owned by Sir Henry Ingilby, Yorkshire (c. 1450). The best MSS. are the two earliest. In matter all of the five agree. Cotton lacks the first eight stanzas. The other MSS. have 28 stanzas ababababcdddc, of which the first eight lines are alliterative long lines, the ninth has one iambic foot with feminine ending, the tenth and eleventh and twelfth have three stresses, and the thirteenth has two stresses. The original is apparently Scottish. The poem should be connected with the other pieces of the 'alliterative revival' (see page 240).

The story is told sympathetically and effectively. The poet dwells much on the loveliness of his heroine, and introduces a lengthy catalogue of the birds and fruits and plants in Susannah's garden. The stanza is melodious, and has caused suggestion that the piece was intended to be sung. It is of interest that a *Ballad of Constant Susanna* was current in Shakespeare's day, and that Sir Toby Belch sang the first and sixth lines of it.

The fact that, in a long digression in his fifth book defending 'Huchown of the Awle Ryale,' Wyntoun says that 'Huchown' 'made the gret Gest of Arthure, And the Awntyre off Gawane, The Pystyll als off Swete Swsane,' has led some to ascribe the present piece to this 'Huchown' [9]. Further, the *Awntyrs of Arthure* (see page 61) has been supposed to be the 'Awntyre off Gawane,' and the 'Gret Gest' to be the alliterative *Morte Arthure* (see page 36). These identifications are very questionable, and ascription of the pieces to 'Huchown' is probably incorrect. Much has been written on 'Huchown' by several writers; but their rather intemperate claims leading to assignment to 'Huchown' of about forty thousand lines of the extant alliterative Middle English verse, have been received very unfavorably. To 'Huchown' have been ascribed also the *Gest Historiale of the Destruction of Troye*, *Golagrus and Gawain*, *Gawayne and the Grene Knight*, the *Wars of Alexander*, *Titus and Vespasian*, *Purity*, *Erkenwald*, *Patience*, the *Pearl*, *Wynnere and Wastoure*, and the *Parlement of the Thre Ages*. The only reliable material on 'Huchown' is still what is in Wyntoun. That 'Huchown' wrote this *Pistill* is possible; that he was Sir Hugh of Eglinton (as has been urged) is unlikely; that he wrote any of the other extant Middle English pieces, has been supported by no good evidence.

PURITY and PATIENCE [10], two West Midland alliterative poems, the one consisting largely of Bible stories, the other of the story of Jonah, are discussed with the *Pearl* (see page 583).

THE SOUTHERN TEMPORALE [11] contains much Old Testament story. But these items are so bound up with legendary material, that they are to be considered with the legends and ₩ith the stories of the Virgin and Christ (see pages 320 ff.).

THE STORY OF ADAM AND EVE [12] so developed, both independently and in relation to the story of the Rood, as to necessitate consideration of it with the legends (see page 319).

THE SURTEES PSALTER [13], so called from its publication by the Surtees Society, is extant in MSS. Cotton Vespasian D VII (c. 1350; oldest and purest text); Egerton 614; Harley 1770; Bodley 425 and 921; and Corpus Christi College Cbg. 278. The MSS. except Cotton are of 1350-1400; the *Psalter* is probably of 1300-1350. All the MSS. show much evidence of Northern composition, the first three containing some Midland traits. The original is regarded as of the North, probably Yorkshire, though argument has been made for the Midland. The *Psalter* consists of translation of 150 Psalms from the Vulgate. The MSS. fall into two groups, externally differentiated by use in Cotton of short couplets throughout, and in the other MSS. generally of couplets but in certain Psalms (*e.g.*, 26, 44, 61) of a stanza ababcdcd.

ROLLE'S COMMENTARY ON THE PSALTER [14] is, except for a few omissions and additions, a close prose translation of Petrus Lombardus' *Commentarium in Psalmos*. Perhaps because Peter's work was frowned on, Rolle does not mention his Latin original, and gives the impression that his writing was made up from passages from the Fathers. The English piece had great popularity. At least twenty-three MSS., most from the fifteenth century and the best Northern, are extant. The prologue of sixty long alliterative lines in couplets, says that the work was undertaken by Rolle at request of Margaret Kirkby, a nun (see page 445). The expression is unidiomatic and lacking in flexibility. See under the *Canticles*, below.

LOLLARD REVISIONS OF ROLLE'S PSALTER [15]. In the latter part of the fourteenth century a revision of Rolle's *Commentary* was made to suit the needs of Lollards, but was still palmed off as Rolle's. The prologue is kept, the text of the Psalms is little modified; but in the commentary gradually more and more matter of the Wycliffite type is added, the expansion becoming extensive and Rolle's comments being practically lost. The MSS. (early 15th century) agree in *Psalms* 1 to 89. Thereafter they fall into two groups. In the first of these groups (represented by at least five MSS., of which Trinity College Cbg. B, V, 25 alone has the whole *Psalter*) there is little added matter after *Psalm* 89. In the second group (represented by MS. Royal 18 C XXVI, *Psalms* 89-117) the additions after *Psalm* 89 are extensive.

Still later, the Lollard *Psalter* was cut down, the controversial matter and attacks on the clergy being eliminated or generalized. This text is in MS. Trinity College Dublin 71 (A, 2, 1) of 1450-1500.

THE CANTICLES [16], a dozen hymns taken from the Old and New Testaments, were regularly appended to the *Psalter* for church services. Versions of Canticles 1-7 with commentaries, are a part of Rolle's *Psalter* in all complete MSS. of that work. These appear to be certainly by the hermit, though perhaps they were retouched later. Versions of all the twelve hymns with commentaries, are found in later or interpolated MSS. The last five Canticles with their commentaries are probably of Wycliffite production.

Versions of eleven Canticles are in the *West Midland Prose Psalter* and in the first Vernon *Psalterium Beate Mariæ* (see page 404).

THE WEST MIDLAND PROSE PSALTER [17] is in

MSS. Br. Mus. Additional 17376 (c. 1340-1350), Magdalene College Cbg. Pepys 2498 (late 14th or early 15th century), and Trinity College Dublin A, 4, 4 (c. 1400). Because the later MS. of Shoreham's poems chances to be bound up with Additional (see page 349), the *Psalter* was formerly wrongly attributed to the Kentish poet. The work contains all the Psalms, eleven Canticles, and the Athanasian Creed. It was made from a glossed version of the Vulgate. A verse of the Latin is followed by the English rendering, then comes the Latin and then the English, and so on. Some suggestion has been made that the work is from the French. Perhaps Rolle's *Psalter* antedates this so-called 'earliest' complete English *Psalter*.

JEROME'S PSALTERIUM ABBREVIATUM [18] is represented by an English version in MSS. Hatton 111 (1350-1400) and Bodley 416 (c. 1400). Jerome omits wholly a number of Psalms, and usually represents each of the rest with extracts of several verses. Bodley ends with *Psalm* 141 verse 8. Hatton abridges the Latin original, and Bodley (probably the copyist) makes still further omissions.

A COMMENTARY ON PSALMS 90 AND 91 [19] is in MSS. Cbg. Univ. Libr. Dd I 1 (North Midland; 15th century) and Hh I 2 (15th century). The commentary on *Psalm* 91 is in MS. Harley 2397 (c. 1400). The text is based on Rolle's version (see page 401) with variations from it, and is commented on verse by verse at length. Its mystic trend, and absence of allusion to or attacks on contemporary conditions, point to the school of Rolle rather than to that of Wycliffe.

A PARAPHRASE OF PSALM 50 [20] from the Vulgate, is in MS. Auchinleck f. 280 v (c. 1330-1340), in groups of four four-stress verses in couplets, with the Latin preceding each group. But 95 lines are extant.

THE SEVEN PENITENTIAL PSALMS [21] are extant in an English verse paraphrase in the fifteenth-century MSS.

Digby 18 f. '38 r, Rawlinson A 389, Ashmole 61 f. 108, and Digby 102 f. 128. The dialect is declared to be East Midland. After a prologue of eight lines (in Digby 18 and Rawlinson only) follow 952 four-stress verses abababab, each stanza headed by the Latin original. The Digby prologue ascribes the piece to 'Richard Hampole'; the Rawlinson prologue says the author was 'Richarde Maydenstoon in Mary ordre of þe Carme.' As Rolle did not write in East Midland, and as Maidenstone was of Kent (see his *De Concordia inter Ricardum Secundum et Civitatem London;* see pages 399, 416), probably both ascriptions are incorrect. In MS. Vernon f. 113 (1370-1380) are the last 138 verses, with the Latin abbreviated, of the paraphrase of *Psalm 51*, representing verses 407-544 of the English Penitential Psalms. Another copy of this paraphrase of *Psalm 51* in MS. Br. Mus. Additional 10036 f. 96 v (beginning 15th century), has all the 160 verses complete.

Another English version of the Penitential Psalms [22] ascribed in a sixteenth-century hand to 'Frater Thomas Brompton, sacræ Theologiæ Doctor, fr. minorum pauperculus confessor,' and dated 'Anno 1414,' is in MS. Sloane 1853 (15th century). Another less complete late fifteenth-century copy is in MS. Harley 1704. Sloane contains 124 stanzas ababbcbc of four-stress verses. The piece opens with a strophe stating that on a winter midnight the author rose, prayed to Jesus for help, and confessed his sins. Most of the other stanzas are preceded by the first words of the Latin original. Each stanza ends with 'Ne reminiscaris, Domine!'

The Penitential Psalms and the fifteen Gradual Psalms [23] are in the *Primer* or *Lay-Folks' Prayer-Book* (see page 356) in MS. Cbg. Univ. Libr. Dd XI 82 (c. 1420-1430).

PSALTERIUM BEATE MARIÆ [24] is the title of each of two pieces in MS. Vernon (1370-1380). The former is a paraphrase in 1286 verses of a Latin poem in quatrains by Albertus Magnus, each quatrain being rendered by an English stanza ababcdcd of alternate fours and threes. The whole is a series of utterances of praise to the Virgin. Beginning with

the first Psalm and proceeding successively through the first
148 Psalms, the MS. quotes the Latin opening of each Psalm,
and follows it with Albert's quatrain and the English rendering.   Twelve more stanzas are similarly built on the Canticles.

The second piece is a paraphrase of a Latin original ascribed
to Thomas Aquinas.   It proceeds through the first 50 Psalms,
comprising a total of 392 English verses.   This also is a series
of addresses to the Virgin, each composed of a Latin quatrain
with the English paraphrase ababcdcd in alternate fours and
threes.

2.   THE NEW TESTAMENT

THE LIFE OF JESUS [25], probably originally Southern and translated from the French, is in MS. Magdalene College Cbg. Pepys 2498 (late 14th or early 15th century).   It
tells the story of Christ from the Conception to the Resurrection.   The piece is divided into 112 short prose sections or
'gospels,' really a paraphrase, with apocryphal matter, of the
text of the Gospels for Sundays and Festivals, arranged in
chronological order.

THE SOUTHERN TEMPORALE [26] contains the
whole or parts of the stories of the Virgin and of Christ, from
the prophets to Doomsday.   The pieces are partly the product
of a working over of the Gospel lessons (see page 299).

A PROSE VERSION OF SELECTED PARTS OF THE
NEW TESTAMENT [27] is in MSS. Selwyn College 108,
L, 1 (Southern, with Northern traits in *Acts;* c. 1400); Cor-
pus Christi College Cbg. Parker 434 (probably a copy of
Selwyn; c. 1400-1450); Cbg. Univ. Libr. Dd XII 39 (North-
ern East Midland, nearest MS. to Northern original; latter
part of 14th century); Douce 250 (Southern transcript of
a Midland text, Northern traces in *Acts, Peter, James,* and *I
John;* c. 1400); and Holkham Hall 672 (soon after 1400).
Selwyn and Parker have a prologue, *Acts,* most of the Epistles,
Matthew 1-6.13.   Dd has only *Acts.*   Douce has the version

of *Acts* and *Matthew* in Selwyn, Parker, and Dd; but its
Catholic Epistles are from a different version, from which
were borrowed *II-III John* and *Jude* of Selwyn and Parker.
Holkham Hall has the Catholic and the Pauline Epistles as
in Selwyn and Parker.

The collection as a whole falls into three parts. The first
consists of a prologue, *Peter, James, I John,* and the Pauline
Epistles, in a dialect with chiefly South-Western traits; it
is apparently from a version by a man of Kent or the South-
East; and it appears to have formed the original collection.
The second part comprises a collection of mostly Southernized
additions from a Midland version originally of the North or the
North-East Midland; the extant items are the Catholic Epistles, *Acts, Matthew* 1-6.13; *Acts* is the closest to the original
dialect; *II-III John, Jude, Acts,* and *Matthew* seem to be
borrowed from a still earlier version.

The two most complete MSS., Selwyn and Parker, have a
prologue that recounts the chief incidents from the Creation
through the Flood. Then they present a dialogue in which a
monk and a nun, ignorant but inquiring, are instructed by a
brother superior, who on pressure informs them of the story of
Israel to the entrance of the Promised Land, and tells of the
moral, the civil and the ceremonial laws. Thereafter the piece
is dramatic in form. After a break, versions of the various
books of the Bible are recited by the superior. Each piece is
introduced and concluded with connective dialogue or with
address by the priest to the nun. So, like the *Ancren Riwle,*
Rolle's *Psalter* and *Form of Perfect Living* and *Ego Dormio,*
A Luue Ron, the *Wohunge of Ure Louerd,* several versions of
the Benedictine Rule, and other pieces, the collection was
written at least partly for the benefit of nuns.

A COMMENTARY ON MATTHEW, MARK, AND
LUKE [28], composed in the North at about 1350, is largely
borrowed. It voices a low opinion of the clergy, but has little
controversial matter. *Matthew* is in MS. Cbg. Univ. Libr. Ii
II 12 and MS. Egerton 842; *Mark* and *Luke* are in Corpus
Christi College Cbg. Nasmyth XXXII. The expression is awk-

ward, the translator evidently fearing to depart far from his original.

A COMMENTARY ON MATTHEW, LUKE, AND JOHN [29], erroneously assigned to Wycliffe, is of considerable extent, and apparently was issued at three different times. The translation is similar to the Early Wycliffite translation (see page 410). The commentary is made up almost wholly of borrowed extracts. It has been suggested that perhaps the pieces are by the author of the collection of tracts *The Pore Caitif* (see page 482).

A VERSION OF THE PAULINE EPISTLES [30] from the North or North Midland of 1350-1400, is in MS. Corpus Christi College Cbg. 32 (15th century). Paragraph by paragraph the Latin is followed by the close English rendering, with some verbal glosses. The epistle to the Laodiceans is in Latin only.

CLEMENT OF LANTHONY'S HARMONY OF THE GOSPELS [31] (c. 1150) was turned into a fourteenth-century English version preserved in a number of MSS. The translation of the texts is said to differ little from the Earlier Wycliffe version of the Gospels. To this harmony additions were projected. At the end of MS. Royal 17 C XXXIII is a set of translations giving an epitome of Bible doctrines. At the end of MS. Harley 1862 is a similar collection in 166 chapters.

THE BODLEY VERSE PIECES [32]. In MS. Bodley 425 f. 66 v (14th century) are short couplet versions of *John* 1.1-14 ('In beginninge worde it was,' 40 lines); of the Annunciation according to *Luke* 1.26-38 ('In þat time, als was ful wel,' 48 lines); of the Nativity according to *Matthew* 2.1-12 ('When þat Iesus was born yhing,' 50 lines); and of the Commission of the Eleven Apostles according to *Mark* ('In þat time and in þat lande,' 34 lines). The pieces are evidently metrical versions of the Gospels for certain days. The first three correspond to the Gospels for Homilies 17, 7, and 25 of the Harley 4196 form of the Northern Homily Cycle (see page 291); the second and third correspond to Homilies 4 and 13 of the Vernon version of that cycle, and to Homilies 19 and 7 of the original version (see page 288). The similarities in verse-form, in dialect, in matter, and in expression, between these pieces and the Northern Homilies, suggest a common original.

THE RAWLINSON STROPHIC PIECES [33]. The Bodley pieces form indirectly or represent transitional material to the series of four pieces in MS. Rawlinson Poetry 175 (Rawl. F 175) f. 132 (Northern; c. 1350). These pieces all belong to the 'With an O and an I' group (see page 236), repeating 'With an O and an I' in the first half of the next to last line of each strophe. The strophes are aaaaaa of four-stress verses that as a rule have three stresses alliterated. The narrative manner yields somewhat to that of the hymn. The pieces are 'Luke in his lesson,' 48 lines; 'Matthew his manhede,' 48 lines; 'Marke of his myghtes,' 30 lines; and 'Joh'n of his heghnes,' 30 lines.

A BALLAD OF TWELFTH DAY [34], 'Wolle ye iheren of twelte day,' is in MS. Trinity College Cbg. B, 14, 39 (13th century), which contains *Judas* (see page 312) by Child listed as by several centuries the earliest recorded English ballad. The present piece, styled by its editor 'a thirteenth-century literary imitation of a popular ballad,' consists of 80 four-stress lines normally abababab written as 40 long lines. It tells of the visit of the Three Magi, from their first seeing of the Star to their return home.

THE WOMAN OF SAMARIA [35], 'Þo ihesu crist an eorþe was,' is a paraphrase of the Gospel narrative of Jesus at the well. It consists of 77 septenary verses in couplets (the last eight lines aaaa) in MS. Jesus College, Oxford 29 f. 251 v (South-West; c. 1275). It has been suggested that the piece is an antecedent of the Southern Legendary.

THE PARABLE OF THE LABORERS [36] is related in
'*Of a mon Matheu þohte,*' 5 stanzas aabaabccbccb, the *b* lines
of three, the rest of four, stresses, in MS. Harley 2253 f. 70 v
(Southern with Midland traits; c. 1310).   The first four
stanzas relate the parable with much direct discourse; the fifth
applies the story to the poet's own restless state.

THE PASSION OF OUR LORD [37] consists of 353
couplets of seven-stress verses with cæsura in MS. Jesus College Oxford 29 f. 217 (South-West; c. 1275).   The piece
briefly recounts the incidents of the Temptation, and the general course of Christ's life up to the Last Supper; then it
relates in detail with warm feeling all the incidents through
the Passion, the Death, the Burial, and the Resurrection; then,
more briefly, it tells of the Ascension, Pentecost, the general
preaching of the Gospel, and the persecutions by Nero and
Dacian.

The Passion and the Resurrection are treated in various
manners, sometimes independently, sometimes as parts of
larger works (see Southern Legendary, page 321; Northern
Homily Collection, page 320; *Cursor Mundi*, page 339; and
Index).

A LERNYNG TO GOOD LEUYNGE [38], in MS. Digby
102 f. 121 v (beginning 15th century) in 20 stanzas abababab,
is a paraphrase of the Sermon on the Mount.

THE APOCALYPSE OF ST. JOHN [39] with a commentary, formerly erroneously attributed to Wycliffe, is preserved in some 16 MSS., all of Berger's first class.   The oldest
of these is Harley 874 (1340-1370).   The text is in groups of
from three to five verses, each group followed by its commentary.   The latter is usually a close translation of the thirteenth-century Norman commentary on the Apocalypse.   But
there are at least three different translations.   The second
(MSS. Harley 1203 and 171) is basis of the third (MS. Harley 3913).   The first was probably not known to the authors
of the others.   This first version is represented by three classes

of MSS. (a) Harley 874, Magdalene College Cbg. Pepys 2498, Trinity College Cbg. 50; (b) St. John's College Cbg. G 25; (c) Royal 17 A XXVI, Rylands (Manchester) R 4988, Laud 235 and 33. The Harley 3913 rendering is that of the so-called Later Wycliffe version (see below). Apparently still to be grouped are MSS. Trinity Coll. Dublin A, 4, 4, Phillipps 7219 and 10170, and Rawlinson C 750 (a fragment).

Here should be mentioned the treatment of the matter of the Apocalypse in the *Pearl*, lines 865 ff. (see page 581).

THE GOSPEL OF NICODEMUS [40], in English, is discussed under Legends (see page 326).

3.   The Wycliffe-Purvey Translations of the Bible

Wycliffe and his immediate associates were the producers of two English versions of the Scriptures [41]. The so-called Early Version was completed probably at about 1382, at latest before 1384. The Later Version was completed perhaps in 1388, at least by 1400.

Just what part Wycliffe himself had in these translations, is a matter of debate. It is commonly accepted that Nicholas of Hereford had charge of the Old Testament part of the Early Version. The translators' original copy of this version and a transcript of it (MSS. Bodley 959 and Douce 369) both break off at Baruch 3.19; the transcript ends with a note, 'Explicit translacionem Nicholay de herford.' The translators' copy is in five hands. It appears most acceptable to assume that a number of coadjutors participated in the work. This Early Version of the Old Testament, though especially careful, is awkward and often not clear; as a whole it follows the Latin expression too closely. The rest of the version is better in these respects.

The Later Version is generally assumed to be largely by John Purvey, an active Wycliffite. This is an accurate translation, and is much more idiomatic and easy than is the Early Version. Its popularity is attested by preservation of over a hundred and fifty MS. copies of it.

CHAPTER IX

DIALOGUES, DEBATES, CATECHISMS

From the earliest times, among most peoples the dialogue of one type or another has been an agreeable literary form and an acceptable medium for the conveyance of truth. In the Orient it was a favorite. Its prominence in Greek and Roman literature is suggested by mere mention of the names of Xenophon, Plutarch, Plato, Cicero, and Lucian. Its part in pastoral composition is well known. The early Christian writers found it a most effective means for doctrine. In it, through simple interchange of speech, or catechisms, or battle pieces after the *Psychomachia* type, or debates between two personages real or imagined, a long line of mediæval writers of Latin found voice for their matters up to the time of the failure of that tongue in literary use. From the twelfth century on, the folk, the court, and the learned, cherished the dialogue in all the languages of Western Europe. There is scarcely need to allude to its prominence in Provence and North France in the *partimen*, the *tenson*, the *feigned tenson*, and the *jeu parti*. It had influence on the beginnings of modern drama.

In Middle English of before 1400 a few pieces in forms of dialogue survive. They may be grouped into three general classes: 1. *Dialogues*; 2. *Debates*; 3. *Catechisms*.

1. Dialogues

THE DEBATE BETWEEN THE BODY AND THE SOUL [1], so-called, has had a remarkably wide and long popularity. Versions are extant in Latin, Greek, French, Provençal, German, Dutch, Spanish, Italian, Danish, and English. The various versions fall into two general classes: first, those in which only the Soul speaks, chiding the Body for the evil life it has led; second, those in which the Body, accused, retorts with accusations of the Soul as responsible. The writings of the second class are the more numerous. They appear to descend from a Latin poem of the later twelfth century, perhaps written in England, and ascribed variously to St. Philibertus, St. Bernard, and Walter Mapes. There appears to be a dependence between the two classes.

In English there are extant the speech of the lost Soul to its Body in the Exeter Book; the speech of the saved Soul to its Body in the Vercelli Book; the Worcester Cathedral fragments respectively of 46, 45, 50, 50, 52, 50, 56 alliterative lines of the twelfth century in a South-Western dialect; a fragment of 25 South-Western alliterative verses of the twelfth century in MS. Bodley 343 f. 170 r (c. 1150-1175), given the titles *The Grave* and *Fragment on Death;* a fragment of 24 lines, a mixture of short couplets and alliterative verses, many defective, in MS. Trinity College Cbg. B, 14, 39 (13th century), a part of an address of a Soul to its Body.

There are also six texts in four-stress verses abababab, all from one original MS. containing an argument between the Soul and the Body, in MSS. Laud 108 f. 200 v (part I, c. 1290), 490 verses, the last four French; Auchinleck f. 31 v (c. 1330-1340), 592 verses with end defective; Royal 18 A X f. 61 v (1350-1400 or after 1400), 536 verses; Vernon f. 285 v (1370-1380), 496 verses; Br. Mus. Additional 22283 (1380-1400), first 198 verses of Vernon; and Digby 102 f. 136 v (beginning 15th century), 536 verses. This piece has a narrative frame, with very short narrative connectives between the speeches, which are of irregular length.

The poet tells that, as he lay just before dawn of a winter's day, he saw lingering by the bier the spirit of a knight who had led an ill life. The Soul asked at length where were the glory and possessions that the Body had enjoyed (see page 389); the Body had brought her to Hell. The Body replied that the Soul had had the control, and was responsible. The Soul declared the decay and dispersion the Body should suffer, and its then repellant condition; and she asserted that the Body had not obeyed her. Then trooped in a thousand and more devils, whose appearance and behavior the poet describes with much detail. These tortured the Soul with

ingenious torments.   The Soul cried out to Christ, but the devils
declared such appeal vain.   So she was cast into the devils' pit
through an opening in the earth, which closed again over her.
Sweating with fear, the poet cried out for God's mercy when he
should die.   Let men seek shrift and repentance.   Christ's mercy
surpasses all sin.

Another working over of the argument between the Soul and
the Body, with insertion of matter from the widely treated
Signs before Judgment (see page 328), is in MSS. Digby 86 f.
195 v (1272-1283) in 69 stanzas abababab, and Harley 2253
f. 57 r (c. 1310) in 248 verses usually alternating four and
three stresses, and usually abababab.   The speeches are each of
four lines, one line of which is sometimes narrative connective.

In a dark place the poet stood listening to a 'strif' between a
Soul and its Body on a bier.   The Soul chides the Body for cheating
and falseness; points out its loss of worldly treasures; declares
worms shall devour it; and asks why did it not bethink it of Christ
by night and by day?   To these several speeches the Body replies
that it deemed its joys lasting; now Death holds it fast; worms
possess it; well does it know it shall rot; let the Soul fare away,
the Body suffers enough; chiding avails not.   The Soul describes
seriatim the signs before Doomsday, and then the Judgment.
Finally, the poet tells that the Soul went to Hell, and that the
Body rots endlessly in the earth.   He reminds that the dead are
soon forgotten; worldly gear avails not, and is soon lost.   Were
not Christ's mercy greater among us, we should all come to a sorry
end.

All the treatments are remarkable for their dignified and
solemn impressiveness.   On the 'ubi sunt' formula used in these
versions, see page 389.

A blaming of the Body by the Soul makes up a large part of
Death in MSS. Cotton Caligula A IX and Jesus College Oxf.
29 (see page 392).   In MS. Porkington 10 (~~Phillipps 8336~~;
c. 1460) is the *Vision of Philibert* in seven-line stanzas.

THE VICES AND VIRTUES [2], a Kentish or South-
Eastern bordering on Kentish prose piece of about 1200, is the
earliest extant Middle English dialogue.   It is in MS. Stowe
240 (c. 1200); the beginning is lost; in print it covers 75
pages.

A Soul confesses to Reason its sins—sorrow, sloth, pride, disobedience, swearing, and eight others—with careful explanation,
the matter being grouped into sections each headed with the name
of the sin under discussion.   At the end, the Soul asks Reason for
direction to become reconciled with Christ.   Reason urges cherishing of the three Christian Virtues, which it describes severally.   On
promise of the Soul to cherish these, Reason urges humility, fear,
pity, knowledge, etc.   The Soul bidding it proceed, Reason dilates
on the Christian Virtues as chief components of the Temple of God,
whose foundation is the Soul.   The Body now protests and explains
that, though Christ ennobled the Body by entering into human flesh,
the Body and the Soul are of different natures.   Reason shows both
should work in accord.   Then it discourses on Peace, Prudence,
Foresight, Righteousness, and twenty-three other virtues.   In conclusion, it recommends the Soul to practice its counsels, and to
thank and praise God.

This dignified and elevated piece is, then, really a series of
expositions of the topics indicated, each topic isolated and
labeled, the whole united by the loose dialogue device. Of
much interest is the allegorical section on *Mercy*, wherein is a
dialogue between Mercy, Truth, Pity, Peace, and Patience
based on 'Misericordia et veritas obviaverunt sibi,' etc., from
the *Psalter*.

THE DIALOGUE BETWEEN THE VIRGIN AND
CHRIST ON THE CROSS [3], 'Stond wel, moder, vnder
rode,' is in MSS. Harley 2253 f. 79 r (c. 1310; Southern) in 66
lines, and Digby 86 f. 127 r (1272-1283) in 54 lines, all lines
four-stressed aabccb.   Brandl assigns the poem to the South-
East Midland.   Stanzas 1-9, though differently arranged,
correspond closely in the two MSS.   They are pure dialogue
without narrative, Christ speaking from the Cross lines 1-3
of each stanza, Mary replying in lines 4-6.

Christ urges Mary to cease weeping, and to look gladly on Him,
her tears are to Him worse than death; He is redeeming Adam and
all his kin; now Mary knows the sorrow of women who bear children; His time is come, He must go to Hell for her sake.   Mary
replies that she cannot be glad; at her heart is the sword that
Simeon promised; let Him not blame her; may she die before Him;
He helps all in need; she suffers so that she well-nigh dies.—Harley
adds two stanzas of narrative stating that at the Resurrection Mary's
sorrow was turned to joy; and concludes with prayer for her intervention and for Christ's intercession.

The poem is truly dramatic, and has much genuine pathos. Similarity is seen to the *Stabat Mater* in the first line and in the strophe-form, and to *'Jesu Cristes milde moder'* in matter (see page 518). With the piece should be compared the Christ on the Cross lyrics (see page 515).

A DISPUTISON BI-TWENE CHILDE JESU AND MAISTRES OF THE LAWE OF JEWUS [4] is in MSS. Vernon f. 300 (1370-1380) and Br. Mus. Additional 22283 (1380-1400). The piece is Kentish of about 1275-1300 in 215 four-stress verses abababab, lines 57-68 being ababababab. There are commonly three alliterative syllables in the line. The poem consists of direct discourse with short narrative connectives.

It tells of Christ in the Temple—of his discomfiting of the hostile Hebrew sages, first, by His knowledge of the letter A as symbolizing the Trinity and the Deity, since it is the chief letter and made with three strokes; next, by expounding the prophecies and nature of His birth; then, by defending His divinity. Romans who were there knew by prophecy that He was Christ, and honored Him.

THE LAMENTATION OF MARY TO ST. BERNARD [5] is in two versions. The former, independent of the latter, is lines 23945-24658 of the *Cursor Mundi* (see page 339) in stanzas of tail-rime aabaab. It is from a Latin sermon of St. Bernard, especially as preserved in the Antwerp edition of 1616. Its introductory address to the Virgin (ll. 23945-68) is the property of the *Cursor* poet, with some ideas from Bernard. The rest is chiefly an inartistic reproduction, with expansions and some additions, of Bernard.

The second version is in MSS. Cotton Tiberius E VII f. 82 (c. 1400), 712 verses; Vernon f. 286 (1370-1380), 736 verses; Rawlinson Poetry 175 f. 76 (c. 1350), 712 verses; Cbg. Univ. Libr. Dd I 1 f. 21 (15th century), 764 verses; Trinity College Oxf. 57 f. 167 (late 14th or beginning 15th century), 548 verses, incomplete; and Laud 463 (or L 70; end of 14th century), 859 verses. This version is in four-stress verses ababab. It is based on the sermon ascribed to St. Bernard that was used for the first version. Additions are from the Gospels, especially *St. John.* The matter is dealt with in French poems in MSS. Cbg. Univ. Libr. Gg I 1 and Royal 19 C II. As Dd has two final stanzas opening, 'This ryme mad an hermyte. . . . Barfot he wente in gray habite . . . ,' the piece has been ascribed to Rolle (see page 446). It has been assigned also to Maidenstone (see page 404) and Nassyngton (see page 463). Kribel and Brandl locate the poem in the South-East of the Midland, Horstmann and Fröhlich in the North.

All the MSS. but Trinity open with four stanzas stating the author's desire to help the ignorant. Christ's Passion brought Mary unspeakable grief. Once, in a church, Bernard besought her to tell how she sorrowed, for he would have his heart melted. Mary acquiesces. Bernard asking specific questions between the stages, as an eye-witness and sorrowing mother she tells, with affecting detail born of warm imagination and sympathy, the story of the Passion from Gethsemane up to the Resurrection. Bernard thanks her; what he has heard will protect him from evil.

With the dialogues should be connected the various pieces on the themes of *Christ on the Cross* and the *Compassion of Mary* (see pages 515 ff.).

In MS. Sion Coll. Arc. L. 40, 2ª+² (15th century) is said to be 'A Legend of the Virgin Mary's Sorrows, as supposed to be revealed by her to St. Bernard in a Dialogue with him.'

THE DISPUTE BETWEEN MARY AND THE CROSS

[6] (according to the *Apocrypha*, say the MSS.) is in MSS. Vernon f. 315 v (1370-1380), 528 verses, and Royal 18 A X f. 126 (less complete), 372 verses. There is much alliteration. The stanzas are abababababcdddc, the *c* lines of three, the rest of four, stresses. Vernon 1 and 40 and Royal 2 and last are aabaabaabaabcdddc, the *a* and *b* verses of two stresses, the rest normal. Royal prefaces an introductory stanza, and omits stanzas 11, 16, 17, 19, 22, 24-32 of Vernon. The piece is of the South-West Midland of about 1350, and belongs to a large group of Laments of Mary (see page 515), of which are extant several versions in Middle Dutch by Mærlant, one in Provençal, and a number in Latin. A Latin piece, 'Crux, de te volo conqueri,' in 98 lines by Philippe de Grève (*obiit* 1236) has many parallels with Vernon 1-147; all the matter

of its first 72 lines is in Vernon. In the first 478 lines the English piece proceeds by interchange of long speeches, with single-
line connectives. It has no poetical merit, and is too long
drawn out.

Mary chides the Cross for defiling and torturing her Son. The
Cross shows it did all for good. Mary urges Paul's declaration of
the cruelty of the Jews and the lamentation of the prophets; why
did the Cross rend her Son? The Cross shows it did so to save
Man. Mary declares Christ's sufferings and her grief; why did
not the Cross crack? The Cross replies that it bore Christ to tame
the Devil, to give baptism, and at Doomsday to accuse Christ's
tormenter. The writer states that Mary kissed the Cross, and that
she uses it to bring men from Hell; the Cross was deaf and dumb,
but had speech and hearing given it to set back the Devil.

A DISPUTISON BY-TWENE A CRISTENEMON AND
A JEW [7], in MS. Vernon f. 301 (1370-1380), consists of 20
stanzas aaabcccbdddbeeeb, the *b* lines of two or three stresses,
the others of four. The piece is actually a very realistic story
with very free use of dialogue.

Two clerks of divinity, one an Englishman, the other a Jew, at
Paris disputed vainly all one day. The Christian maintained sal-
vation by the Cross and the Virgin Birth. The Jew argued for one
God who had no son. For this the Christian promised him Hell.
The Jew wagered he would show his opponent Christ on the Cross.
Through a cleft in the earth they came to a fair manor like Para-
dise, with lovely gardens, singing birds, and fair flowers; and all
Arthur's Table Round were there. At a nunnery they were splen-
didly feasted; but the Christian would not eat. There they saw
Christ on the Cross. The Christian exhibited a mass-wafer that
he had secretly brought. The building burst, the show vanished.
The Jew acknowledged that his craft was devilish, and that God
is three in one; and he was christened. The Christian was Sir
Walter of Berwick, whom the Pope made a penitencer.

The story illustrates the magic fairy castle of the romances.
The *Disputison* seems based on a form in Thomas Cantimpre's
Bonum Universale de Apibus (*De Falso Demonum Apparata*,
1256-1263), which is a variation of an incident in the eighth-
century *Life* of St. Wulfram.

With the dialogues should be connected '*In a fryht as y con
fere*' (see page 495), '*My deþ y loue*' (see page 495), and the

pieces on Christ on the Cross and the Compassion of Mary
(see pages 515 ff.).—To be noted here are Trevisa's dialogues
(see page 206).

2. DEBATES

THE OWL AND THE NIGHTINGALE [8], from about
1220 and Dorsetshire, is in MSS. Cotton Caligula A IX f. 233
r (before 1250) and Jesus College Oxf. 29 (Bodleian Library)
f. 229 r (c. 1275). The two MSS. are from a common original,
which was a copy. The poem consists of 897 short couplets,
two of the lines being omitted in one MS. and two others in
the other. The Nicholas of Guildford chosen as umpire by
the birds (ll. 191, 1746), can hardly be the author. The John
of Guildford who wrote his name in some verses in the Jesus
MS. now extant only in a copy by Thomas Wilkins on another
part of the MS., can be claimed as author on only most questionable evidence. A recent attempt has been made to identify
Nicholas with a 'Nicholaus submonitor capituli de Gudeford'
in 1220, and a 'Nicholaus capellanus archidiaconi' testator of
a document at Salisbury in 1209.

In a hidden nook of a valley the poet heard an Owl and a Nightingale debate long and loud. From a flowery beech the Nightingale
looked scornfully at the Owl on her old stump, and bade her begone
for her loathly singing. At nightfall the Owl replied; had she the
Nightingale in her claws, the latter would sing a different song.
The Nightingale answers that all birds are .enemies of the Owl
because of her monstrous aspect, her vile food, and the filthy habits
of her offspring. Furious, the Owl seeks to entice her opponent
from her safe shelter in the beech. But the Nightingale declares
cunning is better than fighting; let them argue for precedence.
Master Nicholas of Guildford is chosen arbiter; but at once the
Nightingale chides the Owl as blind, a creature of the dark, and
hence evil. The Owl retorts that she is of the hawk's kind; abuse
does not prove baseness, the wise ignore it; her voice is powerful
and ringing, more agreeable because *it* is not active all night long;
she can see by day, but prefers to fly by night. Hard put to it,
the Nightingale accuses the Owl of singing only where woe is;
her own song ever rejoices, and when hard days come she flies
away. The Owl replies that she sings in Winter when friends
foregather, and especially at Christmas; the Nightingale is full
of lust, and sings but to encourage lust; the Owl sings to hearten

the distressed; her opponent is but a chatterbox, fond of dirty perches by night and evil food, while she herself rids barns and churches of mice, and has fine clean abodes in the woods; her birds are no fouler than are other younglings. Much put out, the Nightingale exclaims that she sings merrily to remind of the bliss of Heaven; she is not powerful, but she is clever, and a single effective art is more than many inferior ones. Nay, retorts the Owl, it is not singing, but repentance and sorrow for others, that leads to Heaven; her song helps men to these—the Nightingale never helps so, and never sang in any of the distressed places like Galway or Ireland. The Nightingale defends her noble office of singing in the garden while lovers are abed; life is not to be made up of lamenting; song would be pure waste in Galway or Ireland. The Owl exclaims, 'You entice to lasciviousness, one of your kind was torn to pieces for such.' 'The man who did the deed paid for it heavily, to the honor of all my kindred,' cries the Nightingale; 'I may sing where I will, but all folk seek thy life; birds hate thee for thou art horrible of appearance and forbodest evil—cursed be thou!' 'Curse thyself!' replies the Owl; 'I foreknow all ill-fortune, and I beneficently forewarn men of it; your arguments bring you but shame.' 'You practice witchcraft,' says the Nightingale, 'you must purge yourself of it, for you are accursed everywhere; I do not entice to spouse-breaking, I encourage lawful love, and warn those who would go amiss—but every good may be turned to evil.' 'The ladies turn to me in distress, and I encourage them,' cries the Owl; 'true, men seek my life, but in return I do them good—even when slain I make a good scarecrow.' 'You confess! you boast of your own shame!' exclaims the Nightingale;—and she sang out so loud that a host of birds assembled about them, and chanted in mockery of the Owl. The Owl declared she would summon all the hook-billed and sharp-clawed birds; but she reminded her opponent of the agreement to arbitrate. The Wren bade preserve the King's peace, and submit to the judge. All flew off to the home of Nicholas at Portishom in Dorset—and the poet knows no more of the matter.

So, the poem presents, in narrative frame with short narrative comments, an actual debate, where argument is met by argument. The fact that the contention is concerning superiority of personal worth, distinguishes the poem among the Middle English contention pieces. Though in Provençal, Latin, and French up to 1250, never more than one of the two contestants is bird or beast, in the *Owl* not only the principals but all the actors and many of the persons in the illustrations and by-incidents, are lower animals. All of this reminds of the popularity of stories and of descriptions of characteristics and properties of animals in the period—of fables, bestiaries, and works on natural history such as Neckam's *De Naturis Rerum* (see pages 180 ff.). The *Owl* is the predecessor of a long line of animal contests, such as the *Thrush and the Nightingale* (see page 421), the *Fox and the Wolf* (see page 183), the *Cuckow and the Nightingale* (see page 423), Dunbar's *Merle and the Nightingale,* Henryson's *Lion and the Mouse,* etc.— No direct source for the whole or a part of the poem (except several of the proverbs) has been traced. The Provençal *partimen, tenson,* and *feigned tenson* had no direct influence on the form. Little direct influence of the North-French *tenson* or *jeu parti* or *feigned tenson* can be suspected. It is rather, to narrative French poems imitative of the Latin duels that one should look for possible French influence. Individually and as a class the Latin contentions, especially the duels, are closest in characteristics to the *Owl.* Probably many of the traits in the English poem originated in the poet's own mind. Most of the similarities to other pieces are such merely in the bare fact of general similarity; the embodiment, the use, the prominence, and the extent of influence, of the characteristic, are always unlike those in the other pieces.

Of striking vigor and originality of mind, possessing a sane critical judgment founded on a considerable culture, and endowed with astonishing poetical gifts for his time and environment, the poet produced a work that seems the earliest and, from many points of view, the best, original long poem of a wholly imaginative character written in English before the time of Chaucer. The poem is beneath all didactic; but it is literature. It is very frank, impartial, judicial. As is true of all that is general and universal, the matter and the presentation of the piece could in its day and now be appropriated to perhaps many local and contemporary conditions; but they could be assigned definitely to no one alone, and not to the local or the contemporary alone. Neither the teaching nor the method of presentation is that of the learned or the priestly writer in English of the date. They are both rather representative of the popular element, they are based on practical experience, breadth of view and common-sense, sane humor, and a desire to please. Life was to the author precious for its own sake as well as a means to Heaven. The verses are full of minute touches that could come only from an appreciative and sympathetic lover of Nature and the lower animals, and of human life and character. As the poet did not allow himself to be drawn into a narrow or ascetic view of life, so he did not follow slavishly any foreign fashion or (apparently) translate or paraphrase a foreign original. From other writings he seems to have got but very general suggestion for the form of the poem. From the syllable-counting French short couplet he obtained suggestion for a regularity needed to control the disintegrating Teutonic accentual line; and thence he produced graceful, free verses that are unequaled in English before Chaucer. He was indebted to the dialectical spirit of the period, but he wrote pure literature. His theme, the discord between the apparently irreconcilable elements Duty and Pleasure, Seriousness and Joyousness, was an old one. But theme and treatment grew here out of the poet's own immediate experience. His authority was the popular wisdom crystallized into the proverbs of which he was fond (see page 376). While he apparently leaves the problem unsolved, he gives the solution as far as it can be given—there is good in all that is used rightly. Further, the poem is notable in its period for its embodiment of the distinctly national tone and spirit that were beginning to grow out of the amalgamation of the French and the English, the learned and the popular, in the island. It is characterized by appreciation of the lighter graces and pleasures of life; sympathy with æsthetic appeal; sureness and precision of presentation; sustained unity of plan and execution; artistic finish; aptness, deftness, spontaneity, spirited dramatic conception and effortless execution; arch humor; independence of attitude; freedom in theory and in practice; naturalness in plan and in effect; sane common-sense; sound ethics and right morals; a dominant seriousness, and steadfastness and devotion to higher purpose.

THE THRUSH AND THE NIGHTINGALE [9] is in

MS. Auchinleck (1330-1340), 74 verses of the beginning of the poem, and MS. Digby 86 f. 136 (1272-1283), 192 verses. The piece is in stanzas aabccbddbeeb, the *b* verses of three, the rest of four, stresses. Especially in lines 1-48, the two texts agree closely in matter. The poem is Southern, probably of the reign of Edward I, and was influenced by the *Owl and the Nightingale*. Its opening is similar to that of '*Lenten ys come wiþ loue to toune*' (see page 494). The matter is not new (see page 234). The piece is animated, dramatic, and realistic. Except for one place in Digby, the speeches proceed alternately without connective narrative. Auchinleck has indication of the speaker at the head of each speech.

On a beautiful May morning full of song of birds and blooming flowers, the poet hears debate a Thrush and a Nightingale. The former attacks women as treacherous, fickle, workers of woe, ready ever to do shame. The latter defends them as peace-makers, as sweet companions of men; none is wicked, all are meek and mild, still they keep themselves pure, they give their mates the dearest joy. The debate proceeds with interchange of personal recriminations, until the Nightingale reminds that Christ was born of Mary. The Thrush at once acknowledges he has been wrong; he will never again say ill of maid or of wife; he will leave the land, he cares not whither he shall go.

THE DEBATE BETWEEN THE HEART AND THE EYE [10], of considerable currency in Latin and in French in the period, is represented (1) by five English couplets following a Latin prose condensed text and a French version of nine verses, in MS. Merton College 248 f. 132 r col. 2 (late 14th century); and (2) by four English couplets in Johannis de Grimstone's commonplace book compiled in 1372 and preserved as MS. Advocates' Libr. Edinburgh 18, 7, 21 f. 99 v.

In these versions there are two exchanges of speeches: the Heart accuses the Eye of being the ready gate through which enter sin and evil thought; and the Eye replies that the Heart is responsible— for it has not exercised its power to restrain the Eye. In the final lines, Reason, as arbiter, judges that the Eye weep, and that the Heart sorrow and repent.

The resemblances in the first two lines of the two versions are probably due to dependence on a common Latin original.

Both of the English pieces belong, not to the commoner courtly type of the *Debate between the Heart and the Eye*, but to the rarer theological type, in which sin, and not love, is the theme. The condensed treatment in the two pieces has well been said to produce resemblance to the *exemplum*.

A DISPUTISON BITWENE A GOD MAN AND THE DEUEL [11], dating from about 1350, is in MSS. Vernon f. 288 (1370-1380) and Br. Mus. Additional 22283 (1380-1400). It consists of 987 verses in unequal groups of short couplets alternating with unequal groups of couplets of doggerel lines of from five to eight stresses. The piece is in dialogue with narrative introduction (ll. 1-38 not in Additional) and conclusion, and with brief connectives. The Devil speaks in short couplets; the Man, except at the end, in the doggerel.

On his way from Church the Good Man related to a handsome emissary of the Devil the gist of the sermon he had just heard on the Deadly Sins. The Devil sought to make the Man revolt against God for letting folk suffer, and then to make him believe the Sins not reprehensible. All the arguments the Man met at length. The Devil becoming mad with wrath, the Man suspected his nature. He compelled him to show himself black and stinking foully, and ordered him back to Hell. Then he went home thanking God.

The arguments of the Devil are well put, and the replies of the Man are ordered, sensible, and personal, despite accord with conventional teaching. Much effective doctrine is cleverly enunciated. Of interest is the bit of satire against the fashion in dress of the time.

THE BOOK OF CUPID or THE CUCKOO AND THE NIGHTINGALE [12], ascribed by Thynne to Chaucer, is dated by some as early as 1389-1390, by others after 1400. The body of the poem consists of 58 stanzas of pentameter verses aabba in MSS. Fairfax 16 f. 36 v, Bodley 638 f. 11 v, Cbg. Univ. Libr. Ff I 6 f. 22 r, Bodley Tanner 346 f. 97 r, and Bodley Selden B 24 f. 138 v, all of the fifteenth century. Cambridge adds two seven-line stanzas. Tanner appends a 'balade with envoy,' Fairfax the *balade* alone. The piece shows influence of the *Legend of Good Women,* the *Parlement of Foules,*

and the *Owl and the Nightingale,* among other works.   The
'Clanvowe' mentioned at the end of Cambridge, is now generally
accepted as the author of the poem.   It is debated whether he
was Sir John Clanvowe, who was long in the public service and
who died before March 4, 1392, or Sir Thomas Clanvowe, probably son of John.

Feeling the supreme power of the God of Love and of the Spring-
time, the poet determined to seek the Nightingale.   Sitting by a
stream in a flowery land, and listening to the song of birds, he
fell asleep and dreamed.   So, he heard a Cuckoo and a Nightingale
contend, first concerning their song, then concerning their bur- .
den.   The Cuckoo opposed Love and lovers, the Nightingale favored
them.   The Nightingale fell to weeping.   The poet drove away the
Cuckoo.   The Nightingale declared fealty to him, and counseled
him as to his behavior.   Then she summoned the birds of the dale,
and told of the chiding with the Cuckoo.   They all determined
on a parliament on St. Valentine's Day.   The Nightingale gave
thanks, and flew away;—and the poet awoke.

The poem is graceful and pleasing.   Perhaps it afforded
some suggestion for Milton's *To a Nightingale.*   Wordsworth
effectively paraphrased it.

3.   CATECHISMS

With exception of *Ypotis* and *Inter Diabolus et Virgo,* the
Middle English catechisms are dialogues between a learner and
a master.

ELUCIDARIUM *sive Dialogus de Summa Totius Christianæ Theologiæ* [13], composed in three books of Latin prose
perhaps before 1092 by Honorius Augustodunensis (Honoré
d'Autun), was turned into English.   A close translation of
Book I Caps. 23-25 and Book II Caps. 1-6, is in MS. Cotton
Vespasian D XIV ff. 163 v and 159 (c. 1125) in a hand different from that of the rest of the MS.

A Tretis þat Is Clepid Lucidarie, of the late fourteenth or
early fifteenth century, is in MSS. St. John's College Cbg. G
25 (15th century) and Cbg. Univ. Libr. Ii VI 26 f. 158 (15th
century).   It is a version of the first and a part of the second
book of the *Elucidarium,* and makes in print 34 pages.   Eleven

final questions and answers exhibiting Wycliffite views, are added to the first book, and two to the second.

From the *Elucidarium* are seven riming questions and answers in MS. Ashmole 59, which was written by Shirley in the first half of the fifteenth century.—Another 'echo' in two short couplets is in MS. Rawlinson F 35 f. 205 in a hand of 1450-1475.

QUESTIONES BY-TWENE THE MAISTER OF OXENFORD AND HIS CLERKE [14] (prose, making in print two pages) is in MS. Harley 1304. In matter and expression it is commonly close to the Old English prose *Salomon and Saturnus* (MS. Cotton Vitellius A XV; not to be confused with the very different Old English verse *Salomon* in MSS. Corpus Christi Coll. Cbg. 41 and 422) and *Adrian and Ritheus* (MS. Cotton Julius A II). The two Old English pieces have much matter and phrasing in common, and probably represent fragmentarily parts of one original. The materials and the form have been shown to have been widely popular. As do the other two pieces, Harley consists of a series of questions and answers between a master and a learner. Here each question is a single brief sentence; each answer usually is one sentence.

Among much else, the clerk learns God's location at the first Creation, God's first speech, the derivation of the name 'Heaven,' a definition of God, the elements of which Adam was composed, the derivation of his name, his age and stature when created, God's favorite flowers and bird, etc.

In MS. Lansdowne 762 (1500-1550) is an abbreviated version of the *Questiones* close to the 'dialogue' of *Salomon and Saturnus*.

YPOTIS [15], the story of the *Wise Child* or *L'Enfant Sage*, is a series of questions and answers between the Emperor Hadrian of Rome and the child Ypotis or Epictetus. The theme took rise from the Latin dialogues *Adrian et Epictitus* and *Disputatio Adriani Augusti et Epicteti Philosophi*, and had great popularity in the Middle Ages. Many versions were composed in Latin, Provençal, French, Cymric, Catalan, and Castilian. In English exist eleven MSS., of which the earliest are Vernon (1370-1380) and Br. Mus. Additional 22283 (1380-1400). The piece consists of 311 short couplets. Suchier has found the English most closely related to the Provençal; but as direct Provençal influence is not found elsewhere in Middle English, the version is probably from a lost French text. The original English was probably from between the East Midland and the South-East, but not from Kent. The piece attempts to present in a short space a large body of theological dogma, to make it palatable by locating it in a narrative framework, and to give it credence by putting it in the mouth of the sage child (identified later with the Child Christ) and by declaring St. John the Evangelist to be the author of the original account. The piece has no intrinsic literary value, but its doctrines and explanations of doctrine are of interest.

INTER DIABOLUS ET VIRGO [16] consists of 22 irregular short couplets in MS. Rawlinson 328 f. 174 v (15th century). The matter, perhaps the piece, is earlier than 1400.

The Devil declares to a maiden that, if she will be his faithful leman, he will teach her all the wisdom in the world. He asks her a series of questions; these she must answer correctly, or be his lover. Through prayer, the maid is able to give the right replies. Then she bids the fiend be still, she will speak no more with him.

CHAPTER X

SCIENCE, INFORMATION, DOCUMENTS

Scientific and documentary composition of all sorts in the period was for the most part not in English. Yet there survive in the vernacular a few technical treatises, medical recipes, pieces on virtues of plants, statements of the characteristics of countries or of districts, glosses, specifications of measures, writings on natural philosophy, charms, interpretations of dreams and natural phenomena, documents, etc. For convenience these are all dealt with in the present chapter.

1. Treatises on Hunting

THE TREATISE ON HUNTING [1] of Twici, Court-Huntsman of Edward II, is extant in French in MSS. Phillipps 8336 (here 1350-1400) and Caius College Cbg. 424 (late 14th century); and in English in MS. Cotton Vespasian A XII (c. 1420). It was written originally in Norman French in or before 1328. The English version has 35 introductory pentameter verses with irregular rime, followed by 11 short prose sections giving directions for hunting the hare, the hart, the buck, and the boar. The colophon ascribes the work to 'Twety' and 'Johan Gyfford.'

THE MASTER OF GAME [2] is to be mentioned here, though it was written probably between 1406 and 1413 by Edward III's grandson, Edward, second Duke of York. The piece is in prose, and is preserved in two versions, the original one in nineteen MSS., the other in five MSS. Some of the MSS. have many illuminations. Thirty-one of the thirty-six chapters are translations, with illustrations, of Gaston de Foix's *Livre de Chasse*, which was begun, according to its preface, May 1, 1387. The five original chapters afford much valuable evidence as to the changes in hunting since the Conquest.

2. MEDICAL AND PLANT TREATISES

PERI DIDAXEON [3], in MS. Harley 6258 f. 83 v (12th century), is a collection of medical recipes in captions, breaking off in the midst of Caption 67. The source is indirectly or partly the *Practica* of Petrocellus or Petronius Salernitanus, written about 1035. The English piece is perhaps of the beginning of the twelfth century.

MEDICINA DE QUADRUPEDIBUS [4], found also in several earlier MSS., is in MS. Harley 6258 f. 44 (12th century). This prose piece gives instructions for medical use of the badger, the fox, the hare, the goat, the ram, the boar, and the wolf; and it adds several special cures for physical ills.

THE SCIENCE OF CIRURGIE [5] is an English prose version of Lanfranc's elaborate treatise. It was composed perhaps between 1387 and 1400, and is preserved in MSS. Ashmole 1396 (? c. 1380) and Br. Mus. Additional 12056 (c. 1420).

THE HENSLOWE MS. RECIPES [6] are in a manuscript of before 1400 that was in 1899 in the possession of Professor J. G. Henslowe, formerly Lecturer on Botany at St. Bartholomew's Hospital Medical School. It is a collection of medical recipes in English prose inserted among Latin recipes.

RECIPES IN THE BRITISH MUSEUM [7]. In Vol. 101, Class Catalogue of MSS. of the British Museum there are various entries of collections of medical recipes in Latin, French, and English, from the ninth to the eighteenth century. About fifty are in English, and about forty in Latin, of the fourteenth century. Parts of the English recipes (originally Northern) of MSS. Harley 2378 (Southern), Sloane 2584 (Midland, near 1400), and Sloane 521 (c. 1400, by a scribe of Norman birth, in Kent), have been edited.

STOCKHOLM RECIPES [8]. A list of 28 brief recipes and charms for physicians, of probably the end of the fourteenth century and the South-East Midland, is in MS. Royal Library Stockholm Med. Miscell. XIV (15th century). Of these Items 10, 25, 26 are Latin, and Item 24 is French. All the items are in prose—except Item 27, which is ababacac of four-stress lines.

PHILLIPPS RECIPES [9]. A more extensive originally Northern prose collection of medical recipes, is on a fragment of a fourteenth-century MS. (No. 335) formerly owned by J. O. Halliwell-Phillipps. The MS. has several short additions of the end of the fourteenth or the first of the fifteenth century. The last recipes seem to go back to Old English medical collections.

STOCKHOLM-ADDITIONAL VERSE RECIPES [10]. In MSS. Royal Library Stockholm Med. Miscell. XIV (15th century) and Br. Mus. Additional 17866 f. 5 r (early 15th century), is a group of medical recipes in short couplets. The two MSS. vary considerably from each other. The Stockholm MS. consists of 496 verses of prescriptions, followed by 965 verses of a medico-botanical nature. In the Additional MS. the medico-botanical section comprises 753 verses, and precedes 370 verses of prescriptions. Both MSS. show traces of a Northern dialect.

FIFTEENTH-CENTURY RECIPES [11]. A collection of medical recipes of considerable extent is in MSS. Br. Mus. Additional 33996, Sloane 3153, Royal 17 A III, Royal 19, 674, Harley 1600, and Sloane 405. The matter was written down perhaps by several hands in 1400-1450. Additional at least was probably of the Southern East Midland, with its second part of a more Northerly character.

Other collections or short scraps of the fifteenth century are listed by Heinrich in his edition of the above collection, and others may be found in *Reliquiæ Antiquæ*.

THREE OF JOHN OF ARDERNE'S TREATISES [12] were turned into English. That on *Fistula in Ano* was translated into English prose largely in abstracts, and written in the fifteenth-century MSS. Sloane 6 and 76 and 277 and 563 and 8093, and Emmanuel College Cbg. 69, and in the sixteenth-century MS. Sloane 2271. Printed, this piece covers 104 pages.—An English version of John's *De Judiciis Urinarum* is in MS. University Libr. Glasgow 328 (14th century); and one of his *Hoc Est Speculum Phlebotomiæ* is in MS. Emmanuel College Cbg. 69.

A TREATISE ON BLOOD-LETTING [13], 45 four-stress couplets, has been printed from a fourteenth-century MS. formerly owned by C. W. Loscombe, now MS. Ashburnham CXXX.

THE VIRTUES OF HERBS [14] are dealt with in 64 four-stress couplets comprising the first parts of a piece in a fourteenth-century MS. formerly owned by C. W. Loscombe, now MS. Ashburnham CXXX.

THE HERBARIUM APULEII [15] is extant in an English prose version in MS. Harley 6258 f. 31 (c. 1150; neighborhood of London), and in several other early MSS.

3. GLOSSES

MODERN COMPILATIONS OF GLOSSES OF PLANT-NAMES [16] from the tenth to the fifteenth century, excepting the fourteenth, have been printed by Earle. Henslowe has drawn up an alphabetical glossary of medicinal and other plants mentioned in fourteenth-century works.

THE DIGBY 172 GLOSS [17]. An Anglo-French and early Middle English gloss of 1150-1200 is in MS. Digby 172.

THE RAWLINSON G 57 GLOSSES [18]. In MS. Rawlinson G 57 (beginning 12th century) are some Latin and

English glosses—at ff. 1-5 on the *Disticha Catonis*, and at ff. 6-27 on the *Ilias Latina*.

THE STOWE 57 GLOSSES [19]. In MS. Stowe 57 ff. 156, 158 (c. 1200) are inserted some French and English equivalents of Latin names of animals, making what is intended to be a trilingual gloss, though in several cases the French equivalents, and in one the English, are wanting.

AN ENGLISH-FRENCH LEGAL GLOSS [20] was made c. 1130-1150, and was copied very widely, both separately and in chronicles or in collections. Between 30 and 50 copies are said to survive. It has been printed from MSS. Cotton Julius D VII f. 127 (c. 1250) and Cotton Galba E IV f. 46 (1285-1331); with the chronicles of Roger of Hoveden, Bartholomeus de Cotton, and Higden; and in the Chartulary of St. Mary's Abbey, Dublin, the Muniments of the Guildhall, London, and the Red Book of the Exchequer.

THE CAMBRIDGE-ARUNDEL GLOSS [21]. An English-French gloss is in a MS. of Walter de Biblesworth of the reign of Edward II in the Cambridge University Library. Another copy is in MS. Arundel 220 (early 14th century).

THE CAMBRIDGE EE GLOSS [22]. In MS. Cbg. Univ. Libr. Ee IV 20 f. 162 (c. 1340) is *Nominale siue Verbale in Gallicis cum Expositione eiusdem in Anglicis*. The piece consists of 888 verses, and gives the French, with the English equivalents, for parts of the body, natural noises and acts of men and women, assemblies, building a house, utensils, winds and storms, breaking things, a few puns, some red things, etc.

HARLEY 978 AND ADVOCATES' GLOSSES [23]. The Anglo-French and the English equivalents of certain Latin names of plants are in MS. Harley 978 f. 24 r (c. 1265).—In MS. Advocates' Libr. Misc. 18, 5, 16, Edinburgh, are a series of English, or French, or English and French, equivalents of Latin plant-names.

4.   GEOGRAPHY, TRAVEL, ETC.

A GEOGRAPHY IN VERSE [24] is in MS. Royal 13 D I f. 287 (14th century).   Headed *Recapitulatio Omnium Terrarum Civitatumque Tocius Mundi*, in rude irregular lines with little regard for rime, the piece devotes 26 verses to enumeration of the countries of Asia, 23 to the lands of Africa, and 29 to those of Europe.   It is merely a rude list of names.

A DESCRIPTION OF DURHAM [25] (*De Situ Dunelmi et de Sanctorum Reliquiis quæ ibidem Continentur Carmen Compositum*) in 21 alliterative verses, is in MS. Cbg. Univ. Libr. Ff I 27 (12th century; probably Northern) at the end of Simeon of Durham's *Chronicle*.

THE CHARACTERISTICS OF COUNTIES [26], a set of 21 four-stress couplets in MS. Harley 7371, and of 25 like couplets in a Rawlinson MS., is an interesting jingle, amusing in its brief statement line by line of the names and the special popular characterizations of the counties severally.   The Rawlinson text prefixes an introductory couplet, expands several characterizations into two verses, and rearranges or displaces some of the shires.   The piece reminds of the Warwickshire Seven Towns rimes.

THE SHIRES AND HUNDREDS OF ENGLAND [27], in MS. Jesus College Oxford 29 f. 267 (c. 1275), gives the extent of England, the number and names of shires, bishoprics, and archbishoprics, and offers some details of the facts in former times.   In print the piece makes up 58 lines of prose.

A LIST OF 108 ENGLISH TOWNS [28], the name with the special attribute or product of each in a short verse, is in MS. Douce 98 ff. 195-96 (14th century).   The list is not earlier than 1295.   Worcester is entered for its verse-makers, 'Rymeour de Wyrcestre.'

THE STATIONS OF ROME [29], ostensibly composed to inform prospective pilgrims of the nature, the locations, and

the virtues, of the various holy places in Rome, was written
in short couplets at about 1275-1300, probably in the South-
East Midland. It is extant in MSS. Cotton Caligula A II f.
81 (1400-1450) and Lambeth 306 f. 152 v (15th century).
The two MSS. are very close to each other; Cotton ends at
line 553, Lambeth at line 914. Another abbréviated version
in MSS. Vernon f. 314 (1370-1380) and Br. Mus. Additional 22283 (1380-1400), consists of 367 short couplets,
with an added prologue of 39 couplets lauding the glorious
origin of Rome, and urging the reader to visit the city for his
pardons. A later prose version is in MS. Porkington 10 f.
132 (Phillipps 8336; c. 1460). A Northern version is in MS.
Advocates' Libr. Edinburgh Jac. V, 7, 27 (now 19, 3, 1; 15th
century). So the piece seems to have had a considerable popularity, though it was composed probably less as a guide-book
than with the under-purpose of winning pilgrims to Rome, and
away from the shrines at Santiago and Jerusalem. The latter
places must have had powerful patronage to vie with the thousands of years of pardon that the *Stations* promised at any
of the host of Roman shrines that the writer enumerates the
virtues of.

THE STATIONS OF JERUSALEM [30] consists of 848
irregular four-stress verses, sometimes in couplets, sometimes
abab, sometimes abcbdbeb, sometimes in *laisses* on one rime.
It is in MS. Ashmole 61 f. 128 (15th century) in a defective
state, with many evident modifications of the original. The
date is difficult to determine. The piece purports to be from
personal experience. It begins with departure from Venice,
and proceeds stage by stage to Jerusalem, with description of
the holy places on the way, and with narrative of the events of
the New Testament connected with each.

THE TRAVELS OF SIR JOHN MANDEVILLE [31]
has been among the most popular of Middle English writings.
Some three hundred MSS. of the work survive, and there are
said to be more copies of it dating from the fourteenth or the
fifteenth century than there are of any other book except the

Scriptures. Before 1500 it had been printed in German, Dutch, Italian, Latin, and English; and it came to be translated into practically all European tongues. Versions in French, Latin, and English were by 1400 credited to Sir John Mandeville.

It seems now agreed that the work was originally in French. The versions manifest ignorance of English conditions, that (it is declared) no Englishman would show. The French prologue alone states that, though he should have chosen Latin, the author wrote in French so as to be more widely understood. The Latin MSS., and all the English MSS. but Cotton, imply that their text is the original. Cotton says that the author translated the book from Latin into French, and thence into English 'that every man of my nation might understand it.' There are extant a number of French MSS., all apparently representing one version, the best and oldest of them being MS. Nouv. Acq. Franç. 4515 in the Bibliothèque Nationale and of date of 1371. Five Latin versions survive, of the most popular of which there are 12 MSS., all of the fifteenth century. This vulgate Latin version was translated from French at Liège.

The English versions contain blunders such as could not come from an original author's own hands. They seem to be from separate revisers. They are three in number, represented respectively by (1) MS. Cotton Titus C XVI, Midland and close to a good French original, the MS. perhaps 1410-1420; (2) MS. Egerton 1982, Northern, perhaps 1410-1420, from a Latin original and also a French one that differed from any extant; and (3) some defective MSS. The third version was especially popular in the fifteenth and sixteenth centuries, and was often printed up to 1725. It appears to be from a French original (though it may be from the version represented by Cotton), is shorter than the other two English versions, and is imperfect. The second and the third English versions assign Mandeville's journey to 1332, and the writing of the book to 1366; the best French and Latin texts, and

the Cotton English version, assign the journey to 1322, and
the writing to 1355 or 1357.

In the prologue the author declares himself to be Jehan de
Mandeville, Knight, of the town of St. Albans, born and bred
in England. He states that he gives an account of his actual
travels begun from England in 1322 (1332). He pretends
that his work is a guide-book for those who would travel to
Jerusalem (cp. *Stations of Rome, Stations of Jerusalem,* pages
432-33), written from his own experiences. He exhorts the
reader to regard for the Holy City where Christ suffered for
men. Then the work exhausts the various routes, direct and
circuitous, to the City, with all the marvels to be encountered
in the districts that must be traversed. Then follows a lengthy
second part dealing with the East outside of Palestine—the
lands of the great Cham and of Prester John, India and China
and the other 'islands' of the Orient. The astounding wonders
that the book records, have become matters of common knowledge, and need not be detailed here.

It is now generally admitted that the original author did
not write from personal travel, for it has been shown that his
geography and his marvels were practically all derived from
earlier works. The book is a remarkably clever composite
made by a writer of wide acquaintance with books of travel
and natural history ranging from before the time of Pliny to
the fourth decade of the fourteenth century. The first part
was derived largely from Albert of Aix's eleventh-century story
of the first Crusade, William of Boldensele's account (1336)
of his Eastern travels in 1332-1333, and from other writings
of the twelfth and thirteenth centuries, such as *Pêlerinages por
Aler en Iherusalem,* the continuation of William of Tyre, and
Jacques de Vitry. The second part is from Friar Oderico de
Pordenone's account (written in 1331) of his embassy to the
Great Khan, with materials from the Armenian Hayton, who
dictated his travels in 1307, John of Carpini's *Historia Mon-
golorum,* the wonders of the *Legenda Aurea,* the writings of
Isodore and Bartholomeus, the *Trésor* of Brunetto Latini, Vin-
cent of Beauvais' *Speculum,* the *Letter of Prester John,* the

Letter of Alexander to Aristotle (see page 98), Solinus' compendium of Pliny, and other works. A source has been shown for practically every statement of the *Travels* that is not evidently purely imaginary. The work is a curious mixture of fable, of what was fact in the writer's day, and of what was fact recorded centuries before the author's time. Perhaps the writer believed more of what he tells about than his general forgery would lead one to credit.

Until the later years of the nineteenth century the work was accepted as by Sir John Mandeville of St. Albans, who in 1322 (1332) departed from England, and journeyed through the East until in 1343 he became ill at Liège. The vulgate Latin version asserts that at Liège, at the suggestion of his physician John *ad Barbam*, he undertook the account of his travels, finishing the work in 1356 or 1357. But this fact was not recorded in the earliest French MS. of 1371. This MS., moreover, was bound up with a treatise on the plague by the Liège physician 'Maistre Jehan de Bourgoigne autrement dit à la Barbe.' Jean d'Outremeuse of Liège is said to have stated in his *Myreur des Histors* (the statement now extant only in a copy of before 1720) that in 1372 a Jehan de Bourgogne or Jean à la Barbe on his death-bed confided to him that he was John de Mandeville, 'chevalier, comte de Montfort en Angleterre et seigneur de l'isle de Campdi et du chateau Perouse,' and that he had been a fugitive from England in 1322 because he had killed a man of rank. Outremeuse stated that Mandeville was buried in the church of the Guillemins. In later centuries several persons speak of having seen the tomb bearing a coat of arms that is now recognized as that of the Tyrrells, but they do not agree as to the inscription on the tomb. The church was destroyed in 1798. The differences between Outremeuse's story and that of the Latin *Travels*, the character of the titles he assigns to Sir John, and various other facts, make Outremeuse's account very questionable. Curiously, a John de Mandeville was a rebel under Edward II, and was pardoned in 1313; and a Johan de Bourgoyne was a minor figure in another rebellion, was pardoned in 1321, and, on revocation of his pardon in 1322, fled from England. In the list of persons pardoned with de Bourgoyne was a 'Johan Maugevilayn'; and the name in the list preceding Maugevilayn's is 'Johan le Barber.' It is of importance that Outremeuse declared he inherited Mandeville's library, that he wrote work in much resembling the *Travels*, and that only the Latin version of the *Travels* tells of Ogier the Dane, who was hero of an epic by Outremeuse. We probably do best to conclude that the Liège physician's true name was de Bourgogne, and that he wrote the *Travels* under the assumed name of de Mandeville. Possibly d'Outremeuse is responsible for the Latin *Travels*.

The *Travels* deserves the popularity that it has enjoyed. The Cotton and Egerton versions are among the notable pieces of English prose. The writers of each of these versions were of exceptional ability. Each produced work that has scarce any mark of translation, and that, indeed, appears to come directly from the hand of the author himself. Each of these versions, as do the others, presents to us with remarkable skill, a personality, that of the apparently fictitious Sir John Mandeville. The versions exhibit great capacity in adapting the genuine to the fabulous. Their plausibility is astonishing. The writer of the original and his followers knew well how to create impression of truth by skilful statement of collateral circumstantial detail. Though the work starts out as a guide for journeys to Jerusalem, it soon puts aside the pretense, and assumes a distinguished place in Middle English prose by actually seeking chiefly to amuse. This aim it accomplishes through offering interesting information. The Cotton and Egerton versions are admirable in style, steady, smooth, direct, and natural—by far superior to most of the contemporary prose.

5.· NATURAL SCIENCE

THE INFLUENCE OF PLANETS [32] was made the theme of seven strophes (several defective) aabbcc, the *a* and *b* verses of five stresses, the *c* verses of one stress and six stresses respectively. The lines are very uneven and rude. The piece is in MS. Rawlinson 939 f. 3 (c. 1350).

THE DISTANCE BETWEEN EARTH AND HEAVEN [33] is indicated in MS. Rawlinson 939 f. 5 (c. 1350) in 27 verses ascribed to 'Rabbi Moses.' The piece was used in the Galba *Pricke of Conscience,* lines 7651-86 (see page 447).

A FRAGMENT ON POPULAR SCIENCE [34], so-called, consisting of 394 verses abab of fours and threes, has been printed from MS. Harley 2277 f. 127 (c. 1300). The piece is really the conclusion (ll. 391 ff.) of an account of the legend of St. Michael in the Southern Legendary as represented in MS. Laud 108 f. 132 r. (see pages 294, 300). The lines present interesting information concerning movements of heavenly bodies, the planets, the sun, the moon, the elements and their influence on mankind, lightning, thunder, rain, snow, the formation of the child in its mother's womb, etc. The piece is probably of the Midland and 1275-1300.

DE PROPRIETATIBUS RERUM [35], by the Franciscan Bartholomeus Anglicus, was turned into English by John of Treves, translator of Higden's *Polychronicon* (see page 204). The English was completed February 6, 1398. It was printed with omissions by de Worde in 1491, and by Berthelet in 1535. It presents interesting, and often amusing, accounts of the elements; the spirits animating man; the colors; the metals; the motions of planets; the conditions of men; the relations of family life; mediæval society under chivalry; daily life in the Middle Ages; physiology; geography real and legendary; and natural history of trees, birds, fishes, and beasts.

EMB ÞUNRE [36], a prose piece making in print some 15 lines, is in MS. Cotton Vespasian D XIV f. 103 (early 12th century). It tells of the significance of thunder in each of the months of the year.

Here should be mentioned the several small collections [36a] of popular knowledge printed by Cockayne and Förster, but all probably not of our period.

6. MISCELLANEOUS PIECES

EIGHT MISCELLANEOUS RECIPES [37] in English for making colors, making iron hard as steel, etc., are in MS. Harley. 2253 f. 52 (c. 1310). As several leaves are cut out of the MS. after the last of the eight, the recipes may be but the first of a considerable collection.

MIDDLE ENGLISH MEASURES OF WEIGHT [38] are briefly stated in MS. Cotton Claudius E VIII f. 8 r (14th century; perhaps of Norwich).

A DEFINITION OF ROBBERY [39], under the heads of 'aperte thefte,' 'pryve thefte,' 'covert thefte,' and stealing by a wife or a man of religion, is the theme of 25 four-stress couplets in MS. Sloane 1785 (14th century).

THE CONSTITUTIONS OF MASONRY [40], composed in Southern short couplets in 1350-1400 by an ecclesiastic, carries back Masonry to Euclid and King Æthelstan, and urges right education of children, training in table-etiquette, attendance at church, devotion to the Virgin, fostering of the Seven Arts, and cherishing of courtesy in general.

THE SEVEN AGES OF THE WORLD [41], a development of Bede's *De Sex Ætatibus Sæculi* at the close of his *De Temporibus*, in MS. Cotton Caligula A XV f. 139 extends from the Creation to the end of the world, on a Biblical basis; in the Hyde Register comes down to 1031; and in MS. Arundel 60 f. 149 is carried to 1099. It is prose, and in print covers about a page.

7. CHARMS

'WENNE, WENNE, WENCHICHENNE' [42] is a charm in 13 alliterative verses in MS. Royal 4 A XIV. It is probably a modernized copy (c. 1150) of an Old English charm.

NAMES OF A HARE [43] (*Les Noms de un Levre en Eng-leis*) is the title of an odd piece in MS. Digby 86 f. 168 (1272-1283). The first 10 lines state that when a man meets a hare, he must lay on earth whatever he bears, bless him with his elbow, and say a prayer in worship of the hare. Then follow 44 lines of names of the hare, evidently to be recited. There-after are the 10 final lines: When this is all done and said, the hare's power is laid, and the man may go where he will—'have good-day, Sir Hare; may God so let you fare that you come to me dead or ready to be eaten.'—The verses have from two to four stresses each, and rime—now in couplets, now in *laisses*.

TWO CHARMS FOR TOOTH-ACHE [44] are in MS. Thornton f. 176 (1430-1440). Both are in four-stress verses; one has 7, the other 21, couplets. A Latin charm follows them in the MS.

8.   Dream Books

A METRICAL TREATISE ON DREAMS [45] is in MS. Harley 2253 f. 119 (c. 1310). The piece, probably of 1250 or 1250-1275, consists of 319 four-stress verses, all in coup-lets, except lines 177-216 which are on one rime. It is a free version of a Latin original of a class represented in the Vienna MS. 271. It purports to be based on a collection of inter-pretations of dreams made by David, the prophet, when he interpreted the dreams of princes in the city of Babylon. It consists of a series of brief general statements of chief features of dreams, and the meaning of each. The work has, of course, no poetical quality; but it is interesting in connection with the dreamlore so treasured through all ages in all peoples, and especially with the matter that repeatedly occurs in a number of the excellent English works of the period, such as the *Nun's Priest's Tale* and the *Owl and the Nightingale*.

A PROSE DREAM BOOK [46] of the fourteenth century is in MSS. Sloane 1609 f. 29 (c. 1400; best text and closest to original), Trinity College Cbg. O, 9, 37 f. 26 (15th century), and Royal 12 E XVI f. 1 (fragments; 15th century). It is a verbal translation from the Latin of the same group of texts as the original of the English *Metrical Treatise* in Harley 2253 (see above). It consists of a series of 124 subjects of dreams, with interpretation of each in a single phrase, all alphabetically arranged. MS. Trinity adds items carrying the total up to 178.

9. DOCUMENTS

EARLY CHARTERS [47]. A number of charters, deeds, and the like, of 1050-1093, are extant.

EARLY WILLS [48]. Several wills of 1050-1097 have been preserved.

HEMING'S ACCOUNT OF WULFSTAN AND WORCESTER [49] is a short passage in MS. Cotton Tiberius A XIII. The piece is from after 1095.

A LETTER OF EADWINE [50], monk and child-master to Ælfsige, Bishop of Winchester, regarding a vision in which St. Cuthbert appeared, and of date 1056-1070, is preserved in the Hyde Register and in MS. Br. Mus. Additional 15350 f. 14.

THREE NORTHUMBRIAN DOCUMENTS [51] of about 1100 have been preserved and printed. They are a grant by Gospatrick, the laws and rights of Archbishop Thomas I of York, and a deed of gift of Bishop Ranulf of Durham (1099-1128).

WRITS OF GILBERT OF WESTMINSTER [52]. In the so-called Doomsday of Westminster (c. 1306) is a writ of 'Gisilberd,' Abbot of Westminster, of about 1100. A similar writ of 'Gisilberd' is in *Monasticon* 1. 310.

A NORTHUMBRIAN LETTER [53] of Gospatrick, of the latter part of the eleventh century, has been printed.

A PROCLAMATION OF HENRY III [54] of 1258, some 260 words, is extant. It was originally issued in English, French, and Latin versions.

A CHARTER OF EDWARD II [55] (*Charta Sancti Edwardi Regis, de Concessione Ballivæ Suæ*) is in MS. Cotton Julius F X. It consists of 22 verses of irregular length aaaabbbbbccddeefgghhii. The charter is of the Hilary Term of 1324, and merely indicates the King's commission of the keeping of his forest of the Hundred of Chelmer and Dansing to Randolph Peperking, with record of the witnesses.

THE USAGES OF WINCHESTER [56] have been printed from a French version in the archives of Winchester College (MS. 1250-1300), and two English texts in the Guildhall at Winchester (one, 14th century; the other, first years of Henry VI).

A DEED OF 1376 [57], in South-Western English, preserved in British Museum Harley Charters 45, A, 37, is declared to be the oldest private legal instrument in Middle English.

TWO WILTSHIRE DOCUMENTS [58], one of 1375 and one of 1381, are in the British Museum.

THE FIRST PETITION TO PARLIAMENT IN ENGLISH [59], made by the Mercers of London in 1386, consists of about 1350 words in the London dialect, and is preserved in a MS. in the Public Record Office.

AN APPEAL OF THOMAS USK [60], made before the Coroner of London in connection with the election of Sir Nicholas Brember to the office of Mayor in 1384-1385, is extant in the Public Record Office.

THE SCOTTISH DOCUMENTS OF 1385-1440 [61], some of the phases of whose language have been investigated, are of value to students of the vernacular.

ENGLISH WILLS [62]. The fifty earliest wills in English preserved in the London Court of Probate, extend from 1387 to 1439, and have been printed.—In MS. University College Oxf. 97 is a will of Robert Folkyngham, dated 1399.

ENGLISH GUILD RECORDS [63]. A number of valuable fourteenth-century (most of c. 1389) documents in English relating to guilds, have been edited from the originals in the London Public Record Office (Miscellaneous Rolls, Tower Records).

LADY PELHAM'S LETTER [64], written to her husband, Sir John Pelham, in 1399, is extant.

CHAPTER XI

ROLLE AND HIS FOLLOWERS

In this chapter will be discussed the writings probably by 1. *Rolle and Unnamed Followers;* 2. *Walter Hilton;* 3. *William Nassyngton;* and 4. *Juliana Lampit.*

1. ROLLE AND UNNAMED FOLLOWERS

Richard Rolle of Hampole is one of the most considerable figures in the religious history of the fourteenth century in England. His character was impressive, his life extremely romantic; his activity as originator and oral promulgator of his mystic doctrines, made him one of the notable forces of his century; he wrote well both in Latin and in English works that, though contemned by many of the learned, gave him a high reputation in his day, and a long influence after his death; if he composed the short poems ascribed to him (see pages 451, 504, 394, 515), he was an excellent religious lyrist; perhaps he wrote in the vernacular a version of one of the more imposing long religious poems of the period; and he was eminent as a writer of English prose.

Rolle [1] was born at about 1300 at Thornton-le-Dale a few miles from Pickering in Yorkshire, of a family apparently in good circumstances. He was educated at home, and later was sent to Oxford under patronage of Thomas de Neville, afterwards Archdeacon of Durham. But the logic and the philosophy of the theologians at the newly aroused University were unsatisfying to the visionary youth, to whom the heart and the inner light were ever transcendent; and Richard returned home. Soon, determined to give himself to the life of contemplation that seemed to him the ideal training, he left Thornton clad in a makeshift hermit's costume contrived from a hood

of his father's, and two garments, one gray, one white, begged
of his sister. For some years he lived on the estate of Sir
John Dalton, by whose bounty he was clothed and fed. There,
as far as the conditions permitted, he led a semi-hermit life
of meditation, and during some years passed stage by stage
through the inner experience and development of the *calor,* the
canor, and *dulcor* (as he styled them) of submission to Divine
Love. So, in meditation, in reading, and in prayer, he matured
the theory of Love as the beginning of all, the means, and the
end, that he was to preach throughout his after-life. Following the deaths of Dalton and his wife, under whose patronage
he had lived peacefully for a number of years, Rolle for some
time wandered from place to place, amid much misunderstanding and friction. Though he was never a member of the clergy,
and though he had technically the rights only of a layman, he
became a missionary, moving actively among the people and
talking his beliefs as he might. The personality and the earnestness that had won the Daltons, and the worth of his doctrine, gained him esteem and reverence. Soon he was accepted
as adviser and instructor by some younger clergy. Moreover,
he took to writing—first in Latin, then, for extension of influence, as well in English. His reputation grew; miraculous acts
were attributed to him. But misunderstanding brought him
many foes; his works that are apparently of this date com-
plain bitterly of hostility.

After a time Rolle settled in the county of Richmond at
about a dozen miles from Anderby, where Margaret Kirkby
was living a semi-hermit life much like his own. Margaret
seems to have had great influence on his writing, especially on
that in the vernacular. To this 'dilecta sua discipula,' as he
styled her in the prologue of his English *Commentary on the
Psalms* (see page 401), he gave spiritual counsel, and several
times afforded miraculous aid in sickness. To her he addressed
his *Form of Perfect Living* and his *Ego Dormio.* This close
friendship, apparently maintained largely by correspondence,
seems to have continued until death.

Finally, when he was about fifty years old, Rolle went to

Hampole in the South of Yorkshire near Doncaster, where was a Cistercian nunnery to which he seems to have become a spiritual counselor. Here he is assumed to have written a *Pricke of Conscience.* Here he dwelt until his death in September, 1349.

It was presumed that his devout and influential life would win him canonization; but, though apparently he was actually orthodox, he was never elevated—perhaps because of the novelty of his doctrines and the eagerness of the Lollards in appropriating them. The information concerning his life is afforded by the *Officium* and the *Legenda* prepared in anticipation of his canonization, and by his own works—especially his *Incendium Amoris.*

The English work most surely to be attributed to Rolle, is, in style as well as in thought, dominated by feeling rather than logic. Inspiration, rather than method and judgment, characterizes the pieces. As wholes the treatises are rambling and loose, the arrangement in them is often poor. The sentences, however, are commonly constructed with much elaboration. Balance, antithesis, alliteration of prominent words, and repetition of words and phrases, are striking elements of Rolle's work. Indeed, so marked are these features that a critic has declared his writings to be the 'earliest original prose exhibiting a style anticipatory of the highly developed Euphuism of Lyly and his school.'

Rolle's popularity led to influence on what has been styled a school of writers, to the wide copying of his works, and to assignment to him, during the next two centuries, of a number of writings found anonymous in MSS. It is likely that many of the pieces have been improperly so assigned to him, that some accepted as his by critics at the present time, are really by other writers, and that he wrote some extant pieces to which his name is not attached [2]. The whole matter needs to be gone over thoroughly from its beginnings [3]. The information available for determining the authorship and the relationships, and, in some cases, even the nature, of the works, is confused and notably deficient. Assertions and investigations have been based on limited and imperfect knowledge, and

on very questionable assumptions. The most comprehensive
list of both the Latin and the English pieces to be considered
in making up a list of Rolle's compositions, is that given by
Horstmann.

With the Latin works we are not immediately concerned here.
The English pieces connected with Rolle's name will be dis-
cussed under the heads: I. *Writings Accepted as by Rolle;*
II. *Writings Probably by Followers of Rolle.*

I. Writings Accepted as by Rolle

THE PRICKE OF CONSCIENCE [4] is a comprehensive
poem of religious information and instruction belonging to the
general class of the *Handlyng Synne* and the *Aȝenbite of Inwyt*
(see pages 343, 345). But, while these latter pieces are rather
objective, dealing with the nature and the effects of the Sins
and the Virtues, the *Pricke* is more introspective, being concerned with the experience past, present, and future, of the
Soul itself.

The poem is discussed here rather than with the *Handlyng
Synne* and the kindred works, because it is usually assumed
to be by Rolle. The available information regarding it is very
defective and confused. At least thirty-one of its MSS., many
Southern and of c. 1350, have been compared. While the treatments in these MSS. have been classed roughly in four general
groups, even there the variations are most extensive and
baffling both as respects length (from one book to seven books)
and omission and modification of material. The common titles
in the MSS. are *Stimulus Conscientiæ* and *Pricke of Conscience,*
sometimes both in one MS.; but, to the confusion of students,
other titles are employed—*e.g., Treatise of Knowing Man's
Self, Speculum Huius Vitæ, Key of Knowing,* and *Clauis Scien-
tiæ.* Latin versions varying much from each other, and apparently short, are extant. The relations between the Latin and
the English versions are at present as uncertain as is our
knowledge of the number, the nature, and the relations to each
other, of the several English texts. It is possible that a Latin
text, perhaps by Grostête, was the original basis for the ver-

sions. Miss Allen has indicated that but four of the MSS., and
these not the best, ascribe their texts to Rolle; that the traditional assignment to Rolle rests chiefly on a late statement by
Lydgate in the *Falls of Princes;* that the substance, the attitude, the manner, and the method of the *Pricke,* do not accord
with, and actually contradict, those of accepted mystical works
of Hampole; that the English *Pricke* is probably a translation
or a rehandling; and that perhaps the work is to be connected
with Nassyngton (see page 463).

The *Pricke* has been edited from the accepted best MS.,
Cotton Galba E IX (Northern; first of 15th century), in 4812
couplets. In contrast with the regularity usual among Northern writers, these verses have four stresses with irregular number of unstressed syllables.

A prologue shows that God is the beginning and the end of all;
that Man, His chief work, was made in His likeness; that self-
knowledge is necessary, but is interfered with by popular favor,
beauty, fervor of thought, and wealth. The work proper is divided
carefully into seven parts. Part I deals with the Wretchedness
of the State of Man, much of it from Innocent III's *De Contemptu
Mundi,* Bk. I Chs. 2, 3, 5-12, and Bk. III Ch. 1, with omissions:
Man in the flesh has a wretched beginning, a foul middle life, a
disgusting old age, and is finally food for worms. Part II, on the
World and Worldly Life, is drawn, among other sources, from
Bartholomew de Glanvilla's *De Proprietatibus Rerum:* there are
the upper and greater world of the planets and the stars, and the
lower and lesser world containing the Earth and Man; the Earth
is a wilderness, a battle-field, the servant of the Devil and the
opponent of God; Man is a pilgrim; worldly success is a sign of
damnation. Part III is on Death, the fear of Death, the reasons
for this fear, the conditions at the time of death. Part IV is on
Purgatory, its location, its torments, the causes for its existence,
the sins that send to Hell, the venial Sins and their remedies, the
proper attitude toward Purgatory, and the powers of the Mass and
of the Church as regards Purgatory. For this matter Aquinas'
Compendium Theologicæ Veritatis was a part source. Part V is
on the Signs of Doomsday—the destruction of Rome, the coming
of Antichrist, the Fifteen Signs, and the Judgment. The passage
on the Signs (see page 328) is short (ll. 4738-4815), but this Part
is the most elaborate of the seven. Part VI treats the Pains of
Hell, fourteen in number. Part VII is on the Joys of Heaven:
the nature and the geography of the various heavens are described;
then are shown the life of the soul in Heaven, the physical constitution of the Holy City, and a parting picture of the correspondent

torments in Hell. Material for this part was drawn from Honorius d' Autun's *Elucidarium*. The poem is called *Pricke of Conscience* because, if a man read and understand its matters, his conscience will be stirred to dread and meekness, and he will be led to a right life.

In contrast with the *Aʒenbite*, the *Pricke* draws its materials from many sources, both Latin and English, and is ultimately based on much reading. It combines into a whole most of the elements of knowledge especially in use among the ecclesiastical writers of the day. A part of the description of the heavens reminds of the passage in the legend of Michael (see page 438). The expression is free and effective, and in some places remarkably modern. Though the style is simple, striking passages are not infrequent. But all the matter is abstract, remote from every-day life, arid, depressing, and so to us of scarce any appeal, especially as compared with the *Handlyng Synne*. Yet the extraordinary number of MSS. preserved, and the extent of its influence and of borrowing from it, indicate that the *Pricke of Conscience* was far more acceptable in its own and the next century than was Mannyng's work.

Of þo Flode of þo World (218 verses) and *þo Whele of Fortune* (112 verses), paralleling the *Pricke of Conscience*, lines 109 ff. and 1273 ff., are in MS. Royal 17 B XVII ff. 101, 103 (West Midland; 1370-1400).—A treatment, often in similar terms, of some of the topics of the *Pricke of Conscience*, is in 768 irregular four-stress verses ababab in the same MS. f. 36.—In MS. Thornton f. 276 v (1430-1440) are 50 couplets of four-stress lines that correspond to the *Pricke*, lines 438-551. In the fifteenth-century MSS. Rawlinson C 285 f. 39 and Cbg. Univ. Libr. Dd V 55 f. 92 v are 14 short couplets, '*þai þat withoutene lawe dos syne*,' extracted from the *Pricke*, lines 6071 ff. (see page 391).

THE FORM OF PERFECT LIVING [5], a rhythmical prose epistle of some ten thousand words to Margaret Kirkby, is preserved in at least three Northern MSS., a number of MSS. in other dialects, in selections in a number of others, in several early printed texts, in a Latin version, and in several

Latin fragments. MSS. Cbg. Univ. Libr. Dd V 64 f. 101 (late 14th or early 15th century) and Rawlinson C 285 f. 40 (early 15th century), both Northern, appear to offer the best text. The piece consists of six chapters on the form of living in general, and six on Love (*Amore Langueo*).

The chapters deal with the following: the three great sources of ill in life—lack of spiritual strength, use of fleshly desires, exchange of the enduring for the transitory; the blessedness of the recluse's life, and temptations in visions; holiness, the despising of worldly things and the being better than one seems; entire devotion to Christ; the source of defilement of the heart, the means of purification and holding to purification and devotion to God's will; the heart ever to be filled with love and praise of God; the three degrees of Love; the cherishing of the name and the thought of Jesus; the nature of Love, how to recognize Love, how most to love; the Seven Gifts of the Holy Ghost; the superiority of the Contemplative Life.

Corresponding to Chapter XI is the piece on the Seven Gifts concluding *Of Grace* in MS. Arundel 507, and written separately in MS. Thornton (see page 452).

A paraphrase of the first part of the *Form*, in 431 short couplets, possibly by Nassyngton (see page 464), is in MS. Cotton Tiberius E VII f. 85 v.—See also page 459.

The Libel of Richard Hermyte of Hampol of the Amendement of Mannes Lif, Other ellis of the Rule of Goode Livyng, which is said to be in MS. Worcester Cathedral Libr. 172 (late 15th century) in twelve chapters of prose, is perhaps a madeover version of the *Form*.

EGO DORMIO ET COR MEUM VIGILAT [6] is in MSS. Cbg. Univ. Libr. Dd V 64 f. 122 (late 14th or early 15th century; Northern), Rawlinson A 389 f. 77 and f. 95 v (beginning 15th century), Vernon (1370-1380), and Arundel 507 f. 40 (14th century; abridged and imperfect). The Vernon text is apparently similar to the second Rawlinson text, which is not from the first Rawlinson. The tract consists of about 3500 words of prose. In several of the MSS. it is written as a continuation of the *Form of Perfect Living*. It is directed to a nun ('cuidam moniali Zedyngham,' says the colophon of Dd);

it urges all-devoted love to the Heavenly Lover, and the eschewing of all fleshly and worldly desires; and it adds a meditation on the Passion, and a concluding lyrical rimed Song of Love 'that thou shalt delight in when thou art loving Jesus Christ.'

A COMMANDMENT OF LOVE TO GOD [7], some 3000 words of prose, is in MS. Cbg. Univ. Libr. Dd V 64 f. 129 (late 14th or early 15th century; Northern; best MS.), and in Southern texts in MSS. Rawlinson A 389 f. 81 (15th century; good copy), Vernon (1370-1380; much altered), Cbg. Univ. Libr. Ii VI 40 (15th century), Ff V 40 (15th century), and Dd V 55 (c. 1400; defective). The colophon of Dd V 64 declares the piece 'scriptus cuidam sorori de Hampole.' The tract urges implicit obedience to the command to 'love our Lord in all our heart, in all our soul, in all our thought'; explains the three degrees of Love dealt with in the *Form* (see page 450); and insists on rejection of all pride and vanity, and neglect of all worldly things in devoted love and contemplation of Christ.

THE COMMENTARY ON THE PSALTER [8], generally accepted as Rolle's, is discussed on page 401.

MEDITATIO DE PASSIONE DOMINI [9], generally accepted as Rolle's, is extant in two texts, neither of which is in the Northern dialect. The former consists of about 5000 words, the first part much abridged, in MS. Cbg. Univ. Libr. Ll I 8 f. 201 (14th century); the latter contains about 7000 words in the later MS. Cbg. Additional 3042. The piece rests on the *Privity of the Passion* (translated from Bonaventura, see page 456), parts of which work it repeats at times. With intense longing the writer utters his gratitude to Christ for His love and sacrifice, his vivid realization of the scenes of the Passion, and his consecration to the Savior. The work is one of the most poetical of the Middle English Passion writings, and so is to be associated with the beautiful *Talkyng of the Love of God* (see page 458).

Possibly by Rolle are some of the lyrics [10] in MSS. Thornton, Cbg. Univ. Libr. Dd V 64, and Cotton Galba E IX (see pages 504, 505, 394, 515).

II. Writings Probably by Followers of Rolle

Some of the following pieces may be by Rolle; but most, if not practically all, are probably by writers under Rolle's influence.

'A GRETE CLERK ÞAT MEN CALS RICHARD OF SAYNT VICTOR' [11], a fragment of about 120 words, the beginning of a prose piece, is in MS. Cbg. Univ. Libr. Dd V 64 f. 142 v. (late 14th or early 15th century).

TWO GROUPS OF LYRICS [10], one in MS. Cbg. Univ. Libr. Dd. V 64, and one in MS. Thornton (see pages 504, 505), may be by Rolle.

OF GRACE [12] and OUR DAILY WORK [13] have similarities in style, plan, and thought to Rolle's accepted work. They are in MSS. Arundel 507 ff. 41 and 54 v (c. 1400) and Thornton (1430-1440), with works by Rolle. In Arundel the versions are abridged, as are the versions of *Ego Dormio* and the *Form* (see page 450).

Of Grace (A 2700, T 3200, words) indicates the three kinds of Grace in Holy Writ; the necessity of Grace with full accord of Man's Free-Will, for spiritual health; and the operations of Grace on Man's soul. In Arundel is joined a short passage on the *Seven Gifts of the Holy Ghost*, corresponding to Chapter XI of the *Form* (see page 450), and written separately in Thornton.

Our Daily Work (A about 11000 words, T about 6000 words in different arrangement) states and elaborates at unequal length the three needs of Man—honest work without waste of time, work with free spirit as the work demands, and demeanor honest and fair and loving of God and inspiring of good wherever it is. There is frequent quotation of the Latin Scriptures, Isodore, Gregory, and Augustine, and once of Seneca, with illustration from Bible records and by short narrative bits.

'FOR ALS MYKIL AS MANNES SAULE' [14], a prose

bit of some 100 words in MS. Arundel 507 f. 36 (c. 1400), declares Man's obligation to serve God, and his lack of desert.

A MEDITATION ON THE PASSION AND OF THREE ARROWS OF DOOMSDAY [15], about 3300 words of prose, is in MSS. Rawlinson C 285 f. 64 (beginning 15th century), Arundel 507 f. 48 (c. 1400), and Cbg. Univ. Libr. Ff V 40 (15th century). The piece belongs to the class of the various Middle English treatises on the Passion and the Fall, and is not at all an apostrophe like the other *Meditation* by Rolle (see page 451). It is an exhortation to think on the incidents of the Passion, which are enumerated in order. Then the reader is bidden to consider Doomsday and the three arrows that God shall shoot—the summons to resurrection, the arraignment and the condemnation.

OF THREE ARROWS ON DOOMSDAY [16] consists of some 1500 words of prose in MSS. University College Oxf. 97 f. 316 (end of 14th or beginning of 15th century), Laud 174, Harley 1706, Cbg. Univ. Libr. Ff V 45 and Ff II 38 and Ff VI 55, Tanner 336, and Douce 13. It has been styled an imitation of the Rawlinson *Three Arrows* (see above), and has been ascribed to Wycliffe as well as to Rolle. It is probably Southern.

TWELVE PROSE PIECES [17], ranging from 100 to 2500 words each, are written with works probably by Rolle in MSS. Rawlinson C 285 f. 57 v (Northern; beginning 15th century) and Cbg. Univ. Libr. Ff V 40 (Southern; 15th century). None of these, except perhaps the *Meditation and of Three Arrows* (see paragraphs above) is Rolle's. The pieces are *How to Know if You Love Your Enemy*, *What Most Helps a Man's Knowing*, *On the Name of Jesus*, *Sentences from Gregory*, *How an Anchoress Shall Behave*, *St. Anselm's Admonitio Morienti*, *Sentences*, *Of the Ten Commandments*, *Nine Points Best Pleasing to God* (also in MSS. Vernon and Harley 1704), *Meditation on the Passion and of Three Arrows*, *Against Boasting and Pride*, and *Sayings of the Fathers*. Item 8 is from Gaytryge's *Sermon* (see page 348). Items 11 and 12 may be by Walter Hilton (see page 463). Items 1, 2, 5 are from Hilton's *Scale of Perfection* (see page 461).

THE NINE POINTS BEST PLEASING TO GOD [18] (see Item 9 just above) is in short couplets in the fifteenth-century MSS. Harley 2409, Cbg. Univ. Libr. Ff I 14 and Ii IV 9, and is probably a version of a Latin text in MS. Caius College Cbg. 140 f. 132. A prose piece of about 1100 words on the theme, is in MS. Harley 1706 (15th century).

THE PASSION OF CHRIST [19] is made the centre of a small group of quotations (400 words of prose) from Bonaventura, Rolle, Bernard, *et al.*, in the fifteenth-century MSS. Rawlinson C 285 f. 39 v and Cbg. Univ. Libr. Dd V 55 f. 93.

TWO PROSE ANECDOTES [20] from Cæsarius Heisterbachensis' *Dialogus Miraculorum,* are in MS. Harley 1022 f. 1 v (end of 14th century).

THE RULE OF THE LIFE OF OUR LADY [21], some thousand words of prose, in MSS. Harley 1022 .f. 64 (end of 14th century) and Bodley 938 f. 202, is a translation of Bonaventura's *Meditationes Vitæ Christi,* Chapter III.

BENJAMIN MINOR [22], some 6000 words of prose, is a free and abridged translation of Richard of St. Victor's *De Præparatione Animi ad Contemplationem Dictus Benjamin Minor* or *De Studio Sapientiæ.* It is in MSS. Harley 1022 f. 74 (end of 14th century) and 674 and 2373, and is said to be in the Southern MSS. Cbg. Univ. Libr. Ii VI 39 f. 120 (14th century) and Kk VI 26 and Ff VI 33, and Arundel 286. This ingenious piece is an allegorization of Jacob (God), Rachel (Reason; her maiden, Bala, being Imagination), and Leah (Affection; her maiden, Zelfa, being Sensuality), and the offspring of Jacob (Reuben, Fear of Pain; Simeon, Sorrow for Sin; etc.). By telling of the birth of the various children, the piece shows how in men spring Fear, Sorrow, Hope, Love, Double Sight in Imagination, etc.

'WYTHDRAGH þɪ ÞOGHT' and 'THRE POYNTZ' [23] are two short prose scraps following *Benjamin Minor* in MS. Harley 1022 f. 80 v (end of 14th century).

A GROUP OF PROSE TRACTS [24] is in MSS. Harley 674 and 2373, and others, associated with *Benjamin Minor*. All are of about 1350, and are possibly by one author. They are *An Epistle of Prayer, An Epistle of Discretion in Stirrings of the Soul, A Treatise of Discerning of Spirits, The Divine Cloud of Unknowing* (sometimes ascribed to. Hilton and Exmeuse, see page 460), *Dionise Hid Divinity* (a paraphrase of Dionysius' *Mystical Theology*), and *An Epistle of Privy Counsel.*

MEDITACIO SANCTI AUGUSTINI [25], in MSS. Douce 322 (15th century), Harley 1706 (15th century, here a copy of Douce), and Cbg. Univ. Libr. Hh I 12, is a translation in rhythmical prose (some 1800 words) of a Latin piece, not St. Augustine's, partly preserved in MS. Magdalèn College Oxf. 93. The treatise is a consideration of the infinite mercy of.God, with prayer for its continuance to the meditator.

NARRACIO: A TALE ÞAT RYCHERDE HERMET [made] [26], some 200 words of prose, is in MS. Harley 1022 (end of 14th century) a part of *Encomium Nominis Iesu* (see page 463), but is a separate piece in MS. Thornton (1430-1440).

TWO PROSE ANECDOTES [27], 'Rycharde hermyte reherces' and 'Allswa he reherces,' each some 200 words, one on 'unperfitte,' the other on 'verraye' Contrition, from Cæsarius Heisterbachensis, are in MS. Thornton f. 194 (1430-1440). The former has been traced to Rolle's Latin *Forma sive Regula de Modo Confitendi.*

MORALIA RICHARDI HERMITE DE NATURA APIS [28] follows the above. It attributes to the bee three curious habits (two on authority of Aristotle), said to illustrate human practice.

A PROSE ANECDOTE [29], 'Alswa Heraclides,' of some 175 words from Heraclides Paradisius, follows the *Moralia.* It is said to be used by Rolle 'in Ensampill.' It tells of a girl who for ten years shut herself up, and took her food through a hole in a wall, because her beauty had tempted a youth.

THREE SHORT PROSE EXPOSITIONS [30] follow the above—one of the *Commandments,* one of the *Seven Gifts of the Holy Ghost* (see Chapter XI of *Form of Perfect Living,* page 450; and *Of Grace,* page 452), and one on *Delight in Christ.*

A TRACT ON THE PATER NOSTER [31] is in MS. Thornton f. 209 v (1430-1440; see page 353).

THE PRIVITY OF THE PASSION [32], an abridged prose translation (some 12000 words) of Bonaventura's popular *Meditationes Vitæ Christi,* Chapters 74-92, is in MS. Thornton f. 179 (1430-1440). After prefatory exhortation on the efficacy for edification of meditation on the Passion, the piece narrates in detail the incidents from the rising from the Last Supper to the apparitions of Christ after the Resurrection. The narrative is divided to correspond with the Hours of the Cross. It is to be connected with the *Meditations on the Supper* (see page 358) that is sometimes incorrectly assigned to Mannyng.

A translation of all of Bonaventura's *Life of Christ* was made early in the fifteenth century by Nicholas Love, under title *The Mirrour of the Blessed Lyf of Iesu Crist.*

AN EPISTLE ON SALVATION BY LOVE OF THE NAME OF JESUS [33], some 1500 words of prose, is in MS. Thornton f. 229 (1430-1440). It has Rolle's idea of the various ranges and qualities of bliss in Heaven. It is in Caption 45 of the Vernon copy of Hilton's *Scale of Perfection* (see page 460).

ON PRAYER [34], 3000 words of rhythmical prose with alliteration, the end missing, is in MS. Thornton f. 233 (1430-

1440). Several scholars have accepted it as Rolle's. It treats of the sources, nature, and influence of prayer.

A treatise similar to the above in rhythmical prose with alliteration, probably originally Northern, is said to be in MS. Royal 18 A X f. 8 (1350-1400, or after 1400).

SIX THINGS TO WIT IN PRAYER [35] is in MS. Thornton f. 237 (1430-1440). It consists of about 3200 words of prose, the beginning being missing; and is evidently a part of a more extensive piece. A much shorter passage on the theme is in *Our Daily Work* (see page 452).

A PRAYER TO CHRIST [36], 'Ihesu Christe goddes sune of beuene,' makes up some hundred words of prose in MS. Thornton f. 212 (1430-1440).

'HE ÞAT DEVOTELY SAYSE' [37] is a prose introduction (200 words) to a Latin prayer in MS. Thornton f. 176 v (1430-1440).

'NOW IHESU GODDIS SONNE' [38] is a prose prayer for the Seven Gifts of the Holy Ghost, in MS. Thornton f. 178 (1430-1440).

THE TWELVE PROFITS OF TRIBULATION [39] consists of some 7500 words of prose in MSS. Royal 17 B XVII f. 49 v (1370-1400; West Midland) and Laud 210 f. 99 (c. 1370; Southern). It is a close translation of Peter of Blois' *Duodecim Utilitates Tribulationis,* and was probably originally Northern.

A later Midland translation, perhaps derived from the above and combined with other elements, is represented in the fifteenth-century MSS. Royal 17 A XXV, Cbg. Univ. Libr. Ii IV 9, Harley 1706 f. 54, Rawlinson C 894, Royal 17 C XVIII, and Corpus Christi College Oxf. 220.

Another treatise on Tribulation is said to be in MSS. Cbg. Univ. Libr. Ji VI 40 and Bodley 938.

OF THE DOUBLE COMING OF CHRIST [40], in MS. Royal 17 B XVII f. 67 (1370-1400, West Midland), is a prose translation (about 1000 words) of Bernard's *De Adventu Domini*, Sermo VI. In the MS. it is followed immediately by several Latin pieces ascribed to Rolle.

A SERIES OF BRIEF COUNSELS [41] on 'Truth, Hope, Love, Grace, Honor,' etc., makes up about 500 words of prose in MS. Royal 17 B XVII f. 100 (see above).

A TALKING OF THE LOVE OF GOD [42], probably of Northern origin, is in MS. Vernon f. 367 (1370-1380; Southern). Intended to be written as prose, it is made up chiefly of alliterative long lines, with rimed couplets, tirades, and strophes. It consists of some 12000 words. Its editor has styled it, with little exaggeration, 'one of the pearls of Old English literature.' It is a rhapsody of passionate love and devotion, a long-sustained series of intense lyrical outbursts as the writer contemplates the beauties and the perfections of the Heavenly Lover, his own unworthiness, Christ's incarnation and passion for him, the sorrows and joys of the Virgin, and the assurance of salvation and of Christ's boundless love. Though perfervid and too material and fleshly in its expression and suggestion, the piece deserves far more consideration than apparently has been given it.

THE MIRROR OF SINNERS [43], a free abridged translation of the *Speculum Peccatoris* ascribed to Augustine, Bernard, and Rolle, consists of some 1800 words of originally Southern prose in MSS. University College Oxf. 97 f. 253 (15th or end of 14th century), Br. Mus. Additional 22283 (1380-1400), Laud 174, Harley 1706 (15th century), Cbg. Univ. Libr. Ff V 45 and Ff VI 55, Tanner 336 (15th century), Douce 13 (14th century). The piece expounds in detail the sentence: 'Would that they knew and understood, and provided for, the last things.'

A MEDITATION OF THE FIVE WOUNDS OF CHRIST [44] comprises some 650 words of prose, probably originally Southern, in MSS. University College Oxf. 97 f. 262 (15th or end of 14th century) and Br. Mus. Additional

22283 f. 61 v (1380-1400). In the Oxford MS., Rolle's *Form* (see page 449) follows it.

A FULL GOOD MEDITATION FOR ONE TO SAY BY HIMSELF ALONE [45] makes up some 1200 words of prose in MSS. (see above) University College Oxf. 97 f. 305, Br. Mus. Additional 22283, and Laud 174. The piece explains carefully the behavior of the penitent suppliant before, during, and after the utterance of the prayer itself.

A MEDITATION BY ST. ANSELM [46], especially on the Judgment, comprisês some 1200 words of prose in the MSS. just named.

With the four pieces just mentioned is found in several of the MSS. *Of Three Arrows on Doomsday* (see page 453).

'THOU SCHALT LOVE THI LORD THI GOD OF AL THŸN HERTE' [47] is the text of a discourse of 1200 words in MSS. University College Oxf. 97 (15th or end of 14th century) and Laud 210 (c. 1370).

THE DESERT OF RELIGION (see page 371) is ascribed in the MSS. to Rolle.

CONTEMPLATIONS OF THE DREAD AND LOVE OF GOD [48], in the fifteenth-century MSS. Royal 17 A XXV f. 13, Harley 2409 and 1706 f. 154, and Cbg. Univ. Libr. Ii VI 40 f. 4, was printed in 1506 by de Worde as Rolle's. The piece consists of some 18000 words. The MSS. all appear to be Southern.

THE REMEDY AGAINST THE TROUBLES OF TEMPTATIONS [49] was printed as Rolle's by de Worde in 1508 and 1519. The matter really comprises three pieces. The first, *Four Profitable Things*, consists of some 350 words from Chapter III of Rolle's *Form* (see page 450). The second is the title piece. It consists of some 9200 words in ten chapters. The versions in MSS. Harley 1706 f. 115 and Cbg. Univ. Libr. Hh I 11 (both Southern) are said to differ much from that of de Worde. The third is a *Meditation in Saying Devoutly the Psalter of Our Lady*, translated from Alanus de Rupe. It consists of some 2500 words.

'ON FOURE MANERS MAY A MAN WYT' [50] con-sists of some fifty words of prose among the lyrics (see page 505) in MS. Cbg. Univ. Libr. Dd V 64 (late 14th or early 15th century) indicating how to determine freedom from deadly sin.

'GASTLY GLADNESS IN IHESU' [51], some hundred words of prose among the Cbg. Dd lyrics (see page 505), is on spiritual gladness, joy of heart, and love of Christ.

It may be mentioned that Rolle's *De Emendatione Vitæ* (*On the Mending of Life*) [52] was given at least five different Eng-lish translations before 1450. Of these at least ten MSS. are known.

2. WALTER HILTON

Walter Hilton [53] is said to have been to the spiritual life of the late fourteenth century something of what Rolle was to that of the earlier part of the century. Unfortunately, we know little about him, and of English works but three can be surely named as his. In MS. Harley 6576 he is said to have died March 24, 1395-1396. In MS. Cbg. Univ. Libr. Ee IV 30 f. 4 he is styled 'canonicus de Thurgarton qui obiit A. D. 1395 decimo Kal. Apriles circa solis occasum.' At Thur-garton near Newark in Nottinghamshire was a house of Augustinians. Judged from the writings apparently surely his, Hilton was characterized less by mystic, fervid enthusiasm, than by a forceful, logical power that finds expression in a clear, smooth, direct prose.

THE SCALE OF PERFECTION [54] (*Scala Perfec-tionis*), an extensive prose work apparently certainly Hilton's, is preserved in eight Harleian MSS., three Rawlinson MSS., MS. Lansdowne 362, MSS. Cbg. Dd V 55 and Ff V 40, and others. As some of the MSS. begin with address to 'sister,' others to 'brother,' others to 'brother and sister,' the assumption that the work was intended for anchoresses, as was the *Ancren Riwle* (but see page 361), is questionable. Though perhaps it was composed for the recluse, its doctrine is capable of broader application.

The work falls into three books. After a brief passage on the Active Life and the Contemplative Life, the *Scale* discusses the kinds of Contemplation, the good and the evil appeal of the senses, the objects of activity of the Contemplative Man, the aids to Contemplation—Humility, Faith, Hope; Prayer, its kinds, its manner; Meditation; Temptations and their remedies; knowledge of the Soul, cleansing and restoring the Soul's dignity, the Seven Sins and their remedies; Man the image of God after the soul, how is restored and reformed the image misshapen by sin, how the reforming must be by Faith and Feeling, how such Feeling is to be understood, and the manner of reforming of the Soul.

The number of extant MSS. suggests that the work had a wide circulation. The Carthusians esteemed it highly, and early in the fifteenth century a Carmelite turned it into Latin. De Worde printed it in 1494, 1519, and 1525, and Pynson in 1506. Dom Serenus Cressy printed a modernized text in 1659 that was reissued in 1672 and 1679. Father Guy printed an edition in 1869. Reprints of Cressy's text were made in 1870 and 1908 for general reading with approval of the Roman Church.

Chapters 70, 91, 82 of the *Scale* are reproduced in three pieces of MS. Rawlinson C 285 f. 57, 'Be whàte takynes,' 'What thyng helpes,' 'How ane Ankares' (see page 454).

AN EPISTLE ON MIXED LIFE [55], consisting of some 7500 words of prose, is in MSS. Vernon f. 353 (oldest MS., 1370-1380), Additional 22283 (1380-1400), Thornton (only Northern text; beginning missing; 1430-1440), Harley 2254 (beginning missing), and others. It was printed by Julian Notary in 1507, de Worde in 1525 and 1533, and Pynson in 1516, each time being ascribed to Hilton. MS. Vernon begins, 'Here beginneþ a luitel Boc þat was writen to a worldli lord . . . ,' and has twenty chapter divisions. MS. Thornton has no chapters. The later MSS. and the prints modify the Ver-

non numbering and location of chapters. They add an epilogue and an introductory passage. Notary's text is headed,
'This is a deuout boke compyled by mayster Walter Hylton to
a deuout man in temperal estate, how he sholde rule him.'
Apparently originally, as in MS. Vernon, the piece was
directed to a devout worldly lord, to teach him to conduct himself in love to God and to his fellow Christians.

The tract examines carefully the nature of and the authority
for the Active Life and the Contemplative Life, and shows where
and when and how each should be followed, recommending to prelates and to worldly lords that rule other men, the pursuit, on
proper conditions, of the mixed life by example of Christ and holy
men of high degree.

OF ANGELS' SONG [56] consists of some 2000 words of
prose in MSS. Cbg. Univ. Libr. Dd V 55 (Northern; c. 1400)
and Ff V 40 (Southern; 15th century), and Thornton f. 219
(headed 'The Anehede of Godd with Mannis Saule'; Northern;
c. 1430-1440). Method and style favor authorship by Hilton,
and contradict ascription to Rolle made on the basis of association in MSS. with works of Hampole. As early as 1521,
Pepwell assigned the piece to Hilton.

Very logically the tract demonstrates that souls fit for Heaven
must be purified, spiritualized, and made accordant with God and
responsive to the spiritual. God comforts souls in Heaven with
the song of angels, which is not heard, but is felt by the responsive.
Purity of soul and perfectness in love fit one to hear the angels'
song.

PROPER WILL [57], some 1000 words of prose, is in
MSS. Cbg. Univ. Libr. Dd V 55 (Northern; c. 1400) and Ff
V 40 (Southern; 15th century) and Ff VI 31 (Southern).
Following in several MSS. the *Commandment of Love to God*
(see page 451), it has sometimes been assigned to Rolle; but
its method and style contradict Rolle's authorship, and favor
composition by Hilton. Logically and with argument the
piece shows that self-will must be forsaken and made 'common'—that is, it must be made accordant with the will of God,
of all good men, and of the sovereign.

ENCOMIUM NOMINIS JESU [58] or *The Virtues of the Holy Name of Jesus*, some 1800 words in MS. Harley 1022 f. 62 (end of 14th century) and 1600 words in MS. Thornton f. 192 (1430-1440), is a translation of the Latin *Encomium*. By Thornton it is improperly attributed to Rolle. The style perhaps justifies ascription to Hilton.

Ecstatically the piece exclaims that the name of Jesus is full of infinite virtue; love of that name fills with boundless joy; joy and salvation are born only of that joy. In Harley the piece is enforced by a story (written separately in the other MS., see page 455) of the author's temptation through the image of a woman just after he had abandoned the secular life.

OF DEADLY AND VENIAL SIN [59], 600 words of prose reminding of a passage in the *Pricke of Conscience* (ll. 3356 ff., see page 447), is in MS. Cbg. Univ. Libr. Dd V 55 (Northern; c. 1400). It has been suggested that Hilton wrote the piece. The author attempts to distinguish for an inquiring brother the difference between the two classes of sin.

Horstmann suggests that Hilton wrote *Against Boasting and Pride* and *Sayings of Fathers* [60], Items 11 and 12 of the group in MS. Rawlinson C 285 f. 57 ff. (see page 454).

3. WILLIAM NASSYNGTON

William Nassyngton [61] is named in some MSS. as author of a version of de Waldeby's *Speculum Vitæ*, *A Treatise on Trinity and Unity*, and a paraphrase of a part of Rolle's *Form of Perfect Living*. As the copies of his work in the Royal MSS. are dated 1418, Nassyngton probably flourished at about 1375. MS. Thornton declares him 'quondam aduocati curie Eboraci.' He has little originality or poetical faculty; he is a translator with a knack for fluent verse.

THE MIRROR OF LIFE [62], in MSS. Cotton Tiberius E VII f. 1 (c. 1400), Cbg. Univ. Libr. Ll I 8 (14th century), etc., has been discussed with the other pieces associated with the *Mirror of St. Edmund* (see page 348).

A TREATISE ON TRINITY AND UNITY [63] consists of 216 short couplets in MS. Thornton f. 189 (Northern; 1430-1440). The material is derived largely from St. Edmund's *Speculum*. The piece is in the form of prayer to God, exalting Him as Creator, Redeemer, and Judge, and offering a *résumé* of the facts of the Creation, the Incarnation, the Passion, and the Judgment.

A METRICAL FORM OF LIVING [64], in MS. Cotton Tiberius E VII f. 85 v (c. 1400), is possibly by Nassyngton. It consists of 431 short couplets, and is a version of the first part of Rolle's *Form of Perfect Living* (see page 450).

Because they occur in MS. Cotton Tiberius E VII after the pieces just mentioned, Horstmann suggested that perhaps Nassyngton wrote the Tiberius *Lamentation of St. Mary on the Passion* (see page 415), the metrical *Gast of Gy* (see page 170), and the expanded version of the Northern *Evangelia Dominicalia* (see page 291).

4.   Juliana Lampit [65]

FOURTEEN REVELATIONS OF DIVINE LOVE [66] *Made to a Devout Servant of Our Lord, Called Mother Juliana, an Anchoress of Norwich*, is in MS. Sloane 2499, an Amherst MS., and a MS. in the Bibliothèque Nationale, Paris. The author was probably Juliana Lampit, who had a cell at the east end of the churchyard of St. Julian's at Norwich, who was thirty and a half years old in 1373, and who is said to have lived until 1443. The second of the 83 short chapters of this prose work, states that the revelations took place on May 14, 1373. The last chapter says that 'fourteen year after and more' the writer obtained from the Lord a spiritual interpretation of the revelations: Love was His meaning; Love showed her the revelations; and the revelations were shown for Love. The revelations are evidences of His love, consisting largely of manifestations of phases or facts of the Passion. The piece is a beautiful embodiment of the achievement and the assurance of a beautiful spirit.

CHAPTER XII

WYCLIFFE AND HIS FOLLOWERS

John Wycliffe [1] was born at Hipswell near Richmond in
Yorkshire at about 1320. Probably he became a student, and
later a scholar or fellow, of Balliol College, Oxford, of which
he is said to have been Master in 1361. Probably in May,
1361, he obtained the rectorship of Fillingham in the diocese
of Lincoln. This he resigned in 1368 for a benefice at Ludgershall near Oxford. In 1366 or 1374, in his tract *Determinatio
. . . de Dominio contra Unum Monachum*, he appeared as
supporter of the secular power against the Church. In 1372
he became doctor of theology. In 1374 he went to Bruges as
ambassador to the Papal delegates at Ghent for the English
government. Shortly after this his appointment to the prebend of Aust at Westbury was confirmed by the government.
Apparently he failed to obtain a prebend at Lincoln to which
he was 'provided' by the Pope. Soon after his Westbury confirmation he resigned his benefice at Ludgershall to accept that
of Lutterworth in Leicestershire with which his name is always
connected.

On the mission to Bruges Wycliffe came to personal
acquaintance with the Duke of Lancaster. His preaching and
teaching of his doctrines of the rights of the secular lords, and
of opposition to the Church and the clergy in their efforts for
worldly power, won for him from John of Gaunt and Lord
Percy an approval that stood him in good stead when in February, 1377, he appeared before the Archbishop of Canterbury
at St. Paul's to answer a charge of heresy. The violence of
the Duke and Percy and the populace, brought Wycliffe off
unsentenced. Papal bulls were issued against him and his
doctrines. The University of Oxford was ordered to bring
him before the Archbishop of Canterbury and the Bishop of

London. In the summer of 1377, consulted by the counselors
of the King and the Parliament as to exportation of money to
foreign holders of English benefices, Wycliffe wrote his powerful paper against such payment, and composed another on
dominion. The Papal accusations were brought forward at
Oxford; the authorities declared Wycliffe's ideas sound, but
their expression liable to misinterpretation. In 1378 he was
brought before the Archbishop and the Bishop at Lambeth;
but the widow of the Black Prince forbade procedure against
him, and the citizens violently put an end to the trial. A second trial at Lambeth led merely to a request that, because of
the scandal they produced, Wycliffe's doctrines be not preached.

Soon the schism headed by Urban VI and Clement VII led
Wycliffe to question the fundamental principles of the ecclesiastical system. Now he gave himself to efforts to instruct the
people in the vital issues of Christian religion. He instituted
his 'poor priests,' who, living in poverty and clad in russet
gowns, went about on foot preaching to rich and poor all over
the country. Everywhere in his writings he urged the prime
authority of the Scriptures as true in itself and as opposed
to ecclesiastical systems and laws. Moreover, he incited, probably he supervised, and perhaps he participated in, the making
of an English version of the whole Bible. This was finished at
about 1382, at latest by 1384. A revision was completed after
his death (see page 410).

In 1381 Wycliffe began to become clearly unorthodox in his
views regarding the Eucharist. These views were condemned
at Oxford, and he was forbidden to teach them at that place.
In the same year the rising of the peasants was connected by
many with his preaching and with that of his poor priests.
In May, 1382, Archbishop Courtenay summoned the 'Earthquake Council,' which condemned a list of twenty-four views or
theses of Wycliffe and his followers. But Wycliffe remained a
power at Oxford. Now, by aid of royal injunction, after great
difficulty, the ecclesiastical authorities obtained repression of
Wycliffiteism at Oxford. Yet Wycliffe's hold on popular regard was such that he was able to withdraw and to live at

Lutterworth unharmed. There, apparently, he preached some of his extant sermons, perhaps worked at and certainly directed the translation of the Bible, probably composed some of his most fiery invectives against the Pope and the friars, and in 1382 wrote a petition to Parliament against them. That he ever recanted, as has been declared, is scarcely to be credited. He became partly paralyzed in 1382 or 1383. After another stroke, he died at Lutterworth on December 31, 1384.

The eminence of Wycliffe has caused to be associated with him many writings [2]. Most of these are assigned to him on the basis of similarity of idea with pieces probably his; some are assigned on one or more of the additional bases that they are well written, or have been attributed to him in the MSS. or by early writers, or occur in MSS. that contain much work of his or probably by him. The matter is complicated by the facts that Wycliffe had among his associates a number of men of excellent training and of much natural ability, and that his ideas were held and, no doubt, expressed by many kindred spirits.

The many Latin and the English pieces connected with Wycliffe's name, are characterized by recurrence of certain ideas, of which the following are most prominent: attacks in the whole Church hierarchy, from the Pope (Antichrist) down to the lowest orders; attacks on privy auricular confession, the friars' doctrine of the Eucharist, the new intoning and chanting in services, the endowment of the clergy and possession of property by them, the elevation of ecclesiastical law above Christ's law, Papal infallability, misuse of anathema, the use and right of absolution and indulgence, abuse of tithing, simony, checking of preaching of poor priests and failure of friars and regular clergy to preach, and the Church's teaching of and resort to war; and insistence on the rule of poverty and preaching as the only true rule for priests, on the God-given right of dominion by laymen with its corollary of lay correction and subjection of the clergy, and on the supreme authority of the teaching and the life of Christ as represented in the Scriptures.

It is with the English pieces that we are concerned.

The Wycliffite translations of the Bible [3] are dealt with on page 410.

On the following pages the works usually attributed [4] to Wycliffe or his followers [5] are mentioned under the heads: 1. *Accepted Writings of Wycliffe;* 2. *Additional Probably Genuine Works of Wycliffe;* 3. *Wycliffite Writings;* 4. *Writings Not by Wycliffe.*

The canon is made up from agreements of the lists of Vaughan, Shirley, Arnold, Lechler, and Matthew. But slight consideration shows that the actual reasons offered in support of Wycliffe's authorship, are, in the cases of many works included in the first class or the second, of little weight. The *Sermons* are the bases from which must be argued composition in English by Wycliffe. The whole matter needs to be gone over again. After careful study of some of the pieces, Jones has assigned to Wycliffe *De Papa, The Seven Works, The Ten Commandments, Five Questions, Ave Maria* (first text), and *The Church and Her Members;* and has denied to him *De Officio* and *Of Confession* (both from Latin works by Wycliffe), *Of Dominion, De Blasphemia, Of the Leaven, Of Prelates, Of Clerks Possessioners, How Men Ought to Obey Prelates, The Office of Curates, The Order of Priesthood, Three Things, The Clergy May Not Hold Property, How Satan* (the last seven to be classed together), *Faith, Hope, and Charity, Lincolniensis, Vita Sacerdotum* (the last three with alliteration, and to be classed together, the last two in a Western dialect), and *Of the Seven Deadly Sins* (with alliteration, and in a Western dialect).

1. ACCEPTED WRITINGS OF WYCLIFFE

The accepted (see the remarks above) writings of Wycliffe fall into four groups: I. *Sermons;* II. *Didactic Works;* III. *Statements of Belief, etc.;* IV. *Controversial Works.*

### I.	Sermons

THE SERMONS [6] of Wycliffe printed fill two large volumes. They fall into three classes: (1) On the Gospels for

Sunday, for the *Commune Sanctorum*, and for the *Proprium Sanctorum*, 123 items; (2) on the Week-Day Gospels, 116 items; (3) on the Epistles for Sundays, 55 items. All of these classes, or one or more of them, are said to occur in a number (19) of MSS. that have been enumerated by Arnold. The chief MS., Bodley 788 (end of 14th century), contains them all.᳠

The sermons average in print from two to three pages each. Much of each sermon on the Gospels consists of a paraphrase, or an expanded narrative, or a translation, of the Scriptural matter. The translations are not those of the so-called Wycliffe versions (see page 410). There often follows an interpretation that is sometimes mystical. Commonly the comment is running. The concluding comments (some of them directions to preachers) in certain of the earlier Gospel sermons, suggest that perhaps some or all of this class were composed for use of priests rather than for oral delivery. The sermons on the Epistles differ from the rest in that they contain less narrative, and are confined more to exposition of the text, to interpretation, comment, and application.

Wycliffe's emphatic opposition to story-telling by preachers, prevents appearance of *exempla* in the sermons. Through the pieces, in marked contrast to the practice in other similar writings that we have discussed (see pages 278, 279, 282, 303), runs a steady series of comments on and applications to conditions and topics of debate of the day. The attacks are not on social or political conditions; they are confined to ecclesiastical or religious matters. There is persistent and intense attack on the friars and on abuses in the Church. Assaults are made on the selling of pardons, the false new consistory law by which is supplanted the law of Christ, the value of pardons and dispensations, the Church's right of absolution, the granting and the abuse of indulgences, the value of pilgrimages, the Church's and the friars' false doctrines of the Eucharist, endowments of the clergy and holding of property by the Church, the overgrown authority of the Pope, auricular confession, the Pope's right to legislate for the Church, Papal infallibility, the utility of cloistered orders, the methods of

canonization, ecclesiastical zeal for temporal power, the preaching of war, the crusade of le Spencer, the Church's use of the
temporal sword, and much else.   Constant are the comments
and applications attacking the Pope—that Antichrist; the
friars—those wolves in the sheepfold, those tares in the field,
those limbs of the devil, those modern Pharisees; the whole hierarchy, Pope, canons, monks, curates—the false Christs of the
Gospel prophecy.   Persistently friars and clergy are inveighed
against as substitutors of a new, false, worldly order for the
order of Christ; as lovers of this order and its rules above the
order and law of Christ; as covetous, incorrigible, worldly; as
conceivers and expounders of heresy and false doctrine; as idle;
and as silencers of preaching by the faithful priests.

The manner of the sermons is direct, the expression concise.
The language fulfils the urging of one of the pieces that the
people be addressed in a speech that is not strange to them.
The sermons are pithy, vigorous, often fiery; they everywhere
evince profound conviction, zealous assurance, and ardent
enthusiasm.

WYCKLYFFE'S WYCKETT [7] is a separate piece
printed early and apparently extant in no MS.   It is a sermon
presenting Wycliffe's special views as to the nature of the
Host.

VÆ OCTUPLEX [8] and **OF MINISTERS OF THE
CHURCH** [9] are found in every complete MS. of the Sermons except Douce 321.   *Væ Octuplex* is an exposition of
Matthew 23, 'Wo be to ʒou, scribes and Fariseis.'   In detail,
each of the eight accusations against the Scribes and the Pharisees is applied against the friars and the prelates.—*Of Ministers of the Church* is an exposition of *Matthew* 24, 'Jesus wente
out of þe temple; and his disciplis came to him to shewe him
hilding of the temple. . . .'   The author will expound this
Gospel in the mother tongue, especially because it is not all
read in church.   He interprets and applies all the details of
the passage, item by item, to conditions of religion, especially
to the Church of the day.

A set of fifty-four other sermons on the Sunday Gospels [10], and five others on great festivals, have been incorrectly ascribed to Wycliffe.

II. Didactic Works

THE TEN COMMANDMENTS [11] (see pages 351, 354) severally are stated with exposition in two versions, one in MS. Bodley 789, the other (fuller, but less individual and forceful) in MSS. Laud 524 and University College Oxf. 97. Printed, the matter makes ten pages. The Bodley version has the familiar Wycliffe notions as to priests who do not preach, dominion resting on Grace, and urging to read the Scriptures.

TWO EXPOSITIONS OF THE PATER NOSTER [12] [13], item by item, are assigned to Wycliffe (see pages 351, 353, 479). One is in MSS. Bodley 789, Lambeth 408, Cbg. Univ. Libr. Dd XII 39 f. 72, Trinity College Dublin C V 6, and Harley 2385. The other (less full) is in MS. Harley 2398, a MS. at Wrest Park, and a MS. formerly owned by a Mr. Corser.

THE AVE MARIA [14], with comments (in print 2 pages) perhaps by Wycliffe, is in all the MSS. of the earlier *Pater Noster* (see also pages 350, 479, 530).

EXPOSITIONS OF THE APOSTLES' CREED [15], THE FIVE OUTER WITS [16], THE FIVE INNER WITS [17], in MS. Lambeth 408, all unimportant, have been ascribed to Wycliffe.

A COMMENT ON THE DEADLY SINS [18], in MSS. Bodley 647 (West Midland), Douce 273, and Trinity College Dublin C V 6, is perhaps by Wycliffe. The piece (in print some 50 pages) deals elaborately with each Sin in its several forms, with application to contemporary conditions and various orders of society.

TREATISES ON THE SEVEN WORKS OF MERCY BODILY and THE SEVEN WORKS OF MERCY GHOSTLY [19] (in print 15 pages) are written as one tract in MS. New College Oxford 95 (15th century). They are also in MS. Trinity College Dublin C V 6 (15th century). The work was composed probably not long after May, 1382. The first part discusses chiefly almsgiving and tithes; the second urges chiefly the need for preaching, and the shameful neglect of it.

FIVE QUESTIONS ON LOVE [20], in MS. New College Oxford 95, is a short reply (2 pages in print) to five inquiries as to Love: What, where is Love? How love God medefully? How know if one loves as God wishes? In what condition of life may one love God best?—The inevitable attack on friars is prominent. Copies of a Latin version of the piece are in Vienna and Prague.

ON THE SUFFICIENCY OF HOLY SCRIPTURES [21], in MS. Trinity College Dublin C III 12, is a brief argument (one page in print) for defending the supreme authority of the Scriptures against Antichrist's clerks.

OF WEDDID MEN AND WIFES AND OF HERE CHILDREN ALSO [22], in MSS. Corpus Christi College Cbg. 296 (last of 14th or beginning of 15th century), Cbg. Univ. Libr. Dd XII 39 f. 3 (latter part of 14th century), and Br. Mus. Additional 24202 f. 29 (14th century; see page 483), is perhaps Wycliffe's. The piece (in print some 13 pages) gives counsel as to the purpose and the justification of marriage, marriage of priests, continence as the highest state, what constitutes a true marriage, the relations and duties of the parties, and duties of parents to children. Much knowledge of homely practical conditions, and insight into human nature, are shown. One of the three great failings of married folk, is the wives' wasting of money on begging friars.

DE STIPENDIIS MINISTRORUM [23] (in print a page and a half) is in MSS. Corpus Christi College Cbg. 296 and

Trinity College Dublin C III 12. It indicates the qualifications. to be looked for in seeking priests, and inveighs against incensing and intoning.

A SHORT RULE OF LIFE [24], in MSS. Corpus Christi College Cbg. 296 and Laud 174, is possibly Wycliffe's. The piece (in print 3 pages) gives general directions for thanks and prayer on awaking; suggestions for right conduct in the day; and special counsels to priests, to lords, and to laborers. In Laud a paragraph on the Judgment is added.

III.   Statements of Belief, a Letter, a Petition

TWO STATEMENTS AS TO BELIEF CONCERNING THE EUCHARIST are in Knyghton's *Chronicle* ascribed to Wycliffe. The first [25], apparently an abstract from Wycliffe's *Confessio* of 1381, is quite orthodox; the second [26] (also in MS. Bodley 647) declares belief in consubstantiation, and dates from the middle of 1382. Both pieces are very short.

A LETTER TO POPE URBAN [27] (in print two pages), probably originally in Latin, is in MSS. Bodley 647 and New College Oxf. 95. It was composed probably in 1384, when paralysis prevented Wycliffe from going to Rome as the Pope had suggested. The writer is willing to bear all reasonable correction. He boldly declares that the Gospel is the heart of God's law; and that the Pope is more by virtuous living than by worldly possessions, and is to be followed as he follows Christ.

A PETITION TO THE KING AND PARLIAMENT [28] (in print 14 pages), in MSS. Corpus 296 and Trinity Dublin C III 12, is perhaps addressed to the parliament assembled May 6, 1382. It urges permission to members of religious orders to withdraw at will; the King's right to deal with the temporal interests of the Church; dependence of giving of tithes and offerings on the merit of the clergy; and the giving

of free course to the teachings of Christ on the Eucharist, and
the stopping of the contrary.

IV.   Controversial Works

SIMONISTS AND APOSTATES [29] or DE DUOBUS
GENERIBUS HÆRETICORUM (in print a page and a
half), in MS. New College Oxf. 95, is perhaps a somewhat early
piece of Wycliffe's.   It condemns simony as universal in the
Church, and warns against apostasy in preferring Man's law
to God's.

CHURCH TEMPORALITIES [30] (in print four and a
half pages), in MS. Corpus 296 and in a Dublin MS. (not distinguished by Arnold), is of about 1378, and probably Wycliffe's.   It offers three reasons why secular lords should
deprive the Church of its temporal holdings, and should compel the clergy to lead holy and unselfish lives of Christian
poverty.

DE PRECATIONIBUS SACRIS [31] (in print over 9
pages), in MSS. Corpus 296 and Trinity College Dublin C
III 12 and C V 6, is of about 1379 and probably Wycliffe's.
It declares the efficacy of prayers of righteous priests, and the
injuriousness of prayers of evil priests.   Finally, it attacks
intoning or chanting of prayers.

LINCOLNIENSIS [32] (in print 2 pages), in MS. Bodley
647, is of about 1382, and is perhaps by Wycliffe.   Poor
priests have been imprisoned because their pure lives have been
a reproach to the friars; the powerful laymen should have
them freed.

VITA SACERDOTUM [33] (in print some 8 pages), in
MS. Bodley 647, appears to be of 1382 or 1383.   Possession
of temporal power and property by the clergy, is contrary to'
Christ's command of poverty; the God-given power of lords
and great men, should be used gradually to deprive the church
of its worldly holdings.

DE PONTIFICUM ROMANORUM SCHISMATE [34] (in print 24 pages) is in MS. Trinity Dublin C III 12, and dates probably from the end of 1382. The Great Schism is used to attack the temporal aims and means of the Church, particularly the authority of indulgences; the true successors of Peter and the Apostles must live their life; resort to war by the clergy is denounced.

THE GREAT SENTENCE OF CURS EXPOUNDED [35] (in print 66 pages), in MS. Corpus 296, is of 1383. The clergy are declared subject to anathema on some score of counts, the Pope being the most culpable offender.

THE CHURCH AND HER MEMBERS [36] (in print some 26 pages) is in MS. Bodley 788 with the Sermons, and in MS. Trinity Dublin C V 6. The tract is a general attack on the Church as unusually corrupt, and on the Pope as Antichrist. Practically all the chief Wycliffite contentions are thoroughly presented and maintained.

FIFTY HERESIES AND ERRORS OF FRIARS [37] (in print 35 pages), in MSS. Bodley 647 and Corpus 296, and in a Trinity Dublin MS. (not distinguished by Arnold), is probably of the latter half of 1384. Perhaps the list of twenty-four accusations against Wycliffe in the Council of London, suggested the idea of this list, each item of which is carefully exposed in a section of its own. The points of attack are those familiar through the other pieces.

DE BLASPHEMIA, CONTRA FRATRES [38] (in print 27 pages), in MS. Bodley 647, is probably Wycliffe's. Its three parts declare blasphemous, and suggest remedies for, the friars' doctrines of the Eucharist, of begging, and of sharing the merits of their order by letters of fraternity.

DE APOSTASIA CLERI [39] (in print 11 pages), in MS. Trinity Dublin C V 6, is perhaps by Wycliffe and perhaps of before 1381. It attacks religious orders as such, and is given largely to exposure of evils of Church endowment.

SEVEN HERESIES [40] (in print 5 pages), in MSS. Douce 274, Harley 2385, and Trinity Dublin C V 6, is probably by Wycliffe and after 1381. Each under its own caption, are ·presented the seven heresies of the friars and the clergy of Rome against the seven petitions of the Lord's Prayer.

OCTO IN QUIBUS SEDUCUNTUR SIMPLICES CHRISTIANI [41] (in print 6 pages), in MSS. Corpus 296 and Trinity College Dublin C III 12 and C V 6, explains eight sources of deception of simple Christians.

2. ADDITIONAL PROBABLY GENUINE WORKS OF WYCLIFFE

The following writings have been regarded as probably by Wycliffe (see remarks on page 468).

CONFESSION AND PENITENCE [42] (in print 19 pages) is in the fifteenth-century MSS. Ashburnham XXVII and Trinity Dublin C V 6 f. 127 v. The piece declares need of confession, opposes privy confession, urges general public confession, admits silent confession; and it also asserts that Peter's keys are really knowledge of God's law, and teaching, preaching, and reproving.

DE DOMINIO DIVINO [43] (in print 10 pages), in MS. Trinity Dublin C III 12 f. 188, is probably Wycliffe's, but signs of translation from Latin have been detected in it. It opposes Church ownership and endowments, and the judging of the clergy only by ecclesiastical courts. It bases its argument on dominion and correction by laymen, through inalienable gifts of God.

DE SACRAMENTO ALTARIS [44] (in print one page) is in MS. Bodley 788 f. 96 (end of 14th century) and Trinity Dublin C III 12. The author poses as a defender of the Church; the new orders are heretics, for they deny that the bread is Christ's body, and attribute their heresy to the Pope and the Papal authorities; the Host is God's body in form of bread.

OF FAITH, HOPE, AND CHARITY [45] (in print 8 pages), in MSS. New College Oxf. 95 f. 124 (15th century) and Trinity Dublin C III 12, is probably Wycliffe's. It defines Faith and Hope and their opposites, and Charity with Paul's enumeration of its properties. The friars are incidentally shown to be without the virtues; but the piece is chiefly evangelical.

TRACTATUS DE PSEUDO-FRERIS [46] (in print 28 pages), in MS. Trinity Dublin C V 6 f. 81 (1400-1450), is very possibly Wycliffe's. Some friars are good, but friars generally fulfil 'Jude's and James' and John's warnings and prophecies against vain religion and apostasy.

DE PAPA [47] (in print 23 pages) is in MS. Ashburnham XXVII f. 25 (15th century), and probably by Wycliffe about 1380. The tract opposes holding of lordship and worldly possessions by the Church, and meets the arguments for such holding. .

3. WYCLIFFITE WRITINGS

The following pieces are by Wycliffites, some of them perhaps by Wycliffe (see remarks on page 468). In Matthew's edition of them, a synopsis is prefixed to each. In the following notices, MS. Corpus Christi College Cbg. 296 (last of 14th century or early 15th) is indicated by X, and MS. Trinity College Dublin C III 12 (copy of original of X), by AA.

OF THE LEAVEN OF THE PHARISEES [48] (in print 20 pages) is in X and AA. Reference to Bishop le Spencer's crusade dates it about 1383. The tract is weak in style, but reflects some of Wycliffe's representative doctrine: the orders are like the Pharisees, guilty of all the sins of omission and of commission, and they should be exposed.

DE OBEDIENTIA PRÆLATORUM [49] (in print 10 pages) is in X and AA. It is probably by some poor clerical follower of Wycliffe. The author speaks from bitter personal experience of the improper commands and conduct of prelates, of 'poor priests,' of preference of Man's curses to God's, and of Man's law to be obeyed only as it accords with God's law.

THE RULE AND TESTAMENT OF ST. FRANCIS [50] (in print 12 pages) is in X and AA. It recites the rules of St. Francis. Then it shows that the friars break them, for they fail in obedience, in poverty, in charity. It has been suggested that *Fifty Heresies of Friars* (see page 475) is a later amplification of this tract.

OF PRELATES [51] (in print 52 pages) is in X and AA. It appears to have references to le Spencer's crusade, but was written probably not long after Wycliffe's death. It presents a number of familiar accusations against the clergy.

SPECULUM DE ANTICHRISTO [52] (in print 3 pages) is in X and AA. It is perhaps by Wycliffe, and dates from before the attempts to repress the 'poor priests.' It meets the arguments of Antichrist and his clerks against preaching.

OF CLERKS POSSESSIONERS [53] (in print 24 pages) is in X and AA. The tract enumerates the evils to which the practice of possessioners gives birth.

HOW THE OFFICE OF CURATES IS ORDAINED BY GOD [54] (in print 20 pages), in X and AA, mentions le Spencer's crusade of 1838 as a past matter. The piece attacks the evil worldly life of curates.

FOR THE ORDER OF PRIESTHOOD [55] (in print 14 pages), in X and AA, attacks specifically a number of abuses in the life of priests; then it declares the nobleness of the priest's office, and urges priests and lords to amend the evils.

THREE THINGS DESTROY THE WORLD [56] (in print 6 pages) is in X and AA. The three things are shown to be false confessors (friars), wicked (especially ecclesiastical) lawyers, and cheating merchants—but the first are the worst.

OF FEIGNED CONTEMPLATIVE LIFE [57] (in print 8 pages) is in X and AA. It attacks pretense of contemplation in order to escape preaching; contemplation is for Heaven. It opposes singing and too much ritualism in services, and reprobates worldly aims of priests.

AN EXPOSITION OF THE PATER NOSTER [58] (in print some 4 pages), only in X, may be another piece of its kind by Wycliffe (see page 471). It comments on each clause of the Prayer, and concludes with praise of the Prayer.

A TRACT ON THE AVE MARIA [59] (some 5 pages in print; see page 530) is in X and MS. Sidney Sussex College Cbg. Δ, IV, 12. The piece explains the constitution of the *Ave*, and gives the lessons from it. It discourses on vanity in dress, the decay of proper conduct and ideals among gentle folk, gross amusements at Christmas, the bad example set in courts, Eve the bringer of ill, and Mary the bringer of good. After a Wycliffite passage on the immanence of God, the tract concludes with comment on the *Ave*.

HOW SATAN AND HIS CHILDREN TURN WORKS OF MERCY UPSIDE DOWN [60] (in print some 10 pages), in X and AA, contrasts Christ's with the priests' attitude toward the Works of Mercy, and discusses the temptations of the senses and proper use of the senses. The piece shows intimate and intense realization of the distresses of the poor, and urges forcefully evils of imprisonment for debt.

HOW RELIGIOUS MEN SHOULD KEEP CERTAIN ARTICLES or HOW MEN OF PRIVATE RELIGION SHOULD LOVE MORE THE GOSPEL [61] (in print some 5 pages), in X and AA, is a list of forty-four suggestions for proper conduct. Most of these injunctions are negative.

OF SERVANTS AND LORDS [62] (in print 17 pages), in X and AA, was composed possibly by Wycliffe, and soon after Tyler's rebellion. The tract expounds the duties of servants, and earnestly disclaims for the 'poor priests' the false socialistic teachings of the day. But it declares the duties of lords, and inveighs against their oppression of the poor. It attacks the common false conduct of prelates, confessors, lawyers, merchants, servants, and particularly the clergy.

WHY POOR PRIESTS HAVE NO BENEFICE [63] (in print 9 pages) is in X and AA. This well-written piece declares that simony prevents 'poor priests' from benefices; patrons appoint only capable secular agents; 'poor priests' cannot take office, because to hold their place they must waste the people's money, protect the vicious powerful, and feast their patrons—they can do more good unbeneficed. The grounds for the institution of the system of 'poor priests,' are well presented.

HOW ANTICHRIST AND HIS CLERKS TRAVAIL TO DESTROY HOLY WRIT [64] (in print 8 pages), in X and AA, was composed probably when the 'poor priests' needed support in their appeals to God's law in justification of their order. The tract states and meets each of the four false notions: that the Church is of more authority than the Gospels; that St. Augustine says he would not believe the Gospel unless the Church told him to do so; that men know the Gospel only through the Church; and that men believe the Gospel without knowing why.

HOW SATAN AND HIS PRIESTS . . . CAST BY THREE CURSED HERESIES TO DESTROY ALL GOOD LIVING AND MAINTAIN ALL MANNER OF SIN [65] (in print 11 pages) is in X and AA. The piece presents and meets three prevalent heresies: that Holy Writ is false; that a lie is lawful; and that to denounce sins of the great is uncharitable.

OF POOR ·PREACHING PRIESTS [66] (in print 5 pages), in X only, is probably of 1377, and certainly from before 1400. It presents a list of three general and thirteen special needs for reformation of the clergy, and eighteen needs for secular improvement.

THE CLERGY MAY NOT HOLD PROPERTY [67] (in print 43 pages) fills MS. Lambeth 551 (c. 1450). The tract opposes the efforts of the clergy for secular property, and their right to ownership of any such property. Finally, it opposes holding of secular office by priests.

DE OFFICIO PASTORALE [68] (in print 50 pages), in MS. Ashburnham XXVII (15th century), corresponds closely in many places with a Latin tract of the same name, which is not later than 1378. The piece is possibly by Wycliffe. It declares that priests should live Christ's rule of poverty; tithes should not be paid to bad priests, or when churches are wrongly endowed. It discusses the papal authority as to residence and appropriation, the efforts to check translation of the Bible, the obligation of priests to preach, litigation by the clergy, the conditions of preaching, qualities of the good parson, sects and the Church Militant, the new orders and the Apostles, the evils of absenteeism, the Pope the source of evil, etc.

4. Writings Not by Wycliffe

The following pieces are Wycliffite, but not by Wycliffe (see remarks on page 468).

ON THE TWENTY-FIVE ARTICLES [69] (in print 41 pages), in MS. Douce 273, lists and then meets severally twenty-five accusations against the poor priests. The piece was composed before the death of Pope Urban (1389), who is mentioned as reigning, and after the opening of Parliament in 1388—at least four years after Wycliffe's death.

SPECULUM VITÆ CHRISTIANÆ [70], Shirley's Item 11, is probably not at all Wycliffe's. Articles 1 and 7 have been shown to be from a manual of religious instruction written in English in 1387 by direction of Thoresby, Archbishop of York (see page 355).

ANTICHRIST AND HIS MEYNEE [71] seems to be much later than the lifetime of Wycliffe.

AN APOLOGY FOR LOLLARD DOCTRINES [72] (in print some 113 large pages) is in MS. Trinity College Dublin C V 6 f. 164 (15th century). The piece explains elaborately and severally thirty points of belief held by Lollards.

THE LAST AGE OF THE CHURCH [73] was formerly erroneously regarded as the earliest of Wycliffe's writings. It is in a MS. in the University Library Dublin (late 14th or early 15th century), and consists of about 1700 words.

THE PORE CAITIF [74] or PAUPER RUSTICUS or CONFESSIO DERELICTI PAUPERIS is a series of tracts for instruction of the poor. It has comments on the *Apostles' Creed* and the *Pater Noster*. Then follow various treatises— *Sweet Sentences Exciting Men and Women to Heavenly Desire, Virtuous Patience, Of Temptation, The Charter of Heaven* (see page 370), *Of Ghostly Battle* (see page 372), *The Name Jesus*, etc. Copies are in the British Museum, the Lambeth Library, the Library of Trinity College Dublin, the Bodleian Library, the Cambridge University Library, and the Bibliothèque Nationale. MS. Ashburnham Additional 27 d is perhaps the oldest MS. and of the fourteenth century. MS. Ashmole 1286 is of about 1400. The other MSS. appear to be later.

THE BRITISH MUSEUM ADDITIONAL 24202 TRACTS or TENISON WYCLIFFITE TRACTS [75] are twelve prose pieces in MS. Br. Mus. Additional 24202 (14th century). The MS. was for a time at St. Martin's-in-the-Fields, London, and in 1861 was purchased for the British Museum from the library of Archbishop Tenison. From it only Item 2 has been printed. Other copies of Items 8, 10, and 11, have been edited. The MS. was recently relocated and identified through the efforts of Professor Albert S. Cook. An edition of the pieces is now in preparation. According to the British Museum Catalogue of Additional MSS., the tracts are as follows:

1. THE BISCHOPES OTHE THAT HE SWERIS TO

THE POPE [76], Urban VI (1378-1389), in 23 articles; with condemnatory remarks on the oath itself, and the several articles, f. 1.

2. A TREATISE OF MIRACLIS PLEYINGE or SERMON AGAINST MIRACLE-PLAYS [77], f. 14. In general object this piece reminds of *Against the Minorite Friars* (see page 236), but it has none of the violence of that poem.

The writer urges the irreverence of dealing with Christ and holy matters in plays, and the inevitable ill effect of plays on the attitude of men toward Christian themes. He presents at length the arguments offered in favor of the performances—they often convert the unbelieving; they move to compassion and devotion; they often effect what the actual good deeds of God and of men cannot effect; they afford to those who must have recreation a valuable and serious amusement; they are as justifiable as are paintings of Biblical incidents; and they are 'quick,' while paintings are dead. Each of these points in turn the writer meets vigorously, honestly, and humanly, and with effective appeal.

3. AGAINST DICE [78], ff. 21-24.

4. AGAINST EXPOSING RELICS FOR GAIN [79], f. 24.

5. ON THE KNOWLEDGE OF THE SOUL [80], beginning 'Dere sister in Crist sithen charite alle thing leeueth as seith the apostle,' f. 25.

6. A TRETYSE OF YMAGES [81], against their use, f. 26.

7. A TRETISE OF PRISTIS [82], f. 28 v.

8. OF WEDDID MEN AND THER WYUIS AND THER CHILDERE, f. 29, has been discussed on page 472.

9. ON TITHES AND OFFERINGS [83], f. 34.

10. THE SEVEN SACRAMENTIS, by John Gaytrigg, f. 35 v, has been discussed on page 348.

11. THE SEVEN UERTUES, by John Gaytrig, imperfect at the end, f. 36 v, has been discussed on page 348.

12. A TREATISE PRINCIPALLY AGAINST THE RELIGIOUS ORDERS [84], f. 37. This is a fragment, extending from the middle of the 16th to the beginning of the 39th chapter. In the 33rd chapter Wycliffe is quoted, with the Bishop of Lincoln (Robert Grostête), Bradewardyn (Archbishop of Canterbury, 1349), the Archbishop of Armagh (Richard Fitz-ralph), and Kilmyngton (Geoffrey).

CHAPTER XIII

PIECES LYRICAL IN IMPULSE OR IN FORM

The marriage of Eleanor of Guienne and Henry II made, England a centre of commercial and social and religious intercourse for Western Europe. The English court became for a number of decades the home of many of the Provençal singers, and of a majority of the writers in French. To and from the Continent passed the wandering clerks with their Goliardic songs. To the influences of these lyrists as they filtered from class to class, were added those of the Latin hymns and liturgical pieces and sacred poems. Clear evidence of the working of all these forces (of the Provençal through the French) on the native popular impulse, is evident not only in the metres and stanzas of the extant English pieces, but as well in their motives and even in their phrasing. Courtly lyrics in English were developed only in the period of Chaucer, and then apparently were composed by but few.

In the present chapter the terms 'lyric' and 'lyrical' are applied only to pieces that are chiefly expressive of personal emotion or of emotion imagined as personal, or that are phrased or constructed to impress as of one of these classes. Regard for practical general usefulness has led to avoidance here of an attempt to differentiate what is lyrical chiefly in impulse and essential nature, what is lyrical in form, and what is lyrical in both impulse and form. Yet, elastic as is such a basis for discussion, in a number of specific instances in Middle English (an experience one encounters somewhat on any basis in any field) it is by no means easy on it finally to determine between what is, and what is not, lyrical. Throughout the period, fondness for composition in verse and in stanzas, led to treatment in strophic form of practically every kind of material, irrespective of its impulse, its nature, or its purpose.

Yet it will probably be admitted without much dissent that most of the pieces included in this chapter are lyrical.

Except in so far as they duplicate or parallel earlier texts, the poems in MSS. Lambeth 853 (c. 1430) and Sloane 2593 (15th century), some of which may be of before 1400, are not discussed here. Because of difficulty in ascertaining their dates, and because of the lateness of the extant texts, ballads are not treated in this book.

For convenience, the political and satirical pieces have been discussed in Chapter IV (see pages 208, 227). The lyrics of Chaucer are considered with that poet's other works (see pages 628 ff.). Pieces that obviously are, or were regarded as being, chiefly homiletic or monitory, or of the proverb or precept type, or for use in church services (included in the *Lay-Folks' Mass-Book*, the *Lay-Folks' Prayer-Book*, *How to Hear Mass*, the *York Bidding Prayers*, *Of the Sacrament of the Altar*, *Prayers at the Levation*, and *Patris Sapiencia* and other *Horæ*), are treated in their appropriate chapters (see pages 375 ff., 385 ff., 350 ff., 354). Individual lyrics in the service pieces just mentioned, are not discussed apart from those pieces, as wholes. Prayers in stanzas, several of them in rhythmical prose, are included with the lyrics because of their personal nature; and there are included also some few monitory pieces evidently regarded by the makers of Middle English collections as appropriate companions for lyrical writings.

The pieces are grouped as 1. *Secular*, and 2. *Religious*. The claims advanced for Rolle's authorship of the religious lyrics in MSS. Cbg. Univ. Libr. Dd V 64 and Thornton, make desirable the discussion of these poems in isolated groups. Moreover, the 'Vernon-Simeon refrain lyrics' seem best discussed as a group. Further, despite opposition to such arrangement, it has seemed wisest to hold to the common groupings of *Christ on the Cross and the Compassion of Mary*, *Hymns and Prayers to God, Christ, the Trinity*, and *Hymns and Prayers to the Virgin*. Yet, whenever an item of any one of these groups would fall appropriately into another group, the piece is mentioned in the discussion of the latter. The items of each group are located loosely according to supposed chronology, the arrangement being modified to bring together the items that are similar in theme.

After application of these limitations, there remain over two hundred pieces. The following four paragraphs show how the poems occur in the MSS. The numbers following the name of the MS. are the *Note-Numbers* (see Preface) in the discussions after the titles of the respective lyrics.

I. *Before 1300:* MSS. containing lyrics of Godric (†1170), 27; Thomas of Ely's *History* (c. 1166), 1; Cotton Titus D XVIII, 171 (South-West, 1200-1250); Rawlinson G, 22 (East Midland), 4 (c. 1225); Lambeth 487, 169 (South-West, 1200-1250); Cotton Nero A XIV, 170, 172, 206, 207 (all South-West, 1200-1250); Royal 17 A XXVII, 206 (South-West, 1200-1250); British Museum Additional 27909 (1225-1250), 200; Harley 978 (late 13th century), 6 (Southern, 1225-1250); Cotton Caligula A IX (South-West, before 1250), 201; Cotton Cleopatra B VI (c. 1250), 136, 176, 183; Tanner 169* (soon after 1250), 129 (West Midland); Egerton 613 (Southern, c. 1250), 164, 189, 191, 203; Jesus College Oxf. 29 (South-West, c. 1275), 29, 43, 51, 141, 160, 173, 201, 210; Digby 86 (Southern, 1272-1283), 7, 31; Douce 139, 5 (c. 1270); Liber de Antiquis Legibus, Guildhall, London, 30 (c. 1270); Arundel 248 (Southern, 1250-1300), 42, 127, 128; Cbg. Univ. Libr. Hh IV 11 (13th century), 179; Trinity College Cbg. B, 14, 39 (Southern, 13th century), 188, 189, 201, 205, 210; Arundel 292 (North-Midland, late 13th century), 32, 175; Caius College Cbg. 44 (13th century), 178; Digby 2 (Southern, 13th century), 28, 124, 199; Corpus Christi College Oxf. 54, D, 15, 14 (before 1300), 193, 194; Göttingen Theol. 107 (? 1300-1350), 214; *Cursor Mundi* MSS. (see page 339), 120.

II. *1300-1350:* Bodley 42 (1300-1320), 116 (version attached to Durham Cathedral A III 12 of uncertain date); College of Arms E. D. N. 27, now Arundel 27 (Edward II), 8, 9; Lincoln's Inn Hale 135, 25 (soon after 1300); New College Oxf. 88 (beginning 14th century), 115 (Southern); Harley 2253 (the best MS. collection of Middle English lyrics— eight political, fourteen secular, eighteen religious—copied by a scribe of Leominster Abbey, Hertfordshire; Southern, c. 1310), 3, 12-24, 33, 46, 125, 134-35, 137-38, 157-58, 163, 165, 191, 197, 204, 209; Harley 913 (Kildare MS., by emigrants to Ireland from South-West England, 1308-1318, before 1325), 48, 49, 114, 140; Arundel 57 (Kent, c. 1350), 177; Rawlinson D 913 (Southern, 1300-1350), 10.

III. *1350-1400:* Bodley 692 (14th century), 11; Trinity College Cbg. B, 15, 17 (late 14th century), 168; Rawlinson Poetry 175 (Northern, c. 1350), 110; Vernon (the great collection of religious works; containing the longest list of lyrics in Middle English; Southern, 1370-1380), 69-75, 76, 77-79, 83-93, 96, 97, 102-04a, 113, 121, 131-32, 139, 142-46, 148-52, 156, 166, 174, 184-87, 195, 212, 213; British Museum Additional 22283 (Simeon MS.; sister MS. of Vernon, much of which it duplicates; Southern, 1380-1400), 69-75, 76, 77-79, 83-93, 96, 97, 102-06a; Royal 17 B XVII (West Midland or Midland, 1370-1400), 159, 161a; Laud 622 (South-East Midland, 1380-1400), 47; Ghent Univ. Libr. 317 (14th century insertion), 198; Harley 2316 (1350-1400), 107, 153, 155, 202; Harley 7322 (14th century), 119, 123; Harley 1022 (Northern, end of 14th century), 52; Bodley 425 (Northern, 14th century), 44, 130, 192; Arundel 507 (Northern, Durham, 14th century), 117; Harley 7358 (14th century), 50; Halliwell 214 (14th century), 180; Barton (14th century), 132; Douce 128 (14th or 15th century), 161.

IV. *After 1400:* Cbg. Univ. Libr. Gg IV 32 (Henry IV), 181; Cotton Galba E IX (Northern, early 15th century), 108, 109; Cbg. Univ. Libr. Dd V 64 (Northern, late 14th or early 15th century), 58-60, 62-67, 111-12; Cbg. Univ. Libr. Gg IV 27 (early 15th century), 26 (3 pieces); Ashmole 343 (earlier 15th century), 81; Douce 126 (1400-1450), 167, 181; Garrett (1400-1450), 82, 95, 99; Lambeth 853 (c. 1430), 76, 156; Thornton (Northern, 1430-1440), 53-57, 61, 68, 139, 156, 215; Douce 95 (15th century), 19a; Rawlinson B 408 (c. 1450),

147; Rawlinson A 389 (Southern, 15th century), 156; Cotton
Caligula A II (15th century), 80, 94, 98; Bodley Engl. Poetry
e I (15th century), 101; British Museum Additional 31042
(15th century), 118; Cbg. Univ. Libr. Hh IV 12 (15th century), 122; Cbg. Univ. Libr. Ee I 12 (15th century), 26a;
Cbg. Univ. Libr. Ff V 48 (15th century), 196; Porkington 10,
now Phillipps 8336 (c. 1460), 34-41 (before 1330); Trinity
College Cbg. O, 9, 38 (15th century), 82; Harley 2382 (15th
century), 196; Chetham 8009 (15th century), 196; Bannatyne (1568), 82; British Museum C, 11, a, 28 (? 15th century), 196; Lord Mostyn's MS. 186 (? 15th century), 154;
Ashmole 1393 (? 1425-1450), 190; Advocates' Libr. Edinburgh Jac. V, 7, 27 (now 19, 3, 1; 15th century), 70a; Balliol
College 354 (early 16th century), 84a.

1. Secular Lyrics

The secular lyrics of the period are few as compared with
the religious lyrics, though as a body they are superior in
quality to the latter. Practically all are political or erotic.
The political pieces have been discussed already (see pages
208 ff.). The following poems are direct, sincere, spontaneous,
of genuine lyrical impulse and power. As one reads them one
is distressed at the loss of the host of other admirable lyrics of
which these are but the scattered, and sometimes fragmentary,
chance survivors.

The use of elements of Nature for setting, for comparison,
or for real or assumed source of original motive or impulse, is
prominent in the poems (see Nos. 2, 4, 5, 6, 8, 9, 10, 14, 17,
18, 20, 23, 25, 26). Alliteration is frequent and, especially in
MS. Harley 2253, often overdone, with resultant obscurity.
In Nos. 9, 17, 18, 25, 26 is employed the form of the *chanson
d'aventure* (see also page 508, and Index), according to which
the poet tells that he went out a-pleasuring in a wood or the
fields, or went to church, where he met a fair maid or a distressed lady, or a penitent man, or heard monks or a bird singing—and then relates what he learned from the personage
encountered. The motive of the return of Spring, the *reverdie,*

is used in Nos. 6, 14, 20, 23, 25 (see also pages 492, 495, 498, 527). A reflection of the formulated code of Love is seen in No. 25. The *estrif* or dialogue between lovers, is imitated in Nos. 19, 20. After a French fashion, in Nos. 21, 24, and 3 sts. 3-4, successive stanzas are connected by repeating in the first line of a second stanza a word or a phrase from the last line of that preceding (see *Repetition*, Index). The refrain (see pages 504, 507, etc.) is used in Nos. 6, 12, 13, 22; in No. 13 a folk-song refrain occurs, without regard for appropriateness of matter. The tone and the motives of some of the love pieces, especially poems of MS. Harley 2253, are close to those of the French *trouvère*. Yet even here, what the poet would utter is unsophisticated, personal, close to the life, and full of direct details—especially as compared with the French; and all the pieces are characterized by a prevailing frankness of spirit and expression. Fortunately, the notation of the musical accompaniments for several of the poems, has been preserved.

THE CANUTE SONG [1] is quoted by Thomas of Ely in his *History of the Church of Ely*, Chapter 15 (c. 1166-1117), as composed by Canute on the Ouse while he listened to the monks of Ely singing:

> 'Merie sungen þe munaches binnen Ely
> þa Cnut ching reu þer by:
> Roþeþ cnites noer þe land,
> And here we þes munaches saeng.'

LYRICS IN ROMANCES [2], on Nature themes and some-times on Love, are at the head of each of the sections of *Arthour and Merlin* (see page 43) and *Kyng Alisaunder* (see page 102), and at the beginning of the second part of *Richard Coer de Lyon* (see page 152).

'MON IN ÞE MONE STOND AND STRIT' [3] consists of 40 four-stress lines abababab with alliteration, in MS. Harley 2253 f. 114 v (c. 1310). Humorously it presents at an early period (reign of Edward I) in England the ancient notion of the Man in the Moon, that has been a theme of popular

imagination in many lands.   Here is the man leaning on his
fork, on which is a bush of thorn because he was confined to the
moon for collecting twigs on a Sunday.

'MIRIE IT IS WHILE SUMER ILAST' [4] (c. 1225)
consists of seven lines ababbba (ll. 2, 4 of 2, l. 7 of 3, the rest of
4, stresses) with its music, in MS. Rawlinson G 22 f. 1 v (13th
century).—It's a merry time while Summer lasts with birds'
song, but the cold blasts and fierce weather approach.   Alas!
how long the night is! and how with much wrong I sorrow and
fast!

'FOWELES IN THE FRITH [5], The fisses in the flod,
And I mon waxe wod; Mulch sorwe I walke with For best of
bon and blod,' five verses in all, is with its music in MS. Douce
139 f. 5 (late 13th century).   It is of about 1270.

THE CUCKOO-SONG [6], 'Sumer is icumen in,' Southern
of 1200-1250 or perhaps 1200-1225, in MS. Harley 978 (late
13th century), consists of 12 lines abcbbdbebbbb (ll. 3, 8 with
medial rime; ll. 5, 10 of 2, ll. 2, 4, 9 of 3, the rest of 4, stresses)
following its refrain couplet.   The poem exclaims that the
cuckoo's song is typical of Spring; all the creatures are filled
with renewed love-longing.   The note is that of the folk-song,
but the piece is an adaptation of the *reverdie* (see page 489;
Index).   The poet has caught the very spirit of the season.
The musical accompaniment, the *Reading Rota* or *Roundel*,
apparently by John of Fornsete of Reading, is notable not
only for its extraordinary intrinsic merit, but also for its historical importance as probably a unique specimen of its class,
marking an astonishingly high attainment for its period and
for the 'First English School of Music.'

'LOVE IS SOFFT, LOVE IS SWET, LOVE IS GOED
SWARE' [7], in MS. Digby 86 (1272-1283) consists of 28
Southern alliterated verses of six or seven stresses aaaabbbb-
ccccddddeffggghhiiiii.   Pathetically it admonishes that while
Love is sweet, it brings much pain and sorrow.

COLLEGE OF ARMS FRAGMENTS. Two scraps of South-West Midland love songs of the popular type are in MS. College of Arms E. D. N. 27, now Arundel 27 (time of Edward II). The former [8], '*A levedy and my love leyt,*' is eleven normally ? seven-stress verses, aaabcacacdd. Lines 1-3 have rime of the cæsural stresses; line 4 has three stresses; each half of lines 1-6 has two or three alliterative syllables. Defects in the text and use of popular stock-phrases, make lines 1-6 obscure. These verses consist largely of details of Nature setting. Lines 7-11 advise to let a lass have her way until she is won. The rhythm is very catching.

The second fragment, '*As I stod on a day*' [9], is narrative in the first person of the *chanson d'aventure* or *pastourelle* type (see page 489; Index). It consists of three stanzas (31 verses of six or seven stresses, parts of the piece lost) apparently originally ababababcc. There is some alliteration.—On a morning the poet met under a tree a splendidly dressed maiden. He made love to her, but she played him off. Inflamed, he became more ardent; but the lady bade him go where he might speed better.—The opening reminds of the supernatural introduction to *Thomas of Erceldoune* (see page 224).

THE RAWLINSON FRAGMENTS [10]. The first leaf (1300-1350) of MS. Rawlinson D 913 (a collection of odd leaves and fragments) is probably out of a minstrel's note-book. It contains bits of eleven, perhaps twelve, popular Southern songs, two of them French. All the scraps long enough for judgment exhibit the primitive popular use of repetition, and apparently all were rude pieces for singing by the roadside or at the ale-house. All are catching jingles, with no sign of reflection or of the learned touch. They are very valuable as direct evidence of existence of many similar early pieces in the vernacular.

The first sings in eight short lines that 'the hawthorn blows sweetest of every kind of tree,' and 'my love, she shall be the fairest of earthkind.'—The second and the third are but single lines: 'Þe Godemon on is weie,' 'Ichaue a mantel i-maket of cloth.'—The fourth is an illegible line, perhaps two lines.—

The fifth and the sixth are French.—The seventh, perhaps the earliest English dance-song extant, is seven verses: 'Icham of Irlaunde, ant of the holy londe of irlande: gode sire pray ich ʒe, for of saynte charite, come ant daunce wyt me, in irlaunde.'— The eighth, *'Maiden in a mor lay,'* tells in 18 verses of a maiden who in a moor lay full seven nights and a day, her meat was the primrose and the violet, her drink the cold water of the well-spring, her bower the red rose and the lily-flower. The following piece of 18 verses may belong to the eighth. Its sense is obscure, but runs to declaration of what the lover would do for his leman.—The ninth tells in four very imperfect lines that all night the singer lay by the rose; the rose he dared not steal, but the flower he bore away.—The tenth is three lines: Ionet's hair is all gold, and Iankyn is her lover.—The eleventh consists of eleven defective lines claimed as the oldest extant English drinking-song.

'JOLY CHEPERTE OF ASCHELL DOWN [11], Can more on love than al this town,' are the only legible verses of a poem in MS. Bodley 692 (14th century).

ALYSOUN [12], in MS. Harley 2253 f. 63 v (c. 1310), consists of four stanzas ababbbbc (*a* of 4, *c* of 3, stresses; *b* of 3 or 4 stresses with feminine ending) with a refrain dddc (*c* of 3, *d* of 4, stresses). The refrain is closely bound in sense to the rest of the verses; the poet declares in it his delight at his heaven-sent fortune that his love is turned from all others, and fixed on Alysoun. The piece is one of the most charming of Middle English songs. After a Spring-time opening, the singer asserts his love-longing for the fairest of all things; he describes her brown brow, her black eye, her laughing lovesome face, her small and well-turned waist, her neck whiter than the swan. He tosses and turns at night with love; he is all worn out with watching, weary as water in a weir—if she have not pity on him, he shall die.

'ICHOT A BURDE IN BOURE BRYHT' [13], with a folk-song refrain, 'Blow, norþerne wynd,' etc., not at all connected in sense with the poem proper, is in MS. Harley 2253

f. 72 (c. 1310). It consists of ten stanzas aaabcccb (*b* of 3, the others of 4, stresses). Each line has two or three alliterative syllables; assonance is prominent. The poem is very artificial. With many figures the lover details the physical beauties and the excellences of his lady; he made his plaint to Love; Love advised appeal to the lady before he falls as mud from boot; for her love he droops and waxes wan, worn with depression and vigils.

'LENTEN YS COME WIÞ LOUE TO TOUNE' [14], in MS. Harley 2253 f. 71 v (c. 1310), is full of the Spring. It has three stanzas aabccbddbeeb (*b* of 3 stresses with feminine ending, the others of 4 stresses). Alliteration of two or three syllables to the line, is the rule. Verse by verse, the poet declares the new life of plants and beasts and birds, of the sun and the moon, in the new Spring. He is in accord with them—he loves, and he would have his lady's favor. The setting is that of the *reverdie* (see page 489; Index). With the first lines should be compared the first of the *Thrush and the Nightingale* (see page 421). The poem is Southern, probably from North-East Midland.

IOHON [15], 'Ichot a burde in a bour ase beryl so bryht,' in MS. Harley 2253 f. 63 (c. 1310), has five stanzas aaaaaaaabb of long alliterative lines. The piece is probably originally West Midland, and is very artificial. It consists of praises of the lady—a series of comparisons line by line, the first stanza to various gems, the second to flowers, the third to birds, the fourth to spices, the fifth to famous personages of history.

'WIÞ LONGING Y AM LAD' [16], in MS. Harley 2253 f. 63 v (c. 1310), forty three-stress verses aabaabbaab, is possibly by the author of *Iohon*. Effectively the poet pictures to his lady his distress for love of her; he grieves, he groans, he is growing mad; he shall die if she does not pity him; but he will ever remain faithful—will she not have mercy? She is very lovely, lily-white and red as rose; Heaven would be his who were once her guest.

'MOSTI RYDEN BY RYBBESDALE' [17], *The Beauty of Ribbesdale,* in MS. Harley 2253 f. 66 v (c. 1310), is of the South-West Midland, and consists of 84 lines aabccbddbeeb (*b* of 3, the rest of 4, stresses), with extensive alliteration. The poem has the form of the *chanson d'aventure* (see page 489; Index). As the poet rode by Ribbesdale, he found the fairest lady ever made. With fine care he describes definitely and sharply all her physical beauties, concluding (as did the author of '*Wiþ longing y am lad*') that Heaven would be his who might have her in his arms.

'IN A FRYHT AS Y CON FERE FREMEDE' [18], *The Meeting in the Wood,* of the West or South-West Midland, in MS. Harley 2253 f. 66 v (c. 1310), consists of 48 four-stress verses in stanzas, the second and seventh abab, the rest abababab. The verses have from two to four alliterative syllables. The piece is of the *chanson d'aventure* type (see page 489; Index), with similarities to the *estrif*. As he fared through a wood the poet accosted a lovely lady, who bade him go his way. The last six stanzas are a dialogue between the two. The blandishments of the poet are naught in face of the lady's desire for a 'man without guile.'

'MY DEþ Y LOUE, MY LYF Y HATE' [19], another *estrif* between a lover and a lady, consists of 36 seven-stress North-East Midland verses aaaa in MS. Harley 2253 f. 80 v (c. 1310). In his successive speeches the lover praises the lady's beauty, and declares his distress now she no longer favors him; he has wandered over the world for love of her. Gradually, from calling the clerk 'fool,' and warning him of danger of discovery by her kin, the lady melts—she is his to do his bidding.—A similar piece [19a] in alternate French and English lines is said to be in MS. Douce 95 f. 6 (15th century).

'WHEN þE NYHTEGALE SINGES' [20], in MS. Harley 2253 f. 80 v (c. 1310), consists of 20 seven-stress verses aaaa (ll. 17-20 aaab with medial rime in *b*).—In April the nightingale sings, leaf and grass and flower spring, and Love drinks the poet's heart's blood. All the year he has endured; shall he not have one word, one kiss? Between Lincoln and Lindsay, Northampton and London, he knows none so fair as is his lady; will she not love him a little?—The poem has been assigned questionably to the poet of '*My deþ y loue.*'

'A WAYLE WHYT ASE WHALLES BON' [21], in MS. Harley 2253 f. 67 (c. 1310), consists of 55 verses in the Burns stanza with overmuch alliteration. There is a tendency to link successive stanzas by repeating in the first line of a second a word or idea in the last of the preceding (see *Repetition*, Index). The poet praises his lady with the gray eyes, the curved brows, and the comely mouth, and laments his sad state. Would that he had her favor!

'LUTEL WOT HIT ANYMON' [22], in MS. Harley 2253 f. 128 (c. 1310), consists of five stanzas ababbb with a re- frain couplet of long verses. Probably from a tendency to write songs after some popular air or familiar words, the piece agrees in stanza, in minor details of expression, and in first line, with a religious lyric (see page 503).—The lady has cast off the lover for revealing their secret love. He pleads inno- cence; he grieves that he is shut out of her bower;—he greets her as often as dewdrops are wet, as stars are in the sky, as grasses are sour or sweet.

'IN MAY HIT MURGEþ WHEN HIT DAWES' [23], *Advice to the Fair Sex*, of the North or the North-East Mid- land, in MS. Harley 2253 f. 71 v (c. 1310), consists of four stanzas aabccbddbeeb (*b* of 3, the rest of 4, stresses, with double or triple alliteration). After a Springtide opening, the poet declares his admiration for ladies, especially for her who is the best from Ireland to Ynde. Stanzas 2-4 warn ladies against treachers who are everywhere.

'WEPING HAUEþ MYN WONGES WET' [24], in MS. Harley 2253 f. 66 (c. 1310), consists of six Southern from West Midland stanzas abababbcdcd (*a* and *b* of 4, the rest of 3, stresses). The successive strophes are connected by repetition (see *Repetition*, Index); alliteration is used very elaborately and intricately. With mocking gravity the poet declares that he has spoken against ladies in many verses, and broken the rules of the book of ladies' love (perhaps an imitation of the Provençal *Leys d'Amors*). A certain Richard has attacked him in championship of ladies. The poet confesses guilt, professes penitence, and ironically extols the glory of Richard, the honored of maidens. In MS. Digby 86 f. 111 (1272-1283) is a French poem by a Norman Richard said to have contended with a rimer of England. If the two Richards are one, the French would locate the English poet at Lindsay.

'NOW SPRINGES THE SPRAI! [25], Al for loue i am so seke That slepen i ne mai!' is the refrain of a charming love poem written as prose on a fly-leaf of the legal MS. Lincoln's Inn Hale 135 (late 13th century). It is conjectured to be West Midland of soon after 1300. Reconstructed, it consists of three stanzas ababbba (ll. 1, 3, 6 of 4, the rest of 2, stresses; st. 2 ends baa). The first line 'Als i me rod this ender dai' is that of '*Ase y me rod*' in MS. Harley 2253 (see page 536). Riding a-pleasuring (see *chanson d'aventure*, page 489; Index) the poet heard a maid singing. In her pleasant arbor she told him her lover had changed his love; if she might, she would make him rue it.

MS. CBG. UNIV. LIBR. GG IV 27 [26] (c. 1400) contains three non-Chaucerian lyrics, '*In may whan euery herte is lyȝt*,' '*De Amico ad Amicam. A celuy que pluys eyme en mounde*' (French and English), and '*Responcio. A soun treschere et special*' (French and English), which may be of before 1400.

THE FALSE FOX [26a], discussed with the animal tales, was intended to be sung (see page 184).

MS. Sloane 2593 (15th century) contains some pieces that may be of before 1400 (see page 486).

2. Religious Lyrics

For convenience (see page 486) the religious lyrics are grouped here as follows: I. *Miscellaneous Religious Lyrics;* II. *Thornton Lyrics;* III. *Cambridge Dd Lyrics;* IV. *Vernon-Simeon Lyrics;* V. *Christ on the Cross and the Compassion* of *Mary;* VI; *Hymns and Prayers to Christ, God, the Trinity;* VII. *Hymns and Prayers to the Virgin.*

The metrical paraphrases of the *Pater Noster, In Manus Tuas,* the Latin liturgical pieces, and the pieces included in the *Lay-Folks' Mass-Book* and the like, are discussed with the service pieces (see pages 351, 354).

The pieces in MSS. Lambeth 853 (c. 1430) and Sloane 2593 (15th century), some of which may be of before 1400, are discussed in these sections only where they duplicate or parallel earlier texts.

Nearly two hundred religious lyrics are dealt with in the following pages. Wholly or largely translation or paraphrase of Latin versions, are Nos. 34-42, 54, 55, 74, 103, 104, 104a, 106, 106a, 108, 114-16, 129, 130, 131, 142, 175-82, 192, 206, and perhaps 127-28; Nos. 157-59 are imitations of the Latin. Nos. 188-90 consist of mixed Latin and English; No. 197 is English and French. A French analogue or source for No. 143, and the French original for No. 30, are extant. The close connection between the religious and the secular lyrics, is seen in the similarities between Nos. 46 and 22. A number of poems reflect the fondness for employment of five stanzas exhibited in the French love lyrics. The stanza-forms and the metre exhibit influence of both the French secular verse and the Latin hymns and religious lyrics. The secular and the French Nature setting is used in Nos. 163-65, 204; the *reverdie* (see page 489) in Nos. 163-64. The *chanson d'aventure* (see page 489; Index) supplies the form for Nos. 69, 70, 79, 84, 97, 103, 137, 204, 209. Refrains (see pages 504, 507) are employed in Nos. 46, 52, 69-71, 73-87, 89-91, 93-103, 105, 118, 186; to the 'With an O and an I' refrain group (see page 236) belong Nos. 60, 61, 161, 167. The French device of connecting successive stanzas by repeating in the first line of a second a word or a phrase from the last line of the preceding, is employed in Nos. 28, 33, 124, 135, 199, 134 sts. 1-2, 204 sts. 3-4 (see *Repetition*, Index). Alliteration, often of as many as four syllables to a line, sometimes carried through several lines, and often unpleasing as well as productive of obscurity, is used very steadily.

Theological dogma appears scarcely at all in these pieces. The monitory motive (see pages 385 ff.) manifests itself in fondness for dwelling on the transitoriness of the world, of beauty and strength, of wealth, of power, of love; on failure of friends and kin; and on the vanity of all human endeavor. Favorite themes are the essential sinfulness of Man, and remorse for an ill-spent life. Even the lullabies (see pages 394, 504) are composed of such matter. As Penitential Lyrics, reflecting closely various of the phases of penitence, have been classed Nos. 147, 132, 84, 200, 135, 134, 38, 143, 61, 139, 137, 199, 193, 201, 189-90, 204, 40, 104, 41, 162, 28, 106, 142, 101, 148, 57, 150, 152, 27, 202, 195-96, 185, 213, 194, 191, 188, 184, 211. But the consciousness of sin is a much more prominent theme than this list would indicate. These penitential poems are said to draw their material and much of their phrasing chiefly from the Liturgy, and scarce at all from Latin hymns or sacred lyrics. Favorite, too, is insistence on the imminence of Death, the dread of Judgment, the need to escape Hell. The prevalence of such themes makes the prayers generally trite, though now and then an individual note is struck. Most, of the poems end with a line or a couplet of prayer for intercession by Christ, or, more frequently, by the Virgin. It is of interest that, though the saints in a body are invoked in the midst of several pieces along with the members of the Trinity and the Virgin, only No. 29 is addressed to a saint. The hymns or poems of praise of Christ or the Virgin, are much more varied and personal. Some are full of mystical fervor. The most notable results are attained in the pieces dedicated to worship of Christ as the Heavenly Lover (*e.g.*, in Nos. 157-59, 170, 171, 173, 174), and to the cult of the Virgin—both among the early and persistent motives of the Middle English lyric. Yet, as might be expected, and as was done in French, to these pieces are carried over frequently elements of structure, phrases of address, and enumeration of physical qualities, that are characteristic of, and often in themselves scarcely distinguishable from, some in the French secular lyrics. Withal, however, despite frequent borrowings and conventionalisms and triteness, these religious poems as a group are evidently sincere attempts at expression of real personal feeling.

I.   Miscellaneous Religious Lyrics

LYRICS OF ST. GODRIC [27].   In various MS. accounts (*e.g.*, Douce 207, end of 13th century; Harley 322, 12th century) of St. Godric (died 1170) three English bits are ascribed to the saint.   Though alliteration appears in them, the Old English measure is breaking up in favor of a more regular movement, and rime is used.   '*Sainte Marie uirgine,*' a prayer for protection and for aid to the joy of God and of Heaven, consists of eight lines aabb.   It looks forward to the thirteenth-century cult of the Virgin.   The musical notation for it survives.—The second bit is a couplet: 'Crist and sainte Marie swa on scamel (Lat. *scamellum*) me iledde, þat ic on þis erde ne silde wið mine bare fote itredie.'—The third bit is 'Sainte Nicholæs, godes druð, tymbre us faire scone hus, at þi burth, at þi bare; sainte Nicholæs, bring vs wel þare.'

'NO MORE WILLI WIKED BE' [28], *A Resolve to Reform*, consists of three stanzas aaabab (*a* of 4, *b* of 3, stresses) in MS. Digby 2 f. 15 (early 13th century).   The poet will leave his sins, and will become a friar minor devoted to good works and to Christ who died for him.

AN ANTHEM TO ST. THOMAS THE MARTYR [29], 'Haly thomas of beoue-riche,' five short couplets in MS. Jesus College Oxf. 29 f. 258 v (c. 1275; South Midland), praises the saint, and asks his help.

THE PRISONER'S PRAYER [30], 'Ar ne kuthe ich sorghe non,' 44 verses in irregular stanzas that were probably originally tail-rime, is with its Norman-French original and with music of about 1270 in *Liber de Antiquis Legibus*, Guildhall, London, f. 160 v.—Formerly the poet knew no sorrow; now with companions he lies in prison guiltless. He prays Christ for succour, and asks forgiveness of the guilty. Let none trust life; Death brings all low. May the Virgin intercede for him!

'WORLDES BLIS NE LAST NO THROWE' [31], written in four-stress lines, is in MS. Digby 86 f. 163 (1272-1283), 70 lines ababcccbcb under title *Chauncon del Secle;* in MS. Arundel 248 f. 154 r (Middle South, 1250-1300), 60 lines; and in MS. Rawlinson 18 f. 105 v (1250-1300), 70 verses with music. With all the ascetic vigor of the period the song declares the vanity and transitoriness of earthly effort and attainment, and urges consideration of the Passion and the doing of good works. The handling of the verse is interesting.

THE LAMENT OF THE MONK [32], 'Un-comly in cloystre i coure ful of care,' on the comparative difficulty of learning secular and church music, consists of 52 long alliterative North Midland lines aaaa (sometimes longer *laisses*) in MS. Arundel 292 f. 71 v (late 13th century). With homely wry humor the poor monk describes his vain efforts to master the words and the music amid the chidings of his teacher.

'MIDDELERD FOR MON WES MAD' [33], of the South-East Midland, consists of 77 verses abababcbc (*c* of 3, the rest of 4, stresses) in MS. Harley 2253 f. 62 v (c. 1310). There are from two to four alliterative syllables to the line, and successive stanzas are connected by repetition of a word or a phrase (see *Repetition*, Index). The expression is obscure. The piece is a pessimistic utterance of ill done, and of a world all amiss.

THE LYRICS OF WILLIAM HEREBERT, a Franciscan

(died c. 1330), in MS. Porkington 10 (Phillipps 8336; c. 1460), are eight paraphrases of Latin service hymns.

'*Herodes, thou wykked fo*' [34] is a rendering of the *Hostis Herodes impie* in four triplets of seven-stress verses followed by a couplet, each section headed by the Latin catch-phrase.

'*The Kynges baneres beth forth y-lad*' [35] is a rendering of the *Vexilla regis prodeunt* in 28 four-stress verses aabb, each quatrain headed by the Latin catch-phrase.

'*Wele, heriȝyng and worshype bee*' [36] is a version, in six couplets of seven-stress verses, of *Gloria laus et honor tibi sit, rex Christe redemptor* for the Palm Sunday processional. The Latin catch-words follow each group.

'*My volk, what habbe y do the?*' [37] is a version of the *Popule mi, quid feci tibi*, 32 lines in couplets and triplets each followed by the first line as refrain (see Christ on the Cross, page 516).

'*Loverd, shyld me vrom helle deth*' [38] consists of 14 seven-stress verses aaabbaccaddcee. It is a version of the Response and Versicles following the ninth lesson in the *Exsequiæ Defunctorum*, Use of Sarum.

'*Thou, wommon, boute vere*' [39] consists of 57 three-stress verses aabccb, the last nine lines aabccbddb.—How could Mary be mother of her Father and Brother, and sister and mother of the poet? With the figure of the *Charters of Christ* (see page 369), the poet shows that Christ wrote the charter of His love with the inkhorn of His wounds; by the Spear and Crown and Nails and Cross, He is bound to aid Man.

'*Heyl, levedy, se-stoerre bryht*' [40], a version of the *Ave Maris Stella* (see page 532), consists of 12 short couplets and one final couplet of seven-stress verses.

'*Come, shuppere, Holy Gost*' [41] renders the *Veni, Creator Spiritus* (see page 520) in 7 couplets of seven-stress verses.

'GABRIEL FRAM EVENEKING' [42], in MS. Arundel 248 f. 154 r (Southern; 1250-1300), consists of 5 stanzas ababccddefef (ll. 2, 4, 11, 12 of 3, ll. 7, 8 of 2, the rest of 4, stresses; ll. 2, 4, 7, 8 have feminine ending). It is a free translation, closely following the stanza-form of the *Angelus ad*

Virginem written with it in the MS. and mentioned in the *Miller's Tale.*

'FROM HEOUENE INTO EORÞE' [43], another Annunciation piece, is a fragment of 18 verses written in two separated parts of MS. Jesus College Oxf. 29 ff. 261 and 254 (c. 1275).

A NARRATIVE OF THE ANNUNCIATION [44], in 24 short couplets in MS. Bodley 425 f. 67 v (Northern; 14th century), employs much direct discourse.

Fifteenth-century Annunciation songs [45] are printed by Wright: *Regina cele letare, Nowell, Nowell,* and *Nowel, ol, el, el,* in MS. Sloane 2593; and *Ecce ancilla Domini* in the Advocates' Library, Edinburgh.

'LUTEL WOT HIT ANYMON' [46], a Southern Redemption poem with Midland remains, consists of 5 strophes ababbb (ll. 1, 3 of 4, ll. 2, 4 of 3, ll. 5, 6 of 5, stresses) with a refrain couplet (7 + 6 stresses), in MS. Harley 2253 f. 128 (c. 1310). The whole is declarative. The poem agrees in stanza-form, in some details of expression, and in first line, with a secular lyric (see page 496).

A SONG OF JOY ON THE COMING OF CHRIST [47], 'Off ioye & blisse is my song,' consists of 172 seven-stress verses in couplets in MS. Laud 622 f. 71 (c. 1380-1400). It pleasingly exults in the Redemption which Dayid and the prophets foreknew and longingly prayed for.

'LOUE HAUIÞ ME BROȜT IN LIÞIR ÞOȜT' [48], styled by an editor *A Rime-beginning Fragment,* is in MS. Harley 913 f. 58 (1308-1318, before 1325), the Kildare MS. (see page 228).—Love of sin has brought the poet to care and unhappiness; he will try to go the right course ere he dies.—The piece, perhaps incomplete, appears to be an exercise in a complicated form. It consists of 12 lines abababab-cdcd (*a* and *c* of 4 stresses, *b* and *d* of 3 stresses with feminine ending). Lines 1 and 9 have rime of the second stress with the fourth; the final word of each line is the first of the next.

TWO LULLABIES, one [49] in MS. Harley 913, the other [50] in MS. Harley 7358, belong with the religious lyrics, but because of their themes have been discussed with the monitory pieces (see page 394).

'ÞEO SUÞE LUUE AMONG VS BEO' [51], *The Duty of Christians*, consists of 15 stanzas abababab (*a* of 4 stresses, *b* of 3 stresses with feminine ending) in MS. Jesus College Oxf. 29 f. 266 (c. 1275). It urges true love among Christians, and honor and fidelity to Christ the Redeemer, the Creator, the King: though Doom is at hand, the righteous need not fear.

'ÞURGH GRACE GROWAND IN GOD ALMYGHT,' [52], with refrain 'In one es alle,' consists of 56 four-stress verses with much alliteration ababcdcd in MS. Harley 1022 f. 65 v (end of 14th century) following *The Rule of Our Lady* (see page 454). It sings of the glory and sacrifice of Christ; bids recognize the vanity of worldly things, beware of the hideous torment of Hell, trust in the Trinity, and win the reward of well-doing.

Other poems that on the basis of form might well be discussed here, are listed with the monitory pieces (see pages 385 ff.). Note the late *Treatise of Parce Michi Domine* (page 394).

MSS. Lambeth 833 and Sloane 2593 contain poems some of which may be of before 1400 (see page 486).

II.   Thornton Lyrics

In MS. Thornton (Northern; c. 1430-1440) are twelve lyrical poems mixed in with pieces by Rolle or his followers, and by some critics ascribed to Rolle (see page 451). They may be of before 1400. Alliteration is used freely. The poems have little grace, and exhibit little skill; but they are sincere and full of the real passion that characterizes Hampole. All except 8 and 10 (which are in Cbg. Dd V 64 also) and 11 and 12, are addressed to God, Christ, or the Trinity.

The first four of the pieces immediately follow (f. 191 r) William Nassyngton's poem on the Trinity (see page 464). They are '*Lorde Ihesu Cryste, godd almyghty*' [53], '*Almyghty god in trinite*' [54], '*Lorde God alweldande*' [55], and '*Ihesu that diede on the rude*' [56]. The first consists of 23, the second of 4, the third of 10, couplets of four-stress verses. The fourth has two stanzas, abcbdbeb (*b* of 3, the rest of 4, stresses) and ababcbcb (each of 4 stresses). The second and the third paraphrase prayers in St. Edmund's *Speculum* (see page 346). The first two are thanksgiving to God for His mercies. The third commends body and soul to God, and prays for protection and for unity with Christ. The fourth begs defense, and aid to cherishing of Christ's love.

'*Ihesu criste, Saynte Marye sonne*' [57], the fifth poem (f. 211), 80 four-stress (*b* sometimes three-stress) verses abab, repeats matter in the *Meditation on the Passion*, Rolle's *Ego Dormio*, and '*All vanitese forsake*' (see pages 451, 450, 507). With passionate longing the poet prays Christ to preserve him as He has redeemed him, and to fill his heart with His indwelling love.

The lyrics '*Fadir and sone and haly gaste*,' '*When Adam dalfe*,' '*Ihesu Criste, haue mercy one me*,' '*Ihesu, thi swetnes*,' and '*þi joy be ilke dele*,' are in other earlier MSS., and for convenience are discussed with the other texts (see respectively pages 522, 506, 526, 507). '*The begynyng es of thre*' is discussed with the *Pricke of Conscience* (see page 449). '*Erthe owte of erthe*' is discussed with the other versions among the monitory pieces (see page 387).

III.   Cambridge Dd Lyrics

In MS. Cbg. Univ. Libr. Dd V 64 (Northern; late 14th or early 15th century) are twelve lyrical poems mixed with pieces possibly by Rolle. Some of them may, then, be by the hermit. They are over-alliterated. As are the Thornton pieces, Items

8 and 10 of which they repeat, they are characterized less by art than by emotional sincerity.

'VNKYNDE MAN' and 'LO, LEMMAN SWETE,' also in MS. Vernon, are discussed with the Cross poems (see page 516.)

'MY TREWEST TRESOWRE' [58] consists of 28 loose four-stress verses abab. With intense feeling the poet apostrophizes Christ, exclaiming on His sufferings; he begs His influence that he may dwell with Him ever. The piece is over-alliterated, there usually being four occurrences of the letter within the line.

'IHESU, ALS ÞOW ME MADE & BOGHT' [59] is the beginning of three separate stanzas aaaa, four-stress; abab, four-stress; aaaa, six-stress. These pray Christ for union with Him, for grace and perfect love, and for security from ill-conduct.

'WHEN ADAM DELF AND EVE SPAN' [60] is on the inherited sinfulness and misery of Man, the transitoriness of physical strength and beauty, the inevitableness of the Grave and of Doomsday. It consists of 72 verses alternately of four and three stresses, usually abcbdbebfghg. Predominantly there is medial rime in the odd verses. The ninth line opens with the refrain 'With I and E,' or 'With E and I,' or 'With E and O,' connecting the poem with the 'With an O and an I' group (see page 236).—Another copy [61] in MS. Thornton f. 213 f. (see page 505) has two added stanzas and at the end a prayer of three short couplets, 'Ihesu Criste, haue mercy one me.'

'ALL SYNNES SAL ÞOU HATE' [62], 48 verses abab-abab (*b* of 3, *a* of 4, stresses), counsels use of reason, following the King's way; reminds of the rewards of earthly suffering; and pictures the awfulness of Doomsday, with the beginning then of the joy of the distressed.

'MERCY ES MASTE IN MY MYNDE' [63], in 48 four-stress lines ababababcdcd, sings the mercy of God and the poet's trust in and gratitude for the mercy he shall receive at the last day.

'IHESU, GOD SON, LORD OF MAGESTE' [64], 48 verses of six or seven stresses aaaa, often with rime of cæsural stresses aaaa, is a prayer for submission and devotion to Christ's love, with contemplation of His Passion and Resurrection. It has similarities to Rolle's *Ego Dormio* (see page 450).

·'LUF ES LYF ÞAT LASTES AY' [65], 192 verses of three or four stresses abababab or ababcbcb, is a glowing effort to tell what Love is, and should be compared with *What is Love?* in Rolle's *Form* Chapter IX (see page 449).

'HEYLE, IHESU, MY CREATOWRE' [66] consists of seven stanzas similar in form to the above. It passionately declares realization of Christ's love, and devotion in love to Him; and asks aid to love Him aright. There are echoes from Rolle's *Ego Dormio* (see page 450).

'ALL VANITESE FORSAKE' [67] and 'THY JOY BE ILK A DELE' [68] consist of 120 and 72 three-stress verses abababab. They are written as one poem in MS. Thornton f. 222, where the second (with two added stanzas) precedes the first (with the conclusion missing). The themes are the vanity and the transitoriness of the world and its elements, and devotion to love of Christ.

IV.   Vernon-Simeon Lyrics

In the sister MSS. Vernon ff. 407 r-412 v (Southern; 1370-1380) and Simeon (Br. Mus. Addit. 22283) ff. 128 v-134 r (Southern; 1380-1400) is a group of 28 short East Midland poems—each, except 4, 17, 21, 27-28, with a refrain. MS. Simeon has two additional items, 29 and 30, of which 29 has a refrain. Varnhagen's Simeon 31 is really stanzas 3 ff. of 30. The poems exhibit much alliteration, often three alliterative syllables to a verse; but effort at alliteration does not lead

to obscurity as it does in Harley 2253. The verses are of
four stresses, except in 27-28, where four and three stresses
alternate. All the poems are in stanzas—18 (Nos. 2, 3, 5, 8,
10, 11, 13, 14, 15, 17, 18, 19, 20, 22, 23, 24, 26, 30) are
ababbcbc; No. 4 and No. 21 sts. 3-8 are abababab (sts. 1-2
ababcdcd); 8 (Nos. 1, 6, 7, 9, 12, 16, 25, 29) are abababab-
bchc; 2 (really one poem, Nos. 27 and 28) are ababababcdcd.
Nos. 1, 2, 11, 13, 24, 26, adopt the form of the *chanson d'aventure* (see page 489). The poems are much more finished and
sophisticated than are those of the other groups, except some
pieces of Harley 2253; and they are correspondingly less
intense and direct of emotion. All are religious or religious-
moral. Nos. 8, 26, 27-28, 30-31, are largely translation or
paraphrase from Latin. In contrast with the other religious
lyrics, there is recurrent (Nos. 1, 9, 14, 19, 20, etc.) reflection
of the evil state of the times, so much the theme of the later
fourteenth century; and now and again appears something of
the bitterness of the *Proverbs of Hendyng* (see page 377).
There is a not inconsiderable variety of themes, some but too
well-worn: *e.g.*, the vanity and transitoriness of worldly things
and of human relationships (Nos. 6, 7, 10, 12, 24); the imminence of Death and the need of repentance and shrift (Nos. 1,
3, 4, 6, 23, 24, etc.); the need of mercy and the glorification of
the mercy of God (Nos. 1, 12, 13); the need of charity and of
control of the tongue (Nos. 15, 22); the nature of Love (No.
4); the problem of truth-telling in a lying age (Nos. 9, 14);
the defense of Woman (No. 16) and of the clergy (No. 21);
praise of the Virgin and of Christ (Nos. 16, 17, 18); and the
need of humility, patience, endurance, and gratitude to God
(Nos. 2, 5, 11, 13, 15).

1. 'BI WEST, VNDER A WYLDE WODE-SYDE' [69],
with refrain 'How merci passeþ alle þinge,' comprises 192
verses. It is of the *chanson d'aventure* type (see page 489).—
By a woodside the poet saw, among many wild beasts and
birds, a merlin holding a bird that thought mercy passes all
things. Set free the next day, the bird sang of the supremacy
of mercy. The poet tells that at Doomsday God will reproach

for neglect of the deeds of mercy.   Unlike the lower creatures, we depart from nature.   Meed and pride prevail; with oaths we rend God.   Knights and clergy are rooted in ribaldry. Christ must be made King, and mercy passes all.   The merlin held the bird for warmth, and let it go next day.   May God grant us repentence and respite and shrift.

2.   'IN A CHIRCHE, ÞER I CON KNEL' [70], also of the *chanson d'aventure* type, with refrain variants on 'And al was Deo Gracias,' consists of 88 verses.—Hearing a clerk and a choir sing 'Deo Gracias,' the poet asked a priest what it meant.   He learned that it was thanks for the Redemption.   He left the church, declaring he too ever would sing that song. Amend and do well; fear naught; thank God for all.   Be modest, pure, courteous.   If you be an officer, judge right-eously.—Another text [70a] is in MS. Advocates' Library Edinburgh Jac. V, 7, 27 (now 19, 3, 1).

3.   'NOU BERNES, BUIRDUS, BOLDE AND BLYÞE' [71], with refrain variants on 'Aȝeyn mi wille I take mi leue,' has 64 lines.   The poet thanks his friends for their kindnesses; against his will he must leave them and this world.   At death friends avail not; Heaven or Hell awaits the soul; let us keep our lamps burning in anticipation.

4.   'DEUS CARITAS EST' [72] consists of 56 verses. It warns of Doomsday.   Who dwells in Love dwells in God, and God in him.   Let Love do what is needed; let us love and be shriven, and may Christ bring us to bliss.

5.   'MI WORD IS DEO GRACIAS' [73], with refrain variants on 'I sey not but Deo gracias,' has 48 lines.   In good and ill, in sickness and in health, the poet thanks God.   When rich he was sought out; now, poor, he is deserted;—yet he thanks God.

6.   'IN A PISTEL ÞAT POUL WROUȜT' [74], with refrain variants on 'For vche mon ouȝte him self to knowe,' consists of 108 verses.—Paul bade every Christian know him-

self. See how few are your good deeds, how many your sins. Know God as Maker and Redeemer. Know that you must die, and that your body must decay. Worldly glory fades as Arthur and Hector are laid low. Repent, trust Conscience, beg mercy.

7. 'WHON MEN BEOþ MURIEST AT HEOR MELE' [75], *A Song of Yesterday*, consists of 180 four-stress alliterative verses abababbcbc with a final refrain line bidding think on yesterday, on what is gone. With much effect the author declares the vanity of earthly conditions, the transitoriness of all possessions, and the approach of Death, that comes not by stealth, but ever with many warnings.

8. 'I WARNE VCHE LEOD þAT LIUEþ IN LONDE' [76], 104 verses with refrain variants on 'To kepe wel Cristes Comaundement,' is a paraphrase of the Commandments with an introductory and a final stanza (see page 354). Another copy [76a] is in MS. Lambeth 853 (c. 1430).

9. 'þE MON þAT LUSTE TO LIUEN IN ESE' [77] has 96 verses with refrain variants on 'For hos seiþ þe soþe, he schal be schent.'—He who would live at ease and win Heaven, must learn to feign and flatter. Dependents flatter their lords instead of reproving them. To cure a wound, a physician must examine it; but physicians are lacking. Friars · suffer for telling the people of the fruits of their misdeeds. The world is out of joint, and will run its ill course. As none dares tell the truth, I will make merry. Learn the lesson: who tells the truth shall suffer.

10. 'FRENSCHIPE FAILEþ & FULLICH FADEþ' [78], comprises 72 verses with refrain variants on 'And þere, fy on a feynt frend!'—There are few faithful friends and many glosers. Rich, you will be sought; poor, you will be hated and mocked. Trust yourself best. There is more truth in a hound than in some men. Let each so govern himself that, if friends fail, his own deeds will raise him. Trust no earthly friendship, put your love in Christ.

11. 'BI A WEY WANDRYNG AS I WENT' [79], 136
verses with refrain variants on 'Euere I þonke god of al,' is of
the *chanson d'aventure* type (see page 489).   Another version [80] is in MS. Cotton Caligula A II f. 68 v (15th century),
omitting stanzas 2, 6-10, 16.   The Cotton text, excluding its
stanzas 10 and 11, is in MS. Ashmole 343 f. 169 r [81] (earlier
15th century).—As, almost mad for sorrow, the poet wandered
along a way, he read on a wall counsel ever to thank God for
everything.   Job suffered, but he gave thanks; and God rewarded him.   So, despite all ill, disappoint the Devil by thanking God—and Heaven will be yours.—Other versions [82] of
the piece are in the fifteenth-century MSS. Trinity College
Cbg. O, 9, 38, Sloane 2593, Garrett in Princeton University
Libr., and in the Bannatyne MS. (1568).

12. 'I WOLDE WITEN OF SUM WYS WIHT' [83],
with refrain variants on 'Þis world fareþ as a fantasy,' consists
of 132 verses.   It dilates on the vanity and the transitoriness
of the world, the generations, and individual men.   Who but
God knows?   Everyone thinks the rest rave.   Let us make
merry and slay care, and worship God, and keep our con-
sciences pure, and pray for mercy: this world is but a fantasy.

13. 'AS I WANDREDE HER BI WESTE' [84], of the
chanson d'aventure type (see page 489), with refrain variants
on 'Ay, merci, God, and graunt-merci,' comprises 96 verses.—
By a forest's side the poet heard a man alternately asking
God for mercy, and giving Him thanks.   He gave thanks for
his creation, for his five wits, and for time to repent in.   He
asked mercy for commission of the Seven Sins; and he prayed
for knowledge of God's will, and for pity at his death-day.—
A variant [84a] is in MS. Balliol College 354 f. 145 r (early
16th century).

14. 'HOSE WOLDE HIM WEI AVYSE' [85] has 72
verses with refrain variants on 'We schal wel fynde þat treuþe
is best.'—Cherishing of Truth and hatred of Falsehood are
best on earth for men of all classes, and the only means to win
Heaven.   Lords should cherish Truth; lawyers should not

destroy it. Should we but hold to Truth, it would liberate
us from sin and make us the flower of chivalry. That Truth
once reigned, Spain and Brittany bear record. Though Falsehood rule for a while, as he is most cherished to the North and
the West, we shall hunt him as the cat does the mice.

15. 'HOSE WOLDE BEÞENKE HIM WEEL' [86],
with refrain variants on 'For charite is no lengor cheere,' consists of 112 verses.—If a person considered well the falsehood
in the world, he would mourn that love is no longer dear. Who
trusts a relative is tricked. None can judge of the inner life
of another; each sees himself in others. Let those who would
give blame, look to themselves and leave judgment to God.
Good words lie as light on the tongue as do the worst. Lock
your words in your chest, and let Conscience keep the key.

16. 'IN WORSCHUPE OF ÞAT MAYDEN SWETE'
[87], with refrain variants on 'Of wimmen comeþ þis worldes
welle,' consists of 120 verses. It praises women, and defends
them against the common malicious abuse by men. For similar
treatments of the theme, see pages 422, 233; Index, *Women.*

17. 'OFF ALLE FLOURES FEIREST FALL ON' [88]
consists of 104 verses in praise of the Virgin. The poet declares her fairest of all flowers, like the Rose; lovely, peerless
of pris, pure, wise, and true as steel. He must have her love.
On this New Year, he greets her with five *aves,* and begs her
help to build a bower in Heaven where he may see her.

18. 'MARIE MAYDEN, MODER MYLDE' [89] con-
sists of 136 verses with 'fflourdelys' at end of each stanza.—
Mary is the Fleur de Lys, Christ is its blossom. The flower
began at the Annunciation, sprang up at the Crucifixion,
spread at the Burial. . . . When Christ ascended, the flower
was seen; since then our peace has been granted. Fairest of
all blooms is the Fleur de Lys, and we should pray to it.

19. 'A, DERE GOD, WHAT MAI ÞIS BE?' [90], with
refrain variants on 'Þat selden iseiȝe is sone forȝete,' consists

of 112 verses. The poem deals with Edward III, his sons, and Richard II. It is discussed with the political pieces (see page 217).

20. 'YIT IS GOD A CURTEIS LORD' [91], with refrain variants on 'Þat þei ne haue warnyng to be ware,' comprises 88 verses on the earthquake of 1382. It has been discussed on page 237.

21. 'CRIST ȜIUE VS GRACE TO LOUE WEL HOLICHIRCH' [92] consists of 64 verses exalting the office of the clergy, maintaining their conduct, and urging obedience to them.

22. 'QWEEN OF HEUENE, MODER AND MAY' [93], with refrain variants on 'And fond euermore to seye þe best,' consists of 56 verses. It urges control of the tongue, whatever be the conditions, and constant saying of the best that can be said. In MS. Cotton Caligula A II f. 68 (15th century) is a piece [94] with a like refrain, but having only stanzas 2, 3, 5 in common with this text. In MS. Garrett, Princeton University Library, f. 45 r (15th century), is another version [95] in 80 lines, agreeing in but three stanzas with Vernon-Simeon.

23. 'ILKE A WYS WIHT SCHOLDE WAKE' [96], with refrain variants on 'And mak no tarijng til to-morn,' consists of 72 verses. It bids set to work at once for Heaven; wealth passes; Death must come; share with the poor.

24. 'BI A WODE AS I GON RYDE' [97], of the *chanson d'aventure* type (see pages 489, 508), has 96 verses with refrain variants on 'Ffor þi sunnes amendes make.'—In a wood the poet heard a bird singing, 'Make amends for thy sins.' He found three causes for the bidding: everyone shall die, none knows when, and none knows where he shall go (see *Three Sorrowful Tidings*, page 392; '*Wanne I ðenke ðinges ðre*,' page 392). Be generous; be just, however high is your office.— Another version [98] of the same length, but with variations in

order, is in MS. Cotton Caligula A II; another [99] is in MS.
Garrett, Princeton University Library, f. 49 r; a shorter version [100] is in MS. Sloane 2593; and another [101] is in MS.
Bodley Engl. Poetry e I. All these MSS. are of the fifteenth
century.

25. 'WHON ALLE SOÞES BEN SOUHT AND SEENE'
[102], with refrain variants on 'But suffre in tyme and þat is
best,' consists of 80 verses.—Good is ever balanced with ill; to
endure is precious. Oppressed, be humble and so win pity. Of
high degree, have mercy. In council with lords, speak wisdom;
if they chide, be still. In company with the foolish, be silent
till you may depart.

26. 'IN SOMER BIFORE ÞE ASCENCIUN' [103], of
the *chanson d'aventure* type (see pages 489, 508), with the
refrain 'Mane nobiscum, Domine,' which is the Versicle for the
Fourth Sunday after Easter, comprises 80 verses.—At his
devotions at evensong on a Sunday, the poet heard the words,
'Mane nobiscum, Domine.' The risen Christ was not recognized by his two disciples; the night is nigh, the light of day
fades. Then follows a paraphrase of the *Pater Noster*. Be
with us, without Thee we have no might, we can but cry to
Thee; the fiend is at hand, the flesh is frail, dwell in us and
preserve us from sin.

27. 'HEIL, STERRE OF ÞE SEE SO BRIHT' [104] is
discussed with the other versions of the *Ave Maris Stella* (see
page 532).

28. 'IN GOD FADER HERYNG SIT' [104a], *A Prayer
to the Trinity*, 24 verses, is really the conclusion of No. 27,
representing stanza 7 of the Latin.

29. 'WHO SO LOUETH ENDELES REST' [105], with
refrain variants on 'But he sey soth, he schal be schent,' consists of 72 verses.—Unless we speak truth we shall suffer at
Doomsday. God asks but truth and kindness united. Tell the
truth, maintain the right; so you may win bliss above. The
poem should be compared with No. 9.

30. 'I ÞONK ÞE, LORD GOD, FUL OF MIHT' [106], *A Morning Thanksgiving and Prayer to God*, consists of 88 verses. The poet gives thanks for preservation through the night, asks aid for the day, gives his five wits into God's care, confesses, and asks mercy and time for repentance. Stanza 1 paraphrases St. Edmund's *Oratio in Mane*. The poem follows the form for morning devotions suggested in the *Speculum* (see pages 346 ff.), and is close to the paraphrase prayer in Rolle's *Our Daily Work* (see page 452).

31. Again it must be noted that Varnhagen's No. 31, '*Lord god þat þis day*' [106a], is really stanzas 3 to end of No. 30.

V. Christ on the Cross and the Compassion of Mary

The Complaint of Christ from the Cross, and as well the Compassion of Mary with the Lament of Mary or *Planctus Mariæ*, were frequently treated in the various tongues from an early time. It has been shown that their influence on the Drama was notable. They were made the themes of a number of English lyrical pieces.

A. Christ on the Cross

'MEN RENT ME ON RODE' [107], in MS. Harley 2316 f. 25 r (1350-1400), is a fragment of 24 irregular verses aaaa 1 and 3 of 2, 2 of 3, 4 of 4, stresses; 2 and 4 with feminine ending, written as prose. From the Cross Christ reminds of His sufferings, and bids think of Him and sin no more.

'BIDES A WHILE AND HALDES ȜOURE PAIS' [108] and 'MAN, ÞUS ON RODE I HING FOR ÞE' [109], are in stanzas aabccb (*a* and *c* of 4, *b* of 3, stresses) in MSS. Cotton Galba E IX f. 48 v (early 15th century) and Rawlinson Poetry 175 [110] (c. 1350). The former is a version of the *Popule mi, quid feci tibi*, in 3 stanzas. Lines 1-3 bid hearken to Christ. In the rest of the piece Christ bids the passers-by behold Him on the Cross, and repent and ask mercy.—In the six stanzas of the second poem Christ from the Cross declares to the sinner His sacrifice for Man, and promises His mercy to the repentant.

'MY VOLK, WHAT HABBE Y DO THE?' is William Herebert's version of the *Popule mi, quid feci tibi* (see page 502).

'VNKYNDE MAN' [111] and 'LO, LEMMAN SWETE' [112] are excellent pieces, perhaps by Rolle (see pages 444, 505), in MSS. Cbg. Univ. Libr. Dd V 64 f. 134 (see page 506) and Vernon [113]. In both, Christ addresses the beholder. The fifteen short couplets of the former poem bid see His wounds, remember the years of His sacrifice, love Him and draw from sin. The six lines (aabccb, fours and threes) of the second bid see how He has given His life, and urge to love Him. Horstmann thinks these pieces afforded material for the Charters of Christ (see page 369).

'BIHOLD TO þı LORD, MAN' [114], in MS. Harley 913 f. 28 (1308-1318, before 1325), is the opening of an English paraphrase of the first four of five parts of a Latin prose piece, 'Respice in faciem Christi tui.' Parts 1 and 2 are respectively 16 and 2 irregular long lines in couplets; Parts 3 and 4 are 4 and 8 irregular short couplets. Part 1 bids Man see on the Cross his Lover bloody and wan. In the last three parts Christ bids behold His sufferings for which Man gives no thanks.

'MAN AND WYMAN, LOKET TO ME' [115], 10 irregular four-stress Southern lines in couplets in MS. New College Oxf. 88 f. 179 (beginning 14th century), is a paraphrase of a part of the Harley Latin passage (see just above), but is older than the Harley version. Christ bids Man behold His wounds for him. On the next page are five irregular lines aaabb, in which the Soul declares the Lord has called long, and it has delayed ever.

'WIT WAS HIS NAKEDE BREST' [116], in MS. Bodley 42 f. 250 (c. 1300-1320), consists of two couplets of verses of six or seven stresses describing Christ on the Cross. This is followed by the opening of the above Harley Latin passage, with an English paraphrase in three irregular couplets bidding Man behold Christ suffering on the Cross.—The first two couplets are also on a piece of vellum (of uncertain date) pasted in MS. Durham Cathedral A III 12.

'SYNFUL MAN, LOKE VP AND SEE,' [117], in MS. Arundel 507 f. 10 (14th century), consists of 8 four-stress verses abababab, in which Christ bids the sinner behold Him on the Tree, and repent, and forsake sin.

'MAN, TO REFOURME' [118], in MS. Br. Mus. Additional 31042 f. 94 v (15th century), consists of 120 five-stress verses ababbcbc with a refrain voicing the general purport of the address by Christ to Man: 'Looke one my woundes, thynke one my passioun.'

'ȜE ÞAT BE ÞIS WEY PACE' [119] is two short couplets in MS. Harley 7322 f. 154 (in a 14th-century piece). Christ bids the sinner stop, and behold His face; is any pain like His?

THE CURSOR MUNDI LINES 17111-17270 [120] (see page 415) have a discourse between Christ and Man, in which Christ from the Cross reminds of what He has suffered for Man. Then follow the author's grateful, prayerful exclamations, which are interspersed with imagined words of exhortation and encouragement from Christ.

A LUYTEL TRETYS OF LOUE: OF GODES PASSYON [121] consists of 96 four-stress verses aaaa. in MS. Vernon (1370-1380). Christ informs Man's soul of His sufferings for its redemption, and requires that it come with love to His arms and to Heaven's bliss. The last 20 lines are a prayer for preservation and ultimate bliss.

THE CHARTERS OF CHRIST (see page 369) contain treatment of the theme.

'WHI ART THOW FROWARD, SITH I AM MERCI-

ABLE' [122] is the refrain of 40 five-stress verses ababbcbc in
MS. Cbg. Univ. Libr. Hh IV 12 f. 85 r (15th century).   In
four stanzas Christ reminds of His sacrifices and His pity.   In
the fifth stanza the hearers declare that they are mindful, and
pray for mercy.

'HO ÞAT SIÞ HIM ON ÞE RODE' [123], in MS. Harley
7322 f 7 (in a 14th-century piece—see page 396), consists
of 9 lines abcbdbefb (ll. 2, 4 of 3, the rest of 4, stresses).—
Whoever sees on the Cross his Lover Christ, and Mary and
John standing by, should grieve and forsake his sins.

'HI SIKE AL WAN HI SINGE' [124] has 60 three-stress
lines ababccbccb or -ddb in MS. Digby 2 f. 6 r (13th century).   Successive stanzas are connected by repetition (see
page 490; Index).   The singer expresses his sorrow as he pictures his Lover suffering on the Cross, and his wonder that men
ruin their souls redeemed at such cost.—The same, with rearrangement and with dialectical variations [125], is in MS.
Harley 2253 f. 80 (c. 1310).

THE DEBATE BETWEEN MARY AND THE CROSS
(see page 416) contains treatment of the theme.

A fifteenth-century lament [126] of Christ over men's sins,
is in Wright's *Songs and Carols.*

B.   *The Compassion of Mary*

'JESU CRISTES MILDE MODER' [127], in MS.
Arundel 248 f. 154 (c. 1250-1300), consists of 66 Southern,
perhaps South-East Midland, verses aabccb in fours and threes,
that remind of the Tanner Compassio (see page 519).   The
poem consists chiefly of address to Mary, indicating Christ's
suffering, but particularly developing the Mother's grief.
Then is declared her joy at the Resurrection.   A prayer for
the Virgin's intercession, ends the whole.   There is much similarity of matter to the Digby 86 and Harley 2253 *Dialogue
between the Virgin and Christ* (see page 415).

'ꝧE MILDE LOMB ISPRAD ON RODE' [128], in MS.
Arundel 248 f. 154 v (c. 1250-1300), consists of 48 four-stress
Southern, perhaps originally South-East Midland, verses aaabcccb with the music. As is that which precedes it, the poem
is probably from Latin, though an original of but stanza 4
has been indicated. The piece is largely narrative, a mixture of
Passio Christi and *Compassio Mariæ.*—Christ suffered on the
Cross. Mary, grieving, stood beside Him with John. Christ
reminded her of her rejoicing at His birth; she must bear her
sorrow while He died for men. John cared for her.

A COMPASSIO MARIÆ [129], of which the first part is
missing, comprises 43 four-stress West Midland verses aabccb
in MS. Tanner 169* f. 175 (soon after 1250) with music. The
fragment follows with much freedom the last seven stanzas of
a Latin *De Beata Maria Virgine.* Addressing the Virgin, the
poem declares sympathetically her grief at the Passion and her
joy at the Resurrection, and ends with prayer for salvation.
The piece has resemblances to '*Jesu Christes milde moder*' (see
above), but the two are probably independent compositions.

Also of the thirteenth century is the handling of the theme
in the *Dialogue between Mary and Christ on the Cross* (see
page 414). Of the fourteenth century are the treatments in
Meditations on the Passion of Christ (see page 451), *Meditations on the Supper of Our Lord* (see page 358), *Christ's
Testament* or the *Charter of Christ* (see page 369), the
Lamentation of Mary to St. Bernard (see page 415), the
Cursor Mundi lines 23945-24658 (see page 415), the *Lamen-
tatio S. Mariæ* (see page 415), the *Dialogue between Mary and
the Cross* (see page 416), and lines 36-42 of the Cbg. Gg
Assumption (see page 330).

The fifteenth century was especially fruitful of treatments
[129a]. The Virgin in monologue speaks of her grief in
Hoccleve's *Lamentation of Green Tree* from De Guilleville's
Pélerinage de l'Ame; in the *Virgin's Complaint* ('As resoun
rewlid') and the *Virgin's Complaint and Comfort* ('As reson
hathe rulyd') ; in '*Lysteneth, lordynges*'; in the *Virgin's Lament*

over *Her Dead Son* ('Who cannot weep'); in the *Lamentation of the Virgin* ('Off alle women,' three texts); in Kennedy's *Passion*, stanzas 168 ff.; in the Bodley 596 prose *Lamentation of Our Lady;* and in Banister's (died 1490) *Dream of the Passion and Compassion.* The theme is treated in dialogues, *et al.*, in '*Mary moder, cum & se*' and '*His body is wrappyd,*' where John, Mary, and Christ speak; in Jacob Ryman's '*O my dere sonne,*' between Jesus and Mary; in Kennedy's *Passion*, stanzas 147 ff., between Mary and the Cross; in *Mary's Speeches to Bridget* in MS. Lambeth 432 f. 76.—Of the late fifteenth or the sixteenth century may be mentioned four pieces in MS. Balliol College 345: '*A babe is born,*' '*When yet my swete sone,*' '*Bowght & sold full traytorsly,*' and '*Thys blessyd babe.*'

Purely dramatic treatment of the sorrows of Mary may be found in the *York Plays* Nos. 34, 36, 43; the *Towneley Plays* Nos. 22, 23, 29; the *Chester Plays* No. 17; the *Hegge Plays* Nos. 28, 32, 34, 35; and the Bodley *Burial of Christ.*

VI. Hymns and Prayers to God, Christ, the Trinity

For convenience, are discussed on page 505 the Thornton poems '*Lord Ihesu Cryste,*' '*Almyghty god in trinite,*' '*Lorde god alweldande,*' '*Ihesu that diede,*' '*Ihesu criste, Saynte Marye sonne*'; and on pages 505-07 the Cbg. Univ. Libr. Dd poems '*My trewest tresowre,*' '*Ihesu, als þow me made,*' '*Mercy es maste,*' '*Ihesu, god son,*' and '*Heyle, Ihesu, my creatowre.*'

THE IN MANUS TUAS versions are noted on page 350.

THE VENI CREATOR SPIRITUS is extant in three English versions of before 1400 that follow line for line its eight stanzas (the seventh is dropped in modern use): '*Come, shuppere, Holy Gost,*' one of William Herebert's pieces (see page 502); '*Cvm, maker of gaste þou ert*' [130], in MS. Bodley 425 f. 93 (14th century), 32 four-stress verses as in the original; '*Cum, lord vr makere, Holigost*' [131], in MS. Vernon (1370-1380), 32 four-stress verses abab.

'SWETE IHESU CRIST, TO þE' [132], *A Confessioun to Ihesu Crist*, consists of 49 short couplets in MS. Vernon (1370-1380).   The poet confesses guilt of all the Seven Sins and against the Commandments, with all his five wits; but he has never forsaken God.   He asks penitence of Christ, and intercession of Mary and all the saints.—On a fourteenth-century leaf taken from a binding by the Rev. J. R. Barton, is a Kentish version [133] of 36 lines, corresponding (with omissions) to lines 1-44 of this text.

'I ÞONK þE, LORD GOD, FUL OF MIHT,' *A Morning Thanksgiving and Prayer to God*, is No. 30 of the Vernon-Simeon lyrics (see page 515).

√ 'GOD, ÞAT AL ÞIS MYHTES MAY' [134], probably originally Southern of 1250-1300, consists of 56 four-stress verses abababab in MS. Harley 2253 f. 106 r (c. 1310).   To God the poet confesses his guilt and unworthiness; he submits him to the mercy of Christ.   The piece is sincere; but the rime-system and the end-stopped lines make it little melodious.

√ 'HE3E LOUERD, ÞOU HERE MY BONE' [135], in MS. Harley 2253 f. 72 r (c. 1310), consists of six stanzas aabaab-ccbccb (*b* of 3 stresses with feminine ending, the rest of 4 stresses) each with an after-stanza abaab (*a* of 4 stresses, *b* of 3 stresses with feminine ending), and an extra final similar stanza abaab.   Most of the lines have double or triple alliteration.   Successive stanzas are connected by repetition (see page 489; Index).   The piece springs warm out of experience.— Fool the poet has been, and base, in the days of youth and prosperity; he who was wildest and boldest and most welcome, now has staff for steed, and goes halting and loathed into hall. Of all sins he has been guilty; death is near.   The remedy is praise of Christ and submission to Him.   The poet is ready. May God give us light to see the saints, and Heaven for our reward!—Similarities to the pieces on Old Age (see page 391) and to the debates between the Body and the Soul (see page 411) may be seen.

'[ ]IDDE HUVE WITH MILDE STEVENE' [136] consists of six irregular couplets with alliteration introducing the *Pater Noster*, etc. (see page 350), in MS. Cotton Cleopatra B VI f. 201 v (c. 1250). It asks God to feed and foster the lord of the house and all loyal servants, with all other Christians.

'IESU CRIST, HEOUENE KYNG' [137], Southern perhaps from West Midland, in MS. Harley 2253 f. 75 v (c. 1310), consists of a stanza aabccbddb (*b* of 3, the rest of 4, stresses) asking mercy of Christ; and twelve lines aabccb (*b* of 3 stresses with feminine ending, the rest of 4 stresses) declaring the world offers but distress, and urging conduct that will win Heaven. Line 10 introduces the *chanson d'aventure* form (see pages 489, 508).

'IESU, FOR þI MUCHELE MIHT' [138], Southern from West Midland, consists of five stanzas ababccdeed (*b* and *d* of 3, the rest of 4, stresses) in MS. Harley 2253 f. 79 v (c. 1310). From introductory address to Christ, the piece becomes homiletic. The poet is overcome with remorse for sins. Doomsday is nigh. If we believe and abandon folly, we shall have bliss.

'FADUR AND SONE AND HOLIGOST' [139], *An Orisun of þe Trinite*, consists of 104 four-stress verses ababababab in MSS. Vernon (Southern; 1370-1380) and Thornton f. 211 v (Northern; c. 1430-1440; omits ll. 7-8, 15-16). The poet prays for protection from Hell and aid at death, and asks mercy and time for repentence. Hall has ventured to assign this poem to Laurence Minot (see page 217). Other prayers to the Trinity are noted on pages 341, 514.

'SWET IESUS, HEND AND FRE' [140], in MS. Harley 913 f. 9 r (1308-1318, before 1325), consists of 15 complicated but skilfully handled stanzas aaababbab (*b* of 3 stresses with feminine ending, the rest of 4 stresses) with internal rime in the last two *a* lines. Stanza 15 ascribes the poem to Michael Kildare, a friar minor (see page 228). The piece is really a

chiding of the rich for devotion to vanities, and an urging to
amendment.

'LOUERD CRIST, ICH þE GRETE' [141] is in MS.
Jesus College Oxf. 29 f. 265 (South-Western; c. 1275). It is
a rude jingle of 32 couplets of irregular four-stress verses with
cæsura. It acknowledges Christ's mercy in the Incarnation and
the Passion, and His example of obedience and good deeds;
and it asks aid to believe and to follow Him.

'LORD, MY GOD AL MERCIABLE' [142], *An Orysoun
to God þe Fadur*, makes up 45 short couplets in MS. Vernon
(1370-1380). It is a version of a prayer of Thomas Aquinas,
Oratio solita recitari singulo die ante imaginem Christi, 'Con-
cede mihi, misericors Deus. . . .' Earnestly it asks full submission to God's will, and devotion to right living.

'LORD, SWETE IHESU CRIST' [143], *An Orysoun to
God þe Sone*, in MS. Vernon next after the piece just mentioned, consists of 40 verses of six or seven stresses aaaa. The
metre is poor; the utterance is hackneyed, but sincere. The
poet declares he should love Christ for His sufferings; he has
sinned; he prays for forgiveness for himself and his friends.
A French analogue or source is said to be in MS. Bodley 57 f.
6, with a variant in MS. Digby 86 f. 200 v, both ascribed to
St. Edmund. Similarities to Edmund's *Speculum* (see page
346) have been noted.

'INWARDLICHE, LORD, BISECHE I þE' [144], *An
Orisoun for Negligens of þe X Comaundemens*, comprises 14
short couplets in MS. Vernon (1370-1380).

'LORD, I ȜELDE ME GULTI' [145], *A Confessioun for
Necligence of þe Dedes of Mercy*, consists of 24 lines aabccb
(*b* of 3 stresses with feminine ending, the rest of 4 stresses)
also in MS. Vernon.

'LORD, SUNGED HAUE I OFTE' [146], *An Orysoun for
Sauynge of þe Fyve Wyttes*, 12 lines aabccb (*b* of 3, the rest

of 4, stresses), is with the above in MS. Vernon. Sin through all the senses is confessed, and pardon is asked.

'I KNOWLECH TO GOD, WITH VERAY CONTRICON' [147], 77 five-stress lines ababbcc in MS. Rawlinson B 408 (c. 1450), is a later piece to be connected with the three next above.

'GOD, þAT ART OF MIHTES MOST' [148], *A Prayer for the Seven Gifts of the Holy Ghost*, 30 lines aabccb (*b* of 3, the rest of 4, stresses) in MS. Vernon (1370-1380), asks in turn for each of the Seven Gifts, with final lasting joy.

'TO LOUE I-CHULLE BEGINNE' [149], *A Mourning Song of the Love of God*, also in MS. Vernon f. 299, consists of 256 three-stress lines abab.abab. With much feeling, the poet abjures the world for devotion to Christ; reviews the Passion; asks intercession of Mary; and prays for the thrusting of Christ's love deep into his heart. The shortness of the lines, and the frequency of the rimes, spoil the effect of the piece. One should compare with the poem the *Prayer to the Five Wounds* (see below [152]).

'IHESUS þAT DIȜEDEST VPPON þE TRE' [150], *An Orisoun to þe Fyue Woundes of Ihesus Christus*, 48 lines aabccb (*b* of 3, the rest of 4, stresses), also in MS. Vernon, prays for mercy and grace in the name of the Wounds successively, a stanza with a *Pater Noster* being given to each.

'IESU, þAT ART HEUENE KYNG' [151], 32 four-stress verses abab, also in MS. Vernon, beseeches Christ to draw the poet from earthly desire; to pardon all who have been good to him; and, in the name of the Five Wounds, to make him love Him as he should.

'IHESU CRIST, MY LEMMON SWETE' [152], *A Preyer to þe Fiue Woundes*, also in MS. Vernon, consists of 16 verses abcbdbeb, ababcbdb. Stanza 1 is a variant of the last stanza of '*To loue I-chulle beginne*' (see above [149]). The opening of stanza 2 reflects the first lines of '*Ihesus þat*

diȝedest' (see above) in MS. Vernon. A variant of stanza 2
is the opening of Thornton lyric No. 4 *'Ihesu that diede'* (see
page 505). Stanza 1 with slight variations occurs as second
of a set of poetical scraps in MS. Harley 2316 f. 25 (1350-
1400), *'Jhesu Cryst, myn lemman swete'* [153]. An interesting adaptation of stanza 1 to the Virgin and her joys and
sorrow, is *'Ladye mary, mayden swete'* [154] abcbdbdb in
Lord Mostyn's MS. 186 (? 15th century).

'HE YAF HIMSELF AS GOOD FELAWE' [155], one of
a number of poetical scraps in MS. Harley 2316 f. 25 (1350-
1400), is a hymn of 8 four-stress verses abababab, declaring
that Christ gave Himself as a good fellow, a good nurse, a
good shepherd; we shall know Him when He gives Himself as
reward in Heaven.

'IHESU, þɪ SWETNESSE WHOSE MIHT HIT SE'
[156], perhaps originally Northern, a hymn in stanzas abababab, is in MSS. Vernon (1370-1380; 120 lines), Lambeth 853
(c. 1430; 120 lines), Thornton f. 14 (the best MS.; 1430-
1440; 113 lines), and Rawlinson A 389 f. 104 (15th century).—All earthly love is bitter beside the sweetness of Christ;
He is God, Man, Savior, never-failing Friend; the poet can
never repay Him, but he can love and serve Him truly.

THE IESU DULCIS MEMORIA is imitated in several
pieces.
   'Suete Iesu, King of Blysse' [157], in MS. Harley 2253 f.
75 (Southern; c. 1310), consists of 60 four-stress verses
aaaa.—'Suete Iesu' (the opening of each stanza), light and
remedy of my heart, food of my soul, thou hast shown me how
sweet is Thy love; woe is to him who knows it not or abandons
it. Thou didst redeem me on the Cross where Thy mother sorrowed as witness; save me, and let me take the Sacrament ere
I die.—Stanzas 1-3 correspond to the last 12 verses of *Les
ounsse peines de enfer* in MS. Digby 86 f. 134 (see page 332).
   'Iesu, Suete is þe Loue of þe' [158], on f. 77 v of the same
MS., consists of 50 similar stanzas perhaps intended as a

rosary. It expands the matter of the former piece, elaborates
that on the Passion and the Compassion, and adds much.—I
am espoused to Thee, but I have sinned and am ever unworthy;
make me worthy; cause me to serve Thee; I long for Thee; care
for my soul at death, and bring me to Thee.

'*Here begynnus þo passion of Ihesu*' [159], 356 four-stress
verses aaaa in MS. Royal 17 B XVII f. 13 v (1370-1400; here
Southern), combines and expands the above two. pieces, with
a greatly enlarged account of the Passion, the Seven Words
on the Cross, and inserted single stanzas to Mary at intervals of some fifty lines. Each stanza, except those to the
Virgin, opens with 'Swete Ihesu.' In MS. Vernon f. 297 (c.
1370-1380; Southern), the Royal text is in turn enlarged to
444 verses, '*Swete Ihesu, now wol I synge.*' The monotony of
the repetitions is broken by the action in the Passion matter.
The poems are throughout contemplative, full of intense personal longing and devotion. It has been suggested that each
of the versions is from a Latin original; that the expansions
imply Northern origin; and that the similarity of theme with
Rolle's work, may admit of Rolle's having connection with
them.

See also '*Marie, ȝow quen*' in MS. Harley 2316 (see page
535).

'LOVERD, SHYLD ME VROM HELLE DETH' is one
of the pieces of William Herebert (see page 502).

'NAUEþ MY SAULE BUTE FUR AND YS' [160] is a
fragment of ten lines in MS. Jesus College Oxf. 29 f. 262 (c.
1275), urging prayer to God for salvation.

'IN GOD FADER HERYNG SIT,' styled *A Prayer to the
Trinity*, is really the conclusion of Vernon-Simeon lyric No.
27 (see page 514).

'AS þOU FOR HOLY CHURCHE RIȝT' [161], in MS.
Douce 128 f. 258, consists of two stanzas ababcded (*b* and *d*
of 3, *a* and *e* of 4, stresses) and abababcded (all but *c* of 3

stresses). The *c* lines (2 stresses) are the 'With an O and an I' refrain (see page 236). The writer prays for joy to the Savior who suffered on the Cross; for he dwells alone, his friends are few, his foes walk thick. The MS. is of the fourteenth and fifteenth centuries.

'IHESU MYNE, GRAUNTE ME þɪ GRACE' [162], ultimately from *Isaiah* 7. 15-16, consists of three short couplets in MS. Royal 17 B XVII (1370-1400) asking time and power to make amends for sin and to do God's will.

'WHEN Y SE BLOSMES SPRINGE' [163], in MS. Harley 2253 f. 76 (c. 1310), mingles with religious matter secular nature and love elements in 50 three-stress verses (*a, c, d* with feminine ending) ababccbddb.—Bursting of blossoms and song of birds fill the poet with longing for Him in whom is all his joy. Yet thought of His Passion brings sadness. May Christ aid to repent and to love Him aright, and may Mary give might to endure for Him.

'SOMER IS COMEN AND WINTER GONE' [164]' an adaptation of the *reverdie* (cp. *Thrush and Nightingale,* '*Lenten ys come*,' pages 421, 494), in MS. Egerton 613 f. 1 v (Southern; c. 1250), consists of 80 lines ababccdefe (ll. 1, 3, 6 of 4, ll. 2, 4, 5 of 3, ll. 7, 10 of 1, ll. 8, 9 of 2, stresses).— The birds sing joyously; but I grieve because of a gentle child who sought me out in the woods and on the hills, and found me bound because of an apple from a tree. He broke the bonds with His wounds.—Then follows treatment of the Passion and the Compassion, the Harrowing of Hell, the Resurrection, and the Ascension. Despite the forced figure, the piece is pleasing—certainly graceful and melodious.

'WYNTER WAKENEÞ AL MY CARE' [165], in MS. Harley 2253 f. 75 v (c. 1310), consists of 15 verses aaabb (l. 5 of 6, the rest of 4, stresses), in which the subjective and the objective, nature and the inner man, mingle into one, and transform an old theme.—Winter revives all my care, the green becomes fallow, the leaves fall; so I mourn that all the world's joy comes to naught; all passes but God's will.

'GOD, Þat AL HAST MAD OF NOUHT' [166], *A Confessioun of Wyrschip in Orysoun*, comprises 8 short couplets in MS. Vernon (1370-1380). The poet thanks God for creating and redeeming Man for love; asks right love to Him, protection from sin, and guidance to Heaven.

'GODYS SONE Þat WAS SO FRE' [167], in MS. Douce 126 f. 90 (1400-1450), consists of 60 verses abababababcded (*a* of 4, *c* of 2, the rest of 3, stresses). The *c* verse is the refrain 'With an O and an I' (see page 236). The poem exalts Christ's Passion for Man, who will not know Him. The poet's will is changed, he will serve the lovely lady who bore Him. The transition to the Virgin is abrupt.

'CRIST MADE TO MAN A FAIR PRESENT' [168], in MS. Trinity College Cbg. B, 15, 17 (late 14th century), consists of 44 four-stress verses, 1-10 on one rime, the rest usually aaaa.—Love has given Jesus His bloody wounds and His death, so that it no longer has a home. But Love has won the poet's heart to faithfulness to Christ.

ON UREISUN OF OURE LOUERDE [169], in MS. Lambeth 487 f. 65 r (1200-1250), consists of about 1200 words of alliterative rhythmical lyrical prose. It is an earlier but incomplete version of *On Wel Suiðe God Ureisun of God Almihti* [170], some 1350 words of similar prose in MS. Cotton Nero A XIV f. 123 v (1200-1250). The piece is of the South-West of 1200-1250. It is a notable prayer of passionate realization of the sweetness and softness and brightness of Christ, and of beseeching for purification and union with the Heavenly Lover. In its ardor, the piece largely loses the spiritual in the physical.

THE WOHUNGE OF URE LAUERD [171], about 3500 words of alliterative rhythmical lyrical prose, of the South-West of 1200-1250, is in MS. Cotton Titus D XVIII f. 127 r. As do the writers of the *Ureisun* (both versions), the poet exalts with a rhapsodic enthusiasm the beauty, the grace, the gentleness of Christ, much as if He were an elevated and perfected earthly lover. He ecstatically glorifies and laments His Passion, extols His harrowing of Hell, and gives over his body and his soul to absolute possession of the Heavenly Spouse.

Efforts made to show that the three pieces just mentioned are by one author who was a woman, and that the pieces were influenced more or less by English writings like the *Ancren Riwle* and *Hali Meidenhad* (see pages 361, 272) with which they have some points of agreement, are scarcely convincing. It has been shown that the pieces were probably largely influenced by French clerical writers in Latin, like Hugo de St. Victor and Anselm of Canterbury.

A LOFSONG OF URE LAUERDE [172], some 1200 words of alliterative rhythmical prose in MS. Cotton Nero A XIV f. 128 r, likewise of the South-West of 1200-1250, is a prayer for purification, for defense from the Devil, and for help in weakness; and a declaration of abnegation of mankind, and of desire for union with Christ alone and for a being filled with absolute devotion to Him. To this piece is appended a prose Creed (see page 353).

A LUUE RON [173], 'A mayde cristes me bit yorne,' is ascribed to 'Frater Thomas de Hales de ordine fratrum Minorum ad instanciam cuiusdam puelle deo dicate' at the head of its text in MS. Jesus College Oxf. 29 f. 260 (c. 1275). This notable piece is of the South-West. It consists of 210 four-stress verses abababab (st. 1, ababcbcb), with a final couplet.—A maid of Christ besought the poet to make a love song; he will teach as best he can. He preaches the vanity of the world: worldly love is fleeting and inconstant; where are Paris and Helen, and Amadas, and Tristram, and Hector, and Cæsar? He will direct to a Lover whose vassal is King Henry; He sends an invitation to be known to Him; His dwelling is fairer than Solomon's; there is all bliss, the sight of Him is all joy; He has given the maid a jewel, virginity, that heals all love-wounds, that shines bright in Heaven. Choose the Lover who is the best. Learn and recite this rime to other maidens, and obey what it teaches.—On the use of the 'ubi sunt' formula here, see page 389.

OF CLENE MAYDENHOD [174], 136 verses in MS. Vernon f. 299 (1370-1380), is to be associated in matter with *Hali Meidenhad* (see page 272). With some minor modifications, it has all the groups of matter of *A Luue Ron* in the order of that poem. With the latter it has close similarity in phrasing, and identity of wording of ideas similar or identical, identity of stanza-form, identity in one or both of the rime-sounds, and frequently identity in rime-words. On the use of the 'ubi sunt' formula here, see page 389.

MS. Lambeth 853 (c. 1430) contains other pieces, some of which may be before 1400 (see page 486).

VII   Hymns and Prayers to the Virgin

THE AVE MARIA occurs in the following English versions: MSS. Arundel 292 f. 3 r (1200-1250), four lines [175] aaaa; Cotton Cleopatra B VI f. 201 v (c. 1250), four irregular four-stress lines [176] aabc; Arundel 57 f. 94 r (c. 1350), Kentish prose [177]; Caius College Cbg. 44 (13th century), prose [178]; Cbg. Univ. Libr. Hh VI 11 (13th century), three short couplets [179]; and Halliwell 219 (14th century), prose [180]. See also the groups of versions of the Creed, the *Pater Noster*, etc. (see pages 350; and see 471, 479).

Two very interesting renderings of the *Ave* are in MSS. Douce 126 [181] (15th century) and Cbg. Univ. Libr. Gg IV 32 (time of Henry IV) [182]. The former consists of 17 stanzas aaaa of verses of six or seven stresses. When read consecutively, the first words of the successive stanzas form an English translation of the successive seventeen Latin Words: 'Hayle, Mary, Grace, full of, Lord, with Thee, blessed, thou, in, women, and, blessed, fruit, womb, thine, Jesus, Amen.'—The latter piece, 15 stanzas abababab of four-stress verses, practices the same device. Latin and French *aves* of similar form exist.

'MAIDEN AND MODER ÞAT BAR ÞE HEVENE KING' [183], a prayer in five couplets of verses of six or seven stresses, follows the *Ave* in MS. Cotton Cleopatra B VI f. 201 v (c. 1250).

'HEIL BEO ÞOU, MARIE, MYLDE QWEN OF HEUENE' [184], 56 six-stress verses aaaa in MS. Vernon (1370-1380), beseeches Mary to help from sin and to bring to eternal bliss.

'MARIE MODUR, QWEN OF HEUENE' [185] consists of 17 short couplets in MS. Vernon. The poet prays Mary to let him not die in sin, but to save him and his friends.

'HEIL BEO ÞOW, MARIE, MOODUR AND MAY' [186], in MS. Vernon, comprises 132 four-stress lines abababababbcbc. Each stanza consists of a series of 'hails' and epithets of flowery and exaggerated glorification, closing with 'Do prey for vs to þi sone so fre. Aue.'

'MAYDEN, MODUR, AND COMELY QWEEN' and 'HEIL BEO ÞOW, MARIE, MODUR OF CRIST' [187], printed as one by their editor, are in MS. Vernon. Both are aabccb (*b* of 3, the rest of 4, stresses). The former in 24 lines blesses the Virgin for aiding the singer at point of death. The conclusion has been taken to suggest that the poet at least intended to add a passage on the Five Joys (see page 537).— The second piece [187a] consists of 384 verses, each stanza ending with an *ave*. Stanzas 1-26 hail Mary with epithets and declarations covering the history from her birth to the turning of the water into wine. The rest are an elaborate series of 'blessings,' item·by item, of the details of Mary's anatomy, her strength and morals and steadfast thought and sweetness and fairness and life and soul, and her body in general.—The detailed blessing of the Virgin may be traced to a Latin practice at least as early as the 12th century.

'SEINTE MARI, MODER MILDE' [188] consists of 6 stanzas ababaacdc (ll. 1, 3, 5, 6, 8 of 4 stresses, ll. 2, 4 of 3 stresses with feminine ending, ll. 7, 9 of one stress with feminine ending), the *b* and *c* lines Latin, in MS. Trinity College Cbg. B, 14, 39 (Southern; 13th century). In graceful verse the poet declares Mary's power in taming his wild impulses, begs Christ not to let Man be lost after His sacrifice, and prays Mary to help him to turn to her from the world and all his sins.

'OF ON ÞAT IS SO FAYR AND BRIƷT' [189] consists of 5 stanzas ababccded (*a, c, e* of 4, *b* of 3, stresses, *d* of one stress with feminine ending), the *b* and *d* lines Latin, in MSS. Egerton 613 f. 2 (Southern; c. 1250) and Trinity College Cbg. B, 14, 39 (next after '*Seinte Mari*'; Southern; 13th century). In charming verse, with great feeling and genuine lyrical impulse, the poet prays for Mary's intercession, and praises her; her Son will not refuse her requests. The Latin is generally an essential part of the sentence. In MS. Ashmole 1393 (c. 1425-1450) is a song [190] with music, made up of the first four lines of each stanza of this poem, with two added quatrains.

'BLESSED BEO ÞU, LAUEDI, FUL OF HOUENE BLISSE' [191] comprises 36 seven-stress verses aaaa in MSS. Egerton 613 f. 2 (Southern; c. 1250) and Harley 2253 f. 81 r (Southern with Midland traits; c. 1310). The Egerton text is probably the earlier, though it is not the archetype of Harley. It is the more corrupt, probably having been written down from memory. The poem is a prayer for aid from sin and to salvation.

THE AVE MARIS STELLA, DEI MATER ALMA is extant in several English versions [192].

'*Heile sterne on þe se so bright*,' in MS. Bodley 425 f. 93 v (Northern; 14th century), consists of 28 four-stress verses aaaa, following beautifully the Latin, stanza for stanza.

'*Heyl, levedy, se-stoerre bryht*,' in MS. Porkington 10, is one of the poems by William Herebert (see page 502).

'*Heil, sterre of þe See so briht*,' 144 verses ababababcdcd (alternately 4 stresses and 3 stresses with feminine ending), is Nos. 27 and 28 of the Vernon-Simeon lyrics (see page 514).

The piece quotes the stanzas of the Latin, after each giving an expanded English paraphrase of two stanzas, the first stanza closer to the original than the second. It has not the grace of the former two versions.

'EDI BEO þU, HEUENE QUENE' [193], praising the Virgin in 64 four-stress lines abababab, is preserved with music in MS. Corpus Christi College Oxf. 54, D, 5, 14 f. 113 v (before 1300). This is not a version of '*Blessed beo þu, lauedi,*' and is much more graceful than that poem.

'MODUR MILDE, FLUR OF ALLE' [194] is in the MS. with '*Edi beo þu*' f. 116 v, in three stanzas of like form to be sung to the same music. The singer prays for salvation from sin, and for intercession with Christ.

'MARIE, MODUR AND MAYDEN, EUERE WEL þE BE' [195] is in MS. Vernon (1370-1380) in 26 couplets of six-stress lines with medial cæsura. The poet prays for aid from sin, for spiritual food, for protection of friend and foe. Another version [196] of the piece, greatly condensed in 27 short couplets often with much the same rimes, is in MS. Cbg. Univ. Libr. Ff. V 48 (15th century). Other texts of the shorter version are in the fifteenth-century MSS. Harley 2382, Chetham 8009 f. 121, and British Museum C, 11, a, 28 f. 97. Perhaps the Vernon version is a copy with the lines of the original lengthened.

'MAIDEN, MODER MILDE, OIEZ CEL OREYSOUN' [197], probably of the West Midland, is in MS. Harley 2253 f. 83 (c. 1310) in 48 three-stress verses abababab. The *a* lines are English, the *b* lines are French. The poem begins with a prayer to the Virgin, but at stanza 3 it shifts to a narrative of the Passion from the arrest to the rejoicing of Pilate at the death of Christ.

'QWEN OF HEWYN, JOY THE [198], Alle saftys honur the, He ros als he sayd the, Leuedy pre for hus we bid the,' four English lines, are in a group of mixed English, French, and Latin verses by a fourteenth-century hand in MS. Ghent University 317.

'HAYL, MARI, HIC AM SORI' [199], in MS. Digby 2 f. 6 v (13th century), consists of 5 stanzas aaaaabab (*b* of 3, *a* of 4, stresses) with medial rime in the first and the third, and once in the fifth, line. Successive stanzas are connected by repetition (see page 489; Index). The singer fears punishment for his sins; he asks grace for penance, salvation from the fiends, and sight of Mary's face.

'LEUEDI, SAINTE MARIE, MODER AND MEIDE' [200] consists of 11 stanzas aaaa of verses usually seven-stressed, in MS. Br. Mus. Additional 27909 (1225-1250). The piece is full of real feeling, but was probably not intended to be sung. It has ideas and phrases similar to some in the *Poema Morale* (see page 385). It is really a confession and a declaration of repentance, with prayer for aid.

'ON HIRE IS AL MI LIF ILONG' [201], in MSS. Cotton Caligula A IX f. 246 v (South-West; before 1250) and Jesus College Oxf. 29 (South-West; c. 1275), consists of 5 stanzas ababaababa (ll. 1, 3, 5, 6, 8 of 4, l. 10 of 2, stresses, ll. 2, 4, 7, 9 of three stresses with feminine ending).—By bearing Christ, Mary brought Man salvation. She brought help; Eve brought woe. All earthly things are vain. The poet will repent and amend. Will not Mary punish him in this life?—MS. Jesus has not the last 19 lines. In MS. Trinity College Cbg. B, 14, 39 (Southern; 13th century) is another copy with different arrangement of stanzas.

'THOU WOMMON BOUTE VERE' is one of the poems of William Herebert (see page 502).

'IN WORSCHUPE OF ÞAT MAYDEN SWETE' is No. 16 of the Vernon-Simeon lyrics (see page 512).

'OFF ALLE FLOURES FAIREST FALL ON' is No. 17 of the Vernon-Simeon lyrics (see page 512).

'MARIE MAYDEN, MODER MYLDE' is No. 18 of the
Vernon-Simeon lyrics (see page 512).

'MARIE, 3OW QUEN! 3OW MODER! 3OW MAYDEN
BRIHT!' [202] consists of two couplets, one five-stress verse,
and three four-stress verses, among some poetical scraps in
MS. Harley 2316 f. 25 (1350-1400.) It asks protection in
sin, in sorrow, in want. A variant is in the Vernon version of
'*Swete Ihesu, now wol I synge*' (see pages 525-26, and the other
texts of the *Iesu dulcis memoria* there).

'LADYE MARY, MAYDEN SWETE' is an adaptation of
part of '*Ihesu crist, my lemmon swete*' (see page 524).

'LITEL UO IT ENIMAN' [203], in MS. Egerton 613 f.
2 v (Southern; 1250), consists of 3 couplets of verses of from
five to seven stresses, on the love of the Virgin.

'NOU SKRINKEÞ ROSE & LYLIE FLOUR' [204] con-
sists of 6 stanzas aabaabcbcb (*a* and *c* of 4, *b* of 3, stresses) in
MS. Harley 2253 f. 80 (c. 1310; Southern from Midland). It
adapts to religious ends the *chanson d'aventure* and the secular
love lyric with nature setting (see page 489).—Now the rose
and the lily so sweet in Summer, are shriveling; no queen is so
mighty, no lady so fair, that death shall not take her. A-pleasuring one morning out of Peterborough, the poet thought of his
foolish life, and besought the Virgin to intercede for us all.
She is the best leech from Catenas to Dublin: all the sick she
brings to bliss. Woman with thy beauty, think on God's
storms; though white and bright, thy blooms shall fade.

'NU ÞIS FULES SINGET HAND MAKET HURE BLIS'
[205], twelve couplets of six-stress verses sometimes with rime
at the cæsura, is in MS. Trinity College Cbg. B, 14, 39 f. 81 v
(13th century).—Now the birds are singing and the grass
is springing up and the boughs are putting out leaves, I will sing
of a maid that is 'makeless,' whom the King of kings chose as
mother. The poem glorifies Mary's motherhood in virginity.—
Curiously, couplets 2 and 10 appear as couplets 1 and 5 of

the charming *Christ and His Mother,* 'I sing of a maiden that is makeless,' in MS. Sloane 2593 (15th century).

ON LOFSONG OF URE LEFDI [206], some 750 words of alliterative rhythmical lyrical prose in MS. Cotton Nero A XIV f. 126 v, and some 350 words (end missing) in MS. Royal 17 A XXVII f. 70, is of the South-West of 1200-1250. It must be grouped with *On Ureisun,* the *Wohunge of Ure Lauerd,* and *A Lofsong of Ure Louerde* (see pages 529, 530). It is a prayer to Mary, a confession of great abasement through sin, and a petition for intercession in the name of the sufferings of Christ. It is a somewhat full version of the Latin *Oratio ad Sanctam Mariam* of Archbishop Marbod of Rheims (1035-1128), whose connection with England is shown by a piece written to Matilda, wife of Henry I.

ON GOD UREISUN OF URE LEFDI [207], 171 long verses with much alliteration, is in MS. Cotton Nero A XIV f. 120 v. It is from Berkshire or Wiltshire, of 1200-1225. It has been urged that Edmund Rich, Archbishop of Canterbury, to whom has been assigned the oldest *Assumptio Mariæ* (see page 330), was probably author of this piece. There seems little ground for the theory that the poem was influenced rather by English than by Latin writings. The poet exults in the power and the glory of Mary in Heaven, where she is Queen with Christ. She is the singer's love, his life. He beseeches her to cleanse him of sin and to preserve him from the Devil—. to give him her mercy and her love.

THE FIVE JOYS OF THE VIRGIN [208] were of extreme importance in the history of the Church. The Joys vary in number, 5, 7, 8, 12, 15. In Middle English poetry (except in Harley 2253) they are five—the Annunciation, the Nativity, the Resurrection, the Ascension, and the Assumption.

'*Ase y me rod þis ender day*' [209], in MS. Harley 2253 f. 81 v (c. 1310), consists of 10 South-East Midland strophes normally aaabcb (*b* of 3, the rest of 4, stresses). After a graceful *chanson d'aventure* (see page 489) opening in praise of the Virgin and in declaration of the poet's love, are recounted the Joys—here the Annunciation, the Nativity, the Epiphany, the Resurrection, and the Ascension of Mary.

'*Seinte Marie, levedi brist*' [210], in MS. Trinity College Cbg. B, 14, 39 (13th century), consists of 60 South Midland or South-Western four-stress lines aabaabccbccb. It is in form of a prayer to the Virgin; each of the stanzas addresses Mary, and, in the memory of one of the Joys, asks mercy, grace, pardon, Heaven's bliss, and salvation.

'*Leuedy, for þare blisse*' [211], in MS. Jesus College Oxf. 29 f. 254 (c. 1275), has 56 four-stress verses ababababb. It is a prayer to the Virgin constructed as is that just mentioned, with one of the stanzas asking for help to Heaven, and one asking Christ for Mary's prayers to cleanse and give everlasting light.

'*Haue Ioye, Marie*' [212], in MS. Vernon (Southern or South-Midland; 1370-1380), has 6 stanzas aabccb (*b* of 3, the rest of 4, stresses.) It is a prayer constructed after the fashion of those just mentioned, with stanza 6 asking the Trinity for Mary's sake to grant enduring joy.

'*Marie, Modur, wel þe bee*' [213], *Orisoun to þe Fyue Ioyes*, in MS. Vernon, has 8 similarly formed stanzas. It is a prayer like the preceding, with two general introductory stanzas and one final one.

'*Haile be þu, Mari, maiden bright*' [214] is a treatment of the Five Joys in the Göttingen MS. of the *Cursor Mundi* (see page 339). This consists of 13 stanzas aaabb (*a* of 4, 1. 4 of 2, 1. 5 of 6, stresses), the metre of the *Celestin*. It has two introductory, and four concluding, stanzas.

A Preyere Off The ffyve Ioyes [215], in MS. Thornton f. 177 v (Northern; c. 1430-1440), is a prose prayer of 700 words to Mary in the name of her Five Sorrows and Five Joys.

William of Shoreham's Poem 5 deals with the Five Joys (see page 350), as do two fifteenth-century carols [216].

Perhaps the Vernon '*Mayden, Modur, and comely Queen*' contained a set of verses on the Joys (see page 531).

A fifteenth-century hymn to the Five Joys [217], comprising five stanzas ababbcbc and an envoy aaaaa, is in MS. Bodley Rolls 22 (1400-1450).

THE FIFTEEN JOYS OF OUR LADY and THE FIFTEEN JOYS AND FIFTEEN SORROWS OF OUR LADY [218], in fifteenth-century MSS., have been ascribed to Lydgate.

THE SEVEN JOYS OF MARY IN HEAVEN are treated in 6 stanzas aabccb (*b* of 3, the rest of 4, stresses) directed to be addressed to the Virgin by the devout, in the sermon (see page 303) on the Assumption in Mirk's *Festial* (c. 1400).

Robert Fabyan ends each of the seven parts of his *Chronicle* with a stanza on the Seven Joys. In 1508 'D. T. Mylle' wrote a piece [219] on the theme.

MS. Lambeth 853 (c. 1430) and MS. Sloane 2593 (15th century) contain pieces some of which may be of the fourteenth century (see page 486).

CHAPTER XIV

DRAMATIC PIECES

In the following pages, though the dates of most of them are uncertain, and though most in their present form are late, will be considered, for the sake of completeness, all the extant pieces in English intended for acting, and of a general class earlier than moralities. The Bibliographical Notes direct to full information as to the probable development of the mediæval Continental and English drama, and to the history of its performance.

Probably there were represented in England most, if not all, of the stages in the development of the mediæval religious plays, from the liturgical drama for Easter (the *Depositio*, the *Elevatio*, the *Visitatio;* the tropes *Quem quæritis, Victimæ paschali, Planctus,* and *Peregrini;* and the homiletical material of the *lectiones* for Easter) and for Christmas (the *Pastores*, the *Stella,* and the *Prophetæ* or *Processus Prophetarum*), to the secularized spoken vernacular cosmic cycles of Old and New Testament plays. But fewer British specimens, at least of the earlier of these various stages, are preserved than there are of similar Continental compositions.

Of pieces exhibiting the transition from the Latin to the vernacular, there are extant in English only the *Shrewsbury Fragments* and *Caiphas;* sequences of the Easter Day service were utilized in the Bodley *Resurrection.* Of plays actually dealing with miracles, there are only the speeches of the chief personage of *Dux Moraud* and the Croxton *Sacrament*—the latter concerned with a contemporary miracle. To saint-plays the only approaches are the very mixed Digby *Magdalene* and the *Conversion of St. Paul*. The *Interludium de Clerico et Puella* is a unique secular interlude of the end of the thirteenth,

or the beginning of the fourteenth, century, perhaps based on
a still older interlude.

Because of the facts that have just been stated, to avoid
misconception, the Middle English plays on Biblical subjects
are, throughout this chapter, styled 'mysteries.'

Of cycles of drama performed by the English trade-guilds,
are preserved the Chester, the York, and the Towneley plays,
and the two true Coventry plays; probably the Newcastle
Noah, the Norwich *Grocers' Pageant,* and the Digby *Massacre
of the Innocents;* perhaps part of the *Ludus Coventriæ;* possibly the Brome *Abraham;* and barely possibly the Dublin
Abraham. Apparently no parts of the cycles of Beverly, Lincoln, London (played by 'parish clerks), and the several other
towns known to have had plays, are extant.

Evidently the favorite time for the performance of guild
plays, was Corpus Christi Day, instituted by Pope Urban IV
in 1264, and confirmed by Clement V at the Council of Vienne
in 1311. The Coventry, the York, and the Newcastle plays,
and originally the Chester cycle, were given on this festival.
In the sixteenth century, the Chester plays were performed at
Whitsuntide, and at least once at Christmas. The Norwich
play, at first given perhaps on Corpus Christi, also was shifted
to Whitsuntide. The changes in these instances were probably partly to avoid the clash with the Corpus Christi procession. The latter probably had much influence among the other
festival processions in the evolution toward the performance of
plays on movable 'pageants.' The full cycle was performed in
one day at Coventry and at York, in an afternoon at Newcastle, and in equal parts on three days in the sixteenth century at Chester. The fifteenth-century Bodley *Burial and
Resurrection,* begun as a 'treatise' for reading, is marked for
playing of one part on Good Friday afternoon, and of the
other on Easter Day after the Resurrection. A series for performance partly one year and partly the next, is met with in
a portion of the *Ludus Coventriæ* and in the Digby *Massacre
of the Innocents.* As in the Chester cycle, apparently some

plays were in a later period isolated and presented as separate pieces for special occasions.

In the crafts' series, usually a single guild, often several united, played a single play. In some instances, as in the true Coventry plays, several guilds acted one play that was a group of plays or scenes. Changes in the lists, the proclamations, and the MSS. of the extant pieces, show that frequently guilds changed plays. Sometimes elements of the nature of the craft coincided with features of the story that it played—as when watermen acted the *Flood;* goldsmiths, the *Magi;* bakers, the *Last Supper;* and cooks, the *Harrowing of Hell.*

With few exceptions, the extant craft plays were written to be played on wagons or 'pageants,' evidently one play to a 'pageant,' that moved from fixed station to fixed station through the city. At York there were from twelve to sixteen stations; at Coventry not more than three or four have been determined. The records indicate that but few wagons were used at Coventry; the two extant plays exhibit the practice of performing a number of scenes by one group of actors on a single wagon. It has been held commonly that the *Ludus Coventriæ* plays were performed on a single stage. Whether the Newcastle *Noah* and its cycle were so performed, has been debated.

The use of songs accompanied by music, and introduced as an essential part of the action, is seen in some of the plays— as in those of York and Coventry; and as an accompaniment to the action, in at least the Norwich play. The MS. of the Digby *Conversion* has later marginal directions for a dance at intervals in the action; and the epilogue of the Digby *Massacre* calls for music, and summons the virgins present to dance.

Of the 'banes' or banns or proclamations announcing performance of the play or the cycle, a number of copies have been preserved. Some of these are in verse; and some call for music at a stage, or at stages, or at the end, of the recitation of them. In some of the pieces is seen the popular 'Expositor' or 'Doctor'—as in the Chester and the Brome plays; or his representative, such as 'Contemplacio' in the *Ludus Coventriæ.*

In the Coventry plays question-and-answer passages by 'prophets' assist exposition.

The scope of the cycles may be seen from the lists of the plays in the discussion of each of the several extant groups. It is necessary here merely to mention that, in the full cycles in their most developed forms, the pieces covered the Biblical and apocryphal history from the Creation of the World to Doomsday.

The theory that some of the plays, especially the Chester group, the *Ludus Coventriæ*, and the Brome play, are directly from French pieces, has not been established. The Bodley *Burial and Resurrection* seems to have been begun for reading, in course of composition to have been written as for acting, and to have been left as for either acting or reading. Leach has offered much evidence to show that the common ascription of the English Corpus Christi plays or guild plays to monkish authors, is incorrect, and that one should look for the origin of these plays among the common townspeople or the secular clergy who lived and worked in their midst.

In their present state all the plays present more or less corrupted forms that exhibit sometimes defects due partly or wholly to failure of the memory of actors from whose recitation the texts were on some occasion taken down; sometimes incongruities of matter, manner, and versification, that are results of revisions to adapt plays to new conditions; and sometimes confusion caused by repeated unfinished 'editorial' effort at standardizing the form. These imperfections and inconsistencies have afforded materials for investigations of age, development, and authorship, of passages and plays and cycles, that have demonstrated what other evidence would suggest—that almost every one of the extant pieces and groups is the product of an extended evolution, and of the efforts of a number of hands working at different times. Further, study of the many similarities in theme, arrangement, treatment, and phrasing, have shown that in some cases this development was not merely in isolation, but that different groups and localities were sometimes in a remarkable degree interrelated by dependence on common original sources, or by borrowing one from another, either directly or indirectly.

All the extant criticisms of the drama that were written in English before 1400, are hostile to the plays. These passages are in Mannyng's *Handlyng Synne* (ll. 4643 ff.), *Pierce the Ploughmans Crede* (ll. 78, 107), the *Treatise of Miraclis Pleyinge* (see page 483), the Wycliffite *Ave Maria* (see page 479), and *Against the Minorite Friars* (see page 236).

THE SHREWSBURY FRAGMENTS [1] are in MS. Mus. iii 42 f. 38 (beginning of 15th century) in the Shrewsbury School. They consist of the English text, with cues, of a single actor's part in each of three plays, with conventional Latin phrases of the service concerned. The liturgical nature of the plays is shown by the facts that they occur in the midst of a collection of Latin anthems; that the Latin portions are given notes for singing (the English are not noted); that the second play is headed 'Hic incipit Officium Resurrectionis in die Pasche,' and the third 'Feria secunda in ebdomada Pasche, discipuli insimul cantent'; and that several of the Latin passages are identical with like parts of the liturgical plays composed wholly in Latin.

The heading and perhaps a speech or two speeches, of the first group, are missing. The lines are, however, obviously those of the third shepherd in the *Officium Pastorum*. The piece is a development of the liturgical *Pastores*, which was originally an *Introit* trope for the third Mass at Christmas. It has been urged that the complete play would probably be about as long as the correspondent in the York cycle. The last stanza is very close, with verbal agreements and like rimes, to the last stanza of the extant York text, but has one verse with a reading apparently older than the York parallel.

The second group of lines are those of the third Mary of the *Officium Resurrectionis*, which was a development of the *Quem quæritis in sepulchro*, the Resurrection trope located variously by different churches, in some between the third respond and the *Te Deum* of the Easter Matins—the germ whence sprang all modern drama. The verses present a version that holds to the two scenes of the earlier form of the liturgical plays on the theme. Three of the Latin couplets are almost identical with three in the Dublin *Dramatic Office* for Easter, which is preserved in a fourteenth-century MS. The end of the York correspondent suggests reflection of a play very similar to this Shrewsbury fragment.

The third group are the lines apparently of Cleophas in the *Officium Peregrinorum,* a version of the important *Peregrini,* a liturgical drama on the Journey to Emmaus that was established by the twelfth century, and was attached to the *Processio ad Fontes,* a regular part of Vespers during the Easter week, and another vital factor in the development of the liturgical drama. The heading shows that the present piece was intended for Easter Monday.

The fragments end with a Latin couplet that is apparently the opening of a fourth play on the Incredulity of Thomas.

The pieces are immensely valuable, for they exhibit an otherwise unrepresented stage in the development of the drama in England and in English. They are apparently still liturgical plays, performed probably in the church; exhibiting both Latin and English lines in the single pieces, and so the transition from the Latin to the English; and showing the plays in progress of advance from the sung Latin to the spoken English.

Professor Skeat, who first printed the plays, suggested that they were perhaps from the lost Beverly cycle. Perhaps, as has been suggested, it is more than coincidence that the themes of the pieces are those of the plays given in Lichfield Cathedral. The language of the fragments is that of the North—'just that of the York plays,' says Professor Skeat.

CAIPHAS [2], styled *Ceremonial Verses for Palm Sunday* by Wright, is in MS. Sloane 2478 f. 43 r (early 14th century), and consists of 168 verses .of tail-rime aabccb of the South-West at about 1300. The last stanza, formerly illegible, has been brought out by the use of reagents. All the other items in the MS. are Latin religious pieces. Though *Caiphas* has been little noticed, it exhibits a very interesting stage in the growth of liturgical drama—use, in the Palm Sunday procession, of a person who not only is a singer of a Latin trope, but is also a speaker, expositor, and exhorter in the vernacular and in Latin.

In the English tail-rime Caiphas addresses the assemblage, who are bearing palms; announces that he will soon sing a little song; states that all should be glad his prophecy has come true—namely, that it were better that one man died than that all were lost; and (?) sings in Latin the *Expedit unum hominem mori*. Then he states that he has 'a tale' to tell of Christ and the palms—he would have leave of the Dean to read and sing of this ere he goes. So, in Latin verses, he asks the Dean for permission. Evidently he obtains this, for it is apparently he that delivers a short Latin prose exposition of the significance of the procession and the palms. Next, in English verses, he announces that he is the bishop to whom the Jews looked for counsel, and (?) sings the *Pontifex anni illius qui consilium dederat iudeis*. He tells in English verse that he and Annas undertook to buy Jesus for the pieces of silver, and (?) sings the *Tamen expedit*, etc., and explains its sense. He declares that he knew not what his prophecy meant; and urges the audience to fight Man's Three Foes (see Index), to make amends with sorrow of heart and shrift, and so to meet Christ bearing palms. He tells of the Entry into Jerusalem, and (?) sings the *Benedictus qui venit in nomine domini*. He explains the significance of the palms as signs of shrift; sings the *Expedit* once more; warns all that have come to the service unshriven, to make amends at once; dismisses the congregation; and bids the (?) choir sing.

The use of the tail-rime, a favorite measure of the mystery writers, will be noticed. Brown has indicated that the mention of the Dean connects the piece with a secular cathedral church; that the dialect confines the lines to Salisbury and Wells alone of such churches (Chichester, Salisbury, Wells, Exeter, and Hereford) in the South of England; that Caiphas' rôle at Salisbury apparently was confined to singing with two other clerks the *Expedit* at the third station of the procession before the west door of the church; and that the ritual at Wells probably offered more opportunity for the introduction of the single singer and speaker, and so of the matter, of *Caiphas*.

DUX MORAUD [3] is of much importance to the student of drama. It is written in a fourteenth-century hand on the margin of an assize roll of Norfolk and Suffolk of 1250-1300, in MS. Bodley Engl. Poet. f 2 (Bodl. Addit. 30519). It consists of 268 verses, some illegible, in stanzas ababababcdddc, the ninth line of one stress and the other lines of three and four stresses. With these stanzas is intermingled tail-rime aabccb or aaabcccb. The verses are in twenty-two sections disconnected in sense, so that formerly the sections were regarded as single pieces. They are apparently the consecutive speeches of a single personage of a play, Dux Moraud, who in the first section introduces himself elaborately after the mystery fashion. The story is close to that of the *Incestuous Daughter.* When the verses are read with that tale, the sense of *Dux Moraud* becomes clear. If the lines be what they seem, they represent a drama unique in Middle English—a miracle-play in the stricter sense of the term, antedating the cycles of the usual English type (see page 539).

INTERLUDIUM DE CLERICO ET PUELLA [4], in the dialect of South Yorkshire or North Lincolnshire, is in MS. Br. Mus. Additional 23986 (early 14th century). It consists of 42 short couplets, the beginning of an interlude. There is no narrative; each speech has a marginal indication of the speaker. There is, first, a scene in which the clerk makes love to the girl in her home, and is repulsed. In the next scene, unfinished, Mome Elwis, a procuress, welcomes the clerk, apparently into her house. The clerk tells his case, and asks the procuress' aid. Mome Elwis protests her pious and godly life. Here the fragment ends.

The piece is unpolished; its language is rude. Its chief interest consists in its presentation of a very early specimen of secular English drama, dating from the end of the thirteenth, or the beginning of the fourteenth, century. Ten Brink suggested that the author was acquainted with *Dame Siriʒ* (see page 178). There are verbal resemblances and identity of lines in the two pieces. Heuser has contended that the *Interludium* and *Dame Siriʒ* have as common basis an interlude in couplets of the border between the North and the East Midland, composed in the thirteenth century.

THE CHESTER PLAYS [5] are preserved in MSS. Hg,

Hengwrt 229 (1475-1500; probably a prompter's copy), in the possession of Mr. Wynne of Peniarth; D, Devonshire (written in 1591 by Edward Gregorie), in the library of the Duke of Devonshire; W, Br. Mus. Additional 10305 (1592; signed at end of each play, 'George Bellin'); h, Harley 2013 (1600; some plays signed 'George Bellin' or 'Billinges'; a verse 'banes' prefixed; and a separate copy of a prose proclamation of 1544 by the Clerk of the Pentice, added); B, Bodley 175 (1604; written by 'Guilelmus· Bedford,' with a complete 'banes'); H, Harley 2124 (1607; two hands, one that of 'Jacobus Miller'); and M, Manchester Free Library (end of 15th or beginning of 16th century; three and a half stanzas of the *Resurrection*). MS. Harley 1944 (1609) has some additional lines of the 'banes'; and MS. Harley 2150 f. 85 v (a copy of the White Book of the Pentice; revision of the version of 1544-1547) has a copy of the 'banes.' Investigation indicates that B best represents a common source of D, W. h, and B, and that H varies much from these MSS., offers a better text than do they, and is probably related to Hg.

In addition to the 'banes' or banns or proclamation, there are extant twenty-five plays, as follows:

1. Tanners: *Fall of Lucifer;* 2. Drapers: *The Creation and Fall*, and *The Death of Abel;* 3. Water-leaders and Drawers in Dye: *The Deluge;* 4. Barbers and Wax-chandlers: *Lot*, and *Abraham and Isaac;* 5. Cappers and Linen-Drapers: *Balaam and his Ass;* 6. Wrights and Slaters: *The Salutation* and *The Nativity;* 7. Painters and Glaziers: *The Adoration of the Shepherds;* 8. Vintners: *The Three Kings;* 9. Mercers: *The Offering* and *The Return of the Kings;* 10. Goldsmiths and Masons: *The Slaughter of the Innocents;* 11. Blacksmiths: *The Purification;* 12. Butchers: *The Temptation* and *The Woman Taken in Adultery;* 13. Glovers: *Lazarus;* 14. Corvysors: *The Entry into Jerusalem;* 15. Bakers: *The Betrayal of Christ;* 16: Fletchers, Bowyers, Coopers, Stringers: *The Passion;* 17. Ironmongers: *The Crucifixion;* 18. Cooks: *The Harrowing of Hell;* 19. Skinners: *The Resurrection;* 20. Saddlers: *The Pilgrims to Emmaus;* 21. Tailors: *The Ascension;* 22. Fishmongers: *Pentecost;* 23. Cloth-workers: *Ezechiel;* 24. Dyers: *Antichrist;* 25. Weavers: *Doomsday.*

One of the banns inserts an *Assumption* for Whitsunday, which was performed in 1477, and played separately in 1488,

1497, and 1505. The late banns and the MSS. unite the *Scourging* and the *Crucifixion*.

The basic type of stanza for the cycle is aaabaaab, the *b* verses of three, the others of four, stresses. Difficulty in riming led often to use of aaabcccb, and sometimes to a considerable breaking-down of the stanza. In Play 1, stanzas abab and abababab of four stresses, appear, the latter several times made up of long alliterative lines.

The sixteenth-century banns (the earliest being of 1544) assign the plays to the mayoralty (1268-1277) of John Arneway. That of 1544 states that Sir Henry Frances, 'somtyme monk of this dissolved monastery,' devised the plays and obtained from Clement (IV, 1265-1276; V, 1305-1316; VI, 1342-1352) grant of pardon for those who saw the play in proper mood. The banns of 1551-1572 state that Arneway 'sett out in playe The devise of one done Randall, moonke of Chester abbe.' The *Breauarye* of Rogers (1609) assigns the cycle called the Whitsun Plays to 'Rondoll, a monke of ye Abbaye of St. Warburge in Chester'; and, in a list of mayors under the year 1328, it adds 'Higden' to 'Rondoll,' the name of the author. Chambers has sought to meet the objection that Arneway was mayor long before the lifetime of Higden or Frances, by showing that in 1327-1329 Richard Erneis or Herneys was mayor. Ranulph Higden, author of the *Poly-chronicon* (see Index, *Higden*), was a monk of St. Werburgh's from 1299 to 1364. Frances or Francis is mentioned in 1377 and 1382 as senior monk of the abbey. Discovery of the use in several instances in the *Polychronicon* and the Chester plays of the same material that might have come in each case from the same sources, has caused Hemingway to accept the authorship of Higden, and the Harley 2124 dating of 1388, for the pieces. Ten Brink and Pollard date the plays 1340-1350. Gayley opines 'that at the latest some of the Chester plays were in existence during the first third of the fourteenth century, and that the present form . . . represents, in general, a revision which may have been made about the end of the fourteenth or the beginning of the fifteenth century.'

The earliest notices of the plays are references to the plays of the Bakers and the Saddlers in charters of these crafts that are dated 1462 and 1471. The performances were at first on Corpus Christi Day; but during the sixteenth century they were at Whitsuntide, and once at least at Christmas. The changes of date were due perhaps to effort to avoid a clash of the procession and the plays. The performances, at first annual, were given after 1546 at intervals of from three to seven years; the last presentation of the group as a whole occurred probably in 1575. The Chester use of 'pageant' is peculiar in that it usually concerns the play; the wagon is, at Chester, commonly styled 'carriage.' The records show that sometimes single plays were used for special occasions.

Though it is admitted that indirectly French mysteries may have had some influence on the Chester plays, the present tendency is to reject the theory (based on Play 2, l. 17, and Play 1, l. 209; on the occurrence of a number of French phrases in the plays; on some agreement with the French *Viel Testament* in sequence and motive; and on the treatment of subjects not found in the other English plays, but found in French plays) that the plays are derived directly from the French. Of the accepted sources may be mentioned the Vulgate Bible, Josephus, the *Legenda Aurea*, Tatian's *Harmony*, Comestor's *Historia Scholastica*, the apocryphal New Testament, Augustine and Gregory and Jerome directly and indirectly, Latin hymns, and perhaps English legends and sermons—with influence, perhaps, of Latin liturgical plays, French plays, older English plays, English religious lyrics, and English works dealing with Bible history, but perhaps not the *Cursor Mundi*. Davidson's theory (based on the statement of MS. Harley 2124 that Higden—not Francis—went thrice to Rome before he could obtain permission to give the plays in English) that the plays were originally in Anglo-Norman, appears to be untenable. There are strong resemblances between Chester Play 19 (Jesus' speech in the *Resurrection*) and Towneley Plays 26 and 38. It has been claimed, accordingly, that Chester here is derived from Towneley, and, again, that it is from an older York version. Chester Play 7 and the Towneley *Prima Pastorum* have strong similarities. The Chester *Abraham* is apparently as close a borrowing as the stanza of Chester would permit, from an early fourteenth-century version of the Brome play (see page 569). The Chester *Christ in the Temple* (11) may be from an original of York Play 20, with which and with Towneley 18 it has close agreements. The Chester *Doubting of Thomas* (20) is said to have the same sources as York 42 and Towneley 28.

The Chester plays are uneven in quality. The handling is often crude. The cycle would seem to present an attitude preceding the popularizing tendencies exhibited especially in the York and the Towneley cycles. A liturgical flavor is often evident. Exposition and explanation of the stories and their significance characterize this group, as intention to present a vivid picture of the incidents is most evident in the York and the Towneley cycles. There is prevalent the earlier didactic tendency; in several of the plays a 'Doctor' or 'Expositor' (a stock figure in much of the earlier English drama) explains the moral or symbolic sense of the action. As Ten Brink has noted, to this same inclination are probably due the treatment of subjects (such as Lot, Balaam, Ezechiel, and Melchisadek) not encountered in the other cycles, and also a specially extensive use of apocryphal materials. Yet it will probably be granted that the plays do not exhibit the over-didacticism of the *Ludus Coventriæ*. Moreover, there is in them a general primitive epical dignity and severity, and a degree of really religious spirit, not evinced in the other cycles. At times, vigorous and striking impressions are given, and in some places (as in the first of the *Shepherds*, and in *Balaam*) efforts at crude comic effect, and attempts at homely actuality, are cultivated with much success.

There are extant sixteenth-century notices of several other plays, apparently late, that were performed at Chester—that by the 'colliges and prestys' on Corpus Christi Day, noticed in the White Book for 1544-1547; in 1529, *King Robert of Sicily;* in 1563, a *History of Æneas and Queen Dido;* in 1578, a 'comedy' by the 'schollers of the freescole'; and in 1589, *King Ebrauke with All his Sons.*

THE YORK PLAYS [6] are in MS. Br. Mus. Additional 35290, formerly MS. Ashburnham 137 (c. 1430-1440). The Scriveners' play (Play 42) alone is on four leaves of parchment (early 16th century) given by Dr. Sykes to the York Philosophical Society. As it supplies a line and several important words wanting in Ashburnham, the Sykes MS. is not a copy of Ashburnham.

In the *Liber Diversorum Memorandorum Civitatem Ebor. Tangentium*, Roger Burton, the town-clerk, entered two detailed lists of the plays and the crafts that were to perform them. The first list contains fifty-one plays, and is dated 1415. The second list, not dated, gives short titles for fifty-seven plays. The more authoritative character of the 1415 list, is indicated by the fact that on it were entered the modifications to suit the changes of the crafts in later years. MS. Additional contains forty-eight plays and one fragment.

The plays as they stand in MS. Additional, and the names of the crafts concerned with them, are as follows:

1. Barkers: *The Creation* and *The Fall of Lucifer;* 2. Plasterers: *The Creation, to the Fifth Day;* 3. Cardmakers: *God Creates Adam and Eve;* 4. Fullers: *Adam and Eve Put in the Garden;* 5. Coopers: *Man's Disobedience and Fall;* 6. Armorers: *The Expulsion;* 7. Glovers: *Sacrificium Cayme et Abell;* 8. Shipwrights: *The Building of the Ark;* 9. Fishers and Mariners: *Noah and his Wife, The Flood, Its Waning;* 10. Dealers in Parchment and Bookbinders: *Abraham's Sacrifice;* 11. Hosiers: *The Departure of the Israelites from Egypt, The Ten Plagues, The Passage of the Red Sea;* 12. Spicers: *The Annunciation, The Visit of Elizabeth;* 13. Pewterers and Founders: *Joseph's Trouble about Mary;* 14. Tile-thatchers: *The Journey to Bethlehem, The Birth of Jesus;* 15. Chandlers: *The Angels and the Shepherds;* 16. Masons: *The Coming of the Three Kings to Herod;* 17. Goldsmiths: *The Coming of the Kings, The Adoration;* 18. Shoers and Curers of Horses: *The Flight into Egypt;* 19. Girdlers (makers of small articles of metal work) and Nailers: *The Massacre of the Innocents;* 20. Spurriers and Makers of Bits: *Christ with the Doctors;* 21. Barbers: *The Baptism of Jesus;* 22. Smiths: *The Temptation;* 23: Curriers of Leather: *The Transfiguration;* 24. Capmakers: *The Woman Taken in Adultery, The Raising of Lazarus;* 25. Skinners:

The Entry into Jerusalem; 26. Cutlers: *The Conspiracy;* 27. Bakers:
The Last Supper; 28. Shoemakers: *The Agony and Betrayal;* 29.
Bowyers and Fletchers (featherers of arrows): *Peter's Denial, Jesus
before Caiaphas;* 30. Makers of Tapestry and Coverers of Couches:
The Dream of Pilate's Wife, Jesus before Pilate; 31. Litsters:
The Trial before Herod; 32. Cooks and Carriers of Water: *The
Second Accusation before Pilate, The Remorse of Judas, The Pur-
chase of the Field of Blood;* 33. Tilemakers: *The Second Trial be-
fore Pilate;* 34. Shearers of Cloth: *Christ Led to Calvary;* 35. Pin-
makers and Painters: *Crucifixio Christi;* 36. Butchers: *Mortificacio
Christi* and *Burial;* 37. Saddlers: *The Harrowing of Hell;* 38.
Carpenters: *The Resurrection, The Fright of the Jews;* 39. Wine-
drawers: *Jesus' Appearance to Mary Magdalene;* 40. Sledmen:
The Travelers to Emmaus; 41. Hatmakers, Masons, Laborers:
The Purification, Simeon and Anna; 42. Scriveners: *The Incredulity
of Thomas;* 43. Tailors: *The Ascension;* 44. Potters: *The Descent
of the Holy Spirit;* 45. Drapers: *The Death of Mary;* 46. Weavers:
The Appearance of Mary to Thomas; 47. Hostlers: *The Assumption and Coronation of the Virgin;* 48. Mercers: *Judgment Day.*
Finally, in a hand of the (?) end of the fifteenth century, is a
fragment, Innholders: *The Coronation of Our Lady.*

The writing of the MS. is chiefly of the first half of the fifteenth century, probably 1430-1440. The fragment appended
later was probably meant to supersede Play 47. The first two
plays and a late copy of the third, are on a quire inserted at
the beginning of the MS. a few years after the body of the
volume was written down. Not until 1558 were entered *Adam
and Eve* (4), an old play; an addition to *Sacrificium Cayme et
Abell* (7); and the *Purification* (41), which perhaps was later
than the rest of the pieces, and displaced an earlier treatment
of the same subject. Blank spaces are left after Plays 22 and
23, respectively for the Vintners' *Marriage at Cana,* and the
Ironmongers' *Jesus Eating with Simon the Leper and Mary
Magdalene.* The archives of the Corporation indicate a play
Fergus or *Portacio Corporis Mariæ,* which, according to York
records, came after Play 45, and was 'laid apart' in 1485; and
also a passage, *Suspencio Iudæ,* that in 1422 was an episode of
Play 33.

Miss Smith has dated the original cycle 'as far back as 1340
or 1350, not long after the appearance of the *Cursor.*' The
variations in the lists, and the changes in the MS. already
noted, show that the texts were modified, or in some cases dis-

placed, at various times. Corrections, notes, and glosses in the MS., indicate that the Council's direction of 1568 that the book of plays be 'perused and otherwise amended,' or its similar order of 1579 that the book be 'corrected,' was carried out somewhat. Metrical tests indicate that Plays 2, 8, ? 9, 10, 11, 20, 23, 24, 27, 35, 37, and 44, and the parts of 12, 15, and 17 that show connection with the Northern septenar stanza, are survivals of a parent cycle. It has been urged that all that approaches the comic in the cycle, is of a second period, in which shone the originator of the comic features of *Cain and Abel, Noah's Flood,* and the *Shepherds;* and that the more realistic elements of the cycle are from a third period, in which was active a special author that wrote Plays 26, 28, 29, 31, and 33, probably composed Play 32, and perhaps had a hand in Plays 36, 37, and 38.

The earliest notice of the plays, that of 1378, implies that at that date the plays were of long standing, and that each was supported by a craft, and was acted by it on Corpus Christi Day on a movable wheeled pageant-wagon whose station was appointed in advance. The performances at York were at from twelve to sixteen stations. The Corpus Christi procession and the plays occurred all on one day. Records of 1394, 1397, 1399, and 1417, confirm these implications. In 1426 the procession occurred on the day after the feast, and the plays on the festival. Performances continued more or less irregularly after 1535, because of substitutions of the *Creed Play* and the *Paternoster Play,* and the occurrence of pestilence and war; and on at least one occasion the plays were given on Whitsunday. Though the Bakers chose pageant-masters as late as 1656, the latest actual performance recorded is that in 1579, or one in 1580.

In the extant pieces alliteration is used frequently. The metre exhibits much variety, apparently governed somewhat by difference in date and in authorship, and somewhat by effort at accord with the character and the rôle of the speaker—dignified for God and Christ, and swelling and sounding for the villains. Not infrequently the stanzas vary within single plays. Twenty-two different forms of stanza occur. These range from abab to ababababcdcccdee. The one predominant form is ababababcdcd, which occurs in thirteen plays. The preference is to employ not over four rime-sounds in a stanza; only one play has stanzas of six rime-sounds, and only three others have stanzas of five rime-sounds; and nineteen plays have stanzas of but three rime-sounds. Except the short 'tags,' which are used in fourteen plays, the lines are of four or three stresses. References for details regarding the verse are given in the Bibliographical Notes.

It has been well remarked that, among the authors of the English plays, those of the York cycle are of notable independence and originality. Possibly the general design, and probably some details, of these plays, underwent influence of the *Cursor Mundi*. Materials were drawn from the Vulgate Bible (which is followed closely), the *Pseudo-Evangelium Matthæi*, the *Pseudo-Evangelium Nicodemi* (both parts), the *Evangelium de Nativitate Mariæ*, the *Transitus Mariæ*, the *Legenda Aurea*, the Northern English metrical *Gospel of Nicodemus* (for parts of Plays 30, 33, 36, 37, and 38); perhaps one of the English accounts of the Assumption, and possibly the *Speculum Humanæ Salvationis*, Comestor's *Historia Scholastica*, and some French texts. Miss Foster has pointed out similarities through verbal reminiscence or resemblance of outline between the *Northern Passion* so-called (see page 287) and Plays 26-29, 32-36, and 38. She suggests that indeed the *Northern Passion* and the English *Gospel of Nicodemus* 'would appear to supply the basis for the whole plays, the sources being used to supplement each other.' Taylor has noted similar themes in the plays and some vernacular lyrics. Cady has argued for the possibility of a common liturgical source in the Christmas series of the York, the Towneley, and the true Coventry cycles, and a common liturgical source for the York and the Towneley Resurrection series; and he has suggested a common liturgical source for the York and the Towneley Passion series.—The probable influence of the York plays on other plays is noted on pages 550, 557, 563, 567, 571.

When considered from all the points of view of age, extent, quality, and influence, the York plays and the originals that they represent, are the most important of the English cycles. It appears likely in some instances, and certain in others, that either in themselves or in earlier antecedents the plays influenced directly each of the other great English groups that are preserved. The plays of the assumed first or formative period have little individuality, and scarcely any reflection of real life; yet they do exhibit strongly the old liturgical character and purpose of merely making clear the incidents dealt with. But the pieces of the later periods are virile and spirited, fresh and vigorous, with a power that is rude and gentle by turns. For these periods have been claimed the notable humor of Cain, of the quarrel between Noah and his wife, of the scene between the Beadle and Pilate, of the Shepherds, and the like; and the remarkably realistic treatment of the subjects, that, with the home-spun and often coarse humor, achieves an obvious prime purpose of vivifying and actualizing the stories by presenting them in terms of the vulgar life of the day. Much of the characterization and exposition of conduct and motive, is admirable—as in the cases of Caiaphas and Annas and Judas, the uneducated, shy Joseph, Mary in the flight to Egypt, the domestic side of Pilate and his wife, the Janitor, and others.

Here should be mentioned the lost *Play of the Paternoster* referred to by Wycliffe in his *De Officio Pastorali*, Ch. 15 (1378), which was performed by a Corpus Christi Guild that as such had nothing to do with the Corpus Christi plays. So, too, should be mentioned the *Creed Play*, also lost, bequeathed in 1446 by William Revetor to the Corpus Christi Guild for performance every tenth year. The age of the play may perhaps be guessed at from the fact that in 1455 the MS. was so worn that the guild had it copied. Apparently the latest performance was in 1535. The MS. was heard of last as in the hands of Dean Hutton in 1568.

THE TOWNELEY PLAYS [7] are preserved in a MS. (1450-1500) formerly in the library of Towneley Hall, and now in that of Major Coates of Ewell, Surrey. The oft-.

repeated association of the cycle with Widkirk or Woodkirk, and with the 'Black Canons' of an abbey at that place, may be due to some tradition in the Towneley family; it seems to rest entirely on a description of the MS. by Douce in a bookseller's catalogue of 1814, and on a description in another such catalogue of 1883. Headings in the MS., and topographical allusions in representatives of all the stages of growth of the cycle, seem certainly to connect the group with Wakefield, though no record of plays at that place is preserved.

The cycle consists of thirty-two plays, as follows:

1. Barkers of Wakefield: *The Creation;* 2. Glovers: *Mactacio Abel;* 3. *Processus Noe cum Filiis* (Flood) Wakefield; 4. *Abraham* (end missing); 5. *Isaac* (only the last 35 couplets); 6. *Jacob;* 7. *Processus Prophetarum;* 8. Litsters (Dyers): *Pharao;* 9. *Cesar Augustus;* 10. *Annunciacio;* 11. *Salutacio Elizabeth;* 12. *Una Pagina Pastorum;* 13. *Alia Eorundem;* 14. *Oblacio Magorum;* 15. *Fugacio Josep & Marie in Egiptum;* 16. *Magnus Herodes;* 17. *Purificacio Marie* (end missing); 18. *Pagina Doctorum* (beginning missing); 19. *Iohannes Baptista;* 20. *Conspiracio;* 21. *Coliphizacio;* 22. *Flagellacio;* 23. *Processus Crucis;* 24. *Processus Talentorum;* 25. *Extraccio Animarum;* 26. *Resureccio Domini;* 27. *Peregrini* (assigned to the Fishers in a later hand); 28. *Thomas Indie;* 29. *Ascencio Domini, et cetera* (incomplete); 30. *Iudicium;* 31. *Lazarus;* 32. *Suspencio Iude* (incomplete).

Only the crafts of Plays 1, 2, 8, and 27 are known. *Lazarus* (31) is in an early sixteenth-century hand, and should follow Play 19. The *Suspencio Iude* (32) should follow Play 22. Twenty-six leaves of the MS. are lost—twelve after Play 1, probably ·containing the *Fall;* and twelve after Play 29, probably containing *Pentecost.* Ten Brink's conjecture that Plays 5 and 6 represent a much earlier late thirteenth-century play, has not been accepted.

That, as the mixed verse-forms suggest, the cycle is a composite one, has been admitted generally. It has been recognized, too, that two groups stand out in the plays—one of pieces that in matter, metre, and phrasing have very strong likenesses to or identity with certain of the York plays; and one of extraordinary vigor, realism, and comic power.—Davidson felt that the present cycle is the work of one editor, who sought to write now in couplets, and now in quatrains.—Hohlfeld perceived a word for word borrowing from York of Plays 8, 18, 25, 26, and 30 (York 11, 20, 37, 38, and 48); imitation of whole plays and borrowing of passages, in Plays 10, 14, and 15; imitation of whole plays in Plays 16 and 20; imitation of parts, and verbal borrowing of others, in Play 22; imitation of parts in Play 21; parallel passages in Play 23; and absence in York of Plays 5, 6, 9, and 24. From the close agreement in details, and the general imitation, Hohlfeld concluded that the original matter was sometimes borrowed directly from York (in some instances from memory), and was sometimes written independently, but ever with close following of Scriptural sources; and that a second author, who regarded little the Scriptural sources, wrote the more admirable realistic series of humorous plays.—Pollard thought that the cycle exhibited at least three stages of growth extending perhaps from about 1360 to about 1410, 'though subsequent editors may have tinkered here and there and allowance must be made for continual corruption by the actors.' His first group is distinguished by presence of a simple religious tone, the majority of the items being in tail-rime of six lines, fours and threes, with some couplets—Plays 1, 5, 6, 7, 9, and 11, and parts of 10, 17, 23, and 28. Plays 7, 9, 10, and 11 he accepted as certainly by one writer. Pollard's second stage is that of borrowing from a York version Plays 8, 18, 25, 26, and 30 (York 11, 20, 37, 38, and 48), the York plays probably being brought home by Wakefield men that acted at York, and being written down from memory or recitation. The norm of the metre of Plays 8, 18, and 25 is ababababcdcd, *a* and *b* of four, *c* and *d* of three, stresses; that of Play 26 is fundamentally aabab, *a* of four, and *b* of two, stresses; that of Play 30 is ababab of four stresses with variants. Pollard's third stage is the work of a single genius, a writer of great vigor, realistic power, and notable humor. The pieces were composed probably not after 1410, and perhaps as early as 1380-1390, in a stanza aaaab-cccb (ll. 1-4 of 4 stresses with rime of the cæsural stresses, l. 5 of 1 stress, ll. 6-9 of 2 stresses), sometimes divided by critics to make ababababcdddc. These pieces make up a fourth of the total of the verses of the cycle, and comprise Plays 3, 12, 13, 16, and 21. To the same writer Pollard assigned Plays 22, 24, and 2.—Gayley has followed Pollard generally. To the second group he adds, as adapted, Plays 10, 14, and 15; and, as seemingly 'based on early alternatives of York plays, discarded about 1340,' 'still others like 4, 19, 27.' To the 'Wakefield Master' (the writer of Pollard's third group) he ascribes parts of Plays 2, 30, 16, 20, 22, 29, and 23, all showing some York parallels; the whole of Plays 3, 12, 13, and 21; and occasional parts of Play 24, and perhaps of Plays 23 and 27. The nine-line stanza is Gayley's ultimate test.

Cady has urged exemplification in the cycle of Chambers' general theory of cyclic growth, a theory of three periods— liturgical (development within the liturgy of plays on Christ's Birth, Resurrection, and possibly Passion), transitional (secularization of the plays by translation into the vernacular, and by enlargement within existing scenes, or by addition of scenes from Biblical or apocryphal sources—the cycle finally extending from the Creation to the Judgment), and final (complete secularization, the plays being in the hands of guilds, acted now by one trade, now by another, and revised and rearranged as conditions demanded, but holding to the cyclic form). He suggests that the Towneley plays that are perhaps from a liturgical source are Plays 11-16 inclusive (from the Christmas play in perhaps a late form), and 26-28 inclusive (from the Resurrection play and its immediate sequents); that the source of the Towneley Christmas series is that of the York and the Coventry parallel plays; and that there is a common source for the Towneley and the York Resurrection series. He suggests that many difficulties regarding the Passion scenes in Towneley may be explained by considering these scenes and the York Passion group, as derived from a late liturgical Passion play. Cady has also shown good reasons for supposing that the couplet and the quatrain revisions are by two distinct editors—not one, as Davidson held; and that Pollard's third group actually antedated his second. Further, on the bases of metrical form (the nine-line stanza; see above) and of pres-

ence of humor and high dramatic quality, he assigns to the
'Wakefield Master' Plays 3, 12, 13, 16, and 23; scenes in Plays
20, 22, and 30; and isolated stanzas in Plays 2, 23, 27, and
29. Cady suggests that Plays 13, 16, 20, and 30, as well as
2 and 24, appear to be based on older plays already in the
cycle. The pieces of this writer he finds to manifest a tendency
to add unaccented syllables, and so to lengthen the line to an
unusual extent; and to use alliteration little except to intensify
the bombast of such persons as Herod and Pilate and their
heralds, or to enhance the serious or solemn effect of some other
speeches.

Leach has noted indications that the original plays were in
Latin, the titles of acts, the stage-directions, and the first
stanza of Pilate's speech, being in Latin, and the other stanzas
of this speech being mixed Latin and English. Other details
regarding the verse of the cycle may be had in the studies of
Pollard, Davidson, Cady, Bunzen, and Gayley.

On the sources of the plays the writings mentioned in the
Bibliographical Notes, should be consulted. Miss Foster has
said that general similarity of outline and identity of rimes and
of wording show Plays 20, 22, 23, and 26 to be based on the
so-called *Northern Passion* (see page 287). But in a later
study she says the influence is confined to Play 20. Probable
indebtedness for the comic part of the *Prima Pastorum* (Play
12) has been noted to a tale of the 'foles of Gotham' (see l.
180), a form of which is in Hazlitt's *Shakespeare Jest Book*.
The monologue of Christ in Play 26, lines 226 ff., has resemblances to the Middle English *Harrowing of Hell*, and closer
ones to the *Cursor Mundi*, lines 17113-89.

As compared with the other cycles, the group exhibits remarkable freedom and astonishing constructive power in its
expansion of the most meagre Scriptural materials, in its making over of older pieces, and in its interpolating of original
scenes whose color and intensity are taken right out of the
common life of the lower English folk. The plays are notable
for their spontaneous, broad humor, which, however incongruous and coarse it may sometimes be, is representative of the

realness, the vitality, and the immediate contact with humanity, that underly all the features of the pieces. Though they are
hearty, vigorous, and rough, they are also on occasion equally
gentle and tender. Repeatedly, for fairly drawn persons or
for mere figures in other cycles, they present real characters
like those of Cain, Noah and his wife, Caiaphas, and what has
been styled 'the first humorous low comic character in the
English drama,' the ploughboy, Garcio.

But the general tendency among critics to declare the
Towneley plays as a group to be superior to the other English cycles, is qualified by recognition that this superiority is
due to the merits of the so-called 'Wakefield Group.' The
pieces that represent the earliest of the contributions to the
cycle have no striking qualities, and exhibit the tone and the
spirit that we are wont to expect of the earlier forms of the
religious drama not long after its liberation from the liturgy.
The pieces that represent the York borrowings are the products of earnest effort, but are uninspired and little distinctive.
The 'Wakefield Group' is recognized as presenting the best of
the dramatic pieces in English of the period. The *Second
Shepherd's Play*, which is recognized as containing the first
actual comic plot in the English drama, and which ever rises in
mind foremost when one thinks of the older English plays, exhibits all these qualities, and reaches the high-water mark of the
early dramatic achievement. Nor is there absent from this
play a manifestation of that satirical vein—reflective of the
spirit of the later fourteenth century, but certainly here also
the direct outgrowth of personal feeling—which, in several
parts of the cycle, as in the interpolated scenes of the *Judgment*, exposes vice and selfishness and meanness, the follies of
fashion, and the weaknesses of religionists, while it pities the
distressed poor and scores their vicious rich oppressors.

THE LUDUS COVENTRIÆ or HEGGE PLAYS [8] will
be found in MS. Cotton Vespasian D VIII (on f. 100 is the
date 1468). The earliest known owner of the MS. was Robert
Hegge (†1629) of Durham, from whom the plays are sometimes named in order to keep them distinct from the true Cov-

entry plays, with which apparently they had no connection. Halliwell's arrangement (said by Chambers to be 'clearly wrong') makes a total of forty-two plays in the group; Chambers' division makes forty-three plays. Miss Block, who is closely familiar with the MS., states that Halliwell's numbering is that of the MS., except that Halliwell inserts the number 17, which is missing in the MS., and so from that point has numbers just one behind the MS., until by dividing Play 26 into two parts he causes his numbers to coincide thereafter with those of the MS. The prologue was not written for the cycle as it now stands. It assumes division to produce forty plays; does not divide as does either Halliwell or Chambers; would exclude consideration of the *Assumption* (the next to last play), which is said to be in a hand of the time of Henry VIII; and omits also Plays 8, 13, 18, and 26, as listed below. Perhaps it is later than the extant copy of the plays, and intended for an abbreviated performance.

According to Chambers, the plays are as follows—Halliwell's numbers are given in parentheses where they differ from those of Chambers:

1. *Fall of Lucifer* (H, first of 1); 2. *Days of Creation, Fall of Adam* (H, part of 1, 2); 3. *Cain and Abel;* 4. *Noah's Flood;* 5. *Abraham and Isaac;* 6. *Moses;* 7. *The Prophets;*—a prologue by Contemplation (H, 8); 8. *Joachim and Anna* (H, 8); 9. *Mary in the Temple;* 10. *The Betrothal of Mary;* 11. A scene of *Contemplacio, Virtutes, Pater, Veritas, Misericordia, Iusticia, Pax, Filius—The Annunciation;* 12. *The Doubt of Joseph;* 13. *The Visit to Elizabeth;*—departure of *Contemplacio,* 'With Ave we begunne, and Ave is oure conclusyon'; 14. *The Trial of Joseph and Mary;* 15. *The Nativity;* 16. *The Shepherds;* 17. *The Magi;* 18. *The Purification;* 19. *The Slaughter of the Innocents* (H, part of 19); 20. *The Death of Herod* (H, part of 19); 21. *The Dispute in the Temple* (H, 20); 22. *The Baptism* (H, 21); 23. *The Temptation* (H, 22); 24. *The Woman Taken in Adultery* (H, 23); 25. *Lazarus* (H, 24); 26. *The Conspiracy of the Jews* (H, 25); 27. *The Entry into Jerusalem* (H, 26); 28. *The Last Supper* (H, 27); 29. *The Mount of Olives* (H, 28);—*Contemplacio,* 'an exposytour in doctorys wede,' introduces a new group (H, part of 29); 30. *Herod's Wishing to See Christ* (H, parts of 29, 30); 31. *The Death of Judas, Christ before Pilate and Herod* (H, part of 30); 32. *The Dream of Pilate's Wife* (H, 31, part of 32); 33. *The Crucifixion* (H, part of 32, 33); 34. *Longinus;* 35. *The Harrowing of Hell,*

The Resurrection; 36. *Quem quæritis;* 37. *Hortulanus;* 38. *Peregrini;* 39. *The Incredulity of Thomas* (H, part of 38); 40. *The Ascension* (H, 39); 41. *Pentecost* (H, 41); 42. *The Assumption of Mary* (H, 41); 43. *Doomsday,* end missing (H, 42).

Cotton's librarian, Richard James, wrote on a fly-leaf of the MS., 'Contenta Novi Testamenti scenice expressa et actitata olim per monachos, sive fratres mendicantes: vulgo dicitur hic liber Ludus Coventriæ sive ludus Corporis Christi: . . .' Similar statement was made by Dugdale. But it seems certain that this cycle never actually had connection with Coventry. The association of the Gray Friars with the plays seems little tenable, though the seventeenth-century *Annals* of Coventry state that in 1492-1493 Henry VII saw plays acted at their establishment, or by them. Ten Brink has been followed by Pollard and others in assigning the dialect and the scribal peculiarities of the MS. to the North-East Midland. The idea has been advanced that the MS. is the lost play-book of Lincoln. It has been urged that the conclusion of the prologue, 'A Sunday next, yf that we may, At vj. of the belle we gynne oure play, In N. towne, wherefore we pray, That God now be ʒoure spede,' shows that, at least at the period of the prologue, the plays were in the hands of a strolling company— 'N. towne' being a common name ('N.' for 'Nomen,' as in the Catechism, Marriage Service, etc.). For 'N.,' 'Northampton' and 'Norwich' have been suggested. The notion that the Coventry friars took the plays on the road, seems not acceptable.

It is held commonly that the plays were performed on a fixed stage. Thompson saw evidence that they are from an original for which movable pageants, each presenting a group of plays, were provided. Chambers suggests that the unusual number of scenes devoted to the Virgin points to performance of the cycle on St. Anne's Day, and not on Corpus Christi Day. The declaration of Contemplation in the prologue to the group that opens with *Herod* (Chambers 30, Halliwell 29), 'We intendyn to procede the matere that we lefte the last ʒere. . . . The last ʒere we shewyd here how oure Lord for love of man Cam to the cety of Iherusalem mekely his deth to take,' etc., shows that probably only a part of that portion of the cycle was acted in a single year (cp. the Digby *Massacre*, see page 575).

The cycle exhibits few, if any, clear signs of borrowing from others of the extant cycles. There are slight resemblances to passages in York and Towneley. Ten Brink has remarked on similarities in treatment of like themes in the true Coventry plays. The MS. shows much more evidence of modification in course of development of the cycle than has been indicated in our statement of its contents. Ten Brink has noted the composite nature of the cycle, its groups of plays of apparently different origin associated without effective effort, if any, toward unification of the whole. Gayley conjectures that the composite cycle may in general be assigned to the first half of the fifteenth century, some parts of it being of much earlier date.

It has been pointed out that in the cycle, and in certain plays in particular, we have a closer reflection than in any other of the cycles, of the liturgical drama. The ecclesiastical atmosphere, and the theological and scholastic purpose and manner and matter, are oppressively evident. Obvious is the frequent dependence on the liturgy, hymns, and paraphrases of Scripture. Argument has been offered that some such source or sources must have been used directly or indirectly for both the *Ludus* and the Chester plays. The sources of the *Ludus* are in great part the Vulgate Bible, Tatian's *Harmony*, the *Golden Legend*, the apocryphal Gospels, the *Gospel of Nicodemus*, the *Protevangel of James*, the *Birth of Mary*, and the *Transitus Mariæ*. Use of writings of Cardinal Bonaventura of Padua, especially his *Meditationes Vitæ Christi*, has been urged. Miss Foster has found verbal resemblances 'throughout the whole series of plays' to the *Northern Passion*, and has noted likeness in order of elements to the *Passion*. The influence of the *Passion* she attributes to the reviser B, the writer in quatrains and eight-line stanzas, accepted by some critics.

In the prologue and some dozen of the plays the stanza is abababab cdddc, the *c* verses of 3, the others of 4, stresses; the octave here is sometimes ababbaba or ababcdcd. Alliteration is used much. There also occur aaabcccb of fours and threes; ababbcbc of four-stress tumbling verse; ababbcbc of four stresses; a little of abab of four stresses; aaabcccb of fours and threes; aaabcccb of twos; aabaabbcbc of fours; ababbcbc or ababcbcb of fives; abab of four-stress tumbling verse; abab of fives; aabccb of twos and ones or twos; and some use of seven-stress verses in stanzas.

Miss Foster has urged that the cycle went through at least three stages of development: first, that of the original cycle (even then composite), determined by the use principally of stanzas aaabaaab of fours and threes, and abababababcdddc, and by the list of the prologue of the original cycle; second, that of revision in quatrains and ababbcbc, of moderate length, with insertion of plays from the *Entry into Jerusalem* to the *Crucifixion*, and rewriting of *Longinus* and the *Burial;* and, third, the addition of the scholastic and theological amplifications and adornments, with revision in quatrains and ababbcbc, with excess of stressed syllables, the purpose being formation of three small cycles, one for a year.

Miss Dodds has argued that 'the Prologue including the last stanza, was originally written for a cycle of plays belonging to N——town.' She has felt that later it was expanded with descriptions of interpolated plays. To the original cycle of N——town plays she assigns Halliwell's Plays 1-7, 20-24, 36-42 (*i.e.*, to the end of the *Prophets, Christ and the Doctors* to *Lazarus* incl., the *Three Maries* to the end incl.). At about 1468, she judges, with the old cycle five others were amalgamated, all the plays being selected to convey instruction and to honor the Virgin. So were interpolated the group on the Girlhood of the Virgin (Halliwell's Plays 8-13 incl.; based on the apocryphal *Book of the Virgin* and *Protevangelion of James*), suitable for St. Anne's Day; probably from a trade-guild cycle, the *Trial of Joseph and Mary* and *Joseph and the Midwives* with the *Birth of Christ* (Halliwell's Plays 14-15; apocryphal), as part of the history of the Virgin; a Christmas series (Halliwell's Plays 16-19 incl., close to the Bible with addition of the *Death of Herod*) to the end of the *Death of Herod*, in which is inserted the *Purification* from a source other than any of those already mentioned; and an Easter play from the *Council of the Jews* to the end of the *Resurrection* (Halliwell's Plays 25-35 incl.). Miss Dodds suggests that the whole could not have been acted often; that it would take six days to act; that it was probably arranged for some particular occasion; that the MS. drifted in the sixteenth century to Durham, though the compilation was made in the Midlands; and that the slight evidence points to Bury St. Edmunds as the home of the MS.

Miss Block, who is most closely familiar with the MS., feels that we have not 'to do with a simple expansion of the proclamation (or prologue) to correspond with the interpolation of a group of six new plays (8-13) into an existing cycle, but with some revisions of a compilation already containing a group of Mary plays'; and that there is reason to feel that the compiler drew from two Mary series for this cycle. She notes that the MS. suggests that it is of a composite nature, and contains two series of Passion plays written each in a separate section by a scribe at a period different from that of the other; and that so, perhaps, in the MS. the groups stand as they were presented separately, and not as adapted as part of a cycle. She argues that the MS. shows that 'the compilation was subsequently used for acting purposes, and that different groups were selected for performance.' Moreover, she finds evidence in the MS. that 'suggests an ecclesiastical rather than a civic origin.' She concludes as follows: 'that the cycle comprises a number of groups, that the MS. itself is made up of separate portions containing distinct groups, that the plays continued apparently to be used in separate groups . . . , that the compiler and the later reviser had both alternative versions of the plays to draw from, all these facts give support to the theory that these plays formed part of the repertory of some body of actors of clerical character, who gave yearly performances of plays in connection with different festivals of the Church.. . . .'

THE COVENTRY PLAYS [9], which apparently had no connection with the so-called *Ludus Coventriæ,* are the *Shear-*

men and Tailors' Pageant and the *Weavers' Pageant.* The former is represented only in the text of Sharp's prints of 1817 and 1825, the MS. of Robert Croo, dated 1534, having been destroyed in the fire at the Free Reference Library at Birmingham in 1879. The *Weavers' Pageant* is preserved in another MS. written by Croo in 1534 (until Craig's rediscovery of it supposed to have been burned with the other MS.) and two leaves (contemporary with Croo's copy, and correspondent with ll. 1-58, 182-233 of it) of an earlier version, the property of the Clothiers and Broad Weavers' Company of Coventry, and apparently now with the Corporation MSS. in St. Mary's Hall. It should be noted that later songs (several in each), to be sung at appropriate places in the action, were appended to the texts of the plays.

The *Shearmen and Tailors' Pageant* consists of two plays comprising in all 900 lines. The first play ends with line 331, and covers the Annunciation, the Nativity, and the Shepherds. Then follows a colloquy between two 'prophets' on the Nativity, its meaning, and its claims for acceptance, which is probably a prelude to the next play. The second play (ll. 475 to end) deals with the Magi and Herod, the Slaughter of the Innocents, and the Flight into Egypt. It would appear, then, that in this pageant two crafts were associated in two immediately connected plays. As is usual with the extant English mystery, the metre and the manner of the pageant are mixed, evincing various stages of growth and revision. It has been urged that some of the 250 lines or so of abab four-stress verses, which contain the gist of the story, represent the oldest extant parts of the work, though some of the quatrains are probably late. Perhaps another general stage is represented by the 550 lines or so that are on a basis of the Chester aaabaaab or aaabcccb, lines 4 and 8 of three, and the rest of four, stresses. A stage or several stages still later may be represented by the 49 lines of rime-royal, and the 35 lines ababbcc of four stresses—the last two lines of each of these two kinds of seven-line stanza often riming with the first and the third lines of the next stanza. Davidson held that there was a common source for the *Nativ-*

ity, the Chester *Salutation,* and York Play 12, and felt that
the Coventry play may be directly from a church play or from
an older York play.

The *Weavers' Pageant* evidently followed next after that of
the Shearmen and Tailors. Its 1192 lines fall into three parts:
the first, the dialogue of two 'prophets' on the Star in the
East (ll. 1-176), whose original form was probably ababbcc of
eight syllables, though some of the second prophet's speeches
were probably always irregular; the second, on the Presentation in the Temple (ll. 177-721) in quatrains abab of eight syllables, which, when isolated, give the gist of the story, and
among which were inserted the eight- and seven-line stanzas
and variants from the periods of the like forms in the Shearmen's piece; and the third, on the Dispute in the Temple (ll.
722-1192), predominantly in stanzas of four-, six-, and eight-
syllable lines with alternate rime, with some seven-line stanzas
(see above) and some possibly still later Chester stanzas aaabaaab or aaabcccb.—The fragments of the other version of the
Weavers' piece are in rime-royal. Its editor is disposed to
think it was originally in quatrains. He judges it to be from no
very early form of the play, but to be, at least in places, somewhat nearer to the source (Luke 2. 22) than is the completer
MS.; and thinks that it is the version, or a transcript of it,
that Croo 'translated.'

The *Dispute in the Temple* has been shown to be ultimately
the same play as that in the York, the Towneley, and the
Chester cycles. But here it is longer than in any of the other
groups. The latest investigation confirms the earlier opinion,
that the original of the *Dispute* was Northumbrian, and grew
up in York; and concludes that, on the way to Coventry, the
play was influenced perhaps by Towneley or by influence
affected by Towneley, and that the Chester and the Coventry
versions do not interdepend.

The themes of but four or five other pageants or groups of
plays belonging to this cycle, have been determined, and these
only partly. By 1450, probably some ten groups were being
performed. The combinations of crafts were varied repeatedly.

Unlike other localities, Coventry seems to have had a marked preference for New Testament subjects. No reference to Old Testament plays is found in the records.

The earliest notice of plays at Coventry is in a deed of 1392—mention of the 'domum pro le pagent pannarum.' Performances are referred to frequently in the fifteenth century. The plays were given annually, all on Corpus Christi Day. Unlike the practice in other places, here but few wagons were used, each pageant treating a number of incidents. Only a few stations for wagons have been determined. Each craft here had its own play-book. It is said that in the sixteenth century the Coventry plays were probably the most famous in England. But toward the end of the century they fell off. Though they were probably revived in 1591, the Coventry *Annals* record that in 1628 they had 'bine put downe many yeares since.'

Apparently one or more of the revisers made over the plays with a very free hand, and with little skill or taste. Much of the text is greatly corrupted. Carelessness or effort at brevity has led to omission of important essentials of action and motivation. The extended didactic explanatory question-and-answer scene between the 'prophets' in the midst of the first play, is very tedious, as is the set of questions and answers between the 'prophets' narrating and explaining the Nativity and its significance, at the opening of the Weavers' play. There is no humor in the pieces. Little spontaneity or naturalness is exhibited in the action or the dialogue. Excessive fondness for learned words and bookish expression, mars the speech. The most human elements are certain features of Joseph's regret at his unjust accusation of Mary, the pitiable need of warming the Child with the breath of the beasts, and the dialogue between Mary and the Boy in the Temple.

THE BROME *ABRAHAM* [10] is in the *Book of Brome*, a commonplace book of 1470-1480, the property of the owners of Brome Manor in Suffolk. Ten Brink assigned the original to Suffolk, not far from the Norfolk boundary. The mixture of metrical features shows that the piece as extant is not in its original form, which may be as old as the later fourteenth century. The play consists of 465 lines, most frequently abab, usually of four, and sometimes of five, stresses—perhaps the original stanza. About half as frequently occur stanzas abaab, probably marking a not consistently carried out attempt at revision.

The play has no title in the MS., and no prologue. There appears to be no satisfactory indication as to whether or not it was performed as a part of a cycle. A hortatory epilogue is spoken by a 'Doctor.'

Study of the marked resemblances between the Chester *Abraham* and this play, has led some students to the conclusion that the former is borrowed from an early, perhaps a fourteenth-century, version of the latter. The theory of direct dependence of the Brome play on French mysteries, is not received favorably.

The naïve innocence of the child Isaac (not the York man of thirty years), his growing fearfulness as he suspects the purpose of the mission up the mountain, and his simple, gentle resignation when he hears the will of God, with Abraham's transition from the comparatively cool traditional patriarch to the agonized parent torn between his duty to God and his human pity and his father-love, are presented with a variety of pathetic and tragic appeals that put the piece far in advance of the other English plays on the subject.

THE BODLEY *BURIAL AND RESURRECTION* [11]

is in MS. Bodley E Museo 160 f. 140 (early 15th century). Schmidt says the piece has a mixture of Northern and East Midland forms; Morris assigns it to the North, with a West Midland scribe; Ten Brink ascribes it to the North and 1430-1460. The play consists of 1631 verses aabccb or aabaab, sometimes aaabcccb, of fours and threes. The Virgin's complaint is chiefly ababbcbc. The piece appears to have been begun for reading, for it is headed, 'This is a play to be playede, on part on gud friday after none, & þe other part opon Ester day after the resurrectione, In the morewe. but at [the] begynnynge ar certene lynes which [must] not be saide if it be

plaiede, which [a line cut off]'; at the head of the prologue it is
styled 'this treyte or meditatione'; at lines 1-3 'a soule that list
to singe of loue' is asked to 'rede this treyte'; and a number of
connections before speeches (*e.g.*, 'Mawdeleyn saide,' 'Than
said Iosephe,' and the like) were entered in the first 419 lines,
and later crossed out. But after line 419 the piece progresses
as a play, with only indications of the speakers' names to mark
off speeches.

The *Burial* opens with a long lament by Joseph of Arimathea and
the three Maries (ll. 16-391); Nicodemus appears, and with the
others takes Christ's body from the Cross (ll. 392-449); Mary
enters with John, and laments (ll. 450-832); and the body is buried
(ll. 833-64).

The *Resurrection* consists of a *Quem quæritis* (ll. 867-1133;
see page 539); a lamentation of Peter, Andrew, and John (ll.
1134-1467); Jesus and the Maries in the garden (ll. 1468-94);
a second appearance to the Maries (ll. 1495-1556); singing of the
Victimæ paschali from the Easter Sunday Mass, and participation
by John, Peter, and Andrew in sung Latin dialogue from the Easter
Sunday Matins and the Tierce or nine o'clock Mass; announcement
of the Resurrection; on (ll. 1557-86); the visit of the Apostles
to the sepulchre, their singing of the *Scimus Christum surrexisse*,
and their departure (ll. 1581 to end).

The use of the *planctus* or lament of Mary (see page 518)
and of some of the sequences of the Easter Day services, are
to be noted, as are the parallels to the several meditations on
the Passion (see Index). Similarities to the *Cursor planctus*
have been pointed out. It has well been noticed that the play
is especially lyrical in its concentration on the feelings, and
the revelation of feeling, of the personages. Now and again
narrative is well introduced into the laments. There is little
action in the *Burial*. The apparent attempt at preparation of
a piece for either reading or acting, called for originality. The
influence of the Chaucerian school is evident now and again,
especially in the verse.

THE NEWCASTLE-UPON-TYNE *NOAH'S ARK* [12]
is preserved in the text of its first editor, Henry Bourne, the
MS. apparently being lost. The text of the MS. is conjectured
to date about 1425-1450. The play deals only with the build-

ing of the Ark, and does not include the embarkation. It consists of 206 lines, which are greatly corrupted. The verse is predominantly abab of fours and threes. After line 76 there are several extensions in ababab, and several variants of tailrime. Davidson has judged that the original stanza was ababab of four-stress verses; but that this is a play of two or more types of stanza, some portions having been added in another type. Critics do not agree as to whether the play was one of the Corpus Christi cycle. Chambers thinks it was for 'a spring or summer folk-feast.' Brotanek felt that it was influenced by the York correspondent, since at York the Noah material was in two plays, and since he found some slight parallels between the Newcastle and the York plays. Waterhouse suggests that the Newcastle play may have been influenced by some Northumbrian play between the York and the Newcastle plays. The Newcastle play is more elaborate than the York and the Towneley pieces on the subject. An angel as well as God appears in the warning scene; and Noah's wife and the Devil have a colloquy immediately afterward. These additions are due, no doubt, to desire to enhance spectacular and comic appeal—as is the Devil's assurance to the wife that he will be with her in the Ark. Holthausen pointed out a parallel to the use (which has been criticised adversely) of the angel, in Alcimus Ecdicius Avitus' *De Diluvio Mundi*, and felt that the direct or indirect use of this Latin piece would not be doubted. The Devil recites a short epilogue. Brandl calls attention to the approach to the Morality-play in the use of the Devil, who appears in none of the other English mysteries. Davidson felt that this use suggests French influence.

THE DUBLIN *ABRAHAM* [13] is in MS. Trinity College Dublin D, IV, 18 f. 16 v. A list of mayors and bailiffs of Northampton is carried in the same hand up to 1458. The play, as well as this copy, is probably not much earlier than this date. The piece consists of 369 lines. The most common stanza is aaabcccb, with occasionally aaabaaab, of fours and threes. Perhaps for suggestion of dignity, stanzas of nine, twelve, thirteen, and seventeen verses, variants of ababababcdddc, are sometimes used. Verses of three, four, six, and seven, and sometimes five, stresses, are employed.

The play was probably not performed in Dublin, though a series of what were probably Scriptural dumb-show accompaniments of a Corpus Christi procession were actually given in that city. Indeed, the play was probably played alone, not as part of a cycle. From its contents and its nature, Brotanek conjectured that it was played at Northampton, or in the neighborhood of that city; and he suggested a connection with the mention of 'N——towne' at the end of the *Ludus Coventriæ* banns (see page 562). But records of plays at Northampton are lacking.

The play seems to stand apart from the other English Abraham plays, and to have closer resemblances to the extant French treatments. Much is made of the domestic element, and Sarah (who in the other English pieces is only an influence) is here an active personage on the stage, and contributes much to the effect of the piece.

THE CROXTON *SACRAMENT* [14] is in MS. Trinity College Dublin F, IV, 20 (here 1450-1500). Statement in the colophon, and allusion in lines 56-60 of the prologue, date the play after 1461. The language, which is much corrupted, has been said to be probably of the East Midland. The end of the banns declares of the piece that 'At Croxston on Monday yt shall be sen.' Unfortunately for identification, there are Croxtons in Norfolk, Cambridgeshire, Leicestershire, Cheshire, Lincolnshire, and elsewhere. In verses 540, 541, 'the Tolkote' and 'Babwelle Mylle' are mentioned. The latter is said to be near Bury St. Edmunds. The MS. bears the initials 'R. C.'

The piece consists of 927 verses, several of them Latin. The most common stanza is abab, normally of four stresses, but with variants of three and five stresses. Commonly the *b* lines rime with the first and third lines of the next stanza, giving a combined stanza ababbcbc. Several groups (ll. 409-520, in most part; 542-72) are ababbcbc. Five-line stanzas abbba or ababb occur, as sometimes do couplets and *laisses* on one rime.

The play tells of how Sir Aristorius of Eraclea in Aragon

sold the holy wafer to a Jew; how the Jew and his associates boiled and tormented Christ in the wafer; how finally Christ burst the building; and how the Jews were converted. It is said to be based on a French legend from about 1290. But there are many and marked variations from this in the play. Most of the piece is repulsive. The humor is extremely broad and in bad taste. The play has special interest because it is unique (but see *Dux Moraud*) among the older English plays in its presentation of a miracle, and at that a contemporary miracle, as its actual basis. It exhibits also, in its manner of using the 'Doctor,' an interesting adaptation of a feature of the Maytime folk drama.

THE DIGBY PLAYS [15] are four plays connected with each other only by chance association in one MS., Digby 133. All the three with which we are concerned are probably of the fifteenth century; the hands of the MS. are probably of the early sixteenth century, though Furnivall suggested '?1480-90.' The *Conversion of St. Paul* (f. 37) has an insertion, in a second hand, of a scene between the devils Belial and Mercury. After 'Poeta' at the head of the prologue, a later hand has added 'Myles Blomefylde.' 'M.B.' is on *Mary Magdalene* and *Wisdom*, as well as on the *Conversion*. Schmidt has discovered a Miles Blomefylde, a monk of Bury in 1525. Blomefylde was probably an owner of the MS. *Mary Magdalene* (f. 95) is said to be in the second hand of the *Conversion*, and the *Massacre of the Innocents* (f. 146) to be in the first hand. The *Massacre* is headed, 'candelmes day & the kyllynge of the children of Israell, anno domini 1512,' and has at its end, 'Anno domini Millesimo cccccxij.' At the end of the *dramatis personæ* is, 'Ihon Parfre ded wryte thys booke.' These passages are said to be in a hand later than that of the text.—Because it is a morality (see page 539), *Wisdom*—which is in a hand different from those of the other plays—is not dealt with here.

The *Conversion of St. Paul* is assigned by Schmidt to the East Midland, with a Southern scribe. It consists of 663 verses generally in rime-royal, often with the rime of the last line carried over to the next stanza. Couplets occur in some passages. The piece is on material not represented in the other extant plays. In general outline and in many details, it follows the Scripture closely. The scenes of the horseboy and the devils give comic relief, the latter scene being evidently a late interpolation to lighten the dreary concluding part. The action breaks off at a vital point, to be finished by statement in the last epilogue. Of much interest is the division of the piece into three 'stations' suggestive not only of the separate parts of a cycle, but of the acts of the classical and the later drama. But the division is on the basis of content, and probably not at all on that of external conditions of performance. Each 'station' has a prologue and an epilogue by the 'Poeta.' At the end of the first prologue, and at the ends of the first and second 'stations,' a later hand has added the direction, 'Daunce.'

In the first 'station' Saul boasts of his renown and his persecution of the Christians. He obtains the letters for further persecution, and, after his servant and the hostler have engaged in a humorous dialogue, departs for Damascus. The second part exhibits the vision on the road; the warning of Ananias; and the baptism of Saul. The third division presents the revelation of the facts to the priests at Jerusalem by Saul's knights; the interpolated scene between the devils in Hell; Saul's sermon to the people, and his visit to the priests at Damascus; the preparations of the priests to kill Saul; Saul's declaration that he shall be let down over the wall; and, in the last epilogue, tells of his escape.

Mary Magdalene is said by Schmidt to be of the West Midland, with a Kentish scribe. Furnivall judged it to be East Midland. It consists of 2144 verses in a great variety of stanzas. The piece is an interesting mixture of saint-play, mystery, and morality. It is a dramatization of legendary accounts of Mary, overloaded with a multiplicity of features introduced on a basis of inclusion, not on one of selection, from a mixed mass of material. The chief sources are said to be the Bible, and a version of the legend apparently independent of the *Legenda Aurea* and the English versions (see page 306). In the MS. the play is not divided into scenes. It implies a stationary setting with very elaborate properties—among which are an arbor, a castle, a temple, a wilderness, a tavern, and a movable ship. There are over sixty persons, including allegorical figures like the Seven Sins.

The *Massacre of the Innocents*, 'candelmes day & the kyllynge of the children of Israell,' is by Schmidt said to be Midland, with a Southern scribe. A later hand has added to the title 'anno domini 1512.MlDxij.' In what is said to be the hand of the historian Stow, is added after this last, 'the vij booke,' suggesting that in the annotator's mind the play was seventh of a group. That the piece was one of a series, parts of which were played in separate years, is indicated by the prologue (ll. 25 ff.), which states that the next preceding year a play on the Adoration of the Shepherds and the Wise Men had been given; and by the epilogue (ll. 561 ff.), which promises for the next year 'the disputacion of the doctours to shew in your presens.' This practice is similar to that followed with some of the pieces of the *Ludus Coventriæ* (see page 563). It is of importance that the epilogue summons the minstrels to their best efforts, and invites the virgins present to dance (see the *Conversion*). The 'Poeta's' prologue (ll. 2, 51) shows that the piece was meant for St. Anne's Day (July 26), as were the lost Lincoln plays and perhaps at least part of the *Ludus Coventriæ* (see page 562).

The play consists of 566 lines almost always ababbcbc of five stresses, except for a few rime-royal stanzas (an interpolation of 25 lines after l. 80; and ll. 315-28, 358-64). As often in the plays, the *c* rimes are sometimes used for the first and third lines of the next stanza. The verse is lame; the work generally is not very effective; and the characterization, as well as the comic features, is weak.

The piece is really a double one on the Massacre of the Innocents and the Purification in the Temple. It presents Herod's rage, and his order for the slaughter; the humorous scene of his braggart messenger Watkyn's desire for knighthood, and his fear of the women; the Flight into Egypt; the Massacre; the wrath of the mothers; Herod's fear, and his death; and the Purification—the last in 178 lines.

THE NORWICH GROCERS' PLAY [16] of the *Creation of Eve, and the Fall*, exists in two versions. These are preserved in an eighteenth-century copy from the *Grocers' Book*. The *Grocers' Book* is lost; the copy is in the Record Room of the Castle at Norwich.

The first version was written into the *Book* in 1533. It consists of 90 lines, chiefly rime-royal, with a gap after the Lord's call to Adam following Eve's offer of the apple. It concludes with the expulsion from Eden and a 'most dullfull song' (Chambers suggests, the 'newe ballet' paid for in 1534). The second version consists of 153 lines, also on a rime-royal basis, with some longer five-stress tumbling verses. It is said in the copy to be 'newly renvid & accordynge unto þe Skripture, begon thys yere A° 1565. A° 7 Eliz.' It has a prologue and an alternative prologue, for use as the play was performed first in its series, or after other plays. It is said to be not at all indebted to the earlier version. A prolocutor is added. Probably by morality influence, after the expulsion, Dolor and Misery appear, and announce themselves as Adam's constant associates; and the Holy Ghost comforts and consoles Man. To the text is appended a stanza of praise of the Lord. It is of importance that music (vocal and probably instrumental) accompanied parts of each of the versions. The texts seem to have no special resemblance to other plays on the same theme.

The earliest notice of plays at Norwich is in a letter of Whetley to Paston in 1478, which seems to imply performance on Corpus Christi Day. But in the sixteenth century the performances were given at Whitsuntide. Evidently plays were maintained in the city until after 1565. A list of twelve plays, probably of 1527, is extant.

Besides the Corpus Christi procession there was at Norwich a procession of the Guild of St. Thomas à Becket on July 7 to St. Thomas' chapel in the wood—where interludes were played. From at least 1408, there occurred on April 23 the Riding of the Guild of St. George.

THE CORNWALL PLAYS [17], in the Cornish tongue, it is not necessary to deal with here. They are (a) *Origo Mundi, Passio Domini, Resurrexio Domini;* (b) *The Life of St. Meriasek;* (c) *Creatio Mundi;* and (d) *Passio Domini.*

UNIDENTIFIED PLAYS [18]. Chambers has quoted Hastings' notice of a cycle of plays in a MS. owned by a Mr. Nicholls; and Hazlitt's note of 'a fragment of a large sheet on which was printed . . . an English Miracle-Play,' owned by 'a gentleman at Leipsic.'

CHAPTER XV

THE *PEARL* POET; GOWER

The discussion of the *Pearl, Patience,* and *Purity* in the same chapter with Gower, is due merely to desire to avoid unnecessary chapter divisions.

1. THE *PEARL* POET

In MS. Cotton Nero A X (now A X + 4), in a hand of the fourteenth or early fifteenth century, along with *Sir Gawayne and the Grene Knight* (see page 54), are three other notable poems, the *Pearl, Patience,* and *Clannesse* or *Purity.* The *Pearl* is an elegy; *Patience* and *Purity* are metrical homilies consisting chiefly of paraphrase of Bible story. The language of the pieces is West Midland. On the bases of preservation in one MS., and of asserted similarity of interests, themes, powers, and vocabulary and language in general, the four poems have usually been assigned to one author commonly styled 'the Gawain Poet' [1]. The poems were written probably somewhere about 1370, certainly under influence of the West Midland 'alliterative school' (see page 240). The evidence for authorship by one writer is very questionable, especially when one realizes the amount of excellent poetry composed in the West Midland in the period. Vain efforts have been made to identify the assumed single writer with that fourteenth-century Bacon, 'Huchown of the Awle Ryale,' and with Ralph Strode, Chaucer's 'philosophical Strode' (see page 660). It has been urged that the author of the *Pearl* is the poet of the alliterative *Erkenwald* (see page 310). Productive of interesting and valuable discoveries concerning form and content of the poems, but little convincing as regards the immediate object of the investigations, have been the various efforts of students to determine the relative chronology of the four pieces. Productive and futile in like kind, have been the several efforts to construct from the matter of the poems the life history of the supposed single writer.

THE PEARL [2]. We have already seen that *Sir Gawayne and the Grene Knight* is the jewel of Middle English romance literature. The *Pearl* is the best of the lyrical-narrative English pieces of the fourteenth century, one of the very best Middle English poems. Because of its elaborate and finished artistic form, the brilliance and vigor of its imagination, and the sincerity and profundity of its passion, it has a force and a depth of appeal encountered not at all in kind, and scarcely ever in degree, in the other English writings of our period.

The external form of the poem is the most elaborate and ingenious in Middle English. The piece consists of one hundred and one stanzas, apparently intended as one hundred. These are grouped into twenty sections, each, except the fifteenth (sts. 71-76), of five stanzas. The last line of the poem is reminiscent of the first (cp. *Sir Gawayne* and *Patience*). The last line of each stanza of a section is a refrain for the section. Section is bound to section, and stanza to stanza, by repeating in the first line of the second element a prominent word or phrase (usually inclusive of the last word) in the last line of the former element. The stanza consists of twelve lines of four accents abababababcbc, with usually two or three alliterative syllables to the line, with a well-marked cæsura in each line, and with an irregular number of unstressed syllables employed with pleasing grace. It has been suggested that possibly the author was influenced to the stanza, and to the use of repetition and refrain as connective devices, by some of the contemporary Southern Vernon-Simeon lyrics (see pages 507 ff.) or by some of the earlier West Midland Harley 2253 poems (see pages 488). The stanza of the *Pearl* is used more skilfully than are those of the lyrics in question. For uses of complicated stanzas with alliterative lines, see *Alliteration*, Index; and for use of repetition to connect stanzas, see *Repetition*, Index.

The vocabulary of the poem is drawn very liberally from French and Scandinavian, as well as English. This catholicity, due partly to the exigencies of alliteration and stanzaic form, contributes largely to the obscurity of the language that has influenced the publication recently of a number of modernizations.

His precious pearl without compeer the poet let fall in the grass. He sought in vain for it, and mourned heart-broken. On the high holiday of August (the definite dating is not uncommon in fourteenth-century writing), as he lingered about the spot, he threw himself on the ground, and, lulled by the sweet odors of the flowers, fell asleep.

In a vision the poet finds himself in a shimmering land of cliffs and rocks and fair woods and holts, where rapturous birds of brightest hue sing sweetest melodies. Faring through a magnificent forest, he comes to a lovely glimmering stream, bordered with fair flowers, its pebbles precious gems. Along the stream he goes, full of solace, seeking passage across to the paradise that he dreams to be on the farther side. Then, on the other bank he beholds a cliff of crystal, and beneath it a gracious maiden all in glistering white. She raises her face, and he is filled with wonder at her loveliness. As he gazes, she rises, a beauteous vision in garments all wrought with pearls, on her head a pearl-crusted coronet, her golden hair pouring over her shoulders. She advances to the strand, and, removing her crown, bows graciously and addresses the poet. Is she his pearl, he asks, whom he has lost and mourned? She raises her face, and gazes on him with her gray eyes; and she puts on her crown. She chides him: he chooses the worser way; like all fair flowers, she has faded to grow more; a pearl of price she has become. The poet asks forgiveness, he has thought her dead; he will keep her fast in these groves; he loves the Lord and His laws, and would be with her. He has spoken words ill-advised, she declares; this is not her dwelling-place, he may not remain with her, he may not cross the stream; the Lord promised we should arise, the righteous man should have faith, and not trust to reason or the senses; he cannot cross the stream before he has left his body in cold clay, and been met by Christ for the crossing. Must he remain mourning? the poet asks; what avails treasure but to cause man grief because he must lose it? Lamentation for loss avails not, she replies; he must abide God's will—and He may pity and give comfort as He deems fitting. The poet declares submission to God's mercy, and asks comfort of her; she has been his joy and his grief, but, now he sees her, his sorrow wanes; he is mortal, Sorrow's mate, she can be little moved at his distresses—but will she not tell him of her present life? he is full of joy at her bliss. Now his humble speech is gladsome to her, she says; his mood what

Christ loves in those who appear before Him; she is wedded to the Lamb, and is a queen in bliss. 'Queen!' he cries—'it is Mary, the Phœnix of Araby, who is Queen!' The maiden kneels in homage to the Queen of Courtesy; Empress, the Mother rules Earth, Heaven, and Hell, none would usurp her place; but in this realm each is a queen or a king, each would wish each other's crown five times as fair as it is—but Mary rules all; all are members of the body of Christ, as Paul said, and all are in loving union. 'But thou art over young,' the poet declares, 'to have so high honor; how could those who battle long and suffer years of penance come to greater state? Strange it is that thou, who didst live but two years on earth, and knewest not *Pater Noster* or Creed, art crowned a queen; countess surely had been enough!' The maiden beautifully tells him the parable of the Workers in the Vineyard. But the *Psalter* declares that reward shall be according to merits, the poet urges. God's generous grace is like a deluge from a dike, she replies; as life is long, demerits increase; Adam brought Man to sin; through Christ he was redeemed, and the repentant is ever given Grace; God saves the righteous and the harmless, as the Psalmist shows; Christ loved the children and promised them the Kingdom, only the children should enter His realm; the man sold his all and bought the pearl without price; long has she borne it on her breast. 'Whence thy form, thy mien, thy beauty?' the poet cries; 'Pygmalion could not conceive of thee, or Aristotle devise thy virtues!' 'Christ chose me for His bride, and made me clean, and crowned me,' she replies. 'Tell me,' he asks, 'the name of Him who has espoused thee; how has so many a maid won His favor?' She answers, 'Spotless I am, but not peerless; twelve times ten thousand, the Apocalypse says, are His brides. In Jerusalem was the Christ slain, a Lamb brought to the slaughter; He broke the seals, and opened the Book. He is lovely beyond compare, and each pure soul is His mate in bliss that shall never diminish.' And she tells of John's vision of the brides of the Lamb of Jerusalem singing before God's throne the song of the spotless host to their spotless Lord. 'Of Christ's household art thou, but what is the Jerusalem of which thou speakest?' asks the poet. 'It is the New Jerusalem, the City of God, the site of Peace,' she replies. The poet would come into that place. She answers, 'Thou mayst see the outer form, but mayst enter only by His Grace if thou be spotless.'

The poet speeds through the thicket until he beholds a fair burg on a hill, brighter than a sunbeam. It is all of burnished gold, aflame like gleaming glass, glittering with gems, based on twelve strong pillars each of precious stone, as John declared. On each of its four sides are three gates of pearl. The poet sees through the walls. The city is filled with light. On the throne is High God. From beneath it flows a swift river brighter than sun or moon, surging clear and mighty through the city. Chapel nor temple is there; God is the Church and the Priest, Christ is the

Sacrifice. The gates are ever open, but only the spotless may enter. By the river stand twelve fair trees that blossom and bear twelve times each year. Like a quail in a daze, the poet stands amazed; had a man in the body seen that sight he had died. Then the poet beholds a fair procession of hundreds of thousands of virgins decked with pearls, each bearing the pearl of delight on her breast. With seven golden horns the Lamb proceeds before them, His robes all white agleam with pearls, His pierced side bleeding, but His face full with gladness. As He nears the throne, the joy grows, the Elders fall prostrate before Him, legions of angels scatter incense and sing songs of gladness. Among the throng the poet sees his 'lyttel quene.' He seeks to plunge into the stream—and he awakens in the arbour, to lament the impetuousness that caused him to contradict the Prince's pleasure. If the maiden be blessed as he has dreamed, all is well with him in this 'doel doungoun'; and he commends his Pearl to God's care.

The *Pearl* has generally been regarded as an elegy expressive of the poet's experience in consequence of loss of a beloved daughter at the age of two years. The arguments that have been made to show that it is primarily an allegory, 'an artistic arrangement of a situation by which certain theological and religious opinions could be effectively presented,' appear to have been opposed successfully. It is indeed true that the poem exhibits much religious opinion and theological matter. It has been shown that the poet is orthodox in attitude toward the two great fourteenth-century problems of Predestination and Free-Will and Salvation by Grace or by Merits, but that he is heretical in his view that the rewards of the saved are equal, not graded. It would appear that his attitude is rather against controversy, is not schismatical, and is not that of the theologian. It is easy to believe that the poem is the impassioned personal utterance that one might expect of grief in face of actual loss of a loved one.

The poet adopts the popular mediæval device of a vision of the other world (see page 331). The influence of Romance poetry indicated in the metre, is obvious through the piece. The poet takes over directly or indirectly from the *Roman de la Rose* and its imitators the device of falling asleep out of doors and of a visit to a beautiful place. But the personification of abstractions characteristic of these works, does not appear in the verses. The poet seems rather averse to use of symbolism and allegory, though the figures of the pearl lost in the grass (soon becoming a matter of epithets) and of the pearl as emblematic of the purity and virginity of the maiden (familiar in the legends of St. Margaret), are adopted. Such adoption would be natural in an elegy. About three hundred lines are paraphrase or quotation from the Bible, introduced for authority, or, more especially, for picturesque effect. Similarities in the *Pearl* to the fourteenth Eclogue of Boccaccio, have been pointed out; but indebtedness of the English poet to the Italian has been opposed. The comparison of the Virgin (ll. 429-31) to the Phœnix has been set against Chaucer's likening of Blanche to the Phœnix in the *Book of the Duchesse* (ll. 981-84), and several other similarities between the *Pearl* and the *Duchesse* have been noted—none of these implying indebtedness. The poem manifests markedly a number of traits of the Northern alliterative poetry—vigor of diction, moral earnestness, great descriptive power, an attraction to the grander and more severe aspects of Nature, and a lingering fondness for splendor and richness, for sensuous details, for color, for precious metals, for gems. Passages (especially ll. 257-360) of a homiletic character or tone occur. Influence of the familiar mediæval debate (see page 418) is apparent in the dialogue between the maiden and the poet.

The poem is one for any age to be proud of. It exhibits to us a true poet and true man—a person of high refinement, of extensive cultivation, of great and elevated imagination, of warm response to physical beauty, of fine artistic sense, of intense feeling, deeply religious, absolutely sincere, devout, strong, sound, sane, thoroughly human.

PATIENCE [3]. The homiletic poems *Patience* and *Purity* might have been discussed with the homilies (see page 271 or the Bible paraphrases (see page 397). In each of the poems the unrimed alliterative long line is used masterfully. It has been pointed out that in *Patience* the sense of the verses marks them off into groups of 4 or of 5 + 3 or of 3 + 5; and that in *Purity* there is at the beginning and the end a tendency to a four-line grouping. *Patience* consists of 531 verses, made up of the prologue (ll. 1-60), the main narrative (ll. 61-524), and the conclusion (ll. 525-31). The last line is practically identical with the first.

The prologue has, first, eight verses urging the nobility of Patience, and the necessity for practicing it; then follow (ll. 9-56) exposition of the Beatitudes ascribed to Matthew, and comment on them with especial stress on Poverty and Patience as of the poet's experience and to be endured without complaint; finally (ll. 57-60), the poet declares that he will relate the story of Jonah as example of the evil of Impatience. Then the main body of the poem tells the story of Jonah from his commissioning to Ninevah by God to his casting into the sea; next, through his experience with the whale to his final submission to God and reception of God's explanation of His purposes and His relations to Man. Thence, in the last seven verses, the poet returns to the theme that the story is meant to enforce—be patient in pain and in joy; who rends his clothes too hastily, oft must sit among worse to sew them up again; when Poverty oppresses me, it behooves me to endure; for Patience is a noble virtue, though it is often unpleasant. So, as in *Purity,* the poem closes, as it begins, with a verse expressing the point of the piece.

Attention has been called to Tertullian's *De Patientia* Ch. X, where the Beatitudes are introduced, and Patience and Poverty are stressed, in a fashion similar to that in the prologue of *Patience.* The story of Jonah is probably chiefly from the Vulgate Bible, whose details are incorporated into the poem. Resemblances to, and possible dependence on, Tertullian's hexameter poem *De Jona et de Nineva*, have been noted and urged. Recently it has been argued forcefully that the poet had not read *De Jona*.

The poem, like *Purity,* is notable for its vigorous narrative, its realistic detail, its spirited descriptions. The author of each of the pieces is full with his theme, and writes with enthusiasm and with power. In many respects the two poems are worthy successors of the Old English alliterative narratives.

PURITY [4] or CLANNESSE, less vivid, less concise, and less finished than *Patience*, consists of 1812 long alliterative lines in thirteen sections varying in length.

The poet commends Purity. Then, for warning and encouragement, in great detail with much comment and with application, he tells the parable of the Marriage Feast. Then he relates the story of the Fall of the Angels and the Fall of Man; the evil conduct of the children of Adam up to the Flood; the Flood and the Ark; the visit of the Angels to Abraham; the destruction of Sodom and Gomorrah, with a description of the Dead Sea; the purity of Christ and of the Virgin, and their potency for Man's salvation; the conquest of Nebuchadnezzar; the evils wrought by Nebuchadnezzar; and the impiety and the punishment of Belshazzar.

In his passage on the Virgin and Christ, the poet introduces the declaration of 'Clopyngnel' in 'his clene Rose' of how a lady should be loved. For some details he is dependent on the French text of the *Travels of Mandeville* (see page 433). A possible source of lines 265-68, 459-64, 695 ff., is Comestor's *Historia Scholastica* Chs. 31, 34, 52. General similarity of incidents of lines 781-1051 to Tertullian's *De Sodoma*, with possible use (see above) of the same writer's *De Jona* in *Patience*, has suggested the theory of a general influence of the former poem.

2. GOWER

The poet John Gower [5] probably had no connections with Wales or with the family of Gowers of Stitenham in Yorkshire, with which he has been associated. He was of the Gowers of Kent: the arms on his tomb accord with those of Sir Robert Gower buried in Brabourne Church, Kent; in 1382 a manor known to have been Gower's at a later date, was granted to John Gower 'Esquier de Kent'; and the executors of Gower's will were Kentish. But few scraps of record concerning the poet are available. He was born perhaps about 1330. Much that has been asserted of his life, is based on false inference (as that he was a member of the Temple), or on confusion resulting from identity of names (as in the case of the Kentish John Gower of Aldyngton and Kentwell, apparently a vicious relative of the poet), or on both (as, perhaps, in the matter of the deed of 1373 executed at Otford).

Apparently, the earliest, sure record of the poet is of May, 1378, to the effect that Geoffrey Chaucer gave to John Gower

and Richard Forester a general power of attorney during his
absence abroad (see page 613). There is record, August, 1382,
of a grant of the manors of Feltwell in Norfolk, and Multon in
Suffolk, to John Gower, Esquire, of Kent, and to his heirs. Of
the same month is a record of Gower's grant of these two
manors to Thomas Blakelake (Parson of St. Nicholas, Feltwell) and others, for life, at a rental of forty pounds, to be
paid quarterly in the Abbey Church, Westminster. In February, 1384, this grant was repeated. In 1393 (perhaps the
autumn) Henry of Lancaster gave a collar worth twenty-six
shillings and eight pence to 'an esquire John Gower,' on account
of a collar given him by the Earl of Derby. A representation
of this collar is on the effigy of Gower in St. Savior's Church.
On January 25, 1397-1398, was issued a license for the marriage of John Gower and Agnes Groundolf, parishioners of
St. Mary Magdalene, Southwark, in the oratory of John Gower
within his lodging in the Priory of St. Mary Overey, Southwark.
Various inferences have been drawn from this late marriage.
A short Latin poem appended to his *In Praise of Peace* (see
page 590), states that in the first year of Henry IV, Gower's
eyesight failed; and another MS., apparently a revision, says
that, in the second year of Henry, he had become blind, so that
he gave up writing. The fact of his blindness is suggested by his
dwelling on the blessings of light in the Latin epistle to Thomas
Arundell, Archbishop of Canterbury, prefixed to the All Souls
MS. of the *Vox Clamantis*. His will, now in the Lambeth
Library, is dated August 15, 1408, and was proved October
24, 1408—whence it is inferred that he died in October of that
year. The will indicates that Gower had been a considerable
benefactor of the Priory of St. Mary Overey, and that he was
well off. His prominence in the eyes of the Priory is shown by
his holding of apartments within the Priory, and by his being
given a tomb in the most prominent part of the Church of St.
Savior's (Southwark Cathedral)—*i.e.*, in the Chapel of St.
John the Baptist. The tomb is still extant, but was moved in
1832 and again in 1894. It now stands on the supposed site

of the Chapel of St. John, but is much modified from its original form.

The conclusions that Gower was a member of the clergy, that he was a lawyer, and that he was a physician, must be dismissed. His expressions may cause belief that he was a widower when he married Agnes Groundolf. If anything is to be made of his utterances and attitudes in his writings, he would seem to have been more closely identified with the merchant class than with any other. He appears to have been a simple man of fine integrity, of strong and advanced religious views, of settled conviction concerning the evils in the Church, and possessed with a most earnest desire to help the world.

The head of the effigy of Gower in Southwark Cathedral rests on the representations of three volumes labeled, *Speculum Meditantis, Vox Clamantis, Confessio Amantis*. These are the works [6] on which he felt his fame to depend. The uncertainty of the language, and the feeling of many of the *literati* of the period in England, are reflected in the fact that each of these poems is in a different tongue. It is of a good deal of interest that the French *Speculum*, or, more properly, *Miroir de l'Omme*, is preserved in but one MS., and that identified only in 1895 by G. C. Macaulay; that the Latin *Vox* is in ten extant MSS.; and that the English *Confessio* is in over forty MSS.

THE MIROIR DE L'OMME [7], known usually by its Latin name of *Speculum Meditantis*, appears to be Gower's earliest great undertaking. It is a tremendous poem in 28603 (originally about 31000) regular octosyllabic verses aabaabbbabba, some leaves being lost, in MS. Cbg. Univ. Libr. Addit. 3035 of the latter part of the fourteenth century. The Latin note that occurs with variations in most of the MSS. of Gower's works, says that the poem 'is divided into ten parts, and, treating of vices and virtues, as also of the various conditions of men in the world, endeavors rightly to teach the way by which the sinner who has trespassed, ought to return to the knowledge of his Creator.' Its editor has pointed out that the work is a combination of manual of vices and virtues (see pages 342 ff.), of attack in the evils of contemporary society (see pages 227 ff.), and of compendium of Scripture history and legend directed to the glorification of the Virgin (see page 340). But unlike the *Somme des Vices et des Vertus*, the *Aӡenbite*, the *Parson's Tale*, and the *Manuel des Péchiez* and its successors, it is not merely devotional and utilitarian, not merely a manual of instruction; it is literary, exhibiting much successful effort at unity and regularity.

The first 18,000 lines are allegory telling of the birth of Sin from the Devil, of the offspring of these two, and of the struggle of the Devil and Sin and their various descendants pitted against Reason and Conscience, and the Seven Virtues, and their offspring, in effort to win the Soul of Man, and so to defeat the Plan of Salvation. This is all much in the manner of the various Old French *Batailes* and *Mariages* of the general Contention class (see page 411). Then, to determine the victor, Gower reviews human society from the time of Rome. All states and conditions he finds possessed with Sin. Now (l. 26605) he turns to the ultimate cause of this evil condition. All he finds due to Man, and none to Nature; Nature and the lower animals are good. So, Man should repent, and be reconciled to God. This can be only by intercession of Mary. So he concludes with a life of the Virgin from her birth to the Assumption, with praises to her under various names.

MINOR FRENCH POEMS [8]. In addition to the *Miroir*, Gower wrote in Anglo-French *Cinkante Balades* and *Un Traitié selonc les Auctours pour Essampler les Amantz Marietz*. The former comprises fifty-one love *balades* with a dedication to Henry. IV. The items were composed probably at various times through the poet's life, and not all in his early youth. The pieces are impersonal and unimpassioned, and are apparently written as a series of treatments of various possible situations of lovers, in some cases women; but they have been praised for their charm and grace, and for the fanciful and clever variations of their common themes. The *Traitié* consists of eighteen *balades* with envoys, written apparently just before Gower's marriage, and so probably in 1397. They present the nature and nobility of Marriage, and the evil of unfaithfulness to the bond. The group is dignified and elevated in its views; but its execution, though good, is a falling off from the *Cinkante*

Balades. Much material used in his earlier pieces is used here by Gower in illustration.

THE VOX CLAMANTIS [9], preserved in ten MSS., consists of 10265 Latin elegiac verses in seven Books, each with a prologue. The whole work is a great cry of apprehension in face of the evil conditions of the day.

After a pleasing prologue of a fair summer's day, the First Book presents in form of a dream-allegory a vivid picture of the violence of the Peasants' Rebellion of 1381, with which, as a Kentish man, Gower must have been very familiar. The people are presented as transformed into raging beasts. This matter, the most interesting of all the work, may be an afterthought, for the Second Book and the rest are independent of it, and the Laud MS. has only the prologue and the first chapter of Book I, while Books II-VII are there numbered I-VI. The real matter of the *Vox* is the theme of the last ten thousand lines of the *Miroir de l'Omme*— a presentation of the baseness of human society as cause of the evils in the world. The Second Book prepares for the more specific message of the work. The Third and Fourth Books are given over to the corruption of the clergy and the religious orders; the Fifth Book, to the debasement of the ideals and the practice of the Knights, and the evil conduct of the Laborers; the Sixth Book, to the knavery of Lawyers. The Seventh Book presents the *Miroir* doctrine of Man the Microcosm, affected with all the Seven Sins, debasing the world; and it dwells on the inevitable coming of Death, and the need of repentance to escape punishment, with laments for the evil state of the land, and prayer for pity.

The agreement of Gower with the views of Wycliffe and the Lollards in regard to the clergy and the religious orders, and the rebellious peasantry, as well as in much else of his doctrine, is notable. Gower did not hesitate to give blame where he thought it was due, and ventured quite openly to lecture Richard as to his duties and his official and personal conduct. Yet, as the prologue to the *Confessio* shows, Gower was not sympathetic with the Lollards as a class, and took special occasion to warn his readers against them and against any hope that they would be the means of reform. The *Vox* would seem, in its complete extant form, to have been composed soon after the Peasants' Rebellion of 1381. The MSS., four of which are contemporary with Gower and contain corrections by the same hand (perhaps the author's), show modifications due to change of view. It is apparent from these that Gower had at first strong confidence in Richard, but that, as time went on, the ill-conduct of the King alienated him so far that in the later changes in this work, and in the minor Latin poems, he turned to correction and reprehension and emphatic condemnation of Richard.

THE MINOR LATIN POEMS [10] comprise three groups—one of political pieces against the ills of the times and the abuses of Richard's rule, a second on the accession of Henry IV, and a third consisting of short occasional pieces evidently of Gower's last years. The political pieces must be remembered as expressions in Latin of much the same attitudes toward much the same conditions, as are seen in the political poems in English of the end of the century (see page 208).

THE MINOR ENGLISH POEMS are *In Praise of Peace* and, possibly, the *Balade Moral of Gode Counseyle*. The former poem [11] is in a MS. at Trentham Hall, in 385 pentameter verses ababbcc. The poet congratulates Henry on his rightful succession; reminds him of the views of old books on war and peace; urges the blessings of peace; shows the causes of war, how war is against Christ's commandments, and how knighthood, instituted to aid the needy, is failing in its purpose; tells of the schisms in the Church, of the warfare between Christian nations, and of the miscreants who prosper in violence because of the divisions; and reminds of the transitoriness of all fame of arms. Peace, declares Gower, is like a sacrament, and it must be partaken of with a true heart; where Mercy reigns, there is Grace also; may Henry and all rulers cherish peace. At the end of these verses is the Latin poem stating that, in the first year of Henry IV, blindness has come upon the author, so that he must cease to write (see page 586). So the *Praise* is probably Gower's last poem in English, and of date about 1399.

Balade Moral of Gode Counseyle [12], beginning 'Passe forthe, thou pilgryme,' a series of maxims for conduct in 35,

English pentameter verses ababbcc, is in MSS. Ashmole 59 f. 17 v, Rawlinson C 86 (last stanza omitted), and Br. Mus. Additional 29729 f. 6 v. It has been ascribed to Gower, but is probably not his. In the last MS. it is assigned to Benedict Burgh under the title 'A leson to kepe well ye tonge.'

THE CONFESSIO AMANTIS [13], the work by which Gower's fame is preserved, is extant in some forty-three MSS. which represent three recensions, with three groups of the first, two of the second, and one of the third. A list of these and a description of the MSS., are given by Macaulay and Spies; these are too long for reproduction here. The first recension was completed probably in 1390; the second, probably between June 21, 1390, and June 21, 1391 (Bk. VIII 2973 margin); the third, not later than June 21, 1393 (Prologue 25).

In general, the differences between the versions are as follows. The first recension is distinguished by the fact that its conclusion praises Richard as an excellent ruler, and presents the book to him. The second version has additional passages in Books V (6395 ff., 6981 ff., 7032 ff.) and VII (2328 ff., 3163 ff.), a rearrangement of the matter in Book VI, and a rewritten conclusion omitting the praise of Richard, with (in some MSS.) a new preface and a dedication to Henry of Lancaster. The third recension agrees with the first as regards the added passages of the second version, and retains the revised preface and the revised conclusion of the second. This change of Gower's attitude toward Richard was due probably to realization of misplaced faith. All his writings indicate that the poet was an upright and true spirit, and that at all times his aim was right and justice and the welfare of his nation and of Man.

Further, the first recension has (VIII 2941-57) an eulogistic passage on Chaucer that in most MSS. of the later versions disappears with the rest of the first conclusion. On this and on Chaucer's Man of Law's headlink (see pages 613, 699) has been based a theory that Gower took offense at the Man of Law's 'attack.' But it has not yet been demonstrated that the passage in Chaucer has any connection with Gower. Lydgate did not take the passage as condemnation of Gower, for he adapted Gower's *Canace* for the *Falls of Princes.* Chaucer's confidence in Gower is shown by his power of attorney to him (see pages 585, 613); and his friendship is indicated in the dedication of *Troilus and Criseyde* to moral Gower and philosophic Strode (see page 660). Gower's passage of praise of Chaucer from the mouth of Venus, is the beginning of the first recension's conclusion that was later omitted. Possibly the passage on Chaucer was dropped out by accident from some of the early copies of the revision; possibly it was omitted because of feeling of irrelevance of the material to the matter of the substituted later conclusion.

The MSS. with the first conclusion, and some with the second, have a passage (Prologue 35 ff.) telling that, one day when Gower was on the Thames, Richard invited him into his barge, and in their talk bade the poet undertake in English some new writing that the King might read. It is not at all necessary to suppose, as some have done, that imitation of or rivalry with Chaucer begot Gower's enterprise or his plan, any more than it is necessary to suppose that because Chaucer and Gower dealt in some cases with the same stories (see pages 688, 699) one was seeking to outshine the other. Actual indebtedness of either poet to the other has not yet been proved.

The *Confessio* is in short couplets, in its longest form some 34000 verses, making up eight Books and a Prologue.

The Prologue declares that the poet would go the middle way and write a book of pleasure as well as of instruction. The Prologue is really a repetition of much of Gower's earlier declarations of the decay of the times, for which the temporal rulers, the Church, and the Commons are responsible: four ages of Nebuchadnezzar's dream are fulfilled, this is the fifth and worst.

But at the opening of Book I Gower definitely puts aside part of his usual moral intention. He cannot set all these ills right; he will change the nature of his writing. Accordingly, he will deal with a universal theme, Love, which none can resist or find a remedy for, and which he himself has known. So he tells of how, on a May morning, weary of life, he, the lover, wandered into a wood. Throwing himself on the ground, he prayed Cupid and Venus for mercy. Looking up, he saw the twain. Cupid passed him by scornfully. Venus asked his name and his affliction. He stated

that he had served her, and would have his reward. She declared
there are many pretended lovers, and would learn the whole truth—
but he must confess to Genius, her priest. The priest bade the
lover tell all, not in response to questions, but in unprompted confession. Genius would speak of Love; but as a priest he should
make clear the nature of the Vices or Deadly Sins, and aid the lover
by applying the doctrines to Love.

The piece is carried on through confession and inquiry by the
lover, and through instruction and exposition by the priest, with
exemplification of each point through at least one story, and often
through a number of tales. By his direction, the lover confessed.
He was instructed concerning the sins of the Five Senses, then the
Deadly Sins. Book I 575 to end, deals with Pride and its five
ministers, Hypocrisy, Inobedience, Presumption, Avantance, and
Vain-glory; and with Humility, the opposite of Pride. Book II
is given to Envy in form of Sorrow for another's Joy, Joy for
another's Grief, Detraction, False Semblant, and Supplantation
(Gaining by another's Loss); and to Charity, the remedy for Envy.
Book III deals with Wrath and its five servants, Melancholy,
Cheste or Contention, Hate, Contek, Homicide, and Foolhaste, the
chamberlain of Contek; and with Mercy, the opposite of Wrath.
After verse 2196, is introduced, rather gratuitously, in response to
the lover's inquiry, a discussion of the lawfulness of war (see
Gower's *In Praise of Peace*) and of crusades against the Saracens.
Book IV ostensibly deals with Sloth and its brood, Lachesce,
Pusillanimity, Forgetfulness, Negligence, Idleness, Somnolence,
and Tristesce. In the discussion of Idleness, much space is given
to the opposites, Prowess in arms, Gentilesce, and Labour—which
last leads to introduction unnecessarily of some three hundred and
fifty verses on the history of the Useful Arts. Book V is sup-
posedly devoted to Avarice and its servants, Covetousness, False
Witness and Perjury, Usury, Ingratitude of Unkindness, Ravine,
Robbery, and Stealth; and to the remedy, Largess or Liberality.
Incidentally is introduced matter on Jealousy (444-725), to which
is attached a very remote body of matter on the various Religions
of the World (726-1970). Book VI is on Gluttony with its two
branches, Drunkenness and Delicacy. As the book has but 2444
verses, one wonders why Gower did not develop the other branches
of Gluttony, and why he gave up half the book to a rather irrelevant discussion of Sorcery. The story of Nectanabus, illustrative
of Sorcery, is used to introduce the next book. Book VII is in
fact a lecture to the King. It presents Aristotle's counsel to Alexander on the three chief branches of Philosophy, namely Theoric,
Rhetoric, and Practic. Book VIII, perhaps directed to the King,
discusses the Laws of Marriage and Incest. From line 2029 is
the Conclusion. The priest counsels the lover to cease to love, and
to become subject to Reason. After a debate, the priest agrees to
deliver to Cupid and Venus the lover's petition (in pentameter

verses ababbcc). Venus appears in response, learns that he is John Gower, promises remedy, and mocks his age and advises him to withdraw. Cupid and a great company of the famous lovers of the world, appear and entreat Venus in behalf of the poet. Cupid draws the arrow from his heart; Venus anoints the wound, and gives him a mirror in which he sees his wrinkles and dim eyes— and Reason rules him. The poet admits that he knew not what Love is, and, on request, is absolved of his Confession and excused from Love's court. Venus gives him a string of black beads marked in gold 'Por reposer,' and bids him dwell with Moral Virtue where are his books; he and she shall never again be together. In the first version (ll. 2940 ff.) she bids him greet for her her servant the poet, Chaucer, and tell him that in 'his later age' he shall put a cap to his work by writing a testament of love. Then follow a farewell to Venus, a prayer for the King, lengthy commendation of him and dedication of the book to him, and finally a farewell to Earthly Love, and a commendation to Heavenly Love. / The other versions conclude (ll. 2940 ff.) with a farewell to Venus; a prayer for England; a declaration of the evils of dissension among the various orders, and the duty of a king; assertion that Gower has done his best, despite sickness and old age and lack of curious skill, to fulfil his promise of a book between 'ernest and game'; a request for kindly grace; and a farewell to Earthly Love, and a wish for Love that is Heavenly.

That Gower had at command a number of copyists, is suggested by the existence of several contemporary MSS. wholly or partly in the same hand, and of several contemporary MSS. each with corrections by the same hand. The survival of so many MSS. both of the *Vox* and the *Confessio*, evinces Gower's acceptableness to the age. Preservation of a Castilian translation of the *Confessio* dating from the beginning of the fifteenth century (Libr. Escurial G, ii, 19), and referring to, and perhaps based on, an earlier Portuguese translation, marks the book as probably the first extensive English work to be translated into a modern tongue, and indicates Gower's international reputation. In 1483 Caxton printed a composite text from three MSS. In 1532, and again in 1534, Berthelette printed a copy somewhat like Bodley 294, supplying missing elements from Caxton, with warm compliments on the directness and simplicity of Gower's language in contrast with the false refinements of the love-poets of the day. Ben Jonson in his *English Grammar* cited Gower as standard for use of language more frequently than he mentioned any other writer. Shakespeare admittedly took the plot of *Pericles* from the *Confessio,* and introduced the poet as the Prologue for four of the five acts of the play. Long lists of passages have been gathered attesting the high esteem of Gower as an English poet during the two centuries after his death. He was then regularly mentioned side by side with Chaucer and with Lydgate as one of a great trio. But, as time went on, Gower's repute waned, partly because of more just critical estimation, partly because of his juxtaposition to Chaucer, and partly because Chaucer's epithet 'moral' (*Troilus* V), applied to him properly and with approval by contemporary and later writers, became in later periods repellant, just as moralizing and instruction became unpopular in those periods. Finally, for long Gower's name has been synonymous with didacticism, prosing, and dullness. But recently some of the few who have actually read or read at his work, have come to recognize in him certain high merit in his kind. Perhaps, after a time, it will not be heretical to speak of this merit. Meanwhile, it surely behooves us to realize that Gower was tremendously acceptable to his age; that he is very representative of that age in English literature, and in many respects more truly representative than is Chaucer; that condemnation of the *Confessio,* on the bases on which he has been condemned, means largely condemnation of the great part of Middle English writing; and that to judge him by the standard of Chaucer, whose work was far in advance of his age and in much different from his age, and to condemn him for deficiency of qualities exhibited by Chaucer—this, though from the universal point of view in large degree just, is, from the point of view of the times and of history, distinctly unfair.

The fundamental core of the *Confessio* is the treatment of the old theme of the Seven Deadly Sins (see Index, *Seven Sins*), with a great number of stories as illustrations. Anticipatory of this in English, is, of course, Robert of Brunne's *Handlyng Synne* (see page 342). But the purpose of Robert, and of practically all the other treatments, was finally, as well as fundamentally, didactic; Gower's purpose was, as he declares, to steer the middle course between instruction and pleasure. The general frame-idea of the confession of the lover to the priest, Genius, may have been obtained from Langland, or, more probably, from the confession of Nature to her priest, Genius, in the *Roman de la Rose.* Possibly the *Legend of Good Women,* possibly notices of the plan of the *Canterbury Tales,* helped to immediate suggestion of the grouping of a variety of stories in one frame. But the idea of such a grouping was common property already long exploited in such fruits of Oriental suggestion as the *Seven Sages* (see page 186), *Barlaam and Josaphat* (see Index), and the *Disciplina Clericalis.*

The Prologue, with its complaints on the times, and the conclusion of the later recensions to the same effect, are little relevant, and are largely a working over of matter of the *Vox Clamantis.* Repeatedly in the body of the poem occur digressions and irrelevant passages, such as those noted in the synopses of Books III-VII; sometimes matter is but superficially connected with that to which it is attached; often the application of a story to the theme of Love is not made evident, though the illustration of the sin in question is clear; and the sub-division of the Sins is too minute. Yet in all these defects one must recognize common traits of mediæval writing.

Gower undertook and completed one of the most extensive collections of the period in a modern tongue. The stories are notable not only for their number, but also for their variety and for the cleverness of their combination. As would be expected, they are drawn most frequently from Ovid (*Metamorphoses, Heroides, Fasti*), and next from the Vulgate Bible. But the sources are widely various; among them are principally Josephus Flavius, Peter Comestor, Methodius' *Revelations,* Augustine's *De Civitate Dei,* Isidore of Seville, Gregory's *Morals* and *Homilies,* Hyginus' *Fabulæ,* Livy's *Annals,* Statius' *Thebais,* Servius' commentary on Virgil, Horace (slightly), Valerius Maximus, the *Historia Alexandri,* the *Vita Barlaam et Josaphat,* the *Roman des Sept Sages,* Godfrey of Viterbo, Brunetto Latini, Nicholas Trivet, Benoît de Sainte More, and Guido delle Colonne.

Gower presented the fruits of his extended reading with great narrative power. He arranged and proportioned the material as he would, commonly with good judgment; and he frequently introduced effective novel modifications. His narrative is interesting, simple, lucid, and often notably picturesque. Having begun a tale, he proceeds evenly and without digression to the end, often, indeed, sacrificing somewhat the moral application for which it was originally largely intended, and certainly exhibiting a sustained personal interest and a control that, though fundamental conditions of ideal story-telling, are sometimes missed in even his greatest contemporary.

In his tales he evinces frequently no mean satirical power. His treatment of Love and Love-matters is not wholly conventional or remote or abstract; it often manifests warmth and individuality. Not only in the conceptions of the speakers of the poem, but in the reflected personality of the beloved lady, the work exhibits appreciation of elevated ideal love.

The style is always direct, simple, unartificial, even plain; but it·is rarely bald. The language is pure and lucid. Yet, as one studies its effects, one sees that they are the results of care, of an art that does not obtrude; and one comes to realize why Jonson cited Gower as standard more frequently than any other English writer.

One must recognize in Gower one of the great English masters of the octosyllabic couplet, a greater master than any of his predecessors or contemporaries, or than any of his successors for several centuries. His verse is smooth, easy, fluent. The beats are regular, the syllables of even count. Sometimes, but not often, the metre is too regular. Gower had attained remarkable skill and facility in shifting of the pause, in use of the run-on line, in splitting of the couplet by a full stop, and in employment of the sentence and the paragraph, rather than the line, as unit-basis. Of wrenched accent he has comparatively little; he is especially careful for purity of rime; he has studied the possibilities of the inflectional ending and of elision for rhythm; and he is not driven to frequent use of slurring.

Rightly Gower has been declared to exhibit talent rather

than genius, to be over-anxious to instruct, to lack brilliancy, to have attained his achievements by labor rather than by inspiration, to manifest unwavering effort toward control and regularity, and to have sought correctness rather than elevation.   These are not ill characteristics, if they are not over-developed. Perhaps Gower developed them more commendably, especially if his times be considered, than has been realized.   Had the next succeeding generations carried on what he gave to them, they would have done well.

CHAUCER

Geoffrey Chaucer is the greatest English writer between the Norman Conquest and the age of Elizabeth. He was the first courtly poet in English, the first to equal the French in any of the fields in which they shone, the first to feel and to utilize any of the splendid achievements of Italian poetry. He had genius as well as talent; he was a conscious artist, not merely an industrious writer. Such is his eminence that we are ever tempted to estimate him, not by his compatriots or his contemporaries, but by the best writers of the classical and the modern literatures.

Chaucer was not a deliberate reformer of the English language. He used the current dialect of his native city. In this dialect he wrote with the care and consistency of a literary artist. He did not labor to reduce or to normalize inflection, or to expand the vocabulary by introduction of foreign terms; it has been shown that, passage for passage, *Piers Plowman* contains a somewhat greater proportionate use of foreign elements than does Chaucer, and that, on like themes treated in a like spirit, the proportion of native elements in the two writers would probably be about the same. Chaucer's conscious effort in this field consists in his persistent loyalty to the vernacular, in face of the temptations of Latin and French. By producing a large body of excellent literature in London English, as unpurposed consequences he assisted toward the dominance of that dialect, he made composition in the native tongue respectable in any class of society, and, being widely imitated for over a century, he affected the literary language and helped to establish a standard speech.

For smoothness, facility, grace, variety, and novelty, Chaucer was the greatest English metrist up to the time of

Shakespeare, and is to be classed among the most notable writers of English verse in any period. His achievement is the greater from the paucity of forms in earlier English verse, and from the comparatively unsettled state of the language that he had to use. In the *House of Fame*, the *Duchesse*, and perhaps the *Romaunt*, he employed the short couplet—long familiar from the *Roman de la Rose*, and practised admirably in the *Owl and the Nightingale*; in *Sir Thopas* he used the tail-rime popular in the later romances; and perhaps it was he who wrote the two tetrameter quatrains abab of the *Proverbs*. He introduced into English the pentameter couplet in the *Legend* and most of the *Canterbury Tales*, and *terza rima* in the *Compleint to his Lady*. In addition to these, he first in English used the following stanza forms: aabba, envoy of the *Purs*; ababaa, envoy of *Womanly Noblesse*; ababcb, envoy of *Clerk's Tale*; ababbcc or *rime royal*, in many pieces—in three stanzas on one set of rimes with refrain in *Purs*, *Lak of Stedfastnesse*, *Gentilesse*, *Truth*, and the *Legend* lines B249-69; ababbab in part of *Fortune*; ababbcbc (the 'Monk's Tale stanza'), in *ABC, Monk's Tale, Former Age, Bukton*—in three stanzas on one set of rimes with refrain in *Fortune, Venus, Rosemounde*; aabaabbcc in the complaint in *Mars*; in *Anelida*, aabaabbab with and without internal rime, and aaabaaab bbbabbba; aabaabbab in three stanzas on one rime in *Womanly Noblesse*; aabaabcddc in *Compleint to his Lady*; aabaabbaab in envoy to *Venus*; and the roundel in the *Parlement* lines 680 ff., and *Merciles Beaute*.

In numerous and often extensive digressions Chaucer exploits his knowledge. Formerly there prevailed the mistaken notion that he was learned. His writings show that he read widely, but apparently generally with carelessness. Professor Lounsbury has pointed out his suspicious familiarity with only the beginnings of many of the books that he was acquainted with. He probably owed much to some of the many current collections of extracts. He seems to have read with ease Latin, French, and Italian; but he was prone to misconception of details. Many of his deficiencies in these respects are characteristic of the age. Perhaps he had but brief glimpses of some of the books he met with; perhaps often he was forced to depend on memory because few volumes were accessible to him. Nevertheless, here, as elsewhere, he was not profound or thorough. His favorite works were both parts of the *Roman de la Rose*, Boethius's *De Consolatione Philosophiæ*, Boccaccio's *Teseide* and *Filostrato*, and Ovid. The last, his 'owne book' (*Fame* l. 712), was his chief Latin dependence, of use to him throughout his career. The *Roman* was of constant influence on him from his earliest poems. The Boethius afforded most of his philosophical notions. The various sources from which he drew are enumerated in the discussions of his individual works (see pages 628 ff.).

His writings indicate that Chaucer had interest in the science of his day. He had considerable acquaintance with astronomy and mathematical calculation based on it, and with the kindred field of astrology; he had knowledge of the jargon and some of the practices of alchemists; dream-lore was familiar to him; he knew of the theory of sound as a mode of motion, and suggested a notion of the world's being round. His use of materials from such sources indicates neither mastery of the subjects nor lack of it. As regards prognostication by dreams or by astrology, he was distinctly skeptical; yet frequently in his pieces he introduced and discussed it for motivation. Alchemy, at least in its practitioners, he appears to have rejected. In his attitude in these concerns he seems to have been at the forefront of his age.

As regards theology, two topics appear repeatedly in his work—the purpose of evil and reconciliation of its existence with the fact of an almighty and loving God, and the problem of free-will and God's foreknowledge. Sometimes Chaucer's discussion of these topics is grave; not infrequently, in itself or in its context, it is humorous. He offers no conclusions, expresses no fixed opinions of his own. He is content to put the case; his expression shows no vital spiritual concern, but suggests, rather, intellectual interest.

The attitude exhibited here is characteristic of Chaucer's

work, and is representative of the qualities at the root of all his
successes and failures. He is a genius, but always a conscious
artist; with scarce a single variation, the man yields to the
man of letters. His work is always the product of poise and
control; it holds aloof; it is tolerant; it is cool; it is the utterance of an amused spectator, not a participant. Consequently,
in the last analysis it impresses inevitably as superficial and
remote. Yet there is perhaps no large body of work that is
more permeated with the personality of its author. In season,
and out of season, Chaucer interrupts his work to explain or
to comment in his own person, or to put forward in the mouth
of one of his creatures notions that are of interest to him or
that will exploit him in the eyes of his reader. But his personality is more pervasive, more subtly evinced in the tone and
manner and attitude of his work. Chaucer's work has no
vision; it is scarcely at all interested in the human heart or the
ways of the soul. It has but limited emotional range, and it
shows little enthusiasm. Consequently, though Chaucer wrote
graceful and pleasing stanzas, he had success with but the
form of lyrics—his best lyrical effects are incidental bits of a
line or two in his narratives. Though again and again he introduced into his pages passages of a meditative cast, and though
he struck out several excellent pieces in *Gentilesse* and *Fortune*,
the materials in such places are chiefly borrowed, and as a
reflective poet he is thin and tame. It is true that on every
occasion he rises admirably to sentimental treatment of the
pathos of injured innocence and helplessness; but of more
intense feeling in response to less mild appeal, and of anything
approaching profound passion or really tragic conception, he
has nothing.

So is to be expected the fact, that, among a nation of writers
who had been and were concerned especially for the welfare
of their fellows and society, in a period when the literature was
responding particularly to the impulse of great political and
religious and social needs and movements, Chaucer exhibits
scarcely a sign of any reforming spirit, or indeed any direct
reflection at all of these needs and movements. This is particu-

larly noticeable, because, from soon after his majority, he became more and more intimately connected with public affairs; because his welfare was dependent on patronage bound to vary with political changes; and because the *Canterbury Tales* show positively that he did know much of the conditions of the times. Yet in all his work there is not an allusion to English politics; there is not a single patriotic utterance. He *says* his Physician made his money during a plague. We are told that the revelers in the *Pardoner's Tale* held forth in a pestilence, and we hear the bell of the carriers of corpses—but the scene is laid in Flanders. We find in the works no response to the terrible afflictions wrought in England by the five pestilences of the poet's lifetime, not even a picture of any phase of them. The Peasants' Uprising is merely drawn on for an allusion to vivify the hullabaloo of the widow's household in pursuit of Reynard. The dependence of the poet's fortunes on royal and noble patrons may have made wise a diplomatic silence in regard to contemporary conditions; but the silence remains. Like Chaucer's success in cultivation of the enigmatical and unscrupulous John of Gaunt, and his apparent readiness to the end of his days in adapting his muse to occasion for personal profit, that silence does not enhance our regard for the poet. True it is that in the Prologue to the *Legend*, in *Lak of Stedfastnesse*, and in the *Former Age*, Chaucer speaks out against the King and the times; but his habitual reticence—perhaps one may say, caution—arouses suspicion that, did we know better the circumstances of these poems, and the dates of the last two, we should find in these instances no exception to the poet's regard for the main chance. Moreover, it seems a fact that strife and misery and ugliness were ungrateful to the man, as dwelling on their sources and their significance and their fruits, was unpleasing to the artist. The cancer on the Cook's shin was merely a striking distinguishing feature of his personal appearance.

With regard to the conditions among the representatives of the Church Chaucer was less reticent, but only in his last years. Slyly he exposed the worldliness and hypocrisy of monk and friar and pardoner and summoner. But it is the individuals that he exposed, not what fostered and lived by such agents. He did not take the matter to heart. He has no word against the system, no condemnation of the personages. He expresses no indignation. As always, he was interested and amused; as always when dealing with reprehensible or vicious personages, he has a good word to say for these folk, makes them likable after all. It is an interesting fact that the two model pilgrims of the *Tales*, the Parson and the Plowman, are composites of conventional motives connected with these figures.

Chaucer is often condemned for his amiable treatment of his false ecclesiastics and of others less culpable because they are not masqueing in the garb of the Church, and for his questionable tales. But one must not lose sight of the facts that there is a mellower, larger humanity that can see the admirable side by side with the ill in a given case, and that Chaucer participates to a notable degree in this; that damning of baseness and evil is often less productive of change and less a hindrance to imitation, than is mere exhibition of the evil; that humor is commonly more effective than abuse; that certainly, in presentation of reprehensible personages, Chaucer does preserve a right moral balance—none can get a false impression of the nature and the significance of the ill; and that in the ribald tales the ribaldry appears in its true colors, while the emphasis and point of each such narrative is not in the ribaldry, but in the characters of the actors, in the cleverness of the intriguers, and in the inevitable relation of *dénouement* as effect to character as cause. Appreciation of the merits of Chaucer's choice and treatment of these themes, may be aided by comparison with his directly didactic efforts in the *Melibeus*, and in the tales of the Monk and the Parson. It should be noted that the preachments that occur in his tales, are largely for characterization, and are usually of actually humorous effect, at least are given a humorous turn. The links of the tales of the Monk and the Parson, produce something of this effect for even these pieces.

As regards religious views, Chaucer is as non-committal as

he is regarding most others. We have remarked on his handling of the problems of evil and free-will. Much vain effort was
formerly expended in arguing that he was a Lollard, or at
least of strong Lollard leanings (see page 746). Upon slight
and ambiguous remarks it has been maintained that he was
distinctly skeptical regarding religious and spiritual issues
and the dogmas of the Church. Actually little is to be made
of all this. Chaucer is notable for deficiency in reverence.
His tone and attitude are uniformly such as to cause one who
would not make allowances for them to feel that he was skeptical in regard to almost all that he touched. Apparently, he
was quite in accord with the general tenets of the Church, while
incongruities and abuses in her theories and practice he beheld
with the amused tolerance with which he regarded other
objects.

On two themes he did speak out—the one religious and social,
the other social and political. It is not uncharacteristic that
the Wife of Bath is a mouthpiece on each topic. Through the
Wife and the Host (D1 ff.; B3140 ff., 4640 ff.) he delivers
a most effective sane protest against the doctrine of celibacy.
Through the Wife (D1109 ff.), and in his poem *Gentilesse*, he
presents what for his time is a striking declaration—that true
nobility is not at all born of wealth or subject to inheritance;
it is the fruit of virtue and noble living. But the *Canterbury
Tales*, the work that we regard as most representative of the
man himself, exhibits yet greater evidence of his democratic ✓
spirit than is afforded by such utterances. The mere grouping together, as heroes for a vast work, of a mixed body of
persons of all classes such as are the Canterbury pilgrims, and
the determination to constitute that body almost wholly of folk
other than nobles and largely of the common walks of life—
these, in themselves, were notable enterprises. More so was the
association of all these personages on an absolutely common
level, and the subjection of them to the authority of an innkeeper.

Frequently it has been well said of Chaucer, we go to him to
be amused, to be entertained, to watch the shows of things.

>He is the poet of the eye, not of the heart or the soul. He is
not concerned with causes or effects. He was limited in his
powers, and he wisely confined himself within his powers.
Repeatedly he deliberately claims exemption from responsibility—he says he is a reproducer, he merely exhibits things
as they are. He does reflect the externals of things as they
appear to a neutral observer of marvelous acuteness of vision
who is at his best when face to face with what gratifies his
whimsical fondness for eccentricities of humor, incongruities
in conduct, and inconsistencies in human nature. His real
greatness is attained in the poems that enable him to practice
this faculty and attitude—the *Troilus* and the *Canterbury
Tales*. Without doubt, had he not composed these two works,
he would have stood unique among the English poets up to
1400, because none had attempted what he had accomplished in
his other poems. But these other writings, with all their merit,
are but admirably imitative of the pale, conventional artificiality of the courtly French poets. However charming and
graceful they are, they are remote from life, and could never
have any permanent appeal.

Chaucer's limitations, native and self-imposed, gave him
freedom to the practice of powers that put him in the third or
the fourth class of great poets. Unlike his predecessors in English poetry, he was ever conscious of what he was about; he was
thoroughly acquainted with many of the principles of his art
as principles, and with many of his own attainments and imperfections. Because of incidental utterances concerning his work,
which accumulated make up a considerable body of vital theory,
he has been styled the beginner of English literary criticism.

His control and aloofness gave Chaucer extraordinary power
and versatility in narrative. Though in the *Miller's Tale* he
shows great skill in interweaving two lines of action, he regularly develops one plot, with one central interest, led with simplicity and directness (despite occasional pause for comment
or exhibition of learning) to an effective climax. A recent
critic has declared, '*Troilus* and *Cressida* and *The Knight's
Tale* aside, there is no one of his narratives which does not find

its place at the head of some story kind long popular with English readers.'

Conjoined with his narrative power is his descriptive faculty. He has little apparent regularity in arrangement of description. He seeks ever definiteness. He restricts himself to a minimum of striking and picturesque details. Suggestion is his chief means. Through this and his simplicity, his parsimony, and his precision, he has created to the eye and to the mind a host of images astonishing for their variety as well as their vividness.

The qualities that gave him eminence in narrative and description, assisted and were assisted by his dramatic power. As an analyzer and expositor of less profound features of character, he has few equals. In the elaborated study of the personages of the *Troilus,* in the brief sketches of the Canterbury pilgrims sustained and filled in by the links between the tales, and in some of the tales themselves, he has given us characterizations that, as groups or as individuals, have been rarely surpassed in their kind. His people are real people, not puppets, not caricatures. He is most skilful in utilization of situation, always has plenty of action, and is a master of dialogue. Consequently, he has been hailed as a real precursor of the Elizabethan drama.

Accompanying and clothing these excellences, are his verse, of which we have already spoken, and his style. In its maturity his style is always simple and natural, always effortless—indeed unnoticeable, because it is so perfectly adapted to each turn of subject. In its precision, elegance, and finish, it is to be classed with the finest achievements in the language.

Chaucer's mature work must remain a treasured possession of mankind. The source of its lasting appeal is multifarious. It is the vividness, the brightness, the sharpness, and the clarity of its presentation. It is its variety, the breadth of its range and tone. It is its excellence of selection, its suggestiveness, its exhibition of significant and speaking features of its themes. It is the spontaneity of conception and of composition, the vivacity, that but rarely yield place to any slowness of spirit or drag in execution. It is the poet's genuine interest, without anxiety or fussiness. It is his thorough enjoyment of his situations, his people, and his stories. And, with all this, it is the reflection at every turn of the poet's own attitude and personality, his enveloping sense of the comic, his whimsicality, his slyness, his covert strokes, his glances of humor, of irony, of satire—the clear and fresh atmosphere of a hearty, healthy, sound, catholic nature whose large experience has left it sweet and right.

1. LIFE [1]

The name Chaucier ('shoemaker' or 'hosier') is not uncommon in the thirteenth and fourteenth centuries. It appears in East Anglia from 1275. After about 1250, it occurs steadily in London, especially as connected with Cordwainer Street or the Ward of Cordwainer Street.

Geoffrey Chaucer's grandfather was Robert Chaucer, who in 1310 was appointed 'one of the collectors in the Port of London of the new customs upon wines granted by the merchants of Aquitaine,' and who had a small messuage in Ipswich. In 1307 Robert had married a widow, Mary Heyroun, probably by birth a Stace. By her he had a son, John, who was to become father of the poet. Robert died before 1316. In 1323 Mary married Richard le Chaucer, a vintner in Cordwainer Street Ward, a person of some means, and probably a relative of Robert. On December 3, 1324, John Chaucer was seized by the Staces in an effort to marry him to Joan de Westhale. A plea in Parliament in 1328 for diminution of fine, shows that the attempt failed, that the Staces were mulcted originally £250 (£3700 present money), that in 1324 John was less than fourteen years old, and that in 1328 he was unmarried. Richard's will, probated July 20, 1349, leaves his house and tavern, along with other property, to pious objects. So, perhaps, in 1349 John was in prosperous circumstances. In 1338 John Chaucer, in attendance on the King in Flanders, obtained letters protecting him from suit in his absence. In 1348 he was deputy to the King's Butler in the port of Southampton.

He was a vintner, and owned a house in Thames Street, which Geoffrey disposed of in 1380 (see page 613). In 1349 he was executor of the estate of his half-brother, Thomas Heyroun. In the same year occurs mention of his wife Agnes, relative and heiress of Hamo de Co(m)pton. A conveyance of January 16, 1366, indicates that he was alive at that date; but that he died soon afterwards, is shown in a deed of May 6, 1367, where Agnes, lately wife of John Chaucer, citizen and vintner, is said to be wife of a vintner, Bartholomew atte Chapel.

Probably Agnes was the mother of Geoffrey, though she may not have been John's only wife. Her marriage in 1367 may indicate that she was not wedded to John until a number of years after 1328, at which date John was unmarried. The date of Chaucer's birth is unknown. It was certainly after 1328. The poet's testimony in the Scrope-Grosvenor suit in October, 1386, to the effect that he was then in age 'forty years or more,' and that he had then borne arms 'twenty-seven years,' fits the record of his first campaign in 1359, and suggests birth at about 1340. This date is generally accepted as the birth-date. That a 'Catherina, soror Galfridi Chawcer militis, celeberrimi Poetæ Anglicani,' married Simon Manning de Cobham in Kent, is noted in MS. Harley 1548 f. 29.

The earliest records of the poet are in some remnants of household accounts (now MS. Br. Mus. Addit. 18632) of Elizabeth, Countess of Ulster and wife of Lionel, Duke of Clarence and third son of Edward III. These state that in London in April, and on May 20, 1357, Chaucer was given clothing; and that in December, when the Countess was at Hatfield in Yorkshire, he was allowed twenty shillings 'for necessaries at Christmas.' The probability of Chaucer's residence with the Countess in Yorkshire, has suggested that perhaps it was here that he came to the notice of John of Gaunt, the Countess' half-brother, then at Hatfield; has been used to account for the Northern expression in the *Reeve's Tale;* and has been seized upon in argument for Chaucer's authorship of the extant *Romaunt of the Rose.*

Between December 4, 1359, and January 11, 1360, Chaucer

made his first expedition; he set off with Edward III to France.
He was taken prisoner near Reims. On March 1, 1360, the
King contributed £16 (£240 in present money) toward his
ransom. In May, with the King and his sons, he returned to
England. Later, during the peace negotiations at Calais,
probably with Lionel, in whose service he still remained, he
went back to France. Almost immediately after this he carried letters from Calais to England. Soon (perhaps shortly
after the death of the Countess of Ulster in 1363) he entered
the King's service. On June 20, 1367, designated as *dilectus
vallectus noster*, he was granted by the King a pension of 20
marks (about £200 present money) for life. In 1368 he is
mentioned as seventeenth in the list of thirty-seven esquires of
the Royal Household. Such a position usually required personal provision of entertainment by narrative, music, and song,
and the performance of such more important services as the
King called for. In 1369 Chaucer was again in military service in France, perhaps with John of Gaunt; but on October
8 he received personally his semi-annual pension. Little
credence is now given Chaucer's supposed unsuccessful love-
suit of this period, inferred from the plaint in the *Pite* and
from the declaration in the *Duchesse* (1369) of unhappy love-
sickness 'suffered this eight yere.' These passages are regarded
now as conventional.

That Chaucer was already married in 1366, seems probable.
On September 12 of that year, a Philippa Chaucer, in the service of the Queen, was granted for life an annual stipend of
ten marks. In 1374 and at times later, Philippa Chaucer
received her pension through Geoffrey Chaucer, her·husband.
The term *domicella* in the grant is a title, and did not imply
unmarried condition. It is barely possible that Philippa was
by birth of the Chaucer family, and that her name does not
imply marriage to the poet by 1366. On September 1, 1369,
Geoffrey and Philippa were given cloth for mourning for the
Queen. Other payments were made both to Geoffrey and
Philippa in this year.

The year 1370 inaugurated the period of Chaucer's diplo-

matic career. On June 20 he received letters of protection
till Michaelmas from suits during his absence abroad in the
King's service. In 1371 and 1372 he received his pension in
person in London. In 1372, 1373, and 1377 he received what
appears to be a squire's usual allowance of £2 for clothes. On
August 30, 1372, John of Gaunt gave Philippa a pension of
£10 for service past and future to his wife Constance; and he
presented to her a 'botoner' and six silver-gilt buttons as a New
Year's gift for 1373. On November 12, 1372, Chaucer received a commission with James Provan and John de Mari to
treat with the Genoese concerning choice of a port in England
as a commercial base. Chaucer's accounts for the journey
extend from December 1, 1372, to May 23, 1373. On November 22, 1373, he received his pension in person. On this mission Chaucer probably made his first direct acquaintance with
Italy, and probably with Italian literature. It has been
argued that he was sent on the mission because of previous
knowledge of Italian; and, again, it has been urged that his
acquaintance with Italian literature dates from the second
visit of 1378. He visited Florence as well as Genoa. The
facts that he was in Italy during Petrarch's residence at Arquà
near Padua, and that his Clerk says he learned the tale of
Griselda at Padua of Petrarch (see page 726), have led to
argument that Chaucer visited Padua and met Petrarch there.
That the poets did meet, has been shown to be unlikely.

On January 20, 1374, the King remitted the advance of £10
made to Chaucer at the beginning of the war in 1369. On
June 13, 1374, John of Gaunt gave Chaucer a pension of £10.
Success of the mission to Genoa may be inferred from the
King's grant of a pitcher of wine daily to Chaucer on April
23, 1374. On May 10, 1374, from the Corporation of London
Chaucer leased for life the dwelling above the gate of Aldgate.
Here he lived at least up to 1385; he still had possession in
October, 1386. On June 8, 1374, he was appointed Comp-
troller of the Customs and Subsidy of Wools, Skins, and
Tanned Hides in London, with the requirement that he keep
the books and perform the other duties in person. On Novem-

ber 8, 1375, he received the wardship of Edward Staplegate of Kent, whence he obtained £104, for which he was afterwards sued; and on December 28 he was granted custody of certain land during the minority of William de Solys, an infant one year old—an office that apparently proved not very profitable. On July 12, 1376, he was granted a fine of £71 4s. 6d. paid by John Kent for evading duty on wool to Dordrecht. On December 23, 1376, to Sir John de Burley and to Chaucer was paid a sum for secret service to the King. In February, 1377, Chaucer went to Flanders on secret service with Sir Thomas Percy, on February 12 receiving letters of protection until Michaelmas, and on February 17 £10 for expenses. On April 11, at the Exchequer, he received in person £20 as reward for his various journeys abroad on the King's service. On April 28 he was given letters of protection until August 1 while on the King's service abroad; and on April 30 he was paid £26 13s. 4d. on account for this service, which would appear to be connected with the mission of Sir Guichard d'Angle and others appointed April 26 to negotiate peace with France. On May 31, 1377, John of Gaunt granted Chaucer an annuity of twenty marks, and Philippa (as one of the damsels of the chamber of Constance) an annuity of ten marks.

Chaucer's steady advance in prosperity was not checked by the death of Edward III in June, 1377. On January 16, 1378, he was joined with Sir Guichard d'Angle (now Earl of Huntingdon) and several others, on a mission to negotiate a marriage of Richard II and a daughter of the King of France. On March 9, with John Beverle, Chaucer was a surety for Sir William de Beauchamp on matters relating to Pembroke Castle. On March 23 Chaucer's annuity of twenty marks was confirmed, and on April 18 his allowance of a pitcher of wine daily was commuted to a pension of twenty marks. On March 26 Philippa's annuity of ten marks was confirmed. In the spring of this year Chaucer made his second visit to Italy on a mission with Sir Edward de Berkeley to Barnabo Visconti, Lord of Milan (dealt with in the *Monk's Tale*), and Sir John Hawkwood, the famous free-lance. On May 10, he received protection until Christmas; on May 21 he gave power of attorney to John Gower, the poet, and Richard Forester, to hold during his absence from England; and on May 28 he received £66 13s. 4d. as wages and expenses. The account for this mission ends with September 19. The power of attorney to Gower is evidence of friendship between the poets, and of Chaucer's confidence in Gower's judgment and integrity. It contributes somewhat against the notion (see pages 591, 699) of later ill-feeling between the poets—a notion based on supposed slighting reference in the Man of Law's headlink to Gower's treatment of the story of Canace, and on omission in some MSS. of the *Confessio* (see page 591) of parts of Gower's remarks about Chaucer. The second visit to Italy, extending over several months, contributed largely to the Italian influence on Chaucer's work, and was in its fruits one of the most important experiences of his life.

On May 1, 1380, a Cecilia de Chaumpaigne, probably a daughter of William Chaumpenys, a London baker, yielded her rights of action against Chaucer '*de raptu meo.*' Just what was Chaucer's connection with the matter, has not been determined. There are various records of payment of the pensions of Chaucer and Philippa, and of payment of arrears for past services and for service as Comptroller. In a deed dated June 19, 1380' preserved in the Guildhall with date 1381-1382, Chaucer ('me galfridum Chaucer, filium Johannis Chaucer, vinetarii Londonie') gave up his interest in his father's house to Henry Herbury, vintner. On May 8, 1382, he was appointed to the additional office of Comptroller of the Petty Customs of London, with permission to perform the duties by deputy. Perhaps for some years, when not on special missions, Chaucer had been somewhat closely bound by his required personal performance of the duties as Comptroller of Customs. A passage in the *House of Fame* is commonly taken to refer to this situation, and to indicate that he found it irksome (see page 659). On February 17, 1385, he was permitted to commit the duties to a permanent deputy. If, as has been urged, and as is possible, this relief came through the Queen, her influence does not appear in the extant petition to Richard, which is signed by Robert de Vere, Earl of Oxford, favorite of the King. This new-found leisure Chaucer may have employed to begin the *Legend of Good Women* and the *Canterbury Tales*.

But soon he came into new offices. On October 12, 1385, he was made Justice of the Peace for Kent, an appointment that suggests that he had been dwelling in Greenwich. On February 19, 1386, Henry, son of John of Gaunt, Sir Thomas de Swyneford, and others, and Philippa Chaucer, were admitted as brethren and sister of Lincoln Cathedral Church. This suggests further inference as to Philippa's connection with the Swyneford family. During October, 1386, he sat in the Parliament of Westminster as one of the two knights of the shire for Kent, probably as a member of the King's party. On October 15 he gave the evidence (see page 609) in the Scrope-Grosvenor suit that is so valuable toward the dating of his birth. During this session he gave up the house over Aldgate that he had held since May, 1374.

The tide of politics was turning. John of Gaunt was displaced, the King was deprived of power. A commission was appointed to investigate the customs offices. Probably because of some political affiliation, on December 4, 1386, Chaucer lost his Comptrollership of Customs, and on December 14 the Comptrollership of Petty Customs. His own and his wife's pensions were continued. From the fact that her pension was paid for the last time on June 18, 1387, it is inferred that Philippa died in the latter part of that year. Argument that the poet's wedded life was unhappy, has been based on the letter of some of his expressions concerning the married state; but it has been pointed out that most of these passages are in works assigned to a period later than the supposed date of Philippa's death, and that passages of the sort were stock jests of the age. On May 1, 1388, perhaps pressed for ready money, Chaucer made over two of his pensions to John Scalby, retaining his pension of £10 granted by John of Gaunt in 1374. It is urged that perhaps this transfer indicates merely that Chaucer was capitalizing his income, since such transfers were not uncommon and were often profitable to the assigner. Whatever was his financial situation, the poet was freed for application to the *Canterbury Tales*, which perhaps progressed rapidly in this period.

Soon Fortune smiled again.   In May, 1389, Richard came of age, and deposed the commission.   John of Gaunt returned to England.   On July 12 Chaucer was made Clerk of the King's Works, an office calling for supervision of royal properties in the metropolis and in a number of places outside of London, and paying about £550 in present money.   On March 12, 1390, Chaucer was associated with five others in a commission to repair the banks of the Thames between Woolwich and Greenwich.   He was paid for erecting scaffolds for the jousts at Smithfield in May.   Between June, 1390, and June, 1391, the Earl of March, grandson of his former patron, Prince Lionel, appointed him Sub-forester of North Petherton Park, Somersetshire; in 1397-1398 he was reappointed.   In July, 1390, he was ordered to repair St. George's Chapel at Windsor.   On September 6 he was twice robbed of King's money by one gang of highwaymen, at Westminster and at Hatcham in Surrey. On confession of one of the robbers, Chaucer was excused repayment of the money.   On January 22, 1391, the poet appointed John Elmhurst his deputy for the duty of attending to repairs at the palace of Westminster and at the Tower.   On June 17 Chaucer was ordered to surrender his accounts, etc., to John Gedney, and apparently at the same time lost his other clerkship.   Payments to him as 'late Clerk of the Works' continued to 1393.

Now perhaps Chaucer was in straits.   Probably in 1393, and perhaps in residence at Greenwich (as a MS. note opposite I. 45 indicates), the poet wrote his *Envoy to Scogan*.   Perhaps by intercession of Scogan (see *Envoy* 1. 48), on February 28, 1394, the King granted Chaucer a pension of £20 payable semi-annually.   Chaucer's straitened circumstances may be shown by his obtaining of several 'loans' from the Exchequer in 1395, and by the fact that one of the loans is but £1 6s. 8d.; but these 'loans' may be merely payments on pension in arrears.

Possibly in 1395-1396 he was in attendance on the Earl of Derby. On April 6, 1396, he was made one of the attorneys for Gregory Ballard, in connection with properties in Kent. In 1396 and 1397 his pension was collected very irregularly. Since it was received for him by John Walden in October 26, 1397, conjecture is offered that the poet was then in poor health. In the Easter term of 1398 Isabella Buckholt sued Chaucer for £14 1s. 11d.; but in the Michaelmas and Trinity terms the poet was reported by the sheriff 'non est inventus.' On May 4, the King granted Chaucer protection for two years from suit by enemies, that he might not be hindered in attending on many urgent affairs of the King. On June 4, 1398, William Waxcombe took his pension to Chaucer. On July 24 and 31 the poet applied to the Exchequer for advanced loans of 6s. 8d.; and on August 23 he personally received a similar loan of £5 6s. 8d. On October 13, 1398, he petitioned the King, 'for God's sake and as a work of charity,' to permit him to be given a hogshead of wine. In response the King granted him a hogshead annually for life, the grant being graciously post-dated December 1, 1397. On October 28, 1398, Chaucer personally received £10 from the Exchequer. Better days were at hand.

On September 30, 1399, Henry of Lancaster was declared King. With characteristic promptness, Chaucer presented his claims to the new monarch in his *Compleint to his Empty Purse*, perhaps an older composition touched up and capped with a new envoy for the occasion. On October 13, Henry granted him forty marks per year 'over and above those twenty pounds' that had been given him by Richard, and that are said in Henry's grant already to have been confirmed by the new King. On October 18 there passed under the Great Seal Henry's confirmation of Richard's two grants of £20 and a butt of wine yearly. This patent states that Chaucer had 'casually lost' both the patents of Richard. On October 21 another confirmation was made to Chaucer of Richard's patents, and as well of Henry's of October 18. On December 24 he leased a tenement in the garden of St. Mary's Chapel, Westminster, for as many of fifty-three years as he should live. He drew money from the Exchequer on February 21, 1400, and on June 5 a sum was sent him by Henry Somere, Clerk of the Receipt of the Exchequer. According to a tradition indicated by the inscription on a tombstone of gray marble placed near his grave in 1556 by Nicholas Brigham, Chaucer died October 25, 1400. The record of June 5 is the latest extant; his pension was not paid in October.

The poet was buried in Westminster Abbey. In his *Survey*, Stow says his tomb is in the cloister near the body of his friend, Henry Scogan. The arms on the present tomb in the Poet's Corner are those of Thomas Chaucer, who has been claimed to be Chaucer's son. Thomas succeeded Geoffrey as Forester of North Petherton, but not until 1416-1417. The importance of the possible relationship consists in the facts that the arms of Roet or Rouet occur repeatedly on Thomas Chaucer's tomb as his paternal coat; that this would indicate that if Philippa were Thomas' mother she was a Roet; that hence Philippa may be sister of Katherine de Roet of Hainault, long the mistress, and from 1396 the wife, of John of Gaunt; and that hence may be seen a special reason for the continued favor of John to Geoffrey. The argument becomes very attenuated, and the relationship between Thomas and Geoffrey is not established.

The prologue to the *Treatise on the Astrolabe*, composed about 1391, states that the piece was made for 'Litel Lowis my sone' who then was of the 'tendre age of ten yeer.' Beyond this and Lydgate's mention (see page 652), we know nothing of Lewis.

For knowledge of Chaucer's personal appearance we are indebted to the portrait in the Hoccleve MS. Harley 4866, and to the *Sir Thopas* headlink (see page 706).

2. Works

I. The Chaucer Canon [2]

BASES FOR ASCRIPTION. The Chaucer canon is established through ascription of writings as follows: (1) in a chain

of passages in Chaucer's works (Man of Law's headlink, Prologue to *Legend,* 'Retraction' at end of *Parson's Tale,* and .
Chaucer's Words unto Adam), based on acceptance of
Chaucer's authorship of the *Canterbury Tales;* (2) in declarations by John Lydgate (in the Prologue of the *Falls of Princes*
and in the translation of Deguilleville's *Pèlerinage de la Vie
Humaine*) ; (3) in statement of authorship attached to pieces
in MSS. copied by John Shirley or copied under his influence;
and (4) in the copying of pieces near to works declared to be
Chaucer's in MSS. by Shirley or influenced by him, or in other
MSS. containing pieces that are in the MSS. asserted to be
by Chaucer or that are on one or more of the other bases
accepted as Chaucer's.

Further, ascription is tested in each case by agreement with
the peculiarities of language and versification of works shown
to be Chaucer's especially by evidence afforded by the first class
of testimony just mentioned. These verse and linguistic tests
cannot be enumerated here. They may be found through reference to the bibliographical list on the Canon, appended to this
book.

WORKS CLAIMED BY CHAUCER. Common tradition
and the assertion of John Lydgate justify ascription of the
Canterbury Tales to Chaucer. Using the *Tales* as basis, we
obtain a chain of four passages in works by Chaucer, that
determine his authorship of a number of pieces. .

In the Man of Law's headlink (B47-76) the Man of Law
declares that 'Chaucer' has told tales 'of olde tyme'; that he
has told of more lovers than Ovid mentioned in his *Epistles;*
that 'In youthe he made of Ceys and Alcion'; and that since
then he has told of women who were noble wives and lovers, in
'his large volume' 'cleped the Seintes Legende of Cupyde.' The
list of ladies dealt with shows clearly that this 'Legende' is the
Legend of Good Women.

In the Prologue of the *Legend of Good Women* (A241 ff.
B315 ff.) Chaucer has the God of Love accuse him of heresy
against his law in writing against Love and in derogation of
women; has him declare as special evidence, 'Thou hast trans-

lated the Romauns of the Rose'; and has him ask (A-text),
'Hast thou nat mad in English eek the book How that Crisseyde
Troilus forsook?' or assert (B-text), 'And of Criseyde thou
hast seyd as thee liste.' In the same piece Chaucer has the
Queen of Love, in defending him from the God's accusations,
declare (A405 ff., B417 ff.) that he has written the *Hous of
Fame*, the *Deeth of Blaunche the Duchesse*, the *Parlement of
Foules*, 'al the love of Palamon and Arcyte of Thebes,' 'hymns'
such as are called 'Balades, Roundels, Virelayes,' a translation
of Boethius in prose, 'of the Wreched Engendring of Man-
kinde' (not mentioned in B-text) according to Pope Innocent,
'the Lyf also of Seynt Cecyle,' 'goon sithen a greet whyl
Origenes upon the Maudeleyne,' and 'many a lay and many a
thing.'

At the end of the *Parson's Tale* is the 'Retraction,' in which
the author asks mercy of God, especially on account of his
'translacions and endytinges of worldly vanitees, the whiche I
revoke in my retracciouns; as is the book of Troilus; The book
also of Fame; The book of the XXV (Skeat prefers 'nynetene') Ladies; The book of the Duchesse; The book of seint
Valentynes day of the Parlement of Briddes; The tales of
Caunterbury, thilke that sounen in-to sinne; The book of the
Leoun; and many another book, if they were in my remembrance; and many a song and many a lecherous lay; . . .
But of the translacion of Boece de Consolacione, and othere
bokes of Legendes of seintes, and omelies, and moralitee and
devocioun, that thanke I oure lord Jesu Crist and his blisful
moder, and alle the seintes of hevene; . . . .' Though until
comparatively recently much doubt was felt as to Chaucer's
authorship of this 'Retraction,' scholars now appear tacitly to
admit it as authentic (see page 747).

The second of its seven verses shows that *Chaucer's Words
unto Adam* was written by the author of a *Boethius* and a
Troilus.

SURVIVORS OF WORKS CLAIMED BY CHAUCER.

Of the pieces that Chaucer himself claims, there are preserved
the *Canterbury Tales*; the *Legend of Good Women* (not com-

pleted) ; a version of part of the *Roman de la Rose,* of which
part A is commonly, and part C sometimes, now assigned to
Chaucer; *Troilus and Criseyde;* the *Hous of Fame* (not finished) ; the *Parlement of Foules;* the *Book of the Duchesse;*
the *Life of St. Cecilia,* modified in the *Second Nun's Tale;* and
the prose translation of Boethius. The account of Ceyx and
Halcyone that makes up 158 lines of the proem of the
Duchesse, may be the piece named in the *Legend,* its extent
winning it separate mention; but the lines may well be a worked-
over version of the earlier piece. The *Palamon and Arcyte*
was long held to be a version in seven-line stanzas of Boccaccio's *Teseide.* It was felt that this version was drawn on for
the first seventy lines of *Anelida and Arcite,* for lines 183-294
of the *Parlement,* and for three stanzas of *Troilus,* and was
used as a basis for the *Knight's Tale.* It is now to be accepted
that the present *Knight's Tale* is practically the earlier *Palamon and Arcite* (see page 692). The *Wretched Engendring
of Mankind,* evidently a version of part or all of Pope Innocent
III's *De Miseria Conditionis Humanæ,* is lost; perhaps parts of
it were drawn on or worked over for some lines of the Man of
Law's prologue (B99-121) and *Tale* (B421-27, 771-77, 925-
31, 1135-41). *Origenes upon the Maudeleyne,* a version of the
homily on Mary Magdalen falsely attributed to Origen, is
apparently quite lost—as is also the *Book of the Lion,* supposed to be a version of Machaut's *Le Dit du Lion.* The 'othere
bokes of Legendes of seintes, and omelies, and moralitee and
devocioun,' mentioned in the 'Retraction,' have been lost as
such. It is probable that Chaucer wrote many lyrical pieces, as
he states in the Prologue to the *Legend,* and as he intimates in
the 'Retraction.' In so far as these survive at all, they are
represented by the minor pieces noted below, and by the poems
inserted in the *Duchesse,* the *Parlement,* and the *Legend.*

WORKS ASCRIBED BY LYDGATE. In the Prologue of
his *Falls of Princes,* Lydgate, the poet's lover, imitator, and
contemporary (?1370-?1445), ascribed to Chaucer *Trophe*
(apparently *Troilus and Criseyde,* see page 664), a translation of Boethius, a treatise on the Astrolabe 'to his sonne that

called was Lowis,' 'Daunt in English,' *Ceio and Alcion,* 'the death also of Blaunche the duches,' a translation of the *Roman de la Rose,* the *Parlement of Foules, Origen upon the Maudelayn,* 'of the Lyon a booke,' *Anelida and Arcite,* the *Brooch of Thebes,* the *Legend of Good Women,* the *Canterbury Tales,* the tales of *Melibeus* and *Griselda,* the *Monk's Tale,* and 'ful many a fresh ditee, Complaintes, ballades, roundles, virelaies.'

In his translation of the *Pèlerinage* Lydgate ascribed to Chaucer a version of a hymn to the Virgin by Deguilleville, and left a blank space (MS. Cott. Vitell. C XIII f. 256) for the scribe to insert the poem. The piece was never copied in. Evidently it is Chaucer's extant *ABC* (see page 628).

Of the pieces mentioned by Lydgate and not by Chaucer, there survive the *Treatise on the Astrolabe,* the *Anelida,* the *ABC,* the *Melibeus,* the *Griselda (Clerk's Tale),* and the *Monk's Tale.* The *Daunt in English* has not been identified, but has been assumed to be the *Hous of Fame,* or to be represented in that poem (see page 653); yet the phrase has been declared to be, not the title of a writing, but an epithet characterizing Chaucer as 'Dante in English.' The *Brooch of Thebes* has been identified with the *Compleynt of Mars* (see page 635).

ASCRIPTIONS IN SHIRLEY MANUSCRIPTS. John Shirley, an admirer of Chaucer, said by Stow to have died October 21, 1456, at the age of 90 years, himself copied out works of Chaucer in MSS. Br. Mus. Addit. 16165, Ashmole 59, Sion College $\frac{\text{L 40. 2a}}{3}$, Trin. Coll. Cbg. R, 3, 20, and Harley 78 (four leaves); and evidently influenced the copying of MSS. Br. Mus. Addit. 5467, Harley 7333, Harley 2251, and Br. Mus. Addit. 34360 (the last two made up from one lost Shirley MS.). There are ascribed to Chaucer in MS. Trinity, *Fortune* (also in Ashmole 59), the *Compleynt of Mars,* the *Compleint of Venus* (also in Ashmole 59), *Chaucer's Words unto Adam, Truth* (two copies), *Lak of Stedfastnesse, Gentilesse* (also in Ashmole), part of *Anelida;* in MS. Addit. 16165, *Boethius,* the *Complaint of Anelida,* and a *Balade* marked as Chaucer's but not printed with his works; in MS. Sion College,

ABC; in MSS. Harley 78 and Addit. 34360, the *Compleynt unto Pite* and the doubtful continuation, *Compleynt to his Lady* or *Ballad of Pity;* in MS. Harley 7333, *Anelida,* the *Compleynt of Mars,* the *Parlement of Foules,* the *Compleint to his Empty Purs, Gentilesse,* and *Lak of Stedfastnesse;* in MS. Harley 2251, *Compleint to his Empty Purs* and *Fortune;* in MS. Harley 2251 and Addit. 34360, the *Purs* accompanied by a continuation lamenting imprisonment, which continuation occurs in Harley 7333 without ascription to Chaucer.

ASCRIPTIONS IN OTHER MANUSCRIPTS. Other MSS. ascribe other pieces to Chaucer: MSS. Cbg. Univ. Libr. Gg IV 27, Fairfax 16, Pepys 2006 Magdalene Coll. Cbg., the *Envoy to Scogan;* MS. Fairfax, the *Envoy to Bukton;* MS. Cbg. Univ. Libr. Ii III 21 and Hh IV 12, the *Former Age;* MSS. Fairfax and Harley 7578, *Proverbs* (in Shirley's Addit. 16165, but not ascribed to Chaucer); and MS. Rawlinson Poetry 163, *To Rosemounde.* These are generally accepted as Chaucer's. Strong doubts have been expressed as to the *Proverbs.*

DOUBTFUL PIECES. Of the *Romaunt of the Rose* in the Hunterian MS. V, 3, 7, in, Glasgow, Section A is commonly, and Section C sometimes, accepted as Chaucer's (see page 649).—On the bases of form and of content some critics now assign to Chaucer several pieces of doubtful authenticity, none of which except *Womanly Noblesse* is ascribed to Chaucer by the MSS. These poems are: MS. Pepys 2006, *Merciles Beaute;* MSS. Fairfax 16, Cott. Cleop. D VII, Harley 7578, *Newfanglenesse* or *Against Women Unconstant;* MSS. Fairfax, Harley 7333, Bodley 638, *Compleint d'Amours* or *An Amorous Compleint;* MS. Addit. 16165, *Balade of Compleint* (Skeat, who first claimed this poem, later rejected it); MS. Addit. 34360, *Womanly Noblesse;* MS. Harley 7578, *Complaint to my Mortal Foe* and *Complaint to my Lodesterre.*

REJECTED PIECES. The many other pieces formerly ascribed to Chaucer but now rejected, need not be spoken of

here. None beyond the writings mentioned above, is now favored by critics as authentic. A list of the rejected pieces is
given in Skeat's *Oxford Edition* and in his *Minor Poems,* in
Lounsbury's *Studies,* and in Hammond's *Manual.*

II. Chronology of the Works

Many of the views offered as to the chronology [3] of
Chaucer's works, rest upon very uncertain bases and upon
slender arguments. In the following paragraphs an attempt is
made to exhibit some of the more prominent conclusions, from
those of Ten Brink, who first threw real light on the matter,
to those of scholars now investigating the dating. Uncertainty.
of the critics' actual views, and allowance for error in regard
to them, are imposed by chronologists' lack of directness or
their contradictions in statement, their change of opinion from
time to time, and their dispersal of statement through scattered
writings. Further details as to dating are given in the remarks
on the individual works (see pages **628 ff.**).

PERIODS OF WORK. Since Ten Brink's *Chaucer Studien*
in 1870, it has been customary for convenience to divide
Chaucer's work into three periods that are with some variation
in terminology styled respectively the 'French and Latin,' the
'Italian,' and the 'English,' periods. Many students have followed Furnivall, who in 1871 distinguished a period of 'Decline'
dating from 1390. Recognition of a period of 'Transition'
connecting the 'French' and the 'Italian' periods, has well been
urged. Critics generally have felt that the Italian influence
followed the first journey to Italy in 1373; some have felt that
it preceded that journey; others have urged that it followed
the second journey in 1378. In accepting these groupings one
must remember that the Italian influence on Chaucer held in
the last period or periods; that the Latin and the French influences survived until Chaucer's death—Ovid remained ever
powerful, Latin writings were always drawn on to de Lorris
succeeded Jean de Meun, and Deschamps and the *fabliaux*
followed Machaut. And one must remember that the name

'English' is applicable to the third period merely because the
poet then dealt with English life and character; (that the
French influence of the first period was dominating and productive of imitation; and that the Italian influence was inspira-
tional and emancipatory.)

TEN BRINK'S VIEWS are here gathered from his *Studien*
(1870) and the English version (1892) of his *English Literature*. In brackets are noted his additions made in *Englische
Studien* (1892) just before his death. First Period: before
1370, 'numerous erotic poems'; after September 12, 1369,
Duchesse; 1370-1372, *Pite*. Second Period: 1373—, *St. Cecile*
['before 8 June 1374']; translation of Innocent's *De Miseria*
[1387-1388]; *Palamon*; 1379, *Mars*; about 1380, *Romance of
the Rose* (not the Glasgow piece); about 1381, Boethius
(greater part and end, at earliest); 1382 early, *Parlement*;
Troilus (dedicated to Gower and Strode probably 5 or 6 years
after 1378); 1384, *Fame*. Third Period: 1385, *Legend* [Gg
prologue being the later one and soon after Man of Law's
headlink and hardly before 1393]; *Physician's Tale*; [1387-
1388, translation of Innocent's *De Miseria*]; after 1387, *Griselda*; 1390, Prologue to *Wife's Tale* (original form); *January
and May*; General Plan of *Canterbury Tales*; [*Man of Law's
Tale* several years before its headlink, and dated 1391]; after
1390, *Knight's Tale*; *Anelida*; *Squire's Tale*; 1390-1400, all
the *balades* except that in Prologue to *Legend*; 1391, *Astrolabe*; after 1391, *Fortune*; 1393, *Envoy to Scogan*; about
1394, *Venus*; *Envoy to Bukton* (contemporary with Wife of
Bath); beginning 1398, *Stedfastnesse*; 1398, *Purs*. Ten Brink
dated the *Parson's Tale* at the end of Chaucer's career, and
Canterbury Fragment B² among the latest tales; and felt that
the *Shipman's Tale* was originally for the Wife.

FURNIVALL'S DATING in his *Trial Forewords* 1871 (in
brackets are noted the variant datings given in the general
'Table of Events' at his pages 17 ff.) and in his article in the
Athenæum 1871 II 495, are—First Period (before Italian
travels): early [?1367], *ABC*; 1366-1368 [probably 1367-

1368], *Pite* (perhaps with the *roundel* 'So hath your beauty
. . .'); 1369, *Duchesse.*—Second Period (after first visit to
Italy): [1373, Prologue to *Clerk's Tale*]; 1373, *St. Cecile;*
?1374, *Parlement;* [?1375], *Mars;* [?1375-1376], *Anelidu*
(? before *Boece*); [?1376] *Boece* and *Former Age* [later];
Troilus [? finished 1382]; [?1383], *Lines to Adam; ?* 1383-
1384, *Fame* (before February 17, 1384-1385).—Third Period:
1384-1385 ('Addition,' dated 1872, says 1387), *Legend*
[?1385 Prologue, rest probably at various times] (pp. 10,
125, Gg prologue 'not far from 1386'; p. 112, Gg prologue
'before 1382 or at some later time when Chaucer had lost favor
at Court. Anne died on June 7, 1394'); 1386 [? central period
of *Canterbury Tales*, best tales near this time, the dull ones
earlier or later] off and on to death, *Canterbury Tales* (1373
to 1400), probably *Second Nun's Tale* about 1373, free and
easy tales 'while young blood was still hot in his veins'; 1387,
revised *Knight's Tale;* 1386-1387 [1386], *Truth;* [?1387-
1388], *Proverbs;* 1388, General Prologue to *Tales* (p. 9, General Prologue and links after most of the tales); 18 April 1388,
date of 'Headlink of the *Persones Tale* and therefore of the
other, or many of the other, links, and the General Prologue.'—
Fourth Period (Decline): 1391, *Astrolabe;* ?1392, *Venus;*
?1393, *Envoy to Scogan;* [?1394-1395], *Envoy to Bukton* and
Gentilesse; ?1397, *Lak of Stedfastnesse;* ?1398, *Fortune;* 1399,
September, *Purs; Manciple's Tale*, late; up to death [?1400],
Parson's Tale.

KOCH'S DATING as presented in his *Chronology* (1890),
follows. First Period (French Influence): ?1366-1367,
Romaunt of the Rose (not the Glasgow text); ?1368, *ABC,
Maudeleyne;* 1369-1370, *Duchesse.*—Second Period (Italian
Influence): ?1373-1374, the amorous complaints, [after 1372]
Pite, [1374] *St. Cecily, Wreched Engendryng*, etc.; ?1375-
1376, *Palamon;* ?1377-1378, *Boece* begun (Astronomical,
Latin, Italian studies?); 1379, *Mars.*—Third Period (Cen-
tral): 1380-1381, *Troilus* (view in 1909, 1382 before *Parle-
ment*), *Boece* finished, *Adam Scriveyn, ? Merciles Beaute, ?
Newfangelnesse, ? Rosamounde* [1380-1384, the last three

poems]; 1382, *Parlement;* 1383-1384, *Fame, ? Anelida;* 1384-
1385, *Legend,* ? General Prologue, Knight's, Miller's, Reeve's,
Cook's [?] tales, Man of Law's Prologue?; 1385 (18-20 April)-
1390, *Canterbury Tales;* 1386-1387?, Man of Law's, Doctor's
Clerk's, Monk's tales, *Melibeus;* 1388, (? *Fortune,* etc.);
1389-1390 [1391]?, Wife's, Summoner's, Shipman's, Merchant's tales, etc.?—Fourth Period (Decline): 1391-1392,
Astrolabe, ? Parson's Tale; 1393-1394, *Envoy to Scogan,
Venus;* 1393-1399?, *Fortune, ? Former Age, ? Gentilesse,
? Stedfastnesse, ? Truth;* 1396, *Envoy to Bukton;* 1399 Sept.
30-Oct. 3 (?1400), envoy of *Purs.* These datings must be
modified somewhat from Koch's late reviews indicated in the
Bibliographical Notes.

SKEAT'S LIST, 'arranged, *conjecturally,* in chronological
order,' in the Oxford Chaucer, follows: *Maudeleyne, Leoun,
Ceys* (first version), *Romaunt, ABC;* 1369, *Duchesse; St.
Cecile* (first version); *Monk's Tale* (parts of first version);
about 1372-1373, *Clerk's Tale* (first version); *Palamon* (first
version); *Compleint to his Lady; Amorous Compleint; Pite;
Anelida; Melibeus* (first version); *Parson's Tale* (first version); *Wretched Engendring* (first version); *Man of Law's
Tale* (first version); 1377-1381, *Boethius;* ?1379, *Mars;* 1379-
1383, *Troilus; Words to Adam; Former Age; Fortune;* 1382,
Parlement; 1383-1384, *Fame;* 1385-1386, *Legend;* 1386,
Canterbury Tales begun; 1387-1388, Central Period of *Tales*
(tales of Nun's Priest, Wife, Friar, Summoner, Merchant,
Squire, Franklin, Canon's Yeoman, Manciple, 'among the latest
written'—*i.e.,* 'later than 1385'); 1389 etc., *Tales* continued;
1391, *Astrolabe;* ?1393, *Venus;* 1393, *Envoy to Scogan;*
1396, *Envoy to Bukton;* 1399, envoy of *Purs;* perhaps between
1380-1396, *Merciles Beaute, Rosamounde, Against Women
Unconstaunt, Purs* (first version), *Lak of Stedfastnesse, Gentilesse, Truth, Proverbs.*

POLLARD'S DATING, in his *Primer,* 1893 and 1903, and
the *Globe Chaucer,* 1898, assumes that the Italian influence began with the year 1378. His arrangement is as follows. French

and Latin Period to about 1380: Uncertain whether before or after *Duchesse*, are *ABC*, *Pite*, *Romaunt of Rose*, *Lion*; 1369-1370, *Duchesse*; 1370-1380, *St. Cecyle* (usually assigned to 1374, perhaps earlier), *Griselda* (after 1373), *Constance* (toward close of 1369-1379), *Twelve Tragedies* (original of *Monk's Tale*, after 1373; Globe, toward close of 1369-1379), *Mars* (probably towards 1380); about 1380, *Compleynt to his Lady*, *Anelida*.—Italian Period, 1380-1385: 1380-1383, *Boece*, *Troilus*, *Lines unto Adam*, *Rosemounde*; 1382, *Parlement*; 1383-1384, *Fame*; 1384-1385, *Legend* (Globe, begun 1385.)—English Period, 1385-?: after 1385, *Canterbury Tales*—Prologue, talks on road, nineteen out of twenty-three tales (Globe, 1386-1388, 1387 acceptable); any time after 1382, ?1386-1389, *Former Age*, *Fortune*, *Truth*, *Gentilesse*, *Lak of Stedfastnesse*; 1391, *Astrolabe*.—Period of Decline, 1391-1400: 1393, *Envoy to Scogan*; ?1393, *Venus*; 1396, *Envoy to Bukton*; 1399, *Purs*. The *Knight's Tale* is the *Palamon*, and precedes the Prologue to the *Legend*; the tales of the Franklin and the Squire are of the period of the *Knight's Tale*; the dull Physician's and Manciple's tales are of the less happy period preceding the General Prologue; and the *Prioress' Tale* follows the conception of the general Canterbury plan.

LOWES' CHRONOLOGY seems to be about as follows: 1369, *Duchesse*; 1369-1379, perhaps *Second Nun's Tale*, body of *Monk's Tale*, tales of Man of Law, Clerk (close and envoy after Wife's Prologue), Doctor, Manciple,—probably *Romance of Rose*, a number of the minor poems extant, the lost *balades*, *roundels*, *virelays*, etc.,—presumably *Maudeleyne*, translations used later for *Melibeus* and *Parson's Tale*; 'very late seventies,' *Fame*; most, perhaps all, of individual Legends; *Anelida*; about 1382, *Palamon*; early 1382, *Parlement*; *Boethius* immediately before, perhaps overlapping, *Troilus*; 1382-1385, *Troilus*, Bk. 1 soon, rather than long, after January 14, 1382; about middle of 1386, B Prologue of *Legend*; 1393, *Envoy to Scogan*; worked over in time of *Tales*, *Wretched Engendering*; 1393-1396, Marriage Group of *Tales*; 1393 or early 1394, Wife's Prologue, before A Prologue to *Legend*; *Mer-*

chant's Tale close to Wife's Prologue; soon, rather than long, after June 7, 1394, A Prologue to *Legend; Squire's Tale* in hand with A Prologue; reference to *Legend* in Man of Law's headlink perhaps due to recent revision of Prologue to *Legend;* 1396, *Envoy to Bukton.*

TATLOCK'S CHRONOLOGY appears to be as follows: 1376, 1377, or earlier, first version of *Troilus*—after 1380, second version; about 1379, completed *Fame;* probably 1381, *Parlement;* 1386-1387, before latter part of 1387, *Legend* (A Prologue about latter part of 1394, B Prologue 1386; probably most or all of the Legends followed the Prologue); 1383-1384, *Anelida;* 1384-1386, *Knight's Tale* (*Palamon,* slightly revised later as *Knight's Tale*); 1387, commencement of *Canterbury Tales;* 1387-1400, *Tales* as a whole; 1387, first part of General Prologue, whole written immediately after conception of general plan; after 1387, *Clerk's Tale,* not before B Prologue to *Legend,* story first known to Chaucer after 1378; after 1387, *Monk's Tale,* probably written for *Tales,* at least second part not before 1386; after 1386 and before 1390, probably 1388, *Physician's Tale;* 1388-1394, *Melibeus,* after *Knight's Tale* and B Prologue to *Legend,* and before *Man of Law's Tale;* 1388-1394, in following order, Wife of Bath in General Prologue, *Shipman's Tale* (1388-1393), Wife's Prologue (earliest possible date 1388, date tentative), *Melibeus* (before 1394), *Merchant's Tale* (shortly after *Melibeus,* very probably not after 1394), Prioress' Prologue, *Wife's Tale;* 1396, *Envoy to Bukton.*—Tatlock appears to hold that the Italian influence began after the second journey to Italy in 1378.

III.   Minor Poems

The following poems of Chaucer, classed generally as 'Minor Poems,' are arranged alphabetically. Included are four poems of doubtful authenticity, but accepted by some scholars.

ABC [4] is so named because its 23 stanzas of pentameter lines ababbcbc ('Monk's Tale stanza,' see page 600) successively begin with the letters of the alphabet in their usual order. Preserved in thirteen MSS., it is ascribed to Chaucer in the two Pepys copies and by Shirley's hand in the Sion College MS. It has merit merely as an exercise in verse-making, being but a free translation of an ABC prayer to the Virgin in *La Pèlerinage de la Vie Humaine* composed by Deguilleville in stanzas of twelve octosyllabic lines on two rimes, in 1330 or 1331. It is probably the piece by Chaucer that Lydgate intended to insert in his version of Deguilleville (see page 621). The theme and the handling suggest the beginner in poetizing. Little weight is allowed Speght's declaration in the first printed text of 1602 that the poem was 'made, as some say, at the request of Blanch, Duchesse of Lancaster, as a praier for her priuat vse.' If made for Blanche, the poem dates from between 1359 and 1369. It is regarded as one of Chaucer's earliest pieces (see pages 624 ff.).

AGAINST WOMEN UNCONSTANT or NEWFAN-GELNESSE [5] is with Chaucerian poems in MSS. Fairfax 16, Cotton Cleopatra D VII, and Harley 7578, without statement of authorship. Stow in his edition ascribed it to Chaucer. It is an attractive piece. Its manner is Chaucerian, but its authenticity has been strongly questioned. Skeat suggested that the idea of the poem and also the refrain are from 'Chaucer's favorite author, Machaut.' The *balade* comprises three stanzas ababbcc, the whole poem being on three rime-sounds. Through various comparisons the poet reproaches his lady for fickleness.

AN AMOROUS COMPLEINT or COMPLEINT D'AMOURS [6], in MSS. Fairfax 16, Bodley 638, Harley 7333, is in Chaucer's manner; but its authenticity is questioned. Skeat printed it first in 1888. Koch assigned it conjecturally to 1374. A heading states that the poem was 'made at Windsor.' It consists of 91 verses ababbcc. The poet laments his sad state through love for a lady, there is but death for him; yet it is not she that is to blame, it is her beauty and his eye; he beseeches her to read his plaint and forgive his importunity; he will ever be faithful—so he sends her the poem on a St. Valentine's Day.

ANELIDA AND ARCITE [7], or THE COMPLEYNT OF FEIRE ANELIDA AND FALS ARCITE, is preserved in a number of MSS., is ascribed to Chaucer by Shirley in MSS. Trinity R, 3, 20 and Additional 16165, and is named in Lydgate's list of Chaucer's works (see page 621). The poem is incomplete in 357 lines. It comprises, first, a Proem of three rime-royal stanzas from the opening of Boccaccio's *Teseide;* and next, twenty-seven similar stanzas (ll. 22-49 partly from Statius' *Thebais* XII 519 ff., and ll. 50-70 from the *Teseide*) presenting part of the 'story.' To this succeeds the Complaint in fourteen stanzas in four groups: (1) a Proem of nine pentameter lines aabaabbab; (2) six stanzas, of which the first four are pentameter aabaabbab, the fifth stanza is of 16 lines aaabaaabbbbabbba with its lines 4, 8, 12, 16 pentameter, the rest tetrameter, and the sixth stanza is aabaabbab pentameter with internal rime of the second and fourth stresses in each line; (3) another group of six stanzas, identical in form with that immediately preceding; (4) a conclusion of one stanza, corresponding to the form of the Proem to the Complaint. A rime-royal stanza concludes the fragment.

The story opens with the triumphant progress toward Athens of Theseus with Hippolyta and her sister Emelye, after the conquest of Scythia. Then are rapidly sketched the desolating of Thebes and Creon's winning of neighboring peoples to dwell in that city. Of these was the beautiful Anelida, Queen of Armenia. She was courted and won by the treacherous Theban, Arcite, to whom she became wholly devoted. Wearying of her, Arcite turned to another lady; to cover his treason, he accused Anelida of faithlessness. Though his new lady was very 'dangerous,' he was most subject to her. So the situation affords example of man's dissatisfaction with love he may have, and his desire for what is withheld. At first overwhelmed with grief, Anelida wrote her complaint and sent it to Arcite. After the quotation of the complaint, a stanza tells that Anelida vowed prayer to Mars in his temple, and promises to describe the building of the temple.

Effort to connect the poem with a contemporary love-affair, has proved unsuccessful. The Complaint proper (ll. 211-350) has been declared to be an exercise in difficult verse-forms, an elaboration of the *Compleint to his Lady;* and the 'story' frame has been said to be a later addition. The Proem ends (l. 21), 'First folow I Stace, and after him Corinne.' Perhaps 'Corinne' is but an invention of Chaucer. It has been urged recently that the Complaint proper is from Ovid's *Heroides;* that 'Corinne' is from Ovid's mistress, Corinna, addressed in the *Amores;* and that Chaucer's copy of Ovid contained, first, the *Amores* styled *Corinna,* and, next after it, the *Heroides*— whence a confusion of titles.

The character of Arcite is that of the false tercelet in the *Squire's Tale* Part II; Anelida is like the falcon in the same piece. The *Teseide* is source of stanzas 1-3, 8-10, of *Anelida,* of sixteen stanzas of the *Parlement,* of the *Knight's Tale,* and of the *Troilus* V 1807-1827. The promise at the end of *Anelida* is fulfilled in the building of the temple in the *Knight's Tale.* Hence, it is argued that all these pieces were written at about the same time—*i.e.,* 1380-1385 (see pages 620, 692).

The poem is pleasing. The fact that it is incomplete, prevents satisfactory judgment of the story. The Complaint proper is perhaps Chaucer's most successful lyrical effort, because of the graceful and melodious handling of the difficult metrical form, and because of the sustained pathos and the impression of sincerity achieved through what is largely a conventional type.

A BALADE OF COMPLEYNT [8], in the Shirley MS. Additional 16165, was claimed for Chaucer by Skeat in 1888, but was later given up by him. It has never received any considerable acceptance as authentic. It consists of three stanzas ababbcc. The poet declares his subjection to his lady, and his fidelity to her; he begs that she will accept his ditty, and will not let him remain too long in his plight.

THE BOOK OF THE DUCHESSE [9] is so styled in two (Fairfax 16, Bodley 638) of its three (third is Tanner 346) MSS., none of which ascribes it to Chaucer. But Chaucer claims 'the Deeth of Blaunche the Duchesse' in the Prologue

of the *Legend* (see page 619); line 948 says of the heroine,
'gode fayre Whyte she hete'; Lydgate (see page 621) ascribes
to Chaucer 'the death also of Blaunche the Duches'; the MSS.
of the *Book* contain other pieces by Chaucer; and the contents
and the style accord with the known tests (see page 618) of
Chaucer's work.

That the dream in the poem is an allegory, is hinted (ll. 278-
90). The name 'Whyte' (l. 948) shows the heroine to be
Blanche. That the husband was John of Gaunt, Duke of Lancaster and Earl of Richmond, is suggested by the *'long castel
with walles whyte . . . on a riche hil'* (Richemounde) of lines
1318-19, to which at the end of the poem the King (? Edward
III, complimentarily styled 'th' emperour Octovien' at l. 368)
retires with his hunters. Blanche, wife of John of Gaunt,
Chaucer's steady patron through his mature years, died September 12, 1369, both she and her husband being then twenty-
nine years of age. In line 455 the black knight is said to be
twenty-four years old, a discrepancy due perhaps to intention
to confuse, or perhaps to desire not to be too exact, or perhaps
to a scribal error of V for X in XXIX. As the point of the
poem consists in exhibition of the black knight as inconsolable,
and as such exhibition could have been little acceptable to John
after his second marriage in 1372, the piece must have been written soon after the death of Blanche—probably at the end of
1369. The fact that its date can be so closely reckoned, makes
the poem of great importance as basis for determining the chronology of Chaucer's other works.

The *Book* is in short couplets, often with initial truncation,
often with feminine ending—a measure that was employed elsewhere by Chaucer in the *Fame*, and that occurs in part of the
Glasgow *Romaunt*. The black knight recites two lyrics, one
(ll. 475-86) of tetrameter verses aabbaccdccd, the other (ll.
1175-80) of six similar verses aabbaa.

The poem consists chiefly of a dream (ll. 291-1323) enveloped
in a story of the poet's experience (ll. 1-290, 1324-34). The poet
has been long oppressed with insomnia and melancholy, the culminating effects of a love-sickness from which he has suffered 'this
eight yere' and for which 'ther is phisicien but oon.' Wakeful one

night, he reads in 'a romaunce' (evidently Ovid's *Metamorphoses*) the story of Ceyx and Halcyone. Wonderstruck at what he learns therein of gods able to bring sleep, he cries out of the gifts he would bestow on Morpheus and Juno for exercise of their power on him. Immediately he falls into a slumber, in which he has the dream that gives the poem its title.

The poet dreams that he was awakened by the joyous song of birds, to find himself in a splendid sunny chamber, whose walls were covered with paintings of the story of Troy, of various mythological personages, and 'bothe text and glose of al the Rómaunce of the Rose.' He joined a hunting party in the train of the Emperor Octovien, and ultimately was led by a whelp into a wood. There he came upon a man in black greatly dejected, and heard·him repeat a lament for loss of his lady. He addressed the knight, who at great length told of his grief, inveighed again Fortune who had bereft him of his lady, described the beauty and the worth of his beloved, recounted the details of their courtship, and finally, in response to question, declared she was dead. Hereupon the hunting-party appeared, giving up the chase, and riding back to a long castle with white walls on a rich hill. A bell in the castle struck twelve.—And the poet awakes in his bed, his hand still holding the book of the story of Ceyx and Halcyone.

The verses on the poet's love-sickness, with the *Pite* ·(see page 638), have been taken to indicate an actual protracted, unsuccessful love affair of Chaucer. The passages are now generally regarded as merely conventional (see page 610). The theme and the extent of the narrative of Ceyx and Halcyone (ll. 62-220) have led to assumption that the verses are survivors (perhaps in modified form) of the perhaps originally independent poem 'of Ceys and Alcion' that the Man of Law's headlink assigns to Chaucer's youth (see page 618). Skeat felt ·that lines 215-20, in which the poet breaks off without relating the lovers' transformation into halcyons, give a hint at suppression of part of the original piece.

The whole framework of the lovelorn poet, the sleeplessness and the dream, and most of the details of the piece, with the pictures on the walls of the chamber, are from the *Roman de la Rose* and the works that begot it and were influenced by it. Kittredge has shown that probably much of the plan,, and certainly a great many details, of the *Book*, are due to Guillaume de Machaut's *Le Jugement dou Roy de Behaingne*, and much detail to Machaut's *Remède de Fortune, Lay de Confort*, and

Motets. Some resemblances between the *Duchesse* and the fourteenth-century French love-poem *Le Songe Vert,* have been pointed out. Ten Brink showed that for the story of Ceyx and Halcyone Chaucer drew on Ovid's *Metamorphoses* XII 410-748 and Machaut's *Dit de la Fontaine Amoureuse.* Froissart's *Paradys d'Amours,* long regarded as influenced by the *Duchesse,* is now accepted as a source for the English poem; it probably afforded the much-discussed name *Eclympasteyre* (1. 167).

The *Duchesse* is the earliest original longer poem of Chaucer, and the piece from which one must measure the poet's development. Scholars have pointed out that it is often irregular in metre; is overburdened with accessories; lacks unity and proportion in its proem (most of which is a complete story practically independent of the rest of the poem), in its diffuseness of style, and in the tediousness of the knight's speeches; shows poor taste in its artificiality and conceits, and in the knight's unjustified exhibitions of learning and his pedantic explanations; is everywhere dependent on well-worn conventions; and has many other deficiencies. Yet one must remember the relative position of the poem in the history of English literature, and as well in the development of Chaucer's art. Whatever be its defects, it stands well as compared with earlier Middle English poems. It is graceful in manner and in effect, and has many charming passages. Much of the description (as of the conditions to which the poet awakes on the May morning, and of the beauties of body and spirit of the lady) has been commended highly. One must not pass over the dramatic effect of the interview with the black knight and its abrupt conclusion, or the spirited give and take of the dialogue with which the narrative of the knight is relieved. Some of the qualities of the knight's speeches are appropriate to his supposed state of mind. Dependent as he is on the school of the *Roman,* Chaucer gave his personages and his setting a reality little met with in the work of that school.

CHAUCER'S WORDS UNTO ADAM [10] is in MS. Trinity College Cbg. R, 3, 20, where Shirley heads it 'Chauciers wordes. a. Geffrey vn-to Adame his owen scryveyne.' A late copy is in MS. Cbg. Univ. Libr. Gg IV 27. This single stanza of rime-royal declares with comic seriousness the poet's labors in correcting the errors due to carelessness and haste of 'Adam scriveyn,' and wishes him the scab if, should it become his duty to copy 'Boece or Troilus,' he copy not true to the author's making. The stanza is generally dated shortly after Chaucer's *Boethius* and *Troilus*.

THE COMPLEYNT OF MARS [11], preserved in seven MSS., is ascribed to Chaucer by Shirley. Through its heading in Harley 7333 (also originally in the first copy in Pepys 2006, see page 622), and through the passage on the brooch of Thebes (ll. 245-71), it has been identified with the complaint 'of the broche which that Vulcanus at Thebes wrought' ascribed to Chaucer by Lydgate (see page 621). With exception of two and a half lines (13-15), the poem is supposed to be sung by a bird.

It opens with a proem of four rime-royal stanzas sung in the early morning of St. Valentine's Day. The bird bids its fellows rejoice, and warns lovers to part if they would escape detection through the light of Phœbus; then it urges each bird to take its mate in accord with the festival, and declares that in honor of the feast it will recite the complaint of Mars separated from Venus by the Sun.—Next follow eighteen rime-royal stanzas in which, through a mingling of mythology and elaborate astronomical lore, the bird tells of the subjection of Mars to Venus; of their union, of Phœbus' coming upon their chamber, of the flight of Venus to escape detection and of her reception into the tower of Cyllenius or Mercury, of Mars' vain efforts toward reunion with the goddess.—Then it recites the complaint of Mars: this consists of sixteen stanzas aabaabbcc of pentameter lines, that fall into six groups— a proem of one stanza, and five sets of three stanzas each. The complaint is a declaration of devotion to his love, a description of a lady in fear and woe, a declaration of the instability of happiness, the story of the brooch of Thebes, and an appeal for sympathy.

Whatever be its actual significance, the piece is in glorification of illicit love. At the head of the poem in MS. Trinity, Shirley states that it was made at command of John of Gaunt; and at the end he records that 'some men sayne' that it was made with respect to 'my lady of York, doughter to the kyng of Spaygne, and my lord of Huntyngdoun, some tyme duc of

Excestre.' This lady was Isabel, sister-in-law of John of
Gaunt, who was 'somewhat wanton in her younger years' but
repented late in life; and the Lord Huntingdon was John
Holande, half-brother of Richard II. It has been suggested
that the passage on the brooch of Thebes is perhaps in allusion
to a "Tablet of Jasper which the King of Armonie gave her,'
bequeathed to John of Gaunt by Isabel in a will dated December
6, 1382. As Isabel arrived in England in 1372, it has been
conjectured that the piece was written soon after that date,
perhaps in 1374. The poem is remarkable for the astronomical details that it presents. Students have ascertained that
Mars and Venus were in conjunction on April 14, 1379.
Though Chaucer seems to point to April 12 as the date of conjunction, this has been used to date the piece 1379 or 1380.
So, on the basis of Shirley's statements and the astronomical
data, along with a linking of the opening lines with the *Parlement of Foules*, the poem has been questionably assigned variously to 1374, 1377-1379, 1379, 1380. On the other hand,
the *Mars* has been styled 'only a *jeu d'esprit* in versified
astrology.' Certainly, if Shirley's interpretation be correct,
the poem puts neither John of Gaunt nor Chaucer in an enviable
position. As a Valentine's Day poem it should be connected
with the *Parlement*.

THE COMPLEYNT OF VENUS [12] occurs in seven
MSS., usually in connection with the *Mars*, but separately in
MSS. Ashmole 59 and Cbg. Univ. Libr. Ff I 6. Shirley attributes it to Chaucer in Ashmole and Trinity. It consists of three
balades each of three stanzas ababbccb with identity of rime-
sounds and repetition of the last line between stanzas in each
balade, and a final envoy aabaabbaab. The pieces are conventional treatments of conventional love-themes, one on the
worthiness of the lover, the second on disquietude from jealousy, the last on satisfaction in constancy. The verses are
not a complaint, and are not spoken by Venus. They are a
rather free version of three *balades* of Sir Otes de Graunson of
Savoy, whose 'curiositee' Chaucer says in his envoy he has
sought 'to folowe word by word.' The chief merit of the piece

is the reproducing of the complex rime-order of the French. Association in the MSS. with the *Mars*, has led to suggestion that the Venus addressed as 'Princess' in the envoy is Isabel of Spain, the Venus of the *Mars*. .Were this accepted, the poem would be dated before Isabel's death in 1394. The poet's complaint of his age in the envoy has led to dating after 1390.

A COMPLEINT TO HIS LADY [13] or BALADE OF PITY, is in MSS. Harley 78 and Additional 34360. In Harley, Shirley copied it right after the *Pite* (see page 622) with only a dividing line between the two, and the pages throughout are headed 'The Balade of Pytee. By Chauciers.' Apparently the piece is merely a set of experiments in verse-forms— four conventional laments of unsuccessful love. All are in pentamèter verses—the first, two rime-royal stanzas; the fourth, nine stanzas aabaabcddc; the second and third, respectively ten and nineteen lines of *terza rima*. These sections of *terza rima* exhibit apparently the only uses of this form in English before Wyatt and Surrey. As they were written obviously under influence of Dante, they date after Chaucer's visit to Italy in 1373.

THE COMPLEINT TO HIS PURS [14], in seven MSS., is ascribed to Chaucer by MS. Harley 7333 and three other MSS. It is a pleasing bit of humorous application of conventional love-phrasing, not to a lady, but to an empty purse. It occurs in three forms: three rime-royal stanzas with like rime-sounds and final refrain line, followed by an envoy aabba; the three stanzas without the envoy; and the three stanzas without the envoy and with a set of rime-royal stanzas on imprisonment. There is a general impression that the envoy is Chaucer's latest composition, and was added to the stanzas, which are of earlier date. This notion is supported by a statement in Harley 7333 that the poem is 'A supplicacion to Kyng Richard by Chaucier.' The phrasing of line 23 shows that the piece is directed to Henry IV, who was formally acknowledged King by Parliament, September 30, 1399. As Chaucer was granted an additional pension October 13, 1399, the envoy would appear to have been written for presentation between September 30 and October 12—preferably the earliest of these days. Machaut addressed a similar appeal to John II in 1351-1356. A closer prototype is Dechamps' similar *balade* with a somewhat similar refrain, composed in 1381 for presentation to Charles VI on his accession, and made up of three rime-royal stanzas and an envoy of six lines. It is a plausible assumption that 'this toune' (l. 17) is Greenwich (see page 615). In December, 1399, Chaucer again leased a house in London.

THE COMPLEYNT UNTO PITE [15], in nine MSS., comprises 119 lines of rime-royal (perhaps the first use of this stanza in English) consisting of one stanza of proem, seven stanzas of narrative, and nine stanzas of complaint. Shirley's attribution of the poem to Chaucer in MS. Harley 78, is confirmed by internal evidence.

> After years of suffering, the poet ran to Pity to ask vengeance on Cruelty of Love. Though, strangely, none but he knew her to be dead, he found Pity buried in a heart, with Bounty, Beauty, Lust, Jollity, and all their associates standing about the bier unitedly unsympathetic to him. So he did not present his bill of complaint. But he now quotes it: addressing himself to Pity, he complains that, 'under color of womanly Beauty,' Cruelty displaced Pity; he urges Pity to claim her own, and to extend mercy to him, who without such relief must suffer till death.

The piece imitates the conventional French love poetry. Very possibly it is but a translation. Skeat suggested a parallel between the struggle of Pity and Cruelty and that of Pietas and Tisiphone in Statius; but the matter was not uncommon. Possibly the piece is somewhat autobiographical; but more probably it is chiefly or wholly conventional, as is the passage on the poet's eight-year love-sickness in the *Duchesse* (see page 633). Beyond the form and the content, which would point to youthful composition, evidence for dating the poem is lacking. Scholars assign it to various dates from 1367 to 1373.

THE FORMER AGE [16] or THE GOLDEN AGE is attributed to Chaucer in both its MSS., Cbg. Univ. Libr. Ii III

21 and Hh IV 12. Koch grouped the poem with *Fortune,
Truth, Gentilesse,* and *Lak of Stedfastnesse,* as one of a cycle
of free translations from Boethius. The group has been dated
variously between 1380 and 1394-1398. It consists of 64 lines
in the 'Monk's Tale stanza' (see page 600). As MS. Ii notes,
it is based on Boethius' *De Consolatione* Bk II metre 5. But
only about 20 lines are directly from Boethius, the rest being
Chaucer's own, with probable influence of the *Metamorphoses*
I 89-112 and the *Roman de la Rose* 8395-492. The piece
is a graceful and pleasing glorification of the Golden Age as
free from all the distress and baseness and strife of the poet's
day. Its late printing in 1866 was no slight addition to the
Chaucer canon.

FORTUNE [17] is attributed to Chaucer in four of its ten
MSS., and by Shirley in two (Ashmole 59, Trinity Cbg. R, 3,
20) of them. It comprises three *balades* (each of three stanzas
ababbcbc with rime-sounds, rime-arrangement, and final verses,
identical), and an envoy ababbab. The first *balade* is a complaint against Fortune; the second, an answer to the first. The
first stanza of the third *balade* is another complaint, and the
second and third stanzas are an answer to this. The envoy is
Fortune's appeal to 'Princes,' after the conventional form,
asking aid for the poet. The material reflects directly the
teachings of Boethius, but seems to be based on no particular
passage. Parallels in idea may be found in the *Consolation*
II prose 1-5, 8, and metre 1; probably some suggestions came
through the *Roman de la Rose,* whose lines 4853-994 the poet
certainly knew. But, however much Chaucer's philosophy was
due to the *Consolation,* the piece is no mere echoing of Boethius.
The powerful verse masterfully handled, is the utterance of a
noble emotion to whose experience the fickleness and the might
of Fortune are familiar, but which they cannot control; the
poet is master of his fate, and is able to wring from the blows
of Fortune goods that cannot fail. The poem offers no direct
hints for dating. Suggestion has been made that it would fit
well with Chaucer's supposed ill-fortune in 1386. Koch has
connected it with *Former Age, Lak of Stedfastnesse, Gentilesse,*

and *Truth*, in a Boethius cycle; the five poems have been dated as early as 1380 and as late as 1394-1398.

GENTILESSE [18] or TRUE NOBILITY, preserved in seven MSS. independently, is quoted as Chaucer's in a poem by Henry Scogan (see page 642) in MS. Ashmole 59. It is ascribed to Chaucer by Shirley in MSS. Ashmole 59 and Trinity Cbg. R, 3, 20, and by MS. Harley 7333. It is a *balade* of three stanzas ababbcc, with identity of rime-sounds and final line from stanza to stanza. Like the other four of the 'Boethius cycle' (*Truth, Lak of Stedfastnesse, Fortune,* and *Former Age*) the poem is a product of the philosophy of Boethius, here particularly as found in Bk. III prose 6; and it was influenced by the *Roman* lines 18807 ff. As have those other poems, it has been dated variously between 1380 and 1394-1398. The noble lines declare a conviction more rare in Chaucer's day than in our time, that the source of true nobility is virtue (cp. *Wife's Tale* D1109, and *Franklin's Tale*): 'Vertu to sewe and vyces for to flee' is the only means to beget nobility, and none can inherit it.

LAK OF STEDFASTNESSE [19], in some nine MSS., is ascribed to Chaucer by Shirley in MS. Trinity Cbg. R, 3, 20. It is a *balade* of three rime-royal stanzas with the last line of each as a refrain, with an envoy to 'King Richard' in the same stanza-form, and with all four stanzas on the same rime-sounds. MS. Harley 7333 (under Shirley's influence) asserts that the piece was sent to 'kynge Richarde the secounde þane being in his Castell of Windesore,' and Shirley's MS. Trinity says it was made by Chaucer 'in hees laste yeeres.' Consequently, scholars have generally dated the piece between 1393 and 1399, during which period Richard was steadily degenerating. Some preference has been shown for 1397 or 1398. Suggestion has been made that a date—say 1389—when the young King was first undertaking his duties, would be the only time at which one who depended on royal favor would have wisely ventured to send the piece to the King. Influence of the philosophy of Boethius is evident, but direct indebtedness to the *Consolation* has not been shown. In the poem, Chaucer, who is notable for unwillingness to spurn at the times, speaks out emphatically of the evils of the age, and bids the King desire to be honorable, to cherish the folk, to hate extortion, to permit no ill in the realm, to dread God, to practice the law, to love truth and worthiness, and to wed his people again to steadfastness.

LENVOY DE CHAUCER À BUKTON [20], ascribed to Chaucer in its only MS., Fairfax 16, consists of four stanzas ababbcbc, the last an envoy. To Bukton, whom he has promised counsel regarding marriage, the poet gives familiar, humorous advice warning of the well-known perils of the bond—though 'Bet is to wedde, than brenne in worse wyse.' Let Bukton read the Wife of Bath on the subject, and may God grant him to live in freedom. The matter on marriage carries on the 'sovereignty theme' of the *Canterbury Tales*. It has been shown that lines 13-16 are paralleled in *Polycraticus* VIII 11 by John of Salisbury just after he has quoted some of Chaucer's favorite passages from Jerome and Theophrastus that were used in the Marriage Group (see pages 686, 719, 722, 731, 736, 744). The general tone of the piece, the mention of the Wife's Prologue, and the possible hint in line 8 that, when writing, the poet was a widower, all suggest a late date. Study of the procedure of Deschamps in his utterances concerning marriage, and recognition of the conventional attitude of contemporary writers toward the subject, suggest that one be careful in attributing autobiographical significance to the envoy or to any other part of the piece. The allusion in line 23 to the dangers of capture in Friesland, is perhaps to be connected with the participation of some Englishmen in an expedition against that country begun August, 1396, and ended at about October. Lowes has argued that line 23 would have little or no point after the expedition; he dates the Wife's Prologue 1393 or early 1394. Tyrwhitt identified Bukton as Peter de Buketon, King's escheator for the county of York in 1397. Tatlock prefers Robert Bukton, esquire to the Queen in 1391, 1393, 1394, and holder of various offices thereafter;

and .shows that Robert wedded Anne, noblewoman, of the diocese of Norwich, between October, 1396, and January, 1397.

LENVOY DE CHAUCER À SCOGAN [21] is attributed to Chaucer in all three of its MSS., Cbg. Univ. Libr. Gg IV 27, Fairfax 16, Pepys 2006. The Scogan addressed is supposed to be Henry Scogan, who was a tutor to the two sons of Henry IV, and who, in his *Moral Balade* to the princes, quoted bodily Chaucer's *Gentilesse* and styled the poet 'my maistre.' The first fourteen lines culminating in mention of 'this deluge of pestilence,' are taken as concerned with the terrible storms of September, 1393. Mention of Michaelmas (l. 19) suggests that the piece was written toward the end of the year. The hint of Chaucer's dwelling at Greenwich (ll. 45-46), to which he was probably called by his commission of 1390 to repair the banks of the river, fits in well with this date, as do also the poet's allusions (ll. 27-42) to his age. All the MSS. have notes explaining 'the stremes heed' (l. 43) as Windsor, and 'thende of which streme' as Greenwich.

The poem consists of seven rime-royal stanzas, the last an envoy. Chaucer playfully chides Scogan for quickly giving up his lady when he found she would not favor him; all the country is flooded with Venus' tears because of his faithlessness. Love will make vain the devotion of all men who, like Scogan and the poet, are 'hore and rounde of shape.' The envoy asks Scogan to use his influence for the poet's advancement. The request may have contributed to the granting of Chaucer's pension of 1394. The figure of the muse rusting (ll. 38-40) is probably due to the prefaces to Alanus de Insulis' *Anticlaudianus*. Moore suggests that the poet's muse was rusting just before the activity that resulted in the Marriage Group of the *Canterbury Tales* (see page 684; Index).

MERCILES BEAUTE [22], in MS. Pepys 2006 with much Chaucerian work, is a triple *roundel* comprising 39 verses, composed, conjectures Koch, at about the time of the *Parlement* and *Troilus*. The MS. does not assign the poem to Chaucer, but the manner is his. Lowes has practically established the authorship in showing that the poem is 'an adaptation, now close, now with a masterly freedom of hand,' of two poems of Deschamps, one a *rondeau*, and one a *virelay* that in its MS. follows two *balades* of the *marguerite* group (see page 668), one of which Chaucer may have known. Deschamps' message and request to Chaucer (see page 669) show that the latter knew some of the French poet's pieces under conditions suggesting turning some of them into English. Other English contemporaries seem not to have known Deschamps' work. In the first two parts Chaucer sings with great skill the conventional lover's distress; in the last part he turns the whole into a joke.

THE PARLEMENT OF FOULES [23] or PARLEMENT OF BRIDDES is in fourteen MSS. that fall into two groups styled by Miss Hammond A and C. It is included in the lists of pieces by Chaucer in the Prologue to the *Legend* A407, in the 'Retraction,' and in Lydgate's prologue to the *Falls of Princes*. It consists of 699 pentameter lines, all rime-royal except a thirteen-line *roundel* (ll. 680-92). Root has urged that the divergences of the A group of MSS. indicate revision by Chaucer up to line 250. The piece is of the dream-vision type illustrated in the *Duchesse*, and prominent in the *Roman de la Rose* and numerous other mediæval French writings. Like the *Duchesse*, the poem consists of a proem, a 'story,' and a conclusion.

After four stanzas of introduction, the poet tells of reading 'Tullius of the dreme of Scipioun' (Cicero's *Somnium Scipionis,* a part of the *De Republica*) of which he gives a general epitome (ll. 32-84); then he relates how he fell asleep, and how Scipio appeared to him (ll. 85-112; ll. 99-105 are from Claudian). After an invocation to Cytherea (ll. 113-19), the poet begins the 'story' or dream proper (ll. 120-692). Scipio led him through a gate with an inscription modeled after that on the entrance to Hell in the *Divine Comedy* (ll. 120-68; other parallels to Dante are at ll. 85, 109, 169), into a park full of many varieties of trees (evidently influenced by the tree passages in the *Roman*) and containing a lovely garden in which multitudes of birds were singing and stringed instruments were making sweet accord (ll. 169-210). Here he came upon Cupid and his daughter Voluptas and all their train (ll. 211-29), and beheld a temple of brass dedicated to Venus, which he describes elaborately in a passage to be compared with the account of the temple to Venus in the *Knight's Tale* (ll. 230-94). Most of the description of the park and the temple (ll. 170-294) is from Boccaccio's *Teseide*.—Now follows the real subject of the poem, the matter of which is Chaucer's own. The poet turned back and beheld the Goddess Nature sitting on a flowered hillock, surrounded by birds of every kind assembled on this St. Valentine's Day to choose their mates. Many of the birds he enumerates, following with modification Alanus de Insulis' *De Planctu Naturæ*, as he indicates in line 316. With a lovely female formel eagle on her hand, Nature declared that the royal tercel eagles should be the first to choose; thereafter, according to their respective ranks, the other orders of birds should elect. Three tercel eagles successively pleaded suit for the formel eagle, but with little demonstration of superiority of any one of them. The other orders cried out at the delay, the goose finally protesting for the water-fowl, the cuckoo for the worm-fowl, and the turtle for the seed-fowl (ll. 414-518). Nature quieted the tumult by bidding the kinds to select representatives who should choose the mate for the formel eagle. But the electors could not agree (ll. 519-616). Nature declared that the formel eagle should choose for herself, at her request granted her a year for consideration, and gave each of the birds its mate (ll. 617-72). All united in singing a graceful *roundel* in glorification of Nature and the season for mating (ll. 673-92). When the song was done, the cries of the birds awakened the poet. At once he fell to his books;—on them he pores always, in hope of again having such another dream (ll. 693-99).

The poem is generally accepted as a courtly compliment to Richard II and his Queen. The female eagle is taken to be Anne, who was daughter of the Emperor Charles IV and sister of King Wenceslaus of Bohemia. The birds of prey are taken to represent the nobles, the worm-fowl the *bourgeois*, the water-fowl the mercantile class, and the seed-fowl the agricultural interests. Anne was wedded to Richard on January 14, 1382. The year for consideration is regarded as symbolizing the year or more of negotiations between Richard and Wenceslaus for the union. The three tercel eagles were long accepted as Guillaume de Bavière, betrothed to Anne in 1371; Friedrich of Meissen, betrothed to her in 1373; and Richard, who became her suitor in 1380. But recently Emerson has offered excellent evidence to show that they were, rather, respectively Richard, Friedrich, and Charles VI of France. Charles was a suitor for Anne in 1379-1380. The reference to the planet

Venus as in the north-northwest (l. 117), is said to suit the early summer and the astronomical conditions of 1380 and 1382. This has been taken to indicate not only that the wooing before Nature in the poem took place in the summer of 1380, but that the poem was itself begun at that date. As the negotiations for the marriage of Richard and Anne were inaugurated in 1380, as Anne was expected in England in October, 1381, as the year for consideration is mentioned, and as the poem does not refer to the marriage or actual betrothal, it is held probable that the *Parlement* was completed in 1381. Apparently the *Palamon* was written at about this time (see pages 623 ff., 692), with materials from the *Teseide*. It has been suggested that, finding some of the *Teseide* not desirable for the *Palamon*, Chaucer utilized it for lines 176-294 of the *Parlement;* but it has been argued that the *Palamon* is of 1381 or the first of 1382. Suggestion has been made that the closing lines of the poem are a hint to Richard for farther favors.

But recently, in face of all this, Manly has urged that the astronomical allusion fits 1374, 1382, or 1390; and that, if the *Parlement* is a compliment, it is a poor one to either Richard or Anne—for it stresses the lady's uncertainty and leaves her still undecided. He urges that the poem is a conventional love-vision, in which the central situation is a *demande d'amours* or love discussion or debate (the problem, as often in such situations, being of three branches) presented before a parliament of birds presided over by a representative of the god or the goddess of Love (in this case Dame Nature). For all of the features he finds conventional parallels. The ancient popular cult of St. Valentine was taken up by the courtly poets after 1350 or 1375. The *Mars* (see page 635) is a Valentine poem. Manly holds that the *Parlement* is a Valentine poem written perhaps for a *court amoureuse* such as was instituted at Paris on Valentine's Day, 1400, that it finds its sufficient explanation in this fact, and that it is unnecessary to look for an historical situation to give rise to the poem or to be shadowed in it. Emerson has strongly opposed the arguments of Manly.

The *Parlement* is of much interest as showing the poet under the French influence of his youth, and as well the Italian influence of his so-called second period. It exhibits the tendency to disproportion of treatment and lack of unity, that appears in much of Chaucer's work, especially that of his earlier years. There is the same difficulty in getting to his story. There is the same obsession of working in material from reading: the epitome of Cicero is extraneous, the elaborate description of the garden, though pleasing, is unnecessary. But having once got over these elements, Chaucer tells a story that, in its machinery and execution, is admirable. Remote as may appear the pleadings of the wooers, the poet presents the behavior of the lower birds with a consistency, with a dramatic realism, that he first prepared for in the *Duchesse* and maintained and developed through his greater pieces, and with a humor that is one of his most familiar qualities. In these latter respects the poem prepares for the *Nun's Priest's Tale.*

THE PROVERBS [24] are ascribed to Chaucer by MSS. Fairfax 16 and Harley 7578. But, since Shirley does not assign them to him in the other MS., Additional 16165, some scholars have doubted Chaucer's authorship. Each proverb is four four-stress lines abab, the first two lines presenting a question or objection, the last two an answer. Correspondence of lines 7-8 with *Melibeus* l. 2405, has led some to date the stanzas near that tale.

TO ROSEMOUNDE [25] is on a fly-leaf next after the end of the *Troilus* in MS. Rawlinson Poetry 163. The poem is followed by 'Tregentil' and 'Chaucer,' *Troilus* by 'Tregentyll' and 'Chaucer.' The piece is widely accepted as authentic. It is a *balade* in three stanzas ababbcbc, with the same rime-sounds, and with the final line as refrain, repeated from stanza to stanza. As it partakes of the seriousness, the humor, and the irony of the *Troilus*, next to which it stands in the MS., it has been dated between 1380 and 1385. Line 20 appears to be from Froissart.—The poet is overcome with the beauty of the lady; yet her dancing and her voice are as balm to his

wounds. Never was pike so smothered in dressing as he is
immersed and wounded in love—he is truly Tristram the
second, he is ever her thrall, though she will give him no favor.

TRUTH [26], in some sixteen MSS., is declared to be
Chaucer's by Shirley in both his copies in MS. Trinity R, 3,
20. One of these copies styles it 'Balade that Chaucier made
on his deeth bedde.' This assertion is not generally accepted
as true to fact; but it is held that the poem was written late.
The *balade* consists of three rime-royal stanzas and an envoy,
each with the rime-sounds of the others, the last line of each
being a refrain. The envoy occurs only in MS. Additional
10340. By some it has been held to be spurious; but recently
it has been declared that Shirley's omission of the envoy shows
that he knew little about the poem.

The piece has been praised highly; not, however, without
dissent. It is based on the philosophy of Boethius, and is
grouped with *Gentilesse* and the three other short Boethius
pieces (see page 639).—Flee from the crowd, it bids; be content with what thou hast, strive not as does the crock against
the wall; strike not back at the world; here is not thy home—
know thy country, look up, hold the high way, follow thy soul,
and Truth shall surely set thee free.

Recently Miss Rickert has shown that the difficult address
'Thou Vache' in the envoy, may be directed to Sir Philip la
Vache or de la Vache, who married Elizabeth, daughter of
Chaucer's friend, Sir Lewis Clifford (see page 669); and she
has urged that the details of *Truth* are all applicable to incidents in the life of Sir Philip. Consequently, she dates the poem
1386-1390.

WOMANLY NOBLESSE [27] is headed 'Balade that
Chauncier made' in its MS. Additional 34360 that was written
perhaps under influence of a Shirley MS. Scholars differ as
to its authenticity. Skeat printed it first in 1894. It consists of three stanzas aabaabbab, the same rimes being used
from stanza to stanza. It ends with an envoy acacaa. It is
a very pleasing effort at expression of conventional love-matter

in a difficult form.—The poet is the captive of the lady's virtues and beauty, he will ever be true; will she not alleviate his
distress with some favor?

IV.　'The Romaunt of the Rose'

THE ROMAUNT OF THE ROSE [28], an English translation of about a third (ll. 1-5169, 10716-12564) of the
Roman de la Rose, consists of 7698 lines of short couplets
preserved only in MS. V, 3, 7 in the Hunterian Museum,
Glasgow.

The *Roman de la Rose,* a dream-vision allegory, is the work
of two poets quite unlike in personal character and ideal.
Guillaume de Lorris, born about 1200, originated the general
plan of the poem, and, probably between 1225 and 1230, composed the first 4067 lines of it in the short couplet. Guillaume
was an idealist, quiet and gentle of nature, noble in purpose,
fully in accord with the spirit of Chivalry—a lover of beauty,
a worshipper of woman as almost divine. His poem is an *ars
amandi,* a story of love—a dream on a May morning of wandering in the flower-decked fields among the singing birds, of a
splendid garden of Love full of birds and trees and flowers, of
the Fountain of Narcissus, of the lovely rose-tree whence he
would pluck the bud that symbolizes his lady, and of the many
abstract elements of courtly love and conduct and their opposites personified as actors in the story. Jean de Meun, probably between 1268 and 1277, took up the story where Guillaume
left off, and carried it to the length of 22047 verses. He
adopted Guillaume's theme of the quest of the Rose, his
machinery, and his verse-form. But these are to Jean but a
vehicle for the conveyance of a varied body of ideas with
which he was full. For the gentle loveliness, the reverential and
devoted aspiration and faith, of Guillaume's lines, Jean's continuation exhibits domination of intellect. It is rational and
logical; its language is direct and forceful. Jean is fond of
irrelevant, extended excursions on philosophical and theological
themes. He is a satirist, nothing of the devotee. Woman and

the clergy he makes objects of bitter attacks. The *Roman ⟩* contained little that was new; its authors merely wove into admirable verse ideas and elements of form that they had found common. This, with the twofold character of the work, gave the poem a tremendous and widespread influence during at least two centuries after it appeared. Chaucer mastered thoroughly all parts of it. In his poems up to his death its influence was potent—in the earlier pieces the influence was that of de Lorris, in the more mature work it was that of de Meun.

The God of Love in the Prologue to the *Legend* (A255, B329), rests his accusation of 'heresye ageyns my lawe' on the facts that Chaucer has 'translated the Romauns of the Rose' and has written also of the love of Troilus and Cressida. The 'Retraction' at the end of the *Parson's Tale* does not mention the translation. Lydgate (see page 621) says that Chaucer 'did his businesse' 'To translate the Romaynt of the Rose.' That Chaucer probably did not complete the translation, would appear from the facts that the original is very long; that Chaucer was ready to tire of an extended task, and to turn to more interesting work; and that, if he had translated the whole, the popularity of the *Roman* and of Chaucer himself would surely have caused the piece to be preserved. Yet the accusation of the God of Love would point to Chaucer's completion of translation of at least parts of Jean's addition (*i.e.*, those dealing with woman's faithlessness) that are not in the extant *Romaunt*.

That any of the extant translation is Chaucer's is doubtful. In 1870 Child pointed out that the rimes and the style vary from Chaucer's practice; that there is a break at verse 5814; and that thereafter the work improves. In 1874 and 1878 Skeat put the *Romaunt* among the doubtful pieces, a proceeding which Furnivall approved in 1878. From 1878 on Ten Brink rejected the poem. In 1880 Skeat argued against its authenticity because of its variation from Chaucer's practice in riming, its use of Northern forms, and the differences in its vocabulary from that of Chaucer. Cook and Fick offered some arguments against Skeat. In 1887 Lindner contended that the part after line 5810 is not by the author of lines 1-5809. In 1892 Lounsbury defended Chaucer's authorship of all the translation, and was answered by Kittredge. In 1893 Kaluza showed that the piece is really three fragments—A, lines 1-1705; B, lines 1706-5810; C, lines 5811 to end. Much discussion has followed; but Kaluza's division has been accepted. It is commonly recognized that, in rime, vocabulary, and dialect, A is not discordant with Chaucer's practice; that B is less close to the original, and contains most of the Northern forms and unusual rimes; and that C has but few of the un-Chaucerian rimes and expressions. It is generally agreed that B is not by Chaucer. Most critics accept A as his, and some accept C.

As Chaucer's translation is mentioned in both texts of the Prologue to the *Legend*, it was composed before 1386. That this Prologue connects the translation with the *Troilus*, is due probably to the heretical attitude toward woman's love adduced against both pieces, rather than to any closeness in dates of the two poems. The general feeling is that Chaucer's version of the *Roman* was made in his youthful period, before the *Duchesse*, and probably between 1360 and 1368.

V.   'Boethius,' and the 'Astrolabe'

THE TRANSLATION OF BOETHIUS *De Consolatione Philosophiæ* [29] is preserved in nine MSS., with a somewhat disguised version in a tenth. The 'Retraction' at the end of the *Parson's Tale* names a 'Translacion of Boece de Consolacione.' The Prologue to the *Legend* says that Chaucer 'hath in prose translated Boece.' *Chaucer's Words unto Adam* mentions 'Boece or Troilus.' Shirley's copy in MS. Additional 16165 ascribes the extant version to Chaucer.

Anicius Manlius Torquatus Severinus Boethius was born at Rome about A. D. 480, of a family that had held public office from before the beginning of the Christian era. Long a senator, he was made sole consul through the favor of Theodoric in 510. Boethius gave himself to study as well as to politics, and became the most learned man of his age. He sought to make accessible the whole range of Greek philosophy; despite his public duties, he actually succeeded in translating much of the Greek philosophers and adding comment thereon. Suspecting the Senate of treason, Theodoric made Boethius the scapegoat. After imprisonment, he was put to death in 524. While in prison, he wrote his greatest work, the *De Consolatione*, said to have had more influence in the Middle Ages than any other one book except the Bible. Its effect on English literature is observable from the beginnings. Alfred translated it. Oddly, despite the facts that the work is essentially pagan in thought, and that it offers a consolation not a matter of faith but of reason, its author was accounted among the saints. The work is a dialogue between the author in prison and the personification of Philosophy, who appears to him and seeks to console him in his distress. It is in five Books, each divided into Chapters that are alternately in prose and metre. The metres vary in kind. The prose passages present the arguments; the metrical parts are for ornament and recreation. Chaucer was greatly affected by the teachings of the book, his philosophy in all his later years being largely that of the *Consolation*. The list of passages in the English poet reminiscent of or directly owed to Boethius, is a long one; already the Boethius group of five minor poems has been mentioned (see page 639). The translation of the whole work is of interest chiefly because of this influence.

Chaucer made his version from the Latin, probably using a MS. with glosses—seemingly Trivet's Latin commentary, or matter from Trivet. Possibly he had access to the French translation associated with Jean de Meun. A fourteenth-century MS. containing all three of these works together, is in Paris (MS. Latin 18424). Attention has been called to the numerous and often gross blunders made in translating the Latin, and to the contrast between the fluent grace of Chaucer's verse and the common awkwardness of this prose; and regret has been expressed that the poet turned the metres of the *Consolation* into prose, instead of utilizing for them the power in verse that he showed in the *Former Age*, his rendering of the fifth metre of the second Book (see page 638).

Conjectural dates varying between the extremes 1373 and 1386, have been assigned to the translation. Mention in the Prologue to the *Legend*, dates it before 1386 at latest. Influence of Chaucer's visits to Italy would seem to have fostered the work. The prominence of the thought of the *Consolation* in the *Troilus*, has led to a feeling that the translation was made at about the date of that poem.

THE TREATISE ON THE ASTROLABE [30] is preserved in more than twenty MSS. There is said to be MS. authority for connecting it with that which Lydgate said (see pages 617, 620) Chaucer wrote 'to his sonne that called was Lowis.' In a charming, familiar prologue the author addresses 'Litel Lowis my sone,' who is of the 'tendre age of ten yeer'; and he tells that he has written for the boy this explanation of the Astrolabe in five parts. Of the five, but the first and a portion of the second have been preserved; perhaps the treatise is another of the works that Chaucer left unfinished. The piece has merit merely as a specimen of Chaucer's prose, as an excellent example of good exposition, and, through its prologue, as an illustration of the poet in the rôle of affectionate parent concerned for the progress of his child. Chaucer declares, 'I nam but a lewd compilatour of the labour of olde Astrologiens.' His source was the Latin *Compositio et Operatio Astrolabie* of Messahala, an Arabian astronomer of the end of the eighth century. The use twice (II 1.6; 3.18) of the 'yeer of oure lord 1391, the 12 day of March,' as an example for the reckonings, gives justification for assumption that at least the second part of the treatise was written on or soon after that date, which perhaps in present reckoning means March 12, 1392. Moore has shown that the calendar of Nicholas of Lynne mentioned in the prologue, was, as its preface states, composed in 1386 for use in 1387; and that so the prologue could not have been written before 1387. As the treatise directs that the calculations be made 'after the latitude of Oxenford,' it has been suggested that perhaps Lewis was at the time a student at Oxford. The facts that Lewis was ten years old at the date of the prologue, and that the abduction of Cecilia de Chaumpaigne occurred apparently early in 1380 (see page 613), have led to the venturesome suggestion that possibly Lewis was son of Cecilia.

VI.   'The Hous of Fame'

THE HOUS OF FAME [31] consists of 2158 lines in MSS. Fairfax 16 and Bodley 638, and of 1843 lines in MS. Pepys 2006. Apparently the poem was left unfinished as it stands in the two longer copies. These break off in the midst of a page, the former having the next three leaves, and the latter the next leaf, blank. The MSS. do not ascribe the poem to Chaucer. At line 729 the eagle addresses the poet as 'Geffrey.' The *Hous of Fame* is listed among Chaucer's works in the Prologue to the *Legend* (A405, B417). It is the 'Book of Fame' of the 'Retraction' (*Parson's Tale* 1086), and is possibly the 'Daunt in English' mentioned as Chaucer's in Lydgate's *Falls of Princes* (see page 621). Shirley's heading to the *Temple of Glass* in his MS. Additional 16165, shows that he knew the extant poem as the *Hous of Fame*. The poem is in short couplets, and is divided into three Books.

After an introductory discussion of dreams, followed by an invocation of Morpheus, the poet proceeds to tell of a wonderful dream that he had on the night of December 10th. He was in a temple of glass dedicated to Venus and adorned with representations of all the story of the *Æneid*. These he describes in an epitome of the *Æneid,* dwelling especially on the episode of Dido. But the beauty of the temple did not hold him; he declared that he knew not who made the images, nor where he was, nor in what country— he would go out and see if he could find anyone who would inform him. Issuing forth, he found himself in a desert waste. Fearful, he prayed for Christ's aid from 'fantom and illusioun.' Then he became aware of a golden eagle descending from close to the sun.—In Book II, after a short exhortation to attention, and an invocation of Venus and the Muses, the dream is continued. As the poet wondered at the eagle's beauty, the bird descended. It caught him in its claws, and bore him away. The eagle declared that, because of his unrewarded long studies and eager zeal to serve Love in verse, and because of his almost hermit-like life of isolation from happenings in the world, Jupiter had ordered it to bear him to the House of Fame, where he should have the recreation of hearing tidings of all sorts. It told that the house is situated between heaven and earth and sea, and that all sounds come thither; and it explained how this can be. High up in the air, it offered to tell him of the constellations; but the poet declined the favor. The eagle set his charge on the path to the House. In the House was a great rumbling, explained by the eagle as all the speeches of men, each of which comes thither and takes on the appearance of the person who has uttered it. The eagle bade the poet go forward, it would await his return.—Book III, properly the account of the House of Fame, opens with an invocation to Apollo. The poet climbed with difficulty to a castle built on a hill of ice whose southern side was engraved with names partly melted away by the heat of the sun, but whose northern side, despite the storms and the cold, preserved its names intact. In niches of the pinnacles were statues of famous minstrels and tellers of tales; in another place stood a throng of famous musicians; and in another, a host of celebrated jugglers and musicians. In a splendid hall, heralds cried out, and the poet beheld sitting in state the Lady Fame. The walls and floor of the hall were of gold graven with names; the pillars that lined the room were surmounted with statues of Statius, Homer, Dictys, Dares, Lollius (l. 1468, see page 664), Guido, Geoffrey of Monmouth, Virgil, Ovid, Lucan, and Claudian. The Lady waxed from less than a cubit's stature till she towered to the skies; she had a host of eyes and ears. She heard the petitions of nine companies of folk of varying merit, and rewarded them with complete arbitrariness, Æolus dismissing them with the trumpet of Fame or of Slander as she willed. A man to whom the poet declared that he came not for fame but for tidings, led the visitor to the House of Rumor or of Dædalus, sixty miles long, made of varicolored basket-work, its walls full of holes, and its many doors ever open. The house whirled rapidly round and round. The eagle bore the poet in through a window. The building was filled with people of all classes telling news, some of which flew out at the openings, often false news and true news flying conjoined. Each particle went direct to Lady Fame, who did with it as she pleased. The poet listened to the various stories. He stood looking at a crowd of people who were eagerly seeking to hear one in a corner tell tidings of love. At last he saw a man who seemed of great authority, but whom he will not name.—Here the poem breaks off.

The general notion of a House of Fame Chaucer owes to the *Metamorphoses* XII 39-63, a passage that the eagle refers to at line 712, characterizing the work as 'thyn owne book.' The details of this notion were developed carefully. Ovid afforded hints for a number of scattered passages. To Virgil the poem owes the epitome of the *Æneid* (I 140-467), and much of the description of Lady Fame (III). Chaucer drew also from Alanus de Insulis' *Anticlaudianus* (mentioned l. 986), his favorite *Somnium Scipionis* with the commentary of Macrobius, Boethius, Martianus Capella's *De Nuptiis Philologiæ et Mercurii*, Boccaccio's *Amorosa Visione*, and perhaps a short Latin piece in rimed leonine elegiacs on Troy ('Pergama flere volo'), and other works. The several efforts to trace suggestions for the poem to folklore, have made little headway. Until recently the slight parallels with the *Divine Comedy* have been overstressed, and the French influence has been underestimated. The *Hous* and the *Divine Comedy* have each three books, each preceded by an invocation. The invocation to Apollo in the *Hous* Book III imitates that in the *Paradiso* I 13 ff.; that to the Muses in Book II imitates the opening of the *Inferno* II. In each poem the poet finds himself in a great wilderness. Virgil and Beatrice act as guides and instructors to Dante; in the *Purgatorio* IX an eagle carries the poet upward. Some slight passages of the *Hous* follow Dante's sense and wording. But the poems are essentially different, and the *Hous* really owes little material to Dante. Chaucer's indebtedness is in the way of hints independently developed and thoroughly wrought into the work. He owes to Dante rather general culture and inspiration. One need not consider the notion of a parody of Dante in the *Hous*.—Miss Cipriani has shown that the great part of the prologue is due to the *Roman de la Rose*, and that the influence of that poem is very strong throughout the piece. Sypherd's and Fansler's studies confirm this. Sypherd has argued that, like the *Duchesse*, the *Parlement*, and the Prologue to the *Legend*, the *Hous* was written under the determining influence of the French love poetry.

The poet's purpose and the meaning of the poem, are matters of debate. Some scholars hold that, unlike Chaucer's other dream-visions, the poem was not written for an occasion or as an effort toward personal advancement. Others see in it an appeal for liberation from the drudgery of personal service at the Custom House (ll. 641 ff.). Some regard the man in authority (ll. 2155 ff.) as Richard II, who was to aid the poet in his difficulties. Some feel that the piece is not at all a love poem. Sypherd argues that it is written in honor of Love, after the French style illustrated in the *Roman* and Froissart's *Paradys d'Amours;* that in Book III Chaucer's effort at description of the abode of Fame caused enlargement and modification of his conception of Fame or Rumor that had been derived from classical sources, by making her presiding deity over earthly reputation, a function familiar in the goddesses of Love and Fortune; and that Chaucer returns to his original idea in the House of Tidings where he is to hear news of Love. Imelmann has argued that the *Hous* is a love poem, a bid for royal favor, being written to celebrate the approaching wedding of Richard and Anne, as the *Parlement* was composed in honor of their betrothal; that the eagle is Richard; and that the tidings sought are news of the actual relations between the royal pair. Mañly has argued that the poem is not allegorical, and has declared himself 'disposed to believe that the poem was intended to herald or announce a group of love stories and to serve as a sort of prologue to them.' So he would regard the *Hous* as the first of Chaucer's experiments in grouping stories, of which the *Legend* was a second, and the *Canterbury Tales* the successful final effort. Sypherd opposes this theory, and holds that the 'poem exists for the sake of the story of this wonderful journey to the house of tidings.'

An interpretation offered with individual variations in details, is that the piece is a revelation of the poet's personal experience and of his ideals of life and of poetry, at a critical point, perhaps a turning-point in his poetical and personal career. Brandl has recently so far accepted this conception as to characterize the poem as a landmark in the history of English autobiography. Interpretations of this class make the visit to the Temple of Venus represent the poet's fruitless devotion to Love, or to the study and the composition of love poetry, and his departure therefrom to represent his realization of the uselessness and the unreality of such devotion. Some of these urge that contact with Italian influence, especially with Dante, had made the poet desire higher and nobler objects and effort; some, that it had caused him to long for closer contact with the actual affairs of human life. Some feel that the desolate waste represents the poet's recognition that the love cult is remote from real life, others feel that it signifies the hopeless and helpless state of the poet after he had left his former interests and before he attained the newer ones. The eagle who is to rescue him from the waste and to conduct him to knowledge of more tidings, is commonly taken as Philosophy (see reference to Boethius, l. 972), though it is argued that in Book III such an interpretation will not hold. This class of interpretation goes on to note that at the House of Fame the poet finds that fame or disfame or oblivion is not according to merit, and is but fleeting; so he declares that he is willing to be forgotten after death (ll. 1872 ff.); what he seeks is rumor or tidings affording acquaintance with the present life of men. So he is conveyed to the House of Rumor where he may have his desire.

Unhappily, each of these interpretations neglects or slurs some one or more, or some aspects, of prominent elements of the poem. For solution of the problem, certain facts must be regarded persistently. The poem is incomplete. Book III was to be the last (l. 1093), and has already 1068 lines for 508 and 582 of the other Books. Apparently the actual theme is not reached until the poet arrives at the House of Dædalus (cf. ll. 1874 ff., 1884 ff., 1894-95), the place of the eagle's promise (ll. 672 ff., 1890 ff., 2000 ff.; cp. ll. 662-63). For the theme, then, Book I is unnecessary; and, once introduced, its matter is over-emphasized and treated disproportionately. Book II is too long drawn out. Perhaps in these Books, and indeed in the third, after the fashion of earlier and contemporary allegory, and after Chaucer's common practice, much of the matter was inserted as consequence of incidental suggestion, and not intended to count toward the allegory (granted allegory) or the purpose.—'Fame' is used in two senses: 'rumor' or 'report of facts or acts' (ll. 711-883, 1070-83, 1907-2158), and 'good repute' or 'renown' (ll. 1110-1882).

The progressive expressions, 'mo tydinges' (l. 675) and 'most tydinges' (l. 2025), may indeed have significance.—Again, there are some scattered humorous allusions to the poet's personal life, all (ll. 560, 574, 660, 995), except possibly one (ll. 1348-49) in Book II, notable for number rather than intrinsic significance. But the eagle speaks two important personal passages. The former (ll. 614-99) declares Jove's perception of the poet's unrewarded service of Love in his writings, and his hermitlike application to it, without tidings of Love or of aught else domestic or foreign that God has made. So he shall visit the House of Fame as a *recreation* (ll. 654, 664-65); nothing is said of *distraction* from or change of habitual activity, or of any enlarging of capacity through experieuce. The poet appears little desirous of coming into contact with life itself; he declines the eagle's offer of explanations of the stars and of their mythology (ll. 991 ff., 1000 ff.)—he is satisfied with what he has read in books, and his eyes might be injured if he looked at the stars themselves. Again, the poet declares (ll. 1873 ff.) that he has come to the House, not for Fame, but for 'som newe things, I not what, Tydinges . . . of love or swiche thinges glade'; ever since he has had wit he has known some folk desire fame. In the second of the long personal passages (ll. 2000 ff.) the eagle promises that at the House of Dædalus the poet shall 'most tydinges here'; and represents him as *still* afflicted, and to be offered diversion through novel sights and hearing of rumors or news. Obviously, the words 'tyding' and 'tydinges,' often eked out with 'newe thinges,' are of vital importance (cf. ll. 644, 648, 675, 1027, 1886, 1888, 1894, 1907, 1955, 1957, 1983, 2010, 2025, 2045, 2066, 2072, 2109, 2111, 2124, 2134, 2143). At line 675, the tidings are of love; at lines 1886-88, they are of love or 'swiche thinges glade'; at the end, the folk in the corner are telling 'love tydings.' The 'tyding . . . herd of som contree that shal not now be told for me' (l. 2134), seems to have significance, and may be connected with the eagle's 'fer contree' (l. 647).—The evident inconsistency and obscurity in use and significance of prominent features of the poem, may indicate that the poet had no very clear design; that, in larger and smaller details, he did not hold effectively or faithfully to any such design; that he was run away with by a plenitude of materials; and that he gave up the piece without seeing, and perhaps *because* he did not see, his way to a satisfactory or consistent conclusion.

The date of the poem is as much a matter of debate as are its meaning and purpose. The obvious Italian influence fixes the *terminus a quo* at 1373. The poem precedes the Prologue to the *Legend,* which names it (A405, B417), and so is before 1386 at latest. The *terminus ad quem* has usually been accepted as the date of Chaucer's permit to employ a deputy, February 17, 1385. This acceptance is based on the first long personal passage (ll. 652 ff.). Chaucer's appointment to the Customs Office was made in June, 1374. But certainly the eagle's words cannot fairly be construed into a complaint of the poet's labors over his accounts; and it is argued that, since all that is said of the duties is that when the poet's labor is done and he has made his reckonings, he goes directly home to pore over more books, the statement may possibly apply—though not so well—to the period after the appointment of a deputy and up to the date of the loss of the offices (December, 1386), or even to other reckonings—this especially because the eagle is putting the poet's excessive application as strongly as possible. The use of the short couplet and the general treatment of the poem, have led to a common conclusion that 1385 is a fitting latest possible date. The evident significance of the repetition of the date, the 10th day of December (ll. 63, 111), Chaucer's persistent interest in astronomical studies and application of them in his work, and the fact of Jove's influence in the dream, led Ten Brink to assign for the beginning of the poem a Thursday (Jove's day), which would fall on December 10th in 1383. Koch, who at first spoke most favorably of this conclusion, has since, with others, indicated that it is but a clever conjecture. Yet Koch and Tatlock and a number of other scholars, hold apparently to the date 1383-1384. Lowes has shown the apparent untenableness of the idea that the 'comedie' that at the end of the *Troilus* Chaucer speaks of wishing to write, is an anticipation of the *Hous*. He has argued for the date 1379, and Sypherd has supported him; but these arguments apparently have not been accepted as at all conclusive. Heath, who held that the poem was begun some years before 1383, suggested that Book III was written later than the other books (*i.e.*, after the *Troilus*). Recently, after locating the poem before the *Troilus*, Imelmann has sought on very fragile bases to date the dream between December 10, 1381, and the arrival of Anne in England later in the month—he holding (see page 656) that the poem is in honor of the wedding, as the *Parlement* is of the betrothal, with Richard. There appears to be a growing feeling that the piece should be dated much earlier than Ten Brink put it. Kittredge dates it before the *Troilus*. Root would like to locate at least Books I and II soon after the second visit to Italy. Emerson feels that the piece was written 'not long after the first Italian journey.' Certainly much of the form and the manner of the *Hous* accords with the earlier pieces, and there are many links with the *Duchesse*. But it has been noted that its humor (one of the most pleasing features of the poem) points toward that of *Troilus*, and suggests that the *Hous* preceded *Troilus*, perhaps not closely.

VII.   'Troilus and Criseyde'

TROILUS AND CRISEYDE [32] represents Chaucer's chief contribution to the Troy Story (see page 106). It consists of five books comprising 8239 verses of rime-royal, exclusive of the twelve-line Latin Argument of Statius' *Thebais* (Bk. V, in the MSS. written after l. 1498, by Skeat put after l. 1484). The poem is mentioned in the list in the Prologue to the *Legend* (A265, B332) along with the translation of the *Roman*, and in the 'Retraction' at the end of the *Parson's Tale*. The work was dedicated to 'moral Gower' and to 'the philosophical Strode' (V 1856-57). The latter is Ralph Strode, perhaps related to N. Strode, who, in the Latin

appended to the *Treatise on the Astrolabe* Part II § 40, is
mentioned as the tutor at Oxford of Chaucer's son, Lewis.

The *Troilus* is preserved in a number of MSS., which make
clear the existence of two versions of the poem. The former
version is illustrated in MSS. Phillipps 8252, Harley 2392,
Cbg. Univ. Libr. Gg IV 27, Harley 3943, and St. Johns Coll.
Cbg.; the latter, in MSS. Corpus Christi Coll. Cbg., Harley
2280, and Campsall. The latter version differs from the
former version in phrasing at numerous places, at such points
departing farther from the Italian original. It adds Troilus'
hymn to Love (III 1744-71), from Boethius; his long soliloquy
on Free-will (IV 953-1082), largely from Boethius; and the
ascent of his soul to Heaven (V 1807-27), from the *Teseide*.
McCormick's theory of a still earlier version represented in
MS. Phillipps 8252, Tatlock has not accepted.

The story of Troilus and Cressida is a mediæval product.
Homer merely mentions once Troilus, a son of Priam (*Iliad*
XXIV 257). Virgil gives four verses to his death (*Æneid* I
474-78). Cressida (Benoît's Briseida) is probably a combination of Homer's Briseis, slave of Achilles (*Iliad* I 184), and
Chryseis, daughter of Chryses (*Iliad* I 182). Dictys and Dares
give more prominence both to Troilus and to Briseida, but do
not associate their lives with each other. The story of their
love appears first in Benoît de Sainte-More's *Roman de Troie*,
where a series of passages, comprising in all some 1500 lines,
is devoted to the lovers. In Benoît a King Pandarus is merely
mentioned as one of the Trojan parliament. In his *Historia
Trojana* Guido delle Colonne gives an epitome of Benoît's tale,
adding extended denunciations of women. Boccaccio took the
story from Benoît and Guido, recomposing it as an independent
work of 5704 lines, the *Filostrato*. In his hands the tale
becomes a realistic, immoral portrayal of the voluptuous love
of Italy, a foil to the conceptions and treatments of love by
Dante and Petrarch. Troilo is the principal personage, a representation of Boccaccio himself; he is sentimental and passionate, and intended to receive the reader's thorough sympathy. Greseida is a young widow of considerable experience,

corrupt in character and very capable at the love-game.
Boccaccio makes Pandarus not only an essential but a determining force in the story, one of the three foremost characters,
a cousin of Greseida, the devoted assistant of his friend, a
young, gay go-between, of whose behavior the narrator
cordially approves.

Since Chaucer's version puts little stress on incident, and consists of psychological analysis and revelation of character and
nature chiefly through conversation and meditation, any abstract
must be quite inadequate to represent its real nature.—(I) Calchas,
the great diviner, foreknowing the fall of Troy, fled to the Greeks,
leaving behind his lovely daughter, Criseyde, a widow. The King's
son, Troilus, a professed woman-hater, saw the lady at worship, and
was instantly overwhelmed with love for her. He took to his
chamber in shame and love-sickness. His friend Pandarus, uncle
of Criseyde, undertook to make all well. Troilus did great deeds
in the field.—(II) On a fair May morning, in her garden, Pandarus told Criseyde of Troilus' love and distress, and urged her
to pity him. From her chamber-window, Criseyde saw the hero
riding back from battle, and was affected. With Pandarus' aid,
Troilus wrote the lady a letter. In reply Criseyde engaged to be
as a sister to the hero. After a dinner at the house of Deiphobus,
Pandarus brought Criseyde to the bedside of Troilus, who was pretending exhaustion for love.—(III) Criseyde kissed the youth,
and took him into her service. Finally, on a stormy night at his
house, Pandarus skilfully arranged so that Criseyde came to her
lover's arms.—(IV) The Greeks offered Antenor in exchange for
Criseyde. The Trojans accepted. Pandarus urged Troilus to withhold the lady; but need for secrecy prevented this. At a most
passionate final meeting, Criseyde proposed a plan by which she
would escape from the Greeks and return to Troy in ten days.
Troilus urged elopement, but Criseyde feared disgrace.—(V)
Diomede escorted Criseyde to the Greeks, on the way pleading his
love for her. Among the Greeks, Diomede pressed his suit. On
the tenth day after her departure from Troy, Criseyde gave him a
steed and a brooch that she had received from Troilus, and bade
him wear her token. But she lamented greatly her falseness.
Troilus waited in vain for her return. To a letter she replied that
she would come as soon as she could. Cassandra interpreted a dream
of Troilus as showing that Diomede had Criseyde's love. The hero
refused to believe this, and wrote many letters to the lady. She
replied feebly, and finally broke off the correspondence. At last,
on the captured armor of Diomede Troilus found his brooch. The
two heroes often met on the field, but neither slew the other. Troilus
wrought vengeance on the Greeks, and at last fell by the hand of
Achilles.

The poem is the one extensive piece that Chaucer finished. With exception of the *Canterbury Tales*, it is his masterpiece. It is remarkable for the originality of its treatment of motives and character, the consistency of its execution, its finish, the excellence of its verse, the brilliancy of its characterization, its analysis of feeling, and its semi-ironical humor. Professor Price showed that the poem is mainly direct discourse, that it falls into fifty scenes of astonishing variety connected by link-passages composed of reflections on the story, or made up of the narrative or description necessary for understanding of the purely dramatic parts. For Boccaccio's 5704 lines, it has 8239 verses. The prolixity of a number of passages may be due to a desire to develop motive and character. Chaucer's characteristic aloofness is apparent. He sympathizes with none of his chief personages. Boccaccio's sentimentality and pathos give way to intellectual analysis by a semi-ironic humorist. The lovely Criseyde is a heartless and artful intriguer, most clever in her assumed rôle of innocent, but really not the victim of the machinations of her uncle. With all his commendable idealism, Troilus is not presented for the reader's admiration. He is mighty in arms, but has little experience of men or of conduct; he is an undeveloped, love-sick youth, not at all the master of his fate, a person of little volition, and the plaything of Pandarus. Pandarus is Chaucer's supreme humorous character. He is an incarnation of intellect without any moral sense, a master of intrigue delighting in the deft manipulation of the strands of his plots. Yet withal he is a most attractive personage because of his subtle humor, his inexhaustible good-nature, his knowledge of the world, and his clever adaptability. And one must not forget his real loyalty to Troilus.

It has been shown that the *Filostrato* is the source chiefly followed in the poem, 2730 of its 5704 lines affording material for 2583 verses, or about five-sixteenths, of the *Troilus*. From time to time during more than half a century, the question of whether it is Benoît's *Roman de Troie* or Guido's *Historia Trojana* that was Chaucer's secondary source, has been discussed. It seems that the poet probably drew much more extensively from Benoît than from Guido, who supplied material for but few passages. Probably Boccaccio's *Filocolo* was used, especially in Book III, and particularly there for lines 512-1190, where Chaucer departs widely from the account of the *Filostrato*. Book III 813-33, 1625-29, 1744-68, are from Boethius II prose 4. 86-120, 4-10, metre 8; much of Book IV 947-1085 is from Boethius V. Book V 1-14, 1807-27, are from parts of Boccaccio's *Teseide* (see page 692). Part of the last stanza of Book V is from Dante. Troilus' love-song at I 400-20 is a translation of Petrarch's *Sonnet 88*. Scattered passages show influence of Ovid, Statius, the *Roman de la Rose*, and other works; and there are several bits probably indirectly from Horace. Book I 1065-69 is probably from Geoffrey de Vinsauf. The use at II 19 ff. of the early fourteenth-century Italian allegorical poem *L'Intelligenza*, suggested by Koeppel, has been seriously questioned by Kittredge. In his list of Chaucer's works Lydgate speaks of the *Troilus* as 'a translacion of a booke which called is Trophe in Lumbard tong' (see page 620). In the *Monk's Tale* (B3307) is 'At bothe the worldes endes, seith Trophee, in stede of boundes, he a piler sette.' What 'Trophee' represents, is one of the Chaucer *cruces*. The argument of the *Thebais* of Statius in twelve Latin hexameters after V 1498, is prior to Chaucer, and has been dated not much after the sixth century. Much debate has arisen from 'myn autour called Lollius' in I 394, where the song is quoted from Petrarch's *Sonnet 88;* 'as telleth Lollius' in V 1653, when the incident is in *Filostrato;* and the *Hous of Fame* 1468, where Chaucer joins 'Lollius' with Dares and Tytus (Dictys) as a writer on the story of Troy. It is unsettled whether the use of this name 'Lollius' is a result of an attempt at mystification; or is due to confusion by Chaucer; or is a substitution for Boccaccio to conceal indebtedness; or is an attempt to gain authority by ascription to a supposed ancient writer; or is an error due to mistaken inference from Horace's 'Troiani belli scriptorem, maxime Lolli' quoted in John of Salisbury's *Polycraticus* VII ix, that Lollius was a writer on

Troy; or is a representation of 'Lælius,' a name of Petrarch, Chaucer supposing Petrarch wrote the *Filostrato* (Chaucer never names Boccaccio); or is due to some combination of several of these causes.

The obvious use of Boethius, and the connection of *Troilus* and a version of Boethius in the *Words unto Adam* (see page 634), have led to general assumption that the translation and the *Troilus* were composed close together. For many years the date of the *Troilus* was assigned variously between 1374 and 1384. Tatlock's argument in 1903 and 1907 for 1376 (1377), on the basis of Gower's assumed allusion to the poem in his *Miroir de l'Omme* (ll. 5245-56), was effectively met by Lowes in 1905 and 1908, and by Kittredge in 1909. In 1908 Lowes argued that 'Right as our firste lettre is now an A' (I 171) is a reference to Anne newly become Queen, and that the first Book was begun after the date (January 14, 1382) of Anne's marriage to Richard. Koch and Kittredge have approved of this explanation and this dating. In 1907 Tatlock dated the revision of the poem after the Cecilia Chaumpaigne episode in 1380 (see page 613). In 1911 Professor C. Brown adduced evidence to show that IV 169-210 are largely Chaucer's own, and contain allusions to Jack Straw's rebellion in 1381—so confirming Lowes' dating. Scholars feel that the *Troilus* was completed before the Prologue to the *Legend* was begun, and before the regular plan of the *Canterbury Tales* was entered on—that is, before the end of 1385.

VIII. 'The Legend of Good Women'

THE LEGEND OF GOOD WOMEN [33], so designated in both versions (A473-74, B483-84) of its own Prologue, is preserved in a number of MSS. It is mentioned (see pages 618, 619) in the Man of Law's headlink (l. 61) as 'the Seintes Legende of Cupyde,' and in the 'Retraction' as 'The book of the XXV (Skeat alters to *nynetene*) Ladies.' The *Legend* evidently was left unfinished. It consists of a Prologue, of which there are two versions, the legends of ten ladies in nine

pieces (the last unfinished), Cleopatra, Thisbe, Dido, Hyp-
sipyle and Medea (one piece), Lucretia, Ariadne, Philomela,
Phillis, and Hypermnestra. The A version of the Prologue is
in only MS. Cbg. Univ. Libr. Gg IV 27; it consists of 545 lines.
Prologue B has 579 lines. The legends, independent of the
Prologues, comprise 2144 verses. With exception of the *balade*
(A203 ff., B249 ff.) the poem is in pentameter couplets.

The two versions of the Prologue differ much in the phrasing
and the location of parallel passages, and in the setting of
similar elements. In B there are 124 lines not in A, and in A
there are 90 lines not in B. The *balade* in B is not sung by the
company, as it is in A. In A Alceste is named (l. 179) much
earlier than (l. 432) in B. The time of the vision is in B the
first day of May, in A at almost the last of the month. The
following is a synopsis of B.

After a passage on the value of books and on the poet's devotion
to them, follow verses on his love of May and its flowers, especially
the daisy. Then the author humbly asks help of the 'marguerite'
poets who have left him but the gleanings of the field; and he
praises his lady.—On the first morning of May, he went out among
the flowers and the rejoicing birds, and gave himself to honoring
the daisy. ' Toward evening, when the daisy had closed its petals,
he went home to his 'litel herber.' There he dreamed that in a
meadow whither he had gone to seek the daisy, he saw the God of
Love, and with him his Queen, whose headdress suggested the
appearance of the daisy. In her honor follows a *balade*. The
royal pair were attended by a train of nineteen ladies, and a host
of other women, all 'trewe of love.' After a song of praise to
woman's faith and to the daisy, all sat down in the meadow. The
poet remained kneeling close by. Him the God of Love chided
for translating the *Romance of the Rose* and for writing of Cressida. The Queen, who declared she was Alceste, whilom Queen
of Thrace, defended the poet, and named a list (see page 619) of
his works that glorified her sex. She directed that the poet devote
the most of his time during the rest of his life to writing in praise
of women true in loving. When completed, the book should be given
with her compliments to the Queen at Eltham or at Shene. The
God directed the poet to deal first with Cleopatra, and with Alceste
after the other stories were written. The poem should treat ladies
in the company whom the poet knew of, especially those of them
mentioned in his *balade*. The poet at once took up his books, and
set to work. We are not told that he awoke.—The nine extant
legends follow, without links.

According to the Prologue (A542-43, 538-40; B566, 548-50) Chaucer was to write first the story of Cleopatra, and at the end to add a poem on Alceste, the Queen of Love. Despite the views of many scholars, the directions at B554 ff. (not in A) need not be taken to include treatments of any specific number of ladies, or of all, or of no others than, the nineteen ladies who are the principals of the host of good and true women (B285-90, A188-93) in the train of Alceste. It matters not that the *balade* mentions two men, or that it names but eighteen women (A also Alceste). It is no contradiction of the God's directions, that the extant legends treat Medea and Philomela who are not named in the *balade*. Chaucer was to write of ladies in the *balade*, or of others, that he knew about. The disagreement of the Man of Law's headlink (ll. 62 ff.) with both the *balade* list and the set of extant legends, may be due to later revision or to the fact that the link list is only a general indication of contents, perhaps indicative of intention at a later date to proceed farther with the *Legend*. Only the B Prologue has the God's directions concerning the *balade* and the ladies to be written about. Interestingly, in the *balade* list is Canace, whose story is so emphatically rejected in the much-discussed passage of the Man of Law's headlink (see page 699).

The sources of the *Legend* are various. Ovid's *Heroides* contributed to the general conception of the work, and were drawn on largely for materials. Probably Boccaccio's *De Claris Mulieribus* and *De Casibus Virorum et Feminarum Illustrium*, the models for the *Monk's Tale*, were suggestive of a series. For the nine stories Chaucer seems to have used many sources, reading up on each heroine, and adopting whatever appealed. For *Cleopatra* he probably drew somewhat from Florus' *Epitome Rerum Romanorum;* and perhaps he used a Latin translation of Plutarch's *Antony*, Orosius' *Historia*, and the *De Claris Mulieribus*. For Thisbe he seems to have drawn only from the *Metamorphoses* IV 55-166. The material for *Dido* came from the *Æneid* I-IV, but lines 1355-65 are from the *Heroides* VII 1-8. Much of the *Hypsipyle and Medea* is from the *Metamorphoses* VII and *Heroides* VI and XII, but more is from Guido's *Historia Trojana;* perhaps Statius' *Thebais,* possibly Hyginus' *Fables 14* and *15,* and Boccaccio's *De Claris Mulieribus* and *De Genealogia Deorum,* were used. The *Lucretia* is chiefly from Ovid's *Fasti,* and from Livy's *Historia,* with perhaps Augustine's *De Civitate Dei;* to all of these Chaucer refers. The *Ariadne* came from the *Metamorphoses* VII 456-58, *Heroides* X, and perhaps *Fasti* III 461-516; perhaps a Latin translation of Plutarch's *Theseus,* Boccaccio's *De Genealogia,* the *Æneid,* and Hyginus' *Fabulæ,* were used. The *Philomela* is perhaps from the *Metamorphoses* VI 424-605 alone. The *Phillis* is mainly from the *Heroides* II, perhaps with use of another source unknown, and with slight suggestions from the *Æneid.* The *Hypermnestra* is mainly from the *Heroides* XIV, and evidently Chaucer had read up Boccaccio's *De Genealogia.* Similarities have been observed between Gower's *Confessio Amantis* I 4 and the Prologue lines 17-28, and the *Confessio* I 45-48 and the Prologue; but these are held to indicate no direct connection, if any connection, between the works. Gower's III 357-67 with its list of lovers, however, and his treatment of Cleopatra's death, seem certainly reminiscent of Chaucer's poem. In 1913 Schofield argued that, for the description of the sea-fight in the *Cleopatra,* 'the poet was influenced by what he had read of sea-battles, and perhaps had Jean de Meun's *Art de Chevalerie* before him, but he probably gained most of his information from oral accounts of recent conflicts and discussions by navy men.'

With its dream-vision allegory, its court of love, its Mayday setting, the Prologue was composed under influence of the French love-allegories. Resemblances to the poet's situation in the Prologue are in Machaut's *Le Jugement dou Roy de Navarre* and the anonymous *Trésor Amoureux.* The use of the daisy with its symbolizing of Alceste, and, through her, possibly of Queen Anne, is due to contemporary French 'marguerite' poems. These were inaugurated by the *Dit de la Marguerite* of Guillaume de Machaut, who was followed by Froissart in his *Dittié de la Flour de la Margherite* and *Paradys d'Amours* and several other poems, by Deschamps in his *Lay de Franchise* and a group of *balades*, and by other poets. The first pieces of the cult appear to have been concerned with ladies named 'Marguerite'; but later poems were written of ladies not bearing that name. Chaucer knew the work of Machaut, Deschamps, and Froissart. A *balade* of Deschamps, 'O Socrates plains de philosophie,' addressed to the 'Grant translateur, noble Geffroy Chaucier,' states that its author sent it with others of his poems by Clifford (Sir Lewis Clifford) as agent, with a request that Chaucer send in return some of his own. The *Lay de Franchise* may have been one of these pieces. However much the Prologue was indebted to specific pieces, it is clear that much of it is the fruit of very clever imitation of French 'marguerite' poems, whose authors are the 'lovers' addressed with such unnecessary humility in lines 68 ff. On the influence of Deschamps' *Miroir de Mariage* see page 686 and the references there.

The dating of the various parts of the *Legend* has been much discussed. Close dating of the two Prologues is very important because of the lists of Chaucer's works that they contain. Fortunately, the items in the two lists agree except for the *Wretched Engendering of Mankind*, which is named only in A, and which is preserved, if it survives at all, only in scraps in other poems (see page 620). The direction of the Queen of Love in B496-97, that when completed the Legend shall be given to 'the quene . . . at Eltham, or at Shene,' dates that passage, and hence probably the rest of B, between Richard's marriage to Anne in January 14, 1382, on the one hand, and, on the other, the death of Anne (June 7, 1394) and the consequent destruction of the palace, or Richard's aversion to it, in 1394. If Deschamps' *Lay de Franchise* actually influenced the *Legend*, the earlier Prologue followed May 1, 1385, for which date the *Lay* was written. Apparently Sir Lewis Clifford could have brought Deschamps' poems to Chaucer before the late spring or the summer of 1386; if the *Lay* was among these poems, the earlier Prologue must have followed that date. Again, in October, 1386, Chaucer gave up the lease on the dwelling above the city gate of Aldgate, that he had received on May 10, 1374. The fact that in October, 1385, he was made Justice of the Peace for Kent, may account for the yielding of the lease. In both Prologues he goes to sleep at home 'in a litel herber that I have'; but an arbor (a shaded space with green terraces) would hardly be connected with a house over a city gate. On February 17, 1385, Chaucer was permitted to appoint a deputy comptroller, and so allowed freedom for writing. It is urged that after beginning the *Canterbury Tales* in 1386 or 1387, Chaucer would hardly turn to the lesser design. The evidence in general points to completion of the earlier Prologue in 1385 or 1386, perhaps rather in 1386.

The question of which Prologue is the earlier has been discussed at length. In 1392 Ten Brink urged that A is the later version, written not before 1393. Koch opposed Ten Brink's view, but Koeppel and Kaluza supported it. In 1904 and 1913 Lowes argued, and in 1907 Tatlock reargued, that the B version was composed in 1386, and the A version about the middle of 1394. Despite the opposition of Koch and French, this last view seems sure of acceptance. By those who accept this dating the King's extravagant grief for the loss of Anne on June 7, 1394, is urged as the cause for the omission in A of the dedicatory lines in B496-97. By those who hold that Alceste represents the Queen, the King's extraordinary grief is urged as adequate cause for the very considerable revision to the inferior A version, the object of the revision being to remove all signs for identification of Alceste. It must be admitted that all the various theories often depend directly or ultimately on suppositions rather than on demonstrated facts.

From Ten Brink's *Studien* (1870) to 1904, Alceste of Prologue B was accepted as Queen Anne. In 1904 Lowes, and in 1909 Kittredge, made the identification difficult to accept. In 1907 Tatlock defended it. Lydgate's statement in the prologue to his *Falls of Princes* that the *Legend* was written 'at the request of the quene,' has been questioned, but has been favored recently by Tatlock and C. Brown. Ten Brink's suggestion that B was written in gratitude to Anne for his release from official duties in February, 1385, appears to be merely interesting conjecture. The Earl of Oxford's signature on Chaucer's extant petition for a deputy, does not show, however, that the Queen did not at all assist the poet in the matter.

In 1909 and 1910 Root argued that the *Hypsipyle and Medea* was written after the Man of Law's headlink, whose earliest date could be 1390. He suggested that the *Cleopatra* was written before 1390, the *Lucretia* after Gower's *Confessio* Book VII and perhaps after the publication of the whole *Confessio* in 1390; that *Phillis* followed *Ariadne* and perhaps also *Dido* and *Hypsipyle and Medea;* that the pieces were written probably in the order in which they stand in the MSS.; and that, since the *Medea* is fourth in the list, most of the pieces were written after 1390. Kittredge opposed Root, and was replied to by him. In 1905 Lowes argued that *Ariadne* and *Phillis* preceded *Palamon and Arcite,* and that most, perhaps all, of the legends preceded the Prologue to the *Legend;* that the *Hous of Fame* antedated the *Ariadne;* that the *Troilus* is close to the Prologue; and that *Palamon* and the *Hous* preceded the *Troilus.* In 1907 Tatlock maintained that 'most or all of the Legends were written after the Prologue.'

The Prologue is the most valuable and interesting part of the poem. Only genuine enthusiasm could give the cluster of imitations the freshness and spontaneous delight, the ease and grace, that put it among the most pleasing work of Chaucer. Much of its charm lies in its personal details. Nowhere else has the poet so directly and unmistakably let us into his own personal interests, his love of books, his love of the fresh out-of-doors. But students have pointed out again and again that, though much in them is admirable, the separate stories of the ladies are comparatively inferior; that the poet seems to be interested only by fits; and that, as the pieces progress, they evince increasing weariness. Perhaps the lack of variety made them a burden; perhaps as Chaucer read more he found that the ladies were not such attractive models of excellence as he had supposed.

IX. 'The Canterbury Tales'

A. The Tales in General

ORIGIN AND SOURCES OF THE PLAN [34]. Already
in dealing with the miscellaneous tales in English (pages 164,
185) we have remarked on the popularity, in the three languages current in England, of collections of pieces of a kindred nature assembled and sometimes united on some one of
several easily recognized bases.   These were encyclopædias
made up of writings of a single kind, fables, saint's legends,
homilies, etc.; groups of narratives preceded by an introduction, either narrative, as in the *Legend of Good Women,* or
expository of purpose, as in the *Monk's Tale;* groups of pieces
fitted together as integral components of a continuous narrative, as in the *Cursor Mundi;* or pieces illustrative of a large
general theme introduced at the beginning of the whole and
sustained between the individual items by a narrative, as in the
Confessio Amantis.   The widely cherished *Seven Sages of
Rome* (see page 186) and the *Confessio* (see page 591), however, illustrate also a still different type of union, that of the
Canterbury Tales; in them the tales are told incidentally by
personages in a large narrative whole that is introduced by a
prologue, gathered up in a conclusion (designed, but not
actually written, in the *Tales*), and sustained from tale to tale
by narrative links.

Until recently the plan of the *Canterbury Tales* has been
regarded as unique among the works of this last class in English of our period, in the respect that it and its components
were not intended to illustrate a large single *motif* or topic
after the fashion of the *Seven Sages* and the *Confessio.* But
emphasis on the Marriage Group (see page 684) has led the
way, and has given some countenance, to suggestion (see page
687) that the *Tales* was intended more or less, and must have
been recognized by Chaucer's contemporaries, as a 'curious
blending (as in Gower's "Confessio") of the *motif* of Love
with that of the *Seven Deadly Sins.*'

The fact that Boccaccio's *Decameron* unites its hundred tales through the single enveloping story of the lords and ladies at Florence, that is maintained in a narrative introduction, narrative links, and a narrative conclusion, has produced contradictory assertion and discussion regarding indebtedness of Chaucer to that work for the general idea of his framework. It is admitted as possible that in Italy Chaucer went over the *Decameron* hastily. But no uncontradicted evidence, and none that uncontradicted would approach conclusiveness, has been offered to show that he drew from the *Decameron*, or even that he knew of the existence of that book. The tale of Griselda, though treated in the *Decameron*, is drawn from Petrarch (see page 726) ; and the *Franklin's Tale* is more probably based on the *Filocolo* than on the *Decameron* version of the story (see page 736). Again, it has been suggested that the conception of the framework of the *Tales* may possibly have been aided by Boccaccio's *Ameto*, if Chaucer were acquainted with it, or perhaps by the *Questioni* episode of Boccaccio's *Filocolo*, a work certainly used for the *Troilus*. But did one grant actual indebtedness to any or to all of these works or of the earlier English pieces, one would have to admit that the resemblances between the Canterbury design and that of any one or all of the others together, were but general and slight, and that Chaucer's transformation of the elements were no less extraordinary than if he had invented them wholly. The elements of resemblances are indeed such as a capable artist acquainted with various *types* of mediæval literature might conceive of independently.

Recently Young has pointed out very close similarities (suggested earlier by Hinckley) between the plan and details of the *Tales* and the *Novelle* of the Italian Sercambi. Sercambi's work consists of a narrative introduction, a series of tales, etc., connected by narrative links and comments on the items, and a narrative conclusion. The framework is that of a journey by a company of persons of various walks of life, with members of the clergy, who travel together through a great number of Italian cities while awaiting the subsidence of a pestilence in

Lucca in 1374. As they are gathered in a church preliminary
to their departure, a prominent citizen, Aluisi, proposes that
they have a leader. He himself is elected to the office. He at
once suggests songs, conversations, and discourses, to amuse
the party on the way, and appoints Sercambi the story-teller.
The work proceeds with the tales, etc., and the narrative connectives recording progress of the journey and reporting the
comments of the company on the items of entertainment. The
Novelle would appear to have been written soon after 1374.

DATE OF PLAN [35]. Though the conception of the
pilgrimage plan for the *Tales* has been assigned to various
dates, most scholars now are agreed on 1385-1387, with preference for 1387. More and more the *Legend* is being accepted
as begun in 1385 or 1386, and regarded as left unfinished not
only because Chaucer tired of it (see page 671), but because
he put it aside to develop the newly acquired Canterbury
design.

CHAUCER'S TRIP TO CANTERBURY? [36]. It is
unnecessary to suppose with some scholars that the notion of
the pilgrimage grew out of an actual pilgrimage to Canterbury
by Chaucer in 1385-1387. Nothing in the tales calls for first-
hand acquaintance with experiences on pilgrimages. Chaucer
had lived all his life in London, and, especially during his residence in Greenwich from 1385, must have seen many bands of
pilgrims start on their way. Moreover, he must already have
acquired sufficient familiarity with the conditions on the road,
from his various journeys over the route on his way to the
Continent.

GENERAL PLAN [37]. The *Canterbury Tales* is a story
of a pilgrimage to the shrine of Thomas à Becket. The general
design is outlined in the Prologue. At the Tabard Inn in
Southwark the poet was accepted into fellowship by a company
of 'wel nyne and twenty,' (actually thirty) other pilgrims.
These were a Knight, a Squire, a Yeoman, a Prioress, a Nun
(the Prioress' 'chapeleyne') with her three priests, a Monk,

a Friar, a Merchant, a Clerk of Oxford, a Man of Law, a Franklin, a Haberdasher, a Carpenter, a Weaver, a Dyer, an Upholsterer, a Cook, a Shipman, a Doctor, a Wife of Bath, a Parson, a Plowman, a Miller, a Manciple, a Reeve, a Summoner, and a Pardoner. All accepted a proposal of their Host, Harry Bailly (A4358; the name perhaps from that of 'Henry Bayliff ostyler' named in the Subsidy Rolls for Southwark, 1380-1381, and of Henry Bailly, representative in Parliament for Southwark in 50 Edw. III and 2 Rich. II—*i.e.*, 1376-1377 and 1378-1379), that, to pass the time on the journey, each of the party should tell two stories going and two returning; that the Host should accompany them as absolute governor and judge; that on their return they should assemble at supper at the Tabard, the teller of the best tales to be entertained at the general expense; and that any who failed in any respect to obey the Host should pay all that the company spent on the pilgrimage. So, with description of the various personages, runs the Prologue. It concludes with an account of the start on the next morning, and of the drawing of lots by which it was determined that the Knight should tell the first story. Accordingly, the Knight tells his tale, and the others follow.

The plan as outlined in the Prologue evidently calls for a narrative conclusion telling of the events at the end of the pilgrimage, for one hundred and twenty-four tales (four by each of the pilgrims and four by Chaucer), and for narrative links between the tales. But this plan was not fulfilled, and it was modified as Chaucer progressed with his enterprise (see page 676).

THE FRAGMENTS OR GROUPS [38]. The work is preserved to us in nine fragments, which, since the Chaucer Society's Six-Text Edition, have been distinguished by the letters of the alphabet from A to I inclusive. Fragments B, E, F, G, are sub-divided as B^1, B^2, E^1, E^2, F^1, F^2, G^1, G^2, for closer designation of the divisions in some of the MSS. The Fragments are constituted as follows: A, Prologue, tales of Knight, Miller, Reeve, and Cook, with the connective links; B^1, Man of Law's headlink, prologue, tale, and endlink (last known

as *Shipman's Prologue*); B², tale of Shipman, tales and links
of Prioress, *Thopas, Melibeus,* Monk, Nun's Priest, and endlink of Nun's Priest; C, tale of Physician, Words of the Host,
and prologue and tale of Pardoner; D, prologues and tales of
Wife of Bath, Friar, and Summoner; E¹, prologue and tale
of Clerk; E², prologue, tale, and epilogue of Merchant; F¹,
prologue and tale of Squire; F², words, prologue, and tale of
the Franklin; G, tale of Second Nun, and prologue and tale of
Canon's Yeoman; H, prologue and tale of Manciple; I, prologue and tale of Parson.

The extant work consists of twenty-one complete tales and
three (*Sir Thopas,* and the tales of the Cook and the Squire)
incomplete tales. Of the twenty-four, two are told by Chaucer,
and one by the Canon's Yeoman, who was added to the company at Boghton under Blee. Of the thirty original pilgrims,
but twenty-one actually tell stories.

Some MSS. have inserted after the *Cook's Tale* the *Tale of
Gamelyn* (see page 25), headed 'The Cokes Tale of Gamelyn.'
This piece is evidently not by Chaucer. It is little appropriate
for the Cook, though very appropriate for the Yeoman; following the *Cook's Tale* it would give excellent variety and contrast. Hence students have inferred that Chaucer had the tale
by him in his MSS., intending to write it over for the Yeoman;
and that it was found in the MSS. next after the imperfect
Cook's Tale, which perhaps the rewritten *Gamelyn* was to follow, and was copied by some of the scribes in that place with the
blundering label 'The Cokes Tale.'—The so-called *Ploughman's
Tale* or *Complaint of the Ploughman,* appears in the edition of
1542, but in none of the MSS. In its present form it is of
the sixteenth century, but some elements of it may be from
a fourteenth-century Lollard piece (see page 268).—Hoccleve's *Tale of the Ploughman,* the legend of the Virgin and her
Sleeveless Garment, is in the Christ Church College Oxford MS.
CLII after the *Squire's Tale,* and also in MS. Ashburnham 133
with other Hoccleve pieces.

CHANGES IN THE GENERAL PLAN OUTLINED

[39]. As has been stated (page 675), the plan outlined in the

Prologue was modified. The Canon and his Yeoman join the party at Boghton, and the latter tells his tale (see page 740). The statements in the Parson's headlink (I16, 19, 25, 27-28, 47; see page 744) would seem to indicate that the plan of telling two tales on the way to Canterbury, was altered to the telling of but one. If the 'Retraction' see pages 619, 746) be genuine and really intended to follow the *Parson's Tale* (I1081), then when he wrote it Chaucer must have given up the idea of an epilogue telling of the supper at the Tabard and the dispersal of the pilgrims, and, unless he altered the place indications in the links (see page 682), must have given up also the notion of the return journey to London. If all this be accepted, the plan as modified would call for but thirty-three tales in all—*i.e.*, thirty by the regular company, two by Chaucer (*Thopas* and *Melibeus*), and one by the Canon's Yeoman; so, nine tales would be unwritten, and two more (Squire's and Cook's) incomplete, *Thopas* being intended to be left as it is.

Again, the 'wel nyne and twenty in a companye' (A24) may indicate an original number of pilgrims differing from that of the Prologue as it stands. But the disagreement in the numbers may be due (as Skeat suggested) to scribal filling out of defects at A163-64, or (as Hammond suggested) to the fact that the 'wel nyne and twenty' was intended as a round number (see pages 692, 712).

THE LINKS [40]. The links between the tales are of two sorts, Headlinks and Endlinks, the former preparing for the next story, the latter containing an epilogue or comment on the story preceding. Sometimes a link fulfils both these offices. Such are the links Knight-Miller, Miller-Reeve, Reeve-Cook, Shipman-Prioress, Prioress-*Thopas*, *Thopas-Melibeus*, *Melibeus*-Monk, Monk-Nun's Priest, Physician-Pardoner, Wife-Friar, Friar-Summoner, Clerk-Merchant, Squire-Franklin, and Second Nun-Canon's Yeoman. There is merely a headlink before each of the following: Man of Law, Squire, Clerk, Manciple. Physician, Wife, and Second Nun, have no headlink; Cook, Pardoner, Summoner, and Franklin, have no endlink.

The pieces in the last three of the groups just mentioned, occur at the unconnected beginning or end of one of the Fragments.

In some of the MSS. the Nun's Priest has an endlink, and the Merchant and the Pardoner have epilogues (see pages 731, 718). The Man of Law's endlink, usually known as the *Shipman's Prologue* (B1163-90), is discussed at page 702; the conclusion of the *Parson's Tale* is discussed at page 746.

Spurious links (see discussion of separate tales) are in some MSS. as follows: Cook-Gamelyn, Merchant-Wife, Franklin-Physician, Canon's Yeoman-Physician, and Pardoner-Shipman. There is a spurious prologue to *Thopas*, a four-line introduction to the Wife, a passage of eight lines at the end of the Squire, and a passage of four lines at the end of the Cook's fragment.

GAPS [41]. There are some gaps between the Fragments, due to omissions of tales or of links or of both. At least the greater part of the *Cook's Tale* and some connective narrative, are lacking between Fragments A and B. At least a part of a link is missing between the members of each of the following pairs of groups: F and G (see G555, 588-89), D and E, ?E and F (see page 725), G and H, and H and I (see H2, 16, I5). Fragment C has no connecting links at its beginning or its end, and has no indications of time or of place. Of course, tales were to be inserted at several, perhaps most (but not between H and I), of the points just noted.

ORDER OF THE FRAGMENTS [42]. The proper arrangement of the extant tales is matter of debate. Apparently, Chaucer worked with groups of tales in separate booklets. The MSS. differ as to the order of the Fragments A to I, and differ as to arrangement in some of their components (as in B, E, F, G). Of course A must be the first of the Fragments, and I was meant to be the last (see I16, 19, 25, 47). The editors of the *Tales* have paid little attention to the order in the MSS., and have arranged the tales and the Fragments according to indications of time and place in the texts (see page 681). On such bases, Furnivall adopted for the Six-

Text Edition the order AB¹B²CDEFGHI, but later accepted Shipley's (1895) order ACBDEFGHI. Koch agreed with Furnivall's first order, but in 1913 declared that he no longer accepted it. For uniformity of numbering Skeat adopted for his editions Furnivall's first order, but urged that the right order is ABDEFCGHI; and just before his death he urged AB¹DEF (E and F one Fragment) GCB²HI. Ten Brink and recently Tatlock, as well as Skeat, have urged that E and F should be held as one Fragment. Fleay had previously suggested Shipley's arrangement, but put F before D. Apparently, the present tendency is strongly toward Shipley's order.

The really troublesome Fragments are C and B². C has no headlink or endlink, and no indications of time or place. Furnivall 'lifted up' B² to follow B¹ on the basis of similarity of phrasing in B46 and B1165, on address 'ye lerned men in lore' (taken as the Man of Law and the Parson) in B1168, and on the necessity for arrival at Rochester (B3116) to precede the allusion to arrival at Sittingbourne (D847). The present preference is for ACB¹B²D, etc.

THE MANUSCRIPTS [43]. But few persons have made any general study of the MSS. The list of MSS. usually given comprises 66 items. To these must be added three more, recently acquired by the British Museum, and a number that contain a single tale or two tales. Skeat in his *Oxford Chaucer*, and Miss Hammond in her *Manual*, have given lists. Neither includes the Plimpton MS. described by Tatlock.

In his *Oxford Edition*, on the basis chiefly of order of tales with admittance of personal judgment, Skeat accepted the four following types for classification of the MSS.: I, AB¹DEF· CB²GHI, order of Ellesmere and its allies, the order adopted by Tyrwhitt for his edition; II, AB¹DEFGCB²HI, order of Harley 7334; III, AB¹F¹DEF²GCB²HI, as in Lansdowne 851; IV, AB¹F¹E²DE¹F²GCB²HI, as in Harley 7333.

In his *Evolution of the Canterbury Tales* Skeat accepted five groups of MSS., typically represented as follows: Hengwrt; A, Petworth; B, Lansdowne; C, Harleian 7334; C*, Ellesmere. The characteristics of these groups Skeat presented by a very complicated symbolism that he explained somewhat in his *The Eight-Text Edition,* etc. The classification can best be seen by referring to these works. The *Evolution* as a whole has not been well received.

Following Bradshaw's suggestion of classification according to the links or the prologues to the separate Fragments, Miss Hammond made the following groupings of the MSS. (the hyphens show the presence of the links or prologues): (1) Ellesmere Group—$AB_1DE\text{-}FCB^2GHI$; (2) Harley 7334—$AGamelynB^1DE\text{-}FGCB^2HI$; (3) Selden—$ADE^1\text{-}E^2\text{-}F^1F^2B^1\text{-}B^2G\text{-}CHI$; (4) Corpus-Harley 7333, Group—(a) Harley 7333, Trinity R, 3, 15—$AB^1\text{-}F^1E^2DE^1F^2GCB^2HI$; (b) Corpus-Sloane 1686-Lansdowne—$AGamelynB^1\text{-}F^1DE^1E^2F^2G\text{-}C\text{-}B^2HI$; (c) Harley 1758, etc.—$AGamelynB^1\text{-}F^1\text{-}E^2DE^1\text{-}F^2G\text{-}C\text{-}B^2HI$; (d) Petworth, Cbg. Mm—$A\text{-}GamelynB^1\text{-}F^1\text{-}E^2DE^1F^2G\text{-}C\text{-}B^2HI$; (e) Hatton, Cbg. Ii—$A\text{-}GamelynB^1\text{-}F^1\text{-}E^2\text{-}F^2DE^1G\text{-}C\text{-}B^2HI$.

THE HARLEY 7334 TEXT [44]. Some scholars, notably Pollard and Skeat, have favored the theory that MS. Harley 7334, with its unique readings, some good and some bad, represents revisions or a general revision by Chaucer after copies of the *Tales* were in circulation. Other students, notably Koch and Tatlock, have opposed this theory.

BASES OF EDITIONS [45]. Practically all editions of the *Canterbury Tales*—all except several of single items (*e.g.,* Liddell's *Prologue* and *Knight's Tale,* Koch's *Pardoner's Tale*)—have taken as foundation the Six-Text Edition of the Chaucer Society. This followed MSS. Ellesmere, Cbg. Univ. Libr. Gg IV 27, Hengwrt 154, Corpus Christi Coll. Oxf., Petworth, and Lansdowne 851. Later the Society printed the unique MS. Harley 7334, and MS. Cbg. Univ. Libr. Dd IV 24 with gaps filled in from MS. Egerton 2726. Koch has published a detailed comparison of the eight MSS. The Ellesmere MS. has been published in facsimile.

MODIFICATIONS AS REGARDS INDIVIDUAL PIECES [46]. For hints of changes in the poet's plans in regard to individual pieces, see the remarks on the *General Prologue, Cook's Tale, Man of Law's Tale, Wife's Prologue and Tale, Shipman's Headlink, Shipman's Tale, Melibeus, Monk's Tale, Nun's Priest's Prologue, Clerk's Tale, Merchant's Prologue,* and *Second Nun's Tale* (see pages 690, 697, 698, 700, 722, 723, 703, 704, 708, 710, 711, 727, 728, 729, 739, 744). Further changes in arrangement are suggested by the variations (some apparently not due to scribes) in the MSS. in respect to presence, as well as nature, of links between tales (see page 678, and remarks on individual links hereafter).

USE OF EARLIER MATERIALS [47]. It has been suggested that for the *Canterbury Tales* Chaucer in some instances drew upon earlier work that he had by him. See the remarks on the tales of the Knight, the Man of Law, the Prioress, the Monk, the Clerk, and the Second Nun.

DATES OF THE INDIVIDUAL PIECES [48]. For the conjectured dates of composition of the individual pieces, see the remarks on the separate items, and the Chronology (pages 689 ff., 623 ff.).

DATE OF THE PILGRIMAGE [49]. The day on which the pilgrimage is supposed to have been made, is fixed by the distinct declaration in the Man of Law's headlink (B5) that the morning (apparently the second of the journey) was that of the 18th of April. So the meeting at the Tabard was conceived of as occurring on the 16th of April, or April 24 in present reckoning. Calculations based on the astronomical data at the opening of the Parson's headlink (see page 745), have led Scherk to conclude on April 28, 1393, Koch on April 18, 1391, and again April 20, 1386, Ehrhart on April 6, 1388, as date for that piece. Skeat has emphatically rejected these calculations as based on false interpretations of the statements of the text. Skeat prefers 1387, when April 17 fell on Wednesday and so left four week-days clear for the journey.

INDICATIONS OF TIME AND PLACE [50]. There are the following definite indications of *time* in the *Tales:* (1) *Pro-*

logue 1-8, a little after the middle of April; (2) *Reeve's Prologue* A3906, 'half-way prime,' or about 7.30 a.m.; (3) *Man of Law's Headlink* B1-15, ten o'clock a.m. April 18 (Ellesmere MS., 28th; Harley, 13th; Hengwrt, 18th); (4) *Squire's Tale* F73, 'it is pryme,' or about 9 a.m.; (5) *Parson's Headlink* I5, 'foure of the clokke it was tho.' Other time indications are in C321-22, E4, E1170, E1685-86, G555, G588, H2, H16, and I1.

  ˙ The following are the definite indications of *place:* (1) *Prologue* A826, 'the watering of St. Thomas'; (2) *Reeve's Prologue* A3906-07, 'Lo Depeford,' 'Lo Grenewich'; (3) *Monk's Prologue* B3116, 'Lo Rouchestre stant heer faste by'; (4) *Wife's Prologue* D847, the Summoner threatens to tell several tales against friars before he comes to Sittingbourne; (5) *Summoner's Tale* D2294, 'we been almost at toune'; (6) *Canon's Yeoman's Prologue* G555, 'Er we had riden fully fyue myle At Boghton under Blee,' the Canon and his Yeoman ride up; (7) *Manciple's Prologue* H1-3, the Manciple begins his tale at 'Bob-up-and-down under the Blee'; (8) *Parson's Prologue* I16, 19, 25, 47, 62-63—the last tale is told by the Parson after 4 p.m., apparently near Canterbury.

THE DURATION OF THE PILGRIMAGE [51] has been discussed on the basis of the time and place indications. The idea of a journey of one day, and that of a journey of two days, are not now regarded as at all tenable. Furnivall suggested a journey of four days or of three and half days, and was followed by Skeat, Shipley, Pollard, and others. This gives Dartford, Rochester, and Ospringe, as the three lodging-places. Koch and Tatlock have favored a three-days' journey, Koch with lodging at Rochester and Ospringe, and Tatlock with lodging at Dartford and Ospringe. The notion of a journey of four or of three and a half days, presumes lodging after Fragments A, B, and E; or, if C be located after A, it presumes lodging after C, B, and E. The three-day journey would presume lodging after A and E; or, if C were shifted to follow A, it presumes lodging after C and E.

    The general view is that all the extant tales were for the

outward journey. Ten Brink favored the beginning of the homeward journey for the *Manciple's Tale*.

GROUPS AND MOTIFS [52]. Whatever Chaucer intended when he first adopted his framework, the Prologue and the links and the tales show relationships beyond the merely artificial bonds produced by the general setting. It has long been the practice to assume adaptation of the individual tales to the character of their narrators—an assumption to which there are obvious exceptions. But consideration has shown that the nature and the contents of at least certain sections of the *Tales*, are actually determined by the interplay of the personalities, the views, and the conduct, of the pilgrims one upon another, and that, coincidently with the exhibition of this interplay, there are treated more or less extensively certain definite *motifs*. Whether the design of exposing these *motifs* begot the interplay, or the need of plot-basis for exposition of the interplay gradually developed and led to the treatment of the *motifs*, and how far the treatment of any of the *motifs* is merely accidental, can, in the present state of the *Tales* and of our knowledge, scarcely be determined.

QUARREL MOTIFS [52]. For long the quarrels of the Miller and the Reeve, the Friar and the Summoner, and the Manciple and the Cook (hinted), arising from the antipathy and the conduct of these persons toward each other, and producing effort by each to apply his tale to the shame of his opponent—these have caused the respective rivals and their tales and links to be classed as '*quarrel groups*.' It has been suggested that originally Chaucer intended the Wife and the Merchant to form another such group (see page 722). The Cook's promise of a tale of an innkeeper in payment for the Host's jests on him (A4344 ff.), suggests another quarrel notion not worked out.—On quarrel *motifs* see pages 694, 697, 704, 722, 743.

BOND OF CONTRAST [52]. Again, Fragment B², comprising the tales and links of the Shipman, the Prioress, *Thopas*,

Melibeus, the Monk, and the Nun's Priest, is recognized as forming a close sequence united beyond other sections by the bond of *literary contrast.*

THE MARRIAGE GROUP [52]. But of much more importance is the *'Marriage Group.'* The nexus of this Group is a debate as to which of the two, husband or wife, should have the mastery. The Group, according to Kittredge, its most pleasing expositor, consists of the tales and links of Fragments D, E, and F. The Wife's Prologue begins the Group, being 'not connected with anything that precedes.' Here and in her tale the Wife declares and maintains that women should have sovereignty over their husbands. Her notions, her account of her personal conduct in wedlock, and her gibes, offend the views of some of her auditors, and insult others, especially the Clerk, who is outraged not only by her tenets and her treatment of her last husband, a clerk, but by the thrusts that she directs at him himself and at his brotherhood. At the conclusion of her tale, the quarrel between the Friar and the Summoner forms 'a comic interlude.' This ended, the Clerk has his opportunity. Cleverly he defends himself and his brotherhood from the slurs of the Wife, and rebukes her conduct and her views with the story of Griselda, which exemplifies ideals antithetical to those of the Wife; and he drives home his point with his ironical envoy urging wives to proceed and rule their husbands—and make them miserable, as the Wife of Bath made hers. Impelled by bitter personal experience, the Merchant catches up the Clerk's last words, and launches into a mock encomium of the wedded state, with furious irony enforcing his attack on the Wife and the conduct of the system that she represents. Then, after the *Squire's Tale,* which is an interlude of 'pure romance,' despite the Host's efforts to divert him from the theme of which he has already had enough, the Franklin tells his tale of 'gentilesse' in marriage, expressly repudiating the Wife's contention, as well as rejecting the opposite—his solution is that neither husband nor wife shall be subject, each shall love and serve the other in patient forbearance. So the discussion ends—according to Kittredge, with 'no connection between the *Franklin's Tale* and the group that follows.'

Lawrence has urged that if 'the Wife's Prologue and Tale opens the specific discussion of marriage, the "Melibeus" is the beginning of the remarks that prepare its way'; that in the *Melibeus* the theme of conjugal sovereignty is first clearly sounded, the tale is a prose counterpart of the *Wife's Tale*, the wife in each inducing her husband to give to her control in domestic affairs, and extricating the husband from embarrassment; that the Host's comments on the *Melibeus* based on experience with his own shrewish wife, continue the remarks; that the Monk's 'tragedies' constitute a serious interlude corresponding to the comic interlude of the Friar and the Summoner at the later point; that the *Nun's Priest's Tale* takes up the implied challenge of the Host ignored by the Monk, and illustrates just the converse of the point made by the *Melibeus*—give confidence to your wife's counsel, and you will suffer; and that locating Fragment C between A and B (see page 713) places the Wife's Prologue right after the *Nun's Priest's Tale*, and, through that tale and the priest's final exclamations against woman's counsels as cause of Adam's fall, affords motivation for the Wife's enunciation of her doctrine.

Koch has opposed use of the term 'Marriage Group,' because of the theme of marriage, of good and ill influence of wives on husbands, in the tales of the Miller, the Shipman, and the Manciple, and in the *Melibeus*. Lawrence has urged in defense that, though marriage is dealt with in these tales, the influence of wife on husband is not in the least emphasized in them as a theme of discussion; and that what gives unity to the Marriage Group and its prelude, is the debate as to which of the two should have the mastery, husband or wife.

Tupper has urged extension of the term 'Marriage Group' beyond the four tales, because of 'the large use of preceding motives by the Wife, the Merchant's indebtedness to the "Tale of Melibeus," the protracted debate on wifely counsels in Group B,' and 'the continuation of the marriage theme into the tales of the Second Nun, the Manciple, and the Parson.'

Lowes has shown remarkable association of the tales of the Merchant, the Parson, and the Franklin, the prologue and tale of the Wife, and the *Legend of Good Women* Prologue A, through indebtedness to Deschamps' *Miroir de Mariage* Chs. 14-25, 33-40, and Jerome's *Epistola adversus Jovinianum* (see pages 673, 643 and references there). He would associate with the Marriage Group the Miller's remarks about women good and bad, and the relations of the carpenter and his wife in his *Tale;* 'the *Clerk's Tale,* at least part'; and the *Manciple's Tale.* He points out that 'the theme was still in Chaucer's mind' when the *Envoy to Bukton* was written.

The dates of the Marriage Group proper as it stands are according to Lowes and Tatlock, from the end of 1393, or early in 1394, to 1396.

On the Marriage Group see pages 627, 641, 642, 672, 684, 699, 709, 720, 727, 733, 735, 737.

LOVE MOTIF [52]. Recently Tupper has urged that the *Tales* are 'as genuinely tales of love as the anecdotes of Gower under Venus's sway in the "Confessio Amantis." ' He has argued that Venus had special domination over pilgrimages; the mid-April days of the Canterbury pilgrimage are dominated by the planet Venus; Venus is the *deà ex machina* in the *Knight's Tale,* which illustrates chivalric devotion; the Reeve's and Miller's tales illustrate the churl's attitude toward love, an intent announced at the end of the Miller's Prologue; the Love *motif* makes relevant the explanation in the headlink of the Man of Law that, once having adequately portrayed Love's martyrs, Chaucer need not treat them in the *Tales,* and also the poet's assertion that he will not touch incestuous passion though such would be appropriate for a complete treatment of Love; the *Man of Law's Tale* is of the love of a stately wife and mother; the *Shipman's Tale* of the unfaithful wife was primarily intended to illustrate Envy, and was inserted here in afterthought as an antitype to the story of Constance; the *Prioress' Tale* falls under the Love plan only by its stress on virginity; *Sir Thopas* parodies the stock motives of conventional romance; *Melibeus* exalts wifely counsels, and is offset

by the shrewishness of the Host's wife (B3081 ff.), and rebutted
by the treachery of Delilah in the *Monk's Tale;* the actually
chief theme of the *Nun's Priest's Tale* is the mock-romantic
uxoriousness of Chanticleer. Tupper pointed out that by the
arrangement of Fragments ACBD, etc., the *Wife's Tale* becomes twelfth of the twenty-four. So he maintained that the
Wife is 'the key-stone of the arch of the Canterbury Tales,'
because she incarnates the ruling 'influence' upon pilgrimages,
she bears an obvious likeness to the wives of the tales of the
Miller, the Reeve, and the Shipman, and she epitomizes in her
prologue and tale all the opinions of her fellows on the woman
question. He noted that the Marriage Group follows the
Wife's Tale, and held that its theme is carried over into the
tales of the Second Nun, the Manciple, and the Parson; the
Pardoner utters his views as to unlawful love; though the Friar
and Summoner do not tell stories of love, their wantonness
toward women is often indicated; in the *Canon Yeoman's Tale*
is the parallel between the priest's devotion to alchemy and a
knight's service for his lady, and the hint of the Canon's relation to his wife shows that he could tell another story; the
Second Nun apotheosizes Virginity in designed opposition to
the Wife's octogamy; and the *Manciple's Tale* is a return to
the cuckold theme, and prepares for the *Parson's Tale,* chiefly
stressing Lechery.—It will be seen that in much of this matter
one is rather put to it to find an intentional and dominant
Love *motif* in the *Tales,* or, granted the Marriage Group, much
more of treatment of Love than would be found in almost any
collection of twenty-four tales.

SINS MOTIF [52]. Later Tupper called attention to the
prominence, 'not casual, but organic,' of the Seven Deadly
Sins (see pages 699, 701, 714, 717, 720, 723, 725, 738, 740,
743, 745, 746) in the *Tales.* Locating Fragment C after F, he
found together 'the Physician's version of Gower's theme of
Lechery in the *Confessio Amantis,*' 'the Pardoner's long attack
upon Avarice and Gluttony . . . followed by its tale that
admittedly illustrates both,' and the Second Nun's Prologue on
Idleness, 'introducing that antitype of Sloth St. Cecilia.' He

noted also Gower's themes of Pride (Inobedience) in the *Wife's Tale*, Wrath (Chiding) in the *Manciple's Tale*, and Envy (Detraction) in the *Man of Law's Tale*. He indicated that each of the four stories also used by Gower, is accompanied by a preachment against the sin in question; that the Pardoner, the Wife, the Manciple, and the Physician, each incarnates the sin that he condemns; that a lawyer was regarded as especially liable to Envy and Avarice; that the Friar-Summoner tales represent 'Wrath in its general aspect,' and their conduct illustrates Wrath; that, in the *Parson's Tale*, evidently intended as the concluding piece, the discourse on the Seven Sins is especially prominent; that each of the tales under discussion is undeniably indebted to the Sins treatise in the *Parson's Tale* (see page 745); that 'all the evidence tends to show that the Sins *motif* belongs to the latter part of our collection'; that 'the device of the Sins apparently came to the poet late'; that Chaucer's and Gower's use in four instances of the same tales for the purpose of illustrating identical divisions of the Seven Sins, argues indebtedness of one of the poets to the other, the debtor really being Chaucer; that to Chaucer the Sins *motif* is merely a device that appealed at intervals through its popular effectiveness, its potent suggestions of irony, and its value as a framework in separate instances; that the term 'Sins Group' is to be avoided as indicating 'an ordered sequence, a coherence between these stories that is entirely lacking'; and that the *motif* appears in the *Wife's Tale*, and is developed (1) by blending it skilfully with the Love *motif* in the four Gower tales (as Gower also blends it) and in the *Second Nun's Tale*, (2) by making it dominant in the tales of the Friar, the Summoner, and the Pardoner, neglecting the Love theme for the illustration of the Sins, as Gower does in many *exempla* of the *Confessio*, and (3) by abandoning it in the Marriage Group tales of the Clerk, the Merchant, the Squire, and the Franklin. Tupper feels that Chaucer's treatment of the Sins *motif* is complete, and that he carried back the *Cook's Tale* from a position following the *Manciple's Tale* (see page 697).

Recently Lowes has replied at great length to Tupper, 'on the basis of those authorities alone which he himself cites,' that

'Tupper's interpretation, in its postulates and its conclusions, is 'inconsistent with mediæval modes of thought'—inconsistency with mediæval modes of thought being, according to Tupper, a great cause for blindness to the Sins *motif* hitherto, and for dissent of critics from his views; that the ' "definitely fixed limits of variation among the branches" [of the Seven Deadly Sins], which Mr. Tupper postulates, simply does not exist'—indeed, that in the Middle Ages the '*confusion* of the categories is, to say the least, as essential a fact as their *rigidity*.' In detail Lowes discusses and rejects Tupper's arguments regarding individual tales, and shows how on Tupper's principles other tales could be added to those in his list. He concludes (1) that 'Chaucer makes abundant use of the Seven Deadly Sins,' for he 'dealt with life' which 'is a labyrinth of the Vices and the Virtues,' but he calls the Vices freely by their names—to deny a formal schematizing of the Seven Deadly Sins in the *Canterbury Tales*, is by no means to gainsay this; (2) that 'Chaucer is thoroughly mediæval in his use of *exempla*,' but the range of the *exempla* is not to be declared 'coterminous with the Seven Deadly Sins, and their application limited by the confines of the categories'; (3) that Chaucer's irony is 'independent of any formal schematizing of a group of Tales'; (4) and that Chaucer at the height of his powers did not revert from 'the glorious liberty he had attained, to the more or less schematic tendencies of his earlier period,' but that 'the development was the other way.'

Koch also has opposed Tupper's views.

B. *The Individual Fragments*

In the following pages the constituents of the individual Fragments are discussed in the order in which they are regularly printed.

Fragment A [53]

Fragment A comprises the General Prologue, and the tales of the Knight, the Miller, the Reeve, and the Cook, with the links between them.

THE GENERAL PROLOGUE [54]. An April prelude, an alluring introduction to the reader, breathes the spring-time atmosphere that environs not only the Prologue, but as well the *Knight's Tale,* and that reflects the essential spirit of all the tales. Then follows the narrative (19-34) of the assembling at the Tabard Inn, and of the poet's association with the company. To a few lines of comment and explanation (35-42) succeeds the account of the individual pilgrims (43-714), one of the greatest pieces of descriptive verse in litera-ture, and probably the greatest extended piece descriptive of persons and manners. The nature and the arrangement of the elements in the single sections of the passage, are determined by no fixed principle. Much is made of external personal appearance—of color, striking or representative details of dress or equipment, and bearing. But, vivid as are the pil-grims, the great feature in each case is the inner character or nature of the personage, and, perhaps more than this, his manners and habitual conduct. There is little abstract state-ment. Traits or qualities are exhibited by indication of char-acteristics of appearance and demeanor that might be noted by a temporary associate such as the poet is supposed to have been. But much more frequently they are shown through details that could be had only through the convention of omnis-cience—details regarding possessions, rank, standing in the community, habitual behavior, past acts and achievements, and opinions. It is through his skilful utilization of these, his large personal reaction on them, that Chaucer was enabled to present in the Prologue figures that are not only individual and as well typical for his own day, but also representative of human nature and conduct in all time.

Next follows the poet's clever humorous apology (715-46) that he enforced in the Miller's headlink (A3167-86): his duty is to record the facts exactly as they were; he must not be held responsible for irregular conduct or ribald speech or failure to deal with folk according to their degree; it is the pilgrims themselves who must be indicted. Then we make the acquaint-ance of the Host, and learn of the incidents of the evening, and

of the plan for telling tales on the journey, that has already
been outlined (see page 674). The last lines (822-58) recount
the assembling of the company the next morning, and, at the
watering of St. Thomas, the Knight's drawing of the lot for
the first story.

The general plan for the *Tales,* its analogues, and the date
at which Chaucer supposed it to occur, have already been
discussed (pages 672, 674, 681).

The figures and the characters of the individual pilgrims,
are generally assumed to be original as they stand, to be the
products of the poet's imagination developing the fruits of wide
reading and of personal experience with men. Suggestions for
some of the personages have been traced to earlier works. For
instance, some features of the Prioress have been found in the
Roman de la Rose, and of the Wife in the *Roman* and Deschamps' *Miroir de Mariage;* and the Parson is claimed as a
tissue of conventions, and as perhaps due in part to use of
Renclus de Moiliens' *Roman de Carité.* The Plowman reflects
much of the current ideal made popular through *Piers Plowman* and its kindred pieces. Biographies of actual contemporary persons have been used to prove the close reflection of
the life of the day in Chaucer's men and women.

The Prologue is regarded by some scholars as composed
before any of the tales were written in their final form, by
others as written somewhat later, and by still others as among
the last of the Canterbury pieces. Chaucer's apparent modification (see page 676) of the general plan outlined in the
Prologue, would seem to point to composition of the Prologue
earlier, perhaps much earlier, than the date of the modification.
Some of the links seem to imply previous composition of the
Prologue. The passage on protection of commerce between
Middleburgh and Orewelle (ll. 276-77), would seem to point to
conditions of control of trade in 1384-1387. This implies composition after 1384, but gives no *terminus ad quem.* Some
hold that at one date or more the Prologue was modified and
was augmented to accord with changes and additions connected
with later links and tales—*e.g.,* that the characterization of

the Wife was modified or rewritten at the date of the Wife's
Prologue as a result of the conception developed in composition of that prologue; that lines 163-64, with their omission
of the characterization of the Second Nun and of that of the
Nun's Priests (see page 711), each of whom is assigned a tale,
are due to a later addition of those two figures to the company,
or to description of the Nun 'in too strong strokes' and subsequent withdrawal of the passage, perhaps with intention to
substitute another personage—in any case, to failure properly
to fill out the passage (see page 677) ; and that the personages
introduced as a group at lines 542-44, were a later addition.
The possible omission at lines 163-64 Skeat connected with the
fact that Chaucer is said to have joined 'wel nyne and twenty'
pilgrims (l. 24) at the Tabard, though there were really
thirty.   He felt that the discord arose from a later change of
plan.   But the 'wel nyne and twenty' may be merely a round
number.

THE KNIGHT'S TALE [55].   On very unsubstantial
bases Ten Brink advanced, and Koch and others supported, the
frequently repeated theory that the *Palamon and Arcite* mentioned in the Prologue of the *Legend* (see page 619) was in
seven-line stanzas.   This theory was rejected by Hempl, Pollard (later view), Mather, and Root, and seems to have been
disposed of by Tatlock.   Tatlock has argued effectively
against the idea that the *Troilus* V 1807-27 and V 1-7, 8-11,
the description of the Temple of Venus in the *Parlement* (ll.
183-294), and much of the opening of *Anelida and Arcite* (ll.
1-70), which with the *Palamon* were drawn largely from Boccaccio's *Teseide*, represent sections of a lost *Palamon* or were
parts of such a work (see page 620).   He has urged the probability that the *Palamon and Arcite* (which he dates at about
1385) and the *Knight's Tale,* are practically identical, allowance being made for a few slight changes (as in A875-92) to
adjust the poem in 1388-1390 to the Canterbury plan.   Emerson accepts the *Knight's Tale* as the *Palamon,* and offers evidence to date it 'the last of 1381 or first part of 1382.'
Pollard dates the poem 1383 or 1384.   Lowes holds for an

earlier form of the poem from about 1382, after the *Fame* and the greater number of the stories of the *Legend*, and before the *Troilus*. Kittredge has shown that Clanvowe quoted the tale before 1392, perhaps before 1391.

The tale is an adaptation of Boccaccio's *Teseide*, for whose 9896 lines Chaucer has but 2250 lines, of which 270 are translated, 374 more bear a general likeness to the *Teseide*, and 132 more exhibit a slight likeness to the Italian. To be noted is the condensation of the original here, in contrast with the great expansion of Boccaccio in the *Troilus*. Statius' *Thebais* was drawn on for descriptive suggestions, and Boethius for moralizing material.

Two Theban cousins, Palamon and Arcite, held prisoners in Athens, behold through a window, and fall in love with, Emelye, sister of their conqueror, Theseus. At once their former affection becomes enmity. Arcite is ransomed, but is forbidden Athenian territory. He returns disguised, and serves as page of the chamber to Emelye. Palamon escapes from prison, and encounters Arcite a-maying. A duel is arranged for the next day. Theseus and his retinue come upon the combatants. Theseus decrees a joust between the parties, each supported by a hundred knights, the date one year thence, the prize the hand of Emelye. At the joust, Palamon is made prisoner; but the victorious Arcite, Mars' favorite, is, through the interposition of Venus and Pluto, mortally injured by his horse. After a long period of mourning, Theseus arranges the marriage of Palamon and Emelye.

The tale is the longest, and from many points of view the best, of the Canterbury poems. Chaucer put it first perhaps partly because of its merit, perhaps partly because of the rank of the Knight. Possibly he intended the Knight to win the supper that was to be given in honor of the best teller of tales. The poem is most appropriate to the supposed narrator. It is the only tale of chivalry in the series, if we except the unfinished *Squire's Tale*. While (as was common in romances) pagan and Christian, ancient and mediæval, elements are commingled in it, its themes and general spirit are mediæval—it is a tale of knightly prowess, but more of knightly love. Of the four figures that stand out, the two knights are contrasted in appearance and in rôle, as their chief champions and their religious affiliations are contrasted; but they are scarce at all distinguished from each other in character. Emelye is but the conventional beautiful object of desire, with no individuality, grieving and loving on the meet occasion. She speaks but once. Theseus is the most individualized—a spirited, dominating personality, with a will of his own, opinions, and large views, and much of Chaucer's own humor. He was needed merely to fulfil the part of the Shakespearean Duke or Prince—but, just as did Shakespeare in *Midsummer Night's Dream,* Chaucer became interested in him, and developed him, and perhaps let himself speak out through him. The conduct of all the personages, except perhaps of Theseus, is purely conventional. The descriptive and pictorial features are the prominent elements. Thirty-four per cent (in Part I forty-eight per cent) of the lines, are direct discourse. The poem is a series (1) of striking situations and dramatic scenes, and (2) of splendid descriptive passages. The first two Parts consist more largely of the former; the last two Parts are made up chiefly (forty-seven per cent and forty-one per cent) of the latter. The springtime, early morning, atmosphere encompasses the whole (each of the incidents takes place in May and in the morning)—a lovely and rare atmosphere in perfect keeping with the fine, clear, somewhat remote, delicate grace and elevation of all the story. Notable are the characteristically Chaucerian passages of comment, and the equally characteristic touches of subtle humor in situation and in turn of speech.

THE MILLER'S PROLOGUE [56]. All the company are delighted with the Knight's tale. Pleased with this beginning, the Host turns to the Monk for the second story—but the drunken Miller has another 'noble tale' with which to quit the Knight. Despite the Host's reluctance, he gets permission to proceed. He protests that his drunkenness must be excuse for any objectionable speech; he will tell of how a clerk set the cap of a carpenter and his wife. At once Oswald the Reeve, who is a carpenter, bursts out against any such defaming of men and shaming of women. So, the first of the 'quarrel groups' (see page 683) opens. The Miller declares he means no harm; there are pure wives, but none can tell what his own is. The poet slyly adds his humorous defense (cp. A725-42) of the ribald tales he is about to tell: he must tell the tales just as they were narrated, and is not responsible for their matter or their words. Root has noted similarities between this apology and the 'Conclusione dell' Autore' of the *Decameron*.

On the basis of similarity between A3154-56 (which lines are in only three MSS.), Deschamps' *Miroir de Mariage* 9097-100, and the A Prologue to the *Legend* 275-79, Lowes concludes that 'in the Miller's Prologue Chaucer recalled the A-version of the Prologue to the *Legend*, and with it (and even more definitely) the phraseology of the *Miroir de Mariage* itself' (see page 686).

THE MILLER'S TALE [56]. The poet wisely declares the Miller's to be a churl's tale, and advises the delicate to turn over the page and choose another. The story is a combination of two originally separate jests—that of the man who let himself be scared by prediction of a second Flood, and that of the lover, who, expecting to kiss his sweetheart's lips, was grievously disappointed in his success, and avenged himself with a hot coulter. Chaucer's tale is supposed to rest on a lost French *fabliau*. Hans Sachs and Schumann tell a similar tale. An analogue to the second jest is in a collection by Masuccio di Salerno of the latter half of the fifteenth century. There is extant a fourteenth-century Dutch version of the combined jests, that is a transitional form between Chaucer and Masuccio.

The art of the *Miller's Tale* is masterful; the story is admirably told, the elements of the two plots are most skilfully interwoven, and the characters and the personalities of the actors are presented with remarkable vividness and spirit. As is usual in his morally objectionable tales, in contrast with the practice of most narrators of such matter, Chaucer does not write for the dirtiness of the story; what he stresses is the jest itself, and the qualities of the tricksters and the butts, on which the conception and the execution of the jest depend.

THE REEVE'S PROLOGUE [57]. The company are much amused at the Miller's account of the adventures of Alison and Nicholas and Absolon and the Carpenter. Even the 'sclendre colerik' (A587) Reeve appears actually to enjoy the fun—but he must grumble a bit. Moreover, one victim in the tale is a carpenter who is in some personal respects much like himself. He declares he could requite this jest with a ribald 'blering of a proud milleres ye'; but he is old and failing, 'grastyme is doon'—and he launches into a discourse on the wretchedness of old age. Indignant at the sermoning, and at sermons from a reeve, the Host bids him get on with his tale—Deptford is in sight, and Greenwich, and it is half-way prime (see page 682). Disregarding his previous ·professions, the Reeve proceeds.

THE REEVE'S TALE [57]. More indecent than the Miller's story is Oswald's tale of Simkin, the miller of Trumpington, who took advantage of two clerks, and was repaid with the debauching of his proud wife and cherished heiress, with a beating, and with the loss of some of his wares. The direct source of the tale is supposed to be a lost French *fabliau*. An analogue of common origin is found in the *Decameron* Day 9 Tale 6. Another is in the French *fabliau De Gombert et des Deux Clers* by Jean de Boves. The closest version is in the French *fabliau Le Meunier et les II Clers* in a Berne MS. A later English treatment is *A Mery Jest of the Mylner of Abyngton.*

Like its companion, the *Miller's Tale*, the tale of the Reeve is a masterpiece of narrative art. The action is well bound together, the whole carefully constructed, each incident and act planned for in advance. The characterization is remarkable—even the horse has individuality. The action all grows out of character. Once more the nature of the people and the humor of the jest, are the centres of emphasis. Largely contributing to the realism of the piece are its definiteness of detail; its precise indications of time and place; the circumstantial elaboration of the original situation; the naming of persons, places, and even the horse; the sketching in of minor features of environment—the fen, the arbor, the barn; and the details of the interior of the mill and the dwelling. The use of contrast and surprise is effective, as is the employment of the Northern dialect for the clerks (see page 609).

THE COOK'S PROLOGUE [58]. The Cook, Hodge of Ware, is in ecstasies over the Reeve's story—he will himself tell 'a litel jape that fil in our citee.' With a knowledge not sustained in a later link (H 5 ff.; see page 743), the Host taunts him with his cheating dealings, and then bids him tell on. The Cook promises as good as he gets; before they part he will tell a tale of an innkeeper that will requite the Host. So, preparation is made for the Cook's second tale called for by the original plan (see page 675), and suggestion is given of another 'quarrel group' (see page 683) not worked out.

THE COOK'S TALE [58] was carried only so far as line 58. The figure of the prospective hero, Perkin Revelour, is well drawn, and the excellent exposition apparently is about complete. The tale was probably to be of the type of the Miller's and the Reeve's that immediately preceded it. Ten Brink suggested that it was recognition of this fact that caused Chaucer to break off, and that the piece stands here at the end of Fragment A just as he left it. Tupper has urged that the tale was moved back to its present place for neighborhood to the other two; that it was originally intended to follow the *Manciple's Tale* since the Manciple's Prologue (H11 ff., 28-29) implies that the Cook's tale is not yet told; and that at that time Chaucer had come to his modified plan of one tale per pilgrim on the way. But Root takes the demand for a tale by the Cook to prove that when the Manciple's Prologue was written, Chaucer still had the plan of two tales going and two returning. Yet the passage (H11, 15; see also 'This cook' H20) would indicate that the Host had scarce laid eyes on the Cook before (unless he is jesting); while the Cook's Prologue (A4344 ff.) shows that he knew his name and his methods of dealing, and that the Cook must have impressed himself on him when he promised a tale against an innkeeper to pay him back. Skeat suggested that the Manciple passage indicates that the Cook's fragment was meant to be suppressed.

The Tale of Gamelyn, inserted in some of the MSS., where it is assigned to the Cook (see page 676), is discussed on page 25.

FRAGMENT B¹ [59]

In all the MSS. except Selden, Fragment B consists of two sections: B¹ (B1-1190), which regularly follows A or AGamelyn, but in Selden follows F²; and B² (B1191-4652), which regularly comes late (see pages 679, 680). B¹ consists of the headlink, prologue, tale, and endlink of the Man of Law, the endlink being usually styled the *Shipman's Prologue.*

B¹ is marked off from A by the break at the end of the *Cook's Tale,* and by its opening on a morning (B1-17), evidently the second of the journey. It is supposed that the pilgrims lodged at Dartford or at Rochester (see page 682).

THE MAN OF LAW'S HEADLINK AND PROLOGUE [60]. The day is the eighteenth of April (B5-6). The Host rouses the company: it is ten o'clock, time passes, they should be at their stories; let the Man of Law begin. The Lawyer will keep forward, though he knows 'no thrifty tale' (B46, cp. B1165; see page 703). 'Chaucer,' he declares, is cunning in rimes, and 'of olde tyme' has told many a story of love—'in youthe' of Ceys and Alcion, and since then of noble wives and lovers in his 'Seintes Legende of Cupyde'; but he has not dealt with vicious passion. So, the Lawyer will treat of no evil love; he cares not that he cannot vie with Chaucer in rime; he will 'speke in prose' (B96). He opens with a prologue on the miseries of poverty; his tale was told him by a merchant many years gone by. The prologue and the tale are in rime-royal.

Several important points are encountered in this link. It contains one of the three passages (see page 618) in Chaucer's works asserting authorship—here of *Ceys and Alcion* and the *Legend of Good Women.* But the list of heroines does not agree with that of the *Legend* itself (see page 667). Evidently, in the Lawyer's list Chaucer is speaking only in general terms.

It has been suggested that the treatment in the *Legend* of only eight of the names in this list, indicates that Chaucer was still at work on the *Legend* when this passage in the headlink was written, or that at this time he was intending to take up the *Legend* again and was planning how to continue it.

The lawyer's declaration that Chaucer has written no word 'of thilke wikke ensample of Canacee' or of Apollonius of Tyre (B77 ff.), has been the source of much discussion. Since in the *Confessio* (III 143, VIII 271) Gower tells as *exempla* the stories of these personages, it has been urged that Chaucer was here attacking or taunting him. With this has been associated Gower's later omission of his compliment to Chaucer (see page 591); and thence have been built up theories that a quarrel between the poets originated from the Lawyer's words. The argument becomes very thin. What little we know of relations between the poets is of friendship (see pages 585, 591). It is argued that Gower's treatment of Apollonius omits the vicious episode alluded to by the Lawyer; that the stories of Canace and Apollonius were widely known in the period; that Canace is dealt with in Ovid, whose treatment of love-tales is in the Lawyer's mind (B54); and that the date of publication, 1390, of the *Confessio* would seem to preclude allusion in the Lawyer's headlink. Moreover, Canace is one of the approved ladies in the *Legend ballade* (see page 667). On the other hand, it is urged that Gower and Chaucer perhaps exchanged MSS. or talked over plans of work; that the Lawyer's headlink and tale postdated the *Confessio,* as did other Canterbury tales (*e.g.,* the Marriage Group); and that the *Lawyer's Tale,* though taken from Trivet, shows some signs of possible influence by Gower's treatment of the story of Constance (see page 701). The whole question of whether either poet is debtor to the other, is a pretty one. The notion of a quarrel is a far-fetched inference.—One must bear in mind Tupper's argument (see Lowes' opposition, page 687) that four stories used by Gower as *exempla* of Deadly Sins, are used by Chaucer as *exempla* of the same sins (the *Lawyer's Tale* illustrating Envy), and thence that Chaucer is indebted to Gower for these parallels.

A number of critics have felt that the tale is inappropriate to the Lawyer. Tupper has argued that the Poverty of the prologue is Impatient Poverty, a vice that is opposed to the virtuous Wilful Poverty, and that is characterized by 'grucching,' which is a phase of Envy; and he has pointed out the association of Envy with merchants (see B132,135) and lawyers in the Middle Ages and up to Elizabeth's day. Lowes has opposed or qualified Tupper's inferences (see page 688). The headlink is in couplets; the prologue and the tale are in rime-royal. The Lawyer's declaration, 'I speke in prose, and lat him rymes make' (B96) has been said to mean 'I usually speak in prose'; but it is commonly regarded as referring to the tale that is to be told. Thence scholars have inferred that at one time Chaucer intended to have the Lawyer tell a prose tale, and failed to correct this passage when he assigned him the *Constance*. The prose tale is assumed by some to be the *Melibeus*. Lowes points out that the story of Constance is one of a noble wife, such as the Lawyer says (B56) he will not tell. He urges that the Lawyer's prose tale was to be a version of Pope Innocent's *De Contemptu Mundi*, a version of which is claimed by Chaucer in the list in the A Prologue to the *Legend* (see page 618). The mention of Chaucer's incapacity in verse (B47-48) has by some been taken to indicate that at least that part of the headlink was originally intended to follow *Sir Thopas*, and intended to attain point by reminiscence of Chaucer's failure in that tale (B2109 ff.).

The Poverty materials in the actual prologue to the *Lawyer's Tale* (B99 ff.), are commonly regarded as due to Innocent's treatise, and have been taken as based on Chaucer's version of it assumed to be earlier than this prologue. Lowes connects this Poverty prologue, the insertion in the A Prologue to the *Legend* (dated by him soon after June 7, 1394) of the claim of a version of Innocent's work, and the passage on the *Legend* in the Lawyer's headlink; and infers that the translation falls in the Canterbury period, and not in the earlier period often assigned to it—that is, he puts it after the B Prologue to the *Legend*, 1386, and before the A Prologue,

1394. Pollard dated the tale toward the close of 1369-1379. Skeat felt that the Poverty lines (B99-121) and the passages from the *De Contemptu* in the tale (B421-27, 771-77, 925-31, 1135-41), were inserted at about 1387 as part of a revision made of an independent tale of before 1385 and probably of about 1380. This theory of a revision has been strongly opposed. As the *De Contemptu* is used in the prologue and the tale here, and is quoted elsewhere only in the tales of the Pardoner and the Monk (both dated late by him), Tatlock dates these passages from Innocent late, accepting a date after 1386 and before 1394. He accounts the evidence good that the *Constance* was written 'well within the Canterbury period, certainly after the first Prologue to the *Legend*.' This location he believes to be indicated by failure of the B Prologue to mention the Constance. He dates the tale as probably after 1390, because he believes that Gower as well as Trivet was used for it.

THE MAN OF LAW'S TALE [60]. The Constance theme is an extensively treated one, and is related to the Griselda, Florence, and Eustace stories (see pages 112 ff.). The tale of Constance is based on the story of 'la pucele Constaunce' in the English Nicholas Trivet's Anglo-Norman *Chronicle* composed at about 1334. Chaucer abbreviated the story, modifying only details, and omitting little of any importance. He added from Boethius B813-19, and from Pope Innocent B421-27, 771-77, 925-31, 1135-41. His own additions, apparently the best parts of the tale, are B190-203, 270-87, 295-315, 330-43, 351-71, 400-10, 421-27, 449-62, 470-504, 631-58, 701-14, 771-84, 811-19, 825-68, 925-45, 1037-43, 1052-78, 1132-41. On his theory of revision (see above), Skeat ascribes to a later date B190-203, 295-315, 358-71, 449-62, 631-58, 701-14, 827-68.

The possible influence of Gower, the date, and the connection with a Sins *motif*, are discussed with the headlink and the prologue (see page 699).

Constance, daughter of the Emperor of Rome, weds the Sultan of Surrie on condition that he and his become Christians. The

Sultan's mother is enraged at this defection, and has her son and all the other Christians slain at a feast. Constance is set adrift alone on a vessel. Eventually she arrives at Northumberland. Constance's virtue withstanding his desire, a knight slays her host-ess, and puts the knife in the heroine's hand as she lies asleep. At the trial, the villain is stricken down from Heaven. King Alla weds Constance. In Alla's absence, a boy is born. By substituting false letters, the furious mother-in-law, Donegild, produces orders to set the mother and the child adrift on a vessel plenteously victualled. Alla returns; on learning the facts, he slays his mother. Constance comes to a heathen land, providentially is saved from the lust of a steward, sails past Gibraltar, and ultimately is helped to Rome by her uncle. With the uncle and the aunt she and the child live long, unrecognized. Alla comes to Rome, is entertained by the uncle, at a feast recognizes his boy, and later is united to Constance. At a dinner given by Alla to the Roman Emperor, Constance reveals herself to her father.

The tale is quite improbable; stock features are common in it; the plot is but a string of incidents that might be added to infinitely; most of the items might be omitted; and the promi-nent *motifs* of the tale are repeated. Yet all this is to be expected of mediæval narrative, especially of a pious tale or an approach to a saint's legend. The piece is rightly one of the most esteemed of the Canterbury series. Again and again in it Chaucer is at the height of the pathos in which he excels. Constance is the incarnation of purity, of constant faith, of sublime patience. As in all his tales of innocence distressed, Chaucer develops the personality of the chief figure, and makes that the centre of interest as well as of action, and in itself the adequately unifying element of the whole story.

THE SHIPMAN'S PROLOGUE [61]. The Man of Law's endlink, usually styled the 'Shipman's Prologue,' is definitely assigned to the Squire in eighteen or twenty MSS. In two more MSS. titles assign it to the Squire, but there B1179 has the name 'Somnour.' Harley 7334 assigns it to nobody, but names the 'Somnour' in B1179, and follows the link with the *Wife's Tale*. Only Selden both styles the link 'Shipman's Prologue,' and follows it with the *Shipman's Tale*. The rest of the MSS., the best or among the best of all, are said to omit the link. Miss Hammond suggests that perhaps the Sum-

moner was at one time intended to follow the Man of Law.
Skeat's latest views were that the Shipman's Prologue was composed with the Shipman in view, but became useless because no
Shipman's tale had been written; that the present *Shipman's
Tale* was originally meant for the Wife (see page 722); that
when the present *Wife's Tale* was written, the old Wife's tale
was attached by a link (B1625-42) to the *Prioress' Tale* and
styled *Shipman's Tale;* that the old Shipman's Prologue
(B1163-90) was experimentally prefixed to the *Squire's Tale*
with an intention (unfulfilled) of altering some of the later
lines; that a new Squire's Prologue (the present F1-8) was
written; and that the old Shipman's Prologue (B1163-90) was
practically abandoned, and so does not appear in many of the
best MSS.

In eleven MSS. and in the black-letter editions there is a
spurious Shipman's Prologue of twelve lines connecting the
Tale with the *Pardoner's Tale*. A spurious link of six lines
heads the *Tale* in MS. Lansdowne.

FRAGMENT B² [62]

Fragment B² comprises the tales of the Shipman, the Prioress, *Sir Thopas, Melibeus*, the Monk, and the Nun's Priest, and
the accompanying links (B1191-4652). The Fragment follows
next after B¹ in only MS. Selden, but there B¹ follows F². A
glance at the MS. arrangement of the Fragments on page
679, will show that regularly except in Selden, B¹ comes early
and B² late.

Following Bradshaw's suggestion, in the Six-Text Edition
Furnivall 'lifted up' B² (see page 679) to follow B¹. Skeat
adopted this arrangement for his editions. The reasons for
this order are, first, that so Rochester (B3116) is made to
precede (see page 682) the reference to Sittingbourne (D847);
and, second, that the Man of Law's Prologue (B46), 'I can
right now no thrifty tale seyu,' is echoed in the comment on the
Lawyer's Tale in the Shipman's Prologue (B1165), 'This was
a thrifty tale for the nones.' Skeat finally came to feel (see
page 679) that B¹ should follow A, and that the last five

Fragments should be GCB²HI, as in his MSS. Groups II, III, IV and in Miss Hammond's Group IV (see page 680).

THE SHIPMAN'S TALE [63] is a *fabliau*, but not so coarse as those of the Miller and the Reeve.

The wife of a merchant of St. Denis asks from a priest, Dan John, a cousin and close associate of her husband, the loan of a hundred francs for finery. The priest borrows the money of the merchant. In the merchant's absence in Flanders, he gives it to the wife. The wife grants the priest her favors. When the husband returns, the priest informs him that he has paid his wife the money he has borrowed. The woman admits receiving and spending the money; she will pay her husband as she can.

Koch assigns the tale to 1389-1390, Tatlock to 1388-1393 (see pages 625, 628). The domestic character of the story has caused some critics to regard the tale as not especially appropriate for the Shipman. The plural first personal pronouns in B1202-04-08-09, and line 1364, show that the tale was originally written for a married woman, evidently the Wife of Bath, the only matron in the company; and that, when it was assigned to the Shipman, the opening was not thoroughly revised. Tatlock suggested that Chaucer originally intended a quarrel between the Wife and the Merchant, caused by a merchant's being the butt of the story, just as the Miller-Reeve quarrel was caused by the *Miller's Tale* being against a carpenter (A3861). Close parallels exist between the Shipman's and Merchant's tales (B1199, E1315, probably from the *Parson's Tale* I1068; B1559, E2322, probably from the *Roman de la Rose*), and the *Shipman's Tale* and the Wife's Prologue (B1194-209, 1363-67; D337-56, 257-62).

The First Tale of the Tenth Day of the *Decameron* is similar to the story told by the Shipman. But Skeat, Ten Brink, and others agree with Tyrwhitt's judgment that Chaucer got his matter from some French *fabliau*, greatly modifying his original. Skeat calls attention to 'Qui la' (B1404), the laying of the scene near Paris, mention of France (B1306, 1341' 1384), and the merchant's departure for Bruges (B1448).

THE PRIORESS' HEADLINK AND TALE [64]. The

gracious and gentle personality and conduct of the Prioress have a powerful effect on the Host. With the most courteous deferential diffidence he ventures to request of her a tale, if so be that she would be so kind—will she vouchsafe?

The character of her tale and her way of telling it, bear out our conclusion that the affectations of the Prioress are on the surface. Her story is of 'yonge Hugh of Lincoln,' the little chorister who loved to sing the *Alma Redemptoris Mater,* who was murdered by the Jews and cast into a pit, and who was found through his song which persisted until in the church the abbot raised the miraculous grain from his tongue. This pathetic story, rightly one of the best known and most cherished of the tales, illustrates once more Chaucer's wonderful power in treatment of simplicity and innocence, and his tendency, in all the tales calling for such treatment, to draw the interest from the mere story or the accessories, and to centre it on the nature and the personality of the principal personage.

The poem is in rime-royal. Like the *Second Nun's Tale,* this story by the Prioress is really a legend. Attention has been called to the similarity between the invocations at the head of the two tales. Stanza 3 of the *Prioress' Tale* reminds of stanza *M* of the *ABC* (see page 628).

The notion of Jews murdering Christian children is common in all Christian countries from the fifth century to the very present. Many mediæval treatments of the theme of the Prioress were made. After a study of twenty-nine versions of the story, Brown assigns Chaucer's tale to the '*Alma Redemptoris* "Magical Object" Version' of the C Group of the treatments, represented also in the Vernon miracles (see page 166), Alphonsus a Spina's *Fortalicum Fidei,* and in a text in MS. Trinity College Cbg. O, 9, 38. The actual original of Chaucer is not extant. Brown concludes that the tale owes to the original practically the whole framework, as well as many minor details and some phrases.

The general view appears to be that the tale is late. Skeat assigned it 'probably' to 'the later period'; Pollard put it after the conception of the Canterbury plan; Lowes sets it 'certainly late.' This is held despite the formerly favored but now rejected theory that stanzaic form implies early composition of a Canterbury tale.

THE PROLOGUE TO SIR THOPAS [65]. The company are greatly affected by the Prioress' story. That the Host himself is moved, is suggested by his use of rime-royal as he turns to Chaucer for a tale. Beyond the Hoccleve portrait (see page 617), with which its details agree admirably, the following passage has been our only source of direct information as to Chaucer's personal appearance and manner. Here we learn that he was stout and 'small and fair of face.' In demeanor and appearance he is 'elvish,' not gossiping with his fellows, but riding silently, and thoughtfully staring on the road. From him the Host expects 'som deyntee thing.' It is possible that the long-cherished notions based on this passage will be given up for the interpretation that what we see of the poet here is not habitual, but is due to the mood begotten by the *Prioress' Tale,* and that the usual impression got from this passage is not in keeping with the conception of Chaucer as 'leading spirit in arrangeing the party' (A30-34) and as holding intimate intercourse with the Monk while slyly ridiculing his remarks (A182). The substitute conception will by many be received reluctantly.

SIR THOPAS [65] is one of the most delightful bits of the *Canterbury Tales.* It is neither a bitter assault nor a serious satire. It is but a scrap of burlesque thrown off in a playful moment, mimicking the fondness for insignificant detail, the diffuseness, the vapidity, the galloping movement with little actual progress, that are characteristic of the decadent romances. So slyly and skilfully has Chaucer made his imitation that the absurdities that are in almost every stanza, dawn on one but gradually. Six romances, one unidentified, are named in the piece. Of these *Guy of Warwick* (see page 15) presents the greatest number of parallels of expression and of content with *Sir Thopas.* But that Chaucer was making *Guy* or any other single romance his butt, is little acceptable.

Apparently he wrote in an off-hand fashion, from his general impressions. The fragment exhibits eight stanza-forms, of which the common basis is the tail-rime aabccb or aabaab. The variations are by addition of multiples of three lines, or by use of a 'bob.' Clearly, despite the suggestions of some students, the object of the variations was not to illustrate the various romance stanzas, or to exhibit Chaucer's capacity in handling verse-forms. The poet let himself go in the spirit of the mood, exuberantly running on here, and adding a quirk there, as facility in rime or the swing of the jingle invited.

THE PROLOGUE TO MELIBEUS [66]. The Host soon sickens of this 'drasty speche' and 'rym dogerel.' It becomes unbearable from the moment he learns that Sir Thopas 'drank water of the wel.' Despite Chaucer's protest that the other personages have been permitted to finish their tales uninterrupted, the Host commands the poet to tell in prose something in romance style, or at least something affording amusement or doctrine. So Chaucer tells of Melibeus a 'moral tale vertuous.' It is often forgotten that the Host invites the Monk also (B3982, 3995) to begin again after he has been interrupted. It is to be noted that Chaucer speaks (B2147, 2154) of *Melibeus* as if it were a written piece (see also A1201, G78, 1957 and 1081).

THE TALE OF MELIBEUS [66] is dull reading; but the mere fact that Chaucer troubled to translate it, would show that it had much appeal for the period. In protesting against possible misapprehension of his accuracy, Chaucer not only asserts that there are several versions of the piece, but supposes it likely that his modifications will be noted by the company, who are probably familiar with some version (B2130-54). The interest of the *Melibeus* is largely in the fact that with the *Boethius*, the *Astrolabe*, and the *Parson's Tale*, it exhibits Chaucer's ability in prose. The tale is a close translation of the French *Le Livre de Melibee et de Dame Prudence*, made perhaps by Jean de Meun from the Latin *Liber Consolationis et Consilii* of Albertano of Brescia (see pages 731, 744).

Melibeus, the mighty and rich, finds that his foes have entered his house, and beaten and wounded his wife, Prudence, and his daughter, Sophie. He is furious; but his wife counsels patience. He summons a great congregation of folk, and puts the case to them: shall he keep peace, or make war? The personages in turn give contradictory advice, with a leaning to war. In the colloquy that follows their departure, Prudence counsels Melibeus at great length, citing the authority of various sages. Melibeus agrees that Prudence have private conference with their foes. These subject themselves to her arbitrament. Her kindred and old friends are summoned to judge the case; they counsel peace. The foes submit to Melibeus, who finally, by advice of his wife, forgives them.

The appropriateness of the *Melibeus* as a narrative for the Man of Law, the fact that the Man of Law promises a tale in prose (B96), and the appearance of '*the* tale of Melibee' (B3079) in many MSS. of the early type for the later '*my* tale of Melibee,' all assist the idea that the tale was written first for the Man of Law and not for Chaucer, the endlink (Monk's Prologue) being composed when the *Melibeus* was still assigned to that personage. Lowes has argued that the prose for the Man of Law was the translation of Innocent (see page 700).

It has been pointed out that the *Melibeus* is a prose counterpart of the *Wife's Tale*, and that the piece seems to open the preparation for the sovereignty discussion begun by the Wife (see page 685).

Omission of a passage in the French reflecting on youthful kings, caused Tatlock to infer composition of the *Melibeus* after the death of Edward the Black Prince on June 8, 1376. Tatlock dates the tale before the *Troilus*, and before the *Man of Law's Tale*. Koch put the tale at 1386-1387, Mather at 1373-1378, Skeat at 1372-1377 with a later revision, Pollard after 1385.

THE MONK'S PROLOGUE [67]. The opening of the Monk's Prologue is made over from, or is made over into, the 'merye wordes of the Hoste' or *Verba Hospitis*, a rejected stanza at the end of the *Clerk's Tale* in several MSS., apparently originally intended to end that piece (see pages 727, 728).

The inference that the two groups of lines, and so their contexts, were composed at about one date, does not follow.

Whatever be our estimate of the *Melibeus*, the Host was delighted with it, especially because it presents a woman of patience in striking contrast with his militant wife. He launched into a vividly realistic picture of the virago and her habitual conduct. This has been regarded as sustaining the theme of the relationship between husband and wife introduced in the *Melibeus*, and carried on by the Nun's Priest, to be developed into the sovereignty theme of the Marriage Group opened formally by the Wife (see pages 684, 720).

The pilgrims are approaching Rochester (B3116), by some critics regarded as the lodging-place for the first, by others for the second, night (see pages 681, 682). Twitting him with his prosperous appearance and evident physical lustiness, the Host turns to the Monk for a story. With dignified patience the Monk disregards the Host's remarks, and quietly disappoints his expectations of a merry tale. He will recount the life of St. Edmund, or tell first some 'tragedies,' of which he has a hundred in his cell. 'Tragedies,' he explains, are stories of persons of great prosperity who fell and ended wretchedly.

THE MONK'S TALE [67]. But the Monk really gives his audience no choice, for he plunges at once into the story of Lucifer, and proceeds through the others of his seventeen pieces. Collections of such pieces were long popular: examples in English are Lydgate's *Falls of Princes*, the *Mirror for Magistrates*, and Drayton's tales. Chaucer's general plan and some of his material came from Boccaccio's *De Casibus Virorum et Feminarum Illustrium* and *De Claris Mulieribus*. For the separate pieces he draws his material chiefly from the Vulgate Bible, Ovid, Boethius, the *Roman de la Rose*, Dante's *Inferno*, and Guido delle Colonne, with traces of Seneca's *Tragedies*, and possible influence of Innocent's *De Contemptu Mundi*. The Monk apologizes for failure to observe chronological arrangement for his stories. But if the Bible be taken as basis, with filling in of secular heroes by the way, the order is not very irregular—except in some of the MSS. in the cases of the

four modern persons, Pedro of Spain, Pedro of Cyprus, Barnabo, and Ugolino. In some MSS. these last four pieces are at
about the middle of the *Tale* between Zenobia and Nero. Here
the editions of Skeat, Pollard, and others, locate them, in order
to connect more reasonably B3953, 3956, and the Nun's
Priest's Prologue B3972 (not in the earlier form of that prologue), and also to bring the repetition (B3951) of the definition of 'tragedy' to the end, a more appropriate place for it
and one that corresponds to the location of the earlier definition at the opening. MSS. Ellesmere, Hengwrt, and others,
put the modern pieces last, as if they were added later to the
rest. Barnabo's death in 1385 is said to be the latest historical event alluded to in the *Tales*. It is generally agreed that
most of the Monk's stories were written early as beginnings of
a collection after the form of the *De Casibus*, that Chaucer
became wearied of the undertaking and put it aside, and that
later he used the pieces for the *Monk's Tale*, adding the four
modern sections. The tales are in pentameter ababbcbc, styled
from use here the 'Monk's Tale Stanza.' This stanza was used
also in the *ABC*, the *Former Age*, and *Lenvoy à Bukton*, and
is the basis on which by adding a final *c* alexandrine the 'Spen-
serian Stanza' was formed.

Questionably, the stanza-form has been taken to point to
early composition of the original parts (see page 727). The
pieces must have followed Chaucer's first acquaintance with
Italian writings. The *Ugolino* and the *Nero* B3667, from
Dante, call for knowledge of the *Inferno*. The amalgamation
of Brutus and Cassius has suggested that the *Cæsar* preceded
knowledge of Dante. The confusion of 'Busirus' and Diomedes
of Thrace, indicates that Chaucer was not yet thoroughly
familiar with Boethius. The *Crœsus* also may be later, for the
earlier form of the Nun's Priest's Prologue has not the allusion
to it. Kittredge pointed out that the *Crœsus*, in idea and
expression, accords with the proem (B3181 ff.), enforcing the
moral of Fortune's deceit and malice that gives the tragedies
their structural unity. He assigns the tragedies to about
1374, with insertion of the Barnabo stanza in January, 1386.

The Ugolino section, he and Tatlock do not regard as later than the other sections. Tatlock thinks it probable that the *Monk's Tale* was written for the *Canterbury Tales;* he would put 'the whole second half of the poem' 'not earlier than 1386.'

Despite the admirable account of Ugolino, the excellence of which is probably due to Dante's powerful treatment, the *Monk's Tale* is dreary work, and one is greatly relieved when the Knight, seconded by the Host, stops the narrator. It is of interest that the Host appears ready to give the Monk another chance (B3983, 3995), as he permitted Chaucer to tell a second tale. But the Monk declines.

THE NUN'S PRIEST'S PROLOGUE [68]. A number of MSS. (Harley 7333, Hengwrt, Corpus, Petworth, etc.) have what appears to be an earlier form of this prologue, consisting of 34 lines with but 22 lines correspondent to the regularly printed B3957-98. The shorter form of prologue omits the host's mocking paraphrase (B3972-75) of parts of the last stanza of the *Crœsus* (B3951 ff.), so suggesting addition of the *Crœsus* after this first form of prologue (see page 710), and also later revision of the prologue to its longer form as printed. Further, noting that the nearly related Caxton and Trinity R, 3, 15 texts have 'Host' for 'Knight' in the first line of the prologue, Miss Hammond suggests that this may point to a revision of the prologue very soon after the completion of the earlier version, and that when the *Nun's Priest's Tale* was put after the *Monk's Tale* and the *Melibeus*, the fact that the Host had interrupted Chaucer (B2109) would cause the poet for variety to make the change in this prologue from 'Host' to 'Knight.' The implication in the prologue to the *Melibeus* (B2116-18) that nobody had been interrupted before Chaucer, indicates composition of the earlier form, and so of the later, of the Nun's Priest's Prologue after the prologue to the *Melibeus* or later than the intended location of it after that prologue, and so after *Melibeus*. The double form of this present prologue has suggested that the *Nun's Priest's Tale* was added to Fragment B at a time later (but not much later) than the date of the first formation of Fragment B. The difficulty that

Skeat saw in the meagre statement about the Second Nun and
her three priests in the General Prologue (see pages 677, 692),
and the postponement of the description of the Nun's Priest
to the latter's epilogue, may contribute to the idea that the
Nun's Priest's Tale and the lines of the General Prologue
(A163-64) are insertions.

THE NUN'S PRIEST'S TALE [68] is related by one of
the three priests associated with the Second Nun, chapeleyne
to the Prioress. As we learn nothing of him in the General
Prologue, it has been suggested that assignment of this great
tale to a person of little prominence was to emphasize the
failure of the lordly Monk. But the Host's remarks in the
Nun's Priest's endlink (B4637 ff.), afford the description of
the Priest that could have been put in the General Prologue—
that of a personality from whom the tale might well be expected, a powerful physique, a great neck, a broad chest, a
sanguine complexion, and eyes keen and bright as a sparhawk's.

The tale is one of the best known of the Canterbury series,
and is in all respects the best of the several treatments of beast
material in English of our period (see page 183). The story
of the cock and the fox is in the *Roman de Renart* and the
Reinecke Fuchs. The immediate source of Chaucer's tale is
not accessible. Miss Peterson has shown it to be probably a
version of the Reynard epic closer to the *Reinecke Fuchs* than
to the *Roman*.

In the enclosed yard of a poor widow with two daughters, the
proud Chauntecleer dwells with his harem, chief of whom is Pertelote. He dreams of a strange creature that 'would have had him
dead.' Pertelote declares that dreams have no significance; she
ascribes them to physical causes, and learnedly explains the origins
of the several kinds; and finally she prescribes for her spouse laxa-
tive herbs. With *exempla* and authorities Chauntecleer maintains
at great length the prophetic force of visions; he will have no medi-
cines. Later, as he is strutting about the yard with his dames, he
catches sight of a col-fox, the foe of his dreams. Reynard subtly
soothes his fears, and, by declaring his admiration of the song of
the Cock's father, persuades Chauntecleer to sing so loud that he
must shut his eyes. Then the Fox seizes him, and bears him off,
with the widow and her girls and the dogs and all the creatures in

loud pursuit. Cunningly the Cock proposes that Reynard bid
defiance to his pursuers. As the Fox opens his mouth to reply,
Chauntecleer escapes.

The plot is slight, the incidents are few. The stress is comparatively little on the incidents or on the relations between the
Cock and the Fox, usually the important features in treatments of the theme. Here the interest is in the characterization of the Cock and his spouse in human terms, while skilfully
one is never let forget that they are fowls; in the humorous
satire, in terms of the barnyard, of the human husband's lordly
self-satisfaction; in the marvelous burlesque of the relations
and attitudes and behavior toward each other of husband and
wife in the bosom of their domesticity; in the astounding exhibitions of learning by the parties; and in the mock-heroics of
the apostrophe to the Fox, the outcry against Destiny, and the
lamentations of the widowed hens. The story is a masterpiece
in a kind of work difficult to do and, when undertaken, difficult
not to overdo—an exquisite achievement that alone would make
a reputation for a poet.

FRAGMENT C [69]

Fragment C, comprising the *Physician's Tale*, the *Words of
the Host*, and the *Pardoner's Tale*, is the most difficult Fragment to place in the series. It has no genuine headlink, though
there exist three spurious prologues to the *Physician's Tale*.
It has no indication of time or place, and no connection with
any following matter. The Fragment occurs between Fragments F and B² in MS. Harley 7335 and the Ellesmere family
of MSS., and between Fragments G and B² in all the rest
except Selden, where it appears between Fragments G and H.
In the Six-Text Edition it was pushed up to follow Fragment
B², which was pushed up to follow Fragment B¹. Here it has
been printed in all editions since. Skeat steadily held that C
should follow F; he printed it after B² only for concord with
the standard of numbering set by the Six-Text Edition. The
present tendency is to locate it either after F or preferably
after A (see page 679).

THE PHYSICIAN'S TALE [70] is one of Chaucer's stories of afflicted innocence.

Appius, a lascivious judge, enamored of the lovely Virginia, and realizing that the power of her friends would prevent him from his desire, bribed a churl, Claudius, to claim the maiden as his servant stolen from him while a child. Despite the proofs of the father, Virginius, Appius decreed the maid to Claudius. After a pitiable interview with Virginia, to save her from shame the father decapitated her, and bore her head to the judge. The people defended him. Appius committed suicide in prison. At Virginius' request, Claudius was given his life, but was sent into exile.

The ascription to 'Titus Livius' in the first verse, and the general matter and the outlines of the story, are from Jean de Meun's version in the *Roman de la Rose* (Méon's edition ll. 5613-82). Chaucer holds fairly closely to the general story of the French. He introduces the description (C5-65, 105 ff.) of the lovely maiden, with the pathos and grace that he ever exhibits in presentation of helpless innocence and purity; the passage of advice as to education of children (C66-104), another instance of his readiness to thrust doctrine into narrative; and the piteous interview between the father and Virginia after the judge's decree (C207-53). It has been pointed out that the two long pathetic passages so introduced turn the emphasis upon Virginia, and that they direct it from the story of injustice and its punishment, which is the great feature in the *Roman*, and as well from the tragic situation of the father and the political moment of the tale, which are stressed in Livy. This emphasis on the heroine and development of her personality, is in accord with Chaucer's procedure in the other pathetic tales of Constance, Hugh of Lincoln, and Griselda.

Tupper has urged that Chaucer's comment at the end (C277-86) makes of the story proper an *exemplum* of Lechery (see l. 206), and that in the *Confessio* Book VII Gower tells the story as an *exemplum* of Lust. These facts Tupper has used to support his suggestions of the Sins *motif* (see page 687). All of this is opposed by Lowes (see page 688).

Kittredge has connected lines 72-85 with the third Duchess of Lancaster, so pointing to the date 1386 or later; Ten Brink has connected them with the death of Chaucer's wife, that left

him with his children to educate alone. Ten Brink felt that
the close of the tale is what Chaucer might well write under
impression of the tragic events of the first part of 1388. Tatlock believes that if the tale had preceded the B Prologue to
the *Legend*, it would have been mentioned therein. He argues
that, while Chaucer used the *Confessio* for the *Man of Law's
Tale*, he had not read Gower's story of Virginia when he wrote
the *Physician's Tale*. So he locates the poem at 1386-1390,
probably at about 1388, as perhaps 'the first story written
expressly for the Canterbury Tales.'

THE WORDS OF THE HOST [71] (C287-328; not to be
confused with the *Verba Hospitis* at the end of the *Clerk's
Tale*, see pages 727, 728) is the rather inappropriate title of
the link between the *Physician's Tale* and the Pardoner's Prologue. The Host is outraged at the fate of Virginia, and prays
blessing on the Physician for his story. Then he bids the Pardoner to tell at once some mirth or jape to lighten his distress.
The Pardoner is very willing—as soon as he has had a draught
and eaten a cake. Perhaps here the party stop at the wayside
inn (C321). The 'gentles' are alarmed; they will have no
ribaldry, but 'some moral thing.' The Pardoner acquiesces; he
will think on 'some honest thing' while he drinks.

THE PARDONER'S PROLOGUE AND TALE [72]. The
Pardoner was given the next to longest treatment in the General
Prologue. His own lengthy prologue and his tale are devoted
largely to exhibition of his character and habitual conduct.
The prologue is to be compared with the Wife's Prologue for
length and power. It is in Chaucer's best humorous style.
With engaging impudence the speaker deliberately opens his
hypocrisy and thorough rascality to his fellow-pilgrims, revealing not only the rottenness of his principles, but laying bare
the artful method by which he imposes on the superstition and
gullibility of folk. And he illumines his theme, and imposes on
the very audience to whom he illumines it, by delivering a specimen of the discourse through which he wins and compels offerings to his false relics. The evil of covetousness is ever his

subject, and the getting of money by any means is ever his aim. He will tell the party a moral tale that is wont to bring him in a good collection.

The Pardoner sketches admirably the life of a group of young revelers in Flanders. Then, seizing the occasion, before the tale is begun, the rascal stops, to discourse to the company for some hundred and eighty lines on Gluttony and Drunkenness, Gambling, and Swearing, with *exempla* such as he has previously declared the lewd folk dote on.--His tale is of three revelers who in plague-time set out from an inn on a drunken quest of Death who has just borne off one of their associates. They meet an aged man, who directs them to a tree under which they shall find him whom they seek. On the spot designated they discover a heap of gold. One of them goes to an inn for drink, and poisons the wine. The others plan his death. On his return, they murder him, but die of the poisoned liquor.

The story itself is one of Chaucer's most extraordinary achievements, a narrative of notable power for any period. Its effect arises largely from its suggestiveness; from the terrible setting of pestilence, the atmosphere of imminent death, that environs all; from the remarkable care for detail, yet economy of effort; from the close realness of each element of its setting and its action; from the dramatic quality lent by these features, and by the fact that the story is largely in direct discourse; from the shocking awfulness of the rioters' blasphemous drunken hardihood; from the pathetic yet ominous figure and discourse of the old man, and the contrast he presents to the chief actors; from the rapidity of the action; and from the inevitableness of the incidents and the outcome.

The story is of Eastern origin. It has been widely treated from a very early date to the present time. A version of it, apparently not the source of Chaucer's piece, is the Tenth Tale of the Sixth Day of the *Decameron*. The treatment closest to the Pardoner's is the second (that in the edition of 1572) of two versions in the *Cento Novelle Antiche*. Chaucer's actual original is not yet identified. Koeppel has shown that many of the moral reflections of the Pardoner (C483-84, 491, 505-07, 513-16, 517-20, 521-23, 534-36, 537-46, 551-52, 560-

61) are from Innocent's *De Contemptu Mundi.* Perhaps all these passages are from Chaucer's prose version of the *De Contemptu* (see pages 619, 620). The considerable use of Innocent's work in the Man of Law's Prologue and Tale (see pages 700, 701), may point to closeness in dates of composition of the latter pieces and the *Pardoner's Tale.* Much matter on Avarice and Gluttony uttered by the Pardoner, is from the *Parson's Tale,* which must have preceded the tale of the Pardoner.

Koch dates the tale 1389-1390. Skeat put it among the latest written of the tales—*i.e.,* after 1385. Miss Hammond regards it as of about the date of the assignment of the present Constance story to the Man of Law (see page 700), the period of the hypothetical insertion (see page 692) of the subsidiary group, Pardoner, Summoner, Reeve, Miller, and Manciple.

The Pardoner's final comment (C895 ff.) makes the tale an *exemplum* of Avarice, perhaps because there is but one theme in the world for him. Tupper has argued that the tale is an *exemplum* of Avarice and Gluttony, and is to be connected with the other tales on Sins (see pages 687-88). Lowes has declared the two sins to be 'either one too many or three or four too few.'

THE PARDONER'S ENDLINK [72] is, in the MSS. and the printed texts, the concluding lines of the *Tale.* The Pardoner's revelation of self, and his tragic narrative, have indeed relieved the company of the depression caused by the story of Virginia. But the tale of the revelers itself calls for relief. This Chaucer gives in this endlink. With brazen impudence, despite his revelations of his own viciousness, the worthlessness of his wares, and the contempt he feels for his gulls, the Pardoner in all gravity bids the pilgrims step up and pay their money and enjoy the virtues of his relics. The Host, furious, bursts out in a torrent of abuse against him. The Pardoner sulks in silent rage. The Knight reconciles them; they kiss; and all ride on their way.—So ends Fragment C, without connection with the following tale.

Fragment D [73]

Fragment D comprises the Wife of Bath's Prologue, the Friar-Summoner dispute at its end, the *Wife's Tale,* and the headlinks and tales of the Friar and the Summoner. The Fragment has no headlink or endlink. In some MSS. it follows the *Man of Law's Tale* without headlink; in MSS. Barlow, Laud 739, and Royal 18, it follows the *Merchant's Tale* with a spurious sixteen-line link; in others it follows the *Squire's Tale*—in MS. Lansdowne with eight spurious verses and four more introducing the Wife. The location of the Fragment in the various MSS. may be seen on page 679; it occurs between B^1 and E, F^1 and E, E^2 and E^1, F^2 and E, and in Selden between A and E.

Time and place in the Fragment are indicated in the Summoner's promise (D846-47) of 'tales two or three of freres ere I come to Sidingbourne' (see page 682); and in the Summoner's last line (D2294), 'My tale is doon, we been almost at toune.'

THE WIFE OF BATH'S PROLOGUE [74]. Chaucer gave the Wife as prologue for exposition of her views and exhibition of her character, 828 lines, much more than he allotted to many of the tales, and over twice as much as to the Wife's own tale. The prologue is an elaborate discourse rejecting celibacy as theoretically admirable and most desirable for saints, but not practicable or directed by Scripture for general application; urging the use of all that Heaven has given; and defending the Wife's practice in five marriages. This is related with the Wife's account of her experience of wedlock and her methods of handling her spouses—three old and rich, the fourth a reveler who led her a life of jealousy, and the fifth a clerk. The various points of the discourse are illustrated and enforced with *exempla* and citations from Scriptural and secular sources, that may be supposed due to influence of the fifth husband. In this prologue Chaucer attains the most admirable characterization and what is generally the best work, in the *Canterbury Tales.* The Wife is frankly animal in nature, openly militant, of keen insight, witty, jovial, and hearty; she is kindly and companionable, with many admirable traits that possibly would have developed in more favorable marital conditions. With his usual skill in such matters, the poet makes her a very engaging personage, yet at the same time leaves us under no misapprehension as to the real nature of the person or of her conduct. The suggestion is very questionable, that the Wife was intended as a disappointed woman, beset with· a haunting fear that her life and her principles were all awry.

For certain elements of his conception of the Wife and her methods (A445 ff., D1 ff.) Chaucer was indebted to the old woman, La Vielle, and to the declarations of the old married man, Le Jaloux, in the *Roman de la Rose*. Without doubt other prominent features were derived from Deschamp's *Miroir de Mariage*. The discourse on celibacy and much of the Wife's account of her treatment of her old husbands, are based on Jerome's quotation of *Aureolus Theophrasti Liber de Nuptiis* in his *Epistola adversus Jovinianum*. Side by side with Jerome, for this matter Chaucer apparently had Deschamps' *Miroir* that itself drew here from the *Epistola*. Further, Chaucer used *Epistola Valerii ad Rufinum de non Ducenda Uxore*. The three Latin works were included in the volume that the Wife's last husband loved best (D671-75).

For further discussion of the Wife's Prologue, see the remarks on the *Wife's Tale*.

THE WIFE OF BATH'S TALE [74] exhibits the Wife in a finer aspect than does her Prologue.

In the olden days of King Arthur the land was full of *faerie*. But now there are no fays, because of the friars. A knight of Arthur violated a maid. He was delivered over to the Queen. She gave him life provided that, after a search of a year and a day, he told her what women most desire. His quest was vain, until in a fairy-dance a crone promised him the secret if he would marry her. He agreed, and at the appointed time he gave the proper answer: Women desire most the *sovereignty* over their husbands that they have over their lovers, and to be in *maistrie* over them. The crone claimed her betrothed. In their chamber she discoursed to her reluctant spouse on true *gentilesse* as not of wealth or inheritance, but of God and virtuous living; on the worth of 'wilful poverty'; and on the advantage of having an old and ugly wife. Would

he have her old and foul, but true and humble; or would he have
her young and fair, and take his chance as to the rest? 'Choose
yourself,' the knight replied; 'I put myself in your wise governance.'
'Then have I got maistrie of you?' she asked.   At his kiss she became
a young and lovely maiden.

The tale is a treatment of the theme of the Knight and the
Loathly Lady dealt with from the Orient to Iceland.   The
Wedding of Gawain and Dame Ragnell and the *Marriage of
Sir Gawain* (see pages 67, 69) offer other versions.   The *Tale
of Florent,* the version used in the *Confessio* I as *exemplum*
for the Inobedience or second phase of Pride, has generally been
regarded as not having influenced Chaucer.   Tupper notes
that in the *Parson's Tale* (I 390) Inobedience is the first division of Pride; and he regards the prologue and tale of the Wife
as an *exemplum,* or as illustrative, of Inobedience (see page
687).—The discourse on *gentilesse* (D1109 ff.) has been
attributed to Boethius' *De Consolatione* III prose 6 and metre
6, to Dante, to the *Roman de la Rose* (Méou's edition) 6603-16,
18807-19096, etc.   Compare the *balade Gentilesse* (see page
640), and the *Franklin's Tale.*

The prologue and tale of the Wife open the definite discussion that is the *motif* of the Marriage Group consisting of the
tales and the links of Fragments D, E, and F, and prepared for
by the remarks in the *Melibeus,* the Host's comments on the
Melibeus, and the *Nun's Priest's Tale* (see page 684).

The greater part of the Wife's Prologue is devoted to what
at the time was a revolutionary protest against the Church's
doctrine of Virginity (see also Host B3133 ff., 4637 ff.); let
those be virgin who will; our parts and powers are given us
for use; chastity is perhaps ideal; she has married and enjoyed
freely, she will have her fling to the very end.   But this is not
all.   Her account of her life with her last husband, the clerk,
becomes more and more vehemently a protest.   This is directed
first against the mediæval views of woman's character and conduct, as those views were exemplified in her fifth spouse's personal attitude and in his favorite books; and, secondly, against
the accepted idea of subjection as the wife's proper relation
to her husband.   All leads to the climax of her account, her

outwitting of the clerk, and winning of dominance over him. The Prologue ends with the key-words of the discourse and of the Marriage Group: 'whan that I badde geten unto me, *By maistrie*, al the *soveraynetee*. . . . After that day we hadden never debaat' (D817-22). *Maistrie* and *soveraynetee* is the theme.—Moreover, the Wife tells her tale to enforce her demand that after marriage the woman shall have the sway that she has had over her lover. The answer that preserves the Knight's life is 'Wommen desyren to have sovereyntee As well over hir housband as hir love, And for to been in maistrie him above' (D1038-40); and the knight wins happiness in marriage by putting himself in his wife's 'wyse governance'—giving her, as she emphasizes it, 'maistrye' (D1231-36). The Wife concludes her tale with prayer. that women be sent 'Housbondes meke, yonge, and fresshe abedde, And grace t'overbyde hem that we wedde,' and that Heaven may 'shorte hir lyves That wol nat be governed by hir wyves' (D1260-62).

In the course of her talk the Wife determines two of the other speakers on the theme. The Clerk she offends not only by her views, but also (despite her earlier deprecation in D125) by her account of her treatment of her last husband, a clerk of Oxford (D525 ff.), and still more by her gibes against clerks in general (D688-91, 707-10). The *Clerk's Tale* is a reply to her (see pages 684, 728). Moreover, the discourse on *gentilesse* (D1109 ff.), with her views, sows the seeds in the Franklin's mind for his tale on *gentilesse* and patience in mutual forbearance as the true means to bliss in marriage (see page 735).

Two other interesting connections are to be noted. The Friar laughingly breaks in with a remark on the Wife's 'long preamble' (D830-31). The Summoner takes him up, and promises before they come to Sittingbourne some tales of friars that will make him grieve. So the *motif* for the next two tales is prepared. The Wife says nothing at the moment; but, after a few verses of her tale, she has her gibe at the limitors and other holy friars (D866 ff.). The matter comes to nothing, however, for, at the end of her tale, the Friar is too preoccupied with the Summoner to follow up her challenge.

.. The other connection is with the Merchant. Evidently,. at
one time Chaucer intended to have the Wife tell the present
Shipman's Tale (see page 703). This story of the cheating of
the merchant of St. Denis and his wife, would have afforded to
the Merchant much the same incentive for quarrel as the
Miller's Tale .afforded the Reeve. It has also a passage
(B1416-24) that may have been intended as a gibe at the
Merchant, who, according to the General Prologue, was in
debt (A280-82). Hence it has been inferred that Chaucer
earlier planned between the Wife and the Merchant a quarrel
somewhat parallel to those of the Miller and the Reeve, and the
Summoner and the Friar (see page 683). √

Lowes' association of the several tales of the Marriage
Group and the A Prologue to the *Legend* through influence on
them of Deschamps' *Miroir de Mariage* and Jerome's *Epistola
adversus Jovinianum,* has been noted (see pages 641, 686).
Accordingly, Lowes dates the Wife's Prologue either early in
1394 or some time in 1393, at any rate before the A Prologue to the *Legend;* and he dates the *Merchant's Tale* as
rather closely following the Wife's Prologue. Tatlock has
dated the *Merchant's Tale* 'shortly after *Melibeus,* very probably not later than 1394'; the *Melibeus* between the Wife's
Prologue and the *Merchant's Tale* (a location that Lowes
opines seems to be right), and probably very shortly before the
Merchant's Tale; and the *Wife's Tale* after the *Merchant's
Tale.* The Wife's Prologue precedes *Lenvoy à Bukton* (1396)
which alludes to it—as does the *Merchant's Tale* (E1685-87).
Skeat dates the tales of the Nun's Priest, the Wife, the Friar,
the Summoner, the Merchant, the Squire, the Franklin, the
Canon's Yeoman, and the Manciple 'among the latest written'—
i.e., 'later than 1385.' The close similarities between the description of the Wife in the General Prologue (A445 ff.), and
the matter and the expression of the Wife's Prologue, may
indicate composition of the two at nearly the same time, the
Wife's Prologue being the later. It would seem likely that the
Friar-Summoner matter was all worked out at the same time
as the Wife's Prologue and the General Prologue. That the

married woman who was in Chaucer's mind early, was somewhat of the kind of the Wife, is indicated by the nature of the present *Shipman's Tale* that evidently was intended for her. The extent and the elaborateness of the Wife's Prologue, have led Ten Brink and Legouis to suppose that it was originally an independent piece.

THE FRIAR'S PROLOGUE [75]. The Friar-Limitor disapproves of the Wife's 'school-matter' and citation of 'authorities.' But he does not take up her challenge (D866-81). He has been hostilely eyeing the Summoner, and now falls to abuse of the latter's profession. He is bidden to tell his tale, with promise of requital in the Summoner's narrative.

THE FRIAR'S TALE [75] is notable for its realistic detail, and as well for its bits of exquisite humor, all cleverly assuming the viciousness and contemptibleness not only of the summoner in the tale, but of the calling itself. It is these, and not the fate of the summoner in the story, that infuriate the Canterbury member of the profession. Tupper (opposed by Lowes) argues that the tale is an *exemplum* of the Cursing phase of Wrath, and that the quarrel of the Friar and the Summoner illustrates Wrath in general (see page 687).

The tale is of an evil summoner given to bribery and extortion. On his way to mulct a poor widow, he meets a yeoman, and swears brotherhood with him. The yeoman reveals that he is a fiend, and on inquiry tells of the methods of fiends in their practice on men. When, at the cottage, the summoner attempts to extort a gift from the widow, she commends his soul and body to the Devil. Accordingly, on being assured that she is in earnest, the fiend bears the evil officer off to Hell.—Let us beware of the torments of that place; Christ will preserve us.

No direct source for the tale has been discovered. An analogue is *Narratio de Quodam Senescallo Sceleroso* in the Latin collection of *exempla* for sermons by John Herolt, a Dominican of Basle, who flourished about 1418. Another similar Latin story *De Aduocato et Diabolo*, is in the *Promptuarium Exemplorum* made early in the fourteenth century. The former

piece gives indications of the nature of the anecdote that
Chaucer used.

THE SUMMONER'S PROLOGUE [76].　At the very
opening of his tale the Friar so enraged the Summoner that he
broke in on him, and had to be checked by the Host.　Now
'lyk an aspen leef he quook for yre.'　He opens with a tremendous stroke, the anecdote of the friar who was ravished to Hell
in a vision, and who found there the favorite nest of friars—
the tail of the Devil, where they abode twelve thousand strong.
A jest analogous to this is in Cæsarius of Heisterbach's *Dialogus Miraculorum* (Cologne 1851) 7, 59.　The Friar is overwhelmed; it is only after the Summoner has begun his tale,
that he recovers.　Then he breaks in (D1761), just as at a
similar place (D1332-37) his opponent had interrupted him.

THE SUMMONER'S TALE [76] follows the prologue
without comment by any person.

A hypocritical friar of the marshy country of Holderness in
Yorkshire, lectures a sick man on the evil of Wrath, and insistently
begs a gift for his order.　The angry invalid grants the request with
a very unsavory benefaction that is to be shared with twelve other
friars.　The friar has recourse to the lord of the district, with little
result except appreciation of the pretty problem of how to share the
gift.　To the delight of all except the friar, the squire Jankin offers
a solution.

The tale has scarcely any plot, and little action.　Most of it
is in direct discourse; it is essentially dramatic.　The piece is
sustained by the remarkably realistic talk between 'the sick
man, his wife, and the friar; the sermon of the friar; the scene
between the friar and the lord and his wife; and the lord's
rhapsody on the friar's problem.　Its great quality, its unifying element, is its revelation of the rascally hypocritical
friar, a marvel of characterization.　Here again, as in the tales
of the Miller and the Reeve, definiteness in the location of the
scenes, and minute details of environment, of action, of demeanor, of turns of phrase, contribute cleverly to the effectiveness of the narrative.

No direct source for the tale has been found.　The latter

part, following the receipt of the gift, seems to be Chaucer's own. The earlier part appears to be largely original. An analogue to the first part has been found in *Li Dis de la Vescie à Prestre*, or *The Story of the Priest's Bladder*, by Jakes de Basiu or Basieux. A somewhat similar story is said to have been told of a bequest of Jean de Meun to the Jacobin friars. The friar's sermon is from the *Parson's Tale* 1534, 564 ff., but mainly from Seneca's *De Ira*. Tupper (opposed by Lowes) sees in the Friar's and the Summoner's conduct, as well as in their tales, illustration of the Sin of Wrath (see page 687).

Koch dated the tale 1389-1390. Skeat put it among the 'tales latest written'—*i.e.*, after 1385. Miss Hammond supposes it added to the original plan with the Reeve-Miller group, which she regards as possibly a later conception (see page 692).

In MSS. Petworth, Sloane 1685, Royal 18, Rawlinson Poetry 149, and Laud 739, the tale stops at line 2159, with four added lines styled spurious by Furnivall. Lounsbury thinks it not impossible that the last 136 lines of Fragment D as they appear in the other MSS. and in the modern printed texts, are a later addition by Chaucer.

Fragment E [77]

Fragment E consists of E¹, the headlink, prologue, tale and envoy of the Clerk, followed in some MSS. by a seven-line stanza of comment by the Host; and E², the headlink and tale of the Merchant. Ten Brink favored union of E and F as one Fragment. Skeat opposed this, but finally approved it; Tatlock favors the union (see page 679).

The location of E¹ and E² in the MSS. may be seen from Skeat's and Hammond's tables on pages 679, 680. Together they occur between D and F¹ (with a link between E and F) or D and F²; separated they occur in the orders F¹E²DE¹F²G and F¹E²F²DE¹G, with various modifications of the links.

THE CLERK'S HEADLINK AND PROLOGUE [78].

The Host turns to the Clerk, who has been riding as coy and

still as a maid newly wed sits at table.   He bids him leave
study and tell a 'mery thing of adventures,' eschewing figures
and 'high style'—and not to preach.   The Clerk proposes a tale
he learned at Padua of a worthy clerk now dead, 'Fraunceys
Petrark, the laureat poete'; in 'high style' Petrarch wrote for
his tale a proem in which he described its geographical setting
and the course of the Po.

This prologue, then, was composed at least partly after the
death of Petrarch, July 18, 1374.   The Clerk's statement that
he had learned the story from Petrarch, has been carried on to
suggest that Chaucer himself met Petrarch on the mission to
Genoa in 1373.   Such a meeting is possible, but there is no
proof of it (see page 611).   Giovanni di Lignano spoken of
as dead (E34 ff.), died in 1383.

THE CLERK'S TALE [78].   The story of the patient
wife, the Griselda saga, has been treated widely in various
literatures.   At times it occurs in combination with one or several of the Constance, Florence, and Eustace stories (see page
112).   The immediate source of the *Clerk's Tale* is *De Obedientia et Fide Uxoria Mythologia*, a translation of the story of
Griselda made from the Tenth Tale of the Tenth Day of the
Decameron by Petrarch in 1373, after April.   Comparison of
the three versions shows that Chaucer did not use the *Decameron* for his poem.   The *Clerk's Tale* is as follows:

> Urged by his people to provide an heir, Walter, Marquis of
> Saluces in Italy, weds the daughter of Janicula, the poorest of his
> subjects.   Griselda swears never willingly in deed or thought to dis-
> obey her husband.   A daughter is born.   To test his wife's patience,
> Walter has the child removed from her, leading her to suppose it
> slain.   Six years later, Griselda submits to removal of her two-
> year-old boy.   When the daughter is twelve years of age, Walter
> has false documents of divorce sent as from the Pope.   When this
> and the Marquis' will to wed another wife are roughly announced
> to Griselda, she submits and even voluntarily prepares the wedding-
> feast and decks the bridal apartments for her successor.   Satisfied
> at last, Walter tells her that all has been but a test.   The pretended
> bride is their daughter.   The boy is restored.

At least part of the Clerk's Prologue was composed after
the death of Petrarch, July 18, 1374, and after that of

di Lignano in 1383 (E29-38). Commonly there is favored a version of the tale dating from soon after Chaucer's return from his first Italian journey in 1373. Skeat thought the main part of the tale was written in 1373 or 1374, and that E1051-64 and the envoy were written later. Koch judged E1170-212 to be later additions for better connection with the *Merchant's Tale*. Tatlock urged that Chaucer first became acquainted with the story in 1378, the date of the second journey to Italy; accepted Mather's argument that if the tale had preceded the Prologues to the *Legend* (dated 1386, 1394) it would have been mentioned there with the other works adduced in defense of the poet's treatment of women; remarked rightly that closeness of translation and use of stanzas are not good evidence as to date; and dated the tale 'after 1387.' Ten Brink connected the comment on the fickleness of popular enthusiasm (E995-1001) with the behavior of the Londoners at and after the banquet to Richard on November 10, 1387; but Tatlock cites similar situations in 1376, 1381, and 1393. Miss Hammond suggests that Chaucer's 'heigh style' (E41, 1148; cp. E18) for Petrarch's *alto stilo* and *alio stilo,* means composition probably before the pun on 'high style' in the *Squire's Tale* (F105-06). She suggests that the agreement between the wording and ideas of the *Verba Hospitis* or *Words of the Host* (see Skeat's editions, note to E1162; and see below) and of the *Melibeus* endlink (B3079 ff.; see page 708), indicates that the *Verba,* which was perhaps the original endlink of the *Clerk's Tale,* is earlier than the *Melibeus*-Monk link (B3079 ff.). So, she suggests, the tales of the Monk and Nun's Priest may have been added to the Fragment B before the present Clerk's Envoy was written, the envoy antedating the rearranging of the envoy and the writing of the Merchant link (E1213 ff.) to meet it. Lowes dates the tale 'perhaps 1369-79,' and the close of the tale and the envoy after the Wife's Prologue, which he places 'early in 1394, or at some time in 1393.'

The Friar and the Summoner have been too much occupied with their quarrel to proceed with the Wife's theme of sov-

ereignty in marriage. But to the quiet Clerk there are, as has
been seen (cp. pages 684, 721), both personal and professional
grounds for remembering it. His tale is a reply to the Wife.
It is a tale told him by a worthy *clerk* (E27, 32). It is a tale
of marriage and married life. Its initiation is the invitation
to Walter to bow his neck 'under that blisful yok of soveraynetee, noght of servyse, which that men clepeth spousaille or
wedlok' (E113-15). From an early point, the theme is Walter's determination to dominate (E351 ff.), and the story becomes an exemplification of the submissive and patient wife as
opposed to the Wife of Bath's ideal. So, in the face of the
Wife's declarations, the Clerk demonstrates that a clerk *can*
speak well of women (D688-91). To make the point clear,
and to emphasize the intent of the story, the Clerk explains
(E1142 ff.) that it would be 'importable' (unbearable; so,
?not to be performed by a woman in actual life, or ?not to be
tolerated by the world in general) for a wife to do wholly as
Griselda did; she is an extreme example; Petrarch wrote the
story to urge each person according to his degree to be patient
in adversity. Then he applies the matter to the Wife: 'for
the wyves love of Bathe, Whos lyfe and al hir secte god mayn-
tene In heigh *maistrye*' (E1170-72), he will sing a song. His
song is his ironical envoy (E1177-212), a *tour de force* of six
stanzas ababcb with identity of rime-sounds from stanza to
stanza: Griselda is dead, and all her kind; let women stand
to their rights, and permit no dominance by men—be fierce as
a tiger, scold like a mill-clapper; fear not, revere not thy
husband, but torment him with jealousy; gad about, spend
freely, be merry, and let him grieve. So the Clerk ironically
urges, in contrast with the behavior of Griselda, practice of
conduct identical with what the Wife has commended and
herself acted out.

In some of the best MSS. a rime-royal stanza (see Skeat's
editions, note to E1162) of comment by the Host, usually
styled *Verba Hospitis* (not to be confused with the *Words* at
C287 ff.), follows the envoy, and agrees closely with the opening
of the Monk's Prologue (B3079 ff.; see pages 708, 727, 732).

Skeat thought Chaucer originally intended to end the *Clerk's Tale* at E1162, and to append this stanza. The MSS. vary as to the arrangement of stanzas 4-6 of the envoy. Tyrwhitt adopted, and the later editors have followed, the order of some MSS., that makes the sense and the phrasing of the last line (E1212) suggestive of the first (E1213) of the Merchant's Prologue.

THE MERCHANT'S PROLOGUE [79]. Carried away by his emotions, the Merchant catches up the final words of the Clerk's ironic compliment. He knows well what wives now are: he has been married but two months, yet he has experienced to the full the curse of matrimony—his wife would *overmatch* the Devil. 'Since you know so much of this, tell us about it,' exclaims the Host. 'Gladly,' replies the Merchant—but he will reveal no more of his own fate. So, cleverly the new speaker is introduced, and further discussion of *sovereignty* is prepared for.

That at an earlier time Chaucer meant the Merchant to reply to the Wife as a result of a quarrel between them, has been mentioned (see page 722). The similarities between E1213 ff. and the Clerk's explanation and envoy (E1142 ff.), and the Merchant's reference to 'Grisildis grete patience' (E1224), show that finally Chaucer intended the Merchant to follow the Clerk.

THE MERCHANT'S TALE [79]. The first part of the *Merchant's Tale* is the rich old January's consideration of marriage, and his discourse on wedlock, with the debate between Placebo, the time-server, and Justinus as to whether it is well that January marry (E1245-688). The second part deals with the wedding of January and May, and the love-sickness of the squire, Damian, for May (E1689-2056). The third part tells of the dotard's becoming blind, his jealous watchfulness, May's outwitting him with Damian up the pear-tree, his discovery of the culprits through restoration of his sight by Pluto, and May's rehabilitation through the partisanship of Proserpine (E2057-418).

The tale is a bitter retort to the prologue and tale of the Wife. The opening encomium on marriage has been declared 'one of the most amazing instances of sustained irony in all literature.' So effective is it that by some writers it has been quoted as sincere praise. The whole piece is bitter, almost savage, satire, that not only far surpasses anything else of the sort in Chaucer, but is astonishingly contrary to his characteristic attitudes and methods. The sentiments are not the poet's own; they are the Merchant's, as under stress of the trials of the past two months he lets himself go, retorting on the provocation of the Wife in the tone suggested by the Clerk's ironical envoy. The 'blissful' life of wedlock is his text (E1259, 1284, 1340, 1347, etc.). The problem of obedience, of mastery in the married state, is his theme; it is ever in the mind of January before his marriage (E1287, 1333, 1357, 1361, 1378, 1428); it is the point of the quarrel between Pluto and Proserpine (E2276, 2312), which ends in the former's defeat, acknowledged in words similar to the words of the Wife (D425-27). Resemblances have been traced between the Wife's old husband and January, between January and Walter, and between May and the Wife (*e.g.*, E2187-206, 2368-415 and D443-50, 226-34). The words of Pluto parallel those of Jankin (E2237-53, D641-785), Proserpine's parallel the Wife's (E2264-310, D226-34 and 35-43). Moreover, the Merchant catches up other passages from the Wife's discourse —*e.g.*, E1423-28, D601-16 and 45 and the rejected lines following 44 (see Skeat's editions, text-note on D44); cp. D165 and 1270-77; E1670-73, D489-90. To clinch the whole matter, are the lines, awkwardly introduced so that one is not sure whether they are the Merchant's or Justinus', 'But lat us waden out of this matere. The Wyf of Bathe, if ye han understonde, Of mariage, which we have on honde, Declared hath ful wel in litel space' (E1684-87).

In addition to the humor of the ironical discussion of marriage, and of the revelation of the Merchant, the prominent features of the tale are the character and the impotent lewdness and folly of the principal personage, and his sentiments and demeanor as illustrative of them. Compared with these, plot and incident afford but slight interest. Yet, bitter as is the Merchant's exposure of the disgusting dotard, the serious and tragic possibilities of the tale were ignored for a wryly comic treatment. Once more, as in the tales of the Miller, the Reeve, and the Summoner, character and cleverness are supreme over objectionableness of theme in a questionable tale.

The general setting for the pear-tree episode, the marriage matter, and certain scraps (especially E1267-392, 1400-68), are chiefly from Deschamps' *Miroir de Mariage* that for some scattered passages was drawn on side by side with the *Melibeus*, the *Parson's Tale*, Albertanus of Brescia's *Liber Consolationis et Consilii* and *Liber de Amore*, and Theophrastus, who was used for the Wife's Prologue and the A Prologue to the *Legend* (see pages 641, 669, 686). Reminiscences of Boethius are evident. Apparently the conception of all the first two parts of the tale (E1245-2056), is Chaucer's. All the *plot* of the first part is due to the *Melibeus*. Of the *plot* of the third part, apparently only the bare idea of the pear-tree episode was borrowed. The actual original of the widely narrated pear-tree story that Chaucer used, has not been traced; the version in the Ninth Tale of the Seventh Day of the *Decameron*, is not a source. Chaucer's own is the fairy machinery (E2219-2319, etc.), with its contest for supremacy between Pluto and Proserpine further illustrating the sovereignty theme.

Skeat dates the tale after the *Melibeus*, the *Boethius*, and the *Wife's Tale*, and 'among the latest written'—*i.e.*, 'after 1385.' The parallels and indebtedness indicate that the *Merchant's Tale* followed the *Melibeus* and the *Parson's Tale*. As it draws from much the same sources, discusses much the same matter, and refers to the Wife's Prologue (E1684-87), it appears to have followed that piece. Tatlock puts it probably just after the *Melibeus*, and the *Melibeus* after the Wife's Prologue, a location approved by Lowes.

THE MERCHANT'S EPILOGUE [79]. As the Merchant was moved by the tale of the Clerk, the Host is moved by the Merchant's narrative. He cries out against his wife's shrew-

ish tongue and 'heep of vyces mo,' and his being bound to her.
He has already given a pretty clear idea of her disposition
and of the relations between them (B3081 ff.). But he dares
not dilate on her vices, lest some woman (probably the gossip
Wife) report to his spouse.

FRAGMENT F [80]

The break between Fragments E and F is very slight. The
Host is speaking in both the Merchant's Epilogue and the
Squire's Prologue. As has been said (see page 725), Ten
Brink assumed, and Skeat and Tatlock have urged, that prop-
erly the two Fragments should be regarded as one.

Fragment F consists of the Squire's Prologue of eight lines,
the unfinished *Squire's Tale*, the 'Words of the Franklin to
the Squire,' and the prologue and tale of the Franklin. There
is no endlink to the Fragment.

The normal position of the *Squire's Tale* in the MSS., is
between the tales of the Merchant and the Franklin, the location in the prints since the Six-Text Edition. But in many
MSS. the tale follows that of the Man of Law, being connected
thereto by the passage usually styled 'Shipman's Prologue'
(B1163-90), whose line 17 in such MSS. has 'Squire' for
'Shipman.' Theories as to the history of this link and this
location for the *Squire's Tale*, have been noted already (see
page 702).

The *Franklin's Tale* normally occurs after the Squire's, with
the Words of the Franklin as a link. But often it occurs after
the *Merchant's Tale*, to which it is united by combination of
the Merchant's Epilogue (E2419-40) and the Squire's Prologue (F1-8) with 'Squire' displaced by 'Franklin.' It occurs,
too, after the *Clerk's Tale*, preceded (a) by the united Merchant's Epilogue and Squire's Prologue, and no connective
with the Clerk; or (b) by two seven-line stanzas, one from the
Merchant's Epilogue, the other made up from the Squire's
Prologue, assigned to the Franklin; or (c) by the above two
stanzas preceded by the Words of the Host (see Skeat's

editions, text-note on E1162).   It is found also after the
Pardoner's Tale, with only its own prologue intervening.

THE SQUIRE'S TALE [81] has no bearing in the argument concerning sovereignty in marriage.   It has been styled
an interlude of 'pure romance,' and corresponds to the comic
Friar-Summoner interlude earlier in the Marriage Group.   It
is a story of chivalry, of magic, and of luxuriant fancy, one
of the happiest of Chaucer's adaptations of tale to narrator.
The Host demands (F2) a tale of love—the Squire conforms
to the demand.

> Cambinskan, King of Tartary, had two sons, Algarsyf and Cam-
> balo; and a lovely daughter, Canacee.   On the King's birthday, a
> knight brought to the court as gifts from the King of Araby, a
> steed of brass that would bear its rider where he desired; a glass
> mirror that distinguished friend and foe, forewarned of evil, and
> revealed treason in love; a gold ring that gave power to discourse
> with fowls and plants; and a sword that pierced any armor, and
> that healed with its flat side.   On a morning, Canacee with the ring
> encountered a female falcon, who narrated her courtship by a terce-
> let, her yielding of her love, and her lover's abandonment of her.
> Canacee took the bird home with her, and tenderly cared for it.
> Chaucer promises to tell later how the tercelet was recovered
> through Cambalo.   Now he will tell of great haps and battles—of
> Cambinskan's conquests; of Algarsyf's winning of Theodora; of the
> lover of Canacee, who for her fought thrice with her brothers.   But
> the fragment breaks off before any of this is told.

Spenser wrote a continuation of the story in the *Faerie
Queene* IV 3.30 ff., omitting Cambinskan and the falcon; and
in *Il Penseroso* Milton celebrated the tale with the memorable
allusion to the story that was 'left half-told.'

No single source for the *Squire's Tale* has been found.
Effort to connect the poem with the *Travels* of Marco Polo
has failed.   Froissart's *Cléomadès* appears to offer the closest
analogue to the magic feature.   That the tale probably grew
from Chaucer's fancy working on accounts of magic eked out
with reminiscences of traveler's tales of wonders of the East,
is supported by the fact that the piece is unfinished.   The poem
has frequently been likened to Coleridge's *Cristabel* in that
apparently it could not be finished effectively, because the tale

depends on the magic element, and because further treatment
of the magic would necessitate its application to and association with the definite and the commonplace. Brandl's theory
that the tale is an allegory of conditions at the English Court,
Cambinskan being Edward III, and Canacee representing Constance, second wife of John of Gaunt, has been rejected.

Skeat dated the tale among the latest of the series—that is,
after 1385; and indicated the resemblance of the falcon episode, in tone and situation, to the *Anelida.* Wülcker approved
of dating 'about 1393.' Lowes pointed out parallels that may
indicate that the tale and the A Prologue to the *Legend* 'were
in mind not far from the same time.' This last Miss Hammond
regards as very probable.

THE WORDS OF THE FRANKLIN, [82] etc., let us
into the secret desire of the Franklin's heart and its great dis-
appointment, and prepare for the tale that follows. 'Well and
like a gentleman hast thou acquitted thee,' he exclaims to the
Squire; 'I would my son were like thee! Wealth without virtue
is naught. The boy cares not for virtue, but prefers to gamble
and lose all he has, and would rather talk with a page than
with a gentle person from whom he may learn *gentilesse.'*
Gentilesse the Franklin would possess, and he would have his
son a gentle-man.—'Straw for your *gentilesse!*' cries the Host;
and he bids the Franklin tell a tale. So Chaucer again varies
his manner of introducing a new narrator.

THE FRANKLIN'S TALE [82]. Much has been made of
an impression that, in contrast to the tales of the Knight, the
Squire, the Reeve, the Miller, and others, the tales of the Merchant and the Franklin are not appropriate to their narrators,
and therefore were assigned to them as result of a conception
later than that of the characterizations in the General Prologue. But it is surely unnecessary to imagine from the General Prologue that the Franklin was merely a rustic squire
limited to the delights of the table. Nor is it necessary to take
as more than modesty his preliminary protest (F716 ff.) that

he is but an ignorant man of rude speech, who never learned aught of rhetoric and figures.

Alveragus and Dorigen of Armorica live several years in happy wedlock, in which love is sustained by absence of claim of mastery on either side. Alveragus is forced to make a journey to England. A young squire, Aurelius, falls in love with Dorigen, pleads his suit, and is repulsed. But to soften her refusal, yet still to yield nothing, Dorigen tells him she will be his if he removes all the rocks from the coast of Brittany. At first the youth abandons himself to despair; but, through a brother, he obtains the services of an astrologer of Orleans. The magician makes it appear that all the rocks are gone. Dorigen knows not what to do. Alveragus returns; broken-hearted, he declares that word pledged must be kept. The lady goes to Aurelius; but, moved by her own and her husband's nobility, the squire will not violate her 'agayns franchyse and alle gentillesse' (F1524). Affected by the magnanimity of the other parties, the magician forgives Aurelius the sum that is due for his services.

So, while seeming not to protest against the Host's scorn for *gentilesse*, the Franklin quietly tells a tale in which *gentilesse* is the motive of almost every vital act of each of the principals (see F709, 754, 1524, 1527, 1574, 1595, 1608, 1611).— Moreover, the tale is the final formal treatment of the question of whether husband or wife should have sovereignty or mastery. The Franklin accounts for the perfect domestic bliss of Alveragus and Dorigen by deliberate enunciation of a theory of married life quite different from all that had been expressed, and nobly fitted to end the discussion. He directly rejects the Wife's solution, and as directly that of the other side. When Dorigen, who was of higher estate, accepted her lover, she did so with full intent to submit to such lordship as men have over their wives (F742-43). But Alveragus voluntarily swore that he would have but 'the name of soverayntee'; he would 'take no maistrye agayn hir wil ne kythe hir jalousye,' and as husband would follow her will as a lover should his lady's. Dorigen accepted his proffer born of *gentilesse*, and pledged ever humility and fidelity to him (F754-59). So, declares the Franklin, commenting carefully and at length on the situation—so it should be; friends must obey each other if they will long hold company; love will not be constrained by mastery; he who is.

most patient in love is supreme; patience vanquishes when rigor
shall never attain (F761 ff.).

The spirit and the tone of the poem are in perfect accord
with its noble sentiment. The relations of the lovers are presented most sympathetically and admirably. The picture of the
devoted wife in a 'derke fantasye' (F844) brooding over the
wave-washed rocky coast, is remarkable—as is the very strikingly different characterization of the gentleman scientist.
Though one must regard as decidedly unfortunate the long
enumeration of other virtuous women abused by lust (F1367-
458), such matter is to be expected in plaints of the period.

Chaucer's opening (F709 ff.) and the setting (F729, 806,
808, 992), would lead us to suppose that he was following a
Breton *lai* of the sort used for *Sir Orfeo, Lai le Freine,* etc. (see
pages 124 ff.). No such piece has been discovered. Schofield
has offered little to prove his theory that a legend of the British Alviragus, who is dealt with in Geoffrey of Monmouth's
Historia, was current in South Wales, was taken to Brittany,
and was put into writing by a poet of the school of Marie de
France. The story is ultimately from the East. A similar
tale is the Fifth Novel of the Tenth Day of the *Decameron.*
This is repeated in the fourth of the *Questioni d'Amore* in Boccaccio's *Filocolo,* which Rajna and others regard as the source
of the *Franklin's Tale.* The question (F1622) with which the
Franklin concludes, 'Which was the moste free (generous),
as thinketh yow?' is paralleled at the end of each of the versions by Boccaccio. One wonders if Chaucer could possibly
have intended the unwritten endlink of the Franklin to be made
up at all of discussion of the question, somewhat after the
nature of what follows in the Italian texts, and what was so
popular in French and Provençal.

The list of the various victims (F1367-458) is from
Jerome's *Epistola adversus Jovinianum* Chs. 41, 43, 44-46, a
work utilized considerably for the Wife's Prologue (see page
722) and the A Prologue to the *Legend* (see page 669). This
helps to confirm the impression created by the style and the
manner of the poem, the conditions of its appearance in the

MSS., and its relations with the other members of the Marriage Group—namely, that the *Franklin's Tale* in its present form is one of the latest of the tales, and of date between 1394 and 1396, at least late in the period of the Marriage Group (see page 686).

FRAGMENT G [83]

Fragment G has no headlink or endlink. It consists of the prologue and tale of the Second Nun,. and the headlink and tale of the Canon's Yeoman. In the MSS. G usually comes between Fragments F² and C, or B² and H; in Selden it is between B² and C; in Hatton and Cbg. Ii, it is between E¹ and C (see pages 679, 680). G554 shows that the Canon's Yeoman's Prologue was intended to follow next after the *Second Nun's Tale;* and G556 indicates that the company were at Boghton under Blee, which is five miles (from Ospringe; see pages 688-89) on the last morning's journey toward Canterbury (G588-89). Consequently, G must precede H immediately (see page 742).

THE SECOND NUN'S PROLOGUE [84]. As Skeat pointed out, the so-called Second Nun's Prologue is merely such an introduction as was suitable for a legend. Beyond the rubrics of the MSS. there is no authority for attributing the story of St. Cecilia to the Second Nun: she is not mentioned in the prologue or the tale; and G554, which connects the Canon's Yeoman's Prologue with the *Cecilia,* says merely, 'When ended was the lyf of seint Cecyle.' One is probably right in identifying the Second Nun with 'Another Nonne,' chapeleyne to the Prioress (A163-64). The facts here quite accord with the notion that A163-64 (on the Nun and her three priests) were perhaps a later addition, and were at least left incomplete (see pages 677, 692). With this agrees the fact that the Nun's Priest is given a tale, though he had appeared but as one of the 'preestes three' in the General Prologue; and that the description of him is given only in the epilogue to his tale (B4640 ff.; see page 712), after which Fragment B breaks off with the link unfinished.

The so-called Second Nun's Prologue consists of three parts. The first of these, the four stanzas against Idleness, is scarcely to be assigned to influence of Jehan de Vignay's introduction to his French version of the *Legenda Aurea,* for it has been shown that Chaucer probably did not use the *Legenda* at all for the tale. The stanzas here are of a sort adapted for writing but not for oral delivery. Brown suggests that they were introduced merely in accord with a convention of beginning a piece with lines against Idleness. Tupper finds in them an appropriate introduction to a treatment of Cecilia, who was notable for her industry and was styled 'the busy bee' (cf. G195), and also concord with his theory (opposed by Lowes) that the tale was inserted into the Canterbury series to fill out the Idleness *motif* in the Sins treatments (see page 687).

The second part of this prologue is the *Invocatio ad Mariam,* G29-77. Brown has shown that this was composed as one piece, that it is an interweaving of Dante's *Paradiso* XXXIII 1-21 and XXXII 133-35, with material from several Latin hymns; and that the passage (G36-56) regarded as showing special influence of Dante, cannot be an insertion added after making acquaintance with Dante. On basis of style, skill in transition, and failure to mention Cecilia within the *Invocatio,* Brown argues that the *Invocatio* is possibly a later addition to the prologue. The influence of the *Paradiso* on the *Hous of Fame* and the *Troilus,* and Ten Brink's proof that the *Invocatio* preceded the *Troilus,* lead Brown to locate the insertion not long before the *Troilus.*

The third part of the prologue is the Envoy to the Reader (G78-84) and the *Interpretatio* of the name 'Cecilia' (G85 ff.). Such etymologies occur in several saint's legends. From the heading of the interpretation one would infer that the tale is from Jacobus Januensis' or Jacobus a Voragine's *Legenda Aurea* (see page 306); but Kölbing has shown that the source is a Latin life (not extant) closely related to the *Legenda,* but in some features closer to Simeon Metaphrastes' life printed at Louvain, 1571.

THE SECOND NUN'S TALE [84] of St. Cecilia (see Index) is generally regarded as originally a separate and early piece. The inappropriate 'sone of Eve' applied to herself by the Nun (G62), and the phrase 'yow that reden that I wryte' (G78), show that the poem was not originally intended for recitation or for recitation by a woman, and that it was not finally revised for the *Tales*. For other evidence, see the discussion of the Nun's Prologue. Both texts of the Prologue to the *Legend* state that Chaucer had 'mad the Lyf also of seynt Cecyle' (see page 619); so the tale antedates 1386. Furnivall dated it 1373; Ten Brink, not before 1373, and not after June 8, 1374; Koch, after *Pite* in the spring of 1374; Koeppel (strongly opposed), after the *Troilus*. Kittredge thinks 1373 or 1374 is 'a little too early,' but would not accept a date later than the *Troilus* or the *Palamon*, or the *Hous of Fame*. The general tendency is to date it 1373, at the beginning of the Italian influence on Chaucer, because of immaturity of style, and apparent closeness to the original, and because G36-44, 50-56, are largely from the *Paradiso* of Dante. But style and supposed closeness to the original, are not strong bases for argument, and Brown has offered reasons for taking the Dante passages as part of a larger insertion in the prologue (see above). Moreover, the parts of the prologue are of a sort readily to be composed separately or as additions to the tale. Further, the fact that the tale is in rime-royal, is very questionable evidence of early composition.

The maiden Cecilia, of noble Roman stock, is pledged to virginity. Wedded to the young Valerian, she persuades him to her ideal, and so directs him that through the good Saint Urban he beholds the angel that ever guards her. The angel gives to Cecilia a crown of roses, to Valerian one of lilies; these may be seen only by the chaste; Valerian shall have whatever boon he asks. He asks that his brother Tiburces have grace to know the truth. This is granted; and the brother is taken as 'ally' by Cecilia, and is christened. Heaven performs for them many miracles. The brothers are arrested, and convert their jailors. Tiburces and Valerian refuse to sacrifice to the pagan gods, and are decapitated. Their jailor, Maximus, is beaten to death. Arrested, Cecilia defends her faith, and defies and lectures the pagan lord, Almachius. Vainly they try to destroy her in a bath of flames. Then they cut her neck half in two. After lying three days preaching the faith, she gives her property to Urban, and dies. She is buried in the church named for her.

The story is told with great sincerity and devotion, and, though it appears to be in Chaucer's earlier style, with much of that sympathy for goodness in distress that is a notable element in his work. As in the tales of the Nun's Priest, the Man of Law, and the Prioress, it is personality rather than incident that is the chief interest. Here Cecilia does not appear as inventor of the organ whose melody brought an angel down. Of the organ we hear only that, before the wedding, while the organs (the plural form is kept) are playing, Cecilia sings in her heart prayers for preservation of her maidenhood. The angel is her protecting spirit, ever present but visible only to chaste believers. Lowes has shown that the core of the legend in general and as Chaucer conceived of it, was virginity and martyrdom symbolized in the crowns of roses and of lilies (G220-21). Tupper (opposed by Lowes) has argued that the Idleness introduction (G1 ff.) and the treatment of Cecilia, who was well known for her special virtue of 'lasting bisinesse,' (G98, 116-17, 195), show that the legend was introduced into the *Tales* as antipathetic to the Undevotion phase of Sloth, in furtherance of a Sins *motif* (see page 687).

THE CANON'S YEOMAN'S PROLOGUE [85] was intended to follow the 'Lyf of seint Cecyle' (G554), apparently on the last morning before the arrival at Canterbury (G556, 588-89). The tale is generally regarded as among the latest written. Skeat calls attention to its originality, and to the careless ease of its rhythm, which sometimes becomes almost slovenly, as if some of it were written in haste to be revised later. The prologue and tale come late in the MSS., are but incompletely connected with the *Second Nun's Tale*, and conclude Fragment G, with no endlink. Moreover, their insertion is commonly regarded as a marked departure (see page 677) from the plan of the General Prologue. The notion that Chaucer added the prologue and tale in a moment of resent-

ment against some alchemist who had cheated him, seems quite
uncalled for.   In themselves and in the manner of their introduction, these pieces afford admirable variety—a variety that,
with the surprise of their appearance, would account adequately
for their introduction.   Indeed, it would account for a possibly
later insertion of them, when already the burden of his undertaking had apparently caused Chaucer to cut down the number of tales from one hundred and twenty-four to thirty-one
or thirty-two, or possibly to fewer still (see page 677).   Kittredge urges that there is no evidence except the silence of the
General Prologue to indicate that the Canon and his Yeoman
are afterthoughts, and reminds that the design for their introduction could not have been mentioned in the General Prologue
without spoiling the very effect aimed at in their sudden
appearance.

At Boghton, after rapid riding, the Canon and his Yeoman
overtake the pilgrims, whom they have seen set forth that
morning from their inn (apparently at Ospringe, see page
682).   The Yeoman is communicative, and needs but little
encouragement from the Host to open himself, half in mockery,
half in admiration, concerning the alchemistic powers and the
cheats of his master.   Unable to silence him, the Canon rides
off 'for verray sorwe and shame.'   Then the Yeoman bursts
out against the rogue; he will declare all he knows.

THE CANON'S YEOMAN'S TALE [85] is in two parts.
The first is the Yeoman's half-serious, half-ironical attempt at
exposition of the materials and methods by which the alchemist
honestly seeks to make gold.   His own confusion of mind in
the matter, and his furious resentment and awe working on the
jargon that his master has made familiar to him, produce an
amusing jumble of 'termes' 'clergial' and 'queynte.'   Admirable
is the concluding description of the scene at the breaking of
the crucible, when the gulls try to explain the cause of their
loss, and the canon encourages them, and perhaps himself, to
try again—the next time he shall succeed.   This prepares for
the second part, the realistic account of how the London
canon—not *his* canon, the Yeoman is careful to say—posing

as an alchemist, by legerdemain cheated a credulous priest of forty pounds.

The chief interest of the tale is in the Yeoman's mixed feeling of bitterness and admiration toward his master, who for seven years has systematically victimized him with visions of gold, exhausted his brain with mathematical calculations, and worn out his body and scorched his face with blowing the fire. This is the *motif* that runs under all the piece, and that again and again breaks forth most ludicrously. The several interruptions at the beginning of the narrative portion, and the comments at the end, both so characteristic of Chaucer, are very appropriate to the nature and the mood of the Yeoman. Once the tale is under way, however, there are no interruptions, and the story proceeds swiftly. The narrative is very dramatic, with much direct discourse; and the poem is remarkably realistic, of the class of Jonson's *Alchemist*, in comparison with which it suffers little.

No source for the tale has been pointed out. The piece is probably a product of the poet's own knowledge of alchemy, of human nature, and of the cheats to which credulity and cupidity open the way. Whether or not, as did many of his contemporaries, Chaucer believed in the claims of alchemy, cannot be shown. The poem indicates that he had been interested sufficiently to acquaint himself considerably with details of the art. Possibly the second part of the piece is from an occurrence of the day within the poet's own personal knowledge; but it may well be from an anecdote long current.

FRAGMENT H [86]

Fragment H consists of the prologue and the tale of the Manciple. In the MSS. regularly, as next to last of the series, it precedes Fragment I. It is not perfectly connected with Fragment G.

THE MANCIPLE'S PROLOGUE [87] opens with the pilgrims at Bob-up-and-doun under the Blee (H1-3), on the last morning of the journey to Canterbury (H16; I1, 16, 25, 47).

In our remarks on the *Cook's Tale* (see page 697), are noted the problems connected with the Host's expressions to the Cook here, and his directions to him to tell a tale (H5 ff.), with their implications of change of plan and shift of position for the *Cook's Tale*. Little support has been given Ten Brink's remark that the *Manciple's Tale* was written more probably for the journey homeward.

Having been drinking heavily overnight, the Cook is in a dazed condition, so that, when called on for a tale, he is incapable. The Manciple takes his place, but chides him with the very violence that in his following narrative he warns against. Full of impotent wrath, the Cook falls from his horse; he is mounted again only with the greatest effort. The Host reproves the Manciple for his violence, and warns of probable retaliation by the Cook on his becoming sober. So is suggested another 'quarrel group' (see page 683). The Manciple mollifies the Cook with a draught from his gourd; and, with his usual thrift, the Host commends the wisdom of bearing with one a supply of good drink, the general peacemaker.

THE MANCIPLE'S TALE [87] is of the adultery of the wife of Phœbus with a fellow of low rank; the betrayal of the lovers by the white crow, a pet of the husband; the angry Phœbus' execution of his wife; his grief; and, finally, his retaliation on the crow by plucking him and casting him out of doors. The Manciple's homiletic turn evinced in his prologue, is manifested in all the tale. Of the 258 lines, 130 in four sections (H146-54, 160-95, 207-37, 309-62) are exhortations on keeping wives close, on difference in rank or estate as creating no real difference in guilt, and on jangling or prating scandal. The first theme is illumined by several 'ensamples' (H187); and the whole story is itself declared by Tupper (opposed by Lowes) to be an 'ensample' (H309) against Jangling, which is a phase of Wrath (see page 687). Note the return to the cuckold theme of the Miller-Reeve group (see pages 694 ff.).

The tale is a remaking of the fable of Apollo and Coronis in Ovid's *Metamorphoses* II 534-632, with addition of the exhortation. The theme of the Tell-Tale Bird was brought afresh from the East in the Middle Ages, and incorporated into the *Seven Sages* (see page 186) ; but this version is not Chaucer's. The tale of Phœbus and the White Crow is sketched with comment in 43 lines as third *exemplum* under Cheste or Chiding, the second phase of Wrath, in Gower's *Confessio* III. It is interesting that the mother's persistent repetition of 'my sone' in the final exhortation in Chaucer, is paralleled in the 'father's' repetition of 'my sone' in Gower at all this point. The concluding lines of application of the 'ensample' (H317 ff.) are mostly from the *Parson's Tale* (1647 ff.), and Albertanus of Brescia's *De Arte Loquendi et Tacendi*, with matter from the Vulgate Bible and perhaps Seneca or the *Sentences* of Publilius Syrus. For the other passages of exhortation Chaucer drew on Theophrastus, Boethius, the *Roman de la Rose*, and the *Gesta Romanorum*.

The parallels with Gower, and the apparent dependence on the *Parson's Tale*, suggest a later date for the poem. Koeppel urged that it preceded the *Squire's Tale*. Miss Hammond suggests (see page 692) that the Miller-Reeve group to which the Manciple belongs (A542-44), is an afterthought pieced into the original form of the General Prologue; but she puts this tale with the group that she regards as the first composed.

FRAGMENT I [88]

In the MSS. Fragment I is regularly the last Fragment, and follows H. It consists of the prologue and tale of the Parson, with the 'Retraction' at the end of the tale.

THE PARSON'S PROLOGUE [89] opened at 4 p.m. (12 ff.) and was to follow next after the *Manciple's Tale* (H) which must have been finished in the morning (H16). Furnivall urged that Chaucer left a blank space in I1, where the scribes later inserted the Manciple's name. In MS. Hengwrt the name is on an erasure. MS. Christ Church has the Canon's Yeoman precede the Parson, and has his name in I1. Ultimately Chaucer would probably have inserted tales between H and I, and have changed the wording of H16 or I1, or of both. The day is the last of the journey to Canterbury, the *Parson's Tale* the last of the stories to be told (ll6, 19, 25, 47, 62). The astronomical indications (l2 ff.) have been used for evidence of the year of the journey; but the calculations seem to have been based on misinterpretation of the text (see page 681). The indications of change of plan from two tales to one on the way, are discussed on page 676.

THE PARSON'S TALE [89]. The Parson refuses to tell 'fables and such wretchedness,' he will relate 'morality and virtuous matter'; he is 'a Southern man,' he cannot alliterate and he values rime little—he will tell in prose. The troop observe that it is fitting 'to enden in som vertuous sentence.' Despite the Host's urging that he 'beth fructuous, and that in little space,' he delivers a lengthy discourse on Penitence, into which he introduces a treatment of the Seven Deadly Sins (§§23-84; see pages 687 ff.) longer than the main piece. Until 1901 it was assumed that the chief source of the tale was Frère Lorens' *Somme des Vices et des Vertus*. But in 1901 Miss Peterson showed that the Penitence matter is from an untraced version of Raymund of Pennaforte's *Summa Casuum Pœnitentiœ*, a work written especially for guidance of confessors as to the new regulations for confession ordained by the Lateran Council, 1215-1216; and that the Sins matter is from an untraced version of Guilelmus Peraldus' *Summa seu Tractatus de Viciis*. Many able critics, Ten Brink, Lowell, and others, have questioned the authenticity of the tale, or have urged interpolation by a hand or by hands other than Chaucer's. Possibly the Sins and the Penitence part were written separately. But it has been shown that the Sins bulk large in various *summœ* and *penitentials*, and that Confession of the Deadly Sins is one of the great mediæval divisions of Penance. That Chaucer wrote the tale, seems now generally accepted, and is the conclusion of the latest studies. Koeppel showed that many of its passages appear in somewhat changed form in the tales of the Pardoner (and his prologue), the Summoner, the Wife (and her prologue), the Physician, the Clerk, the Knight, the Second Nun, the Merchant, the Nun's Priest, and the Manciple, and in the *Melibeus.* There are also parallels in the *Troilus* and *Fortune.*

Ten Brink apparently would date the tale at the end of the poet's career, though he doubted its authenticity. Koeppel would put it (in a first form) 'in the eighties'; Skeat put it probably before 1380, at much the same time as the *Melibeus,* a few paragraphs near the end being later insertions. The dating of the parallel passages in the pieces just mentioned, must be used for final decision as to the date of the tale.

In the treatment of the Sins in the tales, and the introduction into other tales of free borrowings of thought and word from the Sins passage, Tupper finds strong confirmation of his belief (opposed by Koch and Lowes) that Chaucer used deliberately the Sins *motif* in a number of the tales composed in the later years of the poem (see pages 687 ff.).

The Host's exclamation, 'I smelle a loller in the wind' (B1173), and the similarity at first thought between the Parson of the General Prologue (A477 ff.) and the 'poor priests' of Wycliffe, have fostered contention that the Parson was meant as a Wycliffite, and that Chaucer was a Wycliffe sympathizer. This view never made much headway. The Parson of the General Prologue is a composite of conventional attributes of parsons in literature preceding Chaucer, and possibly a development of suggestions from Renclus de Moiliens' *Roman de Carité.* The *Parson's Tale* is most orthodox, its ultimate basis, the *Summa Casuum,* being a specially important orthodox instruction book (see above). And it has well been urged as quite in accord with Chaucer's method of humor, to have the most worthy cleric of the company accused of heresy.

CHAUCER'S RETRACTION [89]. At the close of the *Parson's Tale* a section now styled 'The Retraction' announces, 'Here taketh the makere of this book his leve,' apologizes for the defects of 'this litel tretis,' and continues: 'I biseke yow mekely for the mercy of god, that ye preye for me, that Crist have mercy on me, and foryeve me my giltes:—and namely of my translacions and endytinges of worldly vanitees, the whiche I revoke in my retracciouns: . . .' Then the writer gives the

list of his works that has already been noted (see page 619).
The question of the authenticity of this passage is of importance, since the section aids in determining the Chaucer canon,
and, more, since it presents to us the strange picture of Chaucer, under what seems to be the pressure of narrow tenets,
apologizing for and condemning most of what he had labored
for in literature.   Moreover, the Retraction being genuine, it
would appear that actually Chaucer had finally meant to end
the *Canterbury Tales* with the *Parson's Tale,* and so had·
changed his plan from two tales to one on the way to the shrine,
and had given up the return journey.   In recent years the ͻ
general trend of opinion has been in favor of authenticity.
Tatlock has shown that 'before Chaucer's day there was a well-
marked though slim literary tradition for writing Retractions,' which would make Chaucer's writing of one 'a little more
intelligible,' and that perhaps we stress too far the author's
disavowal added (just as was Spenser's in the Platonic *Hymns,*
and Herrick's in the *Hesperides*) to one of the very works that
he condemned but did not reform.   In thinking of the matter,
one must not forget the conduct of Ruskin and Ibsen and
Tolstoi.

BIBLIOGRAPHICAL NOTES

BIBLIOGRAPHICAL NOTES

Though they seek to indicate *all the really valuable prints, editions, and discussions of the several writings and classes or types* of writing composed in Middle English between 1050 and 1400, these bibliographical notes cannot pretend to be quite complete. The limitations of the notes on Chaucer are stated at their head. In some few cases *early editions or prints now of little general value and noted in the later editions,* are not mentioned here. Usually the introductions and the notes in the editions, are not indicated separately, for it is assumed that the student will *always examine those introductions and notes* without specific reference to them here. The entries in the following pages include, it is hoped, *all* the *pertinent articles* (some minor reviews and notices of works being excepted) *in the periodicals and series* (except those starred) that are listed in the Table of Abbreviations below, *up to September, 1915.* It is believed that there is in the periodicals and series starred little of value, as judged on the bases indicated for these notes, that is not entered in the notes. Additional materials are included from periodicals and series other than those in the Table. For space, but *a limited number of the more important notices and reviews of the editions and of the monographs,* are admitted. References to the *general* works on Versification and Language noted on page 760, are usually not entered under the individual items, it being presumed that the student interested will examine those works regarding the piece in question. Effort has been made to include all studies of the language of single pieces or groups. Writings on *general* linguistic problems or features, are entered only as they deal with the individual piece. Limitation of space has prevented more extended indication of the contents and nature of each bibliographical item, than has been given.

In accord with the purpose of this book, the bibliographical notes are *primarily for the writings in English;* but references sufficient to put the student in touch with the French and the Latin literature connected with each class or type or piece, are given.   Yet there will be noticed an occasional yielding to a temptation to include, for possibly greater helpfulness, some isolated items that properly are within the provinces of only the Romanic or General Germanic bibliographer.   Often such entries must appear to be arbitrarily made; they must be taken merely as suggestive.   Very full information for the Romanic and Germanic fields may be had in the *Jahresbericht der Germanischen Philologie,* Gröber's *Grundriss,* and Vollmöller's *Kritischer Jahresbericht.*

The *references for the individual class or type or group,* are entered *at the head* of the notes for the class or type or group. The *special treatments of the individual writing* are noted in the bibliography of that writing.   In each such case *the notes for the class or type or group, should be consulted.*

Acad* . *Academy*, London 1869—.

AEB *Altenglische Bibliothek*, ed. Kölbing, Heilbronn 1883—.

AELeg 1875 *Altenglische Legenden*, ed. Horstmann, Paderborn 1875.

AELeg 1878 *Sammlung Altenglischer Legenden*, ed. Horstmann, Heilbronn 1878.

AELeg 1881 *Altenglische Legenden, Neue Folge*, ed. Horstmann, Heilbronn 1881.

AESprPr *Altenglische Sprachproben*, ed. Mätzner, Berlin 1867.

AJPhil *American Journal of Philology*, Baltimore 1880—.

AllgLtbl* *Allgemeines Literaturblatt*, Vienna, 1891—.

Angl *Anglia, Zeitschrift für Englische Philologie*, Halle 1877—.

AnglAnz *Anglia Anzeiger*, Halle 1880—.

AnglBbl *Beiblatt zur Anglia*, Halle 1890—.

AnglForsch *Anglistische Forschungen*, ed. Hoops, Heidelberg 1901—.

AnzfDA* *Anzeiger für Deutsches Alterthum*, Berlin 1875—.

Arch *Archiv für das Studium der Neueren Sprachen und Literaturen*, ed. Herrig *et al.*, Elberfeld and Iserlohn 1846—, Braunschweig 1849—.

Archæol* *Archæologia*, London 1770—.

Ashton *Romances of Chivalry*, Ashton, London 1890.

Athen* *Athenæum*, London 1828—.

Ausg u. Abhdl *Ausgaben und Abhandlungen aus dem Gebiete der Romanischen Philologie*, Marburg 1881—.

Berliner Beitr *Berliner Beiträge zur Germanischen und Romanischen Philologie*, Berlin 1893—.

Billings *A Guide to the Middle English Metrical Romances*, A. H. Billings, New York 1901.

Böddeker *Altenglische Dichtungen des MS. Harl. 2253*, ed. Böddeker, Berlin 1878.

Bonner Beitr *Bonner Beiträge zur Anglistik*, Bonn 1898-1908.

Bonner Stud *Bonner Studien zur Englischen Philologie*, Bonn 1909—.

Brandl *Mittelenglische Literatur*, in Paul's *Grundriss der Germanischen Philologie*, 1st ed. Strassburg 1893, 2^1.609 ff., Index 2^2.345.

BrynMawrMon *Bryn Mawr College Monographs*, Bryn Mawr 1905—.

Cbg Hist *The Cambridge History of English Literature*, Vols. 1-2, Cambridge 1907, 1908.

Ch&Sidg *Early English Lyrics*, ed. Chambers and Sidgwick, London 1907, new ed. 1912 (refs. to 1907 ed.).

Chambers *The Mediæval Stage*, E. K. Chambers, Oxford 1903, 2 vols.

ChS *Publications of the Chaucer Society*, two series, 1868—.

ColUnivSt *Columbia University Studies in English* and *in Comparative Literature*, New York 1899—.

Courthope *History of English Poetry*, W. J. Courthope, Vol. 1, London 1895.

Ctbl *Literarisches Zentralblatt*, Leipzig 1850—·

de Julleville Hist *Histoire de la Langue et de la Littérature Française*, Vols. 1-2, Paris 1896.

DLz* *Deutsche Literaturzeitung*, Berlin 1880—·

DNB *Dictionary of National Biography*, ed. Stephen and Lee, New York and London, 1885-1900.

EETS *Publications of the Early English Text Society*, Original Series, 1864—.

EETSES *Publications of the Early English Text Society*, Extra Series, 1867—.

Ellis EEP *Specimens of Early English Poetry*, ed. G. Ellis, London 1811, 3 vols.

Ellis Spec *Specimens of Early English Metrical Romances*, ed. G. Ellis, London 1805, 3 vols.; revised Halliwell, 1 vol. Bohn ed. 1848 (latter ed. referred to).

Erl Beitr *Erlanger Beiträge zur Englischen Philologie*, Erlangen 1889—.

Ency Brit *Encyclopædia Britannica*, 11th ed.

ESt *Englische Studien*, Heilbronn, Leipzig, 1877—.

ETB *Englische Textbibliothek*, ed. Hoops, Berlin (dates under individual items).

Furnivall EEP *Early English Poems and Lives of Saints*, ed. F. J. Furnivall, Berlin 1862 (Transactions of Philological Society of London 1858).

Gayley *Plays of Our Forefathers*, C. M. Gayley, New York 1907.

Germ *Germania*, Stuttgart 1856-8, Wien 1859-92.

GRMSchr *Germanisch-Romanische Monatsschrift*, Heidelberg 1909—.

Gröber *Grundriss der Romanischen Philologie*, Strassburg 1888-1902, new issue 1897-1906, 2nd ed. 1904— (Vol. 2¹, 1902, referred to).

Hammond *Chaucer: A Bibliographical Manual*, E. P. Hammond, New York 1908.

Hartshorne AMT *Ancient Metrical Tales*, ed. Hartshorne, London 1829.

HarvStN *Harvard Studies and Notes in Philology and Literature*, Boston 1892—.

Hazlitt Rem *Remains of the Early Popular Poetry of England*, ed. W. C. Hazlitt, London 1864-6, 4 vols.

Herbert *Catalogue of Romances in the Department of MSS. of the British Museum*, J. A. Herbert, London 1910 (Vol. 3 of Ward's Catalogue).

Hist Litt *Histoire Littéraire de la France*, Paris 1733-1898.

Jahresbericht *Jahresbericht über die Erscheinungen auf dem Gebiete der Germanischen Philologie*, Berlin 1879—, Leipzig 1883—.

JbREL *Jahrbuch für Romanische und Englische Sprache und Literatur*, ed. Ebert and Lemcke, Berlin and Leipzig 1859-76.

JEGP *Journal of English and Germanic Philology*, Evanston, Illinois, 1903-5, Urbana, Illinois, 1905—.

JGP *Journal of Germanic Philology*, Bloomington, Indiana, 1897-1903.

JPhil* *Journal of Philology*, Cambridge, England, 1868-1907.

KielerSt *Kieler Studien zur Englischen Philologie*, Kiel 1901—.

Kild Ged *Die Kildare-Gedichte*, ed. W. Heuser, Bonn 1904 (Bonner Beitr 14).

Körting *Grundriss der Geschichte der Englischen Literatur von ihren Anfängen bis zur Gegenwart*, G. Körting, 5th ed. Münster 1910.

Krit Jahresber* *Kritischer Jahresbericht über der Fortschritte der Romanischen Philologie*, Zweiter Teil, ed. Vollmöller, München u. Leipzig 1892-3, Leipzig 1896-7, Erlangen 1897—.

Legouis *Chaucer*, E. Legouis, Engl. trans. by Lailavoix, London 1913.

LitBl *Literaturblatt für Germanische und Romanische Philologie*, Heilbronn, Leipzig, 1880—.

Manch Univ Publ *Manchester University Publications*, English Series, Manchester 1909—.

Manly Spec *Specimens of the Pre-Shakespearean Drama*, ed. J. M. Manly, 2nd ed. Boston 1900, Vol. 1.

MarbSt *Marburger Studien zur Englischen Philologie*, Marburg (dates under individual items).

Minor Poems *Chaucer: The Minor Poems*, ed. W. W. Skeat, 2nd ed. Oxford, 1896.

MLN *Modern Language Notes*, Baltimore 1886—.

MLQ *Modern Language Quarterly*, London, March, 1898-December, 1904.

MLR *Modern Language Review*, Cambridge, England, 1905—.

Morley *English Writers*, H. Morley, Vols. 3-5, London 1888-93.

Morris Spec *Specimens of Early English*, Part 1 ed. R. Morris, Oxford 2nd ed. 1887; Part 2 ed. R. Morris and W. W. Skeat, Oxford 4th ed. 1898.

MPhil *Modern Philology*, Chicago 1903—.

Münch Beitr *Münchener Beiträge zur Romanischen und Englischen Philologie*, München 1890—.

N&Q* *Notes and Queries*, London 1849—.

OMETexts *Old and Middle English Texts*, ed. Morsbach and Holthausen, Heidelberg (dates under individual items).

Oxf Ch *The Works of Geoffrey Chaucer*, ed. W. W. Skeat, Oxford 1894—, 6 vols., extra 7th vol. of Chaucerian Poems.

Palæstra *Palæstra, Untersuchungen und Texte*, Leipzig, Berlin, 1898—.

Paris Litt Franç *La Littérature Française au Moyen Âge*, G. Paris, 4th ed. Paris 1909.

Patterson *The Middle English Penitential Lyric*, ed. F. A. Patterson, New York 1911.

Paul Grundriss *Grundriss der Germanischen Philologie*, H. Paul, 1st ed. Strassburg 1891-1900, 3 vols.; 2nd ed. not completed (references are to 1st ed. unless 2nd ed. is indicated).

PBBeitr *Beiträge zur Geschichte der Deutschen Sprache und Literatur*, ed. Paul and Braune, Halle 1874—.

Percy Soc *Publications of the Percy Society*, London 1840-52.

PFMS *The Percy Folio MS.*, ed. Furnivall and Hales, London 1867-9, 4 vols.

PMLA   *Publications of the Modern Language Association of America,* Baltimore 1884-1901, Cambridge, Massachusetts, 1902—.

QF   *Quellen und Forschungen zur Sprach- und Culturgeschichte der Germanischen Völker,* Strassburg 1874—.

RadMon   *Radcliffe College Monographs,* Boston 1891—.

Rel Ant   *Reliquiæ Antiquæ,* ed. T. Wright and J. O. Halliwell, London 1845, 2 vols.

RevCelt   *Revue Celtique,* Paris 1870—.

RevCrit*   *Revue Critique d'Histoire et de Littérature,* Paris 1866—.

RevGerm   *Revue Germanique,* Paris 1905—.

Rickert RofFr, RofL   *Early English Romances in Verse: Romances of Friendship,* Vol. 1; *Romances of Love,* Vol. 2, Edith Rickert, London 1908.

Ritson AEMR   *Ancient English Metrical Romances,* ed. J. Ritson, London 1802, 3 vols. (this ed. referred to); revised Goldsmid, Edinburgh 1884.

Ritson APP   *Ancient Popular Poetry,* ed. J. Ritson, 2nd ed. London 1833.

Ritson AS   *Ancient Songs from the Time of Henry III,* ed. J. Ritson, London 1790; new ed. 1829, 2 vols.; revised *Ancient Songs and Ballads,* W. C. Hazlitt, London 1877, 1 vol. (this ed. referred to).

Robson   *Three Early English Metrical Romances,* ed. J. Robson, London, Camden Society, 1842.

Rom   *Romania,* Paris 1872—.

RomRev   *Romanic Review,* New York 1910—.

Root   *The Poetry of Chaucer,* R. K. Root, Boston 1906.

Roxb Club   *Publications of the Roxburghe Club,* London 1814—.

SATF   *Publications de la Société des Anciens Textes Français,* Paris 1875—.

Schipper   *Englische Metrik,* J. Schipper, Bonn 1881—.

Schofield   *English Literature from the Norman Conquest to Chaucer,* W. H. Schofield, New York 1906.

Scott Antiq   *The Scottish Antiquary, or Northern Notes and Queries,* Edinburgh 1886-1903.

Scott Hist Rev*   *Scottish Historical Review,* Glasgow 1904—.

ShJhb   *Jahrbuch der Deutschen Shakespeare-Gesellschaft,* Berlin 1865—.

Skeat Spec   *Specimens of English Literature, 1394-1579,* ed. W. W. Skeat, Oxford, 6th ed.

StEPhil   *Studien zur Englischen Philologie,* ed. Morsbach, Halle (dates under individual items).

STS   *Publications of the Scottish Text Society,* Edinburgh 1884—.

StVL   *Studien zur Vergleichenden Literaturgeschichte,* Berlin 1901-9.

Ten Brink   *Early English Literature, English Literature,* trans. Kennedy, *et al.,* London and New York 1887-92, Vol. 1, Vol. 2 Parts 1-2 (referred to as *Vols.* 1-3).

Thoms   *A Collection of Early Prose Romances,* ed. W. J. Thoms, London 1828; part ed. Morley, Carlsbrooke Library, London; whole, revised ed. London (Routledge).

Ward   *Catalogue of Romances in the Department of MSS. of the British Museum*, H. L. D. Ward, London 1883-93, 2 vols. (See Herbert, for Vol. 3).

Ward Hist   *A History of English Dramatic Literature to the Death of Queen Anne*, A. W. Ward, new ed. London 1899, 3 vols.

Weber MR   *Metrical Romances of the XIII, XIV, and XV Centuries*, ed. H. Weber, Edinburgh 1810, 3 vols.

Wiener Beitr   *Wiener Beiträge zur Englischen Philologie*, Vienna 1895—.

Wright AnecLit   *Anecdota Literaria*, ed. T. Wright, London 1844.

Wright PPS   *Political Poems and Songs from the Accession of Edward III to that of Richard III*, ed. T. Wright, London, Rolls Series, 1859-61, 2 vols.

Wright PS   *Political Songs of England from the Reign of John to that of Edward III*, ed. T. Wright, Camden Society, London 1839 (this ed. referred to); revised, privately printed, Goldsmid, Edinburgh 1884, 3 vols.

Wright SLP   *Specimens of Lyric Poetry Composed in England in the Reign of Edward I*, ed. T. Wright, Percy Society, London 1842.

Wülker   *Geschichte der Englischen Literatur*, R. Wülker, Leipzig 1896, 2 vols.

YaleSt   *Yale Studies in English*, New York 1898—.

Yksh Wr   *Yorkshire Writers*, Library of Early English Writers, ed. Horstmann, London 1895-6, 2 vols.

ZsfDA*   *Zeitschrift für Deutsches Alterthum und Deutsche Litteratur*, Leipzig, Berlin 1841—.

ZsfDPh*   *Zeitschrift für Deutsche Philologie*, Halle 1869—.

ZsfFSpruL*   *Zeitschrift für Französische Sprache und Literatur*, Oppeln 1879-91, Oppeln and Leipzig 1891—.

ZsföGymn*   *Zeitschrift für die Österreichischen Gymnasien*, Vienna 1850—.

ZsfRPh   *Zeitschrift für Romanische Philologie*, Halle 1877—.

ZsfVL   *Zeitschrift für Vergleichende Litteraturgeschichte*, Berlin 1887—.

WORKS CONTAINING GENERAL BIBLIOGRAPHICAL NOTES

Booker   *A Middle English Bibliography—Dates, Dialects and Sources of the XII, XIII, XIV Century Monuments and Manuscripts exclusive of the Works of Wyclif, Gower, and Chaucer and the Documents in the London Dialect*, Heidelberg 1912 (crit. MLN 29.153).

Brandl in Paul's *Grundriss der Germanischen Philologie*, 1st ed. $2^1.609$ ff.; in 2nd ed. $2^1.1073$ ff. on O. E. Literature to 1133.

Cambridge History of English Literature 1.497 ff., 2.491 ff.

Edwardes, M. *A Summary of the Literatures of Modern Europe*, London 1907, 39 ff.

Geddie *A Bibliography of Middle Scots Poets*, STS 61.
Körting *Grundriss der Geschichte der Englischen Literatur*, 5th ed.
 Münster 1910, §3 and §6, and §§69 ff.
Schofield *English Literature from the Norman Conquest to Chaucer*, New
 York and London 1906, 466 ff.

SOURCES OF INFORMATION ON PUBLICATIONS

Varnhagen *Systematisches Verzeichniss der Programmabhandlungen, Dis-
 sertationen, u. s. w., aus dem Gebiete der Romanischen und Englischen
 Philologie*, 2nd ed. Leipzig 1893.
*Jahresbericht über die Erscheinungen auf dem Gebiete der Germanischen
 Philologie*, Berlin 1879—, Leipzig 1883—·
*Jahres-Verzeichniss der an den Deutschen Universitäten Erschienenen
 Schriften*, Berlin 1887—·
*Jahres-Verzeichniss der an den Deutschen Schulanstalten Erschienenen
 Abhandlungen*, Berlin 1890—·
Fock *Bibliographischer Monatsbericht über Neu Erschienene Schul-, Uni-
 versitäts-, und Hochschulschriften*, Leipzig 1889—·
Catalogue des Thèses et Écrits Académiques Françaises, Paris 1885—·
*Catalogue des Dissertations et Écrits Académiques Provenant des
 Échanges avec les Universités Étrangères . . . par la Bibliothèque
 Nationale, Paris* 1882—·
A List of American Doctoral Dissertations Printed in 1912, C. A. Flagg;
 in 1913, A. M. Stephens; Library of Congress 1913, 1914.
Publishers' Weekly, New York 1872—; cumulated quarterly; cumulated
 annually in *Annual American Catalogue* 1886—·
Monthly Cumulative Book Index, Minneapolis 1898-1913, White Plains and
 New York 1914; cumulated annually; cumulated in *United States
 Catalogue of Books in Print to January 1, 1912*.
Publishers' Circular, London 1837-72; *Publishers' Weekly* 1872—; cumu-
 lated annually in *English Catalogue of Books*, London 1863—, see its
 Index of Subjects.
Bibliographie de la France, Paris 1811—, weekly.
Catalogue Générale de la Librairie Française depuis 1840, Rédigé par Otto
 Lorenz, Paris; continuation by D. Jordell, Paris 1849—; *Répertoire
 Bibliographique*, D. Jordell, Paris, monthly.
Kayser *Vollständiges Bücher-Lexikon*, Leipzig 1834—, see its Subject
 Indexes.
Heinzius *Allgemeines Deutsches Bücher-Lexikon*, Leipzig 1850-92, covers
 years 1700-1892.
Hinrichs *Wöchentliches Verzeichnis der Erschienenen und der Vorbe-
 reiteten Neuigkeiten des Deutschen Buchhandels*, Leipzig 1893—; to this
 is published a *Monatsregister;* cumulated in *Halbjahrs-Katalog,*
 1798—, see its Register; cumulated every four and five years, 1846—,
 1851—.
See the notices in AnglBbl, *Anglia Bücherschau*, MLN, MLR, etc.

GENERAL HISTORIES AND WORKS OF REFERENCE

See in Table of Abbreviations: Brandl, Cbg Hist, Courthope, DNB, Herbert, Körting, Morley, Schofield (crit. JEGP 6.507; ESt 38.78; MLN 22.186; Athen 1907.1.94; Rev Germ 4.472; Gött. Gel. Anzeiger 1907. No. 11; ZsfFSpruL 32.116; LitBl 28.241; espec. AJPhil 1907.460), Ten Brink, Ward, Wülker.

Baldwin, C. S. *An Introduction to Medieval English Literature*, New York 1914.
Brandl in Paul's *Grundriss der Germanischen Philologie*, 2nd ed. 2¹.1073 ff. on O. E. Literature to 1133.
Dale *National Life and Character in the Mirror of Early English Literature*, Cambridge 1907, Chs. 4 ff.
Edwardes, M. *A Summary of the Literatures of Modern Europe*, London and New York 1907.
Jusserand, J. J. *A Literary History of the English People*, Vol. 1, London 1894.
Ker, W. P. *English Literature, Medieval*, New York and London 1912.
Pollard, A. W. in Chambers' *Cyclopedia of English Literature*, new ed. 1901-3, 1.31-119, 150-62.
Saintsbury, G. *The Flourishing of Romance and the Rise of Allegory*, New York 1897.
Saintsbury, G. *A Short History of English Literature*, London and New York 1898.
Snell, F. W. *The Age of Chaucer*, London 1901; *The Age of Transition*, 2 vols., London 1905; *The Fourteenth Century*, New York 1899.
Warton *History of English Poetry*, ed. W. C. Hazlitt, 3 vols., London 1871.

PUBLISHING SOCIETIES

Abbotsford Club, Bannatyne Club, Camden Society, Chaucer Society, Early English Text Society, Hunterian Club, Maitland Club, Percy Society, Roxburghe Club, Scottish Text Society, Spalding Club, Surtees Society, Warton Club.

SERIES OF EDITIONS OR MONOGRAPHS

Albion Series, Boston; Belles Lettres Series, Boston;— and see Table of Abbreviations—AEB, AnglForsch, Berliner Beitr, Bonner Beitr, Bonner Stud, BrynMawrMon, ColUnivSt, ETB, Erl Beitr, HarvStN, KielerSt, Manch Univ Publ, MarbSt, Münch Beitr, OMETexts, Palæstra, QF, RadMon, StEPhil, Wiener Beitr, YaleSt.

READERS, COLLECTIONS OF SELECTIONS

Cook *A Literary Middle English Reader*, Boston 1915.
Emerson *Middle English Reader*, New York and London 1905, new ed. 1915.

Kluge *Mittelenglisches Lesebuch,* 2nd ed., Halle 1912.
MacLean *An Old and Middle English Reader,* London 1894.
Mätzner *Altenglische Sprachproben,* Berlin 1867.
Morris *Specimens of Early English* (1150-1300), 2nd ed. Oxford 1887.
Morris and Skeat *Specimens of Early English* (1298-1393), 4th ed. Oxford 1898.
Skeat *Specimens of English Literature* (1394-1579), 6th ed. Oxford.
Sweet *First Middle English Primer,* Oxford 1884.
Wülcker *Altenglisches Lesebuch,* 2 parts, Halle 1874-9.
Zupitza *Alt- und Mittelenglisches Übungsbuch,* 11th ed. Wien und Leipzig 1915.

COLLECTIONS OF MODERN RENDERINGS

Pancoast and Spaeth *Early English Poems,* N. Y. 1911, 95-173.
Rickert *Early English Romances in Verse,* London 1908, 2 vols. (see Table of Abbreviations).
Shackford *Legends and Satires,* Boston 1913.
Weston *Romance, Vision and Satire,* Boston 1912.
Weston *The Chief Middle English Poets,* Boston 1914.

For modernizations of *individual* works or authors, see under individual items.

VERSIFICATION

See Körting Grundriss §85.6.
Kaluza *A Short History of English Versification,* London and New York 1911.
Luick in Paul Grundriss, 2nd ed. 2^2.141; Angl 38.269.
Schipper *Englische Metrik,* Bonn 1881—; *Grundriss der Englischen Metrik,* Wien und Leipzig 1895; in Paul Grundriss, 2nd ed. 2^2.181; *History of English Versification,* Oxford 1910.
Saintsbury *History of English Prosody,* Vol. 1, London 1906; *Historical Manual of English Prosody,* London 1910; *History of English Prose Rhythm,* London 1912.

See the general statement at the head of these Bibliographical Notes, page 751.

LANGUAGE

See Körting Grundriss §85 and §3 and §6.
Einenkel *Streifzüge durch die Mittelenglische Syntax,* Münster 1887.
Emerson *History of the English Language,* New York 1894. New edition in preparation.
Jespersen *Growth and Structure of the English Language,* 2nd ed. Leipzig 1912.
Jordan *Die Mittelenglischen Mundarten,* GRMSchr 2.124.
Kaluza *Historische Grammatik der Englischen Sprache,* 2 vols., Berlin 1900-1; 2nd ed. 1906-7.
Kluge in Paul Grundriss, 2nd ed. 1.926.

Lounsbury *History of the English Language*, rev. ed. New York 1894, 1901.

Luick *Historische Grammatik der Englischen Sprache*, Leipzig, two parts issued by end of 1914.

Morsbach *Mittelenglische Grammatik*, Halle 1896 (but part published).

Skeat *Principles of English Etymology*, Series 1 and 2, Oxford 1887 (2nd ed. 1892), 1891.

Skeat *Notes on English Etymology*, Oxford 1901.

Skeat *English Dialects*, Cambridge, England, 1911.

Stratmann *Mittelenglische Grammatik*, Crefeld 1885.

Sweet *History of English Sounds*, Oxford 1888.

Sweet *New English Grammar*, 2 vols., Oxford 1892-8, 1900-3.

Toller *Outlines of the History of the English Language*, London 1900.

Wyld *A Short History of English*, London 1914 (phonology and inflexions; see bibliogr. at page 14.)

DICTIONARIES

Mätzner *Altenglische Sprachproben*, Wörterbuch, *A-Misbileven*, Berlin 1878-1900.

Mayhew and Skeat *A Concise Dictionary of Middle English*, Oxford 1888.

Stratmann *Middle English Dictionary*, revised and enlarged by A. Bradley, Oxford 1891.

The Oxford or *New English Dictionary*, ed. Murray and others, Oxford 1888—.

CHAPTER I—ROMANCES

Billings *Guide to the M. E. Metr. Rom.* (English and Germanic Legends, Cycles of Charlemagne and of Arthur), synopses, gen. summary of crit., bibliogrs., N. Y. 1901 (crit. JGP 4.112; MLN 18.55; AnglBbl 15.353); Blackwell, H. D., *Guide to the M. E. Metr. Rom.* (Cycle of Antiquity, Romances of Adventure), Yale diss. 1903, unprinted, in Yale Univ. Libr., synopses, gen. summary of crit., bibliogrs.; Körting §§86-126; Cbg Hist 1.270-356, and *passim* (bibliogr. 513-24); Edwardes *Summary of the Lits. of Mod. Eur.*, L. 1907, English 94-109, French 150-3, 167-92; Schofield 145-319 (bibliogr. 476); Ward Vols. 1, 2; Herbert Vol. 3; Ellis Spec. abstracts; Dunlop *Hist. of Prose Fiction*, revised L. and N. Y. 1888, 2 vols.; Ten Brink 1.119, 164, 180, 225, 234, 253, 327, 336; Rickert RofFr and RofL, introds.; Morley 3.120, 251, 264, 375; Dixon *Engl. Epic and Heroic Poetry*, L. 1912; Ker *Epic and Romance*, L. 1897, 2nd ed. L. 1908; Gross *Sources and Lit. of Engl. Hist.*, new ed. L. 1915; Spence *Dict. of Med. Rom. and Rom. Writers*, L. 1913 (synopses, short notices of writers, works, personages); Saintsbury *Flourishing of Rom.*, N. Y. 1897 (gen. view); Clark *Hist. of*

Epic Poetry, Edbg. 1900; Ludlow *Pop. Epics of the Mid. Ages,* L. 1865;
Gautier *Bibliogr. Gén. des Chansons de Geste,* Paris 1896; Paris, G., Litt
Franç §§18 ff. (see bibliogr.); Paris, G., *Med. Fr. Lit.,* L. 1903; Hist Litt 30;
Gautier *Les Épopées Françaises,* 2nd ed. Paris 1878-92; de Julleville Hist
1.49-344 (see its bibliogr. 168-70, 252-3, 340-4); Lanson *Hist. de la Litt.
Franç.,* Paris 1909; Gröber *Grundriss der Rom. Phil.,* 2nd ed. 2¹·Register;
Nutt *Influence of Celtic upon Med. Rom.,* L. 1899;— Söchtig *Zur Technik
Ae. Spielmannsepen,* Leipzig diss. 1903; Kahle *Die Clerus im Me. Versro-
man,* Strassburg diss. 1906 (crit. AnglBbl 20.38); Geissler *Religion u. Aber-
glaube in den Me. Versromanzen,* Halle diss. 1908; Hübner *Die Frage in
Einigen Me. Versroman,* Kiel diss. 1910 (crit. ESt 43.264; AnglBbl 23.308);
Voltmer *Die Me. Terminologie der Ritterlichen Verwandtschafts- u. Stan-
desverhältnisse nach den Höfischen Epen u. Romanzen des 13 u. 14 Jhdts.,*
Kiel diss. 1911; Lawrence *Mediæval Story,* N. Y. 1911; Witter *Das
Burgerliche Leben im Me. Versroman,* Kiel diss. 1912; Peebles *Blood-
Brotherhood in the M. E. Rom.,* prgr. MLA 1913; Lausterer *Der Syntakt.
Gebr. des Artikels in den Älteren Me. Rom.,* Kiel diss. 1914.— See below
under individual groups and works.— Gen. bibliogr. in preparation as a
Univ. of Chicago diss. by Miss L. A. Hibbard.

1.   ENGLISH AND GERMANIC LEGENDS

Billings 1; Schofield 258; Ten Brink 1.148, 225; Körting §§87-92; etc.
See first items above.   Deutschbein *Stud. zur Sagengeschichte Englands,*
Cöthen 1906 (crit. LitBl 28.280); Creek *Character in the Matter of England
Romances,* JEGP 10.429, 585.

On the Waltheof Story, see Paul Grundriss 2nd ed. 2¹.1084; the Wade
Story, see *ibid.* 1085-6; the Hereward Story, see *ibid.* 1087-9, Noack
Sagehistorische Untersuchungen zu den Gesta Herewardi, Halle diss. 1914.

[1] KING HORN.   Ed. all texts, Hall, Oxf. 1901 (crit. JEGP 4.529;
ESt 32.124; Arch 113.193; Athen 1902.2.822);— Cbg., Michel *Horn et
Rimenhild,* Paris 1845; EETS 14 (emendations ESt 3.270), revised 1901
(crit. JGP 4.529; Athen 1902.2.822); AESprPr 1.209; Morris Spec 1.237;—
crit. text, Wissmann, QF 45 (coll. AnzfDA 9.182; introd., QF 16; for
crits. see Billings 11, Hall's ed. xv);— Harley, Ritson AEMR′2.91 (coll.,
QF 45.i; AnzfDA 9.182);— Oxf., Horstmann, Arch 50.39 (coll. AnzfDA
9.182).— On MSS., Hall ed. vii.— Selections: Zupitza Übungsbuch; Cook
Reader 11. Mod. rend., Hibbard *Three M. E. Rom.,* L. 1911; Weston *Chief
M. E. Poets* 93.— Brandl §22; Körting §87; Ten Brink 1.149, 227, 3.10; Ward
1.447; Billings 1; Paris Litt Franç §27 (see its bibliogr.).— On ll. 701-4,
Angl 19.460.   Metre: Wissmann, QF 16, 45; Wissmann, Angl 5.466; Schip-
per *Engl. Metr.,* Ab. 3. Cap. 9.; Schipper, AnglAnz 5.88; AnglAnz 8.69;
Jahresbericht 1882, item 1003; Paul Grundriss 2¹.1038, 1005; AnglBbl
13.332; West *Versification of K. H.,* Johns Hopkins diss. 1907.— McKnight
Germanic Elements in the Story of K. H., PMLA 15.221; Wissmann
Studien zu K. H., Angl 4.342; Wissmann *K. H., Untersuchungen,* QF 16
(crit. LitBl 4.132; Ctbl 1883.61; ESt 1.351, 5.408, 6.150, 153; AnzfDA 4.149,
9.181; RevCrit 1876. No. 240); Deutschbein *Stud. zur Sagengesch. Englands,*

Cöthen 1906 (crit. AnglBbl 18.1; MLR 2.176; LitBl 28.280); Hartenstein *Stud. zur Hornsage*, KielerSt 4 (crit. Ctbl 1902.1534; DLz 1902.2717; Neu Phil. Rund. 1902.549; LitBl 24.372; AnglBbl 15.333); Morsbach *Die Angebl. Originalität des . . . K. H., Beitr. zur Rom. u. Engl. Phil., Festgabe für W. Förster*, Halle 1902, 297 (crit. JEGP 4.539; ESt 31.281); Schofield *Horn and Rimenhild*, PMLA 18.1 (crit. JEGP 4.540); Northup *K. H., Recent Texts and Studies*, JEGP 4.529; Breier *Zur Lokalisierung des K. H.*, ESt 42.307; Schofield *Home of K. H.*, etc., PMLA 17.xxix; Heuser *Horn u. Rigmel, eine Namen-Untersuchung*, Angl 31.105; Deutschbein *Beiträge zur Horn- u. Haveloksage*, AnglBbl 20.16, 55.— French: ed. Michel *Horn et Rimenhild*, Paris 1845; Brede and Stengel, Ausg u. Abhdl 8. See Mettlich *Bemerkungen zu d. Agn. Lied. . . . K. H.*, Münster prgr. 1890, Kiel 1895 (see ESt 16.306); Gautier *Bibl. des Chansons de Geste*, 129; author, Rom 15.575; Gröber 2¹.573, 776.

[2] HORN CHILDE AND MAIDEN RIMNILD. Ed. Ritson AEMR 3.282; Hall, ed. *King Horn*, Oxf. 1901; Michel, ed. *Horn et Rimenhild* 341; Caro, Breslau diss. 1886, ESt 12.323 (emendations, Angl 14.309).— Brandl §52; Ten Brink 1.248; Körting §87; Billings 12; Schofield 264.— Schofield *Story of Horn and Rimenhild*, PMLA 18.1 (crit. JEGP 4.540).— Author, Rom 15.575.— See under *King Horn.*— On verse, see Wilda under *Eustace-Constance*, etc., page 781.

[3] HIND HORN. Ed. Michel *Horn et Rimenhild* 393; Child *Ballads* 1.195 (1882). See QF 16.121; ESt 1.335, 360, 12.335; PMLA 18.1; Rom 34.142.

[4] KING PONTHUS. Ed. PMLA 12.1.— Rom 26.468; AnglBbl 1897.197; Billings 3, 12. Gröber 2¹.1196.

[5] LAY OF HAVELOK. Ed. Laud, Madden, Roxb. Club 1828; Skeat, EETSES 4 (coll., Angl 13.194); Holthausen, OMETexts L. 1901, 1910 (crit. Arch 108.197; RevCrit 1902.176; JGP 3.510; Arch 108.197; Ctbl 1901.1689; DLz 1901.346; AnglBbl 14.164; Museum 1905.296; LitBl 23.14); Skeat, Oxf. 1902 (crit. MLQ 5.154; Neu Phil. Rundschau 1903.473; Scott Hist Rev 1905.1.446; N&Q 9th Ser. 10.400; DLz 1903.1296; AnglBbl 14.10);— Cbg. 4407 (19), described and printed, Skeat, MLR 6.455.— Emendations and Notes: Angl 1.468, 7.145, 13.197, 15.499, 17.441; ZsfDA 19.124; ESt 1.423, 5.377, 16.299, 17.297, 442, 19.146, 27.391, 29.368; Wittenbrink (see below) §2; *Engl. Misc. Pres. to Dr. Furnivall*, Oxf. 1901, 176;— on l. 247, Angl 29.132; Angl 15.499, 17.442; AnglBbl 11.306, 359, 12.146, 23.294; l. 1006, ESt 32.319; l. 2333, Trans. Phil. Soc. 1903-4, 163 (see ESt 19.148); ll. 2495-7, *ibid.* 1903-4, 161; ESt 30.343; l. 2461, Arch 107.107; Arch 110.100, 425, 128.194; on ll. 300 ff., 641-3, 646 ff., 686 ff., 2084 ff., Scott Hist Rev 1904.1.55-57; *Havelok's Lament*, MLN 21.23, see 7.134; *Minor Notes*, MLR 4.91.— On Laud, Skeat ed.; Hall, ed. *King Horn;* Skeat *Twelve Facsimiles of O. E. MSS.*, Oxf. 1892, plate vii.— Selections: Zupitza Übungsbuch; MacLean Reader 85; Morris Spec 1.222; Wülcker Lesebuch 1.81 (emendations, ESt 17.297); Emerson Reader 75; Cook Reader 17. Mod.

rend., Hibbard *Three M. E. Romances Retold,* L. 1911; Hickey, Cath. Truth Soc., L. 1902; Weston *Chief M. E. Poets* 110.— Kupferschmidt (on Gaimar and the *Lay*), Rom. Stud. 4.411 (see Rom 9.480); Brandl, AnzfDA 10.322; Kölbing, ed. *Amis and Amiloun,* introd. xxxi; Storm, on *Havelok* and *Anlaf,* ESt 3.533 (orig. pr. Christiania 1879); Ludorff *Über die Spr. des Ae. Lay H. þe D.,* Giessen diss. Münster 1873; Hupe *Havelok-Studien,* Angl 13.186; Wittenbrink *Zur Kritik u. Rhythmik des Ae. Lais v. H. d. D.,* Burgsteinfurt 1891, prgr. (crit. ESt 16.299; AnglBbl 2.244); Hohmann *Über Spr. u. Stil. . . . ,* Marburg diss. 1886; Wohlfeil *The Lay of H. the D.,* Leipzig diss. 1890; Hales, Athen Feb. 23, 1889 (repr. *Folia Litteraria* 1893, 30);— Schmidt *Zur Heimatbestimmung des H.,* Göttingen diss. 1900; Gollancz *Hamlet in Iceland,* L. 1898; Ahlström *Studier i den Fornfranska Lais-Litteraturen,* Upsala diss. 1892; Putnam *The Lambeth Version of H.,* Johns Hopkins diss. 1900; Putnam, PMLA 15.1; Zenker *Boeve-Amlethus,* Berlin 1905 (Ch. 5; see ShJhb 42.287); Deutschbein *Stud. zur Sagengesch. Englands,* Cöthen 1906, 96-168; DNB, *Olaf Sitricson;* Brie *Zum Fortleben der Havelok-Sage,* ESt 35.359; Heyman *Studies on the Havelok Tale,* Upsala diss. 1903; Putnam *The Scala-Chronicon Version,* Trans. Amer. Phil. Assoc. 34.xci; Björkman *Nordiska Vikingasagor i England,* Nordisk Tidskrift 1906.437; Wolff, A. K., *Zur Syntax des Verbums im Ae. Lay of H. the D.,* Leipzig diss. 1909; Deutschbein *Beiträge zur Horn- u. Havelok-sage,* AnglBbl 20.16, 55; Creek *Author of H. the D.,* ESt 48.193.— Brandl §52; Wülker 1.81, 97, 105; Morley 3.267; Ward 1.423; DNB 42.82; Ten Brink 1.149, 232; Cbg Hist 1.520; Billings 15; Schofield 266; de Julleville Hist 1.344.— French: ed. Madden, Roxb. Club 1825, 105; Michel, Paris 1833; Wright (see below) appendix 3; Hardy and Martin *Rerum Brittannicarum Medü Aevi Scriptores,* L. 1888, Vol. 1;— Gaimar's version, Madden as above, 147; Petrie *Monumenta Historica Britannica,* L. 1848, 1.764; Wright for Caxton Soc., L. 1850, Vol. 2; Hardy and Martin, as above. Gröber 2¹.471, 473; Ward 1.423, 940.

[6] GUY OF WARWICK. Ed. Additional, Phillips, Middle Hill 1838, repr. Turnbull (see below) xxviii;— Auchinleck, Turnbull, Abbotsford Club 1840;— Cbg., EETSES 25.26 (text crit., ESt 13.136);— A, a, Caius, EETSES 42, 49, 59 (see Angl 11.324);— Sloane, Zupitza, Sitzungsber. d. Kais. Akad. d. Wiss., Phil. Hist. Kl., 74.623 (see Germ 21.351, 365; ESt 2.248). Abstract, Ellis Spec 188.— Brandl §§37, 53, 80; Körting §89; Ten Brink 1.150, 182, 232, 246; Wülker 98, 105; Ward 1.471; DNB; Schofield 271, 477; Billings 24; Hist Litt 22.841; Gröber 2¹.776, 1195; de Julleville Hist 1.344.— On MSS. and relations of versions, see eds. of Cbg. and Sloane; Zupitza *Zur Literaturgesch. des G of W.,* Wien 1873; Tanner *Die Sage v. G. v. W.,* Heidelberg diss., Heilbronn 1877 (crit. Angl 2.191; ESt 2.246); Wilda *Über die örtliche Verbreitung der 12zeiligen Schweifreimstrophe in England,* Breslau 1888, 46; Kölbing *Amis and Amiloun and G. of W.,* ESt 9.477; Weyrauch *Die Me. Fassungen der Sage v. G. of W. u. ihre Af. Vorlage,* Breslau diss. 1899, full form Breslau 1901 (crit. Arch 110.444; ESt 1903.405; DLz 23.669; Bull. Crit. 23.228); Penn *On the Dialect of the Auch. and Caius MSS.,* PMLA 20.xxviii; Deutschbein *Stud. zur Sagengesch. Englands,* Cöthen 1906, 214; Liebermann *G. of W's Einfluss,* Arch

107.107; Reeves *The So-Called Prose Version of G. of W.*, MLN 11.404.—
On late versions, see Ward 1.494; Brown *Source of a G. of W. Chapbook*,
JGP 3.14; Crane *Vogue of G. of W. from the Close of the Middle Ages to
the Romantic Revival*, PMLA 30.125.

[7] GUY AND PHILLIS. Ed. PFMS 2.201, 608; Ritson AS (1877)
314. See Zupitza, Crane, under [6].

[8] GUY AND COLEBRANDE. Ed. PFMS 2.527 (see Germ, Neue
Reihe, 22.193). See Zupitza, Crane, under [6].

[9] GUY AND AMORANT. Ed. PFMS 2.136; Percy's *Reliques* Bk. 8,
No. 2. See Zupitza, Crane, under [6].

[10] LYDGATE'S GUY. Ed. Harley, part, PFMS 2.520;— Laud,
Zupitza, Sitzungsber., as above under [6], 649 (chief vars. from Lans-
downe, Kölbing Germ 21.365);— Harvard, and vars. of Leyden from
Zupitza, Robinson, HarvStN 5.177. Ward 1.494. See EETSES 107.xviii.

[11] LANE'S ROMANCE. Only introd. printed, PFMS 2.521.

[12] WILLIAM OF PALERNE. Ed. Madden, Roxb. Club 1832;
EETSES 1 (text-crit., ESt 4.99, 280). Selections: Morris Spec 2.138;
Wülcker Lesebuch 2.76; Hartshorne AMT 256. Fragm. of prose print of de
Worde, Arch 118.318.— Brandl §73; Körting §91; Ten Brink 1.329; Schofield
312; Billings 41.— On verse, Angl 11.566; see under *Alliteration*, page 800.
Interp. notes, Angl 26.367. Kittredge *Arthur and Gorlagon*, HarvStN
8.150; Smith *Hist. Study of the Werwolf in Lit.*, PMLA 9.1; Hertz *Der
Werwolf;* Baring-Gould *Book of Werwolves;* Grimm *Deutsche Mythol.;*
relation to French source, ESt 4.197; Schüddekopf *Spr. u. Dialekt . . . .*,
Erlangen 1886 (crit. ESt 10.291; DLz 9.1755); Pitschel *Zur Syntax . . . .*,
Marburg diss. 1890; Nicholson *An Unknown Engl. Prose Version of W.
of P.*, Acad 1893. No. 1088. General story: Paris Litt Franç §§51-2, 67; de
Julleville Hist 1.254 (bibliogr. 344); Hist Litt 22.829; Gröber 2¹.487, 529.
French, ed. Michelant, SATF 1876.

[13] SIR BEUES OF HAMTOUN. Ed. A, Turnbull, Maitland Club
1838 (coll. with MS., ESt 2.317; Kölbing's ed.); Kölbing, EETSES 46, 48,
65 (crit. Angl 11.325; ESt 19.261, 24.463; Rom 23.486). On MS. Chetham,
ESt 7.198. Analysis, Ellis Spec 239. Mod. rend., Hibbard *Three M. E.
Romances Retold*, L. 1911.— Brandl §§30, 53, 164; Ten Brink 1.150, 182,
246; Wülker 1.98; Körting §90; Billings 36.— Schmirgel *Stil u. Spr. des Me.
Epos Sir B. of H.*, Breslau diss. 1886 (repr. in Kölbing's ed.); see under
Alliteration, page 800; allit. in Auch., ESt 19.441; Gerould, on Eustace leg.,
PMLA 19.335; Matzke *Leg. of St. George*, PMLA 17.508, 18.99, 19.449;
Deutschbein Stud. zur Sagengesch. Englands, Cöthen 1906, 181; Kölbing
Zu Sir B. of H., ESt 2.317.— Gröber 2¹.572, 811; Krit Jahresber; Gautier
Bibl. des Chansons de Geste, 69; Paris Litt Franç §27 (see its bibliogr.).
Stimmung ed. *Der Agn. Boeve de Haumtone*, Halle 1899; Stimmung ed.
Der Festlandische Bueve de Hamtone, Fassung 1, (all MSS.) Gesellschaft
für Rom. Lit. 25, 1911; Zenker *Boeve-Amlethus*, Lit. Hist. Forschungen

32, Berlin 1905; Boje *Über den Af. Roman v. B. de H.*, Beihefte z. ZsfRPh
19, Halle 1909; Hibbard *Nibelungenlied and Sir B. of H.*, MLN 26.159;
Wolf *Gegenzeitige Verhältnis der Ger. Fassungen des Festlandischen B. de
H.*, Göttingen diss. 1912; *Die Eustachiuslegende* . . . , Arch 121.340;
Robinson *Celtic Versions of Bevis*, ESt 24.463; Hist Litt 18.748; Hoyt
Home of the Bevis Saga, PMLA 17.237; Kölbing *Ein Schlusswort zu Ceder-
schiölds Ausgabe* . . . , PBBeitr 24.414; Kölbing *Stud. zur Bevissage*,
PBBeitr 19.1; on Icelandic versions, ZsfVL NF 10.381; N&Q 8th Ser.
11.207, 208, 385, 396, 10th Ser. 8.390, 434, 473; Matzke *The Oldest Form of
the B. Leg.*, promised in MPhil; Kuhl *Das Gegenseitige Verhältnis der Hds.
der Fassung II des Festlandischen Beuve de Hantone*, Göttingen diss. 1915.

[14] ATHELSTON. Ed. Hartshorne AMT; Rel Ant 2.85; ESt 13.331,
14.321. Mod. rend., Rickert RofFr 67.— Brandl §80; Billings 32.— Wilda
Über die örtliche Verbreitung der 12zeil. Schweifreimstrophe, Breslau
1888, 61.— Gerould *Soc. and Hist. Reminiscences in* . . . *A.*, ESt 36.193.—
On early ballads on Æthelstan, see Paul Grundriss 2nd ed. 2¹.1087.

[15] TALE OF GAMELYN. Ed. Skeat Oxf Ch 4.645, 5.477; Skeat,
Oxf. 2nd ed. 1893;— several MSS., ChS 8, 9, 10, 13; Six-Text Ed. of Chaucer. Mod. rend., Rickert RofFr 85.— See Hammond *Chaucer: A Bibliographical Manual* 425 for bibliogr.— On name, Arch 119.33, 123.23.— Schofield 279; Ten Brink 2.183, 3.271; Morley 5.321; Ward 1.508; Cbg. Hist
2.221; ESt 2.94, 321.

2. ARTHURIAN LEGENDS

Bibliogrs. in Gröber Grundriss, 2nd ed. 2¹, see Register at p. 1254 and
under individual names; Paris Litt Franç §§53 ff.; de Julleville Hist 1.340;
Krit Jahresber; Ency Brit, *s. v. Arthur, Lancelot, Tristram, Merlin,
Perceval, Holy Grail, Gawain;* Körting §101 anm.; Cbg Hist 1.513; Weston,
as below; notes to later pieces, Brown, below; Billings 85.— See under
individual items below.

Paris Litt Franç §§ 53 ff.; Hist Litt 30.1; Rom 10.464; Gröber 2¹.288,
363, 469, 495, 551, 585, 996, 1195; de Julleville Hist 1.255; Ten Brink 1.134,
140, 164, 171, 187; Sommer's Malory, 1890, Vol. 3.; Rhŷs *Arthurian Legend*,
Oxf. 1891; Maccallum *Tennyson's Idylls of the King and Arthurian Story*,
Glasgow 1894; Wülcker *Die Arthursage in der Engl. Lit.*, Leipzig 1895;
Saintsbury *Flourishing of Romance*, N. Y. 1897, 86; Ker *Epic and Ro-
mance*, 1897, Ch. 5; Newell *King Arthur and the Table Round*, Boston
1897; Newell *Arthurian Notes*, MLN 17.258; Nutt *Celtic and Med.
Romance*, L. 1899; Nutt *Les Derniers Travaux Allemands*, RevCelt 12.181;
Brown *Round Table before Wace*, HarvStN 7; Lot *Nouvelles Études*, Rom
1901.1; Dickinson *King Arthur in Cornwall*, N. Y. 1900 (crit. MLN 17.429);
Kittredge *Arthur and Gorlagon*, HarvStN 8.149; Briggs *King Arthur in
Cornwall*, JEGP 3.342; Weston *King Arthur and his Knights, A Survey*,
L. 1905; Fletcher *Arthurian Material in the Chronicles*, HarvStN 10 (crit.
ZsfVL 17.170; for others, see Jahresbericht 1907.15.34, 1908.15.32; AnzfDA
32.103); Paton *Studies in Fairy Mythol. of Arthurian Rom.*, RadMon 13
(crit. ESt 34.377; Rom 34.117; MLN 19.80; MLQ 7.110; RevCrit 59.4); Mott

The Table Round, PMLA 20.231; Hoeppner *Arthurs Gestalt in der Lit. Englands im Mittelalter*, Leipzig diss. 1892; Maynadier *The Arthur of the English Poets*, Boston 1907; Curdy *Arthurian Lit.* (versions to date), Rom-Rev 4.125, 265; Jones *King Arthur in Hist. and Leg.*, Cbg. 1911 (crit. AnglBbl 24.298); Loth *Contributions à l'Étude des Romans de la Table Ronde*, Paris 1912 (see Arch 130.445); Schofield 159, 475; Billings 85; Körting §101; Cbg Hist 1.270;— summary, RevCelt 13.475; Rhŷs *op. cit.* 370; Weston *op. cit.*— On Avalon, see Billings 205; MLN 14.93.

I. The Whole Life of Arthur

[16] NENNIUS. Ed. Mommsen *Mon. Germ. Hist.*, Berlin 1898, 13.111. Trans., Giles *Six Old Engl. Chronicles*, L. 1848, new ed. 1901. de la Borderie *L'Histoire Britonum*, Paris and L. 1883 (summary of older crit.); Zimmer *Nennius Vindicatus*, Berlin 1893; Zimmer, Neues Arch. d. Gesellsch. f. Ältere Deutsche Geschichtskunde 19.436; Mommsen, same place 19.283; Thurneysen, ZsfDPh 1897.— See bibliogrs. in DNB, *Nennius;* Ency Brit, *Nennius.* Cbg Hist 1.273; Gröber 2¹.150.

[17] GEOFFREY OF MONMOUTH. Ed. Schulz, A. (San Marte), Halle 1854. Trans., Giles *Six Old Engl. Chronicles*, L. 1848, new ed. 1901; Evans, L. 1903; Everyman's Libr.— Ward 1.203; Cbg Hist 1.284; DNB, *Geoffrey of M.* (bibliogr.). Fletcher *Arthurian Material in the Chronicles*, HarvStN 10; Fletcher *Two Notes on Hist. Reg. Brit.*, PMLA 16.640; Jones *G. of M. and the Arthur Legend*, Quar. Rev. July 1906.

[18] WACE. Ed. Le Roux de Lincy, Rouen 1836-8, 2 vols. See Rom 9.594, 16.232, 604; Paris Litt Franç §93 (see its bibliogr.); Cbg Hist 1.293; Gröber 2¹.635. Arthur matter, trans. Everyman's Libr. No. 578.

[19] LAYAMON. See p. 792.

[20] ARTHUR. Ed. EETS 2.— Brandl §70; Körting §101; Schofield 255; Wülker 1.110; Billings 190. On verbs, QF 63.49.

[21] MORTE ARTHURE. Ed. Halliwell, L. 1847; EETS 8 (revised 1871;— on text, AnglAnz 8.227); Banks, N. Y. 1900 (crit. ESt 35.101; AnglBbl 12.235; N&Q 1900.6.520; Athen 1900.3821; Scott Antiq 17.51), notes on glossary, MLQ 6.64; Björkmann, OMETexts, Heidelberg 1915. Selection: Wülcker Lesebuch 2.109. On text, Angl 8.227; AnglBbl 24.250; verse, text, Angl 39.253. Mod. rend., parts, verse, Weston *Romance, Vision and Satire*, Boston 1912, 139;— whole, prose, *Morte Arthur*, Everyman's Libr.— Brandl §75; Körting §103; Ten Brink 3.49; Sommer's Malory 3.148; Schofield 253; Billings 181.— Wülcker *Die Arthursage* (see above), 12; Branscheid *Die Quellen des M. A.*, AnglAnz 8.179; on verse, Luick, Angl 11.585; Mennicken *Versbau u. Spr. in Huchowns M. A.*, Bonner Beitr. 5 (crit. AnglBbl 12.33, 104, 203; ESt 30.269); Lübke *Awntyrs off Arthure* (see p. 771), 30; Griffith *Malory, Morte Arthure, and Fierabras*, Angl 32.389; Reiche *Untersuchungen über dem Stil der Me. M. A.*, etc., Königsberg diss. 1906; Bruce *Development of the Mort Arthur Theme in Med.*

Rom., RomRev 4.403; Seyferth *Spr. u. Metr. des Me. Ged. 'Le M. A.' u. seine Verhältnis zu 'The Lyfe of Ipomydon,'* Berliner Beitr. 1895; Neilson *Baulked Coronation of Arthur*, N&Q 9th Ser. 10.381, 403; Neilson *M. A. and the War of Brittany*, N&Q 9th Ser. 1902.161; Neilson *The Viscount of Rome in M. A.*, Athen 1902.2.602; Neilson *Three Dates in M. A.*, Athen 1902.2.758; Neilson *Huchown's M. A. and the Annals of 1327-64*, Scott Antiq 16.229 and Antiquary 38.73, 229.— On ll. 1166-9, 3776-9, Scott Hist Rev 1904.1.55-7.— See under *Huchown Discussion*, page 826; *Alliteration*, page 800.

[22] LEGEND OF KING ARTHUR. Ed. PFMS 1.497; *Percy Reliques* Bk 7. No. 5; Child *Ballads* (1857) 1.106.

II. Merlin and the Youth of Arthur

[23] MERLIN STORY. Mead *Outlines of Hist. of Saga of Merlin*, EETS 112, introd.; Taylor *Pol. Proph. in England*, N. Y. 1911, Chs. 1-3; San Marte *Die Sagen v. M.*, 1854; Billings 114 (see its bibliogr.); Sommer ed. *Vulgate Fr. Merlin*, 1894; Paris and Ulrich ed. Huth *Merlin*, SATF 1886, introd.; Ward 1.278, 371, 384; Ency Brit, *Merlin;* DNB, *Merlin* (see its bibliogr.); Gröber 2^1.193, 371, 406, 489, 725, 909, 997, 1006; Paris Litt Franç §54 (see its bibliogr. to §§54, 60, 57-63); de Julleville Hist 1.342 (bibliogr.); Krit Jahresber; Maynadier *The Arthur of the Engl. Poets*, Boston 1907, Chs. 3, 6; Weston *Legend of Merlin*, Folk-Lore 17.2.30; Lot *Études sur Merlin*, Annales de la Bretagne, Apr., July, 1900 (see Rom 30.473); Gaster, Folk-Lore 16.pt 4; Schofield 248; Rhŷs *Arthurian Legend*, Oxf. 1891; Paton *Story of Vortigern's Tower*, RadMon 1910 (*Studies in Engl. and Comp. Lit.*); Ward, on Merlin Silvester, Rom 22.504; on *Prophetia* and *Vita*, Ward 1.207, 278.— See under *Prophecies*, p. 797; *Geoffrey of Monmouth*, p. 767.

[24] ARTHOUR AND MERLIN. Ed. version A, Turnbull, Abbotsford Club 1838;— version L, 1st 16 and last 28 lines, PFMS 1.420, 479;— version D, 1st 25 and last 12 lines, PFMS 1.420-1;— version P, *ibid.* 1.417;— versions A, L, D, with var. of P, Kölbing, AEB, Leipzig 1890 (crit. Arch 87.88; Ctbl 1892.573; LitBl 12.265; ESt 16.251; Rom 20.378; AnglBbl 2.105; ZsfVL 5.409). Abstract, Ellis Spec 77. Mod. rend., part, Weston *Chief M. E. Poets* 119.— Brandl §36; Körting §109; Ten Brink 1.244, 3.10; Schofield 251; Cbg Hist 1.298, 353, 446; Billings 111.— EETS 10.xvi, 112.lv; Gaster *Jewish Sources of and Parallels to E. E. Metr. Rom. of King A. and M.*, L. 1887; Dunlop *Hist. of Fiction*, 1.146.— See *Merlin Story*, above.

[25] PROSE MERLIN. Ed. EETS 10, 21, 36, 112.— Richter and Stecher *Beitr. zur Erklärung u. Textkritik*, ESt 20.397, 28.1; EETS 112.lxiii. Körting §109 anm.

[26] LOVELICH'S MERLIN. Ed. EETSES 93, 112. Selections: Furnivall *Seynt Graal*, Roxb. Club 1861-3, Vol. 2 end; EETSES 20, 28; Kölbing ed. *Arthour and Merlin* (ll. 1-1638).— Schofield 250; Billings 123; Kölbing *op. cit.*, xvlii, clxxx.— See under *History of the Holy Grail*, p. 774.

III. Lancelot and the Last Years of Arthur

Weston *Legend of Sir Lancelot du Lac*, L. 1901, see the footnotes for most of the literature (crit. ESt 32.113; Athen 1901.2.274; RevCelt 1901.349; AnglBbl 14.168; MLQ 4.134; ZsfVL 15.168); Paris Litt Franç §§60-2 (see its bibliogr.); Paris, Rom 10.465, 12.459, 16.100; Sommer's ed. Malory 3.176; Billings 195; Rhŷs *Arthurian Legend* 127, 145, and *passim;* Maynadier *The Arthur of the Engl. Poets* 84; Hist Litt 30; Gröber above under *Arthurian Legends;* Krit Jahresber; Paton *Studies in the Fairy Mythol. of Arthurian Rom.;* Paris, P., *Romans de la Table Ronde* Vol. 3; Petit *Bibliogr. der Meddelnederlandsche Taal-en Letterkunde,* Leiden 1888; Weston *King Arthur and his Knights* 38; Ency Brit, *Lancelot;* Ward 1.345; de Julleville Hist 1.341 (bibliogr.); Bruce *The Dev. of the Mort Arthur Theme in Med. Romance,* RomRev 4.403 (see its notes for bibliogr.);— Fr. *Vulgate Lancelot,* ed. Sommer for Carnegie Institution, Washington 1910-2.

[27] LANCELOT OF THE LAIK. Ed. Stevenson, Maitland Club 1839; EETS 6 (revised 1870); STS, New Series 2. Selection: Wülcker Lesebuch 2.115.— Brandl §138; Körting §108; Billings 192; Schofield 239.— Weston *Leg. of Sir Lancelot;* Weston *The Three Days' Tournament,* L. 1902.— Ed. Fr. *Vulgate,* see above. Analysis of Fr., Paris, P., *Romans de la Table Ronde* 3; Dunlop *Hist. of Fiction* 1.179.—See general *Lancelot* bibliogr., above.

[28] SIR LANCELOT DU LAKE. Ed. PFMS 1.84; Percy *Reliques* Bk. 2. No. 9.— Billings 200 note.

[29] LE MORTE ARTHUR. Ed. Roxb. Club 1819; Furnivall, L. and Cbg. 1864; EETSES 88; Hemingway, Boston 1912; print., *Morte Arthur,* Everyman's Libr., 95. Abstract, Ellis Spec 143. Mod. rend., parts, Weston *Chief M. E. Poets* 262; abr. parts, Newell *King Arthur and the Table Round* 2.99.— Brandl §125; Körting §103 anm.; Billings 200; Schofield 238, 255; Ward 1.405.— Mead *Sel. from Malory's Morte Darthur,* Boston and L. 1897 (notes); Sommer's ed. Malory 3.220, 249; Seyferth *Spr. u. Metr. des Me.* . . . *Le M. A. u. seine Verhältniss zu The Lyfe of Ipomydon,* Berliner Beitr. 8; Branscheid, AnglAnz 8.220; on sources and rel. to Malory, Angl 23.67 (replied to, Angl 29.529; counter-reply, Angl 30.209; see Rom 1901.478); Griffith *Malory, Morte Arthure, and Fierabras,* Angl 32.389.

[30] KING ARTHUR'S DEATH. Ed. PFMS 1.501; Percy *Reliques* Bk. 7. No. 4; Child *Ballads* (1857) 1.40.— Billings 208 note.

IV. Gawain

Weston *Legend of Sir Gawain,* L. 1897 and 1900 (see espec. 1.282;— see its bibliogr.); Weston *Legend of Perceval,* L. 1906, 1.282 (on English poems); Weston, Ency Brit, *Gawain;* Weston *Sir G. and the Grail Castle,* L. 1903; Hist Litt 30, 33.29; Gröber above under *Arthurian Legends;* Krit

Jahresber; Rhŷs *Arthurian Legend;* Maynadier *The Arthur of the Engl. Poets,* index; Maynadier *Wife of Bath's Tale,* L. 1901; Rom 33.333.

[31] SIR GAWAYNE AND THE GRENE KNIGHT. Ed. Madden *Syr Gawayne,* Bannatyne Club 1839; EETS 4 (revised 1869, and by Gollancz 1897, 1912;— on text, Knott, MLN 30.102). Selections: AESprPr 1.311; Cook Reader 53. Mod. rend. prose condensed, Weston, L. 1898; verse, Weston *Romance, Vision, and Satire,* Boston 1912, 1; lit. rend., Kirtlan, L. 1912. Abstract, Hist Litt 30.71.— Brandl §74; Körting §105; Ten Brink 1.337; Cbg Hist 1.363, 525; Ward 1.387; Hist Litt 30. 71; Weston *Leg. of Sir G.,* 85; Billings 160.— On verse, Rosenthal, Angl 1.417; Fuhrmann *Die Allit. Sprachformeln in Morris' E. E. Allit. Poems and Sir G.,* Kiel diss. 1886; Luick, Angl 11.572; Kuhnke *Die Allit. Langzeile in . . . Sir G. . . . ,* Königsberg diss. 1899, and in Kaluza's *Stud. zur Germ. Alliterationsvers* 4, Weimar 1900 (crit. AnglBbl 12.33, 65); Fischer *Die Stabende Langzeile in den Werken des Gawaindichters,* Bonner Beitr 11 (crit. AnglBbl 12.33, 17.41); Trautmann *Zur Kenntnis u. Gesch. der Me. Stabzeile,* Angl 18.83 ff.; Thomas *Die Allit. Langzeile des Gawayn-Dichters,* Jena diss. 1908;— Fick *Zum Me. Ged. von der Perle,* 5, Kiel diss. 1885 (text emendations); Knigge *Die Spr. des Dichters v. Sir G. .̇ . . ,* *der Sogen. E. E. Allit. Poems . . . ,* Marburg diss. 1885; Schwahn *Die Conjugation in Sir G. . . . u. den Sogen. E. E. Allit. Poems,* Strassburg, prgr. 1884; Kullnick *Stud. über den Wortschatz in Sir G.,* Berlin diss. 1902; Schmittbetz *Das Adjectiv im Verse v. Syr G.,* Bonn diss. 1908; Schmittbetz, Angl 32.1, 163, 359; Wright, on vocab., ESt 36.209; Brett *Notes on Sir G. . . .* (linguistic and etymol.), MLR 8.160, 10.188; Reiche *Untersuchungen über den Stil der Me. Allit. Ged. Morte Arthure . . . ,* Königsberg diss. 1906;— Trautmann *Über die Verfasser u. Entstehungszeit Einiger Allit. Ged. . . . ;* Leipzig 1876 and Angl 1.117; Thomas *Sir G. and the Gr. K., a Comp. with the Fr. Perceval, Prec. by an Investigation of the Author's Other Works.* Zürich diss. 1883; Steinbach *Über den Einfluss des Cr. de Troies auf die Altengl. Lit.,* Leipzig diss. 1885, 48 (crit. LitBl 5.211; ESt 12.91); Chambers *Sir G. and the Gr. K.,* ll. 697-702, MLR 2.167; Bruce *The Breaking of the Deer in Sir G. . . . ,* ESt 32.23; Hamilton *Capados and the Date of Sir G. . . . ,* MPhil 5.365; Jackson *Sir G. and the Gr. K. Considered as a 'Garter' Poem,* Angl 37.393; Chambers *Med. Stage* 1.117, 185 (Gr. K. a 'form of fertilization spirit'); Hulbert (on 'Beheading Game'), MPhil 13.49. See under *Pearl; Patience; Purity* or *Clannesse; Huchown Discussion; Alliteration,* below, Ch. IV head of Sect. 2. II.

[32] THE GRENE KNIGHT. Ed. Madden *Syr Gawayne,* Bannatyne Club 1839, 224, 352; PEMS 2.56.— Brandl §113; Schofield 217; Billings 209.

[33] THE TURKE AND GOWIN. Ed. Madden *Syr Gawayne,* as above, 243, 355; PFMS 1.88.— Brandl §125; Hist Litt 30.68; Schofield 218; Billings 211.

[34] SYRE GAWENE AND THE CARLE OF CARELYLE. Ed. Madden *Syr Gawayne,* as above, 187, 344.— Brandl §125; Hist Litt 30.68; Schofield 218; Billings 215.

[35] THE CARLE OF CARLILE. Ed. Madden *Syr Gawayne*, as above, 256, 365; PFMS 3.275.— Schofield 218; Billings 217.

[36] AWNTYRS OFF ARTHURE. Ed. Douce, Pinkerton *Scotish Poems*, L. 1792, 3.197;— Thornton, Laing *Anc. Pop. Poet. of Scotl.*, 1822, new ed. Small 1885, revised by Hazlitt 1895, 1.4; Madden *Syr Gawayne*, as above, 95, 326;— Ireland, Robson *Three E. E. Metr. Rom.*, L. 1842;— all MSS., Amours *Scot. Allit. Poems*, STS 27. Mod. rend., Weston *Romance, Vision, and Satire*, 109.— Billings 173; Brandl §75; Ten Brink 1.336; Hist Litt 30.96; Gröber 2¹.519; Schofield 218; Cbg Hist 325, 347; Körting §102.— Lübke *The Aunters of Arthur . . .* (MSS., metre, author), Berlin diss. 1883; on verse, Luick, Angl 12.452; on author, Trautmann, Angl 1.129; Athen 1903.1.498, 626, 657, 689, 754, 816, 2.221; Neilson *Crosslinks betw. The Pearl and The Awntyrs*, Scott Antiq 16.67; on MS. Lambeth, Bülbring, Arch 86.385.— See under *Huchown Discussion*.

[37] GOLAGRUS AND GAWAIN. Ed. Pinkerton *Scotish Poems*, L. 1792, 3.65; Madden *Syr Gawayne*, as above, 131, 336; Trautmann, Angl 2.395; Amours *Scott. Allit. Poems*, STS 27 (on l. 704, Acad 45. No. 1131. 13). Facsimile ed. Edbg. 1827 of Edbg. ed. 1508.— Brandl §133; Körting §106; Hist Litt 30.41; Schofield 220; Billings 168.— Noltemeyer *Über die Spr. . . .* , Marburg diss. 1889; Hahn *Zur Verbal- u. Nominal-Flexion*, 1889; Bearder *Über den Gebrauch der Praepositionen*, Halle, 1894; Trautmann, on author and source, Angl 1.109, 2.402; Luick, Angl 12.438; Neilson *Hist. in the Rom. of G. and G.*, Proc. Roy. Phil. Soc. of Glasgow 1902; interp. notes, Skeat, Scott Hist Rev Apr. 1904, 296; on ll. 265, 809, Scott Hist Rev 1904.1.55-7. See Thomas, M. C., under *Sir Gawayne and the Gr. K.*, 87; and under *Huchown Discussion*.

[38] AVOWYNGE OF KING ARTHUR. Ed. Robson *Three E. E. Metr. Rom*, L. 1842.— Brandl §75; Hist Litt 30.111; Schofield 222; Billings 178.— Kittredge, on de Garlandia, MLN 8.502; Greenlaw *Vows of Baldwin in A. of A.*, PMLA 21.575. See Thomas, under *Sir Gawayne and the Gr. K.*

[39] YWAIN AND GAWAIN. Ed. Ritson AEMR 1.1, 3.219, 437; Schleich, Oppeln and Leipzig 1887 (crit. LitBl 6.262; DLz 11.394; ESt 12.83; Angl 14.319; Ctbl 41.1417). Coll. with MS., ESt 12.139. Text, ESt 15.429, 24.146. Mod. rend., part, Weston *Chief M. E. Poets* 228.— Brandl §64; Körting §104; Dunlop *Hist. of Fiction* 1.266; Schofield 230; Ward 1.392; Billings 153.— Source, Schleich *Ywain u. Gawain . . .* , prgr. Berlin 1889 (crit. Angl 12.479; ESt 15.429); Weston *G. and G., and Le Chev. au Lion*, Mod. Quar. of Lang. 2.98, 3.194; Steinbach *Über den Einfluss des Cr. de Troies*, Leipzig diss. 1885. See Kölbing *Riddara Sögur*, Strassburg 1872, introd.; Brown *Ywain, A Study in the Origins of Arthurian Rom.*, HarvStN 8; Brown *The Knight of the Lion*, PMLA 20.673.— French *Yvain*, ed. Foerster, 3rd ed., Halle 1906; Gröber 2¹.501; Krit Jahresber; see Paris Litt Franç §57 (see its bibliogr.).

[40]-[41] WEDDYNGE OF SIR GAWEN. Ed. Madden *Syr Gawayne*, as above, 297.— *Marriage of Sir Gawain*. Ed. Madden *op. cit.* 288; PFMS 1.105; Percy *Reliques* Bk. 7. No. 2; Ritson AEMR 1.cx; Child *Ballads*

(1857) 1.288.— Brandl §113; Hist Litt 30.97; Billings 217; Schofield 224.—
Clouston *Orig. and Analogues*, ChS 2ser. 22.483; Skeat Oxf Ch 3.447;
Maynadier *The Wife of Bath's Tale*, L. 1901; Görbing *The Ballad 'The
Marriage of Sir G.,'* Angl 23.405.— See under *Wife of Bath's Tale*.

[42] JEASTE OF SYR GAWAYNE. Ed. Madden *Syr Gawayne*, as
above, 207, 348. Brandl §113; Schofield 228; Billings 213.

[43] LIBEAUS DESCONUS. Ed. Caligula, Ritson AEMR 2.1 (coll.
in Kaluza's ed. xii;—repr. Goldsmid, Edbg. 1891); Hippeau *Le Bel Inconnu*,
Paris 1860, 241;— Percy, PFMS 2.405;— crit. text, Kaluza AEB, Leipzig
1890 (crit. ESt 17.118; Rom 20.297; ZsfVL 5.412; Ctbl 23.792; DLz 6.172;
LitBl 14.325). Mod. rend., Weston *Sir Cleges; Sir Libeaus Desconus* . . . . ,
L. 1902 (crit. AnglBbl 15.332).— Brandl §70; Körting §107; Hist Litt
30.171 (espec. 185); Ward 1.400; Schofield 226; Cbg Hist 1.329; Billings
134.— Origin, etc., ESt 1.121, 362; Hist Litt 30.171; Rom 15.1; Mennung
*Der Bel Inconnu des Renaut de Beaujeu in seinem Verhältniss zum
Lybeaus Desconus*, Halle diss. 1880 (crit. Rom 20.299; LitBl 3.84).— Schofield *Studies on The L. D.*, HarvStN 4 (crit. Moyen Âge, Oct. 1896; Rom
26.290; RevCrit 1897.1.258).— Author, Sarrazin ed. *Octovian*, Halle 1885,
xxv; Sarrazin, ESt 22.331; DNB, *Chestre, Thomas;* Kaluza, ESt 18.165; see
under *Sir Launfal*, p. 783. Broadus *The Red-Cross Knight and L. D.*,
MLN 18.202. On verbs, QF 63.30.— Gröber 2¹.513; Krit Jahresber.

V. Perceval

Weston *The Legend of Sir Perceval*, L. 1906-9, 2 vols. (see bibliogr. end
of Vol. 2;— crit. Ctbl 60.1690); Billings 134; Nutt *Studies on the Leg. of
The Holy Grail*, L. 1888; Hertz *Die Sage von Parzival u. dem Graal*,
Breslau 1882; Hertz *Die Sage von Parzival*, Stuttgart 1884; Golther
*Chrestiens Conte del Graal in seinem Verhältniss zum Wälschen Peredur
u. zum Engl. Sir P.*, Sitzungsber. d. Münch. Akad., Phil. Hist. Kl. 1890.2.
203; Golther *Ursprung u. Entwicklung der Sage vom P.* . . . , Bayreuther
Blätter No. 7. 1891; Heinzel, Sitzungsber. d. Wiener Akad., Phil. Hist Kl.
130.50, 51, 112 (Engl. and Kyot, and source of Kyot and Chrétien); Harper
Leg. of the Holy Grail, PMLA 8.77 (also MLN 8.316); Maynadier *The
Arthur of the Engl. Poets*, 107; Strucks *Der Junge Parzival* (in Wolfram,
Chrétien, Engl. *Sir P.*, Ital. *Carduino*), Münster diss. 1910 (crit. LitBl
33.393); Newell *Leg. of the Holy Grail*, Cbg. Mass. 1902; Windisch *Das
Keltisch Brittanien*, Abhdl. d. Phil. Hist. Kl. d. Kgl. Sächs. Ges. d. Wiss.,
29.No. 6, Leipzig 1912; Woods *A Reclassification of the Perceval Ro-
mances*, PMLA 27.524; Ency Brit, *Perceval;* on Caradoc, Rom 28.214;
Paris, *P., Les Romans de la Table Ronde;* Paris Litt Franç §§59-60 (see
its bibliogr.).— Ed. Chrétien, *Perceval*, Potvin, Mons 1866-71;— abstracts,
Nutt *op. cit.;* Birch-Hirschfeld *Die Sage vom Graal*, Leipzig 1877; Harper,
PMLA 8.89.— See under *Holy Grail*.

[44] SIR PERCYVELLE OF GALLES. Ed. Halliwell *Thornton Romances*, L. 1844, 1; Morris, Kelmscott Press 1895; Campion and Holthausen, Heidelberg 1913. Coll. of Halliwell's ll. 1-1060 with MS., ESt

12.139. Abstract, Lady Guest *Mabinogion*, 1849, 1.398; Hist Litt 30.255; Nutt *Studies on . . . Holy Grail* 37. Mod. rend., Weston *Chief M. E. Poets* 236.— Brandl §79; Körting §108 note; Dunlop *Hist. of Fiction* 1.172; Cbg Hist 1.327; Gröber 2¹.504; Schofield 229; Billings 125.— On verse, Luick, Angl 12.437; Paul• Grundriss 2².168. Steinbach *Über den Einfluss des Cr. de Tr. auf die Ae. Lit.*, Leipzig diss. 1885 (crit. LitBl 5.211; ESt 12.89); Ellinger *Über die Sprachl. u. Metr. Eigentumlichkeiten in . . . Sir P. of G.*, Troppau prgr. 1889; Ellinger *Syntakt. Untersuchungen . . .*, Troppau prgr. 1893 (crit. AnglBbl 4.363); Griffith *Sir Perceval of Galles, A Study of the Sources . . .*, Chicago diss. 1911 (see its bibliogr.;— crit. Rom 1911; RomRev 4.125; JEGP 11.635; RevCrit 46.454; Ctbl 1912.265; LitBl 33.393; AnglBbl 23.260).— See above, Harper, Golther, Paris, Strucks, Heinzel, Newell, Woods, Weston.

VI. The Holy Grail

Birch-Hirschfeld *Die Sage vom Graal*, Leipzig 1877; Nutt *Studies on the Leg. of the H. G.*, L. 1888 (see Paris, Rom 18.588); Nutt *Legends of the H. G.*, L. 1902; Paris Litt Franç §§57, 59, 60 (see its bibliogr.); Paris Hist Litt 30; de Julleville Hist 1.341; Gröber 2¹.502, 724, 996, 1195; Krit Jahresber; Heinzel *Ueber die Fr. Graalromane*, Denkschr. d. Kaiserl. Akad. d. Wiss., Phil. Hist. Kl. 40, Vienna 1891 (crit. LitBl 2.50; AnzfDA 18.253; ZsfRPh 16.269); Harper *Leg. of the H. G.*, PLMA 8.77; Harper, MLN 8.316; Hagen *Der Gral*, QF 85 (see *Jahresbericht* 1900.19.37); Wechssler *Die Sage vom Hl. Gral*, Halle 1898 (see its bibliogr.; see *Jahresbericht* 1899.19.33); Kempè *Leg. of the H. G.*, EETSES 95; Kroner *Die Longinuslegende*, Münster diss. 1900; Wechssler *Untersuchungen zu den Graal-Romanen* (de Borron's *Estoire*), ZsfRPh 23.135; Newell *The Leg. of the H. G.*, Cbg. Mass. 1902; MacDougall *Orig. of the Leg. of the H. G.*, L. 1903; Staerck *Über der Ursprung der Grallegende*, Tübingen u. Leipzig 1903; Vercoutre *Un Problème Litt. Résolu* (origin), Paris 1901; Vercoutre *Orig. u. Gen. de la Lég. du Saint-Graal*, Paris 1905; Tunison *The Graal Problem*, Cincinnati 1904; Fremond *Ein bisher nicht Benutzte Hds. der Prosa-Romane Jos. v. Arimathie u. Merlin*, Bausteine zur Rom. Phil. 398, Halle 1905; Klob *Beitr. zur Kenntnis der Span. u. Portug. Gral-Lit.*, ZsfRPh 26.169; Kralik *Die Gralsage . . .*, Ravensburg 1907; Weston *The Grail and the Rites of Adonis*, Folk-Lore Sept. 1907.283; Wesselofsky *Zur Frage über die Heimat der Leg. vom Hl. Gral*, Arch. f. Slav. Phil. 23.321; Dostal *Die Heimat der Gralsage*, prgr. Kremsier 1914; Maynadier *The Arthur of the Engl. Poets* 106; Sterzenbach *Ursprung u. Entwicklung der Sage vom Hl. Gral*, Münster diss. 1908; Iselin *Der Morgenländische Ursprung der Grallegende . . .*, Halle 1909; Junk *Gralsage u. Graldichtung des Mittelalters*, Wien 1911; Schroeder *Die Wurzeln der Sage vom Hl. Gral*, Akad. Wien 1910; Peebles *The Leg. of Longinus in Eccles. Tradition and in Engl. Lit.*, Bryn Mawr diss. 1911 (crit. Ltbl 33.393; Acad. 1912.1.494; Arch 128.435); Kröner *Die Longinuslegende*, Münster diss. 1900; Weston *The Quest of the H. G.* (gen. survey of theories), L. 1913. Nitze *The Fisher-King in the Grail Romances*, PLMA 24.365; Waite *The Hidden Church of the Holy Grail*, London 1909.— Billings 99; Körting §101 anm.,

110; Ten Brink 1.171; Schofield 240; Ward 1.340; Ency Brit, *Grail.*—
Abstracts of de Borron's *Joseph* and *Grand St. Graal*, Nutt *op. cit.* 64a,
52; Birch-Hirschfeld *op. cit.* 150, 9.— On Glastonbury, PBBeitr, 3.326;
EETSES 44.xxiii; Rhŷs *Arthurian Leg.* Ch. 14; ZsfRPh 19.326.— See under
Perceval.

[45] JOSEPH OF ARIMATHIE. Ed. EETSES 44.187.— Brandl
§73; Körting §110; Ten Brink 1.332; Dunlop *Hist. of Fiction* 1.159; Schofield 247; Billings 96.— On verse, Luick, Angl 11.569; and see under
Alliteration, page 800.— See under *Holy Grail*, above.

[46] HISTORY OF THE HOLY GRAIL. Ed. Furnivall *Seynt Graal*,
Roxb. Club 1861-3, 2 vols.; EETSES 20, 24, 28, 30, 95 (see introd. in 95).—
Brandl §113; Schofield 246; Billings 109.— Fr. orig. printed in Roxb. ed.—
Skeat *The Translator of the Graal*, Athen 1902.2.684, 758; Bradley *Henry
Lovelich the Skinner*, Athen 1902.2.587.— See under *Holy Grail; Joseph of
Arimathie; Prose Merlin.*

[47] PROSE LYFE OF JOSEPH, *DE SANCTO JOSEPH, HERE
BEGYNNETH, A PRAYSING*. Printed in EETSES 44.— Körting §110
anm.; Billings 109.

VII. Tristram

Michel *Tristan, Rec. de ce qui Reste des Poèmes Relatifs à ses Aventures*, L. 1835-9; Villemarqué, Arch. des Missions Scient. 5.97; Novati *Studj
di Fil. Rom.* 263; Thomas' *Tristan*, ed. Bedier SATE 1902-5, 2 vols. (crit.
LitBl 1907.60); Vetter *La Lég. de Tr. d'après le Poème Fr. de Thomas*,
Marburg diss. 1882 (crit. ESt 7.349); Röttiger *Der Tr. des Thomas* (crit.
and lang.), Göttingen diss. 1883; Béroul's *Tristan*, ed. Muret SATF 1903;
on *La Chèvre*, Rom 16.362; see espec. the lists in Rom 15.481, 16.288, 17.603,
18.322, 510; Paris, G., *Poèmes et Lég. du Moyen Âge*, 113; Paris Litt
Franç §56 (see its bibliogr.); Gröber 2¹.470, 489, 490, 492, 499, 593, 726,
999, 1006; Bossert *Tr. et Iseult, Poème de Gotfrit de Strassburg, Comparé
à d'Autres Poèmes . . .*, Paris 1865; Heinzel *Gottfrits v. Strassburg Tr.
u. seine Quelle*, ZsfDA 14.272; Behaghel, Germ 23.223, 24.187; Brynjuleson
Saga af Tr. och Isond, Kopenhagen 1878 (see Rom 8.276); Suchier, ZsfDPh
18.81; Sarrazin *Germ. Sagenmotive im Tristanromane*, ZsfVL '1.262; Sarrazin, RomForsch 4.317 (geogr. and hist.); MacNeill ed. *Sir Tristrem*
introd.; Golther *Die Sage v. Tr. u. Is., Stud. über ihre Entstehung u.
Entwicklung im Mittelalter*, München 1887 (crit. AnzfDA 14.233; Rom
17.603; ZsfVL 1890.161); Wesselofsky *Matériaux et Recherches pour
Servir à l'Histoire du Roman et de la Nouvelle*, Petersburg 1889 (crit.
Rom 18.303); Golther *Zur Tr.-Sage*, ZsfRPh 12.348 (crit. Rom 18.322);
Paris *Tr. et Is.*, Bouillon 1894; Paris, Rev. de Paris 1894.138 (crit. RevCelt
15.407; see Rom 24.154); Golther *Bemerkungen zur Sage u. Dichtungen
von Tr. u. I.*, Zs. f. Frz. Spr. u. Litt. 22.1.— Gen. rev., Freymond, Krit
Jahresber 1.408; Röttiger *Der Heutige Stand der Tristanforschung*, 1897;
Bossert *La Lég. Chiv. de Tr. et Is.*, Paris 1902; Greg *Pre-Malorean
Romances* (Lancelot and Tr. identical?), MLQ 3.38; Golther *Tr. u. Is. in
den Dichtungen des Mittelalters u. den Neuen Zeit*, Leipzig 1907; Mayna-

dier *The Arthur of the Engl. Poets* 153; Schoepperle *Tristan and Isolt, A Study of the Sources* (see ESt 48.299); *Les Auteurs de Tristan et de Horn,* Rom 15.575; see Rom 15.481-602; Brandl §51; Körting §118; Ten Brink 1.237; Hist Litt 19.687; Billings 85 and notes; de Julleville Hist 1.259 (bibliogr. 340); Schofield 201; Ency Brit, *Tristram;* Krit Jahresber.

[48] SIR TRISTREM. Ed. Scott, Edbg. 1804 *et seq.;* Kölbing, Norse and Engl. versions, Heilbronn 1878-82 (see ESt 2.533, 6.463, 7.189, 13.133;— crit. LitBl 1880.93; AnzfDA 5.405, 8.331, 10.331; Mag. f. d. Lit. des In- u. Ausländer, Jhg 50.455; Jen. Ltzt 1879.35; Arch 64.201; Ctbl 23.738; ZsföGymn 1884.210; ZsfRPh 4.170; AnglAnz 6.48; Rom 8.281; Gött. Gel. Anz. 1879.447; Jen. Belege 1880.16; Rev. des Langues Romanes 3 Ser. 3.131; Rom. St. 4.192; DLz 23.813); MacNeill STS 1886 (crit. ESt 10.287; Athen 1887. No. 3090.92). Notes, ESt 13.133. Selection: AESprPr 1.234. Mod. rend., Weston *Chief M. E. Poets* 141.— Brandl §51; Körting §118; Ten Brink 1.238; Hist Litt 19.687; Schofield 208; Billings 85.— See under *Tristram* above, espec. Michel 1.xxxiv; Heinzel, ZsfDA 14.272; Heinzel, AnzfDA 8.212; Bossert *Tr. et Is.* 88; Vetter 32.— Deutschbein *Stud. zur Sagengesch. Englands,* Cöthen 1906, 169; Skeat *Romance of Sir Tr.,* Scott Hist Rev Oct. 1908. On l. 1875 ff., Scott Hist Rev 1904.1.55-7.— On MS. Bibl. Nat. 12576 (Fonds Franç.) ff. 165-71, Athen 1903.2.62.

3. CHARLEMAGNE LEGENDS

Gautier *Les Épopées Françaises,* Paris 1878-82, espec. Vol. 3; Müntz, Rom 14.321; Gautier *Bibl. des Chansons de Geste,* Paris 1897; bibliogr. in Paris Litt Franç §§15, 18-32; Gröber 2¹.447, 461, 535, 792, see Register; Krit Jahresber; de Julleville Hist 1.Ch.2 (bibliogr. 168);— Paris Litt Franç §§15, 18-32; Paris *Hist. Poétique de Ch.,* 2nd ed. Paris 1905 (English, espec. 154 ff.); Rajna, Rom 13.598; Paris, Rom 11.149 (latter on Engl. pieces); Ten Brink 1.122, 124-5; Saintsbury *Flourishing of Romance,* N. Y. 1897, 22; Ker *Epic and Romance* Chs. 1, 4; Weston *The Romance-Cycle of Ch.,* L. 1901 (see its bibliogr.); Billings 47; introd. to EETSES 36-41, 43-5, 50; Ward 1.546-707; Ency Brit, *Charlemagne;* Church *Stories of Ch.,* L. 1902; Bulfinch *Legends of Ch.,* L. 1905; Ludlow *Pop. Epics of the Mid. Ages,* L. 1865; Kirchhoff *Zur Gesch. der Karlssage in der Engl. Lit. des Mittelalters,* Marburg diss. 1913; Bedier *Les Légendes Épiques,* Paris 1908-13, Vols. 3, 4.

I. Firumbras

[49] SOWDONE OF BABYLONE. Ed. Roxb. Club, L. 1854; EETSES 38 (crit. AnglAnz 5.69; Arch 63.460;— notes, Angl 15.200).— Brandl §125; Körting §95; Billings 47; Paris *Hist. Poétique,* as above; Gautier *Les Épopées Franç.* 3.366.— Abstract, Ellis Spec 379. Gröber, *Verhandlungen der 28sten Versammlung Deutscher Schulmänner,* Leipzig 1873 (crit. JbREL 11.219); Hausknecht *Ueber Spr. u. Quelle . . . ,* Berlin diss. 1879 (crit. LitBl 1.100; Arch 63.460; Rom 8.479; ZsfRPh 4.163). *Destruction de Rome,* Rom 2.1, 28.503; Gautier, Paris, as above. See under *Sir Firumbras.*

[50] SIR FIRUMBRAS. Ed. EETSES 34 (crit. ESt 18.270; Rom 9.149; LitBl 1.374). Selection: Zupitza Übungsbuch; MacLean Reader 111.— Brandl §70; Körting §94; Billings 52.— Carstens *Zur Dialektbestimmung des Me. Sir F.*, Kiel diss. 1884 (crit. Angl 4.308; AnglAnz 7.4; LitBl 1884.388; Ctbl 1885.390); on verbs, QF 63.35; Reichel *Die Me. Sir F. u. ihr Verhältnis zum Af. u. Prov. Fierebras*, Breslau diss. 1892; Reichel *Zur Textkritik*, ESt 18.270; Angl 4.308, 7.160; Griffith *Malory's Morte Darthur and Fierebras*, Angl 32.389; continental infl. on lang., Heuser, Bonner Beitr 12.178 (crit. ESt 34.101); Jarnik *Studien über die Komp. der Fierebrasdichtungen*, Halle 1903.— French *Fierebras*, ed. Kroeber and Servois *Anc. Poétes de la France*, Paris 1860.— Paris *Hist. Poètique* 154 ff.; Gautier *Bibl.* 97; Gröber *Die Handscriftlichen Gestaltung der Fierebras*, Leipzig 1869 (crit. RevCrit 1869.2.121; Rom 24.1); Bédier *La Composition de Fierebras*, Rom 17.22; Gautier *Les Épopées Franç.* 3.381; Gröber 2¹.539, 541, 545, 1194; Paris Litt Franç §§24, 37; Krit Jahresber.— Provençal, ed. Bekker, Berlin 1829.

[51] CHARLES THE GRETE. Ed. EETSES 36, 37.

II. Otuel

See under *Otuel*, below.

[52] ROLAND AND VERNAGU. Ed. Nicholson, Abbotsford Club 1836; EETSES 39.35 (text-notes, Angl 21.366; Wächter, below, 36).— Brandl §§52-3; Körting §100; Ten Brink 1.245; Billings 58.— Abstract Ellis Spec 346, 373.— Orig. legends, Gautier *Les Épopées Franç.* 3.283; Gautier *Bibl.* 170 ff.; Paris *Hist. Poétique* 53, 337; Rom 9.29, 11.149 ff., 13.208. Wächter *Untersuchungen über die Beiden Me. Ged. R. and V. und Otuel*, Berlin diss. 1885; on metre, Kaluza ed. *Libeaus Desconus* lvii.— On verse and location, see Wilda under *Eustace-Constance*, etc., page 781.

[53] SEGE OF MELAYNE. Ed. EETSES 35 (crit. Rom. 9.151; emendations, ESt 5.467, 13.156).— Brandl §79; Rom 11.151; Ward 1.953; Körting §98; Billings 63.— Dannenberg *Metr. u. Spr. der Me. Romanze The S. of M.*, Göttingen diss. 1890.— Gautier *Les Épopées Franç.* 2.304, 407; Gautier *Bibl.* 201.

[54] OTUEL. Ed. Nicholson, Abbotsford Club 1836; EETSES 39.65 (text-notes, Angl 21.369). Abstract, Ellis Spec 357.— Brandl §37; Körting §96; *Hist. Poètique;* Ten Brink 1.245; Billings 67; Hist Litt 26.269; Rom 11.151.— (See Wächter, under [52]). Treutler *Die Otinelsage*, ESt 5.97 (crit. ZsfRPh 5.582); Gragger *Zur Me. Dichtung 'Sir O.,'* Graz 1896; Rajna, Rom 18.35; Koeppel *Eine Hist. Anspielung in 'The Rom. of O.,'* Arch 107.392.— French *Otinel*, ed. Guessard and Michelant *Anc. Poétes de la France*, Paris 1859.— Gautier *Les Épopées Franç.* 3.397; Gautier *Bibl.* 135; Gröber 2¹.545; Krit Jahresber.

[55] DUKE ROWLANDE AND SIR OTTUELL. Ed. EETSES 35.53 (crit. Rom 9.150).— Körting §97; Brandl §79; Billings 71; Ward 1.954.— Engler *Quelle u. Metrik der Me. Rom. Duke R. . . . .*, Königsberg diss. 1901.— See under *Otuel*.

[56] FILLINGHAM OTUEL. Abstract, Ellis Spec 357, 373.— Billings 60; Paris *Hist. Poétique.*

III. Detached Romances

[57] SONG OF ROLAND. Ed. EETSES 35.107 (text-crit., Angl. 4.317).— Brandl §113; Körtiṅg §93; Ten Brink 1.244; Schofield 151; Paris *Hist. Poétique* 155.— Schleich *Prolegomena ad Carmen de Rolando Anglicanum,* Burg 1879 (crit. Angl 3.401; LitBl 1.334); Schleich *Beitr. zum Me. Roland,* Angl 4.317; Wichmann *Das Abhängigkeitsverhältnis des Ae. Rolandsliedes zur Af. Dichtung,* Münster diss. 1889.— Paris Litt Franç §33 (see its bibliogr.); Paris, Rom 11.151; Gautier *Bibl.* 170 ff., 190, 192-3; Gröber 2¹.463; Krit Jahresber. See under *Charlemagne,* above.

[58] TAILL OF RAUF COIL3EAR. Ed. Laing *Sel. Rem. of Anc. Pop. Poetry of Scotland,* Edbg. 1821, revised by Hazlitt, L. 1895, 1.212; EETSES 39; Amours STS 39; Browne, W. H., Baltimore 1903 (crit. ESt 36.256; AnglBbl 17.65; Scott Hist Rev 2.458).— Brandl §135; Körting §99; Billings 79; Rom 11.150.— Tonndorf *Rauf Coilyear,* Halle diss. 1894, full print Berlin 1894; Angl 1.129.

[59] TEN BALLADS. First seven printed in Percy *Reliques;* eighth in PFMS 2.550-94; ninth in Hazlitt Rem 1.11; tenth in Rel Ant 1.147.

[60] FOURE SONNES OF AYMON. Ed. EETSES 44-5.— French, Rev. des Langues Romanes 49.97, 219, 368, 50.97, 217, 344, 51.67, 143, 289, 407, 52.16, 130, 193;— mod. rend. of ed. of 1480, J. d'Albignac, Paris 1908. Gautier *Bibl.* 158; Gröber 2¹.547; Krit Jahresber.— Mod. version in English, Steele, L. 1897.

[61] HUON OF BURDEUX. Ed. EETSES 40, 41, 43, 50.— Gautier *Bibl.* 132; Paris Litt Franç §25; Gröber 2¹.549; Krit Jahresber.

4. LEGENDS OF GODFREY OF BOUILLON

Paris Hist Litt 22.350, 25.507; Paris Litt Franç §29 (see its bibliogr.); Paris *Nouvelle Étude sur la Chanson D'Antioche,* Paris 1874; Pigeonneau *Le Cycle de la Croisade et de la Famille de Bouillon,* St. Cloud 1877; Petit *Bibliogr. der Meddelnederlandsche Taal-en Letterkunde,* Leiden 1888, 465; Gautier *Bibl. des Chansons de Geste* 77; Rom 21.62, 30.404, 34.206; de Julleville Hist 1.Ch.2 (bibliogr. 169); Gröber 2¹.471, 575; Krit Jahresber; Tiedau *Gesch. der Chanson d'Antioche des Rich. le Pèlerin u. des Graindor de Douay,* Göttingen diss. 1912.

[62] CHEVALERE ASSIGNE. Ed. Utterson, Roxb. Club 1820; EETSES 6.— Brandl §73; Ward 1.708; Billings 228; Schofield 315.— On verse, ESt 16.174; on text, Angl 21.441; *Bibl. Norm.* 3.lxx; Krüger *Zur Me. Rom. Ch. As.,* Arch 77.169; on an early notice, Arch 107.106; *Der Ursprung der Schwanrittertradition in Engl. Adelsfamilien,* ESt 29.337. On origin of legend, ZsfDA 38.272; ZsfRPh 21.176; Rom 19.314, 26.581; Germ 1.488.— See under *Godfrey,* above.

[63] HELYAS, THE KNIGHT OF THE SWAN. Copland's text, pr.
Thoms 3.1, repr. 691;— de Worde's text, pr. Grolier Club, N. Y. 1901.

[64] GODEFROY OF BOLOYNE. Ed. EETSES 64·

5. LEGENDS OF ALEXANDER THE GREAT

Meyer, P., *Alexandre le Grand dans la Litt. du Moyen·Âge*, Paris 1886,
2 vols.; Budge *Hist. of Alex. the Great*, Cbg. 1889; Budge *Life and Exploits of Alex. the Great*, L. 1896; Ward 1.94; Ency Brit, *Alexander-
Romance;* Paris Litt Franç §44 (see its bibliogr.); de Julleville Hist 1.229
(bibliogr. 252); Gröber 2¹.579, 817; Krit Jahresber; Saintsbury *Flourishing
of Romance* 148; Morley 3.286; Cbg Hist 1.518 (bibliogr.); Körting §111
anm.; introds. to EETS eds.; Ausfeld *Zur Kritik des Griech. Alexander-
romans*, Bruchsal prgr. 1894; Loomis *Alex. the Gr's Celestial Journey*, prgr.
MLA 1914; Hertz *Aristoteles in den Alexanderdichtungen d. Mittelalters*,
München 1889; Nöldeke *Beitr. zur Gesch. d. Alex.-Romans*, Vienna 1890;
Becker *Die Bramahnen in der Alexandersage*, Leipzig 1889;— on Latin,
Knizel ed. Lamprecht's *Alexander*, introd.; Landgraf *Die Vita Alexandri*,
Erlangen 1885; Rom 4.7; Muller ed. *Pseudo-Callisthenes*, Didot 1846, repr.
1877; Ausfeld *Die Orosius Recension der Hist. de Prœliis*, Badischen Gymn.
1886;— Carraroli *La Leggenda di Alessandro Magno*, Turin 1892 (see
Rom 11.253, 23.260); Taylor *Class. Her. of the Mid. Ages*, N. Y. 3rd ed.
1911, 39, 360, 390; Fuchs *Beiträge zur Alexandersage*, Giessen prgr. 1907.—
On O. E. versions, see Wülcker Grundriss 504-5; Körting §68a; Paul Grundriss 2nd ed. 2¹.1132-3.

[65] LYFE OF ALISAUNDER or KING ALISAUNDER. Ed. Weber
MR 1.3. Text-notes, ESt 13.138, 17.298. Selections: Laud, Warton *Hist.
Engl. Poet.*, ed. Hazlitt 1871, 2.206, 4.102;— AESprPr 1.244; Wülcker
Lesebuch 1.85; Morris Spec 1867, 52.— Brandl §36; Ten Brink 1.241;
Schofield 300; Körting §111C; Meyer *op. cit.* 2.294; Hist Litt 24.501; MLN
15.90; Hildebrand *Die Af. . . . Le Roman de Toute Chevalerie . . . u.
die Me. Kyng Alisaunder*, Bonn diss. 1911. Author, Kölbing ed. *Arthour
and Merlin* lx. Cpd. with Lamprecht's *Alexander*, ed. Weisman 1851,
1.lxxxi, 2.405, and ed. Knizel 1885, introd.

[66] ALLITERATIVE ALEXANDER FRAGMENTS. Fragment A,
Alisaunder: ed. EETSES 1.177. Brandl §73; Körting §111B; Ten Brink
1.333. Trautmann *Über Verfasser u. Entstehungszeit Einigen Allit. Ged.*,
Halle 1876; on verse, Angl 1.415, 11.553; Deutschbein *Zur Entwicklung des
Engl. Alliterationsverses*, Halle 1902.— Fragment B, *Alexander and Dindi-
mus:* ed. Stevenson, Roxb. Club 1849; EETSES 31. Brandl §73; Körting
§111B; Ten Brink 1.333. Trautmann *op. cit.;*— on verse, Deutschbein
op. cit.; Angl 1.415, 11.553.— Fragment C, *Wars of Alexander:* ed. Stevenson, Roxb. Club 1849; EETSES 47. Brandl §§73, 125; Körting §111A;
Schofield 301. Facsimile of leaf of MS. Ashmole, Skeat *Twelve Facsimiles*,
Oxf. 1892, 34. Acad Jan. 14, 1888; Hennemann *Untersuchungen über . . .
Wars of A.*, Berlin diss. 1889 (crit. DLz 1890.92; AnglBbl 13.219); Hennemann *Interpretation of Certain Words and Phrases*, MLN 5.4; Bradley

Athen 1900.2.826; Neilson *W. of A.*, Athen 1902.1.784; on verse, ESt 16.169; Steffens *Versbau u. Spr.* . . . , Bonner Beitr 9 (crit. AnglBbl 17.40; Arch 113.183); on Dublin MS., ESt 3.531; Reiche *Untersuchungen über den Stil der Me. Allit. Ged. Morte Arthure*, etc. (see under *Morte Arthure*).— See Hertz, Becker, Meyer, Carraroli, above;— see under *Huchown Discussion*, page 826; *Alliteration*, page 800.

[67] CAMBRIDGE ALEXANDER-CASSAMUS FRAGMENT. Ed. Rosskopf *Editio Princeps des Me. Cassamus* . . . , München diss., Erlangen 1911.

[68] THE PROSE ALEXANDER. Ed. EETS 143.— *Thornton Romances*, Camden Soc., xxvi.

[69] SCOTTISH ALEXANDER BUIK. Ed. Laing, Bannatyne Club 1831. Schofield 302. Hermann *Untersuchungen über das Schott. Alexanderbuch*, Berlin 1893 (crit. LitBl 17.9).— Scott. Notes and Queries July 1895, 17; Aug., 46; Nov., 85; Feb. 1896, 132; May, 187. French *Vœux de Gadres* and *Vœux du Paon*, ed. Bannatyne Club 1831. Gröber 2¹.818, 891; Krit Jahresber.— See Barbour's *Bruce*.

[70] GILBERT HAY'S BUIK. Selections: Hermann *The Forraye of Gadderis, The Vowis*, Berlin 1900 (crit. ESt 33.259). Hermann *The Taymouth MS. of Sir G. H's Buik*, Berlin 1898. Schofield 304; DNB, *Hay, Gilbert.*

[71] FOUR FRAGMENTS OF AN OLD PRINT. Ed. ESt 13.145. See ESt 14.392; Körting §111 ft-note.

6. LEGENDS OF TROY

Dunger *Die Sage vom Troyanischen Kriege* . . . , Leipzig 1869; Joly *Benoît de Sainte-More et le Roman de Troye*, Paris 1870-71; Körting *Dares u. Dictys*, Halle 1874; de Julleville Hist 1.188 (bibliogr. 252); Constans *Le Roman de Troie*, SATF 1904; Greif *Die Mittelalterlichen Bearbeitungen der Trojanersage*, Ausg u. Abhdl 61, Marburg 1886 (crit. Rom 14.630; ZsfVL 2.118); on British, French, Norman treatments, Heeger, München diss. 1886 and Landau prgr. 1891 (see LitBl 1891.305); Wesselofsky *Matériaux et Recherches pour Servir à l'Histoire du Roman et de la Nouvelle*, St. Petersburg 1889 (see Rom 18.303); Piper *Höfische Epik*, Stuttgart 1893-5, 1.282; Sommer *The Recuyell of the Historyes of Troye*, L. 1894, 1.xvlii (general view; crit. Rom 1894.292; Athen 1895, Feb. 9; N&Q 8th Ser. 6.459); Griffin *Dares and Dictys, Introd. Study of the Med. Versions* . . . , 1907 (crit. Ctbl 59.656); Ency Brit, *Troy, Dares, Dictys, Phrygius, Dictys Cretensis* (see the bibliogrs. there); Morley 3.207; Ward 1.1; Hist Litt 29.455; Gröber 2¹.583, 1147, 1197; Krit Jahresber; Taylor *Classical Heritage of the Mid. Ages*, N. Y. 3rd ed. 1911, 39, 360, 390 (bibliogr.); Taylor *The Mediæval Mind*, N. Y. and L. 1911, 1914, Ch. 32, Sec. 4; gen. bibliogr., Wager ed. *Seege of Troye* (see below) 117; Paris Litt Franç, bibliogr. to §45.

[72] GEST HISTORIALE. Ed. EETS 39, 56. Selections: Wülcker
Lesebuch 2.80; ESt 29.384; Zupitza Übungsbuch; MacLean Reader 104.—
Brandl §125; Körting §112; Morley 6.241. Bock *Zur D. of Tr.,
eine Sprach- u. Quellenuntersuchung,* Halle diss. 1883; Brandes *Die
Me. D. of Tr. u. ihre Quelle,* ESt 8.398; Greif, Körting, *op. cit.* above;
Wager *op. cit.* below;— author, Trautmann, Angl 1.123; EETS 1.ix;
Brandes *op. cit.* 410; ESt 11.285;— dialect, Luick, Angl 11.405; Reiche
Untersuchungen über den Stil der Me. . . . Morte Arthure, etc., Königs-
berg diss. 1906. *G. H.* and *Laud Troy-Book* compared, ESt 29.384. Athen
1900.1.751. See under *Huchown.*

[73] SEEGE OF TROYE. Ed. Harley, Lincolns Inn, Zietsch, Arch
72.11;— Harley, Wager, N. Y. and L. 1899 (crit. MLN 15.188; Arch
106.182).— Körting §112a; Brandl §70; Ward 1.84; Sommer *op. cit.* xvii;
Schofield 289.— Zietsch *Über Quelle u. Spr. . . . ,* Göttingen (Kassel) diss.
1883 (crit. Acad. No. 649.241); Greif *op. cit.* §§168-172; Granz *Über die
Quellengemeinschaft des Me. . . . S. . . . of Tr. u. des Mhd. Gedichtes . . .
des Konrad v. Würzburg,* Leipzig diss. 1888 (crit. Angl 11.327; ZsfVL
5.127); Bülbring *Gesch. des Ablauts der Starken Zeitwörter . . . ,* Strassburg 1889, 34; Fick *Zur Me. Rom. S. of Tr. I bis IV,* Breslau diss. 1893.—
Full bibliogr. in Wager's ed.

[74] LAUD TROY-BOOK. Ed. EETS 121, 122 (crit. JEGP 5.367).
Körting §112b. Wülfing *Das Bild u. die Bildliche Varneinung,* Angl 27.555,
28.29; Kempe, notes, ESt 29.1; Wülfing, ESt 29.374; Greif *op. cit.* §69.

[75] LYDGATE'S TROY-BOOK. Ed. EETSES 97, 103, 106.— Körting
§112 anm.; Ten Brink 2.224; Brandl §103; Ward 1.75, 78; DNB, *Lydgate;*
Schofield 289.— Skeat, Acad May 7, 1892; N&Q 7th Ser. 12.146, 215; Bergen
Descr. and Genealogy of the MSS. and Prints of L's T-B., Müncher diss.
1906. See ESt 29.382.— See [79], below.

[76] SCOTTISH TROY FRAGMENTS. Ed. Horstmann *Barbours
Legendensammlung,* Heilbronn 1881, 2.215 (see AnzfDA 11.334).— Bearder
Über den Gebr. der Praepositionen, Halle 1894. Brandl §76; Körting §112c;
Ten Brink 3.53, 58; Schofield 290.— Author, Angl 9.493; ESt 10.373; EETS
39, 56.x. See ESt 29.382 ff.; Prothero, *Memoir of H. Bradshaw,* London
1888, 133. See Cbg. Antiq. Soc. 3.117; Bradshaw's *Collected Papers,* ed.
Prothero, 1888.— See Barbour's *Bruce; Scottish Legend Collection.*

[77] RAWLINSON MISC. 82 PROSE TROY PIECE. Ed. PMLA
22.157; with prose *Thebes,* Arch 130.40, 269.— Wager *Seege of Troye*
xxvii.

[78] THE RECUYELL OF THE HISTORYES OF TROYE. Ed.
Sommer, L. 1904, 2 vols.

7. LEGENDS OF THEBES

Gröber 2[1].582; Paris Litt Franç §47 ·(see bibliogr.); de Julleville Hist
1.173, 252; Ency Brit, *Thebes, Romances of;* Constans, below; Krit Jahresber.

[79] LYDGATE'S SIEGE OF THEBES. Ed. EETSES 108 (crit. ESt
46.98); pr. by de Worde, and added by Stowe to 1561 ed. of Chaucer, pr.
thence with Chaucer to time of Chalmers. Prologue, ed. Hammond, Angl
36.360.— On Bath MS., ESt 10.203.— On date, etc., Schick *Lydgate's
Temple of Glass*, EETSES 60; Bergen *The MSS. and Prints of L's Troy-
Book*, Bungay, Chaucer Press 1906, München diss.; Koeppel *L's S. of Th.;
eine Quellenuntersuchung*, München diss., Oldenbourg 1884; Fiedler *Zum
Leben L's*, Angl 15.391 (crit. LitBl 1885.284); MacCracken *The L. Canon*,
Trans. Lond. Phil. Soc. 1907-9, appendix, and EETSES 107.introd.— Ten
Brink 2.221; Brandl §101; Körting §164; Morley 6.101; Wülker 1.179;
Ward 1.87; Courthope 1.321; Cbg Hist 2.225, 527 (bibliogr.); DNB, *Lyd-
gate* (bibliogr.).— French: Constans *La Légende d'Œdipe*, Paris 1881 (crit.
Rom 10.270); Constans *Roman de Thèbes*, Paris 1890 (see Rom 21.107);
Constans, Rev. d. L. Rom. 35.612; bibliogrs. in Gröber, Paris, de Julleville,
as above.— See under *Lydgate's Troy-Book*.

[80] RAWLINSON MISC. *D* 82 SIEGE OF THEBES. Ed. Arch
130.40, 269.

8. EUSTACE-CONSTANCE-FLORENCE-GRISELDA LEGENDS

Gerould *Forerunners, Congeners, and Derivatives of the Eustace Legend*,
PMLA 19.335; Ogden *Comp. Study of Guillaume d'Angleterre*, 1900;
EETSES 51.xxi; Steinbach *Der Einfluss Crestien de Troies auf die Ae.
Lit.*, Leipzig 1886, 41; Gough *The Constance Saga*, Palæstra 23 (crit. ESt
32.110); *Die Eustachiusleg. Chr. Wilhelmsleben . . .*, Arch 121.340; see
under *Eustace*, p. 810;— Wilda *Über die örtliche Verbreitung der Zwölf-
zeiligen Schweifreimstrophe in Engl.*, Breslau diss. 1887; EETSES 99.xcix,
xxxii; Westenholz *Die Griseldis-Sage in der Literaturgeschichte*, Heidelberg 1888 (crit. ZsfvL 2.111); Wannemacher *Die Griseldissage auf die
Iberischen Halbinsel*, Strassburg diss. 1894 (crit. LitBl 1895.415); Siefken
Der Konstanze-Griseldistypus in der Engl. Lit., Rathenow 1904 (part
printed as *Das Geduldige Weib . . .*, Leipzig diss. 1904); on Griselda
story, Wheatley *Folklore Tracts* Ser. 1.4; see *Patient Grisell* in PFMS
3.421; see under *Eustace* (page 810), *Chaucer, Clerk's Tale, Man of Law's
Tale*. Däumling *Studie über den Typus des Mädchens ohne Hände inner-
halb des Konstanzezyklus*, München diss. 1912.

[81] SIR ISUMBRAS. Ed. Utterson *Sel. Pieces of E. E. Pop. Poetry*,
L. 1817, 1.77; Halliwell *Thornton Romances* 88; Schleich, readings of all
MSS., Palæstra 15 (crit. AnglBbl 12.333; Öst. Lit. Bl. 12.209; LitBl 23.16;
Ctbl 1902.16; Le Moyen Âge 5.418); text of Naples frag., ESt 3.200; text
of Univ. Coll., ESt 48.329. Text-notes, Arch 88.72, 90.148. Abstract, Ellis
Spec 479.— Körting §94 anm.; Brandl §79; Ward 1.760; Schofield 313.—
Gerould, PMLA 19.365, 20.529; Adam, EETSES 51.xxiv; Sarrazin ed. of
Octovian xliv; Wilda *op. cit.*; on date, Bonner Beitr 12.97. See Perrould
The Grateful Dead, Folk-Lore Soc. 1907.

[82] SIR EGLAMOUR OF ARTOIS. Ed. Halliwell *Thornton Romances*, 121; Schleich (all variants), Palæstra 53 (crit. RevCrit 62.153;

Arch 118.441; AllgLtbl 17.399; Ctbl 58.737; ESt 39.433; AnglBbl 17.291);
Cook, N. Y. 1911; fragm. of old print, Arch 95.308.— On Egerton, see ESt
7.193.— Brandl §79; Körting §113 anm.; Ward 1.766; Schofield 313.—
Abstract, Ellis Spec 527; Ashton 257. Zielke *Untersuchungen über Sir
E. of A.*, Kiel diss. 1889; Schleich *Über die Beziehungen v. E. u. Torrent,*
Arch 92.343; EETSES 51.xxvii; *E. and Emare,* EETSES 99.xlvii; Gerould,
PMLA 19.439; Siefken *op. cit.* 44.

[83] SIR TORRENT OF PORTYNGALE.   Ed. Halliwell, L. 1842;
EETSES 51 (crit. LitBl 11.17; ESt 12.432, 15.1). Coll. of MS., ESt 7.344;—
on text, Angl 17.401; note, ESt 13.136. Körting §113 anm.; Brandl §125;
Schofield 313.— Adam *Über Sir T.*, Breslau diss. 1887; Schleich *Über
die Beziehungen v. Eglamour u. T.*, Arch 92.343; Gerould PMLA 19.439;
Siefken *op. cit.* 48.— See Wilda, above.

[84] OCTOVIAN.   Ed. Sth version, Weber MR 3.157; Sarrazin AEB
3 (crit. ESt 9.456; LitBl 7.137);— Nth version, Halliwell, Percy Soc.
1844 (Cbg. MS.); Sarrazin *op. cit.* (both MSS.).— Körting §113; Brandl
§§70, 79; Ward 1.762; Schofield 184, 313.— Streve *Die Octaviansage,*
Erlangen 1884; Kaluza *Thomas Chestre*, ESt 18.165; Kaluza ed. *Libeaus
Desconus* clxiii; Bülbring *Gesch. des Ablauts des Starken Verben*, QF 63.30;
Eule *Untersuchungen über die Nordengl. Version des Octovian*, Berlin
diss., Burg 1889; Brockstedt *Floovent-Studien*, Kiel 1904; Settegast
Floovent u. Julian, Halle 1906; Siefken *op. cit.* 40. French *Octavian*, ed.
Volmöller, Heilbronn 1883. Gröber 2¹.798; Krit Jahresber.— DNB, *Chestre,
Thomas.*— See under *Sir Launfal, Libeaus Desconus.*

[85] SIR TRIAMOUR.   Ed. Utterson *Sel. Pieces of E. E. Pop. Poetry,*
L. 1817, 1.5; Halliwell, Percy Soc. 1846; PFMS 2.78; Bauszus, Königsberg
diss. 1902 (only introd.). Abstract, Ellis Spec 491; Ashton 171.— Brandl
§113; Schofield 313.— Siefken *op. cit.* 54.— On Macaire and the dog,
Guessard ed. *Macaire;* Baugert *Die Tiere im Af. Epos*, Ausg u. Abhdl,
Marburg 1885, 177; Gröber 2¹.543, 811; Gautier *Bibl.* 143; Krit Jahresber.

[86] KING OF TARS.   Ed. Vernon, Ritson AEMR 2.156;— all MSS.,
Krause, ESt 11.1 (crit. Angl 15.195-6; AJPhil 11.378).— On 'Auch., ESt
7.179.— Abstract, Warton *Hist. Engl. Poetry*, 1840, 1.188.— Brandl §38;
Körting §114 anm.; Ward 1.767; Schofield 312; Ten Brink 1.252.— Source
and notes, Angl 15.195.— Parallels, Zielke's ed. *Sir Orfeo*, Kölbing's *Sir
Beues* introd. xlv ff.

[87] LE BONE FLORENCE.   Ed. Ritson AEMR 3.46; Victor and
Knobbe, Text, Marburg 1893, Introd., 1899 (crit. Arch 110.446; DLz
1900.442; AnglBbl 10.129; ESt 29.123).— Brandl §79; Körting §86 vorbem.;
Schofield 313.— Knobbe *Über die Me. . . . Le B. F. of R.*, Marburg diss.
1899 (crit. ESt 19.123); Siefken *op. cit.* 34. General: Wenzel *Die Fassungen der Sage v. Fl. de R.*, etc., Marburg diss. 1890 (crit. LitBl 13.266);
Freymond, LitBl 1890.266.— Hist Litt 26.335; Ward 1.711; Gröber 2¹.798,
910, 919; Gautier *Bibl.* 102; Paris Litt Franç §27; Krit Jahresber.

9. Breton Lais

Kittredge, AJPhil 7.176; EETSES 99.xxviii; Schofield 179. See Paris Litt Franç §55 (see its bibliogr.); Rom 8.33, 14.606; de Julleville Hist 1.285, 340; Gröber 2¹.496, 591, 593; Krit Jahresber.

[88] LAI LE FREINE. Ed. Weber MR 1.357; *V*arnhagen, Angl 3.415; Laurin *Essay on Lang. of Lay le Freine*, 27. Mod. rend., Rickert RofL 46. Abstract, Ellis Spec 538. Text, ESt 10.41; Angl 13.360.— Brandl §29; Körting §133; Ten Brink 1.259; Schofield 192.— Marie's *Lais*, ed. Warnke, 2nd ed. 1901. Gröber 2¹.527, 595; Krit Jahresber. See par. preceding.— See Westenholz, Siefken, Wheatley, Wilda, *et al.*, under *Eustace-Constance-Florence-Griselda Legends*; Chaucer's *Clerk's Tale*, *Man of Law's Tale*.

[89] SIR ORFEO. Ed. Harley, Ritson AEMR 2.248;— Ashmole, Halliwell *Illustr. of the Fairy Mythol. of A Midsummer Night's Dream*, L. 1845, 36, repr. Hazlitt *Fairy Tales*, L. 1875; Scott Antiq 16.30;— Auchinleck, Laing *Sel. Rem. of Anc. Pop. Poetry of Scotland*, 1822, rev. Hazlitt 1895, 1.64 (see ESt 7.189); readings of all MSS., Zielke, Breslau 1880 (crit. ESt 5.166; AnglAnz 5.13; LitBl 2.135);— Auch. completed from Harley, after Zielke, Cook Reader 88. See incorrect notices of Digby 86 in lists of MSS. needing copying for EETS, in covers of Pubs. of EETS.— Mod. rend., Weston *Chief M. E. Poets*, Boston 1914, 133; Rickert RofL 32;— adaptation, Hunt, E. E., Cbg. Mass. 1910.— Brandl §29; Körting §133; Ten Brink 1.260; Ward 1.171; Hist Litt 29.499; Gröber 2¹.593; Schofield 184.— Ker *Engl. Lit., Med.* 121; on prol., MLN 21.46; Kittredge, AJPhil 7.176; ESt 10.42; ZsfFrSpr 20.154; Wirl *Orpheus in der Engl. Lit.*, Wiener Beitr 40.— Hertz *Spielmanns Buch*, Stuggart 1886, introd.— *King Orfeo*, ed. Child *Ballads* (1857) 1.215.

[90] EMARE. Ed. Ritson AEMR 2.183; Gough, L. 1901 (crit. Arch 110.196; ESt 30.294; LitBl 24.89; AnglBbl 13.46); Rickert EETSES 99 (Chicago diss. 1907;— crit. ESt 40.413). Coll. of Ritson, ESt 15.248. On ll. 49 ff., AnglBbl 13.46.— Brandl §80; Ward 1.418; Schofield 189. Gough *The Constance Saga*, Palæstra 23 (crit. ESt 32.110); Gough *On the M. E. Mctr. Rom. Emare*, Kiel diss. 1900; Lücke *Das Leben der Constanze bei Trivet, Gower, u. Chaucer*, Angl 14.77.— See under *Eustace-Constance-Florence-Griselda Legends*, p. 781; Chaucer's *Clerk's Tale*, *Man of Law's Tale*.

[91] SIR LAUNFAL or LAUNFALUS MILES. Ed. Ritson AEMR 2.1 (repr. Goldsmid, Edbg. 1891); Halliwell *Illustr. of the Fairy Mythol. of A Midsummer Night's Dream*, L. 1845, repr. Hazlitt *Fairy Tales, Legends, and Romances*, L. 1875, 48; Erling, Kempten 1883; Kaluza, ESt 18.165. Mod. rend., Weston *Chief M. E. Poets* 204; Rickert RofL 57.— Körting §125; Brandl §§70, 113; Billings 144; Schofield 181.— On Chestre, ESt 18.165; Sarrazin's ed. *Octovian*; Kaluza's ed. *Libeaus Desconus*; DNB, *Chestre, Thomas*. Münster *Untersuchungen zu Th. Chestre's Launfal*, Kiel diss. 1886; see Kolls, below.— On verbs, QF 63.30.— See Wilda, under *Eustace-Constance*, etc.— Marie's version, ed. Warnke, 2nd ed. 1901. Engl.

prose rend., Weston *Four Lais of M. de F.,* L. 1900. Gröber 2^1.595; Krit Jahresber. Schofield *Lays of Graelent and Launfal,* PMLA 15.121 (crit. Rom 29.487); Schofield *Lay of Guingamor,* HarvStN 5.221 (crit. Rom 27.323); Cross *The Celtic Fée in Launfal, Kittredge Anniv. Papers* 1913, 377.

[92] SIR LANDEVAL. Ed. Kittredge, AJPhil 10.1; Zimmermann, Königsberg diss. 1900.

[93] SIR LAMBEWELL. Ed. PFMS 1.144; Kolls *Zur Lanvalsage,* Berlin 1886 (crit. Ctbl 14.491; DLz 29.1092; Rom 15.644).

[94] SIR LAMWELL. Ed. Douce, Malone, PFMS 1.522, 533; Kolls *op. cit.;*— Cbg., Furnivall *Captain Cox,* 1871, xxxi; Furnivall *Robt. Laneham's Letter,* New Shakespeare Soc., 1890.

[95] SIR DEGARE. Ed. Utterson *Sel. Pieces of E. E. Pop. Poetry,* L. 1817, 1.113 (from Copland's print);— Auchinleck, Laing, for Abbotsford Club 1849;— Percy, PFMS 3.16. On Egerton, see ESt 7.192-3; on Auch., see ESt 7.185. Abstract of Copland, Ellis Spec 574; Ashton 103.— Brandl §50; Hist Litt 24.505; Ten Brink 1.252-4; Schofield 186. Kaluza ed. *Libeaus Desconus* cliv.

[96] SIR GOWTHER. Ed. Royal, Utterson *Sel. Pieces of E. E. Pop. Poetry,* L. 1817, 1.157;— both MSS., Breul, Oppeln 1886 (crit. AnzfDA 14.205; ESt 12.78; Rom. 15.160; Angl 7.6; LitBl 1.16; DLz 1886.1458).— Brandl §80; Billings 227; Ward 1.416, 419; Schofield 187.— Ravenal *Tydorel and Sir G.,* PMLA 20.152; Potter *Sohrab and Rustum,* L. 1902; Weston *The Three Days' Tournament,* L. 1902; see Ward 1.728.— See Breul for study and bibliogr. of Robert the Devil. Repr. of de Worde's *Robert,* Hazlitt Rem 1.217; Thoms 167.— See Wilda, under *Eustace-Constance,* etc., page 781.

[97] EARL OF TOULOUS. Ed. Ritson AEMR 3.105; Lüdtke, *Sammlung Engl. Denkmäler* 3, Berlin 1881 (crit. ESt 7.136; LitBl 3.179).— Mod. rend., Rickert RofL 80.— Brandl §80; Schofield 196.— Bolte *Graf von Toulouse,* Bbl. der Lit. Ver. 1901.172. Parallels, Child *Ballads* (1886) 2.33.— See Wilda, under *Eustace-Constance,* etc., page 781.

10. Miscellaneous Romances

I. Romances of Greek or Byzantine Origin

Schofield 305; Ten Brink 1.114, 169-71. See bibliogr. in Taylor *Class. Her. of Middle Ages,* 3rd ed. 1911, 361.

[98] APOLLONIUS OF TYRE. On O. E. version, Körting §68a; Wülker *Grundriss der Ags. Lit.* §622; Paul Grundriss 2nd ed. 2^1.1132.— Gower *Confessio Amantis,* Bk. 8 (see p. 866). English *Gesta Romanorum,* ed. Madden, Roxb. Club 1838; EETSES 23.— Ward 1.161; Schofield 306.— Gröber 2^1.1197; Krit Jahresber.

[99] FLORIS AND BLAUNCHEFLUR. Ed. Auchinleck, Hartshorne AMT 81; Laing *A Peniworth of Witte*, Abbotsford Club 1857;— Cbg., Cott., Trentham, EETS 14, re-ed. 1901 (crit. Athen 1902.2.822);—all MSS., Hausknecht, *Sammlung Engl. Denkmäler 5*, Berlin 1885 (crit. AnglAnz 8.150; ESt 9.92, 389). Mod. rend., Rickert RofL 1. On text, Angl 1.473; ESt 3.99.— Brandl §38; Körting §114; Ten Brink 1.236; Schofield 306; Cbg Hist 1.343.— See espec. Hausknecht's and EETS introds.; Rom 28.348, 439, 35.95, 335. Reinhold *Floire et Blancheflor, Étude de Litt. Comparée*, Paris 1906; Johnston *Orig. of the Leg. of F. and B.*, Matzke Mem. Vol., Leland Stanford, 1911; Ernst *Floire et Blantscheflur: Studie zur Vergl. Literaturwissenschaft*, Strassburg diss. 1912; Körting ·*Encykl. der Rom. Phil.*, 2.497, 3.320; Herzog, Germ 29.137; Herzog *Die Beiden Sagenkreise von F. u. B.*, Vienna 1884; Paris Litt Franç §51 (see its bibliogr.); Gröber 2¹.490, 527, 859; Ward 1.714; Krit Jahresber.— French, ed. Du Méril, Paris 1856.

II. Composites of Courtly Romance

[100] SIR DEGREVANT. Ed. Halliwell *Thornton Romances* 177. Collation, ESt 12.140. Mod. rend., Rickert RofL 106.— Brandl §79; Körting §86 vorbem.; Schofield 311.— ESt 3.100.

[101] GENERYDES. Ed. Helmingham, Furnivall, Roxb. Club 1865;— Cbg., Wright EETS 55, 70. On text, ESt 17.23, 49; Angl 1.481, 23.125, 249; Arch 106.351; Holthausen *Beitr. zur Textkritik der Me. G. Rom.* (EETS ed.), Gothenburg 1899 (crit. DLz 1900.1443).— Brandl §108; Körting §116; Schofield 310.— Zirwer *Untersuchungen zu den Beiden Me. G.-Rom.*, Breslau 1889; Settegast *Quellenstudien zur Galloromanischen Epik*, Leipzig 1904, 232.

[102] PARTHENOPE OF BLOIS. Ed. Univ. Coll., New, parts of Rawl., Buckley, Roxb. Club 1862;— *Vale Royal*, Roxb. Club 1873;— Robarts, Angl 12.607;— Br. Mus., Robarts, Bödtker, EETSES 109.— Brandl §113; Körting §103 anm. 2; Schofield 307.— See Angl 12.607; ESt 14.435. Kölbing *Beitr. zur Vergl. Gesch. der Rom. Poesie u. Prosa des Mittelalters*, Breslau 1876, 80; Weingartner *Die Me. Fassungen der Partonopeussage u. ihr Verhältniss zum Af. Orig.*, Breslau 1888.— French, ed. Crapelet, Paris 1834; Massmann, 1847. See Paris Litt Franç §51 and bibliogr.; Gröber 2¹.586; Ward 1.698; Krit Jahresber.

[103] IPOMADON. Ed. all three pieces, Kölbing, Breslau 1899 (crit. AJPhil 10.348; LitBl 1890.142; Athen 1889. No. 3220; Ctbl 1889.1779; DLz 1889.1681; ESt 13.432);— *Lyfe of Ipomydon*, Weber AEMR 2.279;— fragments, ESt 13.153. On text, ESt 14.371, 38.131. Notes, ESt 38.131, 14.371, 386. Syntax, ESt 18.282. Abstract, Ellis Spec 505.— Brandl §§80, 125; Körting §103 anm. 2; Ward 1.728-56; Hist Litt 24.504; Schofield 310.— On Chetham, ESt 7.199. Kirschten *Überlief. u. Spr. d. Rom. The Lyfe of I.*, Marburg diss. 1885; Seyferth *Spr. u. Metr. des Me. Str. Ged. Le Morte Arthur u. sein Verhältnis zu The Lyfe of I.*, Berliner Beitr 8

(crit. Ctbl 1895.1562); Weston *The Three Days' Tournament*, L. 1902.—
Hue de Rotelande's *Ipomedon*, ed. Kölbing and Koschwitz, Breslau 1889.
Gröber 2¹.585; Ward 1.728; Krit Jahresber.— Carter *Ipomedon, an Illus-
tration of Romance Origins, Haverford Essays* 1909.—Furnivall *Capt.
Cox's Ballads* cxlii.—

[104] SQUYR OF LOWE DEGRE. Ed. Copland's text, Ritson AEMR
3.145; Hazlitt Rem 2.21;— Percy, PFMS 3.263;— all texts, Mead, Boston
1904 (crit. AnglBbl 17.7). Mod. rend., Rickert RofL 153.— See Mead
for bibliogr.— Brandl §113.— Tunk *Studien zur . . . Sq. of L. D.*, Breslau
diss. 1900; Weyrauch *Zur Komposition, Entstehungszeit, u. Beurteilung der
. . . Sq. of L. D.*, ESt 31.177; Jefferson *A Note on the Sq. of L. D.*, MLN
28.102.

III. Romances on Historical Themes

[105] RICHARD COER DE LYON. Ed. Cbg., Weber MR 2.1;—
Auchinleck, Turnbull and Laing *Owain Miles*, Edbg. 1837;— all MSS.,
Brunner *Der Me. Versroman über Richard Lowenherz*, Wiener Beitr. 42
(crit. N. Y. Nation July 30, 1914.138). On Auchinleck, ESt 7.178, 190,
8.115, 11.497 note, 13.138;— on Cbg., ESt 14.321, 337. Selections: Wülcker
Lesebuch 1.95 (crit. ESt 17.299); Rom 26.356, 362. Abstract, Ellis Spec
282. Mod. rend., parts, Weston *Chief M. E. Poets* 123, 126.— Brandl §36;
Körting §122; Ten Brink 1.242; Ward 1.944; Schofield 314.— Author,
Kölbing ed. *Arthour and Merlin* lx.— Jentsch, ESt 15.161; Jentsch and
Needler, ESt 16.142; Needler *R. C. de L. in Literature*, Leipzig diss. 1890
(crit. DLz 1891.418; Rom 26 below; Ctbl 1891.272); Rom 9.542; Paris Litt
Franç §§69, 88, and bibliogr.; Paris *Le Roman de R. C. de L.*, Rom 26.353
(crit. AJPhil 20.339); Gröber 2¹.661, 665, 675, 765; Krit Jahresber.

[106] TITUS AND VESPASIAN or DESTRUCTION OF JERUSA-
LEM. On French *Destruction* or *La Venjance Nostre Seigneur (Sauveur)*,
Suchier, Halle diss. 1899; ZsfRPh 24.161, 25.94; Rom 16.56; RevCrit
1882.1.346; Notices et Extraits 33.1.70; Paris Litt Franç §140; Gröber
2¹.658; Krit Jahresber; Ward 1.176.— On English in general, Hulme,
EETSES 100.xxii and note; Brandl §73; Körting §110 end; Schofield
378.— *Bataile of Jerusalem* or *Vengeaunce of Goddes Deth* or *Sege of
Jerusalem* (Couplet Version): Ed. five London and Oxf. MSS., Herbert,
Roxb. Club 1905 (crit. Arch 122.159);— Magd. Pepys 37, Arch 111.285,
112.25. On MSS., Ward 1.187; EETS 69.7; Arch 108.199.— Brandl §70;
Arch 122.159; Bergau *Untersuchungen über Quelle u. Verfasser*, Königsberg diss. 1901 (crit. Arch 108.199); Hulme *op. cit.— Distructio Jerusalem*
or *Sege of Jerusalem* or *La Sege de Jerusalem* or *Distruccio Jerusalem*
(Alliterative *V*ersion): Ed. Laud, Steffler, Emden 1891 (crit. AnglBbl
2.244). On MSS., Ward 1.180, 185, 928; Arch 86.384.— Brandl §73; Kopka
The Destruction of Jerusalem, Breslau diss. 1887; PFMS 3.xxx; Warton
Hist. Engl. Poetry, ed. 1840, 2.105; Reiche *Untersuchungen über den Stil
des Me. Ged. Morte Arthure*, Königsberg diss. 1906.

IV. Romances from Family Tradition

[107] MELUSINE. Ed. Br. Mus. MS., EETSES 68.— Körting p. 133 note; Ward 1.687.— Köhler *Der Ursprung der Melusinersage*, Leipzig 1895 (crit. ZsfVL 10.256; Ctbl 1895.1598; Euphorion 3.245); Desaivre *La Légende de Mélusine*, Niort 1885; LitBl 1887.346; de Julleville Hist 1.344 (bibliogr.); Gröber 2^1.1082; Krit Jahresber.— See under *Parthenay*.

[108] ROMAUNS OF PARTHENAY or LUSIGNEN. Ed. EETS 22, new ed. 1899. Abstract, Ashton 1.— Körting p. 133 note; Brandl §108; Schofield 316.— Hattendorf *Spr. u. Dialekt des . . . Romans of P.*, Leipzig 1887.— See under *Melusine*.

[109] KNIGHT OF CURTESY. Ed. Ritson AEMR 3.172; Hazlitt Rem 2.65. Mod. rend., Rickert RofL 141.— Brandl §113.— *Le Chatelain de Couci*, de Julleville Hist 1.343 (bibliogr.). Lorenz *Die Kastellanin von Vergi in der Literatur*, Halle 1909 (see Krit Jahresber 12.2.45). *La Chastelaine de Vergi*, ed. Raynaud, Paris 1910 (crit. RomRev 2.214), 2nd ed. 1912 (crit. RomRev 6.112).

V. Legendary Romances of Didactic Intent

[110] AMIS AND AMILOUN. Ed. Auchinleck, Weber MR 2.367;— all MSS., with Fr., Lat., and Norse texts, Kölbing, AEB 2, Heilbronn 1884 (crit. and notes, ESt 9.175, 456, 477, 13.134; Angl 8 Anz 27; AnzfDA 13.92). Abstract, Ellis Spec 584. Selection: Cook Reader 81. Mod. rend., Weston *Chief M. E. Poets* 174; Rickert RofFr 1.— Brandl §52; Körting §115; Ten Brink 1.250; Ward 1.674; Schofield 309; CbgHist 1.350.— Kölbing *Zur Überlieferung der Sage von A. u. A.*, PBBeitr 4.271, ESt 2.295, 5.465; PBBeitr 4.282; Ayres *The Faerie Queene and A. and A.*, MLN 23.17 (see for bibliogr.).— French, ed. Hofmann, Erlangen 1882 (see introd. and bibliogr.). *Morris*, mod. rend. of Fr., *Old Fr. Romances*, L. 1896, 25. Gröber 2^1.458, 549, 570, 993, 1088; Krit Jahresber; Gautier *Les Épopées Françaises* 2.308; Gautier *Bibl.* 52, 212; Paris Litt Franç §27; Schwieger *Die Sage von A. and A.*, Berlin 1885 (crit. ESt 9.149; Rom 14.319); Kölbing ed., xcvi.— See Wilda under *Eustace-Constance*, etc., page 781.

[111] SIR AMADACE. Ed. Auchinleck, Weber MR 3.241;— Ireland, Robson *Three E. E. Metr. Rom.* 27; Stephens *Ghost-Thanks*, Copenhagen 1860. Mod. rend., Weston *Chief M. E. Poets* 216; Rickert RofFr 49.— Brandl §75; Körting §86 anm.; Hist Litt 24.505; Schofield 322; de Julleville Hist 1.343 (bibliogr.).— Hippe *Untersuchungen zu d. Me. . . . . Sir A.*, Arch 81.141 (same as diss. of 1888;— crit. Rom 18.197); Perrould *The Grateful Dead*, Folk-Lore Soc., extra vol., 1907.— See on *Amadas et Idoine*, Hippeau, Paris 1863; Gröber 2^1.531; Krit Jahresber; Paris Litt Franç §66.— On origin, Rom 18.626; Paris, *Furnivall Misc.*, 1901, 386.

[112] SIR CLEGES. Ed. Auchinleck, Weber MR 1.331;— both MSS., Treichel, ESt 22.345;— Ashmole, McKnight *M. E. Humorous Tales in*

Verse, Boston and L. 1913, 38 (*q. v.* for bibliogr. and analogues). Mod.
rend., Weston *Sir Cleges, Sir Libeaus Desconus,* L. 1902 (crit. AnglBbl
15.332).— Brandl §114; Körting p. 157 note 2; Schofield 322.

[113] ROBERD OF CISYLE.   Ed. Harley, Utterson, Private Print,
1839; Cbg Ff II 38, Halliwell *Nugæ Poeticæ,* L. 1844;— from Utterson and
Halliwell, Hazlitt Rem 1.264;— Vernon and Trinity, readings of all MSS.,
AELeg 1878.209;— three Cbg. MSS., Horstmann, Arch 62.416;— crit. ed.
Nuck, Berlin diss. 1887 (text notes, ESt 13.136). Selections: Cook Reader
167. Abstract, Ellis Spec 474. Mod. version, Longfellow *King Robert
of Sicily.*— Brandl §40; Ward 1.763; Schofield 314.— Madden *O. E. Versions of the Gesta Romanorum,* 1838. On dramatic versions, see Ward
Hist. Engl. Dram. Lit. 1.93; Collier *Hist. Engl. Dram. Poetry,* L. 1831,
1.113, 2.128, 415.— Version of Jean de Condé, *Dits et Contes de Baudouin
de Condé et son Fils,* ed. Scheler, Brussels 1866, 2.355, 455. Gröber 2¹.843.

CHAPTER II—TALES

Canby *Short Story in English,* N. Y. 1909, see its bibliogr. at p. 351;
Crane *Mediæval Story Books,* MPhil 9.225; Crane *Mediæval Sermon-
books and Stories,* Proc. Amer. Philosoph. Soc. 1883, No. 114.49; Herbert,
passim; Mosher *Exemplum in Early Religious and Didactic Lit. in Eng-
land,* N. Y. 1911, see its bibliogr. at p. 140.— Eds. of Jacobus de Vitriaco,
Crane *Exempla or Illustr. Stories,* L. 1890; Frenken *Die Exempla des
Jacob von Vitry,* Berlin diss. 1914; Greven *Die Exempla aus den Sermones
Feriales et Communes,* Heidelberg 1914. See Crane *Recent Collections of
Exempla* (on Frenken, Greven, Klapper, Hilka, Welter), RomRev 6.219.
On the *Lai,* see *Breton Lais,* above, Ch. I Sect. 9.

1. PIOUS TALES

I. Miracles of the Virgin

Ward 2.587; Herbert, *passim;* Canby *op. cit.* 15, 352; AELeg 1881, 329;
Crane, RomRev 2.235; G. Paris Litt Franç §141; Gröber 2¹.648, 917; Krit
Jahresber; Mussafia, Sitzungsber. d. Wiener Akad. d. Wiss., 1886, 1887-8,
1889, 1891, 1898; Löwinski *Die Lyrik in den Miracles de Nostre Dame,*
Berlin 1900 (crit. LitBl 24.207); Patzer *The 'Miracles de Nostre Dame' and
the 14th Century,* MLN 20.44; Schofield 480.

[1] VERNON MIRACLES.   Ed. EETS 98.138; Arch 56.221.   Schofield
327.

[2] OTHER MIRACLES.   See Ward 2.735; AELeg 1875, vi, xxvi note;
AELeg 1881, 1.

[3] LAMBETH SKETCHES.   Ed. Angl 3.319.   AELeg 1881, 329.

[4] HOW THE PSALTER OF OUR LADY WAS MADE. Ed. Auch., Laing *A Peniworth of Witte,* Abbotsf. Club 1857;— Digby, EETS 117.776; AELeg 1881, 220 (with var. of Auch.).—Brandl §40; MLN 4.274.

[5] THE CLERK WHO WOULD SEE THE *V*IRGIN. Ed. AELeg 1881, 499. See Arch 82.465.— Mirk, EETSES 96.234.

[6] EFFICACY OF AVE MARIAS. Ed. MLN 4.274.

[7] DE MIRACULO BEATE MARIE. Ed. AELeg 1881, 503. See Arch 82.465.

[8] THE GOOD KNIGHT AND THE JEALOUS WIFE. Ed. AELeg 1881, 329.— Schofield 327.

II. Other Tales

[9] GAST OF GY. Ed. Cott., Tib., Rawl. (at xvii fragm. of Caius), Schleich, Palæstra 1 (crit. DLz 1899.987; LitBl 21.330; Ctbl 1899.824; AnglBbl 10.65; Arch 106.179);— Tib., *V*ern., Yksh Wr 2.292.— *Revelation of Purgatory,* ed. Yksh Wr 1.383.— Schofield 329.

[10] TRENTALLE SANCTI GREGORII. Ed. *V*ernon f. 230, ESt 8.275; EETS 98.260 (with var. of *V*ernon f. 303);— Cott., EETS 15 (revised).114; EETS 98.260;— Harley, ESt 40.351 (see Ward 1.171);— Lamb. var. from Cott., EETS 15 (revised).114;— Advocates', Turnbull *Visions of Tundale,* Edbg. 1843; Angl 13.301;— Garrett, ESt 41.362;— Crit. text (all readings, exc. Garrett) of version 1, and text of Cbg. Kk, Kaufmann ErlBeitr 3 (crit. LitBl 11.301). Sources, Angl 13.105.— Brandl §40; Körting p. 153, n. 2.

[11] NARRATIO DE *V*IRTUTE MISSARUM. Ed. Rel Ant 1.61.— Brandl §71.

[12] NARRATIO SANCTI AUGUSTINI. Ed. Rel Ant 1.59.— Brandl §55.

[13] SMITH AND HIS DAME. Ed. Hazlitt Rem 3.201; AELeg 1881.322.— Brandl §114; Schofield 330.

[14] EREMYTE AND THE OUTELAWE. Ed. Fillingham, Park Brydges *Restituta,* L. 1816, 4.91 (see ESt 16.434);— Addit., ESt 13.165 (text-note, Angl 13.359).— Brandl §71; Körting §130 p. 153; Schofield 328; Kittredge, ESt 19.177.— See Crane *Exempla of Jacques de Vitry,* L. 1890, Nos. 72, 165; de la Marche *Légendes et Apologues Tirés du Recueil Inédit d'Étienne de Bourbon,* 1877, Nos. 26, 284;— *Chevalier au Barizel,* Barbazon *Fabliaux* 1.208.— Rohde *Die Erzahlung vom Einsiedler u. Engel,* see Jahresbericht 1894 p. 322.

[15] CHILD OF BRISTOWE. Ed. Wright, Retrospective Rev., New Ser. Pt. 6; Hazlitt Rem 1.110; AELeg 1881, 315.— Brandl §129; Schofield 329.

[16] TALE OF AN INCESTUOUS DAUGHTER. Ed. Hartshorne AMT 151; AELeg 1881, 334 (Cbg. with Ashmole readings); Arch 79.421

(see 82.204).— Schofield 329. Thum *Über die Me. Fromme Erzahlung
'A Tale of an Incestuous Daughter,'* Rostock diss. 1893 (crit. LitBl 16.123).

[17] LAMENT OF THE SOUL OF BASTERFELD. Ed. Thornton,
AELeg 1881, 528;— Ashmole, AELeg 1881, 367; EETS 15 (revised).123;—
Rawl. with var. of others, Leonard *Zwei Geschichte aus Hölle,* Zürich diss.
1891 (crit. AnglBbl 2.321.)

[18] AGAINST BREAKING OF WEDLOCK. Ed. Leonard *op. cit.*
above;— Cbg. Ff V, Hartshorne AMT 169;— Ashmole, AELeg 1881, 368;—
Rawl., Arch 79.419;— Lambeth, EETS 15 (revised).126.

[19] LEGEND OF THE CRUCIFIX. Ed. AELeg 1881, 339.— *Handlyng Synne,* EETS 119.130.— See under *The Cross,* p. 812.

2. HUMOROUS TALES

Bédier *Les Fabliaux,* 3rd ed. Paris 1912; de Julleville Hist 2.56 (see
its bibliogr. 2.103); Hist Litt 23.69; Gröber 2'.Register p. 1261; Krit
Jahresber; Rev. des Deux Mondes Sept. 1893; Pilz *Die Bedeutung des
Wortes Fablel,* Stettin 1889; Fromentin *Essai sur les Fabliaux Français,*
Sainte-Étienne 1887; Hermann, F., *Schilderung u. Beurtheilung . . . in der
Fabliaudichtung,* Coburg diss. 1900.— Morley 3.336, 378; Cbg Hist 1.407;
Schofield 118, 323, 338, 348, 479; PMLA 21.200, 23.1, 329; MPhil 2.477;
Canby *Short Story in English* 46; McKnight *M. E. Humorous Tales,* Boston
1913, introd. and its full bibliogr. at p. 81 (crit. MLR 10.237).

[20] *DAME SIRI3.* Ed. AESprPr 1.103; Wright *Anec. Lit.* 1844, 1;
Zupitza Übungsbuch, 6th ed. (crit. ESt 31.268); McKnight *M. E. Humorous
Tales,* Boston 1913, 1; Cook Reader 141.ᴵ On text, ESt 5.378; l. 62, MLR
1.325.— Brandl §49; Körting §80; Ten Brink 1.255; Schofield 321; Cbg
Hist 1.408; Schipper §168.— Elsner *Untersuchung zu dem Me. Fabliau
'Dame Siriz,'* Berlin diss. 1887. See Angl 30.306. Bibliogr. of analogues,
etc., McKnight *op. cit.* 83.

[21] PENIWORÞ OF WITTE. Ed. Cbg., Ritson APP 67;— Auch.,
Laing *A Peniworth of Witte,* Abbotsf. Club 1857;— Cbg. with use of
Auch., Hazlitt Rem 1.193;— all readings, Kölbing ESt 7.111.' Notes, ESt
8.496, 9.178, 11.216, 13.135; Angl 14.308.— Brandl §39; Ten Brink 1.261;
Schofield 325; Canby *Short Story* 52.— French piece, ed. Montaiglon et
Renaud *Recueil Général,* 1878, 88.

[22] LATER PIECES. Editions of most of these are noted in Brandl
§114. See texts in Hazlitt Rem.

3. FABLES, BESTIARIES, ANIMAL TALES

I. Fables

Dressel *Zur Gesch. der Fabel,* Berlin 1876; Moll, ZsfRPh 9.161; Jacobs
The Fables of Æsop, L. 1889, introd., espec. 1.158, 180; Warnke *Bibl. Norm.*
6; McKnight, PLMA 23. 497; Keidel *Manual of Æsopic Fable Lit.,* Balti-

more 1896; Keidel notes on med. Span. and Port. fables, ZsfRPh 25.721;
Plessow *Gesch. der Fabeldichtung in England,* Berlin diss. 1906 (crit. LitBl
30.191; AllgLtbl 17.431; Neu Phil. Rundschau 1908.329;— see Jahresbericht
1907.15.41, 1911.16.43); de Julleville Hist 2.1 (see its bibliogr. 2.55); Ward
2.149, 272; Herbert 3.31; Ency Brit and Johnson's *Univ. Cyclop., s.v. Fable;*
Gröber 2¹.409, and Register at 1261; Krit Jahresber. Smith *The Fable and
Kindred Forms,* JEGP 14.519.

[23] ENGLISH FABLES. See Canby *Short Story in English* 34, 354;
and espec. Moll, Jacobs, Plessow, above.

II. Bestiaries

Bibliogr. of Physiologus, AnglBbl 10.274, 12.13, 338;— de Julleville
Hist 2.162 (see its bibliogr. 2.214); Gröber 2¹.136, 257, 322, 386, 483, 710, 727;
Krit Jahresber; Ency Brit; McKenzie *Unpub. MSS. of Ital. Bestiaries,*
PMLA 20.380; Lauchert *Gesch. des Physiologus,* Strassburg 1889 (crit.
LitBl 11.53; ZsfDPh 22.236; RevCrit New Ser. 27.464; ESt 14.123; Beitr.
zur Allg. Ztg. 1889, No. 339).

[24] BESTIARY. Ed. Wright *Altdeutsche Blättern,* 1837, 2.99; Rel Ant
1.208; EETS 49.1; AESprPr 1.55. Selections: Morris Spec 1.132; Cook
Reader 316. Mod. rend., parts, Weston *Chief M. E. Poets* 325; Shackford
Leg. and Sat. 101.— Brandl §21; Körting §78; Ten Brink 1.196; Schofield
336; Schipper §79.— Hallbäck *Lang. of M. E. Bestiary,* Lund diss. 1905.

III. Animal Tales

Jonckbloet *Étude sur le Roman de Renard,* Groningen 1863; *Ueber die
Thierbücher des Mittelalters,* Arch 55.241; Thoms. *Hist. of Reynard the
Fox,* Percy Soc. 12; P. Paris *Les Aventures de Maître Renard et d'Ysen-
grin,* Paris 1861; Kröhn *Bär und Fuchs,* Helsingfors 1888; Kröhn *Mann
und Fuchs,* Helsingfors 1889; Hist Litt 22; Gröber 2¹.409, 473, 626, 895;
Potvin *Le Roman du Renard,* Paris 1861; ZsfRPh 15.124, 374, 16.1;
Jacobs *Fables of Æsop,* L. 1889; Sudre *Les Sources du Roman de Renard,*
Paris 1892; G. Paris *Le Roman de Renard,* Paris 1895; Büttner *Stud. z. d.
Roman de Renart u. d. Reinhart Fuchs,* Strassburg 1891; Ward 2.368; de
Julleville Hist 2.14 (see its bibliogr. 55); Willems *Étude sur l'Ysengrimus,*
Paris 1895; Foulet *Le Roman de Renard,* Paris 1914 (crit. N. Y. Nation
99.751); McKnight *M. E. Humorous Tales* 85, bibliogr. of discussions and
editions; Krit Jahresber.— Fiske *Animals in Early Engl. Eccl. Lit.,* PMLA
28.368.

[25] FOX AND THE WOLF. Ed. Wright, Percy Soc. 8; Rel Ant
2.272; Hazlitt Rem 1.58; AESprPr 1.130; McKnight *M. E. Humorous
Tales* 25; Cook Reader 188. Mod. rend., Weston *Chief M. E. Poets* 275.—
Brandl §29; Körting §133; Ten Brink 1.258; Ward 2.388; Herbert 3.31
(see 39, 44, 47, etc.); Schofield 334. Canby *Short Story* 51; Skeat, on
writing of MS., MLQ 3.31; McKnight, PMLA 23.497. Gen. bibliogr.,
McKnight *M. E. Hum. Tales* 87.

[26] FALSE FOX. Ed. Rel Ant 1.4.

4. UNIFIED COLLECTIONS OF TALES

Ward and Herbert, *Vols.* 2 and 3.— English *Gesta Romanorum* ed. Madden, Roxb. Club 1838; EETSES 33.

[27] *SEVEN SAGES OF ROME.* For gen. bibliogr., see Campbell's ed. below.— English versions: Ed. Auch. with beg. and end of Cott., Weber MR 3.1 (coll. with MS., ESt 6.443);— Cbg. Dd, Wright, Percy Soc. 16 (coll. with MS., ESt 6.448);— Cott., Bannatyne Club 1837 (with var. of Rawl.); Campbell, Boston 1907 (crit. MLN 24.153). On Rawl., PMLA 14.459; on Asloan, ESt 25.321.— Specimen and analysis, Ellis Spec 405. Selections: Auch., AESprPr 1.254; Cook Reader 141;— Arundel, PMLA 14.94;— Rawl., PMLA 14.460;— Egerton, Petras *op. cit.* below, 54;— Cbg. Ff, Halliwell *Thornton Romances* xliii; Wright, Percy Soc. 16.lxx; Petras *op. cit.* 60. Mod. rend., parts, Weston *Chief M. E. Poets* 281.— Brandl §§36, 64; Ten Brink 1.261; Körting §117; Ward 2.199; Schofield 344.— Gröber 2¹.280, 321, 528, 605, 727, 991, 994; Krit Jahresber; G. Paris, *Deux Redactions des Sept Sages,* Paris 1876; Petras *Über die Me. Fassungen . . .* , Breslau diss., Grünberg 1886 (crit. Rom 14.631; ESt 10.279); Buchner *Historia Septem Sapientum* (with source of Scot. version), Erlangen 1889 (crit. ESt 25.321; Rom 19.494); Buchner *Beitr. zur Gesch. der Sieben Weisen Meistern,* Arch 113.297; Campbell *Study of Rom. of the Seven Sages with Spec. Ref. to the M. E. Versions,* Baltimore diss. 1898, and PMLA 14.1 (crit. ZsfVL 14.217; Rom 28.166; AnglBbl 10.38); Campbell *Source of Story of 'Sapientes,'* MLN 23.202; Fischer *Beitr. zur Lit. d. Sieben Weisen Meister,* Greifswald diss. 1902 (crit. Arch 113.29); Smith *Verse Version of the Sept Sages* (Fr.), RomRev 3.1.

CHAPTER III—CHRONICLES

Schofield 349; Gross, C., *Sources and Lit. of Engl. Hist.,* L. and N. Y., 2nd ed. 1915, *passim.*

[1] OLD ENGLISH CHRONICLE. Ed. Thorpe, Rolls Ser. 2 vols. 1861; Earle, 1865, revised Plummer and Earle, Oxf. 2 vols. 1892, 1899. Selections: Morris Spec. 1.9; Emerson Reader 1; Cook Reader 235. Mod. rend., Gomme, Bohn ed. 1909.— Körting §14 note, §67; Wülcker *Grundriss · · · Ags. Lit.* §507; Paul Grundriss 2nd ed. 2¹.1118 ff., 1078, 1083.

[2] PROSE FRAGMENT. Ed. Angl 1.195. See Angl 3.33. Paul Grundriss 2nd ed. 2¹.1125.

[3] LAYAMON'S BRUT. Ed. both MSS., Madden, L. 1847 (crit. Athen 1847.954; Qtrly Rev. 82.325; Gent's Mag. n. s. 28.273, 29.487, 600, 30.22). Selections: Thorpe *Anal. Anglo-Saxonica,* 1834, 154; Corson *Handbook of A. S. and E. Engl.,* 121; Kluge Lesebuch 61; Zupitza Übungsbuch; AESprPr 1.21; Morris Spec 1.64 (see Angl 25.318; MLN 1.137); Emerson

Reader 181; Cook Reader 219. Mod. rend. Arthur Material, Everyman's Libr. (crit. JEGP 11.486); selections, Weston *Chief M. E. Poets* 1.— Körting §81; Brandl §18; Ten Brink 1.187; Ward 1.268; Morley 3.202; Schofield 350; Cbg Hist 1.260; DNB; Courthope 1.124. Wright *Biogr. Brit. Lit.*, I.. 1846, 439; Kemble *Dialogue of Salomon and Saturnus*, L. 1848, 127; Bouterwek *Caedmon's Bibl. Dichtungen*, 1854, 1.lvi; Hardy, *J. D., Descr.. Cat.*, L. 1862, 1.352; PBBeitr 1.65, 66, 259; EETSES 4.xxx.— MSS. and Text: Zessach *Die Beiden Hdschr.* . . . , Breslau diss. 1888 (see JEGP 10.281); Luhmann *Die Überlieferung von L's Brut*, Halle diss. 1905, full print StEPhil 22 (crit. DLz 28.2725; JEGP 7.136; Neu Phil. Rundschau 1907.478; AllgLtbl 17.399); ESt 3.269, 4.96, 5.373; on Cott. 13857, Arch 114.164; Monroe in *Studies . . . in Celebration of 70th Birthday of J. M. Hart*, N. Y. 1910, 377; Bartels *Die Zuverlässigkeit der Hdschr. v. L's Brut u. ihr Verhältniss zum Original*, StEPhil 49 (see ESt 48.439; AnglBbl 25.296).— Date: Madden ed.; Imelmann *infra* 9.— *Verse*: Guest *Hist. Engl. Rhythms*, ed. Skeat, index; Angl 2.153; AnglAnz 5.111, 8.49; Kluge, PBBeitr 9.445; Zetsche *Ueber den Ersten Teil der Bearbeitung des 'Roman de Brut' des Wace durch Robert Mannyng of Brunne*, Leipzig diss. 1887, cap. 2; Regel *Allit. im L.*, Germ. Stud. 1.171; Schipper §67; Schipper *Grundriss* §34; Paul Grundriss 2¹.999; Hamelius *The Rhetorical Structure of L's Verse, Mélanges Godefroid Kurth*, Lüttlich 1908; Brandstädter *Stabreim u. Endreim in L's Brut*, Königsberg diss., Heidelberg 1912.—Sources: PBBeitr 3.524 (summary, Rom 7.148); Kölbing ed. *Arthour and Merlin*, cxxvii note; Fletcher on L. and Geoffrey of Monmouth, PMLA 18.91; Imelmann *Laʒamon, Versuch über seine Quellen*, Berlin diss. 1906 (crit. ZsfVL 16.488; AnglBbl 18.110; Arch 118.179; RevCrit 1907.pt.6); Brown *Welsh Traditions in L's Brut*, MPhil 1.95; Brown *Round Table before Wace*, HarvStN 7.183 (see Imelmann 23; crit. Rom 1900.634, 1901.1); Bruce *Some Proper Names in L's Brut*, MLN 26.65; Fletcher, HarvStN 10.*passim.*— Language: *his* for -*es* gen., Phil. Soc. Trans. 1864.28; pl. -*es* for -*en*, *ibid.* 57, 1865.75; inorganic *h*, Phil. Soc. Trans. 1865.90; Ellis *Early Engl. Pronunciation*, 1869, 2.496, 497; Hadley, *J., Essays Phil. and Crit.*, 1873, 233 (on poss. gen.); Fr. suffixes, Phil. Soc. Trans. 1895-8.399; *ie* sound, AJPhil 15.58; *æ* im L., ESt 2.118, 3.403; Regel *Spruch u. Bild in L's Brut*, Angl 1.197; *Das Paragogische n in L's Brut*, Angl 3.552; Sturmfels *Der Af. Vokalismus*, Angl 8.201; *Open and Close ē in L.*, Angl 16.380; Callenberg *L. u. Orm nach ihren Flexions-Verhältnissen Verglichen*, Arch 57.317 (Jena diss. 1876; see Germ 22.93); Lucht *Lautlehre der Älteren L.-Hdschr.*, Palæstra 49 (Berlin diss. 1905; crit. AllgLtbl 17.399; AnglBbl 17.227; Arch 119.449; JEGP 7.136; Neu Phil. Rundschau 1907.478); on verbs, Lange *Das Zeitwort in d. Beiden Hdschr. v. L's Brut*, Strassburg diss. 1906; Böhnke *Die Flexion des Verbums in L's Brut*, Berlin diss. 1906; Funke *Kasussyntax bei Orrm u. L.*, München diss. 1907; Hoffmann *Das Gram. Genus in L's Brut*, Halle diss. 1909, full print StEPhil 36 (see Arch 130.432); Luhmann *Die Überlieferung v. L's Brut nebst einer Darstellung d. Lat. Vok. u. Dipth.*, Halle diss. 1905, full print StEPhil 22; Monroe *French Words in L.*, MPhil 4.559; Kühl *Der Vokalismus der L.-Hs. B.*, Halle diss. 1913; Lichtsinn *Der Syntaktische Gebr. des Infinitivs in L's Brut*, Kiel diss. 1913.— Miscellaneous: Giles Galfredi Monumetensis *Hist.*

Brit., Caxton Soc. 1844, xix-xxiv; Kolbe *Schild, Helm u. Panzer zur Zeit L's*, Breslau diss. 1892 (see Jahresbericht 13.355); Krautwald *L's Brut Vergl. mit Waces Roman de Brut in Bezug auf der Darstellung der Kulturverhältnisse Englands*, Breslau diss. 1887 (see ESt 13.84); Hart, MLN 14.158; Fiske *Chess in Iceland*, 1905, 76; ll. 28320 ff. and *Hildebrandslied* ll. 63 ff., MLN 21.110; Seyger *Beiträge zu L's Brut*, Halle diss. 1912; on L's King Bladud, MLN 25.263, 26.127, N. Y. Nation Oct. 28, 1909, 404; Sayce *Y Cymmrodor* 10.207 (see *Hart Anniv. Vol.* 381); Langschur *Beiträge zur L.-Forschung*, prgr. Jägernsdorf 1913; Cook *L's Knowledge of Runic Inscriptions*, Scott Hist Rev 11.370.— On L. literature to 1908, JEGP 7.139.— On 'Brut' meaning 'chronicle,' Acad No. 1035.233.

[4] ROBERT OF GLOUCESTER'S RIMED CHRONICLE. Ed. Hearne, Oxf. 1724, repr. 1810, 2 vols.; Wright, Rolls Ser. 2 vols. 1887. Selections: AESprPr 1.155; Morris Spec 2.1; Wülcker Lesebuch 1.51; Emerson Reader 203. Mod. rend., selections, Weston *Chief M. E. Poets* 20.— Notes, Angl 26.364.— Körting §119; Brandl §32; Ten Brink 1.275; Schofield 358; Cbg. Hist 1.374; DNB.— *Verse:* Schipper §114; Trautmann, Angl 2.153; Rosenthal, Angl 1.414; Wissmann *King Horn*, Strassburg 1876; Pabst *infra* 12. Brossmann *Über die Quellen . . .*, Breslau diss., Striegau 1887; Ellmer *Über die Quellen . . .*, Halle diss. 1886, fuller in Angl 10.1, 291; on verbs, QF 63.16; Pabst *Die Sprache . . .*, Berlin diss. 1889 (crit. AnglBbl 1.92; LitBl 12.123); Pabst *Die Flexionsverhältnisse bei R. v. Gl.*, Angl 13.202, 245; Strohmeyer *Der Styl . . .*, Berlin 1891; Strohmeyer *Das Verhältniss der Hdschr.*, Arch 87.217. See Angl 10.308, 13.202.

[5] SHORT METRICAL CHRONICLE. Ed. Royal, Ritson AEMR 2.270, revised 3.18 (coll. with MS., ESt 15.249). Körting p. 135 anm. 2; Brandl §32; Schofield 361. Sternberg, ESt 18.1, 356. On verbs, QF 63.15.

[6] THOMAS BEK OF CASTELFORD'S CHRONICLE. Not edited. See Perrin *Ueber Th. C's Chronik von England*, Göttingen diss., Boston 1890. Brandl §55; Schofield 360; Cbg Hist 1.377.

[7] ROBERT MANNYNG OF BRUNNE'S RIMED STORY. Ed. Part 2, Hearne, Oxf. 1725, 2 vols.;— Part 1, Furnivall, Rolls Ser. 2 vols. 1889;— Lambeth to birth of Christ, Zetsche, Angl 9.43;— Rawl. fragm., ESt 17.166. Selections: AESprPr 1.297; Wülcker Lesebuch 1.61; Zupitza Übungsbuch. Mod. rend., selections, Weston *Chief M. E. Poets* 25.— Körting §120; Brandl §55; Ten Brink 1.297; Schofield 361; Cbg Hist 1.390; DNB, *Mannyng.*— Zetsche *Ueber den Ersten Teil der Bearbeitung . . . durch R. M.*, Leipzig diss. 1887; Preussner *R. M. of Br's Übersetzung von Pierre de Langtoft's Chronicle u. ihr Verhältnis zum Originale*, Breslau diss. 1891; Preussner *Zur Textkritik*, ESt 17.300; Thummig *Ueber die Me. Übersetzung der Reimchronik P. L's durch R. M. of Br.*, Leipzig diss. 1891 (also Angl 14.1); Hellmers *Über die Sprache R. M's u. über die Autorschaft der . . . Medit. on the Supper of our Lord*, Göttingen diss. 1885; Boerner *Die Sprache R. M. of Br's*, Göttingen diss. 1904, full print StEPhil 12 (crit. ESt 39.375; Arch 115.223; LitBl 1906.450). See Imelmann *Laӡamon*, Berlin diss. 1906, 104.

[8] THE BRUCE. Ed. Pinkerton, L. 1790; Jamieson, Edbg. 1820; Innes, Spalding Club, Aberdeen 1856, L. 1868; Skeat, EETSES 11, 21, 29, 55; Skeat, STS 31, 32, 33; MacKenzie, L. 1909 (with extensive bibliogr.). Selections: AESprPr 1.373; Morris Spec 2.203; Zupitza Übungsbuch; Mac-Lean Reader 107; Wülcker Lesebuch 2.60; Emerson Reader 165; Mac-Kenzie *Selections, for Schools*, 1909; Cook Reader 237; *et al.* Mod. rend., Eyre-Todd, G., Glasgow and L. 1907 (crit. ESt 40.103); Macmillan, M., Stirling 1914; selections, Weston *Chief M. E. Poets* 26.— Körting §121; Ten Brink 3.52; Brandl §76; Morley 6.2, 10, 41, 120; Schofield 317; Cbg Hist 2.101, 115, 127; Ency Brit, *Barbour;* DNB, *Barbour.*— See extensive bibliogr. in Geddie *Bibliogr. of. Mid. Scots Poets*, STS 61.61.— Bibliogr. notes, Scott. Notes and Queries Aug. 1895.— Baudisch *Ueber die Charaktere im Bruce*, Marburg prgr. 1886 (crit. ESt 11.308); Kolkwitz *Die Satzgefüge in Barbours Bruce u. bei Henry Wallace*, Halle diss. 1893; Henschel *Darstellung der Flexionslehre in J. B's Bruce*, Leipzig diss. 1886; Regel *Inquiry into the Phonetic Peculiarities of B's Br.*, prgr. Gera 1877; Craigie *B. and Blind Harry as Literature*, Scott. Rev. 22.173; Bearder *Über den Gebr. des Praepositionen*, Halle 1894; Heuser *Ai and ei . . . in der Cbg. Hds.*, Angl 17.91; Bain *Cal. of Documents relating to Scotland*, 3.ix; on the legends and Troy fragments, Angl 9.493, ESt 10.373, Athen 1897.1.279; Neilson *'Cornbote' in B's Bruce*, N&Q 9th Ser. 10.61, 115, 253; Neilson *John Barbour, Poet and Translator*, L. 1900 and Phil. Soc. Trans. 1900 (crit. ESt 30.281; Athen 1901.1.170; Scott Antiq 15.166; Hist. Rev. 1901.405); Neilson and J. T. T. Brown *J. B. vs. John Ramsay*, Athen 1900.2.647, 683, 725, 760; Brown *The Wallace and the Bruce Restudied*, Bonner Beitr 6 (crit. ESt 30.281; AnglBbl 11.336; Athen 1900.1.170; Arch 107.419; MLN 16.49; Ctbl 1901.1891; Rom 1900.292; Scott Antiq 15.166; MLQ 1902.73; DLz 1901.2331); *Barbour's Bruce and the Buik of Alexander*, Scott Antiq 16.206 (see Arch 107.419); *Sword of Bruce*, N&Q 10th Ser. 8.261, 334, 370; *The MS. Book of Cupar*, Athen 1901.1.147, 243; Mühleisen *Untersuchungen über die Verwandtschaft der Überlieferungen v. B's Bruce*, Bonn diss. 1912; Maxwell *Early Chronicles*, 1912, 234; Mühleisen *Textkritische, Metr. u. Gram. Untersuchungen v. B's Bruce*, Bonn 1913.— See under *Scottish Legends; Scottish Troy Fragments; Scottish Alexander Buik.* .

[9] TREVISA'S TRANSLATION OF HIGDEN. Ed. Babington and Lumby, Rolls Ser. 9 vols., 1865-86. Selections: AESprPr 2.243; Morris Spec 2.235; Wülcker Lesebuch 2.205; Emerson Reader 220.— Rolls ed., introd.; DNB, *Trevisa, Higden;* Körting §143; Brandl §67; Cbg Hist 2.82, 503.— On verbs, QF 63.37; Pfeffer *Die Sprache des Polychronicons John Trevisas* (Tiberius MS,), Bonn diss. 1912.— *Dial. betw. Master and Clerk*, Smith *Lives of the Berkeleys*, Vol. 1, ed. MacLean, Gloucester 1883.

[10] THE BRUT OF ENGLAND. Ed. Brie, EETS 131, 136 (crit. Ctbl 1906.429; DLz 1906.152; Arch 117.413).— On Lambeth 491, Arch 86.383.— Brie *Gesch. u. Quellen der Me. Prosachronik 'The Brute of England' oder 'The Chronicles of England,'* Marburg, N. G. Elwert 1905 (crit. AnglBbl 20.9; AllgLtbl 17.241).

CHAPTER IV—WORKS DEALING WITH CONTEMPORARY
CONDITIONS

1. POLITICAL PIECES

I. Non-Prophetic Writings

Wright PPS 1, introd.; Ten Brink 1.314; Courthope 1.185; Schofield
363, 368; Cbg Hist 1.411.

[1] SCRAPS IN MATTHEW PARIS. Ed. MLR 4.509.

[2] STANZA IN WYNTOUN. Print in Cbg Hist 2.116.— Brandl §58;
Murray *Dial. Sth. Scotl.* 28.

[3] PIECES IN FABYAN. Ed. Ellis *New Chronicles of England and
France by Robt. Fabyan,* L. 1811, 398, 420, 440. Arch 111.408; *Chronicon
de Lanercost,* ed. Stevenson, Edbg. 1838, 166; Hemingburgh's *Chronicle,*
ed. Hamilton, L. 1848, 2.99.

[4] PIECES IN MANNYNG AND LANGTOFT. Mannyng's *Chron-
icle,* ed. Hearne, Oxf. 1725, Pt. 2.266, 273, 276, 277, 278, 279, 281, 282, 330.
Langtoft's *Chronicle,* Rolls Ser. 2.222, 234, 244, 248, 252, 254, 260, 266, 364,
and Wright PS 275, 286, 292, 295, 298, 300, 305, 308, 318, 322.— Comparison
by Thummig, Angl 14.14.— Brandl §§55, 77; Schofield 363.— See Arch
111.408.

[5] SONG AGAINST THE KING OF ALMAIGNE. Ed. Wright PS
69; Böddeker 95; Percy *Reliques* Bk. 4, No. 1; Ritson AS (1877) 11;
AESprPr 1.152.— Ten Brink 1.314; Brandl §25; Schofield 364.

[6] SONG ON THE FLEMISH INSURRECTION. Ed. Wright PS
187; Ritson AS (1877) 44; Böddeker 112.— Brandl §35; Ten Brink 1.315;
Schofield 364.

[7] SONG ON EXECUTION OF SIR SIMON FRASER. Ed. Wright
PS 212; Ritson AS (1877) 25; Böddeker 121.— Brandl §35; Ten Brink
1.315; Schofield 364.

[8] ELEGY ON DEATH OF EDWARD I. Ed. Percy *Reliques* Bk. 4,
No. 2; Wright PS 246 (Fr. orig. at 241); Zupitza Übungsbuch; Böddeker
140 (Fr. orig. at 453);— fragments in Cbg 4407 (19), MLR 7.149.— Mod.
rend., Weston *Chief M. E. Poets* 32.— Brandl §45.

[9] SONG ON THE TIMES OF EDWARD II. Ed. Wright PS 195;
Kild Ged 131.— Brandl §28.

[10] ON THE KING'S BREAKING OF MAGNA CHARTA. Ed.
Wright PS 253; Wülcker Lesebuch 1.74.— Schofield 365; Ten Brink 1.318.

[11] PERS OF BIRMINGHAM. Ed. Ritson AS (1877) 60; Kild Ged
158.— Brandl §45.

[12] LAURENCE MINOT. Ed. Wright PPS 1.58; Scholle QF 52 (introd. Strassburg diss. 1884;— crit. ESt 8.162; LitBl 6.187; Angl 7.111); Hall, Oxf. 2nd ed. 1897, 3rd ed. 1915. Selections: AESprPr 1.320; Wülcker Lesebuch 1.77; Morris Spec 2.126; Zupitza Übungsbuch; Cook Reader 421.— Brandl §57; Körting §138; Ten Brink 1.322; Morley 4.258; Cbg Hist 1.398; Schofield 365.— Bierbaum *Über L. M. u. seine Lieder*, Leipzig diss. Halle 1876; Dangel *L. M's Gedichte*, Königsberg prgr. 1888; DNB, *Minot*.

[13] BATTLE OF HALIDON HILL. Ed. Hall ed. of Minot 39, 99-101;— see under *Brut of England*, page 795.— Schofield 367.

[14] ON THE DEATH OF EDWARD III. Ed. Addit. with var. of Vernon, Wright PPS 1.215;— Vernon, EETS 117.715; Cook Reader 425. On MSS., Angl 7.281. Liebau *König Edward III von England*, Angl Forsch 6.1901.— Brandl §82.

[15] LETTERS AND SPEECHES OF REBELS IN 1381. Ed. *Walsingham*, Rolls Ser. 2.33; Skeat *Piers Plowman*, Oxf. 1886, 2.lv; *Knighton*, Rolls Ser. 2.138; Maurice *Engl. Pop. Leaders*, 1875, 2.157; Trevelyan *England in Age of Wycliffe*, 3rd ed. 1900, 203.— Brandl §82.

[16] REBELLION OF JACK STRAW. Ed. Wright PPS 1.224; Rel Ant 2.283.

[17] ON KING RICHARD'S MINISTERS. Ed. Wright PPS 1.363; Archæol 21.

[18] SIEGE OF CALAIS. Ed. Rel Ant 2.21.

[19] FIFTEENTH-CENTURY PIECES. Ed. ESt 23.438; EETS 124; Wright PPS 2.— *Crowned King*, ed. EETS 54.523. Brandl §116; Körting §123 II.

II. Prophetic Writings

Taylor *Political Prophecy in England*, N. Y. 1911, with its bibliogr. at pp. 1-2 and in its notes (crit. ESt 46.137; RevCrit 74.409).— *Merlin Prophecies*, N&Q 9th Ser. 8.103, 234, 287, 386; Brandl §128; Ward 1.292.

[20] 'HATEST THOU URSE.' In William of Malmesbury *Gest. Pont.* Cap. 115. Morley 3.241; Paul Grundriss 2nd ed. 2¹.1096.

[21] HERE PROPHECY. Ed. Hales, Acad 1886.2.380 and *Folia Literaria 55*; Morley *Engl. Wr.* 3.200.— Brandl §19; Paul Grundriss 2¹.1010; Cbg Hist 1.242; Schofield 368.

[22] ADAM DAVY'S FIVE DREAMS. Ed. EETS 69.11; Emerson Reader 227.— Brandl §39; Schofield 367; Cbg Hist 1.397.— Taylor *Pol. Proph.* 92.

[23] PROPHECY OF THE SIX KINGS. Ed. Hall *Poems of L. Minot*, 2nd ed. 1897, 101;— *Brut* version, EETS 131.73; Halliwell's *Shakespeare* 9.401.— Ward 1.309; Taylor *Pol. Proph.* 4, 48, 99, 157, 160.

[24] BALLAD ON SCOTTISH WARS. Ed. Ritson AS (1877) 35;
Langtoft's *Chronicle*, Rolls Ser. 2.452.— Brandl §77; Ward 1.299; Hall's
Minot 76; Taylor *Pol. Proph.* 65.

[25] THOMAS OF ERCELDOUNE. Ed. Cbg. with coll. of Lincoln and
Cott., Jamieson *Pop. Ballads and Songs*, 1806;— Thornton suppl. from Cbg.,
Laing *Sel. Rem.*, 1822, revised by Hazlitt, L. 1895, 1.81;— Scott *Minstrelsy
of the Scottish Border;*— Cbg., Halliwell *Illustr. of Fairy Mythol. of Midsummer Night's Dream*, 1845;— Prophecy of birth of Edward, Rel Ant
1.30;— Thornton fitt 1, Child *Engl. and Scott. Ballads*, ed. 1882, 1.317;—
all texts, EETS 61; Brandl *Sammlung Englischer Denkmäler* 2, Berlin
1880. Selections: Cook Reader 70.— Brandl §77; Körting §124; Morley
3.280; Ward 1.328; DNB; Schofield 208, 368.— Angl 14.310; EETS 61.
introd.; Burnham *Study of T. of E.*, PMLA 23.375; Taylor *Pol. Proph.*
62; Saalbach *Entstehungsgeschichte der Schott. Volksballade Thomas
Rymer*, Halle diss. 1913 (crit. AnglBbl 24.366).— Mod. pageant, Dixon
Thomas the Rhymer, Glasgow 1911.

[26] PROPHECIES ASCRIBED TO À BECKET. Ed. Cbg., EETS
42.23;— Hatton (ll. 1-28) Taylor *Pol. Proph.* 165; (all) Arch 102.352.—
Brandl §73; AELeg 1881, 527; Hall's *Minot* 76; Taylor *Pol. Proph.* 58, 62.—
On verse, see *Alliteration*, page 800.

[27] TWO NORTHERN ALLITERATIVE PROPHECIES. Ed.
EETS 42.18, 32. Ward 1.312; Taylor *Pol. Proph.* 57; Brandl *The Cock in
the North*, Sitzungsber. d. Königl. Preuss. Akad. d. Wiss., Berlin 1909,
1160.— See under *Alliteration*, p. 800.

2. SATIRE AND COMPLAINT

Tucker *Verse Satire in England before the Renaissance*, N. Y. 1908 (see
its bibliogr. at pp. 228 ff.; crit. Ctbl 61.24; RevCrit 68.407; LitBl 31.318;
AnglBbl 21.2); Wright *Anglo-Latin Satirical Poets*, Rolls Ser. 2 vols.
1872; Fairholt *Satirical Songs*, Percy Soc. 27; Haessner *Die Goliardendich-
tung u. die Satire im 13Jhdt. in England*, Leipzig diss. 1905; Manitius *Die
Engl. Satire des 12Jhdts.*, Allgem. Zeitung, Beil. 1906.193; Wright *Latin
Poems Commonly Ascribed to Walter Mapes* 16; Wright PS and PPS;
Previté-Orton *Pol. Sat. in Engl. Poetry*, Cbg. 1910, 7-30.

I. Works Not in Alliterative Long Lines

[28] HWON HOLY CHIRECHE. Ed. EETS 49.89.— Brandl §16; Ten
Brink 1.316; Schofield 370; Cbg Hist 1.251; Tucker *Verse Sat.* 53; Wells ed.
Owl and Nightingale xix.

[29] LAND OF COCKAYGNE. Ed. Hickes *Thesaurus* 1.231; Furnivall
EEP 156; Wright *Altdeutsche Blättern* 1.396; AESprPr 1.147; Kild Ged
141. Selection: Cook Reader 367. Mod. rend., parts, Shackford *Legends
and Satires* 128; Weston *Chief M. E. Poets* 279; Ellis EEP 1.82.— Brandl
§29; Ten Brink 1.259; Morley 3.354; Körting §133; Schofield 325, 369, 461;

Tucker *Verse Sat.* 57; Cbg Hist 1.407.— Poeschel *Scharaffenland,* PBBeitr 5.381, 413.— French *fabliau,* ed. Barbazan *Fabliaux et Contes,* new ed. Méon, Paris 1808, 4.175.   Gröber 2¹.905; Hist Litt 23.149.

[30] SONG OF THE HUSBANDMAN.   Ed. Wright PS 149; Böddeker 100; Wülcker Lesebuch 1.71.— Brandl §28; Ten Brink 1.317; Cbg Hist 1.413; Schofield 369; Tucker *Verse Sat.* 60.— Mod. rend., Shackford *Legends and Satires* 131.   ESt 2.502, 17.297; Arch 90.144.

[31] AGAINST THE PRIDE OF LADIES.   Ed. Fairholt, Percy Soc. 27.40; Wright PS 153; Böddeker 105.— Brandl §28.

[32] ON THE RETINUES OF THE GREAT.   Ed. Wright PS 237 (cf. 153); Wülcker Lesebuch 1.73; Böddeker 134 (cf. 106).— Brandl §28; Schofield 369; Tucker *Verse Sat.* 62.

[33] SATIRE ON CONSISTORY COURTS.   Ed. Wright PS 155; Böddeker 107.— Brandl §57; Schofield 369; Tucker *Verse Sat.* 56.— On l. 64, ESt 3.102; on ll. 37 ff., MLN 2.70.

[34] SONG ON THE TIMES.   Ed. Wright PS 251.

[35] ON THE EVIL TIMES OF EDWARD II.   Ed. Wright PS 323; Percy Soc. 28.1.— Brandl §28; Ten Brink 1.318; Schofield 370; Tucker *Verse Sat.* 64.— Skeat ed. *Tale of Gamelyn,* Oxf. 1884, xii, 2nd ed. 1893.

[36] SONG OF NEGO.   Ed. Wright PS 210; Kild Ged 139.— Schofield 370.

[37] SATIRE ON THE PEOPLE OF KILDARE.   Ed. Rel Ant 2.174; Furnivall EEP 152; Kild Ged 150.— Brandl §28; Schofield 373; Cbg Hist 2.563; Tucker *Verse Sat.* 59.

[38] PRAISE OF WOMEN.   Ed. ESt 7.101; Arch 108.288 (with French source and bibliogr., nachtrag Arch 110.102;— crit. DLz 1902.1829).— Brandl §41; Schofield 486.— See ESt 7.386, 8.394, 11.216, 13.135, 19.149; Angl 13.358, 14.308.   Heider *Untersuchungen zur Me. Erotischen Lyrik,* Halle diss. 1905, 14.— See *Of Women's Horns,* Rel Ant 1.79; *What is Woman,* ibid. 1.168; *Song on Woman,* ibid. 1.248; *Praise of Women,* ibid. 1.275.

[39] TUTIVILLUS.   Ed. Rel Ant 1.257.

[40] MADDAMYS ALLE.   Ed. Rel Ant 2.117.

[41] SATIRE AGAINST THE BLACKSMITHS.   Ed. Rel Ant 1.240; Arch 101.395.— Brandl §41.

[42] AGAINST THE MINORITE FRIARS.   Ed. Rel Ant 1.322; Wright PPS 1.268; Angl 27.302 (see 283); Cook Reader 364.

[43] AGAINST THE FRIARS.   Ed. Wright PPS 1.263; Cook Reader 361.— Brandl §77.

[44] ON THE EARTHQUAKE OF 1382. Ed. Wright PPS 1.250.— Tucker *Verse Sat.* 93.

[45] ON THE TIMES. Ed. Harley, Fairholt, Percy Soc. 27.44;— Trinity and var., Wright PPS 1.270.— Brandl §77; Tucker *Verse Sat.* 93.

[46] DISTICH ON THE YEAR 1391. Ed. Wright PPS 1.278.

[47] NARRACIO DE DOMINO DENARII and SIR PENNY. Ed. Cott., Ritson APP 103; ESt 21.204;— Caius, Rel Ant 2.108;— Cott., Sloane, and Scottish version, Wright *Lat. Poems . . . W. Mapes* 359, 361, 362 (French version and Lat. orig., 355-6). Mod. rend., Cott., Shackford *Leg. and Sat.* 134.— Brandl §128; Schofield 372.

II.   Works in Alliterative Long Lines

On Middle English Alliterative *Verse*, Paul Grundriss 2nd ed. 2¹.160, see bibliogr. 177, 178; Schipper *Grundriss* §32; Angl 1.1, 414, 5.240, 10.105, 11.392, 553, 12.437, 13.140, 15.229, 18.83; AnglAnz 8.49; AnglBbl 5.87; ESt 16.169, 30.270, 34.99; Arch 105.304, 113.183; Bonner Beitr 11.1, 139, 12.103; Skeat in Hales and Furnivall *Percy Folio MS.*, 3.xi; Lawrence *Chapters on Allit. Verse*, London 1893; Kaluza *Stud. zum Germ. Alliterationsvers*, 1894, 1; Amours, STS 27; Cbg Hist 2.1; Deutschbein *Zur Entwicklung des Engl. Alliterationsverses*, Halle 1902; Pilch *Umwandlung des Ae. Allit.-Verses in den Me. Reimvers*, Königsberg 1904; Reiche *Untersuchungen über den Stil d. Me. Allit. Ged. . . . ,* Königsberg diss. 1906; Thomas *Die Allit. Langzeile des Gawaindichters*, Greifswald diss. 1908; Schuhmacher *Studien über den Stabreim in der Me. Alliterationsdichtung*, Bonn diss. 1913. See under [51] below; *Pearl Poet; Sir Gawayne and the Gr. Kt.*

For bibliogr. of works below, see Cbg Hist 2.491.

[48] WORCESTER CATHEDRAL FRAGMENT. Ed. Th. Phillips *Fragm. of Ælfric's Grammar*, 1838, 5; Angl 3.423; Wright *Biog. Brit. Lit.* 1.59.— Brandl §9; Paul Grundriss 2nd ed. 2¹.1133; Brüll *Ælfrics Lateingr.* 1904, 3; Arch 106.347.

[49] PARLEMENT OF THE THREE AGES. Ed. Gollancz, Roxb. Club 1897 (crit. ESt 25.273-89; Athen 1901.2.559); Gollancz, L. 1915.— See Cat. Br. Mus. Addit. MSS., MS. 33991.— Brandl §75; Cbg Hist 2.42; Schofield 316.— On verse, see *Alliteration*, above.— See under *Huchown Discussion.*

[50] WYNNERE AND WASTOURE. Ed. Gollancz in *Parl. of the Thre Ages*, 1897, 88 (ESt 25.273, discussion and abstract).— On date, Athen 1901.2.157, 254, 319, 351.— On verse, see *Alliteration*, above.— Schofield 372, 403; Cbg Hist 1.372, 2.42.

[51] VISION CONCERNING PIERS PLOWMAN. Ed. A-text, Skeat, EETS 28;— B-text, Crowley 1550, repr. 1561; Wright, L. 1842, 2 vols., rev. 1856, new ed. 1895; Skeat, EETS 38; Skeat Prol. and Passus I-VII,

Oxf. 9th ed.; *Davis* Prol. and Passus I-VII, Univ. Tutorial Ser. 1896;—
C-text, Whitaker, L. 1813; Skeat, EETS 54;— ABC-texts, Skeat, 2 vols. Oxf.
1886;— parallel extracts from 45 MSS., EETS 17. Crit. ed. of A-text in
preparation by Prof. Knott of Univ. of Chicago. Skeat notes and gloss
to the three texts, EETS 81. Skeat's eds. crit. RevCrit 1879. Nos. 44-5;
AJPhil 1887.347; Acad No. 769.70; Athen No. 3099.380; N&Q 7th Ser. 3.99;
Nth. Br. Rev. Apr. 1870.— Mod. rend., B-text Prol. and Passus I-VII,
Warren, L. and N. Y. 1895, repr. 1899, 1913 (crit. AnglBbl 6.166); Skeat,
Kings Classics, L. 1905; Everyman's Library;— A-text, and Prol. of B-text,
Weston *Romance, Vision and Satire* 239, 317.

Selections: Wülcker Lesebuch 2.76; Morris Spec 2.176; Cook Reader
334; *et al.*

Brandl §66; Körting §145; Morley 4.285; Ten Brink 1.351; Cbg Hist 2.1
(bibliogr. 2.491); Courthope 1.200.

MSS.: Skeat EETS 17, 28, 38, 81; Skeat Oxf. ed. 2. Facsimile of one
page of Laud Misc. 656, EETS 38; of Laud Misc. 581, Skeat *Twelve Facsimiles*, Oxf. 1892.— See Texts, below; Kron, General Studies, below.

Texts: Angl 15.222; MLR 3.171, 4.357, 5.1, 340; MLN 23.156, 231; Arch
100.155, 334; ESt 5.150; MPhil 12.389.

Argument: PMLA 9.403.

Verse: Schipper §95; Angl 1.414, 11.429, 13.140; Paul Grundriss 2nd
ed. 2.141-80; Schneider *Die Me. Stabzeile im 15 u. 16 Jhdt.*, Bonn diss. 1902
(Bonner Beitr. 12.102); MLR 4.478; Bonner Beitr 11.139; PFMS 3.xi. See
under *Alliteration* above, p. 800.

Language: Bernard *Gram. Treatise on the Lang. of W. L.*, Bonn diss.
1874; Wandschneider *Zur Syntax des Verbs in Langleys Vision*, Kiel diss.
1887 (crit. LitBl 8.518); Teichmann *Die Verbalflexion in W. L's Buch . . . ,*
Aachen prgr. 1887; Klapprot *Das End -e in W. L's Buch . . . Text B,*
Göttingen diss. 1891; Sellert *Das Bild in P. the Pl.*, Rostock diss. 1904;
Jones *Imaginatif in P. P.*, JEGP 13.583.

General Studies: Kron *William Langleys Buch von Peter dem Pfluger,*
Erlangen 1885, Chs. 1-2, Leipzig 1885 (crit. Acad No. 714.26; DLz 7.518);
Jusserand *Les Anglais au Moyen Âge, L'Épopée Mystique de Will. Lang-
land,* Paris 1893, Engl. trans. rev. 1894.

Education, Character, Views of Author; Reflection of Times: Jack
Autobiographical Elements in P. P., JGP 3.393; N&Q 7th Ser. 11.108, 235;
Hopkins *Char. and Opinions of W. L.*, Kansas Univ. Quar. Apr. 1894.234;
Hopkins *Education of W. L.*, Princeton Coll. Bull. Apr. 1895; Mensendieck
*Charakterentwicklung u. Ethisch-Theolog. Anschauungen des Verfassers
v. P. the P.*, Giessen diss., pr. L. and Leipzig 1900 (crit. AnglBbl 12.292;
DLz 1901.1434; ESt 31.285); Gebhard *Langlands u. Gowers Kritik der
Kirchlichen Verhältnisse ihrer Zeit*, Strassburg diss. 1911; Gunther *Eng-
lisches Leben im 14Jhdt. Dargestellt nach The Vision of W. . . . ,* Leipzig
diss. 1889; Traill *Social England* 2.225; Keiller *Infl. of P. P. on the Macro
Play Mankind*, PMLA 26.339. See Skeat eds., Jusserand, above.

Comparisons: with Dante, Courthope 1.160, 200; Bellezza *Langland and
Dante*, N&Q 8th Ser. 6.81;— Owen *Piers Plowman, A Comparison with
. . . French Allegories*, Univ. of London Press 1912, 1915; Traver *The Four
Daughters of God*, Phila. 1907, 147.

Miscellaneous: Bellezza *L's Figur des 'Plowman' in der Neuesten Engl.
Lit.*, ESt 21.325; Brown and Neilson on Huchown, see this bibliogr.,
p. 826; on source of B XVIII 1-68, Acad 1890.1.11.

Authorship Controversy: Hopkins *Who Wrote P. P.?* Kansas Univ. Quar.
Apr. 1898; Jack *Autobiographical Elements in P. P.*, JGP 3.393; Manly
The Lost Leaf of P. the P., MPhil 3.359; Bradley *The Misplaced Leaf of
P. the P.*, Athen 1906.1.481; Bradley *The Word 'Moillere,'* MLR 2.193;
Manly *Piers the Plowman and its Sequence*, Cbg Hist 2.1; *same*, reissued
with forewords by Manly, Bradley, Furnivall, EETS Extra Issue 135b;
Hall *Was 'Langland' the Author of the C-Text of 'The Vision of P. P.'?*
MLR 4.1; Jusserand *P. P. the Work of One or of Five*, MPhil 6.271 (see
CritRev 67.485); *same*, reissued EETS Extra Issue 139b; Chambers and
Grattan *The Text of P. P.*, I, *The A-Text*, MLR 4.357; Manly *The Author-
ship of P. P.*, MPhil 7.83; *same*, reissued EETS Extra Issue 139c; Deakin
The Alliteration of P. P., MLR 4.478; Jusserand *Piers Plowman, The Work
of One or of Five—A Reply*, MPhil 7.289; *same*, reissued EETS Extra
Issue 139d; Chambers *The Authorship of P. P.*, MLR 5.1; Bradley *The
Authorship of P. P.*, MLR 5.202; the preceding two articles, reissued
EETS Extra Issue 139e; Mensendieck, ZsfVL 18.10; Hall *The Misplaced
Lines, P. P.*, MPhil 7.327; Macaulay *The Name of the Author of P. P.*,
MLR 5.195; Mensendieck *The Authorship of P. P.*, JEGP 9.404; Dobson,
Marg., *An Examination of the Vocabulary of the 'A-Text,'* Angl 33.391;
Chambers *The Original Form of the 'A-Text,'* MLR 6.302; Owen *Piers
Plowman*, L. 1912, *passim*; Bradley *Who Was John But?* MLR 8.88;
Rickert *John But, Messenger and Maker*, MPhil 11.107; Moore *Studies in
Piers Plowman*, MPhil 11.177, 12.19; Lawrence, crit. of Cbg Hist Vol. 2,
JEGP 8.607; Brown *The 'Lost Leaf' of 'P. the P.,'* N. Y. Nation Mar. 25,
1909; Knott *The 'Lost Leaf'* . . . , N. Y. Nation May 13, 1909; Knott
The A-Version . . . , MPhil 12.389.

[52] COMPLAINT OF THE PLOUGHMAN or PLOUGHMAN'S
TALE. Ed. Thynne's *Chaucer* 2nd ed. 1542, *et al.;* Wright PPS 1.304;
Skeat Oxford Chaucer 7.149. Date, etc., Athen 1902, July 12. Hammond
Chaucer Bibliogr. 444, 540. Brandl §68; Cbg Hist 2.44, 491, 494; Ten Brink
2.204.— *Jack Upland.* Ed. Gough 1536 or 1540; Speght's *Chaucer* 1602;
Wright PPS 2.16; Skeat Oxf. Chaucer 7.191. Cbg Hist 2.45, 494.— *Reply
of Friar Daw Thopias* and *Rejoiner of Jacke Upland.* Ed. Wright PPS
2.39; *Friar Daw*, ed. Cook Reader 336. Cbg Hist 2.45, 494.— *Crowned
King.* Ed. Skeat, EETS 54.523. Cbg Hist 2.46, 494.— *Death and Liffe.* Ed.
PFMS 1.199. See AnglBbl 23.157. Cbg Hist 2.46, 494.— *Scottish Feilde.*
Ed. PFMS 3.49. Mod. rend., Arber's *Dunbar Anthol.*, Oxf., 126. Cbg
Hist 2.46, 494.

[53] PIERCE THE PLOUGHMAN'S CREDE. Ed. Wolfe, L. 1553;
Rogers, L. 1561; Wright ed. *Piers Plowman, q.v.;* Skeat, EETS 30; Skeat
Spec. 3.1; Skeat, Oxf. 1906.— Selection: Cook Reader 352.— Brandl §68;
Ten Brink 2.201; Körting §146; Cbg Hist 2.44, 493. Verse 372, MLR
4.235.— See under *Alliteration*, page 800.

[54] RICHARD THE REDELESS. Ed. Wright, Camden Soc., 1838; Wright PPS 1.368; Skeat, EETS 54.469; Skeat Oxf. ed. *Piers Plowman* 1.603.— Brandl §66; Körting §122; Ten Brink 2.202; Cbg Hist 2.41, 493.— Title, Athen 1906.1.481. Verse, Angl 1.420, 11.438. Ziepel *The Reign of Richard II and Comments upon an Alliterative Poem* . . . , Berlin 1874 (crit. Ctbl 1874.1051; Acad 1874.1.640, 2.322).— See under *Alliteration,* page 800.

CHAPTER V—HOMILIES AND LEGENDS

See Horstmann AELeg 1881, introd.

1. SERMONS OR HOMILIES

Mosher *The Exemplum in England,* N. Y. 1911, 44 ff. and its bibliogr. (crit. MLN 27.213; ESt 47.81; AllgLtbl 27.213; Ctbl 63.1322; RevCrit 74.409; AnglBbl 24.4); de Julleville Hist 2.216 ff. and its bibliogr. at p. 269; Crane *Med. Sermon-Books and Stories,* Amer. Phil. Soc. Proc. 1883, No. 114.49; Schofield 379; Ten Brink 1.199, 211, 280. See above, Ch. II head.

I. Independent or Isolated Sermons or Homilies

[1] HALI MEIDENHAD. Ed. EETS 18.— Brandl §15; Körting §74; Ten Brink 1.199; Schofield 380; Cbg Hist 1.254, 259.— See under *Katherine; Margaret; Juliana;* below.

[2] SAWLES WARDE. Ed. first version, EETS 34.245; Wagner (diss. 1907), Bonn 1908 (crit. AnglBbl 23.65). Selection: Morris Spec 1.87 (see Angl 25.319).— Ed. second version, EETS 23.263.— Brandl §15; Körting §74; Ten Brink 1.204; Schofield 386; Cbg Hist 1.252, 396.— Williams *Lang. of S. W.,* Angl 29.413; Konrath, ESt 12.459; Vollhardt *Einfluss d. Lat. Geistl. Lit.,* Leipzig 1888, 26 (crit. Angl 11.349; espec. ESt 13.79).

[3] LUTEL SOTH SERMUN. Ed. EETS 49.186; Wright, Percy Soc. 11.80.— Brandl §20; Ten Brink 1.211; Schofield 385.

[4] A SARMUN. Ed. Furnivall EEP 1; AESprPr 1.115; Kild Ged 88.— Brandl §27; Schofield 461.

[5] SPECULUM GY. Ed. EETSES 75 (crit. LitBl 10.330; AnglBbl 11.290; ESt 28.431); Yksh Wr 2.24.— Körting §144 note 2; Schofield 389.— Weyrauch *Die Me. Fassungen der Saga von G. of W.,* Breslau diss. 1899.

[6] LUYTEL SARMOUN OF GOOD EDIFICACIOUN. Ed. EETS 117.476.— Schofield 483.

[7] SERMO IN FESTO CORPORIS CHRISTI. Ed. 3 MSS., Arch 82.167; EETS 98.169.— Brandl §62; Schofield 389.

[8] SEVEN MIRACLES. Ed. EETS 98.198, 123.309. AELeg 1881, lxviii, lxxiii, lxxxii.

. [9] SERMON AGAINST MIRACLE-PLAYS. See under *British Museum Additional 24202 Tracts* below, page 843.

[10] FEAST OF ALL SAINTS. Ed. Arch 79.435.

II. Groups or Cycles of Sermons or Homilies

[11] BODLEY HOMILIES. Ed. EETS 137 (with trans.).

[12] LAMBETH HOMILIES. Ed. EETS 29.1.— Selections: Morris Spec 1.17 (see Angl 25.317); Zupitza Übungsbuch; MacLean Reader 59.— Brandl §20; Körting p. 144 note; Ten Brink 1.156; Cbg Hist 1.244.— Vollhardt *op. cit.* 18; Cohn *Die Sprache in* . . . , Berlin diss. 1880; Mosher *Exemplum* 44.— *Pater Noster*, see other refs., pp. 816-7.

[13] TRINITY COLLEGE HOMILIES. Ed. EETS 53.3;— Items 15-8, Morris Spec 1.26 (see Angl 25.318); Items 3 and 27, Rel Ant 1.128; AESprPr 2.42.— Crit. notes, ESt 15.306.— Krüger *Spr. u. Dialekt der Me. Hom. in d. Hds. B. 14. 32* . . . , Erlangen diss. 1885; Vollhardt *op. cit.* 6.67; Mosher *op. cit.* 44.— Körting p. 144 note.

[14] THE ORMULUM. Ed. White, Oxf. 1854, 2nd ed. Holt, Oxf. 1878, 2 vols. (crit. ESt 2.494). Coll. of MS., ESt 1.1 Selections: Morris Spec 1.39; AESprPr 1.1; Zupitza Übungsbuch; MacLean Reader 63; Sweet *First M. E. Primer* (with grammar).— Brandl §23; Körting §72; Ten Brink 1.193; Schofield 382; Cbg Hist 1.246, 419, 432; Morley 3.232; Mosher *op. cit.* 49.— Monicke *Notes and Queries on the ·O.*, Einladungsschrift, Leipzig 1853.— Author and Name: Arch 117.28, 119.33, 123.23.— Date: Athen 1906.1.609, 2.43, 73, 104.— Sources: ESt 6.1.— Versification: Schipper Engl. Metr. 101; Paul Grundriss (ed. 1) 2¹.1047; Menthel, AnglAnz 8.73; Saintsbury *Hist. Engl. Pros.* 1.38.— Orthography: AnglAnz 7.94, 208, 18.371; Acad Feb. 25, 1890; Effert *Einfache u. Doppelte Kons. im O.*, Bonn diss. 1885 (cp. Angl as above, and ESt 9.113); Sachse *Das Unorganische e im O.*, Halle diss. 1881 (crit. ESt 6.266, 9.113); Bülbring *Die Schreibung eo*, Bonner Beitr 17 (crit. Neu Phil. Rundschau 1906.329; MLN 22.250); Bülbring, AnglBbl 17.135; Lambertz *Die Spr. des O. nach d. Lautl. Seite Untersucht*, Marburg diss. 1904; Napier *Hist. of the Holy Rood-Tree*, L. 1893 (crit. ZsfDA 39.1; Arch 92.7; AnglBbl 5.98; Gött. Gel. Anz. 1894. No. 12; AnzfDA 21.61); Callenberg *Layamon u. Orm nach ihren Lautverhältnissen Verglichen*, 1876; Björkmann *Orrms Doppelkonsonanten*, Angl 37.351; McKnight *O's Double Cons. Again*, ESt 26.455; Napier *Notes on the Orthogr. of O.*, Acad Mar. 15, 1890, repr. with alterations Oxf. 1893; Deutschbein *Die Bedeutung der Quantitätszeichen beim O.*, Arch 126.49, 127.308.— Language: Sweet *First· M. E. Primer* (grammar); Kluge *Das Frz. Element im O.*, ESt 22.179; Brate *Nordische Lehnwörter* im O., PBBeitr 10.1; Henrici *Otfrids Mutter u. Orrms Bruder*, ZsfDA 22.231; Weyel *Der Syntakt. Gebr. des Infin. im O.*, prgr. Meiderich 1896; Reichmann *Die Eigennamen im O.*, StEPhil 25 (see AllgLtbl 17.399); Holthausen

Wel and Well im O., AnglBbl 13.16; Zenke *Syn. u. Anal. des Verbums im O.*, Göttingen diss., Halle 1910, StEPhil 40 (crit. JEGP 10.646; Arch 131.461); Thüns *Das Verbum bei O.*, Leipzig diss. 1909; Funke *Kasus-Syntax bei Orm u. Laʒamon*, München diss. 1907.

[15] FIVE KENTISH SERMONS. Ed. EETS 49.26;— Items 1 and 2, Morris Spec 1.141 (see Angl 25.320); Item 2, Zupitza Übungsbuch; Mac-Lean Reader 81.— Brandl §1; Morsbach *Me. Gram.* 10; Körting p. 145 note; Ten Brink 1.283; Cbg Hist 1.246. On verbs, QF 63.24.

[16] COTTON VESPASIAN HOMILIES. Es. EETS 34.216;— *Bispel*, Morris Spec 1.1 (see Angl 25.316).— Brandl §15; Körting §74; Schofield 386, 459.— On *Bispel*, Vollhardt *op. cit.* 24; ESt 13.79.

[17] WYCLIFFE'S HOMILIES. See below, page 842.

2. Collections or Cycles of Homilies and Legends
Intermixed

See espec. AELeg 1881, introd. Schofield 379, 389; Ten Brink 1.264.

[18] NORTHERN HOMILY CYCLE. See AELeg 1881, lvii-lxxxix; AELeg 1875, iii note; Retzlaff *Untersuchungen über den Nord. Legenden-cyklus des MSS. Harl. 4196 u. Cott. Tib. E VII*, Berlin diss. 1889; Gerould *The North Engl. Homily Collection*, Oxf. diss. 1902 (see its bibliogr.;— crit. JGP 4.542; LitBl 28.242; DLz 1906.992); Gerould, source of orig. homilies, MLN 22.95 and ESt 47.84; Weber, O., *Lang. of the Metr. Homs.* (Small's ed.), Bern diss. 1902; on Addit. 38010, Herbert 3.715; on Harl. and Tib., Herbert 3.331; Wetzlar *Spr. sowie Glossar d. Nordengl. Homi-liensammlung d. Edbg. Royal Coll. of Phys.*, Freiburg diss. 1907; Foster *The Mystery Plays and the 'Northern Passion,'* MLN 26.169; Foster *A Study of the M. E. Poem . . . 'The Northern Passion,'* Bryn Mawr diss., London and Bungay 1914; on Tale 38, *Hermit and St. Oswald*, Gerould, PMLA 20.529 and *Nth Engl. Hom. Coll.* 73-5.— Brandl §62; Ten Brink 1.290; Körting §130AII; Cbg Hist 1.379; Schofield 384.

Editions: Royal Coll., Small *Engl. Metr. Homilies*, Edbg. 1862; 2 items, AESprPr 1.278; 2 items (coll. with Gg), Morris Spec 2.83; *Signs of Doom*, Emerson Reader 148;— Ashmole 42 and Gg, *Alexius*, AELeg 1881, 174;— Cbg. Dd, *Erasmus*, Arch 62.413;— Ashmole 42, *Peter and Paul*, AELeg 1881, 77;— Vernon, *Proprium Sanctorum*, Arch 81.82, 299; *Narrationes* from *Temporale*, Arch 57.241 (see AELeg 1875, xxvi note); *Theophilus*, ESt 1.16;— Harl. 4196 and Tib., *Proprium Sanctorum* (exc. Items 9, 12, 15), AELeg 1881, 1 (see DLz 1881.754; AnzfDA 8.98; LitBl 2.397; ZsfdöGymn 1882.684); *Barlaam and Josaphat*, AELeg 1875, 226; *Cecilia*, Lovewell, YSt 1898 (crit. ESt 26.394), mod. rend. Weston *Chief M. E. Poets* 72;— Harl. 4196, *Cecilia*, ESt 1.235 (text-notes, AnzfDA 4.252); selections, Angl 27.290; *Story of Rood, De Invencione S. Crucis, De Festo Exaltacionis*, EETS 46.62, 87, 122; from *Passion*, Arch 57.78;— *In Festo Corporis Christi*, Vernon, Harl. 4196, Dd, EETS 98.169; Arch 82.167;—

Theophilus, Vernon, Harl. 4196, Tib., ESt 1.16 (see 1.186, 2.281); see Kölbing *Beitr. zur Gesch. d. Rom. Poesie u. Prosa des Mittelalters,* Breslau 1870;— *Northern Passion,* text of Dd, Addit. 31042, Gg V 31, Harl. 4196, and collations of Ii IV 9, Ff, Gg I 1, Ashmole 61, Tib., Foster EETS 145 and 147.

[19] SOUTHERN LEGEND COLLECTION. See AELeg 1881, xliv-lvii; AELeg 1875, i-xxxvii; EETS 87. vii-l; on Stowe, Angl 7.405; on Corpus and Tanner, Angl 1.392; on Laud, Arch 49.395 and EETS 87. introd.; Mohr *Sprachliche Untersuchungen zu den Me. Legenden aus Gloucestershire,* Bonn diss. 1889; Knörk *Untersuchungen über die Me. Magdalen-Legende,* Laud 108, Berlin diss. 1889; Schmidt, Wm., *Über den Stil der Legenden des MS. Laud 108,* Halle diss. 1893;— Brandl §110; Körting §130; Ten Brink 1.268; Schofield 393; Cbg Hist 1.378.

On *Brandan:* Schirmer *Zu Brandanuslegende,* Leipzig 1888 (espec. Celtic; see Angl 11.327; Rom 18.203); Zimmer *Brendans Meerfahrt,* ZsfDA 33.129, 257; Goeje *La Légende de S. Brandan,* Leyden 1890; Steinweg *Die Hdschrl. Gestaltungen d. Lat. Navigatio Brandani,* Halle diss. 1891; O'Donoghue *Brendaniana, St. Brendan the Voyager in Story and Legend,* Dublin 1893; Kleinschmidt *Das Verhältnis des 'Baudouin de Sebourc' zu dem 'Chevalier au Cygne,' 'Marco Polo,' 'Brandan,'* . . . , Göttingen diss. 1908; Balz *Die Me. Brendanlegende des Gloucester Legendars,* Berlin diss. 1909; Brown, A. C. L., *St. Brandan and the Sea-God Bran,* prgr. MLA 1914. Ward 2.516. Gröber 2¹. Register, *Brendan.*

On *Barlaam and Josaphat:* Ward 2.111; Jacobs *Barlaam and Josaphat, Engl. Lives of Buddha,* L. 1896 (see appendices for bibliogr.;— N&Q 8th Ser. 9.320); Unger, ed. *Barlaams ok Josaphats Saga,* Christiania 1851; Liebrecht *Die Quellen des B. u. J.,* JbREL 2.314; Conybeare *The B. and J. Legend,* Folk-Lore 7.2; Braunholz *Die Erste Nichtchristliche Parabel des B. u. J.,* Halle diss. 1884; Kuhn, Abhdl. Bav. Akad. Science, Munich 1893 (extensive bibliogr.); Kuhn, Acad 1896.1245-6; Kleinschmidt *Das Verhältnis des 'Baudouin de Sebourc'* . . . , Göttingen diss. 1908; Heuchenkamp *Die Prov. Prosa-Redaktion . . . B. u. J.,* Halle 1912.— Brandl §§48, 71.— See under *Northern Homily Cycle, English Prose Translation of Legenda 1438, Caxton's Golden Legend.*— Gröber 2¹. Register.

On *Cecilia:* Lovewell, YSt 1898.
On *George:* see under *George,* p. 810.
On *Guthlac:* Bönner Beitr 12.

Editions: Laud 108, whole, EETS 87 (see Angl 11.543); *Passion,* Horstmann *Leben Jesu,* Münster, Regensburg 1873 (see AELeg 1875, xi note; on verbs, QF 63.21); *Childhood of Jesus,* AELeg 1875, 1 and Arch 82.107 (see Brandl §31); *Alexius,* Arch 51.101; *Magdalen,* AELeg 1878, 148;— see below *Brandan, Cuthbert, Purgatory of St. Patrick;*— mod. rend. of *Brandan,* Weston *Chief M. E. Poets* 57.

Laud 108 and Bodley 779, *Cuthbert,* Surtees Soc. 87 (1889).

Harley 2277, Items in Furnivall EEP as follows, *Barnabus* 34, end of *Theophilus* 40, 42, *Dunstan, Swithin* 43, *Kenelm,* end of *Miracle of St. James* 57, *Christopher* 59, *The 11000 Virgins* 66, *Edmund the Confessor* 71, *Edmund the King* 87, *Katherine* 90, first part of *Andrew* 98, *Lucy* 101,

Miracle of St. John 106, *Judas* 107, *Pilate* 111;— last of *Michael*, Wright
Pop. Treatises on Science 132 (see *Fragment on Popular Science, infra*, p.
835);— *Becket*, Black for Percy Soc. 1845 (on verbs, QF 63.21); AESprPr
1.177; mod. rend., *Chief M. E. Poets* 41;— *Brandan*, with de Worde's 1527
ed. from trans. of *Legenda*, Wright, Percy Soc. 48 (1844);— *Dunstan* and
Christopher, AESprPr 1.171, 194;— *Dunstan*, Morris Spec 2.19 (on verbs,
QF 63.21); mod. rend., *Weston op. cit.* 37;— *Katherine, Judas*, Wülcker
Lesebuch 1.12, 18;— *Margaret*, EETS 13.24.

Ashmole 43, *Juliana*, EETS 51.81;— *Advent*, AELeg 1875, 64;— *Cecilia*,
Lovewell, YSt 1898; Furnivall *Orig. and Anal. of Some of the Canterbury
Tales*, ChS 2ser. 10.208;— see below under *Brendan; Birth of Jesus;
Purgatory of St. Patrick*.

Ashmole 43 and Egerton, *Birth of Jesus*, AELeg 1875, 64.— Brandl §31.

Cotton Julius D IX, see below under *Purgatory of St. Patrick; Guthlac*.

Egerton, *Advent and Christmas Gospels*, AELeg 1875, 65;— see below
under *Purgatory of St. Patrick*.

Vernon, *Alexius*, Arch 56.394;— *Barlaam and Josaphat*, AELeg 1875,
215 (Brandl §48);— *Gregory*, Arch 55.407; *Susanna*, Angl 1.85.

Lambeth 223, and Trinity Cbg., *Magdalen*, Arch 68.52 (Brandl §31).

Bodley 779, later addits. Items 67-108 incl., exc. 70, 74, 77, 80, 83-4, 86,
90-1, Arch 82.307, 369;— *Barlaam and Josaphat*, AELeg 1875, 113 (Brandl
§71; notes, Angl 14.318);— *Margaret*, Arch 79.411 (see AELeg 1881, 489,
225);— *Cecilia*, Lovewell *op. cit.;— Cuthbert*, Surtees Soc. 87 (1889; with
Laud 108);— see below under *Guthlac*.

Laud L 70 (*i.e.*, 463; see AELeg 1875, xxxii), *Celestyn*, Angl 1.55 (text-
notes, Angl 14.310;— Brandl §71).

Laud L 70 and Trinity Oxf., *Alexius*, Arch 56.401.

Purgatory of St. Patrick, Ashmole 43, Cott. Jul., Egerton, Laud 108,
AELeg 1875, 151. See page 815.

Brendan, Balz *Die Me. Brendanlegende des Gloucester-Legendars*, Berlin
diss. 1909.

Guthlac Bodley, Cott. Jul., 26 ll. of Corpus, Bonner Beitr 12.18;— Cott.
ll. 1-24, 105-24, and Corpus ll. 1-24, Birch *Mem. of St. Guthlac;— see
AELeg 1875, xxvi, xxxiv; Angl 1.392; Bonner Beitr 12, for general acct.

[20] FESTIAL OF JOHN MIRK. Ed. whole, EETSES 96;— *Alkmund*, AELeg 1881, cxxiv;— *Wenefreda*, Angl 3.314. General, MSS., contents, AELeg 1881, cviii-cxxvii. Angl 3.293.— On Harl. 1288 and 2250,
Herbert 3.681, 705. Mosher *Exemplum* 107.— Brandl· §72; Körting §130
IV; Schofield 395; DNB, *Mirk*.

. 3. LEGENDS

AELeg 1875 and 1878 (crit. LitBl 2.397; ESt 3.125; ZsfdöGymn 31.152,
392), AELeg 1881 (crit. ZsfdöGymn 33.684; Angl 5.21), introds.; EETS
87. introd.; Horstmann *Leben Jesu*, Berlin 1873, introd. Lovewell *Life of
St. Cecilia*, YSt 1898, has at p. 132 a bibliogr. of Legends (crit. ESt 26.394).
Körting §130.— Gröber 2¹.Register p. 1266 *Heiligenleben*, p. 1271 *Legenden,
Legendensammlung*, p. 1274 *Mirakel, Mirakelsammlung;* Krit Jahresber.

I. Collections or Groups of Legends

[21] SMALLER *VERNON* COLLECTION. Ed. Items 1-7 with Latin orig., AELeg 1878, 3;— *Barlaam and Josaphat,* AELeg 1875, 215;— *Eufrosyne,* ESt 1.300; AELeg 1878, 174. AELeg 1881, lxxxix-lx and note; AELeg 1875, xxiv.

[22] SCOTTISH COLLECTION. Ed. Horstmann, Heilbronn 1881-2, 2 vols., Item 29 omitted, but printed AELeg 1881, 189 (crit. LitBl 2.397, 3.398, 101, 5.102); Metcalfe, STS 1896, 3 vols.;— *Alexius,* Arch 62.397;— *Machor,* AELeg 1881, 189;— *Cecilia,* Lovewell, YSt 1898;— *Ninian and Machor,* Metcalfe, Paisley 1906.— AELeg 1881, lxxxix.— Brandl §76; Körting §130; Schofield 394; Cbg Hist 2.119, 146.— Fiby *Zur Laut- u. Flexionslehre in B's Schott. Legenden,* Brunn 1889;— Dublin Rev. April 1887; Bearder *Über den Gebr. der Praepositionen,* Halle 1894 (*John, Cecilia*). Author: Angl 9.493; ESt 10.373; Baudisch *Ein Beitrag zur Kenntnis der Früher Barbourzugeschr. Legendensammlung,* Prgr. d. Offentl. Unterrealschule in Wien 1903 (see ESt 35.103);— see under *Barbour's Bruce,* p. 795, and Huchown Discussion, p. 826. See Prothero *Memoir of H. Bradshaw,* London 1888, 143, and Addendum xi.

[23] LEGENDS BY LYDGATE. On MSS., eds. etc., see MacCracken *The Lydgate Canon,* EETSES 107. introd. Items 67, 74, 110, 113 (ed. p. 193), 116, 119 (ed. p. 145), 120 (ed. p. 161), 123 (ed. p. 173), 126 (ed. p. 154).

[24] LEGENDA AUREA. Latin of Jacobus, ed. Graesse, Dresden and Leipzig 1846, 2nd ed. 1850.— See Tiedemann, Palæstra 87.

[25] ENGLISH PROSE TRANSLATION OF LEGENDA, 1438. Ed. *Barlaam and Josaphat,* Horstmann, Sagan 1887 (crit. ESt 3.190;— see Arch 62.233). AELeg 1881, cxxx; Körting §130 A VI; RomRev 2.323.

[26] CAXTON'S PROSE GOLDEN LEGEND. Ed. part reprod. of ed. of 1483, Holbein Soc. 1878; Ellis, Kelmscott Press 1892, 3 vols.; *Winifred,* Angl 3.293 (see Angl 4.310);— *Catherine of Senis,* Arch 76.33, 265, 353;— *The Cross,* EETS 46.154, 161;— *Barlaam and Josaphat,* Jacobs, L. 1896. Mod. rend., Temple Classics, L., 7 vols.; *Brandan* and *Margaret,* Shackford *Legends and Satires* 53, 73.— AELeg 1881, cxxxv; Butler, P., *Legenda Aurea: A Study of C's G. L. with Spec. Ref. to its Rel. to the Earlier Engl. Prose Trans.,* Baltimore 1899 (crit. AnglBbl 14.360).

[27] OSBERN BOKENAM'S LIVES OF SAINTS. Ed. Roxb. Club 1835; Horstmann, Heilbronn 1883 (crit. ESt 7.143; ZsfdöGymn 1885.121; DLz 33.1162).— Brandl §110; Körting §130 A V; DNB.— AELeg 1881, cxxviii; Hoofe *Lautuntersuchungen,* ESt 8.209; Willenberg *Die Quellen v. O. B's Leg.,* Marburg diss. 1888 (see ESt 12.1); Horstmann *Über O. B. u. seine Legendensammlung,* Wiss. Beilage zum Prgr. des Königstädtischen Realgymn., Berlin 1883.

[28] DOUCE GROUP. Ed. Angl 8.102.— On Belgian Saints, Angl 8.103 note; on St. Elizabeth, source and text, Angl 39.356.

[29] NOVA LEGENDA ANGLIÆ.   Ed. Horstmann, Oxf. 1891, 2 vols.— Capgrave's *Katherine*, EETS 105.   Brandl §110.

[30] STOWE LIVES OF WOMEN SAINTS.   Ed. EETS 86.

II. Legends Treated in at least One Separate Piece

See statement in the text, page 308.

A. Legends of Saints

[31] ALEXIUS.   Ed. Vernon, Laud 108, Naples, Schipper QF 20 (crit. ESt 2.489);— Laud L 70 (*i.e.*, 463), Schipper *Die Zweite Version der Alexiuslegenden*, Wien 1887;— Laud 108, Arch 51.101;— Cbg. Gg II 6, see *Scottish Collection;*— Laud 622, Laud 108, Laud 463, Titus, Vernon, Trin. Oxf., EETS 69.17;— Laud 622, Titus, Arch 59.71, 96;— Vernon, Trin. Oxf., Laud 463, Arch 56.391, 401;— Ashmole 42, Cbg. Gg V 31, AELeg 1881, 174 (see 527);— see under *Caxton's Golden Legend.*   On Cosin's text and Durham MS., EETS 69.99.— Brandl §§71, 54, 40; Körting §130 Bb.— Schneegans, MLN 3.247, 307, 495; Keidel, MLN 8.296; Körting *Studien über Altfrz. Bearbeitungen der A-Leg. mit Berücksichtigung Deutscher u. Engl. Alexiuslieder*, Trier, prgr. 1884; Blau *Zur Alexius-Legende*, Leipzig 1888 (crit. Rom. 18.299); Nöldeke *Zur A-Leg.*, Zs. d. D. Morgenl. Ges. 53.256; Rösler *Die Fassungen der Alexius-Legenden mit bes. Berücksichtigung Me. Versionen*, Wiener Beitr 21, espec. p. 79 ff. (crit. ESt 37.134, *q.v.;* Ctbl 1906.1564; Arch 116.398; Athen 1905.2.860);— old Germ. and Fr. versions, Arch 73.290. Gröber 2¹· Register, *S. Alexis*.

[32] ANNA.   On Chetham, see ESt 7.196; Brandl §110.

[33] ANTONIUS.   Ed. Angl 4.109.— See Arch 87.60.

[34] CECILIA.   Ed. Ashmole, Bodley 779, Cleop., Tib., Gg II 6, and vars. of Laud 108, Cbg. R, 3, 25, Lovewell, YSt 1898 (crit. ESt 26.394);— Laud 108, EETS 87;— Harl. 4196, ESt 1.229;— Caxton and Ashmole 43, *Orig. and Anal.*, ChS 2ser.10. See under the several collections mentioned. ESt 1.215, 2.281; Arch 87.265; Germ 21.437; Angl 14.227; ZsfDA 16.165; Köpke, *Passionals* 629.

[35] CHRISTINA.   See under collections mentioned. Arundel 168, ed. AELeg 1878, 183. Gerould, MLN 29.129. Gröber 2¹.933, 939.

[36] CHRISTOPHER.   See under collections mentioned. Thornton, ed. AELeg 1881, 454.— Brandl §78.— Wiese *Zur Christophlegende, Festgabe für H. Suchier*, Halle 1900. Gröber 2¹· Register, *S. Christoforus*.

[37] CUTHBERT.   See under collections mentioned. Howard, ed. Surtees Soc. 87 (crit. ESt 19.121). Lessmann *Stud. zu dem Me. Life of St. Cuthbert*, Breslau diss., Darmstadt 1896; Lessmann, ESt 23.343, 24.176.

[38] DOROTHEA.   See under collections mentioned. Lambeth 432, ed. Angl 3.319 (notes, Angl 4.311). On Chetham, ESt 7.195. Harley,

Arundel, ed. AELeg 1878, 191.— Peterson *The Dorothea Legend,* Heidelberg diss. 1910 (crit. ESt 44.257).

[39] EDITHA AND ETHELDREDA.   See under *Southern Legend Collection.*   Faustina, *Editha,* ed.   Black *Chronicon Vilodunense,* 1830; Holthausen *St. Editha, sive Chronicon Vilodunense* · · · , Heilbronn 1883 (crit. ZsfdöGymn 37.445; DLz 17.616; AnzfDA 10.391; LitBl 5.200; Angl-Anz 7.31).   Faustina, *Etheldreda,* ed. AELeg 1881.282 (note, 528).— Fischer *Zur Spr. u. Autorschaft,* Angl 11.175 (see Angl 12.528); on verbs, QF 63.45; Heuser *Die Me. Leg. v. St. Ed. u. St. Ethel.,* Erlangen diss. 1887 (lang. and author; see Angl 11.175, 12.578).

[40] ERASMUS.   Ed. Cbg., Arch 62.413;— Harley, Bedford, AELeg 1878, 198, 201.

[41] ERKENWALD.   Harley, ed. AELeg 1881, 265 (see 527).   Knigge, diss. 1885.— Brandl §74.— On verse, see *Alliteration,* page 800.— See *Caxton's Golden Legend.*

[42] EUSTACE.   See under collections mentioned.   Ed. Digby, AELeg 1881, 211 (crit. Ang. 3.400);— Laud 108, EETS 87.393;— Partridge, Roxb. Club 1873; AELeg 1881, 472.— Brandl §40; Körting §89 note 3.—See page 781, *Eustace . . . Legends.*— Ott. ed. OFr. *Eustace* in MS. Nat. Bibl. fr. 1374, Erlangen 1912.— Gröber 2¹· Register, *Placidas.*

[43] GEORGE.   See under collections mentioned.   Huber *Zur Georgslegende,* Festschrift zum 12 Neuphilologentage, Erlangen 1906, 175; Matzke *Contribs. to the Hist. of the Leg. of St. G.,* PMLA 17.508, 18.99; Friedrich *Der Gesch. Hl. G.,* Münster Sitzungsber. 1899.2.159; Matzke *The Leg. of St. G., its Dev. into a Roman d'Aventure,* PMLA 19.449; Taylor *St. G. for England,* 2nd ed. London 1911; Ency Brit; Sandkühler *Der Drachenkampf des Hl. G. in Engl. Legende u. Dicht. vom 14 bis 16 Jhdt.,* München diss. 1913.— Ælfric's *Lives,* EETS 76 and 82.307.— Gröber 2¹.642, 1218.

[44] GREGORY.   Ed. Vernon, Arch 55.407 (see ESt 3.101; crit. Germ 21.437);— Cleopatra, Arch 57.59;— Auchinleck, Turnbull *Legendæ Catholicæ,* Edbg. 1840; Schulz, F., Königsberg 1876 (crit. Germ 21.437);— Keller *Me. Gregoriuslegende,* Heidelberg 1914.   On Rawlinson, see ESt 32.1, 33.335.   Körting §130 Bb; EETS 87, xix note 2; AELeg 1881, xlii; Kostermann *Über Spr., Metr., u. Stil der Me. G-Leg. des Auch. MS.,* Münster diss. 1882; Neussell *Über die Altfrz., Mhd., u. Me. Bearbeitungen . . . ,* Halle diss. 1886; Keller *Einleitung zu einer Krit. Ausgabe der Me. G-Leg.,* Kiel diss. 1909; Keller *Die Me. G-Leg.,* ed., see above.— Gröber 2¹.401, 479, 647, 762, 932.   See under *Trentalle S. Gregorii,* p. 789.

[45] JEROME.   See under collections mentioned.   Lambeth 432, ed. Angl 3.319 (notes, Angl 14.311).   Benedict *Leben des Hl. Hieronomus,* Leipzig 1881.

[46] JOHN THE EVANGELIST.   See under collections mentioned.— Thornton, ed. EETS 26.87; AELeg 1881, 467.   Bearder *Über den Gebr. der Praepositionen,* Halle 1894.   See under *Alliteration,* page 800.

[47] JUDAS AND PILATE. See under *Southern Legend Collection.*
Harley 2277, Furnivall EEP 107.

[48] JUDAS. See under *Southern Legend Collection.* Trinity, ed. Rel.
Ant 1.444; AESprPr 1.113; Child *Ballads* 1.242; Cook Reader 471.—
Brandl §16; Schofield 378, 461.

[49] JULIANA. See under collections mentioned, and *Katherine* and
Margaret. Ed. Royal, Bodley, EETS 51; Morris Spec 1.96 (see Angl
25.319). On text, ESt 4.93.— Brandl §14; Körting §74; Ten Brink 1.199,
392; Cbg Hist 1.255; Schofield 390.— On verbs, QF 63.3, 21; Backhaus
Über die Quelle der Me. Leg. v. d. Hl. J., Halle diss. 1899; Kennedy *The
Leg. of St. J.,* 1906; Bruhnöler *Über Einige Lat., Engl., Frz. u. Deutschen
Fassungen der J-Leg., mit ein Abdruck des. Lat. Textes Dreier Münchener
Hss.,* Bonn diss. 1912.— Gröber 2¹.645, 932.

[50] KATHERINE. Ed. Royal (with Latin), vars. of Bodl. and Tit.,
EETS 80 (crit. Angl 8 Anz 175; DLz 7.226;— note, ESt 9.174);— Titus,
Morton, Abbotsford Club 1841; Hardwicke, Cbg. Antiq. Soc. 1849. Einen-
kel *Ueber den Verfasser der Neuangelsächsischen Leg. v. K.,* Angl 5.91
(see EETS 80, xviii; Angl 5.86; DLz 1882.99; LitBl 12.435); on verbs, QF
63.3; Stodte *Ueber die Spr. u. Heimat der Katherine-Gruppe,* Göttingen
diss. 1896; Victor *Zur Textkritik u. Metr. . . . ,* Bonn diss. 1912 (crit.
AnglBbl 23.226).— Brandl §14; Körting §§130 Bb, §74; Schofield 390;
Ten Brink 1.199, 392; Cbg Hist 1.255.— Versification: AnglAnz 8.49; Paul
Grundriss 2¹.1003; Angl 5.91; EETS 80.xxi; Schipper *Engl. Metr.;* see
general refs. below.— Ed. Auch. and Caius, AELeg 1881, 242—see Brunner,
Wiener Beitr 42.3.— Ed. Cbg. Ff, AELeg 1881, 260; Halliwell *Contribs.
to Ear. Engl. Lit.,* L. 1844.— On Harley 5259, Herbert 3.199.— On Chetham,
ESt 7.196.— Ed. Capgrave, EETS 100. Körting p. 151 note; Brandl
§110.— 15th-cent. hymn by Rich. Spalding, ed. Angl 30.523.— See under
Southern Legend Collection (Laud 108, ed. EETS 87.92); *Scottish Collec-
tion; Bokenham; Mirk; Caxton's Golden Legend.*— General: AELeg 1881,
xlii; Manger *Die Frz. Bearbeitungen der Leg. der Hl. K. v. Alex.,* Zwei-
brücken 1901; Knust *Gesch. der Leg. d. Hl. K. v. Alex. u. d. Hl. Maria
Ægyptiaca,* Halle diss. 1889, Halle 1890 (crit. DLz 34.1237); *Varnhagen
Zur Gesch. der Leg. der Hl. K v. Alex., nebst Lat. Texten,* Erlangen 1891;
Varnhagen, same titel, Festschrift, Leipzig 1901; Varnhagen *Passio S.
Cath. Alex. Metr.,* Erlangen 1891; Paulson *Legenden v. d. Hl. K. v. Alex.,*
Lund 1891; Paulson *Fragm. Vitæ S. Cath. Alex. Metr. ex Libro MS.
Edidit,* Lund 1891; EETS 80. introd.; Körting §§74, 130 Bb, Brandl §14.—
Gröber 2¹.273, 398, 430, 641, 989, 1146, 1218.

[51] MARY MAGDALENE. See under collections mentioned. Ed.
Laud 108, AELeg 1878, 108; EETS 87;— Auchinleck, Turnbull *Leg.
Cathol.,* 1840; AELeg 1878, 163;— Durham, Arch 91.207, 95.439. On
Cosin's MS., see EETS 69.99.— Ed. *Lamentatyon,* B. Skeat, Cbg. 1897
(crit. JGP 3.125).— On Harley 6211, Angl 8.372 note.— AELeg 1881,
xlii.— Knörck *Untersuchungen über die Me. M-Leg. des MS. Laud 108,*
Berlin diss. 1889.— Brandl §40; Körting §130 Bb (see p. 153 note 4).
Gröber 2¹.643, 931, 987, 1220.— See under *Digby Plays.*

[52] MARGARET. See under collections mentioned. Ed. Royal, Bodley 34, EETS 13.1 (on text, ESt 4.93; on strong verbs QF 63.3);— Trinity Cbg. B, 14, 39, Hickes *Thesaurus* 1.224; EETS 13.34 (on verbs, QF 63.16); AELeg 1881, 489 (on MS., MLN 29.155);— Auchinleck, Turnbull *Leg. Cathol.*, 1840; AELeg 1881, 225;— Bodley 779, Arch 79.411;— Harley 2277, EETS 13.24 (on verbs, QF 63.22); AESprPr 1.200;— Ashmole 61, AELeg 1881, 236;— Brome Hall, Smith, L. T., *A Commonplace Book of the Fifteenth Century*, Norwich 1886;— Lydgate, AELeg 1881, 446;— on Cosin's MS., EETS 69.99.— Brandl §§14, 103; Körting §§74, 130 Bb.— Cockayne *Narratiunculæ* 39; Krahl *Untersuchungen über Vier Versionen der Me. M-Leg.*, Berlin diss. 1889 (crit. LitBl 12.158; Angl 15.504); Vögt *Über die M-Leg.*, PBBeitr 1.281; Spencer on development, from Leipzig diss. 1889, MLN 4.393, 5.121, 141, 213; Hart, MLN 4.502; on Engl. versions, Brandl, ZsföGymn 1882.686; foreign versions, see refs. in LitBl 12.159; Germ 31.289; ZsfDPh 12.468; Gröber 2¹.641, 932, 1223.— See under *Katherine, Juliana*, above.

[53] MARINA. Ed. Vernon, Arch 57.259;— Harley, AELeg 1878, 171; Böddeker 254.— Brandl §48; Körting §130 Bb.— See under *English Prose Legenda, Caxton's Golden Legend*, above.

[54] THEOPHILUS. Ed. Rawlinson, ESt 32.1 (correction ESt 33.335;— see MLN 18.145);— Forrest version, Angl 7.60.— Körting §130 Bb; Ward 2.586; Morley 4.273.— Sandison *The T-Leg. in Dramatic Form*, prgr. MLA 1914.— See under *Southern Legend Collection, Northern Homily Cycle*, above.— Gröber 2¹.Register p. 1283; Krit Jahresber.

[55] THOMAS À BECKET. See under collections mentioned, and under *Political Prophecies*, p. 798.— Wade's epic, ed. ESt 3.409.— Jaeger *Thomas à Becket in Sage u. Dichtung*, Breslau 1909; AELeg 1881, 527.— Gröber 2¹.Register p. 1255.

[56] WERBERGE. Ed. EETS 88 (crit. Angl 11.543).

[57] WOLFADE AND RUFFYN. Ed. AELeg 1881, 308 (see 529).

B.   *Other Legends*
a. The Cross

Meyer, Wilh., *Die Gesch. des Kreuzholzes vor Christus*, Abhdl. d. Kais. Bayer. Akad. d. Wiss. 1 Cl. Vol. 16.103, München 1881 (see its bibliogr.); Morris *Legends of the Holy Rood*, EETS 46; Mussafia *Sulla Leggenda del Legno della Croce*, Wien 1869; Napier *Hist. of the Holy Rood-Tree*, EETS 103. introd. (see its bibliogr., up to 1894); Ency Brit, *s.v. Cross;* Gröber 2¹.Register p. 1270; Krit Jahresber.

[58] HISTORY OF THE HOLY ROOD-TREE. Ed. EETS 103.

[59] SOUTHERN LEGENDARY ROOD POEMS. Ed. Laud, EETS 87.1;— Ashmole, Vernon, vars. of Harley, EETS 46.19.—AELeg 1875, vi, viii note, xi, xii note 3, xvi and note 4, xxii, xxviii, xxix, xxxii-xxxiii, xlvii-xlviii, l.

[60] CURSOR MUNDI ROOD VERSION. Ed. Fairfax ll. 21347 ff., EETS 46.108;— all MSS., EETS 59, 62, 66.

[61] CANTICUM *DE* CREATIONE. Ed. Angl 1.287; AELeg 1878, 124.— Brandl §40; Körting §130 B.— Bachmann *Die Beiden Metr. Versionen des Me. C. de C.*, Hamburg 1891, prgr. 724 (crit. ESt 16.304; AnglBbl 2.243).

[62] NORTHERN HOMILY CROSS STORY. Ed. EETS 46.62, 87, 122.

[63] CAXTON'S VERSION. Ed. EETS 46.154, 161.

b. The Saga of Adam and Eve

Bibliogr. in ESt 16.304.

[64] EARLIER *V*ERSION OF CANTICUM DE CREATIONE. Ed. AELeg 1878, 139; Laing *A Peniworþ of Witte*, Abbotsf. Club 1857; Emerson Reader 64 (ll. 445-780). See Bachmann under *Canticum*, above.— Brandl §40.

[65] ÞE LYFF OF ADAM AND EUE. Ed. AELeg 1878, 220.

[66] THE LIFE OF ADAM AND EVE. Ed. Arch 74.353.— *Prose Life of Adam*, ed. Arch 74.345.— Later pieces, see AELeg 1881, cxxxv note.

c. Old Testament Story, and Christ and Mary

[67] SOUTHERN LEGENDARY MATERIAL. See introds. of AELeg 1875, 1878, 1881, and EETS 87. On MS. St. John's Coll., AELeg 1881, li; EETS 87.xxiv.— Ed. Laud 108 Item 8 (141 ll.), *Later Life of Christ*, Horstmann *Leben Jesu*, Münster 1873 (Brandl §31); Laud 108 Item 9, *Infancy of Christ*, AELeg 1875, 1 (on source and text, Arch 127.318;— see Angl 14.312; Arch 49.377; ESt 2.115);— Egerton 1993 Item 2, Ashmole 43 Item 86, AELeg 1875, 65.— For other pieces, see under *Southern Legend Collection*, above.

[68] THE FALL AND THE PASSION. Ed. Harley 913, AESprPr 1.124; Furnivall EEP 12; Kild Ged 106.— Brandl §27.

[69] LA ESTORIE DEL EUANGELIE. Ed. *V*ernon, ESt 8.254; EETS 98.1;— Dulwich, Bodley, PMLA 30.529, 851.

[70] CHILDHOOD OF CHRIST. Ed. Harley 3954, AELeg 1875, 3;— Harley 2399, AELeg 1878, 101 (see ESt 2.117);— Addit. 31042, Arch 74.327.— Brandl §54; Schofield 377.— Reinsch *Die Pseudo-Evangelien von Jesus u. Marias Kindheit*, Halle diss. 1879; Landshoff *Kindheit Jesus*, Berlin diss. 1889; Rom 18.128; Gast *Die Beiden Redaktionen des Evangile de l'Enfance*, Greifswald diss. 1909.— See under *Southern Legendary Material*, above.

[71] RESURRECTION AND APPARITIONS. Ed. Ashmole 61, Arch 79.441.

[72] HOLY BLOOD OF HAYLES. Ed. AELeg 1881, 275 (see 528).

[73] GOSPEL OF NICODEMUS. Ed. *Vespasian*, MPhil 1.79 (see Straub *Lautlehre der Jungen Nic.-Version*, Würzburg diss. 1908;—all strophic MSS., EETSES 100 (see its general bibliogr.);— Harley 4196, Arch 53.389 (see Arch 57.78);— Mt. Sion, Arch 68.207;— Galba readings, Arch 57.73;— Klotz *Das Me. Stroph. Evan. N. mit einer Einleitung Krit. Herausgegeben*, Königsberg diss. 1913. Craigie *Gospel of N. and the York Mystery Plays, Furnivall Misc.*, 1901, 52; Young, Trans. Wisc. Acad. of Sciences, Arts, and Letters 16.889-947; Wülcker *Evangel. Nicod.*, 1872.— Brandl §60.— O. E. *Versions*, ed. Hulme, PMLA 13.457, and MPhil 1.579; text-note, MLR 10.233.— See Paul Grundriss 2nd ed. 2¹.1118.— Gröber 2¹.656, 934; Krit Jahresber.

[74] HARROWING OF HELL. Ed. all versions, EETSES 100 (see its general bibliogr.; crit. ESt 40.263); *Varnhagen*, Erlangen 1898;— Harley, Collier *Five Miracle-Plays*, 1836 (25 copies); Laing *Owain Miles*, etc., Edbg. 1837; Halliwell, L. 1840; Mall, Breslau 1871 (with var. of other MSS.); Pollard *Engl. Mir. Plays*, 4th ed. Oxf. 1904, 166; Böddeker 264.— Young, Trans. Wisc. Acad. of Sciences, Arts, and Letters 16.889-947; Kretzmann *A Few Notes*, MPhil 13.49; Chambers *Med. Stage*, 1.80, 83, 2.74.— Brandl §§31, 43; Körting §134; Ten Brink 2.242; Ward *Hist. Engl. Dram. Lit.* 1.90.— Becker *Die Sage von der Hollenfahrt Christi in der Afrz. Lit.*, Göttingen diss. 1912.

[75] FIFTEEN SIGNS BEFORE JUDGMENT. Ed. *Cursor* version (ll. 444-723), JbREL 5.191; EETS 66.1282, 68.1616 (note of Royal text, Small *Engl. Metr. Hom.*, Edbg. 1862, introd.);— North. Hom. version, Small *op. cit.* 25; Furnivall EEP 162; Emerson Reader 148;— (on Trin. Cbg. R, 3, 25, and Lambeth 223, see AELeg 1881, 1; EETS 87.xx, xxii, xlvii);— *Pricke of Conscience*, Morris, 1863, ll. 4738 ff.;— Mirk's *Festial*, see p. 807;— *Chester Plays*, ed. Wright 2.147;— *Castel of Love*, EETS 98.403;— Harley 913, Wright *Chester Plays* 2.219; AESprPr 1.120;— Furnivall EEP 7; Kild Ged. 96;— Digby 86, Stengel *Cod. Manu Scriptum Digby 86*, Halle 1871, 53;— Laud 622, EETS 69.92;— Trin. Cbg. B, 11, 24, EETS 24.118;— Harley 2255, Wright *op. cit.* 2.222; see AnglAnz 24.55; EETSES 107.xvii;— Cbg. Ff, Angl 3.534 (see ESt 19.148; Angl 13.360, 17.442);— Caligula, Angl 3.543 (see Angl 13.361, 17.442);— *Vespasian*, Angl 11.369;— Brome, Smith, L. T., *A Commonplace Book of the Fifteenth Century*, Norwich 1886; ESt 9.3.— Brandl §31.— Arch 46.33, 124.73; Haupt's Zeitschrift 3.523; PBBeitr 6.413; MLQ 1.pt.2; Grau *Quellen u. Verwandtschaften der Älteren Germ. Darstellungen des Jung-sten Gerichts*, StEPhil 1898; Arch. f. Litgesch. 9.117.

[76] LYDGATE'S LIFE OF MARY. Ed. Ear. Relig. Poetry, 2, L. 1871. See AELeg 1881, 376.

[77] ORIGIN OF FESTIVAL OF CONCEPTION OF MARY. Ed.

Edbg., Small *Ear. Metr. Hom.*, 1862, xv;— Cott. with readings of Edbg., Ellis, H., *Domesday* Book 2.99;— *Cursor* texts, EETS 68.1416. EETS 87. xvii.

[78] ASSUMPTION OF OUR LADY. See EETS 14 (revised 1901); Hackauf ed., below; Brandl §§21, 31, 40, 54; Schofield 376; Cbg Hist 1.258.— Short-couplet version, ed. Cbg. Gg, Addit. 10036, part of Harl. 2382, EETS 14 (revised;— crit. *J*GP 4.529; ESt 31.281; Athen 1902.2.822)— see ESt 7.195, 348;— crit. text., Hackauf, ETB 8 (also diss. 1902;— crit. ESt 33.255; Ctbl 1903.851; Neu Phil. Rund. 1903.351; LitBl 15.292). MS. notes, ESt 33.179; notes, ESt 3.93; sources, ESt 35.350. Gierth *Über die Älteste Me. Version der A. M.*, Breslau diss. 1881, repr. ESt 7.1.— On MS. Chetham, ESt 7.196.— Auchinleck version, ed. ESt 8.427 (notes, Angl 13.358).— Sth Leg. version, see EETS 14 (revised).lii; ESt 8.461; AELeg 1875, xxxiv, 1881, xxxix, 1; Hackauf *op. cit.* iv.— Nth Hom. version, ed. Cott., Harl. 4196, AELeg 1881, 112 (see AELeg 1881, lxxviii). Retzlaff *Untersuchungen über den Nordengl. Legendencyklus*, Berlin 1888. See espec. Hackauf, v.— *Cursor* version, ed. EETS 66.1148. EETS 14 (revised).liii; Haenisch, introd. to *Cursor*, 42.— Lambeth 223 version, see EETS 14 (revised).liii; AELeg 1881, xlvii and notes; Hackauf *op. cit.*

d. *V*isions, and *V*isits to the Under-World

Becker *Med. Visions of Heaven and Hell*, Baltimore 1899 (crit. AnglBbl 13.196); Huber *Beitrag zur Visionsliteratur*, Beil. zum Jahresber. des Hum. Gymn. Metten, 1902-3 (on Monk of Eynsham).— *Monk of Evesham.* See Becker 93, and Huber; Ward 2.493. Ed. in Roger of Wendover, Rolls Ser. ed., 1.246, Bohn's ed. 2.148.— *Vision of Thurcill.* See Becker 96; Ward 2.506. Ed. in Roger of Wendover, Rolls Ser. ed., 1.497, Bohn's ed., 2.221.— See Index, *Dream-Visions;* Baake *Die Verwendung des Traummotivs in der Engl. Dichtung bis auf Chaucer*, Halle diss. 1906; Arnold, M., *Die Verwendung des Traummotivs in der Engl. Dichtung von Chaucer bis auf Shakespeare*, Kiel diss. 1912.

[79] VISION OF ST. PAUL or THE ELEVEN PAINS OF HELL. Ed. Laud, Arch 52.35;— Jesus, EETS 49.147;— Digby, Arch 62.403;— Vernon-Addit., EETS 98.251, 117.750;— *V*ernon, EETS 49.223; ESt 1.293;— Douce, EETS 49.210;— Lambeth, EETS 29.41;— Addit. 10036, EST 22.134. See *De Pœnis* in preface to *Pricke of Conscience*, see p. 838.— Brandl §§16, 40; Ten Brink 1.213; Körting §130 B; Ward 2.397; Cbg Hist 1.130, 252.— Brandes *Visio S. Pauli*, Halle 1885; Becker *op. cit.;* ESt 7.34 (sources).— Gröber 2¹.21, 143, 481, 658, 866; Krit Jahresber.

[80] ST. PATRICK'S PURGATORY. Ed. Laud, Egerton, ˈAshmole, var. of Jul., AELeg 1875, 151;— Caligula, Auch., ESt 1.57 (see Angl 3.60);— Brome, ESt 9.3;— Laud, EETS 87.199;— Auchinleck, Laing *Owain Miles*, etc., Edbg. 1837. Selection from Calig., Wülcker Lesebuch 2.23. Mod. rend. of Auch., Shackford *Leg. and Sat.*, Boston 1913, 33; Weston *Chief M. E. Poets*, 83.— Brandl §§34, 40; Körting §130 B; Ward 2.435, 748; DNB, *Patrick.*— On verbs, QF 63.20. Wright, T., *St. Patrick's Purgatory*, L.

1844; de *Vere* Legends of *St. P.*, L. 1872; Eckleben *Die Älteste Schilderung vom Fegefeuer des Hl. Patricius*, Halle 1885; Krapp *Leg. of St. P's Purg.: its Later Literary Hist.*, Baltimore diss. 1900; Becker *op. cit.* 87; ESt 1.57; de Félice *L'Autre Monde*, Paris 1906 (crit. DLz 29.398). Lat. text, Rom. Forsch. 6.139. Gröber 2¹.277; Krit Jahresber.

[81] *VISION OF TUNDALE.* Ed. Royal, Turnbull *Visions of Tundale*, Edbg. 1843;— Composite text based on Royal, Wagner, A., Halle 1893 (crit. ESt 19.269; Angl 20.452; AnglBbl 4.129; LitBl 15.259).— Selection from Cott., Wülcker Lesebuch 2.17.— Körting §130 B; Schofield 399; Ward 2.416, 746.— Mussafia in Sitzungsber. der Kais. Acad. d. Wiss., *Vienna* 1871, 67.157; Wagner *Visio Tnugdali, Lat. u. Altd.*, ed. Erlangen 1882 (see Angl 6.63); Wagner *Zu Tungdalusvision*, Angl 20.452; Peters *Die Version des Tundalus*, Prgr. des Dorotheenstädt Realgymn. Berlin 1895; Becker *op. cit.* 81.— French texts, pr. Friedel and Meyer, Paris 1907. Gröber 2¹.277, 401; Krit Jahresber.

CHAPTER VI—WORKS OF RELIGIOUS INFORMATION AND INSTRUCTION, AND AIDS TO CHURCH SERVICES

1. COMPREHENSIVE WORKS

[1] CURSOR MUNDI. Ed. EETS 57, 62, 66, 68, 99, 101. Selections: Morris Spec 2.69; Zupitza Übungsbuch 84; Emerson Reader 126.— Interp. notes, Angl 26.365.— Brandl §60; Körting §127; Ten Brink 1.287; Morley 4.121; Schofield 375; Cbg Hist 1.381.— Hupe *Genealogie u. Überlieferung der Hdss. des Me. C. M.*, Altenburg 1886 (see ESt 11.235, 12.451; Angl 11.121; AnglBbl 1.133); Hänisch *Inquiry into the Sources*, Breslau diss. 1884; see studies in EETS 99, 101; Barth *Der Wortschatz des C. M.*, Königsberg diss. 1903; Hornung *Die Schreibg. der Hds. F.*, Berlin diss. 1906; Brown, C., *The C. M. and the Southern Passion*, MLN 26.15.— On MS. Bedford, Herbert 3.307; Cat. of Addits., Br. Mus., 1900-1905, 266.— Traver *Four Daughters of God*, Phila. 1907, 39.

[2] HANDLYNG SYNNE. Ed. Furnivall, Roxb. Club 1862; Furnivall, EETS 119, 123 (with French). Selections: Morris Spec 2.50; Cook Reader 300.— Körting p. 137 n. 1; Brandl §55; Cbg Hist 1.384; Ten Brink 1.299; Schofield 411.— Hellmers *Über die Sprache R. M.'s*, Göttingen diss. 1885; Börner *Die Sprache R. M. of Br.*, Halle 1903, pr. StEPhil 12; Börner *Reimuntersuchung über die Qualität der Betonten Langen E-Vokale bei R. of Br.*, StEPhil 50.298; Kunz *R. M. of Br's H. S., Vergl. mit der An. Vorlage*, Königsberg diss. 1913; Herbert 3.272, 303, 310.— See under Mannyng's Chronicle, p. 794.— On Englissh's work, see Herbert 3.313.— On *Septem Miracula*, see p. 804 [8].

[3] PRICKE OF CONSCIENCE. See p. 838.

[4] AƷENBITE OF INWYT. Ed. Stevenson, Roxb. Club 1885; EETS 23. Selections: AESprPr 2.58; Wülcker Lesebuch 1.112; Zupitza Übungsbuch; MacLean Reader 95; Morris Spec 2.98;. Emerson Reader 215.— Brandl §34; Körting §139; Ten Brink 1.283; Cbg Hist 1.395; Schofield 386, 409.—Text-notes, ESt 1.379, 2.27; Evers *Beitr. zur Erklärung u. Textkritik,* Erlangen diss. 1888. Child *Verse as Prose in Aƶenbite,* MLN 10.64; Konrath on Latin source of parallel to *Sawles Warde,* ESt 12.459 (see *Sawles Warde,* p. 803); Peterson RadMon 12; on verbs, QF 63.27; Jensen *Die Verbalflexion im A. of I.,* Kiel diss. 1908; Foerster *Die Bibliothek des Dan Michael,* Arch 115.167; Dolle *Graphische u. Lautliche Untersuchung von . . . A. of I.,* Bonn diss. 1912.— See Meyer *Notice sur le MS. 27 de la Bibl. d'Alençon (Somme le Roi),* Bull. SATF, No. 2, 1892.

[5] MIRROR OF ST. EDMUND. Ed. Thornton, EETS 26.15; Yksh Wr 1.218;— see Halliwell *Thornton Romances,* Camden Soc., xxv. On Vernon and Cbg. Ff, see Yksh Wr 1.219.

[6] HOW A MAN SCHAL LYUE PARFYTLY. Ed. EETS 98.221.

[7] PRICKE OF LOVE. Ed. EETS 98.268.

[8] MIRROR OF LIFE. Ed. ll. 1-370, with analysis of whole, ESt 7.417, 468 (coll. with MS., ESt 12.468).—Yksh Wr 2.274; DNB, *Nassyngton;* Brandl §78; Allen *Notes on the Speculum Vitæ,* Prgr. MLA 1914; Allen, RadMon 15.163 ff. (on MSS., Author).

[9] DAN GAYTRYGE'S SERMON. Ed. EETS 26.1 (Thornton MS.);— Rawl., Yksh Wr 1.104, Item 8. On MS. Br. Mus. Addit., see page 843 [75], below.— Brandl §78. Paues *A Fourteenth Cent. Bibl. Version,* Cbg. 1902, lxxi note.

[10] WILLIAM OF SHOREHAM'S POEMS. Ed. Wright, Percy Soc. 1849; EETSES 86 (crit. ESt 33.406; Arch 113.194). Selections: Morris Spec. 2.63; Wülcker Lesebuch 1.21; AESprPr 1.260.— Brandl §34; Körting §131; Ten Brink 1.281; Cbg Hist 1.394; Schofield 387; Schipper §164. Text criticism: Angl 4.200, 26.365; ESt 2.36, 3.164, 21.153, 42.205, 43.1; LitBl 2.60, 11.372; AnzfDA 5.257; Jahresbericht 13.354; Paues *A Fourteenth Cent. Bibl. Version,* 1902, lvi; Konrath *Beitr. zur Erklärung u. Textkritik des W. v. S.,* Berlin 1878 (crit. LitBl 1.60); Danker *Die Laut- u. Flexionslehre der Mittelkent. Denkmäler,* Strassburg diss. 1879. On verbs, QF 63.25. On 'Lok-Sunday,' HarvStN 1.88.— On Poem 2, see Jacoby *Vier Me. Geistl. Gedichte,* Berlin diss. 1890; Latin orig. in Mone *Lat. Hymnen* 1.106.

2. The Seven Sins, The Pater Noster, The Creed, Etc.

[11] THE SEVEN SINS, THE PATER NOSTER, ETC., IN GROUPS. Ed. Arundel 292, Rel Ant 1.234; AESprPr 1.49; Arch 128.367-8;— Cleopatra, Rel Ant 1.22;— Cbg. Hh, Rel Ant 1.169;— Harley 3724, Rel Ant 1.57; Patterson *M. E. Pen. Lyric* 108;— Caius, Rel Ant 1.282;— Auchinleck, ESt 9.42 (notes, Angl 13.358);— Arundel 57, Rel Ant 1.42;— Halliwell

219, Rel Ant 1.38;— Laud 463, Kild Ged 185;— Cbg. Gg, Rel Ant 1.159;— Makculloch, see G. Smith *Spec. of Middle Scots* lxviii;— Sarum, ESt 1.214; MLR 3.69;— Arundel 20, part, Kild Ged 206;— Laud 416, part, Kild Ged 207;— Harley 1706, part, Kild Ged 205;— Harley 2346, see Herbert 3.674;— Rawl. B 408, EETS 129.5; Rawl. B 408 *Pater Noster,* Patterson *M. E. Pen. Lyric* 108;— Garrett, ESt 41.362;— Univ. Coll., see Yksh Wr 2.449, 455.— On O. E. versions, Paul Grundriss 2nd ed. 2¹.1114.

[12] SEVEN SINS ALONE. Ed. Harley 957, Rel Ant 1.260;— Vespasian, JbREL 6.332;— Harley 913, Kild Ged 116; Furnivall EEP 17;— Tiberius, see AELeg 1881, lxxviii;— Laud 463, Kild Ged 185;— Jesus, Rel Ant 1.136;— Balliol, Angl 26.224;— Cbg. Ff, EETS 15(revised).224.

[13] PATER NOSTER ALONE. Ed. Lambeth, EETS 29.55 (see Brandl §20; Cohn 1880, p. 81);— Vitellius, Rel Ant 1.204;— Corpus 54, D, 5, 14, EETS 53.258; Patterson *M. E. Pen. Lyric* 110;— Auchinleck, ESt 9.47;— Sarum, ESt 1.215; MLR 3.69;— Corpus 296, EETS 74.197;— Trinity, see AELeg 1881, xxii; see EETS 87.xxii;— Thornton, Yksh Wr 1.261;— Harley 4172, see Yksh Wr 1.443;— Galba, see Yksh Wr 1.261 note, 443;— Lydgate pieces, see EETSES 107.xxiii, trans. pr. *ibid.* 18;— *How the Plowman Learned his Pater Noster,* ed. Hazlitt Rem 1.209. Brandl §116. See Angl 2.388.— See Cook *Evol. of Lord's Prayer,* AJPhil 15.59.

[14] CREED ALONE. Ed. Blickling, MLN 4.276;— Nero, EETS 34.217;— Lambeth, EETS 24.101.

[15] COMMANDMENTS ALONE. Ed. Harley 913, Furnivall EEP 15; Kild Ged 113; AESprPr 1.128;— Cbg. Ff, EETS 49.200;— Trinity, Arch 104.302;— Vernon, Addit., Lambeth, EETS 24.106; see Arch 7.281;— Lambeth 853, EETS 24.104;— Royal, Harley 218, see Herbert 3.674; Thompson, E. M., *Wycliffe Exhibition* (1884) 52;— Harley 5396, see Kild Ged 205;— Harley 665, Arch 85.44;— Jesus, Rel Ant 1.49;— Ashmole 61, Arch 85.46;— St. John's, *Studies in Philology* 6, 8, Univ. of N. Carolina 1910;— Thornton, Yksh Wr 1.195; EETS 20.9.

3. Service Pieces and Offices of the Church

Wordsworth and Littlehales *The Old Service Books of the English Church,* L., n.d.

[16] LAY-FOLKS' MASS-BOOK. Ed. Gg, ESt 33.1;— Advocates', Turnbull *Visions of Tundale,* 1843; ESt 35.28;— the other MSS., EETS 71.1;— Royal, Yksh Wr 2.1; from Royal, *A General Confession* and *A Prayer after the Levation,* Patterson *M. E. Pen. Lyric* 70.— Brandl §60.

[17] LAY-FOLKS' CATECHISM. Ed. both versions, EETS 118;— Thoresby's version only, *Yorkshire Anthology* 287; Thoresby's *Vicaria Leodensis* 213; extracts EETS 71.118. See Arnold *Sel. Engl. Works of Wyclif* 3.vi; DNB, Thoresby. See *Speculum Vitæ Christianæ,* below, Ch. XII [70].

[18] PRIMER or LAY-FOLKS' PRAYER-BOOK. Ed. EETS 105 and 109, and ES 90.— Brown ChS 2ser 45.126; MLN 30.9.

[19] HOW TO HEAR MASS. Ed. EETS 71.128; EETS 117.493. Selection: *Form of Confession,* Patterson *M. E. Pen. Lyric* 47.— Brandl §55; Schofield 389.

[20] MERITA *MISSÆ*. Ed. EETS 71.148. Brandl §129.

[21] YORK BIDDING PRAYERS. Ed. EETS 71.64.— *Horæ,* ed. EETS 71.82.— *Order for Nuns,* ed. EETS 71.90.— Select lyrics, ed. Patterson *M. E. Pen. Lyric* 66, 67, 72.

[22] PRÆPARATIO EUCHARISTIÆ. Ed. EETS 71.122.

[23] SACRAMENT OF THE ALTAR. Ed. EETS 124.103.

[24] TWO PRAYERS AT THE LEVATION. Ed. EETS 98.24;— second prayer, Patterson *M. E. Pen. Lyric* 70.

[25] ATHANASIAN CREED. Ed. Hickes' *Thesaurus* 1.233; Angl 29.405.

[26] PASSION OF CHRIST. See this bibliogr. under works mentioned.

[27] ABC POEM ON THE PASSION. Ed. EETS 15 (revised).171; ll. 1-42, Rel Ant 1.63.

[28] MEDITATIONS OF THE SUPPER OF OUR LORD. Ed. Harley with var. of Trinity and notes on Bedford, EETS 60.— Herbert 3.306; Thien *Über die Engl. Marienklage,* Kiel 1906, 32; Cat. of Addits., Br. Mus., 1900-5, MS. 36983.

[29] LOVE'S MYRROUR. Ed. Powell, Edbg. 1908. Traver *Four Daughters of God,* Phila. 1907, 43.

[30] PATRIS SAPIENCIA. Ed. *V*ernon and Bodley, EETS 98.37;— Bodley, EETS 46.222;— Caius, Angl 27.311.

[31] SYMBOLS OF THE PASSION. Ed. EETS 46.170.

[32] FORM OF CONFESSION. Ed. Yksh Wr 2.340.

[33] ON THE *V*ISITING OF THE SICK. Ed. Univ. Coll., Yksh Wr 2.449;— St. John's Coll.; Maskell *Monum. Ritual.* 3.413.

[34] BOOK OF THE CRAFT OF DYING. Ed. Yksh Wr 2.406.

[35] SE*V*EN QUESTIONS TO BE ASKED. Ed. EETS 15(revised).69.

[36] EXITACION OF CUMFORT. See Angl 3.319.

[37] FESTIVALS OF THE CHURCH. Ed. EETS 46.210.— Brandl §46.

[38] INSTRUCTIONS FOR PARISH PRIESTS. Ed. EETS 31 (revised 1902). Selections: Cook Reader 287.— Brandl §72; Schofield 395; DNB, *Mirk.*

[39] POINTS AND ARTICLES OF CURSING. Ed. EETS 31 (revised).60.

4. INSTRUCTION FOR THE LIFE OF MONKS AND NUNS

[40] ANCREN RIWLE. Ed. Nero with some var. of Titus and Cleo-
patra, Morton for Camden Soc. 1853;— Pepys 2498, Pahlsson *The Recluse,*
Lund 1912 (crit. AnglBbl 25.75);— Robartes, JGP 2.199. Selections: Rel
Ant 1.65, 2.1; Sweet *First M. E. Primer* 19; Morris Spec 1.110; AESprPr
2.5; Emerson Reader 197; Cook Reader 296. Mod. rend., in Morton's ed.,
repr. in King's Classics, L. 1905.— Brandl §§15, 60; Körting §75; Ten
Brink 1.200; Cbg Hist 1.255; Schofield 403; Inge *Studies in Engl. Mystics,*
L. 1906, 38.— Collation of Morton's text with New MS., JbREL 15.179;
notice of Caius MS., Angl 3.34 (see ESt 3.535); notice of Pepys MS., ESt
30.344; Mühe *Über den in MS. Cotton Titus . . . Text der A. R.,* Göttingen diss. 1902; date of Caius, ESt 9.116, 19.247; MLR 4.433; Language of
Morton Text, PBBeitr 1.209; on verbs, QF 63.6; Bramlette *Orig. Lang. of
A. R.,* Angl 15.478; Dahlstedt *The Word-Order of the A. R.,* Sundsvall
1903 (crit. ESt 34.78); Ostermann *Lautlehre der. Germ. Wortschatzes in
der von Morton Hg. Hds. der A. R.,* Bonner Beitr. 19 (crit. LitBl 28.199;
AnglBbl 18.105; Neu Phil. Rundschau 1906.531); Redepenning *Syntakt.
Kapitel aus der A. R.,* Rostock diss. 1906; Williams *Lang. of Cleopatra
MS.,* Angl 28.300; Heuser *Die A. R.—ein aus Ags. Zeit Überliefertes
Denkmal* Angl 30.103 — replies in Angl 31.399, MLR 4.433, ESt 38.453;
Landwehr *Das Gram. Geschlecht in der A. R.,* Heidelberg diss. 1911;
Macaulay *The Ancren Riwle,* MLR 9.63, 145, 324, 463—the most thorough
study, based on examination of all the MSS.

[41] RULE OF ST. BENEDICT. Ed. Common version, Wülcker *Bibl.
der Ags. Prosa* 2; ESt 24.161;— Wells, Wülcker *op. cit.* 2.102;— Wells
and Winteney, Schröer, Halle 1888;— Interlinear, EETS 90;— Winteney,
Schröer, Halle 1888;— Northern Prose and ritual (Lansdowne), EETS
120.1, 141;— Northern Metre (*Vespasian*) ESt 2.60 (see Angl 14.302; ESt
23.284); EETS 120.48 (ritual 145);— Caxton, EETS 120.119. Selections
(Vesp.): Cook Reader 293.— Brandl §78; Schofield 408.— On language of
North. Metre, ESt 2.344; on Lansdowne, language, Angl 31.276, 398, 543;
Fehr *Das Benediktiner Offizium u. die Beziehungen zwischen Ælfric u.
Wulfstan,* ESt 46.337; Rohr *Die Spr. der Ae. Prosabearbeitungen d. B. R.,*
Bonn diss 1912. General view, EETS 120.introd., and 90.introd.

[42] RITUAL FOR ORDINATION. See preceding item.

[43] INFORMACIO ALREDI ABBATIS. Ed. ESt 7.304.— Schofield
409.

[44] EPISTOLA AD SIMPLICES SACERDOTES. Ed. Yksh Wr
2.62.

5. ALLEGORICAL WORKS OF INSTRUCTION

[45] CASTEL OF LOVE. Ed. Vernon-Addit., Weymouth, Phil. Soc.
1864;— Vernon, EETS 98.355;— Var. of Addit. from Vernon, EETS
117.751;— Bodley Addit. (see Angl 12.311, 14.418), Halliwell 1849 (pri-

vately);— Var. of Bodley Addit. from Vernon, EETS 98.394, 403;— Egerton, Cooke, Caxton Soc. 1852, 133 (see Angl 14.393); Angl 14.415; EETS 98.407;— Ashmole, AELeg 1881, 349;— *Cursor* version, EETS 59.549, 68.1664.— Brandl §§40, 55; Schofield 133, 386.— Traver *Four Daughters of God,* Phila. 1907, 29, 39.

[46] ABBEY OF THE HOLY GHOST. Ed. Thornton, EETS 26.48; with readings of Laud, Vernon, Harley 2406 and 1704, Yksh Wr 1.321.

[47] CHARTER OF THE ABBEY. Ed. Laud with vars. of Vernon and two Harley MSS., Yksh Wr 1.337.— Cpd. with Hegge play, Traver *Four Daughters of God,* Phila. 1907, 126.

[48] CHARTERS OF CHRIST. Ed. all texts, Spalding, BrynMawr-Mon 1914 (crit. AnglBbl 26.24);— Harley 2382, *Vernon,* Royal, EETS 117.137;— Harley 2382, *Vernon,* Arch 79.424.— Spalding *op. cit., passim;* Migne Ser. Lat. xv Col. 1837, etc.; *Expos. Ev. sec. Luc.* Lib. x 131; d'Ancona *Origini del Teatro Italiano* 1.132 note; EETS 46.210 l. 184; Rel Ant 2.227; Thien *Über die Engl. Marienklagen* 82; Perrow *The Last Will and Testament as a Form of Literature,* Trans. Wisconsin Acad. of Sciences, Arts, and Letters 17.682.

[49] TESTAMENT OF LOVE. Ed. Skeat *Oxf. Chaucer* 7.1 (crit. Acad 1893.1.22; Athen 1897.1.184, 215). See ESt 23.438; N&Q 10th Ser. 1.245; Skeat *Oxf. Chaucer* 7.xviii, 5.xii note; Hammond *Chaucer: A Bibliogr. Manual* 458.

[50] DESERT OF RELIGION. Ed. Arch 126.58, 360 (addendum, Arch 127.388).

[51] TREATISE OF GHOSTLY BATTLE. Ed. Yksh Wr 2.420.— *Milicia Christi,* see Yksh Wr 2.421.— See notice of *A Treati agenst Gostly Temptaciouns,* in Worcester Cath. Libr. MS. f 336, MPhil 4.69.

[52] QUATREFOIL OF LOVE. Ed. *Furnivall Miscellany,* Oxf. 1901, 112.— See Gollancz *Parl. of the Thre Ages,* Roxb. Club 1897, introd.

CHAPTER VII—PROVERBS, PRECEPTS, AND MONITORY PIECES

1. PROVERBS AND PRECEPTS

[1] SCATTERED PROVERBS. Specimens, ed. Skeat *Ear. Engl. Prov.,* Oxf. 1910 (crit. DLz 31.939; N&Q 11th Ser. 1.319; AnglBbl 20.289).— Wright *Essays on Subjects connected with the Lit., Pop. Superstitions, and Hist. of England,* L. 1846, 1.124; Wahl *Die Engl. Parömiographie vor Shakespeare,* Prgr. d. Handelschule zu Erfurt 1879; Hohmann *Ueber Spr. u. Styl des Ae. Lai Havelok the Dane,* Marburg diss. 1886, and Arch 107.107; Haeckel *Das Sprichwort bei Chaucer,* Erlangen 1890 (see LitBl

12.16), nachträge AnglBbl 2.169, 3.276, 4.330; Kissel *Sprichwort* . . . *bei Sir David Lyndesay*, Nürnberg 1892; Zupitza, Arch 90.241; Walz *Das Sprichwort bei Gower*, Nördlingen 1907; Skeat *Prov. of Alfred*, Oxf. 1907, xlvi; Williams *Gnomic Poetry in Anglo-Saxon*, N. Y. 1914.

[2] TRINITY COLLEGE COLLECTION. Ed. ESt 31.1.

[3] PROUERBES OF DIUERSE PROFETES. Ed. *Vernon*, EETS 117.523;— Harley, Arch 104.304.— Schofield 423 (see MLN 1907.188).

[4] DOUCE COLLECTION. See Foerster *Die Me. Sprichwortsammlung in Douce 52*, Festschrift zum 12 Neuphilogentage in München, Erlangen 1906, 40.

[5] PROVERBS OF ALFRED. Ed. Trinity, Jesus, Rel Ant 1.170; EETS 49.102;— Trinity, Kemble *Dial. of Salomon and Saturnus*, L. 1848, 226;— all texts, Skeat, Oxf. 1907, with full bibliogr. (crit. Athen 1907.2.268; AnglBbl 20.289; DLz 28.2725; N&Q 10th Ser. 8.139; RevCrit 64.390); Borgström, Lund 1908 (crit. AnglBbl 21.76), 1911. Selections: Morris Spec 1.146; Zupitza *Übungsbuch*. Mod. rend., Weston *Chief M. E. Poets* 289.— Brandl §17; Körting §79; Ten Brink 1.151; Cbg Hist 1.243; Schofield 419.— See PBBeitr 1.243; Angl 3.370; AnglAnz 8.67; Skeat, Trans. Lond. Phil. Soc. 1895-8, 399; Schipper *Engl. Metr.* Theil 1, Ch. 7; Gropp *On the Lang. of P. of A.*, Halle diss. 1879; Arch 90.141.

[6] PROVERBS OF HENDYNG. Ed. Harley, Kemble *Dial. of Salomon and Saturnus*, appendix; Böddeker 285; AESprPr 1.304; Morris Spec 2.35; Rel Ant 1.109;— Cbg. and Digby with comp. of Harley, Angl 4.180;— Cbg. 4407 (19), Skeat, MLR 7.151. Notice of Dover MS., Arch 115.165; on MSS., Angl 5.5.— Mod. rend. Harley, Weston *Chief M. E. Poets* 294.— Brandl §55; Körting §132; Ten Brink 1.313; Cbg Hist 1.243, 405; Schofield 420, 448.—Wright *Essays on Lit. of Mid. Ages* 1. Ch. 4; Kneuer *Die Sprichwörter Hendyngs*, Leipzig diss. 1901 (crit. Rom. 31.476).

[7] WISE MAN'S PROVERBS. Ed. ESt 23.442.

[8] DISTICHS OF CATO. Ed. *Vernon*, Addit., Angl 7.165; EETS 117.553;— Sidney, Rawl., ESt 36.1;— Fairfax, EETS 68.1668. ' On Arundel and Caxton, see EETS 117.553; on Rawl. MS., Arch 95.163; on Chetham MS., ESt 7.197; on Cosin's MS., EETS 69.99.— Brandl §55; Körting §65; Cbg Hist 1.132; Schofield 423.— Nehab, Berlin; Goldberg, Leipzig diss. 1883; Förster in Schanz *Gesch. der Römanischen Lit.*, 2nd ed. München 1905, 38-9.— On O. E. *Cato*, Paul Grundriss 2nd ed. 2¹.1072, 1128; Körting §65.— Gröber 2¹.381, 383, 482, 863, 1066, 1187.

[9] HOW THE WYSE (GODE) MAN TAUGHT HYS SONE. Ed. all versions, Fischer, Erl Beitr 2;— Ashmole, EETSES 8.52;— Cbg. Ff, Hazlitt Rem 1.168;— Lambeth, EETS 32.48.— Brandl §41; Schofield 422, 463, 485.— *Ratis Raving*, ed. EETS 43.26.

[10] HOW THE GOOD WIFE TAUGHT HER DAUGHTER. Ed. St. John's, EETSES 29.523;— Cbg. Kk, EETS 43.103;— Lambeth with readings of Trinity, EETS 32.36;— Norfolk, Gibbs *Hist. of Plasidas*, Roxb.

Club 1873;— Ashburnham, Hazlitt Rem 1.178;— Porkington, Ashmole, EETSES 8.39, 44.— Brandl §41; Schofield 422.— Ostermann *Untersuchungen zu Ratis Raving u. dem Ged.* 'The Thewis of Gud Women,' Bonn diss. 1902, Bonner Beitr. 12.41.— Bernard *De Cura Rei,* ed. EETS 42.1.— On author, see Scottish Antiquary 11.145.

[11] ABC OF ARISTOTLE. Ed. nine MSS. in two versions, Arch 105.296;— Harley 541, Strutt *Sports and Pastimes,* 1841, 398;— Lambeth, Harley 5086, EETS 32.11, 9; coll. Harley 1706 with Lambeth, EETS 32.cxxvi;— Harley 1304, EETS 8.65. See Arch 117.371. Schofield 422.

[12] MISCELLANEOUS SCRAPS. Ed. Cleopatra, Rel Ant 2.14;— Cleopatra, Trinity, Arch 104.303;— Cleop., Rawl., Harl., Kild Ged 183;— Rawl., Rel Ant 1.316;— Harl., Furnivall EEP 161;— Calig., Jesus (*Ten Abuses*), EETS 49.184;— Ashmole, Rel Ant 1.58;— Worcester, Arch 128.76. See Arch 128.72, on the group.

[13] WILL AND WIT. Ed. EETS 49.192.

[14] 'HEUEN IS WONNEN,' ETC. Ed. Yksh Wr 2.64.

[15] 'THYNK OFT WITH SARE HART.' Ed. Yksh Wr 1.156.

[16] CBG. Gᴏ SCRAPS. Ed. Rel Ant 1.159.

[17] ARUNDEL 292. Ed. Rel Ant 1.235; Arch 128.367-8.

[18] 'LEⱱERE IS THE WRENNE.' Ed. Rel Ant 2.107.

[19] HARLEY 2316 SCRAPS. Ed. Rel Ant 2.219. '

[20] BODLEY 622 SCRAPS. Ed. Rel Ant 2.18.

[21] HARLEY 3724. Ed. Rel Ant 1.57.

[22] FIFTEENTH-CENTURY SCRAPS. Ed. Rel Ant 1.92, 205, 207, 251, 314, 316, 323.

[23] SLOANE PIECES. Ed. Rel Ant 2.165; Wright, Warton Club 1856. See Arch 107.48, 109.33; Ch&Sidg 303.

[24] CBG. Kᴋ SONGS, WISDOM OF SOLOMON, KING SOLOMON'S BOOK. Ed. EETS 43.9, 11, 81.

2. Monitory Pieces

[25] POEMA MORALE. Ed. E, e, Furnivall EEP 22;— e, Zupitza Übungsbuch; MacLean Reader 49;— E, EETS 34.288;— L, EETS 29.159;— T, EETS 53.220;— T, J, Morris Spec 1.194 (see Angl 25.325); J, EETS 49.58;— D, Angl 1.6;— M, Angl 30.217;— crit. ed., Lewin, Halle 1881 (crit. AnglAnz 4.88; ESt 5.409). See Angl 3.32, 4.406; MLN 1.14.— Brandl §12; Körting §76; Ten Brink 1.153; Cbg Hist 1.244; Schofield 382.— Jordan *Dialekt der Lamb. Hds. des P. M.,* ESt 41.38. On verse, Schipper §§43, 63, 65; Paul Grundriss 2¹.1047; AnglAnz 8.3. Preusler *Syntax im P. M.,* Breslau diss. 1914.

[26] ERTHE UPON ERTHE. Ed. all texts, EETSES 141;— separate

texts, Kild Ged 176; Ch&Sidg 361; MLR 3.218; Cook Reader 436.—
Kittredge, MLN 9.270.

[27] SIGNS OF *DEATH*. Ed. Jesus, EETS 49.101;— Harley 7322,
Rel Ant 1.64; EETS 15(revised).253.— Brandl §20; Schofield 483.—
Whanne þe ffet, Wonne þin eren, ed. EETS 15(revised).249.— *When þe
hee,* ed. Yksh Wr. 1.156.— *Kinge I sitte,* ed. Rel Ant 1.64; EETS 15(revised).251.

[28] THREE MESSENGERS OF DEATH.   See Folk-Lore Soc. Már.
20, 1899; Acad Mar. 30, 1889.— Ed. *Vernon,* EETS 117.443; Arch 79.432;—
Addit., ESt 14.182.— Notes, Angl 13.359; ESt 16.155.— Brandl §31.

[29] ENEMIES OF MAN.   Ed. Turnbull *Owain Miles,* etc., Edbg. 1837;
ESt 9.440.   Text-notes, Angl 13.359, 15.190, ESt 13.136, 19.149.— Brandl
§40.

[30] SAYINGS OF ST. BERNARD.   Ed. Harley, Wright SLP 101;
Böddeker 225 (see also 459;— on l. 76, see ESt 3.103);— Vernon, Auchin-
leck, Angl 3.285, 291;— Digby, Angl 3.59; Ch&Sidg 163; 'Ubi Sunt,' Cook
Reader 432;— Auchinleck, Laing *Peniworth of Witte,* Abbotsf. Club 1857,
119;— Harley, *Vernon,* Laud, Digby, EETS 117.511, 757.—Brandl §42.—
On 'Ubi Sunt' formula, see MLN 8.65, 94, 253, 24.257, 28.106, 197; Creize-
nach *Verhandlungen der 28ten Versammlung Deutschen Philologen u.
Schulmänner,* Leipzig 1873, 203; Gummere *Beginnings of Poetry* 148.

[31] SAWS OF ST. BEDE.   Ed. Digby, EETS 117.765; AELeg 1881,
505 (with var. of Jesus);— Jesus, EETS 49.72.— Brandl §13.   Wolderich
*Über die Sprache u. Heimat Einiger . . . Gedichte des Jesus u. Cotton
MS.,* Halle diss. 1909, 34.

[32] DOOMSDAY.   Ed. EETS 49.163.— Brandl §20.

[33] ON SERVING CHRIST.   Ed. EETS 49.90.— Brandl §20.

[34] SONG ON DEATH.   Ed. Rel Ant 1.138.

[35] OLD AGE.   Ed. Rel Ant 2.210; Furnivall EEP 148; Kild Ged
167.— Brandl §28.

[36] DEATH.   Ed. EETS 49.168; Percy Soc. 11.70.— Brandl §13; Ten
Brink 1.207; MLN 1890.193.

[37] THREE SORROWFUL TIDINGS.   Ed. Jesus, EETS 49.101;—
Arundel, Rel Ant 1.235; Arch 128.367-8;— Harley, EETS 15(revised).250.

[38] CAMBRIDGE 4407 (19) FRAGMENTS.   See MLR 7.150.

[39] GHENT 317 FRAGMENTS.   Ed. Arch 87.431.

[40] HARLEY 2316 PIECES.   Ed. Rel Ant 2.119.— Herbert 3.573.

[41] MAXIMIAN.   Ed. Harley, Böddeker 245; Rel Ant 1.119;— Digby,
Angl 3.275 (text-notes, Angl 13.360).   Latin orig., ed. Wernsdorf *Poetæ
Lat. Min.* 6.1.269.— Brandl §46; Schofield 443.— Skeat *Oxf. Chaucer* 5.287
note 727, 7.548; Hazlitt's Warton 3.136; Bernhardy *Röm. Lit.* 624; Teuffel
Röm. Lit. 1167.

[42] TREATISE OF PARCE MICHI. Ed. *Douce,* EETS 124.143. See Yksh Wr 2.389 col. 2.

[43] 'AL ES BOT A FANTUM.' Ed. Galba, ESt 21.201; Yksh Wr 2.457;— Cbg., Rel Ant 2.20.

[44] TWO LULLABIES. Ed. Harley 913, Rel Ant 2.177;— Harley 913, Ghent, Ch&Sidg 166, 360;— Harley 913 and 7358, Cbg., Kild Ged 172, 211;— Ghent, Arch 87. 432.

[45] 'WEOLE ÞU ART.' Ed. EETS 49.86.

[46] LONG LIFE. Ed. Cott., Jesus, EETS 49.156;— Laud, Angl 1.410;— *Aȝenbite* copy, Angl 2.71; EETS 23.129;— Kent copy, Angl 3.67; EETS 49.36.— Brandl §11; Ten Brink 1.208.

[47] HARLEY 7322 SCRAPS. Ed. verse pieces, EETS 15(revised).249. See Herbert 3.166.

[48] AUGUSTINUS DE CONTEMPTU. Ed. Yksh Wr 2.374.

[49] CONSILIA ISODORI. Ed. Yksh Wr 2.367.

CHAPTER VIII—TRANSLATIONS AND PARAPHRASES OF THE BIBLE, AND COMMENTARIES

See Mombert *English Versions of the Bible,* 1883, enlarged 1907; Stoughton *Our English Bible,* 1878; Moulton *History of the English Bible,* 1895; Hoare *Evolution of the English Bible,* 2nd ed. 1902; Forshall and Madden *The Wycliffite Versions of the Holy Bible,* Oxf. 1850, introds. 4 vols.; Paues *A Fourteenth Century Biblical Version,* Cbg. 1902, the valuable introd., which is not in the 1904 and 1909 eds.; Ency Brit, *Bible;—* Berger *La Bible Française au Moyen Âge,* Paris 1884.— Cook *Bibl. Quotations in O. E. Prose Writers,* 2 parts, N. Y. and L. 1898, 1903; Smyth *Bibl. Quotations in M. E. Lit. before 1350,* YaleSt 41 (1911).— On O. E. versions, Paul Grundriss 2nd ed. 2¹.1116.

1. THE OLD TESTAMENT

[1] GENESIS AND EXODUS. Ed. EETS 7 revised (crit. AnglAnz 6.1). Selections: AESprPr 1.75; Zupitza Übungsbuch; Wülcker Lesebuch 1.1; Morris Spec 1.163 (see Angl 25.321); Emerson Reader 21. On text: ESt 2.120, 3.273, 4.98, 16.429, 17.292; Arch 90.143, 295, 107.317, 386, 109.126; Angl 15.191, 22.141; MLN 26.50.— Brandl §21; Körting §73; Ten Brink 1.197, 391; Schofield 374; Cbg Hist 1.250.— Authorship, Angl 5.43.— Hilmer *Die Sprache von G. u. E.,* Sondershausen prgr. 1876.

[2] STORY OF JOSEPH. Ed. Heuser, Bonner Beitr 17.83 (crit. Neu Phil. Rundschau 1906.329; MLN 22.250).

[3] STROPHIC *V*ERSION OF O. T. PIECES. Ed. *De Matre* and *De Anthiaco*, parts of Bath MS., Arch 79.447;— Selden, Angl 31.6;— Selden *Genesis* ll. 1-48, Angl 31.4.— Bath MS. descr., ESt 10.203.— Brandl §78.

[4] VERSE *V*ERSION OF O. T. PASSAGES. Ed. EETS 69.96, 82.— Brandl §71.

[5] PETY IOB. Ed. Harley with var., Yksh Wr 2.380;— Douce, EETS 124.120.

[6] 'BY A FOREST SYDE.' Ed. EETS 124.143.

[7] LESSONS OF THE *D*IRIGE. Ed. EETS 124.107.

[8] SUSANNAH or SEEMLY SUSAN or PISTILL OF SUSAN. Ed. Phillipps, Arch 74.339;— *V*ernon, Laing *Sel. Rem. of Anc. Pop. Poetry of Scotl.*, 1822, revised Hazlitt, 1895, 1.45; EETS 117.626; Angl 1.93 (see 55);— Cott. with var. of Addit., Arch 62.406;— crit. text, Köster, QF 76 (crit. ESt 23.85; Ctbl 96. No. 7; Museum 4.6);— all but *V*ernon, Amours STS 27, and 38.189 (1892-7).— Brandl §75; Körting §103; Ten Brink 3.50; Cbg Hist 2.138; Schofield 465.— Brade *Über Huchowns Pystil of Swete Susan*, Breslau diss. 1892.— Swedish piece, AnglBbl 7.373;— ballad in Percy's *Reliques*, and Danish and Swedish pieces, Angl 8.22.— Brown, Athen 1902.2.254.— See under *Huchown Discussion*, below.

[9] HUCHOWN DISCUSSION. Large bibliogr., Geddie *Bibliogr. of Middle Scots Poets*, STS 61.40 ff. Summary, MacCracken *Concerning Huchown*, PMLA 25.507.— The following are the chief discussions of the direct topics, since 1878. See Geddie *op. cit.* Trautmann *Der Dichter H. u. seine Werke*, Angl 1.109; Amours *Scott. Allit. Poems*, STS introds.; Ten Brink 3.50; Morley 3.278, 6.61, 121, 237, 7.144; J. T. T. Brown *Poems of David Rate*, Scott Antiq 12.5; M'Neill *H. of the Awle Ryale*, Scott. Rev. Apr. 1888; G. Neilson *Sir Hew of Eglintoun and H.*, Proc. Phil. Soc. Glasgow 32.111; Neilson *Crosslinks betw. Pearl and the Awntyrs*, Scott Antiq 16.67; Neilson *Three Footnotes, Furnivall Misc.* 1901, 383; Chambers' *Cycl. of Engl. Lit.* 1.171, 174 (1901); Neilson *H. of the Awle Ryale*, Glasgow 1902 (crit. ESt 32.124; AnglBbl 17.16; N&Q 1902.458; Athen 1902. No. 3916); Neilson *Early Lit. MSS.*, 1902, 265; Scott Antiq 17.51; Athen 1900.1.591, 751, 2.826, 1901.1.19, 52, 81, 114, 145, 176, 213, 244, 694, 760, 2.157, 254, 319, 351, 559, and 1902-3 indexes; Neilson *Barbour's Bruce and the Buik of Alexander*, Scott Antiq 16.1206; J. T. T. Brown *The Pistill of Susan*, Athen 1902.2.254; Brown *H. of the Awle Ryale and his Poems*, Glasgow 1902 (crit. ESt 32.124; AnglBbl 17.16); Gollancz *Recent Theories concerning H.*, Lond. Phil. Soc. Nov. 3, 1901 (see Athen Nov. 23, 1901); Cbg Hist 2.115, 133, 510; Björkman *Zur Huchown-Frage*, ESt 48.171. See under *Susannah; Sir Gawayne and Grene Knight; Pearl Poet; Morte Arthure; Golagrus; Barbour; Alliterative Verse.*

[10] PURITY (CLANNESSE) and PATIENCE. See p. 864.

[11] SOUTHERN TEMPORALE. See pp. 806 [19], 827.

[12] STORY OF ADAM AND EVE. See p. 813.

[13] SURTEES PSALTER. Ed. Cott., Surtees Soc., 2 vols. 1843-7;— Cott. with vars. of Egerton and Harley, Yksh Wr 2.129. Selections: AESprPr 1.267; Wülcker Lesebuch 1.9; Morris Spec 2.23.— Brandl §60; Körting §128; Ten Brink 1.285.— On MS. Bodley, Angl 29.385; Wende *Überlieferung u. Spr. des Me. Psalters,* Breslau 1884.— On development of *Psalter,* Wildhagen *Studien zum Psalterium Romanum in England,* Halle 1913. See Ency Brit, *Psalms.*

[14] ROLLE'S COMMENTARY ON THE PSALTER. Ed. Bramley, Oxf. 1884 (crit. Angl 8 Anz 170). See Paues *A Fourteenth Cent. Engl. Bibl. Version,* Cbg. 1902, xxxi (private print; not the issue of 1904 or 1909); ·ESt 10.112; AnglAnz 8.170; Middendorff *Studien über R. R. of Hampole,* Magdeburg 1888 (crit. Angl 11.326).

[15] LOLLARD REVISIONS OF ROLLE'S PSALTER. On Trin. Cbg. and Royal version, see Arnold *Sel. Engl. Works of Wyclif* 3.3; Paues *op. cit.* 1902, xliii.— On Trin. Dublin version, see Paues *op. cit.* 1902, li.— Brandl §78.

[16] THE CANTICLES. Ed. Bramley *op. cit.* 494; Arnold *op. cit.* 3.3. See Paues *op. cit.* 1902, lii-liv.

[17] WEST MIDLAND PROSE PSALTER. Ed. EETS 97 (crit. LitBl 12.372). Selection: Emerson Reader 100.— Körting §128 anm.; Schofield 374. See Paues *op. cit.* 1902, lvi. Hirst *Phonol. of Lond. MS. of Earliest Complete Engl. Prose Psalter,* Bonn diss. 1907.

[18] JEROME'S PSALTERIUM ABBREVIATUM. See Paues *op. cit.* 1902, lxiii. Latin orig., Yksh Wr 1.392.

[19] COMMENTARY ON· PSALMS 90 AND 91. See Paues *op. cit.* 1902, liv.

[20] PARAPHRASE OF PSALM 50. Ed. Laing *Penixorth of Witte,* Abbotsf. Club 1857, 76; ESt 9.49 (on text, Angl 13.359).

[21] SEVEN PENITENTIAL PSALMS. Ed. Dig., Ashm., Rawl., ESt 10.215;— Vernon, EETS 98.12;— Addit., EETS 15(revised).279. Selection: Morris Spec 2.231. On Digby, see EETS 124.vii. Aaler, Berlin diss. 1885, most incorp. in ESt 10.215.— On Maidenstone, see Wright *Allit. Poem on Deposition of Richard II,* L. 1838, vii; ESt 10.232; DNB.

[22] BROMPTON'S PENITENTIAL· PSALMS. Ed. Percy Soc. 7. Selections: Wülcker Lesebuch 2.1.— Brandl §119; Körting §128 anm.

[23] PENITENTIAL AND GRADUAL PSALMS. See p. 819 [18].

[24] PSALTERIUM BEATE MARIÆ. Ed. EETS 98.49, 106.

2. The New Testament

[25] LIFE OF JESUS. See Paues *op. cit.* 1902, lxv.

[26] SOUTHERN TEMPORALE. See p. 806 [19]; Paues *op. cit.* 1902, lxviii.

[27] PROSE VERSION OF SELECTED PARTS. Ed. Paues *A Fourteenth Cent. Engl. Bibl. Version,* private print Cbg. 1902, revised without valuable introd. 1904, cheaper issue of revision 1909.

[28] COMMENTARY ON MATTHEW, MARK, AND LUKE. See Forshall and Madden *Wycliffite Versions of Holy Bible* 1.ix; Paues *op. cit.* 1902, 1904, introds.

[29] COMMENTARY ON MATTHEW, LUKE, AND JOHN. See Forshall and Madden *op. cit.* 1.viii; Arnold *Sel. Engl. Works of Wyclif* 1.iv.

[30] VERSION OF PAULINE EPISTLES. See Forshall and Madden *op. cit.* 1.xiii.

[31] CLEMENT OF LANTHONY'S HARMONY. See Forshall and Madden *op. cit.* 1.x.

[32] BODLEY *V*ERSE PIECES. Ed. Angl 29.396.

[33] RAWLINSON STROPHIC PIECES. Ed. Angl 27.283.

[34] BALLAD OF TWELFTH DAY. Ed. MLR 9.235.

[35] WOMAN OF SAMARIA. Ed. EETS 49.84; Zupitza Übungsbuch; MacLean Reader 78.— Brandl §16.

[36] PARABLE OF LABORERS. Ed. Wright SLP 41; Böddeker 184; Morris Spec 2.46.

[37] PASSION OF OUR LORD. Ed. EETS 49.37.— Brandl §16; Ten Brink 1.212; Schofield 459. Wolderich *Die Sprache u. Heimat Einiger Frühme. Relig. Ged. des Jesus u. Cotton MS.,* Halle diss. 1909, 9.

[38] A LERNYNG TO GOOD LEUYNGE. Ed. EETS 124.96.

[39] APOCALYPSE OF ST. JOHN. See Forshall and Madden *op. cit.* 1.vii; Paues *op. cit.* 1902, xxi; Arnold *Sel. Engl. Works of Wyclif,* Oxf. 1869-71, 1.vi.— Note the Royal E 1732 f. 67 version indicated by Vaughan *Life and Opinions of John de Wycliffe,* 1831, 2.389.— Norman Commentary, ed. Meyer and Delisle, Paris 1901.— See the ed. by Herbert for the Roxb. Cl. 1909, of the splendid French MS. Trin. Coll. Cbg. R, 16, 2.

[40] GOSPEL OF NICODEMUS. See p. 814.

3. Wycliffe-Purvey Translations of the Bible

[41] WYCLIFFITE VERSIONS OF BIBLE. Ed. both versions, Forshall and Madden *The Wycliffite Versions of the Holy Bible,* Oxf. 1850, 4 vols.; Skeat *The New Testament in English according to the Version by J. W. . . . and Revised by John Purvey,* Oxf. 1879; Skeat *The Books of Job, Psalms, Proverbs, Ecclesiastes, and the Song of Songs . . . ,* Oxf. 1881; *The New Testament in Scots,* Nisbet's version of Purvey, STS 3 vols. 1901-5.— Selections: AESprPr 2.243; Morris Spec 2.215; Wülcker Lesebuch 2.144, 166; Cook Reader 398.— Brandl §67; Körting §144; Ten Brink 2.16, 26,

32; Cbg Hist 2.66, 499; Paues *op. cit.* 1902, 1904, introds.; Ency Brit, *Bible;* DNB, *Wycliffe, Purvey, Hereford.*—Matthew *Authorship of the Wycliffite Bible,* Engl. Hist. Rev. 10.91; Carr *Über der Verhältnis der Wyclifitischen u. der Purvey'schen Bibelübersetzung zur Vulgata,* Leipzig diss. 1902; Hollack *Vergleichende Studien zur Hereford Wyclifischen u. Purveyschen Bibelübersetzung u. der Lat. Vulgata,* Leipzig diss. 1903; Förster *Wyclif als Übersetzer,* Zs. für Kirchengeschichte 12.3.4; Tucker *The Later Version of the Wycliffite Epistle to the Romans Compared with the Latin Original,* YaleSt 49 (1914); Wager *Pecock's Repressor and the Wyclif Bible,* MLN 9.193; Grimm *Der Syntakt. Gebr. der Praepositionen bei W. u. Purvey,* Marburg diss. 1892; Ortmann *Formen u. Syntax des Verbums bei W. u. P.,* Berlin diss., Weimar 1902 (crit. ESt 34.79; LitBl 1905.403; Arch 116.397; DLz 1903.1660); Skeat *On the Dialect of W's Bible,* Phil. Soc. Trans. 1895-8, 212; Smith *Syntax der W-P'schen Übersetzung* . . . , Angl 30.413 (see his Marburg diss. 1907); Thamm *Das Relativpronomen in der Bibelübersetzung Wyclifs u. Purveys,* Berlin diss. 1908.— See this bibliogr. under *Wycliffe,* p. 841.

CHAPTER IX—DIALOGUES, DEBATES, CATECHISMS

Knobloch *Die Streitgedichte im Provenzalischen u. Altfranzösischen,* Breslau diss. 1886; Selbach *Das Streitgedicht in der Altprovenzalischen Lyrik,* Ausg u. Abhdl 57; Jeanroy *Orig. de la Poésie Lyrique en France;* Jeanroy *La Grande Encyclopédie, s. v. débat;* Hist Litt 23.216; de Julleville Hist 1.384, 2.208, bibliogrs. 1.403, 2.215; Gröber 2¹.662, 699, 859, 870, 876, 948, 1183; Krit Jahresber; Arch 42.293; Hirzel *Der Dialog, ein Literarhistorischer Versuch,* Leipzig 1895; Wells ed. *Owl and Nightingale,* Boston and L. 1907, liii; Merrill *Dialogue in Engl. Lit.,* YaleSt 1911; Walther *Das Streitgedicht in der Lat. Lit. des Mittelalters,* Berlin diss. 1914.

1. DIALOGUES

Kemble *Dial. of Salomon and Saturnus,* L. 1848; von Vincenti *Die Ae. Dialoge von S. u. S.,* Leipzig 1904; Merrill *op. cit.;* Hirzel *op. cit.;* Two *Notes on O. E. Dialogue Lit., Furnivall Misc.,* 1901; Wells *op. cit.* introd.

[1] DEBATE BETWEEN BODY AND SOUL. General: Angl 2.225; Erl Beitr 1; AESprPr 1.90; Wolf, Wiener Jb. d. Lit. 59.30; von Karajan *Frühlingsgabe* 150; Wright *Lat. Poems Attr. to W. Mapes,* Camden Soc. 1841, 321; Du Méril *Poésies Pop. Lat.* 217; Keller *Romvart* 127; Hist Litt 22.162, 23.283; Gröber 2¹.33, 73, 481, 699, 870, 1179; Krit Jahresber; ZsfRPh 2.40; Kleinert *Über den Streit zwischen Leib u. Seele,* Halle diss. 1880 (crit. Angl 3.569); Wolf *Stud. zur Gesch. der Span. u. Portug. Nationallit.* 54; Arch 91.369, 92.412; JEGP 8.225 (early Lat. homily); PMLA 16.503; Dudley *Egyptian Elements in B. and S.,* BrynMawrMon 8.— English: Ed. Exeter, Grein *Bibl. d. Ags. Poesie* 1.198; Wülker heliotype reprod., Leip-

zig 1894;— Worcester, Phillipps *Fragm. of Ælfric's Grammar,* etc., L. 1838;
Singer *Departing Soul's Address to the Body,* L. 1845; Haufe, Greifswald
diss. 1880 (see LitBl 2.92; Angl 4.237); Buchholz, ErlBeitr 6 (crit. LitBl
12.12);— Bodley, Archæol 17.174; Thorpe *Anal. Anglosaxonica,* L. 1846,
153; Rieger *Alt. u. Angelsächsisches Lesebuch* 124; Schroer, Angl 5.289;
Buchholz *op. cit.*;— Cbg., Laud, Vernon, Harley, Wright *Lat. Poems Attr.
to W. Mapes* 322, 334, 340, 346;— Auch., Laud, Vernon, Digby 102, var.
of Addit., Linow, Erl Beitr 1.24, 25, 66, 67, 106 (crit. LitBl 12.12);—
Laud, AESprPr 1.90;— Royal, Angl 2.229;— Digby 86, Stengel *Codicem
Manu Scriptum Digby 86,* 93;— Harley, Böddeker 233. Mod. rend., Child,
Boston 1908; Weston *Chief M. E. Poets* 304.— Brandl §§10, 20, 42, 46;
Körting p. 61 note; Schofield 426.— On MSS., Angl 2.225.— Kunze *Þe
Desputisoun bitwen Þe Bodi and Þe Soule, eine Text-Kritische Versuch,*
Berlin diss. 1892 (crit. AnglBbl 3.302). Bruce *A Contrib. to the Study of
'The Body and the Soul': Poems in English,* MLN 5.385; Mather on passage
in Wulfstan's *Homilies,* MLN 7.185.

[2] *VICES AND VIRTUES.* Ed. EETS 89.— Brandl §11; Schofield
425.—Morsbach *Me. Gram.* 10. Merrill *op. cit.* 23; Schmidt, G., *Ueber die
Spr. u. Heimat der V. and V.,* Leipzig diss. 1899; Philippsen *Die Deklina-
tion in den V. and V.,* Kiel diss. Erlangen 1911; Meyerhoff *Die Verbalflexion in den V. and V.,* Kiel diss. 1913; Traver *The Four Daughters of
God,* Philadelphia, 1907 (crit. MLN 24.91, 196; Moyen Âge 13.139).

[3] *VIRGIN AND CHRIST.* Ed. Harley, Wright SLP 80; Wülcker
Lesebuch 1.46; Böddeker 205;— Digby, Angl 2.252; EETS 117.763.—
Brandl §42.

[4] CHILDE JESU AND MAISTRES OF THE LAWE. Ed. Vernon,
AELeg 1875, 212 (see xxvii); EETS 117.479. On var. of Addit., Arch
62.413. See Angl 14.319.— Brandl §34; Schofield 425.

[5] LAMENTATION OF MARY TO ST. BERNARD. Ed. *Cursor*
version, EETS 68.1368;— *Vernon,* Cbg., EStB 8.67;— *Vernon* and var. of
Cbg., Trin., Tib., Laud, EETS 98.297;— Tib., Yksh Wr 2.274;— second
version, all MSS., Fröhlich, Leipzig 1902. On copy in Roy. Coll. of Phys.,
Small *Engl. Metr. Hom.,* Edbg. 1862, xiv;— on MS. Sion Coll. Arc L, 40,
2a+2, EETSES 100.xxxi.— Lat. sermon, ed. *Bernard Opp.,* Antwerp 1616,
col. 156; print., ESt 8.85 (with *Vernon,* Cbg.); cf. Migne *Patr. Curs.,* Ser.
2.182. col. 1133, Paris 1879.— Kribel, ESt 8.67; Fröhlich *De Lamentatione
Sancte Marie,* Leipzig diss. 1902; Thien *Über die Engl. Marienklagen,* Kiel
1906, 77.— Brandl §60.— See *Christ on the Cross* and *Compassion of Mary.*

[6] MARY AND THE CROSS. Ed. Vernon, EETS 117.612, 46.131;—
Royal, EETS 46.197. Lat. source, notes of parallels, improvements in
Royal for Vernon, Arch 105.22.—Brandl §46; Schofield 425.— Mone
Schauspiele des Mittelalters 1.39; Dutch and Latin versions, Angl 15.504;
French version, Rom 13.521; Provençal version, SATF 75.— See *Christ on
the Cross* and *Compassion of Mary.*

[7] CRISTENEMON AND A JEW. Ed. Hazlitt's Warton *Hist. Engl.*

Poetry 3.181 (three sts.); AELeg 1878, 204; EETS 117.484. Parallels, MLN 25.141. Bearder *Über den Gebr. der Praepositionen*, Halle 1894.— Brandl §75; Schofield 425.

2. DEBATES

[8] OWL AND NIGHTINGALE. Ed. Cott., some vars. of Jesus, Stevenson, Roxb. Club 1838;— Cott., Wright, Percy Soc. 1843;— Eclectic text, most of MSS. readings, Stratmann, priv. pr., Krefeld 1867 (emendations, ESt 1.212);— both MSS. parallel, Wells, Belles Lettres Ser., Boston and L. 1907, revised 1909 (crit. Neu Phil. Rundschau 1908.402; ESt 41.403; AnglBbl 21.227);— Gadow, crit. text, Berlin diss. 1907, full print Palæstra 65 (crit. Arch 123.235; ESt 42.408; AnglBbl 21.227). Selections: AESprPr 1.40; Morris Spec 1.171 (see Angl 25.323); Manly *Engl. Poetry*, Boston 1907, 7; Cook Reader 321. Mod. rend., Weston *Chief M. E. Poets* 310.— Language: Noelle *Ueber die Spr.* . . . , Göttingen diss. 1870; Sherman *A Gram. Analysis* . . . , Trans. Amer. Phil. Assoc. 1875.69; Oliphant *Old and Middle English* 305; Egge, MLN 1887.1.12; Koch, Angl 25.323; on verbs, QF 63.12; Ebisch *Zur Syntax des Verbums* . . . , Leipzig diss. 1905; Wells *Accidence in O. and N.*, Angl 33.252; Wells *Accent-Markings in MS. Jesus*, MLN 25.108; Wells *Spelling in O. and N.*, MLN 26.139; Breier *Syn. u. Anal. des Konjunktivs in O. u. N.*, StEPhil 50.251.— Versification: Guest *Hist. of Engl. Rhythms*, revised L. 1882, 427; Schipper §121; Börsch *Ueber Metrik u. Poetik in O. u. N.*, Münster diss. 1883; Saintsbury *Hist. of Engl. Prosody*, L. 1906, 1.56; Breier, ESt 42.306; Wells ed. lxiv and notes; Gadow ed., above.— General: Wells ed., bibliogr. 184. Brandl §19; Körting §77; Morley 3.331; Ten Brink 1.214; Courthope 1.131; Schofield 427; DNB, *Guildford, Nicholas de;* Cbg Hist 1.264; Atkins, Athen 1906. 1.86; Breier *Eule u. Nachtigall*, Hannover diss., Halle 1910 (full print, StEPhil 39); Kenyon *Notes on O. and N.,* JEGP 12.572; Brandl *Spielmannsverhältnisse in Frühme. Zeit*, Sitzungsber. d. Kgl. Preuss. Akad. d. Wiss. 1910. xli. 886.

[9] THRUSH AND NIGHTINGALE. Ed. Digby, Rel Ant 1.241; Hazlitt Rem 1.50;— Auch., Angl 4.207.— Brandl §26; Körting §77 anm. 2; Ten Brink 1.309; Schofield 429.— Heider *Me. Erotischen Lyrik*, Halle 1905, 17.

[10] THE HEART AND THE EYE. Ed. MLN 30.197. On general theme, MLN 26.161. Ed. Fr. and Lat., Wright *Lat. Poems Ascr. to W. Mapes* 93, 310; later Engl., Hammond, Angl 34.235.

[11] GOD MAN AND THE DEUEL. Ed. ESt 8.259; EETS 98.329, 117.750.— Brandl §31; Schofield 425. Merrill *op. cit.* 27.

[12] BOOK OF CUPID or CUCKOO AND NIGHTINGALE. Ed. Vollmer, Berliner Beitr 17; Skeat *Oxf. Chaucer* 7.347. Hammond *Chaucer: A Bibliogr. Manual* 420. Skeat *Minor Poems of Chaucer*, 2nd ed. 1896, xxviii; Kittredge, MPhil 1.13 (date and author);— author, Acad 1894.2.67, 1896.1.365; Skeat *Oxf. Chaucer* 7.lvii. Brandl §106; Schofield 429. See Cook, Pub. Conn. Acad. of Arts and Sciences 20.214.

3. Catechisms

[13] ELUCIDARIUM. Ed. Cott. Vesp., Foerster *Two Notes on O. E. Dialogue Lit., Furnivall Misc.*, 1901, 89. See Foerster, Arch. 116.312; Napier, Acad 1890.1.134.— Print of Ashmole and Rawl., *Furnivall Misc.* 101, 104.— Ed. Ii and St. John's, Schmitt, Fr., *Die Me. Version des E. . . .*, Würzburg diss., Burghausen 1909 (see Schmitt *Die Me.,. . . E. des Hon. Aug.*, prgr. Passau 1909). Schörbach *Stud. über das Deutsche Volksbuch Lucidarius*, Quel. u. Forsch. zur Spr. u. Kulturgesch. d. Germ. *Völker* 74, Strassburg 1894. Kemble *Salomon and Saturnus*, Ælfric Soc. 1848, *passim.* Merrill *op. cit.* 21.

[14] QUESTIONES BY-TWENE THE MAISTER OF OXENFORD AND HIS CLERKE. Ed. Harley, ESt 8.284;— Lansdowne, Kemble *Salomon and Saturnus*, Ælfric Soc. 1848, 216; Rel Ant 1.230; Wülcker *Lesebuch* 2.191. See ESt 23.434 note; Merrill *op. cit.* 21.— *Salomon and Saturnus*, both pieces, ed. Kemble *op. cit.* See Kemble; von Vincenti *Die Ae. Dialoge v. S. u. S.*, Leipzig 1904 (see its bibliogr.). Ten Brink 1.88; Wülcker *Grundriss der Ags. Lit.* 3. §§378, 615-6; Körting §§48, 68a; Merrill *op. cit.* 18.—*Adrian and Ritheus*, Ed. Wright *Altdeutsche Blätter* 2.189; Kemble *op. cit.* 198; Ettmüller *Scopas et Boceras*, 1849, 39. Foerster, ESt 23.431. Wülcker *Grundriss* 3. §§88, 617-8; Körting §68a; Merrill *op. cit.* 20.

[15] YPOTIS. Ed. Vernon with var. of Addit., AELeg 1881, 341;— Cott. Calig. with var. of Arundel, Ashmole, Titus, AELeg 1881, 511;— Brome, Smith, L. T., *A Commonplace Book of the Fifteenth Century*, Norwich 1886; see Angl 7.317.— French, ed. Suchier *L'Enfant Sage*, Dresden 1910 (MSS. Addit. 36983, Cbg. Trin. Coll. B, 2, 18).— Suchier *Das Provenz. Gespräch des Kaisers Hadrian mit dem Klugen Kinde Epitus*, Marburg 1906.— Brandl §40; Körting p. 139 note; Schofield 425.— Gruber *Beitr. zu dem Me. Dialog Ipotis*, Berlin diss. 1887 (see Angl 11.642); Gruber, Angl 18.56; Suchier *op. cit.*, espec. French 149, 180, 465—best general study and bibliogr.

[16] INTER DIABOLUS ET VIRGO. Ed. ESt 23.444.

CHAPTER X—SCIENCE, INFORMATION, DOCUMENTS

1. Treatises on Hunting

[1] TWICI'S TREATISE ON HUNTING. Ed. French and English, Dryden, Middle Hill Press 1840 (25 copies); French with trans., Dryden, Daventry 1843 (private print); English, Rel Ant 1.149; French, Caius MS., Baillie-Grohman *Master of Game*, L. 1904, 218; Will. *Twici, The Art of Hunting*, Dryden's text, L. (Simpkin) 1908.— See Baillie-Grohman *op. cit.* 215; Rom Oct. 1884; Sahlender *Der Jagdtraktät Twicis*, Leipzig diss. 1894;

Sahlender *Engl. Jagd, Jagdkunde u. Jagdliteratur*, Leipzig 1895; Sahlender *Das Engl. Jagdwesen in seiner Geschichtlichen Entwicklung*, Dresden and Leipzig 1898; Werth *Altfranzösische Jagdlehrbücher*, Halle 1889; Biedermann *Ergänzungen zu Werths* . . . , ZsfRPh 1897.pt.2.— See Borchers *Die Jagd in den Me. Romanzen*, Kiel diss. 1912.

[2] THE MASTER OF GAME. Ed. Baillie-Grohman, L. 1904 (handsome print, illustr.), *q.v.* for accts. of MSS., bibliogr., of hunting treatises to 16th century—cheaper issue Chatto, L. 1909; the ed. by Mylo and Hahn announced as Palæstra 19, not issued by Sept. 1915. Mylo *Das Verhältnis des Hds. des Me.. Jagdbuches 'M. of G.,'* Berlin diss. 1908; Hammond *Chaucer: A Bibliogr. Manual* 379.

2. MEDICAL AND PLANT TREATISES

[3] PERI DIDAXEON. Ed. Cockayne *Saxon Leechdoms*, Rolls Ser., L. 1864-6, 3.81; Löwenack, Erl Beitr 12 (crit. LitBl 20.65). Schiessl *Laut- u. Flexionsverhältnisse d. . . . . P. D.*, München 1905.

[4] MEDICINA DE QUADRUPEDIBUS. Ed. Cockayne *op. cit.* 1.326 and preface; Delcourt, AnglForsch 40, Heidelberg 1914 (see MLR 10.128).

[5] THE SCIENCE OF CIRURGIE. Ed. EETS 102 (both MSS.). Schofield 465.

[6] HENSLOWE MS. RECIPES. Ed. Henslowe *Medical Works of the 14th Cent.*, L. 1899, 1-74 (notes by Skeat).

[7] RECIPES IN BRIT. MUS. Ed. Henslowe *op. cit.* 76, 123, 132.

[8] STOCKHOLM RECIPES. Ed. Angl 19.75.

[9] PHILLIPPS RECIPES. Ed. Rel Ant 1.51.

[10] STOCKHOLM-ADDITIONAL RECIPES. Ed. Stock., Archæol 30.349; Angl 18.293 (see Angl 21.442);— Addit., Angl 34.163.

[11] FIFTEENTH-CENTURY RECIPES. Ed. Heinrich *Ein Me. Medizinbuch*, Halle 1896 (crit. Ctbl 1896.1674; Arch 99.170; AnglBbl 7.233).

[12] JOHN OF ARDERNE'S TREATISES. Ed. EETS 139 (*Fistula* only).

[13]-[14] TREATISE ON BLOOD-LETTING and VIRTUES OF HERBS. Ed. Rel Ant 1.189, 194.

[15] HERBARIUM APULEII. Ed. Cockayne *Saxon Leechdoms* 1.1; Berberich AnglForsch 5 (includes diss. of 1900;— crit. LitBl 1902.285).

3. GLOSSES

[16] MODERN COMPILATIONS OF PLANT-NAMES. Pr. Earle *English Plant-Names;* Henslowe *Med. Works of the 14th Cent.*, L. 1899, 147.

[17] *DIGBY* 172 GLOSS. Ed. Ellis *Anec. Oxon.* Class. Ser. 1.pt.5.27 (1885); Gröber, Strassburger Festschrift zur *XLVI* Versammlung Deutscher Philologen u. Schulmänner, 1901, 39; Förster, Arch 109.314.

[18] RAWLINSON G 57 GLOSS. Ed. Arch 117.17.

[19] STOWE 57 GLOSSES. Ed. Arch 121.411.

[20] ENGLISH-FRENCH LEGAL GLOSS. Ed. Julius, Rel Ant 1.33; Wülcker Lesebuch 1.120;— Galba, M. Foerster in *Beitr. zur Rom. u. Engl. Phil., Festgabe für W. Förster,* Halle 1902, 205 (*q.v.* for general notice). See texts in Roger of Hoveden *Chronicon,* ed. Stubbs, L. 1869, 2.242; B. de Cotton's *Hist. Anglicana,* ed. Luard, L. 1859, 439; *Chartulary of St. Mary's Abbey,* ed. Gilbert, L. 1884, 1.375; *Munimenta Gildhallæ Londoniensis,* ed. Riley, L. 1862, 3.453; Higden's *Polychronicon,* ed. Babington, L. 1869, 2.92; *Liber Monasterii de Hyda,* ed. Edwards, L. 1866, 42; *Red Book,* ed. Hall, L. 1896, 3.1032.

[21] CAMBRIDGE-ARUNDEL GLOSS. Ed. Rel Ant 2.78 (Cbg.).

[22] CAMBRIDGE Eᴇ GLOSS. Ed. Skeat, Phil. Soc. Trans. 1903-6, appendix 1.*

[23] HARLEY 978 and ADVOCATES' GLOSSES. Ed. Harley, Rel Ant 1.36;— Advoc., Arch 100.158.

4. GEOGRAPHY, TRAVEL, ETC.

Heidrich *Das Geogr. Weltbild des Späteren Engl. Mittelalters* . . . . , Freiburg 1915.

[24] GEOGRAPHY IN VERSE. Ed. Rel Ant 1.271.

[25] DESCRIPTION OF DURHAM. Ed. Rel Ant 1.129. See Paul Grundriss 2nd ed. 2¹.1079-80.

[26] CHARACTERISTICS OF COUNTIES. Ed. Rel Ant 1.269, 2.41; Hearne's *Leland's Itinerary* 5.introd.— Brandl §§52, 59.

[27] SHIRES AND HUNDREDS. Ed. EETS 49.145.

[28] LIST OF 108 ENGLISH TOWNS. Ed. Engl. Hist. Rev. 1901.501. See Arch 107.386.

[29] STATIONS OF ROME. Ed. Cott., Lamb., EETS 15(revised). 143;— *Vernon,* prol. EETS 117.609, body EETS 25.1;— Porkington, EETS 25.30;— Advocates', Turnbull *Visions of Tundale,* 1843. Selection: Cook Reader 261.— Brandl §40; Schofield 461.

[30] STATIONS OF JERUSALEM. Ed. AELeg 1881, 355. On author, Scottish Antiquary 11.145.

[31] TRAVELS OF MANDEVILLE. Ed. Cott., Halliwell, L. 1839 and 1866;— Egerton, Warner, Roxb. Club 1889 (with French text); Laynard, L. 1895; Pollard, L. 1901 (mod. spell.). Selections: AESprPr 2.155; Wülcker

Lesebuch 2.200; Morris Spec 2.164; Cook Reader 2.48.— Brandl §67; Körting §142; Morley 4.279; Cbg Hist 2.90, 505 (bibliogr.); Bormans *Bibliophile Belge* 1866.236; Nicholson, Acad 25.261; Bovenschen *Die Quellen f. d. Reisebeschreibung des J. v. M.,* Berlin diss. 1888, revised for Zs. d. Gesellschaft f. Erdkunde zu Berlin, Bd. 23.Hefts 3 and 4; *Vogels Die Ungedruckten Lat. Versionen M's,* Crefeld 1886; Vogels *Handschriftliche Untersuchungen über die Engl. Version M's,* Crefeld 1891; Montegut *Heures de Lecture,* Paris 1891, 235; Fife *Der Wortschatz des Engl. M.* . . . (Cott. MS.), Leipzig 1902 (crit AJPhil 28 pt.1); Fyvie *Some Literary Eccentrics,* N. Y. and L. 1906; DNB; Ency Brit 9th ed., 11th ed., *Mandeville.*

5. NATURAL SCIENCE

[32] INFLUENCE OF PLANETS. Ed. Arch 106.351.

[33] DISTANCE BETWEEN EARTH AND HEAVEN. Ed. Arch 106.349.

[34] FRAGMENT ON POPULAR SCIENCE. Ed. Harley, Wright *Pop. Treatises on Science,* 1841, 132;— Laud, JbREL 13.150; AESprPr 1.136. Selection: Arch 98.401.— Schofield 432, 461, 486.

[35] DE PROPRIETATIBUS RERUM. Extracts in Steele *Med. Lore,* L. 1893.— See DNB, *Trevisa;* Schofield 433.

[36] EMB ÞUNRE. Ed. Angl. 10.185.

[36a] MINOR COLLECTIONS. Ed. Arch 120.43, 121.30, 128.55, 285, 129.16; Cockayne *Saxon Leechdoms,* L. 1864-66.

6. MISCELLANEOUS PIECES

[37] EIGHT MISC. RECIPES. See Böddeker x.

[38] MIDDLE ENGLISH MEASURES. Ed. Rel Ant 1.70.

[39] DEFINITION OF ROBBERY. Ed. Rel Ant 2.38.

[40] CONSTITUTIONS OF MASONRY. Ed. Halliwell, 1844.— Brandl §72.

[41] SEVEN AGES OF THE WORLD. Ed. Caligula, Angl 11.6; Hyde, W. de G. Birch, *Liber Vitæ, Register and Martyrology of New Minster and Hyde Abbey,* L. 1892, 81;— Arundel, Angl 11.105. Paul Grundriss 2nd ed. 2¹.1125 §128.

7. CHARMS

[42] 'WENNE, WENNE.' Ed. Trans. Roy. Soc. of Lit. 11.463; ZsfDA 31.45; AnglBbl 19.213.

[43] NAMES OF A HARE. Ed. Rel Ant 1.133.

[44] TWO CHARMS FOR TOOTH-ACHE. Ed. Yksh Wr 1.375; Rel Ant 1.126; one piece, Cook Reader 379.

8. DREAM BOOKS

[45] METRICAL TREATISE ON DREAMS. Ed. Rel Ant 1.261; Arch 127.31.— See Cockayne *Saxon Leechdoms;* Arch 125.42 on occidental dream books; Gotthardt *Über die Traumbücher des Mittelalters,* prgr. Eisleben 1912.

[46] PROSE DREAM BOOK. Ed. Arch 127.48.

9. DOCUMENTS

[47] EARLY CHARTERS. Ed. Thorpe *Diplomatarium Anglicum Ævi-Saxonici,* L. 1865, 368-445.

[48] EARLY WILLS. Ed. Thorpe *op. cit.* 581-600.

[49] HEMING'S ACCOUNT OF WULFSTAN. Ed. Hearne *Heming's Chartularium,* 1723, 403; Thorpe *op. cit.* 445. See Keller *Die Lit. Bestr. von Worcester,* 1900, 77. Paul Grundriss 2nd ed. 2¹.1126 §128.

[50] LETTER OF EADWINE. Ed. Addit., Thorpe *op. cit.* 321;— Hyde, Birch *Liber Vitæ, Register and Martyrology of New Minster and Hyde Abbey,* L. 1892, 96. Paul Grundriss 2nd ed. 2¹.1125 §128.

[51] THREE NORTHUMBRIAN DOCUMENTS. Ed. Arch 111.275.

[52] WRITS OF GILBERT OF WESTMINSTER. Ed. first piece (and notice of second) Robinson *Gilbert Crispin,* Cbg. 1911, 37; Arch 133.133.

[53] NORTHUMBRIAN LETTER. Ed. Scott Hist Rev 1.62 (see 353).

[54] PROCLAMATION OF HENRY III. Ed. James *Facsimiles of National MSS.* Plate 19; Lounsbury *Hist. of Engl. Lang.,* revised, 487; AESprPr 2.54; Wülcker Lesebuch 1.119; Emerson *Hist. of Engl. Lang.* 71.— Brandl §25.

[55] CHARTER OF EDWARD II. Ed. Rel Ant 1.168..

[56] USAGES OF WINCHESTER. Ed. all texts, Engeroff *Untersuchung des Verwandtschaftsverhältnisses der Anglo-Französischen u. Mittelenglischen Überlieferungen der U. of W. . . . . ,* Bonner Studien 12. French, ed. Smirke, Archeol. Journal 9.69. English 1, ed. EETS 40.347;— selection, Gross *The Gild Merchant,* Oxf. 1890, 2.254. English 2, selection, Appendix to 6th Report of Royal Commission on Hist. Docs. 602-3.— On verbs, QF 63.23.

[57] A DEED OF 1376. Ed. *Engl. Misc. Pres. to Dr. Furnivall,* Oxf. 1901, 347.

[58] TWO WILTSHIRE DOCUMENTS. See Morsbach *Ueber den Ursprung der Neuengl. Schriftsprache* 3.

[59] FIRST PETITION TO PARLIAMENT. Ed. *Rolls of Parl.* 3.225; Morsbach *op. cit.* 171; Emerson Reader 232.

[60] APPEAL OF THOMAS USK. See Morsbach *op. cit.* 11; Skeat N&Q 10th Ser. 1.245.

[61] SCOTTISH DOCUMENTS. Ackermann *Die Spr. der Ältesten Schot. Urkunden,* Göttingen diss. 1897 (crit. AnglBbl 13.202); Meyer *Flexionslehre der Ältesten Schot. Urkunden,* Halle diss. 1907, see pp. 4 ff. for bibliogr. (crit. Neu Phil. Rundschau 1907. No. 20; DLz 1907.2589).

[62] ENGLISH WILLS. Ed. EETS 78.— Will of Folkyngham, ed. Yksh Wr 2.448; Cook Reader 381.

[63] ENGLISH GUILD RECORDS. Ed. EETS 40. Selection: Cook Reader 387.— Schultz *Die Spr. der 'English Guilds,'* Jena diss. 1891 (crit. LitBl 12.337).

[64] LADY PELHAM'S LETTER. Pr. Hallam *Lit. of Europe,* 4th ed. 1854, 1.54, 166. See Emerson *Hist. of Engl. Lang.* 74.

CHAPTER XI—ROLLE AND HIS FOLLOWERS

1. ROLLE AND UNNAMED FOLLOWERS

[1] LIFE OF ROLLE, ETC. Horstmann *Yorkshire Writers,* 2 vols. L. 1895-6, introds. (crit. Arch 96.368, 99.158; ESt 24.275; AnglBbl 6.354, 7.358; Athen 1897.1.377; Ctbl 1896.349, 1897.658; LitBl 17.404); *Officium de S. Ricardo,* EETS 20; *Brev. Eccl. Ebor.,* Surtees Soc. 1882, Vol. 2; DNB, *Rolle;* Harford ed. *Mending of Life,* L. (Allenson) 1913, introd.; Deanesley ed. *The 'Incendium Amoris' of R. R. of H.,* Manchester 1915, introd.; Brandl §61; Ten Brink 1.291; Körting §140; Cbg Hist 2.49, 497 (bibliogr.); Schofield 105.

[2] CANON. Yksh Wr 2.xxxvi; Kühn *Über die Verfasserschaft der in Horstmanns Libr. of E. E. Wr. Band I u. II Enthaltenen Lyr. Ged.,* Greifswald diss. 1900; Schneider *The Prose Style of R. R. of H.,* Baltimore diss. 1906; *Meditatio de Passione Domini* and *Speculum Vitæ,* ESt 7.454, 468, 12.463; Angl 15.197; MPhil 4.67 (on Worcester Cathed. MS. 172).— See Allen, RadMon 15.115 ff.

[3] CRITICISM. See Horstmann, Kühn, Schneider, ESt, etc., above. Hahn *Quellenuntersuchung zu R. R's Engl. Schriften,* Berlin diss. 1900; Liebermann *Zur Me. Handschriftkunde, Hampole u. Lydgate,* Arch 104.360; Henningsen *Über die Wortstellung in den Prosaschriften R. R's of H.,* Kiel diss., Erlangen 1911; Spurgeon *Mysticism in Engl. Lit.,* Cbg. 1913; ESt 3.406, 10.215.— See under [1], [2] above.— Notice of a new Rolle MS., Arch 110.103; Spurgeon *Mysticism in Engl. Lit.,* Cbg. 1913, 116.— See this bibliogr. Chapter VIII [14], [15].

I. Writings Accepted as by Rolle

[4] PRICKE OF CONSCIENCE. Ed. Morris, Phil. Soc., Berlin 1863.
Selections: AESprPr 1.286; Wülcker Lesebuch 1.30; Morris Spec 2.107.
Abstract, Morley 4.264;— Brandl §61; Körting §140; Ten Brink 1.295;
Schofield 388; Cbg Hist 2.55.— On MSS., ESt 23.1; Trans. Phil. Soc. 1890;
Arch 86.383; MLN 20.210; MPhil 4.67. On ll. 7651-86, Arch 106.349.
Interp. notes, Angl 26.366. Allen *Authorship of the P. of C.,* RadMon
15.115; Allen *Notes on the Speculum Vitæ,* prgr. MLA 1914. Sources:
Köhler *Kleineren Schriften,* Berlin 1901, 3. No. 26; Köhler, JbREL 6.176;
Hahn *Quellenuntersuchungen zu R. R's Engl. Schriften,* Berlin diss. 1900.—
See [1,] [2], [3] above.— *Of þo flode of þo worlde* and *þo whele of for-
tune,* ed. Yksh Wr 2.67, 70.— Royal stanza version, ed. Yksh Wr 2.36.—
Thornton version, ed. Yksh Wr 1.372.— Rawl. and Cbg. couplets, ed. Yksh
Wr 1.129 (see 443).

[5] FORM OF PERFECT LIVING. Ed. Cbg., Rawl., Harl. 1022,
Yksh Wr 1.3;— addits. in Arundel 507, Yksh Wr 1.412, 416, 417, 419. See
Yksh Wr 2.xl and note.— Selection: Cook Reader 265.— *Verse* paraphrase
in Cott., ed. Yksh Wr 2.283.— *Seven Gifts* portion, ed. Arundel 507, Yksh
Wr. 1.136; Thornton, Yksh Wr 1.196.— *Libel of Richard Hermyte,* see
MPhil 4.70.

[6] EGO DORMIO. Ed. Yksh Wr 1.49;— Parts of Arundel 507, Yksh
Wr 1.415.

[7] COMMANDMENT OF LOVE TO GOD. Ed. Yksh Wr 1.61.

[8] COMMENTARY ON THE PSALTER. See Chapter VIII [14],
[15].

[9] MEDITATIO DE PASSIONE DOMINI. Ed. Yksh Wr 1.83, 92;—
Cbg. Ll, ESt 7.415 (*q.v.* for study). See Ullmann and Zupitza, ESt 7.415,
454-468, 12.463; Angl 15.197; Thien *Über die Engl. Marienklagen,* Kiel 1906,
29-32.

[10] THORNTON, CBG. Dd, and GALBA LYRICS. See [51]-[66],
Chapters VII [43], XIII [108]-[109], Index. See Kühn under [2] above.

II. Writings Probably by Followers of Rolle

[11] A GRETE CLERK. Ed. Yksh Wr 1.82.

[12] OF GRACE. Ed. Yksh Wr 1.132, 305.

[13] OUR DAILY WORK. Ed. Yksh Wr 1.137, 310.

[14] 'FOR ALS MYKIL.' Ed. Yksh Wr 1.156.

[15] MEDITATION ON THE PASSION AND OF THREE
ARROWS. Ed. Yksh Wr 1.112.

[16] OF THREE ARROWS ON DOOMSDAY. Ed. Yksh Wr 2.446,
436. See Yksh Wr 2.xliii.

[17] TWELVE PROSE PIECES. Ed. Yksh Wr 1.104 ff.

[18] NINE POINTS BEST PLEASING TO GOD. Ed. verse, Yksh Wr 2.455;— Harley 1706 prose, Yksh Wr 2.375.

[19] PASSION OF CHRIST. Ed. Yksh Wr 1.129.

[20] TWO PROSE ANECDOTES. Ed. Yksh Wr 1.157.

[21] RULE OF THE LIFE OF OUR LADY. Ed. Yksh Wr 1.158.

[22] BENJAMIN MINOR. Ed. Yksh Wr 1.162; printed by Pepwell 1521, latter repr. Gardner *The Cell of Self-Knowledge*, N. Y. and L. 1910.

[23] 'WYTHDRAGH þI þOGHT' and 'THRE POYNTZ.' Ed. Yksh Wr 1.172.

[24] GROUP OF PROSE TRACTS. Items 1, 2, 3, printed Pepwell 1521, repr. mod. spelling Gardner *The Cell of Self-Knowledge*, 1910.— *Divine Cloud*, ed. Collins, L. 1871. See M'Intyre, Expositor Ser. 7, Vol. 4.— On the group, see Jones, R. M., *Studies in Mystical Religion* 336; Gardner *op. cit.* introd.

[25] MEDITATIO SANCTI AUGUSTINI. Ed. Yksh Wr 2.377.

[26] NARRACIO: A TALE. Ed. Yksh Wr 1.192; AESprPr 2.125; EETS 20.5.

[27] TWO PROSE ANECDOTES. Ed. Yksh Wr 1.192; EETS 20.6; AESprPr 2.125; Wülcker Lesebuch 1.116.

[28] MORALIA RICHARDI. Ed. Yksh Wr 1.193; EETS 20.8; AESprPr 2.126; Wülcker Lesebuch 1.117; Zupitza Übungsbuch; MacLean Reader 95.

[29] PROSE ANECDOTE. Ed. Yksh Wr 1.194.

[30] THREE SHORT PROSE EXPOSITIONS. Ed. Yksh Wr 1.195, 196, 197; EETS 20.9, 12, 13; AESprPr 2.128-32.

[31] TRACT ON PATER NOSTER. Ed. Yksh Wr 1.261 (see 443).

[32] PRIVITY OF THE PASSION. Ed. Yksh Wr 1.198 (see 443). See Thien *Über die Engl. Marienklagen* 29-31; EETS 60.xii.

[33] EPISTLE ON SALVATION BY LOVE. Ed. Yksh Wr 1.293 (see 2.xlii note); EETS 20.42; AESprPr 2.150.

[34] ON PRAYER. Ed. Yksh Wr 1.295. See Yksh Wr 2.xli.— Royal treatise, see Yksh Wr 443 note.

[35] SIX THINGS TO WIT IN PRAYER. Ed. Yksh Wr 1.300.

[36] A PRAYER TO CHRIST. Ed. Yksh Wr 1.367.

[37] 'HE þAT DEVOTELY SAYSE.' Ed. Yksh Wr 1.376.

[38] 'NOW IHESU GODDIS SONNE.' Ed. Yksh Wr 1.380.

[39] TWELVE PROFITS OF TRIBULATION. Ed. Royal 17 B, Yksh Wr. 2.45;— Royal 17 A, Yksh Wr 2.390;— Rawl., Yksh Wr 2.391.— On Cbg. and Bodley, see Yksh Wr 2.389 note.

[40] OF THE DOUBLE COMING OF CHRIST. Ed. Yksh Wr 2.60.

[41] SERIES OF BRIEF COUNSELS. Ed. Yksh Wr 2.66.

[42] TALKYNG OF THE LOVE OF GOD. Ed. Yksh Wr 2.345.

[43] MIRROR OF SINNERS. Ed. Yksh Wr 2.436.

[44] MEDITATION OF THE FIVE WOUNDS. Ed. Yksh Wr 2.440, 436.

[45] FULL GOOD MEDITATION. Ed. Yksh Wr 2.441, 436.

[46] MEDITATION BY ST. ANSELM. Ed. Yksh Wr 2.443, 436.

[47] 'THOU SCHALT LOVE THI LORD.' Ed. Yksh Wr 2.454 (see 449).

[48] CONTEMPLATIONS OF THE DREAD AND LOVE OF GOD. Ed. Yksh Wr 2.72.

[49] REMEDY AGAINST THE TROUBLES OF TEMPTATIONS. Ed. Yksh Wr 2.106.

[50] 'OF FOURE MANERS MAY A MAN WYT.' Ed. Yksh Wr 1.73.

[51] 'GASTLY GLADNESS IN IHESU.' Ed. Yksh Wr 1.81.

[52] MENDING OF LIFE. Printed mod. spelling, Harford, L. (Allenson) 1913 (see introd. liv on MSS.).— Misyn's trans. (1434) of *Incendium Amoris* and *De Emendatione,* ed. EETS 106; Comper, F. M. M., *The Fire of Love,* L. 1914.— Yksh Wr 2.389 note.

2. WALTER HILTON

[53] HILTON. DNB; Cbg Hist 2.340; Inge *Chr. Mysticism* 197; Inge *Studies of English Mystics,* L. 1906, 80; Allen RadMon 15.163 ff.; Spurgeon *Mysticism in Engl. Lit.,* Cbg. 1913, 124.

[54] SCALE OF PERFECTION. Ed. Guy, L. 1869. Modernized, Dalgairns, L. 1870, 2nd ed. Westminster 1908.— *Be whate takynes,* etc., ed. Yksh Wr 1.104, 105, 106 (see 443, and 2.xli note).

[55] EPISTLE ON MIXED LIFE. Ed. Yksh Wr 1.264; EETS 20.19. Selection: AESprPr 2.137. Mod. rend., Dalgairns *Scale of Perfection* (see above) 313.— Schneider *Prose Style of R. R.* (see under [2] above) 6.

[56] OF ANGELS' SONG. Ed. Thornton, EETS 20.14; AESprPr 2.133;— Thornton, Dd, Yksh Wr 1.175. Pepwell's text of 1521, mod. spell. printed Gardner *The Cell of Self-Knowledge,* 1910, 61. See Yksh Wr 2.xli note.

[57] PROPER WILL. Ed. Yksh Wr 1.173. See Yksh Wr 2.xli note.

[58] ENCOMIUM NOMINIS JESU. Ed. both MSS., Yksh Wr 1.186;— Thornton, EETS 20.1; AESprPr 1.120. Schneider *Prose Style of R. R.* 6.

[59] OF DEADLY AND VENIAL SIN. Ed. Yksh Wr 1.182. See Yksh Wr 1.173, 2.xli note.

[60] AGAINST BOASTING, SAYINGS OF FATHERS. Ed. Yksh Wr 1.122, 125. See Yksh Wr 1.443, 2.xli note.

3. WILLIAM NASSYNGTON

[61] NASSYNGTON. DNB; Cbg Hist 2.52-3; Allen RadMon 15.163 ff.

[62] MIRROR OF LIFE. See Chapter VI [8]. Allen *Notes on the Speculum Vitæ*, prgr. MLA 1914.

[63] TREATISE ON TRINITY AND UNITY. Ed. Yksh Wr 2.334 (see 2.274); EETS 26.59.

[64] METRICAL FORM OF LIVING. Ed. Yksh Wr 2.283.

4. JULIANA LAMPIT

[65] JULIANA. DNB; Cbg Hist 2.342 note; Inge *Studies of Engl. Mystics*, L. 1906, 50; Spurgeon *Mysticism in Engl. Lit.*, Cbg. 1913, 120.

[66] FOURTEEN REVELATIONS. Ed. Paris MS., Cressy, 1670, repr. 1843;— Sloane, Collins, 1877, for Med. Libr. of Mystical and Ascetical Works;— Paris MS., Warrack, 1901;— modernized after Cressy, Tyrrell, L. 1902; *All Shall Be Well, Selections* . . . , Mowbray, 1908;— Amherst MS., *Comfortable Words for Christ's Lovers*, Harford, L. (Allenson). See Dalgairns *Scale of Perfection*, Westminster 1908, xviii.

CHAPTER XII—WYCLIFFE AND HIS FOLLOWERS

[1] LIFE, ETC. Lewis *Hist. of Life and Sufferings of John Wycliffe*, L. 1720, Oxf. 1820; *Vaughan Life and Opinions of J. de W.*, 2 vols. 1828, 2nd ed. 1831 referred to below; Lechler *Johann von Wyclif u. die Vorge-schichte der Reformation*, 2 vols. Leipzig 1873, Engl. trans. 1878 referred to below, cheaper ed. 1903; Matthew, EETS 74.introd.; Buddensieg *J. W. Patriot and Reformator*, L. 1884; Sergeant *J. W. Last of the Schoolmen and First of the English Reformers*, L. 1893 (see Athen Mar. 26, 1892, Feb. 21, 1893; Acad Apr. 1, 1893); Trevelyan *England in the Age of Wycliffe*, 3rd ed. 1900; Twemlow *W's Preferments and University Degrees*, Engl. Hist. Rev. 1900.529; Rae *J. W., His Life and Writings*, London 1903; Loserth *W's Activity in Eccles. Politics*, Engl. Hist. Rev. 11.319; Loserth *Neue Erscheinungen*, Hist. Zs. 95.271; Loserth *Hus u. Wiclif*, Prag 1884, trans. Evans 1884; Loserth *Stud. zur Kirchenpolitik Englands im 14 Jhdt.*, Sitzungsber. d. K. Akad. d. Wiss. in Wien 1897, 1907; Carrick *W. and the Lollards*, L. 1908; Matthew, Engl. Hist. Rev. 5.328; Cannon, Ann. Rept. Amer. Hist. Ass. 1.451 (bibliogr. for 'poor priests'); Shirley *Fasciculi Zizaniorum Magistri Johannis Wyclif cum Tritico*, Rolls Ser. 1858; Cbg Hist 2.55, 500 (bibliogr.); DNB, with bibliogr.; Körting §144; Ten Brink 2.1.

[2] CRITICISM OF ENGLISH WORKS. Furstenau *J. v. W's Lehren von der Einteilung der Kirche u. von der Stellung der Geistlichen Gewalt*, Berlin 1900; Vautier *J. W., sa Vie, ses Œuvres et sa Doctrine*, Paris 1886;

Rosenkranz *W's Ethischsoz. Anschauung,* Barmen diss. 1901; Heine *W's Lehre vom Guterbesitz,* Erlangen diss. 1903; Loserth *Die Ältesten Schreibschriften W's,* Akad. Wien 1908; Loserth *W's Sendschriften, Flugschriften, u. Kleinere Werke Kirchpol. Inhalts,* Akad. Wien 1910. See Shirley, Arnold, Lechler, *V*aughan, *J*ones, as under individual works.— See Fischer *Über die Sprache J. W's,* Halle diss. 1880; Gassner *Über W's Sprache,* Göttingen diss. 1891.— On W. and Pecock, see Körting §144 note; Cbg Hist 2.500.

[3] WYCLIFFITE TRANSLATIONS OF THE BIBLE. See this bibliogr. Chapter *V*III [41].

[4] CANON OF WORKS. *V*aughan *op. cit.* 2.379; Lechler *op. cit.* 2.553; Shirley *Cat. of the Orig. Works of J. W.,* Oxf. 1865; Arnold *Sel. Works of J. W.,* Oxf. 1869-71, 3 vols., 3.xvii; Matthew EETS 74, *passim;* N&Q 6th Ser. 11 (1885); Jones *Authenticity of Some English Works Ascr. to W.,* Angl 30.261.

[5] COLLECTED EDITIONS OF ENGLISH WYCLIFFITE WRITINGS. Todd *Three Treatises of J. W.,* Dublin 1851; Arnold *Sel. Engl. Works of J. W.,* Oxf. 1869-71, 3 vols.; Matthew *The English Works of W. hitherto Unprinted,* EETS 74.— Modern issues of separate works noted under individual items.

1. Accepted Writings of Wycliffe

[6] SERMONS. Ed. On Gospels, Epistles, etc., Arnold *Sel. Wks.* Vols. 1-2.

[7] WYCKETT. See Lecher *op. cit.* 1.627 note; Vaughan *op. cit.* 2.64.

[8] VÆ OCTUPLEX, and [9] OF MINISTERS. Ed. Arnold *Sel. Wks.* 2.377, 291.

[10] ADDITIONAL SET OF 54 SERMONS ON GOSPELS. See Shirley *Cat.,* Item 1; Arnold *op. cit.* 1.iii.

[11]-[24] DIDACTIC WORKS. Ed. all in Arnold Vol. 3, pages as follows in order of mention in the text of this book: 82, 93, 98, 111, 114, 117, 117, 119, 168, 183, 186, 188 (see Paues *A Fourteenth Cent. Engl. Bibl. Version,* Cbg. 1902, lxxi note), 202, 204 (see Arnold 1.vii).

[25]-[28] STATEMENTS OF BELIEF, ETC. Ed. in Arnold Vol. 3, pages as follows in order of mention in the text of this book: 499, 501, 504, 507.

[29]-[41] CONTRO*V*ERSIAL WORKS. Ed. in Arnold Vol. 3, pages as follows in order of mention in the text of this book: 211, 213, 219, 230, 233, 242, 267, 338 (also Todd *op. cit.* 1851), 366, 402, 430 (also Todd *op. cit.* 1851), 441, 447.

2. Additional Probably Genuine Works of Wycliffe

[42]-[47] ADDITIONAL PROBABLY GENUINE WORKS. Ed. all in EETS 74, pages as follows in order of mention in the text of this book: 325, 282, 356, 346, 294, 458.

3. Wycliffite Writings

[48]-[68] PIECES BY WYCLIFFITES. Ed. all in EETS 74, pages as follows in order of mention in the text of this book: 1, 28, 39, 52, 108, 114, 141, 164, 180, 187, 197, 203, 209, 219, 226, 244, 254, 263, 275, 359, 405.

4. Writings Not by Wycliffe

[69] OF THE TWENTY-FIVE ARTICLES. Ed. Arnold 3.454.

[70] SPECULUM VITÆ CHRISTIANÆ. See Arnold 3.vi; EETS 74.xlix.

[71] ANTICHRIST AND HIS MEYNEE. Ed. Todd *op. cit.* 1851;— see Arnold 1.vi.

[72] AN APOLOGY FOR LOLLARD DOCTRINES. Ed. Todd, Camden Soc. 1842. Siebert *Untersuchungen über 'An Apology'* . . . , Königsberg diss., Charlottenburg 1906.

[73] LAST AGE OF THE CHURCH. Ed. Todd, Dublin 1840. See Forshall and Madden *Wycliffite Versions of the Bible* 1.viii.

[74] THE PORE CAITIF. See Vaughan *op. cit.* 2.385; Spalding *M. E. Charters of Christ,* BrynMawrMon. 1914, 98.

[75] BRITISH MUSEUM ADDITIONAL 24202 TRACTS or TENISON WYCLIFFITE TRACTS. See British Museum Catalogue of Additional MSS., and the references under *Treatise of Miraclis Pleyinge,* below. On *Of Weddid Men,* see Chapter XII [22]; on *The Seven Sacraments* and *The Seven Vertues,* see Chapter VI [9].— Edit. of the tracts in preparation by Prof. R. A. Jelliffe.

[76], [78]-[84] See under [75].

[77] TREATISE OF MIRACLIS PLEYINGE or SERMON AGAINST MIRACLE-PLAYS. Ed. Rel Ant 1.42; AESprPr 2.222. Selections: Cook Reader 278. Schofield 381; Chambers *Mediæval Stage* 2.102. Cook, N. Y. Nation 100.599. Edit. in preparation by Prof. A. S. Cook.

CHAPTER XIII—PIECES LYRICAL IN IMPULSE OR IN FORM

For Political and Satirical pieces, see this bibliogr. under Chapter IV. For works dealing particularly with special classes of Lyric, see the subheads below.

The works noted in the next two paragraphs cover *more than one* of the several classes.

BIBLIOGRAPHY and CRITICISM. Chambers *Some Aspects of Mediæval Lyric,* Ch&Sidg 257 (see 297 for list of MSS. and bibliogr.); Reed *Engl. Lyrical Poetry,* New Haven and L. 1912, 22-98 (see its bib-

liogr.;— crit. MLR 8.389); Rhŷs *Lyric Poetry*, L. 1913, 31-116; Schelling
The Engl. Lyric, Boston 1913, 9-31 (see its bibliogr.); Sandison *The
'Chanson d'Aventure' in Middle English*, BrynMawrMon 1913 (see its
bibliogr.; crit. ESt 48.297); Aust *Beitr. zur Gesch. der Me. Lyrik*, Arch
70.253; *V*arnhagen, notes, Angl 2.225, 3.59, 275, 415, 533, 4.180; Kölbing
Kleine Beitr., ESt 17.296; Schlüter *Ueber die Spr. u. Metr. der Me. Weltl.
u. Geistl. Lieder des MS. 2253*, Arch 71.153, 355; Müller *Me. Geistl. u.
Weltl. Lyrik des XIII Jhdts.*, Göttingen diss. 1910 (crit. ESt 46.141;—
StEPhil 44 has full print); Saintsbury *The Hist. Char. of Engl. Lyric*,
Oxf. 1912; Weichardt *Die Entwicklung des Naturgefühls in der Me. Dich-
tung vor Chaucer*, Kiel diss. 1900. Grossmann *Frühme. Zeugnisse über
Minstrels*, Berlin diss. 1906; on minstrels and songs, Chambers *Med. Stage*,
1.23-86, 160, 272, see index; Ritson AS introd.; Brandl *Spielmannsver-
hältnisse in Frühme. Zeit*, Sitzungsber. d. Preuss. Akad. d. Wiss., Berlin
1911; Schipper *Engl. Metr.;* Schipper Grundriss; Schipper *Hist. Engl.
Versification;* Ten Brink 1.153, 199, 205, 211, 280, 302, 348; Schofield 435;
Körting §§82, 126; Cbg Hist 2.422 (see its bibliogr. at 550); de Julleville
Hist, bibliogr. 1.403; Gröber 2¹.415, 444, 477, 652, 658, 659, 938, 948, 971,
1187, 1190;— on English lyric of 10th to 12th century, Paul Grundriss 2nd
ed. 2¹.1086.

COLLECTED EDITIONS. Heuser *Kildare Gedichte*, Bonn 1904 (crit.
Neu Phil. Rundschau 15.184; Indg. Anz. 18.71; AnglBbl 18.105); Böddeker
Altengl. Dichtungen des MS. Harl. 2253, Berlin 1878 (crit. LitBl 1.214;
ZsfdöGymn 1879; ESt 2.499; Angl 2.507, 15.189; Arch .70.153, 71.253; see
Brandl §26); Chambers and Sidgwick *Early Engl. Lyrics*, L. 1907, new ed.
1912; Furnivall EEP; Ritson AS; Wright PPS, PS, SLP; Rel Ant; Hazlitt
Rem; AESprPr; Stainer *Early Bodleian Music*, Oxf. 1901, 2 vols.; Oxf.
*Hist. of Music, V*ols. 1 and 2, 1901-5; Furnivall *Political, Religious, and
Love Poems*, EETS 15 (revised 1903).— Mod. rends. of sel. pieces, Weston
Chief M. E. Poets 337.— Pieces in MS. Sloane 2593, ed. Wright, Warton
Club 1856; part, Arch 107.48, 109.33; part, Wright *Spec. of Christmas
Carols*, Percy Soc. 1841; part modernized, Dalglish *XIVth Cent. Carols*,
L. 1909;— see Ch&Sidg 303, 330. Pieces in Harley 7322, ed. EETS 15(re-
vised).249. Pieces in Lambeth 853, ed. EETS 24.— For later lyrics, see
Cbg Hist bibliogr. 2.550, and other bibliogrs. above.— On carols and other
pieces probably later than 1400, see also Maitland *Engl. Carols of the 15th
Cent.*, 1891; Wright *Songs and Carols*, 1842; Wright *Songs and Carols of
XV Cent.*, Percy Soc. 1847.

1. Secular Lyrics

See all of general Lyric bibliogr. above. Heider *Untersuchungen zur Me.
Erotischen Gedichte* (1250-1300), Halle diss. 1905.— For Political and
Satirical pieces, see Chapter IV.

[1] CANUTE SONG. Ed. *Hist. of Ely* 2.27; Gale 505.— Morley 3.239;
Cbg Hist 2.451; Ten Brink 1.148; Paul Grundriss 2nd ed. 2¹.1084.

[2] LYRICS IN ROMANCES. See editions of individual romances mentioned.

[3] 'MON IN ÞE MONE.' Ed. Wright SLP 110; Böddeker 176; Ritson AS (1877) 58. Angl 2.137; Grimm *Deutsche Mythologie* 680; Scharnbach u. Müller *Niedersächs. Saga u. Märchen*, Göttingen 1855, 334; Hazlitt *Pop. Antiq. of Gr. Brit.*, 3.160; Baring-Gould *Common Myths of Mid. Ages* 190; Bladé *Contes Pop. Recueillis en Agénais*, Paris 1874, 65; Cerquand *Légendes et Récits Pop.*, Pau 1876, 5; Schneller *Märchen u. Sagen aus Wälschtirol*, Innsbruck 1867, 221.— Brandl §26.

[4] 'MIRIE IT IS.' Ed. Stainer *Ear. Bodl. Mus.* 1.plate 3, 2.5; Ch&Sidg 3.

[5] 'FOWELES IN THE FRITH.' Ed. Stainer *op. cit.* 1.plate 6, 2.10; *Oxf. Hist. of Mus.* 2.101— Ch&Sidg 5.

[6] CUCKOO-SONG. Ed. Ritson AS (1877) 9; Hawkins *Hist. of Mus.* 2.93, 96 (with mus. notes); Ellis, EETSES 7.419 (with mus. notes); Ellis, Phil. Soc. Trans. 1868-9, 103; Grove *Mus. Dict.* (with mus. notes); *Oxf. Hist. of Mus.* 1.326 (with mus. notes); Ellis EEP 1.112; Wülcker Lesebuch 1.105; Ch&Sidg 4; N&Q 9th Ser. 2.7, 109, 176, 234, 512; Cook Reader 406.— Brandl §26; Ten Brink 1.304; Schofield 443.

[7] 'LOVE IS SOFFT.' Ed. Wright *Anec. Lit.* 96.— Brandl §26.

[8]-[9] COLLEGE OF ARMS FRAGMENTS. 'A Levedy' and 'As I stod,' ed. Rel Ant 2.19.— Brandl §49. Sandison *Chanson d'Aventure* 130.

[10] RAWLINSON FRAGMENTS. Ed. Angl 30.173.

[11] 'JOLY CHEPERTE.' Ed. Ch&Sidg 279.

[12] ALYSOUN. Ed. Wright SLP 27; Ritson AS (1877) 49; Morris Spec 2.43; Wülcker Lesebuch 1.108; Böddeker 147; Zupitza Übungsbuch; Poet-Lore 6.2; Ellis EEP 1.109; Ch&Sidg 6; Cook Reader 410.— Schofield 445; Ten Brink 1.308.

[13] 'ICHOT A BURDE.' Ed. Ritson AS (1877) 50; Wright SLP 51; Böddeker 167; Wülcker Lesebuch 1.108; Cook Reader 412.— Schofield 444; Ten Brink 1.305, 307.— ESt 2.504, 17.299.

[14] 'LENTEN YS COME.' Ed. Ritson AS (1877) 54; Wright SLP 43; Böddeker 164; Wülcker Lesebuch 1.106; Morris Spec 2.48; Zupitza Übungsbuch; Ch&Sidg 8; Cook Reader 407.— Brandl §56; Schofield 447.

[15] IOHON. Ed. Wright SLP 25; Böddeker 144.— Brandl §45; Schofield 445.

[16] 'WIÞ LONGING Y AM LAD.' Ed. Wright SLP 29; Morris Spec 1.45; Böddeker 149; Cook Reader 414.— Schofield 445.

[17] 'MOSTI RIDEN BY RYBBESDALE.' Ed. Wright SLP 33; Böddeker 154. See Ch&Sidg 275; Sandison *op. cit.* 133.— Brandl §45.

[18] 'IN A FRYHT.' Ed. Wright SLP 36; Böddeker 158. Sandison *op. cit.* 132.— Brandl §49; Schofield 446.

[19] 'MY DEÞ Y LOUE.' Ed. Wright SLP 90; Böddeker 171; Ch&Sidg 12; Cook Reader 418.— Brandl §56; Schofield 446; Ten Brink 1.306 (mod. rend.).

[20] 'WHEN ÞE NYHTEGALE SINGES.' Ed. Wright SLP 62; Wülcker Lesebuch 1.110; Böddeker 173; Ritson AS (1877) 53; Ch&Sidg 10; Cook Reader 408.— Brandl §56; Ten Brink 1.306; Schofield 446.

[21] 'A WAYLE WHYT.' Ed. Wright SLP 38; Böddeker 161; Zupitza Übungsbuch.

[22] 'LUTEL WOT HIT ANYMON.' Ed. Wright SLP 113; Böddeker 177.

[23] 'IN MAY HIT MURGEÞ.' Ed. Wright SLP 45; Ritson AS (1877) 56; Böddeker 166.— Brandl §56.

[24] 'WEPING HAUEÞ ·MYN WONGES WET.' Ed. Wright SLP 30; Böddeker 150 (see 455-6).— Brandl §26; Schofield 447.

[25] 'NOW SPRINGES THE SPRAI.' Ed. MLR 4.236; reconstructed, MLR 5.104. Sandison *op. cit.* 47, 133.

[26] CAMBRIDGE Gᴏ LYRICS. 'In may,' ed. JEGP 7.105;— *De Amico* and *Responcio*, Ch&Sidg 15, 18 (see notes).

[26a] THE FALSE FOX. See Chapter II [26].

2. Religious Lyrics

See all general Lyric bibliogr. above; *Shoreham*, see Chapter VI [10]; lists under special heads below.

CRITICISM. Stengel *Codicem Manu Scriptum Digby 86*, Halle 1871; Patterson *Middle Engl. Penitential Lyric*, N. Y. 1911 (see its bibliogr.;— crit. MLR 8.215; JEGP 13.624; ESt 47.85); Wolderich *Über die Spr. u. Heimat Einiger Frühme. Relig. Ged. der Jesus u. Cotton MSS.*, Halle 1909, full print promised in StEPhil; Vollhardt *Einfluss der Lat. Geistl. Lit. auf Einige Kleinere Schöpfungen der Engl. Übergangsperiode*, Leipzig diss. 1888 (crit. Angl 11.324; ESt 13.79); Aust *Beitr. zur Gesch. der Me. Lyrik*, Arch 70.253; Holthausen *Beitr. zur Quellenkunde der Me. Geistl. Lyrik*, Arch 116.373; Trautmann, AnglAnz 5.118; Menthel, AnglAnz 8.60; Einenkel *Eine Engl. Schriftstellerin aus dem Anfange des 12 Jhdts.*, Angl 5.265; Lewin *Das Me. Poema Morale*, Halle 1881; Kölbing *Kleine Beitr.*, ESt 17.296; Taylor *The Engl. Planctus Mariæ*, MPhil 4.605; Taylor *Relation of the Engl. Corpus Christi Play to the M. E. Relig. Lyric*, MPhil 5.1 (see both arts. for bibliogr. notes); Corsdress *Die Motive der Me. Geistl. Lyrik und ihr Verhältnis zur Lat. Hymnologie des Mittelalters*, Münster diss., Weimar 1913.

COLLECTED EDITIONS. Furnivall *Relig. Poems from MS. Digby 2*, Arch 97.309 (see Arch 86.290); *O. E. Homilies*, EETS 29-34.54, 159, 190, 288, 53.220, 255; *O. E. Miscellany*, EETS 49 (see Arch 88.369); *Minor Poems of Vernon MS.*, EETS 98, 117; Yksh Wr; Patterson (see above);

Jacoby *Vier Me. Geistl. Ged.*, Berlin diss. 1890 (crit. Arch 87.262, 88.374; LitBl 11.336); Lyrics of Cott. Galba E IX, ESt 21.201.— Later lyrics of Lambeth 853, EETS 24;— Thornton, EETS 26;— Sloane 2593, Wright *Songs and Carols,* L. 1836 (20 pieces); Wright *Songs and Carols . . . ,* Warton Club 1856; part, Fehr, Arch 107.48, 109.33 (see Ch&Sidg 303-4, 330); Dalglish *XIVth Cent. Carols,* L. 1909 (sel., modernized);— Bodley Eng. Poet. E I, Wright *Songs and Carols,* Percy Soc. 1847;— Lambeth 306, Harley 7322, EETS 15(revised).249;— Douce 302, Halliwell, Percy Soc. 14;— Digby 102, ESt 23.438; EETS 124;— etc.— Mod. rends. of sel. pieces, Weston *Chief M. E. Poets* 337.

I. Miscellaneous Religious Lyrics

[27] LYRICS OF ST. GODRIC. Ed. *Libellus. de Vita S. Godrici,* ed. Stevenson, Surtees Soc. 1847; ESt 11.401; Cook Reader 453;— 'Sainte Marie,' Patterson 138.— Brandl §10; Körting §75 note; Schofield 436; Cbg. Hist. 1.244; DNB.— Music, frontispiece of Saintsbury *Hist. Engl. Prosody* 1.— Arch 90.142, 94.125; Engl. Hist. Rev. 17.479. Paul Grundriss 2nd ed. 2¹.1096-7.

[28] 'NO MORE WILLI WIKED BE.' Ed. EETS 117.756; Arch 97.312; Patterson 119.— Arch 86.290.

[29] ANTHEM OF ST. THOMAS. Ed. EETS 49.90.— Brandl §20.

[30] PRISONER'S PRAYER. Ed. Rel Ant 1.274; Phil. Soc. Trans. 1868-69.104; Wülcker Lesebuch 1.105; with French and mus. notes, EETSES 7.429.— Brandl §27.

[31] 'WORLDES BLIS.' Ed. Digby, Wright, *Anec. Lit.* 90 (coll. Stengel *MS. Digby 86* 67);—Arundel, Jacoby *Vier Me. Geistl. Ged.,* Berlin diss. 1890, 39 (with var. of Digby);— Rawl., Arch 87.262; Stainer *Ear. Bodl. Music* 1. plate iv (with facsimile), 2.5. On text, Arch 88.374.— Brandl §42.

[32] LAMENT OF THE MONK. Ed. Rel Ant 1.291.— Brandl §56.

[33] 'MIDDELERD FOR MON WES MAD.' Ed. Wright SLP 22; Böddeker 180.— Brandl §42.

[34] 'HERODES, THOU WYKKED FO.' Ed. Rel Ant 1.86.— Brandl §27.

[35] 'THE KYNGES BANERES.' Ed. Rel Ant 1.87.

[36] 'WELE, HERIƷYNG.' Ed. Rel Ant 2.225.

[37] 'MY VOLK, WHAT HABBE Y.' Ed. Rel Ant 2.225. Jacoby *op. cit.* 30.

[38] 'LOVERD, SHYLD ME.' Ed. Rel Ant 2.226; Patterson 67.

[39] 'THOU, WOMMON, BOUTE *V*ERE.' Ed. Rel Ant 2.227.

[40] 'HEYL, LEVEDY, SE-STOERRE BRYHT.' Ed. Rel Ant 2.228; Patterson 112.

[41] 'COME, SHUPPERE.' Ed. Rel Ant 2.229; Patterson 117.

[42] 'GABRIEL FRAM EVENEKING.' Ed. with Lat. and facsimile, Furnivall ChS 1ser.73.695;— Jacoby *op. cit.* 35.— Brandl §42.

[43] 'FROM HEOUENE INTO EORÞE.' Ed. EETS 49.100.

[44] NARRATIVE OF ANNUNCIATION. Ed. Angl 29.401.

[45] FIFTEENTH-CENTURY ANNUNCIATION SONGS. Ed. first text, Wright *Songs and Carols*, Percy Soc.;— second text, Wright *Songs and Carols*, Warton Club 1856;— *Ecce ancilla*, Turnbull *Visions of Tundale*, Edbg. 1843, 141.

[46] 'LUTEL WOT HIT ANYMON.' Ed. Böddeker ·230; Zupitza Übungsbuch.

[47] SONG OF JOY ON COMING OF CHRIST. Ed. EETS 69.93.

[48] 'LOUE HAUIÞ ME BROȜT.' Ed. Furnivall EEP 21; Schipper *Engl. Metr.* 1.317; Kild Ged 165.

[49]-[50] TWO LULLABIES. See Chapter VII [44].

[51] 'ÞEO SUÞE LUUE.' Ed. EETS 49.141.

[52] 'ÞURGH GRACE GROWAND.' Ed. Yksh Wr 1.161.

On Sloane 2593, Harley 7322, Lambeth 853, see gen. bibliogr. of Lyrics, and of Religious Lyrics, above.

II. Thornton Lyrics

[53]-[57] 'LORD IHESU CRYSTE,' 'ALMYGHTY GOD,' 'LORDE GOD ALWELDANDE,' 'IHESU THAT DIEDE,' 'IHESU CRISTE, SAYNTE MARYE SONNE.' Ed. Yksh Wr 1.363-4;— the last ed. also EETS 26.72; Patterson 131.

III. Cambridge Dd Lyrics

[58]-[59] 'MY TREWEST TRESOWRE,' 'IHESU, ALS ÞOW ME MADE.' Ed. Yksh Wr 1.72.

[60]-[61] 'WHEN ADAM DELF.' Ed. Cbg., Yksh Wr 1.73;— Thornton, Halliwell, *Nugæ Poeticæ*, L. 1844, 39; EETS 26.79; Angl 27.306 (with Cbg. vars.); Yksh Wr 1.367.

[62]-[68] All ed. Yksh Wr 1.74, 75, 76, 78, 79, 81, 370.

IV. Vernon-Simeon Lyrics

[69]-[76], [77]-[79], [83]-[93], [96]-[97], [102]-[106a] These, Vernon Nos. 1-28 and Simeon Nos. 29-30 (29-31), ed. EETS 117.658. Vernon Nos. 1-7 and 9-13 incl., with vars. of Simeon, ed. Angl 7.280. Simeon Nos. 1-2, 4-7 incl., ed. Furnivall EEP 118.— On Nos. 1, 2, 11, 13, 24, 26, see Sandison *Chanson d'Aventure.*— Brandl §42.

[70a] Ed. Turnbull *Visions of Tundale* 161.

[71] Ed. alsò Ritson AS (1877) 65.— Brandl §41.

[76]-[76a] Simeon and Lambeth, ed. also EETS 24.106.

[80] Cott., ed. Halliwell *Sel. from Minor Poems of Lydgate*, Percy Soc. 2.225.

[81] Ashmole, see ESt 41.364.

[82] Trinity, see James *Western MSS. in Libr. of Trin. Coll. Cbg.* 3.497;— Sloane, ed. Arch 109.59;— Garrett, ed. ESt 41.374;— Bannatyne, ed. for Hunterian Club, 125.

[84]-[84a] *V*ernon, ed. also Patterson 54;— Balliol, ed. Angl 26.160; EETSES 101.154.

[94] Cott., see ESt 41.363.

[95] Garrett, ed. ESt 41.363, 371.

[98] Cott., ed. Percy Soc. 2.228.

[99] Garrett, ed. ESt 41.376.

[100] Sloane, ed. Arch 109.45; Wright *Songs and Carols*, Warton Club, 1856, 15; Ch&Sidg 186 (see 306).

[101] Bodley, ed. Percy Soc. 73.44.

[103] *V*ernon, ed. also Patterson 125.

[104] Vernon, ed. also Patterson 112.

V. Christ on the Cross and Compassion of Mary

A. Christ on the Cross

Heuser Kild Ged 125; Cook *The Crist of Cynewulf*, Boston 1900, 208; MPhil 5.8 notes; Spaulding *M. E. Charters of Christ*, BrynMawrMon 1914, x note.

[107] 'MEN RENT ME ON RODE.' Ed. Rel Ant 2.119.

[108]-[109] 'BIDES A WHILE'; 'MAN, ÞUS ON RODE.' Ed. Yksh Wr 2.457. For Latin of the former poem, see *Fortlage Gesänge Christliche Vorzeit*, Berlin 1844, 27; Daniel *Hymnol. Blüthenstrauss* 24.

[110] Rawlinson, see Kild Ged 125.

[111]-[113] 'UNKYNDE MON'; 'LO LEMMAN SWETE.' Ed. Yksh Wr 1.71.

[114] 'BIHOLD TO ÞI LORD, MON.' Ed. Furnivall EEP 20; Kild Ged 128.

[115] 'MAN AND WYMAN.' Ed. Kild Ged 207.

[116] 'WIT WAS HIS NAKEDE BREST.' Ed. EETS 15(revised).243; Kild Ged 209.

[117] 'SYNFUL MAN, LOKE VP AND SEE.' Ed. Yksh Wr 1.156;— see Kild Ged 210.

[118] 'MAN, TO REFOURME.' Ed. specimen, Kild Ged 210.

[119] '3E ÞAT BE ÞIS WEY PACE.' Ed. EETS 15(revised).261.

[120] CURSOR MUNDI 17111 ff. Ed. EETS 62.978.

[121] A LUYTEL TRETYS OF LOUE. Ed. EETS 117.462.

[122] 'WHI ART THOW FROWARD.' Ed. EETS 15(revised).141.— see Gild Ged 126.

[123] 'HO ÞAT SIÞ HIM ON ÞE RODE.' Ed. EETS 15(revised).249.

[124]-[125] 'HI SIKE AL WAN HI SINGE.' Ed. Digby, EETS 117.753; Arch 97.309;— Harley, Böddeker 210; Wright SLP 85; Cook Reader 455. See Arch 86.290.

[126] FIFTEENTH-CENTURY LAMENT. Ed. Wright *Songs and Carols*, Warton Club 1856, 22.

B. *The Compassion of Mary*

Schonbach *Die Marienklagen*, Graz 1874; Mussafia *Stud. zu den Mittelalterlichen Marienleggenden*, Sitzungsber. d. Wiener Akad. d. Wiss. 1891; Otto *Der Planctus Mariæ*, MLN 4.210; Wechssler *Die Romanischen Marienklagen*, Halle 1893 (crit. LitBl 15.404); Brooks *Lamentations of Mary in the Frankfurt Group of Passion Plays*, JGP 3.415; Crowne *M. E. Poems on the Joys and the Compassion of the Blessed Virgin Mary*, Cath. Univ. Bull. 8.309 (1902); Fröhlich *De Lamentatione Sancte Marie*, Leipzig diss. 1902; *The Planctus of the Mir. Plays*, MLN 25.173; Thien *Über die Engl. Marienklagen*, Kiel 1906 (see its bibliogr.;— crit. ESt 37.406, q.v.); Taylor *The Engl. Planctus Mariæ*, MPhil 4.605.— See Gröber 2¹· Register p. 1272; Paris Litt Franç §159. Bull. SATF 1875.61, 1885.49; Meyer *Recueil d'Anciens Textes Bas-Latins . . .* , Paris 1877, 374.

[127] 'JESU CRISTES MILDE MODER.' Ed. Jacoby *Vier Me. Geistl. Ged.*, Berlin 1890, 42; *Oxf. Hist. of Mus.* 2.102 (words and mus. notes of two sts.).

[128] 'ÞE MILDE LOMB ISPRAD ON RODE.' Ed. Jacoby *op. cit.* 37.

[129] TANNER COMPASSIO. Ed. Engl. and Lat., Arch 88.181; trans. and revised, EETS 103.75; facsimile and mus. notes, Stainer *Ear. Bodl. Mus.* 1.plate 5, 2.8.

[129a] FIFTEENTH-CENTURY PIÈCES. Hoccleve, ed. Furnivall *H's Minor Poems*, EETSES 61;— 'As resoun rewlid,' 'As reson hathe rulyd,' ed. EETS 15(revised).233, 238;— 'Lysteneth lordynges,' ed. Wright *Chester Plays* 2.204;— 'Who cannot weep,' ed. EETS 24.126;— 'Off alle women,' ed. Rel Ant 2.213; Wright *op. cit.* ·2.207;— Kennedy's *Passion*, ed. Schipper Denkschr. d. Wiener Akad., phil-hist.kl. 48.1;— Bodley *Lamentation*, ed. Arch 79.454;— Banister, ed. Arch 106.64;— 'Mary moder,' ed. Percy Soc. 4.10;— 'His body,' ed. Percy Soc. 23.38;— Ryman, ed. Arch 89.263;— *Mary's Speeches*, see Angl 3.319;— Balliol, ed. Angl 26.247, 262, 263, 240.— See B. Skeat *Complaynt of St. Mary*, Zürich diss. 1897.

VI. Hymns and Prayers to God, Christ, the Trinity

[130]-[131] 'CVM, MAKER OF GASTE ÞOU ERT.' Ed. Bodley with Latin, Angl 29.408;— Vernon, EETS 98.43.

[132]-[133] 'SWETE IHESU CRIST, TO ÞE.' Ed. Vernon, EETS 98.19; Patterson 50;— Barton, EETS 117.785; Arch 98.129. MLN 25.10 (comparison of texts, attempt to restore Barton).

[134] 'GOD, ÞAT AL ÞIS MYHTES MAY.' Ed. Wright SLP 99; Böddeker 222; Patterson 64.

[135] 'HEƷE LOUERD, ÞOU HERE MY BONE.' Ed. Wright SLP 47; Böddeker 187; Patterson 61. Schipper *Engl. Metr.* 337.

[136] '[ ]IDDE HUVE WITH MILDE STEVENE.' Ed. Rel Ant 1.22.

[137] 'IESU CRIST, HEOUENE KYNG.' Ed. Wright SLP 59; Böddeker 193; Patterson 88.

[138] 'IESU, FOR ÞI MUCHELE MIHT.' Ed. Wright SLP 83; Böddeker 208.— Brandl §46.

[139] 'FADUR AND SONE AND HOLIGOST.' Ed. Vernon, EETS 98.16; Patterson 82;— Thornton, EETS 26.75; Yksh Wr 1.365.

[140] 'SWET IESUS, HEND AND FRE.' Ed. Rel Ant 2.190; Kild Ged 79.— Brandl §42.

[141] 'LOUERD CRIST, ICH ÞE GRETE.' Ed. EETS 49.139.

[142] 'LORD, MY GOD AL MERCIABLE.' Ed. EETS 98.26; Patterson 122. See Aquinas *Opera Omnia* 32.820.

[143] 'LORD, SWETE IHESU CRIST.' Ed. EETS 98.29; Patterson 80 (see 173). DNB, *Edmund (Rich)*; Rom 35.577; Stengel *Cod. Manu Scriptum Digby 86* 102.

[144] 'INWARDLICHE, LORD, BISECHE I ÞE.' Ed. EETS 98.36.

[145] 'LORD, I ƷELDE ME GULTI.' Ed. EETS 98.34.

[146] 'LORD, SUNGED HAUE I OFTE.' Ed. EETS 98.35.

[147] 'I KNOWLECH TO GOD.' Ed. EETS 129.8; Patterson 48.

[148] 'GOD, ÞAT ART OF MIHTES MOST.' Ed. EETS 98.34; Patterson 128.

[149] 'TO LOUE I-CHULLE BEGINNE.' Ed. EETS 117.469.

[150] 'IHESUS ÞAT DIƷEDEST.' Ed. EETS 98.131; Patterson 135.

[151] 'IESU, ÞAT ART HEUENE KYNG.' Ed. EETS 98.48.

[152]-[154] 'IHESU CRIST, MY LEMMON SWETE.' Ed. Vernon, EETS 98.22; Patterson 137;— Thornton, Yksh Wr 1.364;— Harley, Rel Ant 2.119;— Mostyn, Patterson 191; Hist. MSS. Comm. 4.355.

[155] 'HE YAF HIMSELF AS GOOD FELAWE.' Ed. Rel Ant 2.121.

[156] 'IHESU, ϷI SWETNESSE.' Ed. Vernon, EETS 98.45;— Thornton, EETS 24.8;— Lambeth, EETS 26.83.

[157]-[159] IESU DULCIS MEMORIA IMITATIONS. Ed. Harley, Wright SLP 68; Böddeker 191 (Digby at 456);— Harley, *Vernon*, EETS 117.449;— Harley, *Vernon*, Royal, Yksh Wr 2.9.

[160] 'NAUEϷ MY SAULE.' Ed. EETS 49.100.

[161] 'AS ϷOU FOR HOLY CHURCHE RIƷT.' Ed. EETS 46.153; Angl 27.305.

[162] 'IHESU MYNE, GRAUNTE ME GRACE.' Ed. EETS 71.18; Patterson 118.

[163] 'WHEN Y SE BLOSMES SPRINGE.' Ed. Wright SLP 61; Zupitza Übungsbuch; Böddeker 196. Schofield 441; Ten Brink 1.310.

[164] 'SOMER IS COMEN AND WINTER GONE.' Ed. Rel Ant 1.100; EETS 49.197; Wülcker Lesebuch 1.44.— Text-note, ESt 13.136.— Brandl §27; Ten Brink 1.311; Schofield 441.— Note on l. 23, ESt 17.296.

[165] 'WYNTER WAKENEϷ AL MY CARE.' Ed. Ritson AS (1877) 56; Wright SLP 60; Wülcker Lesebuch 1.107; Böddeker 195; Ellis EEP 1.108; Ch&Sidg 169. Schofield 442; Ten Brink 1.311.

[166] 'GOD, ϷAT AL HAST MAD OF NOUGHT.' Ed. EETS 98.32.

[167] 'GODYS SONE ϷAT WAS SO FRE.' Ed. EETS 46.150; Angl 27.304.

[168] 'CRIST MADE TO MAN A FAIR PRESENT.' Ed. Rel Ant 1.166.

[169]-[170] ON UREISUN; ON WEL SUIÐE GOD UREISUN. Ed. EETS 34.183, 200.— Brandl §15; Vollhardt *Einfluss d. Lat. Geistl. Lit.*, Leipzig diss. 1888; Angl 5.265.

[171] WOHUNGE OF URE LAUERD. Ed. EETS 34.269. Selection: Morris Spec 1.124 (see Angl 25.320).— Brandl §15; Vollhardt *op. cit.;* Angl 5.265.

[172] LOFSONG OF URE LAUERDE. Ed. EETS 34.209.— Brandl §15; Vollhardt *op. cit.*

[173] A LUUE RON. Ed. EETS 49.93; Cook Reader 433.— Brandl §13; Ten Brink 1.208; Schofield 439; Gummere *Beginnings of Poetry* 149; DNB, *Hales, Thomas de;* comp. with *Of Clene Maydenhod*, Wells, MLR 9.236.

[174] OF CLENE MAYDENHOD. Ed. EETS 25.appendix; EETS 117.464.— Brandl §42.— Comp. with *A Luue Ron*, Wells, MLR 9.236.

VII. Hymns and Prayers to the Virgin

See gen. bibliogr. of Lyrics, and bibliogr. of Religious Lyrics, above.

Lauchert *Über das Engl. Marienlied im 13 Jhdt.*, ESt 16.124; Schroeder *Marienlyrik*, ZsfDA 25.127; Marüfke *Der älteste Engl. Marienhymnus,*

Breslau diss. 1907; Taylor, MPhil 4.605, 5.1; Schaff *Rise and Progress of Maryolatry*, Contemp. Rev. Apr. 1867.— See Gröber 2¹· Register p. 1272 col. 3.

[175]-[180] .AVE MARIA. Ed. Rel Ant 1.234, 22, 42, 282, 169, 38.

[181]-[182] AVE MARIA. Ed. *Douce*, Cbg., Angl 27.320, 325;— Cbg., Rel Ant 1.159.

[183] ·'MAIDEN AND *M*ODER.' Ed. Rel Ant 1.22.

[184] 'HEIL BEO ÞOU, MARIE.' Ed. EETS 98.30; Patterson 149.

[185] 'MARIE MODUR, QWEN OF HEUENE.' Ed. EETS 98.33; Patterson 143.

[186] 'HEIL BEO ÞOW, MARIE, MOODUR.'˙ Ed. EETS 98.134.

[187]-[187a] 'MAYDEN, MODUR, AND COMELY QWEEN.' Ed. EETS 98.121.— On Latin, Du Méril *Poèmes Pop. du Moyen Âge* 223; Mone *Latein. Hymnen* 1.237.

[188] SEINTE MARI, MODER MILDE. Ed. Ch&Sidg˙ 89; Patterson 148.

[189]-[190] 'OF ON ÞAT IS SO FAYR AND BRIƷT.' Ed. Egerton, Rel Ant 1.89; AESprPr 1.53; EETS 49.194; Patterson 96; Cook Reader 457;— Egerton with vars. of Ashmole and Trinity, Ch&Sidg 346;— Ashmole with mus. notes, Stainer *Ear. Bodl. Mus.* 1.plate 28, 2.65.— Brandl §20; Schofield 439.

[191] 'BLESSED BEO ÞU, LAUEDI.' Ed. Egerton, EETS 49.195; Böddeker 457; AESprPr 1.54; Rel Ant 1.102; Patterson 146;— Harley, Böddeker 215; Wright SLP 93.

[192] AVE MARIS STELLA. Ed. Bodley with Latin, Angl 29.411;— Porkington (Phillipps 8336), Rel Ant 2.228; Patterson 112;— *V*ernon, EETS 117.735, 740; Patterson 112;— Simeon, Angl 7.282.

[193] 'EDI BEO ÞU, HEUENE QUENE.' Ed. with mus. notes, EETS 53.255, 260; ed. Patterson 93.

[194] 'MODER MILDE, FLUR OF ALLE.' Ed. EETS 53.257; Patterson 145.

[195]-[196] 'MARIE, MODUR AND MAYDEN.' Ed. *V*ernon, EETS 98.22; Patterson 141;— Cbg., Rel Ant 2.212;— Harley, Patterson 139;— Br. Mus., Dibdin *Typ. Antiq.* 2.13; ll. 1-20, Flügel *Neuengl. Lesebuch* 10. On Chetham, see ESt 7.197.

[197] 'MAIDEN, MODER MILDE, OIEZ CEL OREYSOUN.' Ed. Wright SLP 97; Böddeker 220; Wülker Lesebuch 1.49; Ch&Sidg 100.— Schofield 439. Interp. note, ESt 17.297.

·[198] 'QWEN OF HEWYN, JOY THE.' Ed. Arch 87.432.

[199] 'HAYL, MARI, HIC AM SORI.' Ed. EETS 117.755; Arch 97.311; Patterson 91. Arch 86.91.

[200] 'LEUEDI, SAINTE MARIE.' Ed. EETS 49.192; Patterson 59.—
Ten Brink 1.206.

[201] 'ON HIRE IS AL MI LIF ILONG.' Ed. Calig., Jesus, EETS
49.158; Wright, Percy Soc. 11.65;—Calig., Patterson 95;— Trinity, Ch&Sidg
94.— Brandl §13.

[202] 'MARIE, ʒOW QUEN!' Ed. Rel Ant 2.120; Patterson 139.

[203] 'LITEL UO IT ENIMAN.' Ed. Rel Ant 1.104.

[204] 'NOU SKRINKEÞ ROSE.' Ed. Wright SLP 87; Böddeker 212;
Ch&Sidg 97; Patterson 98.— Schofield 442; Ten Brink 1.310.— Sandison
Chanson d'Aventure 138.

[205] 'NU ÞIS FULES SINGET.' Ed. MPhil 7.165. Gummere *Pop.
Ballad* 116 note.— 'I syng of a mayden.' Ed. Wülcker Lesebuch 2.7; Cook
Reader 466.

[206] ON LOFSONG OF URE LEFDI. Ed. EETS 34.205, 305.—
Brandl §15; Angl 5.265; Vollhardt *op. cit.*

[207] ON GOD UREISUN OF URE LEFDI. Ed. EETS 29.191;
Marüfke, Breslauer Beitr. zur Litt.-Gesch. 12 (crit. ESt 42.303; AnglBbl
21.79; Neu Phil. Rundschau 1908.525; Ctbl 61.205; DLz 29.2918; AllgLtbl
17.625); Morris Spec. 1.129; Zupitza Übungsbuch; MacLean Reader 69;
ESt 1.169.— Brandl §13; Ten Brink 1.205; Vollhardt *op. cit.*

[208] THE FIVE JOYS OF THE VIRGIN. See Crowne *M. E. Poems
on the Joys . . .* , Cath. Univ. Bull. 8.304; T. E. Bridgett *Our Lady's
Dowry;* Patterson 164 note.

[209] 'ASE Y ME ROD.' Ed. Wright SLP 94; Wülcker Lesebuch 1.48;
Böddeker 217; Cook Reader 462.— Notes, ESt 13.135, 17.296.— Brandl §42.—
Sandison *Chanson d'Aventure* 137. ESt 17.296; ZsföGymn 1875.131.

[210] 'SEINTE MARIE, LEVEDI BRIST.' Ed. Rel Ant 1.48;
AESprPr 1.51.— Brandl §20.

[211] 'LEUEDY, FOR ÞARE BLISSE.' Ed. EETS 49.87; Patterson
151.

[212]-[213] 'HAUE IOYE, MARIE'; 'MARIE MODUR, WEL ÞE
BEE.' Ed. EETS 98.25, 133; Patterson 144, 194.

[214] 'HAILE BE ÞU, MARIE.' Ed. Angl 1.390.

[215] PREYERE OFF THE FFYVE IOYES. Ed. Yksh Wr 1.377.

[216] TWO FIFTEENTH-CENTURY CAROLS. Ed. Wright *Songs
and Carols,* Percy Soc., 21, 68.

[217] BODLEY FIVE JOYS. Ed. Angl 30.523, 547.

[218] FIFTEEN JOYS and FIFTEEN JOYS AND FIFTEEN SOR-
ROWS. Ed. MacCracken, EETSES 260, 268— see introd. xvi, xvii.

[219] D. T. MYLLE'S PIECE. Ed. EETS 15(revised).174.

CHAPTER XIV—DRAMATIC PIECES

GENERAL TREATMENTS OF MEDIÆVAL DRAMA. Mone *Schauspiele des Mittelalters*, Karlsruhe 1846; Hase *Das Geistl. Schauspiele des Mittelalters*, Leipzig 1858, trans. Jackson, 1880; Du Méril *Histoire de la Comédie*, Paris 1864; Klein *Geschichte des Dramas*, Leipzig 1865-86; Reidt *Das Geistl. Schauspiele des Mittelalters*, Frankfurt 1868; de Julleville *Les Mystères*, Paris 1880; Sepet *Le Drame Chrétien au Moyen Âge*, Paris 1878; Sepet *Origines Catholiques du Théâtre Moderne*, Paris 1901; Broadbent *Hist. of Pantomime*, London 1901; Chambers *The Mediæval Stage*, Oxf. 1903, 2 vols. (crit. ESt 33.107; MLQ 6.144; MLN 19.207; ShJhb 40.454; Scott Hist Rev 1.399; N&Q 9th Ser. 15.98; AnglBbl 17.353); Mantzius *A History of Theatrical Art*, London 1903—, Vols. 1-2; Tunison *Dramatic Traditions of the Middle Ages*, London 1907 (crit. ShJhb 44.315; MLN 23.254); Creizenach *Geschichte des Neueren Dramas*, Halle 1911, Vol. 1; Wieck *Der Teufel auf der Mittelalterl. Mysterienbuhne*, Marburg diss. 1887; Jusserand *A Note on Pageants . . .*, *Furnivall Misc.* 1901, 183; Tisdel *The Influence of Popular Customs on the Mystery Plays*, JEGP 5.323; Allen *The Mediæval Mimus*, MPhil 7.329, 8.1; Bourne *Miracle Plays*, MLN 11.124; Crowley *Character Treatment in the Med. Drama*, diss., Notre Dame, Indiana, 1907.— See Gröber 2¹· Register, *s.v. Mistères, Mirakel, Drama; General Bibliographies*, below; Krit Jahresber; Jahresbericht; Brooks JEGP 13.610.

LITURGICAL DRAMA. See Chambers 2.1 (bibliogr. at 2.1), and notes on Chs. 18-19; Sepet, Creizenach, de Julleville, as above; Ward, Pollard, Bates, Davidson, as below. Sepet *Les Prophètes du Christ*, Paris 1878; Reiners *Die Tropen-, Prosen-, u. Präfations-Gesänge . . .*, Luxemburg 1884; Gautier *Hist. de la Poésie Liturgique au Moyen Âge*, one vol. pub. 1886; Hartmann, K. A. M., *Über das Altspan. Dreikönigspiel*, Leipzig 1879; Köppen *Beiträge zur Geschichte der Deutschen Weihnachtsspiele*, Paderborn 1893; Frere *The Winchester Troper*, London 1894; Du Méril *Origines Latines du Théâtre Moderne*, Paris 1849, repr. 1897; Milchsack *Die Lat. Osterfeiern*, Wolfenbuettel 1880; Mantzius *op. cit.* 2.1 (see bibliogr. 361); Wagner *Origine et Développement du Chant Liturgique*, Tournai 1904; Anz *Die Lat. Magierspiele*, Leipzig 1905; Butler *A Note on the Origin of the Lit. Drama*, Furnivall Misc. 1901, 46; Young *Contrib. to the Hist. of Lit. Drama at Rouen*, MPhil 6.201; Craig *Orig. of the O. T. Plays*, MPhil 10.473; Young *Harrowing of Hell in Lit. Drama*, Trans. Wisc. Acad. of Sciences, Arts, and Letters, 16.pt.2; Young, in same, 17.300; Young *Observations on Orig. of the Med. Passion-Play*, PMLA 25.309; Young *Origin of the Easter Play*, PMLA 29.1; Schoenbach, ZsfDA 32.85; Jenney *A Further Word on the Orig. of the O. T. Plays*, MPhil 13.59; Coffman *New Theory concerning the Origin of the Miracle Play*, Chicago diss. 1914.—See next section below.

PRINTS AND EDITIONS OF LITURGICAL TEXTS. Wright *Early Mysteries and Latin Poems of the Twelfth and Thirteenth Centuries*, London 1838; Du Méril *Origines Latines du Théâtre Moderne*, Paris 1849, repr.

1897; de Coussemaker *Hist. de l'Harmonie du Moyen Âge*, Paris 1852; Milchsack *Die Öster- u. Passionsspiele*, Wolfenbuettel 1880; Milchsack *Heidelberger Passionspiel*, Tübingen 1880; de Coussemaker *Drames Liturgiques du Moyen Âge*, Paris 1861; Lange *Die Lat. Österfeiern*, Munich 1887; Froning *Das Drama des Mittelalters*, Erster Teil, Stuttgart, Leipzig, 1891; Gasté *Les Drames Lit. de la Cathédrale de Rouen*, Evreux 1893 (see Krit Jahresber 3.126); Schmeller *Carmina Burana*, 3rd ed., Breslau 1894; Meyer *Fragmenta Burana*, Berlin 1901; Stotzner *Österfeiern*, prgr. 594, Zwickau 1901; Meyer *Les Trois Maries* (Reims), Rom 33.239; Blume *Analecta Hymnica* 40 and 47 and 48 and 49; Gautier *op. cit.*, and Le Monde, Paris, Aug. 17, 1872, 2; Pollard *op. cit.* below, appendix; Manly *op. cit.* below, 1.xix, Dublin and Winchester Offices; Pfeiffer, Jhb. der Stiftes Klosterneuberg 1.3 (Easter); Windakiewicza, Bull. Krakauer Akad. 33 and 34 (Easter); Migne *Patr. Lat.*, 78.678, 769 (Easter); Brooks, ZsfDA 50.297 (Easter); Brooks *Some New Texts of Lit. Easter-Plays*, JEGP 8.463; Brooks *Lit. Easter Plays from Rheinau MS.*, JEGP 10.191; Young *A Lit. Play of Joseph and his Brethern*, MLN 26.33; Young *Some Texts of Lit. Plays*, PMLA 24.294; Young, Trans. Wisc. Acad. of Sciences, Arts, and Letters 16.899 (Easter). See works listed in preceding section.

GENERAL BIBLIOGRAPHIES OF ENGLISH AND CONTINENTAL MYSTERIES. Chambers 1.xiii, 2.407, 2.1-2, 68, 106; Cbg Hist 5.425; Stoddard *References for Students of Miracle Plays and Mysteries*, Univ. of Cal. Libr. Bull. No. 8, Berkeley 1887 (noticed with addits. in LitBl 1888.117; Angl 11.325); Bates *English Religious Drama*, N. Y. and London 1893, 240; Mantzius *op. cit.* 2.361; Klein *A Contrib. to a Bibliogr. of the Med. Drama*, MLN 20.202 (addits. to Stoddard and Chambers); Körting §134; Spencer *Corpus Christi Pageants in England*, N. Y. 1911, 263; Cron *Zur Entwicklungsgeschichte der Engl. Misterien Alten Testaments*, Marburg diss. 1913.

GENERAL TREATMENTS OF ENGLISH MYSTERIES. Hone *Ancient Mysteries Described*, London 1823, repr. n.d.; Sharp *Dissertation on the Pageants or Dramatic Mysteries Anciently Performed at Coventry*, Coventry 1825; Ahn *English Mysteries and Miracle Plays*, Trier 1867; Ebert *Die Engl. Mysterien*, JbREL 1.44, 131; Klein *Gesch. des Dramas*, Vol. 12, Leipzig 1876; Genée *Die Engl. Mirakelspiele u. Moralitäten als Vorlaufer des Engl. Dramas*, Berlin 1878; Meyer *The Infancy of the English Drama*, Hagen 1873; Collier *Hist. of Engl. Dram. Poetry*, 2nd ed. 1879, Vol. 2; Prölss *Gesch. des Neuern Dramas*, Leipzig 1880-83, Vol. 2; Jusserand *Le Théâtre en Angleterre*, 2nd ed. Paris 1881; Zschech *Die Anfänge des Engl. Dramas*, Marienwerder 1886; Davidson *Studies in the English Mystery Plays*, Yale thesis 1892; Pollard *Engl. Miracle Plays, Moralities, and Interludes*, Oxf. 5th ed. 1909, introd.; Ten Brink 2.234; Morley 4.68; Hohlfeld *Die Altengl. Kollektivmysterien*, Angl 11.219; Bates *Engl. Rel. Drama*, N. Y. and London 1893 (crit. MLN 8.228); Clarke, S. W., *The Miracle Play in England*, London 1897; Brandl *Quellen des Weltl. Dramas in England*, Strassburg 1898, introd.: Ward *Hist. of Engl. Dram. Lit.*, new ed. London 1899, 1.1; Symonds *Shakespeare's Predecessors in the Engl. Drama*, London 1902, Ch. 3; Chambers *Med. Stage*, Oxf.

1903, 2.106; Syrett *The Old Miracle Plays of England,* London n.d.; Snell *The Age of Transition,* London 1905, Vol. 1; Moore, E., *Engl. Miracle Plays and Moralities,* London 1907; Jusserand *Lit. Hist. of Engl. People,* 1.Bk.3.Ch.6; Courthope *Hist. of Engl. Poetry* 1.393; Cbg Hist 5.1; Creizenach *Gesch. des Neuern Dramas,* Halle 1911, 1.155, 289, 457; Gayley *Plays of our Forefathers,* London and N. Y. 1909; Wesley *The Engl. Miracle Play,* Lit. and Philos. Soc. of Liverpool Proc. 53, 1899; Hastings *Le Théâtre Français et Anglais,* Paris 1900, trans. London and Phila. 1902; Spencer *op. cit.* above.

LISTS OF CONTENTS OF ENGLISH CYCLES. Stoddard *op. cit.* appendix ; Bates *op. cit.* 241; Chambers 2.408; *Everyman,* etc., Everyman's Libr., 198.— Comparative tabular list, Chambers 2.321; Stoddard appendix; Smith *York Plays,* lxii; Hohlfeld, Angl 11.241.

SUBJECTS OF ENGLISH CYCLICAL PLAYS AND OTHERS. Chambers 2.321; Hohlfeld, Angl 11.241;— see section next preceding.

SYNOPTICAL STATEMENTS OF TEXTS, MSS., CONTENTS, ETC. Bates *op. cit.* 241; Chambers 2.407; Stoddard *op. cit.* 51, 60.

RECORDS OF REPRESENTATIONS OF ENGLISH MYSTERIES. Smith *York Plays,* lxiv; Stoddard *op. cit.* 53; Davidson *Studies,* 95; Chambers 2.329; Gayley 95;— Lieberman, Arch 104.360, 107.106, 108, 123.154, 110.426; v.d. Gaaf, ESt 36.228, reply by Sorg, 37.172, counter-reply, 37.461.

MANNER, METHOD, TIME OF PERFORMANCE. See under individual items below. Chambers 2.69, 329, 407; Smith *Engl. Gilds,* EETS 40; Oliver *Hist. of Holy Trinity Guild at Sleaford,* Lincoln 1837; Green, A. S. *Town Life in the Fifteenth Century,* N. Y. and London 1894, 1.175; Davidson *Concerning English Mystery Plays* (Dublin Plays), MLN 7.339; Leach *The Beverly Town Documents,* Selden Soc. Vol. 14, London 1900, espec. xliii, xlvii, l, lii, lix, 33, 45, 99, 109, 111, 117 (see *Furnivall Misc.* 1901, 205); Bateson *Mediæval England,* N. Y. 1904; Bates *op. cit.* 37, 50; Beatty *Notes on Supposed Dramatic Char. of the 'Ludi' in the Great Wardrobe Accounts of Edw. III,* MLR 4.474; Craig *The Corpus Christi Procession and the Corpus Christi Play,* JEGP 13.589; Spencer *Corpus Christi Pageants in England,* N. Y. 1911 (crit. AnglBbl 23.267; ShJhb 48.337;— see its bibliogr.).

EARLY ENGLISH DRAMA, SPECIAL CRITICISMS. Capes *Poetry of the Engl. Mysteries,* Nineteenth Century, Oct. 1883; Davidson *Studies in the English Mystery Plays,* Yale thesis 1892; Gayley *Earlier Miracle Plays of England,* Internat. Qtrly. 10.108 (largely incorporated into *Plays of our Forefathers*); Gothein *Die Frau im Engl. Drama vor Shakespeare,* ShJhb 40.1; Cushman *The Devil and the Vice in the Engl. Drama before 1605,* StEPhil 6 (crit. ESt 29.427); Leach *Some Engl. Plays and Players,* Furnivall *Misc.* 1901, 205; Cook *A Remote Analogue to the Miracle-Play,* JGP 4.421; Gayley *Representative Engl. Comedies,* Boston and London 1903, 1.introd.; Eckhardt *Die Lustige Person im Älteren Engl. Drama,* Palæstra 17 (crit. Athen. 1903. 1.301; ShJhb 39.313; Mus. 10.331; Arch

112.200; DLz 1904.1127); Symmes *Les Débuts de la Critique Dramatique en Angleterre*, Paris 1903; Matthews *The Mediæval Drama*, MPhil 1.71; Emerson *Legends of Cain*, PMLA 21.831; Taylor *The Engl. Planctus Mariæ*, MPhil 4.605; Taylor *The Relation of the Engl. Corpus Christi Play to the M. E. Rel. Lyric*, MPhil 5.1 (the last two items bound up together as Chicago diss., *Rel. of Lyric and Drama in Mediæval England*, 1907); Röhmer *Priestergestälten im Engl. Drama bis zu Shakespeare*, Berlin diss. 1909, complete in Eberling's *Beiträgen; The Christmas Boys*, N&Q 10th Ser. 7.30, 75; Herrlich *Das Engl. Bibeldrama zu Zeit der Renaissance u. Reformation*, München diss. 1910; Greene *Index to the Non-Biblical Names in the Engl. Mystery-Plays*, Studies in Celebr. of 70th Birthday of J. M. Hart, N. Y. 1910; Royster *Richard III. iv. 4 and the Three Maries of Med. Drama*, MLN 25.173; Foster *The Mystery Plays and the 'Northern Passion,'* MLN 26.169; Foster *A Study of . . . 'The Northern Passion' and its Relation to the Cycle Plays*, Bryn Mawr diss., London and Bungay 1914; Grosch *Bote u. Botenbericht im Engl. Dr. bis Shakespeare*, Giessen diss. 1911; Oerlich *Die Personnamen im Mittelalterlichen Drama Englands*, Kiel diss. 1911; Beatty *The St. George or Mummers' Plays*, Trans. Wisc. Acad. of Sciences, Arts, and Letters 15; Cron *Zur Entwicklungsgesch. der Engl. Mysterien des Alten Testaments*, Marburg diss. 1913; Spaar *Prolog u. Epilog im Mittelalterlichen Engl. Drama*, Giessen diss. 1913; Dollefsen *Namengebung in der Drama der Vorgänger Shakespeares*, Kiel diss. 1914.

EDITIONS OF SELECTED PLAYS. Collier *Five Miracle-Plays*. London 1836 (private print); Marriott *A Collection of English Miracle-Plays or Mysteries*, Basel 1838; Pollard *English Miracle Plays, Moralities, and Interludes*, Oxf. 1909, 5th ed. (crit. ESt 21.162, 20.179; Neu Phil. Rund. 1904.598; ESt 34.103; N&Q 10th Ser. 2.278; MLN 19.207); Manly *Specimens of the Pre-Shakespearean Drama*, Boston 1900, 2nd ed. (crit. Ctbl 1901.110; DLz 20.30; Rev. Crit. 45.511; AnglBbl 10.161; Arch 102.409); Hemingway *English Nativity Plays*, YaleSt 38; (crit. Arch 122.445; Angl-Bbl 22.148; DLz 32.1128; ESt 44.795; MLR 7.546; ShJhb 46.325; LitBl 32.399; Rev. Crit. 68.407).— Modernizations: *Everyman and Other Interludes*, Everyman's Libr., 1909; Child *The Second Shepherds' Play*, etc., Boston 1910 (crit. Arch 124.428).

[1] SHREWSBURY FRAGMENTS. Ed. Skeat, Acad 1890.1.27 (see 1.10); Manly Spec 1.xxvii; Waterhouse, EETSES 104.xv, 1.—Chambers 2.90, 108, 427.

[2] CAIPHAS. Ed. Rel Ant 2.241; Brown, *Kittredge Anniv. Papers*, Boston 1913, 105.— Brandl §27.

[3] DUX MORAUD. Ed. Angl 30.180. See Angl 31.24.

[4] INTERLUDIUM DE CLERICO ET PUELLA. Ed. Rel Ant 1.145; Angl 30.307; Chambers 2.324; McKnight *M. E. Humorous Tales* 21; Cook Reader 476.— Brandl §56; Ten Brink 2.295; Schofield 322; Chambers 2.181, 202; Creizenach *Gesch. des Neueren Dramas*, 1.179; Gayley *Repr. Engl. Comedies* 1.xvii; Jusserand *Lit. Hist. of Engl. People* 1.446.

[5] CHESTER PLAYS. Ed. Addit. with passages from Harley 2013, full cycle, Wright for Shakespeare Soc., London 1843-47, 2 vols., repr. as Vol. 1 of Suppl. to Dodsley's *Old Plays,* 1853;— Harley 2124, Plays 1-13 incl., Deimling, EETSES 62 (crit. ESt 21.162);— Harley 1944 (1609) lines of banns addit. to those in Deimling's ed., EETSES 70.xx; earlier banns from Harley 2150, Morris *Chester in Plantagenet and Tudor Reigns,* Chester 1894, 307;— Plays 3, 10, Banns, Markland for Roxb. Cl. 1818;— Devonshire, Play 24, Collier *Five Miracle-Plays,* London 1836;— Plays 3, 24, Marriott *Engl. Miracle-Plays,* Basel 1838;— Play 17, Wülcker Lesebuch 2.136;— Manchester, part of *Resurrection* (19), Manchester Guardian, May 9, 1883;— Play 3 and part of 4, Pollard *Engl. Mir. Plays,* 8;— Plays 5, 24, Manly *Spec* 1.66, 170; Play 7, Barre, London 1906; Play 3, Cook Reader 487;— Devonshire with vars., Plays 6, 7, Hemingway *Engl. Nat. Plays,* 3; Plays 3, 4, modernized, *Everyman with Other Interludes,* Everyman's Libr., 29, 41.— MSS., Manchester, Acad 574.309;— EETSES 62.vii; Coll. of Devonshire, EETSES 62.xxxi.— Text: Deimling *Textgestalt u. Textcritik der Ch. Pl.,* Berlin diss. 1890 (crit. AnglBbl 2.245); EETSES 62.vii.— Date and Author: Pollard *op. cit.,* xxi; Hohlfeld, Angl 11.223; Davidson *op. cit.* 132; Leach, *Furnivall Misc.,* 230; Hemingway *op. cit.* xx; Chambers 2.147, 348; Gayley 128; Cook, N. Y. Nation 100.599.— Comparison with other plays: with Brome *Abraham,* Harper, Rad Mon 15; Hohlfeld, MLN 5.222; Ungemach, as below; Gayley 132; EETSES 104.liii;— with York, et al., Davidson *op. cit.* 154, 157, 164; Gayley 132; Hohlfeld, Angl 11.260; MLN 19.31; Cady, PMLA 24.459, 466; EETSES 87.xxviii; *Dispute in Temple,* MLN 7.184, 308, and see under *Coventry Plays.*— Performance: Chambers 2.138, 348; EETSES 70.xviii.— Sources: Hemingway *op. cit.* xxiv; Ungemach *Die Quellen der Fünf Ersten Ch. Pl.,* Münchener Beitr. 1 (crit. LitBl 12.86)— opposed by Deimling, Arch 86.429; Utesch *Die Quellen der Ch. Pl.,* Kiel diss. 1909; Hohlfeld, Angl. 11.223; Davidson *op. cit.* 130, 162; Gayley 128, 323; *Planctus,* Taylor, MPhil 4.623; lyrical elements, Taylor, MPhil 5.1; parallels and sources of O. T. pieces, Cron *Zur Entwicklungsgesch . . . ,* Marburg diss. 1913 (see above).— Klein 12.711, 741; Morley 4.79; Pollard xxxvi; Körting §135iii; Brandl §47; Ten Brink 2.274, 3.275; Ward Hist 1.76; Bates 105; Chambers 2.407; Cbg Hist 5.53, 433; Creizenach 296.

[6] YORK PLAYS. Ed. Ashburnham, full cycle, Smith, L. T., Oxf. 1885 (crit. MLN 2.344; DLz 6.1304; Angl 8.159); Play 1, Pollard *Engl. Mir. Plays,* 1; Plays 38, 48, Manly Spec 1.153, 198; Plays 12, 13, 14, 15, Hemingway *Engl. Nativ. Plays* 121; Play 14, Cook Reader 121;— Sykes Play, Croft *Excerpta Antiqua,* 1797, 105; Collier *Camden Misc.,* Vol. 4, 1859.— On MSS., Smith *op. cit.* xi, 455; Chambers 2.409; Acad 1882. No. 530.9.— Text and explan. notes: Zupitza, DLz 6.1304; Hall, ESt 9.449; Kölbing, ESt 20.178; Holthausen, *Festgabe für E. Sievers,* Halle 1896, 30; Holthausen, Arch 85.411; Herrtrich, see below, Ch. 2.— Date: Smith *op. cit.* xlv, xxxi; Gayley 133.— *Verse:* Smith *op. cit.* 1; Coblentz *Some Suggested Rime Emendations,* MLN 10.77; Davidson *op. cit.* 137; Gayley 158.— Parent-cycle: Davidson 137; Foster diss. 1914, 86 (see below); Gayley 157; Coblentz *Rime-Index to the 'Parent Cycle,'* PMLA 10.487.— Sources: Holt-

hausen, Arch 85.425, 86.280; Foster *A Study of* . . . 'The Northern Passion,' Bryn Mawr diss. London and Bungay 1914, 81; Hohlfeld, Angl 11.285; Kamann, Angl 10.189; Smith *op. cit.* xlvii; Craigie, *Furnivall Misc.* 1901, 52; Kamann *Über Quellen U. Spr.* . . . , Leipzig diss. 1887; on *Planctus,* Taylor, MPhil 4.623; lyrical elements, Taylor, MPhil 5.1; Gayley 327; Cbg Hist 5.47.— Comparison with other plays: Towneley, Hohlfeld, Angl 11.219; Herrtrich *Stud. zu den York Pl.,* Breslau diss. 1886, 3; Davidson *op. cit.* 147; Smith *op. cit.* 68, 156, 372, 396, 497; Cady, JEGP 10.580, 11.244; Gayley 161;— Chester, Davidson *op. cit.* 154, 157, 164; Gayley 132; Cady, PMLA 24.459, 466;— Coventry, French, MLN 19.31; EETSES 87.xxviii; var. versions of *Dispute in Temple,* MLN 7.184, 308; EETSES 87.xxviii;— Cron *Zur Entwicklungsgesch.,* Marburg diss. 1913 (see above).— Language: Smith *op. cit.* lxix, liii; Kamann *op. cit.*— Performances: Chambers 2.399; Smith *op. cit.* xxxii.— Morley 4.101; Brandl §63; Ten Brink 2.266, 3.275; Körting §135; Pollard xxx; Hemingway xxxix; Creizenach 291; Gayley 147, 153, 161, 191; Ward Hist 1.65; Bates 90; Chambers 2.409; Cbg Hist 1.51, 434.— On the *Pater Noster* and *Creed* plays: Ward Hist 1.97; Pollard xlii; Chambers 2.403.

[7] TOWNELEY PLAYS. Ed. full cycle, for Surtees Soc., 1836; EETSES 71;— Plays 13, Collier *Five Mir.-Plays,* London 1836; Play 30, Douce, Roxb. Cl., 1822; Play 3, AESprPr 1.360; same, Zupitza Übungsbuch; Play 2, Valke *Der Tod des Abel,* Leipzig 1875; Plays 8, 13, 23, 25, 30, Marriott *Engl. Mir.-Plays,* London 1838, 93; Plays 8, 18, 25, 26, 30, Smith *York Plays* 68, 158, 372, 397, 501 (not complete, for comp. with York items); Plays 3, 5, 6, 13, Manly Spec 1, 13, 58, 60, 94; Plays 10, 11, 12, 13, Hemingway *Engl. Nat. Plays,* 155; Play 13, Cook Reader 524; same abridged, Pollard *Engl. Mir. Plays* 31.— Mod. rend.: Plays 13, 23, 25, *Everyman with Other Interludes,* Everyman's Libr., 1909, 55, 105, 147; Play 13, Child *The Second Shepherds' Play,* etc., Boston 1910.— On MS.: EETSES 71.x; Chambers 2.412.— Text: *Processus Talentorum,* Athen 1909.2.284, 321; ShJhb 41.273.— Name 'Woodkirk,' 'Widkirk': Leach, *Furnivall Misc.,* 1901, 228; Hemingway, *op. cit.* xl.— Verse: Pollard, EETSES 71.xxi; Davidson *Studies;* Bunzen *Ein Beitrag zur Kritik der Wakefielder Mysterien,* Kiel diss. 1903 (crit. AnglBbl 17.161); Gayley 161; Cady *Couplets and Quatrains in T. M. Pl.,* JEGP 10.572.— Sources: Huguenin on Play 4.49 and *Viel Testament,* MLN 14.255; Eaton on Play 13, MLN 14.265; on same, Kölbing, EETSES 71.xxxi, from ZsfVL 11.137; Cady *The Liturgical Basis for the T. Pl.,* PMLA 24.419; Davidson *Studies* 157, 164; Gayley 330; Foster *Myst. Pl. and the 'Northern Passion,'* MLN 26.169; Foster *Study of* . . . 'The Northern Passion,' Bryn Mawr diss. London and Bungay 1914, 86.— Authors and Development: Pollard, EETSES 71.introd.; Davidson *op. cit.* 129, 147; Ten Brink 2.244, 257, 3.274; Coblentz *Rime-Index to the 'Parent Cycle,'* PMLA 10.47; Leach, *Furnivall Misc.,* 1901, 230; Bunzen *op. cit.* 11; Cady *The Wakefield Group in T.,* JEGP 11.244; Cady, JEGP 10.572; Gayley 133, 161 (latter, with slight changes, same as Internat. Qtrly. 12.167; read before Amer. Phil. Assoc., see Trans. 35.lxxxix); Gayley *Rep. Com.* 1.xxiv.— Comparisons with other plays: York, Chester, Coventry, French, MLN 19.31; EETSES 87.xxviii; York, Smith *York*

Plays, see pages above; Davidson *op. cit.* 137, 147, 157, 164; Pollard, EETSES 71.xiv; Hohlfeld, Angl 11.253, 285; Bunzen *op. cit.;* Gayley 161, 331; Cady, as above; Cron *Zur Entwicklungsgesch. der Engl. Myst. Alten Test.,* Marburg diss. 1913.— Date: see under two topics next preceding; Bunzen *op. cit.* 19; Traver *Mus. Terms in the 'Shepherds' Play,* MLN 20.1; Hemingway *op. cit.* xlii.— Analogue: Gerould *Moll of the Prima Pastorum,* MLN 19.225.— Ebert, JbREL 1.44, 131; Hamelius *The Char. of Cain,* Jour. Comp. Lit. 1.324.— Place of Presentation: Pollard, EETSES 71.xii, xxviii; Skeat, Athen 1893.2.779; Peacock, Angl 24.509; Leach, *Furnivall Misc.,* 1901, 228; Chambers 2.415; Hemingway *op. cit.* xl; Gayley 135.— Brandl §81; Körting §135; Ten Brink 2.256, 244, 3.374; Pollard *Engl. Mir. Pl.* xxxv; Cbg Hist 5.53, 434; Morley 4.88; Ward Hist 1.70; Creizenach 294; Klein 12.725, 742.

　　　[8] LUDUS COVENTRIÆ or HEGGE PLAYS. Ed. full cycle, Halliwell for Shakespeare Soc., London 1841;— Plays 1, 2, 3, 4, 5, Dugdale *Monasticon Anglicanum,* 2nd ed. 1830, 6.3.1534; Play 10, Collier *Five Mir.-Plays,* London 1836; Plays 12, 14, Marriott *Engl. Mir.-Plays,* Basel 1838; Play 11, Pollard *Engl. Mir. Pl.* 44; Plays 4, 11, Manly Spec 1.31, 82; Play 5, Wülcker Lesebuch 2.130; Plays 11, 12, 13, 15, 16, Hemingway *Engl. Nat. Pl.* 72. Miss Block is preparing an edition of the cycle for the EETS.— Representation and Locality; Hohlfeld, Angl 11.228; Leach, *Furnivall Misc.* 232; Chambers 2.124, 135, 419; Gayley 135; Thompson, MLN 21.18; Sharp *Diss. On the Pageants Perf. at Coventry,* Coventry 1825; Dormer *Life in an Old English Town;* Kramer *Spr. u. Heimat des Sog. 'L. C.,'* Halle diss. 1892.— Sources: Hohlfeld, Angl 11.219; Falke *Die Quellen des' Sog. 'L. C.,'* Kiel diss. 1908; Taylor, MPhil 4.624, 5.1; Foster *A Study of . . . 'The Northern Passion,'* Bryn Mawr diss. London and Bungay 1914, 89; Traver *Four Daughters of God,* Bryn Mawr diss., Phila. 1907, 125; Gayley 335; Cron *Zur Entwicklungsgesch. . . . ,* Marburg diss. 1913; Bonnell *The Source in Art of the . . . 'Prophets' Play . . . ,* PMLA 29.— Authorship and Development: Chambers 2.135; Leach, as above; Thompson, as above; French, MLN 19.31; Hamelius *De Dood van Kain,* Arch. f. Schweiz. *Volkskunde* 15.49; Dodds *The Problem of the L. C.,* MLR 9.79; Block *Some Notes on the Problem of the L. C.,* MLR 10.47; Hemingway *op. cit.* xxxiii; items below.— Körting §135; Brandl §43; Ten Brink 2.283, 3.276; Ward Hist 1.84; Pollard *Engl. Mir. Pl.* xxxvii; Hemingway xxviii; Gayley 135, 191, 325; Bates 117; Chambers 2.416; Davidson 135; Klein 12.727; Creizenach 298; DNB, *Hegge;* Morley 4.106.

　　　[9] COVENTRY PLAYS. Ed. both plays, Craig, EETSES 87;— *Nativity,* Sharp *Illustr. Papers of the Hist. and Antiq. of Coventry,* Coventry 1817, repr. Fretton, 1871; same repr. Sharp *Diss. on the Coventry Mysteries,* 1825, 83; Marriott *Engl. Mir.-Pl.,* Basel 1838; Manly Spec 1.120 (after Sharp, 1825); Pollard *Fifteenth-Century Prose and Verse* (Arber's *Engl. Garner),* 245; modernized, *Everyman with Other · Interludes,* Everyman's Libr., 59;— *Presentation in the Temple,* Gracie for Abbotsf. Cl., 1836; Holthausen, Angl 25.209 (from Gracie; see AnglBbl 16.65; DLz 1902.2272).— Sharp *Dissertation,* as above; authorship, Leach, *Furnivall Misc.,* 1901, 232; lyrical elements, Taylor, MPhil 5.1; Munro *'Tyrly tirlow'*

and the Cov. . . . Nativity, N&Q 11th Ser. 1.125;— comparison with other plays, Davidson, MLN 7.184; Hohlfeld, MLN 7.308; Hohlfeld, Angl 11.260; Davidson *Studies* 135, 157, 163, 164; French, MLN 19.31; EETSES 87.introd.— Körting §135; Ten Brink 2.280; Bates 129; Ward Hist 1.59, 60; Chambers 2.357 (see refs. there), 422; Gayley 135.

[10] BROME *ABRAHAM.* Ed. Smith, Angl 7.316; Smith *A Commonplace Book of the Fifteenth Century,* Norwich 1886; Rye *Norfolk Antiquarian Misc.* 3.1; Manly Spec 1.41; Waterhouse, EETSES 104.36; Cook Reader 497. Selection: Pollard *Engl. Mir. Pl.* 173.— Mod. rend.: Child *The Second Shepherds' Play,* etc., Boston 1910.— Crit. notes: Angl 13.361.— Relation to Chester: Pollard *op. cit.* 185; Hohlfeld, MLN 5.222; Harper, RadMon 15 (1910); Gayley 126, 132; EETSES 104.liii; Ungemach *Quellen der Ersten Fünf Chester Plays,* Müncb Beitr 1.128; Cron *Zur Entwicklungsgesch.* (as above) 87.— Smith, Antiquary 2.101; *V*arnhagen *De Fabula Scenica Immolationem Isaac . . . ,* Erlangen prgr. 1899.— Chambers 2.426; EETSES 104.xlviii; Ward Hist 1.91; Brandl §120; Ten Brink 2.253.

[11] BODLEY *BURIAL AND RESURRECTION.* Ed. Furnivall, for New Shakespeare Soc. 1882, repr. EETSES 70; Rel Ant 2.214.— Schmidt *Die Digby-Spiele,* Berlin diss. 1884, concluded in Angl 8.393; on *planctus,* Taylor, MPhil 4.628; on lyrical elements, Taylor, MPhil 5.1; Davidson *op. cit.,* 131 note; Chambers 2.129, 431; Ten Brink 2.287; Ward Hist 1.96; Bates 162. See under *Digby Plays.*

[12] NEWCASTLE-UPON-TYNE *NOAH'S ARK.* Ed. Bourne *Hist. of Newcastle,* 1736, 139; Brand *Hist. of Newcastle* 2.373; Sharp *Diss. on the Pageants . . . Perf. at Coventry,* Coventry 1825, 223; Holthausen in *Göteborg's Högskola's Ärsskrift,* and separately, 1897; Brotanek, Angl 21.165 (attempt at restoration of text of MS.; crit. LitBl 19.223; ESt 28.115; see AnglBucherschau 1897); Waterhouse, EETSES 104.xxxv, 19.— Performance: Chambers 2.134, 385; EETSES 104.xxxix; Welford, N&Q 10th Ser. 12.222.— Holthausen *Die Quelle des Noahspiels . . . ,* ShJhb 1900.277.— *V*erse: Davidson *op. cit.* 136.— Körting §135 note 2; Brandl §131; Ten Brink 2.273, 3.275; Ward Hist 1.70, 91; Bates 139; Chambers 2.138, 385, 424; Gayley 140.

[13] DUBLIN *ABRAHAM.* Ed. Collier *Five Mir.-Plays,* London 1836; Brotanek, Angl 21.21 (text-notes, Angl 21.441); Waterhouse, EETSES 104.26. Selection: Smith, Angl 7.321.— On Dublin cycle, MLN 7.339.— Comparisons: Cron *Zur Entwicklungsgesch. . . . ,* as above, 87. Chambers 2.364, 386, 426; EETSES 104.xliii; Davidson 98; Ten Brink 2.278; Ward 1.92; Brandl §120; Bates 138.

[14] CROXTON *SACRAMENT.* Ed. Stokes, Phil. Soc. Trans., Berlin 1860-61, appendix;— with banns, Manly Spec 1.239; Waterhouse, EETSES 104.55.— On text: ESt 16.150, 19.150; Angl 15.198.— Brandl §120; Bates 146; Pollard *Engl. Mir. Pl.,* xliv; Ward Hist 1.98; Chambers 2.145, 363, 427; Creizenach 303; EETSES 104.liv.— On May-Drama, Folk-Drama, Chambers 1.160.

[15] *DIGBY PLAYS.* Ed. Sharp, for Abbotsf. Cl., 1835; Furnivall, for New Shakespeare Soc., 1882, repr. EETSES 70 (with added Bodley *Burial and Resurrection;* crit. Angl 6 Anz 74);— *Massacre,* Hawkins *Orig. of Engl. Drama,* London 1773; Marriott *Engl. Mir.-Plays,* Basel 1838;— *Magdalen* (part), Pollard *Engl. Mir. Plays* 49;— *Conversion,* Manly Spec 1.215.— Schmidt *Die Digby-Spiele,* Berlin diss. 1884, concluded in Angl 8.371; on gloss of EETSES 70, Acad 1882.2.281, 297; lyrical elements, Taylor, MPhil 5.1; Körting §136; Brandl §120; Klein 12.750; Chambers 2.131, 145, 428; Ward Hist 1.92; Creizenach 301; Bates 151; Cbg Hist 5.55;— on *Massacre,* Hone *Anc. Myst.* 170; Collier *Hist. Dr. Poetry* 2.196 note 2.

[16] NORWICH GROCERS' PLAY. Ed. Fitch, R., *Norfolk Archæology,* 1856, also pr. separately; Manly Spec 1.1 (text a); Waterhouse, EETSES 104.8 (both texts).— Explan. note, Prol. st. 2, Parsons, MLN 21.224.— Ten Brink 2.253; Ward Hist 1.91; Chambers 2.386, 425; EETSES 104.xxvi.— On à Becket Procession, Chambers 2.389; on St. George Riding, Chambers 2.389, 1.222.

[17] CORNWALL PLAYS. Ed. (a) Norris *Ancient Cornish Drama,* Oxf. 1859, 2 vols.; (b) Stokes *Bennans Meriasek: The Life of St. Meriasek,* London 1872;— (c) Gilbert (Harley 1867) *The Creation of the World, with Noah's Flood,* London 1827; Stokes (Bodley 219), Trans. Phil. Soc., Berlin 1863, appendix;— (d) (Harley 1782) Gilbert, London 1826; Stokes, Trans. Phil. Soc., Berlin 1860-1.— Peter *The Old Cornish Drama,* a lecture, 1906. Ten Brink 2.279; Ward Hist 1.56; Bates 131; Gayley 126, 142, 333; Cbg Hist 5.16, 435; Chambers 2.127, 433.

[18] UNIDENTIFIED PLAYS. Chambers 2.433; Hastings *Le Théâtre Français et Anglais,* Paris 1900, 167; Hazlitt *Manual for the Collector and Amateur of Old English Plays,* 274.

CHAPTER XV—THE *PEARL* POET; GOWER

1. THE *PEARL* POET

[1] THE *PEARL* POET. See bibliogrs. of *Pearl, Patience, Purity,* below, and *Sir Gawayne and the Grene Knight,* p. 770; Cbg Hist 1.357 (bibliogr. 525); espec. Osgood ed. *Pearl,* Boston 1906, 100 (bibliogr.); Bateson ed. *Patience,* Manchester 1912, introd.; Trautmann *Ueber die Verfasser u. Entstehungszeit Einiger Allit. Ged. des Altenglischen,* Leipzig 1876; Trautmann, Angl 1.117; Brown, C., *The Author of the Pearl Considered in the Light of his Theological Opinions,* PMLA 19.154; *V*eitch *Feeling for Nature in Scott. Poetry,* Edbg. and L. 1887, 1.134; Weichardt *Die Entwicklung des Naturgefühls in der Me. Dichtung . . . ,* Kiel diss. 1900; Palgrave *Landscape in Poetry,* L. 1897, 115; Moorman *Interpret. of Nat. in Engl. Poetry,* Strassburg 1905, 106.— Körting §105; DNB, *Strode, Ralph;* Ency Brit, *Pearl.* See under *Huchown Discussion,* p. 826.

[2] PEARL.   See above, and bibliogr. of *Sir Gawayne and the Grene Knight*, p. 770.— Ed. EETS 1 (1864; revised and repr. 1869, 1885, 1896, 1901); Gollancz, L. 1891 (crit. ESt 16.268; Jahresbericht 1891.353; Acad 1891. No. 999.602, No. 1001.36, No. 1003.76, No. 1005.116, No. 1008.176; Athen 1891. No. 3328.184; AnglBbl 2.111), revised 1897, new ed. 1907 (crit. Arch 132.184); Osgood, Belles Lettres Ser., Boston and L. 1906 (see its bibliogr.;— crit. Arch 123.241; MLR 4.132). Text-notes:;see crits. of Gollancz above; Arch 90.142, 131.154; MPhil 6.197; Acad 38.201, 249, 223.— Mod. rend., Gollancz in ed. 1891; Brown (ll. 158-72, line for line), Poet-Lore 5.434; Mitchell (selections, in verse), N. Y. 1906; Coulton (orig. metre), L. 1906 (see AnglBbl 17.290; N. Y. Eve. Post Aug. 4, 9); Osgood (prose), Princeton 1907; Jewett (orig. metre), N. Y. 1908; Weston *Romance, Vision, and Satire* (orig. metre), Boston 1912.— On ll. 212 ff., Cook, MPhil 6.197.— Brandl §74; Körting §105; Ten Brink 1.348; Cbg Hist 1.357 (bibliogr. 525); Morley 4.144; Snell *Age of Chaucer* 20; Courthope 1.349, 366; Schofield 215, 378; Ency Brit, *Pearl*.— Versification: See general studies, on page 800; Angl 1.119; Schipper 1,223, 317, 421; Schipper *Grundriss* §332; Fuhrmann *Die Allit. Sprachformeln in Morris' E. E. Allit. Poems . . .* , Hamburg 1886; Northup *Study of Metr. Struct. of Pearl*, PMLA 12.326; Paul Grundriss 2nd ed. 2².168, 239; Saintsbury *Hist. Engl. Prosody* 1.106; see under *Sir Gawayne and the Grene Knight*, p. 770.— Language: Fick *Zum Me. Ged. v. d. Perle, Eine Lautuntersuchung*, Kiel 1885 (crit. LitBl 6.495); Morsbach *Me. Gram.* 9, 15. See Schwahn, Knigge, Kullnick, Schmittbetz, under *Sir G. and the Gr. Knt.*, p. 770; and under *Alliteration*, p. 800.— Neilson *Crosslinks betw. Pearl and the Awntyrs*, Scott Antiq 16.67; Schofield *Nature and Fabric of the Pearl*, PMLA 19.154; Brown, C., PMLA as above; Osgood *Is the Pearl an Elegy?* PMLA 21.xxiv; Coulton *In Defense of the Pearl*, MLR 2.39.

[3] PATIENCE.   Ed. EETS 1 (as under *Pearl*); Bateson, Manchester 1912 (crit. MLN 28.171; Athen Oct. 26, 1912; AnglBbl 24.133; MLR 8.396); Gollancz, Oxf. 1913. Selections: Zupitza Übungsbuch 95; MacLean Reader 101; Wülcker Lesebuch 2.27 (crit. ESt 4.500); Kluge Me. Lesebuch 105; Cook Reader 441. Text and interpretation: ESt 4.500, 40.163, 44.165, 47.125 (see 48.172); Angl 11.583; review of Bateson: MLN 29.85.— Mod. rend., part, Weston *Romance, Vision, and Satire*, Boston 1912, 173.— Brandl §74; Ten Brink 1.348; Körting §105; Cbg Hist 1.361 (bibliogr. 525); Schofield 215, 378.— Versification: Schipper *Grundriss* §47; Luick, Angl 11.392, 553; Trautmann, Angl 18.83; Fischer, Bonner Beitr 11 (crit. Angl-Bbl 12.33, 17.41); see Fuhrmann, under *Pearl;* ESt 16.169.   See under *Alliteration*, p. 800.— Language: see under *Pearl* and *Sir G. and Gr. Knt.*, above, p. 770.— On parallels with Tertullian, PMLA 10.242; Liljegren *Has the Poet of 'Patience' Read 'De Jona'?* ESt 48.337.— See bibliogrs. of *Pearl Poet, Pearl, Sir G. and Gr. Knt.*, above, p. 770; and in Bateson's ed. 71.— Emerson *More Notes on P.*, MLN 31.1.

[4] PURITY (CLANNESSE).   Ed. EETS 1 (as under *Pearl*). Selections, Morris Spec 2.151, 161. Mod. rend. ll. 1357 to end, Weston, *Romance, Vision, and Satire* 153.— Interp. notes, Angl 26.368.— Brandl §74; Körting

§105; Ten Brink 1.350; Cbg Hist 1.361 (bibliogr. 525).— Bateson ed. *Patience* 64; debt to Mandeville, PMLA 19.149; Comester as source, Arch 106.349.— Notes, Brett, MLR 10.188; Emerson, MLR 10.373.— Versification: see under *Patience*.— See bibliogrs. under *Pearl Poet; Pearl; Patience; Sir G. and Gr. Knt.; Pistill of Susan; Alliteration*, p. 800.

2. GOWER

Brandl §97; Körting §162; Ten Brink 2.38, 99, 132; Cbg Hist 2.153, 512; Courthope 1.305; Morley 4.150, 169, 201; Brydges, E., *Censura Literaria* 10.346; Brydges, E., *Brit. Bibliographer* 2.1; Corser *Collectanea Anglo-Poetica* Pt. 7.36; Macaulay Oxf. ed. (see crits. below); Spies, ESt 28.161 (see JGP 4.118), 32.251, 34.169; Ker *Engl. Lit. Medieval*, N. Y. 1912, 221; Ker *Essays on Med. Lit.* 101; Br. Quar. Rev. 27.1; Stryenski *Un Poète d'Autrefois*, Rev. de l'Enseignement des Langues Vivantes Aug. 1895; Snell *Age of Chaucer* 101; Ellis EEP 1.169.

[5] LIFE. Leland *Script. Brit.* 1.414; Thynne *Animadversiones;* Todd *Illustr. of Lives and Writings of Gower and Chaucer*, 1810; Nicholas, Retrospective Rev. 2nd Ser. 2.103 (1828); Pauli ed. *Confessio* introd.; Meyer, K., *J. G's Beziehungen zu Chaucer u. King Richard II*, Bonn diss. 1889; N&Q 9th Ser. 9.68, 151, 10.59; Macaulay Oxf. ed. 4.vii; DNB; Cbg Hist 2.153.— On the tomb: Berthelette ed. of *Confessio;* Stow *Survey of London*, ed. 1633, 450; Gough *Sepulchral Monuments* 2.24; Macaulay Oxf. ed. 4.xix.

[6] EDITIONS. Complete works, Macaulay, Oxf. 1899-1902, 4 vols. (crit. Acad 1900.1.180, 1901.2.67, 1903 1.48; RevCrit 1900. No. 36; Arch 105.390, 110.197; Rom 1900.160; ESt 32.251, 35.104; Ctbl 1901.110; Athen 1901.2.305, 385; Literature 1902.161; Class. Rev. 18.62; Quar. Rev. 197.437; AJPhil 1903.24; N&Q 9th Ser. 8.175, 10.418). For eds. of separate pieces, see under individual items below.

[7] MIROIR DE L'OMME. Ed. Macaulay Oxf. ed. 1. Relation to social conditions, Flügel, Angl 24.437; Acad No. 1197.315, No. 1212.71, No. 1213.91; *L'Areine au Mer*, Athen 1901.1.632; Fowler *Une Source Franç. des Poèmes de Gower*, Paris diss. 1905; Lowes *Spenser and the Miroir*, PMLA 29.388.

[8] MINOR FRENCH POEMS. Ed. Macaulay Oxf. ed. 1; Roxb. Club 1850; Stengel, Ausg u. Abhdl 64 (1886).

[9]-[10] VOX CLAMANTIS; MINOR LATIN POEMS. Ed. Macaulay Oxf. ed. 4; Roxb. Club 1850;— Minor poems, Wright PPS 1.346, 356, 360, 417.

[11] IN PRAISE OF PEACE. Ed. Macaulay, as above; Wright PPS 2.4; Skeat Oxf. Chaucer 7.205. On MS. see Macaulay Oxf. ed. 1.lxxix.

[12] BALADE MORAL OF GODE COUNSEYLE. Ed. Arch 101.50 (see 102.213).

[13] CONFESSIO AMANTIS. Ed. Macaulay Oxf. ed. *Vols.* 2, 3; Pauli L. 1859, 2 vols.; Morley, L. 1889 (modernized and incomplete); EETSES 81, 82; older eds., Caxton 1483, and Berthelette 1532 and 1534 (repr. Chalmers *Br. Poets*, 1810). Selections: Macaulay *Sel. from C. A.,* Oxf. 1903; Easton *Readings in Gower*, Halle 1896; Wülcker Lesebuch 2.36; AESprPr 1.349; Morris Spec 2.270; Cook Reader 34.— Spanish version, ed. Birch-Hirschfeld, Leipzig 1909.— On MSS., Macaulay Oxf. ed. 2. cxxxviii; Macaulay, Cbg Hist 2.512; Spies, ESt 28.200 (see JGP 4.118), 32.255, 34.175; notice of a MS. in Quaritch's possession, Arch 110.103.— Sources: Eichinger *Die Trojasage als Stoffquelle für J. G's C. A.,* München diss. 1900; Hamilton *G's Use of the Enlarged Roman de Troie*, PMLA 20.179; Hamilton *Some Sources of the Seventh Book of G's C. A.,* MPhil 9.323; Stollreither *Quellen-Nachweise zu G's C. A.,* München diss. 1901; source like de Vitry's *Exempla*, MLN 19.51; Cbg Hist 2.173; Walz *Das Sprichwort bei G.,* München diss. 1907.— Versification: Hofer *Allit. bei G.,* Leipzig diss. 1890; Schipper 1.279; Hofer *Grundriss*, index; Saintsbury *Hist. Engl. Prosody* 1.319; Easton *Rime in C. A.,* Pub. Univ. Penna. 4. No. 1.— Language: Child *Observations on the Lang. of G's C. A.,* 1868; Ellis *Early Engl. Pron.* Pt. 3.726; Tiete *Zu G's C. A., I Lexicalisches*, Breslau diss. 1889; Fahrenberg *Zur Spr. der C. A.,* Arch 89.389; Spies *Ein Lexicographisches Experiment*, Hamburg 1905; Spies *Engl. Worterbucharbeit*, etc., Arch 116.111; Förg *Die Konjunktionen in G's C. A.,* Heidelberg diss., Tübingen, 1911; Eichhorn *Das Partizipium bei G. in Vergleich mit Ch's Gebrauch*, Kiel diss. 1912.— Gower and Chaucer: *C. A. and Legend of G. W.,* Angl 5.313; *Constance*, Angl 14.77, 147; *Miroir* and *Prologue*, Angl 24.437; *Balades* and Ch., ESt 20.154; Meyer, K., *Zu G's Beziehungen zu Ch. u. King Rich. II*, Bonn diss. 1889 (crit. Athen No. 3220.62; LitBl 11.452; ESt 28.174; Macaulay Oxf. ed. 2.xxii); Rumbaur *Die Gesch. v. Appius u. Virginia*, Breslau diss. 1890; Athen No. 2826.851; Hammond *Chaucer: A Bibliogr. Manual* 75, 152, 278; Dodd *Courtly Love in Chaucer and G.,* Boston and L. 1913.— Gower and Langland: Gebhard *L's u. G's Kritik der Kirchlichen Verhältnisse ihrer Zeit*, Strassburg diss. 1913.— See under gen. head of Sect. 2 *Gower*, above; and Ch. XVI *Sources and Indebtedness, Language and Versification*, Tupper cited in [52], and [60], [70], [74], [84], [87].

CHAPTER XVI—CHAUCER

The following notes are intended to supplement, not to supersede, the entries in Hammond's *Chaucer: A Bibliographical Manual*, which, with the criticisms noted in the next paragraph, the student should consult for each item. Nevertheless, directly or through the references in the writings listed, these notes will introduce not only to practically all the matter concerning Chaucer and his work produced since the publication of the *Manual*, but to all the material of *general* usefulness.

č·ρ·

GENERAL BIBLIOGRAPHY. Hammond ₍Chaucer: A Bibliographical Manual, N. Y. 1908 (see Jahresbericht 1908.15.275, espec. 1909.16.205;— crit. ESt 41.136; AnglBbl 20.225; JEGP 8.619; DLz 30.1191; Athen 1909. 1.556; MLR 4.526; MLN 24.159); Cbg Hist 2.514; Körting §§147-161.

ON RECENT CRITICISM. Koch, ESt 41.113, 46.98, 48.251; Koch, AnglBbl 22.265, 25,327; Koch, GRMSchr 1.490.

HISTORY OF CHAUCER CRITICISM. Spurgeon *Ch. devant la Critique en Angleterre et en France* . . . , Paris 1911 (crit. Ctbl 63.1035; Arch 128.449; DLz 33.870; RevGerm 7.605, 8.75); Lailavoix preface to Engl. trans. of Legouis *Chaucer, L.* 1913; Spurgeon *Five Hundred Years of Chaucer Criticism and Allusion,* Part 1 Text (1357-1900), ChS 2ser. 48.

GENERAL CRITICISM. Pubs. Chaucer Soc (ChS) 1ser. and 2ser., 1868— (list of titles in Hammond 523); Brandl §§83-96; Ten Brink 2.33-206; Courthope 1.247; Morley 5.83; Jusserand 1.267; Wülker 1.146; Root *Poetry of Chaucer,* Boston 1906 (crit. AnglBbl 21.161; JEGP 8.232); Legouis *Chaucer,* Paris 1910 (crit. RevCrit 72.352; RevGerm 7.478; Museum 19.58; MLN 27.119; MLR 6.532; Polybibl. 124.235), refs. hereafter are to the Engl. trans. by Lailavoix, L. 1913; Cbg Hist 2.179; Pollard *Chaucer Primer,* L. 1893-1895-1903-1907; Snell *Age of Ch.,* L. 1901, 121; Snell *The Fourteenth Century,* L. 1899; Lounsbury *Studies in Ch.,* N. Y. 1892, 3 vols.; Hadow *Ch. and his Times,* N. Y. and L. 1914; Kittredge *Ch. and his Poetry,* Cbg. 1915.

SPECIAL CRITICISM. *Ch. and Modernity,* Acad 76.712; Schofield *Chivalry in Engl. Lit.,* Cbg. Mass. 1912, 11; Dodd *Courtly Love in Ch. and Gower,* Boston and L. 1913; Tupper *Ch. and the Woman Question,* prgr. MLA 1914; Heidrich *Das Geographische Weltbild des Späteren Engl. Mittelalters* . . . , Freiburg 1915. See under items following, and individual works.

EDITIONS OF COMPLETE WORKS. For earlier eds., see Hammond 114. Best ed., Skeat *The Complete Works of G. Ch.,* Oxf. 1894, 6 vols. and an extra vol.— referred to as Oxf Ch (see Hammond 144). Single vol. eds., Skeat *Student's Ch.,* Oxf. 1894;— Pollard, Heath, Liddell, and MacCormick *Globe Ch.,* L. 1898.— For eds. of individual works, see under the individual items.

VOLUMES OF MISCELLANEOUS SELECTED PIECES. See Hammond 216 for earlier issues. Sweet *Second M. E. Primer,* Oxf. 1876; Paton *Sels. from Ch.,* L. 1888; Robertson *The Select Ch.,* Edbg. and L. 1902; Greenlaw *Sels. from Ch.,* Chicago 1907; Emerson *Poems of Ch.,* N. Y. 1911; Child *Sels. from Ch.,* Boston 1912; MacCracken *The College Ch.,* New Haven 1913.

MODERNIZATIONS AND IMITATIONS. See Hammond 220 for list to 1907. Tatlock and Mackaye *The Modern Reader's Ch.* (complete works), N. Y. and L. 1912, cheaper issue 1914. For separate pieces, see under individual items below.

SOURCES AND INDEBTEDNESS. See Hammond 73-105, 210.—
Lounsbury *Studies* 2.167-426; Oxf Ch 3.370-504, and notes and introds. to
poems *passim;* Cipriani *Studies in the Influence of the Romance of the
Rose upon Ch.,* PMLA 22.552; Fansler *Ch. and the Roman de la Rose,*
N. Y. 1914 (see its bibliogr.); Forsmann *Einiges über Frz. Einflusse in
Ch's Werken,* prgr. St. Petersburg, Deutsche St. Annenschule, 1909; Bar-
delli *Qualche Contributo agli Studi sulle Relazioni del Ch. col Boccaccio.*
Firenze 1911; Wise *The Influence of Statius upon Ch.,* Johns Hopkins diss.
1911; on Statius, see Hinckley *Notes on Ch.,* Northampton 1907, 96; Koep-
pel *Ch. and Cicero's 'Lælius de Amicitia,'* Arch 126.180; Legouis *Chaucer*
44 and *passim;*— French sources, Lowes, MPhil 8.165, 305; Lowes, MLR
5.33; Lowes, PMLA 29.xxix (and see liv);— Boccaccio, Root, ESt 44.1;
Tatlock, Angl 37.69; Morsbach, ESt 42.43;— Sercambi, Young, *Kittredge
Anniv. Papers* 1913, 405; Hinckley *op. cit.* 2-3;— see Kittredge *et al.,*
under individual works, below; Tupper, MLN 30.9; on Dante's *Convivio,*
Lowes, MPhil 13.19;— on Gower, see refs. under Ch. XV [13] end.

LANGUAGE AND VERSIFICATION. See Hammond 464 ff., 475,
481, 491, 493, 501, 504.— Language: Wilson *Ch's Relative Constructions,*
Stud. in Phil. Univ. Nth Carolina 1 (crit. AnglBbl 21.43); Remus *Die
Kirchlichen u. Speziellwissenschaftlichen Rom. Lehnworte Ch's,* StEPhil 14
(crit. ESt 41.97; see *Museum* 14.292; DLz 28.2589); Frieshammer *Die
Sprachliche Form der Ch. Prosa,* StEPhil 42 (crit. AnglBbl 22.278);
Kenyon *Syntax of the Infin. in Ch.,* ChS 2ser. 44 (crit. AnglBbl 22.279);
Borst *Zur Stellung des Adverbs bei Ch.,* ESt 42.339 (crit. AnglBbl 22.280);
Brown, C., *Shul and Shal in the Ch. MSS.,* PMLA 26.6 (crit. AnglBbl
22.281); Gerike *Das Partizipium Präsentes bei Ch.,* Kiel diss. 1911; Flügel
'Benedicite,' *Mätzke Mem. Vol.,* Leland Stanford Univ. 1911 (see ESt
46.109); Eichhorn *Das Partizipium bei Gower im Vergleich mit Ch's
Gebrauch,* Kiel diss. 1912; Helmeke *Beteuerungen u. Verwunschungen bei
Ch.,* Kiel diss. 1913; Eitle *Die Satzverknüpfung bei Ch.,* AnglForsch 44,
Tübingen diss. 1914; Babcock *Study of the Metrical Use of the Inflectional
e in Middle Engl.,* PMLA 29.59; Hüttmann *Das Partizip. Präs. bei Lydgate
im Vergleich mit Ch's Gebr.,* Kiel diss. 1914; Flügel *Spec. of the Ch. Dict.,*
Letter E, Angl 37.497; Flügel *Prolegomena and Sidenotes of the Ch. Dict.,*
Angl 34.354; Skeat *'Hit': Tense in Ch.,* N&Q 11th Ser. 5.465; Eitle *Die
Unterordnung der Satze bei Ch.,* Tübingen diss. 1914; Wild *Die Sprach-
lichen Eigentumlichkeiten der Wichtigeren Ch.-Hdss. u. die Sprache Ch's,*
Wiener Beitr 44; Foster *Ch's Pronunciation of ai, ay, ei, ey,* MLN 26.76.
Versification: Licklider *Chapters on the Metric of the Chaucerian Tradi-
tion,* Johns Hopkins diss. 1910; Shannon *Ch's Use of the Octosyllabic Verse,*
JEGP 11.277; Klee *Das Enjambement bei Ch.,* Halle diss. 1913; see Bab-
cock, above; Seeberger *Fehlender Auftakt u. Fehlende Senkung nach der
Cäsur in der Chaucerschule,* München diss. 1911; Joerden *Das Verhältnis
von Wort- Satz- u. Versakzent in Ch's C. T.,* StEPhil 55; Vockrodt *Die
Reimtechnik bei Ch. als Mittel zur Chronologischen Bestimmung seiner in
Reimpaar Geschriebenen Werke,* Halle diss. 1914.

NOTES. Oxf Ch 1, 2, 3, 5; Hinckley *Notes on Ch.,* Northampton 1907.
See eds. etc., under individual works or groups, below.

1. Life of Chaucer

[1] LIFE. Hammond 1-49, 305; Oxf Ch 1.ix-lxi (corrections Angl 21.245); Lounsbury *Studies* 1.3-224 (see Angl 21.245); *Life-Records,* ChS 2ser. 12, 14, 21, 32 (see Hammond 42); best summary, Kirk, ChS 2ser. 32.v; Kuhl *Index to Life-Records,* MPhil 10.527; Legouis *Chaucer,* Paris 1910 (see under *General Criticism,* above), refs. below are to Engl. trans. 1913; Kern *Ancestry of Ch.,* Johns Hopkins diss. 1906 (crit. JEGP 10.147); Kern *Ch's Sister,* MLN 23.52; Kern *Deschamp's 'Thureval,'* MPhil 6.503; Hulbert *Ch's Official Life,* Chicago diss. 1912 (crit. MLR 28.189); Coulton *Ch's Captivity,* MLR 4.234; N&Q 9th Ser. 9.134, 10th Ser. 1.28, 4.5; Athen 1906.1.233; MLN 21.224; Delachenal *Histoire de Charles V* 2.241; Emerson *A New Ch. Item,* MLN 26.19, 95; Moore on preceding, MLN 27.79; Emerson *Ch's First Military Service,* RomRev 3.321; Emerson *Ch's Testimony as to his Age,* MPhil 11.117; Moore *Studies in the Life-Records,* Angl 37.1; Rye *Ch. a Norfolk Man,* Acad 75.283 and Athen 1908.1.290 (see Athen 29 Jan. 1881 and ChS 2ser. 21.125), reply Acad 75.425; Redstone *The Ch. Seals,* Athen 1908.1.670; Tatlock *Duration of Ch's Visits to Italy,* JEGPhil 12.118; Hulbert *Ch. and the Earl of Oxford,* MPhil 10.433; Kuhl *Some Friends of Ch.,* PMLA 29.270; Kuhl *Ch. and Aldgate,* prgr. MLA 1914; Rye *Ch.: A Norfolk Man* (only 150 copies), Norwich 1915; Cook *Hist. Background of Ch's Knight,* Pub. Conn. Acad. of Arts and Sciences 20.161; Hales in DNB.— Portraits: Hammond 49; Spielmann, ChS 2ser. 31 (crit. ESt 30.445); DNB, *Chaucer.*— Thomas Chaucer: Hammond 47. Athen 1900.1.116, 146, 1901.2.455; Oxf Ch 1.xlviii.

2. Chaucer's Works

I. The Chaucer Canon

[2] THE CANON. Hammond 51 (add Tatlock *Dev. and Chron.,* ChS 2ser. 37.9), 410-1, 416-7, 436, 440, 449, 460, 462, 515; Oxf Ch 1.lxii-lxiii, 20, 5.ix; Skeat *Minor Poems* vii; Skeat *The Ch. Canon,* Oxf. 1900 (Hammond 55); Pollard *Ch. Primer* 36; Emerson *A New Note on the Date of the Knight's Tale, Stud. in Lang. and Lit. in Cel. of . . . J. M. Hart,* N. Y. 1910; Greg *Ch. Attributions in MS. R, S, 17,* MLR 8.539; Tatlock *Ch's Retractions,* PMLA 28.521.— See entries under individual works, below.

II. Chronology

[3] CHRONOLOGY. Hammond 70-72 (see JEGP 8.621-2); Ten Brink *Chaucer-Studien* 1870; Ten Brink *Engl. Lit.* (trans. 1892) 2.37 ff.; Ten Brink ESt 17.1, 189 (1892); Furnivall *Trial Forewords,* 1871; Furnivall Athen 1871.2.16, 495; Koch *Chronology of Ch's Writings,* ChS 2ser. 27 (dated 1890); Skeat Oxf Ch 1.lxii, 2.xxxvii; Pollard *Ch. Primer* (1903) 46-60; Pollard Globe Ch. xxii; Root *Poetry of Ch.,* vii, *passim;* Lowes, PMLA 19.593, 20.748, 23.285; Lowes, MLN 27.45; Lowes, MPhil 8.165, 305; Tatlock *Dev. and Chronol. of Ch's Works,* ChS 2ser. 37; Emerson *Poems of Ch.,* N. Y. 1911, xviii, xxviii; Vockrodt, under *Language and Versification,* above.— See entries under individual works.

III. Minor Poems

Hammond 325.—Ed. Skeat *Chaucer: The Minor Poems,* Oxf. 1888, 2nd ed. 1893; Oxf Ch 1.20, 261.— For other eds. and selections, etc., Hammond 350-3.— Mod. rend. Skeat, London (Chatto) 1908.— Hammond *On the Editing of Ch's Minor Poems,* MLN 23.20.

[4] ABC. Ed. Oxf Ch 1.58, 261; Minor Poems xlvii, 223. Hammond 354; Root 57; Legouis 63.

[5] AGAINST WOMEN UNCONSTANT or NEWFANGELNESSE. Ed. Oxf Ch 1.88, 409, 5.xv; Minor Poems lxxvii, 199. Hammond 440; Root 58.

[6] AN AMOROUS COMPLEINT or COMPLEINT D'AMOURS. Ed. Oxf Ch 1.89, 411; Minor Poems lxxxi, 218. Hammond 416; Root 79.

[7] ANELIDA AND ARCITE. Ed. Oxf Ch 1.76, 529; Minor Poems lxviii, 102. Hammond 355; Root 68; Legouis 52, 67. Tatlock *Dev. and Chron.,* ChS 2ser. 37.83; Ker *Essays on Med. Lit.* 83, 382; Shannon *Source of Ch's A. and A.,* PMLA 27.461.

[8] BALADE OF COMPLEYNT. Ed. Oxf Ch 1.90, 415, 5.xvi; Minor Poems lxxxiv, 222. Hammond 410; Root 79.

[9] BOOK OF THE DUCHESSE. Ed. Oxf Ch 1.63, 277; Minor Poems lvii, 13. Hammond 362; Root 59; Legouis 72. Sypherd *'Le Songe Vert' and Ch's Dream Poems,* MLN 24.46; Lowes *Illustrations of Ch.* (on l. 1028), RomRev 2.121 (crit. ESt 46.114); Emerson, RomRev 3.354 note; Kittredge *'B. of D.' and Guillaume de Machaut,* MPhil 7.465; Kittredge *Machaut and 'B. of D.,'* PMLA 30.1; Kittredge *Ch. and his Poetry* 37; Shannon *'A Cave under a Rock y-grave,'* MPhil 11.227.— Nadal *Spenser's 'Daphnaïda' and Ch's 'B. of D.,'* PMLA 23.646.

[10] CHAUCER'S WORDS UNTO ADAM. Ed. Oxf Ch 1.78, 329; Minor Poems lxx, 117. Hammond 405; Root 69. Kuhl *A Note on Ch's Adam,* MLN 29.263.

[11] COMPLEYNT OF MARS. Ed. Oxf Ch 1.64, 323; Minor Poems lix, 61. Hammond 384; Root 63; Legouis 66. Browne, W. H., *Notes on Ch's Astrology,* MLN 23.54.

[12] COMPLEYNT OF VENUS. Ed. Oxf Ch 1.86, 400; Minor Poems lxxix, 206. Hammond 404; Root 77.

[13] COMPLEINT TO HIS LADY or BALADE OF PITY. Ed. Oxf Ch 1.75, 360; Minor Poems lxxx, 213. Hammond 411; Root 68.

[14] COMPLEINT TO HIS PURS. Ed. Oxf Ch 1.87, 405; Minor Poems lxxx, 210; Emerson *Sel. Poems* 188; Cook *Reader* 428;— MS. Caius Coll. Cbg. 176 f. 23, MLN 27.228.—Hammond 392; Root 78.

[15] COMPLEYNT UNTO PITE. Ed. Oxf Ch 1.61, 272; Minor Poems lvi, 8. Hammond 390; Root 58.

[16] THE FORMER AGE or THE GOLDEN AGE. Ed. Oxf Ch 1.78, 380; Minor Poems lxxiii, 186; Emerson *Sel. Poems* 164. Hammond 367; Root 70.

[17] FORTUNE. Ed. Oxf Ch 1.79, 383; Minor Poems lxxiv, 189; Emerson *Sel. Poems* 165. Hammond 369; Root 71.

[18] GENTILESSE. Ed. Oxf Ch 1.82, 392; Minor Poems lxxv, 195. Hammond 371; Root 74. Lowes *Ch. and Dante's Convivio,* MPhil 13.19.

[19] LAK OF STEDFASTNESSE. Ed. Oxf Ch 1.84, 394; Minor Poems lxxvii, 197; Emerson *Sel. Poems* 187. Hammond 394; Root 74. Holt, JEGP Apr. 1907; MacCracken, MLN 23.212.

[20] LENVOY DE CHAUCER À BUKTON. Ed. Oxf Ch 1.85, 398; Minor Poems lxxviii, 204. Hammond 366; Root 76. Tatlock *Dev. and Chron.,* ChS 2ser. 37.210; Tatlock, parallel in John of Salisbury, MLN 29.98; Kittredge *Ch's E. to B.,* MLN 24.14; Moore *Date of Ch's Marriage Group,* MLN 26.172; Lowes *Date of E. to B.,* MLN 27.45 (crit. ESt 46.114).

· [21] LENVOY DE CHAUCER À SCOGAN. Ed. Oxf Ch 1.83, 85, 396; Minor ·Poems lxxviii, lxxv, 201; Emerson *Sel. Poems* 188. Hammond 393, 418; Root 75. Kittredge, HarvStN 1.109; Kittredge ll. 38-40 and Alanus de Insulis, MPhil 7.483 (see Hammond 418); Moore *Date of Ch's Marriage Group,* MLN 26.173.

[22] MERCILES BEAUTE. Ed. Oxf Ch 1.80, 387; Minor Poems lxvii, 100; Cook Reader 417. Hammond 436; Root 72; Legouis 62. Lowes *Chaucerian M. B. and Three Poems of Deschamps,* MLR 5.33; Skeat, on l. 26, MLR 5.194.

· [23] PARLEMENT OF FOULES. Ed. Oxf Ch 1.66, 335; Minor Poems lxi, 73; Emerson *Sel. Poems* 156; Drennan, Clive 1914. Mod. rend. Skeat, London 1907.— Hammond 387; Root 65; Legouis 82. Tatlock *Dev. and Chron.,* ChS 2ser. 37.41; on l. 353, Hammond 111, and Cook, MLN 22.146; on l. 693, Jones, MLN 27.95; Emerson *The Suitors in Ch's P. of F.,* MPhil 8.45; Moore *Further Note on the Suitors* . . . , MLN 26.8; Emerson *The Suitors . . . Again,* MLN 26.19; Manly *What is the P. of F?* StEPhil 50.279; Emerson *What is the P. of F?* JEGP 13.566.

[24] THE PROVERBS. Ed. Oxf Ch 1.88, 407; Minor⋅ Poems lxxx, 212. Hammond 449; Root 78. Kittredge, parallels to l. 4, MPhil 7.478.

[25] TO ROSEMOUNDE. Ed. Oxf Ch 1.81, 389; Minor Poems 464. Hammond 460; Root 72. Lowes, on l. 20, RomRev 2.128 (crit. ESt 46.114).

[26] TRUTH. Ed. Oxf Ch 1.82, 390; Minor Poems lxxiv, 193; Emerson *Sel. Poems* 166; Cook Reader 431. Hammond 401; Root 73; Legouis 68. MacCracken, Lambeth 223 text, MLN 23.313; Rickert *'Thou Vache,'* and Manly *Notes,* MPhil 11.209, 226.

[27] WOMANLY NOBLESSE. Oxf Ch 4.xxv, 5.xvi; Minor Poems 466. Hammond 463; Root 79.

IV. 'The Romaunt of the Rose'

[28] ROMAUNT. Ed. Oxf Ch 1.93, 417; repr. Thynne's ed. ChS 1ser. 82 (crit. ESt 46.101); illustr. ed. London, Chatto, 1908. Selection: Cook Reader 389.— Hammond 450; Root 45. Cipriani *The R. of the R. and Ch.*, PMLA 22.552; Lange *Rettungen Ch's. Neue Beitr. zur Echtheitsfrage vom Fragment A*, Angl 35.338, 36.279, 37.146; Fansler *Ch. and the R. de la R.*, N. Y. 1914 (see its bibliogr.); Lange *Zur Datierung* (Fragm. A), Angl 38.477.— Gröber 2¹.59, 734, 1040; Krit *J*ahresber; de *J*ulleville Hist 2.105.

V. 'Boethius,' and the 'Astrolabe'

[29] BOETHIUS. Ed. Oxf Ch 2.vii, 1, 419. Selection: Cook Reader 394.— Hammond 360; Root 80. Fehlauer *Die Engl. Übersetzungen von B's 'De C. Ph.'* (Normannica 2), Berlin 1909.

[30] TREATISE ON THE ASTROLABE. Ed. Oxf Ch 3.lvii, 175, 352.— Hammond 359; Root 85. Moore, on date, MPhil 10.203.

VI. 'The Hous of Fame'

[31] HOUS OF FAME. Ed. Oxf Ch 3.vii, 1, 243; Minor Poems lxx, 118; Emerson *Sel. Poems* xxi, 151.— Mod. rend., Skeat, London 1907.— Hammond 372; Root 123; Legouis 86. Tatlock *Dev. and Chron.*, ChS 2ser. 37.34; Cipriani, PMLA 22.585; Sypherd *Studies in Ch's H. of F.*, ChS 2ser. 39 (crit. ESt 41.113, q.v.); Macaulay *Notes on Ch.* (on 2.421 ff.), MLR 4.18; Hamilton, on Skeat's suppl. note on ll. 358-9, MLN 23.63; Brandl, Sitzungsber. d. Kgl. Pr. Akad. d. Wiss., Ph. Hist. Kl., 1908, xxxv (see ESt 45.398); Kittredge *The Date of Ch's Troilus*, etc., ChS 2ser. 42.53; Hathaway *Ch's Lollius*, ESt 44.161 (on 'Lollius,' see under *Troilus and Criseyde*); Imelmann *Ch's H. der F.*, ESt 45.397; Shannon *Æolus in the H. of F.*, MPhil 11.230; Sypherd *The Completeness of Ch's H. of F.*, MLN 30.65; Manly *What is Ch's H. of F.? Kittredge Anniv. Papers* 73; Fansler *Ch. and the R. de la R.*, N. Y. 1914, table on p. 255; Kittredge *Ch. and his Poetry* 73 ff.; Cook *Skelton's 'Garland of Laurel' and Ch's 'H. of F.,'* MLR Jan. 1916.

VII. 'Troilus and Criseyde'

[32] TROILUS AND CRISEYDE. Ed. Oxf Ch 2.xlix, 153, 461. Hammond 395; Root 87; Legouis 121. McCormick and Root *Spec. Extr. from Nine Known Unpub. MSS. . . . and from Caxton's and Thynne's First Eds.*, ChS 1ser. 89 pt.3 (see•ESt 48.251). McCormick *Another Ch. Stanza, Furnivall Misc.* 1901, 296. Tatlock *Dev. and Chron.* ChS 2ser. 37 (see ESt 41.405); Cook, on sources, Arch 119.40; Cook *Char. of Criseyde*, PMLA 22.531; Wilkins *Criseyde*, MLN 24.65;— on 'Lollius,' Hammond MLN 22.51; Hathaway, ESt 44.161; Young *op. cit.* below, appendix C; Koch, ESt 41.125; Imelmann, ESt 45.406; Hammond 94;— Hamilton *Ch's Indebtedness to Guido delle Colonne*, N. Y. 1903; Broatch *Indebtedness of Ch's T. to Benoît's Roman*, JGP 2.14; Young *Orig. and Dev. of Story of T. and C.*, ChS 2ser. 40 (crit. ESt 41.121); Lowes *Date of Ch's T. and C.*, PMLA

23.285 (crit. ESt 41.126); Hamilton, on the Latin hexameters, MLN 23.127; MacCracken *More Odd Texts*, MLN 25.126; Kittredge *Date of Ch's Troilus*, etc., ChS 2ser. 42 (crit. Arch 124.212; AnglBbl 22.273); Kittredge, on Ch. and *L'Intelligenza*, on 2.614, on 4.1408, and on Ch. and de Vinsauf, MPhil 7.477, 479, 480, 481; Kittredge *The Pillars of Hercules and Ch's 'Trophee'* (see Hammond 98), *Putnam Anniv. Vol.*, Cedar Rapids 1909, 545 (crit. AnglBbl 22.271); Fleschenberg *Daresstudien*, Halle 1908; Hammond *A Burgundian Copy*, MLN 26.32; Brown, C., *Another Contemp. Allusion in Ch's T.*, MLN 26.208; Tatlock, on 3.188, 4.788, 5.1791, MLN 29.97; Kittredge *Ch. and his Poetry* 108 ff.; Kittredge *T. and C. and Guillaume de Machaut*, MLN 30.69.— See under *Legends of Troy*.

VIII. 'The Legend of Good Women'

[33] LEGEND OF GOOD WOMEN. Ed. Skeat, Oxf. 1889; Oxf Ch 3.xvi, 65, 288. Mod. rend., Skeat, L. 1907.— Hammond 378 (see JEGP 8.624); Root 135; Legouis 97. Bilderbeck *Ch's L. of G. W.*, London 1902 (not in Hammond); Lowes *Prol to L. . . . as related to the French Marguerite Poems and the 'Filostrato,'* PMLA 19.593 (crit. ESt 36.142; Acad 1906.1.61); Lowes *Prol. to L. . . . in its Chronol. Relations*, PMLA 20.794 (crit. ESt 37.232; Acad 1906.1.227); Tatlock *Dev. and Chron.*, ChS 2ser. 37 (see AnglBbl 20.136; ESt 41.408); Macaulay *Notes on Ch.*, MLR 4.18; Goddard *Ch's L. of G. W.*, JEGP 8.47 (crit. DLz 31.614; MLR 6.136; Arch 123.474; RevCrit 68.407; ESt 41.411); Lowes *Is Ch's L. . . . a Travesty?* JEGP 8.513; Root *Ch's Leg. of Medea*, PMLA 24.124; Root *Date of Ch's Medea*, PMLA 25.228; Kittredge *Ch's Medea and the Date of the L.*, PMLA 24.343; Kittredge *Ch's Alceste*, MPhil 6.435; Kittredge, on Prol. B562 and *'Marcia Catoun,'* MPhil 7.471, 482; Moore *Prol. to Ch's L. . . . in Relation to Queen Anne and Richard*, MLR 7.488; Cook *Ch's L. . . . Prol. 334*, MPhil 6.475; Lowes *Ch's Etik*, MLN 25.87; Lowes *Ch. and the Miroir de Mariage*, MPhil 8.165, 305 *passim*, and 331, 334 notes; Brown, C., *Lydgate and the L. of G. W.*, ESt 47.59; Schofield *The Sea-Battle in Ch's L. of Cleopatra, Kittredge Anniv. Papers* 139; Lowes *The Two Prologues to the L. of G. W.—a New Test*, ibid. 95; Tatlock *Cleopatra's Serpent-Pit and Ariadne's Crown*, MLN 29.99, 100; Brown *Ch's Serpent-Pit*, MLN 29.108; Jefferson *Queen Anne and Queen Alcestis*, JEGP 13.434; Lange *Zur Datierung der Gg-Prologs . . .* , Angl 39.347.

IX. 'The Canterbury Tales'

A. The Tales in General

GENERAL BIBLIOGRAPHY. Hammond 150; Cbg Hist 2.515; Körting §159.

EDITIONS. See Hammond 202.— Mod. collected eds.: ChS Six-Text ed. of MSS. Ellesmere, Hengwrt, Cbg. Gg, Corpus Oxf., Petworth, Lansdowne 851,— and also Harley 7334, and Cbg. Dd completed by Egerton 2726; *The Ellesmere Ch.*, repr. in facsimile, Manchester Univ. Press 1911, 2 vols.; Oxf Ch Vols. 4 (text), 5 (notes and index to subjs. and words explained),

6 (Glossary); Student's Ch. 419; Globe Ch. 1; Koch *G. Ch's C. T. nach dem Ellesmere MS.*, Heidelberg 1915.— For eds. of selected pieces, see under individual items, and Hammond 213.— See Koch *Textkritische Bemerkungen*, ESt 47.338.

MODERNIZATIONS, etc. See Hammond 220. Tatlock and Mackaye *Mod. Reader's Ch.*, 1912. See under individual items.

GENERAL CRITICISM. Oxf Ch 3.371, 4.vii, 5.ix; Ten Brink 2.138, 57; Root 151; Legouis 136; Kittredge *Ch. and his Poetry* 146 ff.

MISCELLANEOUS CRITICISM. Ewald *Der Humor in Ch's C. T.*, StEPhil 45 (crit. ESt 45.443; LitBl 33.400), see Göttingen diss. 1913; Meyer, E., *Die Charakterbezeichungen bei Ch.*, Halle diss. 1913; Markert *Ch's Canterbury-Pilger u. ihre Tracht*, Würzburg diss. 1911; E. K. *Ch. and Modernity*, Acad 76.712; Schofield *Chivalry in Engl. Lit.*, Oxf. 1913; Kuhl *Place-Names in the C. T.*, prgr. MLA 1914. Ch's Influence on later Literature, Hertwig, Marburg diss. 1908; Tobler, Zürich diss. 1907.

INDEX OF PROPER NAMES AND SUBJECTS (comparisons, similes, metaphors, proverbs, maxims, etc.). Corson, ChS 1ser. 72 pt.2.

[34] ORIGIN AND SOURCES OF THE PLAN. See espec. Hammond 150; Fueter *Die Rahmenzählung bei Boccaccio u. Ch.*, Beilage zur Allgem. Zeitung, 1906, Nos. 65-6; Morsbach, ESt 42.43; Tatlock *Dev. and Chron.*, ChS 2ser. 37.132; Tatlock *Boccaccio and the Plan*, Angl 37.69 (bibliogr. in notes); Oxf Ch 3.371, 6.xcix; Pollard *Primer* 101; Globe Ch. xxvii; Root 151; Ten Brink 2.139, 141; Lounsbury *Studies* 2.229; Legouis 136; Young *The Plan of the C. T., Kittredge Anniv. Papers* 405; on Sercambi, see Hinckley *Notes on Ch.* 2-3.— See Jones *The Plan of the C. T.*, MPhil 13.45.

[35] DATE OF PLAN. Hammond 239, 241; Oxf Ch 2.xxxvi, 3.372; Root 159.— See under *Chronology.*

[36] CHAUCER'S TRIP TO CANTERBURY? Pollard *Primer* 99; Tatlock *Dev. and Chron.*, ChS 2ser. 37.

[37] GENERAL PLAN. On Tabard Inn, see refs. in Oxf Ch 5.4; Hammond 269; Rendle and Norman *The Inns of Old Southwark*, L. 1888.— On Host, Hammond 157.— On Harry Bailly, see refs. in Oxf Ch 5.129; Hammond 269; N&Q 1857.1.228, 1902.1.97.— On the Pilgrims, see under *Prologue* and individual Tales.— On the Pilgrimage and Conditions of the Journey, see refs. in Hammond 269; Jusserand *Engl. Wayfaring Life;* Coulton *Ch. and his England*, L. 1908; Rodenberg *Kent and the C. T. in Engl. Lit. and Social*, 1875, 1; Stanley *Hist. Mem. of Canterbury*, L. 1855; Littlehales, ChS 2ser. 30; Pennell *Pilgrimage to Canterbury*, L. 1885; Belloc *The Old Road*, L. 1904; Ward and Ward *The Canterbury Pilgrimages*, L. and Philadelphia 1904.

[38] THE FRAGMENTS or GROUPS. Hammond 158; Oxf Ch 3.374; Root 152; Pollard *Primer.*— See under *Gamelyn*, p. 766; *Ploughman's Tale*, p. 802.— Hoccleve's *Tale* ed. ChS 2ser. 34; see Hammond 444.— See below under *The Manuscripts;* also under headings of individual Fragments.

[39] CHANGES IN THE GENERAL PLAN OUTLINED. Hammond 239-64 *.passim.* (espec. 255), 269; Oxf Ch 3.374, 380, 384, 5.19.— See under *Canon's Yeoman's Prologue, Parson's Prologue, Retraction.*— See under [46], below.

[40] THE LINKS. Hammond 155-7, 241.— See text and bibliogr. here, at beginning and end of individual Fragments.

[41] GAPS. See text and bibliogr. here, at beginning and end of individual Fragments.

[42] ORDER OF THE FRAGMENTS. Hammond 166; Furnivall *A Temporary Preface,* ChS 2ser. 3, see also Acad 1894.2.86, 1895.2.296; Bradshaw *The Skeleton of Ch's C. T.,* 1871 (see his collected works, 1889); Koch *Chronology,* ChS 2ser. 27; Koch, AnglForsch 38.5; Skeat, Acad 1891.2.96; Oxf Ch 3.379, 434; Skeat, MLR 5.430 (see Corson *Index of the Proper Names,* ChS 1ser. 72.viii); Shipley, MLN 11.290; Ten Brink 2.165, 3.268; Tatlock, MLN 29.141 note 3; Fleay, Acad 1895.2.343. Moore *Position of Group C,* PMLA 30.116.— See below and also text, at heads of the several Fragments.

[43] THE MANUSCRIPTS. Hammond 163-201; Oxf Ch 4.vii; Tatlock on Plimpton MS., MLN 29.140. Skeat *Evol. of the C. T.,* ChS 2ser. 38 (crit. ESt 41.127); Skeat *The Eight-Text Edit. of the C. T.,* ChS 2ser. 43 (crit. AnglBbl 22.267). See under *Harley 7334 Text,* below. Koch *A Detailed Comp. of the Eight MSS. of Ch's C. T.,* AnglForsch 36 (crit. AnglBbl 25.234); Flügel *New Collation of the Ellesmere MS.,* Angl 30.401; Koch *Textkrit. Bemerkungen,* ESt 47.338.— See ChS 1ser. 66-71, 72.— On lang. of MSS., Wild, Wiener Beiträge 44.

[44] THE HARLEY 7334 TEXT. Hammond 177; Pollard, Globe Ch. xxix; Skeat *The Eight-Text Edit. of the C. T., with Espec. Ref. to the Harl. MS. 7334,* ChS 2ser. 43; Koch, AnglBbl 22.267; Tatlock *The Harl. MS. 7334 and Revision of the C. T.,* ChS 2ser. 41 (crit. Arch 124.212; JEGP 9.564; AnglBbl 22.266).

[45] BASES OF EDITIONS. See p. 867, and [43], [44], above.

[46] MODIFICATIONS AS REGARDS INDIVIDUAL PIECES. See under items mentioned in the text here. See under [39], above.

[47] USE OF EARLIER MATERIALS. See under tales of Knight, Man of Law, Prioress, Monk, Clerk, Second Nun.— Hammond 239, 241; Oxf Ch 1.xxxi, 2.xxxvi, 3.380.

[48] DATES OF INDIVIDUAL PIECES. See under individual tales and *Chronology.*— Hammond 239, 241; Oxf Ch 3.381.

[49] DATE OF THE PILGRIMAGE. Hammond 265-6, and refs. there; Globe Ch xxviii; Oxf Ch 3.372, 378, 5.445; Pollard *Primer* 99; Tatlock *Dev. and Chron.,* ChS 2ser. 37.

[50] INDICATIONS OF TIME AND PLACE. See Hammond 160; Oxf Ch 3.378; Pollard *Primer* 107.

[51] DURATION OF THE PILGRIMAGE. Hammond 161-3; Furnivall *Temporary Preface*, 1868, 41-3; Koch *Chronology*, ChS 2ser. 27.59, 63; Koch, ed. *Pardoner's Tale*, ChS 2ser. 35.xxi; Oxf Ch 3.375, 5.415, 132; Shipley, MLN 10.265; Globe Ch xxviii; Pollard *Primer* 109; Tatlock, PMLA 21.478 (see its bibliogr. notes); Root 154.

[52] GROUPS AND MOTIFS. Hammond 254 par. 4-257 par. 6, *et al.*—Marriage Group: Hammond 257; Moore *Date of Ch's Mar. Group*, MLN 26.172; Kittredge *Ch's Discussion of Marriage*, MPhil 9.435; Koch, ESt 46.112; Lawrence *The Marriage Group in the C. T.*, MPhil 11.247; Lowes *Ch. and the Miroir de Mariage*, MPhil 8.165, 305; Tatlock *Boccaccio and the Plan of the C. T.*, Angl 37.94; Tupper *Saint Venus and the Cant. Pilgrims*, N. Y. Nation 97.354.— Love Motif: Tupper article just noted.— Sins Motif: Tupper *Ch. and the Seven Deadly Sins*, PMLA 29.93 (opposed by Koch, AnglBbl 25.327); Tupper *Wilful and Impatient Poverty*, N. Y. Nation 99.41; Tupper *The Pardoner's Tavern*, JEGP 13.553; Tupper *The Quarrels of the Canterbury Pilgrims*, JEGP 14.256; Tupper *Ch. and the Prymer*, MLN 30.9; Lowes *Ch. and the Seven Deadly Sins*, PMLA 30.237.— Kittredge *Ch. and his Poetry* 153 ff., 185 ff.

B. The Individual Fragments

Fragment A

[53] FRAGMENT A. Hammond 265; Root 160; Oxf Ch 3.388. See under *Fragments or Groups* and *Order of the Fragments*, above.

[54] GENERAL PROLOGUE. See Hammond 265; Root 160; Oxf Ch 3.388, 5.1 (notes).— Eds. for school use: McLeod, L. 1871; Zupitza, Marburg 1871, 2nd ed. Berlin 1882; Ten Brink, Marburg 1871; Monfries *Introd. to Study of Ch.*, Edbg. 1876; Willoughby, L. 1881; Meiklejohn, L. 1882; Skeat, Oxf. 1891 . . . ; Pollard, L. 1903; Onions, L. 1904;— with *Knight's Tale*, Carpenter, Boston 1872, 1901; Wyatt, Cbg. 1895; Smith, Cbg. 1908;— with *Nun's Priest's Tale*, Wyatt, L. 1904;— with *Squire's Tale*, Wyatt, L. 1903;— with *Knight's* and *Nun's Priest's Tales*, Morris, Oxf. 1867, re-ed. Skeat 1889; Mather, Boston 1898, and L. 1907; Liddell, N. Y. 1901; Ingraham, L. 1902; *et al.*— Mod. rend., Skeat, L. 1908.— Tatlock *Dev. and Chron.*, ChS 2ser. 37.142; Manly 'A Knight There Was,' Trans. Amer. Phil. Assoc. 38.89; Kittredge, on l. 256, MLN 23.200; Greenlaw, on l. 256, MLR 23.142; Cook, on l. 466, MLN 22.126; Macaulay, on ll. 177, 525, MLR 4.15; Kittredge, illustr. of ll. 449-52, and on ll. 475-7, MPhil 7.475; Hammond, on l. 120, MLN 22.51; Lowes, on ll. 262-3, 467, 286, RomRev 2.118; on l. 164, Hammond 286, and ESt 36.328; Markert *Ch's Cant. Pilger u. ihre Tracht*, Würzburg diss. 1911; Barnouw *De Prolog tot de Kantelberg-Vertellingen* . . . , Onze Euw, 12e Jahrgang 1912.375 (crit. ESt 46.110); Lowes *The Prioress's Oath*, RomRev 5.368; Lowes *Ch. and Li Renclus de Moiliens* (on Parson), PMLA 29.liv; Kuhl *Illustr. of Ch. in the Life of the 14th Cent.*, PMLA 29.xxiv; Kuhl *Ch's Burgesses*, prgr. MLA 1914; Tatlock, on l. 254, MLN 29.141; on l. 411, Tupper, N. Y. Nation 96.640; on ll. 707-10, Young, MLN 30.97; Cook *Beginning the Board in*

Prussia, JEGP 14.375; on ll. 51 ff., Cook *The Hist. Background of Ch's
Knight,* Pub. Conn. Acad. of Arts and Sciences 20.161.

[55] KNIGHT'S TALE. Hammond 270; Root 163; Oxf Ch 3.389, 5.60.—
Eds. for school use: see under *Prologue;* W. and R. Chambers, Edbg. and
L. 1896; Pollard, L. 1903.— Ker *Essays on Med. Lit.* 87; Tatlock *Dev. and
Chron.,* ChS 2ser. 37.45, 226, 231; Hart, on ll. 1033 ff., MLN 22.241; Cook,
on l. 810, MLN 22.207; Browne *Notes on Ch's Astrology,* MLN 23.53;
Hempl, Tatlock, Mather *Palamon and Arcite,* MLN 23.127; Macaulay, on
ll. 297, 309, MLR 4.16; Gibbs, on ll. 975-7, MLN 24.197; Kittredge, on
same, MLN 25.28; Gildersleeve *Ch. and Sir Aldingar,* MLN 25.30; Capone
La Novella del Cavaliere di G. Ch. e la Teseide . . . , Sassari 1909;
Hammond, on l. 1159, MLN 27.92; Emerson *A New Note on the Date of
the K's T., Studies . . . in Celebr. of . . . J. M. Hart,* N. Y. 1910 (crit.
AnglBbl 23.365; JEGP 10.491); MacCracken, on ll. A2024-6, MLN 28.230;
Lowes, on ll. 1534-9, MLR 9.94; Williams *Dryden's Pal. and Arcite and
the K's T.,* MLR 9.161, 309; Tatlock, on l. 1529, MLN 29.142; Egg *Ch's
K's T.,* Marburg prgr., Leipzig 1912; Capone *Marginalia a la Novella del
Cavaliere . . . ; la Concezione de la Storia nel Petrarca e nel Ch.; i
Nibelunghi,* Modica tip. Maltese 1912; Robertson *Elements of Realism in
K's T,* JEGP 14.266; Lowes *Loveres Maladye of Hereos,* MPhil 11.491
(see AnglBbl 25.337); suggestion and date of ll. 1297-1328, Cook *Hist.
Background of Ch's K's T.,* Pub. Conn. Acad. of Arts and Sciences 20.161 ff.

[56] MILLER'S PROLOGUE AND TALE. Hammond 275; Root 173;
Oxf Ch 3.394, 5.96.— Barnuow *The M's T. van Ch.,* Handelingen van het
zesde Nederlandische Philologencongres 1910; Barnuow *Ch's M's T.,* MLR
7.145; Root *Ch. and the Decameron,* ESt 44.1; Lowes *Ch. and the Miroir
de Mariage,* MPhil 8.325.

[57] REEVE'S PROLOGUE AND TALE. Hammond 275; Root 173;
Oxf Ch 3.396, 5.112.— Hart *The R's T.* (study of narrat. art), PMLA 23.1;
Derocquigny, on l. 213, MLR 3.72; Tatlock *Simkin's Ruse,* MLN 29.142.

[58] COOK'S PROLOGUE AND TALE. Hammond 276; Root 179;
Oxf Ch 3.398, 5.128.— Tupper *Ch. and the Seven Deadly Sins,* PMLA 29.113,
125.

Fragment B¹

[59] FRAGMENT B¹. Hammond 277; Root 181; Oxf Ch 3.405, 5.132.—
See under *Fragments or Groups* and *Order of the Fragments,* above.

[60] MAN OF LAW'S HEADLINK, PROLOGUE, AND TALE.
Hammond 277; Root 181; Oxf Ch 3.405, 5.132.— Eds. for school use: R. and
W. Chambers, Edbg. and L. 1884; Morris and Skeat Spec, revised Oxf.
1889; with *Pardoner, Second Nun, Yeoman, et al.,* Skeat, Oxf. 1877, rev.
1889, 1897;— headlink and prol. with *Prioress, et al.,* Skeat, Oxf. 1874 . . . .
Tatlock *Dev. and Chron.,* ChS 2ser. 37.172; Browne *Notes on Ch's Astrology,*
MLN 23.53; Tatlock *Dante and Ch.* (ll. 782-4), MLN 29.97; Tupper *Ch.
and the Seven Deadly Sins,* PMLA 29.99, 102, 118; Tupper *Wilful and*

Impatient Poverty, N. Y. Nation 99.41; Lowes, PMLA 30.310.— See under *Eustace-Constance,* etc., p. 781.

[61] SHIPMAN'S PROLOGUE. Hammond 283; Root 187; Oxf Ch 3.417, 5.165. Skeat, MLR 5.430 (crit AnglBbl 22.280).— Eds. for school use: Skeat *Prioress's Tale,* Oxf. 1874 . . . .

Fragment B²

[62] FRAGMENT B². Hammond 283; Root 187; Oxf Ch 3.417, 5.165.— See under *Fragments or Groups* and *Order of the Fragments,* above.

[63] SHIPMAN'S TALE. Hammond 284; Root 187; Oxf Ch 3.429, 5.168. Tatlock *Dev. and Chron.,* ChS 2ser. 37, 205.

[64] PRIORESS'S HEADLINK AND TALE. Hammond 285; Root 190; Oxf Ch 3.421, 5.173. Lowes *'Simple and Coy,'* Angl 33.440; on 'litel clergeon,' MPhil 3.467 (see ESt 37.231); Gerould *An Early Analogue* . . . , MLN 24.132; Brown *A Study of the Miracle of Our Lady,* ChS 2ser. 45; Tupper *Ch. and the Prymer,* MLN 30.9.— Eds. for school use: Morris Spec, Oxf. 1867, 359; with *Thopas, Monk, et al.,* Skeat, Oxf. 1874 . . . ; Cook Reader 117. See under *General Prologue.*

[65] PROLOGUE TO SIR THOPAS, AND SIR THOPAS. Hammond 287; Root 199; Oxf Ch 3.423, 5.182.— Eds. for school use: see under *Prioress;* Cook Reader 108 (*Sir T.*).— Strong *Sir T. and Sir Guy,* MLN 23.73, 102; Snyder *Note on Sir T.,* MPhil 6.133; Manly *The Stanza-Forms of Sir T.,* MPhil 8.141; Snyder *Sir Thomas Norray and Sir T.,* MLN 25.78; Knott *A Bit of Ch. Mythology,* MPhil 8.135.— Nadal *Spenser's 'Muiopotmos' in Relation to Ch's 'Sir T.' and 'N. P's T.,'* PMLA 25.640.

[66] PROLOGUE TO MELIBEUS, AND MELIBEUS. Hammond 289; Root 203; Oxf Ch 3.426, 5.201. Tatlock *Dev. and Chron.,* ChS 2ser. 37.188.

[67] MONK'S PROLOGUE AND TALE. Hammond 291; Root 203; Oxf Ch 3.427, 5.224.— Ed. for school use: Skeat *Prioress' Tale,* etc., Oxf. 1874 . . . . Tatlock *Dev. and Chron.,* ChS 2ser. 37.164; on ll. 380-82, MLN 21.62, 192; MacCracken *A New MS. of Ch's Monk's Tale,* MLN 23.93; on death of Crœsus, Gelbach, JEGP 6.657; Kittredge *Date of Ch's Troilus,* etc., ChS 2ser. 42.41; Kittredge *Pillars of Hercules and Ch's 'Trophee,'* *Putnam Anniv. Vol.,* Cedar Rapids 1899, 545 (see AnglBbl 22.271); Shannon *Busiris in the M's T.,* MPhil 11.227; Tupper *Ch. and Trophee,* MLN 31.11.

[68] NUN'S PRIEST'S PROLOGUE, TALE, AND EPILOGUE. Hammond 292, 241-3, 261, 101; Root 207; Oxf Ch 3.431, 5.247.— Eds. for school use: see under *General Prologue,* above; Pollard, L. 1908; Winstanley, Cbg. 1915; Cook Reader 198.— Tatlock, on ll. 4372-3, 4565-91, 4571, MLN 29.142-3.— See under *Bestiary,* p. 791.— Nadal *Spenser's 'Muiopotmos' in Relation to Ch's 'Sir T.' and 'N. P's T.,'* PMLA 25.640.

FRAGMENT C

[69] FRAGMENT C. Hammond 293; Root 219; Oxf Ch 3.434, 5.260.—
See under *Fragments or Groups* and *Order of the Fragments,* above.

[70] PHYSICIAN'S TALE. Hammond 294; Root 219; Oxf Ch 3.435,
5.260.— Tatlock *Dev. and Chron.,* ChS 2ser. 37.150; Tupper, PMLA 29.99,
103, *passim;* Tupper, MLN 30.5; Lowes, PMLA 30.305.

[71] WORDS OF THE HOST. Oxf Ch 3.437, 5.264.— Ed. for school
use: Skeat *Tale of Man of Lawe,* Oxf. 1877, rev. 1889, 1897.

[72] PARDONER'S PROLOGUE, TALE, AND ENDLINK. Hammond
295; Root 222; Oxf Ch 3.438, 5.269.— Eds. for school use: Koch crit. ed.,
Berlin 1902 and ChS 2ser. 35 (see Hammond 215, 295); *Tale,* Morris Spec
1867, 345; *Tale,* Emerson Reader 237; Drennan and Wyatt, L. 1911;—
see under *Man of Law.*— Tale and *Prol.* from 45 MSS. and 3 prints, ed.
ChS 1ser. 81, 85, 86, 90, 91, suppls. 1, 2.— Hart *The P. T. and 'Der Dot im
Stock,'* MPhil 9.17; Lowes, on Fr. parallels to ll. 474, 651-3, 656, RomRev
2.113; Tupper *The Pardoner's Tavern,* JEGP 13.553; Lowes, PMLA 30.260.

FRAGMENT D

[73] FRAGMENT D. Hammond 296; Root 231; Oxf Ch 3.445, 5.290.—
See under *Fragments or Groups* and *Order of the Fragments,* above.

[74] WIFE OF BATH'S PROLOGUE AND TALE. Hammond 297
(see JEGP 8.625 note); Root 231; Oxf Ch 3.445, 5.290.— Tatlock *Dev. and
Chron.,* ChS 2ser. 37.198; Kern *De Bronnen van The W. of B's T. en
Daarmed Verwandte Vertellingen,* Verlagen . . . der Kon. Akad. van
Wetenschappen, Afd. Letterkunde, 4de Reeks, 9.3; Lowes *Ch. and the
Miroir de Mariage,* MPhil 8.305; Ayres *Notes on the Discussion of True
Nobility,* PMLA 29.xxi; Tupper, PMLA 29.99, 120, *passim;* Tupper *Ch.
and the Woman Question,* prgr. MLA 1914; Tatlock *The W. of B's Re-
venge* (Prol. 800-10), MLN 29.143; Derocquigny, on l. 415, MLR 3.72;
Lowes *Ch. and Dante's Convivio,* MPhil 13.19; Lowes, PMLA 30.342.

[75] FRIAR'S PROLOGUE AND TALE. Hammond 300; Root 244;
Oxf Ch 3.450; 5.322.— Tupper, PMLA 29.112; Lowes, PMLA 30.278.

[76] SUMMONER'S PROLOGUE AND TALE. Hammond 301; Root
249; Oxf Ch 3.452, 5.330.— Tupper, PMLA 29.112; Tatlock, on ll. D1675-
1706, 1854-68, MLN 29.143-4; Tupper *Jerome and the Summoner's Friar,*
MLN 30.8, 63; Lowes, PMLA 30.278.

FRAGMENT E

[77] FRAGMENT E. Hammond 302; Root 253; Oxf Ch 3.453, 5.342.—
See under *Fragments or Groups* and *Order of the Fragments,* above.

[78] CLERK'S HEADLINK, PROLOGUE, AND TALE. Hammond
303; Root 253; Oxf Ch 3.453, 5.342.— Eds. for school use: W. and R.
Chambers, Edbg. and L. 1883, 1888; Sprague *Masterpieces,* N. Y. 1874;

Sheppard, Barrow, Winckler, Madras 1900; Winstanley, Cbg. 1908 (crit. ESt 42.111); Cook Reader 173 (parts of *Tale*);— see under *Prioress's Tale.*— Tatlock *Dev. and Chron.,* ChS 2ser. 37.156; Hamilton *Date of the C's T.* and *Ch's 'Petrak,'* MLN 23.169, 171; Lowes, MPhil 8.333 note; Kittredge, MPhil 9.440, 444; Jones, H. S. V., *The Clerk of Oxenford,* PMLA 27.106; Hulton *The Clerk of Oxford in Fiction,* London 1909.— See under *Eustace-Constance,* etc., page 781.

[79] MERCHANT'S PROLOGUE, TALE, AND EPILOGUE. Hammond 309; Root 262; Oxf Ch. 3.457, 5.353.— Tatlock *Dev. and Chron.* ChS 2ser. 37.198; Lowes, MPhil 8.168; Holthausen *Die Quelle von Ch's M's T.,* ESt 43.168 (see JEGP 12.77); Kittredge, MPhil 9.450; Tatlock, Angl 37.96.

FRAGMENT F

[80] FRAGMENT F. Hammond 310; Root 266; Oxf Ch 3.462, 5.370.— See under *Fragments or Groups* and *Order of the Fragments,* above.

[81] SQUIRE'S PROLOGUE AND TALE. Hammond 311; Root 266; Oxf Ch 3.462, 5.370.— Eds. for school use: W. and R. Chambers, Edbg. and L. 1882; Pollard, 1899; Goodrich, Madras 1899; Innes, 1905; Winstanley, Cbg. 1908 (crit. ESt 42.111);— see under *General Prologue* and *Prioress's Tale,* above.— Hinckley *The Brazen Horse of Troy* (ll. 209-13), MLN 23.157; Hinckley *Ch. and the Cléomadès,* MLN 24.95; Jones, H. S. V., on *Ch. and the Cléomadès,* PMLA 23.557; Jones, MLN 24.158; Kittredge *Ch. and Geoffrey de Vinsauf* (F99-104), MPhil 7.481; Lowes *Sq's T. and the Land of Prester John,* Washington Univ. Studies I Pt. II No. 1; Cook, Pub. Conn. Acad. of Arts and Sciences 20.161 ff.

[82] WORDS OF THE FRANKLIN AND FRANKLIN'S TALE. Hammond 314; Root 271; Oxf Ch 3.479, 5.387.— Hart *The F's T.* (cpd. with technique of Breton *lais*), *Haverford Essays,* Haverford, Pa., 1909, 185; Lowes, on F1118-20 and Fr., RomRev 2.125; Lowes *Ch. and the Miroir,* MPhil 8.324; Kittredge *Ch's Discussion of Marriage,* MPhil 9.457; Aman *Die Filiation der F's T. . . . ,* Munich diss. 1912; Tatlock, Angl 37.72; Tatlock *Astrology and Magic in Ch's F's T., Kittredge Anniv. Papers,* 1913 (crit. AnglBbl 25.327 ff.); Tatlock *Kayrrud in the F's T.,* PMLA 29.xxvi; Tupper, N. Y. Nation 97.355; Tatlock *The Scene of Ch's F's Tale Visited,* ChS 2ser. 51.

FRAGMENT G

[83] FRAGMENT G. Hammond 315; Root 277; Oxf Ch 3.485, 5.401.— See under *Fragments or Groups* and *Order of the Fragments,* above.

[84] SECOND NUN'S PROLOGUE AND TALE. Hammond 315; Root 277; Oxf Ch 3.485, 5.401.— Ed. for school use, see under *Man of Law.*— Kittredge *Date of Ch's Troilus,* ChS 2ser. 42.41; Brown, C., *Prol. of Ch's Lyf of Seint Cecile,* MPhil 9.1; Lowes *The 'Corones Two,'* PMLA 26.315, 29.129; MacCracken *Further Parallel to the 'Corones Two,'* MLN 27.63; Tupper, PMLA 29.98, 106, 112, etc.; Lowes, PMLA 30.288; Brown, C., *Ch. and the Hours of the Virgin,* MLN 30.231.

[85] CANON'S YEOMAN'S PROLOGUE AND TALE. Hammond
316; Root 280; Oxf Ch 3.492, 5.414.— Ed. for school use, see under *Man of
Law*, above.— Kittredge *The C's Y's Prol. and T.*, Trans. Roy. Soc.
of Lit. 30.87; de Vocht *Ch. and Erasmus*, ESt 41.385; Lowes *The Dragon
and His Brother*, MLN 28.229.

FRAGMENT H

[86] FRAGMENT H. Hammond 317; Root 283; Oxf Ch 3.500, 5.435.—
See under *Fragments or Groups* and *Order of the Fragments*, above.

[87] MANCIPLE'S PROLOGUE AND TALE. Hammond 317; Root
283; Oxf Ch 3.500, 5.435.— School ed. *Prol.*, Skeat *Tale of Man of Lawe*,
etc., Oxf. 1877, rev. 1889, 1897.— Andræ *Zu Ch's M's Prol.*, ESt 45.347;
Tupper, PMLA 29.99, 101, 109, etc.; Lowes, PMLA 30.330.

FRAGMENT I

[88] FRAGMENT I. Hammond 318; Root 284; Oxf Ch 3.502, 5.444.—
See under *Fragments or Groups* and *Order of the Fragments*, above.

[89] PARSON'S PROLOGUE AND TALE, AND THE RETRAC-
TION. Hammond 318, 320; Root 284; Oxf Ch 3.502, 5.444.— School ed.
Prol., Skeat *Tale of Man of Lawe*, Oxf. 1877, rev. 1889, 1897.— Lowes,
MPhil 8.171; Spies *Ch's 'Retractio,'* Tobler-Festschrift 1905, 383-94; Tat-
lock *Ch's Retractions*, PMLA 28.521 (crit. AnglBbl 25.327 ff.); Spies *Ch's
Relig. Grundstimmung u. die Echtheit der P's T.*, StEPhil 50.626; Tupper,
PMLA 29.93, 114; Schlecht *Der Gute Pfarrer in der Engl. Lit. bis zu
Goldsmith's Vicar of Wakefield*, Berlin diss. 1904 (crit. AnglBbl 20.42);
Tupper *A Parallel . . .*, MLN 30.11.

INDEX

INDEX

A number in italics refers to the chief discussion of the item desig_ nated; a starred number refers to the bibliographical note on the item; a number in brackets is a bibliographical note number cited for readier identification of the item.

Lightning Source UK Ltd.
Milton Keynes UK
UKHW010336120219
337137UK00004B/243/P